# Glimpses of Glory

*John Bunyan and English Dissent*

# Glimpses of Glory

## JOHN BUNYAN
## AND ENGLISH DISSENT

Richard L. Greaves

Stanford University Press

Stanford, California

2002

Stanford University Press
Stanford, California
© 2002 by the Board of Trustees of the Leland Stanford Junior University
Printed in the United States of America

Library of Congress Cataloging-in-Publication Data

Greaves, Richard L.
    Glimpses of glory : John Bunyan and English dissent / Richard L. Greaves.
        p.      cm.
    Includes bibliographical references and index.
    ISBN 0-8047-4530-7 (acid-free paper)
    1. Bunyan, John, 1628–1688.    2. Christianity and literature—England—
History—17th century.    3. Dissenters, Religious—England—History—17th
century.    4. Authors, English—Early modern, 1500–1700—Biography.
5. Christian literature, English—History and criticism.    6. Dissenters, Religious—
England—Biography.    7. Bunyan, John, 1628–1688—Religion.    8. Dissenters,
Religious, in literature.    9. Christian biography—England    I. Title.

PR3332.G66      2002
828'.407—dc21                                                          2001055039

This book is printed on acid-free, archival-quality paper.

Original printing 2002
Last figure below indicates year of this printing:
    11    10    09    08    07    06    05    04    03    02

Typeset at Stanford University Press in 10/13 Minion

Frontispiece: *John Bunyan*, by Robert White. ©Copyright The British Museum

TO JUDITH

*for sharing and enriching life's pilgrimage*

# Preface

John Bunyan first attracted my attention in 1962 when I commenced doctoral studies at the University of London under the direction of the incomparable Geoffrey F. Nuttall. Although my scholarly interests have ranged rather widely since that time, I have repeatedly been drawn back to this fascinating seventeenth-century author. Over time some of my views about him have changed, partly because of the work of other scholars, and partly as a result of my research in the puritan, separatist, and nonconformist traditions and 'radical' activity and thought during the late seventeenth century. My assessment of his theological principles, however, has not altered. Nevertheless, as I observed in 1992, the Bunyan to whom I was introduced in the early 1960s changed rather dramatically in the ensuing years. In many ways this biography represents the fruits of nearly four decades of research and reading about early modern Britain. Two friends and colleagues, Jim Forrest and Ted Underwood, urged me to write this biography, and I hope the result in some small way meets their expectations.

In this book I employ current psychological research on major depressive episodes and dysthemia to analyze Bunyan. This represents a substantive change in my thinking about him, for I had long regarded *Grace Abounding to the Chief of Sinners* as little more than a work that was heavily shaped by other spiritual autobiographies, albeit one that rose above its contemporaries in the quality and intensity of its writing. A gift from Robert and Lili Zaller in November 1990, William Styron's chilling *Darkness Visible: A Memoir of Madness*, unexpectedly revealed numerous experiences similar to those described by Bunyan. Intrigued, I began reading recent studies of clinical depression, all the while reflecting on and rereading *Grace Abounding*. Although the use of psychology to study people who have long been deceased is fraught with difficulty, it is a valuable, almost an indispensable tool for biographers, and I have therefore cautiously used it in this work. Bunyan's contemporaries certainly knew about depression, which they typically termed *melancholy*. In fact, in some circles it was a fashionable and probably feigned malady, but obviously that does not negate its reality for others. Those who have plunged into the black depths of seemingly interminable despair will probably recognize a fellow sufferer in Bunyan. I am not suggesting that he experienced depression throughout his life, but the evidence points quite strongly to episodes in the 1650s and again in the early 1660s. I have attempted to indicate how this probable illness affected his writing, including his classic, *The Pilgrim's Progress*. Other scholars, such as Josiah Royce, William James, and Esther Harding, have seen evidence of psychological problems in Bunyan, and Vera Camden and Vincent Newey have commented perceptively on this topic. That Bunyan should have used the insights he gained from this illness so effectively in his writings is a tribute to his literary talent. He not only survived depression, but triumphed over it by creatively utilizing his experience in his work.

This biography also differs from its predecessors in another way, for I have provisionally dated the composition of virtually all Bunyan's writings, including those published posthumously, something that has never been attempted *in toto*. The only exceptions are two broadsides, *Of the Trinity and a Christian* and *Of the Law and a Christian*, both of which are probably undatable. I emphasize that the dates I suggest, which are based on internal and external evidence, are *provisional*, and I offer them as a basis for additional research and modification as appropriate. Dating the posthumously published works is possible only in a relatively detailed history of nonconformity, particularly in the period from 1672 until Bunyan's death in 1688. As far as possible, it is essential to recreate a sense of what he would have learned about the treatment of dissenters, especially on his trips to London, and this I have attempted to do. Although many biographies of Bunyan have been written, this is the first to deal with all of his works in the context of his life and the broader world of nonconformity. Most biographers have mistakenly ignored his minor works, including those that were posthumously published, but these offer invaluable insights into his beliefs and his response to the struggles of dissent to withstand persecution.

As every Bunyan scholar knows, his letters have apparently not survived, and, unlike Richard Baxter and John Owen, references to him in the correspondence of others are rare. We are also handicapped by the apparent loss or destruction of the legal records for the borough of Bedford from 1660 to 1700, including presentments, depositions, recognizances, and jail lists, though such documents, with gaps, exist for the county. Without the borough records, the persecution of Bunyan's congregation cannot be fully reconstructed

In 1988 Christopher Hill remarked that he and I, starting from different perspectives, had reached similar views of Bunyan. In certain respects this assessment is correct, for the Bunyan that emerges in this biography, fully rooted in his historical context, is very different than the one portrayed in the classic biography by John Brown more than a century ago, or in the fine study by Michael Mullett, who concluded that "the authentic Bunyan may actually be closer to the Victorian version," "a Protestant man for all seasons." Although there is much to admire in Mullett's biography, I disagree with such a portrayal.

Over the years various fellowships and grants have facilitated my research. Two recent ones—a resident fellowship at the Rockefeller Center in Bellagio, Italy, and a John Simon Guggenheim Fellowship—were particularly crucial for this book. I am also indebted to the fine archivists at the following libraries: the Bedfordshire and Luton Archives, Bedford; the Bodleian Library, Oxford; the British Library; the Cambridge University Library; the Corporation of London Record Office; Dr. Williams's Library, London; the Friends' Library, London; the Guildhall Library, London; the Henry E. Huntington Library; the Inner Temple Library, London; the London Metropolitan Archive; the Nottingham University Library; and the Public Record Office, London.

During the past four decades I have learned much about Bunyan from my colleagues in the field, and this book is heavily indebted to their research and stimulating ideas. It was my good fortune to have known the leading Bunyan scholars of the late twentieth century, particularly Roger Sharrock, Jim Forrest, Christopher Hill, and Michael Mullett. My debt to Roger, who invited me to edit four volumes in the Oxford edition of Bunyan's works, is particularly substantial. My colleagues in that endeavor—Ted Underwood, J. Sears McGee, Graham Midgley, Owen Watkins, and Bob Owens—have advanced Bunyan studies substantially by their expert editorial work. My successors as president of the International John Bunyan Society, Neil Keeble and Vera Camden, have taught me a great deal, as has John Knott. Paul Seaver, Ted Underwood, and Vera Camden read drafts of the full manuscript and offered perceptive criticism; the shortcomings that remain are, of course, my responsibility. Earlier in my career I was assisted by Gordon Tibbutt and Joyce Godber. Geoffrey Nuttall, whose friendship I deeply cherish, has provided invaluable counsel over the years. Among others whose scholarship and friendship have meant a great deal are Sharon Achinstein, Jacques Alblas, Robert Collmer, Michael Davies, David Gay, Tim Harris, Dayton Haskin, Mark Knights, Anne Laurence, Roger Pooley, Greg Randall, Laura Rosenthal, Eileen Ross, Jonathan Scott, Ken Simpson, Stuart Sim, Dewey Wallace, Robert Zaller, and Arlette Zinck. Amid the stunning beauty of Bellagio, Eileen Higham engaged in helpful discussions about the mood disorder we call depression. Stanley Carpenter answered a variety of questions about military practices in the 1640s, and Donald Foss, dean of the College of Arts and Sciences at Florida State University, has been very supportive. Once again it has been a genuine pleasure to work with Dr. Norris Pope, Editorial Director of Stanford University Press, and John Feneron.

I am deeply grateful for the support and encouragement of my family, especially my mother, my daughters Sherry and Stephany, and my son-in-law, Michael Zaic. My debt is especially great to my wife Judith, who has shared life's pilgrimage, making it so much richer and meaningful. To her I offer these lines from John Donne:

> If our two loves be one, or thou and I
> Love so alike that none do slacken, none can die.

R. L. G.

# Contents

# Abbreviations

——◆◆◆——

| | |
|---|---|
| Add. MSS | Additional Manuscripts |
| Arber, *Term Catalogues* | Edward Arber, ed., *The Term Catalogues, 1668–1709*, 3 vols. (London: For the Author, 1903–6) |
| *Arber,* Transcript | Edward Arber, *A Transcript of the Registers of the Company of Stationers of London; 1554–1640 A.D.*, 3 vols. (London and Birmingham: n.p., 1913–14) |
| *Awakening Words*, ed. Gay, Randall, and Zinck | *Awakening Words: John Bunyan and the Language of Community*, ed. David Gay, James G. Randall, and Arlette Zinck (Newark: University of Delaware Press; London: Associated University Presses, 2000) |
| Backscheider | Paula R. Backscheider, *A Being More Intense: A Study of the Prose Works of Bunyan, Swift, and Defoe* (New York: AMS Press, 1984) |
| Baxter, *Calendar* | *Calendar of the Correspondence of Richard Baxter*, ed. N. H. Keeble and Geoffrey F. Nuttall, 2 vols. (Oxford: Clarendon Press, 1991) |
| *BDBR* | *Biographical Dictionary of British Radicals in the Seventeenth Century*, ed. Richard L. Greaves and Robert Zaller, 3 vols. (Brighton: Harvester Press, 1982–84) |
| BL | British Library |
| BLA | Bedfordshire and Luton Archives |
| *BM* | John Bunyan, *The Life and Death of Mr. Badman*, ed. James F. Forrest and Roger Sharrock (Oxford: Clarendon Press, 1988) |
| Brown | John Brown, *John Bunyan (1628–1688): His Life, Times, and Work*, ed. Frank Mott Harrison (London: Hulbert, 1928) |
| *BS* | *Bunyan Studies: John Bunyan and His Times* |
| *Bunyan*, ed. Collmer | *Bunyan in Our Time*, ed. Robert G. Collmer (Kent, OH: Kent State University Press, 1989) |

| | |
|---|---|
| Bunyan, *Works* (1692) | John Bunyan, *The Works of That Eminent Servant of Christ, Mr. John Bunyan*, ed. Charles Doe (London, 1692) |
| *Calamy Revised* | A. G. Matthews, *Calamy Revised* (Oxford: Clarendon Press, 1934) |
| Capp, *FMM* | B. S. Capp, *The Fifth Monarchy Men: A Study in Seventeenth-Century English Millenarianism* (London: Faber and Faber, 1972) |
| *CB* | *The Minutes of the First Independent Church (now Bunyan Meeting) at Bedford 1656–1766*, ed. H. G. Tibbutt, *PBHRS*, 55 (1976) |
| *CJ* | *Journals of the House of Commons* |
| CLRO | Corporation of London Record Office |
| *CSPD* | *Calendar of State Papers, Domestic* |
| CUL | Cambridge University Library |
| Damrosch, *GP* | Leopold Damrosch, Jr., *God's Plot and Man's Stories: Studies in the Fictional Imagination from Milton to Fielding* (Chicago: University of Chicago Press, 1985) |
| *DNB* | *Dictionary of National Biography* |
| DWL | Dr. Williams's Library, London |
| Foxe, *Acts and Monuments* | John Foxe, *The Acts and Monuments of John Foxe*, ed. George Townsend, 8 vols. (New York: AMS Press, 1965) |
| Frye, *GMS* | Roland Mushat Frye, *God, Man, and Satan: Patterns of Christian Thought and Life in Paradise Lost, Pilgrim's Progress, and the Great Theologians* (Princeton, NJ: Princeton University Press, 1960) |
| *GA* | John Bunyan, *Grace Abounding to the Chief of Sinners*, ed. Roger Sharrock (Oxford: Clarendon Press, 1962) |
| GL | Guildhall Library, London |
| Greaves, *DUFE* | Richard L. Greaves, *Deliver Us from Evil: The Radical Underground in Britain, 1660–1663* (New York: Oxford University Press, 1986) |
| Greaves, *EUHF* | Richard L. Greaves, *Enemies Under His Feet: Radicals and Nonconformists in Britain, 1664–1677* (Stanford, CA: Stanford University Press, 1990) |
| Greaves, *JB* | Richard L. Greaves, *John Bunyan* (Appleford, Abingdon, Berkshire: Sutton Courtney Press, 1969) |
| Greaves, *JBEN* | Richard L. Greaves, *John Bunyan and English Nonconformity* (London: Hambledon Press, 1992) |
| Greaves, *SOK* | Richard L. Greaves, *Secrets of the Kingdom: British Radicals from the Popish Plot to the Revolution of 1688–1689* (Stanford, CA: Stanford University Press, 1992) |
| Greaves, *SR* | Richard L. Greaves, *Saints and Rebels: Seven Nonconformists in Stuart England* (Macon, GA: Mercer University Press, 1985) |

| | |
|---|---|
| Harris, *LC* | Tim Harris, *London Crowds in the Reign of Charles II: Propaganda and Politics from the Restoration until the Exclusion Crisis* (Cambridge: Cambridge University Press, 1987) |
| Harris, *PULS* | Tim Harris, *Politics Under the Later Stuarts: Party Conflict in a Divided Society, 1660–1715* (London: Longman, 1993) |
| Hill, *TPM* | Christopher Hill, *A Tinker and a Poor Man: John Bunyan and His Church, 1628–1688* (New York: Alfred A. Knopf, 1989) |
| HMC | Historical Manuscripts Commission, Reports |
| *HW* | John Bunyan, *The Holy War*, ed. Roger Sharrock and James F. Forrest (Oxford: Clarendon Press, 1980) |
| *JBHE*, ed. Laurence, Owens, and Sim | *John Bunyan and His England, 1628–88*, ed. Anne Laurence, W. R. Owens, and Stuart Sim (London: Hambledon Press, 1990) |
| Jeaffreson | *Middlesex County Records*, ed. John Cordy Jeaffreson, 4 vols. (London: Middlesex County Records Society, 1886–92) |
| *John Bunyan*, ed. Keeble | *John Bunyan, Conventicle and Parnassus: Tercentenary Essays* (Oxford: Clarendon Press, 1988) |
| Keeble, *LCN* | N. H. Keeble, *The Literary Culture of Nonconformity in Later Seventeenth-Century England* (Athens: University of Georgia Press, 1987) |
| Knott, *DM* | John R. Knott, *Discourses of Martyrdom in English Literature, 1563–1694* (Cambridge: Cambridge University Press, 1993) |
| Knott, *SS* | John R. Knott, Jr., *The Sword of the Spirit: Puritan Responses to the Bible* (Chicago: University of Chicago Press, 1980) |
| Lacey | Douglas R. Lacey, *Dissent and Parliamentary Politics in England, 1661–1689* (New Brunswick, NJ: Rutgers University Press, 1969) |
| Lindsay | Jack Lindsay, *John Bunyan: Maker of Myths* (London: Methuen Publishers, 1937) |
| *LJ* | *Journals of the House of Lords* |
| LMA | London Metropolitan Archive |
| Luther, *Galatians* | Martin Luther, *A Commentary on St. Paul's Epistle to the Galatians*, ed. Philip S. Watson (Cambridge: James Clarke and Co., 1953) |
| Luttrell | Narcissus Luttrell, *A Brief Historical Relation of State Affairs from September 1678 to April 1714*, 6 vols. (Oxford: Oxford University Press, 1857) |
| Luxon | Thomas H. Luxon, *Literal Figures: Puritan Allegory and the Reformation Crisis in Representation* (Chicago: University of Chicago Press, 1995) |

| | |
|---|---|
| *Minute Book*, ed. Parsloe | *The Minute Book of Bedford Corporation, 1647–1664*, ed. Guy Parsloe, *PBHRS*, 26 (1949) |
| Morrice | Roger Morrice, "Entr'ing Book, Being an Historical Register of Occurrences from April, Anno 1677 to April 1691," DWL |
| Mullett, *JBC* | Michael Mullett, *John Bunyan in Context* (Keele, Staffordshire: Keele University Press, 1996) |
| *MW* | John Bunyan, *The Miscellaneous Works of John Bunyan*, general editor, Roger Sharrock, 13 vols. (Oxford: Clarendon Press, 1976–94) |
| NUL | Nottingham University Library |
| Owen, *Works* | John Owen, *The Works of John Owen, D.D.*, ed. William H. Gould, 16 vols. (London: Johnstone and Hunter, 1850–53) |
| *PBHRS* | *Publications of the Bedfordshire Historical Record Society* |
| Pepys | Samuel Pepys, *The Diary of Samuel Pepys*, ed. Robert Latham and William Matthews, 11 vols. (Berkeley: University of California Press, 1970–83) |
| *Pilgrim's Progress*, ed. Newey | *The Pilgrim's Progress: Critical and Historical Views*, ed. Vincent Newey (Totowa, NJ: Barnes and Noble, 1980) |
| Plomer, *DBP* | Henry R. Plomer, *A Dictionary of the Booksellers and Printers...from 1641 to 1667* (London: Bibliographical Society, 1907) |
| Plomer, *DPB* | Henry R. Plomer, *A Dictionary of Printers and Booksellers...from 1668 to 1725* (Oxford: Bibliographical Society, 1922) |
| *PP* | John Bunyan, *The Pilgrim's Progress from This World to That Which Is to Come*, ed. James Blanton Wharey and Roger Sharrock (Oxford: Clarendon Press, 1960; reprinted with corrections, 1967) |
| PRO, SP | Public Record Office, London, State Papers |
| "Relation" | John Bunyan, "A Relation of the Imprisonment of Mr. John Bunyan," *ad cal. Grace Abounding to the Chief of Sinners*, ed. Roger Sharrock (Oxford: Clarendon Press, 1962) |
| Sharrock, *JB* | Roger Sharrock, *John Bunyan* (London: Macmillan; New York: St. Martin's Press, 1968) |
| Sim and Walker | Stuart Sim and David Walker, *Bunyan and Authority: The Rhetoric of Dissent and the Legitimation Crisis in Seventeenth-Century England* (Bern: Peter Lang, 2000) |
| Spurr, *RCE* | John Spurr, *The Restoration Church of England, 1646–1689* (New Haven, CT: Yale University Press, 1991) |
| Stachniewsky | John Stachniewski, *The Persecutory Imagination: English Puritanism and the Literature of Religious Despair* (Oxford: Clarendon Press, 1991) |

Swaim                    Kathleen M. Swaim, *Pilgrim's Progress, Puritan Progress: Discourses and Contexts* (Urbana and Chicago: University of Illinois Press, 1993)

Talon                    Henri Talon, *John Bunyan: The Man and His Works*, trans. Barbara Wall (Cambridge, MA: Harvard University Press, 1951)

Tindall                  William York Tindall, *John Bunyan: Mechanick Preacher* (New York: Columbia University Press, 1934)

Underwood, *PRLW*        T. L. Underwood, *Primitivism, Radicalism, and the Lamb's War: The Baptist-Quaker Conflict in Seventeenth-Century England* (New York: Oxford University Press, 1997)

# Glimpses of Glory

*John Bunyan and English Dissent*

# Prologue

On 12 November 1660 John Bunyan, having been warned that he faced arrest if he preached to a small group in an obscure Bedfordshire hamlet, refused to be deterred. "Resolved to see the utmost of what [the magistrates] could say or do" to him, he began the service with prayer, only to be interrupted by a constable who took him into custody.[1] In the weeks and months that followed, he firmly declined the opportunity to be released in return for a promise to cease preaching and devote himself to his brazier's craft. He made this decision notwithstanding the psychological and financial burden on his pregnant wife Elizabeth, his blind ten-year-old daughter Mary, and the latter's three younger siblings. He knew too that his defiance could lead to banishment and, if he subsequently returned to England, the hangman's noose, a fact that weighed heavily on his mind. For refusing to yield to the government, he paid a terrible penalty: The child his wife was carrying died when she went into premature labor upon news of his arrest, and during an imprisonment of more than eleven years he had only a minimal taste of the joy of family life.

Resolved not to sacrifice his convictions, he remained adamantly opposed to the Church of England throughout his career, even when ecclesiastical authorities incarcerated him a second time. For a while the government succeeded in silencing his voice, but he utilized his years in prison to hone his writing skills, transposing his message from the pulpit to the press and lashing out at the established church as antichristian, pharisaical, and alien to the gospel. If prison was the crucible in which his faith was tested, the dissenting tradition provided him with spiritual sustenance and a sense of community, particularly in its struggles to survive persecution by a repressive state seeking to impose religious uniformity.

[1]"Relation," 106.

Still, the Bedford jail was but an external dungeon for Bunyan, who, long before the prison doors closed on him, endured the prison of his own mind. Especially as a young man he battled an equally insidious if unseen foe—the pervasive, interminable waves of black despair that washed over him, plunging him into inky depths from which escape was seemingly all but impossible.

CHAPTER 1

# The Early Years

Of his ancestry Bunyan says only that, as many knew, he was descended from "a low and inconsiderable generation," his "fathers house being of that rank that is meanest, and most despised of all the families in the Land." He referred as well to the "meanness and inconsiderableness" of his parents, neither of whose names he bothered to record (*GA*, §2), and he asked the readers of his third book, *A Few Sighs from Hell, or, the Groans of a Damned Soul* (1658), to embrace his teachings notwithstanding his "low and contemptible descent in the world" (*MW*, 1:248). He was born in a cottage on the eastern border of Elstow, near the hamlet of Harrowden, in November 1628. The register of the Elstow parish church records that the minister, John Kellie, christened him on 30 November, and that he was the son of Thomas Bonnionn, Jr. Bunyan's mother was Thomas' second wife, Margaret, daughter of William Bentley and his wife Mary (née Goodwin). On his father's side Bunyan's ancestors were emphatically *not* among the most despised families in England, for five generations earlier, in 1542, William Bonyon held part of the manor of Elstow from Henry VIII. William's son Thomas, described as a laborer, sold part of this land in April 1548, probably because he, like so many others, was confronted with mounting inflation and shortages of cattle and dairy products. Economic hardship seems to have forced this Thomas off the land to earn a living as a victualer and brewer.[1] Did the Bunyan family remember this event as they gazed on land that had once been theirs?[2] Could smoldering resentment have helped to motivate Bunyan's seething condemnation of "drunk-

---

[1] Brown, 22–24, 32, and the genealogical chart between 20 and 21; *Victoria County History, Bedfordshire*, 3:279; Paul Slack, "Social Policy and the Constraints of Government, 1547–58," in *The Mid-Tudor Polity, c. 1540–1560*, ed. Robert Tittler and Jennifer Loach (Totowa, NJ: Rowman and Littlefield, 1980), 95.

[2] The family name was attached to various property in the Elstow area, including Bonyon's End and two fields known as "Bunyans" and "farther Bunyans." Brown, 23–24.

en[,] proud, rich, and scornful Landlords" in 1658? Was the family's past misfortune in his mind when he wondered if landlords "would not bear the burden of the ruine of others for ever?" (*MW*, 1:316).

Bunyan's grandfather, Thomas Bunyon, grandson of Thomas the victualer, was a petty chapman, an itinerant trader who marketed his wares in local villages and probably Bedford itself. At one point he owned nine acres, but he too sold some of the family lands. Yet he was hardly indigent, for he possessed enough goods to warrant a will, the executor of which was Thomas Carter of Kempston, a "loveinge and Kind Friend" as well as a member of the gentry. In the will, made in November 1641, he bequeathed a cottage to his wife, £5 to his daughter, 6d. each to his grandchildren (including John Bunyan), and the remainder of his goods to his wife. This Thomas manifested a degree of popular anticlericalism, for in October 1617 he had been cited in an ecclesiastical court for calling churchwardens "forsworne men."[3] He may have bequeathed more than material possessions, for his grandson imbibed the anticlerical spirit, castigating "filthy blind Priests" in 1658 and wondering how many souls they had destroyed "by their ignorance, and corrupt doctrine" (*MW*, 1:314).

### "My Heighth of Vanity"[4]: Bunyan's Youth

The son of Thomas the chapman, also named Thomas Bonyon, described himself as a brazier, a term that included pewterers as well as tinkers. The family's slide down the social scale continued, for Thomas' cottage, with its single hearth, was not subject to the hearth tax in 1673–74. In fact, Thomas lived in one of the humbler abodes in Elstow, where thirty-six of the sixty-one homes had two or more hearths.[5] Like his father, Thomas apparently could not write, but he too left a will, signing with a mark, as had his father.[6] Clearly, he was not destitute, nor was he a godly man, for Bunyan later recalled that he did not "learn me to speak without this wicked way of swearing" (*GA*, §27). Yet Bunyan seems to have loved his father and by 1663 was hoping for his conversion. In Bunyan's tract, *Christian Behaviour*, the advice he offered to godly children whose parents were unregenerate must have reflected his own relationship with his father at that time: "Speak to them wisely, meekly, and humbly; do for them faithfully without repining; and bear, with all child-like modesty, their reproaches, their railing, and evil speaking." What a joyous occasion it would be, he reflected, if God used children to teach their fathers to believe (*MW*, 3:39–40).

[3] Ibid., 27–28.
[4] *GA*, §11.
[5] Brown, 33.
[6] Ibid., 28, 293.

Although Bunyan's parents were not godly, they, like many others among the lower orders, valued education,[7] sending him to school to learn reading and writing. In his spiritual autobiography, *Grace Abounding to the Chief of Sinners*, he downplays his learning, claiming to have attained this knowledge "according to the rate of other poor mens children," and even to have forgotten the little he had learned (§3). This, of course, is obviously untrue. In addition to boasting that he had never studied Plato or Aristotle (*MW*, 2:16), he later sneered at boys who attend "the Latin School; they learn till they have learned the grounds of their Grammar, and then go home and forget all" (*MW*, 13:91). If he briefly attended such a school, this contempt may reflect his own experience. Observing that even Bunyan's earliest writings display an ability to write coherently and grammatically, Roger Sharrock plausibly concluded that he may have attended grammar school for a time.[8] If so, he distanced himself from its curriculum, preferring to link classical philosophy and its embodiment in medieval scholastic thought with the traditional divines in the Church of England. In *A Few Sighs from Hell* he damns such clerics because they "nuzzle up [their] people in ignorance with *Aristotle, Plato*, and the rest of the heathenish Philosophers, and preach little, if any thing of Christ rightly" (*MW*, 1:345). An adherent of the basic Protestant tenet that Scripture is understandable to the perspicacious reader enlightened by the Holy Spirit, Bunyan was keenly sensitive to any appearance that he relied on human learning to acquire biblical understanding. As late as 1675 he was at pains to aver his total dependence on the Bible:

> *I have not writ at a venture, nor borrowed my Doctrine from Libraries. I depend upon the sayings of no man: I found it in the Scriptures of Truth, among the true sayings of God.* (*MW*, 8:51)

This, too, was an exaggeration, for, as we shall see, he learned from other Protestant authors. The point to make here is simply that he would not have wanted his readers to attribute his teachings to a grammar-school education, if indeed he received one. His ability to read Martin Luther's meaty commentary on Galatians suggests an educational level above that of a petty school.

At the very least, Bunyan built on the rudimentary education he obtained in a petty school by teaching himself the writing and expository skills necessary to publish. After 1660 he also acquired a degree of legal knowledge on his own; in-

---

[7] J. A. Sharpe, *Early Modern England: A Social History, 1550–1760* (London: Edward Arnold, 1987), 272–75; Margaret Spufford, "First Steps in Literacy: The Reading and Writing Experiences of the Humblest Seventeenth-Century Autobiographers," *Social History* 4 (1979): 407–35.

[8] Roger Sharrock, "'When at the first I took my Pen in hand': Bunyan and the Book," in *John Bunyan*, ed. Keeble, 74.

deed, as early as 1659 he was referring to such legal terms as praemunire and "replieve" (i.e., bail), perhaps as the result of knowledge gained from his earliest legal difficulties (*MW*, 2:139). Prior to his marriage he concentrated his reading on ballads, newspapers, and medieval romances probably acquired from chapmen or at the market in nearby Bedford.[9] In an autobiographical passage in *A Few Sighs from Hell*, he recalled his earlier reading preferences: "Alas, what is the Scripture, give me a Ballad, a Newsbook, *George* on horseback, or *Bevis* of Southampton, give me some book that teaches curious arts, that tells of old fables" (*MW*, 1:333). His reference to manuals on "curious arts" presumably reflects an early interest in alchemy or witchcraft, and he probably read the story of St. George in Richard Johnson's *The Most Famous History of the Seven Champions of Christendome* (1596) (1:400). A medieval chivalric romance, *Bevis of Southampton* tells of a hero who, as a slave, refused to worship his masters' false deity Apoline, and then went on to command an army, escape from a dungeon, repulse two lions in a cave, defeat a thirty-foot giant, invade England, and take vengeance on his father's murderer, who had married his dastardly mother. Perhaps remembering how much he had once enjoyed this tale, Bunyan would include a giant, a dungeon, the monster Apollyon, and lions in *The Pilgrim's Progress*. Rather than forgetting what he had learned, he became an avid reader.

Bunyan provides another valuable clue about his early life and development when he describes his boyish nightmares. As an adult he attributed these terrifying experiences to his youthful propensity to swearing, blasphemy, and lying.

> Yea, so setled and rooted was I in these things, that they became as a second Nature to me; the which, as I also have with soberness considered since, did so offend the Lord, that even in my childhood he did scare and affright me with fearful dreams, and did terrifie me with dreadful visions. For often, after I had spent this and the other day in sin, I have in my bed been greatly afflicted, while asleep, with the apprehensions of Devils, and wicked spirits, who still, as I then thought, laboured to draw me away with them; of which I could never be rid. (*GA*, §5)

Judging from the research of specialists on children's dreams, the "dreadful visions" Bunyan describes can be provisionally dated to his pre-adolescent years, that is, ages 11 to 13. Children's nightmares primarily occur during this period and in two earlier ones, namely, 1½ to 2½ and 4 to 6.[10] Because children's nightmares some-

[9] Margaret Spufford, *Small Books and Pleasant Histories: Popular Fiction and Its Readership in Seventeenth-Century England* (Athens: University of Georgia Press, 1981), 7.

[10] Ava L. Siegler, "The Nightmare and Child Development: Some Observations from a Psychoanalytic Perspective," in *The Nightmare: Psychological and Biological Foundations*, ed. Henry Kellerman (New York: Columbia University Press, 1987), 199, 211. However, an older study undertaken at the University of California, Berkeley (1954), found that the incidence of disturbing dreams declined at ages 9 and 10, and were rare at ages 11 to 14.

times focus on monsters that threaten to take them away, the origins of Bunyan's dreams may lie in an earlier period, but the content as he depicts the nightmares in *Grace Abounding* points to his pre-adolescent years. This is confirmed by his recollection that during the same period he was "greatly afflicted and troubled," both day and night, with the specter of the day of judgment and the prospect of spending eternity with "Devils and Hellish Fiends" in the fires of hell. Writing in his late thirties, Bunyan thought these fears and nightmares had occurred when he was about 9 or 10; they were clearly a defining experience in his youth (*GA*, §§6–7). Either he erred by several years in his dating (which is possible) or he was somewhat atypical in experiencing nightmares at this point in his life.

Psychologists have identified numerous triggers for nightmares, including the death of or separation from a family member, parental abuse, sexual molestation, febrile illness, daytime fears, verbal threats, and concerns associated with physical development, such as puberty's onset.[11] Within a short period, Bunyan lost his mother (died 20 June 1644), his sister Margaret (buried 24 July 1644), and his half-brother Charles (buried 30 May 1645),[12] but these tragedies significantly postdated the onset of his nightmares. An overzealous preacher, a religious broadside, or a printed sermon may have triggered Bunyan's terrifying dreams. He makes it clear that his nightmares were recurrent, which suggests, according to psychologists, that they originated in a time of stress. Such dreams typically cease when the problem that caused the stress is resolved.[13]

To aver that Bunyan experienced severe nightmares is not to suggest that he was psychotic. Such experiences can be carried over into one's waking hours, as happened to Bunyan, without causing a regression in the ego's ability to function. The danger nightmares pose occurs when those having them lose the ability while awake to test the dreams' reality. "The ego's capacity to maintain dream-reality distinctions in the face of intense conflict and anxiety is a hard-won strength and is subject to regression and disruption throughout childhood and adult life."[14] As

---

Cited in Ernest Hartmann, *The Nightmare: The Psychology and Biology of Terrifying Dreams* (New York: Basic Books, 1984), 28–29.

[11] Franklin D. Raddock, "Nightmares, Problem Sleep, and Peculiar Bedtime Behavior in Children," in *The Nightmare*, ed. Kellerman, 135; John E. Mack, *Nightmares and Human Conflict* (Boston: Little, Brown and Company, 1970), 214.

[12] Brown, genealogical chart between 20 and 21.

[13] G. William Domhoff, "The Repetition of Dreams and Dream Elements: A Possible Clue to a Function of Dreams," in *The Functions of Dreaming*, ed. Alan Moffitt, Milton Kramer, and Robert Hoffmann (Albany: State University of New York Press, 1993), 298–99; Domhoff, *Finding Meaning in Dreams: A Quantitative Approach* (New York: Plenum Press, 1996), 195–97.

[14] Mack, *Nightmares and Human Conflict*, 32.

we shall see, Bunyan's tortured conversion experience was almost certainly colored by the recurrence of his pre-adolescent nightmares. When this happened, his current anxiety became associated with his childhood fears, at which point he confronted his old nemesis, the Devil, "not as the competent person [Bunyan] may actually have become, but as the small and helpless child surrounded by a world of . . . dangerous forces that he perceives in much the same way as he did in the earlier period when they confronted him daily with his powerlessness."[15] The key to understanding the great drama that dominates *Grace Abounding* is partly situated in Bunyan's childhood nightmares.

Bunyan's experience with nightmares may be linked to both his later bouts with depressed moods and his unquestionable creativity. According to Ernest Hartmann, "depression often appears to be associated with an increase of nightmares."[16] Moreover, depressed people are significantly more likely to have dreams with a masochistic content than other individuals. Such content includes critical representations of the self, with the dreamer exaggerating his or her negative characteristics, much as Bunyan does in *Grace Abounding*. It can also embrace discomfort, failure to attain goals, disappointment, and lack of affection, all of which are characteristic of Bunyan's psychological turmoil.[17] Masochistic themes are common in the nightmares of people suffering from moderate depression, whereas those experiencing deep depression have nightmares focusing on helplessness or hopelessness.[18] This is not to suggest that nightmares trigger depression, but that depressed individuals are more prone to nightmares than most other people.

Sufferers of frequent nightmares tend to be creative people with an ability to depict their dreams in unusually real terms. They also are typically expressive, likely to have extrasensory experiences, and sensitive to both the inner and the outer worlds,[19] as Bunyan certainly was. Hartmann has depicted such people as having "thin boundaries," by which he means permeable or fluid distinctions

---

[15] Ibid., 212.

[16] Hartmann, *The Nightmare*, 35; cf. 66–67. Here I refer to depression in a general sense. Chapter 2 includes a substantive discussion employing clinical terminology.

[17] Carolyn Winget and Milton Kramer, *Dimensions of Dreams* (Gainesville: University Presses of Florida, 1979), 84–85; Domhoff, *Finding Meaning in Dreams*, 35–37.

[18] Anthony Shafton, *Dream Reader: Contemporary Approaches to the Understanding of Dreams* (Albany: State University of New York Press, 1995), 323.

[19] Harry Fiss, "The 'Royal Road' to the Unconscious Revisited: A Signal Detection Model of Dream Function," in *The Functions of Dreaming*, ed. Moffitt, Kramer, and Hoffmann, 404–5; Domhoff, "The Repetition of Dreams," 301; Ernest Hartmann, *Boundaries in the Mind: A New Psychology of Personality* (New York: Basic Books, 1991), 192–96; Hartmann, *The Nightmare*, 129; Mack, *Nightmares and Human Conflict*, 93–99.

between dreaming and waking, fantasy and reality, past and present, ordinary sensory experience and extrasensory experience, and oneself and others.[20]

> The boundaries are important to the work of creative people who have to be open to new ways and be able sometimes to see things in two ways at once. They must be especially sensitive and open to their inner world and often the outer world as well.[21]

The formation of thin boundaries, according to Hartmann, commences in early childhood and is the result of both genetic and environmental factors.[22] Those who develop thin boundaries become "painfully sensitive to, and in danger from, their own wishes and impulses as well as demands or threats from the world outside."[23] Bunyan's nightmares, his profound waking fear of eternal damnation, and his creativity, taken together, point to thin boundaries. So, too, does the fact that his adolescent years, as characterized in *Grace Abounding*, were stormy and difficult, and that he later suffered from depressed moods.[24]

Unfortunately, Bunyan provides little information about his adult nightmares. So deep was his despair as a boy that he wished there had been no hell or that he could have been "a Devil" capable of tormenting others rather than being tormented, but "these terrible dreams" finally ceased, and he forgot them. "My pleasures did quickly cut off the remembrance of them, as if they had never been," he later wrote (*GA*, §§7–8). The nightmares resumed as religious concerns began to weigh heavily on his mind sometime after his marriage, apparently triggering the recollection of his troubling boyhood dreams. Recalling his spiritual struggle in his late thirties, he provided only hints of his dream world, but the turmoil he experienced clearly affected his sleep. At times he could not "lie at rest or quiet" (*GA*, §165). The temptation "to *sell and part with Christ*" assaulted him as he lay in bed one morning, possibly after a troubled night. Overwhelmed with "great guilt and fearful despair," he arose and went "moping" into a field (§§139–40). He was overcome with this temptation, he says, for a year, during which time he "was not rid of it one day in a month, no not sometimes one hour in many dayes together" unless he was asleep (§133).

---

[20] Hartmann, *The Nightmare*, 136–37; Hartmann, *Boundaries in the Mind*, 20–48. Fiss regards Hartmann's theory as "highly speculative . . . [but] extremely intriguing, because it all points toward a fundamental property of human nature whose importance has so far been insufficiently appreciated." "'Royal Road'," 405.

[21] Hartmann, *The Nightmare*, 129. For a more general discussion of the link between dreams and creativity, see Anthony Stevens, *Private Myths: Dreams and Dreaming* (Cambridge, MA: Harvard University Press, 1995), 278–91.

[22] Hartmann, *The Nightmare*, 130, 157; Hartmann, *Boundaries in the Mind*, 111–21.

[23] Hartmann, *The Nightmare*, 158.

[24] Cf. ibid., 35, 66–67.

Near the end of his spiritual travail, when Bunyan found substantial solace in the Pauline promise of justification by grace, he likened this experience to that of a person who has "awakened out of some troublesome sleep and dream" (§258). Manifestly, he was speaking from recent experience. In the midst of his struggle, he attained momentary comfort one evening from a biblical insight (Jeremiah 31:3), following which he went to sleep. When he awoke, apparently having slept well, he recalled the previous evening's experience. The fact that he remembered this occurrence more than a decade later suggests the importance he attached during his travail to a night's sleep framed with positive religious thoughts (§190). When at last the spiritual struggle was over, he slept well: "That night was a good night to me, I never had but few better; . . . I could scarce lie in my Bed for joy, and peace, and triumph, thorow Christ" (§263).

Apart from the nightmares that had such an important role in shaping his experiences, Bunyan had relatively little to say about his youth. When he wrote *Grace Abounding* many years later, he depicted his youthful deeds in highly deprecatory terms. Prior to his marriage he claims to have been "the very ring-leader of all the Youth that kept me company, into all manner of vice and ungodliness" (§8). He offers no details, but admits that his offenses, had he been apprehended, would have rendered him subject to legal punishment. Although he liked to swear (§258), he may also have imbibed alcohol too freely or perhaps enjoyed sexual intimacy with one or more village maidens. Of such matters we can only speculate. He had an adventurous spirit, as exemplified when he stunned a venomous adder with a stick, forced open its mouth, and extracted a fang (§12). Although he could "sin with the greatest delight and ease" and take pleasure in his friends' evil ways, his conscience troubled him, especially when he saw others read books on Christian piety; this sight, he recalled, "would be as it were a prison to me"—an interesting analogy inasmuch as he was incarcerated when he wrote this passage. As a boy he palpably had at least a shallow understanding of what such works contained and probably sampled some himself. He was troubled as well when the ostensibly pious acted wickedly, particularly a religious man who swore, causing Bunyan's "heart to ake" (§§10–11).

Thus the boyish Bunyan, troubled for several years by horrendous nightmares, struggled with his conscience even as he flaunted the laws in pursuit of sensual pleasures. A self-described ringleader of free-spirited youth, he also found time for reading. As for so many other young people in the early 1640s, his boyhood abruptly ended when he entered military service. Here, perhaps for the first time, he would learn discipline, and here too he would be exposed to the teachings of religious dissidents who challenged the prevailing tenets and practices of the Church of England.

"Kill, Kill, Was in Mine Ears"[25]: Bunyan in the Military

When civil war erupted in England during the summer of 1642, Bunyan was thirteen years old, but on or shortly before his sixteenth birthday he enlisted or was conscripted into one of the armies. The evidence for his service in a parliamentary garrison is persuasive. The muster rolls for the garrison at Newport Pagnell, Buckinghamshire, list John Bunnion (or Bunion) as a member of Lieutenant-Colonel Richard Cokayne's company from 30 November 1644 through 8 March 1645; the rolls prior to this period are not extant. In December 1644 Cokayne's company numbered 128 "Centinells" (privates) in addition to officers. Although the muster rolls for this company terminate on 8 March 1645, Bunyan's name appears with sixty-six others on the rolls for the company of Major Robert Bolton between 21 April and 27 May of the same year. The principal muster rolls for this company do not survive after this period, but Bolton's company was not disbanded until September 1646.[26]

Bunyan was not legally liable for military service until he reached his sixteenth birthday in November 1644, though he may have volunteered before this. In mid-October 1643 royalist forces of Prince Rupert occupied Bedford and Newport Pagnell in an attempt to compel the earl of Manchester to divert troops from his Lincolnshire campaign. Rupert's move cut Parliament's line of communication to the north and threatened the Eastern Association. From their Newport base, which Sir Lewis Dyve commanded, royalist parties launched raids into Cambridgeshire and Hertfordshire. On the 27th, Dyve retreated after the earl of Essex ordered troops from London under the command of Major-General Philip Skippon to advance on Newport Pagnell. Parliamentary soldiers led by Colonel Thomas Tyrell occupied Newport on the 28th, and the Eastern Association secured Bedford with 600 horse. Fighting continued in the area, as on 4 November when forces from Newport and Northampton engaged royalists near Olney, Buckinghamshire. The youthful Bunyan would have witnessed or heard about these events and perhaps been inspired to volunteer.[27]

[25] HW, 3.

[26] Anne Laurence, "Bunyan and the Parliamentary Army," in JBHE, ed. Laurence, Owens, and Sim, 19–20. Bolton was raising a company in late January 1645, at which time officers in other units were transferring some of their men to him. Bunyan, however, was in Cokayne's company until at least 8 March. The Letter Books 1644–45 of Sir Samuel Luke: Parliamentary Governor of Newport Pagnell, ed. H. G. Tibbutt (London: Her Majesty's Stationery Office, 1963), 424.

[27] Clive Holmes, The Eastern Association in the English Civil War (New York: Cambridge University Press, 1974), 103, 105; Frederick William Bull, A History of Newport Pagnell (Kettering, Northants.: W. E. and J. Goss, 1900), 156–57; "The Papers of Sir Will.

Bunyan probably became a member of the Newport garrison sometime after Sir Samuel Luke was appointed governor of the town on 25 January 1644. By 8 June Luke had a commission to raise 1,200 foot for the garrison, which was also supposed to have 300 horse, but inadequate finances and poor cooperation from the Eastern Association plagued his efforts. Four months later, he complained to Essex that he had fewer than 600 troops in the town, and he wanted to enlist 500 more by the end of October. As he explained to his father, Sir Oliver Luke, MP for Bedfordshire, Sir Samuel hoped for a better response from that county, which was expected to pay £750 a month toward the garrison's maintenance; should these funds not materialize, troops from another region could be quartered in the county for its defense. (Indeed, the Committee of Both Kingdoms wanted Manchester to station more troops at Newport Pagnell during the winter.) By 16 November Bedfordshire was nearly £5,000 behind its its payments, though its contingent was 300 greater than the 225 required. These men, however, had completed their two months of service and were "importunate to be withdrawn," at least partly because the county had stopped paying them by 24 November. Three weeks earlier Sir Samuel had warned that without funds from Bedfordshire the soldiers faced starvation, and by month's end he feared mutiny.[28]

Between 12 October and 26 November 1644 Luke welcomed more than 200 foot, with Bunyan likely among them. He may have joined this garrison in part because of family connections; his paternal uncle Edward may have been the Edward Bynion who was the personal servant of Sir Samuel's father, Sir Oliver Luke. In any event, Sir Samuel found the new Bedfordshire contingent interesting; they "make a fair show and tell you strange things," he reported to his father.[29] Was Bunyan's powerful imagination already at work relating strange tales?

---

Boteler, 1642–1655," ed. Herbert Fowler, *PBHRS* 18 (1936): 3; *A Letter from Colonell Harvie, to His Excellency Robert Earle of Essex* (London, 1643), sigs. A2r–A4r; *The Happy Successe of the Parliaments Armie at Newport and Some Other Places* (London, 1643), sigs. A2r–A4v.

[28] Luke, *Letter Books*, 22, 25, 27–28, 37, 54, 56, 74, 82, 84, 91, 94–95, 593; BL, Add. MSS 61,681, fol. 111r; *CSPD, 1644–45*, 66; *An Ordinance of the Lords and Commons Assembled in Parliament: For the Erecting and Maintaining of a Garrison at Newport-Pagnell* (London, 1643), 1–3, 6; Bull, *History*, 160–61, 163. At £750 a month, Bedfordshire's assessment was the highest. Altogether the garrison was supposed to receive £4,000 each month. Through 1644 the parliamentary war effort relied heavily on the excise, which had been introduced the previous year, but beginning in 1645 the monthly assessment surpassed the excise as the primary source of funds. Local regiments and garrisons, and the New Model Army beginning in September 1645, sometimes had recourse to free quarter, but this was very unpopular with the inhabitants because it effectively meant double taxation. Ian Gentles, *The New Model Army in England, Ireland and Scotland, 1645–1653* (Oxford: Blackwell, 1992), 28–31. For Luke see *BDBR*, s.v.

[29] Luke, *Letter Books*, 25, 96, 99 (quoted). For Edward Bynion see ibid., 186, 438, 476.

The conditions under which Bunyan served were grim, and morale must normally have been low, though such trying conditions probably increased the troopers' sense of camaraderie. The foot were fifteen days behind in their pay on 29 November, and few had money with which to purchase food or clothing. In the space of a week, fifteen files of musketeers, dismayed by the lack of pay, left the garrison. Notwithstanding the monetary problems, Luke continued his efforts to attain the assigned goal of 1,200 foot and 300 horse, which further exacerbated conditions. His second-in-command, Lieutenant-Colonel Cokayne, reported to the Bedfordshire Committee in January that the troopers were losing respect for their officers: "We having lived so long and wholly subsisted on our credits, . . . are now become men of no reputation and of no command amongst our own soldiers." The men were pawning their clothes and "bands" for bread. By mid-January no one had been paid for fourteen weeks, though the officers were assisting the troops with loans. Eight months behind in its payments on 22 January, Bedfordshire bore a heavy share of responsibility for the dismal circumstances in which Bunyan served. By late January the townsfolk were refusing to house soldiers in their homes because the troops owed so much money. As space became a problem, soldiers slept "3 and 3 in a bed," and in one pathetic case, two soldiers shared a single pair of breeches, "so that when one was up, the other must of necessity be in his bed." The cavalry had neither boots for themselves nor horseshoes for their mounts, and Luke urgently requested muskets, pikes, and "horsearms"; 150 pairs of pistols and 150 backs and breasts had been sent in November.[30] The royalists tried to take advantage of these conditions after Charles received word on 26 January from supporters in Newport that at most 200 soldiers were in its garrison and that half the defensive works had collapsed. Only inclement weather prevented the king from mounting an assault on Newport, though the scare prompted Parliament to send £500 to Luke.[31]

Because of the shortages in the garrison, two troops and a number of dragoons briefly mutinied in early February 1645, but still the wretched conditions continued. "The great arrears of the monthly tax in Bedfordshire have put our troopers so far behindhand here," complained Sir Samuel a few days later, "that we have been forced to eat up the inhabitants in these 3 hundreds that they neither have horsemeat for any, or corn for themselves to sow."[32] So scarce was food for Bunyan and his comrades that Luke constantly struggled to keep Eastern As-

---

[30] Ibid., 100, 106–7, 119, 121–22 (quoted), 124, 421–22, 600, 602; *CJ*, 3:699. For the problem of shortages of food and clothing for soldiers, see Charles Carlton, *Going to the Wars: The Experience of the British Civil Wars, 1638–1651* (New York: Routledge, 1992), 95–97.

[31] *Weekly Account* (29 January–5 February 1645).

[32] Luke, *Letter Books*, 128–29, 134–35 (quoted); *CSPD, 1644–45*, 287, 319.

sociation troops from foraging in the Newport area, and on one occasion he was even prepared to order his men to take up arms to prevent Manchester's soldiers from quartering at nearby Chicheley.[33] Clothing was in such short supply that some troopers had to borrow attire, while others had to remain in bed during the winter because they had no coats. Not surprisingly, the soldiers sought relief by seizing the money and sometimes even clothing from the growing number of royalist prisoners confined in the town. Relief finally came after Parliament learned of Charles' plans to attack Newport; the House of Commons sent £500, and on 10 February the Lords approved an ordinance to strengthen the garrison. On the 22nd, the Committee of Both Kingdoms, noting the soldiers' "extreame necessity" and Newport Pagnell's dangerous condition, ordered the Bedfordshire Committee to pay arrears. To repair the town's defensive works, Luke requisitioned 600 laborers and twenty-six carts from Bedfordshire. From Buckinghamshire came 100 loads of timber and 2,000 poles, but the construction, though essential, further strained the garrison's meager resources. By March 1645, between 3,000 and 4,000 workers were repairing the fortifications.[34]

The dawning of spring found the garrison in which Bunyan served almost at full strength, with 1,000 foot and 300 horse, but still facing staggering shortages. "The lamentations of the soldiers here," wrote Sir Samuel, "are so great through misery and want, that my pen is not able to express it." His best troop had weapons for only forty men, his cavalry lacked saddles and horseshoes, and his soldiers in general were still short of boots and attire. In April forty-one troopers protested to Sir Samuel that if they quartered in the countryside, the people would cut their throats to obtain relief when royalists approached. At Elstow fair the following month, violence erupted between some of Major Christopher Ennis' men and local folk, inciting fear as soldiers threatened to wreak vengeance. At this time Bunyan was serving in Bolton's troop, but his father may have been among the poor Elstow men whom the soldiers threatened. Relations with some of the local aristocrats were also tense as troopers from the Newport garrison hunted without permission in Salcey Forest, prompting a complaint from Sir Richard Samuel, and poached deer in Robert Lord Bruce's park.[35] Delays in receiving their money continued to plague Bunyan and his fellow troopers, causing the Newport Committee to protest in May about "the extreordinarie clamour of souldiers and work men for want of paie." So serious was the problem that Par-

[33] Luke, *Letter Books*, 79, 97, 117–18, 126, 136, 138, 413–14, 419.

[34] Ibid., 201, 421, 606, 614; *CJ*, 4:70; *LJ*, 7:180, 184; BL, Add. MSS 61,682, fol. 1r; H. Roundell, "The Garrison of Newport Pagnell During the Civil Wars," *Records of Buckinghamshire* 2 (1863): 299–300, 304–5.

[35] Luke, *Letter Books*, 223, 236 (quoted), 246, 514–15, 544, 584; Hill, *Tinker*, 48.

liament itself passed an ordinance in September 1645 to remedy the problem, although difficulties continued.[36]

Boredom and inactivity generally plagued garrison life, much of which was taken up with training and guard duty. Bunyan probably learned how to employ a musket, the use of which increased during the civil wars, especially as manufacturing costs fell. To be effective, muskets had to be fired at close range—near enough for a shooter to see the whites of his target's eyes—but they were unreliable, with a misfire rate of 12 percent (18 percent in wet weather). Bunyan may also have been equipped with a hand gun; in *The Holy War* only a shooter's poor aim saves Lord Understanding from being shot with a harquebus, a small-caliber firearm that required minimal training to use and was accurate up to a hundred meters. Bunyan certainly would have received training in the use of a sword. In warfare, "*the shaking of a sword is fear'd,*" and Mansoul "*saw the swords of fighting men made red.*" Bunyan may never have learned to use a pike, a somewhat cumbersome weapon that was between 16½ and 18 feet in length, made of ash, and had an iron tip. Yet he would have at least observed its use, for the House of Commons directed that 150 pikes (and 250 muskets) be sent to the Newport garrison in June 1645 while Bunyan was almost certainly there. Judging from *The Holy War*, Bunyan found the sword more interesting than the pike, perhaps because the latter was only effective when used by well-ordered, sizable units, whereas the sword, at least in literary works, provided greater visual drama and opportunity for individual daring. In practical terms, swords and guns, not pikes, were needed to guard garrisons. The monotonous routine of drilling and guard duty was broken when troopers went on patrol in search of the enemy or to harass civilians who supported the other side. The danger in going on patrol should not be underestimated, for 47 percent of the estimated deaths that occurred in England during the civil wars happened in minor skirmishes and small-scale sieges. (Major sieges claimed 24 percent, and major battles, 15 percent.)[37]

Although some biographers have assumed that Bunyan never participated in the fighting, this is not necessarily so. He may never have served in the small units that left Newport Pagnell to search for royalists, for these generally comprised only horse. With the rest of the garrison, he would have experienced the

[36] BL, Add. MSS 61,682, fols. 23r (quoted), 27r, 79r; *An Ordinance of the Lords and Commons Assembled in Parliament, for the Maintenance and Pay of the Garrisons of Newport Pagnel, Bedford, Lyn Regis* (London, 1645).

[37] *HW,* 4 (quoted), 61; Geoffrey Parker, *The Military Revolution: Military Innovation and the Rise of the West, 1500–1800* (Cambridge: Cambridge University Press, 1988), 16–17; Carlton, *Going to the Wars,* 99–100, 152, 204, 206–7; *CJ,* 4:165. Three months earlier, in March 1645, the Commons had ordered pistols, carbines, and saddles for the cavalry at Newport. *CJ,* 4:70.

excitement when some of these parties returned with prisoners, as did those led by Captains Thomas Evans and Henry Andrewes in March 1645; the former brought back fifty captives and the latter seventeen.[38] Such scenes may have been in Bunyan's mind when he wrote the passage in *The Holy War* recounting how Lord Willbewill's company captured some of Captain Boanerges' soldiers and took them into Mansoul; "they had not lain long in durance, but it began to be noised about the Streets of the Town," much as news of Evans' and Andrewes' exploits would have circulated rapidly in Newport Pagnell (*HW*, 51–52). Occasionally, the foot left the garrison on military missions, as in January 1645 when the Committee of State ordered 300 of them to march to Farnham, Surrey. Although Cokayne protested to the Bedfordshire Committee that his men were unfit to do so, they went anyway. Commanded by Captain James Bladwell, they traveled via Aylesbury. Most were surprisingly cheerful, perhaps because the venture provided a change from the bleak existence at Newport and offered an opportunity to forage en route. Cokayne was able to supply them with at least fifty pounds of gunpowder, eight skeins of match, and 800 bullets.[39]

Troops from the Newport garrison became involved in two significant engagements in May and early June 1645—the parliamentary siege of Oxford and the royalist attack on Leicester. On 3 May the Committee of Both Kingdoms renewed its order commanding Luke to send 300 foot to Aylesbury where they and 400 foot from Northampton were to rendezvous with troops under Major-General Richard Browne and ultimately with Sir Thomas Fairfax's army. This left Luke with 500 men and concerns that more would leave at the harvest season. He therefore actively recruited new men, notwithstanding serious problems with the pay and support of those already in the garrison. Moreover, on 21 May he had to assign 100 foot to convoy money to Grafton Regis, Northamptonshire.[40] The previous day Fairfax's forces approached Oxford with 5,000 to 6,000 infantry and 4,800 cavalry, capturing a party of horse near the town. On the 25th he mounted batteries and "made some great shot into the Town." A report from the parliamentary army at Oxford filed on 31 May indicated that "many shot[s] have been made, both from us to the citie, and from the citie at us." The parliamentary troops directed the barrage at least in part against Christ Church and the marketplace, "and some hurt is conceived to be done by a cannon Bullet against the Schooles."[41]

[38] Luke, *Letter Books*, 105, 114, 413, 420–21; *Weekly Account* (5–13 March 1645), [4]; *Mercurius Civicus* (20–27 March 1645), 868.

[39] Luke, *Letter Books*, 602–5.

[40] *CSPD, 1644–45*, 453, 458, 460, 472; Luke, *Letter Books*, 261–63, 283, 290.

[41] *Weekly Account* (21–27 May 1645), [1, 7]; ibid. (28 May–4 June 1645), [6]; Luke, *Letter Books*, 286; Maurice Ashley, *The English Civil War*, rev. ed. (Gloucester: Alan Sutton, 1990), 124–25.

While Fairfax besieged Oxford, royalist troops attacked Leicester on 28 May. Soldiers from Newport under the command of Major Ennis defended the "Newe Worke" on Leicester's south side, twice repulsing enemy advances. On the 31st the royalists prevailed, and Sir Robert Pye formally surrendered on 1 June. The defenders sustained heavy losses, but Ennis and at least some of his men were among the survivors.[42] Bunyan's first biographer, who published anonymously, claimed the young soldier barely escaped death in the siege of Leicester. The key passage, found in *Grace Abounding*, is Bunyan's only substantive comment about his military service:

> When I was a Souldier, I with others were drawn out to go to such a place to besiege it; but when I was just ready to go, one of the company desired to go in my room, to which, when I had consented he took my place; and coming to the siege, as he stood Sentinel, he was shot into the head with a Musket bullet and died. (*GA*, §13)

According to the anonymous biographer, Bunyan was summoned to serve with the parliamentary troops who were besieging Leicester in June.[43] As we have seen, however, the attack took place between 28 and 31 May when royalists—not parliamentarians—assaulted Leicester. This biographer therefore erred both in his dating and in his confusion of attackers and defenders. In June parliamentary forces under Sir Thomas Fairfax retook Leicester following their victory at Naseby, but Lord Hastings surrendered without firing a shot,[44] so the sentinel who took Bunyan's place cannot have died in the city's recapture.

As the assault on Leicester reached its climax, on 31 May the Committee of Both Kingdoms ordered the dispatch of another 400 foot from Newport Pagnell to the siege of Oxford, the rather sizable scale of which is indicated by Fairfax's requisitioning of 500 barrels of gunpowder, 600 mortar shells, 1,000 hand grenades, 40 tons of match, 30 tons of bullets, 200 scaling ladders, and 2,000 spades. Following the loss of Leicester, Fairfax lifted the siege of Oxford by 3 June in order to pursue the royalist army. In the meantime the Committee of Both Kingdoms instructed Luke to bolster the Newport garrison with recruits from the country and "fetch in provisions for horse and foot." When the siege was lifted, Luke pressed Major-General Skippon for the return of his infantry, but Skippon

[42] *Weekly Account* (28 May–4 June 1645), [6–7]; Roundell, "Garrison," 354. Ennis was back in Luke's service by 15 June as the result of a prisoner exchange. Roundell, ibid.

[43] *Account of the Life and Actions of Mr. John Bunyan* (London, 1692), *ad cal.* The Pilgrim's *Progress*, 3rd Part (London, 1693), 17–18. This writer further errs in asserting that Bunyan entered the military to support himself and his small family, for his marriage postdated his service in the army. The publication of this biography with the spurious third part of *The Pilgrim's Progress* further undermines its credibility.

[44] Gentles, *New Model Army*, 61.

sent them to Abingdon. In mid-June Luke had fewer than 600 foot and one troop of horse.[45] In these circumstances, Bunyan may well have continued in the service, having no compelling reason to leave. In fact, he may have been among the 700 men from Newport Pagnell who participated in the siege of Oxford (though not on the day his comrade was slain). If so, the Thames might have been the "crick of the Sea" into which he fell and nearly drowned (*GA*, §12). Moreover, if there is any truth to the story about Bunyan's narrow escape when a compatriot took his place during a siege, it must have been at Oxford rather than Leicester.

Bunyan's activities between the spring of 1645 and June 1647 are unrecorded, though he probably continued to serve in Major Bolton's company until it was disbanded in September 1646. After Fairfax raised the siege of Oxford, he marched to Newport Pagnell to rendezvous with Colonel Bartholomew Vermuyden. If Bunyan had been at Oxford, he returned to a garrison that continued to experience financial problems. Cokayne feared the unpaid troops would mutiny in the summer of 1645, and in October the Committee of Both Kingdoms observed that the Newport garrison was in "great arrear of pay and much indebted in the town, which cannot give them further credit." The threat of desertion remained a serious concern. Moreover, because the garrison now had no horse, royalist cavalry roamed the countryside and even entered the town.[46]

In August 1646 Parliament ordered the demolition of the defensive works at Newport Pagnell, with officers and soldiers of both horse and foot assisting in the task.[47] Inasmuch as Bunyan was probably still in the army, he would have participated in the partial dismantling of the fortifications. Such an experience seems to be reflected in *The Holy War*:

> The Prince gave a charge that the three strong holds . . . in *Mansoul*, should be demolished, and utterly pulled down. . . . But this was long in doing, because of the

[45] BL, Add. MSS 61,682, fol. 25r; *CSPD, 1644–45*, 550, 552 (quoted), 560, 570; Luke, *Letter Books*, 299, 301, 305, 309, 321; Carlton, *Going to the Wars*, 167; Roundell, "Garrison," 355; *Weekly Account* (4–11 June 1645), [1]. In contrast to the approximately 11,000 men who besieged Oxford, Essex had attacked Reading in April 1643 with 4,600 men, whereas Prince Rupert had assaulted Bristol three months later with an army of 14,000 to 20,000. Peter Young and Wilfrid Emberton, *Sieges of the Great Civil War, 1642–1646* (London: Bell and Hyman, 1978), 21, 28–29. In late May a troop from the Newport garrison under the command of Major Ennis sustained casualties when it was attacked at Tingewick, near Buckingham. Luke, *Letter Books*, 295, 297.

[46] "Civil War Papers of Boteler," 24; *CSPD, 1645–47*, 208.

[47] *An Ordinance of the Lords and Commons Assembled in Parliament: For the Sleighting and Demolishing of Severall Garrisons Under the Power of the Parliament* (London, 1646); "Civil War Papers of Boteler," 31–32.

largegeness of the places, and because the stones, the timber, the iron, and all rubbish was to be carried without the Town. (*HW*, 118–19)

Unable to pay the arrears of many provincial soldiers as well as New Model troops, Parliament sought volunteers for service in Ireland, where rebellion had been raging since October 1641. Volunteers were offered one month's pay upon enlistment plus arrears and another month's pay at the place of rendezvous, whereas the rest of the troops were disbanded.[48] Bunyan appears to have chosen the latter option.

In March 1647 Parliament decided to send the New Model regiments of Colonels Robert Hammond and William Herbert to Ireland under the former's command, but the majority of the troops refused, demanding a voice in the selection of their commander, payment of arrears, and indemnity for wartime actions. Hammond supported his men in their refusal, but approximately 400, reputedly plied with alcohol by Captain Charles O'Hara, agreed to serve. O'Hara's company, which was part of Hammond's regiment, received orders in late April to march to Olney, Newport Pagnell, and Bedford. Parliament unsuccessfullly commanded Hammond's regiment to disband at Bedford on 13 June, though volunteers for Ireland were to march to Newport and await instructions. As an enticement, volunteers were offered two weeks' pay plus two months of arrears.[49] By this point Bunyan had re-enlisted, for his name appears on the muster roll for 17 June as one of seventy-nine privates in O'Hara's company.[50] He may have done so for financial reasons or out of a sense of adventure. Whatever his motives, he never made it to Ireland, for on 21 July Parliament disbanded the regiment of Colonel Owen O'Connolly, which included O'Hara's company.[51]

The disbandment of O'Connolly's provisional regiment, which ended Bunyan's military career, occurred in the context of the struggle between the political Presbyterians and the New Model Army. In May 1647 the Presbyterians in Parliament had attempted to disband the New Model foot, beginning with Fairfax's regiment, and to split the army by enticing some soldiers to volunteer for service in Ireland. Bunyan, of course, was among them. But this plan was undermined

[48] *An Ordinance of the Lords and Commons . . . for the Sleighting . . . of Severall Garrisons.*

[49] *CJ*, 5:109; *Historical Collections of Private Passages of State*, ed. John Rushworth, 6 vols. (London, 1680–1701), 6:463, 466, 468, 493; *Calendar of State Papers, Ireland, 1647–60*, 751.

[50] Laurence, "Bunyan and the Parliamentary Army," 24, 28.

[51] *LJ*, 9:343; *Calendar of State Papers, Ireland, 1647–60*, 769; Sir Charles Firth and Godfrey Davies, *The Regimental History of Cromwell's Army* (Oxford: Clarendon Press, 1940), 350–51.

when junior officers and many of the rank and file staunchly opposed service in Ireland until issues of arrears, regular pay, indemnity, and compensation for maimed soldiers and families of the slain had been resolved. Fairfax's own regiment mutinied at Chelmsford on 31 May, and several days later the army seized the king by authority of "the soldiery of the army," as Cornet George Joyce told Charles. About 8 June the army formally demanded the impeachment of eleven prominent Presbyterian MPs, who averted a crisis by fleeing on the 27th. Nearly three weeks later, on 16 July, Fairfax successfully sought the House of Commons' approval to unite all land forces in England under one command, which the Commons willingly vested in him. The following day the senior officers submitted the terms for a settlement with the king, the Heads of the Proposals, to the Council of the Army. Now clearly on the defensive, Parliament disbanded Colonel O'Connolly's provisional regiment on the 21st, effectively sealing the triumph of those who opposed going to Ireland before their grievances were settled. Among the victors was Colonel Hammond, whose regiment participated in Fairfax's occupation of London the first week in August.[52]

Because Bunyan had re-enlisted to fight under a commander loyal to Parliament rather than the New Model, he was no longer part of the military as it debated a wider franchise at Putney, fought and won a second civil war, purged the House of Commons, and oversaw the king's execution. The officers under whom Bunyan had served were not among the radicals who played a key role in establishing a republic. After Luke surrendered his command on 26 June 1645 in keeping with the Self-Denying Ordinance, he sat in the House of Commons until Colonel Thomas Pride purged him. O'Connolly salvaged his military career, becoming colonel of the Antrim regiment and serving with Cromwell in Ireland until he died in battle in 1649.[53]

Bunyan's military experience had a lasting impact on him, not least because of the numerous views to which he was exposed as troops moved in and out of the region. Manchester's foot were in Bedford in January 1645, and the following month Luke had to find space in Newport Pagnell to quarter Manchester's dragoons. This was possible because Luke simultaneously loaned a company of foot to the town of Northampton. Moreover, in 1644 Luke had sent 200 men to aid Sir William Waller, following this with 300 men in 1645, both times at the earl of Northumberland's command. In June 1645 Cromwell's forces passed through

[52] Gentles, *New Model Army*, 156–57, 166–67, 169–70, 180; Mark A. Kishlansky, *The Rise of the New Model Army* (Cambridge: Cambridge University Press, 1979), 198–99, 218, 228–34, 243–49; Firth and Davies, *Regimental History*, 351.
[53] Firth and Davies, *Regimental History*, 653–54.

Newport en route to Bedford.[54] Even if Bunyan remained in the Newport garrison throughout his military service, he would have been in contact with troops from other units, though not always on friendly terms. Notwithstanding their common opposition to the royalists, antipathy characterized relations between Sir Samuel's men and those of the New Model Army. Luke himself had no respect for the latter, partly because its officer corps was open to men of talent and thus, in his view, was hardly distinguishable from common soldiers. Nor did he approve of their behavior: "I think these New Modellers knead all their dough with ale, for I never saw so many drunk in my life in so short a time."[55]

## "The Religion of the Times"[56]: Early Religious Influences

During his army years Bunyan was directly exposed to the intense religious struggle between proponents of Presbyterian reform within the established church and radical sectaries, many of whom were outspoken separatists. Sir Samuel was a Presbyterian who had no love for sectaries or the ungodly; indeed, he virtually identified the two, warning that sectaries endangered the kingdom and practiced wickedness in the guise of godliness. On 31 March 1645 he resolved to require all men in Newport Pagnell to take the oath to the Solemn League and Covenant and perform "those services we owe to God and are daily practised amongst us" or be banished from the town.[57] Bunyan, then, may have subscribed to the Covenant.

The chaplain of Luke's regiment was Thomas Ford, a relative, who served from November 1644 until the following spring. Ford had been one of three academics at Oxford who were summoned before Charles I in 1631 and expelled for their outspoken criticism of Arminianism. In March 1645 Ford became a member of the Westminster Assembly, and he was of sufficient stature to preach fast sermons in the House of Commons on 28 May 1645 and the House of Lords on 29 April 1646. As a Calvinist, Ford presumably made his views known during his ministry in Newport Pagnell, where his congregation numbered 1,500.[58] Nor was

---

[54]Luke, *Letter Books*, 121, 129, 247, 313, 421.

[55]Ibid., 279, 311 (quoted).

[56]*GA*, §16.

[57]Luke, *Letter Books*, 215, 226 (quoted).

[58]*BDBR, s.v.* Thomas Ford; Anne Laurence, *Parliamentary Army Chaplains, 1642–1651* (Woodbridge, Suffolk: Boydell Press for the Royal Historical Society, 1990), 127; John F. Wilson, *Pulpit in Parliament: Puritanism During the English Civil Wars, 1640–1648* (Princeton, NJ: Princeton University Press, 1969), 245, 247; Luke, *Letter Books*, 85; BL, Stowe MSS 190, fol. 280; Dewey D. Wallace, Jr., *Puritans and Predestination: Grace in English Protestant Theology, 1525–1695* (Chapel Hill: University of North Carolina Press, 1982), 95;

Ford alone, for seven "able divines" labored in Newport during the fall of 1644, and between them preached two sermons on Sunday and another on Thursday. At the changing of the guard each morning Bunyan would also have heard prayers and the reading of a chapter from Scripture.[59] Ford's sermons and possibly those of other Calvinist ministers may have been Bunyan's first exposure to the predestinarian dogma that would trouble him during his spiritual crisis in the mid-1650s and find expression in his first substantive theological work, *The Doctrine of the Law and Grace Unfolded* (1659).

At Newport Pagnell Bunyan also came in contact with substantially different religious tenets, the propagators of which were sectaries who troubled Sir Samuel Luke. Among them was an unidentified captain and former silk-weaver who refused to subscribe to the Solemn League and Covenant on conscientious grounds.[60] On 13 November 1644 Luke reported to Stephen Marshall, the prominent parliamentary preacher, that he had banned sectarian assemblies in Newport Pagnell, though the dissidents held conventicles near the town several times a week and had "growne soe insolent that if there be not some course taken with them, there will bee noe abiding for any Godly able conscientious Devines in these parts." There were "so many sevrall sorts" of these sectaries, he claimed, that he had insufficient space in his letter to list them.[61] The following March Luke discharged Robert Nicholls from the garrison "for disaffection to the service, and perverseness to all religious exercises." Nicholls may have been the sectary whom the Council of War banished and whose readmission was sought by Cornelius Holland, MP for New Windsor. Luke protested vigorously, insisting that such sectaries denied both the established church and its ministers, likening the church to a den of thieves. "Impiety is grown to such a height in this town that my eyes can no longer endure the sight of it nor my ears the hearing." If he failed to cleanse Newport Pagnell of sectaries, Luke warned Holland, God would destroy it as he had Sodom and Gomorrah. Women, he alleged, were bearing children but claiming they had not had sexual intercourse, and men and women "can take one another's words and lie together and insist it not to be adultery." This libertinism he blamed on sectaries who allegedly undermined traditional morality.[62]

The most prominent sectarian preachers to visit Newport Pagnell while Bun-

---

Nicholas Tyacke, *Anti-Calvinists: The Rise of English Arminianism, c. 1590–1640* (Oxford: Clarendon Press, 1987), 82.

[59] Luke, *Letter Books*, 42.

[60] Ibid., 43.

[61] BL, Stowe MSS 190, fol. 280. For Marshall see *BDBR, s.v.*

[62] Luke, *Letter Books*, 193 (quoted), 197 (quoted), 226. For Holland, see *BDBR, s.v.*

yan was there were William Erbery and Paul Hobson. An Oxford graduate (B.A., Brasenose College, 1623), Erbery had links with the Welsh Independents Walter Cradock, Morgan Llwyd, and Vavasor Powell. During the civil war he served as a chaplain in Skippon's regiment and later, during 1646, in Sir Richard Ingoldsby's regiment when it garrisoned Oxford. During these years Erbery reputedly denied the deity of Christ, advocated universal redemption, and urged his listeners to await the return of the Holy Spirit rather than gather churches and baptize believers. Christ's first command, Erbery insisted, was not to baptize but to await the Spirit and its baptism, for "no preaching the Gospel, nor Baptism with Water in a Gospel-way could be, but by the Holy Spirit sent down from Heaven." Without the infusion of the Spirit there could be neither true baptism nor effectual gospel preaching, both of which he averred the Baptists had failed to attain. Erbery did not limit his attack to the Baptists but castigated "all outward Forms, and *Church-Ordinances*" as "the flesh of the Whore" that resulted from the loss of the Holy Spirit's fire and baptism. His message was a clarion call to recover the baptism and fire of the Spirit that had kept the primitive church pure. "As a popular preacher," Geoffrey Nuttall observes, "Erbury was exceptional."[63] Echoes of his message are found in Bunyan's writings, especially the doctrinal tracts composed between 1672 and 1674.

A Particular (Calvinistic) Baptist and, before the war, a barber-surgeon in London, Hobson had attained the rank of captain by the time he and Captain Richard Beaumont, with Colonel Charles Fleetwood's permission, arrived at Newport Pagnell in June 1645. Hobson already had a degree of notoriety, having been denounced the previous December by Sion College, London, along with such dissidents as John Milton, Roger Williams, the Socinian John Biddle, and the Antinomian John Saltmarsh. The heresiographer Thomas Edwards condemned the conventicles of Hobson, Erbery, and others as "the nurseries of all Errours and Heresies, very Pest-houses." Edwards later reported that soldiers in Beaumont's troop had baptized a horse in the Yaxley parish church, Huntingdonshire, after first urinating in the font. Although Luke permitted Hobson and Beaumont to preach for a week when they first came to Newport, he changed his mind after people attended their meeting rather than the official thanksgiving service for the victory at Naseby. Luke had the two "Annabaptisticall Companions" arrested and sent to Fairfax after they complained of harsh treatment at the hands of Luke's officers. But Fairfax sided with Hobson, who served in his regi-

---

[63] *BDBR*, s.v. William Erbery; William Erbery, *The Testimony of William Erbery, Left upon Record from the Saints of Succeeding Ages* (London, 1658), 300–301, 304; Geoffrey F. Nuttall, *The Holy Spirit in Puritan Faith and Experience* (Oxford: Basil Blackwell, 1946), 99 (quoted).

ment, and Beaumont, insisting that they receive reparations and that the officers responsible for their maltreatment be cashiered.[64]

Given the controversy surrounding Hobson's visit to Newport Pagnell, Bunyan was probably among the curious who heard him preach. Hobson subsequently published the sermons that got him into trouble under the title *A Garden Inclosed, and Wisdom Justified Only of Her Children* (1647). In them he espoused a number of key principles subsequently embraced by Bunyan, thus raising the possibility that he may have exercised a significant, if delayed, influence on Bunyan's thinking. Knowing how to read the Bible in Hebrew and Greek was unimportant, Hobson argued, for the key to understanding it was knowing Christ, "the Originall"; experience rather than reason is "the deepest Fountaine." The authority of truth must prevail over reason, and only those who recognize the supremacy of spiritual truth and experience Christ within themselves are fit to preach. Repudiating the notion of a national church with membership determined by residency in a parish, Hobson regarded the true visible church as a voluntary society of visible saints. Damning the Church of England as "a confused wildernesse," he denounced it as a beggarly religion of the letter rather than the Spirit. As Bunyan would later do, he juxtaposed the Church of England with the church of Christ; the former "breeds and bringeth forth that which opposeth and endeavours to destroy the Church of Christ." He also played down the importance of the sacraments, insisting that church membership is based on oneness with Christ, not submission to ordinances. Hobson may have been the first person to introduce Bunyan to typology, for he contended that the church of the Jews was a type of Christ, and that it had ended with his physical coming. Those who restrained "soules possessed with Truth" from proclaiming it were denounced by Hobson, much as Bunyan would subsequently do on many occasions. Hobson castigated those who "endeavour rather with clubs and staves to make men conformable without light," but he also stressed that "*Christ* never is advanced more by saints, then when men persecute and oppose saints."[65] The themes of two of

[64] Luke, *Letter Books*, 322–24, 328–29, 582–84, 586, 622; Thomas Edwards, *Gangraena* (London 1646), pt. 3, pp. 17–18; BL, Egerton MSS 786, fols. 20r (quoted), 25r; Greaves, *SR*, 134–35, 137–38. In 1647 John Lilburne and Sir Lewis Dyve used Hobson as an intermediary between the king and such radicals as Major Francis White and the Levellers, who were concerned that Cromwell would support the Scots' aim to impose presbyterianism on England. In October of that year, after moving through Dunstable en route to Newcastle, Hobson's regiment demonstrated on behalf of the agitators' demands for radical constitutional and religious reform. Bunyan would surely have heard about this. Sir Lewis Dyve, "The Tower of London Letter-Book of Sir Lewis Dyve, 1646–47," *PBHRS* 38 (1958): 58–59, 91–92, 94. For Hobson see Greaves, *SR*, 133–56; *New DNB, s.v.*; for White see *BDBR, s.v.*

[65] Paul Hobson, *A Garden Inclosed, and Wisdom Justified Only of Her Children* (Lon-

Bunyan's early works, the supremacy of grace over law and the necessity of relying solely on Scripture as a guide to worship were also proclaimed by Hobson.
The affinity between so many of Bunyan's fundamental tenets and Hobson's
views suggests influence.[66]

Perhaps it was also at Newport that Hobson preached a sermon reported to
Edwards in which the theme was one subsequently reiterated in Bunyan's *Grace
Abounding*:

> I was once as legal as any of you can be, I durst never a morning but pray, nor never a
> night before I went to Bed but pray; I durst not eat a bit of Bread but I gave thankes; I
> daily prayed and wept for my sinnes, so that I had almost wept out my Eyes with sor-
> row for sin: But I am perswaded when I used all these duties, I had not one jot of God
> in me.[67]

The thrust of Hobson's message was the insufficiency of traditional religiosity,
but he preached and wrote as well against paedobaptism, insisting that only believers should be baptized. This was the thesis he defended in *The Fallacy of Infants Baptisme Discovered* (1645). Although he espoused the doctrine of predestination, he insisted that the gospel be preached to everyone, as Bunyan would
later do in such works as *Come, & Welcome, to Jesus Christ*.

Bunyan also may have heard a disputation concerning infant baptism between John Gibbs and Richard Carpenter that A. G. Matthews has dated about
1647. In Carpenter's published account of the disputation, *The Anabaptist Washt
and Washt, and Shrunk in the Washing* (1653), he referred to Gibbs as being
"unsetled in *place*, and (it seems), in *person* professing for *Anabaptism*." Since
Gibbs became the vicar at Newport Pagnell on 13 July 1652, his unsettled state had
to have predated this appointment. The son of Samuel Gibbs, a Bedford cooper,
John Gibbs (born 15 June 1627) was seventeen months older than Bunyan. Indeed, the two boys may have been in school together during their early years,
though Gibbs went on to Sidney Sussex College, Cambridge, in 1645 and graduated B.A. in 1648.[68] Carpenter too was a Cambridge man (King's College), though

---

don, 1647), 5–6, 8–9 (quoted), 11–13, 15, 22, 38–39 (quoted), 41, 44–45 (quoted), 90
(quoted), 92 (quoted).

[66]Ibid., 22; P[aul] H[obson], *A Discoverie of Truth: Presented to the Sons of Truth* (n.p.,
1645), 6–8, 75–77. In *The Fallacy of Infants Baptisme Discovered* (London, 1645) he explained the ceremonial law as a type that "did in a dark way hold forth *Christ*" (3).

[67]Thomas Edwards, *Gangraena*, 2nd ed. (London, 1646), 122.

[68] Richard Carpenter, *The Anabaptist Washt and Washt, and Shrunk in the Washing*
(London, 1653), sig. A2v (quoted); *Calamy Revised, s.v.* John Gibbs; Frederick William
Bull, "John Gibbs," *Transactions of the Congregational Historical Society* 10 (1927–29): 82–
83. For Gibbs see also Maurice F. Hewett, "John Gibbs, 1627–1699," *Baptist Quarterly* 3
(1926–27): 315–22.

he apparently left without taking a degree. After converting to Catholicism, he studied in Flanders, France, Spain, and Italy. Ordained to the priesthood in Rome, he went on to become a Benedictine monk at Douay, whence he was sent to England as a missionary. Converting again, he embraced ordination as a minister of the Church of England. When civil war erupted, Carpenter preached as an itinerant and published a 600-page treatise, *The Downfal of Anti-Christ* (1644), in which he argued that the pope is Antichrist and Rome is Babylon, that the party of Antichrist has probably seen its best days, and that Antichrist's destruction will prepare the way for the kingdom of Christ. When the civil war did not have the expected apocalyptic consequences, Carpenter returned to France and his Catholic faith. Unsettled again, he came back to England, became an Independent, and resided at Aylesbury. At this point he confronted Gibbs. Before he died about 1670, Carpenter would once again reconcile himself to Rome.[69]

*The Anabaptist Washt* is less an account of Carpenter's debate with Gibbs than a substantive, 450-page treatise defending paedobaptism.[70] In it Carpenter parades his erudition, citing an army of writers and occasionally quoting in Latin and Greek. The patristics are well represented by Augustine, Jerome, Justin Martyr, Gregory the Great, Ambrose, Tertullian, Gregory Nazianzus, Gregory of Nyssa, Cyril of Jerusalem, Cyprian, Origen, Chrysostom, John of Damascus, and Clement. He dipped into classical sources as well, citing such authors as Plato, Lucian, Virgil, Aristophanes, Oppian, Cicero, and Plutarch. The scholastics were not ignored, for he referred to Thomas Aquinas, Albertus Magnus, Duns Scotus, Peter Lombard, Nicholas of Lyra, Alexander Hales, Jean Gerson, Bonaventure, and William of Ockham. The canon lawyers Gratian and Francesco Zabarella make their appearance, as do the Byzantine exegetes Euthymius and Theophylact, the fourth-century military author Flavius Vegetius, the church historian Bede, the mystic Bernard of Clairvaux, and the Spanish orientalist Benito Arias Montano. For good measure Carpenter sprinkled his arguments with citations of modern scholars, including the Protestants Jeremy Taylor and Daniel Featley, and the Catholics Charles Borromeo and Robert Bellarmine. The effect is ponderously academic, though occasionally laced with a touch of sarcastic humor. Carpenter urged his audience to give more respect to his "Squadron of Worthies" than to "one, lone, lean, leaden, Pagnel-Saint in the Country." He could have hurled only a fraction of these citations at his largely unlearned audience, but in

---

[69] *DNB, s.v.*

[70] In this book Carpenter also attacks the Baptists' leading theologian, John Tombes, as "the *Oracle, Apollo,* Champion, *Achilles, Goliath, Knight-Errant,* or lesse improperly, the *Feather'd Forehorse* of our Anabaptists." *The Anabaptist Washt,* 168. For Tombes see *BDBR, s.v.*

so doing he must unwittingly have swayed them toward Gibbs' simple appeal to the indwelling Spirit. Perhaps here Bunyan first sensed the powerful impact of this unadorned message on most people.[71]

In essence, the debate was a contest between two strikingly different forms of religion—the one rooted in academic learning and tradition, the other relying heavily on the experience of the indwelling Spirit. It was also a confrontation between the formally educated and socially respectable on the one hand and—as Carpenter unfairly depicted Gibbs—a mechanic preacher on the other. During the debate Gibbs renounced his academic training in divinity in favor of an experiential faith, prompting Carpenter to retort: "This empty Anabaptist, having publikely disputed away the *University*, that is, renounced the *University* in his Disputation, and done *publike Pennance* for his inward acquaintance with her; never thriv'd afterwards: and retains nothing now, of *Name* or *Thing*, but a meer presentation of Surface-Learning." Gibbs knew enough about his opponent's past to label him a Catholic, a charge that struck a sensitive nerve in Carpenter, but he reasonably countered that he was not ashamed to embrace truth wherever it was expressed. In turn, he was sufficiently cognizant about Gibbs to parody his humble origins: "I despise no man whose Father is a Cooper; but if such a one shall undertake to Hoope-binde his Hogsheads, or Bucking-Tubs, and not perform it strongly; I shall merrily tell him of it."[72]

The heart of the debate involved a hermeneutical issue that would later be of major interest to Bunyan, to wit, the legitimacy of a figurative interpretation of Scripture. Gibbs had treated water figuratively, as a sign of spiritual regeneration. Carpenter summarized Gibbs' view thus: "The child of the Hoop answers out of the Tub; That by *born of water*, is meant *born of the word*; because the word is in Scripture oftentimes compar'd with water: and that the word meant, demeanes it selfe as an *Instrumentall cause*, the Spirit as an *Efficient*." Carpenter would have none of this, branding Gibbs' thesis "the Hocus Pocus of *desperate Ignorance*" that without cause repudiated a literal or historical interpretation for a figurative one.[73]

We cannot be certain that Bunyan witnessed this debate, nor can a full reconstruction of it be made from Carpenter's lengthy treatise. Yet the gist and flavor of the disputation are knowable, with Gibbs charging Carpenter with being a Catholic, and the latter mocking Gibbs, the cooper's son, for relying on the Spirit rather than his university training. Presumably Carpenter displayed some of his

[71] Ibid., 118.
[72] Ibid., 71 (quoted), 114 (quoted), 168.
[73] Ibid., 45.

erudition in the expectation of swaying the audience, only to discover that the
minimally educated are often less impressed with formal displays of learning than
are university graduates.

Conceivably, Bunyan, perhaps having gone to school with Gibbs, wanted to
hear him debate Carpenter. Gibbs' emphasis on the Spirit's primacy and the virtually inconsequential nature of traditional rites were fundamentally akin to Erbery's message, which Bunyan may also have heard at Newport Pagnell. In any
event, Bunyan later asked Gibbs to write the introduction to *A Few Sighs from
Hell*. By that point, Gibbs and Bunyan clearly would have discussed religious issues, and Gibbs may have been the first person to persuade Bunyan that baptism
by water was unnecessary. Gibbs in turn may have learned this doctrine from Erbery when the latter visited Newport Pagnell, or Erbery may have influenced
Bunyan directly.

Thus during his military service Bunyan would have heard a variety of clash-
ing religious views, none of which seems to have had an immediate impact on
him, though they must have remained in his memory to resurface in the 1650s
when he underwent a traumatic religious experience and subsequently began to
shape his own theology.[74] Did God predestine the elect to salvation, and was Bunyan himself one of the chosen? Or were all people ultimately saved? Was the established church sufficiently reformed, or should the faithful form "gathered"
congregations? Was his baptism as an infant effectual, or were only believers to
be baptized? Indeed, was baptism by water necessary if the Spirit baptized? Above
all, was the formal religiosity of the established church acceptable to God or did
the latter expect a spiritual transformation, and if so, what was its nature? How
far—if at all—Bunyan pondered such questions in his late teens we do not know,
but within a few years after he left the army such issues tormented his mind.
More likely than not, Ford, Erbery, and Hobson planted the seeds of these questions.

Bunyan remembered his military experiences, apparently with appreciation,
to the end of his life; they made effective illustrations of his arguments. *The Holy
War* vividly manifests his interest in and appreciation of military activities. Following Mansoul's salvation, Emanuel displays his "graces" to the town in military
feats that evoke memories of Bunyan's own service in the parliamentary army:

> They marched, they counter-marched, they opened to the right and left, they divided,
> and subdivided, they closed, they wheeled, made good their front and reer with their right
> and left wings, and twenty things more, with that aptness, and then were all as they were

[74]The evidence does not support the claim that "as a young soldier John Bunyan spent
his months there [Newport Pagnell] arguing about religion and refining his radicalism."
Carlton, *Going to the Wars*, 152

*again, that they took, yea ravished the hearts that were in Mansoul to behold it. . . . The handling of their arms, the managing of their weapons of war, were marvellous taking to Mansoul and me.* (HW, 110–11)

In *The House of the Forest of Lebanon* even the Trinity appear in "a military posture" (*MW*, 7:138), and in *A Few Sighs from Hell* Bunyan compares the discharge of the cannon-like Ten Commandments against the souls of the wicked at the last judgment to a military siege, possibly that at Oxford: "Consider how terrible this will be, yea more terrible then if thou shouldest have ten of the biggest peeces of Ordnance in England to be discharged against thy body; thunder, thunder, one after another" (*MW*, 1:364). He repeated the analogy the following year in *The Doctrine of the Law and Grace Unfolded*, warning that one who died under the covenant of works would have these guns fire against his or her soul and

> so rattle in thy conscience, that thou wilt in spite of thy teeth, be immediately put to silence, and have thy mouth stopped; . . . if thou shalt appear before God, to have the Ten Commandments discharge themselves against thee, thou hadst better be tied to a tree, and have ten, yea ten thousand of the biggest pieces of Ordnance in the world to be shot off against thee; for these could go no further, but onely to kill the body; but they both body and soul. (*MW*, 2:49; cf. 141–42)

Moreover, like many veterans, Bunyan was still telling war stories in his twilight years. In *Good News for the Vilest of Men* he reiterated an account of a siege from another veteran, noting that the defenders "came tumbling down from their Fortress, and delivered themselves into their Enemies hands" after seeing mercy extended to a fellow soldier who had been captured. Bunyan used the story to underscore his belief that sinners "would come tumbling" into Christ's arms once they knew of his willingness to save them (*MW*, 11:34). The story also suggests that Bunyan had never been present at the successful conclusion of a siege, for had he witnessed such a surrender, he almost certainly would have added his own experience to this passage.

# CHAPTER 2

# Spiritual and Psychological Crisis

————◆•◆————

Sometime following Bunyan's discharge from the army he married for the first time, but he never recorded his bride's name, her place of residence, or the date of their marriage. Because their first child, the blind daughter Mary, was christened on 20 July 1650, the marriage probably occurred no later than October 1649. The Elstow parish register has no record of the event, suggesting that it may have been a private, informal ceremony[1] or that it took place elsewhere, perhaps because his bride was not a local woman. Her father did not live to see his daughter marry, and indeed may have opposed the union. Three decades later, Bunyan seems to have been recalling his own youthful experience when he described the concerns of a young man who fell in love:

> Suppose a Young Man should have his Heart much set upon a Virgin, to have her to Wife: If ever he Fears he shall not Obtain, it is when he begins to love; now, thinks he, some body will step in betwixt my Love, and the Object of it; either they will find Fault with my Person, my Estate, my Conditions, or somthing.
> Now thoughts begin to work, she doth not like me, or something. (*MW*, 8:345–46)

Before he died Bunyan's prospective father-in-law could plausibly have objected to the wedding on two grounds: Bunyan's penury and his ungodly, profane ways. Indeed, he may have encountered some reluctance on the part of the young woman, who clearly had respect for her father, a man whose piety she frequently cited as an example to Bunyan after they married. "She . . . would be often telling of me what a godly man her Father was, and how he would reprove and correct Vice, both in his house, and amongst his neighbours; what a strict and holy life he lived in his day, both in word and deed" (*GA*, §15). For a time her husband palpably fell short of this standard.

[1] See David Cressy, *Birth, Marriage, and Death: Ritual, Religion, and the Life-Cycle in Tudor and Stuart England* (Oxford: Oxford University Press, 1997), 319–29.

Bunyan would later condemn the type of union—between the godly and the profane—that characterized his first marriage. Although the union between Mr. Badman and his wife differed from Bunyan's in many respects, his depiction of the former echoed his own experience in some ways. Badman sought a spouse to obtain a hefty dowry, whereas Bunyan's bride had only two books, Arthur Dent's *The Plaine Mans Path-Way to Heaven* and Lewis Bayly's *The Practise of Pietie.*[2] Yet the parents of the damsel Badman courted were dead, as was the father and probably the mother of Bunyan's betrothed at the time he married her. Did Bunyan, like Badman, feign piety to win her hand, overcoming her "by his naughty lying tongue?" (*BM*, 67). If so, did he, like Badman, shortly after his marriage hang "his Religion upon the hedge, or rather . . . [deal] with it as men deal with their old Cloaths, who cast them off, or leave them to others to wear?" (69). Badman was an abusive husband, seeking sexual pleasure with strumpets, expecting his wife to entertain them in her home, physically striking her, calling her "Whore, and Bitch, and Jade," and discouraging her from attending church services (70–71). There is no evidence that Bunyan, the self-proclaimed "chief of sinners," ever behaved so despicably, but he lashed out against marriages between believers and unbelievers because of their "unequality, unsuitableness, disadvantages, and disquietments" (73). With his wife repeatedly reminding him of how godly her father had been, the early years of Bunyan's marriage must have had their share of domestic discord.

## "An Exceeding Maze"[3]: The Struggle with Despair

Bunyan was not Mr. Badman, and his wife did not go to her grave pleading in vain for his reformation. On the contrary, the first Mrs. Bunyan was a woman whose strength of character, pious faith, and resolution to tame her husband's irreligious ways played a key role in effecting his rather striking religious transformation. When he later recorded this reformation, he discounted it because it was not grounded in the spiritual regeneration he subsequently experienced, but the change, however formal and ultimately unsatisfying, was pronounced. Bunyan "fell in very eagerly with the Religion of the times," attending church services

[2] A copy of Dent's book, inscribed M. Bunyan on the title-page, was destroyed in the Southeby's fire in 1865. A copy of Bayly's book in the University of Alberta collection has the initials M.B. on the front and back cover. James Gregory Randall has suggested the two books may have been owned by Bunyan's wife, though there is no firm evidence that the M. stood for Mary. However, the fact that the couple's first child was named Mary makes the suggestion plausible. Brown, 53, margin; Randall, "The Bunyan Collection at the University of Alberta," *BS* 2 (Spring 1990): 54. For Dent and Bayly see *DNB, s.vv.*

[3] *GA,* §22.

twice a day, singing and reciting passages as devoutly as his fellow worshipers. He would later recall that he "adored" the priest, clerk, vestments, and everything else associated with the church, including the "High-place" at the church's east end, where the Lord's table was the focal point. He adjudged "all things holy that were therein contained," and thought the priest and clerk must be blissfully happy and blessed because they were God's servants and "principal in the holy Temple, to do his work therein" (*GA*, §16). The vicar of Elstow, Christopher Hall, had taken up his duties in 1639, and, like the large majority of parish clergy, was not compelled to relinquish his living during the religious upheavals of the 1640s and 1650s; indeed, he was still serving the parish in 1664. Although Parliament had proscribed the Book of Common Prayer and imposed the Directory of Public Worship, the traditional liturgy was used in many churches, even in London.[4] Bunyan's description suggests that Hall continued to employ the Book of Common Prayer and wear the traditional vestments. Although Hall or other clerics in the area reputedly lived in debauchery, this did not dissuade Bunyan from reverencing them, even to the point that he "could have layn down at their feet, and have been trampled upon by them; their Name, their Garb, and Work, did so intoxicate and bewitch [him]" (§17).

Whatever his shortcomings, Hall could preach, and Bunyan was particularly moved by a sermon advocating proper observance of the sabbath. He would have heard this sermon in late 1649. To violate the sabbath by labor or by sports, Hall warned, was evil.[5] Notwithstanding his formal religiosity, Bunyan had not relinquished Sunday sports, and the sermon struck a sensitive nerve:

> I fell in my conscience under his Sermon, thinking and believing that he made that Sermon on purpose to shew me my evil-doing; and at that time I felt what guilt was, though never before, that I can remember; but then I was for the present greatly loaden therewith, and so went home . . . with a great burden upon my spirit. (§20)

The sense of guilt was fleeting, and by the time he had finished his mid-day meal he was ready to play tipcat. In this game a player hits a piece of wood with a stick, making it fly into the air, where he strikes it again, driving it as far as he can.

In the midst of the contest, which was probably played on Elstow green, Bunyan was about to strike the piece while it was airborne; at that moment an inner

---

[4] Brown, 55–56; Spurr, *RCE*, 14–15.

[5] *Acts and Ordinances of the Interregnum, 1642–1660*, ed. C. H. Firth and R. S. Rait, 3 vols. (London: His Majesty's Stationery Office, 1911), 2:383–87. (The chronology is discussed later in this chapter.) The sermon cannot have been occasioned by the Rump Parliament's subsequent passage of an act governing sabbath observance on 10 April 1650, according to which the clergy were to read the statute before the morning sermon on the first Sunday after receipt of the act and thereafter every 1 March.

voice cried out, "*Wilt thou leave thy sins, and go to Heaven? or have thy sins, and go to Hell?*" (§22). The voice, he remembered, "did suddenly dart from Heaven into my Soul," an experience that would be repeated numerous times in the ensuing years. On this Sunday afternoon he entered a spiritual maze whose blind alleys and wrong turns would befuddle, frustrate, and discourage him as he sought escape with increasing urgency.[6] But he could not have sensed this as he suddenly stood still, his stick on the ground at his feet, his eyes turned skyward, where, in a spiritual vision, he saw an enraged Jesus looking as if he intended to punish him grievously for violating the sabbath and other sins. Here too for the first time Bunyan experienced the soul-shaking dread that divine forgiveness was no longer possible for such a notorious offender, leaving him without hope of heaven, adrift in a sea of despondency (§§22–23). The emotional scars of his pre-adolescent nightmares of exclusion and punishment seem to have reopened, laying bare his former anxiety. Feeling his "heart sink in despair," he resolved to continue in his sinful ways, thinking he might as well be damned for many offenses as for few. Saying nothing to his companions, he picked up his stick and "desperately" resumed the game (§§23–24). As he hit the playing piece with all his might, he may well have trembled in his conscience at the thought of God striking him for his errant ways.

The rough chronology of Bunyan's experiences between his release from military service in 1647 and his imprisonment in November 1660 can be determined from internal evidence in *Grace Abounding*. At the time of his arrest, he had preached for approximately five years, and he had been "about five or six years awakened" when he was invited to preach by "some of the most able among the Saints" (§§265, 318). This would date the commencement of his preaching about late 1655 or early 1656, which is confirmed by an annotation in the *Church Book*,[7] and his spiritual awakening in 1650 following an encounter with three or four godly women in Bedford (discussed below) (§§37–42). Prior to that awakening he had outwardly conformed to the Church of England for approximately a year (1649–50). This period of conformity was triggered by a sermon on sabbath observance, the religious experience while playing cat, and, a month later, his re-

[6] Michael Davies interprets Bunyan's conversion experience as "learning to follow the thread of the Word through a labyrinth of misunderstandings." My point is that the maze was profoundly spiritual and psychological, not merely exegetical. "Bunyan's Exceeding Maze: *Grace Abounding* and the Labyrinth of Predestination," in *Awakening Words*, ed. Gay, Randall, and Zinck, 104. Graham Ward focuses solely on the literary aspect in asserting that "for Bunyan, salvation was *the ability to read*, the ability to have a mind independent of the text." "To Be a Reader: Bunyan's Struggle with the Language of Scripture in *Grace Abounding to the Chief of Sinners*," *Literature & Theology* 4 (March 1990): 43.

[7] *CB*, 21.

proof by a shopkeeper's wife who found his cursing more than she could bear and a terrible influence on other young people (§§20, 22, 26, 31–32, 65, 76). His spiritual turmoil was not resolved until he had been preaching for about two years, that is, in late 1657 or early 1658. Prior to this he had experienced a period of peace lasting approximately a year (tentatively 1657), and this in turn had been preceded by some two and a half years of turmoil; they can provisionally be assigned to the period from mid-1654 to late 1656, which included the writing of his first book, an attack on the Quakers. Prior to this lengthy time of upheaval, he had enjoyed many weeks of respite (§§194–95, 198, 236, 278). Before this point he had heard an unidentifiable voice while he was in a shop (§174); some twenty years later he could still not explain the incident (discussed more fully below). For this reason, he did not include the episode in the first edition of *Grace Abounding*. It appears in the undated third edition, which was prepared about 1672 (the second edition is not extant).[8] Taken literally, this would date the mysterious episode in 1652, though my provisional chronology makes a date of late 1653 or early 1654 more likely.

This leaves a period of approximately three or four years between his awakening in 1650, the year his blind daughter was born, and the unexplained incident. During this time, according to Bunyan, he experienced more than a year of relative calm during which he searched the Bible for an elusive verse, a period of turmoil that occupied "many months," a time of comfort lasting less than forty days, a disconsolate mood for approximately a year, a respite owing to John Gifford's impact, about a year in which he struggled with the temptation to sell Christ, two years of dejection following his apparent decision to do so, several more months in which he felt his soul was fettered, and travail for yet another year or so as he likened his plight to Esau's sale of his birthright (§§92, 106, 117, 133, 142–43, 145, 219). Of the events that transpired in this period, one, his decision to let Christ go, can be roughly dated. According to Bunyan, it occurred approximately a year and a half after his wife almost gave birth prematurely to their first child, Mary (§§240–42). Since Mary was baptized on 20 July 1650, Bunyan's traumatic decision would have taken place about October 1651.

Altogether, the experiences between the year of relative peace and the episode in which he likened himself to Esau, if we take his timing literally, occupied approximately seven years, though my provisional chronology allows only four. Several factors may explain the apparent discrepancy, including the possibility that the tentative chronology is wrong. More likely, however, Bunyan erred in the

---

[8] *GA*, xxxvii; *Grace Abounding and Other Spiritual Autobiographies*, ed. John Stachniewski and Anita Pacheco (Oxford: Oxford University Press, 1998), 249. Bunyan revised *Grace Abounding* six times between 1666 and 1688.

attribution of time to these episodes, especially if he was depressed; people suffering from this mood disorder typically have an altered sense of the passage of time, which appears to move more slowly than it does for most people.[9] Although Bunyan thought it necessary to locate his experience in time, he periodically seems to have lost his sense of it, as reflected in vague statements about its passage. This, too, is characteristic of depressed individuals. Errors in reporting time are also likely in the material added in later editions, particularly the incorporation of an additional two-year period in his spiritual turmoil (§142), first mentioned in the fourth or fifth edition. If this period was superimposed on the existing time-frame, Bunyan's experiences between the year of relative calm and the Esau episode extended over five rather than seven years, bringing his rough chronology close to the one I have suggested.

During this period Bunyan experienced profound despair that was more than spiritual in nature, as a close reading of *Grace Abounding* reveals. That he was capable of recounting his psychological and spiritual turmoil with reasonable veracity is likely, for modern specialists have ascertained that "in general, depressive patients give a fairly accurate account of themselves."[10] Among Bunyan's contemporaries, Robert Burton and Richard Baxter discussed the illness in depth, and John Napier treated patients for it, many of whom were people of rank or substance; in fact, melancholy became fashionable in the Jacobean period.[11]

In *The Anatomy of Melancholy* Burton distinguished between two types of the malady, the first of which is universally experienced, transitory, and occasioned by such things as illness, grief, passion, discontent, anguish, and need. In contrast, habitual melancholy is "a Chronicke or continuate disease, or setled humor" in which the imagination or reason is "*corrupted*." Among the numerous causes he posited for chronic melancholy were God, the Devil, stars and planets, bad diet, excessive or insufficient sexual relations, excessive or inadequate sleep, covetousness, imprisonment or servitude, the death of friends and family, and terror. He recognized that a tendency to be melancholic could be inherited. In exploring possible religious causes of melancholy, he discussed fear of being reprobate, the adverse impact on tender consciences of meditating about eternal judgment and damnation, misinterpretation of Scripture, and undue self-accusation prompted by a guilty conscience. Some of his criticism was directed against

[9] David Healy, "Dysphoria," in *Symptoms of Depression*, ed. Charles G. Costello (New York: John Wiley and Sons, 1993), 29–30.

[10] M. Hamilton, "The Hamilton Rating Scale for Depression," in *Assessment of Depression*, ed. Norman Sartorius and Thomas A. Ban (Berlin: Springer-Verlag, 1986), 146.

[11] Michael MacDonald, *Mystical Bedlam: Madness, Anxiety, and Healing in Seventeenth-Century England* (Cambridge: Cambridge University Press, 1981), 150–60.

puritan clergy for their preaching about predestination and their stress on divine judgment, which he thought could drive people insane.[12]

Baxter's analysis of the symptoms of depression is strikingly similar in many respects to modern diagnoses. Referring to the malady as *melancholy*, he described it as "this diseased crazynes, hurt, or errour of the *imagination*, and consequently of the understanding." Its symptoms, he said, could encompass excessive sadness (including unexplained weeping), unreasonable fear, self-deprecation, proneness to despair, inability to rejoice in anything, a preference to be alone, inactivity, an inclination to purposeless musing, self-centered thoughts, immoderate scrupulosity, a lack of ability to control thoughts rationally, anorexia, suicidal ideas, and a tendency not to speak. In addition, Baxter noted symptoms with a specifically religious focus, including fear that the day of grace is past, despair over presumed reprobation, excessive sensitivity to sin, often an inability to pray or meditate, temptations to blaspheme, and distress that one has committed the sin against the Holy Spirit. *"Fear and dispair* make them go to *prayer*, hearing, reading, as a Bear to the stake: And then they think they are *haters of God and Godliness*, imputing the effects of their *disease* to their *souls."* Depressed people feel as if voices are speaking within themselves, including those of the Devil or God; some hear voices, see lights and apparitions, or believe they are possessed with demons. Their thinking is akin to that of someone in a maze, and few can be persuaded they suffer from melancholy.[13] Most of the symptoms Baxter describes can be found in Bunyan's account of his spiritual struggles; by Baxter's criteria, Bunyan suffered from melancholy, or depression.

Various other ministers discussed despair in theological terms, but what they described was normally not a mood disorder. The Presbyterian John Howe, for instance, distinguished between "a silent, calm, stupid dispair" of the sort that afflicts the reprobate and "a stormy, rageing dispair," which is less dangerous because those who experience it are sensitive to their spiritual plight.[14] In an age prone to thinking in religious terms, victims of mood disorders could readily be diagnosed as suffering from spiritual despair. The blurring is apparent in the Particular Baptist minister Hanserd Knollys' linkage of spiritual anguish with the lure of suicide: "The convinced sinful sinner . . . begins to be a terrour to himself, and is tempted to chuse strangling rather than life, he is so tormented in his con-

---

[12] Robert Burton, *The Anatomy of Melancholy*, ed. Thomas C. Faulkner, Nicolas K. Kiessling, and Rhonda L. Blair, 3 vols. (Oxford: Clarendon Press, 1989–94), 1:136, 139 (quoted), 163 (quoted), 171–376; 3:412, 414, 416. For Burton see *DNB, s.v.* For the case of a woman who reputedly became mentally ill after reading *The Pilgrim's Progress* see Carroll A. Wise, *Religion in Illness and Health* (New York: Harper and Brothers, 1942), 103–8.

[13] Richard Baxter, *A Christian Directory* (London, 1673), 312–14.

[14] DWL, MS 24.19, fols. 188–89, 196 (quoted).

science, and so tempted by Satan, and terrified with fears of Hell."[15] It would be a mistake, however, to attribute all cases of disturbed moods to religious despair, or to regard all descriptions of melancholy states as evidence of mood disorders.

The efforts of John Fell, bishop of Oxford, to help Lady Frances Hatton, second wife of Christopher Lord Hatton, deal with her melancholy provide additional insight into how the ailment was viewed by some contemporaries, perhaps including those who knew Bunyan in the early and mid-1650s. Most of the letters from Fell to the Hattons do not record the year, but she was complaining of melancholy no later than the spring of 1677, at which time she professed to be weary of life as well as lonely because of her husband's absence and a sense of being overburdened with temporal responsibilities. In the summer of 1678 she attributed her "bad nights" to melancholy and described herself as "the most discontented Creature in the world."[16] In the years leading up to her death in May 1684, the melancholy deepened and was observed by both her husband, who became dejected because of her condition, and Fell, who referred to her malady as a "black dream." As depicted by the bishop, her symptoms, which were recurring, included a disconsolate mood, ill humors, difficulty sleeping, and a loss of appetite; at one point she was not eating three days a week. Fell thought she had inherited the malady from her mother, and during Lady Hatton's pregnancy he warned of the dangers to the fetus, including "Phlegmatic dulness and stupidity" as well as abortion or miscarriage.[17]

In Fell's judgment the cure for melancholy was largely a matter of will-power. He advised Lady Hatton to deal with the condition rationally, seek relief through her faith, master her passions, concentrate on family affairs, spend time outdoors, and engage more frequently in discourse. She must also evaluate herself in relation to others: "Cast up your accounts, and when you have don so, tell me plainly whether you would change your condition with any of the gay ladies of the Age: nay with any one whom you know in the whole world."[18] She had a spousal responsibility, Fell insisted, to be cheerful, for a disconsolate, perverse emotional state adversely affected her husband: "If you will not be cheerful because it is your interest; be sure to be so because it is your Duty."[19] Clearly frustrated with her inability—and seeming unwillingness—to rid herself of her dejected mood,

[15] Hanserd Knollys, *The World That Now Is; and the World That Is to Come* (London, 1681), pt. 1, 15.

[16] BL, Add. MSS 29,571, fols. 376–85, 445–56, 459–66; 29,572, fols. 8, 11, 13 (quoted), 21 (quoted).

[17] BL, Add. MSS 29,582, fol. 33r; 29,583, fols. 29r, 33v, 127r–v, 137r, 141r (quoted), 206r, 212r, 235r–v, 321r–v, 323r–v (quoted).

[18] BL, Add. MSS 29,582, fols. 33v, 115v; 29,583, fols. 43r, 197r–v (quoted), 269r, 287r–v.

[19] BL, Add. MSS 29,583, fols. 118r, 144r, 150r–v, 235r–v (quoted), 411r–v.

the bishop appealed to her love for her husband: "Think with your self how in-human a piece of cruelty it is to afflict a person, who studies nothing but your happiness and satisfaction; and render conjugal affection, which is the highest and most generous endearment, only an instrument of Torment. Since you will not hearken to reason, let passion prevail upon you." In the end, his efforts were futile, and Lady Hatton was still "struling with her fatal agonies" when she died.[20] As the bishop's letters make evident, there was nothing fashionable or contrived about her melancholy, the symptoms of which were akin to those expe-rienced by Bunyan.

By modern standards, was Bunyan depressed? Specialists generally regard major depression and dysthymia (less severe depression) as mood disorders, the essence of which is a disturbed mood, "accompanied by a full or partial . . . De-pressive Syndrome, that is not due to any other physical or mental disorder." "Usually Major Depression consists of one or more discrete Major Depressive Episodes that can be distinguished from the person's usual functioning, whereas Dysthymia is characterized by a chronic mild depressive syndrome that has been present for many years."[21] Unlike normal feelings of sadness, clinical depression is distinguished by its pervasiveness, severity, and persistence.[22] There is no evidence that Bunyan experienced manic or (the less severe) hypomanic episodes, and thus he did not suffer from a bipolar disorder.[23]

Symptoms differ in scope, intensity, and severity from person to person. The symptoms of *dysthymia* (sometimes referred to as reactive, mild, neurotic, or psychogenic depression) typically include affective (emotional) phenomena, such as sadness, loneliness, despair, emptiness, and substantial anger toward others and the world in general; matters of self-esteem, such as self-deprecation, self-loathing, and feelings of inadequacy; motivational changes, such as apathy, low energy, and poor concentration; a sense of pessimism and hopelessness, and so-cial withdrawal. Physical symptoms, such as lethargy, modest changes in sleep patterns, and moderate alterations in diet and weight, are less common than in major depressive episodes. In dysthymia there are no hallucinations or delusions.

[20] BL, Add. MSS 29,583, fols. 170r (quoted), 275r–v (quoted).

[21] John H. Greist and James W. Jefferson, *Depression and Its Treatment*, rev. ed. (Washington, DC: American Psychiatric Press, 1992), 106, 140.

[22] Ian H. Gotlib and Catherine A. Colby, *Treatment of Depression: An Interpersonal Systems Approach* (New York: Pergamon Press, 1987), 4.

[23] Andrew Brink, who believes Bunyan suffered from severe, prolonged depression, avers that his "lengthy conflict had bipolar periodicity" as he alternated between denial and affirmation of life—between despair and hope. "Bunyan's *Pilgrim's Progress* and the Secular Reader: A Psychological Approach," *English Studies in Canada* 1 (Winter 1975): 389, 392–93.

The American Psychiatric Association's diagnostic criteria for dysthymia include a depressed mood; the presence of symptoms during at least a two-year period, with no respite exceeding two months; no evidence of a major depressive episode during the first two years; no history of a manic or hypomanic episode; and at least two of the following: poor appetite or excessive eating, insomnia or hypersomnia, fatigue or low energy, low self-esteem, difficulty making decisions or poor concentration, and feelings of hopelessness. Moreover, dysthymia cannot be caused or sustained by a substance or a general medical condition, or superimposed on another major mental illness, such as schizophrenia or a delusional disorder. Often dysthymia is the consequence of a preexisting, chronic disorder, such as that involving anxiety.[24]

The American Psychiatric Association's diagnostic criteria for a *major depressive episode* (sometimes referred to as endogenous, severe, or psychotic depression) include nine primary symptoms, of which at least five must be present in the same period of at least two weeks and constitute a change from one's prior mode of functioning. The symptoms must include a depressed mood most of the day, nearly every day, or a pronounced diminution of interest or pleasure in all or nearly all activities most of the time. The remaining seven symptoms include almost daily fatigue or loss of energy; feelings of worthlessness or excessive guilt; indecisiveness or a reduced ability to think; recurring thoughts of death or suicide; insomnia or hypersomnia nearly every day; a significant change in appetite or weight not caused by deliberate dieting; and prevalent psychomotor agitation (such as pacing or the inability to sit still) or retardation observed by others. "The episode must be accompanied by a clinically significant distress or impairment in social, occupational, or other important areas of functioning." Moreover, as in dysthymia, a major depressive episode cannot have been initiated and sustained by a substance, be explained as normal bereavement, or result from a general medical condition.[25] For an illness to be classified as a major depressive episode, hallucinations or delusions cannot have occurred for at least two weeks before the symptoms or after their remission. The depressive episode is mild if few or no symptoms in addition to those needed to make the diagnosis are present, and if

[24] *Diagnostic and Statistical Manual of Mental Disorders: DSM-IV*, 4th ed. (Washington, DC: American Psychiatric Association, 1994), 345–49; Jerold R. Gold, "Levels of Depression," in *Depressive Disorders: Facts, Theories, and Treatment Methods*, ed. Benjamin B. Wolman and George Stricker (New York: John Wiley and Sons, 1990), 207–13; Greist and Jefferson, *Depression and Its Treatment*, 138–42; George Winokur, "Controversies in Depression, or Do Clinicians Know Something After All?" in *Treatment of Depression: Old Controversies and New Approaches*, ed. Paula J. Clayton and James E. Barrett (New York: Raven Press, 1983), 153, 156.

[25] *Diagnostic and Statistical Manual*, 317, 320–23, 327.

the symptoms only minimally impair one's occupational tasks, social activities, or relationships with others. The episode is severe if additional symptoms beyond those required to make the diagnosis are present, and if the symptoms significantly impede one's occupational duties, social activities, or relationships with others. A severe episode may be accompanied by hallucinations, including voices castigating the individual for his or her sins, or by delusions. Of note for Bunyan's case is the fact that a major depressive episode may be imposed on dysthymia.[26]

The peak period for depressive episodes occurs between the ages of 25 and 44, with the bipolar variety normally commencing about the late 20s and the unipolar in the mid 20s.[27] Without treatment, a major depressive episode normally lasts

[26] Greist and Jefferson, *Depression and Its Treatment*, 30–32, 116–19, 140–41. The scales devised by specialists to assess degrees of depression provide additional useful insights for the evaluation of Bunyan. The Beck Depression Inventory identifies twenty-one symptoms and attitudes, each of which is assessed according to degree of severity: mood, pessimism, sense of failure, lack of satisfaction, feelings of guilt, sense of punishment, self-hate, self-accusations, self-punitive wishes, weeping spells, irritability, social withdrawal, indecisiveness, body image, work inhibition, sleep disturbance, propensity to fatigue, loss of appetite, weight decline, somatic preoccupation, and loss of libido. Roberta Roesch, *The Encyclopedia of Depression* (New York: Facts on File, 1991), 22–23. The Hamilton Scale focuses on eleven categories of symptoms: a dysphoric mood, including feelings of hopelessness and helplessness, and a tendency to weep; guilt, including illusions of it; suicidal thoughts or attempts; abnormal insomnia; loss of interest in typical activities and a diminution of working capacity; psychomotor retardation, which may include monotony of voice, absence of gestures, and pauses before responding to simple questions; restlessness; psychic and somatic anxiety; somatic symptoms, such as pervasive fatigue, loss of sexual drive, or, in extreme cases, hypochondria; lack of insight into one's illness; and declining weight. Hamilton, "The Hamilton Rating Scale for Depression," 143, 146, 148–51. Cf. Gotlib and Colby, *Treatment of Depression*, 78–81. The Brief Depression Rating Scale essentially covers the same symptoms, with one category devoted to appearance (assessing to what degree, if any, a person appears sad). R. Kellner, "The Brief Depression Rating Scale," in *Assessment of Depression*, ed. Sartorius and Ban, 179, 185. The World Health Organization's Standardized Assessment of Depressive Disorders, which is more comprehensive than the Hamilton and Brief Rating scales, seeks more precision in identifying symptoms but also incorporates additional possible signs, including changes in the perception of time, the subjective experience of memory loss, and a determination of whether feelings of depression are constant or worse in the morning or the evening. A. Jablensky, N. Sartorius, W. Gulbinat, and G. Ernberg, "The WHO Instruments for the Assessment of Depressive Disorders," in *Assessment of Depression*, ed. Sartorius and Ban, 77–78.

[27] *Diagnostic and Statistical Manual*, 341; Gotlib and Colby, *Treatment of Depression*, 8–9 (who state that the average onset of major depressive disorder is the mid to late 30s).

six months or longer, following which the symptoms typically go into full remission. However, in many cases some symptoms continue for as long as two years without a break of two or more months; in such instances the depression is labeled chronic. Efforts to distinguish the symptoms of chronic depression from those of a major depressive episode have had debatable results. One suggested criterion is of particular interest for Bunyan's case, namely, that in chronic depression a stricken person cannot be free of dysphoria for more than two months during a period of two years.

> Chronic depression seems then to be identifiable primarily by enduring negative and dysfunctional cognitive, perceptual, and attitudinal patterns or traits, and by correlated or resulting dysphoric affects and moods. Persons with chronic depression consistently view themselves, the future, and the world through the lenses of . . . [a] depressive triad: negative evaluations of the self, pessimism about the future, and a corresponding sense of the world as barren, depriving, depleting, or rejecting.

Depression may be recurrent. Although some people experience only one episode of major depression, more than half have another episode. A second or later episode does not have to fulfill all the criteria of a major depressive episode for the depression to be regarded as recurrent.[28] Also of note for Bunyan is the fact that when dysthymia precedes the onset of major depressive disorder, the likelihood of "frequent subsequent episodes" increases.[29]

In Bunyan's case, recurring periods of anxiety probably triggered dysthymia.[30] After being reproved by a shopkeeper's wife, "a very loose and ungodly Wretch," he ceased swearing, the rebuke having created anxiety that he might be regarded as a social outcast (GA, §26).[31] Influenced by a religious man, he began reading the historical books of the Bible. Although he resolved to obey the Ten Commandments, he occasionally broke one or another, which troubled his con-

---

[28] *Diagnostic and Statistical Manual,* 341–42; Greist and Jefferson, *Depression and Its Treatment,* 120, 135, 137; Gold, "Levels of Depression," 219–21 (quoted at 221).

[29] *Diagnostic and Statistical Manual,* 347.

[30] Considering the gap of approximately two years between the conclusion of Bunyan's military service and his initial spiritual awakening, it seems unlikely that some of his anxiety was rooted in his military experience. According to Charles Carlton, there are few indications of psychiatric wounds sustained in the war, possibly because men were rarely in prolonged combat, or perhaps because the illnesses were not noticed or recorded. *Going to the Wars: The Experience of the British Civil Wars, 1638–1651* (New York: Routledge, 1992), 224–25.

[31] Elspeth Graham, "'Lewd, Profane Swaggerers' and Charismatic Preachers: John Bunyan and George Fox," in *Sacred and Profane: Secular and Devotional Interplay in Early Modern British Literature,* ed. Helen Wilcox, Richard Todd, and Alasdair Macdonald (Amsterdam: VU University Press, 1996), 310–11.

science (§§28–30). During this year of outward conformity, he began to feel guilty about his delight in bell-ringing, which he, like the Quakers,[32] deemed vain, so he contented himself with watching the ringers. The proclivity to contorted reasoning that plagued his years of spiritual turmoil was initially apparent in his tortured attempt to deal with his love of the bells. Thinking that a bell might fall and kill him as he watched the ringers, he stood under a beam, but then he worried that a plunging bell might hit a wall, rebound, and kill him. He took shelter in the steeple door, prepared to seek safety behind the thick walls should a bell fall from the detached belfry, but then he became afraid the steeple itself would collapse, and this seems to have persuaded him to stop watching the ringers.[33] His love of dancing also troubled his conscience, but it was a year before he finally relinquished this pleasure (§§33–35). He first began to be troubled about this rather simplistic, legalistic approach to Christianity when he traveled to Bedford to ply his trade. There he overheard three or four women discussing religion as they sat in a doorway in the sun. Fancying himself "a brisk talker . . . in the matters of Religion," he listened to them but understood nothing:

> They were far above out of my reach, for their talk was about a new birth, the work of God on their hearts, also how they were convinced of their miserable state by nature: they talked how God had visited their souls with his love in the Lord Jesus, and with what words and promises they had been refreshed, comforted, and supported against the temptations of the Devil; moreover, they reasoned of the suggestions and temptations of Satan in particular, and told to each other by which they had been afflicted, and how they were borne up under his assaults: they also discoursed of their own wretchedness of heart, of their unbelief, and did contemn, slight, and abhor their own righteousness, as filthy, and insufficient to do them any good.

They spoke joyfully and in scriptural language, Bunyan recalled many years later, as if they had discovered a new world. This episode was profoundly important in his life, for it provided the fundamental understanding of the nature of religious experience he deemed valid. It seems also to have given him the idea that God speaks directly to those who believe in him, especially those who struggle to withstand satanic temptations, though it would be some time before he grasped this (§§37–39). As Elspeth Graham has observed, this event is also significant because Bunyan "encounters people who, as poor women, are *more* marginalised than he is, yet who inspire in him a feeling that theirs is a desirable exclusion, an exclu-

---

[32] Richard Farnworth referred to "carnall bells." BL, Add. MSS 39,865, fol. 22v.

[33] Elspeth Graham makes the interesting point that Bunyan was so preoccupied with the bells that he failed to attain a full recognition of what they mean. "Authority, Resistance and Loss: Gendered Difference in the Writings of John Bunyan and Hannah Allen," in *JBHE*, ed. Laurence, Owens, and Sim, 127.

sivity."[34] Now he began to sense that exclusion from the world of wealth, power, and social position was meaningless if he could find inclusion among the godly.

As a result of this encounter, Bunyan began seeking the company of these people, who had been gathered into a separatist congregation by John Gifford in 1650.[35] Here he realized that he lacked "the true tokens of a godly man," but he had a "tender" heart and began to be persuaded by the scriptural passages they proclaimed. "By these things my mind was now so turned, that it lay like a Horseleach at the vein" (§§40–42). Spiritual awakening had begun. In his quest for more knowledge about divine matters, he read some Ranter works, at first not knowing what to make of them, but finally rejecting Ranter concepts after discussions with some of their proponents (§§44–45).[36] With the zeal of a new convert, he immersed himself in the Bible, especially the Pauline epistles. Initially he found them pleasant and sweet, but a reading of 1 Corinthians 12:8–9, with its attestation that the Spirit gives one person wisdom, another knowledge, and yet another faith, prompted doubt and anxiety. Did he have faith, without which he was excluded from the blessings of God (§§46–47)? Anxious to find the answer, he looked for proof, nearly succumbing to the temptation, which he attributed to the Tempter, to attempt a miracle. He would turn puddles into dry places, and arid ground into puddles, but he stopped short, afraid that his inability to perform this miracle would prove his lack of faith. He was now "at a great loss, . . . tossed betwixt the Devil and [his] own ignorance, and so perplexed, especially at some times, that [he] could not tell what to doe" (§§49–52). Anxiety had triggered indecisiveness.[37]

At this point Bunyan had "a kind of Vision" in which he saw the saints in Bedford sitting in the sunshine on a high mountain while he shivered in the snow beneath dark clouds. To reach the saints he had to struggle mightily through a very narrow, straight gap, like a doorway in a wall, finally joining them in the sun's warmth and light. In his interpretation, the mountain was the church, the wall was the word of God that separated the godly from the ungodly, and the gap was Jesus Christ. From this he concluded that only those who are in earnest about leaving the wicked world can find eternal life. Instead of encouraging him, the vision plunged him into "a forlorn and sad condition" (§§53–56).[38] Fresh

---

[34] Ibid., 125.

[35] For Gifford see *BDBR, s.v.*

[36] Bunyan's opposition to the Ranters is discussed later in this chapter.

[37] Bunyan's inability to relax (§§49, 52), his fear that the worst will occur (§§33–34, 49), his terror (§§33–34), his fear of losing control (§52), his fear of dying (§§33–34, 49), and his feeling scared (§49) are symptoms found on the Beck Anxiety Self-Rating Scale.

[38] Instead of "a kind of Vision," the first edition read "in a Dream or Vision." Sharrock describes this experience as a hallucination. Ibid., *GA*, 38.

doubts assaulted his soul, increasing his anxiety about whether he was among the elect and whether the day of grace was over. So great was his disquietude that it was as if "the very strength of [his] body . . . had been taken away by the force and power thereof" (§§57–58). "By these things," he wrote, "I was driven to my wits end, not knowing what to say, or how to answer those temptations." Assailed by doubt and anxiety, as he walked he was "ready to sink," faint of mind, and about to relinquish hope (§§61–62). After weeks of being "cast down," a sentence "fell with weight upon [his] spirit," urging him to examine past generations to determine if anyone trusting in God had been confounded. Encouraged and "lightened," he was certain the words were biblical, but for more than a year he searched the Bible in vain, even seeking the assistance of others. At last he found the passage in Ecclesiasticus 2:10, which temporarily troubled him inasmuch as the book was part of the Apocrypha, not the Protestant canon, but in the end he embraced the sentence as an apt summation of numerous biblical promises. It was easier to do this, he observed, because he had now obtained greater experience of God's kindness and love (§§62–65).[39]

By this time Bunyan had evinced signs of dysphoria (a generalized feeling of anxiety and restlessness), fatigue, poor self-esteem—he referred to himself as "an ignorant Sot" (§48)—and probably a reduced inability to think clearly, but the evidence is insufficient to suggest a major depressive episode, and the elapsed time is inadequate for a diagnosis of dysthymia, assuming the year he spent searching for the Ecclesiasticus passage was one of relative calm. But renewed anxiety, this time focused on the question of whether the day of grace was past, triggered the onset of probable dysthymia. Perhaps, he thought, the godly people of Bedford were all that God intended to save in his region. He was now "in great distress": "I went up and down bemoaning my sad condition, counting myself far worse then a thousand fools." He was angry with himself for not having repented years ago, and debilitating fatigue returned, leaving him "scarce able to take one step more." Respite came when he recalled Jesus' statement that room in his house was still available, and he marveled that Christ should have thought of him when he spoke those words for his sake (§§66–69). During this respite he delved into typology, interpreting Moses' clean beasts as children of God and his unclean ones as offspring of the Wicked One. He would later make extensive use of typology in various works. His biblical study renewed his anxiety that he might

---

[39] Peter J. Carlton has effectively analyzed Bunyan's use of disclaiming locutions in the form of biblical verses that fall or dart in on him to give his writing an air of divine authority. "Bunyan: Language, Convention, Authority," *Journal of English Literary History* 51 (April 1984): 17–32.

not be among the elect, a fear, he said, that made him faint and physically ill. For "many months" this continued, prompting him at last to disclose his inner turmoil to some of the godly in Bedford. When they told Gifford, he invited Bunyan to his house to hear him counsel others about God's dealings with their souls. Here, for the first time, Bunyan "began to see something of the vanity and inward wretchedness of [his] wicked heart." The result cannot have been what Gifford intended, for as Bunyan focused on the lust, corruptions, and wicked thoughts and desires within him, his longing for heaven abated and he "began to hanker after every foolish vanity" (§§71–77).[40]

Now considering himself farther than ever from conversion, Bunyan felt his spirits begin to "sink greatly" until they were "as low as Hell." He was "driven as with a Tempest." When he recounted his despair to the godly, they expressed pity and encouraged him to embrace the divine promises of mercy, but so great was the dysphoria that "they had as good have told me that I must reach the Sun with my finger" (§§78–79). He was now acutely sensitive to sin, even to the point that he "durst not take a pin or a stick, though so big as a straw," for his conscience was "sore, and would smart at every touch." Afraid even to speak, he found himself in "a miry bog, that shook if I did but stir." Self-deprecation was pronounced: Convinced he "was more loathsom in [his] own eyes then was a toad," he sensed inward pollution welling up within him, bubbling out of his heart like water from a fountain. Everyone, he opined, had "a better heart" than he, for only the Devil himself could match his inward wickedness and polluted mind. "I fell therefore at the sight of mine own vileness, deeply into dispair." This, he reported, went on "for some years" (§§82, 84). Bemoaning his plight, he became sated with self-pity. As he dwelt on his guilt, he eschewed relief unless it came "the right way," by Christ's blood. All the while he was "troubled and tossed and afflicted with the sight and sence and terrour of [his] own wickedness," believing himself to be obnoxious in God's sight and very much alone (§§85–88). His mood was clearly depressed, and he manifested symptoms of low self-esteem, feelings of hopelessness, and fatigue; by his own reckoning this period lasted several years and in-

---

[40]Whether feelings of utter depravity are delusional, as some psychologists suggest, or theologically essential is debatable. To the extent that a conviction of the total evil of one's being, which Paul taught, produces a profound sense of shame as distinct from guilt for specific sins, such a conviction can contribute to depression. It is necessary to distinguish between intellectual assent to personal depravity, which is not necessarily threatening to psychological health, and an embrace of that doctrine in a manner that produces an overwhelming, debilitating sense of shame. See Gold, "Levels of Depression," 217–18; David B. Cohen, *Out of the Blue: Depression and Human Nature* (New York: W. W. Norton, 1994), 75.

cluded no respite longer than two months. Dysthymia would not have prevented him from functioning socially and occupationally, and he would have continued to pursue his trade as a tinker.[41]

A respite from the dysphoria came when Bunyan heard an unidentified person preach a sermon on Song of Songs 4:1, interpreting the phrase "my love" as Christ's love, and urging afflicted souls to concentrate on those words. The comfort this brought lasted less than forty days. A week or two after the doubts and anxiety had returned, he heard the words of Luke 22:31, "*Simon, Simon, behold, Satan hath desired to have you,*" "call so strongly" to him that he turned around, expecting to see someone. In fact, he described this verse as rattling his ears loudly and often for a time. Shortly thereafter, he interpreted this experience as a divine warning that a storm was about to descend on him (§§89–95).

Indeed, "a very great storm," which he described as twenty times worse than what he had previously experienced, did engulf him, stripping him of all comfort and plunging him into darkness. Then came "whole flouds of Blasphemies" against God and Scripture, raising doubts as to whether there was a deity and a Christ, whether the Bible was a fable, and whether the Turks had "as good Scriptures" to prove Muhammad was the savior. Why, he wondered, should only those who live in a small corner of the earth know the right way to heaven (§§96–97)? Endeavoring to respond with Pauline passages, he began to wonder if Paul was a subtle, cunning man who deceived people. Some of Bunyan's blasphemous thoughts were too horrific to record, he later decided. Weighed down with their number, continuance, and force from morning to night, he found "room for nothing else." God, he felt, had in his wrath consigned his soul to these blasphemies, to be carried away in a mighty whirlwind (§§98–99). "The noise, and strength, and force of these temptations would drown and overflow," burying all other thoughts. Convinced he was possessed by the Devil and "bereft of [his] wits," he plummeted into deeper despair, likening himself to a child kidnaped by a gypsy, hid under her apron, and taken from friends and country, kicking, screaming, and crying to no avail. (The similitude is reminiscent of his childhood nightmares about devils and wicked spirits that threatened to carry him away.) He also compared himself to Saul (1 Samuel 16:14), thinking he, like Saul, might be possessed by an evil spirit (§§100–102).[42]

Bunyan now struggled with the temptation to commit the sin against the Holy Spirit as the only way to find peace. So intense was the striving that he was prepared to force his mouth shut and even dive headfirst into a "Muckhil-hole."

[41] Greist and Jefferson, *Depression and Its Treatment*, 139.

[42] See Vera J. Camden, "Blasphemy and the Problem of the Self in *Grace Abounding*," *BS* 1 (Spring 1989): 5–21.

Better to have been a dog, toad, or horse, he mused. Although he was "broken to pieces," filled with sorrow, and dejected, he could shed no tears to lament his sins. "This much sunk me; I thought my condition was alone," yet he did not seek relief, thus reflecting the sense of futility common to depressed people (§§103–5).[43] This morose mood persisted for "about a year," during which time he continued to attend church services, but they seem to have exacerbated his dysphoria. As he listened to sermons, blasphemies and despair "would hold [him] as Captive," and when he read, his mind would sometimes be "strangely snatched away, and possessed with other things"; an inability to concentrate can be another symptom of depression (§106).[44] What Bunyan now experienced was close to a hallucination. As he prayed, he thought he not only saw the Devil but also felt him pull his clothing. Satan, he claimed, sought his worship, and he was indeed tempted to pray to a bush, a bull, and a broom. Although he cried to God for mercy, God mocked his prayers, or so Bunyan felt. Discouraged and in "great straights," he knew he was not prepared to die, though living longer would make him even more unfit (§§107–11). At times he found momentary comfort in biblical verses such as 2 Corinthians 5:21, Romans 8:31, and John 14:19, until finally the temptation to blaspheme was gone and he "was put into [his] right mind again" (§§113–16).

The key to his temporary relief, the length of which he does not indicate, was Gifford's ministry; his doctrine, Bunyan attested, "was much for my stability." From Gifford he learned about Christ's life, resurrection, and second coming— all this with a vividness that nearly amounted to contemporaneity: "Me thought I was as if I had seen him born, as if I had seen him grow up, as if I had seen him walk thorow this world, from the Cradle to his Cross" (§§117, 120). Gifford also instructed Bunyan in how to withstand temptation by crying mightily to God rather than trusting others. For Bunyan's soul this lesson was like rain on parched earth, and he prayed for confirmation of divine mercy. At least for a while, he found it in the Bible, in a conviction that Quaker teachings were erroneous, and in his belief that Christ's blood removed his guilt. He also realized, probably much later, that divine forgiveness came only after he had experienced great, even crushing guilt (§§117–18, 123–27). In the glow of his new-found peace, he wished he were eighty so he could die and let his soul be at rest. No longer did he feel he was "trembling at the mouth of Hell." Desirous of reading about the experience of an "ancient" godly man, he happened upon a well-worn copy of Martin Luther's commentary on Galatians, in which he found his own condition "largely

---

[43] Gold, "Levels of Depression," 211.

[44] SADD Symptom Checklist, in A. Jablensky, *et al.*, "The WHO Instruments," 77; Gotlib and Colby, *Treatment of Depression*, 3.

and profoundly handled," as if the book had been written out of his own heart. Unlike contemporary spiritual autobiographers, whom he found imitative as well as inadequate in dealing with the perplexities of inner struggle, Luther, in Bunyan's eyes, had genuinely wrestled with the temptations of blasphemy and desperation that originated in the Mosaic law, death, the Devil, and hell. Reflecting on this many years later, Bunyan still preferred Luther's commentary above any book except the Bible "as most fit for a wounded Conscience," for Luther too had found himself alone and vulnerable before the divine word (§§128–30).[45]

Although the agonizing struggle seemed over, with Bunyan likening his love of Christ to a blazing fire, the worst lay ahead. During the next year he battled a temptation to "sell" Christ, an enticement so all-consuming that he "was not rid of it one day in a month, no not sometimes one hour in many dayes together" unless he was asleep (§§131–33). As he ate, chopped wood, or picked up a pin, the words *sell him, sell him* drove relentlessly through his mind, sometimes as many as a hundred times without ceasing. "For whole hours together I have been forced to stand as continually leaning and forcing my spirit against" the temptation to yield. Sometimes he thought he had succumbed, and for days he was tortured as if he were on a rack. He became agitated, unable to finish a meal without bolting from the table to pray, afraid that delay would displease God. At times he neither knew where he was nor how to regain his composure. Finally, as he lay in bed one morning, with the words, "*Sell him, sell him, sell him, sell him*" racing through his mind, he silently thought, "*Let him go if he will!*" (§§134–39, 219).

Like a bird shot in a treetop, Bunyan's spirit fell, plunging him again into "great guilt and fearful despair." Rising from his bed, he trudged into a field, where, for two hours, he was "like a man bereft of life," without hope and consigned to everlasting punishment. For the next two years, as he reckoned the time, he could focus on almost nothing but damnation; moments of relief were few and, as usual, triggered by various scriptural verses. Still, the overriding passage was Hebrews 12:16–17, with its morose account of Esau's sale of his birthright

---

[45] John R. Knott, Jr., "'Thou must live upon my Word': Bunyan and the Bible," in *John Bunyan*, ed. Keeble, 158. See Dayton Haskin, "Bunyan, Luther, and the Struggle with Belatedness in *Grace Abounding*," *University of Toronto Quarterly* 50 (Spring 1981): 304–12; Haskin, "*The Pilgrim's Progress* in the Context of Bunyan's Dialogue with the Radicals," *Harvard Theological Review* 77 (1984): 87–89; Vera J. Camden, "'Most Fit for a Wounded Conscience': The Place of Luther's 'Commentary on Galatians' in *Grace Abounding*," *Renaissance Quarterly* 50 (Autumn 1977): 819–46. Henry Denne found Luther's commentary useful, but Baxter criticized it because of Luther's negative remarks on good works. Denne, *The Doctrine and Conversation of John Baptist* (London, 1642), 23; Baxter, *A Defence of Christ, and Free Grace* (London, 1690), 46. For Denne see *BDBR, s.v.*

and God's subsequent rejection of his repentance (§§140–41).[46] "These words were to my Soul like Fetters of Brass to my Legs." Fearing he had committed the unpardonable sin, he was "a burthen and a terror" to himself, weary of life but terrified to die. The old desire to be anything or anyone other than himself returned, and he labored "to call again time that was past," vainly yearning for a second chance to withstand the fateful temptation (§§142–50). He turned to the Bible in search of others who might have comparably transgressed and been saved. Though David had committed murder and adultery, he was no comfort, for his offenses were against the Mosaic law, nor was Peter, for it was a greater offense in Bunyan's mind to sell Christ than to deny him. God, he concluded, had prevented Peter, David, Solomon, and Hezekiah from committing the unpardonable sin. Bunyan likened his torment to being wracked on the wheel and wondered why, of all the millions of sins, he had committed the only one for which there was no forgiveness. Not only was he void of grace, but he was bewitched (§§151–54, 157).

The dysphoria and self-deprecation were very pronounced. His spirit was so broken and confounded that he felt helpless and terrified: "My torment would flame out and afflict me; yea, it would grind me as it were to powder" (§§153–55). Sorrow, grief, and horror consumed him, and he became persuaded that "all things wrought for [his] dammage, and . . . eternal overthrow." He was "tossed to and fro, like the Locusts, and driven from trouble to sorrow," perpetually haunted by the ringing of Esau's fall in his ears. In desperation he compared his sin with Judas' betrayal of Christ, finding small comfort in the fact that he, unlike Judas, had not acted intentionally, but this led only to a sense of shame that he was "like such an ugly man as *Judas*" (§§157–60). Bunyan's shift from a sense of guilt to one of shame is significant. Guilt focuses on specific behavior, whereas shame entails a negative evaluation of the entire self and is often accompanied by a sense of powerlessness, inferiority, and worthlessness, feelings that were already present in Bunyan and were reinforced or even intensified by his sense of shame. As June Tangney has noted, "shame is a devastatingly painful emotion that can overwhelm and cripple the self, at least temporarily." Guilt can make one uncomfortable, but those who experience intense shame are prone to depression.[47]

Indeed, Bunyan discovered that "despair was swallowing [him] up." For a time he found Ranter and atheistic views tempting, particularly the notions that

[46] The crucial role of Hebrews 12:16–17 in Bunyan's account is explicated by Vera J. Camden in "'That of Esau': Hebrews 12:16–17 in *Grace Abounding* (forthcoming).

[47] June P. Tangney, "Shame and Guilt," in *Symptoms of Depression*, ed. Costello, 161–77 (quoted at 176).

sin was not grievous and that there was no day of reckoning, but a keen sense of death and judgment made him stop short of embracing such tenets. "Methought the Judge stood at the door, I was as if 'twas come already." Yet he found it very difficult to pray because of the despair; it was, he said, as if a tempest was driving him from God (§§161–63). In this depressed mood, he came upon another book, *A Relation of the Fearful Estate of Francis Spira, in the Year 1548* (1649), the account of the Paduan attorney Francesco Spira, who recanted his Protestantism under pressure from the inquisition and perished in despair. Reading this book, Baxter would later warn, caused or increased melancholy in many.[48] Bunyan discovered that perusing the volume was like rubbing salt into a wound: "Every sentence in that book, every groan of that man, with all the rest of his actions in his dolors, as his tears, his prayers, his gnashing of teeth, his wringing of hands, his twining and twisting, languishing and pining away under that mighty hand of God that was upon him, was as knives and daggers in my Soul; especially that sentence of his was frightful to me, *Man knows the beginning of sin, but who bounds the issues thereof?*" Like a hot thunderbolt, the dreaded Esau passage seared his conscience when he had finished Spira's story (§163).[49]

In describing Spira's psychological and somatic state, Bunyan may as well have been depicting his own. For entire days at a time his body trembled greatly, and he felt "a clogging and heat" in his stomach as his nerves tightened. Tensing muscles in his chest made him think his breastbone was about to split, and he became so agitated that he "could neither stand nor go, nor lie either at rest or quiet." Comparing himself to Cain, he "did . . . wind, and twine, and shrink under the burden." Feeling like a condemned man on the way to his execution, he desperately wanted to hide but could not (§§164–65, 167).[50] His power of reasoning blunted by his depressed state, he tried to rationalize that his offense was not greater than the combined sins of all the saints, and therefore Christ's blood was sufficient to forgive him, but this brought no comfort. Again, he recalled the offenses of David and Solomon, adding Manasseh, who had built altars for idols in the temple, practiced witchcraft, burned his own children as a sacrifice, and shed

---

[48] Baxter, *A Christian Directory*, 312.

[49] So powerful was the impact of Spira's story on Bunyan that he referred to it in three other works besides *Grace Abounding*: *The Barren Fig-Tree* (*MW*, 5:58), *The Heavenly Foot-Man* (5:151, 173), and *The Greatness of the Soul* (9:167). Thomas Beard included a synopsis of the Spira episode in *The Theatre of Gods Judgements* (rev. ed., London, 1631), 73–74.

[50] The recurring somatic symptoms in *Grace Abounding* disprove the suggestion that the Bunyan depicted in this book has a heart and mind "without a body." John Barrett Mandel, "Bunyan and the Autobiographer's Artistic Purpose," *Criticism* 10 (Summer 1968): 239.

the blood of the innocent, but none of them, he concluded, had sold Christ (§§167–68). In a manner that suggests delusion, Bunyan despaired that his single sin was greater than those of the entire world; "no one pardonable, nor all of them together, was able to equal mine, mine out-went them every one." His mind and spirit fled from God, but always in "these flying fits" he would remember Isaiah 44:22, with its call to return to the redeemer. "Indeed, this would make me make a little stop, and, as it were, look over my shoulder . . . to see if I could discern that God of grace did follow me with a pardon in his hand." But no one was there, and in the end Bunyan resumed his flight, the Esau passage haunting his tortured mind (§§172–73). The sectary Anna Trapnel had similarly thought she heard a voice behind her, but looked and saw nothing.[51]

In the second or third edition of his spiritual autobiography, Bunyan added a section describing a strange, possibly hallucinatory experience that he still found perplexing some two decades later. This probably occurred, as previously suggested, about late 1653 or early 1654. He recalled walking to and fro in a shop, agitated and in a "sad and doleful state, afflicting [himself] with self abhorrence for this wicked and ungodly thought" of having sold Christ. Lamenting his "hard hap" and "ready to sink with fear," he displayed anxiety, restlessness, self-deprecation, and diminished interest or pleasure in other things. Coupled with the impaired ability to reason reflected in his delusion that his sin was greater than those of the entire world, he now evinced symptoms suggesting a major depressive episode imposed on recurrent, chronic dysthymia. As he walked in the shop, he heard

> the noise of Wind upon me, but very pleasant, and as if I had heard a Voice speaking, *Didst ever refuse to be justified by the Blood of Christ?* and withal my whole life of profession past, was in a moment opened to me, wherein I was made to see, that designedly I had not; so my heart answered groaningly *No.*

Hebrews 12:25, with its command that he who speaks should not be refused, "fell with power" on Bunyan, strangely seizing his spirit, bringing light, and commanding "a silence in my heart of all those tumultuous thoughts that before did use, like masterless hell-hounds, to roar and bellow, and make a hideous noise within me." He interpreted this experience as "a kind of chide for [his] proneness to desparation" as well as a warning to seek salvation from Christ, and he likened the rushing wind to an angel's visitation, though in fact he was at a loss to explain

---

[51] Anna Trapnel, *A Legacy for the Saints* (London, 1654), 7–8. In another interesting case, John Gibson, en route to Windsor and "in much sadness of spirit," heard a voice in October 1666 calling for England to repent, warning that God would send two more judgments—water and fire—followed by a great famine. CUL, Add. MSS 40, no. 13.

the experience. Roger Sharrock has suggested that Bunyan's account of this episode is as close as he comes to making a mystical statement. The comfort brought by this experience was only momentary, lasting three or four days (§174).[52]

Now in the lowest depths of his depressed state, his "life hung in doubt before [him]" and he was overwhelmed with shame. Prayer was still very difficult, not least because of the Esau passage, and he deemed his situation desperate. He sought the prayers of the godly on his behalf, though he feared they would tell him God had commanded them not to pray for him; indeed, he thought God had already whispered this to some of them, a suspicion that was delusional (§§175–79). Confiding his plight to an older believer proved no help when the latter thought he had sinned against the Holy Spirit, though a Calvinist minister presumably would have responded differently since the elect cannot commit this offense.[53] Bunyan now heard the mocking voice of the Tempter, recommending that he beseech God the Father to mediate between him and Christ (§§180–81). The gospel tormented him, assailing his conscience, and thoughts of Christ were like a piercing sword. Even the sight of saints caused him to tremble and shamed his soul. Christ pitied him, he surmised, but could not forgive him because of the nature of his offense. Such thoughts, he subsequently realized, seem ridiculous to others, and indeed were so, but at this time they were "most tormenting cogitations," bringing only misery. The notion that he had committed such a heinous sin "would so confound me, and imprison me, and tie me up from Faith, that I knew not what to do" (§§182–85). He likened himself to "a broken Vessel, driven, as with the Winds, and tossed sometimes head-long into dispair." "Like those that jostle against the Rocks," he was "more broken, scattered, and rent." So profound was his despair and bitterness that he depicted himself as living among the tombs with the dead, groaning under the burden of guilt and shame. One day he walked to a neighboring town, sat on a bench, and contemplated his "fearful state." When he finally lifted his head he thought the sun only grudgingly gave him light, while even the stones in the street and the tiles on the houses "did bend themselves against [him]," joining together to banish him from the world and abhorring him for his sin. The experience approached the hallucinatory. "Thus was I always sinking, whatever I did think or do" (§§186–88).

Respites were occasional but brief, typically initiated by verses that darted into his mind. He described these lulls as havens in a storm. On one occasion the

---

[52] Roger Sharrock, "Spiritual Autobiography: Bunyan's *Grace Abounding*," in *JBHE*, ed. Laurence, Owens, and Sim, 100.

[53] Cf., e.g., Philip Henry: "A child of God may fall into any sin, but the sin against the holy ghost." CUL, Add. MSS 7338, commenting on Genesis 19. For Henry see *New DNB*, *s.v.*

promise of everlasting love in Jeremiah 31:3 enabled him to go to bed in peace, and when he awakened the next morning the passage was still fresh in his mind (§§188–90). The fact that he thought a good night's rest worth noting suggests that during his turmoil he slept poorly, a symptom characteristic of many depressed people. Following that night of good sleep the turmoil returned with force, the Tempter, as Bunyan described the experience, endeavoring to disrupt his peace more than a hundred times, particularly with the haunting passage about Esau. Somatic symptoms were again pronounced, as Bunyan was "sometimes up and down twenty times in an hour." Equally evident was the almost pervasive self-deprecation: "I saw my sin most barbarous, and a filthy crime, and could not but conclude, and that with great shame and astonishment, that I had horribly abused the holy *Son* of *God*." At last he found some solace in Psalm 130:3–4, which promises forgiveness, and Ezekiel 16:63, which speaks of reconciliation. This respite, which lasted "many weeks," was longer than most (§§191–95).

Anxiety resurfaced as Bunyan worried that his spiritual calm had no grounding in Scripture. Hebrews 6:4–6, 10:26–27, and 12:16–17, he thought, indicated his repentance was unacceptable. "Now was the word of the Gospel forced from my Soul, so that no Promise or Encouragement was to be found in the Bible for me" (§§195–97). Piling metaphor on metaphor to describe the wretched dysphoria, he related how he felt himself sinking into a gulf, likened himself to a house whose foundation had been destroyed, and compared his desperation to that of a child who had fallen into a mill-pit and, drowning, could find no escape. For another two and a half years (about mid-1654 to late 1656), as he reckoned, he continued in this despair, with only brief, occasional lulls (§§198–200, 202). Convinced he had no faith, or even that there was a biblical promise on which to base his faith, he found himself "sticking in the jaws of desparation" (§201). He became preoccupied with the question of whether Christ's blood was sufficient to forgive him, but was unable to find a firm answer. For seven or eight weeks, he recalled, he alternated between hope and despair as many as twenty times a day, clearly preoccupied with this question. Belief in the sufficiency of divine grace and recollections of Esau's parting with his birthright were like "a pair of scales" in Bunyan's mind, with one thought and then the other predominant. For the most part he continued to be "full of sadness and terrour," even when he was in church. His emotions were sometimes jumbled, as when he surmised his understanding had been divinely enlightened: "I was as though I had seen the Lord Jesus look down from Heaven through the Tiles upon me, and direct these words unto me; this sent me mourning home, it broke my heart, and filled me full of joy, and laid me low as the dust" (§§203–8). Unable to ascertain whether the key biblical verses agreed on his salvation, he wondered what would happen if the passages about

Esau's action and the sufficiency of divine grace confronted each other in his heart. His mind became a battlefield on which two heroic warriors vied, with grace finally forcing the Esau account to withdraw, but still Bunyan found no lasting peace. Another struggle ensued, this time between Satan and Bunyan as the latter fought to prevent his adversary from driving John 6:37—Christ's promise to reject none who come to him—from his mind. "We did so tug and strive: he pull'd and I pull'd," but Bunyan was ultimately triumphant. The same contest would be repeated many times in his mind. Even more pervasive was Esau's brooding tale, which tormented Bunyan every day (§§209–16, 250).

During this two-and-a-half-year period, Bunyan joined the Bedford church (discussed below) in 1655. According to the anonymous author of a continuation of his life, published in 1692, he was baptized at this time. At first the celebration of the Lord's supper was comforting because of its emphasis on the forgiveness of sins, but soon he was strongly tempted to blaspheme the ordinance as he had earlier blasphemed God, and to "wish some deadly thing" to those who partook of the bread and cup. For nine months, according to his reckoning, he struggled within himself not to succumb to these "fierce and sad" temptations, apparently with success (§§253–54).[54]

Toward the end of this nine-month period, Bunyan began to preach, initially "at two several Assemblies, (but in private)," where he first discovered his "Gift" and his audience was "affected and comforted" (§266). After accompanying other church members when they went into the countryside to preach, he was "called forth, and appointed to a more ordinary and publick preaching." His first two years of preaching were agonizing, for guilt lay heavily on his conscience and he was "most sorely afflicted with the fiery darts of the devil concerning [his] eternal state" (§§267–68).[55] "I have been as one sent to them from the dead; I went my self in chains to preach to them in chains." Although his guilt and terror accompanied him to the pulpit door, mercifully he was free of the dysphoria while he preached, but before he could descend the pulpit steps, the sense of doom descended again (§§276–77). At times while he preached, he was "violently assaulted" with blasphemous thoughts and tempted to utter them to the congregation, though he never did. On other occasions, before he could finish his sermon he could not remember what he had been or should be saying; his ability to con-

---

[54] "A Continuation of Mr. Bunyan's Life," ad cal. GA, 171. Charles Doe, who knew Bunyan only in the last two year's of the latter's life, asserted that he had made a confession of faith and been baptized into the Bedford church between approximately 1651 and 1653. "The Struggler," in Bunyan, Works (1692), [1]. The catalogue of books appended to this volume states that Bunyan was converted about 1652.

[55] Bunyan borrowed the phrase, "the fiery darts of the devil," from Luther. Galatians, 366.

centrate was clearly impaired. Moreover, when he was about to preach "some smart and scorching portion of the *Word*," he was tempted to change the topic lest he leave no room for his own escape or lay more guilt on his own soul; again, he refused to yield to such enticements (§§293–94). Notwithstanding his inner turmoil, Bunyan preached successfully, awakening some of those who heard him and drawing audiences numbering in the hundreds. Surprised by the response, he found some solace in the tears of those his message touched. In the pulpit he "took special notice of this one thing, namely, That the Lord did lead [him] to begin where his Word begins with Sinners, that is, to condemn all flesh," a message he propounded "with great sence" because of his own internal conflicts. "I preached what I felt, what I smartingly did feel" (§§269–76).

Near the end of his lengthy travail, there suddenly "fell upon [him] a great cloud of darkness" that totally concealed the things of God and so overwhelmed his soul that it could not seek grace. Somatic symptoms accompanied this episode, for he felt as if his loins were broken and his hands and feet were bound in chains. In general he felt physically weak, which made his psychological and spiritual affliction "the more heavy and uncomfortable." This condition lasted three or four days, ending only when yet another sentence "sound[ed]" in his heart, "*I must go to Jesus.*" Neither he nor his wife could ascertain if the words were biblical, but within minutes more words "came bolting in upon me," this time from Hebrews 12:22–24, announcing the arrival of believers in the heavenly Jerusalem. A joyful Bunyan then enjoyed a good night's sleep; "I never had but few better," another indication that his sleep throughout his spiritual and psychological upheaval was probably not good (§§261–64).

Troubled sleep is also suggested in another episode. Bunyan included it near the end of his autobiography, with little sense of chronological context other than that it was springtime, probably in 1657 or 1658. He was so physically ill, "inclining to a consumption," that he thought he might die. As he examined his soul's state, he focused on his "innumerable" transgressions, including "deadness, dulness, and coldness in holy Duties; my wandrings of heart, my wearisomness in all good things, [and] my want of love to God, his wayes, and people." Sensitive to the guilt clogging his soul, he was afraid to live or die. His spirit sinking, he paced the house in a woeful psychological state, but reflection on Romans 3:24, which proclaims justification by grace, gave him hope, and he became "as one awakened out of some troublesome sleep and dream." Once again, he linked spiritual comfort with good sleep (§§255–58).[56]

[56] A late date for this passage is suggested by Bunyan's recollection of his "former experience of the goodness of God to [his] Soul." *GA*, §256. For another of Bunyan's physical illnesses, accompanied by dysphoria that led him to observe that he was "as one dead be-

The conclusion of Bunyan's long nightmare of despair began when he was able to reread the biblical passages that had contributed to his troubled state. His despondent mood had lifted sufficiently to enable him to approach these verses more rationally. He began with Hebrews 6, at first "trembling for fear it should strike me," but he now interpreted falling away in the sixth verse to mean an absolute, public denial of Christ's remission of sins, and that those who committed this grievous offense could never repent. Turning to Hebrews 10:26, he explicated its reference to willful sin to mean the public repudiation of Christ and his commandments. The most crucial passage was the Esau account in Hebrews 12:16–17, "which kill'd [Bunyan], and stood like a Spear against [him]." He now recognized that his offense, unlike Esau's, had not been deliberate, public, and ongoing. Moreover, Esau had wanted to repent only to attain his blessing, which Bunyan interpreted to mean eternal inheritance, not his birth-right, or regeneration (§§223–27). The thunder had now passed and only "the hinder part of the Tempest" remained. Some rain still fell occasionally, he remembered, and this was painful because his "former frights and anguish" had been "very sore and deep." Changing metaphors, he likened his new condition to that of one who had been burned; "I thought every [inner] voice was fire, fire; every little touch would hurt my tender Conscience." As he walked through a field, more words came to mind, reminding him that his righteousness was in heaven. The effect was liberating, marking the end of this depressive episode: "Now did my chains fall off my Legs indeed, I was loosed from my affliction and irons" (§§228–30). Experiencing a sense of union with Christ, he visualized himself as simultaneously in heaven through Christ, whom he regarded as his head and righteousness, and on earth in his own body. Scriptural passages, which had sometimes come like bolts to sear his tender conscience, were now keys to the kingdom of heaven, things of wonder and verity (§§233, 245–46). It was late 1657 or early 1658, and he changed the primary focus of his preaching to Christ's offices and benefits for the world. Instead of fighting blasphemous thoughts in the pulpit, he felt "as if an Angel of God . . . stood by at [his] back to encourage [him]" (§§278, 282).

As he looked back on his epochal strife, Bunyan suggested two reasons to explain it. He had not, he said, prayed for God to keep him from future temptations when he received deliverance from those that were afflicting him. Instead he had

---

fore Death came," see §260. With the exception of the dreamer's sleep that provides the context for the allegory, in *The Pilgrim's Progress* Bunyan equates sleep with spiritual laxity. As in his personal experience, however, at the beginning of the allegory Christian suffers from insomnia because of his concern about his salvation. See Arlette M. Zinck, "'Doctrine by Ensample': Sanctification Through Literature in Milton and Bunyan," *BS* 6 (1995–96): 49–52.

focused only on appeals for liberation and fresh assurances of Christ's love. The second cause, he believed, was his tempting of God. He recalled a time when his wife had been pregnant, suffering severe pain and in danger of giving birth prematurely. Seriously questioning God's existence at this time, he offered a secret prayer to see if there was a deity, beseeching God to end his wife's discomfort as proof that he could discern innermost thoughts. When her pains ceased, Bunyan concluded that there was indeed a God who knew people's secret musings. Later, after he had silently agreed to relinquish Christ, he remembered that God was cognizant of his thoughts. He likened himself to Gideon, who, because he had tempted God, had been sent to fight a hoard of enemies without apparent assistance. "Thus he served me, and that justly, for I should have believed his Word, and not have put an *if* upon the all-seeingness of God" (§§236–43).

The evidence strongly suggests that Bunyan suffered from recurrent, chronic dysthymia on which a major depressive episode was imposed about late 1653 or early 1654.[57] The onset of the illness would have occurred about early 1651 and terminated, by Bunyan's reckoning, in approximately late 1657 or early 1658. There would be at least one further apparent recurrence, triggered by anxiety about late 1663 or 1664 during his imprisonment.[58] During his illness in the 1650s, he suffered from pronounced dysphoria, marked feelings of worthlessness and excessive guilt, periodic fatigue, physical restlessness, feelings of hopelessness, impaired rational ability at times, apparent insomnia, and diminished pleasure in normal activities.[59] He thought periodically about death, even to the point that he was "a terror to myself," yet he was afraid to die because of the judgment he ex-

---

[57] On the basis of a less detailed investigation, William James concluded that Bunyan suffered from "morbid melancholy" and a "neurotic constitution." "He was a typical case of the psychopathic temperament, sensitive of conscience to a diseased degree, beset by doubts, fears, and insistent ideas, and a victim of verbal automatisms, both motor and sensory." *The Varieties of Religious Experience*, ed. Frederick H. Burkhardt, Fredson Bowers, and Ignas K. Skrupskelis (Cambridge, MA: Harvard University Press, 1985), 132, 155, 168. Roger Sharrock observed that Bunyan had a "sick consciousness," and referred to *Grace Abounding* as a "psychodrama." "Temptation and Understanding in *Grace Abounding*," *BS* 1 (Autumn 1988): 9, 12. According to Vera Camden, Bunyan was "notoriously neurotic" and a man whose "anxiety force[d] him into a kind of madness." "'That of Esau': Hebrews 12:16–17 in *Grace Abounding*" (forthcoming).

[58] See Chapter 5.

[59] Jerold Gold describes the depressed patient's "cognitive activities . . . [as] dominated by ideas and images of defeat, death, destruction, and an enduring outlook of futility, hopelessness, and pessimism. . . . The patient's thinking is dominated by the themes of failure, guilt, self-blame and condemnation, hopelessness, and sin." This description clearly fits Bunyan during the period under consideration. Gold, "Levels of Depression," 217.

pected in the afterlife (§149).[60] In the absence of any comments about his diet, it is impossible to know if he underwent any significant weight changes in these years. Anxiety, a recognized symptom of depression in the standard diagnostic instruments, was pronounced, and probably triggered the onset of dysthymia.[61]

Throughout the years of his psychological and spiritual crisis a pattern is discernible. Repeatedly he turned to external sources—other people (§§41, 77, 79, 179–80), the Bible (e.g. §§62–65, 68, 72–76, 92, 113, 151–52), other books (§§129, 163)—to seek reassurance that God cared for him and that he himself was as vile a sinner as he thought. Until the crisis eventually subsided, the reassurance he found was only temporary, and the doubt that ensued became progressively more intense, impelling him to continue seeking yet more reassurance. The words are almost a refrain: "After this, that other doubt did come with strength upon me (§66); "within less than forty days I began to question all again" (§92); "the Tempter came upon me again, and that with a more grievous and dreadful temptation then before" (§132); "though I had been most sweetly comforted, and that but just before, yet when that [story of Esau selling his birthright] came into my mind, 'twould make me fear again" (§216). This pattern is characteristic of depressed people, who seek reassurance that others care about them. Because the reinforcement is transitory, they repeatedly return in quest of such assurance, but this "depressive spiral" increasingly elicits rejection from others. Individuals with low self-esteem, such as Bunyan in the 1650s, find that the reassurance conflicts with their own negative self-assessment, prompting them to "engage in both self-enhancing reassurance-seeking *and* self-verifying negative feedback-seeking." As rejection mounts, high reassurance seekers with low self-esteem may develop a sense of hopelessness, as Bunyan did when he feared he had committed the unforgivable sin. Hopelessness in turn exacerbates the depressive symptoms.[62]

---

[60] Because hopelessness is a strong predictor of suicidal ideation, Bunyan was fortunate that his terror of judgment in the afterlife dissuaded him from attempting suicide. Aaron T. Beck, Robert A. Steer, Maria Kovacs, and Betsy Garrison, "Hopelessness and Eventual Suicide: A 10-Year Prospective Study of Patients Hospitalized with Suicidal Ideation," *American Journal of Psychiatry* 142 (May 1985): 559–63; Thomas E. Joiner, Jr., and M. David Rudd, "Disentangling the Interrelations between Hopelessness, Loneliness, and Suicidal Ideation," *Suicide and Life-Threatening Behavior* 26 (Spring 1996): 19, 23–24.

[61] A. Jablensky, *et al.*, "The WHO Instruments," 77; Kellner, "The Brief Depression Rating Scale," 185; Hamilton, "The Hamilton Rating Scale for Depression," 150.

[62] J. C. Coyne, "Toward an Interactional Description of Depression," *Psychiatry* 39 (1976): 28–40; Thomas E. Joiner, Jr., Mark S. Alfano, and Gerald I. Metalsky, "When Depression Breeds Contempt: Reassurance Seeking, Self-Esteem, and Rejection of Depressed College Students by Their Roommates," *Journal of Abnormal Psychology* 101 (February 1992): 170–71; Joiner, Alfano, and Metalsky, "Caught in the Crossfire: Depression, Self-

A fuller understanding of Bunyan's experience is possible by comparing it to that of the novelist William Styron. Bunyan's symptoms are essentially mirrored in Styron's autobiographical account of his battle with depression, though Styron's is not expressed in religious terms. Like Bunyan, Styron experienced substantive self-deprecation, "fidgety restlessness," a sense of alienation and "unfocused dread," "stifling anxiety," insomnia, feelings of hopelessness and anguish, and "despair beyond despair." As did Bunyan, he periodically shivered and suffered "fits of black despondency." Both men likened their despair to being tortured on a rack, both suffered from malaise, and both sometimes found it difficult to concentrate. Moreover, both used analogies of drowning and suffocation. Styron's "muddied thought processes" are reminiscent of Bunyan's tortured reasoning in his depressed state, and both men felt aggrieved and stricken. For both authors, anguish at times replaced cognition. Like Bunyan, Styron found that the illness made him feel physically sapped and drained. He places considerable emphasis on the sense of loss in depression, a feeling vividly depicted by Bunyan after he thought he had sold Christ and relinquished the opportunity for eternal life. Styron's fear of having been abandoned is similar to Bunyan's metaphor of having been kidnaped and spirited away by a gypsy woman; in both instances the dominant mood is anxiety, which pervades the writing of both authors. Perhaps one of the best brief summations of Bunyan's struggle is Styron's depiction of his own depression as "a state of unrealistic hopelessness, torn by exaggerated ills and fatal threats that bear no resemblance to actuality."[63]

When Bunyan eventually found peace, he experienced a sense of exultation, or what Neil Keeble has described as "immediate and overpowering raptures."[64] "I never saw those heights and depths in grace, and love, and mercy, as I saw after this temptation: great sins do draw out great grace" (§252). He sensed the re-

---

Consistency, Self-Enhancement, and the Response of Others," *Journal of Social and Clinical Psychology* 12 (Summer 1993): 113–16 (quoted at 116); Joiner and Norman B. Schmidt, "Excessive Reassurance-Seeking Predicts Depressive but Not Anxious Reactions to Acute Stress," *Journal of Abnormal Psychology* 107 (August 1998): 533 (quoted), 536.

[63]William Styron, *Darkness Visible: A Memoir of Madness* (New York: Random House, 1990), 76. The other quotations may be found on 12, 31, 44–45, 47, 63. The experience of Kay Redfield Jamison, Professor of Psychiatry at the Johns Hopkins University School of Medicine, is also instructive. A victim of manic-depressive illness, she describes her periods of depression as a time of "unrelenting, day-in and day-out, week-in and week-out, despair, hopelessness, and shame." Depression entails "lack of confidence and self-respect, the inability to enjoy life, to walk or talk or think normally, the exhaustion, the night terrors, the day terrors." This effectively describes what Bunyan himself experienced. *An Unquiet Mind* (New York: Alfred A. Knopf, 1995), 111, 217.

[64]Keeble, *LCN*, 159.

newed appreciation of life characteristic of someone who has recovered from depression. In Styron's words, the "return from the abyss is not unlike the ascent of the poet [Dante], trudging upward and upward out of hell's black depths and at last emerging into . . . 'the shining world'," with its "capacity for serenity and joy."[65] Styron experienced his recovery as re-emergence into light. For Bunyan, too, light was very important, not only in biblical imagery but because of its affect on his mood. Throughout *Grace Abounding*, he contrasts the darkness, cloudy skies, and absence of sunlight, all of which have negative associations, with the light and warmth of the sun, symbolic not only of divine grace but also of psychological and spiritual well-being. *Grace Abounding* is the drama of Bunyan's struggle with depression[66] no less than a record of his spiritual experience. Although it belongs to the genre of spiritual autobiography, it is unique for its candor, its richly detailed account of a striving that was psychological no less than spiritual, and his determination to differ from other spiritual autobiographers by "going down . . . into the deep" (§129).[67] If we read *Grace Abounding* merely as a work of conventional, imitative, stereotypical piety, we miss the significant insight it provides into Bunyan's psychological and spiritual struggles.

---

[65] Styron, *Darkness Visible*, 84. Cf. Cohen, *Out of the Blue*, 106–7.

[66] Styron makes the point that the term "depression" as it is popularly used is so bland and vapid that it fails to convey the profound malevolence of the mood disorder to which it refers (*Darkness Visible*, 36–38). Partly for this reason, clinical terms—dysphoria, dysthymia, and major depressive episode—are useful, especially in distinguishing between the disparate moods. Yet even these terms are largely barren in terms of conveying the depths of human experience. Having employed the clinical terms to analyze Bunyan's condition in this chapter, I shall generally refer in subsequent chapters simply to depression in general, stressing instead Bunyan's potent ability to describe his psychological experience.

[67] The conventionality of *Grace Abounding* is emphasized by Tindall, 31–41; Paul Delany, *British Autobiography in the Seventeenth Century* (London: Routledge and Kegan Paul; New York: Columbia University Press, 1969), 88–89; Dean Ebner, *Autobiography in Seventeenth-Century England: Theology and the Self* (The Hague: Mouton, 1971), 47; Robert Bell, "Metaphorphoses of Spiritual Autobiography," *ELH* 44 (Spring 1977): 108–9; Lynn Veach Sadler, *John Bunyan* (Boston: Twayne, 1979), 35–38; and Anne Hawkins, "The Double-Conversion in Bunyan's *Grace Abounding*," *Philological Quarterly* 61 (Summer 1982): 259, 267–69. The uniqueness of *Grace Abounding* is highlighted by Roger Sharrock in *GA*, xxxi–xxxiii; and Camden, "'Most Fit for a Wounded Conscience'," 819–21, 846. Felicity A. Nussbaum has proposed a compelling interpretation that sees Bunyan altering the traditional pattern of spiritual autobiography by conceptualizing the self in both "the universal allegorical ideal" (the conventional approach) and "the particularized individual." The two approaches compete with and complement each other. "'By These Words I Was Sustained': Bunyan's *Grace Abounding*," *ELH* 49 (Spring 1982): 18–34 (quoted at 19).

Given the fact that Bunyan had no formal ministerial training, *Grace Abounding* served as *de facto* credentials to demonstrate his qualifications to preach and a vindication of the cause for which he was incarcerated. His authority was grounded in his experience, not the academic training of Oxford or Cambridge. "Truth in *Grace Abounding*," avers Keeble, "is an experiential fact as undeniable as physical pleasure or pain. On this authority, Bunyan speaks as incontrovertibly as a Hebrew prophet."[68] He used the length and intensity of his struggle with despair for a tripartite purpose: to establish himself as a truly great sinner who, like Paul, was converted to preach the gospel; to persuade others who doubted or struggled that they too could persevere; and to reassure himself, as he wrote in prison, that the cause for which he had been incarcerated was indeed just.[69] *Grace Abounding* prefigures the internal struggle Bunyan would later develop in his two great allegories, *The Pilgrim's Progress* and *The Holy War*, and depicts a microcosm of the encounter he believed was being waged between the cosmic forces of good and evil.

## "To Joyne in Fellowship"[70]: John Gifford and the Bedford Church

The congregation Bunyan joined had roots extending almost certainly to the 1630s, when the group's first members "in some measure separated themselves from the prelaticall superstition, and . . . agreed to search after the non-conforming men" known as puritans. Their inspiration may have been the events unfolding in London, where in 1616 Henry Jacob had gathered a congregation of visible saints, though simultaneously repudiating schism and recognizing the legitimacy of parish churches and their ministers. This position became known as semi-separatism. Discouraged by controversy within his congregation, in part over the admission of wives and servants who lacked the approval of their husbands and masters respectively, Jacob left for Virginia in 1622, but two years later the church found a new pastor, John Lathrop. The congregation finally split in 1630, when John Dupper (or Duppa) seceded with like-minded believers who insisted on total separation from parish churches. The bishop of London sought to stamp out conventicles in 1632, leading to the arrest of Lathrop and his followers. After two years in prison, Lathrop emigrated to New England, and the congregation did not find a replacement until 1637, when Henry Jessey accepted the pas-

---

[68] Keeble, *LCN*, 206. See also Roger Pooley, "*Grace Abounding* and the New Sense of the Self," in *JBHE*, ed. Laurence, Owens, and Sim, 109–10.

[69] Cf. Michael Mascuch, *Origins of the Individualist Self: Autobiography and Self-Identity in England, 1591–1791* (Stanford, CA: Stanford University Press, 1996), 92.

[70] *CB*, 24.

torate. By 1657 the Bedford church was in contact with Jessey, who may have been one of those to whom visible saints in Bedford had earlier turned for help.[71]

At first the Bedford godly were not even semi-separatists, having no "forme and order as to visible church communion according to the Testament of Christ," but the subsequent account in the Bedford Meeting's church book reported that they zealously sought to edify themselves and spread the gospel, "keeping alwayes a door open and a table furnished and free" for all ministers and lay Christians. Here, then, were the seeds in Bedford of church fellowship that required no specific form of baptism, a practice already being followed by Jessey's congregants in London.[72]

The leader of the Bedford group was John Grew, a churchwarden at St. Paul's in 1635, mayor in 1646 and 1655, a justice of the peace in 1650, and a militia commissioner beginning in December 1650. According to his will, he was a member of the gentry. The church book identifies two others, John Eston (or Easton) senior and Anthony Harrington. Eston served as mayor three times, as justice of the peace, and as a churchwarden at St. Paul's in 1629 and 1639. Although of lesser social stature, Harrington, a cooper, would sit in the Bedford Common Council in 1659. In October 1640 all three men were among the parishioners of St. Paul's who supported their vicar when the High Commission cited him for administering the Lord's supper to worshipers who did not present themselves at the communion rails.[73] Thus the nucleus of the Bedford congregation was socially substantial, quite unlike Bunyan's depiction of them as poor people (GA, §53).

The parliamentary overthrow of the High Commission in 1641 and the outbreak of civil war the following year made possible a rapid increase in the number of Independent, Particular (Calvinist) Baptist, and General (Arminian) Baptist churches. Still, however, Grew and his friends eschewed "seperate and close communion" as a congregation distinct from the parish church, though they continued to meet for fellowship.[74] About 1645, Benjamin Cox, who had reportedly endeavored to establish a separatist church in or near Barnstaple, Devon, in 1642, was ministering in Bedford, though apparently with minimal success, probably because he was by this point a Particular Baptist. In 1643 he had accepted Richard Baxter's invitation to debate the subject of baptism at Coventry,

[71] Ibid., 15 (quoted), 28; Murray Tolmie, *The Triumph of the Saints: The Separate Churches of London 1616–1649* (Cambridge: Cambridge University Press, 1977), 10–12, 15–18. For Jacob, Lathrop, Dupper, and Jessey see *BDBR, s.vv.*

[72] *CB*, 15 (quoted); Tolmie, *Triumph of the Saints*, 25. In contrast to Jessey, John Spilsbury founded a Particular Baptist church in London about the mid-1630s; it required believer's baptism for membership. For Spilsbury see *BDBR, s.v.*

[73] Brown, 13, 81–82.

[74] *CB*, 17.

as a consequence of which he was imprisoned. Two years later, with William Kiffin and Hanserd Knollys he was the co-author of a declaration defending believer's baptism. By 1646 Cox was associated with a Particular Baptist church in London that had seceded from Jessey's congregation in 1641. Cox was seemingly again active at Bedford in 1648, but his insistence on believer's baptism as a condition of church membership did not strike a responsive chord with the semi-separatists.[75]

Their position altered owing to the influence of John Gifford, formerly a major in the royalist army who had been captured at Maidstone, Kent, in June 1648 and condemned to the gallows.[76] With his sister's aid, he escaped on the eve of his execution and made his way to London and shortly thereafter to the Bedfordshire area, where he found shelter with royalists. In time he took up residence in Bedford, where he practiced medicine, drank heavily, gambled, and swore. After losing £15 one evening, he entertained "desperate thoughtes against God," but reading a book by the puritan Robert Bolton made him aware of his wicked ways. Within a month or two—quite unlike Bunyan—he found religious peace and sought the semi-separatists, who at first doubted his conversion, in part because he had once threatened to kill Harrington, whose piety he then despised. Gifford soon felt called to preach, which the semi-separatists initially insisted he must do only to them in private. After Gifford had obtained "some light into the Congregationall way, [and] after some acquaintance also with other ministers," he attempted to organize a separatist congregation, which initially gathered with some hesitation. After many days of prayer and consultation with members of other "societyes," Gifford, Grew and his wife, Eston, Harrington and his wife, and six more women resolved "to walke together in the fellowship of the Gospell" and construct a building in which to worship. Unanimously they selected Gifford as their pastor. The qualifications for membership were those espoused by Jessey's congregation, namely, "faith in Christ and holines of life, without respect to this or that circumstance or opinion in outward and circumstantiall things." As Harrington later recalled, the church was founded in 1650.[77] William Whitbread, who would soon join the congregation, had been active in the war effort as a tax assessor at Elstow.[78]

Recent events had fostered a sense of great expectation among Independents

[75] Richard Baxter, *Plain Scripture Proof of Infants Church-Membership and Baptism* (London, 1651), sigs. b4v-c1r; *DNB, s.v.* Benjamin Cox; *BDBR, s.v.* Benjamin Cox; Tolmie, *Triumph of the Saints,* 26, 61. For Kiffin and Knollys see *BDBR, s.vv.*

[76] Alan Everitt, *The Community of Kent and the Great Rebellion 1640–60* (Leicester: Leicester University Press, 1966), 261–63.

[77] *CB,* 16–17 (quoted), 21.

[78] BL, Add. MSS 61,682, fols. 87v–88r; *CB,* 24, 214.

and Baptists. On 31 January 1649, the day following Charles I's execution, the Independent John Owen preached to the House of Commons, cautioning its members to beware of the blowing wind because it might herald a storm, and exhorting those who were "in God's way" to do his work. The guiding hand of providence had been made manifest by the fate of those—Charles and his supporters—who had resisted the nation's deliverers. In a covering epistle dated 28 February, Owen's millenarian zeal was striking: "The days approach for the delivery of the decree, to the shaking of heaven and earth, and all the powers of the world, to make way for the establishment of that kingdom which shall not be given to another people."[79] He followed this with another fast-day sermon to the Commons on 19 April 1649 in which he reiterated his anticipation: "The Lord Jesus Christ, by his mighty power, in these latter days, as antichristian tyranny draws to its period, will so far shake and translate the political heights, governments, and strength of the nations, as shall serve for the full bringing in of his own peaceable kingdom."[80] Two years later, William Dell, rector of Yelden, Bedfordshire, and master of Gonville and Caius College, Cambridge, boldly proclaimed that the saints were "to reduce the *earth* into conformity with *heaven*, and set up *Gods* Kingdom, here in this *present* world."[81] The small band of believers following "the Congregationall way" in Bedford undoubtedly shared this millenarian spirit, but either they maintained no records in this period—the first entry is dated 24 April 1656—or the earliest minutes were lost.

Like most gathered churches, the Bedford congregation welcomed Cromwell's ouster of the discredited Rump Parliament in April 1653 judging from their positive response to his decision, supported by the Council of Officers, to convoke a nominated assembly. Although the Council never invited the gathered churches to propose candidates for the new assembly, some congregations did, either because individual councilors prompted them to do so or because they acted on their own initiative.[82] A letter from Bedfordshire dated 13 May carried the signatures of thirty-six people, including Dell, Gibbs, John Donne, a relative of Dell and rector of Pertenhall, Bedfordshire; William Wheeler, later rector of Cranfield, Bedfordshire; and several members of the Bedford church, among

[79]Owen, *Works*, 8:129 (quoted), 155 (quoted), 156, 162. For Owen see Peter Toon, *God's Statesman: The Life and Work of John Owen, Pastor, Educator, Theologian* (Grand Rapids, MI: Zondervan, 1973); BDBR, s.v.

[80]Ibid., 8:260.

[81]William Dell, *Christ's Spirit, a Christians Strength* (London, 1651), 5. For Dell see Eric C. Walker, *William Dell: Master Puritan* (Cambridge: W. Heffer and Sons, 1970).

[82]Austin Woolrych, *Commonwealth to Protectorate* (Oxford: Clarendon Press, 1982), 103–20.

them Gifford, Grew, Eston, and Harrington.[83] The John Bunyan who signed this
document may have been the Bedford tinker, although the signature on the letter
is unlike that of Bunyan's later specimens and is more likely that of a Cranfield
yeoman of the same name.[84] This group nominated two men, John Crook of
Beckerings Park and Nathaniel Taylor. The Council of Officers refused to accept
Crook, naming Edward Cater of Kempston, Bedfordshire, instead. Taylor was a
member of George Cokayne's Independent congregation.[85]

In the summer of 1653 the Bedford Common Council presented Gifford to
the rectory of St. John's and the mastership of its hospital following the seques-
tration of the incumbent, Theodore Crowley.[86] Gifford may have ministered to
his congregation of visible saints separately from the wider body of parishioners,
but the epistle he addressed to the former shortly before his death on 21 September 1655 suggests that they worshiped jointly, at least occasionally. "When you are
met as a Church . . . tis not a good practice to be offering places, or seates, when
those who are rich come in." Simultaneously, however, Gifford's letter makes it
clear that the congregation had the right to elect its minister,[87] which was clearly
not the case with the parish living, the patronage of which belonged to the corporation.

In Bunyan's estimation, Gifford's doctrine "was much for [his] stability." He
praised Gifford's determination to deliver the godly

> from all those false and unsound rests that by Nature we are prone to take and make
> to our Souls; he pressed us to take special heed, that we took not up any truth upon
> trust, as from this or that or another man or men, but to cry mightily to God, that he
> would convince us of the reality thereof, and set us down therein, by his own Spirit in
> the holy Word.

Without such inner assurance, the saints would wither in the face of powerful
temptations. Through grace, Bunyan attested, his soul was "very apt to drink in
this Doctrine," especially the difference between experiential and notional knowledge, or effectual and feigned faith (§§117–18). Apart from the Bible and Luther's
commentary on Galatians, Gifford's sermons and pastoral counseling were almost certainly the most influential shapers of Bunyan's religious tenets.

[83] *Original Letters and Papers of State Addressed to Oliver Cromwell*, ed. John Nickolls
(London, 1743), 92–93. For Donne and Wheeler see *BDBR, s.vv.*

[84] See Brown, 95–96, and Frank Mott Harrison's counter-argument (in ibid., 122–23).
The signatures are reproduced between 122 and 123.

[85] Woolrych, *Commonwealth to Protectorate*, 241. For Crook, who became a Quaker in
1654, see *New DNB, s.v.*; for Cokayne see *BDBR, s.v.*

[86] *Minute Book*, ed. Parsloe, 91.

[87] *CB*, 20 (quoted), 21.

Gifford published no books, but his epistle to his congregants outlines many of his essential beliefs. Chief among them, he said, was keeping the "mystery" of the faith with a pure conscience. Membership in the church, he insisted, requires a profession of the work of grace in one's life; the observance of Christ's ordinances, including baptism, the laying on of hands, anointing with oil, and psalm-singing, was not essential. To separate from the church over such matters, he averred, was a great evil. Those seeking membership in the congregation, whether male or female, should declare "that through grace they will walke in love with the Church, though there should happen any difference in judgement about other things." In the church, gifts must be exercised in an orderly manner, and disputes about "externalls" must be shunned. Members who do not speak the truth are to be counseled, and those who walk disorderly must be censured before they are excluded from any ordinance. The deacons, he advised, should always have sufficient means to supply the needs of the poor, and he chided the rich for their niggardly donations. Gifford exhorted the congregation to observe solemn days of prayer and thanksgiving, and to stand (unless physically disabled) when they prayed, as they would if they were in a prince's presence. Prayer itself should avoid "self-affected expressions and all vain repetitions." Gifford recommended caution in choosing a pastor, even if this meant waiting a year or two. Before members could attend services in a parish church, they must receive the congregation's approval. Finally, if the minister should be "laide aside," they must continue to meet as a congregation and "build up one another." The dominant theme of Gifford's missive was holy living and unadorned worship.[88]

Following Gifford's death, the Bedford Common Council resolved on 24 September to present the living of St. John's to William Hayes, rector of St. Agnes, Papworth, Cambridgeshire, but the congregation appealed to Cromwell, protesting that the Council's decision had been reached surreptitiously with a number of members absent. Although the Council reiterated its support for Hayes on 15 October, Cromwell appointed John Burton to the rectory and mastership of St. John's on 16 January 1656 after the Triers reported favorably on his qualifications.[89] The influence of the Independents was manifested two months later when, on 19 March, Major-General William Boteler (or Butler), a proponent of liberty of conscience for all Protestants except Quakers, purged the Bedford Corporation, extruding the mayor, Simon Beckett, and four members of the Council. Beckett's replacement was John Grew, and another member of Burton's flock, Richard Spencely, received a seat on the Council; Eston, moreover, continued his prominent role as a councilor, having acted as provisional mayor until

[88] CB, 18–20.
[89] Minute Book, ed. Parsloe, 91, 93; Brown, 98.

Grew's selection.[90] Having leadership of the corporation in the hands of Bedford church members proved fortuitous when Charles Williams filed a suit against Burton for mastership of St. John's Hospital. In return for a portion of the hospital's revenues for seven years, the Common Council agreed to defend Burton commencing in September 1656. The suit had still not been settled in 1663, well beyond Burton's death, and the stress probably contributed to his declining health in 1659–60.[91]

## "Thred-bare at an Ale-House"[92]: The Ranter Challenge

Among the first religious books Bunyan read were some whose authors were Ranters in his estimation, and for a time in the midst of his religious and psychological crisis he was tempted by their views. He and many contemporaries used the term Ranter opprobriously and imprecisely, but there can be no question as to the belief of Bunyan and others that such people and their unorthodox tenets were real. Sir John Gibson, an Anglican of Welburn, Yorkshire, included the Ranters on his list of twenty-two objectionable "Sects" along with everything from Jesuits, Presbyterians, and Independents to Pelagians, Traskites, soul-sleepers, Socinians, Quakers, Seekers, notionists, healers, and Schwenckfeldians.[93] Recent historians have espoused sharply divergent views on who—if any—were Ranters, and what they believed if they did exist. On the one hand, Jerome Friedman has identified five subgroups of Ranters: philosophical Ranters such as Richard Coppin, "the theologian-philosopher of the Ranter movement," and Jacob Bauthumley; sexual libertines such as Abiezer Coppe and Lawrence Clarkson; revolutionary Ranters such as George Foster and Joseph Salmon; divine Ranters such as William Franklin and Mary Gadbury; and gentleman Ranters such as Captains Francis Freeman and Robert Norwood. Friedman has identified a core of Ranter tenets, including dualism, pantheism, class-oriented anarchism, robust individualism, and a denial of heaven, hell, and ecclesiastical institutions. He believes the Ranters were a movement with sufficient shared tenets to warrant the use of the phrase "consensus Rantism."[94] In contrast, J. Colin Davis has contended that Ranters were not a religious sect but a projection of the anxieties and

---

[90] *Minute Book*, ed. Parsloe, 95–97. For Boteler see *BDBR, s.v.*

[91] *Minute Book*, ed. Parsloe, 104–5, 111–12, 132–33, 171.

[92] *MW*, 1:139.

[93] BL, Add. MSS 37,719, fol. 192v.

[94] Jerome Friedman, *Blasphemy, Immorality, and Anarchy: The Ranters and the English Revolution* (Athens: Ohio University Press, 1987), quoted at 17, 192. For Coppin, Bauthumley, Coppe, Clarkson, Foster, Salmon, Franklin, Gadbury, and Freeman see *BDBR, s.vv.*

concerns of such disparate groups as royalists, Presbyterians, Baptists, and Quakers. Royalists and Presbyterians used the example of reputed Ranters to link freedom of conscience to a collapse of social order, whereas Baptists and Friends cited the alleged beliefs and actions of Ranters to delimit the acceptable workings of the Holy Spirit and justify the development of disciplinary procedures to punish those who strayed beyond these boundaries. In effect, Ranters, according to Davis, were a convenient bugbear by which to personify deviant tenets and licentious behavior. The nucleus of reputed Ranter belief, he avers, was pantheistic Antinomianism, but the only core Ranter who espoused these two concepts was Clarkson. Davis finds no shared Ranter ideology, no Ranter organization, and no close direct links between reputed Ranter leaders.[95]

If Friedman has claimed more unifying links than the evidence warrants, Davis fails to account for the fact that people such as Bunyan had specific individuals in mind whom they identified as Ranters. Bunyan claimed to have read Ranter books and to have had a friend who converted to the Ranters. In his mind, Ranters were not a projection of his anxieties but people who espoused certain beliefs or acted in specific ways. In fact, as we shall see, he used the term Ranter in two strikingly different ways. Contemporaries in general had no uniform conception of what they meant when they employed the term other than their agreement that Ranters were undesirable people because of their heretical beliefs or licentious actions. In the face of such evidence, Ranters are most accurately understood as eccentric dissidents who questioned traditional beliefs about sin, hell, and Scripture, but did not constitute a sectarian group.[96] Some espoused pantheism, some a mysticism in which they identified themselves with God, and some an Antinomianism characterized by a conviction that sin was no longer real for them. In a few cases the espousal of Antinomianism led them to act licentiously in order to manifest their liberation from the law's constraints. Such actions made it easy for contemporaries to label anyone who behaved immorally as a Ranter.

When Bunyan referred to certain unidentified books as having been written by English Ranters, he did so because of the principles they contained. These views cannot have been outrageous because they were "highly in esteem by several old Professors." Moreover, Bunyan, still in the midst of his spiritual travail at this time, could not ascertain the validity of these tenets.

---

[95] J. C. Davis, *Fear, Myth and History: The Ranters and the Historians* (Cambridge: Cambridge University Press, 1986). Davis responded to his critics in "Fear, Myth and Furore: Reappraising the 'Ranters'," *Past and Present* 129 (November 1990): 79–103.

[96] After rethinking the Ranter issue in light of Davis' work, I retract my statement in *MW*, 2:300 that Ranters were a sect.

*O Lord, I am a fool, and not able to know the Truth from Errour; Lord leave me not to my own blindness, either to approve of, or condemn this Doctrine; If it be of God, let me not despise it; if it be of the Devil, let me not embrace it.*

He coupled the report of this experience with an account about a friend who became "a most devilish *Ranter*, . . . pretend[ing] that he had gone through all Religions, and could never light on the right till now" (*GA*, §44). This unidentified companion had made the religious pilgrimage from more conservative to increasingly radical groups until he finally embraced atheism and repudiated conventional moral behavior. The linking of these accounts suggests that the Ranter books mentioned by Bunyan espoused Antinomian tenets, for the common nexus was repudiation of the moral law. Elsewhere he explicitly associated two other concepts with Ranters: a denial of the resurrection, the Ranters' "chief Doctrine," and of "outward Gospel-Worship" (*MW*, 3:156–57, 247). During his spiritual struggles he was tempted to embrace Ranter and atheistical beliefs, including the concept that there would be no resurrection and day of judgment, and the idea "that sin was no such grievous thing" (*GA*, §161). The allure of these tenets was presumably sparked by the Ranter books he read.

Although Bunyan never referred to these volumes by their titles or authors, they were probably Jacob Bauthumley's *The Light and Dark Sides of God* (1650) and Lawrence Clarkson's *A Single Eye All Light, No Darkness; or Light and Darkness One* (1650). Here Bunyan could have found the tenets he described as Ranter—a denial of the physical resurrection, a repudiation of formal worship, and Antinomianism. A native of Leicestershire and a shoemaker, Bauthumley served as quartermaster in the New Model regiment of Colonel Alban Coxe. On 14 March 1650 a court martial cashiered him for blasphemy and ordered that his book be burned and his tongue bored with a hot iron.[97] Clarkson, born at Preston, Lancashire, was a tailor who made a remarkable religious pilgrimage that began in the Church of England and successively moved on to the Presbyterians, Independents, Antinomians (whom he erroneously regarded as a sect), Baptists, Ranters, and Muggletonians. Influenced by Paul Hobson, he became a preacher, first at Great Yarmouth to Colonel Charles Fleetwood's regiment and then in Norfolk and Suffolk. After becoming a Baptist in November 1644, he was subsequently persuaded by the Seekers William Erbery and William Sedgwick that water-baptism had terminated with the Apostles. When he came to London in 1649, the printer Giles Calvert put him in touch with a group calling itself "My One Flesh." At this point, as Clarkson later wrote, he believed that no one could

[97] *BDBR, s.v.*; Davis, *Fear, Myth and History*, 44; Sir Charles Firth and Godfrey Davies, *The Regimental History of Cromwell's Army* (Oxford: Clarendon Press, 1940), 434–35.

be liberated from sin until she or he had first committed that sin. "Till you can lie with all women as one woman, and not judge it sin, you can do nothing but sin."[98] However, as he later reflected, he also clearly distinguished between himself and Abiezer Coppe's "ranting and swearing" company. In this context he published *A Single Eye* and attracted a cohort of female disciples with whom he freely engaged in sexual relations, though he would later insist he had never committed adultery. Following an investigation, Parliament ordered in September 1650 that Clarkson be imprisoned for a month and then banished, and that *A Single Eye* be burned. For unexplained reasons, the government never exiled him.[99]

Bunyan's association of Ranter beliefs with illicit conduct could have been learned from a spate of anti-Ranter tracts (at least one of which was published by his first printer, John Wright)[100] or from an oral tradition that thrived by retelling tales of alleged Ranter misdeeds. Some of the anti-Ranter pamphlets included pornographic illustrations that presumably stoked his moral outrage, such as those depicting a woman kissing the naked buttocks of a man or two nude men with erections dancing with naked women to the accompaniment of a fiddler.[101] He could not, however, have found evidence for the reputed Ranter endorsement of such licentious activity in *The Light and Dark Sides of God*. A pantheist, Bauthumley rejected the idea of an external deity, "as if he were locally in Heaven, and sitting there onely."[102] Because God cannot be confined, heaven is not a specific place but "God at large"; it consists of righteousness, peace, and joy in the Holy Spirit, and is within people. Nor is hell a specific place or the Devil a

[98] Lawrence Clarkson, *The Lost Sheep Found* (London, 1660), 4–25 (quoted at 25); T. L. Underwood, "'For then I should be a Ranter or a Quaker': John Bunyan and Radical Religion," in *Awakening Words*, ed. Gay, Randall, and Zinck, 129, 132. See also *The Acts of the Witnesses: The Autobiography of Lodowick Muggleton and Other Early Muggletonian Writings*, ed. T. L. Underwood (New York: Oxford University Press, 1999), 77–79, 198–99. For Sedgwick and Calvert see *BDBR, s.vv.*; for Calvert see also Plomer, *DBP*, 42–43.

[99] *BDBR, s.v.*; Davis, *Fear, Myth and History*, 68–74.

[100] Wright published *A Blow at the Root* (London, 1650). Bernard Alsop, who was probably related to Benjamin Alsop, co-publisher of *The Holy War* and publisher of four other Bunyan works, issued *The Routing of th[e] Ranters* [London, 1650], *The Arraignment and Tryall with a Declaration of the Ranters* ([London], 1650), John Reading's *The Ranters Ranting* (London, 1650), and *Strange Newes from Newgate and the Old-Baily* (London, 1651). See Davis, *Fear, Myth and History*, 108–9. For Bernard Alsop see Plomer, *DBP*, 3–4.

[101] Reading, *The Ranters Ranting*; anon., *Strange Newes from Newgate and the Old-Baily*; and anon., *The Ranters Religion*.

[102] Jacob Bauthumley, *The Light and Dark Sides of God* (London, 1650), 4–5.

creature. The Devil is "*the old Man*," darkness, and falsehood as well as the spirit of envy, malice, and cruelty.[103] "As the Devill is, and hath his Throne and Seat in every man, so is his Hell."[104] Those who dwell in darkness live in hell, which is within people. If there is neither a physical heaven nor a physical hell, there can be no material resurrection. Because only God is eternal, "in the end, whatsoever is of God, or God in the world at the end of it, they shall all be rapt up into God againe."[105] For Bauthumley, the resurrection is spiritual and inward, the transformation of the believer "into [God's] image by his spirit." The resurrected spiritual body is "nothing but the divine Being, or God in spirit."[106]

Bauthumley stressed the importance of worshiping God in spirit and truth, not outward forms, which he likened to shadows. "The spiritual presence of Christ, or God in the spirit, is the Kingdom of Heaven, into which whomsoever is entered, he ceases from the outward and formal use of outward Administrations and Ordinances."[107] This emphasis on the spiritual as opposed to the formal is reflected as well in Bauthumley's radical understanding of Scripture, which accords primacy to the internal witness of the Spirit rather than the printed word.

> The Scripture, as it is written outwardly, is but an outward witnesse of that which is within; and the spirituality of it wherein the life and being of it doth consist, is made out by a spiritual discovery. I do not go to the letter of Scripture, to know the mind of God; but I having the mind of God within, I am able to see it witnessed, and made out in the Letter; for if I do a thing lawfull from the Letter; yet if I be perswaded in my own spirit I should not do it, I sinne.[108]

The true Bible, he asserted, is "the Law in the spirit," whereas the printed word is only its shadow. Bauthumley expected to be taught by God, not biblical books, for those who use the latter as their authority make an idol of Scripture. If, instead, people would learn from God through the law in their hearts, they "need not run so often to a great Bible, to relieve themselves in straights and doubts as men generally do."[109]

Bauthumley's Antinomianism was framed in this uncompromisingly spiritual framework. Sin is real, but unlike most preachers he stressed not the act but its spiritual underpinnings. Sin is a defect of grace, a deficiency, a deprivation of di-

[103] Ibid., 14 (quoted), 28 (quoted), 29–30.
[104] Ibid., 44.
[105] Ibid., 43, 53 (quoted), 57.
[106] Ibid., 55 (quoted), 58 (quoted), 59–71.
[107] Ibid., sig. A3v and 20 (quoted), 22, 56, 78.
[108] Ibid., 72–73.
[109] Ibid., 75–76.

vine glory, and "a living out of the will of God." Although light and darkness are "all one" to God, "sin is properly the dark side of God which is meere privation of light."[110] Sin is like a cloud between us and the sun; though we are in the shadows or darkness, the sun shines—above the clouds—as brightly as ever. God's countenance does not change toward people because of their sins, but this does *not* mean that we can act as we like; as Paul taught in Romans 6:1, we cannot sin that grace may abound. Although Bauthumley refused to make God the author of sin, he contended that the degree of divine presence within people determines whether they sin: "It is onely the powerfull presence of God in one man more then another, that one man acts not as vilely as another."[111] Indeed, Bauthumley came close to denying human responsibility when he averred that an individual "hath no more power or freedom of will to do evill then he hath to do good."[112] People will not perform evil acts if divine grace teaches them to repudiate worldly lusts and live righteously. Essentially, Bauthumley was not espousing the freedom to live licentiously but logically deducing the consequences of a doctrine of an omnipotent, pantheistic deity. Human beings sin because divine grace does not stop them, but God is able to "turn" their actions to his praise. Bauthumley did not condone sinful behavior, but condemned the spiritual root (e.g. lust) as well as the act (e.g. adultery). If people act in accord with the law of righteousness within them, there is no need for society's laws to compel or restrain them. For Bauthumley the ideal society is one of moral responsibility, not unrestrained licentiousness. He admitted, however, that some who heard his tenets were convinced they would lead to rampant immorality.[113] Indeed, this was Bunyan's conclusion.

Clarkson's *A Single Eye* likewise repudiated formal worship and a physical resurrection. Moreover, he espoused what Davis has aptly described as "practical antinomianism."[114] Like Bauthumley, Clarkson relentlessly followed the logic of divine omnipotency, insisting that all power, whether good or evil, originates with God. In this sense no acts are impure, and all darkness is imagined. Guilt is not the consequence of supposedly evil actions but of a sense of separation from God. Clarkson's goal was the liberation of the self from judgment by experiencing unity with the divine. He came close to recommending that people find free-

[110] Ibid., 10 (quoted), 31–33 (quoted).
[111] Ibid., 34–35, 38 (quoted).
[112] Ibid., 37.
[113] Ibid., 35, 37, 39–40, 76.
[114] Lawrence Clarkson, *A Single Eye All Light, No Darkness* [1650], 11, 13–14; Davis, *Fear, Myth and History*, 62.

dom from sin—from the sense of guilt—by committing the reputedly sinful act: "Till acted that so called Sin, thou art not delivered from the power of sin, but ready upon all the Alarms to tremble and fear the reproach of thy body."[115] Clarkson differed from Bauthumley in this advocacy of practical Antinomianism and in treating sin as a psychological manifestation rather than something objective.[116] *A Single Eye* may have contributed to Bunyan's association of Ranter principles with wanton conduct.

Bunyan's coupling of Ranters and Quakers was not without some justification, especially if he was thinking of Bauthumley as a representative Ranter (*MW*, 1:16, 99–100, 112, 137–40). Like the Friends, Bauthumley repudiated formal worship, stressed the Spirit's primacy over the Bible, denied a physical resurrection, and eschewed a spatial heaven and hell. As were the Quakers, Bauthumley was more concerned with the moral basis of an act than its external manifestation. There were, of course, differences, and the Quaker Edward Burrough was frankly incensed that Bunyan had lumped Friends and Ranters together. No more union existed between them, he averred, than between light and darkness, or good and evil. He rejected their practices, presumably referring to their reputed licentious conduct as well as their false doctrines, none of which he specified. Yet Burrough admitted that, like Bunyan, the Ranters might profess the truth "in words," but such a profession was inadequate because it proceeded from a sinful state. "The *Ranters*, and light *Notionists*, and Thee [John Bunyan] we do deny, in that state wherein they and you do stand, till you turn to the Lord by repentance."[117]

Bunyan henceforth made little of the perceived association of Ranters and Quakers, though he coupled them in passing references in *The Heavenly Foot-Man* (written from about December 1667 to February 1668) and *A Discourse upon the Pharisee and the Publicane* (1685). In the former he warned against "*prying overmuch into Gods Secret Decrees*" or entertaining queries about "some nice, foolish curiosities," which had caused Ranters and Quakers to stumble (*MW*, 10:135; 5:153, 156). He was apparently recalling substantive discussions of divine omnipotency, the relationship between sinful actions and God's will, and probably the nature of the resurrection of the sort found in the works of Bauthumley and Clarkson. Ranters and Quakers were also on his mind when, in *The Pilgrim's*

[115]Clarkson, *A Single Eye*, 13–14, quoted in Davis, *Fear, Myth and History*, 63.

[116]Davis, *Fear, Myth and History*, 61–63. See also A. L. Morton, *The World of the Ranters: Religious Radicalism in the English Revolution* (London: Lawrence and Wishart, 1970), 115–42.

[117]Edward Burrough, *The Memorable Works of a Son of Thunder and Consolation* (n.p., 1672), 138–39 (quoted), 281 (quoted). For Burrough see *BDBR, s.v.*

*Progress*, Christian and Hopeful saw the broken, unburied corpses of those who had denied the physical resurrection at the bottom of a steep hill in the Delectable Mountains (*PP*, 120–21). But when Bunyan deplored the "Ranter-like" tendency to "turn the Grace of God into wantonness" or lashed out against "ranting, swaggering Roysters" in *A Treatise of the Fear of God* (1679), he was using the adjective in its popular, pejorative sense as popularized in anti-Ranter pamphlets (*MW*, 1:381–82; 9:105).[118]

[118]For another reference to Ranters as "Roysters" (roisterers) see *The Ranters Religion* (London, 1650), reprinted in Davis, *Fear, Myth and History*, 160.

# CHAPTER 3

# The Young Preacher

## "A New Upstart Sect"[1]: Bunyan and the Quakers

Bunyan's initial encounter with the Friends occurred during his years of spiritual and psychological struggle. At some point in this period, as he later reflected, he attained an understanding of Jesus' life "from the Cradle to his Cross," his resurrection, his coming again to judge humankind, and his divinity as well as his humanity (*GA*, §§120–22). He attributed these insights to his readings in Scripture, a keen sense of the guilt of sin, and "the errors of the *Quakers* . . . ; for as the *Quakers* did oppose his Truth, so God did the more confirm me in it, by leading me into the Scriptures that did wonderfully maintain it" (§123). From his initial introduction to the Friends, he seems to have found their tenets objectionable, not least because in his judgment they contravened biblical teachings. Nowhere does he identify the first Quakers he met, but his initial exposure to their principles almost certainly transpired between the late summer of 1654 and the spring of 1655. The first major Quaker evangelist to witness in Bedfordshire, William Dewsbury, visited the county following his release from York Castle in July 1654. Among his converts were John Crook of Beckerings Park near Ampthill, a justice of the peace; John Rush of Kempston Hardwicke; and John Samm of Houghton Conquest (*MW*, 1:xxii). Bunyan probably heard one of the Friends who came to Bedfordshire the following March, apparently to plan strategy at Crook's house. There George Fox conferred with John Audland, James Lancaster, Thomas Stubbs, Gervase Benson, Alexander Parker, and others.[2]

Following the conference at Beckerings Park, Friends such as Parker engaged their religious opponents in a series of debates in 1655 and 1656. The first recorded

---

[1] *MW*, 1:184.

[2] William C. Braithwaite, *The Beginnings of Quakerism*, 2nd ed., ed. Henry J. Cadbury (York: William Sessions, 1981), 185–86; *MW*, 1:xxiii. For Dewsbury, Audland, Stubbs, and Parker see *BDBR, s.vv.*

disputation in which Bunyan participated took place at Pavenham on 12 April 1656. Nearly seven weeks later, on 23 May, Bunyan, the minister John Burton, and Richard Spencely (Spencly), a member of the Bedford Corporation, argued with Quakers in St. Paul's, Bedford. Bunyan again debated the Friends on 23 October, this time with the silk-weaver John Child and either John or Samuel Fenne, both of whom were hatters. Bunyan would again contend with the Quakers on 30 January 1657.[3]

These debates provided the milieu in which Bunyan first took up his pen, describing himself on the title-page of *Some Gospel-Truths Opened According to the Scriptures* as an unworthy servant of Christ and a preacher of the gospel. He probably wrote the book during the late summer of 1656 since Burrough's response, *The True Faith of the Gospel of Peace Contended for, in the Spirit of Meekness* (1656), was written prior to the debate on 23 October. *Some Gospel-Truths Opened* was printed for John Wright the younger in London, with a variant imprint, again for Wright, but to be sold by Matthias Cowley, a Newport Pagnell bookseller. Bunyan had probably met Cowley while he served in the Newport garrison. Cowley may have been a member of John Gibbs' congregation, for his infant child would be interred in 1662 without having been baptized in the Church of England.[4] He was probably responsible for calling Bunyan's manuscript to the attention of Wright, who, with his father, was extensively involved in the ballad and chapbook trade.[5] The younger Wright was interested as well in sectarian and, later, nonconformist literature. In October 1668 he, George Larkin (who published *Grace Abounding*), and Richard Royston would be arrested, apparently in connection with the government's investigation to discover the author and printer of *Nehushtan: or, a Sober and Peaceable Discourse* (1668), which vindicated nonconformists who repudiated the Book of Common Prayer.[6] As a prosperous businessman with an interest in sectarian writings, Wright was ideally suited to be Bunyan's first publisher.

Burton introduced Bunyan to his first readers, professing that his epistle was

---

[3] *MW*, 1:xxiv; Edward Burrough, *The Memorable Works of a Son of Thunder and Consolation* (n.p., 1672), 151–52, 304–5; *Minute Book*, ed. Parsloe, 96–97.

[4] Brown, 123; Roger Sharrock, "'When at the first I took my Pen in hand': Bunyan and the Book," in *John Bunyan*, ed. Keeble, 82.

[5] Sharrock, "Bunyan and the Book," 83; Plomer, *DBP*, 198; Plomer, *DPB*, 321; Margaret Spufford, *Small Books and Pleasant Histories: Popular Fiction and Its Readership in Seventeenth-Century England* (Athens: University of Georgia Press, 1981), 66, 83, 89, 94, 98, 263–67 *passim*.

[6] Greaves, *EUHF*, 179. The author was the Presbyterian John Wilson and the printer was Elizabeth Calvert. For Larkin see *BDBR*, *s.v.* and Plomer, *DBP*, 113.

intended not "to set up" Bunyan but to join him in bearing witness to Christ's plain, simple truths. Burton candidly dealt with Bunyan's lack of a university education, insisting that he had been schooled at "the heavenly University, the Church of Christ," which was the alma mater of all true gospel ministers. "Though this man hath not the learning or wisdom of man, yet, through grace, he hath received the teaching of God, and the learning of the spirit of Christ." He contrasted Bunyan, whose success in converting sinners he had observed first-hand, to "many carnal empty preachers both learned and unlearned." The key to Bunyan's success was thus his "spiritual lively faith," which contrasted starkly with "a traditional notional dead faith" (*MW*, 1:11–12). Burton also disarmingly argued that Bunyan's book dealt not with "doubtful controversial things," but with gospel truths that must be believed. There was no room for honest disagreement; one either accepted Bunyan's affirmation of the fundamental teachings of Christ or identified with those who opposed Jesus. For Burton, the latter camp included Socinians, who rejected the divinity of Christ, and Familists, Ranters, and Quakers, who in various ways denied the fulness of Christ's humanity. In particular, Burton accused Quakers of gainsaying that the post-crucifixion Christ is a real man dwelling with God in the heavens (1:7–9).

Bunyan provided his own epistle to the reader, which he composed after completing the body of the work and addressed to a different audience. The bulk of *Some Gospel-Truths Opened* is directed to believers who he fears might be enticed by Quaker or Ranter teachings about the person and work of Christ. The primary readership is neither the unconverted nor his Quaker protagonists. In contrast, Bunyan directed his epistle to the unregenerate, beginning with a powerful evocation of his own experience of despair based on the misguided belief that it was too late to repent. Having thus provided an evangelical framework that warned readers against the Devil's delusions, he denounced Quakers, Ranters, "*Notionists*," and legalists for beguiling "Unstable Souls" (1:14, 16). In particular, he called the readers' attention to two satanic fabrications, namely, that salvation is not completely undertaken for sinners by Christ and that the inner light which all people have can lead them to the kingdom of God. To enable his readers to escape the Devil's snare, Bunyan provided directions, commencing with an admonition to "*examine thine own heart by the rule of the word of God, whether or no, thou hast as yet any beginnings of desiring after religion.*" If readers had been led by divine grace to recognize their lost condition, Bunyan urged them to beware of "*making any stay any where on this side the Lord Jesus Christ,*" but instead to embrace the biblical promises of salvation (1:17, 23–24). This incorporation of an evangelical invitation to the unregenerate would become a hallmark of nearly all his writings.

Bunyan's second work, *A Vindication of the Book Called, Some Gospel-Truths*

*Opened*, differed strikingly from its predecessor. A response to Burrough's *The True Faith*, Bunyan's *Vindication* was printed with variant title-pages for Wright and Cowley. He probably composed his rebuttal between October and December 1656, "some few weeks" after completing *Some Gospel-Truths Opened* (*MW*, 1:134).[7] Unlike *Some Gospel-Truths Opened*, Bunyan's second book was primarily directed against Burrough, though he was also writing to the converted in the hope of keeping them from defecting to the Friends. *A Vindication* was thus a narrow polemical work, yet pastoral in its concern for the spiritual welfare of "those who do beleeve in Christ aright, and lay him for their foundation" (1:217). His response to Burrough had the endorsement of his fellow disputants, Burton, Spencely, and Child, who claimed to have experienced "the Truths" espoused by Bunyan and to have "tried them by the Scripture in the light of the Spirit" (1:121). Not surprisingly, Bunyan failed to persuade Burrough, who replied in *Truth (the Strongest of All) Witnessed Forth in the Spirit of Truth, Against All Deceit* (1657), which he finished in February 1657.[8] Two years later, Fox attacked Bunyan in *The Great Mistery of the Great Whore Unfolded: and Antichrists Kingdom Revealed unto Destruction* (1659).

Although Bunyan, Burton, Burrough, and Fox shared many beliefs, finding common ground was impossible because both parties believed their opponents proceeded from a false faith. People, Bunyan pointed out, can speak one thing but mean something else. For him, truth is found in Scripture, but God reveals it only to those who "have received the spirit of the Lord Jesus Christ." He freely recognized that his Quaker protagonists could cite Bible verses to substantiate their tenets, although their erroneous claims were proof that the Friends were "possessed with a spirit of delusion." Those who have the true Spirit of Christ are "led out" of themselves by it to believe in "*a Christ without, and a resurrection of Christ without, and of intercession of Christ without*" (1:108–10, 140). To disagree with Bunyan's Christology was proof that one was not interpreting Scripture with the aid of Christ's Spirit. Acknowledging that many of Bunyan's words reflected biblical teachings and were consequently true, Burrough nevertheless denounced him for his "lying Spirit," an epithet Bunyan also hurled at Burrough. Essentially, Burrough made the same point Bunyan did: "Though the words be true, yet is thy spirit false, and at best, what thou hast said, is but bearing false witness (as to thy self) of a true thing; I own thy words, and I deny the voice."[9] Burrough candidly insisted he would repudiate Bunyan's "voice" regardless of what he said be-

---

[7] The bookseller George Thomason acquired a copy of Burrough's *The True Faith* on 6 September 1656.

[8] Thomason obtained a copy of Burrough's *Truth (the Strongest of All)* on 5 May 1657.

[9] Burrough, *Memorable Works*, 141 (quoted), 148 (quoted); *MW*, 1:184.

cause he did not speak in the Lord's Spirit.[10] Without that Spirit, Bunyan could not discern truth but instead perverted the Bible. If Bunyan professed to rely on the Spirit rather than traditional education, so did Burrough: "Thou reaches not what the knowledge of things eternal is, by that wisdom in which thou art, I need no man to teach me, but the Lord."[11] Both men were thus reduced to denying that the Holy Spirit enlightened the other.

Notwithstanding their common ground, Bunyan and Burrough disagreed on certain fundamental points. Bunyan was not mistaken when he told Burrough he would have to cease being a Quaker if he accepted many things Bunyan said in *Some Gospel-Truths Opened* (1:186). Later, when Bunyan prepared the fifth edition of *Grace Abounding* (or possibly the fourth, which is not extant), he identified eight errors held by the Friends (*GA*, §124). Two of these—the Quakers' reluctance to accept Scripture as the Word of God and their repudiation of an Anselmic doctrine of the atonement—are largely ignored in the Bunyan-Burrough exchange. Both men favored a plain interpretation of Scripture and stressed the Holy Spirit's role in enlightening the reader's understanding.[12] However, in response to Bunyan's insistence on Scripture as the rule of faith, Burrough countered with the primacy of the Spirit, insisting that there could be no "surer thing for the Creature to look to, to walk to Life, or to come to God by." In his judgment, the Spirit's inner testimony was a more reliable witness to both justification and condemnation than external words. The difference was largely one of emphasis, for Burrough could "have union" with the individual who "walks in the Life of the Scripture."[13] When Fox offered his critique of Bunyan, he stressed not only the necessity of the Spirit's guidance to understand the Bible but also the Spirit's primacy because it was the fount from which Scripture came.[14] Bunyan and Burrough accorded even less attention to the atonement, though the former made passing references to the necessity of Christ having rendered satisfaction to God for the sins of the elect (*MW*, 1:36, 45, 52, 56, 63, 154).

The other six reputed Quaker errors were at the heart of the Bunyan-Burrough debate. Three of these dealt with the fundamental question of the "Christ within" and the "Christ without": Did Jesus physically ascend into the heavens? Are Christ's flesh and blood within the saints? Will Jesus return at the last day to judge the world? Two other issues concerned resurrection: Was it past

[10]Burrough, *Memorable Works*, 302.

[11] Ibid., 278, 287, 292–93, 295 (quoted), 302. See the perceptive analysis of Thomas Luxon (131–36).

[12]Burrough, *Memorable Works*, 143; *MW*, 1:108–9.

[13]Burrough, *Memorable Works*, 295.

[14]George Fox, *The Great Mistery of the Great Whore Unfolded: and Antichrists Kingdom Revealed unto Destruction* (London, 1659), 207. See Underwood, *PRLW*, 20–33.

for "good men," and would the physical bodies of the good and evil be resurrected in the future? The final error, according to Bunyan, was the Quakers' belief that Christ's Spirit is in all people (*GA*, §124).

In one respect, the debate over the Christ within and the Christ without involved a false dichotomy. Burrough did not deny Jesus' life and death, nor did Bunyan question the reality of the Christ within, though each man sometimes argued as if his opponent did. The thrust of Bunyan's argument was that "they hold a false opinion (and principles too) who hold up a Christ within, in opposition to Christ without, who is the Saviour" (*MW*, 1:185–86); yet Burrough advocated no such position, claiming instead that the Friends "own him, which was, is, and is to come, who is within us, and without us."[15] Burrough went one step further, virtually espousing pantheism by asserting that Christ is "not only within, but without, not only without, but within, but is all and in all."[16] This attestation came in Burrough's second attack on Bunyan, to which the latter did not respond, though he almost certainly would have found this virtual pantheism objectionable. If on the main point each man deliberately misstated the other's position, there was a difference in emphasis as well as marked divergences on corollary doctrines. At least in this controversy Bunyan stressed the external Christ, particularly in a soteriological context: "Christ within, or the Spirit of him who did give himself a ransome, doth not work out justification for the soul in the soul; But doth lead the soul out of it selfe, and out of that can be done within it selfe, to look for salvation in that man that is now absent from his Saints on earth" (1:142–43). Bunyan's emphasis was on the death, resurrection, and intercession of Christ—on the divine act of justification as something that first had to be accomplished by Christ and was only then bestowed on the elect through faith (1:109). Burrough, however, was concerned that such stress on the external Jesus could amount to nothing more than cognitive recognition of the historical Christ (as distinct from a saving belief in him), in which case everyone in England could be accounted believers. Burrough's concern, like Bunyan's, was ultimately soteriological: "The knowledge of all things whatsoever without, will not justifie, except Christ be within, and if he be within, the power of his Life, Blood, Birth, &c. is known and received and felt."[17]

[15] Burrough, *Memorable Works*, 282. Cf. Fox, *Great Mistery*, 205–6.

[16] Burrough, *Memorable Works*, 279, 286 (quoted).

[17] Ibid., 151, 287, 291 (quoted). Cf. Fox, *Great Mistery*, 206. Larry Ingle makes the interesting point that Fox's Christology, which was essentially the same as Burrough's, is "a kind of gnosticism," though he rightly adds that Fox based his views on his religious experience, not theological controversies in the primitive church. H. Larry Ingle, *First Among Friends: George Fox and the Creation of Quakerism* (New York: Oxford University Press, 1994), 112–13. The Christology of Isaac Penington the younger was similarly accused of

The unmistakable difference in emphasis was related to the two men's disparate conceptions of the second coming, Christ's presence in the saints, and resurrection, both of Christ and of the saints. Bunyan espoused the physical resurrection of Jesus in "the body of flesh wherewith he was crucified," and believed he was physically present "above the clouds and the Stars" (1:46, 79). The mystery of the conjunction of the divine and the human in Jesus, which both Bunyan and Burrough accepted, was extended by the former into the post-resurrection epoch: "Christ, as God meerly could not go up, being no lesse in one place then in another; but as God man, or in his humane nature he went up." Bunyan was persuaded that Jesus would return, still in his corporal body, to meet his elect when they too were physically resurrected from their graves (1:79, 176, 183, 193). In contrast, Burrough rejected the physical resurrection and ascension of Jesus, insisting that Christ had risen spiritually and "is within, and without also."[18] Physical language was interpreted metaphorically: "The very Christ of God is within us . . . ; and we are Members of his Body, and of his Flesh, and of his Bone."[19] Fox ridiculed Bunyan's contention that Christ would come again to judge humankind at the Mount of Olives, arguing instead that he was already present in everyone, judging each and all.[20] Burrough too derided Bunyan, whose simplistic conception of a physical heaven had prompted him to challenge the Quakers to prove their heaven within could contain a man four or five feet tall. "Carnal sottishness," Burrough sneered.[21]

Bunyan and Burrough sharply disagreed as well with respect to the relationship of Christ's Spirit and conscience. Bunyan clearly distinguished conscience, which he recognized as "a light from Christ as he is God," from the Spirit of Christ. Conscience has the capacity to manifest an eternal deity, reveal and reprove sins, and make people cognizant of their responsibility to serve and obey God. In contrast, Christ's Spirit can reveal "the things of Christ savingly," and in comparison with this Spirit, conscience is "a poor dunghill creature" (1:55–56, 146, 148). Conscience can persuade people of their sins against divine law, thereby rendering them subject to its curse, but only the Spirit of Christ has the capability to deliver the elect from that curse. Moreover, the law, unlike Christ's Spirit, can

---

being Docetic or dualistic because he downplayed the role of Christ's humanity, but see the analysis of Maurice A. Creasey, "Early Quaker Christology with Special Reference to the Teaching and Significance of Isaac Penington, 1616–1679" (Ph.D. diss., University of Leeds, 1956), 279–333. For the Quaker understanding of the person of Christ see Underwood, *PRLW*, 34–50.

[18] Burrough, *Memorable Works*, 282–83, 301.

[19] Ibid., 149.

[20] Fox, *Great Mistery*, 9.

[21] *MW*, 1:183; Burrough, *Memorable Works*, 147 (quoted), 306–7.

mislead sinners by persuading them that regeneration can be attained by following the light of conscience. "Now the soule seeing that there is something within
that convinceth of sinne, doth all on a sudden close with that supposing it is the
spirit of Christ; and so through this mistake is carried away with the teachings
and convictions of its owne Conscience (being misinformed by the Devil) unto
the works of the law" (1:58–59, 148). A sinner can never appease God by fulfilling
the law, but must rely on the living faith that comes only through the gift of the
Holy Spirit. Although conscience can teach people the errors of their ways, it is
soteriologically ineffectual at best and dangerously misleading at worst. If conscientious obedience of the law were sufficient to attain salvation, Bunyan contended, Jesus need not have suffered and died. Only those on whom God bestows
the Spirit can believe and be redeemed (1:158–60, 165). Ultimately, then, Bunyan's
understanding of the differing functions of conscience as a light from God on the
one hand and the Spirit of Christ on the other was inextricably rooted in the Reformed doctrine of predestination to which he had been introduced in Dent's
*The Plaine Mans Path-Way to Heaven* and Bayly's *The Practise of Pietie*.[22] "Christ
as he is God, doth not give unto every man that Spirit that doth lead to eternall
life" (1:199).

Burrough's position was dramatically different. Bunyan, he contended, was
correct in asserting that God has enlightened all humans, and that this light is
sufficient to convince all people of their sins, but Bunyan erred in distinguishing
between the light of Christ given to all, which we call conscience, from Christ's
Spirit. "The Light of Christ, given to every man, *Joh*. 1. 9. . . . is not contrary to the
Spirit of Christ, and to the Grace of God, but is one in their nature . . . ; one they
are, in the union, leading in the same way, unto the same End."[23] Because all have
this light, no one, including Jews, Turks, and heathens, can be excused for not
obeying it. Contrary to Bunyan, Burrough insisted that conscience is capable of
revealing the savior to the soul. For him the element of choice is very real: some
reject the light of their own volition—a position that contrasts sharply with Bunyan's assertion that only the elect receive Christ's Spirit. Burrough also rejected
Bunyan's contention that the Devil counterfeits the work of grace by encouraging
people to believe they can attain salvation by following the inner light. "How
blind art thou in confessing the Light within, even Conscience to be the Light of
Christ as God, and yet sayst, the Devil deceives souls by bidding follow the Light

[22] Arthur Dent, *The Plaine Mans Path-Way to Heaven* (London, 1601), 297–309, 408–9;
Lewis Bayly, *The Practise of Pietie*, 3rd ed. (London, 1613), 55, 171–72, 236–37, 983.
[23] Burrough, *Memorable Works*, 143–44, 294–96 (quoted at 295). Cf. Fox, *Great Mistery*,
209.

within."[24] Conscience cannot deceive because it *is* the light of Christ, and Burrough was consequently outraged that Bunyan likened it to a dunghill.[25] Retorting to Bunyan, Fox went so far as to insist that "he is Antichrist who denyes the light which Christ hath enlightened him withall." By differentiating between the light bestowed on all people and the Spirit of Christ, Bunyan, in Quaker eyes, repudiated the latter and was therefore a child of darkness.[26]

The disparate stances on the relationship of conscience to the light of Christ were related to differing views of the law's role. Burrough and Bunyan concurred that obeying the law would not earn salvation, but the former eschewed the sharp juxtaposition of law and grace favored by Bunyan. According to Burrough, "the law of God is spiritual, and is not contrary, but one with the Spirit of Christ in its union." The law, in other words, is light and is written in the heart of every individual.[27] To attain life eternal, one must obey the law so that God fulfills its righteousness in the believer. This is not to say that salvation can be earned by adhering to the law's precepts, but that as long as one disobeys, "the work of the Law is not finished, nor fulfilled."[28] Christ, asserted Burrough, fulfills the law *in every believer*. As long as the law retains the power to convince sinners of their evil deeds and thoughts, God does not terminate it; on the contrary, law and grace work together, for "the Righteousness of the Law must needs be fulfilled in Judgment, upon you all, and by Christ Jesus in you, if ever you receive the Salvation to your Souls."[29]

Although the Quakers' interpretation was not Pelagian, to Bunyan it was tantamount to rejecting salvation by faith alone. Despite the fact that he did not systematically develop this theme in his first two tracts, it is nevertheless present throughout both works, an underground river that periodically surfaces. In his epistle to the reader in *Some Gospel-Truths Opened*, he avows that God offers grace and mercy freely to every person, but only through Christ. From the outset, Bunyan's evangelical fervor was in tension with his adherence to the Reformed doctrine of predestination. After insisting in the preface that the offer of mercy is extended to everyone, in the first paragraph of the body of the text he espouses a doctrine of election and limited atonement: "God seeing that we would transgress, and break his commandement, did before chuse some of those that would fall, and give them to him that should afterward purchase them actually" (1:28,

[24] Burrough, *Memorable Works*, 144–45, 147–49, 288 (quoted). Cf. Fox, *Great Mistery*, 10, 208.

[25] Burrough, *Memorable Works*, 145, 286, 288–89, 307.

[26] Fox, *Great Mistery*, 13, 209 (quoted).

[27] Burrough, *Memorable Works*, 146. Cf. Fox, *Great Mistery*, 10.

[28] Burrough, *Memorable Works*, 141, 144, 290 (quoted). Cf. Fox, *Great Mistery*, 12–13.

[29] Burrough, *Memorable Works*, 141, 287 (quoted). Cf. Fox, *Great Mistery*, 207–8.

30). By faith alone, Christ's righteousness is imputed to the elect, a doctrine he probably learned from Bayly's *The Practise of Pietie.*[30] This imputation is possible, claimed Bunyan, only because Jesus fulfilled the law *at Calvary*, thereby putting "an end to the Law for righteousnesse" (1:65–66, 153–54). Nothing therefore remains to be undertaken for justification other than for the elect to believe. The law is a useful guide for believers, but not for their justification. Bunyan chastised Burrough for failing to differentiate between "justification wrought by the man Christ without, and sanctification wrought by the Spirit of Christ, within" (1:155–56). The emphasis on the external thus had special significance for Bunyan: the life of the sanctified Christian is possible only because of the physical reality of Jesus' suffering and death, by which God was satisfied and Christ's righteousness could be imputed to the elect.

Bunyan and Burrough stand guilty of rancorous rhetoric. It is tempting to suggest that some of this may be owing to the fact that their tenets were sometimes virtually identical, yet the differences were neither imaginary nor insignificant. The nastiness with which they attacked each other was ultimately grounded in each man's conviction that his adversary was imbued with a spirit antithetical to Christ's. In effect, there are two spirits within, each of which contends for the souls of men and women. The doctrine of predestination might seemingly make this struggle of no consequence, but Bunyan's own religious battles, like those of many Friends, were intense and anything but imaginary. To Bunyan the Quakers marched in the enemy's ranks, and it is therefore hardly surprising that he referred to them as heretics, purveyors of "an outward legall holinesse," liars and deceivers, enemies of God, "painted hypocrites" possessed by the Devil, and blind Pharisees (1:61, 82, 113, 124, 135, 139, 143). Quakers are people "whose consciences are seared with an hot iron, and they being sealed up unto destruction, do some of them call themselves Christ [an allusion to the James Nayler episode], and shew great signes, (as their *Quaking*) and such a legall holiness, as makes the simple admire them, and wonder after them" (1:85). To Bunyan, Burrough was an enemy of truth, "a railing *Rabshakeh*" (referring to Isaiah 36–37), a man guided by Satan's spirit, and one whose "lame arguments thou tumblest over, like a blind man in a thicket of bushes" (1:134, 165, 174). In this context, Bunyan's frequent references to Burrough in *A Vindication* as "friend" effectively mock the Quakers' practice of calling themselves by that term.

Burrough gave as rudely as he got, denigrating Bunyan as a liar, slanderer, distorter of Scripture, hypocrite, exponent of false doctrines, and "Wrester of the right Way of God."[31] Dismissing Bunyan's doctrines as "wonderful trash, and

---

[30] Bayly, *Practise*, 132–33, 308, 693 (mspr. 669), 987–88.
[31] Burrough, *Memorable Works*, 148, 292, 302, 309 (quoted). Cf. Fox, *Great Mistery*, 9.

muddy stuff, unheard of before," Burrough called on him to cast aside his armor and write no more, "for thou mayst understand the more thou strives, the more thou art entangled, and the higher thou arises in Envy, the deeper is thy fall into Confusion, and the more thy Arguments are, the more increased is thy folly." Of Bunyan's book, Burrough sarcastically predicted that it would perish like an "untimely" fig or vanish like smoke.[32]

To some extent, Burrough's prediction proved to be correct, for Bunyan's first two tracts have sparked relatively little attention in his own day or among most of his biographers.[33] Together, however, these early tracts repay closer examination. For one thing, they reveal that Bunyan had considerably more education (however acquired) than he was prepared to admit, a substantial familiarity with Scripture, confidence in expounding it (even to the point of expanding its language to make his points), and a rudimentary knowledge of typology.[34] He even made an obscure reference to one or more biblical commentaries that discuss the views of Jewish scholars: "They say that the word *Scepter* in that 49 of *Gen.* is not meant of a Kingly Government, but the meaning is (say they) a rod, or persecutions shall not depart from *Judah*, till Shiloh come." Although he acknowledged he did not read Hebrew, he claimed to know that the Jewish expositors erred because he had been enlightened by the Spirit to understand Scripture. The biblical passage did not refer, he argued, to persecution but to the fact that a governor of Judah would not leave "till Shiloh come" (1:39–40). He probably found this attack on Jewish hermeneutics in a Protestant commentary.[35] No less revealing is the fact that by 1656 he also had a clear conception of heresy. He was as interested in why God permits heretical tenets as in the doctrines that constitute false belief. Heresies, he concluded, are necessary in order that the truth might be manifested. "The Truth is of that nature, that the more it is opposed, the more glory it appears in" (1:134). For this reason, heretical tenets, such as those of the Quakers, serve a function in the divine scheme. Heretics, Bunyan asserted, are not members of the elect, nor will God forever endure their presence in the church. To be confirmed in the truth is to know that one embraces it

[32]Burrough, *Memorable Works*, 307 (quoted), 309 (quoted).

[33]Cf., e.g., the minimal coverage in Gwilym O. Griffith, *John Bunyan* (London: Hodder and Stoughton, 1927); Harold E. B. Speight, *The Life and Writings of John Bunyan* (New York: Harper and Brothers, 1928); Talon; Sharrock, *JB*; Monica Furlong, *Puritan's Progress: A Study of John Bunyan* (London: Hodder and Stoughton, 1975); and Lynn Veach Sadler, *John Bunyan* (Boston: Twayne, 1979). Hill provides somewhat more attention in *Tinker*.

[34]For early examples of Bunyan's typology, see *MW*, 1:34, 44, 153, 158.

[35]Bunyan's third book, *A Few Sighs from Hell* (1658), also reflects his study of biblical commentaries. *MW*, 1:351.

"freely by the grace of God"; hence heresy helps to demarcate the elect from the reprobate (1:213–14).[36]

Sprinkled throughout Bunyan's first two tracts are the seeds that germinated and grew in some of his later works; in one sense, many of his subsequent writings constitute an extended commentary on the doctrines espoused in the anti-Quaker tracts. Already, in the epistle to *A Vindication*, he lashed out at "*the Dives's*" of all ages, who would someday face judgment and wish they had even "*the least favour*" from the elect (1:130). This would be the topic of Bunyan's third book, *A Few Sighs from Hell*. The theme of his major theological work, *The Doctrine of the Law and Grace Unfolded*, was sketched in the opening pages of *Some Gospel-Truths Opened*, where he first explored the covenant between God the father and God the son (1:31–33.) The related concepts of law and election are also discussed,[37] and he referred as well to the Christian life as a pilgrimage. Here too he made it clear that ignorance of Christ is inexcusable, the theological tenet that explains the harsh fate of Ignorance in *The Pilgrim's Progress* (1:90, 130–31). From the beginning, Bunyan also firmly distinguished between human and divine knowledge; "throw away all thy own wisedome," he advised, though he clearly intended this only in a soteriological context (1:98).

Bunyan's first two tracts also provide examples of the robust colloquial style he later used so effectively in his major works. The lukewarm professor, he wrote, "scandals the Gospel by his loose walking, and naughty carriages." "What is the reason I pray you," he asked, "that there are so many giddy-headed professors in these daies that do stagger to and fro like a company of drunkards?" (1:89, 98). When Burrough failed to respond forthrightly to one of Bunyan's queries, Bunyan quipped, "I see you are minded to famble, and will not answer plainly." "Other lame arguments thou tumblest over, like a blind man in a thicket of bushes"; indeed, "like a man in the dark, in seeking to keep thy self out of one ditch thou art fallen into another." One more example must suffice: sinners, Bunyan cautioned, must not "*bottome thy peace*" on a mere notion of free grace (1:26, 165, 184, 192).

Bunyan's first two works should not be slighted as tedious polemics, semantic quibbling, or the products of an uneducated tinker. By the time he initially took up his pen, he had acquired substantial knowledge of the Bible, studied one or

---

[36] In his next book, *A Few Sighs from Hell*, Bunyan was sensitive to the fact that some godly ministers were being accused of heresy, but *The Doctrine of the Law and Grace Unfolded* does not pursue this theme and contains only incidental references to heretics. *MW*, 1:315, 318; 2:115, 188.

[37] For law see *MW*, 1:44–45, 56, 59–63, 132, 140, 148–49, 154–58, 170, 179, 201, 212; for election see *MW*, 1:155–56, 166, 197–98, 212–14.

more biblical commentaries, begun to explore typology, and formulated doctrinal positions on the person of Christ, the atonement, resurrection, election, and the covenant between God the father and God the son. He had also worked out his position on the nature of conscience and its relationship to Christ's Spirit. Although his first publications are not literary masterpieces or erudite works, they are competent examples of the mid-seventeenth century polemical genre. The debate attracted attention from several contemporaries, including the Particular Baptist minister Thomas Collier, an organizer of the Western Baptist Association, the London stationer Thomas Underhill, and of course Fox.[38]

The debate had a brief afterlife when Roger Williams of Rhode Island cited Fox's attack on Bunyan, Burton, and many other authors in *The Great Mistery of the Great Whore Unfolded*. In *George Fox Digg'd out of His Burrowes, or an Offer of Disputation* (1676), Williams referred to Fox's attack on Bunyan's views on conscience, justification, and Christ's physical presence.[39] Fox and his fellow Friend, John Burnyeat, replied in the second part of *A New-England-Fire-Brand Quenched* (1679), explicitly condemning Bunyan's position on conscience.[40] Bunyan apparently took no note of Fox's renewed criticism or of his appearance in Williams' attack on Fox.

In the meantime, members of the Bedford congregation had further contact with the Quakers in the spring of 1659. By this point Alexander Parker, in a letter dated 4 May to Fox, referred to the church as "Bunian his society." When the Quakers held a meeting in Bedford shortly before this, they had "noe open opposicion," but at a subsequent gathering involving Parker, John Crook, and John Rush, a female member of the Bedford church spoke out against the Quakers. Although Bunyan would later insist that women can play no part in church government, defending one's religious tenets against adherents of a rival group was apparently acceptable conduct. On the 3rd, Crook and Parker held another meeting in the area at which "many of Bunyans people" were present, "and one of them made great opposition but did soe manifest his folly that most people

---

[38] Thomas Collier, *A Looking-Glasse for the Quakers, Wherein They May Behold Themselves* (London, 1657), 4, 9; Thomas Underhill, *Hell Broke Loose: or an History of the Quakers Both Old and New*, 2nd ed. (London, 1660), 19–20, 22, 24–26. Notice came as well from Richard Blome, who quoted Burrough's critique of Bunyan in questions posed to Fox and George Whitehead. Thomas Smith, *A Gagg for the Quakers, with an Answer to Mr. Denn's Quaker No Papist* (London, 1659), 15. For Collier and Whitehead see *BDBR, s.vv.*

[39] Roger Williams, *George Fox Digg'd out of His Burrowes, or an Offer of Disputation* (Boston, 1676), 76–78, 188, 193–94, 297, 324, 327, 329. For Williams' response to Fox's attack on Burton see ibid., 87–88, 90, 421–22. For Williams see *BDBR, s.v.*

[40] George Fox and John Burnyeat, *A New-England-Fire-Brand Quenched. The Second Part* ([London], 1679), 3–4, 8–9, 14. For Burnyeat see *BDBR, s.v.*

cryed against him." The Friends won some converts, for "many were made tender." The fact that the Bedford congregation was already identified among Quakers as Bunyan's group is undoubtedly a result of his prior controversy with Burrough and Fox's attack on him in 1659.[41]

## "These Dangerous Rocks"[42]: Sectarian Ferment

As Bunyan and Burrough engaged in their literary duel, the winter of 1656–57 witnessed mounting friction between Cromwell and Parliament, with many members expressing hostility toward the army, the rule of the major-generals, and a toleration policy that permitted Quakers to flourish and arguably led to James Nayler's "horrid blasphemy," the re-enactment of Jesus' entry into Jerusalem. Willing to terminate the experiment of ruling through major-generals, Cromwell was, for the most part, favorably disposed to a proposed new constitution, the Humble Petition and Advice, presented to him in February 1657. He hesitated, however, because it called for the establishment of a hereditary monarchy. As he mulled his options, senior army officers, civilian republicans, and millenarian zealots known as Fifth Monarchists expressed their opposition. In the Bedfordshire area, a group of approximately a hundred that included Dell, Donne, and various members of the Bedford church, among them Eston, the haberdasher Samuel Fenne, and the laborer Richard Cooper, signed *The Humble and Serious Testimony of Many Hundreds, of Godly and Well Affected People in the County of Bedford, and Parts Adjacent, Constant Adherers to the Cause of God and the Nation*, dated 14 April 1657. Whether Bunyan affixed his signature is not known because only a printed version, without the signatures, has survived, though his support is highly likely. The petitioners professed their belief in the destruction of Antichrist's kingdom and the advancement of Christ's, and they affirmed their support for a commonwealth rather than government by a single person as the best polity to prevent the Stuarts' return.[43] The "contrivers" of the document, according to a signer, were Dell and Donne. Colonel John Okey, an-

---

[41] Friends' Library, London, Swarthmore MSS, 3:133.

[42] *MW*, 1:382.

[43] *A Collection of the State Papers of John Thurloe*, ed. Thomas Birch, 7 vols. (London, 1742), 6:228–30; *The Humble and Serious Testimony of Many Hundreds, of Godly and Well Affected People in the County of Bedford, and Parts Adjacent, Constant Adherers to the Cause of God and the Nation* (n.p., 1657). Two of the signers, the gentleman Thomas Gibbs and the Bedford draper George Hawkins, believed "kingly government would involve the nation in a new war." *State Papers of Thurloe*, ed. Birch, 6:229–30.

other influential backer, was subsequently accused by Charles Williams of supporting the use of St. John's by Gifford, Burton, and Bunyan.[44]

The government detained a number of petitioners, apparently sparking Bunyan's ire; his condemnation of "surly dogged persecutors of the Saints" in *A Few Sighs from Hell* has been plausibly related to this episode by T. L. Underwood. So too was Bunyan's dark allusion in the same work to the dangers facing the godly: "And this I am perswaded of, that would the creatures do as some men would have them, the Saints of God should not walk so quietly up and down the streets, and other places, as they do" (*MW*, 1:258, 284, 399). Bunyan's political sympathies were thus almost certainly hostile to those moderates and conservatives who favored the restoration of monarchy, a step Cromwell ultimately rejected, though he did accept a modified version of the Humble Petition and Advice and was reinvested as lord protector in a ceremony akin to a coronation. His rejection of the crown in early May prompted the Bedford church on the 28th of that month to set apart a day "to praise God for his goodnes in delivering us out of our late troubles, and to seeke God for direction in discoursing with any of our dissenting friends."[45] Bunyan and his associates clearly had no desire for the return of monarchy.

Long before *The Humble and Serious Testimony* the government had been monitoring the activities of at least one prominent signer, Colonel Okey. In late 1654 he and two other colonels, Matthew Alured and Thomas Saunders, condemned the Instrument of Government as covertly monarchical and urged the republic's restoration, for which they were arrested. With Sir John Lawson, a Baptist who had been dismissed from his position as vice-admiral in early 1655 because of alleged Fifth Monarchist associations, Okey negotiated with a group of Fifth Monarchy Men, including John Portman, Arthur Squibb, Clement Ireton, and Thomas Venner, beginning in the winter of 1655–56. At their meeting in July 1656 they sought an alliance based on Sir Henry Vane's *A Healing Question Propounded and Resolved* (May 1656), which opposed military rule and advocated republican government, with a franchise limited to "the honest party," by which Vane meant the adherents of the Good Old Cause. The two groups could not find common ground on the nature of a future government, the Fifth Monarchists preferring a theocracy and the Commonwealthsmen a civilian republic. Nevertheless, when John Thurloe, secretary of state, learned of the meetings, he deemed them subversive and had Okey, Lawson, Portman, Venner, and others

---

[44] Vera Brittain, *Valiant Pilgrim: The Story of John Bunyan and Puritan England* (New York: Macmillan, 1950), 141. For Okey see *BDBR*, *s.v.*

[45] *CB*, 26.

arrested in the summer of 1656. The following year Thurloe seized a list of Fifth Monarchist agents that may have been compiled at the time of the negotiations with Okey and his fellow Commonwealthsmen. It included the names of Vavasor Powell, a Welsh Independent minister, and John Child, a member of Burton's Bedford congregation.[46]

The government suspected a conspiracy, and it was not wrong. Members of Venner's congregation, which worshiped in London at Swan Alley, Coleman Street, had established a secret organization comprising five groups, each with twenty-five members. They printed a manifesto, *A Standard Set Up*, calling for theocratic government, with power in the hands of a sanhedrin chosen by the saints and biblically based laws. They had horses, arms, and armor, and were monitoring the army's disposition. What they could not obtain was support from other Fifth Monarchists, and the uprising failed to materialize when government troops raided the conspirators on 9 April 1657 as they were preparing to take up arms. Venner and other Fifth Monarchists, including Portman, went to prison, while Okey and Lawson, who had no role in the plot, were briefly detained.[47]

Bunyan had no link to Venner's group, but at this point he may well have been a Fifth Monarchist sympathizer. In the spring of 1688, not long before his death, he published *The Advocateship of Jesus Christ* in which he recalled that he "did use to be much taken with one Sect of Christians, for that it was usually their way, when they made mention of the Name of *Jesus*, to call him, *The blessed King of Glory*" (MW, 11:194). The kingship of Christ was a theme stressed by Fifth Monarchists, and the phrase in question highlights the distinction, explained by John Tillinghast, between the kingdom of the saints, who will rule prior to Christ's return, and the kingdom of glory, in which the saints will be glorified in Christ their king.[48] Fifth Monarchist writings have numerous references to King Jesus, the king of saints, the king of kings, and the king of nations.[49] Powell com-

---

[46] Capp, *FMM*, 114–15; *BDBR*, s.vv. Matthew Alured, Thomas Saunders, and John Lawson; *State Papers of Thurloe*, ed. Birch, 6:187. For Portman, Squibb, Ireton, Thurloe, and Powell see *BDBR*, s.vv.

[47] Capp, *FMM*, 117–18; *BDBR*, s.v. Thomas Venner; *New DNB*, s.v. Thomas Venner.

[48] John Tillinghast, *Mr. Tillinghasts Eight Last Sermons* (London, 1655), 61–62; for the kingship of Jesus, see 1–43. For Tillinghast see *BDBR*, s.v. and *New DNB*, s.v.

[49] Mary Cary Rande, epistle to Mary Cary, *The Little Horns Doom & Downfall* (London, 1651), sig. A4v; Cary, *A New and More Exact Mappe or, Description of New Jerusalems Glory*, ad cal. *The Little Horns Doom & Downfall*, 212–28 (mspr. 128); anon., *The Faithfull Narrative of the Late Testimony and Demand Made to Oliver Cromwell . . . in the Name of the Lord Jehovah (Jesus Christ,) King of Saints and Nations* (n.p., 1654); John Spittlehouse, *Certaine Queries Propounded to the Most Serious Consideration of Those Persons Now in Power* (London, 1654), 8–10; Spittlehouse, *An Answer to One Part of the Lord Protector's*

posed a hymn "To Christ Our King," and William Aspinwall averred that Christ would be an absolute king during the fifth monarchy.[50] Similar language was sometimes employed by other religious radicals, including Thomas Goodwin, who preached a sermon on the fifth monarchy (though he denounced the Fifth Monarchists), and William Dell, some of whose parishioners charged in 1660 that he had said Charles I had been "no king to him, Christ was his king."[51] But Bunyan made it clear that his attraction had been to a specific group—a "Sect"—which can only have been the Fifth Monarchists.

The cordial relations between Fifth Monarchists and Commonwealthsmen beginning in late 1655 and extending into mid-1657 were mirrored in the Bedford church, where Child was a Fifth Monarchist. If Charles Williams was correct in accusing Okey of supporting the use of St. John's by the Gifford-Burton congregation, such members as Eston, Cooper, and John Fenne, who signed *The Humble and Serious Testimony*, of which Okey was a prominent supporter, were probably sympathetic to the Commonwealthsmen. For a time, Bunyan himself was close to Child. In October 1656, Bunyan, Child, and either John or Samuel Fenne debated with the Quakers, and on 28 May 1657 the church appointed Bunyan, Child, and John Fenne to visit a man at Houghton Conquest. Child, Spencely, and Burton provided a brief introductory note to Bunyan's second

---

*Speech* (London, 1654), 5; William Llanvaedonon, *A Brief Exposition upon the Second Psalme* (London, 1655), 21–29, 47; John Rogers, *Jegar-Sahadutha: An Oyled Pillar* [1657], 4, 45; anon., *The Fifth Monarchy, or Kingdom of Christ, in Opposition to the Beasts* (London, 1659), 5–6, 17, 23, 49; John More, *A Trumpet Sounded* (n.p., 1654), 2. For two examples from 1664 see PRO, SP 29/96/98, 101. For Cary, Spittlehouse, Rogers, and More see *BDBR*, s.vv.

[50] Powell's poem is reprinted in Louise Fargo Brown, *The Political Activities of the Baptists and Fifth Monarchy Men in England During the Interregnum* (Washington, DC: American Historical Association, 1912), 51; William Aspinwall, *A Brief Description of the Fifth Monarchy* (London, 1653), 3. See also Aspinwall, *Thunder from Heaven Against the Back-Sliders and Apostates of the Times* (London, 1655), 3, 11, 35, 38; Aspinwall, *The Work of the Age* (London, 1655), 11–12; John Canne, *The Time of the End* (London, 1657), 33; Canne, *A Seasonable Word to the Parliament-Men* (London, 1659), 5; *Certain Quaeres Humbly Presented in Way of Petition* (London, 1648 [February 1649]), 6; anon., *A Declaration of Several of the Churches of Christ, and Godly People in and about the Citie of London* (London, 1654); Rogers, *Jegar-Sahadutha*, sig. A2v. For Aspinwall and Canne see *BDBR*, s.vv.

[51] Thomas Goodwin, *A Sermon of the Fifth Monarchy* (London, 1654), 3, 5, 10–11, 16; *Calamy Revised*, s.v. William Dell. In conjunction with John Owen, Philip Nye, and Sidrach Simpson, Goodwin issued a statement repudiating the Fifth Monarchists on 9 January 1654. Bodl., Carte MSS 81, fols. 16r–17v. For Goodwin, Owen, Nye, and Simpson see *BDBR*, s.vv.

work, *A Vindication of the Book Called, Some Gospel-Truths Opened*, published in 1657. The church again assigned visitation responsibilities to Bunyan and Child in February and April 1658.[52] During their work together, Child undoubtedly shared his Fifth Monarchist views with Bunyan.

The ties between the Bedford congregation and various churches in London provide additional evidence of Fifth Monarchist sympathies in the former. On 27 August 1657 Burton's flock set aside the following Thursday for a day of prayer with their coreligionists in England, Scotland, and Ireland as called for by Henry Jessey and others. An avowed millenarian, Jessey was on the fringes of the Fifth Monarchy movement and had close ties to such leaders as Christopher Feake and John Simpson. In 1654 various members of Jessey's church had signed a Fifth Monarchist manifesto, and Jessey himself attended a Fifth Monarchist meeting at Allhallows in December 1656, when Feake condemned the government as "Babylonish"; Jessey, however, urged moderation.[53] As Burton's health began to fail in 1659, his congregants decided in November to write to Jessey, Simpson, and Cokayne, a Fifth Monarchist in the early 1650s and again in the 1660s; a Bedfordshire native, Cokayne was minister at St. Pancras, Soper Lane, London. The same meeting approved the request of one of its female members, who had moved to London, to join Simpson's congregation at St. Botolph's, Bishopsgate. Like Cokayne, Simpson at this point had retreated from his earlier Fifth Monarchist militancy.[54]

Child's break with the Bedford congregation was probably due to the church's apparent pullback from its Fifth Monarchist sympathies in 1658. Two years earlier, he had protested against Burton's participation in a lectureship at Westoning, southwest of Ampthill, Bedfordshire. Westoning's minister at that time was William Rawlins, who would be admitted to the rectorship of Hampstead Marshall, Berkshire, on 2 October 1657 and ejected in 1660. But the dominant clerical figure at Westoning in 1656 was Dell, who purchased substantial land there in the mid-1650s.[55] Dell was a supporter of Okey, whose election to Parliament he had sought in the summer of 1654, as he did that of Nathaniel Taylor, John Crook, Edward Cater, and John Barbor, an agent of the Bedford Corporation; all of them, Dell allegedly said, opposed tithes and taxes.[56] Donne was close to Dell, having studied at Gonville and Caius, and probably also par-

---

[52] *MW*, 1:xxiv, 121; *CB*, 26, 29, 30.

[53] *CB*, 28; Capp, *FMM*, 59, 81, 105, 117. For Feake and John Simpson see *BDBR*, *s.vv.*, and for Simpson see also Greaves, *SR*, 99–132.

[54] *CB*, 34; *BDBR*, *s.v.* George Cokayne; Greaves, *SR*, 121–23.

[55] *CB*, 22; *Calamy Revised*, *s.v.* William Rawlins; Eric C. Walker, *William Dell: Master Puritan* (Cambridge: W. Heffer and Sons, 1970), 175–77.

[56] *CSPD, 1654*, 334.

ticipated in the Westoning lectures. As a Fifth Monarchist, Child must not have liked the tenor of these lectures. For the sake of peace and unity in the Bedford church, Burton agreed to cease participating. However, by October 1658 Child had broken with his former associates in Bedford and moved to London, where he promised to take the advice of Jessey, Simpson, and the Fifth Monarchist John Rogers, all three of whom had opposed the militancy evinced in Venner's conspiracy. But Child changed his mind, telling Burton in a letter that he intended to join "Mr. Harris' congregation," preferably with the approval of the Bedford church. When the latter rejected his request on the grounds that he had not provided "solid Scriptural grounds," Child became a member of Harris' church.[57] This was probably the Particular Baptist congregation of Edward Harrison, which met at his home in Petty France, London.[58]

By late February 1659 Bunyan had spoken to Child, counseling him to explain his actions to some of the brethren, but Child refused unless he could address the entire congregation. When Bunyan tendered such an invitation, Child reneged. At this juncture the church decided to seek the advice of the congregations with which it was affiliated, namely, those of Donne at Pertenhall, Wheeler at Cranfield, and Gibbs at Newport Pagnell; these ministers and other representatives therefore met at Bedford on 16 May 1659. They recommended that Child be asked to submit a written explanation of his refusal to appear before the Bedford church and to include the names of ministers or messengers of churches— presumably those of the Particular Baptists—that had advised him not to comply with Bedford's request. Bunyan, John Fenne, and John Whitman, or any two of them, were to convey this message to Child. By late October Child had "confessed his miscarriage in some things relating to his withdrawing from us" to several brethren, and Bunyan, Fenne, and Whitman were again deputed in October and November to talk further with him.[59] The church book has no additional information about Child, who apparently remained in London.

The Bedford congregation reached its decisions on Child and other issues through discussions aimed at achieving a consensus. Business meetings were held monthly. The church elected its officers democratically, with women sharing the right of selection: "Our brethren and sisters were required to consider what per-

[57] *CB*, 22, 31 (quoted); Capp, *FMM*, 117.

[58] *BDBR*, s.v.; *Association Records of the Particular Baptists of England, Wales and Ireland to 1660*, ed. B. R. White, 3 vols. (London: Baptist Historical Society, n.d.), 3:215. A less likely identification is Thomas Harris, a member of Venner's congregation. Venner was still in the Tower at this time. Harris would subsequently die for his part in Venner's insurrection in January 1661. *Mercurius Publicus* 3 (17–24 January 1661); *Kingdomes Intelligencer* (21–28 January 1661).

[59] *CB*, 31–34.

sons the Lord shall direct them to in the society that they shall judge fit to choose, and . . . they [shall] give in their names in writing." Those unable to attend the meeting could submit absentee ballots.[60] Prior to the monthly meeting on 27 August 1657, the members sought divine guidance in electing officers "according to the order of the Gospell." Bunyan, Spencely, and two others had been nominated to the deaconship and "appointed for tryall," but on the 27th the meeting replaced Bunyan with John Fenne because the former had been "taken off by the preaching of the Gospell." For the more orderly handling of business, the monthly meeting decided in December 1659 that the brethren—probably the elders (pastors) and deacons—should convene the Wednesday preceding the meeting to prepare "the affaires there to be managed." The same meeting resolved that at each subsequent monthly gathering, some of the brethren "to whom the Lord may have given a gift, be called forth and incouraged to speake a word in the Church for our mutuall edification." Henceforth, all church members, both male and female, were expected to attend every third monthly meeting.[61]

The business transacted at the monthly sessions ranged rather widely. Provisions were made to counsel and if necessary discipline errant members, such as Oliver Dicks, who falsely claimed a neighbor's sheep, or Sister Linford, who ceased attending because of a disagreement over baptism. The church withdrew fellowship from recalcitrant offenders, who could be readmitted only after professing "humiliation" for their offenses before the congregation.[62] The monthly meeting was also responsible to see that the needy received assistance, as in November 1656, when many of the congregation's friends were experiencing distress, prompting the meeting to urge its members to contribute according to their ability. The previous month the meeting had established a visitation system, whereby two brethren were appointed each month and charged to visit members, "and to certify us how they doe in body and soule, and to stirre them up to come . . . to us," warning them that they must explain their absence should they fail to appear.[63] In February 1658 the monthly meeting revised the system, appointing one or two visitors for Bedford and one for each village or cluster of villages—at this time, Elstow, Kempston, Wilshamstead/Houghton Conquest, and Oakley/Stevington/Radwell. Although this system ostensibly sought to ascertain "a more perfect account of the state of [the] members," its focus was on absenteeism and members' physical needs. This was a more restricted visitation structure than that developed by Quakers in Ireland in the late seventeenth century, which covered

[60] CB, 26, 31, 32 (quoted).
[61] CB, 28 (quoted), 35 (quoted).
[62] CB, 22, 25, 28, 29.
[63] CB, 23 (quoted), 24.

virtually every aspect of behavior, clothing, home furnishings, and ultimately activities in the shops.[64]

Admission to the Bedford congregation was carefully controlled. Church members visited candidates for membership to ascertain "the truth of the worke of grace in their heartes." If satisfied, the visitors invited the applicants to the next meeting, where they had to wait outside until summoned. Should the meeting decide a candidate was not ready, it delegated members to counsel her or him, and to "indeavour the prevention of any temptation, that by the denyall of admittance [she or he] may be exposed to." Acceptance into the church did not require a particular form of baptism; on the contrary, candidates had to affirm that the congregation was "in union with Christ, though differing in judgement about some outward things."[65] Bunyan would subsequently expound on this principle in *A Confession of My Faith, and a Reason of My Practice* (1672), *Differences in Judgment about Water-Baptism, No Bar to Communion* (1673), and *Peaceable Principles and True* (1674).

In September 1658 the monthly meeting appointed Bunyan, Burton, Grew, Harrington, and Whitman to explore ways to promote unity with the churches of Donne at Pertenhall, Wheeler at Cranfield, and Gibbs at Newport Pagnell. Similar groups met in those congregations, and in February the Bedford monthly meeting deputed Bunyan, Grew, and Harrington to meet with their representatives. The result was a written agreement that apparently is not extant, though it was supposed to have been recorded in Bedford's church book. The minutes do refer to the eighth provision, which called for mutual consultation about difficult matters, as occurred in Child's case. Another proviso stipulated that a church which lost its minister should consult representatives from the other congregations concerning a replacement.[66]

With the Bedford church's approval, Bunyan was preaching no later than August 1657. For preaching at Eaton Socon, Bedfordshire, about midway between Bedford and Huntingdon, he was indicted at the assizes by February 1658, probably following a complaint from the Presbyterian Thomas Becke, the local vicar. The church to which Bunyan preached at Eaton Socon was Independent, with members from nearby Hail Weston, Huntingdonshire, as well. The congregation had ties to Dell, who wrote a letter from Hail Weston shortly after he resigned his mastership at Gonville and Caius in May 1660; his contact likely antedated the

[64] *CB*, 29 (quoted); Richard L. Greaves, *Dublin's Merchant-Quaker: Anthony Sharp and the Community of Friends, 1643–1707* (Stanford, CA: Stanford University Press, 1998), 216–21.

[65] *CB*, 24 (quoted), 26 (quoted), 27.

[66] *CB*, 31–34, 36.

Restoration.[67] It was probably Dell who arranged for Bunyan to preach at Eaton Socon. As we shall see, he certainly invited Bunyan to preach from his pulpit at Yelden, where he was rector, on Christmas day, 1659.

"Scalding Lead"[68]: Professional Clergy and the Rich

Expostulating at length on Luke 16:19–31, Bunyan turned his verbal artillery primarily against the wealthy in his third book, *A Few Sighs from Hell, or, the Groans of a Damned Soul*, printed by Ralph Wood for M. Wright in 1658. The theme had been incorporated in Bunyan's epistle to the reader in *A Vindication of Some Gospel-Truths Opened*, where he promised the saints that at their deaths Jesus would deal with them as he had blessed Lazarus, whereas the Diveses of this world *"would be glad if they might have but the least favour from you, one drop of cold water on the tip of your fingers"* (MW, 1:130). In both the epistle and the body of the same work he also lashed out against the professional clergy, castigating them as examples of pride, wantonness, inebriety, and covetousness. Such clerics run and ride

> after great Benefices, and Parsonages by night and by day. Nay they among themselves will scramble for the same. I have seen, That so soon as a man hath but departed from his Benefice as he calls it, either by death or out of covetousness of a bigger, we have had one Priest from this Town, and another from that, so run, for those tithe-cocks and handfulls of Barley, as if it were their proper Trade, and calling, to hunt after the same. (1:127–28)

Using the language of traditional anticlericalism, Bunyan denounced those clergy who sought personal gain as false prophets—dumb dogs and wolves in sheep's clothing. Cloaking themselves in feigned holiness, such men deluded the people with false doctrines, especially the belief that salvation is attainable by good deeds. He lumped such priests with Quakers and Ranters, all of whom, he said, dishonored Christ (1:205, 216–17). Burrough was quick to charge Bunyan himself with "making Merchandise of Souls" by preaching for hire, and Fox echoed the charge, though Bunyan denied receiving monetary compensation for his preaching.[69]

By the time Bunyan turned to his third book, he was already on record as a

[67] CB, 28–29; A. G. Matthews, *Walker Revised: Being a Revision of John Walker's Sufferings of the Clergy During the Grand Rebellion 1642–60* (Oxford: Clarendon Press, 1948; reissued, 1988), 67; Walker, *Dell*, 173, 219–20.

[68] MW, 1:300.

[69] Burrough, *Memorable Works*, 147 (quoted), 151, 281; Fox, *Great Mistery*, 8; MW, 1:139. Burrough made the same charge against John Burton, claiming he received at least £150 p.a. *Memorable Works*, 302.

critic not only of Friends and Ranters but also of most professional clergy. Simultaneously, however, questions were being posed about his own qualifications to preach. In an epistle to the reader in *A Few Sighs from Hell*, John Gibbs, himself a Cambridge graduate, came to Bunyan's defense, acknowledging his modest formal education and the meanness of his "former employment" as a tinker, but averring that he had been taught by the Holy Spirit and demonstrated his ability to enable others to feel the power of God's word (1:243–44).

> He is not like unto your drones, that will suck the sweet, but do no work. For he hath laid forth himself to the utmost of his strength, taking all advantages to make known to others, what he himself received of God: and I fear this is one reason why the Archers have shot so soarly at him.

The industrious Bunyan, with a strong work ethic at age thirty, was, in Gibbs' estimation, disliked by professional clerics whose slothfulness stood in sharp contrast to his preaching and writing. Gibbs also made it clear that he did not consider Bunyan one of the "light fanatick spirits," perhaps thinking of such tub-preachers as the cobbler Samuel How.[70] Gibbs, however, was not prepared to conclude that *only* the unlettered could efficaciously preach God's word, an acknowledgment Bunyan himself did not make in this book (1:243–44).

To some extent Bunyan was on the defensive in *A Few Sighs from Hell*, answering his unnamed critics, whose numbers, opined Gibbs, were already numerous (1:243). Better, Bunyan argued, "to receive a child of God, that can by experience deliver the things of God" than to flatter and fawn over "a company of carnal Clergy-men." The ability to read and speak Hebrew, Greek, and Latin was unnecessary; indeed, he derisively linked that ability to Pontius Pilate (1:304, 307)! Nor was a university education essential: "carnal Priests do tickle the ears of their hearers with vain Philosophy and deceit, and thereby harden their hearts against the simplicity of the Gospel" (1:345), a point also made by such other sectaries as John Knowles, Thomas Collier, William Dell, and the Quakers.[71] University-educated preachers, Bunyan avouched, succumb to the peril of nuzzling up to Plato, Aristotle, and other heathen philosophers instead of preaching Christ "rightly" (1:345). By their corrupt doctrine and ignorance of the gospel, "filthy blind Priests" preach that which is no better for their listeners' souls than is rat-poison for the body. Entire parishes will follow them to hell, bellowing that they have been misled by lies and fables, and told that God's way is heresy. Bunyan

---

[70] For How see *BDBR*, s.v.

[71] Richard L. Greaves, *The Puritan Revolution and Educational Thought: Background for Reform* (New Brunswick, NJ: Rutgers University Press, 1969), 17–25. For Knowles see *BDBR*, s.v.

pointedly contrasted the carnal clergy's preaching and muttering formal prayers in steeple-houses with the sermons and prayers of the godly in private homes and fields (1:282, 306–7, 314–15).

Not surprisingly, the clergy of the Church of England, many of whom were now Presbyterians, resented these verbal assaults. Well before the restoration of the monarchy and the traditional church in 1660, Bunyan was experiencing what he described as persecution. By this time he was reading John Foxe's *Acts and Monuments*, popularly known as the *Book of Martyrs*, and was clearly impressed by the courage of those who had faced the rack, the gallows, and burning at the stake. He singled out Edmund Bonner, the Marian bishop of London, whom he would later call "that blood-red Persecutor" (1:314, 358; 2:253). Foxe undoubtedly helped influence Bunyan's sense of the saints as a persecuted people, but the recurring references in *A Few Sighs from Hell* to persecution reflected contemporary circumstances as well (1:255–56, 258, 277–78, 284, 291, 318). "Enemies rage and threaten to knock me in the head," he wrote, mindful of his own experience (1:360–61). Opposition was increasing, thanks undoubtedly to his undisguised anticlericalism and his seeming tendency to equate the rich with the ungodly. "*The world rages, they stamp and shake their heads, and fain they would be doing: the Lord help me to take all they shall do with patience, and when they smite the one cheek, to turn the other to them*" (1:248). The sense of persecution undoubtedly increased in April 1657 when Robert Fitzhugh, Bedford's mayor, interrogated John Eston and John Grew, two leading members of the Bedford congregation who had supported a petition opposing the offer of the crown to Cromwell.[72] As we have seen, Bunyan himself was indicted at the assizes for a sermon he had preached at Eaton Socon no later than February 1658, when the Bedford church decided to seek legal counsel on his behalf.[73]

The persecuted saints were role models for Bunyan as he wrote *A Few Sighs from Hell*, with its vivid warnings of the dire fate that awaited those who refused to heed God's call to repent. In developing this message Bunyan relied heavily on the Bible, as he had in his debates with Burrough. For Bunyan Scripture was the word and counsel of God, his "true sayings," including both his promises and his threats. Those who slight the Bible treat God with disrespect. All Scripture, he contended, is inspired and profitable for instruction and reproof, but he cautioned against the "bare search" of the Bible as distinct from "a real application of him whom they testifie of, to thy soul" (1:323–24, 328, 346, 357). Without the aid of divine grace, however, no one can "rightly believe" biblical teachings. Bunyan

[72] *CB*, 15, 17; *State Papers of Thurloe*, ed. Birch, 6:228–30.
[73] *CB*, 29; W. T. Whitley, "Bunyan's Imprisonments: A Legal Study," *Transactions of the Baptist Historical Society* 6 (1918–19): 3.

was aware that all groups in the Christian tradition cite Scripture to buttress their often conflicting tenets, but this he blamed on the Devil, who, he averred, uses subtlety to confuse the ungodly, corrupting biblical interpretations and "rendring them not so point blank the minde of God, and a rule for direction to poor souls" (1:345, 355). Given the tenor of Bunyan's attack on the rich in this work, it is worth noting that he condemns those critics of the Bible who dismiss it as the work of political leaders intent on making poor, ignorant people submit to their government and religion (1:343).

Bunyan bolstered his appeal to biblical authority with examples from his own religious experience, effectively treating the latter as a verification of the former. In *A Few Sighs from Hell* he recounted how he had heard many good sermons in which the preacher expounded the word of God, warning that hell would be his portion, that the Devil would wreak malice on him, and that God would treat him with displeasure. But in his self-proclaimed ignorance, conceit, obstinacy, and rebellion, he had refused to heed the scriptural citations despite the preacher's voice ringing in his ears. The Bible, he thought, was "a dead letter, a little ink and paper," worth 3 or 4s. Once awakened to his plight, he recalled how a line or even a word from the Bible could keep him from eating, sleeping, toiling, or enjoying the company of his friends. From his experience he knew too that once he had come to believe that Scripture is God's word, he could be sorely grieved or perplexed if he thought a biblical passage excluded him from the divine promises (1:332–33, 344, 358; cf. 267). Through the Spirit's work, as he saw it, he came to realize that those scriptural promises contain the ultimate key to spiritual tranquillity: "O I say, when the law curses, when the Devil tempts, when hell-fire flames in my conscience, my sins with the guilt of them tearing of me, then is Christ revealed so sweetly to my poor soul through the promises" (1:360). To question the veracity and authority of the Bible was therefore to undermine the inner peace he had finally discovered. By 1658 he had determined that his own spiritual travails were useful in conveying his message, and in the mid-1660s this awareness convinced him to record his experiences more fully in *Grace Abounding to the Chief of Sinners*.

The principal theme of *A Few Sighs from Hell*, the first work in which Bunyan begins to display his fertile imagination, is an exhortation to repent or face the virtually indescribable torments of everlasting punishment. His text, Luke 16:19–31, provided him with a platform from which to castigate the callous rich, though he did so in qualified terms, stopping short of equating the wealthy with the ungodly. He did assert, however, that the rich were "most liable to the devils temptations, [and] are most ready to be puft up with pride, stoutness, cares of this world, in which things they spend most of their time, in lusts, drunkenness, wantonness, idleness, together with the other works of the flesh" (1:253–54). He wrote scathingly of society's great ones who strut up and down the streets in their new suits, regarding themselves as the only happy people. Feasting on sumptuous dishes, they care for nothing but their bellies. Their dogs, Bunyan wrote indignantly, receive better treatment than the saints, who go hungry and inhabit hovels (1:251–52, 257).[74] Unfeeling landlords either evict godly tenants or discourage them from hearing sermons by threatening to raise their rent. The rich treat the poor man as if he were "scrubbed, beggarly *Lazarus*," "a scabbed creep-hedge" who skulks in hedgerows intent on doing evil, but "it is the rich man that goes to hell" (1:252, 257, 304, 315). So too, Bunyan admitted, would the indigent who reject divine mercy. In the end, degrees of wealth and poverty are not the determining factors of one's eternal destiny, though wealth is an almost insuperable barrier to the well-to-do because it disinclines them to repent. In contrast, he described the saints as beggarly and poor (1:254, 285).

To some degree this concern probably reflected the fact that more than half of the Bedford congregation were of the "meaner sort"; Bill Stevenson's analysis of the hearth-tax returns for 1671–74 shows that 14.8 percent of the Bedford church's eighty-one households were exempt and 37 percent had only one hearth. In contrast, 38.1 percent of nonconformist households in Bedfordshire, Cambridgeshire, and Huntingdonshire were poor. From another perspective, the average number of hearths for Bedfordshire in general was 2.44 compared to 1.9 for the Bedford congregation. Only eight households (9.9 percent) in Bunyan's church had four or more hearths compared to 41.7 percent for the Presbyterians and 16.8 percent for the Quakers in the three counties.[75] The number of poor in the Bedford congregation clearly exceeded the norm, and Bunyan must have been sensitive to their needs, though he was also likely to have been influenced by the plight of the impoverished in society generally. He had witnessed the destitution caused by five successive bad harvests between 1646 and 1650, and in the 1650s commodities prices rose and the plight of the indigent worsened.[76] The popularity of *A Few Sighs from Hell* (henceforth published as *Sighs from Hell*),

[74] Cf. Dent, *Plaine Mans Path-Way*, 191–92a; *MW*, 1:xliv–xlvi. Like many in the puritan and nonconformist traditions (and beyond), Philip Henry made the same point: "a prosperous condition a dangerous condition & so it is, prosperity ensnares, entangles, destroyes, lord give mee neither riches nor poverty." *Diaries and Letters of Philip Henry, M.A. of Broad Oak, Flintshire A.D. 1631–1696*, ed. Matthew Henry Lee (London: Kegan Paul, Trench and Co., 1882), 138; cf. CUL, Add. MSS 7338, commenting on Genesis 12.

[75] Bill Stevenson, "The Social and Economic Status of Post-Restoration Dissenters, 1660–1725," in *The World of Rural Dissenters, 1520–1725*, ed. Margaret Spufford (Cambridge: Cambridge University Press, 1995), 334–38.

[76] Anthony Fletcher, *Reform in the Provinces: The Government of Stuart England* (New Haven, CT: Yale University Press, 1986), 199.

which reached a seventh edition by 1686, may owe something to the continuing plight of the indigent. In 1659–60, for instance, numerous petitions and tracts complained about unemployment, high food prices, and depressed trade, and petitioners from Bedfordshire, Buckinghamshire, and Hertfordshire called in 1659 for the abolition of copyhold tenure.[77]

Over the years Bunyan's view of the rich and mighty would generally mellow, though as late as 1687 his indignation against the idle rich would flare up. In contrast to the stridency of his attack on the well-off in 1658, including a snide aside about the gentry, he came to appreciate that God had a role for the landed aristocracy and even for monarchs. In *The Pilgrim's Progress* Great-heart's master is a peer and Christ is Lord of the Hill, and in *The Holy War* the forces of righteousness are monarchical and hierarchical. King Shaddai and Prince Emanuel number among their supporters Lords Innocent, Understanding, and the sometimes troubled Willbewill, and Bunyan ennobled Self-denial. But in 1658 Bunyan was still not far removed from penury, sensitive about his humble background (which he would later make a badge of honor), and perhaps resentful every time he gazed on the lands that had belonged to his ancestors.

At thirty Bunyan was a man of some bitterness, but he channeled his rage into a vivid description of the fate that awaited the ungodly in a hell which was undeniably material. Hell is for bodies as well as souls, and the resurrection of the dead is therefore physical, contrary to Quaker teaching. As in his controversy with Burrough, Bunyan rejected the view that hell exists only in this life. On the contrary, it is a place of eternal torment where the damned "lie and fry, scorch and broil, and burn for ever," the objects of God's "unspeakable scalding vengeance" (1:266–67, 300, 303, 327, 362, 372, 374, 377–78). The damned, he warned, swim in fire and brimstone. One of hell's defining characteristics is pain—agony far worse than that of a man tied to a stake whose flesh is pulled off, bit by bit, with red-hot pincers for several years. To have one's body filled with scalding lead or to be run through with a red-hot spit is like a flea bite in comparison to hell's agonies. In this place of perdition one's sins "will gripe thee and gnaw thee as if thou hadst a nest of poisonous Serpents in thy bowels" (1:300, 303, 364). Hell's second defining quality, Bunyan opined, is deafening noise, "the intollerable roarings of the damned." Those who mock sin and play with it as a baby does with a rattle will find that in hell these rattles will make a din as if all the devils were screaming (1:302–3, 369). Hades' third characteristic is an agonizing recollection of things past, "a scalding hot remembrance of all thy sinful thoughts, words and actions" (1:291). The guilt of one's sins will weigh ever so heavily, as if

[77] Brian Manning, *Aristocrats, Plebeians and Revolution in England, 1640–1660* (London: Pluto Press, 1996), 124, 126.

one's belly were filled with flaming pitch. So too will the painful recollection of all the times one slighted the gospel (1:272–73). Finally, hell is a place where the damned—children as well as adults—will see their family, friends, and acquaintances in heaven, blissfully enjoying the rewards of their belief in Christ. "O wonderfull torment!" (1:274, 379). This depiction struck terror in the heart of a London apprentice when he read that after spending 10,000,000 years in hell, a damned soul was no nearer the end of torment than when it began.[78]

Woven throughout *A Few Sighs from Hell* is a devastating critique of popular culture, which Bunyan makes the prelude to this horrific Hades. Much of his criticism is directed against the traditional targets of Christian moralists—sexual promiscuity and prostitution, gambling, inebriety, and swearing, the evil to which he had been most inclined as a young man.[79] The ungodly, he wrote in a masterful summation, are prone to "painting their faces, feeding their lusts, following their whores, robbing their neighbours, telling of lies, following of playes, and sports to pass away the time." The inclusion of the theater in this catalogue of popular ills reflects puritan tradition, but Bunyan's blanket attack on games was an extreme manifestation of the puritan concern with idleness and reflected his disquietude about wasting time. Dancing, a traditional part of English life, though disliked by puritans and some Prayer-Book Protestants, was no less acceptable to him (1:279).[80] Nor was hunting, which he lumped with other lusts of the flesh as a time-waster. In bold strokes he painted a scene of town and village life that was anything but idyllic. Wanton people walked the streets, manifesting "filthy carriages," while others haunted whorehouses, gambled, or frittered their time away. The ungodly swore, lied, jested, boasted, flattered, and threatened (1:260, 262, 279, 287, 310–11).

> But for all this, how thick, and by heaps, do these wretches walk up and down our streets? Do but go into the Alehouses & you shall see almost every room besprinkled with them, . . . foming out their own shame. (1:335; cf. 311)

In Bunyan's mind, traditional culture is a trap for the unwary as well as the consciously wicked. Relatively fresh from his own triumph over these temptations, he pressed others not to succumb, even to such apparently harmless pursuits as sports, hunting, and dancing. Time is a valuable commodity, to waste only at the peril of everlasting damnation. Not everyone Bunyan saw on the streets engaged

[78] The anonymous apprentice's account is printed in Charles Doe, *A Collection of Experience of the Work of Grace* (London, [1700]), 11.

[79] *MW*, 1:260–62, 279, 301, 305, 309, 311, 314, 317, 335, 337, 340, 378. Although Bunyan condemned gambling, he cited gamblers' odds to make points. See, e.g., *MW*, 1:245, 339.

[80] Richard L. Greaves, *Society and Religion in Elizabethan England* (Minneapolis: University of Minnesota Press, 1981), 434–35 (games), 446–54 (the theater), 454–57 (dancing).

in such dangerous pursuits; others were "drowned in a selfconceited holiness of Christianity," but such people were no less unacceptable to God. Their sanctimonious good deeds would ultimately vanish like crackling thorns that quickly turn to smoke and ashes in a fire (1:293, 318). It is worth stressing that his critique of contemporary culture was in place well before the Restoration.

Throughout *A Few Sighs from Hell* Bunyan indicated that sinners have a choice in deciding their eternal destiny. Like the instructions Christian found in the parchment-roll he received from Evangelist, Bunyan exhorted his readers to fly to Christ (*PP*, 10; *MW*, 1:335). His few references to election and reprobation barely hint at Calvinist predestinarian dogma and pale in comparison to the leitmotif of free will.[81] "Put not off the tenders" of divine mercy, for the offer of grace may terminate before one dies—a reflection of the fear Bunyan himself had experienced in his religious travails. Consider the proffer of grace, he urged, "while you have day-light, and Gospel-light, while the Son of God doth hold out termes of reconciliation to you" (1:281, 294, 366). By advising his readers to enter the straight gate, he clearly presumed they had the ability—the freedom—to do so. Later he would be more careful to stress that faith is a divine gift: Good-will must open the wicket gate for Christian, and Captain Credence is an officer in Emanuel's army, not a resident of Mansoul.[82] But in *A Few Sighs from Hell*, as in his later sermon *Come, & Welcome, to Jesus Christ* (1678), Bunyan the evangelical preacher earnestly entreated sinners to repent and "hold on in thy race" for eternal life, a theme he subsequently developed in *The Heavenly Foot-Man* (published posthumously in 1698) (1:362).

### "Two Covenants in Their Right Places"[83]: Pulpit Theology

Notwithstanding the differences between *A Few Sighs from Hell*, which generally excoriated professional clerics and the wealthy, and *The Doctrine of the Law and Grace Unfolded*, Bunyan's most substantive theological exposition of covenant theology, the transition between them was almost seamless. The concluding sentence of the former announced the theme of the latter:

> [Scriptural] faith if thou attain unto, will so work in thy heart, that first thou wilt see the nature of the Law, and also the nature of the Gospel, and delighting in the glory of it; and also thou wilt finde an ingaging of thy heart and soul to Jesus Christ, even to the giving up of thy whole man unto him, to be ruled and governed by him to his glory, and thy comfort, by the Faith of the same Lord Jesus. (*MW*, 1:382)

[81] For the predestinarian theme see *MW*, 1:277, 289, 297, 366; contrast these references with statements suggesting free will: 1:289–90, 320–21, 333, 337, 339–40, 366–67, 369–70.
[82] *MW*, 1:301; *PP*, 25; *HW*, 68. See Greaves, *JB*, 69–75.
[83] *MW*, 2:15.

From here it was a natural step to launch into an exposition of Paul's assertion in Roman's 6:14 that believers are under grace rather than the law. Indeed, Bunyan may well have followed his sermons on Luke 16:19–31 with a series on this Pauline passage. According to his successor in the pulpit of Bedford Meeting, Ebenezer Chandler, and Bunyan's friend John Wilson, minister at Hitchin, Hertfordshire, he wrote out his sermons after preaching them, probably commencing with an outline and expanding it, especially for sermons intended for publication.[84] *The Doctrine of the Law and Grace Unfolded* follows a common method of sermon construction, beginning with the "opening" of the biblical text, the articulation of doctrines deduced from that passage, and finally the application or "uses" of this material. Interspersed are rhetorical, anticipated, or actual objections followed by Bunyan's refutations. He would subsequently use this dialogue style in *The Pilgrim's Progress*.

By 1659 Bunyan was becoming increasingly at home in the pulpit, preaching what he "felt, what [he] smartingly did feel." At first, as we have seen, he had been troubled by his own spiritual doubts, so much so that he went "in chains to preach to them in chains." For at least two years he preached notwithstanding the feelings of guilt and terror that accompanied him to the very door of the pulpit. By 1655 he had experienced sufficient inner peace—"sweet discoveries of [Christ's] blessed Grace"—to alter the focus of his preaching, which for the next five years concentrated on Christ's "Offices, Relations, and Benefits" (*GA*, §§276–78). The sermons on Luke 16:19–31 and Romans 6:14 fall in this period, with only the latter fitting comfortably with his description of his broad theme, for *The Doctrine of the Law and Grace Unfolded* expounds on the office of Christ as mediator and the benefits accruing to the godly through the covenant of grace.

Although Bunyan now entered the pulpit with assurance, preaching "as if an Angel of God had stood by at my back to encourage me," he was ill at ease preparing material for the printed page. In part this resulted from the difficulty of adequately expressing his intense spiritual and emotional convictions in print. In the pulpit his message had "been with such power and heavenly evidence upon my own Soul, while I have been labouring to unfold it, to demonstrate it, and to fasten it upon the Conscience of others." He was "more then sure" of what he was preaching, although the doctors and priests condemned him, and he knew his published works would be ready targets for more of their criticism (§§282–83). However, he seems to have been more concerned that at least some of his readers would fault him for his lack of higher learning, though even as he expressed this worry he sneered at "Fantastical expressions, and . . . light, vain, whimsical Scholar-like terms." Instead he hoped his readers would find "a parcel

[84] Ebenezer Chandler and John Wilson, epistle to Bunyan, *Works* (1692), sig. A1v.

of plain, yet sound, true, and home sayings," the credit for which he assigned to Jesus. If knowledgeable Christians found his book difficult, Bunyan suggested that the blame lay with his brevity or his weaknesses (*MW*, 2:16). The principal intended reader, however, was not the mature believer but the unconverted, and for most of this audience his book was probably too meaty. In contrast to the highly popular *Come, & Welcome, to Jesus Christ*, which went through six editions in a decade, *The Doctrine of the Law and Grace Unfolded* was published in only one other edition (in 1685) during Bunyan's lifetime. Nevertheless, this treatise is not a tedious, complacent work, reflecting, as G. B. Harrison charged, a cooling of Bunyan's enthusiasm and the beginning of a concern with "the red tape of Christianity";[85] on the contrary, *The Doctrine of the Law and Grace Unfolded* evinces Bunyan's compelling urgency to reach out to those he believed were facing eternal damnation under the covenant of works. It is a book suffused with existential vigor.[86]

Despite the fact that Bunyan self-consciously deprecated his education in his epistle to the reader, he had by this point read and learned from a number of religious works. Several of these he explicitly acknowledged, namely, Luther's commentary on Galatians, the books by Dent and Bayly acquired when he married, and John Dod and Robert Cleaver's *A Plaine and Familiar Exposition of the Ten Commaundements*, to which he directed readers in a marginal comment in his new book (2:35).[87] As we have seen, he was also reading unidentified biblical commentaries, and he may have been influenced by the sermons of Paul Hobson, William Erbery, Thomas Ford, John Gifford, and John Burton, and perhaps by the views John Gibbs enunciated in his debate with Richard Carpenter. Other in-

---

[85] G. B. Harrison, *John Bunyan: A Study in Personality* (Garden City, NY: Doubleday, Doran, 1928), 69.

[86] Stuart Sim and David Walker propose an intriguing reading of *The Doctrine of the Law and Grace Unfolded*, taking note of the fact that its composition occurred during Richard Cromwell's protectorate, when Parliament voted to restrict religious toleration. They argue, rightly, that Bunyan, concerned about the threat of persecution, was asserting the primary allegiance of those in the covenant of grace to Christ. It should be noted, however, that several of the key passages they quote are scriptural verses Bunyan himself is citing: "Therefore ye blessed Saints, seeing you have received a Kingdom which cannot, *which cannot be moved*: (therefore) *Let us have grace whereby we may serve* (our) *God acceptably, with reverence and godly fear* [Hebrews 12:28]" (*MW*, 2:163). "Be wise therefore O ye poor drooping souls that are the sons of this second Covenant, And *stand fast in the liberty wherewith CHRIST hath made you free, and be not again intangled* (not terrified in your consciences) *with the yoke of bondage* [Galatians 5:1]" (2:169). Sim and Walker, 71–88 (the Bunyan quotations noted here are on pp. 86–87).

[87] The first edition of Dod and Cleaver's work, published in 1603, was entitled *A Treatise or Exposition upon the Ten Commandementes*. For Dod see *DNB*, s.v.

fluences were undoubtedly present as well, the best evidence for which is the fact that Bunyan's exposition of covenant theology generally reflects the views of those we can usefully identify as strict Calvinists in contrast with those of the moderate Calvinists, the Arminians, and to some extent the Antinomians. This is not to suggest that the precise sources of his views on the covenants can be identified, for we are limited to charting his place in the multifaceted tradition of covenant thought.

The notion of the covenant was at once biblical (especially Jeremiah 31:31–34) and pragmatic, for it provided theologians and ministers with an understandable way to reconcile predestinarian doctrine with a sense of human responsibility. Arminians such as the Independent John Goodwin used covenant language even though their theology, with its provision of free will, offered ample scope for anyone to opt for inclusion in the new covenant, aided by divine grace that was readily available to all.[88] In contrast, Reformed theologians and ministers, indebted to Augustine and wedded to a belief in the unconditional predestination of the elect, found the covenants a useful device to stress moral behavior as well as provide a measure of assurance to those plagued, as the young Bunyan had been, with doubts as to whether they were among the elect.

Moderate Calvinists such as Richard Baxter, John Ball, Thomas Blake, and Anthony Burgess stressed the element of human responsibility in the covenant of grace even while insisting that an effectual response was possible only with enabling grace. A covenant, Baxter averred, was a mutual engagement requiring faith, consent, repentance, obedience, and perseverance if believers were to have and continue in this relationship with God.[89] In contrast, strict Calvinists such as John Owen, Samuel Petto, and John Tombes underscored the promissory nature of the new covenant, though this was a matter of emphasis rather than substance. Although entry into the covenant of grace is conditional on the human side, God has absolutely promised to enable the elect to fulfill that condition.[90] Moderate and strict Calvinists also disagreed on whether the covenant made before creation

---

[88] John Goodwin, *Redemption Redeemed* (London, 1651), 456, 458. For Goodwin see *BDBR, s.v.*

[89] Richard Baxter, *Plain Scripture Proof of Infants Church-Membership and Baptism* (London, 1651), 225; Baxter, *An End of Doctrinal Controversies* (London, 1691), 142; John Ball, *A Treatise of the Covenant of Grace* (London, 1645), 7–23. For Ball, Blake, and Burgess see *DNB, s.vv.*

[90] John Owen, *The Doctrine of Justification by Faith Through the Imputation of the Righteousness of Christ* (London, 1677), 268–70; Owen, *Salus Electorum, Sanguis Jesu* (London, 1648), 103–5. Cf. Samuel Petto, *The Difference Between the Old and New Covenant Stated and Explained* (London, 1674), 2–4, 30–35; Bayly, *Practise*, 217. For Petto see *BDBR, s.v.*

between God the father and God the son was in fact the covenant of grace, the strict Calvinists insisting it was, whereas the moderates embraced the opposing view.[91]

Differences between the strict Calvinists and the Antinomians were likewise primarily a matter of emphasis. Both accentuated the divine role in establishing the covenant of grace and, with respect to the elect, its promissory rather than contractual nature.[92] Strict Calvinists and Antinomians also disagreed with moderate Calvinists by rejecting the latter's contention that the Mosaic law is part of the covenant of grace.[93] The Antinomians concurred with the strict Calvinists that the covenant of grace was made between God the father and God the son.[94] These two groups split, however, over the law's place in the Christian life, with strict Calvinists insisting that "the *Moral* Preceptive Part" of the law, as Owen called it, was neither abrogated by Christ nor useless for believers.[95] In contrast, Walter Cradock, though acknowledging that the law's substance was eternal and a rule for saints, claimed Christ had "dissolved those little childish lawes, those beggerly Rudiments." Similarly, John Saltmarsh, while admitting that the law's substance was "a *beam* of *Christ*," likened it to a candle in comparison with "the *Sun* of *righteousnesse*" by which believers were to live.[96]

[91] Owen, *The Branch of the Lord, the Beauty of Sion* (London, 1650), 17; Owen, *Doctrine of Justification*, 268–69; John Tillinghast, *Mr. Tillinghasts Eight Last Sermons* (London, 1655), 10–11; and, for the moderate view, Petto, *Difference*, 18–21; Thomas Blake, *Vindiciae Foederis* (London, 1653), 10–11, 24–25; Baxter, *End of Controversies*, 121, 124–25; Baxter, *Catholick Theologie* (London, 1675), bk. 1, pt. 2, chap. 38.

[92] John Saltmarsh, *Free-Grace*, 2nd ed. (London, 1646), 125–27, 152–54, 188–90; Tobias Crisp, *Christ Alone Exalted* (London, 1690), pt. 1, 81–83; pt. 2, 255.

[93] Owen, *A Treatise of the Dominion of Sin and Grace* (London, 1688), 94; Petto, *Difference*, 120–23; Vavasor Powell, *Christ and Moses Excellency* (London, 1650), 207; Walter Cradock, *Mount Sion* (London, 1649), *ad cal. Gospel-Holinesse* (London, 1651), 260–67; Baxter, *End of Controversies*, 131, 151–52; Blake, *Vindiciae Foederis*, 12; Ball, *Treatise*, 15.

[94] Saltmarsh, *Free-Grace*, 125–27; Powell, *Christ and Moses Excellency*, 4 ff.; Crisp, *Christ Alone Exalted*, pt. 1, 80ff.

[95] Owen, *A Declaration of the Glorious Mystery of the Person of Christ, God and Man* (London, 1679), 158–62 (quoted); Bayly, *Practise*, 516–21; Petto, *Difference*, 170–75.

[96] Cradock, *Mount Sion*, 218; Cradock, *Gospel-Libertie, in the Extensions [and] Limitations of It* (London, 1648), 18 (quoted); Saltmarsh, *Free-Grace*, 146–47 (quoted); cf. 148–52. In Dell's judgment, there were only three laws in God's kingdom: the law of a new nature, the law of the spirit of life in Christ, and the law of love. This view reflected the Antinomian position. The moderate Calvinist Samuel Rutherford labeled Dell an Antinomian. William Dell, *Right Reformation* (London, 1646), 26; Rutherford, *A Survey of the Spirituall Antichrist* (London, 1648), title-page and 187–215. For Cradock and Saltmarsh see *BDBR*, s.vv.; for Rutherford see *DNB*, s.v.

The position Bunyan staked out in *The Doctrine of the Law and Grace Un-folded* mostly accorded with that of the strict Calvinists, although echoes of Luther's commentary on Galatians are noticeable, particularly his pronounced dichotomy between law and grace. In fact, Bunyan's discourse can be read as an extended commentary on Luther's basic thesis that "the doctrine of grace can by no means stand with the doctrine of the law," yet Bunyan departed from the Wittenberg reformer in his development of this theme in the framework of covenant theology. Bunyan also stopped short of affirming Luther's bald assertion that "except thou be ignorant of the law, and be assuredly persuaded in thine heart that there is now no law nor wrath of God, but altogether grace and mercy for Christ's sake, thou canst not be saved."[97] Bunyan was too much of a Calvinist to espouse ignorance of the law, but he firmly believed that salvation was solely a matter of grace, not law.

He defined a covenant as a contract with reciprocal conditions, yet he averred that the parties who made this compact and undertook its terms were God the father and God the son, not, as most covenant theologians contended, God and believers (2:88, 95, 161–62). Because Christ fulfilled all the conditions on his part, the new covenant's benefits could be freely promised to the elect, and in this way Bunyan could stress the promissory nature of the covenant of grace, as did other strict Calvinists. "Though there be a condition commanded in the Gospel; yet he that commands the condition, doth not leave his children to their own natural abilities, that in their own strength they should fulfill them . . . ; but the same God that doth command that the condition be fulfilled, even he, doth help his children by his holy Spirit to fulfill the same condition" (2:80–81, 173, 186). As the undertaker for the elect, Christ has performed all conditions and can therefore by his grace enable the chosen to receive the benefits of his work. The souls of such people are taken from the covenant of works and "planted" in the covenant of grace, that is, in a garden in which God assists the elect to grow in the things of Christ (2:91, 152–53, 164–65).[98] Because the covenant of grace antedated creation, Bunyan believed it was actually the original contract, yet because God had revealed the covenant of works to humanity before the covenant of grace, he followed the customary practice of calling the covenant of works the first and that of grace the second (2:93–94).

Notwithstanding the indisputable Calvinist influence on Bunyan's exposition of the covenants, the spirit of Luther looms large, as reflected in Bunyan's pronounced contrast between the law as "a ministration of death and condemna-

[97] Luther, *Galatians,* 23 (quoted), 67 (quoted).

[98] For explicit references to the elect and the reprobate, see, e.g., *MW,* 2:115–16, 134–35, 199, 214–16, 224–25.

tion" and the gospel as "the ministration of life and salvation" (2:185). This seemingly left Bunyan little if any room in the Christian life for the law, apparently aligning him with the Antinomians. Indeed, Baxter would later condemn *The Doctrine of the Law and Grace Unfolded* along with works by Hobson and Saltmarsh as Antinomian books that "*ignorantly subverted the Gospel of Christ,*" and Burrough had earlier accused Bunyan of slighting the law.[99] With respect to *The Doctrine of the Law and Grace Unfolded*, Baxter's charge of Antinomianism is not without merit. In *A Vindication* Bunyan had espoused the strict Calvinist view of the law, touting it as a rule for all believers to live by, though not for justification in God's sight; if used rightly, it is good. "Obedience to the Law is a fruit of our believing" (*MW*, 1:148, 156–57).[100] He would later return to this emphasis, as in *Questions about the Nature and Perpetuity of the Seventh-Day-Sabbath* (1685), and in *The Holy War* Emanuel would urge Mansoul to "*make thy self by my Law straight steps for thy feet*" (*HW*, 248). Yet *The Doctrine of the Law and Grace Unfolded* contains only a few passing references to this view, as when Bunyan refers to "the right use of the Law" or to "the works of the holy Law of God" (*MW*, 2:178, 181). He was at pains to insist that believers are not subject to the law as it is a covenant of works, implying—but not expounding on—the law's usefulness in Christian living (2:85, 141, 169). Like the strict Calvinists and Antinomians he was unwilling to provide a place for even the moral law in the covenant of grace, though it was valuable as a divine tool: "When God brings *sinners* into the Covenant of *Grace*, he doth first kill them with the Covenant of *Works*, which is the Morall Law, or Ten Commandments." In this treatise, Bunyan envisioned the law's primary usefulness as a mirror in which people can discern their dirty faces (2:13, 137; cf. 157).[101]

At this point in his career, Bunyan's near affinity with the Antinomians on the law's role probably reflects the continuing influence of Luther rather than that of the Antinomians. Simultaneously, Bunyan's growing indebtedness to Calvinist theology was causing some tension between those tenets on the one hand and his pastoral inclinations on the other; he would never fully resolve this tension,

[99] Baxter, *The Scripture Gospel Defended, and Christ, Grace and Free Justification Vindicated Against the Libertines*, pt. 1, *A Breviate of the Doctrine of Justification* (London, 1690), sig. A2r; Burrough, *Memorable Works*, 137, 141–42, 144, 146. Baxter also regarded Walter Craddock, Henry Denne, and Tobias Crisp as Antinomians. *Scripture Gospel Defended*, pt. 2, *A Defence of Christ, and Free Grace*, 55. In criticizing my argument that at times Bunyan displayed Antinomian tendencies, Pieter De Vries ignores the subtle shifts in Bunyan's thinking. *John Bunyan on the Order of Salvation*, trans. C. van Haaften (New York: Peter Lang, 1994), 160.

[100] Cf. Bayly, *Practise*, 241–46.

[101] Cf. Dent, *Plaine Mans Path-Way*, 353.

though he sought to explain it in terms of his own religious experience. In 1659 he was already thinking about composing a spiritual autobiography, a sketch of which he incorporated in *The Doctrine of the Law and Grace Unfolded*, and in time it would serve as a précis for *Grace Abounding*. When God first began to instruct his soul, Bunyan attested, he was one of the world's "black sinners," prone to "making a sport of oaths," lying, and such "soul-poysoning" lusts as drinking, dancing, and playing with the wicked; implicitly underlying most of this activity was wasted time. "The Lord finding of me in this condition, did open the glass of his Law unto me, wherein he shewed me so clearly my sins." In Bunyan's experience the initiative belonged to God, who persuaded him to fellowship with the godly, gave him scriptural promises, and ultimately converted him. His experience, including severe temptations in which he "had the triall of the vertue of Christs blood," accorded with the notion of a covenant of grace in which Christ fulfilled all the conditions for the elect (2:156–60). It was impossible, said Bunyan, for an unbeliever to perform a single condition; faith is solely the gift of God, "the nature of which is to lay hold on Christ," but it is not a cause of or reason for salvation (2:77, 81–82).

Bunyan's pastoral instincts impelled him to do more than explain the workings of the covenant of grace and God's provision of faith to the elect, not as a condition of that pact but as a gift from Christ, who had rendered the requisite obedience. Without this gift, unbelievers could have only a "traditional, historical faith," erroneously supposing they had been born Christians or made such by baptism. Such conceptions were "*fables, fancies*, and wicked slights of the devil" (2:150). Although true faith can only come as a divine gift, Bunyan the pastor prefaced his treatise with a call to the unconverted to fly in haste to Christ, and to be restless until extended "the glorious glory" of the covenant of grace (2:17). Near the end of the treatise he returned to this theme, with its implication that the act of flying or coming to Christ is within the power of his readers. "If thou wouldest be saved thou mayest come to Christ" (2:210, 220, 223–24). From his ministerial perspective Bunyan also clearly suggested that grace is resistible: "If thou do get off thy convictions, and not the right way (which is by seeing thy sins washed away by the Blood of Jesus Christ), it is a question whether ever God will knock at thy heart again or no" (2:17). Notwithstanding Bunyan's fundamental commitment to Calvinist principles, his ministerial duties sometimes carried him into what we might term 'pastoral Arminianism,' not as a matter of dogma but as a reflection of his evangelical concern to convert unbelievers.

Bunyan's earlier spiritual travails enabled him to draw from the well of experience as well as Scripture when, in this treatise, he explored the enigmatic, doubt-inducing issues of the unpardonable sin and possible temporal limits to the day of grace. Essentially, the unpardonable sin was, in his estimation, the de-

liberate, spiteful, and "final trampling the bloud of sweet Jesus" after having received light from Christ and made a profession of faith. Ranters and Quakers,
Bunyan opined, were the closest to perpetrating this sin of anyone he knew. To
those worried that they might have committed this sin, as he had once been, he
offered a pastoral opinion that all those "willing to venture their salvation upon
the merits of a naked Jesus" are not guilty of the unpardonable sin (2:201–10).

Bunyan had also undergone the agony of wondering if, for him, the day of
grace had passed. As in the case of the unpardonable sin, his recollection of that
experience in this treatise prefigured his subsequent recitation of it in *Grace
Abounding*. The question he assigns to an objector in *The Doctrine of the Law and
Grace Unfolded* he had once asked himself: "I am afraid the day of Grace is past,
and if it should be so, what should I do then?" (2:211).[102] It was not an idle query,
for Bunyan believed such a time was indeed past before some people died. Here
again, his 'pastoral Arminianism' manifested itself, for he depicted Christ
knocking at the doors of people's hearts, promising "to come in and sup," by
which Bunyan meant the communication of saving grace (2:211–12). To the soul
that despaired of waiting on God for assurance of divine love, he counseled patience, clearly indicating a human role. "God did not wait longer upon thee, and
was fain to send to thee by his Ambassadours, time after time" (2:213). At least
temporarily, then, he recognized a human ability to resist proffers of grace, another indication of 'pastoral Arminianism.' Nevertheless Calvinist tenets remained the bedrock of his convictions. When his objector wondered what good it
would do to wait for divine assurance if he or she was not one of the elect, Bunyan explained that knowledge of election is possible only after "acquaintance
with God in Christ, which doth come by thy giving credit to his promises, and records which he hath given of Jesus Christ" (2:214–15). As long as a person is aware
of his or her "miserable state," seeks communion with Christ, has "secret per-
swasions" that he or she will attain "an interest" in Christ, is periodically cognizant of divine promises, and observes "some little excellency in Christ," the day
of grace has not terminated (2:212–13).

Bunyan also drew on his experience when he discussed the question of perseverance. The logic of Calvinist theology dictated that once in the covenant of
grace, the elect would persevere in their faith, a view he espoused in this treatise.
"The safe state of the Saints, as touching their perseverance, [means] that they
shall stand though hell rages, though the devil roareth, and all the world endeav-
oureth the ruine of the Saints of God." The Devil can no more entice a believer
out of the covenant of grace than he can pluck Christ from heaven (2:199; cf.

[102] Cf. *GA*, §66.

205).[103] Some people have professed faith in God and ultimately fallen away, but they are bastards rather than true children of God—folks whose faith has been historical, traditional, human in origin, or dead, not a divine gift. Bunyan insisted that the new covenant cannot be broken by believers' sins simply because the covenant has been made between God the father and God the son. Enunciating what would later become a primary motif in *The Pilgrim's Progress*, Bunyan added: "The reason why the very Saints of God have so many ups and downs in this their travel towards heaven; it is because they are so weak in the faith of this one thing," namely, a conviction that their sins cannot rupture the new covenant (2:133–35, 167). The remedy for this weakness, he explained, is to keep a steadfast eye on Christ, the surety, mediator, high priest, and "middle man" of the covenant of grace (2:97, 109, 167, 169).

In this treatise the motif of light once again emerges as a liberating force even as darkness had signaled hell's despair. Utilizing a revealing variation on his usual and more traditional imaging of hell as lit with the fires of perpetual torment, Bunyan here envisions Hades in the darkness that had so blanketed his own sepulchral nights during his years of spiritual turmoil. Again, the parallel with Christ is striking; at the crucifixion "there was not such a terrible *darkness* on the face of the earth then, as there was on his precious *soul*." Hell's torments are "the *eclipsings* of the divine smiles of God," the radiating light (2:107). Although Bunyan normally writes of hell as a place of fiery torment, and thus presumably illumined brightly by the flames, he also referred to it as a "*pit* of utter darknesse," an image especially horrific for one who had suffered from depression. Benjamin Keach attempted to solve this enigma by contrasting hell's "dark fire" with the traditional variety that emits light,[104] but Bunyan offered no comparable explanation. In any event, for him hell was the abode of denizens of perpetual night. In contrast, Christ is light, and the radiance of his countenance enlightens believers who struggle with "the reliques of sin" in their hearts (2:123, 125, 221). The righteousness of Christ in the godly "shines as bright as ever," in sharp contrast to the darkness and blindness in unrepentant sinners. The latter sin against light; indeed, the most serious sin, that against the Holy Spirit, is the supreme offense against light (2:178, 193, 201, 206, 209, 222). In the new covenant is light, and thus spiritual and emotional well-being.

Bunyan employed a variety of readily understood images to illustrate his points. The dominant one is the contract between God the father and God the

---

[103] The Arminians rejected the doctrine of absolute perseverance. Cf. John Goodwin, *The Agreement & Distance of Brethren* (London, 1652), 66–67.

[104] Benjamin Keach, *A Golden Mine Opened* (London, 1694), 62. For Keach see *BDBR*, *s.v.*

son, who shook hands upon concluding it, a simple act that reflected the numerous transactions in which artisans and petty merchants engaged in the seventeenth century (2:101, 118).[105] Another was the homely illustration, noted earlier,
of the law as a mirror for dirty faces. To make his point that people must come to
Christ as sinners, eschewing their own efforts to be righteous, Bunyan resorted to
a medical analogy that Roger Sharrock found "flagrantly brutal" and "deliberately
shocking":[106]

> The clean, and righteous have no need of Christ, but those that are foul and sick.
> Physicians you know if they love to be honoured, they will not bid the Patients first
> make themselves whole, and then come to them: no, but bid them come with their
> sores all running on them, as the woman with her bloody issue, *Mark* 5. And as *Mary
> Magdalen* with her Belly full of Devils, and the Lepers all scabbed.   (2:175–76)

To illustrate Christ's role in entering into the covenant of grace with God the father, Bunyan likened the former to the surety required by a creditor to ensure
that a bankrupt debtor's obligation is repaid, an analogy perhaps most familiar to
the urban middling sort. In Bunyan's analogy, Jesus' blood is the payment agreed
on for the salvation of sinners (2:99–100). Indebtedness also figures in Bunyan's
attempt to explain the fairness of God's insistence on obedience to the law even
though this is impossible for fallen humanity; this is, suggested Bunyan, akin to a
master who gives a servant £10 for a specific purpose, and has the latter imprisoned if he spends the money for something else and cannot repay the funds.
Varying the metaphor, because of Christ's mediating endeavors in performing his
contractual obligations, the elect become inheritors of the divine blessing,
something perhaps especially meaningful to Bunyan, whose ancestors had lost
what would have been his landed inheritance (2:45, 96).

Bunyan's early forays into metaphorical language are also evident in his use of
animals to make his points. Drawing on his rustic background, he likened those
who live and die under the unforgiving, capital penalties of the law, notwith-

[105] For the partial indebtedness of covenant theology to secular contracts see David
Zaret, *The Heavenly Contract: Ideology and Organization in Pre-Revolutionary Puritanism*
(Chicago: University of Chicago Press, 1985), 163–98.

[106] Sharrock, *JB*, 38. More broadly, Michael Mullett contends that Bunyan was using
shock treatment in depicting God's pitiless insistence that unredeemed sinners must suffer
the law's full penalties, though he goes too far in suggesting that Bunyan "set up two
Gods," one a vengeful, irate, primitive, "Moloch-like figure," and the other a deity who
lovingly redeems the chosen. Mullett, *JBC*, 139–40. Bunyan posits the unchangeableness of
justice and love in the divine, resolving the tension in the covenant of grace by enabling
God, as father, to insist on satisfaction and simultaneously sacrifice himself, as son, to
provide the gift of faith through grace. This is the fundamental message of *The Doctrine of
the Law and Grace Unfolded.*

standing their sincere efforts to adhere to its precepts, to a poor horse that toils all day and has only a dirty stable at night for its pains. The lion provided Bunyan with a substantially different image, one that evoked a sense of peril. He likened the sins for which Christ died in fulfilment of the covenant conditions to lions and raging devils. Indeed, divine justice demands complete obedience; once it has been wronged, it cannot pity the offender, "but runs on him like a Lion, takes him by the throat, [and] throws him into prison" (2:40, 122).[107] The analogy is flawed, stirring up images of a charging lion, but ending with the unsatisfactory notion of the lion as a jailer rather a devourer of its prey; Bunyan had much to learn before he could be a skilled allegorist. In any event, he offered his readers hope—a gap made by Christ which enables the elect to escape the lion's ravages, the terrible punishment of the covenant of works. This was the gap Bunyan, during his own spiritual travail, had envisioned and through which he finally made his way to find the comfort and warmth of sunlight (2:223; *GA*, §54).

Bunyan did not intend *The Doctrine of the Law and Grace Unfolded* to console most Christians, for their knowledge of Christ, in his view, is notional rather than "experimental"; unaware of being sick, they have no desire to consult a physician. "That man . . . that hath got but a notion of the Law (a notion, that is the knowledge of it in the head, so as to discourse and talk of it) if he hath not felt the power of it, and that effectually too, he, it is to be feared, will at the best be but a notionist in the Gospel, he will not have the experimental knowledge of the same in his heart; nay he will not seek, nor heartily desire after it, and all because . . . he hath not experience of the wounding, cutting, killing nature of the other." The law, then, is God's tool to prepare sinners to receive the divine gift of faith, the knowledge of which is profoundly experiential; the language of God's children must "feelingly drop from [their] lips" (*MW*, 2:12–14, 143). There are no easy signs to discern this, for those still subject to the covenant of works can include seeming visible saints, who, like some of the virgins in Matthew 25, mistakenly proclaim themselves to be Christ's servants; their numbers can also embrace church leaders, gifted preachers, and prophets. In Bunyan's estimation, most of those who profess the gospel are ignorant of its effectual power. Adherence to a particular ecclesiastical polity, proper forms of outward worship, and gospel ordinances are not proof that one is within the covenant of grace, for all these things may be done in a legal, and thus unacceptable, spirit. The great danger, then, is doing or embracing ostensibly good things, including baptism, the Lord's supper, prayer, and almsgiving, in this legal spirit, for "they are thereby used as a hand by the devil, to pull thee under the Covenant of Works . . . and so [you are]

---

[107] Luther repeatedly likened the law to a prison. *Galatians*, 298, 324–28, 332–33, 336, 356.

most miserably destroyed unawares to [your]self" (2:61–62, 69, 71–75, 181–83). The prospect was frightening, but that was Bunyan's unmistakable intent. His own spiritual struggles had been permeated with fear, doom, and darkness, but he held out hope that his readers could find assurance—not in their membership in a society of visible saints, not by adhering to infant or believer's baptism, not by a regimen of prayer, not by caring for the poor, but where he himself had found it, in the inner testimony of the Spirit. "As thou shouldest be much in praying for the Spirit to testifie assurance to thee, so also thou shouldest look to the end of it when thou thinkest thou hast it; which is this, to shew thee that it is alone for Christs sake, that thy sins are forgiven thee, and also thereby a constraining of thee to advance him, both by words, and works, in holiness and righteousness all the dayes of thy life" (2:216). To pass this test was to have the assurance of election and participation in the covenant of grace. Such assurance ultimately sustained Bunyan during the long prison years that lay ahead.

### "Inchantments, and Witchcrafts"[108]: Quakers and Witches

Bunyan's running feud with the Friends in the mid- and late 1650s involved mutual charges of witchcraft. The first such accusation may have been hurled by Anne Blaykling of Draw-well, near Sedbergh, Yorkshire, who became an itinerant Quaker preacher no later than 1652. For preaching in Cambridge in 1654 she went to prison for six months, after which she traveled to London. There she had an audience with Oliver Cromwell in April 1655, and two months later she was witnessing in western Norfolk. In 1656 she preached in Cornwall and Suffolk.[109] At some point during these years she challenged Bunyan. In *Some Gospel-Truths Opened* he reported only that some Quakers had accused him of witchcraft and conjuration for preaching that Jesus was physically in "heaven above the stars," but in *A Vindication* he identified Blaykling (Blackly) as having made this charge. She also allegedly told him to throw away the Bible, which he declined to do because "*then the Divel would be too hard for me*" (*MW*, 2:61–62, 69, 71–75, 181–83).[110] Others similarly accused Bunyan of being a witch, but in *Grace Abounding* he contemptuously dismissed the charge by lumping it with absurd allegations that he was also a Jesuit and a "Highway-man" (*GA*, §307).

Like Luther and many of his contemporaries,[111] Bunyan took witchcraft seri-

[108] *MW*, 7:215.

[109] *BDBR*, s.v.

[110] Bunyan identified Blaykling after Burrough claimed that no Friend had accused him of witchcraft. Burrough, *Memorable Works*, 147–48.

[111] Luther, *Galatians*, 189–92; James Sharpe, *Instruments of Darkness: Witchcraft in England, 1550–1750* (London: Hamish Hamilton, 1996); Deborah Willis, *Malevolent Nur-*

ously, not least because he found ample biblical evidence of it. Among the greatest sinners to whom God offered mercy, averred Bunyan, was King Manasseh of Judah, who had used witchcraft, consulted wizards, and incinerated his sons as an offering before he repented (2 Chronicles 33:1–13). In Acts 8:9–13 Bunyan found the companion example of Simon, who used sorcery to bewitch the people of Samaria before Philip converted him (*MW*, 2:125, 129, 193). Bunyan cited the account of the Jewish exorcists in Acts 19 to warn his own contemporaries not to use Christ's name "*magically*, and after the manner of Exorcism, or conjuration" (*MW*, 9:267; cf. 2:125, 193). This may indicate the continued employment of exorcism by those who sought to demonstrate the validity of their religious views by casting out demons. Freeman's unsuccessful attempt to exorcize a devil from Ned's father in *The Life and Death of Mr. Badman* reflects this practice (*BM*, 37). Such displays were often deemed fraudulent,[112] though Bunyan's objection was grounded on biblical prescription rather than skepticism. He also followed 1 Samuel 15:22–23 in comparing rebellion against the word of God to the sin of witchcraft (*MW*, 9:20).

In addition to the biblical evidence for witchcraft, belief in its reality was harmonious with Bunyan's view of a cosmos replete with evil spirits. Those who reject the offer of divine grace, he warned in 1658, bring everlasting destruction on themselves "for having some of the devils brats, some hellish lusts, that like so many witches, imps, will suck and draw thy soul from God" (*MW*, 1:367).[113] "Hast thou been a witch?" he asked the readers of *The Doctrine of the Law and Grace Unfolded* the following year (*MW*, 2:201). As Christian confronted death in *The Pilgrim's Progress*, "he was troubled with apparitions of Hob-goblins and Evil Spirits" (*PP*, 157). Having experienced these demons in his pre-adolescent nightmares, Bunyan thought it essential to include a poem on "the Apparition of Evil Spirits" in his *Book for Boys and Girls*. The only cure, he asserted in 1688, is divine grace, the water of life—"the *RIGHT* Holy Water"—which will "drive away *Devils* and *Spirits*, 'twill cure *Inchantments*, and *Witchcrafts*" (*MW*, 6:264; 7:215).

If the cosmos is populated with hobgoblins and evil spirits, it was easy enough to believe that England had its coterie of wizards and witches. Indeed, when Bun-

---

*ture: Witch-Hunting and Maternal Power in Early Modern England* (Ithaca, NY: Cornell University Press, 1995). Lodowick Muggleton attributed belief in witchcraft to fear and lack of faith. *The Acts of the Witnesses: The Autobiography of Lodowick Muggleton and Other Early Muggletonian Writings*, ed. T. L. Underwood (New York: Oxford University Press, 1999), 209–11.

[112] Brian P. Levack, *The Witch-Hunt in Early Modern Europe* (London and New York: Longman, 1987), 113.

[113] He deleted this passage in the second (undated) edition of *Sighs from Hell*. Cf. *MW*, 2:45.

yan debated with Particular and General Baptists in the early 1670s over the exclusion of the unbaptized from communion and church membership, he accused his opponents of treating unbaptized saints as harshly as the openly profane, witches, and wizards (*MW*, 4:234). In his catechism, *Instruction for the Ignorant*, he categorized witchcraft as one of the greatest sins, in the company of adultery, fornication, murder, theft, swearing, lying, covetousness, sedition, and heresy; a similar grouping had been included in *The Doctrine of the Law and Grace Unfolded* (*MW*, 8:15; 2:137). "The chief" among the Diabolonians in *The Holy War* includes Mr. Witchcraft as well as Lords Adultery, Fornication, Murder, Anger, Lasciviousness, Deceit, and Evileye (*HW*, 144–45). For Bunyan, witchcraft was real and an abominable offense against God, and his belief in its verity extended throughout his career.

Among his Bedfordshire contemporaries Bunyan was not unique in his belief in the reality of witches. The Bedfordshire quarter sessions dealt with cases involving Emme Saunders of Little Staughton in 1653 and Richard and Mary Favell in 1662.[114] At Dunstable in 1667, four women—Elizabeth Pratt, Mary Poole, Mary Hudson, and Ursula Clarke—were accused of witchcraft. Alleging that twenty other witches like herself lived in the town, Pratt charged Poole, Hudson, and Clarke with bewitching two children, admitted casting a fatal curse on the cattle and horses of a man who had called her a witch, and averred that the Devil, appearing as a man, had ordered her to do so. According to her accusers, she made a contract with Satan, claimed to have seen him in the form of a cat as well as a man (who went to bed with her), bewitched children to death, blinded a girl, and entered into a private yard through a keyhole in the gate. After the death of a boy who desperately pulled the flesh from his nose and lips in the belief that she had bewitched him, neighbors satisfied themselves that she was a witch by thrusting a pin through her hand and observing that she did not bleed. For their part, Hudson and Clarke reputedly cursed men who had wronged them, causing their deaths. Pratt was imprisoned in the county jail while Bunyan was there, and all four women were physically examined for telltale signs of being witches. On Pratt the inspectors found an abnormal piece of flesh growing on her "privities"; on Poole, abnormal flesh on her left shoulder, an impression on her back, and a blue spot on her privates; and on Hudson, two small teats in her privates.[115]

In Bedford the cordwainer John Wright was accused of witchcraft in March

---

[114] *Bedfordshire County Records: Notes and Extracts from the County Records Being a Calendar of Volume I. of the Sessions Minute Books 1651 to 1660*, ed. Hardy and Page, vol. 2 (Bedford: C. F. Timaeus, n.d.), 24; BLA, MS HSA 1662 W/24.

[115] BLA, MSS HSA 1667 W/21–23, 26, 28, 51–54. Pratt died in prison in early 1667. BLA MS HSA 1667 W/58.

1680. Blaming him for periodic seizures (possibly epilepsy) in the preceding year, Dinah Wiffin, a bricklayer's wife who had occasionally given him alms, claimed to have seen him in her dreams, once when he was about to choke her and again as he was preparing to rape her. She also thought she had seen him at the foot of her bed before the onset of her seizures, and one episode occurred after she glimpsed him in the street. A further accusation was made by a Bedford stationer who claimed Wright had similarly bewitched his sister, causing her to have a seizure. Imprisoned in the county jail, Wright hoped he was not a witch but expressed uncertainty.[116] Clearly, belief in the existence of witches was not unusual in Bunyan's Bedfordshire.

The degree to which Bunyan shared popular notions about witchcraft is apparent by his involvement in the case of a witch's reputed victimization of Margaret Pryor of Long Stanton, Cambridgeshire, in 1659. The story was recounted in a "paper" (possibly a broadside) by Bunyan and in the anonymous tract, *Strange & Terrible Newes from Cambridge, Being a True Relation of the Quakers Bewitching of Mary Philips* (1659). Inasmuch as the latter work contains several errors, including a wrong name for the reputed victim, it probably represents a second- or third-hand account, possibly by a London newswriter or a cleric determined to perpetuate the tradition of defaming sectaries typified by Thomas Edwards' *Gangraena*. No copy of Bunyan's work seems to have survived, but it was refuted by the Quaker James Blackley, a Cambridge alderman, in *A Lying Wonder Discovered, and the Strange and Terrible Newes from Cambridge Proved False. . . . Also This Contains an Answer to John Bunions Paper Touching the Said Imagined Witchcraft, Which He Hath Given Forth to Your Wonderment (as He Saith)* (1659). Further proof of Bunyan's tract is contained in a Quaker broadside published in London on 11 April 1670. It refers to a "railing, slanderous, and lying Pamphlet of one *Bunions*, the *Tinker*, and another, called, Newes from *Cambridge*."[117]

Pryor had left the Church of England in 1657 to attend Quaker meetings. The author of *Strange & Terrible Newes* claims she associated for a few weeks with "two unrefined Quakers," Robert Dickson and Jane Cranaway, before renouncing them. According to Blackley, the Quakers never accepted her as a Friend, and in 1659 he described her as a woman of evil conversation, prone to inebriety and profanity. Ostensibly encouraged by a third party, Pryor made sensational allegations against the Quakers Widow Morlin and William Allen, a barber-surgeon, in the summer of 1659. While Pryor lay in bed with her husband on 20 November 1657, she claimed, Morlin put a bridle in her mouth, transformed her into a bay

[116] BLA, MSS HSA 1680 W/94–97.

[117] *A Testimony from the People of God, Called Quakers, Against Many Lying and Slanderous Books* (London, 1670).

mare, rode her to Maddenly House, and tethered her to a door latch. Morlin then went into the house to join others, presumably Quakers, for a feast of mutton, rabbit, and lamb. The justices of the peace who heard these charges ordered her and the accused to appear before the summer assizes at Cambridge in July 1659, by which point Pryor had dropped her charges against Allen. At the assizes a skeptical Judge Windham, noting that nearly twenty-one months had elapsed since the alleged event, wondered why she had not been ridden again. After Pryor explained that she had avoided further victimization by burning elder bark and her own hair, Windham denounced her as a sorceress and a whimsical woman. The jury took only fifteen minutes to acquit Morlin.[118]

Blackley and four other Quakers, including George Whitehead of Westmorland, having been present at the assizes and at some point questioned Pryor themselves, were well positioned to reply to Bunyan's account and *Strange & Terrible Newes*. The latter work had been rushed into print shortly after the trial. Working swiftly, Blackley completed his refutation of both works on 8 August 1659. His emphasis was on inconsistencies and improbabilities. Lamb, for instance, would not have been available in November. In addition to getting Pryor's name wrong, the author of *Strange & Terrible Newes* claimed her feet and hands had been bruised and left as black as coal, but she told Windham that only her hind feet had been so affected. The anonymous writer also asserted that her sides had been "rent and torn," as if "spur-gal'd," and her smock bloodied. How, Blackley mused, could a horse wear a woman's smock or, as a vegetarian animal, identify various meats? Moreover, the anonymous account claimed that after being "bewitched or inchanted," Pryor, in the shape of a mare, had been ridden from Dinton to a town within four miles of Cambridge. There was no such place as Dinton, Blackley countered, though the original version of the story, which the author of *Strange & Terrible Newes* garbled, probably reported a journey from Long Stanton to Fen Ditton, a few miles northeast of Cambridge. When the witches arrived at their destination, according to the anonymous writer, they dismounted and hung the bridle "upon the Pails," at which point the bit came out of Pryor's mouth and she miraculously returned to her human form, astonishing the neighbors.

Ridiculing *Strange & Terrible Newes*, whose author Blackley suspected was a professional clergyman because of his "Priest like language," was easy enough, but Bunyan apparently made few if any slips in recounting the tale of "*Good-wife Pryor*," as he called her. Since he interviewed her himself, this is hardly surprising. After learning about his controversy with Burrough, did she seek Bunyan out, or did he approach her in search of more ammunition with which to attack the

---

[118]Pryor returned to the Church of England and eventually committed suicide. Ibid.

Quakers? Blackley weighed in with an *ad hominem* assault on Bunyan, "who goes up and down to preach and lookest upon thy self [as] higher then the Priests and many others, In that thou hast also dispersed a paper abroad against the *Quakers*, of what the said *Margaret Pryor* said to thee of her being a horse & ridden upon." Bunyan, charged Blackley, was prone to believe lies and "false dreams," perhaps alluding in the latter case to Bunyan's recounting of his own dreams in his preaching. In any event, Blackley likened Bunyan to the false prophets in Jeremiah 23:32. Not even the magicians and witches of ancient Egypt could turn a woman into a horse, Blackley asserted. Those who think the Devil has this power "make Gods decrees alterable, by which man was set in his own proper place above the beasts; and such would make the Devil a creator, and set him in Gods place." This was a telling theological point, especially against a Calvinist, as Bunyan now was. Blackley also attacked Bunyan for repeating Pryor's claim that she could see the people at the banquet, who "did shine so bright as if they had been Angels." Supposedly they discussed theology, "which was a shame for him [Bunyan] to have uttered, that a horse could understand what was like Angels, or understand Doctrine."

Bunyan's biographers have either ignored his involvement in this episode or dismissed it as insignificant. After discussing it at some length, William York Tindall concluded that Bunyan's pamphlet was an "unfortunate gratification" that apparently "pacified [his] resentment against the Quakers," whereas Christopher Hill remarked that it is fortuitous for Bunyan's reputation that his account has been lost.[119] But Bunyan *was* a believer in witchcraft, as were many of his contemporaries, and we cannot fully understand his struggle against the forces of evil if we fail to include his numbering of witches and evil spirits among them. The credence he gave to Pryor's temporary transformation into a horse places him in a long European tradition of popular belief in metamorphosis, though this seems to have been relatively unusual in England. Witches, some believed, could transform themselves or others into animals, normally wolves. A reputed Lancashire witch claimed in January 1666 that she and her parents had each ridden a black cat nine miles to Warrington, where the cats sucked her mother's breasts until they drew blood. Five years later one of Joseph Williamson's correspondents told him about a supposed witch who had been discovered by cats while they danced in the air; among this woman's reputed feats was impeding the English naval effort during the Third Dutch War, preventing the queen from becoming pregnant, and causing a bull to kill a JP who had been prosecuting Protestants.[120] However, the influential handbook on witchcraft,

[119]Tindall, 47; Hill, *TPM*, 369.
[120]PRO, SP 29/146/68; 29/288/5.

*Malleus Maleficarum*, treated metamorphosis as a contrivance of demonic illusion, and early modern intellectuals tended to follow suit.[121] Bunyan's acceptance of Pryor's metamorphosis thus reflects popular belief rather than the views of intellectuals.

Bunyan's attribution of witchcraft to Quakers was not original. A 1655 tract entitled *Quakers Are Inchanters and Dangerous Seducers* recounted how Mary White of Wickham-skeyth, Suffolk, had been enchanted after listening to Friends. The poor woman reputedly suffered "such violent fits and distempers as that foure or five men could hardly hold her in her bed, and in her said fit she roared and in a raging manner called those about her Devills."[122] Two years earlier, John Gilpin of Kendal, Westmorland, related how Quakers had ensnared him, deluding him into thinking that two swallows were angels, causing him to play a bass-viol notwithstanding his hatred of music, and tempting him to slit his throat to receive the words of life. His behavior became erratic: "I was also by the same power carried out of doores upon my hands and knees into the street, which my Wife and others seeing, endeavoured to hinder me, but *I* told them *I* would not be hindred, but leave Wife, Children, and all to follow Christ." In *The Pilgrim's Progress* Bunyan would praise Christian for making exactly this decision. During his self-proclaimed delusional period, Gilpin "fell into great feare and doubting," worried that it was too late to repent because divine judgment had already been pronounced on him.[123] Bunyan, of course, experienced the same despair during his religious struggle, though he never attributed it to the Quakers. He did, however, envision them and their allies, the witches,[124] as dangerous foes in the battle for the souls of men and women.

## "Throw Away All Thy Own Wisdome"[125]: Pulpit Controversy

In 1659 Bunyan unintentionally sparked a controversy with Thomas Smith, keeper of the Cambridge University library, lecturer in rhetoric at Christ's Col-

[121] Levack, *Witch-Hunt*, 45, 52, 189; Keith Thomas, *Religion and the Decline of Magic* (New York: Charles Scribner's Sons, 1971), 445.

[122] *Quakers Are Inchanters and Dangerous Seducers* (London, 1655), 4–5. See also Braithwaite, *Beginnings of Quakerism*, 53, 67, 107, 220, 487.

[123] John Gilpin, *The Quakers Shaken: or, a Fire-Brand Snatch'd out of the Fire* (Gateside, 1653), 3, 8–10, 12.

[124] The Friends repudiated attempts to link them to witchcraft. [Richard Farnworth], *Witchcraft Cast out from the Religious Seed and Israel of God* (London, 1655); George Fox, *A Declaration of the Ground of Error & Errors, Blasphemy, Blasphemers, and Blasphemies* (London, 1657), 13–41.

[125] *MW*, 1:98.

lege, and professor of Arabic. The clash occurred at Toft, some six miles west of Cambridge, where Daniel Angier (or Aungier) asked Bunyan to preach in his barn. The Angier family had a tradition of nonconformity; when Matthew Wren, bishop of Ely, conducted a visitation of his diocese in 1639, William Angier, the parish clerk at Toft, was presented for having moved the communion table outside the rails. Bunyan had previously preached in Toft, encouraging opposition to the curate, John Ellis, though probably not the violence that ensued when Ellis was beaten with a cudgel and the doors of the parish church were broken open. Bunyan had, however, preached in that church, presumably without the curate's approval.[126]

Preaching in Angier's barn on 1 Timothy 4:6, Bunyan warned that at the day of judgment God would lay four books before all people—those of remembrance, the creatures, the Mosaic law, and the gospel. By the second he intended "this or that cup of bear, or pot of wine whereby a man is drunk, the timber in the wall, &c." Since Bunyan preached this sermon about the time he was writing *The Doctrine of the Law and Grace Unfolded* (1659), that topic was very much on his mind. He told his audience, according to Smith, that Christians would be judged by the law as well as the gospel, citing James 2:12, which, Bunyan opined, refers to the Mosaic law as the law of liberty. To this, Smith objected, contending that James was referring to the gospel, the perfect law, which the Mosaic law was not. He also took offense when Bunyan asserted that he was preaching primarily to unbelievers; how could he know this, Smith protested, since he had previously seen fewer than half the auditors. Such assumptions made decent people "run out of their wits." Indeed, Smith referred to Bunyan's followers as "sad melancholly persons, not looking nor behaving themselves like other folk."[127]

The debate soon focused on Bunyan's right to preach. Smith asked "the Tinker," as Bunyan was reputedly known to his friends, who had sent him, referring to Paul's question in Romans 10:15. When Bunyan replied that he had been sent by the church of Christ at Bedford, Smith retorted that this was impossible because the Bedford group, which consisted "only of women and a few Lay-

[126] Margaret Spufford, *Contrasting Communities: English Villagers in the Sixteenth and Seventeenth Centuries* (London and New York: Cambridge University Press, 1974), 268, 273; *Records of the Churches of Christ, Gathered at Fenstanton, Warboys, and Hexham, 1644–1720*, ed. Edward Bean Underhill (London: Hanserd Knollys Society, 1854), 75; [Thomas Smith], "A Letter Sent to Mr. E. of Taft," *ad cal. The Quaker Disarm'd* (London, 1659), sig. C3v; Matthews, *Walker Revised*, 79. This John Ellis may have been the Mr. Ellis who sought Baxter's counsel in May 1659. Baxter, *Calendar*, 1:390. In 1660 Smith sent a copy of *The Quaker Disarm'd* to William Sancroft, chaplain to the bishop of Durham, who presumably would have first learned of Bunyan if he read it. BL, Harleian MSS 3784, fol. 3r.
[127] Smith, "A Letter," sigs. B4v-C1r.

men," was not a church and had no power to bestow. Only properly ordained men could preach. Bunyan thereupon began asking Smith "very many impertinent diverting questions," such as when had he been converted, what were the signs of that conversion, and what sins had he confessed when he last took communion? Indignant, Smith countered that Bunyan was not his confessor but "the meanest of all the vulgar in the Country." Bunyan gave as good as he got, chastising Smith as a fool and a "giddy pated fellow." Perhaps reflecting Dell's influence, Bunyan caustically attacked Smith's formal learning: "Away . . . to *Oxford* with your hell bred Logick."[128] On the defensive, Smith insisted that logic—right reason—differentiated people from animals and was necessary to interpret the gospels and New Testament epistles, whose authors had employed such modes of thought. In Smith's mind, Bunyan was part of a radical sectarian tradition that threatened the fabric of English society. He warned that those who accepted a tinker's right to preach sanctioned the pulling down of church walls to mend roads and the stripping of bells from steeples; moreover, they regarded the clergy as the "Limbs of Antichrist," their preaching as foolishness, and the sacraments as empty ceremonies. If such people prevailed, down go bishops, universities, schools, hospitals, and all thoughts of good, and "in rusheth *Carneades*'s Philosophy." "Then the poorest hireling in the Town will soon have as much land as you, or your Heir." The commonwealth will collapse, to be replaced by "a Community of Bears Tygers." To avert this disaster, Smith opined, people must not deem a tinker "more infallible then the pure spouse of Christ."[129] Smith's strictures clearly reflected the extent to which conservatives regarded formally uneducated, unordained preachers such as Bunyan as a serious threat to the social order.

Although Bunyan never replied to Smith, the General Baptist Henry Denne, who had preached at Toft on a tour through the region early in 1654, came to Bunyan's defense. Denne was himself a Cambridge man, having attended Sidney Sussex College and graduated B.A. (1625) and M.A. (1628). He also had strong radical credentials, having been a Leveller, a participant in the Burford mutiny in 1649, a defender of the right of laymen to preach, and an opponent of tithes, paedobaptism, and religious persecution. In his pamphlet *The Quaker No Papist, in Answer to the Quaker Disarm'd* (1659), he defended the legitimacy of Bunyan's call as well as the Bedford church's right to select a pastor and other officers. If Smith possessed a superior commission, he should have proved it, Denne

---

[128] He may also have been influenced by Luther, who denounced the "sophistical subtleties of the schoolmen." *Galatians*, 35.

[129] Smith, "A Letter," sigs. B4r, C1r-C4v. For more on the historical context of the debate see Ann Hughes, "The Pulpit Guarded: Confrontations Between Orthodox and Radicals in Revolutionary England," in *JBHE*, ed. Laurence, Owens, and Sim, 31–50.

averred. To underscore his contention that the Bedford congregation had a right to send men of faith, imbued with the Holy Spirit, to preach to unbelievers, Denne used a telling analogy: Is it sinful for shipwrecked men who find heathen on an island to convert them to Christianity? *"You seem to be angry with the Tinker because he strives to mend Souls as well as Kettles and Pans,"* Denne bitingly remarked.[130]

Bunyan's appearance in Dell's pulpit at Yelden also proved to be controversial. Approximately thirty of Dell's parishioners subsequently petitioned the House of Lords on 20 June 1660 for his ejection. Among other things, they accused him of supporting the regicide and the abolition of the House of Lords, favoring republican government, neglecting the administration of the sacraments, failing to baptize numerous children, refusing to sing psalms or read chapters from the Bible during Sunday services, collecting excessive tithes, and expressing a preference to hear a plain, uneducated farmer rather than the best orthodox minister in England. Although the last charge may have been an exaggeration, Dell was manifestly willing to accept godly preachers even if they had no formal theological education. The parishioners complained that Dell had permitted Bunyan to preach on Christmas day 1659, when no orthodox cleric officiated. Although the Lords dismissed the complaint on 25 July, Dell's days at Yelden were numbered, and his successor was installed on 4 January 1661.[131]

Dell's influence on Bunyan was significant. The two men shared a pronounced indebtedness to Luther,[132] and both accorded substantial emphasis to the Holy Spirit's role in the Christian life. Because the worship of God in New Testament times was inward and spiritual, according to Dell, external forms are merely accidental and can vary from church to church. Among believers there is unity in the Spirit, but this cannot be compelled; hence uniformity is wrong because it seeks to restrain the Spirit's freedom, a view with which Bunyan concurred.[133] The importance Dell attached to the Spirit led him to conclude that

[130] *New DNB, s.v.*; Henry Denne, *The Quaker No Papist, in Answer to the Quaker Disarm'd* (London, 1659), sig. A2r–v.

[131] *HMC 6, Seventh Report*, 101–2; *Calamy Revised, s.v.*; Brown, 117–18. Dell seems to have disputed his removal; see Walker, *Dell*, 176, n. 1.

[132] Cf., e.g., examples of explicit indebtedness: Dell, *Right Reformation*, 21; Dell, *Christ's Spirit*, 6, 23–24; Dell, *The Way of True Peace and Unity in the True Church of Christ* (London, 1651), 146, 181–82, 191–92, 204, 229–30, 239; Dell, *A Plain and Necessary Confutation of Divers Gross and Antichristian Errors* (London, 1654), title-page, sigs. a1v-a2r, a3v, and 17, 21, 31, 38; Dell, *A Testimony from the Word Against Divinity-Degrees in the University, ad cal.* Dell, *A Plain and Necessary Confutation*, 7; Dell, *The Tryall of Spirits Both in Teachers & Hearers* (London, 1660), sigs. A3v-A4r and 11.

[133] Dell, *Uniformity Examined* (London, 1646), sigs. A1v, A3r-A4r; Dell, *Right Reforma-*

formal academic training is not required for a minister; without the indwelling Spirit, natural abilities and human learning are insufficient to enable a pastor to preach the word of God. Like Bunyan, Dell made experience rather than a university education the *sine qua non* of a gospel minister. This in turn led him to attack the universities as repositories of darkness because they mixed "heathen" learning with the gospel, but he was willing to recognize the benefits of traditional learning as long as it was not made a precondition of the ministry.[134] As we have seen, Dell's views on education may have influenced Bunyan's remarks in his debate with Thomas Smith.

Other views of Dell would find expression in Bunyan's works. Dell had no kind words for clerics who were idle, negligent, inadequate, or preached for monetary gain. Those who preached the efficacy of the law, "moral" theology, and human works he condemned as false teachers, as he did those whose teachings were philosophical subtleties or speculations.[135] As Bunyan would do, Dell stressed the baptism of the Spirit, referring to it as the baptism of substance in contrast with water-baptism, which he downplayed as merely a sign. Only Christ, he insisted, can baptize with the Spirit.[136] Because this baptism binds all Christians together, Dell rejected any fundamental distinction between clergy and laity; ministers differ from other believers only in their office, not in any substantive way. Like the Bedford church, he believed that a minister's only authority stems from the church, with each community of believers empowered to choose its own officers, including the pastor.[137]

Approximately three months before Bunyan preached in Dell's church, Burton's health began to decline. On 27 September 1659 the monthly meeting decided to set apart 5 October to pray about providing him with preaching assistance. By late November, with Burton's frailty increasingly apparent, the monthly

---

tion, 24–26; Dell, *Way of True Peace*, 178–79, 225–26. The importance of the Spirit is manifest in works such as *Christ's Spirit*, *The Tryall of Spirits*, and *Power from on High* (London, 1645).

[134] Dell, *A Plain and Necessary Confutation*, sigs. A2v, a1r–a2r, a3v and 17, 21, 31–32, 38; Dell, *Christ's Spirit*, 17, 25; Dell, *Tryall of Spirits*, sig. A3v; Dell, *Testimony from the Word*, 2, 9, 35–36; Dell, *Way of True Peace*, 197. See also Christopher Hill, *Change and Continuity in Seventeenth-Century England* (Cambridge, MA: Harvard University Press, 1975), 136–43; Peter Burke, "William Dell, the Universities and the Radical Tradition," in *Reviving the English Revolution: Reflections and Elaborations on the Work of Christopher Hill*, ed. Geoff Eley and William Hunt (London and New York: Verso, 1988), 181–89.

[135] Dell, *Christ's Spirit*, 6; Dell, *Tryall of Spirits*, 27, 29.

[136] Dell, *Way of True Peace*, 175–76; Dell, *The Doctrine of Baptismes, Reduced from Its Ancient and Moderne Corruptions* (London, 1648), 11.

[137] Dell, *Way of True Peace*, 196–200, 211–12.

meeting resolved that the elders and deacons should consider writing to Simp-son, Jessey, and Cokayne for help in locating a suitable assistant. Finally, on 29 March 1660 the meeting asked Wheeler, Donne, Gibbs, and Brother (William?) Breeden to preach each Sunday on a rotating basis, and to celebrate the Lord's supper every three or four weeks. In February it was decided that Breeden would preach should someone else be unable to do so. Bunyan's absence from this list was probably owing to a preaching itinerary that took him throughout the region; this is certainly indicated by the earlier decision to excuse him from the diaconate because of such activities. He was not at the meeting on 25 February when his fellow congregants decided he should "speak a word" at their next gathering.[138] By 25 July 1660 Burton could no longer undertake any pastoral responsibilities, and Donne, Wheeler, and Gibbs were consequently invited to Bedford to advise the congregation on a successor; Burton died shortly thereafter. Compounding the church's plight was its loss of St. John's as a meeting place and the decision of some members to cease attending, apparently because traditional services were again available. The dark cloud of the Restoration was already casting its shadow over the Bedford congregation. In November 1660 the Bedford church invited Wheeler to be its new minister, but, in the face of objections from his church at Cranfield, he declined. Finally, in December 1663 Samuel Fenne and John Whit-man agreed to serve as co-pastors.[139] Well before this, Bunyan was arrested on 12 November 1660 for meeting with a conventicle at Lower Samsell in the hamlet of Westoning, perhaps at Dell's invitation.

[138] CB, 34–35.
[139] CB, 36–39

# CHAPTER 4

# Confronting Persecution

—◦•◦—

Given their commitment to the republic and congregations of visible saints with the right to elect their own ministers and deacons, Bunyan and his friends became increasingly concerned as they watched warring factions weaken the national government in 1659. Bolstered by the acquiescence of Richard Cromwell, who had succeeded his father in September 1658, parliamentary conservatives sought to limit religious toleration and curb the army's political power, but the army retaliated by forcing Cromwell to dissolve Parliament on 22 April. In the face of pressure from junior officers for substantive constitutional and religious reforms, the senior officers recalled the Rump on 7 May. Henceforth, Cromwell was a mere spectator, but mutually contradictory aims doomed the alliance between the army and the Rump. To preserve the republic, its supporters in the Rump wanted to recruit additional members rather than hold a general election, as the officers insisted. The army favored more toleration for religious dissidents than did the Rump, and the latter lacked the financial resources to meet the army's demand for arrears. Against this background, freeholders and others in Bedfordshire, possibly including members of Burton's congregation, petitioned Parliament in June for the abolition of tithes, equal protection for people of "different persuasions of faith and worship," legal reforms, the settlement of the militia on those loyal to the Good Old Cause, security of copyhold, a land register, and electoral reform.[1] Sensing that the government was weak enough to topple, Sir George Booth launched an insurrection in August. The general who suppressed Booth's forces, John Lambert, became the Rump's target in the autumn as part of its planned purge of the high command, but Lambert ex-

[1] *To the Parliament of the Commonwealth of England: The Humble Representation and Desires of Divers Freeholders and Others Well Affected to the Commonwealth of England, Inhabiting Within the County of Bedford* (London, 1659).

pelled the Rump and placed the government in the hands of a committee of safety.

Lambert's decision brought opposition from General George Monck, who commanded the army in Scotland. After Monck threw his support to the Rump, he won the backing of troops in Yorkshire and Ireland. The committee of safety collapsed, the Rump was reinstated, and on 1 January 1660 Monck led his troops across the River Tweed into England. After occupying London on 3 February, he restored the MPs excluded by Colonel Thomas Pride in 1648, and the revivified Long Parliament voted for a general election before dissolving itself on 16 March. This action was in keeping with a declaration from gentry and others in Bedfordshire on 22 February calling for "a Full and Free" Parliament "to compose all our Differences . . . in Church and State."[2] When the Convention Parliament met on 25 April, it received a declaration from Charles (II) at Breda in the Netherlands promising, among other things, liberty for tender consciences. The same month Lambert mounted a desperate but futile military uprising to save the Good Old Cause. Presbyterian attempts in Parliament to impose conditions on Charles before his return to England failed, and on 8 May Parliament proclaimed him king. Eighteen days later he landed at Dover, and on the 29th, his thirtieth birthday, he entered London in triumph.

To suggest that the monarchy's restoration was almost universally welcomed is to subscribe to a myth created by Charles' supporters.[3] In the Bedford congregation there had been obvious relief when Lambert quashed Booth's rebellion, and Bunyan and his friends thanked God for delivering the country from this threat. By year's end, however, they were sufficiently troubled by "the distractions of the nation" to set aside 5 January 1660 for a special day of prayer. After the Long Parliament dissolved itself on 16 March, the Bedford meeting reserved 16 April to pray for the country's affairs as well as Burton's failing health. The minutes suggest no air of thanksgiving for the turn of political events.[4] Indeed, the key issue in the election for the Convention Parliament was monarchy, and as the returns were reported in early April, royalists were clearly in the ascendant. By the latter part of August the congregation had lost the use of St. John's, but the minutes make no further mention of national affairs—not even Charles' return—in 1660. No day of prayer was scheduled to praise God for his restoration

---

[2] *The Declaration of the Gentlemen, Free-Holders and Inhabitants of the County of Bedford* (London, 1659 [1660]).

[3] One of the earliest people to accept this myth at face value was Francesco Giavarina, the Venetian envoy. *Calendar of State Papers, Venetian, 1659–61*, 136. For a modern example see John Miller, *The Restoration and the England of Charles II*, 2nd ed. (London: Longman, 1997), 1.

[4] *CB*, 34–35.

or to seek divine guidance for his rule.[5] In short, no evidence suggests that Bunyan and his fellow congregants were initially pleased with the Restoration.

The country's mood was anything but uniform. Critics of the Stuarts reviled Charles and his brother James, comparing the former unfavorably to Oliver Cromwell, renouncing him as a bastard, sneering at his Scottish ancestry, and allegedly threatening to assassinate him. Some dissidents openly predicted the imminent fall of the restored monarchy, and others worried that Charles would plunge the nation into renewed civil war.[6] Such hostile rhetoric came from clergy as well as laity. Fearing that Charles intended to restore and compel adherence to Catholicism, the Presbyterian John Milward, rector of Darfield, Yorkshire, urged his parishioners in May 1660 to "shew ourselves men, and gird every man his sword upon his thigh, and sheath it in his neighbour's bowell, for I doe beleive too many of us have Popes in our bellies."[7] At Llanthetty, Brecknockshire, the open-communion Baptist Jenkin Jones averred that the saints "should have another turne and if [Charles] would not mind things hee should not long Continue."[8] In a barbed analogy, the Presbyterian Andrew Parsons, rector of Wem, Shropshire, likened the Devil to a king who reneged on his word after he gained the throne, a not very subtle allusion to Charles' failure to assure liberty for tender consciences. The king's word was again the issue when Nathaniel Jones, rector of Westmeston, Sussex, accused Charles from the pulpit of breaking his vow to uphold the Solemn League and Covenant and compelling his subjects to violate it. An unidentified minister addressing a congregation at White's Alley, Coleman Street, London, where Fifth Monarchists and Congregationalists gathered, urged his listeners to pray for Charles' overthrow and proclaimed that the saints would ultimately prevail.[9] At Wapping in September, a preacher who was probably the General Baptist and former Leveller Thomas Lamb called on God to punish Charles: "As thou hast struck one stroke already in the family [i.e., the regicide] Lord strike another."[10]

Accusations of seditious preaching were made in 1660 against such ministers as the Presbyterian Zachary Crofton, the Congregationalist Thomas Jollie, and

[5] Ronald Hutton, *The Restoration: A Political and Religious History of England and Wales 1658–1667* (Oxford: Oxford University Press, 1985), 13; *CB*, 36.

[6] Greaves, *DUFE*, 22–26.

[7] *Depositions from the Castle of York, Relating to Offences Committed in the Northern Counties in the Seventeenth Century*, ed. J. Raine, Surtees Society, vol. 40 (1861), 83. For Milward see *Calamy Revised, s.v.*

[8] PRO, SP 29/8/29.1, 29.2 (quoted).

[9] White Kennet, *An Historical Register and Chronicle of English Affairs* (London, 1744), 324, 543; PRO, SP 29/18/22. For Parsons and Jones see *Calamy Revised, s.vv.*

[10] PRO, SP 29/16/24. For Lamb (d. 1673) see *BDBR, s.v.*

the Fifth Monarchists Wentworth Day, Richard Goodgroom, and Vavasor Powell.[11] When the chancellor, Edward Lord Hyde, addressed the House of Lords in September 1660, he indicated that Charles was receiving frequent reports of seditious sermons in London and throughout the country. "Religious zealots of whatever kind," one of the king's correspondents warned, "are more dangerous than impious people."[12]

### "Sweetly in the Prison"[13]: Arrest, Trial, and Appeal

In Bedford, Bunyan and his fellow believers watched as the Restoration began to take its toll on their friends. Colonel Okey appealed to the council of officers in March 1660 to support a republic, but his opposition to Monck cost him his command. The following month he cast his lot with Lambert, eluded capture, and eventually fled into exile; two years later, English agents apprehended him in the Netherlands and returned him to London, where he was executed on 19 April for his role in the regicide. Had Burton lived, he would have been ejected from his living in the state church, a fate experienced by Donne (by August 1660), Cokayne (by December 1660), Gibbs (by January 1661), Dell (apparently by January 1661), Wheeler (by October 1661), and Jessey (in 1661). Rogers had fled to the Netherlands in January 1660, and Dell resigned his mastership of Gonville and Caius College in May of the same year. Simpson, who defended the regicide from the pulpit in October 1660, continued to preach rather militant sermons in London until magistrates arrested him for seditious speech in November 1661.[14] In Bedford, conservatives began the recovery of the power they had lost to the freemen in 1650 by restricting the council to thirteen in August 1660, and three years later they completed their consolidation of authority by limiting council membership to burgesses.[15]

Although Bunyan and his friends had lost the use of St. John's, they contin-

---

[11] *Kingdomes Intelligencer* (18–25 March 1661); "Extracts," in *The Note Book of the Rev. Thomas Jolly A.D. 1671–1693*, ed. Henry Fishwick, Chetham Society, new ser., vol. 33 (1894), 131; Jeaffreson, 3:306–7; *Mercurius Publicus* 40 (27 September–4 October 1660); Kennet, *Register*, 241–42. For Crofton see *Calamy Revised, s.v.*; for Jollie, Day, and Goodgroom see *BDBR, s.vv.*

[12] *LJ*, 11:175; *Calendar of the Clarendon State Papers Preserved in the Bodleian Library*, vol. 5: 1660–1726, ed. F. J. Routledge (Oxford: Clarendon Press, 1970), 18.

[13] "Relation," 113: "I did meet my God sweetly in the prison."

[14] *BDBR, s.vv.*; *Calamy Revised, s.vv.* for all except Okey; Greaves, *SR*, 128–30; PRO, SP 29/19/26; Greaves, *DUFE*, 93.

[15] *Minute Book*, ed. Parsloe, 138–39, 174; Joyce Godber, *The Story of Bedford: An Outline History* (Luton, Beds.: White Crescent Press, 1978), 68–69, 76–77.

ued to gather for worship in private homes and to conduct their affairs, particularly the search for Burton's successor. They were concerned as well about those who were drifting away, presumably to attend services in parish churches and probably worried about the tendency of some royalists to equate nonconformity with disloyalty.[16] No evidence indicates that the Bedford church was hindered from meeting throughout 1660 notwithstanding the fact that more and more such gatherings were viewed with suspicion and in some cases prohibited.

As a practical matter, local magistrates normally decided whether to ban religious meetings apart from those of the established church. In May 1660, following the suppression of Lambert's uprising, Parliament ordered magistrates to prevent illegal assemblies, and in July lords lieutenant throughout the kingdom received instructions to prevent dissidents from assembling and to confiscate their weapons. Indeed, the houses of the Fifth Monarchist Carnsew Helme at Winchcombe, Gloucester, and the Congregationalist Anthony Palmer, who would shortly become a Fifth Monarchist, at Bourton in the same county, had been searched for arms earlier in the year.[17] In September the House of Lords directed that meetings of Baptists and Friends in Northamptonshire be suppressed on the grounds that they were seditious.[18] Magistrates could also inhibit unwanted religious gatherings by enforcing the Elizabethan statute against conventicles, "An Act to Retain the Queen Majesty's Subjects in Their Due Obedience" (35 Eliz. I, c. 1). Magistrates who were inclined to suppress conventicles had ample means to do so, especially if they deemed such meetings a security threat.

In early November 1660, the month of Bunyan's arrest, Okey and Rogers were in exile and Dell had resigned his mastership, but of the ministers with whom the congregation was close, only Donne had been ejected. Sometime between 1660 and 1662, Donne settled at Keysoe, Bedfordshire, where he ministered to his flock. He was still a free man in April 1662, when the Bedford church asked him to preach to it every third week.[19] In November 1660, then, Bunyan and his pastoral colleagues had no compelling reason to anticipate severe punishment if they continued to preach. Moreover, the Bedford congregation finally accepted the Restoration, as reflected by their decision in October to set aside 12 November to pray that God "would direct our governors in their meeting together."[20]

When Bunyan's friends invited him to preach in a house at the hamlet of

[16] *CB*, 36–37.

[17] *Mercurius Publicus* 19 (3–10 May 1660); PRO, SP 29/8/188; Thomas Crosby, *The History of the English Baptists*, 4 vols. (London, 1738–40), 2:28. For Helme and Palmer see *BDBR*, *s.vv.*

[18] Kennet, *Register*, 246; Huntington Library, MS STT 524.

[19] *CB*, 38.

[20] *CB*, 36.

Lower Samsell on 12 November, the very day devoted to prayer for the nation's governors by the Bedford church, he accepted. Word of his impending visit spread, reaching Francis Wingate, justice of the peace, in nearby Harlington. A royalist, his widowed mother had been heavily fined for her political loyalties, and Wingate would hardly have been sympathetic to Bunyan. Indeed, Wingate shared the suspicion of numerous royalists that nonconforming ministers and their supporters "intended to do some fearful business, to the destruction of the country." When Bunyan arrived at Lower Samsell, a friend told him about a rumored warrant, which, in fact, Wingate had issued. Rather than forgo the service, Bunyan decided to preach, not wanting to set a bad example for recent converts or to nonconformists throughout the country by fleeing. "And further, I thought the world thereby would take occasion at my cowardliness, to have blasphemed the Gospel, and to have had some ground to suspect worse of me and my profession, than I deserved." He even refused to move the meeting time forward to evade arrest, preferring "to see the utmost of what they could say or do unto [him]." Clearly, he had no sense of what the state could and was prepared to do. Having begun the meeting with a prayer, he and his fellow worshipers, Bibles in their hands, were interrupted by a constable and his assistant before he could commence his sermon. As they escorted him out of the house, he managed to speak a few words of encouragement to the congregants, attesting that it was better to suffer for God's sake than to be persecutors. To endure on such an account, he counseled them, was "a mercy."[21]

Because Wingate was away on the 12th, the constable permitted one of Bunyan's friends to engage for his appearance the following morning. At that time Wingate asked the constable what Bunyan and the others had done, where they had met, and what they had with them. According to Bunyan, Wingate expected them to have been armed and was surprised both by the paucity of their number and by the absence of any evidence that they intended to pursue violent courses. Wingate inquired if Bunyan was content to follow his vocation instead of breaking the law. With a humble apology and a promise to tend exclusively to his calling, he would have been released, but instead he told Wingate that he had come to Lower Samsell to urge people to repent, "forsake their sins, and close in with Christ, lest they did miserably perish." He could, he insisted, both preach

[21] Mullett, *JBC*, 73; "Relation," 105–6 (quoted). Bunyan's "Relation," first published in 1765, comprised a series of five letters written to his flock from prison. See Roger Sharrock, "The Origin of *A Relation of the Imprisonment of Mr. John Bunyan*," *Review of English Studies*, n.s. 39 (August 1959): 250–56. Various other dissenters similarly refused to avoid confrontations. In October 1674, for example, Owen Stockton "resolved to proceed in my work" despite advance warning that informers would attend his service. DWL, MS 24.7, fol. 87r. For Stockton see *Calamy Revised, s.v.*

and follow his vocation. Bunyan had thrown down the gauntlet, whereupon Wingate threatened to "break the neck" of such meetings. He was willing to release Bunyan pending trial, but only if his sureties provided bonds that he would cease preaching. This Bunyan refused to do, and Wingate left to prepare a mittimus ordering his imprisonment until the quarter sessions.[22]

In Wingate's absence, Dr. William Lindale (or Lindall), vicar of Harlington and step-father of Wingate's wife, met with Bunyan. A man whose principles were sufficiently malleable to serve the established church through all the vicissitudes from the 1630s to the 1660s, Lindale was adjudged by Bunyan "an old enemy to the truth." A Cambridge doctor of divinity who likely knew about Bunyan's encounter with Thomas Smith, Lindale taunted and reviled Bunyan, accusing him, as had Smith, of preaching without a calling. They traded biblical verses as if they were weapons, Bunyan citing 1 Peter 4:10 as proof that everyone who received a divine gift should minister, and quoting Paul's affirmation in 1 Corinthians 14:31 that all believing men could prophesy. Lindale, however, recalled that a coppersmith named Alexander had vexed Timothy (2 Timothy 4:14), a pointed comparison with the Bedford tinker. Debate turned to invective when Bunyan made an allusion of his own, implicitly comparing the Cambridge doctor to the priests and Pharisees whose hands were stained with Christ's blood. Bunyan, retorted Lindale, was one of those scribes and Pharisees, for he uttered "long prayers to devour widows houses." In his parting shot, Bunyan averred that Lindale would not be so wealthy if he had received as little for preaching and praying as had Bunyan. Fortunately for both men, the mittimus was now ready and the constable arrived to take Bunyan to prison.[23]

The exchange is significant because of its transition from the relatively limited question of Bunyan's right to preach, and thus implicitly of the Bedford congregation's authority to commission him to do so, to the much broader insistence of each disputant that the other's church was false. This was the real meaning of each man's charge that his opponent was numbered among the infamous scribes and Pharisees. In the eyes of each disputant, the other was not part of the true church, nor, by extension, were each man's coreligionists. For this reason, Bunyan could not periodically worship in the Church of England and use the Book of Common Prayer, as had the Bedford semi-separatists in the 1640s. The gulf between the two communions was now impassable in the judgment of these contenders.

Before the constable could convey Bunyan to the county jail, two of the tinker's friends interceded with Wingate, who agreed to see Bunyan again. This

---

[22] "Relation," 107.
[23] Ibid., 107–8.

time Wingate was joined by his brother-in-law, the Bedford attorney William Foster, whose appearance Bunyan painted in terms that evoked Judas' betrayal of Jesus in the garden of Gethsemane: "Coming out of another room, and seeing of me by the light of the candle (for it was dark night when I went thither) he said unto me, who is there, *John Bunyan*? with such seeming affection, as if he would have leaped in my neck and kissed me." But Foster was hardly a model Judas, as Bunyan quickly acknowledged, for he had always opposed God's ways, or so Bunyan charged. Seeking to be reasonable rather than confrontational, Foster offered Bunyan liberty if he ceased to hold conventicles and was willing to "be but ruled." In the ensuing exchange, the two men essentially replayed Bunyan's earlier dialogues with Smith and Lindale regarding his right to preach, with Bunyan adamantly insisting that his conscience compelled him to continue exhorting people to seek Christ for salvation.[24]

Foster shifted the debate's focus by charging Bunyan with proximity to the Catholics because of his literal interpretation of Scripture. "Those [verses] that was to be understood literally," Bunyan countered, "we understand them so; but for those that was to be understood otherwise, we endeavoured so to understand them." This provided the Cambridge-educated Foster with an opening to accuse Bunyan of being unable to understand the Bible because he had no knowledge of Greek, but Bunyan was ready, quoting Matthew 11:25 as evidence that God concealed his truth to the world's learned. Foster had unwittingly provided Bunyan with the platform so beloved by most sectarian preachers to proclaim that "God had rejected the wise, and mighty and noble, and chosen the foolish, and the base." In a narrow sense, this effectively damned his three protagonists—a landed gentleman, a cleric with a Cambridge doctorate of divinity, and an ecclesiastical lawyer. More broadly, such views challenged the pillars of Restoration society. Foster maintained his composure, stressing that those who came to hear Bunyan were poor, simple, ignorant people, and again offering Bunyan his freedom if he would promise not to call people together for illegal worship.[25]

When Foster failed to dissuade Bunyan from holding meetings, Wingate dispatched several of his servants to speak with Bunyan, undoubtedly hoping he might be more receptive to fellow commoners. This approach too was a failure, and after further debate with Foster and Wingate about his right to preach, he was incarcerated, having "God's comfort in [his] poor soul."[26]

Five or six days after the prison doors first closed on Bunyan, his friends sought his release on bail until the quarter sessions. To this end they approached

[24]Ibid., 109–10.
[25]Ibid., 111.
[26]Ibid., 112.

Justice Crompton of Elstow, who was almost certainly the Robert Crompton admitted to the Bedford Corporation as a burgess in March 1662.[27] After reading the mittimus, which accused Bunyan of disparaging the Church of England's government by attending conventicles, Crompton demurred, fearing Bunyan might be charged with other offenses. Bunyan took Crompton's decision well, finding "God sweetly in the prison again, comforting of me and satisfying of me that it was his will and mind that I should be there." He was still comparing his experience with Christ's, noting that God had "dropt" a word in his heart, on this occasion Pilate's realization that Jesus had been brought to him because of the chief priests and elders' envy (Matthew 27:18).[28] Here, then, is another perspective from which to view the yawning gulf Bunyan envisioned between the true church and its antithesis, for the latter's defenders, Foster and Crompton, represented Judas and Pilate respectively, whereas Bunyan was the betrayed victim, the suffering servant.

The quarter sessions convened at Bedford in early January 1661, with Sir John Kelynge (or Keeling) of Southill, who had been imprisoned in Windsor Castle from 1642 to 1660 for supporting the royalist cause, presiding. Assisting him were Sir William Becher (or Beecher) of Howbury, Sir George Blundell of Cardington Manor, Sir Henry Chester of Tilsworth and Lidlington, and Thomas Snagge of Marston Manor. Becher had been knighted the previous November, followed shortly thereafter by Blundell. Chester, Wingate's uncle, would be dubbed a Knight of the Bath at Charles' coronation, and Snagge would subsequently become sheriff of Bedfordshire.[29] The proceedings began with a reading of the indictment, which charged that Bunyan had "devilishly and perniciously abstained from coming to church to hear divine service, and is a common upholder of several unlawful meetings and conventicles, to the great disturbance and distraction of the good subjects of this kingdom."[30] The indictment was based on the 1593 Elizabethan statute, which had been directed against seditious sectaries and disloyal people. The offenses it identified were obstinate refusal to attend services in the Church of England, encouragement of others to do the same, and presence at conventicles.[31] The act did not make preaching without lawful ordination an offense, though doing so at a conventicle clearly was.

When the clerk asked Bunyan to respond to the indictment, he changed the

[27] *Minute Book*, ed. Parsloe, 154.

[28] "Relation," 112–13.

[29] Brown, 142. For the Bechers and Snagges see Joyce Godber, *History of Bedfordshire 1066–1888* (Bedford: Bedfordshire County Council, 1969), 245–46.

[30] "Relation," 113.

[31] *Statutes of the Realm*, 4:841–43.

frame of reference, declaring that he commonly attended the church of God, the head of which was Christ. Bunyan sought to provoke a discussion about the nature of the true church, but Kelynge pressed him to indicate whether he went to services in a parish church. What followed was less like the usual questioning of the accused than a debate, with Bunyan and Kelynge the principal protagonists. The exchanges focused largely on the nature of prayer and Bunyan's right to preach, but the underlying issue involved authority. For Bunyan, divine worship had to conform to the Bible, whereas Kelynge looked to tradition as well. The Book of Common Prayer, Kelynge erroneously attested, had existed since apostolic times, though perhaps he meant only that set forms of prayer had been in use since that period. An overconfident Kelynge finally decided to debate Bunyan on his own terms, asking him for biblical proof that he had been authorized to preach. Bunyan was prepared to cite numerous passages, but settled on 1 Peter 4:10 when Kelynge insisted on taking them one at a time. Seizing the initiative, Kelynge offered to explain the verse to Bunyan, averring that Peter's reference to the divinely bestowed gift means a trade or vocation—"tinkering" in Bunyan's case. In turn, Bunyan argued that the ensuing verse, which refers to speaking the oracles of God, makes it manifest that the gift is preaching, not a secular vocation. Kelynge was willing to acknowledge that the gift included teaching spiritual matters, but only if such instruction were confined to one's family. If it were lawful to do good to some, retorted Bunyan, it was acceptable to assist more. With this, Kelynge, grumbling that he was insufficiently versed in Scripture to dispute its meaning with Bunyan, had heard enough.[32]

Most of the trial involved a dispute over prayer and ultimately the nature of acceptable worship. For Bunyan, the crucial text was Paul's call in 1 Corinthians 14:15 to pray with the Spirit and the understanding. This ruled out the prayers in the Book of Common Prayer because they were human creations, not the result of "the motions of the Holy Ghost, within our Hearts." Prayer begins when the Spirit gives supplicants a sense of what they lack, enabling them to pour out their hearts. Bunyan, notes Thomas Luxon, was suggesting that the heart is like a "uterus in which the Spirit opens up a space felt as desire for the things of God."[33] The Spirit fills this space—the worshiper's heart—with unutterable sighs and groans, so that true prayer is first and foremost something felt deep within oneself. But both Jesus and John taught their disciples to pray, Kelynge pointed out, and it was consequently lawful to instruct people to pray by means of the Book of Common Prayer. Bunyan's response drew a firm line between the recitation of the Lord's prayer with the mouth on the one hand and the Spirit on the other, in

[32] "Relation," 116–18.
[33] Ibid., 114 (quoted); Luxon, 138 (quoted).

the latter case "knowing what it is to be born again, and as having experience, that they are begotten of the spirit of God." Anything else, Bunyan pointedly averred, is babbling. The Spirit, not the Book of Common Prayer, teaches people to pray; indeed, true prayer commences with the Spirit's inner workings, a point Bunyan attempted to drive home to the justices. "It is the *spirit that sheweth us our sins*, and the *spirit that sheweth us a Saviour*: And the spirit that stireth up in our hearts desires to come to God, for such things as we stand in need of, even sighing out our souls unto him for them with *groans which cannot be uttered*."[34]

At best, Kelynge's grasp of Bunyan's argument was superficial. Despite Bunyan's explanation, he failed to understand the grounds of his opposition to the Book of Common Prayer. He admonished Bunyan not to speak irreverently of it, but unlike one of his fellow justices who wanted Bunyan to say no more, Kelynge thought his responses were no threat to the established liturgy. Several justices were manifestly impatient with Bunyan's explanations, deriding him as a man filled with delusions and the Devil. One justice sarcastically asked if his god were Beelzebub, chief of the evil spirits, and another jokingly inquired if he wrote out his prayers and then read them to the congregants. Even Kelynge lost his temper at one point, snidely referring to Bunyan's comments about worshipers sensing God's presence in his services as "pedlers French."[35]

Faced with Bunyan's principled refusal to submit, Kelynge returned to the original question, asking him if he acknowledged the truth of the indictment. Bunyan would confess only that he and his friends had often met to pray and exhort one another, at which times they enjoyed God's comforting presence. Kelynge thereupon sentenced him to prison for three months, after which he would have to cease preaching and attend services in the Church of England or be banished from the realm. Should he return without the monarch's permission after being exiled, he would hang as the 1593 statute prescribed. Defiantly, Bunyan responded that if he were liberated today, he would preach tomorrow. Returned to prison, he found comfort in Jesus' promise to give his followers a voice and wisdom their foes could not resist (Luke 21:15).[36]

At virtually the same time Bunyan was on trial, militant Fifth Monarchists in London under Thomas Venner's leadership mounted an insurrection. At his meetinghouse in Swan Alley, Coleman Street, he issued a clarion call for the saints to take up arms for King Jesus. Their enemies, Venner promised, would be unable to touch a hair on their heads. The saints must not sheath their swords until Babylon has been obliterated, and they must bind kings in chains and no-

[34]"Relation," 114–16.
[35]Ibid., 114–17.
[36]Ibid., 118–19.

bles in fetters. Their mission was global, commencing with the conquest of England and moving on to France, the German states, Spain, and beyond. Venner even printed copies of his manifesto, *A Door of Hope: or, a Call and Declaration for the Gathering Together of the First Ripe Fruits unto the Standard of Our Lord, King Jesus*. From the sixth through the ninth of January the Vennerites battled government forces in the streets of London, crying "King Jesus and the heads upon the gates." Some forty people, about half of them rebels, died in the fighting. Although the number of militants was approximately fifty, frightened Londoners, thinking there were ten times that number, took up arms to defend their homes.[37]

On the 10th, the government issued a proclamation banning all unlawful meetings and ordering magistrates to search for conventicles and arrest those in attendance. Throughout the country numerous nonconformist ministers were apprehended, as were many Quakers. The government was suspicious, without cause, of two men with whom Bunyan would subsequently be associated, the Congregationalist John Owen, in whose house weapons were found, and Matthew Meade, who, with his mentor William Greenhill, were each bound £300 and their sureties a total of £500.[38] Many nonconformists distanced themselves from the Vennerites. Greenhill, Cokayne, Helme, Thomas Goodwin, George Griffith, Nathaniel Mather, and nineteen other Congregationalists denounced the uprising as a scandal, suggesting a possible parallel with the infamous events at Münster in 1534–35 and insisting that church services must not be occasions for plotting. A group of some thirty Baptists, including Henry Denne, William Kiffin, and Francis Smith (Bunyan's future printer), submitted a petition denying any affiliation with Venner's group, repudiating its actions as treasonous, and professing loyalty to the king. A group of Lincolnshire Baptists that included Thomas Grantham sent similar addresses.[39] The Quakers likewise condemned the insurrection, principally in *A Declaration from the Harmles & Innocent People of God, Called Quakers, Against All Plotters and Fighters in the World* (1661), subscribed by Fox, Francis Howgill, Henry Fell, and nine others. Nevertheless magistrates arrested substantial numbers at conventicles in the weeks following the rebellion, including

[37] Pepys, 2:7, 9–11 (quoted at 11); *Mercurius Publicus* 1 (3–10 January 1661); *Kingdomes Intelligencer* (7–14 January 1661); Greaves, *DUFE*, 50–52.

[38] *CSPD, 1660–61*, 470; Bodl., Rawlinson Letters 109, fol. 12r; Greaves, *DUFE*, 53–56; PRO, SP 29/28/43, 56. For Meade and Greenhill see *New DNB, s.vv.*

[39] Joseph Caryl, Philip Nye, *et al.*, *A Renuntiation and Declaration of the Ministers of Congregational Churches and Publick Preachers* (London, 1661); Crosby, *History*, 2:35–42; Kennet, *Register*, 383. A manuscript copy of *A Renuntiation* is in Bodl., Carte MSS 81, fols. 19r–20r. For Griffith see Greaves, *SR*, 77–97, and *New DNB, s.v.*; for Mather, Grantham, Caryl, and Nye see *BDBR, s.vv.*

approximately 400 Baptists and 500 Friends in London alone. "Att all theire meetings [the sectaries] are taken away to prison, all prisons filled," reported one observer. Throughout England some 4,230 Quakers found themselves in prison.[40]

Venner's insurrection thus brought nonconformity under a foreboding cloud of suspicion in the early months of 1661, a distrust fed by the association of former Cromwellian officers and men with sectarian congregations.[41] In this context the Bedfordshire justices sent Paul Cobb, clerk of the peace and a fellow member of the gentry, to obtain Bunyan's submission on 3 April 1661. Cobb took a friendly approach, referring to him as "Neighbour" and inquiring about his well-being before reminding him of the possibility of banishment if he refused to submit by the next quarter sessions, which were imminent. Since his trial Bunyan had been studying the statute under which he was convicted, and he now averred that this law had been enacted to punish those who used religious gatherings as a pretext for evil actions, not the sort of services he had attended. Private meetings devoted solely to worship and mutual edification were not, he argued, excluded by the statute. "My end in meeting with others is simply to do as much good as I can, by exhortation and counsel, according to that small measure of light which God hath given me, and not to disturb the peace of the nation." Referring to the Vennerite uprising, Cobb countered that all nonconformists, including those intent on overthrowing the kingdom, made the same plea for toleration. Like many other nonconformists, Bunyan disavowed the rebellion, protesting the unfairness of asserting that all dissenters would act as Venner's Fifth Monarchists had done. To this he added a carefully worded profession of obedience: "I look upon it as my duty to behave myself under the King's government, both as becomes a man and a christian; and if an occasion was offered me, I should willingly manifest my loyalty to my Prince, both by word and deed."[42] The former parliamentary soldier was thus willing to serve the restored monarchy and obey the state insofar as he could *as a Christian*. This, he would shortly explain, was a significant exception, by which he claimed the right to undertake actions explicitly rendered illegal by statute. Strictly speaking, this was more than passive disobedience.

[40]Greaves, *DUFE*, 58. For Howgill and Fell see *BDBR, s.vv.* In London, Quakers apprehended on suspicion of having supported the insurrection were soon released, but those who had been incarcerated for refusing to take the oath of allegiance or supremacy were not. BL, Egerton MSS 2543, fol. 15.

[41] One Fifth Monarchist meeting in London met at the home of a former cornet (Cole) in the regiment of Colonel Okey, a Bedfordshire man. BL, Egerton MSS 2543, fol. 24. For the nonconformist views and affiliations of various navy men in the Restoration period, see Bernard Capp, *Cromwell's Navy: The Fleet and the English Revolution 1648–1660* (Oxford: Clarendon Press, 1989), 373, 381, 387, 392.

[42]"Relation," 119–20.

Recognizing his limitations, Cobb admitted he was unable to dispute effectively with Bunyan, whose command of the Bible gave him a marked advantage in debating with civil magistrates. Yet Cobb sought a solution that would enable the voluble brazier to gain his freedom. In Cobb's judgment, if Bunyan would eschew conventicles he could do much good by privately exhorting his neighbors, but he must not preach to groups lest he seduce the people. Ultimately, Cobb rested his case on the necessity of a Christian to obey the statute in question. This gave Bunyan an opportunity to distinguish between the letter of the law and its formulators' intent, a surprisingly sophisticated argument for a man of his educational background: "I would not entertain so much uncharitableness of that parliament in the 35th of *Elizabeth*, or of the Queen herself, as to think they did by that law intend the oppressing of any of God's ordinances, or the interrupting any in the way of God; but men may, in the wresting of it, turn it against the way of God, but take the law in itself, and it only fighteth against those that drive at mischief in their hearts and meetings, making religion only their cloak, colour, or pretence." Bunyan buttressed his argument by closely paraphrasing a brief passage from the act. He did acknowledge, however, that he thought many people wanted to overthrow the government, a damaging admission that can only have reinforced Cobb's suspicion of conventicles.[43]

Bunyan made it clear that he was more than willing to hold his meetings in public if the magistrates approved. Neither his doctrine nor his practice, he attested, was erroneous or heretical, but this was not at issue in the Elizabethan statute, which concerned itself with unauthorized meetings. Cobb seems to have suggested that Bunyan's teaching was heretical, though the latter's account records no such charge; still, Bunyan was defensive on this point, offering to recant anything Cobb could prove was heretical but defending truth to the death, implicitly identifying himself with the Marian martyrs. He must preach, for God had given him the requisite gift, and he could not acquiesce to Cobb's plaintive request that he at least cease preaching temporarily. "Sir, said I, *Wickliffe* saith, that he which leaveth off preaching and hearing of the word of God for fear of excommunication of men, he is already excommunicated of God, and shall in the day of judgment be counted a traitor to Christ."[44] In short, having the gift but failing to exercise it was treason in the divine court of justice. There is no evidence that Bunyan read John Wyclif or subsequent Lollard writings, but he could have read about Wyclif in John Foxe's *Acts and Monuments* or learned about him from Dell.[45]

[43]Ibid., 120–21.
[44]Ibid., 122.
[45]Foxe, *Acts and Monuments*, 3:22; William Dell, *A Plain and Necessary Confutation of*

Ever the pragmatic magistrate, Cobb wanted to know how he could tell if someone had received the divine gift of preaching. In his mind the question was rhetorical, for the established church had precedence to determine who possessed such a gift and could exercise it, but Bunyan insisted that only the "infallible" Scripture could answer Cobb's query. To make his point Bunyan stressed the necessity of comparing one biblical passage with another, using Christ's offices of mediator and high priest as examples. The Bible, in other words, "doth . . . sufficiently open itself and discover its meaning," and in this manner Bunyan was prepared to demonstrate scriptural sanction of the matters in contention. For him, Scripture, interpreted comparatively with the Spirit's guidance, was the final authority. When Cobb asked if he would be bound by the church's judgment, Bunyan responded affirmatively, though unlike Cobb he was not referring to the Church of England but to "the church of God," whose "judgment is best expressed in Scripture."[46]

The exchange between Bunyan and Cobb turned in the end to the issue of political obedience. Although members of the Bedford congregation had been variously attracted to republican and Fifth Monarchist principles in the 1650s, Bunyan was now prepared to suggest indifference to civil polity. If he had any lingering preference for theocracy or republicanism, it would have been imprudent to express it while he was a prisoner threatened with banishment. He told Cobb he was conscience-bound to obey all "righteous laws . . . whether there was a King or no," and to suffer the penalty for infringing any statute. He was even willing to provide magistrates with his sermon notes, and he probably would have been delighted to have them take him up on this offer, but there is no evidence they did. While he professed his willingness to submit to the government, whatever its form, his qualification of the type of laws he was willing to obey—*righteous* statutes—left open the door to civil disobedience. Cobb wanted only that Bunyan agree to "be ruled," recalling the oft-quoted Pauline dictum that the powers that be are ordained by God (Romans 13:1). Bunyan reminded him that neither Jesus nor Paul had repudiated magistracy, though both suffered at the hands of the state. "Sir, said I, the law hath provided two ways of obeying: The one to do that which I in my conscience do believe that I am bound to do, actively; and where I cannot obey actively, there I am willing . . . to suffer what they shall do unto me." Realizing the two men had reached an impasse, Cobb sat in silence, his mission a failure. It was undoubtedly with a sense of sadness that he

---

*Divers Gross and Antichristian Errors* (London, 1654), sigs. a1v and a3v, and 47; Dell, *A Testimony from the Word Against Divinity-Degrees in the University*, ad cal. Dell, *A Plain and Necessary Confutation*, 5–6.

    [46]"Relation," 122–23.

left after Bunyan had thanked him for his civility. Here was a member of the gentry whom Bunyan at this point thought well of, closing this section of the account of his incarceration with the uplifting thought, "O! that we might meet in Heaven!"[47]

Principle drove Bunyan. Had he met his friends in the Lower Samsell area in their homes, family by family, Wingate would not have had him arrested. Other nonconforming ministers in Bedfordshire and the contiguous areas continued to hold services, as did his own congregation through late December 1660. In the aftermath of Venner's uprising, the church's monthly meetings (or at least records of them) ceased until August 1661, though there may have been gatherings for worship during this period.[48] Various ministers with ties to the Bedford church, including Dell, Cokayne, Gibbs, and Donne, did not go to prison at this time, nor did they conform. Bunyan paid a very high price for holding the meeting at Lower Samsell, but once he had been arrested, the stakes increased significantly when magistrates insisted on his pledge to cease holding conventicles anywhere. Unlike many other prisoners, he failed to benefit from the pardon issued by the king in connection with his coronation on 23 April 1661. Had he been willing to sue for a pardon—to have admitted he had wrongfully convened the group at Lower Samsell—he would have received his freedom, but this he was unprepared to do. At the same time, he escaped the dreaded banishment that by law could have been imposed at the quarter sessions in April. Because of the possibility that he might sue for a pardon, the justices decided to take no action at this time. He remained in jail, confined mostly with robbers and thieves, though one of his fellow prisoners had been accused of raping a girl under the age of ten.[49]

Bunyan now turned for help to Elizabeth, his second wife, whom he had married in 1659.[50] His first wife had died the previous year, leaving him with three daughters, including the blind Mary, and a son. Elizabeth had become pregnant in 1660, but upon hearing of Bunyan's arrest went into premature labor, giving birth eight days later; the infant died at childbirth or shortly thereafter. At some point between April and August 1661, she traveled to London with a petition

[47] Ibid., 123–25.
[48] *CB*, 37.
[49] "Relation," 125; BLA, MS HSA 1661 S/1.
[50] Nathaniel Ponder gave Elizabeth Bunyan a silver tankard in 1671, seven years before he published *The Pilgrim's Progress*, the first book of Bunyan's he is known to have issued. Frank Mott Harrison has queried whether Ponder and Elizabeth Bunyan were siblings. When Bunyan died, she gave the tankard to Andrew Gifford. For more on Gifford and Bunyan, see Chapter 13. Harrison, "John Bunyan and Andrew Gifford," *Baptist Quarterly* 10 (1940–41): 139, 142.

seeking her husband's release. She presented it to "Lord *Barkwood*," by which Bunyan presumably meant William Russell, fifth earl of Bedford, who patronized nonconformist clergy during the Restoration era, including Richard Baxter and Thomas Manton.[51] According to Bunyan's account, Bedford showed the petition to several of his fellow peers; they probably included Arthur Annesley, earl of Anglesey, another friend of nonconformists, who intervened on behalf of the General Baptist printer Francis Smith the same year, and Philip Lord Wharton, a supporter of various nonconformist ministers, including Theophilus Gale (his children's tutor), George Griffith, John Owen, Lazarus Seaman, and William Jenkyn. Although the peers told Elizabeth Bunyan they could not release her husband, they advised her to petition the judges at the next assizes.[52]

In the meantime Bunyan continued to study the law, sharing his knowledge with Elizabeth and preparing her to appear at the assizes in August. When the justices arrived in Bedford, she presented her petition to Sir Matthew Hale, who had acted as counsel for the earl of Strafford and William Laud, archbishop of Canterbury, before serving the Commonwealth and Protectorate governments. In November 1660 Charles II had appointed him chief baron of the Exchequer. Perhaps most importantly for her husband's plea, though Elizabeth could hardly have known this, was Hale's commitment to "experimental" religion. Baxter would write to Hale in May 1676 as a kindred soul who shared the former's belief in "the regenerating, illuminating, quickening spirit, disposing the soule with fil-iall affections to God." Two years earlier, in 1674, Hale had freed George Fox de-spite pressure to keep him in prison by tendering him the oaths of supremacy and allegiance, and in 1664 he would liberate Friends at Exeter because he did not deem their meetings seditious, which was precisely Bunyan's argument. But in the summer of 1661 Hale was more cautious in dealing with nonconformists, per-haps still sensitive about his service to the interregnum regimes. He treated Eliza-beth kindly when she gave him the petition, promising to do what he could but doubting he could succeed.[53]

[51] "Relation," 127–28; Lacey, 463–64; Baxter, *Calendar*, 2:257, 265. For Manton see *Calamy Revised, s.v.*

[52] Lacey, 459–62, 473–74; "Relation," 127. For Wharton's ties in this period to Gale, Griffith, Owen, Seaman, and Jenkyn see, e.g., Bodl., Rawlinson Letters 49, fols. 28r, 32r, 36r, *et seq.*; 50, fols. 34r, 55r, 61r; 52, fols. 314r, 343r, 349r, 359r, 362r; 53, fol. 19r. For Gale see *BDBR, s.v.*; for Griffith see *New DNB, s.v*; for Seaman and Jenkyn see *Calamy Revised, s.vv.*

[53] "Relation," 125–26; Baxter, *Calendar*, 2:186 (quoted); *The Journal of George Fox*, ed. Norman Penney, 2 vols. (Cambridge: Cambridge University Press, 1911), 2:285; PRO, SP 29/102/137. For Hale's religious views see Alan Cromartie, *Sir Matthew Hale 1609–1676: Law, Religion and Natural Philosophy* (Cambridge: Cambridge University Press, 1995), 139–55.

Afraid that Hale might forget her petition in the press of business, Elizabeth threw another one in the coach of Hale's fellow judge, Thomas Twisden (or Twysden), the following day. Appointed to the King's Bench in July 1660, Twisden had already treated Fox roughly from the bench, and he now responded similarly to Bunyan's wife. After reading the petition, he "snapt her up, and angrily told her that [her husband] was a convicted person" who could be released only if he promised to cease preaching. Undeterred, she presented another petition to Hale as he sat on the bench, provoking an objection from Sir Henry Chester that Bunyan, "a hot spirited fellow (or words to that purpose)," had been legally convicted at the quarter sessions. Hale was therefore unwilling to consider the petition.[54]

There the matter might have ended had not the high sheriff persuaded Elizabeth to make one more attempt. Going to the Swan Chamber inn, she found Hale and Twisden in the company of many justices of the peace and other gentry, including Chester. Although embarrassed and nervous, she pressed Hale to know what would happen to her husband. When he indicated he could do nothing because Bunyan had admitted attending conventicles, she cited three grounds for his illegal incarceration, namely, that he had been imprisoned before the government issued a proclamation against conventicles in January 1661, that he had never been asked whether he was guilty, and that he had not pleaded guilty to the indictment. The first point was irrelevant because Bunyan had been charged under the 1593 statute, which Hale wanted to review, calling for the statute book. In the meantime, when Twisden and Chester debated with Elizabeth, the latter justice emphasized that the proceedings, which had been recorded, were lawful. For her part, Elizabeth based her case on a tenuous distinction between an acknowledgment of guilt and her husband's assertion that he had attended meetings at which preaching and prayer occurred; this "word of discourse," she averred, had wrongly been the basis of his conviction. Twisden was prepared to send for Bunyan, but only if he agreed to stop preaching. This, Elizabeth defiantly said, he could not do as long as he could speak, whereupon Twisden had heard enough, castigating Bunyan as "a breaker of the peace."[55]

In what is arguably Bunyan's most dramatic prose, he recounted his wife's highly personal, emotional plea to Hale. Her husband, she pleaded, wanted only to live peacefully and pursue his vocation in order to support her and their four small children, one of whom was blind. While Bunyan was in prison, she continued, his family was dependent on charity. This struck a responsive chord in Hale,

---

[54] Fox, *Journal*, 1:366; "Relation," 126 (quoted).
[55] "Relation," 126–27.

who remarked that she was very young to have four children. When she explained that she was the children's step-mother and recounted how she had lost her own baby at the news of Bunyan's arrest, Hale expressed pity. Quickly, the callous Twisden interjected, accusing her of using poverty as a cloak and reiterating the old charge that Bunyan made more money on his preaching forays than by his vocation. When Hale asked what his calling was, several bystanders replied that he was a tinker. Angered by what must have been the mocking tone of their voices, Elizabeth shed her deferential demeanor and denounced the proceedings for their perceived bias against commoners: "Because he is a Tinker, and a poor man; therefore he is despised, and cannot have justice." Still sympathetic to her plight, Hale explained that she had three options, namely, appealing to the king, suing for a pardon, or obtaining a writ of error. Even this advice provoked Chester and Twisden, who disputed Elizabeth's claims that her husband preached only the word of God. "God!" snorted Twisden, "his doctrine is the doctrine of the Devil." Although Elizabeth desperately hoped Hale would send for her husband and permit him to speak for himself, the judge counseled her to obtain a writ of error, her least expensive option in his opinion. She left the chamber in tears, less, she told her husband, because of the judges' hard-heartedness than because of the accounting they would have to give at the last judgment.[56]

Elizabeth must have returned to her cottage with a heavy heart, perhaps stopping first at the county jail to tell Bunyan what had transpired. The dismay she now experienced, the child she had lost, the financial struggle she had to endure, and the abjection felt by those unaccustomed to dependence on charity were perhaps in Bunyan's mind when he described Christiana's experiences in the second part of *The Pilgrim's Progress*: "A Dream that I had, of two ill-lookt ones, that I thought did Plot how to make me miscarry in my Journey, that hath troubled me much: Yea, it still runs in my mind, and makes me afraid of every one that I meet, lest they should meet me to do me a mischief, and to turn me out of the way" (*PP*, 205). Although her prison had no bars, as long as her husband was incarcerated, it was no less real.

[56] Ibid., 127–29. According to Tamsin Spargo, Bunyan's account of his wife's challenge to "the political and linguistic legitimacy of state authority" effectively subverted his "own prohibition on women taking an active role in political, public affairs." This is wrong, for her appeals on his behalf were clearly within the bounds of English legal tradition and offered no challenge to the government's authority or legitimacy, nor did *A Case of Conscience Resolved* address such activity. Spargo, *The Writing of John Bunyan* (Aldershot, Hants.: Ashgate, 1997), 40.

"Holding Fast the Good"[57]: The Early Prison Years

Virtually from the onset of his imprisonment, Bunyan continued to write. The state could still his voice but not suppress his pen. In his first prison work he recounted his incarceration and dealings with magistrates in five pastoral letters: his arrest and ensuing exchanges with Wingate, Lindale, and Foster (November 1660); his appearance at the quarter sessions before Kelynge, Chester, and their colleagues (January 1661); Cobb's failed attempt to persuade him to cease preaching (3 April 1661); Elizabeth Bunyan's petitioning of Hale and Twisden (August 1661); and a brief account of how he fared from that time until March 1662. During this period Bunyan composed two other works, his first collection of verse, *Profitable Meditations*, published in 1661, and *I Will Pray with the Spirit*, almost certainly written in 1662.

The printer of *Profitable Meditations* was Francis Smith, a signatory of the 1660 General Baptist confession and a man with links to Henry Jessey, the Particular Baptist Henry Danvers, and the General Baptists Henry Denne and John Gosnold.[58] In May 1661, Smith, the minister George Hammon, and five other Baptists appealed to the king for freedom of conscience in a work entitled *Sion's Groans for Her Distres'd*.[59] With Livewell Chapman, Smith had printed Jessey's *The Lords Loud Call to England*, which recounted the persecution of such nonconformists as Vavasor Powell and Carnsew Helme as well as natural disasters that Jessey attributed to divine judgment. In late 1660 Jessey had discussed prodigies (marvels and monstrosities) in London with Smith and Danvers, and on another occasion he exchanged prodigies with George Cokayne. By the summer of 1661 a nonconformist, probably Cokayne or Danvers, compiled a collection of prodigies that warned of divine judgment and the imminent end of the world, and castigated the debauchery of Belshazzar, the barely disguised Charles II. With Elizabeth Calvert, whose husband Giles was already in prison for printing seditious literature, Smith published the collection of prodigies under the title *Mirabilis Annus, or the Year of Prodigies and Wonders*. When government agents found copies, a warrant for Smith's arrest was issued on 15 August 1661. Apprehended with copies in his possession, he was incarcerated and barred from printing for two years. For his involvement, Jessey went to prison in December, remaining there until the early spring of 1663.[60]

[57] *MW*, 2:42, stanza 2 (1663 ed.).

[58] *Baptist Confessions of Faith*, ed. William L. Lumpkin (Philadelphia: Judson Press, 1959), 235; Greaves, *DUFE*, 213; *BDBR*, *s.vv.* Francis Smith and Henry Danvers; *New DNB*, *s.vv.* John Gosnold, Henry Danvers, and Henry Denne.

[59] Crosby, *History*, 2:98–144. For Hammond (or Hammon) see *BDBR*, *s.v.*

[60] Greaves, *DUFE*, 212–14; *BDBR*, *s.vv.* Francis Smith and Henry Jessey; B. R. White,

*Profitable Meditations* was published at some point between late January 1661, when the government began releasing some of the nonconformists arrested in the aftermath of Venner's uprising, and 15 August, when the warrant for Smith's apprehension was issued. Although Bunyan had limited opportunity to leave the county prison during this period, his trip to London occurred sometime between the August 1661 assizes and 19 March 1662, as will be seen. The manuscript was therefore delivered to Smith by someone other than Bunyan, probably his wife Elizabeth, who had gone there to present a petition to the earl of Bedford. Bunyan probably wrote this collection of poems, his first, to raise money for his family, to pay his jailer, and perhaps to acquire funds for a legal appeal.

Periodically throughout his career Bunyan composed verse, improving considerably over the years. His earliest efforts—*Profitable Meditations, Prison Meditations* (1663), *One Thing Is Needful* (1665), and *Ebal and Gerizzim* (1665)—reveal his indebtedness to the ballads, broadsides, and chapbooks beloved by commoners. During his youth, as we have seen, his literary taste ran to "a Ballad, a Newsbook, *George* on horseback, or *Bevis* of *Southampton*" (*MW*, 1:333), but Graham Midgley sagely remarks that after Bunyan's conversion he probably read religious ballads composed for puritan readers. He was likely influenced as well by Thomas Sternhold and John Hopkins' metrical version of the Psalms, which he would have sung in the Elstow parish church. After his first marriage he regularly went to services where he did "devoutly both say and sing as others did." In time his poetic achievement was to refine the religious verse of the popular ballads and broadsheets, though his initial efforts in *Profitable Meditations* were pedestrian. Midgley aptly describes these poems as "solid versified theology, notably lacking in imagery or similitudes."[61]

In his first published verse, Bunyan was sensitive to anticipated criticism, not because he lacked poetic talent but because some readers might find this medium insufficiently serious for religious discourse. In defense of poetry Bunyan averred that

> *Man's heart is apt in Meeter to delight,*
> *Also in that to bear away the more.*

More easily remembered and more appealing than prose, poetry, Bunyan believed, is a useful device by which to convey the gospel message.

---

"Henry Jessey in the Great Rebellion," in *Reformation, Conformity and Dissent*, ed. R. Buick Knox (London: Epworth Press, 1977), 151–52. For the earlier use of prodigies see Alexandra Walsham, *Providence in Early Modern England* (Oxford: Oxford University Press, 1999), 167–203, 218–24. For Chapman and Calvert see *BDBR*, s.vv. and Plomer, *DBP*, 42–44.

[61] *GA*, §16 (quoted); *MW*, 6:xxix–xxxi, xxxiv–xxxv, xlvii (quoted).

> *When Doctors give their Physick to the Sick,*
> *They make it pleasing with some other thing:*
> *Truth also by this means is very quick,*
> *When men by Faith it in their hearts do sing.* (MW, 6:4)

Most of *Profitable Meditations* comprises a series of dialogues: between Satan and the tempted soul, Christ and a sinner, the doubting soul and Christ, death and a sinner, a saint and death, and a sinner in hell and a saint in heaven. Theologically, many of the themes expressed in these lines echo his religious experience, which he would later recount in more personal terms in his spiritual autobiography. Among these themes are the sin against the Holy Spirit, doubts about election and perseverance, and the temporal nature of the day of grace.[62] There are reminders here of the dark days of Bunyan's earlier psychological and spiritual struggles: "Give way to dispair," Satan tempts the soul. Notwithstanding all the fires in hell, it is a place where eyes lose their sight, where the gloomy blackness of eternal night prevails. "The Grave and Darkness now must be thine home," death tells the sinner.[63] The offense of sinners is against the light, and heaven, by contrast, is an abode where saints enjoy the light.[64]

In his earliest verse Bunyan also expressed several themes that had occupied him in his prose works and polemical confrontations. Thomas Smith and William Lindale, his learned critics, must have been in his mind when he remarked on the limits of traditional education:

> When Man doth study of things here below,
> What pretty Arts will he invent in time?
> He'l find out much, and do it neatly too;
> But yet he doth not see the Gospel shine.

In the school of Christ, God provides the learning that matters.[65] Likewise, the dominant theme of *A Few Sighs from Hell*, the castigation of the wealthy, is reiterated in *Profitable Meditations*. In his discourse with death, the sinner boasts:

> I am the man that hath the World at will,
> Both House and Land, and Chattel very much.

Ignoring his soul, the sinner values his "fine array," prompting death to respond with some of Bunyan's better early poetic lines:

---

[62] Ibid., 6:13, stanza LV; 14, stanzas LVIII, LIX; 15, stanza LXVII; 30, stanza CLII.

[63] Ibid., 6:15, stanza LXV (quoted); 22, stanza CVIII (quoted).

[64] Ibid., 6:14, stanzas LVI, LVIII; 15, stanza LXII; 24, stanzas CXVII, CXIX; 25, stanza CXXI; 31, stanza CLIX.

[65] Ibid., 6:5, stanza VI (quoted); 12, stanza XLIX.

> Thou painted brittle Potsherd, fading Grasse,
> I have command to take away thy breath;
> Thou art as brittle as the *Venice* Glass,
> Thy Life I suddenly must turn to Death.[66]

In the end, gold and silver have neither value nor utility when considering the soul's fate. Bunyan also makes a passing but critical reference to "daubing Preachers," an echo of his criticism of the clergy in *A Few Sighs from Hell.*[67]

Theologically, the poetry in *Profitable Meditations* manifests the unresolved tension between Calvinist dogma and 'pastoral Arminianism'. Bunyan gives poetic expression to the doctrines of election and perseverance, and he depicts Christ coming to sinners with grace and faith to free them from the grasp of sin, death, and hell.[68] But he also suggests that the sinner can reject the divine tender of grace and faith: "Come hither Sinner," Christ says, "I thee good will do." "Be rul'd," Jesus tells the sinner, as Cobb had instructed Bunyan, "turn, and save thee from this Wo."[69] The implication is clearly that the sinner can reject the offer and refuse the command.

Although written in prison, the prevailing mood of *Profitable Meditations* is optimistic. The day of judgment now holds only hope for Bunyan, though not for those who oppress him. The earthly banishment with which they threaten him is more than outweighed by the everlasting exile confronting them:

> . . . you shall be banisht from my face,
> 'Tis Justice now and Judgment you must hear.

Similarly, the wrenching farewell when Bunyan left his wife and children to make his stand for conscience will be the lot of the persecutor (and all unredeemed sinners) when death summons: "You see my Wife and Children weeping stand," the sinner cries out, "Oh! be not merciless."[70] But those who repress the godly will find no mercy, whereas the saints can anticipate triumph, joy, and light. Indeed, some of that bliss can be experienced now, even within the prison's dark rooms as the soul finds solace in spiritual communion. The voice of the saint in heaven is that of Bunyan in his cell:

> O sweet! me thought the world to come did so
> Affect my Soul, and make it long to be

[66] Ibid., 6:21, stanza CII (quoted); 22, stanzas CV (quoted), CVI (quoted).

[67] Ibid., 6:22, stanza CVII; 23, stanzas CIX, CX; 30, stanza CXLIX (quoted).

[68] Ibid., 6:14, stanza LIX; 15, stanza LXVII; 16, stanza LXVIII; 20, stanza XCIV; 28, stanza CXLI.

[69] Ibid., 6:18, stanza LXXXV (quoted); 19, stanza XC (quoted); 21, stanza C.

[70] Ibid., 6:23, stanza CXIII (quoted); 29, stanza CXLV (quoted).

With JESUS, that I nothing else would know,
But how I might his precious Beauty see.[71]

Such faith sustained Bunyan during his early months in prison, helping him maintain a reasonably positive outlook.

He found additional reason to be encouraged in the months following Elizabeth's unsuccessful appeal to Hale and Twisden, for his jailer granted him more liberty than he had enjoyed earlier in the year. Taking advantage of this freedom, he resumed his preaching, exhorting the godly to be steadfast in their faith and to shun the Book of Common Prayer. Semi-separatism was not an option, for the vast chasm between the state church and the congregations of visible saints could not be breached; only the latter were true, gospel churches. Bunyan also had the opportunity in this period to participate in the Bedford congregation's activities. At the monthly meeting on 28 August 1661 the church appointed him to call on Robert Nelson and Sister Manly, who were no longer attending services, and on 26 September he and John Fenne were sent on a similar mission to Sister Pecock. However, he was not among the twelve visitors (all male) assigned at the meeting in late October 1661, suggesting that by this time his jailer was again enforcing his confinement.[72]

During his brief period of freedom Bunyan traveled to London "to see Christians." This journey would have occurred in October 1661, shortly after the quarter sessions met. Those with whom he conferred on this trip were most likely the ministers who had prior links to the Bedford congregation, namely, Jessey, Simpson, and Cokayne; Rogers was in exile. When Bunyan's "enemies" learned of this journey they threatened to indict the jailer and accused Bunyan of having gone to the City to plot an insurrection.[73] Rumors and allegations of conspiracies were rather common in 1661, and the government could not afford to dismiss them out of hand. Venner's insurrection had been real enough, and on 22 April a band of dissidents unsuccessfully attempted to seize the magazine at Berwick. The government employed agents to maintain surveillance, studied informers' reports, and searched the homes of dissidents for weapons.[74] On 30 August the agent Peter Crabb compiled a list of eighteen alleged major conspirators, among whom were Jessey, Simpson, and the Particular Baptist Edward Harrison. Sir Edward Broughton, keeper of the Gatehouse at Westminster, made his own list on 16 September which included Simpson, Kiffin, and the Congregationalists Anthony

[71] Ibid., 6:33, stanza CLXVIII.
[72] "Relation," 129; *CB*, 37–38.
[73] "Relation," 130.
[74] PRO, SP 29/34/84; Greaves, *DUFE*, 65–70.

Palmer and Laurence Wise; at this point Palmer was a Fifth Monarchist, and Wise either was or soon would be.[75] Bunyan's likely contacts in London were thus under surveillance. If he met with them, as seems virtually certain, he would have been observed, and a report of such contact would have been sent to Bedford, sparking his enemies' ire. The timing of his visit was particularly unfortunate, for on 21 October the government discovered an alleged Presbyterian plot. Although it was a fabrication based on suspicions and erroneous allegations, officials used it as a pretext to arrest dissidents throughout England and Wales.[76]

In late October Bunyan was closely confined, "so that [he] must not look out of the door." For having traveled to London he expected to be "very roundly dealt withal" at the next quarter sessions, which convened about 10 January 1662. To his surprise, the justices did not summon him to seek his submission, failing which he could have been banished. He looked forward to the next assizes, which were held on 19 March 1662. On this occasion the judges were Hale and Sir Edward Atkyns, who had been a justice of the Common Pleas during the interregnum and was now a baron of the Exchequer. Atkyns had defended the puritan pamphleteer William Prynne in 1623, and in 1640 the minister Henry Burton and Dr. John Bastwick, both puritan authors, sought his assistance. Before the assizes Bunyan "made friends" with the high sheriff of Bedfordshire and Atkyns, who promised that his case would be heard at the assizes; presumably he had met Atkyns on his trip to London. Bunyan also asked the jailer to include his name on the calendar of felons for the purpose of having his case heard. By the time of the assizes, the clerk of the peace, apparently with the support of the justices of the peace, obtained the calendar from the jailer, blotted out the latter's entry for Bunyan, and replaced it with a notation that he had been lawfully convicted of holding conventicles. The clerk also warned the jailer that if Bunyan received his freedom from Atkyns, the clerk would make the jailer pay the fees Bunyan owed him and charge the jailer at the next quarter sessions with preparing a false calendar. As a result of this maneuvering, Bunyan did not appear before Hale and Atkyns but remained in jail.[77]

As we have seen, during his period of freedom in the late summer and early

[75] PRO, SP 29/40/101; 29/41/56. About this time the names of Jessey, Kiffin, Denne, and Knollys appear on a list of "House preachers" who were under surveillance. CLRO, Conventicle Box 1, no. 1. For Wise see *BDBR, s.v.*

[76] Greaves, *DUFE*, 70–72.

[77] "Relation," 130–31 (quoted); J. S. Cockburn, *A History of English Assizes 1558–1714* (Cambridge: Cambridge University Press, 1972), 246, 275; *DNB, s.v.* Edward Atkyns. The list of eighteen prisoners at the bar for this assize includes Bunyan's name, although the list for the ensuing summer assizes does not. BLA, MSS HSA 1662 W/1; 1662 S/1.

autumn of 1661, Bunyan preached against the Book of Common Prayer.[78] Now, in 1662, he expanded one of his sermons into the tract, *I Will Pray with the Spirit*. Three editions were published in his lifetime, the second in 1663 and the third in 1685. No copy of the first edition survives, but it almost certainly appeared in 1662. No printer is indicated for the 1663 and 1685 editions, and this was presumably the case with the first edition as well. Frank Mott Harrison has suggested that Bunyan did not use a bookseller in order to maximize his income, which he needed to support his family and pay his jailer.[79] However, it would have been difficult for him to arrange for the sale of his books while he was closely confined. A more likely explanation is that the work, perhaps taken to London by Elizabeth, was printed and sold by a bookseller who had already been in trouble for publishing nonconformist works. Francis Smith was not supposed to be selling books at this time, though he would publish Bunyan's *Christian Behaviour* in mid-1663. If Smith did not print *I Will Pray with the Spirit*, the likely candidates were those with whom he had links: Livewell Chapman, Thomas Brewster, Elizabeth Calvert, and Simon Dover, whose widow Joan would publish Bunyan's *Holy City* in 1665.[80] After passage of the Act to License and Control Printing (14 Car. II, c. 33) in 1662, it was necessary to publish Bunyan's *I Will Pray with the Spirit* without the printer's name, for its contents would not have received a censor's approval. Of the possible printers, the most likely was Chapman, who had published Vavasor Powell's critique of the Anglican liturgy, *Common-Prayer-Book No Divine Service*, in 1660, followed by an expanded edition in 1661. The theme of Bunyan's book is compatible with Powell's.

*I Will Pray with the Spirit* is a much expanded exposition of the views on prayer Bunyan enunciated in his exchange with Justice Kelynge. Even the core text, 1 Corinthians 14:15, is the same. A divine ordinance, prayer as defined by Bunyan is "a sincere, sensible, affectionate pouring out of the heart or soul to God through Christ, in the strength and assistance of the holy Spirit, for such things as God hath promised, or, according to the Word, for the good of the Church, with submission, in Faith, to the Will of God" (*MW*, 2:235). Prayer is not babbling over words written on paper, which is mere lip-labor, but feelings that bubble forth from the heart, the unutterable sighs and groans stemming from the Holy Spirit's inner workings. For Bunyan, prayer is petition and the vehicle to

[78]This dating is more precise than my suggestion in *MW*, 2:xli that Bunyan's period of freedom was prior to April 1662.

[79]Frank Mott Harrison, *A Bibliography of the Works of John Bunyan* (Oxford: Bibliographical Society, 1932), xiv–xv.

[80]For Brewster see *BDBR*, *s.v.* and Plomer, *DBP*, 32; and for the Dovers see Plomer, *DBP*, 65.

spiritual communion with God. It is also an essential part of the Christian life, for a believer is a praying person (2:237–40, 246–47, 271, 281).

True prayer is profoundly intense; "every syllable carrieth a mighty *vehemency* in it" (2:239). Without an effectual knowledge of Christ, which only God can reveal, prayer is impossible. For the heart and the tongue to function together in prayer, the Spirit's operation is essential, but the heart is more important than the mouth. The best prayers, Bunyan believed, comprise more groans than words (2:238, 241, 255, 257–58). When the Spirit enlightens the understanding, enabling the supplicant to have a keen sense of sin and divine wrath, "the present sence, feeling, and pressure that lyeth upon his spirit, provokes him to groan out his requests unto the Lord" (2:264). Bunyan sharply contrasts prayer that flows from the soul's anguish with that which is based on nothing more than "bare notion, and naked knowledge" (2:263). Words are incidental, even unnecessary in prayer; the mouth may be hindered, but the Spirit, which stirs up unutterable groans and sighs, is not. In his emphasis on Spirit-motivated, unspeakable groans, Bunyan is very close to the Quakers, but unlike them he does not regard silence as the norm and essential starting place. On the contrary, the Spirit's operations in the heart and soul typically result in spoken words, or at least words framed in the mind and uttered in a verbal though unspoken manner to God (2:257, 267). Prayer must be with the understanding as well as the Spirit, and thus in the vernacular, said Bunyan, which would rule out Latin, though not unspoken sighs and groans. Praying with the understanding, he insisted, also means supplicating God "*experimentally*," with enlightened knowledge, instructed by the Spirit and prepared to come to God "*with suitable arguments.*" Prayer can move God, appealing to his heart and eliciting his forgiveness. Experiential prayer thus has a place for a rational component (2:260–63).

Bunyan offered practical advice on how to pray. Lengthy discourses and eloquent tongues do not please God, he counseled, but a humble, contrite heart does. He warned against praying for effect, an offense for which he cited chaplains in great families (of whom he must have learned second-hand) and all those who sought popular acclaim for their silver-tongued prayers. "Affecting expressions" are not to be used in supplicating God (2:272–74, 277), and he cautioned his readers about the difficulties encountered in prayer: "Oh the starting-holes that the heart hath in the time of Prayer! none knows how many by-wayes the heart hath, and back-lains, to slip away from the presence of God." Every period of prayer is an abbreviated pilgrim's progress, with its own perils and temptations, including pride born of eloquence and hypocrisy caused by trying to impress others (2:257).

In two substantive autobiographical passages Bunyan offered his own experience as an aid to others. Yet he was aware that this might "make your poor, blind, carnal man, to entertain strange thoughts of [him]," for he admitted he found it difficult to pray.

> As for my heart, when I go to pray, I find it so loth to go to God, and when it is with him, so loth to stay with him, that many times I am forced in my Prayers; *first*, to beg of God that he would take mine heart, and set it on himself in Christ, and when it is there, that he would keep it there (*Psal.* 86. 11). Nay, many times I know not what to pray for, I am so blind, nor how to pray I am so ignorant; *onely* (blessed be Grace) *the Spirit helps our infirmities.* (2:256–57)

In the second autobiographical passage he recounts how, in his "fits of agony of spirit," perhaps recalling his despondent periods, he was ready to cease seeking God in prayer. Relief came only when the Spirit, helping him to understand that God has mercy on great sinners, enabled him to cleave to God, "and yet to cry," the tears suggesting not only crying out to God but Bunyan's melancholic state. Chillingly, God "made no answer" for a long time. Hang on, Bunyan urged those who similarly suffered, knowing the utter sense of black despair experienced by the depressed (2:265–66).

For Bunyan, then, prayer was very much a manifestation of his experiential faith. Forms of prayer, including the Book of Common Prayer, were not lesser alternatives to extempore prayer but unlawful. The chasm between the two types of prayer was akin to that between congregations of visible saints and the restored Church of England. Convinced that the Book of Common Prayer was not divinely ordained but a human invention prohibited by God, Bunyan allowed no room for compromise. Without the Holy Spirit's assistance, a thousand prayer books will not enable people to pray as they ought (2:248–49, 268). For Bunyan, forms of prayer, like formal written sermons, are "great cheat[s]" employed by Satan to delude the world (2:259). It is "a very juggle of the Devil, that the Traditions of men should be of better esteem, and more to be owned, than the Spirit of Prayer" (2:283). Referring to Foxe's account of the drafting of the Book of Common Prayer in Edward VI's reign,[81] Bunyan argued that if God had sanctioned a liturgy, Paul and his companions could just as easily have created one as did the authors of the Book of Common Prayer (2:247). Prayer books, Bunyan insisted, cannot elevate the heart or prompt the unutterable sighs and groans that were so much a part of prayer for him. To pray, attested Bunyan, we need neither a surplice-clad bishop nor a book of formulas (2:256, 264). Those who rely on forms are "like a painted man, and their Prayers are like a false voice; they in person appear as Hypocrites, and their Prayers are an Abomination" (2:276).

Bunyan had to explain why the prayer Jesus taught his disciples was not an

---

[81] Foxe, *Acts and Monuments*, 5:719–22.

example of formal prayer. He was unwilling to endorse the mere repetition of the Lord's prayer "in a babling way," for no one can truly call God "Father" without experientially believing that the work of grace has been wrought in oneself (2:252). Moreover, each petition in that prayer must be rendered from the heart and not in a hypocritical spirit. Although he did not explicitly prohibit use of the Lord's prayer, he warned that supplicants who recite it without the requisite faith face condemnation, whereas those who pray with the Spirit and the understanding offer their own groans, sighs, and petitions (2:254–55). One word uttered in faith is better, he avouched, than a thousand prayers read "in a formal, cold, luke-warm way," including recitations of the Lord's prayer without living faith (2:252). If Jesus had intended his prayer to be a set-form, Bunyan contended, the versions in Matthew 6 and Luke 11 would be identical. Moreover, he found no evidence that the apostles had formally used it or recommended that others do so. Jesus, averred Bunyan, provided his prayer to teach people to supplicate to God in faith for things in accord with his will (2:270).

Bunyan would not approve the use of formal prayers to teach children. Instead he recommended that children be told what cursed creatures they are, that they are subject to divine wrath because of original and personal sin, and that the penalty for not obtaining God's forgiveness is eternal damnation. Whether children or adults, people learn to pray by first being convicted of their sins, hence the need to tell them of hell fire, damnation, and salvation. "This will make tears run down your sweet babes eyes, and hearty groans flow from their hearts." It is as natural for someone infused with divine grace to pray as for a nursing infant to seek a mother's breast, he opined (2:268–69, 271).

Although Bunyan must have learned his views on prayer from Gifford, Burton, and perhaps Hobson and Dell, he also consulted or at least heard about books that attacked the non-scriptural passages in the Book of Common Prayer as "absurdities." Because such passages "are at large discovered by others, I omit the rehearsal of them," he remarked in passing (2:283). His staunch opposition to liturgies was not the view of moderate puritans such as Richard Baxter, Edmund Calamy, and William Bates, who discussed the proposed revision of the Book of Common Prayer at the Savoy in London in April 1661.[82] Their willingness to use a prescribed liturgy did not necessarily rule out extempore prayer, as Baxter made clear. In contrast, Congregationalists and Baptists rejected the use of a liturgy, a position previously espoused by early English separatists such as Henry Barrow. In the 1640s the Independents, as Geoffrey Nuttall notes, opposed "*stinted* prayers," using the term almost in a technical sense as an authorized liturgical form. Bunyan himself employed the term when insisting that the Lord's prayer was not

---

[82] For Calamy see Greaves, *SR*, 9–62; for Bates see *Calamy Revised, s.v.*

intended to be "a stinted Form of Prayer" (2:270). Writers such as John Owen, Vavasor Powell, Walter Cradock, John Saltmarsh, and George Fox joined the lists against any liturgy, and Bunyan was firmly in this tradition.[83]

The book Bunyan most likely read on this theme is Powell's *Common-Prayer-Book No Divine Service* (1660; expanded ed., 1661). To bolster his repudiation of the Book of Common Prayer Powell shrewdly referred to the critique by five moderate puritans, Edmund Calamy, Stephen Marshall, Matthew Newcomen, William Spurstowe, and Thomas Young; their *Answer to a Booke Entitled an Humble Remonstrance* appeared in 1641 under the acronym Smectymnuus (the authors' initials), and the work was republished in 1660 with the title *Smectymnuus Redivivus*. Powell went on to cite sixty-eight things in the Book of Common Prayer (seventy in the second edition) that he deemed offensive to good Christians.[84] Bunyan was less likely to have seen the Presbyterian Giles Firmin's *The Liturgical Considerator Considered* (1st and 2nd editions, both 1661), a critique of John Gauden's *Considerations Touching the Liturgy of the Church of England* (1661).[85] Interestingly, Bunyan shared many of the critical points made by Fox in *Something in Answer to the Old Common-Prayer-Book* (1660), and may have seen a copy. Owen's *A Discourse Concerning Liturgies, and Their Imposition* (1662) could not have been among the works to which Bunyan referred because it dealt only with the general question of whether liturgies are lawful, not specific problems in the Book of Common Prayer.[86]

Throughout *I Will Pray with the Spirit*, especially near the end, Bunyan mounted a barbed, frontal assault against his enemies. Inasmuch as such criticism would have harmed his chances to obtain freedom at the assizes in March 1662, he would have composed this book after that date. One passage, in fact, seems to refer to the great ejection of nonconformist ministers on St. Bartholomew's Day in 1662: That the authorities advance human formulas above Spirit-inspired prayer, he argued, "is evident . . . by the silencing of God's dear Ministers, though never so powerfully enabled by the Spirit of Prayer; if they, in conscience, cannot admit of that Form of *Common Prayer*" (2:284). Although some ministers had been ejected as early as 1660, Bunyan probably wrote this passage sometime after the Act of Uniformity (14 Car. II, c. 4) received Charles' assent on 19 May 1662, the same day he signed the Licensing Act.

[83] Greaves, *SR*, 53–54; Geoffrey F. Nuttall, *The Holy Spirit in Puritan Faith and Experience* (Oxford: Basil Blackwell, 1946), 65–73.

[84] Vavasor Powell, *Common-Prayer-Book No Divine Service* (London, 1660), 16–26; ibid., 2nd ed. (London, 1661), 16–28. For Newcomen and Spurstowe see *Calamy Revised, s.vv.*; for Young see *DNB, s.v.*

[85] For Firmin see *Calamy Revised, s.v.*; for Gauden see *DNB, s.v.*

[86] Like Bunyan's tract, Owen's book appeared without a publisher's name.

Bunyan responded to this exercise in conformity with withering criticism, likening those who enforced the Book of Common Prayer to one of the most detested enemies of English Protestants, the Marian bishop of London, Edmund Bonner, "that blood-red Persecutor" (2:253). Again drawing on Foxe, Bunyan denounced the Book of Common Prayer for incorporating material from "the Papistical Mass-Book; being the Scraps and Fragments of the devices of some Popes, some Friars, and I wot not what" (2:239).[87] Bluntly put, the Book of Common Prayer is "Antichristian" and enforceable only by persecution (2:285). In a breathtakingly daring passage, he ridiculed the religious calendar as well as the prescribed behavior of worshipers during the liturgy:

> The wise men of our dayes are so well skill'd, as that they have both the *Manner* and *Matter* of their Prayers at their finger ends; setting such a Prayer for such a day, and that twenty years before it comes. One for *Christmass*, another for *Easter*, and six dayes after that. They have also bounded how many syllables must be said in every one of them at their publick Exercises. For each Saints day also, they have them ready for the generations yet unborn to say. They can tell you also, when you shall kneel, when you should stand, when you should abide in your seats, when you should go up into the Chancel, and what you should do when you come there. All which the Apostles came short of, as not being able to compose so profound a manner. (2:247–48)

These words, among the most potent and sarcastic in the entire corpus of Bunyan's works, stand as eloquent testimony to the depth of his conviction that any attempt to impose barriers to impede the Spirit's freedom contravenes the divine will and must be stringently opposed.

In another passage remarkable for its candor, Bunyan effectively excluded the clergy and defenders of the Church of England from the true church. The gulf between those who endorsed the official liturgy and the saints was unbridgeable:

> All this is too too evident by the ignorance, prophaness, and spirit of envy, that reigns in the hearts of those men that are so hot for the Forms, and not for the Power of prayer: Scarce one of forty among them, know what it is to be born again, to have communion with the Father through the Son; to feel the power of Grace sanctifying their hearts: but for all their prayers, they still live cursed, drunken, whorish, and abominable Lives, full of Malice, Envy, Deceit, Persecuting of the dear Children of God. (2:240)

Although acclaimed as good churchmen for using the Book of Common Prayer, conformist clerics were vile wretches in Bunyan's view.

Clearly incensed by his enemies' success in keeping him in prison, Bunyan lashed out against a government that labeled dissenters "turbulent, seditious, and factious people"—indeed, as heretics and fanatics (2:253). "You count it high Trea-

---

[87] Foxe, *Acts and Monuments*, 6:356–83.

son to speak but a word against the King," Bunyan protested, perhaps because he had done precisely this (2:282). He certainly denounced the doctors of divinity who had established human institutions without biblical warrant and compelled obedience on pain of banishment. Moreover, he lumped bishops with popes for having commanded forms of worship not required by God, and he found fault with magistrates for incarcerating those who believe in praying with the Spirit and the understanding rather than the Book of Common Prayer. Did not conformists frequent alehouses while those who pray with the Spirit find themselves in jail?

> Did God send his holy Spirit into the hearts of his People to that end, that you should taunt at it? is this to serve God? And doth this demonstrate the Reformation of your Church?

Magistrates and conforming ministers, judges and justices, Kelynge and Wingate and Twisden, all were implacable reprobates (2:282–84). In the aptly chosen words of Neil Keeble, *I Will Pray with the Spirit* is "an openly oppositional text,"[88] and its author, defiant and unbent, would remain in prison.

Bunyan's stance was more radical than that espoused by leading Congregationalist ministers in London with whom he became increasingly close—Owen, Cokayne, Griffith, and Meade. With a colleague they drafted a statement explaining why Congregationalists could not participate in worship according to the Book of Common Prayer, which in their judgment enjoined "a false worship of the true God" and was not in accord with New Testament principles. Moreover, they denounced the prayer book because it is "inconsistent with the conduct of the Spirit of God in prayer" and rejects the "promised Aids of the Holy Spirit, with respect unto the prayers of the Church." On this point they were in fundamental agreement with Bunyan. In turn, he would have had no objection to their repudiation of all liturgy on the grounds that it imposed *adiaphora* (non-essentials), diminished the role of the Spirit in worship, and obstructed the church's responsibility to edify its members. Nor would he have found fault with their contention that liturgical worship is conducive to an "ungifted ministry" while silencing "painful ministers," ruining godly families who oppose the liturgy, and destroying souls. "It is not lawfull to be a participant in these things," asserted Owen and his colleagues; "yea the glory of our profession lies in our Testimony against them." But unlike Bunyan, they stopped short of comparing the enforcers of the Book of Common Prayer to Catholic persecutors and associating the Anglican liturgy with the mass. Like Bunyan they made clear their opposition to the government's policy of imposing the prayer book as the only legal means of true worship and punishing those who em-

---

[88] N. H. Keeble, "'Till one greater man / Restore us . . .': Restoration Images in Milton and Bunyan," *BS* 6 (1995–96): 19.

braced other forms.[89] Bunyan's more radical position was in keeping with his confrontational attitude toward the government, which helps to explain why he, unlike his London colleagues, found himself in prison.

Loneliness now began to exact a toll on Bunyan. Once again he turned to verse, but this time his lines are more personal, the emotions closer to the surface, the need for support more openly expressed.

> Friends write to me, that I would hold
> my Head above the Flood.
> And I do wish you also bold
> in holding fast the good.

He was now more sensitive to the fact that he could face exile imminently, perhaps even death, though he still found solace in his relationship with God.

> When they do talk of Banishment,
> Of Death, or such like Things,
> Then to me God sends Hearts content,
> That like a Fountain springs.[90]

Hanging would even be sweet, he boldly proclaimed, if God would appear on the gallows. The more his enemies raged, the greater his spiritual comfort, or so he claimed. Again, he saw his sufferings in Christ-like terms, as when his persecutors gave him gall to drink, or when he expressed a willingness to bear a cross and die with Jesus.[91]

Bunyan's meditations simultaneously reminded his readers—his friends—of why he was in prison and exhorted them to stand fast in the faith. Recalling how he preached grace and faith, not fables devised by cunning men (another slap at conformist clergy), he reflected on his arrest and the ensuing accusations that he was a heretic, a deceiver, and a foe of the church. Against all of this he held his ground:

> . . . having Peace within my Soul,
> And Truth on every side,
> I could with comfort them controul,
> And at their charge deride.[92]

The prison, he admitted, had brought heaviness and grief—potential triggers of another bout of depression—but thus far Christ had provided relief with frequent infusions of grace.

[89] Bodl., Rawlinson MSS D1352, fols. 132r–138v.
[90] *MW*, 6:42, stanza 2 (quoted); 45, stanza 20 (quoted).
[91] Ibid., 6:45, stanzas 18, 21, 22; 48, stanza 48; 49, stanza 51.
[92] Ibid., 6:43, stanzas 8–9; 44, stanzas 10, 14–15, 16 (quoted).

> God sometimes visits Prisons more
> Than lordly Palaces,
> He often knocketh at our Door,
> When he their Houses miss.

Still, Bunyan's enemies called him a fool for lying in prison, taunted him for throwing away his goods and his liberty, and sneered that he disgraced himself by his incarceration with rogues. Some expected he would submit, though such a course, in his eyes, would make him an apostate or a Judas.[93] Throughout these stanzas he sometimes speaks in the singular voice, at other times in the plural, drawing his readers into his suffering, making his stand theirs, and breathing resolve into them. Always, however, his is the experience about which he writes. *Prison Meditations* is spiritual autobiography in verse.

Bunyan battled to make his incarceration not only sufferable but meaningful. Jails, he decided, are schools in which Christ teaches his followers how to die, a grim reminder of the sense of peril that dogged Bunyan's daily life. To survive, he had to live in the conviction that though the body is in prison, the mind is free to study Christ. Jail became a lofty hill from which he could look beyond this world. He could see too that the world is a stage on which people play their parts, the bad raging at the good, the hypocritical turning like weathervanes in the wind. From his cell he felt pain and betrayal as he thought about those he had once regarded as friends but who had now turned against him; such deceivers, he snapped, were vile. So too were those political leaders and magistrates on whom the godly could not count; perhaps the earl of Bedford, who had failed to respond to Elizabeth's plea for assistance, was in his thoughts.

> These Politicians that profest
> For base and worldly ends,
> Do now appear to us at best
> But Machivilian Friends.[94]

In the face of such betrayal, he found comfort in remembering the persecution suffered by good Christians of old. Foxe as well as the Bible was providing critical psychological support, but in a very real sense, during those dark nights in prison he faced his opponents alone, within himself, with "Truth" as his sole companion:

> The *Truth* and *I*, were both here cast
> Together, and we do
> Lye Arm in Arm, and so hold fast
> Each other; This is true.[95]

[93] Ibid., 6:45, stanzas 23–25; 46, stanzas 27 (quoted), 30; 48, stanza 47; 49, stanza 52.
[94] Ibid., 6:43, stanza 5; 45, stanza 24; 47, stanzas 34, 36, 37, 39, 40 (quoted).
[95] Ibid., 6:46, stanzas 31, 33 (quoted).

For Bunyan, the enemies within were always more threatening than the foes without.

Such poetry is powerful and moving.[96] As a versifier Bunyan had improved substantially over the pedestrian lines in *Profitable Meditations*, largely because his own personal experience was now both the core subject matter and the driving force of his poetry. Moreover, as Midgley has noted, he had now established his own poetic hallmark by intricately entwining his diction with scriptural language and imagery. "The true voice of feeling" was shaping his verse (*MW*, 6:xlviii–xlix).

## "Gospelly Good"[97]: Christian Behaviour, a Last Testament

Outwardly defiant, Bunyan anticipated exile according to the terms of the Elizabethan statute under which he was held. The threat was real enough, for the government periodically ordered the transportation of nonconformists abroad.[98] Had he been banished, he clearly intended to return to England, thereby rendering him subject to execution. In the early months of 1663, he therefore composed what he thought might be his final work, *Christian Behaviour; or the Fruits of True Christianity*, the title-page of which identified him as "a Prisoner of *Hope*." Again his printer was Francis Smith. The tone of the book is strikingly positive, and not until the end does Bunyan indicate his expectation of possibly imminent death. From the jail in Bedford on 17 June 1663, he explained that he had composed this work to provoke his readers to faith and holiness "before I die" in order that they might have eternal life and love for one another "when I am deceased." In completing this book, he felt a sense of urgency: "Though there I shall rest from my labours, and be in *Paradise*, as through Grace I comfortably believe, yet it is not there, but here, I must do you good; wherefore I not knowing the shortness of my life, nor the hinderance that hereafter I may have of serving my God and You, I have taken this opportunity to present these few lines unto you for your edification." The hindrance to which he referred was probably his expected exile (*MW*, 3:62).

As Bunyan composed this work, he was at peace with himself, convinced that his death would lead to eternal bliss. The spiritual and psychological turmoil of the 1650s was not forgotten, though he recalled it now only in a general way to provide lessons to others. Although he intended *Christian Behaviour*, with its em-

---

[96] In the last quarter of the seventeenth century one Stephen Thompson found *Prison Meditations* inspirational and copied it into a manuscript volume of verse that also included material by Baxter. Bodl., Rawlinson Poetry 58, fols. 25r–33r.

[97] *MW*, 3:9.

[98] See, e.g., Bodl., Rawlinson MSS C719, fols. 1–6; BLA, MS HSA 1667 W/58.

phasis on good works, as a companion piece to *The Doctrine of the Law and Grace Unfolded* (3:9), with its focus on justification by grace, he also treated it as the logical sequel to his spiritual and psychological struggle, which he would later relate in *Grace Abounding to the Chief of Sinners*. One of the most crucial passages in that conflict was Hebrews 6:4–6, which warns that if the spiritually enlightened fall away, they crucify Christ anew and can never again repent. For the title-page of *Christian Behaviour*, Bunyan selected the two ensuing verses, which explain that the earth which brings forth herbs suitable for those who cultivate it shall be divinely blessed, whereas ground that bears briars and thorns is cursed and will be burned. In terms of his own experience, the point is unmistakable: Those who truly believe and are recipients of divine grace will produce good works, whereas those whose faith is counterfeit will not. Good works, for Bunyan, are a manifestation of election and thus a means of providing the assurance he so desperately craved. From the outset *Christian Behaviour* is rooted in Bunyan's experience.

He drew on that experience to offer spiritual counsel. Once the work of God has begun in someone—once awakening has commenced—it will be opposed by flesh, corruption, and "the body of death"; hence Bunyan warned Christians to take preventive measures by performing good works, something he had not done during the dark days of his spiritual travail. He was recalling his own years of anguish when he cautioned his readers that the Tempter would quicken their lusts and "joyn with them in every assault against every appearance of God in our souls" (3:53). Based on his own experience he concluded that God's "withdrawings" from believers are intended not to weaken them but to try their faith; the same is true, he attested, with respect to whatever God permits Satan or the believers' own hearts to do. Every godly person will struggle because "a body of Death and Sin" remains within, where it perpetually opposes whatever is good; the Christian's soul is thus a battleground for competing forces (3:55). Still drawing on his own background, Bunyan urged the godly not to be discouraged by a sense of their vileness, but instead to keep watch over the wretchedness of their hearts and remember that God knows "every secret turning." Indeed, hearts brimming with good works have little room for satanic temptations. Recalling his own anguish when he felt unfit to die but afraid to live, he informed his readers that the believer "fullest of *Good Works*" is most prepared to live as well as to die (3:56–57). Citing the story of the five foolish virgins in Matthew 25, he reiterated his belief that a time would come when the day of grace will be past, a fear that had once filled him with dread and despair when he thought such a season had already arrived for him. Now he cautioned others not to procrastinate lest their expected heaven be "proved a Hell, and [their] God is proved a Devil" (3:59). For backsliders, he had a special exhortation, drawn like the others from his experience: "I know thou wilt be afflicted with a thousand temptations to drive thee to despair, that thy Faith may be faint, &c. But against all them set thou the Word of God, the Promise of Grace, the Blood of Christ, and the Examples of God's Goodness" (3:61). In providing such counsel, he made *Christian Behaviour* a sequel to his years of internal strife, intending these lessons as perhaps his final bequest.

Although *Christian Behaviour* should be read in part as Bunyan's anticipated last testament, he also meant the volume to serve as a practical guide to Christian living. His primary audience was the newly converted—a reflection of his interest, as he later described it, in preaching in the dark corners of the land, focusing his work on awakening and converting sinners (3:10; *GA*, §§289–90). But he was also concerned about those who were falling away, at least some of whom had been his own converts and were undoubtedly daunted at the prospect of dissenting from the Restoration Church of England (3:59–62). Their loss, he subsequently avouched, was more painful to him than if one of his own children had died. "I have counted as if I had goodly buildings and lordships in those places where my [spiritual] Children were born; my heart hath been so wrapt up in the glory of this excellent work, that I counted myself more blessed and honoured of God by this, than if he had made me the Emperour of the Christian World, or the Lord of all the glory of Earth without it!" (*GA*, §286). It must have been especially painful for him to hear about the apostasy of people he had converted, particularly when his incarceration prevented him from counseling them to remain faithful to the nonconformist cause. *Christian Behaviour* was partly intended to reach such people, though it was primarily aimed at providing recent converts with a primer to help them remain faithful to their new convictions.

To make his handbook effective Bunyan designed it to be different from some of the numerous works of the same genre already on the market. While acknowledging the existence of many large, learned discourses on good works, he averred that all had not *"so gospelized their Discourses as becomes them, and as the Doctrine of the Grace of God calleth for"* (3:9). Sears McGee has plausibly suggested that Bunyan may have been thinking of such popular works as *The Whole Duty of Man Laid Down in a Plain Way for the Use of the Meanest Reader* (1659) and Jeremy Taylor's *The Rule and Exercises of Holy Living* (1650), which were replete with set prayers of the sort Bunyan had attacked in *I Will Pray with the Spirit.*[99] Taylor, moreover, placed more emphasis on Christ as exemplar than redeemer, whereas Bunyan insisted on framing any discussion of good works in the context of God's bestowal of grace and faith (*MW*, 3:xxvii–xxviii). At the same time Bunyan deemed it essential to provide a handbook on good works to refute the unnamed critics who had cast aspersions on his position as Antinomian be-

[99] For Taylor see *DNB, s.v.*

cause it allegedly justified *"looseness of Life"* (3:9). Moreover, he was convinced that insufficient attention to good works in their proper gospel context was partially responsible for disorder in the family and the commonwealth. This was a point perhaps made in part with an eye to the magistrates who would determine his fate, for they would not have disagreed with his fundamental contention that Christians should *"keep their Rank, Relation and Station, doing all as become their Quality and Calling."* Like flowers in a garden, the godly should grow where the gardener planted them, thereby honoring God (3:10). Furthermore, Bunyan, convinced that books dealing with good works were either so scarce or large that few people owned copies, endeavored to produce a volume of modest length to keep the price down and the reading manageable and not tedious. "Multitude of words drown the Memory; *and an Exhortation* in few words, *may yet be so full, that the Reader may find that in the side of a Sheet, which some are forced to hunt for in a whole Quire"* (3:10). In fact, Bunyan's book comprised 140 duodecimo pages compared, for example, to the 386 folio pages in William Gouge's *Of Domesticall Duties* (2nd ed., 1626) or the 175 octavo pages in William Perkins' *Christian Oeconomie* (1609).[100] Unlike Bunyan, Gouge covered various topics that would have been irrelevant to the likely readers of Bunyan's book, such as matters pertaining to the landed aristocracy. Moreover, Bunyan eschewed Gouge's practice of discussing biblical passages that could lead to disparate conclusions about an issue, instead citing only examples that proved his point (3:xxviii–xxix). The result is a work of simplicity, efficiency, and directness that combines maxims of conduct with a theological reaffirmation of the doctrine that those justified by grace must undertake good works.

For Bunyan the corollary of the doctrine of justification by grace is the conviction that the divine gift of faith produces good works. The principal text for his thesis is not Hebrews 6:7–8, which appears on the title-page, but Titus 3:7–8, which proclaims both justification by grace and the performance of good works by those who believe in God. Bunyan is adamant that without faith there can be no good works, for every person lacking faith is evil and no more able to undertake a good deed than briars and thorns can produce grapes or figs. "*Good Works* must come from a good heart" (3:11–12). Consequently, not all works that seem good are necessarily so; faith, not good intentions, is imperative (3:17). He harshly judges those who think they act appropriately or even piously but lack the requisite faith: "The carnal man doth never so much which he calleth good, yet it is rejected, slighted, and turned as dirt in his face again; his prayers are abominable, his plowing is sin, and all his righteousness as menstruous rags" (3:13). In short, Bunyan offered a sweeping indictment of Restoration society and its moral maxims.

[100] For Gouge and Perkins see *DNB, s.vv.*

Now firmly grounded in his own convictions, Bunyan defined faith as a principle of life by which a believer lives, a principle of motion by which the Christian proceeds toward heaven in holy living, and a principle of strength by which the soul overcomes lust, the Devil, and the world. In short, faith alters behavior. It also embraces the divine promise of forgiveness, comforting the soul and providing the believer with assurance of election. Almost certainly recalling his own experience, Bunyan averred that "*faith* is so great an Artist in arguing and reasoning with the Soul, that it will bring over the hardest heart that it hath to deal with." As "a Grace," faith accurately represents everything spiritually relevant to the soul, prompting it to desire a holy life. "A life of Holiness and Godliness in this world, doth so inseparably follow a principle of Faith, that it is both monstrous and ridiculous to suppose the contrary" (3:13–15). Given the importance of light in his psychological and spiritual struggles in the 1650s, Bunyan made a point of linking it to faith. Believers are the children of light and of the day, lights on a hill, and candles on a candelabra. Unlike those who misunderstand the role of good works in the Christian life, the godly do not confuse light and darkness. Children of the light produce good works, whereas fruitless professors will discover at the last judgment that their lamps will be snuffed out like candles in the wind (3:14–15, 20, 58–59).

Bunyan explicitly linked the degree of one's faith to the quantity of good works one performed. Again using the analogy of light, he likened scanty faith to small candles or weak fires that produce light and heat, but only minimally in comparison to substantial faith. In turn, he asserted that while salvation comes by grace, spiritual rewards are earned by good works, and every good deed will result in a heavenly reward (3:16–17). "Be but rich in *good Works*, and thou shalt have more than Salvation," for paradise is anything but a place where all are equal (3:57). If the prospect of such rewards is not sufficient motivation, he warned that those who profess to be Christians but fail to undertake good works will be damned. The person whose "tongue is tipt with a talk and tattle of Religion" has ignored the admonition in James 2:20 that faith without works is dead. The fruitless professor is like a boy who plays with brass or tokens instead of gold or coins (3:58). For a deed to be good it must fulfill strict criteria, that is, it must have biblical authorization, flow from faith, be undertaken at the right time and place, and be done willingly and cheerfully. It must also honor God and edify one's neighbor (3:18–21). Thus Bunyan insisted on an integral place for good works in the Christian life without assigning them a soteriological role, and simultaneously differentiated his position from that of the Antinomians.[101]

[101]Cf., e.g., Walter Cradock, *Gospel-Libertie, in the Extensions [and] Limitations of It* (London, 1648), 43ff.; Greaves, *JB*, 115–16.

In addition to defending himself from charges of Antinomianism, Bunyan made critical references in *Christian Behaviour* to other views and practices he found objectionable. He was scathing in his denunciation of those, surely including the magistrates who had incarcerated him, who zealously prosecuted people whose worship differed from their own: "How hot it hath been, though with no reason at all." He likened them to Nebuchadnezzar, with his fiery furnace, and Darius, with his "*Lyons-Den* for *Nonconformists*"; his dissenting readers would have found it easy to substitute Charles II for Darius. Enforcers and proponents of the state-sanctioned church were palpably in Bunyan's mind when he castigated those who confused the tenets, traditions, and worship of humans with the doctrines and worship of God. Framing his criticism in biblical terms with references to Acts 26:11, Luke 11:53–54, and John 16:1–2, he lashed out at those who "have persecuted men even to strange Cities; have laid traps and snares in every corner, to intrap and to entangle their words; and if they could at any time but kill the persons that dissented from them, they would think they did God *good service*." Read against the background of Bunyan's relation of his imprisonment, this attack referred in part to his own experience, for his accusers had tried, in Luke's words, "to catch something out of his mouth, that they might accuse him," and he was now threatened with the possibility of execution should he be banished and return, in which case those who killed him would think, as John had said, that they served God. For a prisoner to be overly bold was not prudent, so Bunyan quickly shifted his focus to "the *Papists* and their *Companions*" who had "in all Ages *hanged, burned, starved, drowned, wracked, dismembred*, and *murdered*, both openly and in secret . . . under a pretence of God, his Worship, and *Good Works*" (3:17–18). What he was implicitly suggesting, of course, was a link between those who were persecuting him and the Roman Catholics.

When discussing the need for good works to be rightly timed, Bunyan insisted there was a time to act and a time to suffer. "To be hearing when we should be preaching, and doing, that is, yeelding active obedience to that under which we ought to suffer, is not good." In this passage, tucked in the midst of a modest handbook about Christian behavior, he called on his readers to obey God *actively*, whether by preaching or by undertaking other gospel duties, including attendance at dissenting services of worship. Legal prohibitions notwithstanding, he expected fellow nonconformists to join him in suffering if that was the penalty for their active obedience (3:19).

In the context of discussing the right place for good works, Bunyan rather subtly directed criticism against both Anglicans and Quakers. It was wrong, he asserted, to attribute more or less significance to any work than Scripture permitted. Because prelates imposed ceremonies that lacked biblical sanction, he accused them of elevating "things indifferent," or *adiaphora*, "as high as those that are absolutely necessary in the Worship of God." He was willing to stipulate that Christians have liberty to embrace *adiaphora* as long as such things do not "strike at either Faith or Holiness," or are not forcibly imposed on others. Even worse than elevating *adiaphora*, he argued, was to make human traditions more important than those prescribed in the Bible, or to substitute *"darkness for light,"* a phrase on which he did not expound. He may have been thinking of the prelates as well when he condemned both those who made works copartners with Christ and teachers of the law ignorant of what they espoused. More generally, he rebuked those who regarded the ceremonial part of an ordinance, including the sacraments and other acts of worship, as important as its "doctrine and signification." With a broad brush he was criticizing the traditional Christian emphasis, common in some form to Anglicans, Presbyterians, Congregationalists, and General and Particular Baptists, on the importance of external rites, especially baptism, a subject on which he would say much in the early 1670s. Finally, recalling his controversy with Edward Burrough in 1656, he denounced those who regarded "the dictates and impulses of a meer natural conscience, as good, as high, and divine, as the leadings and movings of the Spirit of Christ" (3:20, 24). Thus he thought it important to find space in this modest handbook not only to frame his counsel in the context of the doctrine of grace but also to demarcate his position from those of competing religious groups and to denounce those who persecuted Protestant nonconformists.

Bunyan allocated less than half of his book to the topics for which it is typically remembered: behavioral guidelines for heads of families, parents, masters, wives, children, servants, and neighbors (3:22–44). Three themes run through this section, to wit, the subordination of one group to another—wives to husbands, children to parents, servants to masters—which was a commonplace of such manuals; moderation in apparel, language, eating, drinking, and general behavior; and appropriate speech, to which he accorded significant emphasis, perhaps reflecting the fundamental nature of the spoken word in his ministry as well as his youthful propensity to swearing. He exhorted parents to instruct their children in speech that would persuade them that what they learned was reality, not fable, and in disciplining them they were to eschew unsavory, unseemly words and beware of intermixing chiding terms with levity (3:28–30). Wives were urged to avoid gossip and not speak with "an *idle, talking,* or *brangling tongue.*" If their husbands were unbelievers, Bunyan thought wives should seek their conversion with few words, taking care to use speech that is beseeching and sympathetic, not proud and overbearing (3:32–36). In turn, children were encouraged not to utter "snappish" words to their parents, and, if the latter were ungodly, to "take heed of a parrating tongue" but speak sagely and meekly (3:39–40). Neighbors too were exhorted to shun gossip. Rightly used, speech has the capability to achieve

substantial good, but taken alone it is insufficient to fulfill the Christian's responsibility to perform good works. In many professors, Bunyan complained, there is
"a great deal of tatling and talk about Religion, and but a very little, if any thing,
of those Christian deeds that carry in them the Cross of a Christian in the doing
thereof, and profit to my neighbour" (3:44).

In discussing appropriate behavior for the master of a family, Bunyan drew a
parallel with the pastor of a congregation, expecting both to be doctrinally sound;
capable of teaching, reproving, and exhorting; exemplary in faith and holiness;
and willing to assemble their charges for preaching and prayer. In many respects
the family was a miniature congregation. He was unwilling to permit masters of
families who failed to fulfill their responsibilities to hold offices in the church. In
the performance of their duties, heads of families were expected to ban ungodly,
profane, or heretical books or discourse; he clearly thought the master of a family
must possess sufficient knowledge of gospel fundamentals to discriminate between orthodox and heretical doctrines. He also prompted masters to ensure that
children and servants lived in subjection to Scripture, permitting no behavior
that contravened biblical maxims. If family members and servants refused to attend church with the master, Bunyan recommended that he invite godly men to
his home to preach to them, just as he would summon a medical doctor if they
were ill. In supplying the families' physical needs, moderation was the standard,
and he explicitly admonished masters not to neglect the familial responsibilities
of Bible reading, prayer, and "Christian Conference" (3:22–26).

Bunyan thought highly of marriage, in large measure because a godly husband and wife were a figure or type of Christ and his church. A husband's responsibilities were therefore sweeping in Bunyan's judgment. Christ had instructed,
protected, assisted, and died for his church, and "*so ought men to do for their
Wives,*" he reflected. "Wherefore that husband that carrieth it undiscreetly toward
his wife, he doth not only behave himself contrary to the Rule, but also maketh
his Wife lose the benefit of such an Ordinance" (3:27). Bunyan endorsed the
common view that wives are weaker vessels because of their "frailer constitution," but he also insisted they are subjects and yoke-fellows, not slaves. Moreover, in the husband's absence the wife is to take charge of the household (3:27,
34). The women among Bunyan's readers were narrowly perceived, for he failed
to address the circumstances of single women, including widows and spinsters,
and his remark that wives are "always at home" ignored those who worked
alongside their husbands in shops or assumed their trades following their deaths,
as did Joan Dover, one of his future printers. In this work he offered no counsel
to young people contemplating matrimony, and he ignored the practice of arranged marriage, although he did address the circumstances of spouses, regardless of gender, whose mates are not believers. In both cases his advice was similar,

focusing on the necessity to behave discreetly, patiently, and lovingly, and to seek opportune moments to discuss the gospel. He provided no option of leaving an impious spouse, though he recognized that some wives are "in great slavery by reason of their ungodly husbands"; from Bunyan they received only pity, prayer, and advice to be "more watchful and circumspect in all their wayes." To the wife who objects that her husband is a sot, a fool, and incapable of pursuing his vocation, Bunyan offered no hope, insisting she remember that her husband is her head and lord, that she not exercise authority over him, and that she not disclose her husband's weaknesses to others (3:26–28, 32–36). In short, Bunyan's view of women and marriage was thoroughly traditional.

In his remarks on the parent-child relationship, Bunyan emphasized the pragmatic. Parents have a twofold duty to instruct and correct their offspring. In undertaking the former, he recommended simple words, avoiding "*Whimzies and unprofitable Notions*," taking a gentle and patient approach, and, as noted earlier, utilizing language intended to convince children of the subject-matter's serious nature. For the correction of children, parents can employ the rod if necessary, though he insisted they first use "fair words" and ensure that the children not spend time with rude, ungodly companions. If the rod is necessary, it must be used "in cool blood" with an adequate explanation of the offense and the parent's love; moreover, the child must be told "that if fair means would have done, none of this severity should have been." The key point is that physical punishment must afflict a child's conscience as well as his or her body (3:28–30). Children were, of course, exhorted to obey parents, but Bunyan also expected them to think better of their parents than themselves, to honor them, and to provide for their physical requirements as necessary. If the parents are not believers, Bunyan urged their children to speak to them wisely and humbly, to watch for opportunities "to lay their condition before them," and to bear their reproaches, evil speech, and railing (3:36–40).

In explicating master-servant relations, Bunyan again emphasized the pragmatic, especially with respect to the behavior of masters. If feasible, masters should employ godly servants, but if this is not possible he cautioned them to deal with servants as with children, providing the same spiritual counsel and admonition. He espoused a high standard of behavior for masters: "Know that it is thy duty so to behave thy self to thy Servant, that thy service may not only be for thy good, but for the good of thy Servant, and that both in body and soul." Servants must not be treated as slaves, threatened, misled about their duties when hired, given inadequate wages, or have their stipends reduced. Based on his conversations with servants, Bunyan was incensed that some of those employed by unbelievers enjoyed more liberty to serve God and fairer treatment than those whose masters were godly; "this stinketh." He also cautioned masters to behave in such a manner that servants who leave their service will not have an occasion to scandalize the gospel by tales of inappropriate conduct (3:30–32). In the household he regarded servants as inferior even to children, and he expected them to be content with their station. They should perform their responsibilities not for their employer but for God, who put them in their place. Bunyan regarded a servant's work, rightly undertaken, as possessing substantial dignity: "I conclude, that thy work in thy place and station, as thou art a servant, is as really God's Ordinance, and as acceptable to Him, in its kind, as is Preaching, or any other work for God; and that thou art as sure to receive a reward for thy labour, as he that hangs, or is burnt for the Gospel." Servants in the employ of ungodly masters were reminded that inappropriate behavior not only dishonors God but harms the unbeliever and offends the faithful. Bunyan insisted that servants perform duties for an overbearing master as faithfully as if he were the most pleasant, rational employer in the world, knowing they will be divinely blessed for their suffering "as truly as if [they] wert called upon the stage of this world [the executioner's platform] before men, for the matters of [their] Faith." This they must do until God enables them to "escape" from such employment (3:40–43).

Bunyan intended his counsel regarding *"Good Neighbourhood"* to promote civil, peaceful relations in the community. The foundation is good, sound behavior in one's family, which manifests the gospel's power in the heart. Being a good neighbor also entails courtesy and charity to those in need, including a duty to inquire after the poor rather than waiting for them to request assistance. Bunyan proposed no restrictions on giving solely or even primarily to the godly, nor did he insist that charity be accompanied with spiritual admonitions. Among members of the community he urged the godly to be humble, grave, and gracious, not "light and frothy," and to reprove neighbors for their sins. Self-denial is especially important; rather than injure one's neighbor, he expected the godly to refrain from actions they were otherwise entitled to take. "A Christian in all such things as intrench not the matters of *Faith* and *Worship*, should be full of self-denial, and seek to please others rather than themselves." The godly must be careful not to use offensive language or provoke neighbors to anger, but instead suffer injustice in silence (3:43–44). To Bunyan, community harmony is something to be sought and valued, but not at the expense of excusing the godly from their responsibility to rebuke others for their sinful actions. Such admonitions, if given, undoubtedly created tension among neighbors.

Having completed his survey of appropriate behavior, Bunyan could have concluded his book at this point, but because this might have been his last testament his keen sense of pastoral responsibility prompted him to address three sins he believed were rife in many professing Christians, namely, covetousness, pride, and adultery. Such offenses "spoil both Christian brother-hood, and civil neighbourhood," and thus have substantial bearing on social behavior. Covetousness, opined Bunyan, is the root of sin, for every sinful act commences with an evil desire. He castigated covetousness in a wide array of forms: as dissatisfaction with a comfortable livelihood, a seller's overvaluing of his or her wares, a buyer's undervaluing of the same, reticence to assist the poor, and regret for charitable giving. He similarly deplored manifestations of pride, including the slighting of people who are poor or of lower social status, a refusal to practice self-denial for the benefit of one's neighbors, an unwillingness to heed reproofs for sinful behavior, a thirst for praise, and a reluctance to seek divine assistance in the performance of spiritual duties. "Pride is discovered by mincing words, a made [contrived] carriage, and an affecting the toyes and baubles that Satan and every light-headed fool bringeth into the world." Bunyan likened vain apparel to imitating butterflies, "*painting* the Devil," and "making gay the *spider*" (3:44–49). In his judgment, adultery is "a very predominate and master *Sin*" and "a very taking *sin*" because "it is natural above all sins to mankind." It is pervasive, said Bunyan, because it can be committed unknowingly when a man looks at a woman lustfully, as Jesus taught in Matthew 5:28. Women, too, can be guilty of this offense. In dealing with this sin, Bunyan focused on those who commit it in their hearts rather than outside the marital bed, presumably on the grounds that heading off lustful desires will preclude illicit sexual activity. To this end he admonished his readers to beware of a wanton eye, with its delight in thoughts of immodesty and illicit sexual behavior; indecent speech; and sexually provocative clothing, including "stretched-out necks, [and] naked breasts." Not one to mince words, he unequivocally maintained that "the attire of an Harlot is too frequently in our day the attire of Professors" (3:50–51). As he looked down from the pulpit, was he uneasy because of what he saw?

Bunyan's preeminent interest in pastoral matters is also evident in his closing exhortation to backsliders. Once again, the evangelical face of his Calvinism, which I have termed 'pastoral Arminianism', is manifest. In Calvinist theology, the elect cannot disavow their faith and embrace damnation, for their perseverance is assured, nor can those who only seemingly have faith attain salvation by avoiding the pitfall of backsliding. Bunyan posed the matter as a plea for advice from someone who had once earnestly desired to do God's work but had since lost that yearning. He counseled the backslider to recognize that he or she had fallen from God and to repent and believe. Just as Samson's strength returned as his hair grew back, so would the backslider's faith. "At the first thou wilt find all the wheels of thy soul rusty, and all the strings of thine heart out of tune; as also, when thou first beginnest to stir, the dust and filth of thy heart will, like smoak, trouble thee from that clear beholding the Grace of God, and his Love to thy Soul; but yet wait, and go on, . . . up and be doing, and the Lord will be with thee." But he made it clear that God consigns some backsliders to perdition, periodically even snatching away their lives before they can repent, as he did with Lot's wife. Bunyan was implying that believers could jeopardize their salvation by backsliding, which was, of course, impossible given his doctrine of predestination. He was therefore making a pastoral point, not a theological one (3:59–62).

Thus in what he thought might be his final message, Bunyan sought to motivate believers to undertake good works as a natural consequence of their divinely bestowed faith. The best way to encourage others to perform such deeds, he attested, is to "shew them the certainty of their being by Grace made Heirs of *Eternal Life*" (3:11). Assurance of justification by grace is the strongest incentive to accomplish good works; one does not do such deeds to earn salvation but because one has already received that gift. At the same time, a failure to perform them is an indication that one's faith is counterfeit. He wanted his readers to remember that true religion is not "a *by-business*" but the only essential thing in the world (3:25–26). *Christian Behaviour* is both optimistic and serious in its tone, as befits an intended last testament. Although Bunyan recalled his experiences in the book, he was not preoccupied with his own plight or even with justifying the actions that had seemingly brought death so near. Confident in his own faith, he anticipated a paradise in which he would rest from his labors and be free of the temptations with which he had struggled so mightily (3:15, 62), but new trials, not death, were imminent.

CHAPTER 5

# Millenarian Expectations

———————◆◄►——————

Sometime between completing *Christian Behaviour* on 17 June 1663 and late 1664, Bunyan prepared a broadside entitled *A Mapp Shewing the Order & Causes of Salvation & Damnation*. Although no copy of the first edition is extant, Charles Doe incorporated it in his 1692 folio edition of some of Bunyan's works, and it was republished as a broadside in 1691 and 1700.[1] The inspiration for *A Mapp* came from William Perkins' *A Golden Chaine, or, the Description of Theologie* (London, 1612), which included a table illustrating the causes of salvation and damnation.[2] Perkins in turn had been influenced by a chart illustrating election and reprobation in Theodore Beza's *Tractationes Theologicae*.[3] Perkins explained that his chart was intended as a visual catechism for the illiterate, and Johannes Wolleb indicated that such devices were designed to aid to weak memories.[4] Bunyan's chart begins at the top of the page with a triangle in which four circles are incorporated, the central one representing the son of God, a visual attestation of Christ's centrality in his soteriology. From this triangle a central column extends downward to a circle incorporating Adam, Abel, and Cain—Eve is conspicuously absent—and then onward to a circle at the bottom of the page signifying that God's glory is manifest in both the eternal bliss of the elect and the everlasting damnation of the reprobate. On each side of this central column Bunyan employed twenty-four circles, begin-

---

[1] Arber, *Term Catalogues*, 2:368; 3:195.

[2] William Perkins, *A Golden Chaine, or, the Description of Theologie*, trans. Robert Hill (London, 1612); the diagram is between 470 and 471. This work was published in various editions.

[3] Theodore Beza, *Theodori Bezae Vezelii, Volumen . . . Tractationum Theologicarum*, 3 vols. (Geneva, 1570–82), 1:170.

[4] John Wollebius [Johannes Wolleb], *The Abridgment of Christian Divinitie*, 3rd ed. (London, 1660), title-page.

ning with one for the covenant of grace and another for the covenant of works, to explain the steps in election and reprobation ("*To be Reprobated is to be left out of Gods election*"). In the Ramist tradition, the lines leading to the various circles divide and subdivide, but then return to a single circle. Unlike Perkins, Bunyan included a biblical citation in nearly all of his circles, and he also expanded the text to make the chart more useful as a pedagogical tool (*MW*, 12:418–23).

Hung on the wall of a home, *A Mapp* functioned as a visual reminder of the respective fates that await the saints and the damned, a handy index to pertinent scriptural passages, and a synopsis of the doctrine of predestination.[5] After *The Pilgrim's Progress* was published, readers could use *A Mapp* as a pedagogical tool to heed the pilgrims' advice to learn from the shepherds, whose "Perspective Glass" enabled them to see into the future:

> *Come to the* Shepherds *then, if you would see*
> *Things deep, things hid, and that mysterious be.*  (*PP*, 122–23)

In its own way, *A Mapp* was a "Perspective Glass." Although he had been deprived of access to the pulpit, through *A Mapp* Bunyan found a way to influence and instruct the faithful in the privacy of their homes on a daily basis.[6]

By 1664 incarceration was having a significant impact on Bunyan's psychological state. In his epistle to *The Holy City: or, the New Jerusalem*, a work he composed from about December 1664 through May 1665, he explained that one Sunday, while he was with his ministerial colleagues in their prison chamber, they expected him to discuss something from the Bible in their customary manner.[7] At first his reaction was negative: "At that time I felt my self (it being my turn to speak) so empty, spiritless, and barren, that I thought I should not have been able to speak among them so much as five words of Truth, with Life and Evidence" (*MW*, 3:69). During the year and a half between finishing *Christian Behaviour* and this episode, Bunyan experienced another period of depression, again triggered by anxiety. In several paragraphs near the end of *Grace Abounding* he describes the anguish of

---

[5]Numerous other broadsides were apparently intended at least in part for hanging on walls as convenient guides to spirituality. Cf., e.g., Richard Baxter, *Short Instructions for the Sick* (London, 1665), Christopher Jelinger, *The Resolution-Table* (London, 1676), *The Golden Sayings, Sentences and Experiences of Mr. Vavasor Powell* [London, 1675?], *Most Holy and Profitable Sayings of That Reverend Divine, Doctor Tho. Goodwin* [London, 1680], and *Old Mr. Dod's Sayings* (London, 1671).

[6]Gordon Campbell, "The Source of Bunyan's *Mapp of Salvation*," *Journal of the Warburg and Courtauld Institutes* 44 (1981): 240–41.

[7]The archdeacon of Northampton arranged for a Church of England cleric to preach at the Northampton jail, but I know of no evidence that this was done at the Bedford county prison. BL, Add. MSS 22,576, fol. 24r.

being separated from his wife and children, likening it to the pulling of flesh from his bones. As he supported his family by making long, tagged laces in prison, he often pondered the hardships and misery his family would face if he were exiled or executed. Above all, he worried about his blind daughter Mary, "who lay nearer my heart than all I had besides; O the thoughts of the hardship I thought my blind one might go under, would break my heart to pieces." He imagined her begging, hungry, cold, without adequate apparel, suffering beatings, and facing countless other calamities. It was, he said, as if he were pulling his house down on his wife and children, yet he felt compelled to remain steadfast in his convictions. He would later draw on this experience when, in *The Pilgrim's Progress*, he had Christian leave his family and children to strike out on his journey. But now Bunyan could only find partial solace in his belief that God would care for his family if he ventured everything for God. He reflected too on Hebrews 11:37–38, which describes how the faithful were tormented, stoned, tempted, afflicted, reduced to destitution and wandering, and even killed. "I have verily thought that my Soul and [the Holy Spirit] have sometimes reasoned about the sore and sad estate of a banished and exiled condition, how they are exposed to hunger, to cold, to perils, to nakedness, to enemies, and a thousand calamities; and at last it may be to die in a ditch like a poor forlorn and desolate sheep" (*GA*, §§327–32). Anguish and anxiety challenged his faith as well as his psychological well-being.

In *Grace Abounding* Bunyan describes a period of "many weeks" in which he was "in a very sad and low condition." Although he does not date this period, it occurred while he was still "a young Prisoner, and not acquainted with the Laws." He was concerned at this point that he might face the gallows, a fear he expressed in the conclusion of *Christian Behaviour*. The most likely date for this period of renewed melancholy was sometime during the year and a half following his completion of *Christian Behaviour*. His mood preceding that work, as we have seen, was one of defiance as reflected in his bold attack on the Book of Common Prayer. Thus it was during late 1663 or 1664 that he again battled the Tempter, worrying that he might be in a state of despair at the time of his execution, devoid of any evidence that his soul would attain a better life in the hereafter. Greatly troubled, "I thought with myself, if I should make a scrabling shift to clamber up the Ladder, yet I should either with quaking or other symptoms of faintings, give occasion to the enemy to reproach the way of God and his People, for their timerousness." Ashamed at the prospect of dying with an ashen face and shaking knees, he often reflected about standing on a ladder with a rope around his neck, though he found some comfort in the thought that his last words might convert one of the onlookers. "But yet all the things of God were kept out of [his] sight," and for weeks he knew not what to do. At last he concluded that he would remain resolute, even without comfort and amid recurring temptations. "If God doth not come in, thought I, I will leap off the Ladder even blindfold into Eterni-tie, sink or swim, come heaven, come hell." This bout with a "sad and low condi-tion" ended when another sentence "dropped" on him, asking if Job had served God for naught, followed by Psalm 44, beginning at the twelfth verse, an account of resolution in the face of persecution (*GA*, §§333–36). As late as 1666 Bunyan still experienced doubt and feelings of affliction and oppression that made him abhor himself, as he indicated in the conclusion of *Grace Abounding* (*GA*, 103). Depression can recur, and it is likely that he once again battled the illness in late 1663 and 1664 as the bleak years in prison took their toll.[8]

### "*Out of Babylon*"[9]: The Return of the Holy City

As Bunyan, feeling spiritless and barren, struggled to find something to say to his fellow prisoners, he "providentially" happened upon Revelation 21:11, which lik-ens the new Jerusalem to a piece of jasper as clear as crystal. At first perceiving only "dim glimmerings," he wanted to know more about this city, which he decided to make the subject of his biblical exercise. His presentation, which had much to say about persecution and the church's ultimate triumph, was well-received: "We did all eat, and were well refreshed; and behold also that while I was in the distributing of it, it so encreased in my hand, that of the Fragments that we left, after we had well dined, I gathered up this Basket-full." The more he studied the entire passage, Revelation 21:10–27 and 22:1–4, the more he discovered. After he completed the work, Joan Dover printed it in London in 1665; another imprint appeared the same year, possibly from Dover or Francis Smith, who issued a third imprint in 1669. Bunyan did not regard his contribution as definitive, for he was convinced that oth-ers would be able to discover considerably more by careful study; "much more then I do here crush out, is yet left in the Cluster" (*MW*, 3:65, 70).

Englishmen in the sixteenth and seventeenth centuries expressed substantial interest in the end times. Arthur Dent, whose *Plain Man's Path-Way to Heaven* had been influential in heightening Bunyan's interest in religion, also wrote a book on the last times entitled *The Ruine of Rome* (1603). Since 1645 Bunyan's friend Henry Jessey had been publishing an annual *Scripture Calendar* that dis-cussed current events in light of the book of Daniel, and Bunyan had probably read Fifth Monarchist works at the time he found their tenets enticing. Eschato-logical expectations were prevalent among mainline Protestants as well as radical

---

[8] William James aptly commented that "the iron of melancholy left a permanent im-print" on Bunyan's soul. *The Varieties of Religious Experience*, ed. Frederick H. Burkhardt, Fredson Bowers, and Ignas K. Skrupskelis (Cambridge, MA: Harvard University Press, 1985), 180; cf. 156.

[9] *MW*, 3:94.

millenarians, though the latter were more inclined to predict dates for future events. After John Bale identified Antichrist with the papacy, English Protestants explored the history of Antichrist, developing a scheme whereby apocalyptic images were employed to characterize historical periods.[10] Students of prophecy thought the future could be predicted. After the 1620s, the historical approach to the apocalyptic declined as more and more prophecies were shifted from the past to the future, but millenarian interest continued. Isaac Newton, John Evelyn, Henry More, Robert Boyle, and Thomas Burnet were among those with millenarian beliefs in the late seventeenth century. Richard Baxter contended in 1686 that the millennium had occurred in the past, a position defended in the sixteenth century by John Foxe and others.[11] Bunyan's millenarian interests did not place him in an extremist fringe. Cognizant of the debate about the end times, he staked out his own position by defending a future millennium, eschewing any attempt to predict dates, and identifying Antichrist with the papacy.

Expecting a varied readership, Bunyan provided no less than four epistles to *The Holy City*. In explaining the book's genesis, the epistle to the godly, or nonconformist, reader asked the saints to judge his work charitably, for as in the Bible itself one sometimes finds "nought . . . but words." "Possibly from that which thou mayest cast away as an empty Bone, others may pick both good and wholsom Bits; yea, and also out of that suck much nourishing Marrow." Bunyan's tone was strikingly different in his epistle to the learned reader, whom he expected to deride his book because he lacked formal education. As he told his godly readers, however, he found the Bible and Holy Spirit sufficient to examine even the deepest things of God, citing 1 Corinthians 2:10 as his authority. Nevertheless, he expected criticism from the formally educated because of his plain

[10] For Bale see *DNB, s.v.*

[11] Katharine R. Firth, *The Apocalyptic Tradition in Reformation Britain, 1530–1645* (Oxford: Oxford University Press, 1979), 242, 248–50; Bryan W. Ball, *A Great Expectation: Eschatological Thought in English Protestantism to 1660* (Leiden: E. J. Brill, 1975), 16–54, 233; B. R. White, "Henry Jessey in the Great Rebellion," in *Reformation, Conformity and Dissent: Essays in Honour of Geoffrey Nuttall*, ed. R. Buick Knox (London: Epworth Press, 1977), 144–45; W. R. Owens, "John Bunyan and English Millenarianism," in *Awakening Words*, ed. Gay, Randall, and Zinck, 88–89; William M. Lamont, *Richard Baxter and the Millennium: Protestant Imperialism and the English Revolution* (London: Croom Helm; Totowa, NJ: Rowman and Littlefield, 1979), 27–71; B. S. Capp, "Extreme Millenarianism," in *Puritans, the Millennium and the Future of Israel: Puritan Eschatology, 1600 to 1660*, ed. Peter Toon (Cambridge: James Clarke and Co., 1970), 66–90. Although Paul Christianson's assertion that millenarian interests moved to "the fringes of learned society" after 1653 is overstated, his study is indispensible. *Reformers and Babylon: English Apocalyptic Visions from the Reformation to the Eve of the Civil War* (Toronto: University of Toronto Press, 1978), 244.

language and lack of patristic citations, to which he pleaded that simple words often hit the mark better than scholarly ones, and that pure, naked truth is preferable to vain language. "The Reason why you find me empty of the Language of the Learned, I mean their Sentences and Words, which others use, is, because I have them not, nor have not read them: had it not been for the BIBLE, I had not onely not thus done it, but not at all." Objecting to the spirit of idolatry and whoredom in most of those who valued earthly wisdom, he insisted he was better supplied with a Bible than if he had access to the libraries of Oxford and Cambridge without Scripture. "I am for *drinking Water out of my own Cistern*; what GOD makes mine by the evidence of his Word and Spirit, that I dare make bold with" (3:69–72). This was, of course, hyperbole, for he used Foxe's *Acts and Monuments* in this work, and he had almost certainly read one or more books on Revelation at an earlier date. His comment about his attraction to Fifth Monarchist tenets suggests as much, as does his depiction of learned commentaries replete with patristic citations in the text or the margins.[12] Moreover, his exegesis of the passage from Revelation for his fellow prisoners would have been followed with a discussion in which he undoubtedly received food for thought. Clearly, however, Bunyan did not compose *The Holy City* with erudite commentaries at his side.

The remaining two epistles are shorter, particularly one addressed to the "Captious and wrangling Reader." However such persons came by Bunyan's book, he wanted them to know they had barely been in his thoughts when he composed it. "I intended this Book as little for thee, as the Goldsmith intendeth his Jewels and Rings for the Snowt of a Sow." Such readers should cease their frenzy and act rationally or lay the book aside. Addressed to the Church of Rome, the "*Mother of Harlots*," Bunyan's last epistle was a stinging denunciation of Catholicism, offering neither cosmetics to adorn its wrinkled face nor a crutch to shore up Rome's tottering kingdom, but instead a presage of its sudden, final collapse. "I know that both thy wanton Eye, with all thy mincing Brats that are intoxicated with thy Cup, and inchanted with thy Fornications, will at the sight of so homely and plain a Dish as this, cry, *Foh*! snuff, put the Branch to the Nose, and say, Contemptible!" (3:72–73). Since the likelihood of Catholic readers was slight, Bunyan may have intended this final epistle to reinforce anti-Catholic feelings in his nonconformist audience.

*The Holy City* is a sustained exegetical exercise on Revelation 21:10 through 22:4 in which Bunyan analyzes the passage verse by verse, phrase by phrase. The result is a degree of redundancy as well as an absence of thematic structure. He disarmingly notes the limitations of his exposition: "In my dealing with this Mystery, I shall not

---

[12] Sears McGee suggests that Bunyan's identification of the 12,000 furlongs in Revelation 21:16 as portions or shares for the saints, not inhabitants of the new Jerusalem, may indicate the influence of another commentator. *MW*, 3:xxxv, 124–25.

meddle where I see nothing, neither shall I hide from you that which at present I conceive to be wrapt up therein: onely you must not from me look for much inlargement, though I shall endeavour to speak as much in few words, as my Understanding and Capacity will enable me, through the help of Christ." Given the fact that he was embarking on his first substantive exegetical work and tackling one of the most enigmatic scriptural books, his discretion and modesty were prudent. He was also operating in the belief that the things of God can only be discerned with the Holy Spirit's assistance, and that the more of the Spirit one has, the more one can discover (3:75–76). The implied corollary is that learned commentators without the Spirit's help cannot offer an accurate interpretation of Revelation.

Fundamental to Bunyan's exegetical methodology is his reliance on typology. He had used this hermeneutic methodology in earlier works, especially *The Doctrine of the Law and Grace Unfolded*, but in *The Holy City* it became the basis for his entire book. Typology, which has a history going back to the ancient world, is based on the idea that types or figures foreshadow and signify antitypes. Both are thought to be real. The Hebrews had their own tradition of exegetical typology, whereas for Christians the Old Testament prefigures the New, and the persons, places, and events of the former can be interpreted as types of those in the latter. Pauline exegesis made typology important in the Christian tradition by asserting that Jesus is the messiah referred to in the Hebrew prophecies.[13]

As a method of biblical exegesis, typology is grounded in the interpreter's conviction of Scripture's fundamental unity and harmony, its disparate books having been inspired by the Holy Spirit. Typology is also a manifestation of the hermeneutic principle that the Old Testament must be read in light of the gospel message expressed in the New Testament. As Bunyan understood typology, it is compatible with his hermeneutic principle that readers must seek the plain sense of each passage.[14] Typology is thus the search for correspondence between persons, events, objects, or signs in the Old and New Testaments, with the former prefiguring or predicting the latter. Old Testament types, sometimes called figures or shadows, have their fulfillment in New Testament antitypes. Essentially typology is a system of encoding and decoding literary texts, which in the biblical sphere pertain to the unfolding of God's redemptive plan. Interpreters of scriptural typology believe types and antitypes are historical, unlike biblical allegory, which is concerned with a text's inner, nonliteral meaning.[15] Critics such as

[13] Paul J. Korshin, *Typologies in England 1650–1820* (Princeton, NJ: Princeton University Press, 1982), 4–5, 25–28, 30–31.

[14] Maxine Hancock, "Bunyan as Reader: The Record of *Grace Abounding*," *BS* 5 (Autumn 1994): 71.

[15] Korshin, *Typologies*, 4–5, 8, 75; Joseph A. Galdon, *Typology and Seventeenth-Century*

Samuel Parker and William Sherlock were correct in accusing some contemporaries of imprecisely using such terms as types, parables, emblems, and allegories. Bunyan himself employed such words inconsistently and sometimes used "similitude" to cover all of them. Yet inconsistent usage had long plagued biblical interpreters, going as far back as the Apostle Paul, who in Galatians 4:24 uses "allegory" (ἀλληγορία) to mean "type"(τύπος).[16]

Because Bunyan had an understanding of typology when he wrote *Some Gospel-Truths Opened*, in which he explained that during the age of Moses "God did more gloriously yet break forth with one type after another" (*MW*, 1:34), he probably learned about this subject from Hobson. By the time he began writing *The Holy City*, three major seventeenth-century studies of typology by English authors were available: William Guild's *Moses Unveiled* (1620), Thomas Taylor's *Christ Revealed: or the Old Testament Explained* (1635), and John Everard's *The Gospel-Treasury Opened* (1657). More specialized works included John Weemes' *The Christian Synagogue* (1623) and Christopher Harvey's *The Synagogue, or, the Shadow of the Temple* (1640).[17] Taylor's book appeared in a revised version entitled *Moses and Aaron, or the Types and Shadows of Our Saviour in the Old Testament* in 1653. If Bunyan read any of these works, it was probably Taylor's, for George Griffith, whom Bunyan respected, had signed an epistle to a collection of some of Taylor's works and may have recommended the book to him.

Assuming his readers were familiar with the use of types and antitypes, Bunyan found many of them in the passage he was interpreting as well as in related verses. Of these prefigurations the most important for his purposes was Jerusalem as a type of the church. In *The Holy City* he painstakingly decoded an allegory of church history and its culmination in the building of the new Jerusalem during the millennium. It was a useful lesson in the value of similitudes, which, "if fitly spoke and applyed, do much set off, and out, any point, that either in the Doctrines of Faith or Manners, is handled in the Churches" (3:95–96).[18] He would later put this lesson to good use in writing *The Pilgrim's Progress* and *The Holy War*.

Bunyan dissected virtually every phrase to ascertain its spiritual significance. When, for example, he read that the new Jerusalem had three gates on each of its four sides, he offered a rather strained fourfold interpretation: Three gates on

---

*Literature* (The Hague: Mouton, 1975), 20, 23, 28–29, 34; Graham Midgley, in *MW*, 7:xvi, xxvi.

[16] Korshin, *Typologies*, 6; Midgley, in *MW*, 7:xxiii–xxiv; Galdon, *Typology*, 24–26. The views of Parker and Sherlock are discussed in Chapter 8.

[17] For Everard and Taylor see *BDBR*, *s.vv.* For Guild, Weemes (as Wemyss), and Harvey see *DNB*, *s.vv.*

[18] G. B. Harrison, *John Bunyan: A Study in Personality* (London: Doubleday, Doran and Co., 1928), 106.

each side signify that the gospel summons people with the Trinity's consent and its willingness to receive sinners; that no one can enter the city except by Christ's three offices; that the saints go through three stages in this life, namely, childhood, adulthood, and fatherhood in the church; and that the elect pass through three stages from nature to glory, to wit, the state of grace in this life, the state of felicity in heaven, and the state of post-resurrection glory, or the body and soul's state of grace in this life, the soul's state of glory at death, and the body and soul's state of glory at Christ's second coming. The Old Testament type for the three-fold gates is the three staircases in the temple at Jerusalem that provided access from the lowest to the highest room (3:108–9). Sometimes Bunyan's quest for types and antitypes was contrived, as in the example just cited, which required him to use three staircases as a type for twelve gates.

In *The Holy City* Bunyan enunciated his view of church history for the first time. The broad outline falls into three parts, each of which he interpreted in terms of Jerusalem as a type of the church.[19] (Pre-Christian history had meaning for him only in terms of the fall, which he regarded as a historical event, and the story of the Jews, which he treated as a storehouse of types that prefigure Christian history.) The first phase of church history, the purest state, occurred during the days of Jesus and the apostles, the type for which is Jerusalem during Solomon's reign. In the second stage, for which the type is the Babylonian captivity of the Jews, the church declined and remains in thraldom. During the late stages of this era occur two successive sub-periods, which Bunyan calls altar-work and temple-work. In the final stage, the millennium or period of city-work, the church will return from captivity and rebuild its city and walls, as did the Hebrews in the post-exilic age (3:78–79).[20] As we shall see, according to Bunyan Antichrist's fall will occur at the junction of the second and third periods, though Satan will enjoy a brief revival near the end of the third era, an epoch lasting a thousand years. Christ's return and the last judgment will bring the millennium to a close.

Of the first phase, a time of purity in doctrine and worship, Bunyan says little. He describes apostolic doctrine, whose authors "out-stript all the Prophets that ever went before them," as infallible—"pure, primitive, and unspotted." Those who reject the theology of these foundation-builders despise God. During the

[19] Joachim of Fiore's tripartite scheme of history was substantially different from Bunyan's, for the former viewed the Old Testament era as the time of God the father, the period from Christ to the thirteenth century as that of the son, and the final epoch as that of the Spirit.

[20] McGee suggests that Bunyan's use of the terms altar-work, temple-work, and city-work may have been influenced by John Tillinghast's employment of the expression generation-work. *MW*, 3:xxxviii.

millennium the church's doctrine and worship will be restored to its apostolic, or primitive, state (3:80, 104, 112, 114). He does not make clear how long this initial stage lasted. By the time he wrote, the second era had been under way, he thought, more than a thousand years. Sears McGee suggests the second period began in the fifth century, though it may have commenced as much as several centuries earlier (3:95, 301).

At the outset of the second age Antichrist imprisoned the church in his dungeon. "God did deliver up his People into the hand of the King of *Babylon* . . . in fury and in anger, and . . . for their wickedness he would hide his face from his City" (3:95, 194). Mixing his metaphors, Bunyan described the onset as the scaling of the church's walls, the breach of its battlements, and the entry into its vineyards by the red dragon and the beast with seven heads and ten horns. During this age the Bible was abused, defiled, burned, and almost totally destroyed; for a time "the outward Word of the Gospel," the Bible in the vernacular and biblical preaching, ceased to exist. Theology and worship were corrupted, the Devil having muddied the doctrine of grace, the river flowing with the water of life, by his erroneous opinions; heresy continued to loom large in Bunyan's mind (3:79, 91, 104, 119, 132, 180, 184, 192). The second stage was also characterized by preachers, presumably Catholics and Laudians, who "confounded, and removed to and fro, even like loose and rouling-stones," the offices of Christ, while others attributed them to Antichrist. Bunyan seems to have had in mind those clergy who claimed a priestly role in celebrating the Eucharist (3:133). Yet God, he opined, makes use of some ministers who, though not among the elect, serve him with gifts "for the perfecting the Church under Christ," namely, preaching, prophesying, administering the sacraments, and performing other functions important to the church. Like Judas, Demas, and others, such men, though devoid of saving grace, may receive from God "great knowledge and understanding in the Mysteries of the Kingdom of God, and [he] will also make them for profit and advantage in his Church." Although Bunyan made this statement while discussing gathered churches, he seems to have expressed it broadly enough to recognize the possibility that clergy in other churches, though not personally among the elect, might perform useful service (3:176).

During the church's second period one of its two walls was breached. The wall that remained intact represents the elect's eternal preservation from divine wrath through Christ's benefits, whereas the other wall symbolizes the divine providence that protects the church from its enemies. Between the two walls is a ditch into which members of the church might fall if one wall is breached. This gap, explained Bunyan, was the occasion of the great persecution experienced by the church during the second era (3:99–100). "Now all this befalleth the People of God; they are thrown into the burning fiery Furnace of Affliction and Temptation, and there they are tried, purged, and purified." He likened the church at this time to Esther perfuming herself to be fit for the king's presence (3:139), whereas persecutors were depicted as venomous dragons, ravenous wolves, and ferocious lions. Those who served God in this age did so in much distress, fear, and temptation. Drawing on his own experience, Bunyan described this epoch as "a black and doubtful night of Temptation and Affliction." It was also an era when God provided only a modest measure of gospel light with respect to apostolic doctrine (3:140, 169–70, 194).

Toward the latter part of church history's second age, a time of altar-work took place, signifying the commencement of the Christians' return from the Babylon of Antichrist. This entailed the discovery of Christ's priestly office and the offering of continual prayers and supplications for the church. Those who undertook this work, casting aside the relics of Antichrist that had intruded on Jesus' priestly office, were John Wyclif, John Hus, Martin Luther, Philip Melanchthon, John Calvin, Thomas Bilney, and the Marian martyrs, including Nicholas Ridley, John Hooper, and Thomas Cranmer. "These in their day were stout & valiant Champions for God, according to their light, and did upon the Altar of God, which is *Christ* our Lord, offer up many strong cries, with groans and tears, as every day required, for the compleat recovering of the Church of God." Yet Bunyan insisted these reformers did not lay the foundation of the new temple, the new Jerusalem (3:134, 154).

A period of temple-work, begun by people possessing additional light, follows the time of altar-work. "These men, though they keep the continual Offerings upon the Altar, as the other did, yet they are men also that are for Temple-work, wherefore these begin to search out the Foundations of the Temple of God, that they may rear up the House, as well as build up the Altar." The undertakers of this work are saints making the journey from Babylon. These reformers establish gathered churches of visible saints who separate themselves from the openly profane, the "confused heap of rubbish and carnal Gospelers, that every where like Locusts and Maggots craul up and down the Nations" (3:135). It was a damning indictment of state churches everywhere, regardless of their views on doctrine, worship, and polity. Bunyan likened these first gathered churches to "the coming together of *Ezekiels bones*, cloathed much with flesh and sinews, but greatly void of spirit and life" (3:153). Whatever their weaknesses, he vigorously defended such churches, which admitted only visible saints as determined by their words and lives. Moreover, these congregations excluded those who, once admitted, proved not to be visible saints. Even so, Bunyan acknowledged that not all members of gathered churches were elect, for only God knows people's hearts. Consequently he posited that there are two Books of Life, a longer one recording members of gathered churches, and a shorter one restricted to names of the elect, the "invisible" saints (3:174–78).

During the periods of altar-work and temple-work, the godly, lacking adequate light, are disputatious, especially with respect to "the glorious state of the Church in the latter days: Some being for its excellency to consist chiefly in outward glory; and others swerving on the other side, conclude she shall not have any of this; some conceiving that this City will not be built until the Lord comes from Heaven in Person; others again concluding that when he comes, then there shall be no longer tarrying here, but that all shall forthwith, even all the Godly, be taken up into Heaven." In Bunyan's judgment, this explained the substantial disagreement among even the Protestant nonconformists regarding such matters as the millennium, the second coming, and the last judgment. Of course, numerous other theological differences existed among Christians, "confounding and destroying," but these issues would not be resolved until the millennium (3:94, 115).

In *The Holy City* Bunyan has little to say about Antichrist's fall. Chronologically it precedes the building of the new Jerusalem and thus of the millennium, but he provides no information about the agents or method of Antichrist's collapse. God the father will deliver "the great Red Dragon" into the hands of Christ, who will bind him for a thousand years. When he falls, the gospel will break out "in its primitive glory," and more of the elect, "the *Jewels of God*," will be converted (3:80, 100, 114, 128–29, 143, 150). Bunyan would take up Antichrist's decline in his posthumously published treatise, *Of Antichrist, and His Ruine*.

According to Bunyan, city-work—building the new Jerusalem—will occur at the beginning of the millennium. Although he opted not to suggest a date for this event, he indicated it would happen soon (3:78–79, 92). When the saints return from Babylon, they will march like a mighty army, not the routed forces characteristic of the second epoch: The church "comes in perfect rank and file, *terrible as an Army with Banners*," wrote Bunyan, probably recalling his service in the parliamentary forces. The church's return is purposeful, not "head-strong brain-sick rashness of her own," but the result of divine grace and light leading the church each step of the way. "She will . . . observe both time and order, and will go onely as her God doth go before her; now one step in this Truth, and then another in that, according to the dispensation of God, and the light of the day she lives in" (3:97–98). Because the period of city-work is progressive, the millennium will not inaugurate an era of perfect holiness (3:129). Indeed, the saints will remain imperfect during the millennium. Although the Tempter will no longer be free to assault Christians with his "many dreadful vexing and burning hellish Darts," which assail the soul like arrows, the godly will struggle with their inner lusts. These, however, are "weak, withered Corruptions" and "lean, withered blasted things." In the millennium the godly will have the aid of potent grace, which will strike hard at corruption, leaving it gasping at death's door. Although the elect will not be free of sin, they will no longer combat the Devil's "hellish suggestions" to blaspheme and succumb to despair, which Bunyan had found so arduous in his own years of travail (3:128–30, 153).

Conversions, Bunyan averred, will continue during the millennium. Among the converts will be the Jews, who will find this an especially arduous process. Reflecting the common prejudice that blamed all Jews for the crucifixion, he described "the tempted and doubting Jews, who at the beginning of their return will be much afflicted under the sight and sence of their own wretchedness." With them will come those who are inward Jews, by which he meant Gentiles who by virtue of their conversion are deemed children of Abraham. Thus the millennium will see Jews and Gentiles become one nation in the spirit of the gospel (3:103, 105–7, 115). In asserting that the conversion of the Jews will occur during rather than before the millennium, Bunyan differed from most English Protestant commentators.[21] The conversions of both Jews and Gentiles, in his judgment, will continue even after the city-work has concluded and the new Jerusalem has been built, and only then, at the end of the millennium, will the day of grace finally end (3:82–83, 170). City-work will proceed until the church has attained "a compleat Conquest and Victory over all her Enemies; she shall reign over them; the Law shall go forth of her that rules them, and the Governours of all the World at that day shall be *Jerusalem*-Men" (3:81). This will not happen without strife, however, for "City-work may be trampled under the feet of the wicked and uncircumcised *Gentiles*." In the end, when the new Jerusalem has been completed, "she either draweth and allureth her adversaries to entreat her kindly, and to count it their honour to be under her protection . . . or else she breaks and bruises, and subjects them to her by her Power and Authority" (3:135). At this point every nation will be subordinate to the church; theocracy is both the polity toward which the millennium progresses and the form of government it will ultimately establish throughout the earth (3:82). Only now will the saints at last be free from external persecution (3:128–29, 157, 195).

Bunyan dealt circumspectly with the role of monarchs in the crucial city-work that inaugurates the millennium. In returning from Babylon and rebuilding the church, the saints will not meddle with anyone else's business, he insisted, nor had the church ever been rebellious, a threat to monarchs, or a reducer of their revenues. "The Governours of this World need not at all to fear a disturbance from her, or a diminishing of ought they have." But among the verses Bunyan cited to support his assertion is Isaiah 8:9–10, which warns those who oppose God that they will be broken in pieces, hardly a comforting thought for rulers whose views differ from the church's. Nor was Bunyan's citation of Numbers 21:22–24, which recounts Israel's military defeat of Sihon, king of the Amorites,

[21] On this point I differ from McGee; *MW*, 3:304. For the views of other English Protestants see Bryan W. Ball, *A Great Expectation: Eschatological Thought in English Protestantism to 1660* (Leiden: E. J. Brill, 1975), 148–56.

and its seizure of substantial territory and cities. Bunyan depicted God as harmless and gentle unless he is opposed, in which case he reacts like a lion. Again, the biblical citation is ominous: In Zechariah 12:2–3 Jerusalem cuts its enemies into pieces (3:96–97). Moreover, Bunyan made it clear that while the building of the new Jerusalem is under way during the period of city-work, most monarchs and "great ones" will be serving "Mistris *Babylon*, the Mother of Harlots, the Mistris of Witchcrafts, and Abominations of the Earth." Referring to Revelation 17:14, he evoked the specter of a war in which the rulers

> will be as the horns upon the heads of the Beast, to defend the riding Lady [of Revelation 17:3] from the Gunshot that the Saints continually will be making at her by the force of the Word and Spirit of God. They will be shaking the sharp end of their weapons against the Son of God, continually labouring to keep him out of his Throne, and from having the rule in the Church, and in the World as becomes him who is the head of the body, and over all principality and power.

During this epic confrontation, the saints must patiently endure the hostility and militant opposition of the monarchs, which Bunyan blamed on the mistress of iniquity's instigation and witchcraft. At the beginning of the millennium, most kings and great ones will clearly be enemies of the church, though some, he thought, will help build the new Jerusalem, as Hiram, Solomon, Darius, Cyrus, and Artaxerxes had assisted in constructing and repairing the old (3:166–69).

All this will change, Bunyan avowed, once Antichrist has been chained and the new Jerusalem has been built, for then Christ's love and the city's beauty, not force, will persuade monarchs to embrace the new order (3:97). Henceforth rulers will use their "force and power" to serve the church, turning against Jezebel, the mistress of iniquity:

> *Jezebel*, thy Chamber-companions will shortly, notwithstanding thy painted face, cast thee down headlong out at the *windows*. Yea, they shall tread thee in pieces by the feet of their prancing-Horses, and with the wheels of their jumping Chariots. They shall shut up all bowels of compassion towards thee, and shall roar upon thee like the Sea, and upon thy fat ones like the waves thereof. (3:136, 167)

The imagery is largely that of 2 Kings 9:30–33 and Jeremiah 50:41–42. When the princes finally embrace the church, they will bring their subjects with them, leaving behind only sorcerers, whoremongers, murderers, and liars (3:138). The world will then be like "a crushed bunch of Herbs in which is no Vertue; or like a Furnace full of Dross, out of which the Gold is taken; or like an old crazy and ruinous House, from which is departed all Health and Happiness" (3:138). It is worth emphasizing that in Bunyan's view most monarchs and nobles will *not* embrace the church until well into the millennium; prior to that time they will remain persecutors seduced by the harlot of Babylon (3:166–69, 171).

Once the sovereigns and great ones have entered the new Jerusalem with their subjects, the world will have the doctrinal purity and scriptural worship so valued by Bunyan. Indeed, from the moment of Antichrist's fall, pure apostolic doctrine will hold sway, and upon it "Eternal Safety is built and stands." Apostolic theology is "the Opener, Expounder and Limiter of all Doctrines." The millennium, then, will bring to an end the doctrinal confusion resulting from the disparate views of competing religious groups, and heretics will be destroyed. So important was doctrinal purity to Bunyan that he made it the means through which souls will enter the new Jerusalem and the maintainer of the wall of salvation around the city (3:114, 115, 132, 184). Worship too will be restored to its primitive, pure state and sustained until Christ's second coming. Only then, asserted Bunyan, will it end, not, as the Ranters alleged, in the present age. Moreover, the church will also be "brought into exact Form and Order, lying every way level and square with the Rule, and *Golden Reed* of the New Testament" (3:117, 136, 155–57, 162).

Throughout the millennium, Bunyan declared, ministers will continue to preach, uttering from every scriptural text "most precious and heavenly Fire" and setting the world aflame with love of and delight in the things of God. The substance of their message will, of course, be apostolic doctrine (3:141). Only recipients of spiritual gifts can be ministers in this age, not "every babling fellow" or those who seek "their abilities from the rudiments of the world," a slap at most university-trained clergy. Those without such gifts, who must undergo their own great ejection, "shall be ashamed every one of his vision" and be held in contempt as prevaricators, even by their own parents. The godly "shall be ready to run them through, while they are prophesying in their rough garments," a caustic reference to formal clerical dress (3:147). The ministers of the millennium, whom Bunyan likened to porters and anglers, will vary in gifts and abilities, some being sons of thunder and others sons of consolation, an allusion to Mark 3:17 and Acts 4:36. Ultimately, the ministry will cease after the last of the elect has been converted and the saints have achieved the degree of perfection intended by God during their earthly sojourn (3:104–5, 160, 181).

Near the end of the millennium, according to Bunyan, "raging *Gog* and *Magog*," incited by the Devil, will attack the church in the battle of Armageddon, encamping around the new Jerusalem with the intent of overwhelming it. Other than referring to them as satanic agents, Bunyan does not identify Gog and Magog, the biblical source for which is Ezekiel 38 and 39. This will be Satan's last attempt to "swallow up all in everlasting oblivion," which God will prevent by raining fire and brimstone on the heads of Gog and Magog, destroying them. The duration of this episode will be short; Bunyan describes it as lasting only one evening, though he is almost certainly using the term figuratively, as he often does with temporal expressions. It will then be time for Christ to return again, a

position that marks Bunyan as a postmillenialist, and preside over the last judgment, a theme he would develop in his next book (3:155, 157, 171).

Drawing on his preoccupation with light and darkness as motifs, in *The Holy
City* he employs differing degrees of light to distinguish the stages of church history,
an approach to which his biblical material lent itself. His usage also reflects the importance of light to him as a result of his psychological struggles, and perhaps as
well owing to the likely darkness of the Bedford county jail, where adequate light by
which to write would have been treasured. In *The Holy City* Bunyan associates
darkness with Antichrist; it prevents the godly from recognizing one another's faith
and language, and keeps them separated from each other in judgment and affection. As he knew from his own experience, darkness is "an empty, forlorn, desolate,
solitary, and discomforting state," whereas light brings warmth and pleasure, enabling things to grow and flourish. Light is especially "pleasant to such men that have
for several years been held in the Chains of affliction," a clear reference to his own
periods of oppressive gloom (3:94–95, 135). Understandably, he found light and
darkness useful in explicating the church's history. During the second major era,
for instance, when the church lay in Antichrist's dungeon for more than a thousand
years, it had little light, a third part of the gospel's glory being hidden "by the smoak
of the Pit," or by Antichrist's fog and mist. During the time of altar-work, the light
improved, though it is significantly better during the period of temple-work. As the
time of city-work nears, Christ's light "begins to shine unto perfect day" in the
church, and as the saints make their journey out of Babylon, God's light leads the
way. With judgment, light conveys "sweetness and pleasantness into the Hearts of
those that have the knowledge of them: Every step . . . shall be as it were in Honey
and Butter" (3:90, 92, 134–35, 153–54).

The vision in Revelation on which Bunyan based so much of *The Holy City* is
suffused with light, perhaps explaining why, in part, he found the passage attractive
when he was asked to address his fellow prisoners; he may also have thought it relevant owing to the approach of the year 1666, which some contemporaries believed
had apocalyptic significance because 666 is the number of the beast in Revelation
13:18. Even the title-page of Bunyan's book refers to the new Jerusalem's "Goodly
Light," the source of which is Christ. The church, whose virtues Bunyan compares
to a shining light, gathers the elect within its walls by its beams (3:93, 140–41). He
likens the gates of the new Jerusalem to pearls with a sweet, sparkling light, and the
city's street or way of holiness, he says, manifests perfect light, grace, faith, and
comfort, all of which the inhabitants will enjoy (3:148–49). Given his psychological
experience, the association of light and comfort is suggestive. The street is paved
with gold, which he interprets as an indication of spiritual treasures that beget light
(3:151–52), and the foundations of the city's walls are adorned with precious
stones—apostolic doctrines that "spangle and sparkle" (3:140–41). Embellishing

this theology are gifts and grace that make it shine, casting its golden rays before the nations. Although the radiance of pure gospel worship is glorious, ultimately the city will no longer need the light of the sun and moon, for God himself will be the church's eternal light, and in heaven nights will be no more (3:158, 160–61, 171). The church will "have her Sun at the height; her Light as the light of seven dayes, and shall go no more down for ever." The darkness of night, the pervasive symbol of evil and despair in Bunyan's mind, will be banished forever from the saints' presence, to be replaced by light and warmth, symbolizing happiness and comfort (3:192–93). "'Twil be then alwayes Summer, alwayes Sunshine" (3:196).[22]

Writing *The Holy City*, which required Bunyan to concentrate on the exegetical task and involved a highly optimistic theme, left little time for gloomy introspection and thus brought him from a barren, despondent state to one in which his focus was on light, warmth, and assurance. Throughout the text he refers to the children of God, the elect, with no traces of doubt about his own spiritual status.[23] *The Holy City* is a triumphal work, its author certain of the elect's victory over persecution and secure in the faith that Antichrist, the source of despair, doubt, and blasphemy, will soon be bound with chains for a thousand years. As he drew his book to a close, Bunyan looked forward to "a Golden World" in which the wicked would be ashamed, especially those who had persecuted the church. His work of exegesis had not opened his prison door, but it had uplifted his spirit, and he exultantly quoted the affirmation in Revelation 22:6 that the building of the new Jerusalem "*MUST SHORTLY be done*" (3:196).

## "Now Is the End Come"[24]: The Last Judgment

Thematically, *The Resurrection of the Dead, and Eternall Judgement* is the sequel to *The Holy City*, picking up where the latter concluded and carrying the account from Christ's second coming to the last judgment. Charles Doe was therefore almost certainly correct in assigning a date of 1665 to the only edition known to have been published in Bunyan's lifetime.[25] The new work differs from *The Holy City* in its methodology, for Bunyan largely eschewed the exegetical strategy of decoding types (some of which are scattered throughout the book[26]) in favor of a homiletic

---

[22] Arthur Dent thought Christians would find the study of Revelation comforting as well as preparation for impending trials. *The Ruine of Rome* (London, 1644; 1st published, 1603), sigs. B1v-B3v.

[23] See, e.g., *MW*, 3:87, 90, 108–9, 129, 143, 148–49, 159–60, 162, 177, 182, 186, 189.

[24] *MW*, 3:290.

[25] Doe's list, *ad cal.* John Bunyan, *The Heavenly Foot-Man: or, a Description of the Man That Gets to Heaven* (London, 1698), [76].

[26] See, e.g., *MW*, 3:216, 227, 240–41, 259, 277.

approach. Intending this work for both the godly and the unregenerate, he addressed his readers as if he were preaching from a pulpit (*MW*, 3:203).

The same confident, triumphal tone characteristic of *The Holy City* suffuses
*The Resurrection of the Dead*. Both were composed in a period when Bunyan felt
assured he was among the elect. Indeed, in *The Resurrection of the Dead* he made
effective use of his years of turbulence to describe the affliction faced by some
saints as well as the eternal horrors experienced by the damned. In contrasting
the saints' struggles in this world with their glory in the next, he echoed his own
trials: "While we are here, we are attended with so many weaknesses and infirmities, that in time the least sin or sickness is too hard for us," sapping our strength
and life (3:222–23). Yet afflictions are beneficial because they "make the heart
more deep, more experimentall, more knowing, and profound" (3:238–39). As he
sought to find providential meaning in an imprisonment that was now nearly five
years in duration, he concluded that the elect undergo much hardship and abuse
in order to leave the damned without excuse at the last judgment. "God, by the
lengthening out the life of his people that are scattered here and there . . . in this
world, is making work for the day of Judgment, and . . . will by the Conversion,
life, patience, self-denial, and heavenly mindedness of his dear children, give [the
condemned] a heavy and most dreadful blow" (3:280). In words that have an
unmistakably autobiographical ring, Bunyan drew on his experience to describe
the mental state of the wicked at the last judgment: "Now will the gastly Jaws of
despair gape upon thee, and now will condemnings of Conscience, like Thunderclaps, continually batter against thy weary Spirit" (3:250). When he wrote of the
everlasting punishment of the damned, he used not only the commonplace visions of a fiery hell but also a projection of the mental agonies that had tormented him throughout most of the 1650s. The condemned must eternally suffer
what he had experienced temporally—"tortured consciences." In addition to
physical pain, the wicked will be "flamingly tormented" with *thoughts* of having
rejected divine grace, the very thoughts that had caused Bunyan so much anguish. Knowing how horrific a conscience tortured with despair, desperation, and
shame could be, he deemed this one of the most painful punishments the
damned must endure for eternity (3:289–91).

Bunyan also provided hints of prison life. The example of a felon on his way
to arraignment, shackled in irons, "his Fetters . . . making a noise on his heels"
and his heart full of fear, was drawn from life in the Bedford jail. So too was Bunyan's depiction of the gnawing terror of a criminal about to be sentenced to the
gallows, a dread he shared during the early years of his incarceration (3:248). Felons peering through a grate were reminders of the appalling condition of prisoners in hell, but they must also have reflected his own longing for freedom (3:258).
At times he must have communicated through such a grate to his wife and chil

dren as well as fellow members of the Bedford congregation. Visitors were especially welcome, and he reminded his readers that Christ took pains to recognize those who called on prisoners for the gospel (3:236, referring to Matthew 25:36). Unable to escape the stench that pervaded a seventeenth-century jail, Bunyan attributed foul odors to the wicked and to hell. When the damned are resurrected, their condition will be loathsome, reeking in the nostrils of God as though "they had the most irksome Plague-soars in the World running on them." Hell itself has a "hot scalding stink," like the odor of burning brimstone—the repulsive, sickening stench of burning flesh (3:249–50, 258).[27]

At the outset of his work Bunyan denounced those responsible for his incarceration, though on erroneous grounds. He was in prison, he spuriously argued, because he believed in the resurrection of the dead, something his oppressors professed to allow; hypocritically, however, they prosecuted "*the power of those truths in others, which themselves in words profess*" (3:204). He was on surer footing when he castigated those who persecute the elect on the pretense of holiness, and he surely expressed his own feelings when he averred that the elect in heaven long for the day of Christ's vengeance against his enemies (3:211, 261).

As the text for *The Resurrection of the Dead* Bunyan selected Acts 24:14–15, in which Paul expresses his belief in the raising of the deceased, both just and unjust, and notes that for this faith he was deemed a heretic. Sensing an affinity between himself and Paul, Bunyan explicitly indicated that he shared both the apostle's belief in the resurrection of the dead and his experience of persecution for that commitment. The following year, when he completed *Grace Abounding*, he made this affinity part of the book's title, claiming that he, like Paul, was the chief of sinners. Bunyan opened *The Resurrection of the Dead* with Paul's arraignment, artistically setting the stage for the great trials of the just and the unjust that dominate the book. Paul's profession was Bunyan's, and Bunyan used the condemnation of persecutors in the last judgment to vindicate their joint cause (3:204).

Bunyan attached substantial importance to the doctrine of the resurrection, which he professed to hold in awe. The Bible, he said, centers on this doctrine, the denial of which leads to satanic errors. Chief among these was his belief that repudiating the resurrection means denying Christ rose from the dead; this is tantamount, in his estimation, to destroying the Christian religion. If there is no resurrection, then God has lied, preaching deliverance from sin and death is vain, and those who believe in this doctrine are damned. To reject the precept, argued Bunyan, is to open the floodgates to impiety and "the most outrageous lusts"; for Bunyan the doctrine of the resurrection was, *inter alia*, a means of social control (3:205, 212–14, 227, 247–48). Among those who disavowed this tenet were the Ranters and

[27]Cf. the reference in *The Heavenly Foot-Man* to stinking dungeons. *MW*, 5:164.

the Quakers, though he explicitly mentioned only the former in this tract. Those who say the resurrection has already occurred, as did the Quakers, undermine the faith of those who hear them and simultaneously express a view that "is so far from . . . the Doctrine of God, that it eateth out good and wholesome Doctrine, even as Cankers eat the face and flesh of a man" (3:207, 214, 228).[28] If there is no resurrection, Bunyan reflected, those who suffer, as he obviously did, are the most miserable of all people for they have forsaken present gratification in the expectation of illusory rewards in the hereafter. Echoing Paul in 1 Corinthians 15:32, he asked, "If the dead rise not, what shall I be the better for all my trouble that here I met with for the Gospel of Christ?" For his incarceration to have meaning, the dead must be resurrected. Shorn of this belief, he would have no purpose in his imprisonment and no reason to cause his family to struggle in his absence. This is not to say that he developed his belief in the resurrection while a prisoner to make sense of his suffering, for that faith had been expressed in his earliest, pre-imprisonment works. If anything, confinement strengthened his commitment to this doctrine as the gospel's quintessence and its usefulness in helping believers weather temptation, affliction, and doubt (3:204, 212–14).

In his comments on the timing of the resurrection, Bunyan was strikingly at variance with what he had said in *The Holy City*. In both books, the resurrection occurs following the second coming of Christ. As we have seen, Bunyan argued in *The Holy City* that this would happen at the conclusion of the millennium, which was at least a thousand years in the future. In contrast, in his sequel he told his readers that the time of the resurrection was "*at hand*" (3:203). The millennium plays virtually no role in *The Resurrection of the Dead*, probably because Bunyan assumed he had already said enough on this theme. He does assert that the elect who appear at the last judgment will have imperfections which require purging, a view that is harmonious with the less than perfect state he ascribed to the elect during the millennium in *The Holy City*. Moreover, in *The Resurrection of the Dead* Bunyan asserts that following the last judgment the elect will dwell in heaven with God, not on earth during the millennium. Thus he does not appear to have changed his mind on any (other) substantive point regarding the last times. His assertion of the last judgment's imminence should probably be taken as homiletic license rather than a literal statement of his belief (3:228–30, 243). Whatever the time of the last judgment, he believed it had been divinely determined (3:246).

At the resurrection, according to Bunyan, God will raise the bodies of the

---

[28] Paul's statement in 1 Corinthians 15:50 that flesh and blood cannot inherit the kingdom was regularly cited by opponents of a bodily resurrection, but Bunyan interpreted flesh and blood to mean corruption, weakness, and mortality. *MW*, 3:218–20.

elect and the damned. With respect to their "nature," the bodies of the elect will be the same as those of believers during their earthly sojourn, though their "state" will be far more glorious. The resurrected body differs from the earthly one as the sun's light diverges from the moon's; the former is "sown" in incorruption, glory, and power, the latter in corruption, dishonor, and weakness. God will give the resurrected body beauty, splendor, and luster, turning a natural body into a spiritual one (3:216–22). "The Body when it ariseth, will be so swallowed up of life and immortality, that it will be, as if it had lost its own Humane Nature; though, in truth, the same substantial real Nature is every whit there still" (3:223). To explain this, Bunyan used the analogy of an apothecary who takes something bitter and foul smelling and candies the exterior. At the last judgment, the elect "shall be so candied, by being swallow'd up of Life . . . That we shall be, as if we were all Spirit, when in truth, it is but this Body that is swallowed up of Life." The natural core must remain, according to Bunyan, or it will not be the elect who are in heaven. This candied, "spiritual Body" will be able to ascend to heaven and descend at will, unrestricted by physical constraints. The spiritual bodies of the saints will be like that of Christ, whose body, though comprised of the same flesh and bones that were nailed to the cross, could in its resurrected state be visible or invisible, moving at will through physical objects. Citing the cases of Elijah, Ezekiel, and Philip, Bunyan insisted that God can make such things possible even before the last judgment. In these instances God provided examples of how bodies "thus spiritualized" can act as if they are angels (3:223–25). For Bunyan, God must resurrect the bodies of the elect because believers are members of the risen body of Christ, who purchased them by his death. Moreover, the bodies of the godly are temples of the Holy Spirit that have suffered along with their souls for the gospel and therefore deserve to enjoy heavenly bliss (3:208–10).

Bunyan had much less to say about the nature of the resurrected bodies of the damned. God will raise their bodies because they were partners with their souls in sinning and must be punished. Unlike the elect, who are resurrected in their spiritual bodies, the unjust are raised as "naked lumps of sinful nature," smelling polluted, and as dirty as if they had come from the filthiest hole on earth. All of this suggests bodies that remain quite physical. So too does Bunyan's insistence that the damned will be dispatched to eternal perdition in both body and soul, and that they will suffer the excruciating pain of burning (3:242–43, 249–51, 287).

In this work Bunyan responded to the objection that it is unfair of God to condemn the reprobate because he opted not to predestine them to eternal life. Bunyan refused to permit the accused to use this objection at their trial, insisting that they understood how "God could in his Prerogative Royal, without prejudice to them that are damned, chuse and refuse at pleasure; and besides, they at that day shall be convinced, that there was so much reality, and downright willingness in

God, in every tender of Grace and mercy, to the worst of men; and also so much goodness, justness, and reasonableness in every command of the Gospel of grace, which they were so often intreated and beseeched to imbrace, that they will be drowned in the conviction . . . that they did refuse love, grace, [and] reason" (3:281–82). The wicked are damned because they sinned, insisted Bunyan, not because they were denied saving grace. In sinning they deliberately, knowingly yielded to Satan, turning away from God, and thus the responsibility for their fate rests directly on them. Yet Bunyan the pastor seemed to wrestle with Bunyan the theologian in dealing with this doctrine. On the one hand, he implied that those who are not elect have the ability to respond positively to entreaties that they repent and believe; the damned, he said, refuse to convert during the day of grace and ignore all urging to make their calling and election sure. In the midst of the trial scene, Bunyan interrupted the narrative to include a pastoral plea for unconverted readers to repent and for professed believers to make certain their faith and repentance accord with the Bible; clearly, he assumed his readers were capable of responding positively to his admonitions. On the other hand, he asserted that none can be convinced without the inner working of the Holy Spirit, and this assistance, as he elsewhere explained, is limited to the elect (3:249–50, 259, 273, 275–76).[29]

A book on the last judgment provided Bunyan with an opportunity to put his persecutors on trial, in effect reversing the legal procedures of 1660–61. In John Knott's aptly chosen phrase, this is Bunyan's "cry of blood."[30] Because the outcome of the trial was known to virtually every reader, he faced a daunting challenge in building and sustaining a sense of drama. He succeeded reasonably well by avoiding substantive discussion of theological issues, such as the nature of God or the role of evil in a universe created by an omnipotent deity, and instead vividly imagining what would happen at the last judgment and how the damned in particular would feel. In this way he appealed to people's elemental interest in what occurs after death. Since the late medieval era, paintings of the last judgment on church walls had helped viewers formulate visual images about this subject, and Bunyan's book contributed to the mental imagery by providing an account of what might transpire when Christ formally sentences the damned and welcomes the elect into eternal bliss. In the great trial scene the human element is paramount, and Bunyan, ever the preacher, plays on emotions to persuade the godly to make their calling and election sure, and on the ungodly to repent while they still have time (3:203).

At the last judgment, Bunyan explained, God will raise the saints first. From

---

[29] For the limitation of justifying faith to the elect, see, e.g., *MW*, 2:77–81.

[30] John R. Knott, "Bunyan and the Cry of Blood," in *Awakening Words*, ed. Gay, Randall, and Zinck, 51–67.

the moment of their physical death, the souls of the elect have been with God while their bodies are in their graves. On the day of judgment their shining, spiritual bodies will rise, uniting with their souls for the final accounting before the judgment seat of Christ (3:222, 229). Every sin of each saint will then be "brought fresh upon the stage . . . that [the elect] may see and be sensible for ever, what grace and mercy hath laid hold upon them" (3:233). After the saints confess how they have erred in all these ways, Christ will pronounce their "eternal acquittance" before proceeding to examine each good deed of every saint (3:235). While such acts have no bearing on one's salvation, they will determine the nature of eternal rewards. Bunyan's heaven is not a state of equality but a meritocracy with "places of degrees and honour." A new, spiritual nobility will be created, providing the humble with an opportunity to earn superior eternal status by amassing good deeds during their lifetimes. "Order, as it is comely in Earth, so much more in the Kingdom of the God of Order, in Heaven" (3:241). Unlike degrees of earthly status, which are based on birth and wealth, those in heaven will be determined exclusively by service for God, including the things that most concerned Bunyan—converting souls, counseling believers, and suffering for the gospel. Rewards will be bestowed for all the hidden acts of Christianity, such as seeking divine assistance to suppress one's lusts, praying for more grace and light, and expressing faith in Christ. "There hath not one tear dropped from thy tender eye against thy lusts, the love of this World, or for more Communion with Jesus Christ, but as it is now in the bottle of God; so then it shall bring forth plenty of reward" (2:237). When the awards have been distributed, the saints, garbed in royal apparel and wearing crowns, will take their places on thrones, ready to commence the task of judging the wicked (3:242).

The ungodly's punishment, avowed Bunyan, is reserved until the judgment day. Until then, the wicked man "may go to his Grave in his banner, and rest within his Tomb," a reference to the sometimes lavish funerals of the socially prominent. Bunyan thought that at the time of death the souls of the reprobate are consigned to hell, from which they will rejoin their bodies at the last judgment (3:244, 250). They will then appear in the heavenly court, shackled by their sins and accompanied by the angels of darkness. Before them will be Christ, "the Lord chief Judge," flanked by princes, "Heavenly Nobles," apostles, prophets, and saints, all in their royal attire. As the bar before which the prisoners must stand, "a mighty fire and tempest" will be created by Christ to keep the accused at an appropriate distance. While the prisoners wait "with gastly Jaws," the four books of death and life will be brought to the lord chief judge (3:251).

The first to be opened will be the Book of the Creatures, which lays out the principles of nature by which people can ascertain they are God's creatures, and records how they have acted contrary to those axioms. The three natural principles teach that humans, as rational creatures, can discern the existence of a deity or supreme being; that they should seek after that deity in order to enjoy eternal fellowship with him; and that they should act justly and equitably. "The natural proneness that is in all men, to *Devotion and Religion*, that is, of one kind or another, doth clearly tell us, that they by the Book of nature, which Book is themselves, do read, that there is one great and eternall God." Everyone has transgressed against each of these principles by failing to worship and reverence God sufficiently, by seeking present pleasures rather than future happiness, and by committing contemptible acts and harboring vile affections rather than treating others equitably. After this evidence has been laid out, the second half of the Book of the Creatures will be opened. This portion is concerned with "*the mystery of the Creatures*," by which Bunyan meant the extent to which the entire creation reveals much about God, human nature, and how people should behave. "This Book of the Creatures, it is so excellent, and so full, so easie, and so suiting the capacity of all, that there is not one man in the World, but is catched, convicted, and cast by it." Literacy is not required to read the Book of the Creatures, nor is the Bible necessary to discover a great deal about God and oneself. Bunyan does not indicate if the knowledge gleaned from the Book of the Creatures is sufficient for salvation, for he is only interested in using the natural world to condemn the wicked for having "slighted all the instructions" God gave them in nature (3:252–60).

Although the evidence against the damned is already sufficient for conviction, the Book of God's Remembrance will then be opened. In it God, the master historian and archivist, has recorded every good thing the saints have done and all the evil deeds of his adversaries. "It will be marvellous to behold, how by thousands, and ten thousands, God will call from their secret places, those sins, that one would have thought, had been dead, and buried, and forgotten; yea, how he will shew before the Sun, such things, so base, and so horrid, that one would think, it was not in the hearts of any to commit." Now, for the first time, everyone will know "what Legions of hellish wickednesses" lurk like cockatrices in seemingly decent people. As this great parade of evil takes place, the wicked will remember every sermon they heard, every biblical chapter they read, every twinge of conscience, every admonition to reform, and every unfulfilled vow to repent. Each of these things will afflict the souls of the damned like piercing arrows, biting serpents, and stinging adders. A debilitating sense of shame, which Bunyan knew so well from his own period of turmoil, will wash over each person standing before the lord chief judge. Like a thief whose pockets are examined in the public market, "thou must have . . . the bottom of thy heart searched . . . before thy Neighbour, whom thou hast wronged, and before the Devills, whom thou hast served; yea, before God, whom thou hast despised." From this rite of shame the accused cannot escape (3:260–63).

The Book of the Law, the Ten Commandments, will then be opened, but this, Bunyan says, applies primarily to those with knowledge of it. The "Heathens" will be judged by the law as it was inscribed on their hearts at the creation, that is, the principles recorded in the Book of the Creatures. For those subject to the Mosaic law, it is the most rigorous, for its prescriptions and prohibitions are the plainest. "This Law . . . is the chief, and most pure Resemblance of the Justice and holiness of the Heavenly Majesty, and doth hold forth to all men, the sharpness and keenness of his wrath above the other two [books]." With sinking spirits, the accused will begin to see the fierce wrath awaiting them. When this book is opened, Bunyan expects every damned soul to experience inner thunder and lightning, earthquakes and tempests—turmoil worse than he endured during his agonizing travail. Every act will be measured against the strictness and purity of this law, and "legall Repentance, cold profession, [and] good meanings, thinkings, and doings" will be found wanting (3:263–67).

As the accused, their hearts "throbbing and pricking," desperately contrive to evade their fate, the prosecution will call its witnesses. God will testify that the defendants did not continue in the state of nature in which they were created, that they have been fruitless and impetuous, that he witnessed all the transgressions recorded in the Book of Remembrance, and that the wicked disobeyed divine law. The consciences of the accused will be the second witness, crying amen to what God testified: "Even the Consciences of the most pagan sinners in the World, will have sufficiently wherewith to accuse, to condemn, and to make paleness appear in their faces, and breaking in their loins." The final witness will be the defendants' secret thoughts, the force of which Bunyan knew from his own tortured experience. They include atheism, false views of God or human nature, presumptions of being able to transgress without punishment, and knowingly sinning against light and knowledge. "By the variety of their thoughts, [the wicked] shall be proved unstable, ignorant, wandring Stars, Clouds carryed with a Tempest, without order or guidance, and taken Captive of the Devil at his will," much as Bunyan himself had once been (3:267–71).

These witnesses having made their compelling accusations, the defendants, briny tears flowing like rivers from their eyes, will make their plea. With groans and ghastly countenances, they will tell of having known that God sent a savior to deliver them from their transgressions and of having professed him as such. They will point out that they attended the holy ordinances, that some among them had been preachers who accomplished wonderful works, and that they repudiated the profane world. A great many of the ministers will have been "sparkling wits" who had "the Word and truths of Christ at their fingers ends," but their religion was only in their heads, not their hearts (3:271–72, 281). To put an end to these "cavils and objections" and to ensure that the trial is both legal and convincing, the

Book of Life will be opened. In it is recorded information about election, conversion, and a gospel-conversation as well as the names of the elect. The accused will pore over the pages, vainly seeking their names, their agony compounded when they see the names of their loved ones. As they read about conversion, they will realize that their religious experience was only notional. Alluding to the Gentleman Usher of the Black Rod, who was empowered to detain members of Parliament charged with committing crimes, Bunyan envisions that the defendants will find their names listed "under the black Rod, in the Kings black Book, where he hath recorded all his enemies and Traytors." The rules of evidence are unforgivingly strict: "If thou miss but one letter in thy evidence, thou art gone; for though thou mayst deceive thy own heart with Brass, instead of Gold, and with Tin instead of Silver . . . yet God will not be so put off." Nor will the defendants' actions be found in the last part of the Book of Life, which records the testimonies and worthy acts of the elect after their conversion. Finding nothing in the Book of Life to aid the accused, Christ will close it, pronouncing the defendants sons of perdition (3:272–79). More evidence will be presented, including the unkept vows and promises of those at the bar, and the defendants' condemnation of sin in others while not refraining from it themselves. Additional witnesses could be called, but Bunyan deemed this number sufficient (3:283–85).

The lord chief judge will pronounce the sentence, finding the accused guilty of high treason against God and the murder of their own souls, for which he will sentence them to the everlasting fire prepared for the Devil and his angels. Although shorn of all hope, the guilty will cry out, "being loath to let go all for lost, . . . even as the man that is fallen into the River, will catch hold of any thing, when he is struggling for life, though it tend to hold him faster under the water, to drown him." As the condemned plead for life, they will emit a final, faint groan, uttering the words of Matthew 25:44. When, they will wonder, had they not given Jesus meat and drink, or failed to cloth him and take him in, or been remiss in visiting him when he was sick or in prison? In response, the lord chief judge will make his final pronouncement, ordering the guilty, various monarchs and emperors among them, to depart to their eternal fate. "O heavy day! O heavy Word!" They knew the horrors that awaited them, for throughout the trial they had "a most famous view" of both heaven and hell (3:275, 285–86).

What they saw, as painted by Bunyan, recalling *A Few Sighs from Hell*, was fire, brimstone, the bottomless pit, and "flaming beds." This is a place where they must eat and drink fire, and lie down amid the flames—fire, in Bunyan's estimation, being the most insufferable pain. He went so far as to aver that God delights in burning sinners to ease his mind and satisfy his justice. The damned will be consigned to "the Jaws of eternal desperation," to perpetual darkness, suffering not only indescribable pain but tortured consciences and the flaming torment of anguished thoughts. Although they hope for annihilation, even this will be denied. "A living death shall feed upon them, they shall never be spiritually alive, nor yet absolutely dead." As the godly will receive varying rewards in heaven, so the damned will suffer differing degrees of punishment, though always for eternity. Those who had the most light, conviction, and opportunity to convert will fall the farthest in hell, sinking the deepest "into the Jaws of Eternal Misery." The worst, it seems, is Judas owing to his betrayal of Jesus (3:248, 258, 286–92). Because Bunyan's persecutors were among those who enjoyed the light of the gospel and numerous opportunities to repent, their place in hell will be among the most miserable, painful, and anguish-laden. Nonconformist readers would have understood this point, but a censor or magistrate, assuming he was one of the godly, would have missed it. In stark contrast to the fate of the damned, Bunyan could look forward to ultimate vindication and perhaps one of the more honored places among the saints for eternity. Presumably such thoughts helped him through the dark nights in prison, bereft of his family's company and the comfort of most of his friends.

### "Read My Lines"[31]: Poetry and the End Times

The burst of creative activity that followed Bunyan's recovery in late 1664 from recurrent melancholy included two poetic works, *One Thing Is Needful* and *Ebal and Gerizzim: or the Blessing and the Curse*.[32] Both works deal with the themes of death, judgment, heaven, and hell. Just as *The Holy City* and *The Resurrection of the Dead* are coupled works, so too are the new volumes of verse, as Bunyan explicitly stated in the opening lines of *Ebal and Gerizzim*:

> Besides what I said of the Four last Things,
> And of the weal and woe that from them springs;
> An after-word still runneth in my mind. (*MW*, 6:105)

In his catalogue of Bunyan's works, Doe placed the two poetic books between *I Will Pray* and *A Mapp* on the one hand and *The Holy City* on the other. Although no first edition of either work appears to be extant, Doe's dating is fairly close to the mark. As will be seen, *One Thing Is Needful* parallels *The Holy City* in its concern with the theme of light and darkness, whereas *Ebal and Gerizzim*, like *The Resurrection of the Dead*, is clearly a sequel, brimming with confidence and trumpeting the triumphal spirit of its predecessor. So striking is the parallelism that Bunyan may have worked on the prose and verse volumes in tandem. Certainly his renewed interest in writing, on his own testimony, occurred first in his expo-

---

[31] *MW*, 6:64.

[32] As with *Prison Meditations*, Stephen Thompson copied *One Thing Is Needful* into his manuscript volume of verse. Bodl., Rawlinson Poetry 58, fols. 1r–24r.

sition of Revelation 21:10 to 22:4. Yet *One Thing Is Needful*, which also manifests unmistakable signs of his recent bout with despondency, must have been composed contemporaneously with *The Holy City* or immediately following it. A publication date of 1665 is thus likely.

Although *Ebal and Gerizzim* is the sequel to *One Thing Is Needful*, Bunyan made a significant artistic change in the later work, eschewing the ballad-stanzas, or quatrains, used in his first three books of verse in favor of the more sophisticated iambic pentameter couplet. As Graham Midgley has observed, "Bunyan's handling of this more popular couplet tradition, as with the broadside ballad, was to complicate and give it more sinew, to reduce its areas of tedium, and shape a verse which caught, with a minimum of distortion, his own personal voice" (*MW*, 6:li). Bunyan learned this poetic technique by reading the verse of others, almost certainly while he was incarcerated. Midgley points to Thomas Jenner and Benjamin Keach as possible sources of influence. Bunyan's friend Henry Jessey would later urge readers of *A Looking-Glass for Children* (1672) to ponder Abraham Cheare's lessons; Jessey may have taught Bunyan the value of religious verse to spread his message and suggested that he read Cheare, though the latter's *Words in Season* was not published until 1668, several years after Bunyan composed *Ebal and Gerizzim*.[33] Jenner, whose *The Soules Solace, or Thirtie and One Spirituall Emblems* (1626) was reprinted as *Divine Mysteries That Cannot Be Seene, Made Plain by That Which May Be Seene* in 1651, is a likely source, not least because he used the conversational style of couplet-writing Bunyan adopted in *Ebal and Gerizzim*. Jenner also made extensive use of moral emblems, or similitudes, much as Bunyan later did in *The Pilgrim's Progress* and *A Book for Boys and Girls*. Jenner's similitude about a prisoner facing execution developed a theme Bunyan himself used:

> See therefore what the Prisoners doe, that heare
> Deaths doom; no more themselves deboist they beare,
> But pensively tow'rd execution goe;
> Take patterne then by them, and do thou so,
> Doe not the *Candle* of thy life extinguish
> Before thou *grace* pursue, and *sinne* relinquish.[34]

Keach, whose major poetic works postdate *Ebal and Gerizzim*, is unlikely to have inspired Bunyan's adoption of pentameter couplets. Thus during his recovery Bunyan found cheer and inspiration not only in the twenty-first and twenty-second chapters of Revelation but also, it seems, in the verse of Jenner.

---

[33] For Cheare see *BDBR*, s.v.

[34] Thomas Jenner, *Divine Mysteries That Cannot Be Seene, Made Plain by That Which May Be Seene* (London, 1651), poem 15.

Bunyan wrote *One Thing Is Needful* with his recent troubled state fresh in his memory. From his own experience he knew the blackness of utter despair, the helplessness and irrational grief that characterize the impenetrable depths of depression, and he made this horrific experience a fundamental characteristic of what the damned undergo eternally. Theirs is a state of despair unimaginable except for those who have plunged into deep depression.

> . . . take from them all help and stay,
> And leave them to dispair,
> Which feeds upon them night and day,
> This is the damned's share. (6:95)

Devoid of all hope and remedy, the condemned

> . . . sink
> Into the jaws of misery,
> And Seas of sorrows drink.

Enveloped on every side with oppressive grief and helplessness,

> Headlong into despair they slide,
> Bereft of all relief. (6:93)

Immersed in an everlasting "Gulf of grief and woe," they weep uncontrollably, their "brinish tears" flowing down their faces, their eyes bleary, their loins shaking, and their hearts aching.

> Alas! my grief, hard hap had I,
> These dolors here to find,
> A living death in Hell I lie,
> Involv'd with grief of mind. (6:93, 97)

"To live, and yet be dead" is the experience of the victim of depression, as Bunyan well knew. Hell's ultimate horror is not physical pain but the blackness of eternal depression, the unfathomable despair of those doomed to "cry, Alas, for evermore" (6:95, 102).

As he did in *The Holy City*, Bunyan made much of light and darkness in *One Thing Is Needful*. Hell is a place of eternal night, an abode of utter darkness and "horror strange" (6:70, 90). The chains that bind the damned are those of darkness itself. Searching for images to depict the inky depths of this black despondency, he likened the reprobate to those whose eyes had been blinded by "the steam, and smoak, And flames of Brimstone," yet he heightened their misery by enabling them to see the saints in glory, much as a depressed person, though encompassed in personal blackness, can observe—almost surrealistically—others enjoying the pleasures of life (6:91, 93). While the reprobate are entrapped in perpetual night, the elect bathe in light's warmth, ecstatic in their bliss. So bright is the "exceeding light" of Christ's heavenly countenance "That Angels can't behold his Face" (6:84). The saved

> Shall in that light which no eye can
> Approach unto, behold
> The rayes and beams of glory, and
> Find there his name inrol'd,
> Among those glittering Stars of light. (6:70–71)

In the elect, light and life "Will rise like everlasting springs," enabling their glory to shine forever with a brilliance equal to the sun's. Heaven is thus the antithesis of depression:

> No night is here for to eclipse
> Its spangling rayes so bright,
> Nor doubt, nor fear, to shut the lips
> Of those within this light. (6:84–85, 88)

For Bunyan much of heaven's allure was eternal liberation from ever again plunging into the seemingly interminable despair that can "shut the lips" (6:88). Heaven's bliss—warmth and joy everlasting—stands in stark contrast to the endless gloom and grim hopelessness of hell. Such happiness, such light, such freedom from the threat of renewed immersion in the yawning abyss is the dream of every victim of depression.

In *One Thing Is Needful*, as in *The Holy City*, Bunyan incorporated allusions to his prison life and the struggle with despair it occasioned. Hell, he reflected, was a place where inmates were never bailed, a prison whose locks and bars were the divine decree of eternal reprobation. The long winter nights in the Bedford jail enabled him to envision hell in both physical and psychological terms:

> A Pit that's bottomless is this,
> A Gulf of grief and woe:
> A Dungeon which they cannot miss,
> That will themselves undoe. (6:92–94)

The "brazen bars" through which the damned could watch the saints in glory were an extension of the grate through which Bunyan would have glimpsed his own children as they grew up, largely deprived of his paternal love and supervision. Surely this reinforced his love for them, but no less certainly the experience embodied its own agony as he sensed the acute pain of physical separation. Worse was the state of the condemned in Hades, where gazing on the saints brought no comfort:

> . . . this will not their grief allay,
> But to them torment bee. (6:93)

As painful as incarceration was for Bunyan, he survived by seizing the hope prof-
fered in the gospel. Convinced his torment was temporal, he looked forward to
an eternity not only devoid of hopelessness and blackness but enriched by his
family's reunification:

> Our friends that lived godly here,
> Shall there be found again,
> The Wife, the Child, and Father dear. (6:88)

In addition to recalling his psychological battle with the forces of despair to
convey a sense of hell and heaven, Bunyan began spending more time reflecting
on his earlier spiritual struggles. The outcome of this rumination, whether intended at this time or not, would be the composition of his spiritual autobiography, *Grace Abounding*. Above all, he remembered the encounters waged within
him and the powerful role played by guilt, which had made his "Conscience start,
And quake at every thing." Conscience, as he well knew, was

> . . . the slaughter-shop,
> There hangs the Ax, and Knife,
> 'Tis there the worm makes all things hot,
> And wearies out the life. (6:69, 94)[35]

But the elect triumph through grace, and Bunyan, the pervasive gloom of the
prison notwithstanding, looked forward to the day when he and the other saints
would recount their deliverance

> I' th'open face of Heaven;
> Still calling to remembrance
> How fiercely they were driven
> By deadly foe, who did pursue
> As swift as Eagles fly. (6:77–78)

Indeed, he would soon choose to tell the story of his own struggles with this perilous foe in his spiritual autobiography. He already knew that once in heaven the
saints would realize

> These tempting times that here we have,
> We there shall see, were good. (6:83)

This realization was not only a key to the strength of his spiritual convictions but
a necessary precondition of his decision to recount his "tempting times" for the
benefit of serious readers.

Not surprisingly, some of the stanzas in *One Thing Is Needful* have an unmis-

---

[35] The image may have been adapted from Luther, who likened the pope's vows,
masses, pardons, and purgatory to the "slaughter-house of consciences." *Galatians*, 217.

takable autobiographical ring:

> My Feet to evil I let run,
> And Tongue of folly talk;
> My Eye to vanity hath gone,
> Thus did I vainly walk.  (6:98)

In *Grace Abounding* he would write of that period during his youth when he "went on in sin with great greediness of mind, still grudging that I could not be so satisfied with it as I would" (*GA*, §26). The corresponding stanza in *One Thing Is Needful* captures the same intensity:

> I did as greatly toil, and strain
> My self with Sin to please,
> As if that everlasting gain
> Could have been found in these.  (*MW*, 6:98)

In *Grace Abounding* Bunyan would recall how he had once been in such despair about his presumed reprobation that he had deemed humans "the most doleful of all the Creatures," and had regarded himself as more loathsome than a toad (*GA*, §§84, 87). Again, he had recorded this experience in *One Thing Is Needful*, where he has one of the damned wish he had been created a cockatrice or a toad, and thus without sin.

> A block, a stock, a stone, or clot,
> Is happier than I.  (*MW*, 6:100)

Moreover, although *Grace Abounding* has no comparable passage, his salute in *One Thing Is Needful* to the friend who thrice reproved him for vice is almost certainly autobiographical (6:98).[36]

Bunyan's increasing reflection on his early religious experiences is also manifest in *Ebal and Gerizzim*, particularly its references to the struggles of conscience and the intense battle with temptations. As he sat in the Bedford jail, he called to mind the "lashes of conscience" that had whipped his wounded spirit, but from his own travail he knew his readers should

>                              . . . be bold
> To come to mercies seat, with great access,
> There to expostulate with that justice
> That burns like fiery flames, against all those
> That do not with this blessed Jesus close.  (6:109–10)

---

[36] In certain respects this passage foreshadows Bunyan's account of the woman who castigated him for swearing, but she was "a very loose and ungodly Wretch," not his friend. *GA*, §26.

In a similar vein, he wrote of "the East wind of temptations" that buffet the soul, leaving the believer's graces virtually lifeless and the soul nearly overwhelmed with "the fretting fumes of unbelief." The only remedy is Christ's righteousness, without which sinners are "Opprest with guilt" and their hearts filled with "pride, presumption, or dispair" (6:112–14, 119). Such autobiographical echoes breathe life into Bunyan's verse, giving it an unmistakable air of conviction as well as urgency, for these poems were composed at a time when his thoughts were overwhelmingly on the end times. "God saith, *Convert with speed*" (6:63).

Both volumes of verse encompass vivid imagery. In *One Thing Is Needful* the most powerful representations, reflecting traditional *timor mortis* poetry, deal with death. The door through which all people pass, death is also depicted in Bunyan's verse as an all-conquering king who dares to engage the world, binding even earthly monarchs and driving them from the cosmic battlefield. Death, the great leveler, brings his foreboding cart, filling it with the tightly bound corpses of his prey, whom he carries into his den to lie in darkness and grief everlasting. In a scene reminiscent of *The Iliad* writ large, Bunyan counters this horrific colossus with the heroic figure of a man clad in armor, a helmet on his head, a breastplate protecting his torso, a sword on his thigh, and a shield in his hand. Like the commonplace depictions of St. George confronting the dragon, the Christian strides forth in Bunyan's verse to triumph over death (6:64–67, 70).

> Thus fortify'd he keeps the field
> While Death is gone and fled;
> And then lies down upon his Shield,
> Till Christ doth raise the dead.  (6:71)[37]

In this instance art triumphs over theology, for the imagery suggests a doctrine of soul-sleep at variance with Bunyan's beliefs.

At the time Bunyan wrote this verse the brightness of his outlook contrasted sharply with the grim melancholy from which he had emerged. This juxtaposition of opposites characterizes *One Thing Is Needful*. In addition to the stark images of death already noted, he painted a shockingly repellent figure of death's agent as a

> . . . worm that gnaws,
> And plucks their bowels out.

Fed by excruciating memories of one's every evil deed and thought,

> This ghastly worm is guilt for sin,
> Which on the Conscience feeds,
> With Vipers teeth both sharp and keen,
> Whereat it sorely bleeds.  (6:94)

---

[37] The believer's weaponry reappears in *The Pilgrim's Progress* (54) as that of the pilgrims.

Bunyan also evoked images of "infernall fiends," seas of sorrows, the din of howling and shrieking, the stench of flaming brimstone, and bodies broiling on fiery grates, perhaps indicating that he was again reading Foxe's *Acts and Monuments* (6:91, 93, 96–97).

In striking relief to this cacophony of horror, Bunyan drew on his love of music to pen virtual hymns of joy describing heaven.

> That Wisdom which doth order all,
> Shall there be fully shown:
> That Strength that bears the World, there shall
> By every one be known.  (6:81)

Here are light and life and hope:

> All Mysteries shall here be seen,
> And every knot unty'd:
> Electing love that hid hath been,
> Shall shine on every side.  (6:82)

Heaven's images—warm, alluring, uplifting—range from the light that brings full understanding to crystalline streams of life, the godly reigning as monarchs, and golden chains of love (6:82, 85). Instead of din, heaven's sounds are majestic and free of dissonance:

> The strings of Musick here are tun'd,
> For Heavenly Harmony.  (6:88)

Bunyan's embrace of such imagery reflects his emergence from recurring despair and the renewed joy of one who has rediscovered the ecstasy of light and triumphal optimism. For Bunyan the end times signify hope and the promise of deliverance.

His use of representation markedly increased in *Ebal and Gerizzim* as he employed similitudes to make his points. These two poetic volumes contain the seeds of his great classics, *Grace Abounding* and *The Pilgrim's Progress*. In addition to their didactic purpose, the poems were venues for Bunyan to explore both the relevance of his religious experience to others and the pedagogical value of similitudes. Among the images are a man lost at sea, a man sleeping in a burning house, a man hanging by a thread above hell's abyss, a poor man lying blindfolded among lions, Satan's sieve, cracked coins, a leaking pitcher, filthy rags, and dry ground soaking up rain. Two similitudes convey a sense of power and pathos:

> To see poor sinners yet with sin so bold,
> That like the Horse that to the battell runs
> Without all fear, and that no longer shuns,
> Till down he falls.  (6:126–27)

More vivid is the similitude of the shipwrecked mariner

> . . . that sleepeth in the Sea
> On broken Boards, which without guide or stay,
> Are driven whither winds and water will,
> While greedy beasts do wait to have their fill,
> By feeding on his carkass, when he shall
> Turn over-board, and without mercy fall
> Into the jawes of such as make a prey
> Of those, whom justice drowneth in the Sea.  (6:106)

Try as he might, Bunyan could find no similitudes sufficient to convey the full sense of hell's horrifying nature:

> The fire that doth within thine Oven burn,
> The prison where poor people sit and mourn,
> Chains, racks, and darkness, and such others, be
> As painting on the wall, to let thee see
> By word and figures, the extremity
> Of such as shall within these burnings lye.  (6:125)

For all the emphasis among nonconformists on the primacy of the word, Bunyan recognized its limitations. Rather than driving him into mysticism, this awareness propelled him to seek increasingly more powerful forms of verbal expression, first in the dramatic recounting of his spiritual struggles in *Grace Abounding*, and subsequently in the extended similitudes of *The Pilgrim's Progress* and *The Holy War*.

## "*A Drop of Honey*"[38]: Autobiographical Reflections

Bunyan's outlook as he wrote *The Holy City, The Resurrection of the Dead*, and his poetry about the end times was generally positive. The millennium, he believed, was nearly at hand, and the period of temple-work was about to be supplanted by the building of the new Jerusalem. He was concerned, however, about his converts' resolve to remain loyal to the nonconformist cause, or, as he would have said, the ways of God. For that reason as well as to demonstrate the basis of his ministerial calling, he decided about December 1665 to write a spiritual autobiography. By depicting his own experience he hoped to demonstrate his care for their spiritual welfare, particularly since his incarceration prevented him from fulfilling his normal ministerial responsibilities. Having received encouraging reports of his converts' hungering and thirsting after closer relations with God, their tenderness of heart, and their godly living, he decided to provide additional sustenance in the form of a

[38]*GA*, 1.

drop of honey from a lion's carcass, an allusion to Judges 14:5–8. That passage reports how Samson, with God's help, killed a lion bare-handed and subsequently found that bees had made a nest and produced honey in its carcass. From the strong had come sweetness. Like Samson, Bunyan averred that he too had eaten such honey and found it refreshing. "*Temptations when we meet them at first, are as the* Lyon *that roared upon* Sampson; *But if we overcome them, the next time we see them, we shall finde a Nest of Honey within them*" (*GA*, 1). Surmounting the spiritual turmoil and depressed moods left Bunyan able to recall those traumatic experiences and find spiritual sustenance therein. *Grace Abounding* was thus important as a vehicle for him to revisit his previous trials and to find encouragement in his triumph over them. In this sense, writing his autobiography contributed to his sense of spiritual and psychological well-being.

In the preface to *Grace Abounding* Bunyan described himself as caught between the teeth of lions in the wilderness, and, referring to Song of Solomon 4:8, in a lion's den and on the mountain of leopards. These analogies refer to more than his physical incarceration, for he also continued to confront the possibility of exile and the emotional pain of being separated from his family. Against this experience he juxtaposed his periods of spiritual and psychological turmoil, likening them to the Hebrews' forty years in the wilderness. He had spent so long at Sinai, he said, alluding to Deuteronomy 4:10–11, "to see the fire, and the cloud, and the darkness" in order to relate the works of God to others. In keeping with the commandment in Numbers 33:1–2 to remember how God had led the Hebrews through the wilderness, he decided to recount his own spiritual wanderings in the hope that other people might be prompted to recall God's dealings with their hearts. "*It is profitable for Christians,*" he explained, "*to be often calling to mind the very beginnings of Grace with their Souls.*" Believers were too prone to forget such workings in his judgment. He also continued to see an affinity between himself and Paul, who, when tried for his life, told the judges about his conversion experience, not least because he found reassurance in doing so. Now, as Bunyan looked back on his own travail, he too found such comfort, viewing that tribulation and darkness as if he were David holding the head of Goliath (*GA*, 1–3).

As Bunyan reflected on his spiritual and psychological experiences, he acknowledged that he still struggled in certain respects. He continued to battle disbelief, internal feelings of corruption, forgetfulness of divine love and mercy, and "a leaning to the Works of the Law." Moreover, he still adjudged prayer difficult as his mind wandered and feelings of coldness surfaced, and at times he found it impossible to undertake his spiritual responsibilities. Sometimes he discovered more in a single sentence of the Bible than he "could well tell how to stand under," whereas at other times "the whole Bible hath been to me as drie as a stick, or rather, my heart hath been so dead and drie unto it, that I could not conceive the least dram of refreshment, though I have lookt it all over." He recalled how periods of spiritual ecstasy were sometimes followed within hours by a plunge into darkness, though these experiences seem to have been in the past, not on-going episodes. The worst temptation, he avowed, was questioning God's exis-tence and the gospel's truth; he may have still battled this skepticism as late as 1666, for he uses the present tense in describing it: "When this temptation comes, it takes away my girdle from me, and removeth the foundations from under me." Although he continued to grapple with afflictions and temptations, he was able to turn them to his benefit. They still made him detest himself, but he found in them the motivation to pray, to rely on God, "to watch and be sober," and not to trust the sometimes stormy feelings within himself (102–3).

When Bunyan began to write *Grace Abounding*, he decided against a formal, learned style in favor of one that conveyed the raw emotions, temptations, and despair with which he had battled. Simplicity best suited the gravity of his mes-sage: "God *did not play in convincing of me; the* Devil *did not play in tempting of me; neither did I play when I sunk as into a bottomless pit, when* the pangs of hell caught hold upon me: *wherefore I may not play in my relating of them, but be plain and simple, and lay down the thing as it was.*" If any disapproved, Bunyan chal-lenged them to compose better spiritual autobiographies. In the meantime, he urged his readers to ponder the divine manifestation of grace in his life and to contemplate God's dealings with his people in days of yore. Like David, they should also remember their songs in the night, an allusion to Psalm 77:6, and seek spiritual treasures in their own hearts. If his readers had sinned against light, were tempted to blaspheme, found themselves mired in despair, or felt as though God were fighting against them, Bunyan asked them to remember that he had obtained deliverance from all these problems; so, then, could they. Thus he in-tended *Grace Abounding* as an epistle of hope to the struggling and of edification for all nonconformists (3–4), but simultaneously it also evinced his own opti-mism as he emerged from renewed spiritual and psychological strife.

# CHAPTER 6

# Charting the Pilgrimage

In the year Bunyan published *Grace Abounding* he had a brief respite from prison life. The sources of this information include Charles Doe and the anonymous author of a supplement to the seventh edition of *Grace Abounding*, published in 1692. Some have suggested that the latter author may have been the Congregationalist minister George Cokayne, a longtime friend of Bunyan, though the fundamental inaccuracies in the account make this dubious. According to the anonymous writer, Bunyan had been "confined in *Bedford* Goal for the space of six Years, till the Act of Indulgence to Dissenters being allowed, he obtained his Freedom by the Intercession of some in Trust and Power, that took pity on his Sufferings; but within six Years afterwards he was again taken up, viz., in the Year 1666, and was then confined for six years more, when even the Goaler took such pity of his rigorous Sufferings that he did as the *Egyptian* Goaler did to *Joseph*, put all the care and trust into his Hands."[1] There are problems in this account, including the erroneous dating of the Declaration of Indulgence, which Charles II issued in 1672, not 1666. The statement that Bunyan was rearrested "within six Years" is also mistaken, though this may be an author's or printer's slip for what should have been six *weeks* or *months*. The author relied on information from others as well as what he knew of Bunyan firsthand, and it may be that his source remembered the imprisonment incorrectly or that the author himself misrecorded some of the information. The main point—that Bunyan's lengthy incarceration actually comprised two distinct periods of six years each—seems difficult to misunderstand. Reliable confirming evidence for such a break exists inasmuch as his name is not included on a list of prisoners in the county jail in the summer of 1666. Presumably he received a brief respite from his confinement

---

[1] Charles Doe, "The Struggler," in *MW*, 12:454; anon., "A Continuation of Mr. Bunyan's Life," *ad cal. GA*, 171–72.

owing to the threat of plague, but there was no re-arrest.[2] It was probably during this hiatus in his incarceration that his daughter Sarah was conceived; she married on 19 December 1686 and would have been nineteen if she were born in 1667.[3]

"The Way He Runs"[4]: The Christian Life as Metaphor

Although Bunyan published nothing between *Grace Abounding* in 1666 and his two 1672 works, *A Confession of My Faith, and a Reason of My Practice* and *A Defence of the Doctrine of Justification, by Faith*, his pen remained active. The second edition of *Grace Abounding*, which is not extant, belongs to this period, and the third edition, as we have seen, was prepared about 1672. Although not published until 1698, *The Heavenly Foot-Man: or, a Description of the Man That Gets to Heaven* was almost certainly drafted some three decades earlier. Bunyan never published it, perhaps because he thought it needed revision. His eldest son, John, sold the manuscript to Doe in 1691, and the latter published it in 1698. Bunyan was working on *The Heavenly Foot-Man* when he was inspired to write *The Pilgrim's Progress*, as he indicates in the preface to the latter work:

> . . . I writing of the Way
> And Race of Saints in this our Gospel-Day,
> Fell suddenly into an Allegory
> About their Journey, and the way to Glory. (PP, 1)

Since Bunyan began writing *The Pilgrim's Progress* about March 1668, as we shall see, he must have been working on *The Heavenly Foot-Man* between about December 1667 and February 1668.[5]

*The Heavenly Foot-Man* also contains internal evidence for an early composition date. In the text Bunyan mentions "that little time which I have been a Professor," presumably referring to the period since he joined the Bedford congregation in 1655. He also cites two of his early works, *A Few Sighs from Hell*, which he asks readers to consider seriously, and *The Doctrine of the Law and Grace Unfolded* (MW, 5:152–53, 178). He might also have mentioned *The Resurrection of the*

---

[2] BLA, MS HSA 1666 S/1. See W. T. Whitley, "Bunyan's Imprisonments: A Legal Study," *Transactions of the Baptist Historical Society* 6 (1918–19): 12–14. The more tolerant atmosphere, however brief, also benefitted John Rush, a fellow member of the congregation, who was admitted as a freeman of the corporation on 3 September 1666. BLA, Bedford Corporation Minute Book, 1664–1688, fol. 22.

[3] The suggestion is Monica Furlong's. *Puritan's Progress: A Study of John Bunyan* (London: Hodder and Stoughton, 1975), 85. For Sarah's marriage see Brown, 394.

[4] Title-page, *The Heavenly Foot-Man: or, a Description of the Man That Gets to Heaven* (London, 1698).

[5] Talon proposed a date "shortly after 1666" (316).

*Dead* at one of several places in the text, though he opted not to do so. This fact, coupled with his comment on the brief time he had been a believer, may suggest an even earlier date for the sermon on which *The Heavenly Foot-Man* is based. Conjecturally, the sermon could have been preached in late 1659 or 1660, or have been the sermon he intended to preach at Lower Samsell on the day he was arrested; nothing in the book suggests he was in prison when he wrote it. He certainly kept his sermon notes, for in his account of his incarceration he offered to make them available. Whether the sermon was preached this early or in the mid-1660s, about December 1667 he began to prepare it for publication. When a draft was completed, he set it aside to begin composing *The Pilgrim's Progress*.[6]

Bunyan preached from notes, not a complete text. *The Heavenly Foot-Man* is particularly valuable because it includes, in the guise of a table of contents, the notes he probably used or intended to use in preaching this sermon (5:143–45).[7] This was the method recommended in the preaching manuals of William Perkins and John Wilkins, and the technique Bunyan himself utilized. Graham Midgley plausibly suggests that Bunyan may have studied some of the preaching manuals as well as learned from his fellow ministers. One such manual may have been Perkins' *The Arte of Prophecying* (1592), the guide most commonly used by non-conformists.[8] Authors of these manuals typically recommended a tripartite division for the sermon, consisting of an explanation of the scriptural passage, an account of the doctrines found in it, and the application or "uses" of the doctrine. In *The Heavenly Foot-Man* Bunyan varies this, commencing with the doctrine and then moving to directions, motives, and uses, thus adapting the methodology to suit his text and the intent of his sermon. He clearly felt free to vary his approach rather than slavishly follow the prescriptions of a preaching manual. An unusual feature of *The Heavenly Foot-Man* is his inclusion of a brief synopsis—some 117 words—which he asks readers to memorize (5:165–66).

Bluntly addressing *The Heavenly Foot-Man* to slothful, careless people, Bunyan warned that those who refuse to repent in this world will lose their souls in the next. People who are slothful in spiritual matters, he maintained, do their

---

[6] "Relation," 124. Sim and Walker suggest that Bunyan may have set aside the manuscript because of its subversive content, though the evidence they adduce is modest: the assumption that he was attacking the Church of England because he was in prison, and an allegorical reading of the manuscript that interprets the runner's prize as toleration and references to corruption as an attack on Charles II's court (94–95, 101–3).

[7] The text of *The Heavenly Foot-Man* was probably not substantially expanded beyond the actual sermon, if it was preached, for the sermon in its printed form would take approximately ninety minutes to deliver.

[8] *MW*, 5:xxiii, xxvii; Ebenezer Chandler and John Wilson, epistle to the reader, in Bunyan, *Works* (1692), sig. A1v.

work by the halves, procrastinate in performing their responsibilities, rarely or never do good works, and look for excuses. "Slothfulness *hath these two Evils, first, to neglect the time in which it should be getting of Heaven; and by that means, doth in the second place bring in untimely Repentance.*" By such contrition he was referring to a person who repented after the day of grace had passed, a concern that had plagued him during his own spiritual distress. This season of grace could end before one died, making it highly imprudent to delay faith and contrition (5:137–40).

Throughout *The Heavenly Foot-Man* Bunyan indicates that his readers have the ability to repent before the day of grace is over; the choice is theirs. His audience includes the unawakened: "*If* all this *will not move, I tell you, God will not be slothful . . . to damn you; . . . nor the Devils will not neglect to fetch thee, nor Hell neglect to shut its mouth upon thee*" (5:139). He also addresses the awakened, who are members of gathered churches, indicating they too have a choice with respect to persevering in the Christian life. Bunyan does not talk about the doctrine of predestination, according to which there is no suspense about whether the elect repent in time or whether they remain faithful to the end, but he does warn against "*prying overmuch into Gods Secret Decrees*" (5:156). Theologically, the day of grace cannot terminate before each of the elect has repented and believed, nor can the elect cease persevering and so be damned. From the doctrinal perspective, the basic themes of *The Heavenly Foot-Man* are thus illogical. However, as a sermon directed to both the manifestly unregenerate and the awakened, *The Heavenly Foot-Man* is a prime example of Bunyan's evangelical Calvinism, or 'pastoral Arminianism', the pragmatic manifestation of his stated preference for "awakening and converting Work" coupled with his interest in persuading converts to remain faithful (*GA*, §289).

Bunyan uses the metaphor of a race to discuss the Christian life, placing an emphasis on running to win—on individual effort as distinct from communal experience (*MW*, 5:148). There is no joy in sharing the race with others, only in crossing the finishing line in time to win a prize. He fills his work with admonitions—to start promptly, shed encumbrances, avoid distractions, shun bypaths, ignore temptations to turn aside, refrain from stumbling, and overcome the inevitable fatigue (5:149, 154–55, 157, 161, 165–66). Runners must have a sense of urgency, for the race is long, the time to complete it uncertain, and the racers' ability to continue unknown (5:150). "Think quickly Man, it is no dallying in this matter" (5:178). Losing means blackness, darkness, sorrow, pain, and eternal death. Like a pack of crazed dogs, the Devil, sin, Hell, and the law chase the runners, whose only hope is to find refuge behind heaven's gates before they close (5:150–51). In running this race "*the Will is all*" (5:165). Bunyan consequently urges the competitors to beseech God to inflame their wills for heaven, knowing from his own experience that deterrents and dismay can otherwise persuade a racer to quit (5:162). The strength to compete and finish can only come from God, but the runner must also act: "Get thy *Will* tipt with the Heavenly Grace, and resolution against all discouragments, and then thou goest *full speed* for Heaven" (5:165). Perseverance in this race is not a doctrine but a runner's resolute determination to continue notwithstanding excruciating pain and aching fatigue. "It is an easy matter for a Man to *Run hard for a spurt*, for a Furlong, for a Mile or two: O but to hold out for a Hundred, for a Thousand, for *Ten Thousand Miles*; that Man that doth this, he must look to meet with Cross, Pain, and Wearisomness to the Flesh" (5:161). The metaphor, which Luther also employed in his commentary on Galatians,[9] has dramatic potential, but Bunyan correctly envisioned the much greater possibilities in an allegory of a pilgrimage, which prompted him to lay this manuscript aside.

In *The Heavenly Foot-Man* Bunyan found an opportunity to clarify his position among the various dissenting groups and to reiterate his opposition to Quakers and Ranters. The latter two had fallen prey, he contended, to the temptation to "entertain Questions about some nice, foolish curiosities," which caused them to stumble and fall, leading to their eternal damnation unless God restores them to true faith. He advised his readers to be especially careful of Quakers, Ranters, and "*Free-Willers*," by whom he meant Arminians (5:152–53, 156).[10] Indeed, he was surprisingly critical of most nonconformists:

> Here is one runs a *Quaking*, another a *Ranting*, one again runs after the *Baptism*, and another after the *Independency*. Here's one for *Free-will*, and another for *Presbytery*, and yet possibly most of all these Sects run quite the wrong way.

He even advised his readers not to be overly involved with the Baptists, or "*Anabaptists*," the term he used for himself (5:152–53). As he would make clear in the early 1670s, he was an open-membership, open-communion Baptist, and thus at odds on the ordinance of baptism with both Particular and General Baptists. Undue attention to the form of baptism or church polity, he now argued, constituted a distraction from the race and the runners' ultimate goal.

As he pondered the nature of the race, Bunyan offered some thoughts on how runners should behave in society. Because the Devil and his servants are industrious, so should racers be; the context is spiritual, but Bunyan compared the slothful worker with the laggardly runner, implying the importance of diligence in both spheres. Still, he was not interested in material acquisitions, for heaven,

---

[9]Luther, *Galatians*, 467–68. For Bunyan's use of physical imagery in the metaphor of a race see Nigel Smith, "Bunyan and the Language of the Body in Seventeenth-Century England," in *JBHE*, ed. Laurence, Owens, and Sim, 164–65, 170–71.

[10]Midgley interprets Free-Willer differently. *MW*, 5:187–88.

he insisted, is primarily for the impoverished; as James 2:5 indicates, God has made the poor of this world rich in faith and heirs of the heavenly kingdom. Chiding those who evince little consideration for the plight of the indigent, he observed that "to give, is a *seldom* work." In remarks reminiscent of *A Few Sighs from Hell*, he reflected that heaven would probably have more servants than masters, and more tenants than landlords (5:138, 161, 167–70 *passim*, 177).

Several passages in *The Heavenly Foot-Man* provide valuable insight into Bunyan's frame of mind as he prepared this work. There are no hints of melancholy, but instead clear indications of blissful religious experiences. If the redeemed in heaven could address a lagging runner, Bunyan would have them say: "O if he were here one quarter of an hour, to behold, to see, to feel, to taste and enjoy, but the thousand part of what we enjoy!" (5:168). Bunyan has every expectation of joining them in this spiritual ecstasy. He goes on to describe what this vision means to him:

> Sometimes, when my base Heart hath been inclining to this World, and to loiter in my Journey towards Heaven, the very consideration of the glorious Saints and Angels in Heaven, what they enjoy, and what *low thoughts they have of the things of this World* together, how they would befool me, if they did but know that my Heart was drawing back, hath caused me to rush forward, to disdain these poor, low, empty beggarly things, and to say to my Soul, *come Soul let us not be weary*, let us see what this Heaven is, let us even venture all for it. (5:168)

The same confident tone is characteristic of the entire book and contrasts sharply with his despondent periods. Although he refers to such times, noting that he had been "absolutely distracted," he uses this experience as an example of the importance of trusting Christ's promises to overcome spiritual travail (5:158).

Not even the horrific accounts of martyrdom in Foxe's *Acts and Monuments* could dim Bunyan's optimism at this time. Either he had Foxe at his side as he wrote or a relevant passage was vividly impressed on his mind, for he depicted a scene from one of Foxe's plates in which an early martyr's eyes are being bored out with a sizable augur. He also described martyrs being burned at the stake, stoned, sawn asunder, broiled on gridirons, boiled in cauldrons, thrown to wild beasts, and having their tongues cut out. To him these examples illustrate the worth of the prize for which runners strive (5:162, 167).[11]

A number of ideas with which Bunyan was working in *The Heavenly Foot-Man* provided inspiration for *The Pilgrim's Progress*. The text for the former, 1 Corinthians 9:24, "so run, that ye may obtain," becomes part of Evangelist's

[11] The plate that impressed Bunyan is found at p. 1018 of the first volume of the 1632 edition of Foxe's work, and between pp. 44 and 45 in volume one of the 1641 edition. *MW*, 5:193.

charge to Christian and Faithful: "The Crown is before you, and it is an incorruptible one; so run that you may obtain it" (*PP*, 86). When Christian ignores the cries of his wife and children, he is heeding Bunyan's advice to runners (*MW*, 5:147, 157; *PP*, 10). The Slough of Despond and Hill Difficulty are prefigured in Bunyan's depiction of the race route as including "many a dirty step, many a high Hill" (*MW*, 5:150). Christian has to travel by way of the cross, which he found "at a place somewhat ascending," just as the runner must "go by the Cross" (*PP*, 38; *MW*, 5:159, 162). In *The Heavenly Foot-Man* the runner is exhorted to cast aside everything that might hinder him in the race, but a similar metaphor in *The Pilgrim's Progress* has significant differences, for Christian needs divine assistance to remove the burden of guilt and sin from his back (*MW*, 5:154; *PP*, 38). Bunyan's exhortation to runners to avoid by-paths is the probable model for By-path-meadow in the allegory, and the "Briers and Quagmires" runners meet will reappear in the bog into which Christian falls and the "very dangerous Quagg" he is warned to avoid (*MW*, 5:155, 161; *PP*, 62, 111). Finally, in *The Heavenly Foot-Man* Bunyan tells his audience that some people turn aside to avoid the cross, mistakenly thinking they will find an alternate route to heaven. This is the course Mr. Worldly-wiseman pursues in the allegory (*MW*, 5:162; *PP*, 22).

Thus the simple metaphor of a race became the inspiration for *The Pilgrim's Progress*, the greatness of which is inconceivable without the rich religious experience recorded in *Grace Abounding*. Bunyan's preparation of the second edition shortly before he worked on *The Heavenly Foot-Man* propitiously set the stage for him to begin composing *The Pilgrim's Progress*. The latter half of the 1660s marks the emergence of Bunyan as a creative, powerful writer capable of drawing on his depression, his stormy religious experiences, and the hardships of prison to create two literary masterpieces, *Grace Abounding* and *The Pilgrim's Progress*.

### "Against Our Religion"[12]: The Setting of *The Pilgrim's Progress*

Bunyan laid aside his manuscript for *The Heavenly Foot-Man* to compose an allegory about the saints' way to glory as a means of diverting his attention "*From worser thoughts, which make me do amiss*" (*PP*, 1). Like many other nonconformists, his hopes of toleration had undoubtedly been raised in 1667 as the expiration of the Conventicle Act neared. The statute's termination would occur automatically at the conclusion of the first parliamentary session after 17 May 1667. As it happened, that session did not end until 1 March 1669,[13] but discussion of toleration was widespread in 1667. Bunyan, of course, had been incarcerated under the

[12] *PP*, 96.
[13] PRO, SP 29/258/43.

terms of the Elizabethan act, but he could reasonably hope that implementation of a toleration policy would bring his liberation. Indeed, a letter dated 10 December 1670 from Paul Cobb to Roger Kenyon indicates that Bunyan had been petitioning assize judges for his release: "Benyon [*sic*] hath petitioned all the Judges of the Assize, as they came the Circuit, but could never be released."[14] Bedfordshire records show that he had appeared at the bar in the summers of 1665 and 1668 and the winter of 1669, but he found no mercy, for the judges undoubtedly shared Twisden's hostility toward those who spoke ill of the Book of Common Prayer and refused to use it as well as those who would not attend a parish church "either upon difference of Judgment, Counting our Church Hereticall, or the manner of worship superstitious."[15] Reports circulated in 1667 of parliamentary bills to grant liberty of conscience to all nonconformists, dispense with the Act of Uniformity, and include moderate dissenters in the Church of England, and there was talk as well of a declaration of indulgence. "It seems," wrote Samuel Pepys on 20 January 1668, "there is a great presumption that there will be a Toleration granted."[16] Such reports would almost certainly have reached Bunyan.

Expectations of toleration sustained a setback on 10 March 1668, when the king, responding to pressure from the House of Commons, issued a proclamation against conventicles.[17] The House of Commons subsequently passed a tough bill against unauthorized religious meetings, which one dissenter branded "that Act of violence," but the Lords refused to approve it. In early June Charles promised the bishops more assistance from civil magistrates to repress conventicles, and a month later the Privy Council obtained a judicial opinion that the Elizabethan conventicle and recusancy statutes were still in force and could be used to suppress illegal religious assemblies.[18] The "*worser thoughts*" that prompted Bunyan to write *The Pilgrim's Progress* probably were triggered by reports that the king had yielded to parliamentary calls for a repressive policy, leading Bunyan to conclude that he might never be freed. Undoubtedly dismayed, he found solace, thinking

[14] *HMC* 35, *Fourteenth Report*, Appendix, pt. 4, p. 86.

[15] BLA, MSS HSA 1665 S/1; 1668 S/1; 1669 W/1; Bodl., Rawlinson MSS C719, fols. 15–16 (quoted).

[16] PRO, SP 29/211/55; 29/216/19, 76, 144; 29/217/174; 29/232/187; 29/235/26, 126; BL, Egerton MSS 2539, fol. 119r; Pepys, 9:31 (quoted).

[17] *CJ*, 9:60; William Cobbett, *Cobbett's Parliamentary History of England*, vol. 4 (London, 1808), 413; PRO, SP 29/236/64; London *Gazette* 242 (9–12 March 1668); BL, Egerton MSS 2539, fol. 170r.

[18] Cobbett, *Parliamentary History*, 4:421; PRO, SP 29/239/141.1 (quoted); 29/262/115; Pepys, 9:177, 180–81; *HMC* 25, *Le Fleming*, 64–65.

> . . . to make
> I knew not what: nor did I undertake
> Thereby to please my Neighbour; no not I,
> I did it mine own self to gratifie.  (1)

If he began with the intent to please only himself, he was soon writing with an audience in mind, as we shall see.

Bunyan probably started to compose his allegory in or shortly after March 1668, following Charles' issuance of the proclamation against conventicles. He had completed three-quarters of his manuscript by September 1669, when he began enjoying what would prove to be nine months of relative freedom. A brief respite had occurred in October 1668, when the records of the Bedford church indicate that he and the brothers John and Samuel Fenne were to admonish Robert Nelson for leaving the congregation and other misdeeds. The same month the church appointed Bunyan to reprimand two other men for withdrawing from the congregation.[19] He performed similar duties from September 1669 through May 1670, which probably explains the break in the allegory's first part, denoted by the dreamer's awakening and then resuming his dream (123).[20] Bunyan's modest liberty ended when a new Conventicle Act (22 Car. II, c. 1) went into force on 15 May 1670, signaling a crackdown on dissenters. During the ensuing ten months of close confinement, he almost certainly completed part one of *The Pilgrim's Progress*.

The allegory was not published until 1678. It was entered in the Stationers' Register on 22 December 1677, and licensed and recorded in the Term Catalogues on 18 February 1678.[21] For several reasons Bunyan delayed publication. Censorship must have been a concern, especially in the face of government efforts to control the press. While Bunyan was writing his allegory, Roger L'Estrange, surveyor of the press, was engaged in a crusade to extirpate dissident literature. Two of Bunyan's printers, Francis Smith and George Larkin, felt L'Estrange's sting in the late 1660s, Smith by frequent harassment and Larkin by imprisonment in October 1668. Moreover, Simon Dover, the husband of Joan, another of Bunyan's printers, had died in prison after being convicted of seditious libel.[22] In April 1669 Lord Arlington, a secretary of state, instructed the Stationers' Company to confiscate unlicensed books and pamphlets, incapacitate the presses, and apprehend the printers, and four months later the king ordered the company to assist

[19] *CB*, 39–40.

[20] Brian Nellist argues that the awakening refers to Christian's rebirth, but the rebirth occurred much earlier, at the cross. "*The Pilgrim's Progress* and Allegory," in *Pilgrim's Progress*, ed. Newey, 148.

[21] Arber, *Transcript*, 3:49; Arber, *Term Catalogues*, 1:299.

[22] Greaves, *EUHF*, 167–84; *BDBR*, s.v. Francis Smith.

L'Estrange in his efforts to stamp out the publication of unlicensed material. The attorney general underscored the king's command in September 1670 by threatening to recall the company's charter unless it cooperated more closely with L'Estrange. A month later the government offered not to prosecute Larkin and other printers if they provided information; Larkin's wife helped authorities discover reputedly seditious pamphlets.[23] In December 1671, approximately nine months after Bunyan likely completed the first part of *The Pilgrim's Progress*, Arlington issued another warrant similar to that of April 1669. Others followed, from Arlington in September 1672 and Henry Coventry, secretary of state for the north, in December 1673. Nathaniel Ponder, who would publish *The Pilgrim's Progress* in 1678, went to prison two years earlier for issuing the second part of Andrew Marvell's bitingly satirical *The Rehearsal Transpros'd.*[24] Bunyan's plea to *"let Truth be free"* was especially poignant against this background of censorship (6).

In addition to his likely concern about censorship, Bunyan would have been sensitive about risking his liberty. He was still formally a prisoner when, in May 1671, the security-conscious government ordered troops in London to suppress all illegal and disorderly meetings. Although Charles' Declaration of Indulgence brought toleration in March 1672, parliamentary opposition resulted in its cancellation a year later, by which time the informers authorized by the Second Conventicle Act were once again at work. In February 1675 the Privy Council issued a proclamation calling for the suppression of conventicles, following this with more than seventy letters to justices of the peace urging them to enforce it. The king himself reiterated his desire in March 1676 that illegal meetings be suppressed.[25] Such a manifestly intolerant atmosphere probably contributed to Bunyan's hesitation to publish a book so critical of the Church of England and, more broadly, of Restoration society.

Quite apart from these considerations, Bunyan postponed publication to seek critical appraisal from his friends. What they told him about his *"ends"* gave him pause:

> . . . *some said, let them live; some, let them die:*
> *Some said,* John, *print it; others said, Not so:*
> *Some said, It might do good; others said, No.* (2)

Both the colloquial style and the allegorical method troubled some of his critics,

[23] *CSPD, 1668–69,* 266, 446; *1670,* 486; *HMC 71, Finch,* 2:1–2.

[24] PRO, SP 29/294/172; *CSPD, 1672,* 673; PRO, SP 44/28, fol. 102r; SP 29/366, p. 161.

[25] PRO, SP 29/290/43; 29/334/15; BL, Add. MSS 25,124, fol. 14r; London *Gazette* 962 (4–8 February 1675); BL, Stowe MSS 207, fol. 184r; *CSPD, 1676–77,* 46. For Ponder see *BDBR, s.v.*

who charged that his approach lacked "solidness," blinded readers with meta-phors, and couched the message in "*dark*" language (2–4). In due course he de-cided to publish the book, his critics notwithstanding. The usual assumption is that this decision did not take long to make, but his own words offer no clue:

> At last I thought, Since you are thus divided,
> I print it will, and so the case decided. (2)

Obtaining the reaction of his friends and pondering whether to commit his alle-gory to print probably consumed several years. In the meantime, as we shall see in Chapter Seven, he turned his attention to what must have seemed more pressing concerns, especially his debates with Edward Fowler over justification and various Baptists concerning the conditions of church membership and com-munion. Ponder's legal difficulties in 1676 and Bunyan's own return to prison the same year further delayed publication.

Other considerations also point to Bunyan's first imprisonment rather than the second (1676–1677) as the time of the allegory's composition. In the book, Tempo-rary, who had been "*much awakened once*," had turned away from the true church some ten years previously (151), a caustic comment on those Protestants who had conformed at the Restoration; the episode suggests that Bunyan wrote it about 1670. An early date for the allegory is also likely given the fact that Bunyan pub-lished a significantly expanded second edition in the same year the first appeared. If he wrote most of the first part during his second imprisonment and finished it following his release in late June or July 1677, he would have had less than six months to compose the rest of it, circulate the manuscript among his friends, add his justificatory preface, see the book through the press, prepare a second edition, and shepherd it too through the press.[26] Since the review process alone almost certainly took at least six months (unless he made multiple copies), it must have been undertaken prior to the second imprisonment. At most, during that incarceration he may have made final revisions and composed the preface.[27]

In his preface Bunyan suggests that the decision to write an allegory was un-expected and inspired:

[26] See Roger Sharrock, "'When at the first I took my Pen in hand': Bunyan and the Book," in *John Bunyan*, ed. Keeble, 84; Sharrock, in *PP*, xxxi.

[27] Gwilym O. Griffith and Lynn Veach Sadler have suggested that Bunyan wrote most of part one during his first imprisonment and the rest during the second, but the virtually seamless quality of the allegory mitigates against this. Griffith, *John Bunyan* (London: Hodder and Stoughton, 1927), 220–26; Sadler, *John Bunyan* (Boston: Twayne, 1979), 53. I see no evidence for Jack Lindsay's argument that Bunyan was inspired to write *The Pil-grim's Progress* by his father's death in February 1675. Lindsay, 163–64.

> . . . I writing of the Way
> And Race of Saints in this our Gospel-Day,
> Fell suddenly into an Allegory. (1)

Neil Keeble justifiably deems his preface "the *locus classicus* for imagination in English literature."[28] The allegorical ideas flew, Bunyan said, like sparks from a coal fire, signs of a creative imagination pressing to burst its bounds. The result is not the product of an unlettered tinker, however popular that legend, but a gifted writer who had mastered the art of dialogue,[29] skillfully observed what a later age would call human psychology, and effectively blended common themes from popular romances with his personal experience, Calvinist convictions, and critique of Restoration society and the established church.

The value of allegory for religious purposes is a lesson Bunyan probably learned from Luther, whose commentary on Galatians endorsed allegories and similitudes as devices employed by Jesus because they delight people. "They are, as it were, certain pictures which set forth things as if they were painted before the eyes of the simple, and therefore they move and persuade very much, especially the simple and ignorant." Although allegory is not very persuasive in theological matters, according to Luther, it adorns that which has already been established through invincible arguments. "As painting is an ornament to set forth and garnish an house already builded, so is an allegory the light of a matter which is already otherwise proved and confirmed." Because allegories can be dangerous if mishandled, Luther insisted they must be used only by those with a "perfect knowledge of Christian doctrine," such as Paul, who was "a marvellously cunning workman in handling of allegories." In contrast, Origen and Jerome inappropriately employed them to interpret plainly understood Scripture. Luther's idea of allegory was Galatians 4:22–26, but Bunyan went beyond the use of this device in the Bible to develop his own scripturally grounded, creative allegory.[30]

Although Bunyan may have intended only to divert himself when he first began composing the allegory, he soon determined that the book would have a much wider purpose, partly to entice people to embrace the gospel. Likening himself to the angler and the fowler in their use of creative means to catch their prey, he harnessed allegory in the hope that his

> . . . Book will make a Traveller of thee,
> If by its Counsel thou wilt ruled be. (6)

---

[28] Keeble, *LCN*, 182.

[29] David Seed, "Dialogue and Debate in *The Pilgrim's Progress*," in *Pilgrim's Progress*, ed. Newey, 69–90.

[30] Luther, *Galatians*, 414–23 (quoted at 414, 417).

No less important was his determination that the allegory edify and support those who had already embarked on the pilgrimage. The book is replete with doctrinal instruction, delivered both allegorically and in straightforward passages of a catechetical nature, as in Ignorance's conversation with Christian and Hopeful. Bunyan's periodic recapitulation of previous action likewise serves a catechetical function, and during the course of the allegory Christian develops from catechumen to catechizer.[31] The persecutory imagination that gave rise to the work does not exclude edification but is harnessed to enhance the book's pedagogical mission.[32] Bunyan also intended *The Pilgrim's Progress* as a standard by which his audience could gauge whether they were following the way to salvation with Christian, Faithful, and Hopeful or keeping company with those whose destiny was hell.

> *Would'st read thy self, and read thou know'st not what*
> *And yet know whether thou art blest or not,*
> *By reading the same lines? O then come hither.* (7)

Through the pages of his allegory, with their abundant references to pertinent scriptural texts, Bunyan offered readers and hearers an opportunity to answer the crucial question as to whether they were among the elect. In this sense, *The Pilgrim's Progress* is the most effective casuistic work in English literature. Indeed, eleven editions were printed in the author's lifetime, and double that number by century's end.[33]

Bunyan wrote *The Pilgrim's Progress* not only as a guide to the Christian life but as a contribution to the Restoration crisis of 1667–1673, the crux of which was a debate about liberty of conscience that raised profound questions concerning the limits of the state's authority, the relationship between church and crown, and the rights and obligations of subjects.[34] In their assertion of the autonomy of conscience and the responsibility of Christians to obey God in all matters, nonconformists challenged the Restoration state and the politico-religious settlement imposed in the early 1660s. The dissenters' arguments struck not only at the

---

[31] Dennis Danielson makes a convincing case for catechism's formal role in the allegory. "Catechism, *The Pilgrim's Progress* and the Pilgrim's Progress," *Journal of English and Germanic Philology* 94 (January 1995): 42–58.

[32] For a somewhat different view see Stachniewsky, 179.

[33] Keeble, *LCN*, 128; Charles Doe, "The Struggler," in *MW*, 12:456; Swaim, *PP*, 2. Doe noted that editions had appeared in France, the Netherlands, and New England, and one had been published in Welsh. The allegory's extraordinary success is discussed in the Epilogue.

[34] Portions of the ensuing discussion are drawn from my article, "'Let Truth Be Free': John Bunyan and the Restoration Crisis of 1667–1673," *Albion* 28 (Winter 1996): 587–605.

crown but at Parliament, for it had imposed the so-called Clarendon Code that sought to repress nonconformity. Opponents of toleration warned that it could plunge the country into renewed turbulence: "You that have a mind to see another Rebellion, and another King Murdered," proclaimed one conservative, "I pray & beseech you, Give your votes for a Tolleration."[35]

Some of the greatest works on religious liberty date from these years: John Locke's unpublished "Essay Concerning Toleration" (1667), John Owen's *Indulgence and Toleration Considered in a Letter unto a Person of Honour* (1667), *A Peace-Offering in an Apology and Humble Plea for Indulgence and Libertie of Conscience* (1667), and *Truth and Innocence Vindicated* (1669), William Penn's *The Great Case of Liberty of Conscience* (1670), Slingsby Bethel's *The Present Interest of England Stated* (1671), Andrew Marvell's *The Rehearsal Transpros'd* (1672–73), and John Milton's *Of True Religion, Haeresie, Schism, Toleration, and What Best Means May Be Us'd Against the Growth of Popery* (1673).[36] Focusing on Owen, Bethel, and such lesser known authors as Philip Nye, John Humfrey, and Sir Charles Wolseley, Gary De Krey has identified four principal arguments in defense of conscience. Two of these reconciled the claims of conscience with magisterial authority. The first, expounded by Owen, Nye, and Humfrey, cited natural law to distinguish between the internal sphere of religious belief and worship, where the individual must answer to God, and the external realm of religious order and public morality, in which she or he is accountable to the magistrate. Proponents of this view recognized the crown's right to exercise authority over a religious establishment, accepted the diversity of religious understanding and practice, and endorsed only passive resistance.[37] Humfrey, Bethel, Wolseley, and Owen pro-

---

[35] Bodl., Add. MSS C307, fol. 168r.

[36] Published in the midst of this debate (though written earlier), Milton's *Samson Agonistes* (1671) explores the question of potentially conflicting obligations (to God, law, state, and conscience) and how one makes choices in a society without toleration. Sharon Achinstein, "*Samson Agonistes* and the Drama of Dissent," *Milton Studies* 33 (1996): 133–58. Blair Worden has persuasively argued that *Samson Agonistes* was not written before 1662. "Milton, *Samson Agonistes*, and the Restoration," in *Culture and Society in the Stuart Restoration: Literature, Drama, History* (Cambridge: Cambridge University Press, 1995), 111–36. For Bethel see *BDBR, s.v.*

[37] Gary S. De Krey, "Rethinking the Restoration: Dissenting Cases for Conscience, 1667–1672," *Historical Journal* 38 (1995): 57–60; [John Owen], *Truth and Innocence Vindicated* (London, 1669), 101–8, 156–57, 166, 187–91, 243–49; [Owen], *A Peace-Offering in an Apology and Humble Plea for Indulgence and Libertie of Conscience* (London, 1667), 3, 15–18; [Owen], *Indulgence and Toleration Considered in a Letter unto a Person of Honour* (London, 1667), 9–10, 12; Philip Nye, *The King's Authority in Dispensing with Ecclesiastical Laws, Asserted and Vindicated* (London, 1687), 30–31, 45 (Nye died in 1672); Nye, *The Lawfulnes of the Oath of Supremacy, and Power of the King in Ecclesiastical Affairs* (London, 1683), 19–

pounded a second theory according to which relief for Protestant nonconformists was deemed to be in the political interest of the crown and the country, the religious interest of domestic and international Protestantism, and England's economic welfare. This view was also expounded in a document among Lord Wharton's papers, indicating his interest in this argument.[38] The final two views challenged the crown's traditional ecclesiastical jurisdiction. The third view, espoused by Penn, Nicholas Lockyer, and (with some inconsistency) Wolseley, used natural law and historical right to repudiate the crown's exclusive ecclesiastical jurisdiction and distinguished between the secular order of justice and the internal order of grace. Advocates of this position argued the right of Christians to defend matters of conscience against the Restoration religious code.[39] Proponents of the fourth theory appealed to Hebrew and Christian prophetic imagery to defend their religious convictions, with the Fifth Monarchists insisting that God has a right to rule in matters civil as well as spiritual, and that Christians owe obedience only to godly rulers.[40]

There is no evidence that Bunyan read any of these works or the books that attempted to refute them, such as Thomas Tomkins' *The Inconveniences of Toleration* (1667), Richard Perrinchief's *A Discourse of Toleration* (1668), and Samuel Parker's *A Discourse of Ecclesiastical Politie* (1670).[41] Nevertheless, as Roger Shar-

<hr>

23; [John Humfrey], *A Case of Conscience* (London, 1669), 4–5; H[umfrey], *Two Points of Great Moment, the Obligation of Humane Laws, and the Authority of the Magistrate, About Religion, Discussed* ([London], 1672), 41–44, 72. For Humfrey see *Calamy Revised, s.v.*; for Wolseley see *BDBR, s.v.*

[38] De Krey, "Rethinking the Restoration," 60–63; Jonathan Scott, *England's Troubles: Seventeenth-Century English Political Instability in European Context* (Cambridge: Cambridge University Press, 2000), 371–73; [Slingsby Bethel], *The Present Interest of England Stated* (London, 1671), 13–20, 23–27; [Sir Charles Wolseley], *Liberty of Conscience, the Magistrates Interest* (London, 1668), 3–22; Owen, *Indulgence and Toleration Considered*, 7–8, 17–21; Owen, *Truth and Innocence Vindicated*, 74–81; Owen, *A Peace-Offering*, 13, 19, 31–33; [Owen], *An Account of the Grounds and Reasons on Which Protestant Dissenters Desire Their Liberty* [n.p., n.d.]; Owen, "The State of the Kingdom with Respect to the Present Bill Against Conventicles," [1670], in *Works*, 13:583–86; Nye, *The Lawfulnes of the Oath of Supremacy*, 69; Bodl., Carte MSS 81, fol. 331r–v.

[39] De Krey, "Rethinking the Restoration," 63–65; W[illiam] P[enn], *The Great Case of Liberty of Conscience* ([London], 1670), 3, 19–31, 37–44; [Wolseley], *Liberty of Conscience upon Its True Proper Grounds Asserted & Vindicated* (London, 1668), 3–6, 26–50; [Nicholas Lockyer], *Some Seasonable and Serious Queries upon the Late Act Against Conventicles* [London, 1670], 8–10. For Lockyer see *BDBR, s.v.*

[40] De Krey, "Rethinking the Restoration," 65–67; anon., *The Saints Freedom from Tyranny Vindicated* (London, 1667), 9–11, 17–18, 22–23, 25.

[41] For Tomkins, Perrinchief, and Parker see *DNB, s.vv.*

rock has observed, Bunyan had little difficulty acquiring books in prison. If he traveled to London before he began composing *The Pilgrim's Progress* about March 1668, he could have discussed the issues with Owen. The church minutes, which fall silent in April 1664, resumed in a matter-of-fact manner in September 1668 with a notation that the congregation had admitted two women to fellowship. The casualness of the reference suggests that meetings, if not held throughout much of the period of silence, had probably resumed before September 1668. Bunyan reappears in the records on 30 October, but he may have attended earlier meetings; the minutes for 9 and 25 September record only new members, not any business requiring the mention of older ones.[42]

This raises the intriguing but speculative possibility that Bunyan might have been free during Easter week 1668. If so, had he traveled to London he would have been there when the bawdy house riots erupted on 23 March as a crowd attacked brothels in Poplar. Further assaults ensued on the 24th and 25th, mostly in Moorfields (where Owen and Palmer lived), East Smithfield, Shoreditch, and Holborn. The rioters were apparently protesting the government's intention to suppress conventicles while turning a blind eye to the equally illegal brothels.[43] The riots were an opening salvo in the battle for conscience, for the protestors' slogans included "Liberty of Conscience!" Some rioters were undoubtedly dissenters, and according to a government informer "the generallyty of the Sectaryes" were pleased by the riots.[44] If Bunyan was not in London during the attack on the brothels he would have heard about them, and there may be a faint echo of them in the Vanity Fair episode in *The Pilgrim's Progress* where he includes bawds and whores among the "Delights of all sorts" (88).

As he considered the issues in the crisis over conscience, Bunyan must have pondered how he might lend his voice to those who were championing toleration for Protestants. Sensitive to his lack of a university education he would not have ventured into a weighty discussion of natural law as a basis for freedom of conscience. Nor did he demonstrate substantive concern with interest theory, though he employed a mirror image of it in the Vanity Fair episode, where Faithful and Christian are indicted as enemies to and disturbers of trade. In his response Faithful insisted he had disrupted no one, but Bunyan ignored an obvious place to incorporate a defense of nonconformity on the grounds that it was conducive to economic development (92–93). Given his traditional economic views, it is not surprising that he made no attempt to defend conscience on economic grounds.

[42] *CB*, 39.
[43] Tim Harris, "The Bawdy House Riots of 1668," *Historical Journal* 29 (September 1986): 537–56; Harris, *LC*, 82–91.
[44] Greaves, *EUHF*, 195–97.

He was comfortable with the Bible and had demonstrated facility in theological exposition, and he was interested in biblical symbolism—in what his age called "types"—not in the philosophical realm of natural law or in economic theory. Thus he entered the debate over conscience with an allegory demonstrating the eternal award that awaits the pilgrim who perseveres in adhering to God's way despite all perils, both internal and external. Those who refuse his directions receive a stern warning:

> *Indeed if they abuse*
> *Truth, cursed be they, and the craft they use*
> *To that intent; but yet let Truth be free*
> *To make her Salleys upon Thee, and Me,*
> *Which way it pleases God.* (6)

In a nutshell, this was Bunyan's affirmation of the necessity of toleration. His profession that he wrote only to divert and gratify himself (1) provided him with a defense should the allegorical format suggest unseemly levity to others or, perhaps more importantly, should the work's barely disguised criticism of Restoration society, the aristocracy, the Church of England, and the policy of persecution provoke the authorities' ire.

In a quandary about publishing the allegory when it was finished, he sought the advice of his friends. The usual reading assumes that he sought their criticism in the mid-1670s, shortly before he settled on publication. Perhaps, however, he first shared the manuscript early in the decade, while the debate over conscience raged. Under these circumstances the reaction is understandable: Some thought its publication *"might do good; others said, No"* (2). How, one wonders, might the allegory have been received if published alongside the substantive books of Penn, Bethel, and Marvell? *"At last"* Bunyan decided to publish his allegory, but only in late 1677 against a background of the government's renewed efforts (beginning in 1675) to repress conventicles,[45] a campaign that had briefly returned him to prison. Conscience again had become a pressing issue with significant political overtones. Not surprisingly, Owen reportedly steered Bunyan to his own publisher, Nathaniel Ponder, who issued *The Pilgrim's Progress* following Bunyan's release from jail in June 1677; Owen's voice may have been decisive in persuading Bunyan to publish the work. The topic was timely, for Owen's assistant since 1674, the Scottish minister Robert Ferguson, had published *The Interest of Reason in Religion, with the Import & Use of Scripture-Metaphors* in 1675 in defense of nonconformists who had been accused of "turning Religion into unaccountable

---

[45]BL, Add. MSS 25,124, fols. 33r, 38r; BL, Stowe MSS 209, fol. 237v; PRO, SP 29/369/182; 29/383/54; *CSPD, 1675–76,* 9–10, 61; *CSPD, 1676–77,* 46, 132, 308, 407, 454, 547; *CSPD, 1677–78,* 53.

Phansies and Enthusiasm's, drest up with empty Schemes of speech; and for embracing a few gawdy Metaphors & Allegories."[46]

## "Whither Must I Fly?"[47]: The Pilgrimage

The basic story of *The Pilgrim's Progress* is simple, perhaps deceptively so. In part, Bunyan's genius was framing it in a manner that allowed most Christians to identify with the principal figure, Christian, and thus miss the acute critique of society, government, and the established church embedded in the book. Nonconformists, however, would have readily identified with the struggling, persecuted Christian and recognized Bunyan's searing assessment. His dream commences with the impoverished, burdened figure of Graceless fleeing his wife and young children to escape the heavenly fire destined to destroy their town. Bearing a parchment-roll from Evangelist, Graceless, now called Christian, follows his directions to a wicket-gate, accompanied by his neighbor, Pliable. When both men blunder into the Slough of Despond, Pliable turns back, leaving Christian to escape the bog by providentially supplied steps. Weary of the burden on his back, Christian succumbs to Mr. Worldly-wiseman's advice to seek the assistance of Mr. Legality, only to be terror-stricken by a volcano. Redirected to the wicket-gate by Evangelist, Christian gains entry with Good Will's help. After receiving useful instruction at the Interpreter's house, Christian continues on his travels until he reaches a cross and sepulcher, where the burden falls from his back, and three shining ones give him new clothing, a new roll, and a mark on his forehead. Finding Simple, Sloth, and Presumption asleep, Christian awakens them and warns of the danger they face, and shortly thereafter, he shuns the counsel of two gentlemen, Formalist and Hypocrisie, to rely on tradition. Ascending the Hill Difficulty, Christian pauses to sleep in an arbor, where he temporarily loses his roll. Undeterred by a warning from Timorous and Mistrust of lions ahead, Christian makes his way to the Palace Beautiful, where the damsel Discretion admits him, and Prudence, Piety, and Charity entertain and teach him. After a night's rest in the Chamber of Peace, Christian receives weapons from the young women and resumes his journey. In the Valley of Humiliation he defeats the fearsome monster Apollyon, but only as the latter is about to slay him. Following his

---

[46] Peter Toon, *God's Statesman: The Life and Work of John Owen, Pastor, Educator, Theologian* (Exeter: Paternoster Press, 1971), 161–62; Robert Ferguson, *The Interest of Reason in Religion, with the Import & Use of Scripture-Metaphors* (London, 1675), 278. See Barbara A. Johnson, "Falling into Allegory: The 'Apology' to *The Pilgrim's Progress* and Bunyan's Scriptural Methodology," in *Bunyan*, ed. Collmer, 134–36. For Ferguson see *BDBR*, s.v., and for a discussion of his views on allegory see Chapter 8.

[47] *PP*, 10.

narrow escape he traverses the Valley of the Shadow of Death, with its deep ditch on one side, its perilous quagmire on the other, and its fearsome entrance to hell. As he leaves the valley, he passes a cave inhabited by the giants Pope and Pagan, both of whom prove harmless, and then he overtakes a pilgrim named Faithful. For a time they are accompanied by Talkative, who beguiles Faithful but not Christian.

Reappearing, Evangelist cautions the two pilgrims that they have "not resisted unto blood," and warns them that trouble awaits them in the town of Vanity Fair (86). In fact, their arrival sparks a tumult leading to their arrest and Faithful's trial and execution. After Christian escapes, he and his new companion, Hopeful, soon confront another round of misguided travelers, By-ends, Mony-love, Save-all, and Hold-the-world. Passing through the Plain of Ease, Christian and Hopeful withstand the temptations of Demas and his silver mine before seeing a monument to Lot's ill-fated wife. A river brings welcome respite, but the two pilgrims soon digress into By-path-meadow. For trespassing on Giant Despair's property, they are incarcerated in Doubting Castle, beaten, and exhorted to commit suicide. Escape is possible only when Christian finds the key of promise. Free at last, the pilgrims refresh themselves in the Delectable Mountains, where shepherds caution them about Mounts Errour and Caution and show them a by-way to hell. Christian and Hopeful meet a new traveler, Ignorance, and see another, whom Christian thinks is Turn-away, being escorted to his damnation. This scene prompts Christian to relate the story of Little-faith, who was mugged by the brothers Faint-heart, Mistrust, and Guilt. After being misled by Flatterer, a black man garbed in white, Christian and Hopeful are released from his net by a shining figure carrying a whip, with which he thrashes the errant pilgrims.

Chastened, the travelers easily handle a laughing Atheist, whose twenty-year search for the Celestial City has proven fruitless. Hopeful nearly falls asleep in the Inchanted Ground, but he and Christian make it to the country of Beulah, with its perpetual sunshine, sweet air, and singing birds. Christian, however, becomes despondent when he learns that the River of Death lies ahead. Indeed, as he makes the crossing, waves wash over him and he begins to sink, only to be saved when he heeds Hopeful's exhortation to remain steadfast in his faith. Beyond the river the heavenly gates open, granting them access to the Celestial City amid the glorious sound of trumpets and bells. The gates do not open for Ignorance, who is bound and carried to hell's doorway by two shining agents of God, and on this note the allegorical dream ends.

## "*As I Pull'd, It Came*"[48]: Inspiration and Experience

In crafting his allegory Bunyan drew on a variety of sources, including the Bible, though the notion of believers as pilgrims appears only briefly in Scripture. One key passage is found in Hebrews 11:13, a book that made a substantial impression on him[49]; there the Old Testament saints are described as having been "strangers and pilgrims on the earth." More useful for his purpose was 1 Peter 2:11, which refers to first-century Christians as "strangers and pilgrims." In both passages, the coupling of pilgrims and strangers sets the tone for his allegory, which makes Christian, Faithful, and Hopeful aliens to the world's ways, as reflected, for example, in the Vanity Fair episode and Christian's departure from his family. Of the four references to pilgrimage in the Old Testament, two, both in Genesis 47:9, are synonymous with the span of a lifetime. Exodus 6:4 uses the image of strangers on a pilgrimage to refer to the Hebrews, an idea subsequently reflected in personal terms by the psalmist (119:54). Beyond the pilgrimage theme, much of the allegory's content evinces scriptural influence, as manifested especially in the marginalia's plethora of biblical references.[50] In addition to providing a text within a text, the scriptural quotations enhance the book's claim to authority.

Beyond the Bible, Bunyan was influenced by the venerable notion of pilgrimage in the Christian tradition, passed down in sermons, tracts, and popular custom, and by folklore accounts of heroes, knights and chivalric deeds, monsters and giants, heroic battles, dungeons and dragons, and wondrous escapes. Bunyan, of course, acknowledged his youthful love of the tale of St. George and of *Bevis of Southampton* (*MW*, 1:333). The latter seems to have influenced his depiction of Apollyon, the lions, the cave of giants Pope and Pagan, and possibly Giant Despair. As we have seen, he probably read the story of St. George in Richard Johnson's *The Most Famous History of the Seven Champions of Christendome* (1596), a work that almost certainly influenced his allegory in numerous ways, including the folk-tale motifs and "Johnson's narrative form, a mixture of plot with discussions, set speeches and poems."[51] Among the other works thought to have

---

[48] *PP*, 2.

[49] Brainerd P. Stranahan, "Bunyan and the Epistle to the Hebrews: His Source for the Idea of Pilgrimage in *The Pilgrim's Progress*," *Studies in Philology* 79 (1982): 280.

[50] Maxine Hancock examines Bunyan's use of marginalia to refer, index, interpret, and generalize in *The Key in the Window: Marginal Notes in Bunyan's Narratives* (Vancouver: Regent College Publishing, 2000).

[51] Margaret Spufford, *Small Books and Pleasant Histories: Popular Fiction and Its Readership in Seventeenth-Century England* (Athens: University of Georgia Press, 1981), 7–8; Nick Shrimpton, "Bunyan's Military Metaphor," in *Pilgrim's Progress*, ed. Newey, 212 (quoted).

had an impact on *The Pilgrim's Progress* are Francis Quarles' *Emblemes* (1635), Geoffrey Whitney's *A Choice of Emblemes and Other Devises* (1586), Richard Bernard's *The Isle of Man* (1627), Arthur Dent's *The Plaine Mans Path-Way to Heaven* (1601), and the works of Thomas Adams.[52] Although such material may have influenced Bunyan, deliberate borrowing cannot be proven, and most of the similarities may have resulted from the presence of these themes in folklore and popular Christianity.

In creating his allegory Bunyan drew heavily on his own experience, and in this limited sense the book is autobiographical. But *The Pilgrim's Progress* is not an allegorical rewriting of *Grace Abounding*, as G. B. Harrison averred, or even "an encoded record of the author's life," as Kathleen Swaim has suggested.[53] Most of *Grace Abounding* deals with Bunyan's conversion experience and the preceding events, whereas the greater part of *The Pilgrim's Progress* (some 77 percent) follows Christian's conversion, symbolized by the loss of his burden, his new clothing, the mark on his forehead, and his receipt of a seal-bearing roll (*PP*, 38). In theological terms, *Grace Abounding* deals primarily with election, calling, and conviction, whereas *The Pilgrim's Progress* focuses on sanctification. Roger Sharrock's contention that "each major crisis of the pilgrimage reflects some stage in Bunyan's spiritual struggles"[54] is valid only if we recognize that Bunyan transposed some of the personal religious experiences recorded in *Grace Abounding* to Christian's post-conversion pilgrimage. This is true particularly of the episodes involving Apollyon, the Valley of the Shadow of Death, and Giant Despair and Doubting Castle. More generally, until he reached the Celestial City, Christian's victories, as Vincent Newey has observed, "are all inconclusive—repeated moments of release and of temporary psychological poise along a line of continuing tension,"[55] as in *Grace Abounding*. A literary artist, Bunyan transposed his early religious experiences to illustrate the ongoing struggles of sanctification. Only in

---

[52] Harold Golder, "The Chivalric Background of Pilgrim's Progress" (Ph.D. diss., Harvard University, 1925); Golder, "Bunyan's Giant Despair," *Journal of English and Germanic Philology* 30 (1931): 361–78; Roger Sharrock, "Bunyan and the English Emblem Writers," *Review of English Studies* 21 (April 1945): 107; Sharrock, *JB*, 95–100; James F. Forrest, "Ignorance as White Devil: A Bunyan Debt to Thomas Adams?" *Canadian Journal of Theology* 8 (January 1962): 49–50; U. Milo Kaufmann, "Spiritual Discerning: Bunyan and the Mysteries of the Divine Will," in *John Bunyan*, ed. Keeble, 175–76; Hill, *TPM*, 165–66. For Quarles, Whitney, Bernard, and Adams see *DNB, s.vv.*

[53] G. B. Harrison, *John Bunyan: A Study in Personality* (Garden City, NY: Doubleday, Doran and Company, 1928), 166; Swaim, *PP*, 17.

[54] Sharrock, *JB*, 75.

[55] Vincent Newey, "Bunyan and the Confines of the Mind," in *Pilgrim's Progress*, ed. Newey, 33.

this sense can we deem *The Pilgrim's Progress* "the literary and psychological heir of *Grace Abounding*."[56] By making Christian's post-conversion experience one of recurring spiritual struggle, Bunyan indicated that his own life was not without its periodic trials, doubts, and wrestling with the forces of darkness. *The Pilgrim's Progress* is autobiographical not only because of its borrowing from *Grace Abounding* but also because it stands as a sequel to that work. Christian embodies more than "the terrors and soul-searchings of [Bunyan's] own religious awakening"[57]; he reveals the author's ongoing encounters with the enemies of his faith, both internal and external.

The allegory's indebtedness to *Grace Abounding* is substantial. Hopeful's account of his superficial religious reform prior to his conversion, including assorted acts of piety, reflects Bunyan's "outward Reformation" that so amazed his neighbors but failed to address his religious needs (*GA*, §§29–32). The road to genuine reformation commenced when Bunyan began to experience a conviction of sin and a longing for knowledge about the way to heaven (*GA*, §§37–42); this period in his life must have been in his mind when he had Christian tell Pliable that Obstinate would not have renounced his pilgrimage if he had "felt what I have felt of the Powers, and Terrours of what is yet unseen" (*PP*, 12). The Slough of Despond echoes Bunyan's plunge into despair at the awareness of his vileness (*GA*, §84). Christian's worry that Mount Legality might fall on his head may reflect Bunyan's youthful fear that a church bell would break lose and crush him, and his vision of a gap—Christ—in the wall separating Christians and the world (*GA*, §55) seems to have inspired the allegory's wicket-gate. As Christian wends his way through the Valley of the Shadow of Death, a fiend whispers blasphemies in his ears, making him think they originated in his own mind, an experience Bunyan had undergone a number of times (*GA*, §§100, 101, 107, 200, 253); at last he finds comfort when he realizes, as Evangelist tells Christian, that "all manner of sin and blasphemies shall be forgiven" (*PP*, 22). Just as Bunyan's spiritual turmoil had been lengthy, so Christian's combat with Apollyon lasts "for a long season" (74). At this point in his journey Christian is "preoccupied with the monstrous appearance of evil,"[58] much as Bunyan had been in the early 1650s. The Doubting Castle episode, in which Christian and Hopeful contemplate suicide, must have been inspired in part by Bunyan's recollection of his earlier dread that he had committed the unpardonable sin, at which time thoughts of suicide were in his mind (*GA*, §149).

The echoes of Bunyan's personal experience in *The Pilgrim's Progress* are evi-

[56] Furlong, *Puritan's Progress*, 111.
[57] Sharrock, *JB*, 74.
[58] Knott, *SS*, 148.

dent in yet other ways. Hopeful's observation about his own religious experience reflects Bunyan's remarks in *Grace Abounding* (§§256, 296): "One day I was very sad, I think sader then at any one time in my life; and this sadness was through a fresh sight of the greatness and vileness of my sins" (*PP*, 142–43). Another poignant echo occurs near the beginning of the allegory when Graceless tells Evangelist, "Sir, if I be not fit to go to Prison, I am not fit (I am sure) to go to Judgement, and from thence to Execution" (10). As he faced imprisonment in 1660 and the hardship this would pose for his family, Bunyan wrestled with precisely this concern (*GA*, §§324–31). In his discussion with By-ends, Christian avers that the godly must be willing to be bound in irons (*PP*, 100), another allusion to Bunyan's incarceration. Bunyan may also have drawn on his arrest, trial, and imprisonment in drafting the Vanity Fair account. The allegorical Interpreter, who seeks to "unfold dark things to sinners" (29), is undoubtedly modeled on Bunyan's pastoral experience; indeed, in the prologue to *The Pilgrim's Progress* he defends his work as the explication of truth through "dark" words:

> My dark and cloudy words they do but hold
> The Truth, as Cabinets inclose the Gold. (4)

When Interpreter tells Christian of his own dream, it is the vision of the Last Judgment, the very fear of which had started Graceless and Bunyan on their momentous pilgrimages. The hospitality provided by the shepherds in the Delectable Mountains probably reflects the welcome Bunyan received on his preaching forays outside Bedford. Finally, in depicting Christian's fear as the waters of the River of Death washed over him, Bunyan may have recalled his own near drowning as a youth. Thus, although he has freely transposed his experiences to suit his allegorical needs, *The Pilgrim's Progress* is autobiographical in its inspiration and experiential core.

The impact of Bunyan's personal experience on *The Pilgrim's Progress* is especially evident in the allegory's numerous manifestations of his prior psychological struggles. Indeed, the prologue indicates that he wrote the allegory in part to help the despairing reader "*divert thy self from Melancholly*" (7). As Michael MacDonald notes, "the Puritans produced a literature of anxious gloom in which despair normally preceded conversion."[59] To the extent that Bunyan was fishing for converts with his allegory, his treatment of despair was firmly in the puritan tradition, as various commentators have recognized. Dayton Haskin, for instance, avers that Bunyan made dealing with guilt a major problem for those on "the human pilgrimage," and used Worldly-wiseman and Ignorance as examples of

---

[59] Michael MacDonald, *Mystical Bedlam: Madness, Anxiety, and Healing in Seventeenth-Century England* (Cambridge: Cambridge University Press, 1983), 9.

those who deny guilt's reality.[60] Remarking on Christian's frequent feelings of dread and anxiety, Paula Backscheider notes that his "most acute suffering involves mental anguish combining confusion over his present situation and of his responsibility for his suffering" (70). More generally, she contends that Bunyan was depicting the Christian life as the experience of alternating anxiety and assurance (148). From a theological perspective, John Knott astutely suggests that Christian's recurring trials, each appropriate to a particular stage of the journey, stem from the doubt caused by the godly's inability to have total assurance of faith in this life.[61]

Several critics have recognized that Bunyan's treatment of despair in the allegory goes beyond the typical puritan understanding and reflects mental illness. S. J. Newman candidly refers to Christian's (Bunyan's) psychosis, and David Mills to the neurotic nature of his "self-interested fears" and obsession with guilt. Christian's "creative fear," Mills argues, "always borders on a spiritual despair which threatens to drive him to mental and emotional self-destruction as well as to spiritual damnation."[62] Andrew Brink's stimulating reading of *The Pilgrim's Progress* as "a full-scale allegory of the melancholic temperament" is grounded in his belief that Bunyan suffered from severe depression, and that his "extreme isolation as a lonely pilgrim" led to his quest to discover "new supporting relationships, to be fed, clothed, and confirmed in his being by parental figures" such as the paternal Evangelist and the maternal wicket gate.[63] In assessing what Christian's relations deemed his "frenzy distemper" (9), the symptoms of which were desertion of his family, violent outbursts, an obsession with death, and "a paralysis of will due to irresistible compulsions which have no direction in which to flow," Vincent Newey concludes that he suffered from a genuine neurosis. "There is," Newey contends, "no bolder spectacle of incipient insanity in literature."[64] It is not the case, however, that Bunyan "generalizes the psychosis of an individual into the crisis of a people."[65] Christian's experience is not universal but autobiographical, for Bunyan offers alternative patterns of experience in Faithful and

---

[60]Dayton Haskin, "Bunyan's Scriptural Acts," in *Bunyan*, ed. Collmer, 71.

[61]Knott, *SS*, 143.

[62]S. J. Newman, "Bunyan's Solidness," in *Pilgrim's Progress*, ed. Newey, 236–37; David Mills, "The Dreams of Bunyan and Langland," in ibid., 160, 168, 174.

[63]Andrew Brink, "Bunyan's *Pilgrim's Progress* and the Secular Reader: A Psychological Approach," *English Studies in Canada* 1 (Winter 1975): 386–405 (quoted at 390, 400).

[64]Newey, "Bunyan and the Confines of the Mind," 35. Cf. Stuart Sim's suggestion that "anxiety is arguably Bunyan's most important legacy to literary history." *Negotiations with Paradox: Narrative Practice and Narrative Form in Bunyan and Defoe* (New York: Harvester Wheatsheaf, 1990), 45.

[65]Newman, "Bunyan's Solidness," 236–37.

Hopeful. Faithful's trials transpire not in the Slough of Despond and the Valley of
the Shadow of Death but with Madam Wanton and the first Adam in the Valley
of Humiliation.[66] Unlike Christian, Hopeful nearly succumbs to sleep in the Inchanted Ground, and he has to comfort Christian and dissuade him from suicide
in Doubting Castle. Bunyan would later use the second part of *The Pilgrim's Progress* to drive home his point that not all believers undergo the intense psychological struggles he and his allegorical Christian experienced.

The *Pilgrim's Progress* is neither the product of a psychotic mind nor the depiction of a mentally ill pilgrim but the work of a man who had undergone recurring bouts of depression at least as recently as the early 1660s and perhaps somewhat later. That such an individual could possess extraordinary creative talent is
evident in the lives of such artists as Albrecht Dürer and Vincent van Gogh, Ing-
mar Bergman and William Styron, Jack London and Ernest Hemingway, Hart
Crane, and Albert Camus. Not only are Bunyan's traumatic psychological battles
reflected in *The Pilgrim's Progress*, but they enhance its power as a literary work
through the gripping intensity of the human drama. Because despair, desperation, the forces of darkness, and suicide fascinate as well as repel, we are drawn to
observe them even as our rational being renounces their destructive powers and
their threat to our very being. John Knott has aptly remarked that "Bunyan's
powerful images of physical suffering suggest the force of the assault upon spiritual health nonconformists could expect in prison."[67] I would take this a step
further and contend that Bunyan's potent images of psychological suffering reflect the insidious onslaught on mental and physical health in those who suffer
from depression. Bunyan, we recall, wrote his allegory in part to help those who
suffered from what his age called melancholy. How much he understood of his
own illness we cannot know, but he garnered inspiration and insight from it, as
reflected especially in *The Pilgrim's Progress* and *Grace Abounding*. When he
found Luther's commentary on Galatians valuable because it "so largely and
profoundly handled" his condition (*GA*, §129), it was at least partly because Luther addressed the problem not only of guilt but also of depression—"heaviness
of spirit, desperation and such-like"—which "mightily assail[s]" the person
wrestling with "serious conflicts and terrors" (*PP*, 327). Such people, Luther suggested, are entrapped in a spiritual prison, devoid of inner peace and overwhelmed with mental anguish (462). For those who fight this darkness, life is a

---

[66] Swaim, *PP*, 152. However, she seems to forget this important insight when she asserts
that the first part of *The Pilgrim's Progress* is about "the struggles of the separatist professor" (199). Christian's experience cannot be regarded as typical of all separatists, much
less universal in scope, as Nellist contends. "*The Pilgrim's Progress* and Allegory," 138.

[67] Knott, *DM*, 206.

battle not "with oneself"[68] but within oneself, against the despair and utter black-ness that threaten being itself.

From the outset of his allegory, Bunyan drew on his ordeal with black de-spondency. When Graceless, laden with a heavy burden, becomes sorely dis-tressed, his wife and children hope sleep will "settle his brains" and cure his "frenzy distemper," but he spends the night crying and sighing, his condition worsened by his insomnia, an experience painfully familiar to the depressed. So too is the solitude he seeks as he walks alone in the fields before retiring to his chamber "to condole his own misery," being "greatly distressed in his mind" (9). Bunyan's family had undoubtedly wondered about his sanity, insomnia, and solitude, and his friends may have responded to him as Obstinate did to Grace-less, adjudging the latter one of the "*Craz'd-headed Coxcombs*" and "*a brain-sick fellow*" (11–12). Worldly-wiseman probably echoes the response of Bunyan's neighbors to his distress when he warns Christian that those who read the Bible seriously will become so distracted that "*they run them upon desperate ventures, to obtain they know not what*" (18). Ignorance will subsequently espouse a similar opinion, deeming the beliefs of Christian and Hopeful "*the fruit of distracted braines*" (148). Such points are made frequently enough to indicate the likelihood of Bunyan having heard similar comments during his own travail. As is still the case, depression is often ridiculed or misunderstood by people unaware of its nature as a serious illness.[69]

Christian's weeping, sleeplessness, and seclusion soon lead him into the Slough of Despond, where his sinking reflects the helplessness, and the dirt manifests the self-denigration characteristic of depression. The despair is dead-ening, the burden oppressive, the feeling of being forsaken by God overpowering. So awful is the despondency that even God is unable to prevent some woeful pil-grims from plunging into the morass; this surely is the point of Bunyan's com-ment that 20,000 cartloads of the best material and millions of wholesome in-structions have been unable to obliterate the slough. From his own affliction with grinding hopelessness he knew how distant and helpless God seemingly could be. Fortunate travelers have stepping stones to navigate the slough, a clear indication that not everyone must plummet into despair's unfathomable black depths. Es-cape from the slough brings only partial, temporary relief, and Christian, still a burdened, melancholic man, is counseled by Worldly-wiseman to seek the assis-tance of Mr. Legality, a gentleman with the "*skill to cure those that are somewhat crazed in their wits*" (19). When Christian goes to see him, "musing in the midst

---

[68] As Newey avers. "Bunyan and the Confines of the Mind," 30.

[69] Cf. Stachniewski's harsh assertion that the Slough of Despond "represents a wal-lowing in masochism" (186).

of [his] *dumps*," he fears a nearby mountain will fall and crush him, a manifestation of the irrationality that typically accompanies the illness.

One of the allegory's most chilling reflections of Bunyan's experience is the
caged man seen by Christian at Interpreter's house. Any victim of depression can
recognize the description: "The Man . . . seemed very sad: he sat with his eyes
looking down to the ground, his hands folded together; and he sighed as if he
would break his heart" (34). Bunyan used this emblem to represent someone
who has knowingly committed the unpardonable sin, thereby forsaking all hope,
as he once feared he had done. But he also knew the depths of despair, which he
projected onto this woeful figure. Unlike Bunyan, however, the caged man has
fallen into what Newey calls "a state of psychic arrestment"[70]—depression from
which no recovery is possible. Sharrock has argued that Bunyan's account of the
caged man was influenced by Quarles, whose book of emblems includes a caged
bird fluttering from doubt to despair; by the case of Francesco Spira, mentioned
in *Grace Abounding*; and by that of John Child, who had conformed to the
Church of England before the Restoration and would commit suicide in October
1684.[71] But Child's case is not the source because he did not become depressed
until July 1684.[72] Spira's story is a likely source. Richard Baxter complained that
reading about him had caused many to experience increased melancholy.[73] Luther may also have influenced Bunyan on this point, for in his commentary on
Galatians he observed how many committed suicide because of their inability to
cope with their dread of divine judgment. Luther too was interested in those who
had seemingly renounced their faith and succumbed to the despair of darkness.
"Everyone that falleth from the promise to the law, from faith to works, doth
nothing else but lay upon himself, being weak and beggarly already, such a yoke
as he is not able to bear (Acts xv. 10), and in bearing thereof is made ten times
more weak and beggarly so that at length he is driven to despair, unless Christ
come and deliver him." For Luther the cause of such despair is strictly religious,
namely, one's inability or refusal to understand that the terror of divine judgment has been redirected by Christ's atoning work.[74] Because of Bunyan's psychological struggles and his literary artistry, he made the same point more strikingly with his portrayal of the doomed, brooding, confined man.

The periodic respite that Bunyan had experienced as he wrestled with ener-

[70] Newey, "Bunyan and the Confines of the Mind," 31. Haskin suggests that the man is
in the cage because he has been excessively introspective. "Bunyan's Scriptural Acts," 87.
Dwelling on one's misery is common among depressed people.

[71] Sharrock, in *PP*, 318; Sharrock, "Bunyan and the English Emblem Writers," 111–12.

[72] See Chapter 14.

[73] Richard Baxter, *A Christian Directory* (London, 1673), 312.

[74] Luther, *Galatians*, 153, 333, 387 (quoted).

vating despair—the times of welcome relief enjoyed by most victims of depression—helped him convey Christian's "lightsom" feeling and his joyful leaping when he is eventually free of the burden (38). Such had been the millstone that he, like other depressed individuals, had lost pleasure even in his family (17). When the gloom lifts, Christian bursts into song:

> Thus far did I come loaden with my sin,
> Nor could ought ease the grief that I was in,
> Till I came hither: What a place is this!
> Must here be the beginning of my bliss? (38)

Theologically the answer is affirmative, but experientially the way ahead repeatedly afflicts the pilgrim with renewed despair. Depression is a tenacious foe, as Bunyan well knew. When Christian climbs Hill Difficulty he forgets his roll—the same divine promises that so bitterly eluded him in the Slough of Despond—which triggers renewed sighing and weeping. He manages to make it through the Valley of Humiliation before confronting Apollyon, whose militancy causes him to "despair of life" (59). This "monster of disorder and disorientation, aberrant, abnormal, a conjunction of fragments . . . [whose] essence is perversity,"[75] is especially invidious because he reminds Christian of those searing episodes of despair he previously underwent. The ensuing battle, though theologically framed by Christian's assertion of pardon for his offenses, evokes the desperate struggle mounted by some recovered victims of depression when they sense the onset of another bout. Despite experiencing "a dreadful fall" that nearly enables Apollyon to press him to death (the depressed's sense of being crushed by the weight of unseen forces), Christian recovers in time to repulse his tormentor, but not without again despairing that God has deserted him, a feeling familiar to many in the throes of depression. Such "Combat, no man can imagine" (59–60).[76]

   Shortly after his conflict with Apollyon, Christian enters the Valley of the Shadow of Death, which the prophet Jeremiah (2:6) depicted as a wilderness, a land of pits and desert, and a drought-stricken, uninhabited place. On the left of the traveler's narrow path is perilous quicksand devoid of solid footing, and on the right is a deep ditch into which the blind lead the unseeing. Midway through this terrifying valley is the mouth of hell, spewing flame and smoke, "with sparks and hideous noises" (63). As he makes his way, Christian, hearing doleful voices, fears he will be torn asunder or trampled like mire in the streets, and he becomes so confused when a fiend surreptitiously whispers blasphemies in his ear that he

[75] Frye, GMS, 124.
[76] I would modify Newey's observation about this battle by adding one word: "The defeat of Apollyon is the defeat of the devil [depression] within himself." "Bunyan and the Confines of the Mind," 32.

is unable to recognize his own voice. Disoriented and terrified in the darkness, he hears another voice say that God is with him (Psalm 23:4), "though by reason of the impediment that attends this place, I cannot perceive it" (64). When morning comes, although he is still in the valley he can look back and see the dangers he providentially avoided. Again remembering the profound solitude in which he suffered during the darkest times of his melancholy, Bunyan has Christian profess that he is "much affected with his deliverance from all the dangers of his solitary way" as he views them in dawn's early light (64–65). But more of the valley lies ahead, and if anything Christian deems this portion more perilous because of traps, nets, and pits. If it had still been dark, "had he had a thousand souls, they had in reason been cast away" (65). The message is clear: Bunyan knew from experience that not even the light of reason can comfort the tortured soul in this valley, for only divine guidance can lead the pilgrim to safe passage. Vincent Newey aptly observes that in this place "the shadow side of the psyche—the darkness within, the vortex of deadly fears and imaginings"—threatens to engulf Christian.[77] Although the fiends and hazards are in the mind, they are nevertheless real, and some of the allegory's sheer power to captivate stems from Bunyan's recognition of this fact. Death in this valley is spiritual, the insidious threat to psychological well-being and ultimately the portent of extinction. Loss of faith and deprivation of hope are the twin, virtually inseparable perils. In composing this passage Bunyan had Job in mind, for he too survived this valley, this darkness, this despair.[78] But this is *not* everyone's experience, for throughout Faithful's journey through this valley the sun shines.

Unlike Faithful, Christian manages to escape from Vanity Fair, whose residents adjudged them "Bedlams and Mad" (91), another reflection of the cruel remarks that must have been made about Bunyan when depression wracked his mind and body. With his new companion, Hopeful, the antithesis of melancholy, Christian finds himself in spiritual and psychological trouble again, this time because he ventures into By-path-meadow. A temporary companion, Vain-confidence, leads the way, but in the darkness falls into a deep pit and perishes. Lost in a heavy rain and lightning storm, Christian and Hopeful attempt to return, "but it was so dark, and the flood was so high, that in their going back they had like to have been drowned nine or ten times" (113). Bunyan, of course, nearly drowned as a youth, but the stormy circumstances and the repeated sensation of being engulfed in dark waters go beyond this and strongly suggest the incompa-

[77] Newey, "Bunyan and the Confines of the Mind," 32.

[78] Swaim (*PP*, 101) notes that Job used the phrase "shadow of despair" ten times. Styron prominently quotes Job (3:25–26) on the first page of *Darkness Visible: A Memoir of Madness* (New York: Random House, 1990).

rable agony of the seriously depressed. "For myself," William Styron wrote, "the pain is most closely connected to drowning or suffocation."[79]

The wayward pilgrims, seeking shelter from a storm, blunder onto the grounds of Doubting Castle, the home of Giant Despair. For trespassing, he imprisons them in his dark dungeon, a place "nasty and stinking to the spirit" (114). Vicious beatings follow, prompting their sighs and embittered lamentations. At the urging of his wife, Diffidence, Giant Despair urges the prisoners to commit suicide by knife, rope, or poison, a course of action Christian carefully ponders. Doubt leads to despair as Christian senses that God has deserted him; his hope flags, though Hopeful, a way of personifying Bunyan's own feeling, will not let him take his life. For a time the Bible is no help, and Christian can only recall Job's morose longing to be strangled (Job 7:15). Overcome with despair, Christian feels the crushing weight of unseen forces on him. The dialogue between Christian and Hopeful regarding suicide echoes the inner turmoil within Bunyan when he contemplated taking his own life: "*Now* was I both a burthen and a terror to myself, nor did I ever so know, as *now*, what it was to be weary of my life, and yet afraid to die" (*GA*, §149).[80] The exchange between Christian and Hopeful reflects wrestling with the despair that will, if triumphant, claim one's life. As Styron knew, "faith in deliverance, in ultimate restoration, is absent" in depression, the blackest depths of which Bunyan poignantly captured in Doubting Castle and its tyrannical giant. Just as some depressed people sense at this nadir "a second self—a wraithlike observer" who watches the soul struggle against the forces of despair,[81] so Bunyan made Hopeful serve this function. But unlike those wraithlike observers described by Styron, Hopeful is engaged rather than dispassionate, and through his efforts Christian eschews self-annihilation, even as release continues to elude him.

Hope can sustain but not liberate. Freedom comes only when, on Sunday morning, the day of resurrection, Christian remembers he has a key to the dungeon—the promises that helped him escape the Slough of Despond. Christian's discovery that the key has been with him all the time is neither a flaw in the plot nor a suggestion that the black despondency is self-imposed.[82] From his own experience Bunyan knew his melancholic moods had terminated at some point, though not for any discernible reason. He realized only that as he emerged from

[79] Styron, *Darkness Visible*, 17.

[80] A number of scholars have seen such characters as Hopeful, Faithful, By-ends, and Worldly-wiseman as representations of Bunyan's state of mind. See, e.g., Sharrock, *JB*, 75; Mills, "The Dreams of Bunyan and Langland," 173; Luxon, 171; Backscheider, 68.

[81] Styron, *Darkness Visible*, 62, 64.

[82] As suggested by Nellist, "*The Pilgrim's Progress* and Allegory," 148.

these periods of forlornness he had expressed hope in divine (biblical) promises of forgiveness. For a time the way to normalcy proved to be "*damnable* hard," just as Christian found the key when he turned it in the dungeon lock. In psychological terms, the Doubting Castle episode represents psychic confinement followed by psychic release, the experience of which Bunyan managed to capture so effectively in allegory because he had lived it. This is more than what Leo Damrosch has called release from "an unexpected shift of mood, a sudden recovery of one's better self rather than a gradual process of introspection,"[83] for in Bunyan's experience relief was a process rather than a momentary event.

By the time Christian and Hopeful reach Beulah, which represents psychological well-being and spiritual contentment, Doubting Castle is no longer visible. In this land, where the Celestial City can be seen, shining ones walk, and the sun, the symbolic enemy of depression, never sets. Both pilgrims now hear voices, but this time the message is about imminent salvation (Isaiah 62:11). However, Christian's trials are not yet over, for he still must cross the River of Death, the depth of which varies according to one's capacity to believe in the scriptural promises, and Christian has never been very good at clinging to them. Bunyan knew from experience that despair has a way of returning, and he was true to that experience when he depicted Christian's crossing. As Christian sinks in the deep water, once again enduring the horrific sensation of drowning, he cries to Hopeful:

> Ah, my friend, the sorrows of death have compassed me about, I shall not see the Land that flows with Milk and Honey. And with that, a great darkness and horror fell upon *Christian*, so that he could not see before him; also he in great measure lost his senses, so that he could neither remember nor orderly talk of any of those sweet refreshments that he had met with in the way of his Pilgrimage. But all the words that he spake, still tended to discover that he had horror of mind. (*PP*, 157)

Apparitions of hobgoblins and evil spirits return, bringing back the fathomless, inexplicable inky depths that previously engulfed him. Bunyan was drawing on the experience of his worst periods of forlornness to portray so vividly the final, fearful despair that can afflict even the godly pilgrim. Luther had imputed a similar experience to Christ, who took upon him the sins of others, which "cast him down for a little while, and ran over his head like water" (281). In the end, salvation comes, as always, with the equally unexplainable recall of a biblical promise—Isaiah 43:2. Once again, Bunyan made it clear that Christian's experience is not universal, for Hopeful crosses the river without difficulty.

The Celestial City into which they enter is, as Christian told Pliable near the beginning of the pilgrimage, a place without crying, tears, or sorrow—a place

---

[83] Damrosch, *GP*, 165.

without depression. To a victim of melancholy, such a place is indeed one's special, ultimate hope. Seen in this light, *The Pilgrim's Progress* represents Bunyan's triumph over the crushing despair of his depressed moods. It is an allegory whose theme is the contest between hope and fear, doubt and assurance, dejection and encouragement, darkness and light.

The theme of darkness and light is prevalent in the Christian tradition, not least because of its forceful expression in the Johannine gospel. Among Bunyan's contemporaries the Friends made much of this theme. But darkness and light also characterize the experience of depression and recovery, however temporary. Styron described his recuperation from a particularly deleterious period of utter dejection in these terms: "Although I was still shaky I knew I had emerged into light."[84] Bunyan's handling of the theme in his allegory owes as much to his psychological travail as to Scripture, yet he was careful to accord the latter full credit, writing in the prologue:

> . . . *there springs*
> *From that same Book that lustre, and those rayes*
> *Of light, that turns our darkest nights to days.* (4)

Indeed, the intent of his allegorical method was to facilitate the shining of the light that dispels darkness:

> *Use it I may then, and yet nothing smother*
> *Truths golden Beams; Nay, by this method may*
> *Make it cast forth its rayes as light as day.* (6)

Light, then, is truth or the means of its revelation, whereas darkness signifies ignorance and has the connotation of evil. This is the biblical sense, but in his allegory Bunyan, reflecting his melancholic episodes, also associates light with spiritual happiness and freedom, and darkness with despair and confinement.[85] In both the biblical and the psychological connotations, light equates with the good and darkness with the bad.

In its reflection of Bunyan's experiences of despair and relief, *The Pilgrim's Progress* is a series of episodes that alternate between darkness and light, turmoil and calm, evil and good. At the outset, Graceless' distress occurs near nightfall, but a troubled night leaves him feeling even worse. Unable to see the wicket-gate when Evangelist points to it, Graceless must be shown a shining light, which he follows to the gate. In his subsequent conversation with Pliable, Christian describes heavenly garments that make inhabitants of the Celestial City shine like

---

[84] Styron, *Darkness Visible*, 75.

[85] Earlier, Richard Sibbes had associated spiritual despair with darkness. *Divine Meditations and Holy Contemplations* (Wilmington, DE, 1797), 4.

the sun. In contrast, navigating the Slough of Despond is difficult because the steps often cannot be seen, for "this place doth much spue out its filth" (16). This prompts Worldly-wiseman to warn Christian of the dangers that lie ahead, including darkness as well as hunger, dragons, pain, and death. At the Interpreter's house the master has his servant light a candle to show Christian the way, a reminder that pilgrims need divine light to dispel the gloom. "The taking of the hand in association with the initial lighting of a candle," observes Milo Kaufmann, "suggests that the way is dark, and that Christian may stumble."[86] Despair and darkness are vividly associated in Bunyan's rendition of the "very dark Room" containing the emblem of a man in an iron cage (34), whereas the message of divine forgiveness at the cross is delivered by three shining ones. When Formalist and Hypocrisie choose to follow the ways of danger and destruction, one finds himself in a great and obviously dark wood, while the other ends in "a wide field full of dark Mountains," where he perishes (42). After Christian forgets his roll, he retraces his steps to retrieve it, but this leaves him in darkness well short of the summit when the sun sets; the resultant experience, clearly psychological in nature, is ascribed by Bunyan to Christian's vain sleeping, by which he means his forgetfulness of the divine promises: "*I must walk without the Sun, darkness must cover the path of my feet, and I must hear the noise of doleful Creatures, because of my sinful sleep!*" (45). Diametrically opposed is Christian's restful sleep in the Palace Beautiful, where his chamber, called Peace, faces eastward to welcome the rising sun.

Light and darkness retain their significance, psychological as well as theological, during the latter part of the pilgrimage. The horrific Valley of the Shadow of Death, populated with hobgoblins, satyrs, and dragons, is "as dark as pitch," a place devoid of order, filled with terrible noise, and covered by clouds of confusion and the wings of death (62). So gloomy is it that Christian, unable to see where he steps, nearly plunges into the mire on one side of the path or the deep ditch on the other, a reflection, it seems, of Bunyan's recognition that depression can easily lead to one's destruction. The darkness and confusion, Knott indicates, are associated with deprivation of the sense of divine presence.[87] The marginalia direct the reader to Job 3:5, with its foreboding reference to "the blackness of the day," and 10:22, which depicts "a land of darkness . . . where the light is as darkness." Similarly, Styron writes of feeling "the horror, like some poisonous fogbank, roll in upon my mind."[88] For Christian, the sun finally rises, enabling him

---

[86] U. Milo Kaufmann, *The Pilgrim's Progress and Traditions in Puritan Meditation* (New Haven, CT: Yale University Press, 1966), 63.

[87] Knott, *SS*, 148.

[88] Styron, *Darkness Visible*, 58.

to escape the sepulchral valley. Palpably relieved, he bursts into song:

> *Dangers in darkness, Devils, Hell, and Sin,*
> *Did compass me, while I this Vale was in.* (66)

Bunyan returns to the image of light as truth in the Vanity Fair scene, where one of Faithful's jurors is Mr. Hate-light, but the psychological meaning is again evident when Christian and Hopeful find themselves imprisoned in Doubting Castle. *"With thee I mourn without the light,"* Hopeful says (116–17). The beneficial impact of sunshine on many depressed people is manifest in Bunyan's depiction of Giant Despair, who in sunny weather falls into fits and temporarily loses the use of a hand. From Mount Caution the pilgrims can see Giant Despair's most tragic victims, blinded and stumbling among tombs, the living dead, Styron's "walking wounded."[89] In the Delectable Mountains the shepherds show the pilgrims the by-way to hell, which enables them to glimpse this gloomy, smoky place, hear the fearsome noise like a roaring fire, and smell sulphur's putrid scent. When the pilgrims meet Turn-away from the town of Apostacy, they are in a very dark lane, another example of Bunyan's use of light and darkness in a theological sense.

As Christian and Hopeful near the end of their journey, they enter the country of Beulah, where the sun shines night and day, and where shining ones walk in a land of plenty. From here the pilgrims can see the Celestial City, gleaming so brightly in the sun that they cannot fully behold it. The two men who warn them about the River of Death have countenances that shine "as the light" (156). When the waters of the River of Death engulf Christian, he temporarily loses sight of Christ, the last experience of darkness on the pilgrimage. Having made it through the river, the pilgrims are greeted by two shining figures who take them to the gate of the glistening city, filled with radiant angels. In this place, which shines "like the Sun," Christian and Hopeful receive garments that sparkle like gold (161–62). For the saved, everything is ultimately bathed in light, the antithesis of the murk that overwhelms the depressed. Bunyan's use of light and darkness is less evocative of the Johannine theological imagery than the psychological treatment found in Job.

## *"By Dint of Sword"*[90]: Persecution and Allegorical Warfaring

Although Bunyan's bouts with despair are reflected in and helped shape *The Pilgrim's Progress*, the allegory is not fundamentally about what his age called melancholy. However, it very much concerns Protestant, especially noncon-

---

[89] Ibid., 62.
[90] *PP*, 60.

formist, life in the late seventeenth century. This is evident, for instance, in his treatment of persecution, whether psychological (as in his extended treatment of despair), physical, or social. Persecution is, of course, part of the New Testament pattern of Christian life. As Paul told the church at Corinth, he took pleasure in persecution, for physical weakness is conducive to spiritual strength. Like Paul, Bunyan and his pilgrims glory in their infirmities (2 Cor. 12:9–10). As Leo Damrosch perceptively observes, "Bunyan *needed* prison."[91] When confronted by the persecuting tyrant Apollyon, Christian finds strength in affirming that God permits such ordeals to test the love of Christians and ascertain their resolve to cling to him until the end (58). As Luther explained in his commentary on Galatians, "if we were not exercised outwardly by tyrants and heretics with force and subtilty, and inwardly with terrors and the fiery darts of the devil, Paul should be as obscure and unknown unto us as he was in times past to the whole world" (400).

Rendering the lives of Christian, Faithful, and Hopeful in the context of persecution evinced Bunyan's belief in the necessity of undergoing trials. In depicting this he had to walk a fine line if he expected the book to receive the censor's approval. Persecution, after all, could be read as an indictment of royal and local government, and Bunyan's unmistakable references to Foxe's *Acts and Monuments* must have reminded perceptive readers of what had befallen Protestants in Mary Tudor's reign. Early in his pilgrimage Christian tells Pliable how those who persevere will ultimately see the martyrs. The "Histories" Christian beholds in the Palace Beautiful must have included Foxe (54). As Knott has observed, Bunyan wanted "his readers to identify with the role of martyr, to the point of being prepared to embrace suffering."[92] Consequently, Christian must eschew Worldly-wiseman's advice to avoid danger; indeed, Christian finds himself in peril of another sort when he heeds Worldly-wiseman's exhortation to consult with Mr. Legality and is frightened at the prospect of Mount Sinai falling on him. The theological and psychological dangers of legality threaten those afraid to suffer persecution for remaining faithful to the pilgrimage. To paraphrase Luther, one can suffer in a physical kingdom at the hands of tyrants or in a spiritual kingdom, with both realms being Satan's dominion (435).

Commentators have rightly seen the lions near the Palace Beautiful as symbols of persecution. The animals are sufficiently scary to send Timorous and Mistrust fleeing, and to frighten Christian, who thinks they "range in the night for their prey," an explicit association of darkness and persecution (45). Christian later discovers that the lions are chained and incapable of harming those who stay in the middle of the path. When Faithful treads the same route, the lions are

[91] Damrosch, *GP*, 162.
[92] Knott, *DM*, 200.

asleep because it is midday, when light is plentiful. Henri Talon has interpreted the sleeping lions as a reference to the time of Bunyan's conversion in the mid-1650s, whereas Sharrock thinks Bunyan was alluding to a later lapse in persecution,[93] but the fundamental point is another of Bunyan's affirmations that Christian experience varies; not all pilgrims suffer martyrdom or incarceration. Sharrock may be correct in seeing the two lions as symbols of civil and ecclesiastical persecution,[94] but for allegorical purposes Bunyan needed two lions astride the narrow path. Although they are chained and sometimes asleep, their threat should not be minimized, especially during pilgrims' darker moments. In addition to dissuading Timorous and Mistrust from continuing the pilgrimage, the lions terrify Christian, causing him to fear for his life. To the perspicacious reader the lions evoke the Foxian accounts of martyrs torn asunder by wild beasts. The Stuart state, Bunyan was suggesting, had the capability to destroy nonconformists even though it might be relatively tolerant at the time he wrote. In his preface to *Grace Abounding*, Bunyan had explicitly evoked the image of writing from the lion's den (1).

The assorted giants—Apollyon, Pope, Pagan, and Despair—also represent a varied array of persecution, ranging from the psychological type represented by Despair to the primarily physical kind symbolized by Pope and Pagan. The two varieties can be associated, as when the incarcerated are subjected to isolation from family and often friends, physical discomfort, the howls of shackled inmates, and near-pervasive gloom, leading to despair. Knott is right in seeing Giant Despair as "a caricature of the more tyrannical and abusive jailers in the prison experience of nonconformists."[95] Moreover, although Giant Pagan had long been deceased and Giant Pope was arthritic and elderly, near their cave were the "blood, bones, ashes, and mangled bodies" of earlier pilgrims. Pope permits Christian to pass, but he threatens more burnings in the future; of all the deaths he might have cited, burning is the most important because it evokes memories of Mary Tudor, and by implication warns of what might happen if a Catholic Stuart ascends the throne.

Bunyan's treatment of Catholicism in the allegory reflects sensitivity to conditions in England. When he read Luther's commentary on Galatians, he was reminded how Catholics had excommunicated, banished, and, where possible, killed Protestants, thinking by such acts to serve God (434). Foxe's *Acts and Monuments* provided vivid documentation of such activity. But when Bunyan wrote in the late 1660s, the papacy, preoccupied with the Jansenist challenge and

---

[93]Talon, 189; Sharrock, in *PP*, 325.
[94]Sharrock, in *PP*, 320.
[95]Knott, *DM*, 206.

Louis XIV's aggressive policies, represented no serious threat to English Protestants; hence Giant Pope is chained. The more insidious threat came from what Bunyan saw as Catholic influence in the Church of England and, more broadly, English society. He made this clear in the account of Vanity Fair, where "the Ware of *Rome* and her Merchandize is greatly promoted" (89). Catholicism was a leavening agent, poisoning England. In November 1666, unsubstantiated rumors about a planned Catholic massacre of Protestants had sparked fear, but a year later circumstances had shifted substantially, as reflected in a Privy Council order limiting access to the celebration of mass in the queen's chapel at St. James', the queen-mother's at Somerset House, and the residences of several foreign ambassadors.[96] Such services had been attracting too many people—evidence of the creeping progress of Catholicism Bunyan feared. The Council's action was well-received by nonconformists, though they remained vigilant. Baxter warned against Catholic efforts to impose religious unity because they could lead to massive executions and inquisitions.[97] As Bunyan completed *The Pilgrim's Progress*, concern about Catholicism was mounting, leading to a proclamation dated 22 March 1671 calling for the enforcement of the laws against Catholics and the exile of priests and Jesuits.[98] By the time this proclamation was issued, Bunyan had probably completed his allegory. Between this time and its publication, concern about Catholicism continued, as reflected, for example, in the lectures preached at Southwark; Nathaniel Vincent collected and published twenty-five of them, warning his readers that popery was "one of the *greatest visible Enemies* that Christ has in the world."[99] The intensity of the attack increased in 1677 with the publication of Marvell's *An Account of the Growth of Popery, and Arbitrary Government in England*, which argued that for years the Catholics had plotted "to change the Lawful Government of *England* into an Absolute Tyranny, and to Convert the Established *Protestant Religion* into down-right *Popery*" (3). Bunyan published his allegory before Titus Oates made his allegations of a Popish Plot in August 1678. Curiously, Bunyan made no changes in subsequent editions of *The Pilgrim's Progress* to reflect the intensifying fears of Catholicism, especially in the aftermath of the supposed conspiracy. He must have believed that the most serious threat continued to be the established church, which in his mind was dangerously cor-

---

[96] Friends' Library, London, Swarthmore MSS, vol. 3, fol. 137r; PRO, SP 29/216/148; *HMC* 25, *Le Fleming*, 53.

[97] PRO, SP 29/217/75; Baxter, *The Cure of Church-Divisions* (London, 1670), 276. Baxter wrote this book in 1668 (sig. C2v).

[98] Bodl., Carte MSS 81, fols. 318r, 324r–v; *CSPD, 1671*, 140.

[99] [Nathaniel Vincent, ed.], *The Morning-Exercise Against Popery* (London, 1675), sig. A3r.

rupted with Catholic elements.[100] Its defenders, though professing Protestants, emulated the Catholics in persecuting saints.

In the Vanity Fair episode, the allegory's clearest exposition of the sanctity of a biblically enlightened conscience, Bunyan powerfully expressed his opposition to religious repression.[101] As Knott avers, this section "constitutes the most important statement of the warfare between spirit and flesh" in the allegory,[102] but it is no less an assertion of the struggle between the conscience and a state that sought to define and forcefully impose its religious convictions. The account contains unmistakable references to Bunyan's experience with Bedfordshire justice. Lord Hategood, the trial judge in Vanity Fair, was modeled after Sir John Kelynge and possibly Thomas Twisden, with whom Bunyan's wife had dealt, but not George Jeffreys, as some commentators have suggested.[103] The infamous "bloody assizes" were well in the future, and Jeffreys first received a position on the bench in 1671. Nor should we see what Brean Hammond calls the "kangaroo court" at Vanity Fair as a satire on the state trials of Charles II's reign, for at that level the judicial proceedings were normally fair by prevailing standards.[104]

That the Vanity Fair trial is an evocation of Bunyan's legal difficulties in the early 1660s is apparent from a close comparison of the accusations against Christian and Faithful with the earlier ones against Bunyan himself. Just as Faithful is accused of heresy but promises to recant if he is persuaded of his error (95–96), so was Bunyan.[105] The indictment against Christian and Faithful charges them with making commotion and division (92), just as Bunyan had been accused of promoting disturbances.[106] Christian and Faithful are further indicted for having "won a party to their own most dangerous Opinions" (93), much as Bunyan had been cited for seducing the people.[107] All parties, of course, are reminded that

---

[100] Mullett argues that Bunyan made no alterations to reflect the increased danger of Catholicism because he took a long historical perspective, including his conviction of Antichrist's eventual demise. *JBC*, 196.

[101] This section again draws on my article, "'Let Truth Be Free': John Bunyan and the Restoration Crisis of 1667–1673," *Albion* 28 (Winter 1996): 587–605.

[102] Knott, *SS*, 145.

[103] Sharrock, in *PP*, 327; Brean Hammond, "*The Pilgrim's Progress*: Satire and Social Comment," in *Pilgrim's Progress*, ed. Newey, 120; Knott, *DM*, 204. Sharrock and Hammond also cite Kelynge as a model, as does N. H. Keeble, "'Till one greater man / Restore us . . .': Restoration Images in Bunyan and Milton," in *Awakening Words*, ed. Gay, Randall, and Zinck, 36.

[104] Hammond, "*The Pilgrim's Progress*: Satire and Social Comment," 120.

[105] "Relation," 121–22.

[106] Ibid., 113, 127, 130.

[107] Ibid., 120.

their actions on behalf of the godly cause are illegal.[108] The indictment of Christian and Faithful charges them with disturbing their trade (92), much as Foster had admonished Bunyan to cease preaching and follow his calling.[109] The most substantive parallel occurs in Faithful's defense of himself against an accusation by Mr. Superstition:

> That in the worship of God there is required a divine Faith; but there can be no divine Faith, without a divine Revelation of the will of God: therefore whatever is thrust into the worship of God, that is not agreeable to divine Revelation, cannot be done but by an humane Faith, which Faith will not profit to Eternal Life. (95)

The key here is the principle that nothing can be included in worship unless it conforms to divine revelation, that is, to Scripture. This was a point Bunyan had made to the magistrates, particularly with reference to the Book of Common Prayer.[110] The theological core of the charges against Christian and Faithful on the one hand and Bunyan on the other is thus identical, namely, the believer's right to worship and serve God as a biblically enlightened conscience mandates.

Bunyan also used Vanity Fair to turn one of his persecutors' charges against themselves. "Who is your God?" one of them had asked him. "Beelzebub?"[111] In Vanity Fair Pickthank testifies that Faithful railed against Prince Beelzebub, to which Faithful responds that the prince and his "Rablement" are fit for hell (94–95). Bunyan also seized the opportunity to castigate Stuart justice by having Judge Hategood approvingly cite statutes of an unnamed pharaoh, Nebuchadnezzar, and Darius, all of whom had tyrannically persecuted those who rejected the state religion. The Egyptian case was especially iniquitous because males had been drowned to prevent them from *possibly* disobeying the government. These were damning though implicit parallels with Charles II; to some degree this was unfair inasmuch as the penal legislation of the 1660s had been passed at the Cavalier Parliament's insistence, not the king's.

Another parallel between Bunyan's experience and Faithful's trial is worth noting because it underscores the depth of Bunyan's commitment to conscience and the manifestation of that commitment in *The Pilgrim's Progress.* Just as he had lain in prison under the threat of exile and, if he returned to England, execu-

---

[108] *PP*, 93; "Relation," 110, 113, 124.

[109] "Relation," 110.

[110] Ibid., 114, 116. Diane Parkin-Speer usefully draws attention to the disparities between contemporary legal practice and the trial at Vanity Fair. It is, however, problematic to use a piepowder (fair) court as a model because Vanity Fair is a town with a permanent fair (*PP*, 88) and could be the site of other courts. "John Bunyan's Legal Ideas and the Legal Trials in His Allegories," *Baptist Quarterly* 35 (July 1994): 325–27.

[111] "Relation," 117.

tion, so in Vanity Fair, Faithful's jurors cry out for the death penalty. With his own experience of psychological terror as well as Foxe's stories in mind (particularly the account of George Wishart's martyrdom[112]), Bunyan blackened those who persecuted the godly for being true to their consciences by having them inflict "the most cruel death that could be invented" on Faithful (97). Faithful is scourged, buffeted, lanced with knives, stoned, stabbed with swords, and finally burned at the stake. At first sight this is rhetorical overkill, for whatever sympathy we feel for him is dulled by the excess and then mitigated by his immediate, Elijah-like transportation to glory in a chariot accompanied by a trumpet fanfare.[113] Bunyan sacrificed what could have been the dramatic and emotional impact of a martyrdom to make a fundamental point about the ultimate victory of conscience over persecution. He and his readers believed that those who commit such acts face worse torments in eternal damnation. Conscience will triumph and the persecuted will be avenged. As horrible a place as Vanity Fair seems, we miss a crucial point if we forget that by many standards the town is very decent, populated with residents who are religious, law-abiding, economically prosperous, and valuers of "laudable doings." The accusations against Faithful of disrespect to prince and law as well as disregard for the town's religion represent, as Roland Frye has observed, "apparently solid and high-minded interest in saving the community from corruption, and in preserving its highest values."[114] Persecution and the legal inhibition of conscience are insidious because they are inflicted by an apparently religious, law-abiding society, not devils living in manifest degradation. This was a particularly important point in the battle over conscience.

Although Faithful and Christian make no effort to resist their captors, Bunyan nevertheless interwove a message of defiance throughout the allegory. The repressive, superficially religious society convicts and executes Faithful, but another pilgrim immediately takes his place: "Thus one died to make Testimony to the Truth, and another rises out of his Ashes to be a Companion with *Christian*" (98). The message is clear: No matter how severe, persecution cannot destroy the true church. The defiance—the undeterred resolve of the fully committed pil-

---

[112] Thomas S. Freeman, "A Library in Three Volumes: Foxe's 'Book of Martyrs' in the Writings of John Bunyan," *BS* 5 (Autumn 1994): 50. Cf. Clarence Eugene Dugdale, who argues against the parallel between Hategood and Kelynge but affirms the indebtedness of the episode to the Catholic persecution of Protestant martyrs. "Bunyan's Court Scenes," *University of Texas Studies in English* 21 (July 1941): 65–66.

[113] Knott makes the important point that Faithful's triumph supplies the sense of victory and the church's regeneration that was absent in Bunyan's depiction of the dead martyrs near the cave of Giants Pope and Pagan. *DM*, 203.

[114] Frye, *GMS*, 120.

grim—is also manifested as militancy. In this imagery the pilgrimage is conflict, as wayfaring becomes warfaring. Such imagery is unmistakably biblical, drawing particularly on the Old Testament, but Bunyan was also cognizant of the Pauline command that believers should don God's armor. For Bunyan, as for his pilgrims, the world is the battleground between good and evil, light and darkness. Ostensibly, he restricted militancy to the spiritual realm, but his willingness to stand firm regardless of penal statutes and persecutory acts was by nature a political as well as a religious act in a society whose rulers claimed and exercised the power to compel obedience to their view of right religion. There is no escaping the fact that *The Pilgrim's Progress* is a profoundly political tract in its espousal of a spiritual ethic that combined the value of suffering with the need to resist the state's resolve to pursue its own religious ends. In a state that recognized no clear line of demarcation between the spiritual and the secular, spiritual acts had secular connotations. Worldly-wiseman, Mony-love, Hategood, Love-lust, Pliable, Time-server, and all the other minions who servilely yield to the conformist establishment find no salvation in Bunyan's book.

In the allegory Bunyan first underscores the militancy of the Christian life when Interpreter shows Christian to the door of a palace where many armed men seek to bar entry. As Christian watches, a man of stout countenance draws his sword, dons a helmet, and charges the armed men. They "laid upon him with deadly force; but the Man, not at all discouraged, fell to cutting and hacking most fiercely; so after he had received and given many wounds to those that attempted to keep him out, he cut his way through them all, and pressed forward into the Palace" (33). Bunyan's point is that those determined to win eternal glory must be willing to fight their way through any barrier standing in their way, obviously including laws aimed at prohibiting nonconformists from meeting. So important was this episode that Bunyan recalled it in a dialogue between Christian and Piety (48).

Bunyan gave the church a militant cast in the Palace Beautiful account. Built for the security of pilgrims, the palace was a fortified structure, the master of which, the Lord of the Hill, was "a *great Warriour*, and had fought with and slain him that had the power of Death" (52). Moreover, the lord's servants are a militant people who have subdued kingdoms, "stopped the mouths of Lions, quenched the violence of Fire, escaped the edge of the Sword; out of weakness were made strong, waxed valiant in fight, and turned to flight the Armies of the *Aliens*" (53). Christian is welcomed into this society of kingdom-subduers, shown an armory with enough equipment to outfit as many men as there are stars, and armed from head to foot. In this armory he sees the historic weapons with which the great biblical heroes triumphed over their foes and the sword Christ will wield to slay Antichrist. Graceless, the man in rags, is transposed into a warfaring saint, a knight-errant whose right to bear arms identifies Christian as one of the spiritually armigerous.[115]

On three occasions, the first of which is his battle with Apollyon, Christian uses his weapons. Nearly no match for the beastly giant's fiery darts, Christian finally succeeds in repulsing him with his sword. In crafting this account Bunyan blended Scripture with the story of St. George; like the latter, who was healed by the fruit of a magical tree, Christian recovers from his wounds by applying leaves from the Tree of Life.[116] The episode's impact is to encourage each believer, like an epic hero, to engage in spiritual battle against the forces of evil. His sword drawn, Christian continues on his way, ready for the next enemy. In the Valley of the Shadow of Death, his sword proves to be useless against the flames spewing from hell's mouth and the din of raucous voices. This time the weapon of choice is *"All-prayer,"* with a marginal notation to Ephesians 6:18 and Psalm 116:4 (63). As innocuous as this weapon seems to most modern readers, to Bunyan it was a major distinguishing feature between nonconformist and Anglican worship, as he had forcefully argued in *I Will Pray with the Spirit.* Suitably strengthened with this weapon, Christian has the courage to face down a company of fiends.

Bunyan persistently reminds his readers of Christian militancy. After Faithful wins his battle against Shame, he sings a warrior's song, with its clarion call to others to *"Be vigilant, and quit themselves like Men"* (74). There is an echo here of Hugh Latimer's admonition to Nicholas Ridley as they were about to be burned at the stake: "Play the man." This is also Evangelist's exhortation to Faithful and Christian at Vanity Fair. Resolute defiance of an ungodly state is the unmistakable message and appropriate standard of Christian conduct. Again reflecting militancy, Evangelist will subsequently warn Faithful and Christian that they are "not yet out of the gun-shot of the Devil" (86). In a conversation with Hopeful, Christian describes his encounter with the brothers Faint-heart, Mistrust, and Guilt and their master, the King of the Bottomless Pit. Although armed, Christian finds it "hard work to quit my self like a man; no man can tell what in that Combat attends us, but he that hath been in the Battle himself." The four foes are eventually repulsed by Great-grace, *"the Kings Champion,"* who is unequaled for "such feats of War." This time the message focuses on the varying degrees of faith within believers, their ability to succeed in spiritual combat, and the importance

[115] Michael McKeon develops the feudal analogy in *The Origins of the English Novel 1600–1740* (Baltimore: Johns Hopkins University Press, 1987), 302–11.

[116] A number of commentators have noted the likely influence of Richard Johnson's *The Most Famous History of the Seven Champions of Christendome* (London, 1596) on Bunyan. Sir Charles Firth, in *Bunyan, The Pilgrim's Progress: A Casebook,* ed. Roger Sharrock (London: Macmillan, 1976), 89; McKeon, *Origins,* 302; Shrimpton, "Bunyan's Military Metaphor," 210–12; Mullett, *JBC,* 192.

of relying on Great-grace, who "is excellent at his Weapons, and has [done], and can, so long as he keeps them at Swords point, do well enough with them" (130). Again, Job, the veteran of so much spiritual warfare, served as Bunyan's inspiration: "'Tis true, if a man could at every turn have *Jobs* Horse, and had skill and courage to ride him, he might do notable things" (131, referring to Job 39:19). By their narrow escape at the hands of the King of the Bottomless Pit and his minions, Christian and Faithful are reminded that they are foot soldiers who must wear their armor, especially the shield of faith,[117] and travel in a convoy led by God. Honest neatly encapsulates the twin themes of warfaring and wayfaring when, in part two, he tells Christiana about Christian's wars and travels. Kaufmann perceptively remarks that the setting for *The Pilgrim's Progress* is not a wilderness but "an ordered spiritual realm in which good and evil, though in continual warfare, are in a strife where all battle lines are clearly drawn."[118] Because these spiritual wars are fought in the earthly arena, they have momentous repercussions for the godly in a corrupt state and society.

## "*Turn up My Metaphors*"[119]: Interpreting the Allegory

In *The Pilgrim's Progress* Bunyan provides a critique of the Restoration state, society, and established church. Much of the allegory deals with the conflicting allegiances to two lords so effectively articulated in the Apollyon scene. When Apollyon attempts to persuade Christian to cease serving the King of Princes and return to his former status as Apollyon's vassal, Christian replies that he has sworn allegiance to his new king, whom he cannot forsake without being hanged for treason. "I like his Service, his Wages, his Government, his Company, and Countrey better then thine" (57). This is not about monarchy versus republicanism, but competing allegiances to two sovereigns, the King of Princes and the King of the Bottomless Pit. Accusations of treason figure not only in this episode but also in Pliable's return to the City of Destruction, whose inhabitants want to hang him as a turn-coat, and in the behavior of Faithful, which Lord Hategood adjudges traitorous. Indeed, Faithful freely acknowledges having proclaimed that Vanity Fair's sovereign and his attendants are fit for hell, and that its laws, if not in conformity with the Bible, are diametrically opposed to Christianity. As James Froude has remarked, after Faithful made such allegations it is hardly surprising

---

[117] The reference to Ephesians 6:16 echoes Luther's exhortation to "take unto thee the armour of God, the shield of faith, the helmet of hope, and the sword of the Spirit." *Galatians*, 462.

[118] Kaufmann, *Pilgrim's Progress*, 106.

[119] *PP*, 164.

that he is accused of having preached rebellion.[120] As an indictment of the ungodly Stuart state, the account of Vanity Fair is an extended comment on Luther's pronouncement that "the faithful must bear this name and this title in the world, that they are seditious and schismatic, and the author of innumerable evils" (430–31). Embedded in the story are critical observations about oaths, which are no safeguard against malicious testimony; informers, as represented by Pickthank and possibly Envy; the Clarendon Code, as implicitly likened to the persecutory laws of Nebuchadnezzar, Darius, and a pharoah; and the harsh penalties imposed on some dissenters, as suggested by the excessive punishment meted out to Faithful. Those who supported the Stuart state were branded aliens in God's kingdom, the forces of which would ultimately rout "the Armies of the *Aliens*" of the King of the Bottomless Pit (23, 53).

Bunyan leveled harsh remarks against the landed aristocracy, not least his marginal comment in the Vanity Fair account that "*Sins are all Lords and Great ones.*"[121] Among his friends Prince Beelzebub numbers the peers Old Man, Carnal Delight, Luxurious, Desire of Vain-glory, and Lechery, as well as Sir Having Greedy "with all the rest of our Nobility"; such was the testimony of Pickthank the informer in the court of Lord Hategood (94). According to Pickthank, Faithful villified most of Vanity Fair's gentry and wanted to banish all nobles from the town. Indeed, he admits in court that the gentlemen named by Pickthank are suited for hell. Other peers also populate the allegory's pages, among them Turn-about, Time-server, and Fair-speech. The gentry receive their share of attention through the figures of Worldly-wiseman, Formalist, Hypocrisie, Hold-the-world, Mony-love, Save-all, and Legality. The grandson of a waterman, By-ends married the daughter of Lady Faining, who "arrived to such a pitch of Breeding, that she knows how to carry it to all, even to Prince and Peasant" (99). By-ends is attracted to the "*Gentleman*-like" Demas, the son of Judas, and his silver mine on Lucre Hill (108). But Bunyan was careful not to damn the entire landed aristocracy, not least because he knew that such members of the Bedford church as John Grew, John Eston, Mary Tilney, and William Whitbread of Cardington were members of the gentry.[122] In Faithful's trial, Pickthank testifies

[120] James Anthony Froude, *Bunyan* (New York: Harper and Brothers, 1880), 163.

[121] Dealing with the same theme, Philip Henry took a more moderate approach, indicating only that it is more difficult for the mighty than the humble to pursue godliness: "Very hard for great ones to bee Godly, because their temptations are more and snares." CUL, Add. MSS 7338, commenting on Genesis 13.

[122] Brown, 81–82; *A True and Impartial Narrative of Some Illegal and Arbitrary Proceedings* (n.p., 1670); W. M. Wigfield, "Recusancy and Nonconformity in Bedfordshire Illustrated by Select Documents Between 1622 and 1842," *PBHRS* 20 (1938):179–81; BLA, MSS HSA 1671 W/17; 1678 W/15.

that the accused has vilified most of Vanity Fair's gentry; presumably a few of them are among the townsfolk sympathetic to Christian and Faithful. Evangelist, whom Christian deems "a very great and honorable person," may be a gentleman (18). Christian himself, as we have seen, is transformed into a spiritual knight-errant, warfaring though landless; Great-grace, the king's champion, must be a lord; and by implication the King of Princes has his own nobility. Indeed, the Lord of the Hill has elevated many beggars to be princes, though not in this life. *The Pilgrim's Progress* is about social inversion, not leveling, for God's hand "*pulls the strong down, and makes weak ones stand*" (6). The point was not lost on the conformist Cave Underhill, who in 1681 denounced Bunyan for believing he had the right to "bind Kings in Chains, and their Nobles in Links of Iron."[123] As Christopher Hill has observed, Bunyan's damning indictment of the aristocracy was a key reason for the upper classes' tendency to shun his work for a century and a half.[124]

In *The Pilgrim's Progress* Bunyan's sympathy is unmistakably with the poor, not least because of the rich's sneering contempt of them. Giant Despair mockingly depicts Christian and Hopeful as "sturdy Rogues" (117), a phrase evocative of the social and legal hostility directed toward the sturdy beggars who reputedly shunned gainful employment and preyed on society. The same point is made when Judge Hategood refers to Faithful as a "Runagate" (95). Shame objects to Faithful's religion because few wealthy, mighty, or formally learned people embrace it, and he remarks derisively on "the base and low estate and condition of those that were chiefly the Pilgrims; also their ignorance of the times in which they lived, and want of understanding in all natural Science," an aside perhaps directed at the Royal Society, some of whose members, including John Wilkins, bishop of Chester (1668–1672), were Latitudinarians (72). One of Bunyan's principal lessons in *The Pilgrim's Progress* is that a poor man such as Graceless, who begins his journey in rags, is richer, if he loves Christ, "than the greatest man in the world that hates him" (73). Many of those who will be made princes, says Bunyan, originate in dunghills. Almost proudly, he identifies with the poor, who

[123] [Cave Underhill], *Vox Lachrymae: A Sermon Newly Held Forth at Weavers-Hall, upon the Funeral of the Famous T. O. Doctor of Salamancha* (Frankfurt, 1681; repr., London, 1682), 6–7.

[124] Hill, *TPM*, 221. Thomas N. Corns oversimplifies by depicting the allegory as an attack on "the gentry class and their agents," but he rightly asserts that "texts that value the lives of indigent and counter-cultural itinerants over those of magistrates necessarily invite a political reading, especially when the author vouchsafes that he writes from prison." *Uncloistered Virtue: English Political Literature, 1640–1660* (Oxford: Clarendon Press, 1992), 305–6. In the preface to part two, Bunyan claims his allegory has been well-received among at least some aristocrats (*PP*, 169).

are treated like dirt and befouled by the wealthy. At Vanity Fair the pilgrims are smeared with dirt before being incarcerated, an act of retaliation for Faithful's allegedly having "bespattered most of the Gentry" (95). Bunyan's sense of social identity with the indigent is also evinced in Shame's complaint that "Religion made a man grow strange to the great, because of a few vices . . . and made him own and respect the base, because of the same Religious fraternity" (73).

Bunyan was no fan of the developing capitalist economy because it was founded, in his view, on the acquisitive spirit. The pathetic figure of the muckraker at the Interpreter's house, with his diligent but misguided efforts to accumulate straw, sticks, and dust—symbols of material wealth, loses a crown of grace. In the town of Love-gain in the northern country of Coveting, the schoolmaster, Mr. Gripe-man, teaches his pupils "the art of getting, either by violence, cousenage, flattery, lying or by putting on a guise of Religion" (101). Among his pupils are Mony-love, Save-all, Hold-the-world, and By-ends.[125] In the figure of Hold-the-world Bunyan satirized those, such as Wilkins, the former puritan and present bishop of Chester, who sought an accord between the capitalist spirit and religion.[126] Hold-the-world prefers a religion that will "stand with the security of Gods good blessings unto us; for who can imagin, that is ruled by his reason, since God has bestowed upon us the good things of this life, but that he would have us keep them for his sake" (102). To Hold-the-world's argument that people can legitimately become (more) religious to enhance their business or trade, Christian retorts that it is abominable to use Christ and religion as "a stalking horse to get and enjoy the world" (105). Such, he thinks, is the view of heathens, hypocrites, devils, and witches. Although Vanity Fair was modeled on the centuries-old Stourbridge Fair, Hill is correct in seeing it as a representation of the capitalist spirit,[127] for everything in Vanity Fair is for sale, including husbands and

---

[125] J. W. Draper and U. Milo Kaufmann err in seeing Hold-the-world, Money-love, and Save-all as Scottish Presbyterians, for the latter were staunch Calvinists and opponents of universal redemption. Draper, "Bunyan's Mr. Ignorance," *Modern Language Review* 22 (January 1927): 14; Kaufmann, "Spiritual Discerning," 173.

[126] Wilkins' classic, *Of the Principles and Duties of Natural Religion*, was published posthumously in 1675. I am not suggesting Bunyan read this work, which appeared after he had written *The Pilgrim's Progress*. He may have heard about Wilkins' views, in which case Love-gain could be Chester. For Wilkins see Barbara J. Shapiro, *John Wilkins, 1614–1672: An Intellectual Biography* (Berkeley: University of California Press, 1969). The reconciliation of wealth and piety had deep roots in England; writers as disparate as Richard Hooker, William Perkins, and Thomas Wilcox had espoused this view. See Richard L. Greaves, *Society and Religion in Elizabethan England* (Minneapolis: University of Minnesota Press, 1981), 550–51.

[127] Hill, *TPM*, 225.

wives, children, masters and servants, honors and preferments, trades, houses and lands, lusts and pleasures, bawds and whores, gems and pearls, bodies and souls, and even kingdoms. Profit rules everything.

Bunyan manifests a keen sense of place and its relation to social injustice and religious commitment. As James Turner has observed, "the units of topographical space (heights and depths, lands, fields, hills, houses, and roads) are inseparable in Bunyan's imagination from the social means of their control, from lordships, tenure and sale, trespass actions and enclosure claims." Bunyan's world is "a hostile hierarchy of wealth and power founded on *place*."[128] This sense of place, especially exclusion from property, reflects his sensitivity to the land his ancestors were forced to sell and thus the poverty he and his first wife endured early in their marriage. Devoid of property, Graceless undertakes his journey not only to rid himself of his burden but in search of an inheritance, especially after being disowned by his relatives, Pride, Arrogancy, Self-conceit, and Worldly-glory (71–72). During their travels the pilgrims must be wary of trespassing, a fear that troubles Christian as he retraces his steps to the wicket-gate; "he went like one that was all the while treading on forbidden ground, and could by no means think himself safe" (24–25). The most dramatic trespass leads to Christian and Hopeful's incarceration in Doubting Castle, a fate to which they passively submit; in this episode Giant Despair is an aristocratic property-owner whose power to imprison trespassers echoes the role of the gentlemen justices of the peace who enforced property laws. But trespassing can also violate the laws of the Lord of the Celestial City, as Christian warns Formalist and Hypocrisie, who committed the offense by climbing over a wall rather than commencing the pilgrimage through the wicket-gate. Thus, not all property ownership is bad. Unlike carnal property, which excludes the poor and provides the power base for an oppressive, worldly aristocracy, God's property is held in common by all believers, or at least all have equal access to it. This includes the route to the Celestial City, the hill on which Palace Beautiful is situated, the Delectable Mountains, Beulah, and presumably the Celestial City itself.[129] Although Bunyan never proposed a redistribution of landed estates, the recurring theme of communalism in *The Pilgrim's Progress* may have reminded some readers of the radical mid-century demands espoused by the Diggers. Particularly to the indigent, the promise of a splendid eternal inheritance

---

[128] James Turner, "Bunyan's Sense of Place," in *Pilgrim's Progress*, ed. Newey, 97. Cf. Stachniewski: "Bunyan's imagination is . . . so deeply imbued with the thoughts attached to experience of a discriminatory social structure that it is permanently disfigured, permanently engaged in the attempt to exorcise the fears it entertains" (129).

[129] If property in the Celestial City is held in common, pilgrims cannot receive land tenure upon completion of their journey, as McKeon's feudal analogy suggests. *Origins*, 305.

must have been alluring. Consequently, as Turner notes, Bunyan's allegory, "the symbolic landscape of the landless, remained for two centuries one of the principal possessions of the dispossessed."[130]

*The Pilgrim's Progress* also resonated with the humble because Bunyan gave fresh voice to the tradition of medieval social commentary that excoriated ruthless landlords, parasitic officials, and carnal clerics. By "giving the rich and propertied their allegorical come-uppance,"[131] he appealed to those who suffered at their expense or resented their monopoly of material goods. In the end, the company of lords and gentry satirized by Bunyan would receive their condign punishment, leaving the poor but godly to enjoy eternal splendor. He obviously enjoyed his satirizing, prompting Brean Hammond to characterize *The Pilgrim's Progress* as "a revenge-fantasy directed at Bunyan's own persecutors and captors."[132] Indeed, recapitulating a point he made in *The Resurrection of the Dead*, Bunyan has a shining one tell Christian and Hopeful that the saved will have a voice in the last judgment, for the damned are their enemies as well as Christ's. This, then, is the ultimate revenge. Yet despite the harsh nature of his social criticism, Bunyan was not a social radical, for unlike the Levellers and Diggers he stopped short of calling for substantive reforms in this world.

In addition to satirizing Restoration society, Bunyan directed some of his most withering criticism at the Church of England. Although its adherents were generally honest people who lived "*in credit and good fashion*" in the town of Morality (19) or formally religious folk such as those in Vanity Fair, their common failure was the lack of a genuine sense of sin. Like Mr. Legality and his son Civility,[133] its preachers used the vocabulary of moral virtue, even denouncing sin from the pulpit, yet they would "*abide it well enough in the heart, and house, and conversation*" (81). In the view of conformists, the godly were too "precise," an early term for puritans and the charge Christian's wife and children leveled against him in response to his "great tenderness in sinning against God, or of doing any wrong to my Neighbor" (52). Such a tender conscience, Shame asserts, is unmanly, though he may have been beyond the pale of the established church, for he deemed it "a pitiful, low, sneaking business for a man to mind Religion" (72). The figure of Shame clearly reflects a common, hostile view of nonconformists when he ridicules those who sit "whining and mourning under a Ser-

---

[130]Turner, "Bunyan's Sense of Place," 109.

[131]Hammond, "*The Pilgrim's Progress*: Satire and Social Comment," 125.

[132]Ibid., 129.

[133]For Bunyan's use of Civility to attack the Church of England, see P. J. H. Titlestad, "The 'pretty young man Civility': Bunyan, Milton & Blake and Patterns of Puritan Thought," *BS* 6 (1995–96): 34–43.

mon" and then come "sighing and groaning home" (72–73). Faithful succinctly answers such critics when he avouches that "God prefers a tender Conscience," the phrase Charles II used when referring to nonconformists in the Declaration of Breda (73). Talkative thinks "the appearance of a tender conscience" is "*a foolish timorousness*" (79), but Bunyan, through Faithful, repaid the affront by asserting that Talkative's religion is compatible with alehouses, sexual improprieties, swearing, and covetousness. In damning the Church of England, Bunyan made it clear that theological expertise is insufficient, for Talkative can discuss doctrine rather intelligently but fails to understand that "the Soul of Religion is the practick part" (79). Conformists had the husk of religion but not the kernel.

Bunyan employed a number of allegorical characters to convey his disapprobation of the established church. Worldly-wiseman of the town of Morality, a church-goer who espouses doctrine that saves him from the cross (persecution), first appears in the second edition of *The Pilgrim's Progress* (1678). Sharrock has suggested that Bunyan modeled him after the only Latitudinarian whose work he definitely knew, Edward Fowler,[134] but unlike Fowler Worldly-wiseman is not a minister. Instead he must represent those gentry who readily conformed at the Restoration, finding in Latitudinarianism an antidote to the sharply defined religious principles that had contributed to the upheavals of the 1640s and 1650s. Worldly-wiseman is probably much like Temporary, who was once "*a forward man in Religion*," that is, a puritan who has been "*much awakened once*" (151). After meeting Save-self about 1660, he became a backslider, as did his neighbor, Turn-back. All of these characters retreated to the safety of conformity and in so doing embraced a liturgy that, in Faithful's words, is "*not agreeable to divine Revelation*" and thus is ineffectual (95). In his defense, Faithful reiterates the core of Bunyan's argument against the established church as expressed in *I Will Pray with the Spirit*. From another perspective, Bunyan castigated conformists in the characters of Formalist and Hypocrisie, who rely on a thousand years of religious tradition and their conscientious obedience of the church's laws and ordinances; to Christian they are fraudulent, lacking the signs of election—the coat of righteousness, the mark on the forehead, and the roll containing evidence of salvation.

The town of Fair-speech—another allusion to the rhetoric of moral virtue—is the home of the parson Mr. Two-tongues, his nephew By-ends, and such folk as Lord Turn-about, Lord Time-server, Mr. Facing-bothways, Mr. Smooth-man, and Mr. Any-thing, most of whom are related to By-ends. In a blistering critique of those who conformed at the Restoration and thus explicitly or implicitly sup-

---

[134] Sharrock, in *PP*, xxxv, 314; Isabel Rivers, "Grace, Holiness, and the Pursuit of Happiness: Bunyan and Restoration Latitudinarianism," in *John Bunyan*, ed. Keeble, 56. For Fowler see *DNB*, *s.v.*

ported the persecutory state, Bunyan has By-ends explain that he and his wife, Lady Faining's daughter, differ religiously

> from those of the stricter sort, yet but in two small points: First, we never strive against Wind and Tide. Secondly, we are alwayes most zealous when Religion goes in his Silver Slippers; we love much to walk with him in the Street, if the Sun shines, and the people applaud it. (99)

Deeming his principles profitable and harmless, By-ends follows the winds of fortune, contrasting himself with Christian and Hopeful, who adhere rigidly to their views and dismiss the opinions of others. "Let a man be never so godly, yet if he jumps not with them in all things, they thrust him quite out of their company" (101), a reference to the disciplinary procedures of nonconformist congregations. In this account Bunyan is excoriating those who renounced their earlier adherence to puritan principles, not attacking the Church of England's doctrine.[135] Although Fowler has been suggested as the model for By-ends,[136] the latter, like Worldly-wiseman, is not a clergyman but a cowardly lay turncoat whose views are compatible with Latitudinarianism. Save-all, who thinks Christian and Hopeful are rigid, censorious, and overly righteous, and Mony-love are former classmates of By-ends. In Mony-love, Bunyan struck at ministers such as Fowler who altered their principles, became more studious, and preached more zealously in order to gain a more lucrative benefice.

Of the Anglican figures in the allegory, Ignorance is the last and, for some commentators, the most difficult to explain. Outwardly he is a professing Christian who prays, fasts, renders tithes, gives alms, pays his debts, and has left the country of Conceit to go on a pilgrimage. Stanley Fish argues that he "is merely another in the long line of pilgrims whose great error is to believe too literally in the image of the journey,"[137] but Ignorance's difficulty does not stem from his desire to be a pilgrim but how he began his journey, namely, through a crooked lane rather than the wicket-gate; in theological terms, he relies on the old Adam

---

[135] In making this distinction between the doctrine and practices of the Church of England, Bunyan was in agreement with John Owen. *A Peace-Offering*, 14, 17. See also anon., *The Observator Observ'd* 1 (6 May 1681), 2.

[136] Rosemary Freeman, *English Emblem Books* (London: Chatto and Windus, 1948), 226; Sharrock, in *PP*, 328; Tindall, 60–63; T. L. Underwood, in *MW*, 4:xxiv–xxv. The probable inspiration for By-ends, according to Tindall, was Fowler's discussion of those who undervalue Christ's role as a promoter of holiness by deeming such a function as "at best but a *Bye-one*." Edward Fowler, *The Design of Christianity* (London, 1671), 2. However, Bunyan almost certainly completed *The Pilgrim's Progress* some ten months before he saw Fowler's book.

[137] Stanley E. Fish, *Self-Consuming Artifacts: The Experience of Seventeenth-Century Literature* (Berkeley: University of California Press, 1972), 261.

rather than Christ for his justification. His fate is clear well before the book's end, for Christian tells Hopeful that "*it will certainly go ill with him at last*" (149). Like so many other figures in the allegory, Ignorance need not have received further mention, for his fate is manifest. Yet after Bunyan had seen Christian and Faithful safely through the Celestial City's gates, he returned to Ignorance, whom he dispatched to perdition, his surface piety notwithstanding. His fate has provoked objections from such commentators as Froude and F. R. Leavis, who find Bunyan's treatment of Ignorance unacceptably harsh.[138] In modern terms, Bunyan banished Ignorance to hell because he had not been "born again."[139] As a preacher, Bunyan used Ignorance's fate to make his final appeal to readers whom he hoped to convert, and this fact alone may explain the book's unusual ending.

*The Pilgrim's Progress* is also a polemic work, "made possible on the playing fields of dissent," as Henri Talon notes. A number of commentators have suggested that Ignorance was patterned after Latitudinarians, particularly Fowler,[140] yet since the manuscript was almost certainly written prior to the publication of *The Design of Christianity* (1671), Ignorance can only have personified adherents of the Church of England more generally.[141] That he is a conformist is apparent by his exhortation to Christian and Hopeful "to follow the Religion of your Countrey" (124). Bunyan's use of his final paragraph to castigate the established church suggests substantial provocation, possibly the imposition of the Second Conventicle Act in May 1670 and his return to close confinement. Although incapable of proof, another possibility suggests itself. Since Ignorance's fate had already been indicated, Bunyan did not need the final paragraph. Conceivably, he originally ended the allegory with what is now the penultimate paragraph, expressing the dreamer's wish to be with Christian and Hopeful in the Celestial City. As we shall see in the next chapter, in 1672 Bunyan published *A Defence of the Doctrine of Justification, by Faith*, refuting Fowler's *The Design of Christianity*. Fowler or his

---

[138] Froude, *Bunyan*, 168–69; F. R. Leavis, in *Bunyan, The Pilgrim's Progress: A Casebook*, ed. Sharrock, 208–9.

[139] This is not to suggest that he was a Deist, as Draper has argued. "Bunyan's Mr. Ignorance," 18. James F. Forrest has noted that Ignorance's fate was a consequence of his own willful action. "Bunyan's Ignorance and the Flatterer: A Study in the Literary Art of Damnation," *Studies in Philology* 60 (January 1963): 12–22. Viewing Ignorance's destiny in psychological terms, Stuart Sim avers that he lacked one critical sign of election—anxiety. "'Safe for Those for Whom it is to be Safe': Salvation and Damnation in Bunyan's Fiction," in *JBHE*, ed. Laurence, Owens, and Sim, 153.

[140] Talon, 58, 212; Tindall, 61; Sharrock, in *PP*, 337; Sharrock, *JB*, 337; Luxon, 184; Stachniewski, 211–12; Rivers, "Grace, Holiness, and the Pursuit of Happiness," 66–67; Mullett, *JBC*, 200.

[141] Cf. Gordon Wakefield, *John Bunyan the Christian* (London: Fount, 1992), 89.

surrogate replied in the vituperative *Dirt Wip't Off* (1672). The subtitle of the latter work manifests the *ad hominem* nature of the counterattack: *A Manifest Discovery of the Gross Ignorance, Erroneousness and Most Unchristian and Wicked Spirit of One John Bunyan, Lay-Preacher in Bedford.* After reading this venomous critique, Bunyan may have responded by adding the final paragraph to his manuscript, sending Ignorance, *now* a representation not merely of conformists in general but of Fowler, to hell.

*The Pilgrim's Progress* is informed by Bunyan's theology, which is made more intelligible by the allegorical imagery.[142] To say that the book is a religious rather than a theological work[143] does not mean that the allegorical drama violates the author's doctrinal principles. Gordon Campbell avers that "we should be ill-advised to search for Bunyan's theology in *The Pilgrim's Progress*," for its emphasis on Christian experience "precludes the serious treatment of doctrines that relate to the mind of God rather than the mind of Christian."[144] But the reader who fails to read the allegory as a means of explicating Bunyan's theology misses one of his primary reasons for writing the book:

> My dark and cloudy words they do but hold
> The Truth, as Cabinets inclose the Gold. (4)

The obligation to ferret out the theological principles by decoding the allegory rests on the reader. Campbell bases his case largely on Bunyan's perceived repression of the doctrine of predestination in the allegory,[145] yet this tenet is fundamental to Christian's experience; much of his pilgrimage deals with doubts about his spiritual status, as in the Slough of Despond, the Valley of the Shadow of Death, Doubting Castle, the battle with Apollyon, and crossing the River of Death.[146] Because figures such as By-ends and Ignorance fail to commence the pilgrimage through the wicket-gate, which can only be opened by Christ (hence the Calvinist doctrine of election), they represent the reprobate. Bunyan makes the same point in asserting that the burden can only be removed and the pilgrim given new clothing, a mark on the forehead, and a roll by God. These are acts of divine sover-

[142] Damrosch, *GP*, 159.

[143] Gordon Campbell, "The Theology of *The Pilgrim's Progress*," in *Pilgrim's Progress*, ed. Newey, 257.

[144] Ibid., 257, 260–61.

[145] Ibid., 256–57, 261; Campbell, "Fishing in Other Men's Waters: Bunyan and the Theologians," in *John Bunyan*, ed. Keeble, 151. This is also the view of Nick Davis, "The Problem of Misfortune in *The Pilgrim's Progress*," in *Pilgrim's Progress*, ed. Newey, 198.

[146] The centrality of predestination in the allegory is asserted by Stachniewski, 169; E. Beatrice Batson, *John Bunyan: Allegory and Imagination* (London: Croom Helm; Totowa, NJ: Barnes and Noble, 1984), 40–41; and Kaufmann, "Spiritual Discerning," 181.

eignty, not human will. Although the allegory commences with Graceless' desire to attain salvation, this originated with his reading of the Bible, itself the result of divine initiative, and instructions from Evangelist conveying God's message. As it pertains to eternal life, the crux of that message is that "if we be truly willing to have it, [God] will bestow it upon us freely" (14). This is more than a desire to be formally religious, as Ignorance discovers. Only God can implant the desire to be spiritually reborn within the pilgrim, and only Christ's righteousness, not human effort, can win the traveler's acceptance in God's sight (justification by an imputed righteousness). Mr. Legality and the dangers of Mount Sinai are insufficient to save those who seek eternal life through morality (good works).

"The redeeming literary quality of *The Pilgrim's Progress*" is not "that Bunyan's imagination transcends his theological convictions," as Campbell avers,[147] but that his allegorical images express his doctrine so effectively. At the house of the Interpreter (the Holy Spirit), Christian learns that the dust of original sin cannot be swept away by the law, for only the water of grace is effective. Similarly, the image of a man pouring oil on a fire represents Christ infusing grace in the heart to sustain the regenerative work and thus the believer's perseverance. Christian's coat symbolizes justification by imputed righteousness, a point on which Bunyan would disagree with Fowler. No other means of justification is possible, as Faithful discovers when he is repeatedly knocked down by a man he later learns was Moses, who has no mercy for transgressors of his law. Talkative, as we have seen, can discourse about such things, but he lacks the divinely bestowed grace requisite for salvation. Most of *The Pilgrim's Progress* is about sanctification, the Christian life following justification. This is not a period free of recurring struggle, doubt, and even despair, which is a fundamental point of the allegory. From the moment of justification the believer does not experience perseverance as absolute certainty, but must resolve, as Evangelist tells Christian and Faithful, to run for the crown. "Set your faces like a flint, you have all power in Heaven and Earth on your side" (87). Although the end is certain according to Reformed theology, assurance of that fact is not possible unless one appropriates the divine promises, something Christian has a tendency to forget, even as he crosses the River of Death. At the end, Bunyan believed, will come the resurrection of the body, the denial of which leads in the allegory to the demise of those (notably the Quakers) whose unburied bodies lie mangled at the foot of Errour Hill. Worldly-wiseman, By-ends, and their companions represent the religion of reason or morality as opposed to that of grace, one of Bunyan's most significant theological points.[148] Another is the im-

---

[147] Campbell, "Fishing in Other Men's Waters," 150.

[148] See the excellent discussion in Rivers, "Grace, Holiness, and the Pursuit of Happiness," 47, 63–69.

portance of Christ, who opens the wicket-gate for Christian, makes possible his new garments, pours the oil of grace on the fire in believers' hearts, saves Faithful from Moses' blows, and finally appears to Christian at the crucial moment as he crosses the River of Death.[149]

Bunyan's treatment of the church in *The Pilgrim's Progress* reflects his open-membership, open-communion views. The House Beautiful represents the church, though membership is not essential for salvation because Faithful by-passes it. Since the Palace Beautiful represents a separatist congregation, admission is not automatic; Discretion, Prudence, Piety, and Charity make inquiries of Christian before welcoming him into the house. Despite efforts to discern the truly faithful, the church sometimes admitted the unworthy, prompting Christian to deplore "*Talkative* Fools, whose Religion is only in word, and are debauched and vain in their Conversation, that (being so much admitted into the Fellowship of the Godly) do stumble the World, blemish Christianity, and grieve the Sincere" (85).[150] Bunyan may have been thinking of his fellow church member Humphrey Merrill, who was excommunicated by the congregation in December 1669; Bunyan had been unsuccessful in seeking his repentance and testified to the church about his ill-behavior.[151] For Bunyan, the church was significant for its instructional and sustaining role in the Christian life. Hopeful joins Christian in "a brotherly covenant" (98), much as new members did when they became members of a separatist congregation. In contrast, Ignorance prefers to walk alone (144). From a different perspective, the first part of *The Pilgrim's Progress* is about Christian's millennial vision of the Church Triumphant, expressed as early as his conversation with Pliable; membership in this church is essential. Unless the sprinkling of water to remove the dust is an allusion to baptism,[152] Bunyan ignores this ordinance in the first part of *The Pilgrim's Progress*. The Lord's supper is depicted in Christian's meal at the Palace Beautiful, taken at the Lord of the Hill's table, an obvious allusion to the Lord's table in the separatist tradition. Similar refreshment ensues in the Delectable Mountains and Beulah.[153]

The considerable attention Bunyan devoted to his doctrinal tenets and cri-

---

[149] On the role of Christ in the allegory see Geoffrey F. Nuttall, "The Heart of *The Pilgrim's Progress*," *American Baptist Quarterly* 7 (December 1988): 476–82.

[150] As Paul Davis has demonstrated, talk itself has theological ramifications in the allegory, for pilgrims speak the language of Canaan while others "chatter worldlily." "John Bunyan and Heavenly Conversation," *Essays in Criticism* 50 (July 2000): 217, 221 (quoted).

[151] *CB*, 42.

[152] As suggested by Frye, *GMS*, 154. Fish errs in seeing the River of Death as a reference to baptism. *Self-Consuming Artifacts*, 260.

[153] Cf. Ken Simpson, "'For the Best Improvement of Time: *Pilgrim's Progress* and the Liturgies of Nonconformity," in *Awakening Words*, ed. Gay, Randall, and Zinck, 121–23.

tique of the Church of England and Restoration society should warn us that in composing *The Pilgrim's Progress* he was not transforming his spiritual autobiography into fiction.[154] As allegory, *The Pilgrim's Progress* is myth rather than straightforward fiction, for it endeavors to depict truth by reifying the spiritual realm, delineating theological principles, and offering a critique of society and the established church.[155] In part, allegory enabled Bunyan to circumvent censorship, and he further protected himself by couching allegory in the form of a dream—a vision he claimed merely to have reported.[156] The dream format also enabled him to transform a spiritual quest into easily understood physical terms.[157] The pilgrimage commences with the materiality of the present world, moves through an allegorical journey, and concludes in the higher, ultimate reality of the Celestial City as Bunyan perceived it. For him, Christian's pilgrimage was not fictional but a mythic (or symbolic) portrayal of truth. As John Stachniewski observes, "the blurring of the metaphorical and the actual—the refusal of the distinction—helps to account for the strange power of the persecutory imagination which finds its ideal literary vehicle in allegory."[158] The allegorical dream world is well-suited to convey Bunyan's religious, social, and political message. What John Knott has said of the Vanity Fair scene applies more generally to the book as a whole: "Bunyan gives the episode a mythic character, making it embody central elements of a drama that originated with the primitive church and assimilating contemporary persecution of nonconformists to this larger drama."[159] At root *The Pilgrim's Progress* is Bunyan's way of explaining the varying impact of the drama of salvation on the lives of believers.

The allegory reflects progress in the sense that Graceless makes his way via the Slough of Despond and the Interpreter's house to the cross, where his burden is removed and he receives new raiment, a mark on the forehead, and a roll. The allegory also conveys progress because all three pilgrims eventually reach the Celestial City, the unmistakable goal from the outset. The fact that the obstacles are not fixed and graduated, that there is no direct relationship between surmounting these obstacles and accumulating spiritual credit, and that the pilgrims, notably

---

[154] As argued by Talon, 140; Sharrock, *JB*, 73; and Stachniewski, 170.

[155] David Dawson goes further when he refers to Bunyan's "concern to underscore the factual character of his own allegorical narrative" and embrace "a realism shared by contemporary historical prose narratives." "Allegorical Intratextuality in Bunyan and Winstanley," *Journal of Religion* 70 (April 1990): 199–200.

[156] Fish, *Self-Consuming Artifacts*, 263.

[157] Backscheider, 67.

[158] Stachniewski, 177; cf. 215.

[159] Knott, *DM*, 204–5.

Christian, seemingly fail to become more confident as they near their goal[160] underscores the extent to which Bunyan's intent was to convey a series of truths—about the disparate nature of the Christian experience, the theological tenets in which he believed, and the problems he observed in the Church of England and Restoration society. From his struggles with depression, he perceived that progress of the sort Stanley Fish expected to find was not part of the reality he knew. Despair and doubt are recurrent—in some cases (like Christian's) to the very end. The book's drama is intensified because it mirrors life in its recognition of the unexpected. Fish is on target when he observes that in *The Pilgrim's Progress* "a trial is never further away than the next step or thought, for the perils of the way are generated by a pilgrim's weakness."[161] He might have added that some of the dangers in Bunyan's day were imposed by a persecutory state and an established church. If the pilgrims sometimes seem to go in circles—the City of Destruction and Vanity Fair are arguably the same place—they are not the same people as when they began their journey. Their spiritual condition, loyalties, and goals radically alter, and in this sense they make substantial progress. Only the Christian pilgrim can make such headway, in all cases experiencing the *ultimate* victory of light over darkness, spiritual solace over disquietude, hope over anguish, and mercy over justice no matter how arduous the trials during the journey. *The Pilgrim's Progress* is Bunyan's resounding testament that through faith he would triumph over persecution, doubt, and despair, progressing from the City of Destruction to the Celestial City.

[160] These are Fish's objections. *Self-Consuming Artifacts*, 229. For a critique of his reading see John R. Knott, Jr., "Bunyan's Gospel Day: A Reading of *The Pilgrim's Progress*," *English Literary Renaissance* 3 (Autumn 1973): 443–61.

[161] Fish, *Self-Consuming Artifacts*, 230.

# CHAPTER 7

# The Anvil of Debate

During Bunyan's imprisonment the government waged a sporadic campaign against dissent. Although the Quaker George Whitehead complained that "there was but little Respite from *Persecution* in *twelve Years* Time, from the Year *1660* unto *1672*,"[1] the repression was uneven, coming in waves triggered by Thomas Venner's abortive rebellion, passage of the Quaker and Conventicle Acts (1662 and 1664 respectively), and approval of the Second Conventicle Act (1670). Suppressive efforts also varied from place to place largely because of disparate attitudes toward nonconformity among local magistrates. In August 1665 Henry Muddiman, one of the king's journalists, observed that "the Conventicles are now so hotly pursued, no meeting but presently snapt and the Brethren prosecuted according to the strictness of the Law." The following month the Presbyterian Philip Henry noted that many dissenting ministers were in prison throughout England. Laity suffered as well; in Middlesex alone, 909 conventiclers, 361 of them women, were convicted between 17 July 1664 and 31 December 1665. Many dissenters refused to cease meeting, reckoning the Conventicle Act void, according to one of Arlington's correspondents, because it violated the law of nature; he might have added that they also thought it contravened divine law.[2]

Among the nonconformists who stood their ground was a group that worshiped at Blunham, Bedfordshire, under the leadership of the saddler John Wright. With four of his fellow believers he was in prison with Bunyan in the summer of 1665, and the following January he and some of his coreligionists were arrested, fined, and, upon their refusal to pay, imprisoned ten days, again joining Bunyan in

---

[1] George Whitehead, *The Christian Progress of That Ancient Servant and Minister of Jesus Christ, George Whitehead* (London, 1725), 346.

[2] PRO, SP 29/129/99 (quoted); Philip Henry, *Diaries and Letters of Philip Henry, M.A. of Broad Oak, Flintshire A.D. 1631–1696*, ed. Matthew Henry Lee (London: Kegan Paul, Trench and Co., 1882), 175; Jeaffreson, 3:341–43; PRO, SP 29/137/97.

the county jail. For attending another conventicle, Wright and others were sent back to prison on 30 April 1666, this time for twenty days, having once more refused to remit their fines. After meeting again in June, Wright and others were apprehended, and six of them were committed without bail to the county prison. Also in the Bedford jail by early 1667 were other dissenting leaders in the area, including the ministers William Wheeler of Cranfield, John Donne of Keysoe, and Thomas Haynes as well as Bunyan's fellow church member, William Man. Donne and Haynes had been under sentence of banishment to Barbados since the quarter sessions in July 1666. As Bunyan observed the stepped-up persecution of his fellow dissenters, his resolve to persevere must have been reinforced, but their presence did provide the opportunity for welcome spiritual fellowship.[3]

Tension heightened in 1668 and 1669, particularly as the more confrontational dissenters forced conformists from parish churches, interrupted sermons, took over their pulpits, and in some cases stripped surplices from parsons. Conservatives began documenting such activities as ammunition for parliamentary action against conventicles. So intense were feelings in the House of Commons that Sir William Morice, secretary of state for the north, warned in April 1668 that "the fire of zeal for suppression of Conventicles may be so hot, that it may burn those that cast them in, as well as those that are cast in."[4] The following year the archbishop of Canterbury, alarmed by continuing reports of frequent conventicles, ordered all clergy and ecclesiastical officials in his province to determine how many illegal meetings were held in each town and parish, how many people attended them, who their ministers or leaders were, and who was protecting them. If the ecclesiastical authorities could not suppress the conventicles, they were to seek the assistance of justices of the peace.[5] Bunyan's colleague Samuel Fenne was arrested in 1669 for allegedly having attempted to incite the Bedford congregation to rebellion by denying the king's role as head of the Church of England, but he escaped punishment when the jury returned a verdict of *ignoramus*. Nevertheless both Samuel and John Fenne spent six months in prison with Bunyan the same

[3] W. M. Wigfield, "Recusancy and Nonconformity in Bedfordshire Illustrated by Select Documents Between 1622 and 1842," *PBHRS* 20 (1938): 167–71; BLA, MSS HSA 1665 S/1; 1666 W/16; 1667 W/58. Wheeler and Man had also been imprisoned with Bunyan in the summer of 1665. HSA 1665 S/1. The John Clark under sentence of transportation may have been the man of the same name who joined the Bedford church in 1671. HSA 1667 W/58; *CB*, 70. At the quarter sessions at Bedford on 6 April 1665, constables received orders to arrest conventiclers. Wigfield, *PBHRS*, 20:166.

[4] Pepys, 9:96; BL, Egerton MSS 2539, fol. 162v; *CJ*, 9:58, 60–61; *Debates of the House of Commons from the Year 1667 to the Year 1694*, ed. Anchitel Grey, 10 vols. (London, 1763), 1:97, 103–6, 146 (quoted).

[5] BL, Add. MSS 19,399, fol. 107r-v; 34,769, fol. 70r-v; Harleian MSS 7377, fol. 6r.

year for preaching at a conventicle. During this period William Foster, commissary of the archdeacon's court and chancellor of the diocese of Lincoln, was energetically trying to suppress dissent, convening church courts at Bedford four times between May 1668 and October 1669.[6] His bishop, William Fuller of Lincoln, would subsequently praise him for having been "so zealous in asserting the Rights of the Church and my Jurisdiction," adding that he was "much beloved by the clergy, and obliging [to] the gentry."[7] Religious conditions were so tenuous at this time that Thomas Barlow, the future bishop of Lincoln, attached plausibility to rumors that Owen or Baxter would be appointed to the next available bishopric.[8] Not surprisingly, Bunyan, as we have seen, enjoyed substantial liberty between September 1669 and May 1670. Taking advantage of the lapse of the first Conventicle Act on 1 March 1669, nonconformists were very active during this period. Based on informers' reports, the lord mayor of London calculated that 12,000 people were attending conventicles on a single Sunday in May 1670. Among them was the meeting of Bunyan's printer Francis Smith at Goswell Street, where between 400 and 500 worshiped.[9]

Although the new Conventicle Act became effective on 15 May 1670, nonconformists continued to gather in large numbers in London and elsewhere.[10] Again, efforts to enforce the statute varied depending on the attitude or effectiveness of magistrates. In London the lord mayor called out the trained bands, but constables and other lesser magistrates were generally ineffective; among those arrested were the Congregationalist Anthony Palmer, whom Bunyan knew, and the Quakers George Fox and Alexander Parker. In Somerset, various justices of the peace were absent in the summer of 1670, raising suspicion that as "polititians" they were "not willing to disoblige so considerable a partie."[11] At Bristol, where nonconformity

[6] BLA, MS HSA 1669 S/46; Wigfield, *PBHRS* 20:179; Hill, *TPM*, 145; *Original Records of Early Nonconformity Under Persecution and Indulgence*, ed. G. L. Turner, 2 vols. (London: T. Fisher Unwin, 1911), 1:63; Mullett, *JBC*, 97. A grand jury issued a verdict of *ignoramus* when it had insufficient evidence to send a case to a petty jury.

[7] Bodl., Tanner MSS 43, fol. 25r. Fuller also thanked the aldermen of Grantham for arresting conventiclers. BL, Add. MSS 34,769, fol. 70r.

[8] Bodl., English Letters C328, fol. 509r.

[9] Sir Edward Dering, *The Parliamentary Diary of Sir Edward Dering 1670–1673*, ed. Basil Duke Henning (New Haven, CT: Yale University Press, 1940), 4–6; DWL, MS 89.32; PRO, SP 29/275/104.

[10] PRO, SP 29/275/140 (London); 29/276/127 (Dover); 29/275/162 (Bristol); 29/276/76 (Somerset and Wiltshire); 29/277/165 (Great Yarmouth); 29/275/138 (Chester); 29/275/172 (Hull); 29/278/119 (Whitby).

[11] Bodl., Carte MSS 77, fol. 535r; CLRO, Conventicle Box 1, no. 2; PRO, SP 29/275/158, 173; 29/276/1, 72; 29/277/11 (quoted).

was strong, Sir Robert Yeamans, a councilor, threatened churchwardens, overseers, and constables with prosecution if they failed to enforce the statute, but they
had too few informers.[12] Some constables in Wiltshire preferred to perjure themselves rather than prosecute dissenters, the mayor of Dover ignored conventicles,
and justices of the peace at Great Yarmouth refused to implement the law. Enforcement was also lax at Hull, where many magistrates were nonconformists.[13]
The king stepped up the pressure on London dissenters in June by authorizing officials to seize their meetinghouses for use by the Church of England.[14]

In Bedford the magistrates performed their duty on 15 May 1670 after two informers reported a meeting of Bunyan's congregation at John Fenne's house.
Acting on Foster's warrant, constables arrested twenty-eight people, including
Nehemiah Coxe, the preacher, John and Samuel Fenne, and ten women, all of
whom were fined according to their ability to pay; Coxe joined Bunyan in prison
and was still there in the summer of 1671. Reflecting Bunyan's view, he had asserted "that the Church of England as it now stands is an anti-Christian church
and that this meeteing at which they were now taken is the way of Christ and according to the word of God." Although Bunyan had apparently been present at a
church meeting in early May when the congregation appointed him and Samuel
Fenne to visit a potential member,[15] he was not among those arrested on the 15th,
his relative freedom having ended with the implementation of the Second Conventicle Act. When a constable and a churchwarden refused to help collect the
fines, each was fined £5, and two men who were unwilling to carry goods distrained by another churchwarden were incarcerated. On the 22nd the congregation met again, notwithstanding the threat of doubled fines, and when the worshipers ignored an order to disperse, they were forcibly disbanded. With one exception, the resulting fines ranged from 5s. to £6; Mary Tilney, the widow of a
gentleman, was fined £20 and, after refusing to pay, had goods valued at more
than £40 distrained.[16]

While these events unfolded, Bunyan remained in prison, where he spent part
of his time working on a concordance. According to Charles Doe, "A Pocket
Concordance" was never printed,[17] but this may not be the case. At the end of

[12]PRO, SP 29/276/75; 29/278/149.

[13] PRO, SP 29/278/116 (Wiltshire); 29/287/57 (Dover); 29/277/126; 29/278/171 (Great
Yarmouth); 29/276/4, 65, 113, 176 (Hull); HMC 25, *Le Fleming*, 75 (Dover).

[14]BL, Harleian MSS 7377, fol. 15v.

[15]BLA, MSS HSA 1671 W/6, 15, 84 (quoted); 1671 S/22; *CB*, 52. Coxe was initially imprisoned in the town jail. HSA 1671 W/6.

[16]*A True and Impartial Narrative of Some Illegal and Arbitrary Proceedings* (n.p., 1670);
Wigfield, *PBHRS* 20:179–81.

[17]Doe's list of Bunyan's works is appended to *The Heavenly Foot-Man: or, a Descrip-*

Bunyan's *A Defence of the Doctrine of Justification* (1672), Francis Smith appended a list of some of the books he was selling, including *A New and Useful Concordance to the Holy Bible, According to the Last Translation, Containing the Most Material Scriptures in the Line and Margent of the Old and New Testament, Together with the Chief Acceptations of Special Words, with Notes to Distinguish the Promises, Commands, and Threatnings, Being Plainer, and Much Larger Then Any of This Volume Yet Extant*, published in octavo and duodecimo. Immediately following came this cryptic phrase: "Also to be had bound up with the Bible in both Vollumns. 1. Bunyans. 2. Arminius."[18] T. L. Underwood has identified the terse reference to Bunyan as his missing concordance (*MW*, 1:223). As the subtitle makes clear, the titled work was the 1671 edition of Vavasor Powell's *A New and Useful Concordance to the Holy Bible. Whereunto Is Added, the Chief Acceptations & Various Significations Contained in the Old and New Testament. Unto Which Also Is Added More Than in Any Extant, Marks to Distinguish the Commands, Promises and Threatnings. Also a Collection of Those Scripture Prophesies Which Relate to the Call of the Jews, and the Glory That Shall Be in the Latter Days*. Published for Smith and R. Clark, this volume was completed by N. P. (the Congregationalist Nathaniel Partridge?), J. F. (the Congregationalist John Faldo of London or the Presbyterian John Fairfax of Barking?), and unnamed others, and included an epistle by Edward Bagshaw, an ejected minister who had been incarcerated with Powell in Southsea Castle, and the Baptist Thomas Hardcastle, Powell's brother-in-law, on how to use the concordance.[19]

An edition published two years later by Smith alone includes an epistle by John Owen in which he explains that Powell, who died on 27 October 1670, did not complete his work from the letter 'F' onward, and that other authors finished

---

*tion of the Man That Gets to Heaven* (London, 1698), [73–84]; for the concordance see [84]. Another work has apparently not survived, namely, *A Christian Dialogue*.

[18]A select list of Smith's publications at the end of Thomas Paul's *Some Serious Reflections on That Part of Mr. Bunion's Confession of Faith: Touching Church Communion with Unbaptized Persons* (London, 1673) includes the phrases, "Also to be had bound up with the Bible, in both Volumes. By Mr. *Vavasor Powel*," but without mentioning Bunyan and Jacobus Arminius. The citation of Arminius in the list at the end of *A Defence of the Doctrine of Justification* probably refers to Pierre Bertius' *The Life and Death of James Arminius and Simon Episcopius*, published by Smith in 1672; at the end of this work a select list of books includes *A New and Useful Concordance*, which is available separately as well as "printed on a fine page and bound with the Bible." The reference to Bunyan in the list at the end of *A Defence* may be to the so-called third edition of *One Thing Is Needful* (see *MW*, 6:15–16), which is also advertised at the back of Bertius' book.

[19]For Partridge, Faldo, Fairfax, Bagshaw, and Hardcastle see *Calamy Revised, s.vv.* For Partridge see also *The Records of a Church of Christ in Bristol, 1640–1687*, ed. Roger Hayden, Bristol Record Society's Publications, vol. 27 (1974), 34–42.

the task.[20] This raises the possibility that Bunyan may have been one of those responsible for completing Powell's concordance, in which case he never prepared a comparable work of his own. This would account for Doe's information that Bunyan had worked on a concordance and explain why he knew of no copy. However, Doe's description of Bunyan's work as a pocket concordance is not a good descriptor of Powell's book, the 1673 edition of which was nearly 500 pages in length, nor were the initials J. B. on the list of those who completed Powell's work.[21] The more likely possibility is that Bunyan prepared his own small concordance, but perhaps found no publisher because of Powell's book, or had few buyers because Powell's concordance was superior. Further evidence that Bunyan prepared his own concordance is found in Ponder's advertisement in the eighth edition of *Grace Abounding*, which notes that it was in his shop and would be published with "the twelvs Bible."[22] If Bunyan compiled a concordance, he would have undertaken most or all of the labor in the period between the completion of *Grace Abounding* and about August or early September 1667, when he apparently began working on the second edition of his spiritual autobiography, and he may have returned to the concordance between April and September 1671.

## "A Strict Separation"[23]: Church Membership and Communion

Bunyan entered the lists in the debate over church membership and baptism with *A Confession of My Faith, and a Reason of My Practice*, printed for Francis Smith in 1672. Chronologically *A Confession* preceded *A Defence of the Doctrine of Justification*, with its appended list of books, including *A Confession*, also printed by Smith. Bunyan would therefore have written *A Confession* during the period between the completion of *The Pilgrim's Progress* and his receipt of Fowler's *Design of Christianity* on 13 January 1672, probably starting in October 1671.[24] His motivation for *A Confession* may have been the Bedford church's decision on 24 October 1671 to consider him for the eldership, though the work itself, with its

[20] John Owen, epistle to Vavasor Powell, *A New and Useful Concordance* (London, 1673), sig. A2r–v. The *City Mercury* advertised it in 1676; 14 (3–10 February 1676).

[21] Bunyan may have known Powell, for the latter's diary includes this undated entry: "I received a special Letter this day, from our dear Brother J. B. which suited much with my condition and judgment." *The Life and Death of Mr. Vavasor Powell* (London, 1671), 73.

[22] Ponder's advertisement is in the University of Alberta's copy of the eighth edition of *Grace Abounding*, but not the British Library's copy.

[23] *MW*, 4:185.

[24] The epistle concludes, "Thine in Bonds for the Gospel" (4:136). Mullett erroneously suggests that Bunyan composed *A Confession* after his release. *JBC*, 176. Brown's date of early 1672 is also wrong (223).

epistle to an unidentified man who had questioned his lengthy imprisonment, suggests an external target, at least in part. This hypothesis is strengthened by the fact that the book's main thrust is a defense of those nonconformists who refused to make water-baptism a condition of church membership and communion. The objections to which he responded in the latter part of the book suggest prior experience dealing with those who considered water-baptism essential.

In the first third of *A Confession* Bunyan outlined his basic theological principles, richly documenting them with scriptural citations which he deemed the inspired "words of God" (*MW*, 4:152). These were the tenets, he insisted, for which he had been incarcerated more than eleven years. He acknowledged that he had often pondered his beliefs, the lengthy confinement "*continually dogging of me to weigh and pause, and pause again, the grounds and foundation of those principles, for which I thus have suffered*" (4:135). A thousand times he had re-examined his beliefs, only to be as certain of them in 1671 as he had been in 1660. Nothing in his preaching or writing, he averred, savored of heresy or rebellion, nor did his tenets justify his prolonged confinement and the lingering threat of exile or hanging. Insisting on his right to fellowship solely with visible saints, a position that set him apart from Catholics, Anglicans, and Presbyterians, and his obligation to resist "*superstitious inventions*" in worship regardless of state mandates to the contrary, he adamantly refused to make of his conscience "*a continual butchery, and slaughter-shop*," preferring to suffer instead (4:136). Prison had broken neither his spirit nor his resolve to oppose the Church of England—eloquent testimony to the bankruptcy of religious coercion.

The book's confessional portion embodies a relatively straightforward articulation of Calvinist principles. Bunyan's view of predestination is infralapsarian, for God knew of the fall, "having all things present to, and in his wisdome, [before] he made his choice" of whom to save and whom not (4:146).[25] The infralapsarian stance placed Bunyan in the company of most Calvinists. His emphasis in *A Confession* dealt heavily with election, which he described as free, permanent, without regard to works, and unhindered by any impediment (4:145–46). Grace is therefore irresistible and perseverance assured. He employed biblical language exclusively in referring to reprobation in *A Confession*, citing Romans 11:7: "Israel

[25] Greaves, *JB*, 52, contrary to Mullett, *JBC*, 177, and Gordon Campbell, "Fishing in Other Men's Waters: Bunyan and the Theologians," in *John Bunyan*, ed. Keeble, 147–48. See also Galen Johnson, "Supra or Infra? Clarifying Bunyan's Doctrine of Election," *The Recorder* 6 (Spring 2000): [6–7]; and my response, "Bunyan's Doctrine of Predestination: A Historical Perspective," op. cit., [7–10]. Among early modern theologians, supralapsarians asserted that God's decree to predestine the elect *preceded* the decree to permit or effect the fall, whereas infralapsarians contended that the decree to allow the fall came first. Neither group argued that the decree of election postdated the fall itself.

hath not obtained that which he seeketh for; but the election hath obtained it, and the rest were blinded." Faith is possible only for those in whom the Holy Spirit implants it, namely, the elect (4:144–45). Effectual calling, tendered only to the elect, produces faith, hope, and repentance (4:149–50). On the eve of his attack on Fowler's *Design of Christianity* Bunyan was emphasizing justification by Christ's imputed righteousness, and his *Defense* can be seen as a reassertion and amplification of his statement in *A Confession* (4:140, 143–44).

A short passage on magistracy, apparently added while the work was in progress,[26] draws heavily on Romans 13:2–6, a safe position for one who hoped to win his freedom. While acknowledging that magistracy is divinely ordained and that a "well qualified" magistrate can bestow numerous benefits, Bunyan's final words in this section evoke the nonconformist resolve not to surrender their principles to the dictates of an evil government: "*let us shew our christianity in a patient suffering for well doing, what it shall please God to inflict them*" (4:153). By setting this sentence in italics, the printer, probably following Bunyan's instructions, created the impression that these words were scriptural, like the rest of the italicized words in this section. In 1671 Bunyan was unbowed though prudently cautious. For dissenting readers his message of continued defiance could be readily discerned.

The remainder of *A Confession* delineates Bunyan's conviction that gospel churches should be constituted of visible saints regardless of their views on baptism by water. He had learned this position from John Gifford and Henry Jessey, and a comparable emphasis on Spirit-baptism from William Dell. Gifford's practice had been to accept members based on a candidate's faith and holy living regardless of "this or that circumstance or opinion in outward and circumstantiall things," thereby avoiding "disputings and occasion to janglings and unprofitable questions." The primary purpose of this latitude was practical—the fostering of amity, love, and edification. Not unique to the Bedford church, the practice was followed by congregations at Bury St. Edmunds, Bristol, Cambridge, Nottingham, Hexham, Southwark, and Dublin.[27] This was the position of Jessey, whose leadership in radical religious circles had been recognized by the Bedford congregation since 1657. In *A Storehouse of Provision, to Further Resolution in Severall Cases of Conscience* (1650), he argued for the admission of believers to fellowship and communion regardless of their views on baptism primarily because he found no evidence in the New Testament that excluded any saints from the church on

[26]The paragraph on magistracy does not appear in one of the two extant copies. *MW*, 4:153.

[27]*CB*, 17 (quoted), 19; Geoffrey F. Nuttall, *Visible Saints: The Congregational Way 1640–1660* (Oxford: Basil Blackwell, 1957), 119–20.

baptismal grounds; hence those whom Christ embraces must be admitted to the visible church. The door of membership and communion was open to those whose hearts had been purified by the Holy Spirit as manifested by their repentance and holy living.[28] With other Bedford church leaders, Bunyan would have known of Jessey's views because they had looked to him, George Cokayne, and John Simpson in November 1659 to find an assistant for the ailing John Burton.[29]

Bunyan espoused the same position, calling for the acceptance of any into church membership and communion who profess faith in Christ, repent of their sinfulness, and live a virtuous life. As Jessey had contended, this was the New Testament practice (4:154–55). To make water-baptism a wall to divide believers from one another is unjustifiable, particularly since baptism by water is not essential for salvation (4:171, 174). Like Gifford, Bunyan stressed that love is a greater bond than baptism by water, for Christ's love "hath swallowed up all distinctions" (4:177). Election, not baptism, produces Christians. Because divisions over baptism discriminate between the elect, they are "momentary and hatcht in darkness" (4:178). To bar the unbaptized from communion is to make laws where God has imposed none and therefore persecute some of the godly. Such is "the Nursery of all vain janglings, backbitings, and strangenes among the Christians" and "a Prop to Antichrist" (4:182–83). Bunyan went so far as to suggest that the disputes over baptism had so riven the visible saints as to have caused the judgments under which they suffered, presumably since the Restoration.[30] Faced with a persecuting state, he issued a call to unite: "Close; Close; Be one as the Father and Christ is one" (4:186).

In Bunyan's estimation, water-baptism and the Lord's supper are "shadowish, or figurative ordinances," of excellent use as representatives of Christ's death and resurrection but not fundamentals of the faith. He called them "mystical Ministers" that could instruct believers in spiritual matters, but this did not justify making them essentials, which amounted to idolatry (4:160). He distinguished sharply between the doctrine and practice of baptism, the doctrine "being that which by the outward sign is presented to us, or which by the outward circumstance of the act is preached to the believer: *viz. The death of Christ; My death with Christ; also his resurrection from the Dead, and mine with him to newness of life.*" The heart of water-baptism is baptism by the Spirit, and this, unlike the external practice, is essential. Baptism by water is not an infallible sign of Spirit-

[28] Henry Jessey, *A Storehouse of Provision, to Further Resolution in Severall Cases of Conscience* (London, 1650), 94–98, 109.

[29] *CB*, 34.

[30] In *Differences in Judgment* he claimed the printer had altered "a cause" to "the cause" (*MW*, 4:233).

baptism, whatever its pedagogical value (4:172). Indeed, the gospel can be effectually preached without mentioning baptism (4:180). Water-baptism, which did not
make early Christians church members, is therefore not an initiating ordinance
into Christian fellowship (4:162–63). Nevertheless, baptism must not be taken
lightly, for its essential prerequisite is visible sainthood. Notwithstanding the importance he attached to Spirit-baptism, Bunyan stopped short of Dell, who had
contended that water-baptism is not only inferior to it but no longer of value.
For Dell, water-baptism is but the shadow, and Spirit-baptism, which alone is
part of Christ's kingdom, the substance. "What need hath he of cold *material
water* to be powred on his body, under the pretence of any signe whatever, either
of *Moses* or *John*, when as [the believer] hath the truth, substance, and heavenly
thing it self?"[31] In contrast, Bunyan did not jettison baptism as a rite that ended
with the coming of Christ's baptism by the Spirit.

Much has been written about whether Bunyan was a Baptist.[32] One key passage in *A Confession* makes it clear that he was an open-communion, open-
membership Baptist: The baptismal candidate, he maintained, "must be a visible
Saint before, else he ought not to be baptized," a position Bunyan based on Acts
8:37, 9:17 [–18], and 16:33 (4:164).[33] Shortly after publication of Bunyan's *Confession*, William Kiffin, pastor of the Particular Baptist church at Devonshire Square,
London, explicitly confirmed that Bunyan opposed paedobaptism, favoring instead the baptism of believers.[34] Not only did Bunyan embrace believer's baptism,
but he deemed those who rely solely on Spirit-baptism to be deficient in "light."
Because such light is divinely bestowed, those without it cannot fairly be excluded from the church (4:170, 172). Indeed, those who are baptized without this
light transgress, for in religion nothing must be done "but by light in the word"
(4:175, 178). Here, too, he placed substantial emphasis on the preeminence of
conscience.

Tolerance in baptism did not mean indulgence with respect to admitting the

[31] William Dell, *The Doctrine of Baptismes, Reduced from Its Ancient and Moderne
Corruptions* (London, 1648), 8–10, 17–24, 26 (quoted).

[32] See the following citations in James F. Forrest and Richard Lee Greaves, *John Bunyan: A Reference Guide* (Boston: G. K. Hall and Co., 1982): Armitage, 1888:2; Urwick,
1888:12; Brown, 1889:3; Venables, 1889:7; Whitley, 1911:17; Thomas, 1928:120; Payne, 1944:8;
Kingsley, 1978:29. See also Joseph D. Ban, "Was John Bunyan a Baptist? A Case Study in
Historiography," *Baptist Quarterly* 30 (October 1984): 367–76.

[33] The Joseph Bunyan baptized at St. Cuthbert's, Bedford, on 16 November 1672 was
probably the son of John Bunyan the younger. W. T. Whitley, "The Bunyan Christening,"
*Transactions of the Baptist Historical Society* 2 (1910–11): 256. For a contrary view see
Brown, 222–23.

[34] William Kiffin, epistle to Paul, *Some Serious Reflections*, sig. A3r.

openly profane. On these matters Bunyan was anything but liberal-minded. "Mixed communion polluteth the ordinances of God," violates divine law, provokes judgment, and defiles God's people (4:157, 159). This is why Bunyan and the Bedford congregation required prospective members to give "a faithful relation" of their belief and commitment to holy living (4:160), a practice common to the Congregational and Baptist traditions,[35] and this, too, explains the determination of these churches to expel members whose commitment to holy living failed to last. After all, critics of the separatist churches were not chary about calling attention to the periodic failure of some of their members to live holy lives, and the Anglican Thomas Mariott went so far as to claim that "the Separatists meetings are as mixed as ours, and they are as wicked every way."[36] Bunyan strove to prevent exactly this problem, citing such offenders as idolaters, fornicators, sabbath violators, murmurers, and tempters (4:159). Among those expelled from the church was John Rush of Bedford "for being drunke after a very beastly and filthy maner, that is above the ordinery rate of drunkenness for he could not be carried home from the Swan to his own house without the help of no less then three persons, who when they had brought him home could not present him as one alive to his family, he was so dead."[37] Such conduct contrasted vividly with the standards required for admission to the church and could not be tolerated (4:162). Members of the congregation, expected to live in accord with "moral duties Gospellized," were under perpetual scrutiny by one another, making a gathered church an intensely introspective society. Bunyan advised congregations to use the Ten Commandments as the guide for judging the appropriateness of conduct, thereby avoiding excessive severity and manifesting "christian tenderness" (4:165).

Nor did Bunyan's moderate liberality extend to toleration for corrupt forms of worship. Here again he directed his criticism primarily at the Church of England. Adulterated worship, he averred, had been a cause of the great flood and a plague visited on Israel. Toleration regarding baptism did not justify abandoning the fundamental principle of separatism that demarcated the congregations of visible saints from the established church, with its unfettered embrace of the openly profane (4:158). Communion with members of the Church of England was unthinkable unless they joined a separatist congregation: "If there be a visible Saint yet remaining in that Church; let him come to us, and we will have communion with him." Such a person, Bunyan believed, could not simultaneously belong to two "diametrically opposite" bodies; "he who professeth himself a

---

[35] Nuttall, *Visible Saints*, 110–14.
[36] CUL, Add. MSS 6375, fol. 71v.
[37] CB, 75.

member of a Church of Christ; must forthwith, nay before, forsake the Antichristian one" (4:184). Uncompromising to its core, this position set Bunyan sharply at odds with those moderate nonconformists, such as Baxter, John Howe, John Cheyney, and Philip Henry, who endorsed occasional conformity.[38] It also opened him and like-minded nonconformists to charges of "causelesse" separation and schism, particularly since they shared core doctrinal principles with adherents of the established church. The differences between dissenters and conformists, averred the Anglican Thomas Mariott, amounted to nothing more than "trifles & vanities."[39] For Bunyan, however, the established church was not only Antichrist's congregation but the antithesis of "our discipline, which is not forced, but free" (4:157). Against this enemy he wanted visible saints to unite in the conviction that the Spirit's battles should be fought over fundamentals, not figurative ordinances.

Bunyan's interest in uniting the visible saints—Baptists, Congregationalists, and possibly Presbyterians—was a goal shared in some form by various other dissenters in the late seventeenth century. In the words of Philip Henry, "as Unity promotes so divisions hinder the Progresse of the Gospel . . . most of all, if the falling out bee for Trifles."[40] During the summer and fall of 1674, a group of Congregationalist churches in Yorkshire, Lancashire, and Cheshire, whose leaders included Thomas Jollie and Michael Briscoe, articulated the principles on which their association was based, in part because the Presbyterian congregation of Oliver Heywood wanted to join them. Desirous of petitioning the king for "outward Liberty," this association sought the counsel of John Owen, raising the possibility that he told Bunyan of their activities.[41] Moreover, Wharton's papers contain evidence of another plan, this one a proposal drafted in the early 1680s to unite Presbyterians and Congregationalists.[42] The culmination of such efforts occurred with the organizing of the Happy Union in 1691, bringing Congregationalists and Presbyterians together temporarily, but Bunyan was dead by this time. His vision of unifying the visible saints came to naught, effectively blocked by the harsh opposition of traditional Baptists, the fierceness of whose attack he would find painful.

[38] Keeble, *LCN*, 35–36. For Howe see *Calamy Revised*, *s.v.*; for Cheyney see *DNB*, *s.v.*

[39] Richard Salter, CUL, Add. MSS 1, no. 13 (quoted), resolving the doubts expressed in nos. 14 and 16; Thomas Mariott, CUL, Add. MSS 6375, fols. 70v–71v (quoted at 71r).

[40] CUL, Add. MSS 7338, commenting on Genesis 13.

[41] BL, Stowe MSS 745, fols. 79r–80r. For Jollie see *BDBR*, *s.v.*, and for Briscoe and Heywood see *Calamy Revised*, *s.vv.*

[42] Bodl., Carte MSS 81, fols. 348r–349r. For more on the issue of unity see Chapter 13.

"Like an Eel on the Angle"[43]: Edward Fowler and
the Debate about Justification

Bunyan's final work during his eleven-and-a-half-year confinement was a testy, impolite attack on Edward Fowler's *The Design of Christianity* (1671), a sequel to the latter's Latitudinarian *apologia, The Principles and Practices, of Certain Moderate Divines of the Church of England* (1670). Now vicar of Northill, Bedfordshire, a village southeast of Bedford, Fowler had been chaplain to the dowager countess of Kent and a Presbyterian. By conforming at the Restoration he retained his benefice, which he had held since 1656. As a turncoat in Bunyan's eyes, Fowler, with his "Unstable Weathercock Spirit," had "hop[ped] from Presbiterianism, to a Prelatical Mode; and if time and chance should serve you, backwards, and forwards again: Yea, . . . you can make use of several Consciences, one for this way now, another for that anon" (*MW*, 4:83, 101). His antipathy toward Fowler was not merely a matter of theological differences but the rector's personification of the "rabling counterfeit Clergy" who persecuted nonconformists (4:100). His challenge to Fowler, whom he must have known inasmuch as they ministered in the same area,[44] and whom he blamed, among others, for his lengthy incarceration, was intensely personal, but he was simultaneously defying the very powers of the state in religious matters: "As for your subtile and close incensing the power to persecute Non-conformists, know that we are willing, God assisting, to overcome you with truth, and patience, not sticking to Sacrifice our lives, and dearest concerns in a faithful Witness-baring against your filthy errors, Compiled and Foiled into the World, by your Devilish design to promote Paganism, against Christianity" (4:106).[45]

As soon as Bunyan heard about Fowler's new book, he sought a copy, receiving it on 13 January 1672.[46] Writing studiously, he finished his response, a manuscript of approximately 46,500 words, on 27 February (4:10–11). It was published by Smith as *A Defence of the Doctrine of Justification, by Faith in Jesus Christ.*[47] Plagued by redundancy, the book is replete with caustic references to

---

[43] *MW*, 4:102.

[44] At least two members of Bunyan's congregation, Sister Bunyan and Robert Disher, were from Northill. *CB*, 83, 225.

[45] Sim and Walker (100) challenge my earlier statement that *A Defence* was not a contribution to the debate over conscience, though its discussion of that issue is not its primary theme.

[46] Fowler's book had been licensed on 5 June 1671. Arber, *Transcript*, 2:425.

[47] It does not appear in the Term Catalogues until 21 November 1672, immediately preceding the entry for the reply by Fowler or his surrogate, *Dirt Wip't Off*. Publication of Bunyan's book must have occurred months earlier. Arber, *Term Catalogues*, 1:116.

Fowler, his arguments, and occasionally the Church of England. Seeking no quarter, Bunyan gave none. *The Design of Christianity*, he thundered, was "begun in Ignorance, mannaged with Errour, and ended in Blasphemy" (4:123). Repeatedly he hammered the book as blasphemous, deeming it destructive to Christianity, its principles "Dungish" and "Heathenish," and its doctrine the rotten product of Satan and hell (4:7, 45, 48, 53, 73, 77, 98, 100, 103, 113, 121–22). Filled with "gross Absurdities" and damnable heresies, the book, he charged, reflects Fowler's impiety, idolatry, and muddying the gospel (4:83, 99, 104, 114–15, 123). He heaped invective on Fowler, "a ranting Latitudinarian" who would do anything to avoid persecution (4:102). Linking Latitudinarians, with their emphasis on holy living, and Ranters, with their reputed disdain for traditional morality, blatantly distorted his opponent's teaching, yet in Bunyan's eyes Fowler was a grossly ignorant purveyor of "dunghil Righteousness" whose dirty thoughts and vilifying words ranked him among angels of darkness and ministers of the Devil (4:94–95, 99–100, 113, 121–22). In Bunyan's judgment, Fowler was evil and Ranter-like because he alienated people from God, heretically turning the doctrine of grace into licentious dogma. Despite his gospel vocabulary, his message embodied evil. By such means, he scolded Fowler, "you give [your 'Antigospel Principles'] the Name of Holiness, the Design of Christ, and of Christianity; by which means you remove the Christ of God, from before, and set him behind, *forbidding Man to believe on him, till they have Practiced your things first*" (4:100). Fowler, he opined, was blind as a bat, a dissembler with a snake in his bosom, a corrupter of Scripture, an author of venomous words, and a man with a rotten heart and a deluded brain whose principles were "Pestiferous" (4:11, 22, 35, 39–40, 44, 82, 106). The Northill rector was "Grosely ignorant. 2. Too highly Opinionate. 3. Proud in affection. 4. Liquorish. 5. A Self-Lover" (4:113). As if this rain of insults were insufficient, Bunyan compared Fowler to a litany of enemies that included Quakers, Catholics, Turks, witches, Socinians, heathens, Ranters, and conformists (4:21–22, 28, 36, 44, 46, 68, 80, 98–102, 106, 120–22). At last he drew the book to a close by comparing quotations from Fowler with statements extracted from Edmund Campion (probably taken from Alexander Nowell and William Day's *A True Report of the Disputation . . . with Ed. Campion Jesuite* [1583]) and William Penn's *The Sandy Foundation Shaken* (1668) (4:125–30, 397).[48]

The vituperative language and gratuitous sniping aside, Bunyan's critique of Fowler is incontestably substantive and goes to the core of the fundamental debate among Restoration Protestants over the nature of the gospel. This fact, as well as Bunyan's disdain for a turncoat who represented the church that was persecuting him, explains the vehemence of his rhetoric. Ironically, the Latitudinari-

---

[48]For Campion see *DNB, s.v.*

ans, unlike most Anglican defenders, sought to find a basis for accommodating moderate dissenters in the established church.[49] Fowler, for instance, believed that subscription to the Thirty-nine Articles entailed a pledge not to disrupt the church's peace by contradicting any of them, but recognized the subscriber's right to silent reservation "so long as he does not believ[e] that any one of them contains an errour of so dangerous a nature as that our concern for the souls of men should oblige us to preach against it."[50] If Bunyan knew the Latitudinarians favored accommodation, his determination to highlight the fundamental theological differences between him and other uncompromising dissenters on the one hand and Latitudinarians on the other may have intensified.

For Latitudinarians, natural religion provided a logical basis on which to embrace revelation; reason and revelation, in their view, are compatible. Although persuaded that human nature has been stained by inherited sin, thus making grace essential, Latitudinarians believed that the soul's fundamental principles predispose it to rationality and the ability to discern the morally good. But reason alone is insufficient to turn people from sin to God's ways, making revelation necessary. The Latitudinarians' emphasis was not on human reason's inherent wickedness but its inadequacy to discern fully the truths of God. Human reason differs from divine in scope rather than nature, and faith is not an irrational act but a rational decision to cooperate with divinely bestowed grace. Latitudinarians did not forsake grace for moralism but made it an essential prerequisite for moral reform. Like Anglicans in general, Latitudinarians charted a course that eschewed what they perceived to be the extremes of Socinianism and solifidianism, the reliance on faith alone for salvation. Whereas the former was unacceptable owing to its emphasis on autonomous moral reform, the latter was objectionable because it provided the foundation for Antinomianism. Consequently, Latitudinarians made repentance and obedience conditions for justification. A Latitudinarian hallmark was the emphasis on virtuous living made possible by the infusion of undeserved grace. In short, practical divinity was more important than systematic theology.[51]

Fowler's *Design of Christianity* generally developed these themes, of which four are particularly relevant for the ensuing debate with Bunyan: human nature and its relationship to divine grace; holiness as Christianity's design; Christ's role

[49] W. M. Spellman, *The Latitudinarians and the Church of England, 1660–1700* (Athens: University of Georgia Press, 1993), 157; Isabel Rivers, "Grace, Holiness, and the Pursuit of Happiness: Bunyan and Restoration Latitudinarianism," in *John Bunyan*, ed. Keeble, 49.

[50] BL, Add. MSS 33,498, fols. 71r–72r (quoted at 71r).

[51] Rivers, "Grace, Holiness, and the Pursuit of Happiness," 49–52; Spellman, *Latitudinarians*, 73–74, 81, 83, 86–88, 99–100, 104–5, 111–13, 158–59.

as an exemplar of grace; and the nature of justification and the role of faith, repentance, and holiness. Although Fowler acknowledged the depravity of human nature and the natural state of all humans as one of "imbecillity and great impotence," he also insisted that people are endowed with a principle of reason and freedom of will that enable them to subordinate their *"Brutish Passions and Affections."*[52] People have *"a Divine or God-like Nature, causing an hearty approbation of, and an affectionate compliance with the Eternal Laws of Righteousness; and a behaviour agreeable to the Essential and Immutable differences of Good and Evil."*[53] Humans therefore possess the capacity to cooperate with divine grace and contribute to their own salvation. Fowler explicitly denounced ministers who preached "the Irrespectiveness of God's Decrees, the Absoluteness of his Promises, [and] the utter disability and perfect impotence of Natural men to do any thing towards their own conversion."[54] This is not to say that grace is unnecessary, for without it salvation is impossible. As revealed in the gospel, grace effectually moves people to renounce their sins, delivering them from their power. Without grace there can be no subduing of lust, and only with its assistance can people endeavor to become virtuous.[55] In contrast to Reformed theologians, Fowler averred that grace can be resisted, for all humans possess freedom.[56]

As his second key theme, Fowler asserted that making people virtuous is *"the main and onely design of Christianity."*[57] Because this was the fundamental reason for Christ's earthly life and death, "Holiness *is the only Design of the* Precepts *of the Gospel."*[58] Christ's mission was to save people from their sins, and only secondarily from punishment for them. "The only *direct* scope that Christianity drives at . . . [is] the subduing of sin in us, and our freedom from its guilt or obligation to punishment . . . [is] the consequent of this."[59] Christ's role was to make men and women holy, purifying their natures and instilling virtue in them. The holiness he sought to recreate in people is that which they had lost in Adam, the *imago Dei.*[60] "The Great Errand he came upon was the effecting of our Deliverance out of that sinful State we had brought our selves into, and the putting us again into possession of that Holiness which we had Lost." In fulfilling this mis-

---

[52] Edward Fowler, *The Design of Christianity* (London, 1671), 6, 144–46.
[53] Ibid., 6.
[54] Ibid., 230, 262.
[55] Ibid., 122, 129, 143, 219.
[56] Ibid., 172–73.
[57] Ibid., 98.
[58] Ibid., sig. A3r-v, 13, 18, 28.
[59] Ibid., 14–15, 223–24 (quoted).
[60] Ibid., 17, 36–37, 67–68, 78, 91, 128–29, 134, 224, 271.

sion Jesus' role as exemplar is crucial and much stressed by Fowler. "His whole Life was one Continued Lecture of the most Excellent *Morals*, the most Sublime and exact Vertue."[61] In him one can see the supreme example of morality, affability, courtesy, sociability, appropriate gravity, candor, kindliness, and prudence, making his life the pattern for all Christians to emulate.[62]

For Fowler, the essence of faith, a belief in the gospel's truth that "*includes a sincere resolution of Obedience unto all its Precepts,*" is holiness. Justifying faith must comply with the purpose of Christ's life, namely, making people holy. Faith alone cannot justify because the gospel demonstrates that Jesus died to make people virtuous. It is insufficient to say "*That faith justifieth, onely as it apprehendeth the merits and righteousness of Jesus Christ.*"[63] Lashing out at preachers such as Bunyan who urged their audiences to renounce their virtue and rely on Christ's, Fowler reckoned it "stupid folly" for people to imagine Jesus' righteousness as their own.[64] The gospel's intent is to make believers inwardly and truly righteous. To the extent that Fowler wrote of imputed righteousness he meant that Christ's holiness would "excite men in their endeavours after such a Righteousness as this is."[65] If Jesus' virtue could be imputed to a wicked person in the manner espoused by preachers in the Reformed tradition, "it would signifie as little to his happiness, while he continueth so, as would a gorgeous and splendid garment to one that is almost starved with hunger."[66] In this sense, Christ's righteousness cannot be imputed to wicked people. Grace is magnified not by justifying evil people while they continue in their wicked ways, for this would disparage divine justice, but by renewing or restoring human nature to its state of original holiness. The righteousness that is Christianity's goal is not merely the external application of Christ's virtue but inner transformation manifested in holy living.[67] Consequently, faith is not the condition of justification, as Bunyan believed, since "it compliEth with only the precept of *relying on Christ's Merits* for the obtaining of it: especially when it is no less manifest than . . . that obedience to the *other precepts* must go before obedience to *this*; and that a man may not rely on the merits of Christ for the forgiveness of his sins . . . till he be sincerely willing to be reformed."[68] Unfeigned repentance, diligent endeavors to abstain from sin, and obedience to the gospel are essential prerequisites for justification; reformation

[61] Ibid., 12 (quoted), 39 (quoted).
[62] Ibid., 39, 41, 63, 296.
[63] Ibid., 221 (quoted), 224, 225 (quoted).
[64] Ibid., 214, 262.
[65] Ibid., 226.
[66] Ibid., 120.
[67] Ibid., 5, 119, 130–31.
[68] Ibid., 223.

must precede forgiveness. The covenant of grace, in other words, has conditions which must be fulfilled by people, a position sharply at variance with Bunyan's. Only "holy Souls . . . are capable of having the *Guilt* of their Sins removed, and of being freed from the displeasure and wrath of God."[69]

Bunyan vigorously attacked each of these themes, adjudging them a mass of Scripture-contravening errors. On the fundamental subject of human nature he rejected the possibility of any purity and thus of people's capacity to comply with the external laws of righteousness. "That there is such a Principle in man (since *Adams* fall) . . . by which he may act, or that Christs whole Gospel-design is, *the helping forward such a Principle*, is altogether without Scripture or reason" (*MW*, 4:12–13). Every person's understanding has been darkened, mind and conscience defiled, and will perverted (4:13–14). To act using the principle of reason with which we are endowed is to fall short by "an infinite distance from that, in which it is by God expected, the man must act, that doth ought that is pleasing in his sight." Without faith there is no satisfying God (4:16). Nor was Bunyan prepared to accept Fowler's affirmation of free will with respect to soteriological matters, for humans in their natural state are incapable of discerning things of the Spirit. "Now if he cannot *know* them, from what Principle should he *will* them?" (4:80). In the full force of the Reformed tradition, Bunyan insisted that to preach free grace is to repudiate free will, and he went on to aver that ministers who rightly teach predestination, the absolute nature of divine promises, and the impotency of natural men and women to do anything to facilitate their salvation are proclaiming God's word. Fowler's argument, he contended, was folly (4:104–5).

In Bunyan's judgment, Christ came to give believers his holiness, not restore that which they had lost. Christ is the redeemer who makes satisfaction to God for believers' transgressions, thereby fulfilling the demands of the law, not a mere exemplar to persuade his followers to return to their "Adamitish Holiness" (4:46, 55, 59, 66, 73). Fowler, Bunyan charged, made Jesus a schoolmaster rather than a savior (4:78). Arguing that Jesus seeks to save by leading people back to a holiness they lost was "none other then Barbarous Quakerisme" (4:87). Without saving faith, obedience to the Decalogue or morality's first principles is deemed wickedness by God and constitutes dunghill righteousness (4:98, 106). Bunyan went so far as to insist that any attempt to imitate Jesus' life without faith amounts to rebellion, no matter how sincere (4:121). Ignorance of the gospel is anything but bliss.

The heart of Bunyan's assault on Fowler is his affirmation of a believer's justification solely by Christ's imputed righteousness, thereby freeing the elect from sin's consequences, a theme Luther stressed in his commentary on Galatians

[69] Ibid., 17, 27, 31 (quoted), 80–81, 91–92, 130.

(4:35).[70] The righteousness of which Fowler wrote, Bunyan contended, was pagan holiness, thrown to the dogs by the gospel and valueless with respect to salvation (4:44). Only by Christ's imputed righteousness, not the alleged perfection of their own virtue, can the elect be made holy (4:65, 70). Christ

> hath not designed to Promote, or to Perfect that righteousness that is Founded on, and Floweth from, the Purity of our Humane Nature: for then he must design the setting up [of] Mans righteousness; that which is of the Law; and then he must design also the setting up of that which is directly in opposition, both to the Righteousness, that of God is designed to Justifie us: and *that* by which we are inwardly made Holy. (4:44)

To Fowler's contention that God does not pardon and impute righteousness to the wicked, Bunyan retorted that the beneficiaries of such mercy are indeed real offenders, not "*Painted* Sinners" who make a pretense of pursuing upright ways (4:69). By making repentance precede faith, Bunyan argued, Fowler had confused the gospel sequence of faith, repentance, and holy living. Sanctification is a consequence, not a cause, of justification (4:111, 115). The differences between Fowler and Bunyan were thus fundamental, involving core principles of faith, justification, predestination, and sanctification, thereby convincing Bunyan of the necessity to devote an entire book to refuting his Latitudinarian neighbor.

During the course of his attack on Fowler, Bunyan fired some stinging salvos against the Church of England, continuing the criticism he had mounted in his as-yet unpublished allegory. Much of this was directed at the clergy, as in his scathing denunciation of the "many ignorant Sir *Johns*"(4:82), though he missed the mark if he was thinking of formal education; 95 percent of clerical incumbents in nearby Leicestershire had university degrees in 1670, two-thirds of them master's degrees and thus a theological education.[71] Bunyan was also critical of the "many that have done Violence to their former Light, and that have Damned themselves in their former Anathematizing of others," a group of apostates that included Fowler. Their place in the pulpit, Bunyan surmised, signaled divine judgment on their wayward congregations. Such men live debauched lives, and "after seeming serious Detestings of Wickedness have for the Love of filthy Lucre, and the Pampering their idle Carcasses, made Shipwrack of their former Faith, and that Feigned good Conscience they had" (4:82). With relish, he seized on Fowler's admission that some conformist clerics lived scandalously while others used bombastic language, scholastic arguments, and boyish wit, seeking plaudits "*for their ability in dividing of an hair, their Metaphysical Acuteness, and Scholastick subtilety, or for their Doughty Dexterity in Controversial Squabbles*" (4:103). In *The*

[70]Luther, *Galatians*, e.g., 23, 137–39, 223–29.
[71]Spurr, *RCE*, 170.

*Design of Christianity* Fowler had paraded his erudition, citing such authors as Plato and Cicero, the classical philosophers Pythagoras and Anaxarchus, the Stoics Hierocles and Epictetus, the early Christian authors Origen and Clement of Alexandria, Bishop Simon Patrick, the Cambridge Platonist John Smith, and the reformers Calvin, Peter Martyr, Wolfgang Musculus, and Hieronymus Zanchius. Unimpressed, Bunyan dismissed the classical authors as "Atheistically ignorant of the Religion of Jesus" and the Reformed theologians as irrelevant since he had "neither made my Creed out of them, nor other" (4:38, 122). More generally, he likened the Church of England, with its insistence on a compulsory state religion, to Islam in Turkey, "where *Mahomet* Reigns *as Lord*" (4:101). Proponents of the Church of England, Bunyan asserted, had a "Devilish design to promote Paganism," thus palpably setting them at odds with true Christians (4:106). Yet he was prepared to recognize the validity of some of the Thirty-nine Articles, explicitly identifying three he accepted while accusing Fowler of denying them, namely, those on free will (ten), justification by faith (eleven), and works before justification (thirteen) (4:123–24).

As Bunyan anticipated, Fowler or his surrogate responded in *Dirt Wip't Off* (1672), repaying his vitriolic remarks in kind.[72] The subtitle of *Dirt Wip't Off* refers to Bunyan's gross ignorance, erroneousness, and unchristian spirit. Bunyan, charged the author, was a "*Ranting Antinomian*" with a turbulent and persecuting spirit, a malicious soul, an insolent attitude, and a defaming pen.[73] In the author's mind, faith is not bare reliance on Christ's righteousness, as Bunyan seemingly argued, but a belief in the gospel that implies a believer's adherence to all its precepts. "Christs *individual* Righteousness is not made any mans in a *proper* sense, much less that it is so *merely* because he *believes* it is so"; only those enabled by grace to detect their sins and become inwardly virtuous will benefit from Christ's righteousness.[74] The author was more concerned about Antinomianism and the perceived denigration of holy living than he was in drawing too near Catholicism by according equal emphasis to faith and obedience. Indeed, in his critique of Bunyan he combined the two, referring to "*obediential* faith . . . not as a *meritorious* cause but as a *condition*" of divine pardon. Moreover, if the only inward righteousness in believers is that imputed by Christ, there can be no inner holiness and thus no learning from Christ as the supreme exemplar.[75]

[72] Arber, *Term Catalogues*, 1:116.
[73] *Dirt Wip't Off: or a Manifest Discovery of the Gross Ignorance, Erroneousness and Most Unchristian and Wicked Spirit of One John Bunyan, Lay-Preacher in Bedford* (London, 1672), 2, 27, 40, 46.
[74] Ibid., 31, 48–49 (quoted).
[75] Ibid., 42, 58 (quoted).

Bunyan did not explicitly respond to *Dirt Wip't Off*, though from time to time he sniped at Latitudinarians in later works (e.g., *MW*, 5:125–27; 8:50). As I have suggested, he may have been sufficiently incensed by *Dirt Wip't Off* to add the closing scene, depicting Ignorance's dispatch to hell, to *The Pilgrim's Progress*. In his *Defence of the Doctrine of Justification* Bunyan had referred to Fowler's alleged ignorance, including his reputed errors (*MW*, 4:44, 120–21). Fowler's message of holiness, he maintained, was "ignorant, tottering, promiseless, and Gospelless," and, as we have seen, he deemed the classical philosophers Fowler cited to be "Atheistically ignorant" (4:106, 122). He probably had Fowler in mind when he wrote of "that Learned Ignorant *Nicodemus*" (4:59), for the thrust of his attack embodied the proposition that the formally learned can be ignorant of the gospel. Because Fowler used "Words without Knowledge," Bunyan satirized his "Sophistical Delusive Argument" as "glorious Learning" that enabled him to alter his convictions at will (4:77, 101). He was uncertain whether to attribute Fowler's view of a return to original holiness to ignorance or malice, but he finally decided that his opponent had begun the book lacking knowledge (4:121, 123). Consequently, when he saw himself accused of ignorance on the title-page of *Dirt Wip't Off*, he may have been inspired to add Ignorance's explicit damnation as the conclusion to *The Pilgrim's Progress*.

Many years later, Richard Baxter, looking back on this controversy, remarked that although Bunyan, "an unlearned Antinomian-Anabaptist," had attacked *The Design of Christianity*, he had "never heard that *Bunnian* was not an honest Godly man." Yet Baxter left no doubt that Bunyan had made numerous errors.[76] In contrast, Baxter thought Fowler's book had been a "Plaster" to heal the sore caused by those who abused the doctrine of justification by extolling it at sanctification's expense.[77] Ultimately Baxter had kind words for Bunyan, who by that point was deceased: "*Bunnians* last preachings give me hope that he repented of his Errors; for he Zealously preached but the common acknowledged doctrine of Christ's readiness to receive and pardon converted sinners."[78] In the absence of evidence to the contrary, Baxter's hope that Bunyan changed his mind concerning justification by Christ's imputed righteousness was undoubtedly in vain.

### "Escape the Prison"[79]: Freedom

As Bunyan pondered the government's efforts to repress dissent, he and other nonconformists in the Bedford jail developed a plan to install a network of

[76] Richard Baxter, *A Defence of Christ, and Free Grace* (London, 1690), 49.
[77] Baxter, *How Far Holinesse Is the Design of Christianity* (London, 1671), 20.
[78] Baxter, *Defence*, 49.
[79] *MW*, 4:196.

preachers, teachers, and meeting places in northern Bedfordshire and contiguous areas to withstand persecution. In addition to Bunyan, the key figures in this scheme appear to have been Donne, Coxe, the Fennes, Wright, and Thomas Cooper. Their efforts paid off after Charles issued a Declaration of Indulgence on 15 March 1672, suspending all laws against dissent, though requiring Protestant nonconformists to obtain licenses for their ministers and meeting sites, and not preach sedition or opposition to the Church of England on pain of severe punishment. Not surprisingly, under these conditions Bunyan opted not to risk publishing *The Pilgrim's Progress*, with its searing critique of the Church of England. Owing to George Whitehead's efforts, some 480 imprisoned Quakers obtained their freedom, prompting solicitors for other nonconformists to seek his counsel about getting their clients discharged. He advised them to petition Charles to have their clients' names "inserted in the same Patent with the *Quakers*, which accordingly they did petition for, and obtain."[80]

By this time Bunyan was again enjoying a degree of liberty, for he had participated in the congregation's business in March, June, September, and November 1671. The church was sufficiently optimistic about his future "to seeke God about the choyce of brother Bunyan to the office of an elder" on 24 October 1671. Two months later, on 21 December,

> after much seeking God by prayer, and sober conference formerly had, the congregation did at this meeting with joynt consent (signifyed by solemne lifting up of their hands) call forth and appoint our brother John Bunyan to the pastorall office or eldership. And he accepting therof gave up himself to serve Christ and his church in that charge, and received of the elders the right hand of fellowship.[81]

Although Bunyan was free on 21 December, he was back in prison by 27 February 1672, when he dated his epistle to *A Defence of the Doctrine of Justification* (*MW*, 4:10). About the same time he and five other prisoners—Donne, John Fenne, Thomas and Simon Haynes, and George Farr—petitioned Charles for their freedom. After receiving the petition on 8 May, the Privy Council referred it to the sheriff of Bedfordshire to confirm the reason for their imprisonment. On the 11th, the sheriff attested that the prisoners had been confined for refusing to conform to the Church of England and attending conventicles. Thus, on the 17th the Council instructed the attorney-general to insert their names "into the Generall Pardon to be passed for the Quakers." The pardon was formally issued under the great seal on 13 September 1672, by which point Bunyan had almost certainly

---

[80] Bodl., Tanner MSS 43, fol. 1r; *CSPD, 1671–72*, 203–4; Whitehead, *Christian Progress*, 358–59 (quoted).

[81] *CB*, 63–65, 67, 69, 70–71 (quoted).

been out of prison for four months, for he had received a license to preach on 9 May.[82]

Bunyan's application was part of a document, possibly in his own handwriting, seeking licenses for himself, twenty-six other ministers, and thirty meeting sites, including Josias Ruffhead's barn in Bedford.[83] Of the twenty-six other ministers, six—Donne, Wright, the Fennes, Coxe, and Cooper—had been inmates with Bunyan. The house of another fellow prisoner, William Man, was a designated meeting place. Six churches—Bedford, Keysoe, Cranfield, Stevington, Blunham, and Newport Pagnell—and their associated meetings are included in the application. Of the six, Bedford sought the most licenses for its meetings: Goldington, Oakley, Kempston, Cardington, Stagsend, Haynes, Maulden, and Edworth in Bedfordshire; Gamlingay and Toft in Cambridgeshire; and Ashwell, Hertfordshire. Donne's church at Keysoe, Bedfordshire, also sought licenses for its meetings in Ford End, Bedfordshire, and Upthorpe and Wonditch, Kimbolton parish, Huntingdonshire. The congregation at Stevington, Bedfordshire, where the teachers were Daniel Negus and John Allen, required licenses for its satellite meetings at Turvey and Pavenham in Bedfordshire, and Wollaston and Brafield on the Green in Northamptonshire.[84] John Gibbs' church at Newport Pagnell also sought a license for Olney in the same county, and the church of William Jarvis and Thomas Kent at Cranfield, Bedfordshire, requested a license for its affiliate at Ridgmont, Bedfordshire. Altogether, the application pertained to churches at twenty-six towns and villages in six counties.

Leaders of at least three of the six churches—the Fennes at Bedford, Wright at Blunham, and Donne at Keysoe—had been in prison with Bunyan. Wheeler of Cranfield and Gibbs of Newport Pagnell had been involved with the Bedford congregation during Bunyan's confinement, and the Stevington church had enjoyed close relations with the Bedford congregation since 1656. Probably drawing on the use of visitors to contact church members in outlying communities, Bunyan and his associates developed this plan to assure the survival of dissent in their region and an adequate supply of preachers and teachers. In the ensuing years this organizational scheme furnished the framework for much of Bunyan's min-

---

[82] CUL, Add. MSS 90, fol. 2r; Brown, 176–78.

[83] The document is reproduced in Brown between 216 and 217. Later the same year the church purchased the deed to this property, which comprised part of an orchard containing an "Edifice or Barne" for £50. This building remained in use until 1707. Alan F. Cirket, "The Bunyan Museum, Library, and Free Church, Bedford, *BS* 4 (Spring 1991): 71.

[84] Relations between the Bedford and Stevington congregations continued to be close. In September 1674 the latter church decided to meet at Oakley, which was part of Bedford's sphere, and sometime before 1679 the Stevington congregation permitted Allen and Negus to minister to Bedford's satellite group at Kempston. BLA, MS X239/1, fols. 15, 19.

isterial work and provided a group of supporting teachers who undertook pastoral work when he preached beyond the region or was again imprisoned. As indicated by Bedford's satellite meetings in the application, its primary focus was on the area to the south and east. Between 1670 and 1678, most new members came from this region. Instead of stamping out dissent, the policy of repression prompted Bunyan and his colleagues to develop an organizational scheme that strengthened the roots of their movement at the local level.[85]

Assessing the indulgence's impact in his diocese, which included Bedford, Bishop Fuller underscored the success the nonconformists were enjoying:

> Wee now feel the sad effects of the Declaration. Bold Presbyterians, And Anabaptists with the Quakers are exceedingly increased: Insomuch as if there be not a sodaine stop put to their daring growth: I dread to write the Consequences.

From Sir Joseph Williamson he sought a list of those who had obtained licenses in his diocese, and he wanted to know if those documents permitted them to preach in places not explicitly specified, a point that would have been relevant to Bunyan. "Very many, I heare, exercise [their right to preach] in other places, and generally they Assist one another." The observation was certainly applicable to the network established by Bunyan and his associates.[86]

As Bunyan pursued his ministerial duties in 1672, he apparently prepared revisions for the third edition of *Grace Abounding*. Published by Francis Smith, it was printed without a date.[87] The substantive additions that appear in the third edition cover two broad themes—Bunyan's religious and psychological turmoil in the 1650s and his preaching. The former required painstaking reflection on the past as well as a careful review of the first edition of *Grace Abounding*, and this (with the exception of the mysterious wind episode recounted in §174) is more likely to have occurred while he was still in prison than during his first year of pastoral responsibilities. The new material on preaching, however, is more likely to have been added to the third edition and probably reflects, at least in part, his experiences in 1672. No copies of the second edition have been found, but it was probably prepared in the autumn of 1667, immediately preceding *The Heavenly Foot-Man*. The third edition, which incorporated relatively little new material if this supposition is correct, was probably undertaken in late 1672 or the winter of 1672–73.

The new sections on Bunyan's early experiences are some of the most valuable in *Grace Abounding*. They include the account of his near drowning in a "crick of the Sea," his encounter with an adder, his military experience (§§12–14),

---

[85] Greaves, *JBEN*, 71–87.

[86] Bodl., Tanner MSS 43, fol. 25r.

[87] *GA*, xxxiv–xxxvii. The Term Catalogues record a reprint of the third edition in June 1679. Arber, *Term Catalogues*, 1:363–64.

his delight in bell-ringing and his fear that a falling bell would kill him (§§33–34), his love of dancing (§35), and his association with Ranters and their books (§§43–45). He recounted his conviction that he alone was as wicked as the Devil and his plunge into despair (§§83–84), his difficulty understanding why professing Christians were so concerned about the deaths of family members (§85), and his envy of animals, birds, and fish because they are not plagued with sinful natures (§88). He expanded on hearing a voice crying, "*Simon, Simon, behold, Satan hath desired to have you*" (§§93–94, quoting Luke 22:31), added more detail about being in "the storm or tempest" (§105), and explained the impact Luther's commentary on Galatians had on him (§§129–31) and his compulsion to leave the table to pray while eating (§138). Incorporated as well were passages dealing with Esau's sale of his birthright (§145), fresh detail about his fear of having committed the unpardonable sin (§153), his delusion that there is no last judgment (§161), and his sense of the eternal Judge at his door (§162). He recalled how he had adjudged himself a worse sinner than David, Solomon, and Manasseh (§§169–71), remembered the episode some twenty years earlier of having heard a mysterious voice like a rushing wind (§174), and reported how an "Antient Christian" confirmed his fear that he had committed the unforgivable sin (§180). The vivid imagery of having been driven like "a broken Vessel" through the stormy sea and plunged "head-long into dispair" was added (§186), as were accounts of his fleeting hope that he might receive mercy and his trepidation that Peter, Paul, and John would bar his entry at heaven's gate (§§202, 210). He explained too how terror of damnation had nearly overwhelmed him while he was very ill; "I was as one dead before Death came, and was as if I had felt my self already descending into the Pit" (§260). The addition of these sections indicates that Bunyan, probably still in prison when he wrote them (except §174), was reliving the profound turmoil through which he had come, but he also added a hopeful note by recounting how his apprehension of grace was so great that he "could hardly bear up under it" (§252).

In contrast to the rich new detail about his religious and psychological experience, Bunyan added relatively little about his preaching. In discussing how the Devil roared when "there hath been a work to do upon Sinners," he made a cryptic allusion to the failure of persecution to prevent their conversion: "Often-times when the wicked World hath raged most, there hath been souls awakened by the Word: I could instance particulars, but I forbear" (§89). Since this was probably written within months of his release, such restraint was undoubtedly prudent. As he preached, his concern was to set souls afire for salvation, not "to see people drink in Opinions if they seemed ignorant of Jesus Christ" (§291). He felt thankful he could denounce sin wherever he found it, even if this meant condemning himself, and he was already sensitive to the fact that his gifts belonged to the church, whose servant he was. In the ministry there is no place for pride, he mused, for gifts without grace are not only impotent but dangerous. "The applause, and commendation of every unadvised Christian" endangers souls (§§295, 301–5). Such was his outlook as he took advantage of his liberty to preach and minister.

That freedom enabled Bunyan to preach in Leicester on Sunday, 6 October 1672. According to the borough records, he showed the mayor and two aldermen his license to preach as a Congregationalist. He probably addressed the congregation of Nicholas Kestian, the ejected rector of Gumley, Leicestershire, who had been preaching at Great Bowden in the same county in 1669. In 1672 Kestian was licensed to preach as a Presbyterian in that village, and he received a license as a Congregationalist for his house in Leicester. There were also Baptists in Leicester, including the apothecary Richard Coleman, a Particular Baptist who obtained a license for his house in 1672. Other Baptists, including Richard Farmer, acquired licenses, as did three Presbyterians.[88] Most of Bunyan's known associations were to the south and east, making his trip to Leicester of special interest despite the paucity of information about it.

By this point Bunyan had not acquired a reputation as a prominent dissenter. An anonymous assessment of "The Present State of the Nonconformists" prepared by an Anglican about late 1672 identified the chief Baptist preachers as William Kiffin, Hanserd Knollys, Edward Harrison, John Gosnold, and one Northcott, but made no mention of Bunyan. Several of his closest London associates—Owen, Griffith, and Meade—were included among prominent Congregationalist ministers. The baptismal controversy into which he was about to become embroiled undoubtedly increased his visibility among Baptists, but his reputation outside nonconformist circles was minimal prior to the publication of *The Pilgrim's Progress.*[89]

### "*Union and Communion Among the Godly*"[90]: The Baptismal Controversy

Bunyan's irenic call in his confession of faith for unity among Baptists failed to produce the desired result, instead eliciting attacks by the Particular Baptist Thomas Paul, probably a member of Kiffin's church, and the General Baptist John

---

[88] *HMC 7, Eighth Report*, 440; *Calamy Revised, s.v.* Nicholas Kestian; Turner, *Original Records*, 1:70; 2:758–59, 767, 769; *Victoria County History, Leicestershire*, 4:390–91, 393; 5:45, 120; G. Lyon Turner, "Bunyan's License Under the Indulgence and the Use He Made of It in His Visit to Leicester in October, 1672," *Transactions of the Baptist Historical Society* 6 (January 1919): 129–37; anon., "Early Leicester Baptists," *Baptist Quarterly* 1 (April 1922): 74–77. For Farmer see *BDBR, s.v.*

[89] BL, Stowe MSS 185, fols. 171r–176v; another copy, Stowe MSS 186, fols. 16r–23v.

[90] *MW*, 4:251.

Denne, eldest son of Henry Denne, Bunyan's defender in 1659.[91] A wealthy merchant, the recent sheriff of London and Middlesex, and a prominent member of the
Leathersellers' Company, Kiffin wrote an epistle to Paul's book, *Some Serious Reflections on That Part of Mr. Bunion's Confession of Faith: Touching Church Communion with Unbaptized Persons* (1673).[92] In addition to confirming Bunyan's
commitment to believer's baptism, Kiffin made two fundamental points, insisting
that in the New Testament era baptism was a prerequisite for church membership
and communion, and that Christ's rules cannot be waived in the name of love.[93] It
must have been Kiffin's church, perhaps with others, that sought a conference with
Bunyan while he was in London, possibly to give a manuscript copy of "The Pilgrim's Progress" to one of his friends for a critique. This trip would have occurred
sometime after his release from prison in May 1672 and before the publication of
Paul's book in 1673. The Particular Baptists sent Bunyan an invitation to meet with
them, but he left the City without replying. The Particular Baptists were especially
offended because he had excluded those who insisted on baptism as a condition of
church membership and communion "from having any entertainment in the
Churches, or meetings to which [he] belong[ed]," though they had not banned him
from their gatherings. Moreover, they chastised him for having incited a debate via
the printed word that benefitted only the enemies of truth.[94]

Incensed at such behavior, Paul accused Bunyan of pridefully seeking public
acclaim, blaspheming, writing ignorantly and prejudicially, using "unheard of reproaches," and failing to conform to the law of love and civility.[95] "You have carried it like one of *Machevel's* [Machiavelli's] Schollers," casting much dirt on the
Baptists in the hope of sullying them.[96] Paul even resorted to class snobbery by
sarcastically remarking, "Should all of your rank, take occasion to tell the World
what they do, and do not believe or practice, it might give them more imployment then they can or need to attend."[97] Dismissively, he attributed Bunyan's
confession to an egotistical desire to acquire fame for his "Singular Faith." Kiffin
apparently prompted Paul to compose his critique, for the latter explained that
he wrote because better qualified people were unable to "divert themselves from
more weighty occasions."[98]

[91] For these men see *BDBR, s.vv.*
[92] *Some Serious Reflections* was entered in the Term Catalogues on 7 February 1673. Arber, *Term Catalogues*, 1:126.
[93] Kiffin, epistle to Paul, *Some Serious Reflections*, sigs. A2v-A3v, A5r.
[94] Paul, *op. cit.*, 59–61.
[95] Ibid., 2–3, 41, 58.
[96] Ibid., 42.
[97] Ibid., 1.
[98] Ibid., 1–2.

Paul refuted Bunyan's key baptismal tenets, insisting that water-baptism is a divine command, a manifestation of holy living, and the livery by which gospel believers are known.[99] Want of light is no reason to avoid baptism, for such a principle would excuse obedience to other precepts, resulting in a church of visible sinners; divine commands, including baptism, are binding because of their origin, not someone's light. According to Paul, Bunyan's attempt to differentiate between the doctrine and practice of baptism was invalid because the former is not belief in Christ's death and resurrection but his command to be baptized.[100] Jesus' great commission in Matthew 28:18–20, which his disciples obeyed, calls for teaching and implicitly conversion to precede baptism.[101] A foundation principle, baptism is "an obligation to all following duties," and as a symbol of new birth it must precede the Lord's supper, "the spiritual nourishment of Christ's new-born Babes."[102] Unlike Bunyan, Paul adjudged outward conformity significant because believers' bodies are no less God's than are their souls. Responding to Bunyan's appeal to place edification above baptism in importance, Paul averred that preaching baptism is an essential part of instruction, which itself presupposes the existence of a church with baptism as a prerequisite of membership.[103] Nor would Paul accept Bunyan's entreaty for the primacy of love, for affection cannot replace sound judgment as a basis for Christian behavior. Repudiating Bunyan's assertion that baptismal controversy had brought judgments on nonconformists, Paul mocked him, suggesting that if he were a royal chaplain or had the king's ear, the Baptists would be expelled from England as vipers.[104] His attack on Bunyan left no room for compromise.

Denne's *Truth Outweighing Error* (1673) offers a more copious critique of Bunyan's *Confession* than Paul's work, though making many of the same points. A prominent Baptist in Huntingdonshire and Cambridgeshire, Denne stressed baptism's importance as the initiating ordinance into the church and "*a duty necessarily to be observed by Christians in obedience to God, and in order to Church-Communion.*"[105] To admit people to church membership or communion without believer's baptism is disorderly, sinful, a rejection of divine counsel, and a breach of conscience. For Denne as for Paul, baptism is a foundation principle and fun-

[99] Ibid., 5, 17–18, 52.

[100] Ibid., 7, 15–16, 54.

[101] Ibid., 46–49.

[102] Ibid., 41, 50–51.

[103] Ibid., 23, 26–27. Paul's church, like all separatist congregations, would have required a profession of faith and a commitment to holiness as a condition of membership.

[104] Ibid., 29–30, 43.

[105] John Denne, *Truth Outweighing Error* (London, 1673), 46–47, 50–52.

damental component of Christ's doctrine, which Bunyan wrongfully denied.[106] To be baptized is conformity to divine law, not something circumstantial. "The question is not, who have Light therein, but who ought to have Light therein?"[107] Rightly administered, baptism is a testimony to the initiate's faith and holiness, but Denne was careful to state that the ordinance is valueless unless accompanied by faith and repentance.[108]

As a General Baptist, Denne differed from Bunyan and Paul in repudiating the doctrine of predestination, considering Bunyan's position iniquitous and unjust because it rested on God's reputed ignoring of the qualifications of those he predestined. For God to reprobate some people without respect to their actions would violate the tender mercies promised to everyone in Psalm 145:9. Against Bunyan, Denne averred that *"there is no Person originally so far blinded by the God of Heaven, that they cannot hear, and turn to him."*[109] If God blinds sinners, Denne argued, they cannot be held accountable and their disbelief is no sin. Contrary to Bunyan, Denne proclaimed that the elect are those God foresaw would freely believe and remain obedient to the divine will until the end of their lives, allowing nothing to destroy their faith.[110] In sum, for Denne, God's invitation to all people to obey his will and be saved is "inconsistent with such an absolute Election as is pretended by *John Bunyan.*"[111]

In his counterattack Bunyan focused on Paul's book, for Denne's had not yet been published.[112] Assuming a victim's mantle, he quoted Psalm 120:7 on his title-page: *"I am for Peace, but when I speak, they are for War."* He was willing to forgive Kiffin, whom he apparently knew personally, for writing an epistle to Paul's book, undoubtedly because Kiffin's tone had been mild as he sagely eschewed the sort of personal attack Paul mounted (*MW*, 4:193). No stranger to the use of invective, Bunyan repaid Paul in kind, castigating him for his lack of love and humility, damning his principles as rigid, impertinent, and disruptive, and reproving him for throwing dirt on all the godly in England who differed with traditional Baptists on the subject of baptism (4:195, 248). Yet Bunyan was chary of making foes of all traditional Baptists, some of whom he regarded as moderate; hence he asked them not to look on him as an enemy (4:250–51). Not surprisingly, he took umbrage at Paul's snide reference to his social status, prompting

---

[106] Ibid., 56, 60.

[107] Ibid., 72–73.

[108] Ibid., 44, 121.

[109] Ibid., 22–25.

[110] Ibid., 28–32.

[111] Ibid., 33.

[112] *Truth Outweighing Error* was entered in the Term Catalogues on 24 November 1673, well after Bunyan had completed *Differences in Judgment*. Arber, *Term Catalogues*, 1:146.

him to retort that high birth, wealth, and worldly breeding mean nothing with respect to matters of the soul (4:196). Why, Bunyan asked, should his social rank be
despised or his views be repudiated on that count? On the contrary, "to have gay-
cloathing, or gold-rings, or the Persons that wear them in admiration; or to be
partial in your judgment, or respects, for the sake . . . of flesh and blood, doubtless convicteth you to be of the Law a transgressor" (4:195).

In defending himself against Paul's charge that his *Confession* had incited a di-
visive pamphlet debate, Bunyan pointed to the past sixteen or eighteen years in
which traditional Baptists had endeavored to persuade members of the Bedford
church, including Bunyan himself, to leave it. To a degree they succeeded, "for
some they did rent and dismember from us; but none but those, of whom now
they begin to be ashamed." Such converts to the Baptists have since become "a
stink, and reproach to Religion" (4:197). Ted Underwood has plausibly suggested
that one such person was John Child, who withdrew from the congregation in
1658 to join the congregation of a Mr. Harris, probably, as I suggested in Chapter
3, Edward Harrison.[113] Unfortunately the Bedford church book provides little information about members being lured away by traditional Baptists, though in
1656 a Sister Linford left the church over this issue.[114] Bunyan viewed such ongoing efforts by the Baptists as sufficient grounds for his defense of open-membership, open-communion principles in his *Confession*. Their proselytizing, he
charged, had extended to many churches in the region (4:196–97, 250). For such
behavior, he and his fellow ministers of the same persuasion had banned traditional Baptists from their pulpits. Moreover, when Bunyan and his associates
preached, the Baptists "would either, like *Quakers*, stand with their Hats on their
heads, or else withdraw till we had done" (4:249).

From Bunyan's account, it is unclear whether such confrontations continued,
but relations were tense enough to dissuade him from meeting with members of
Kiffin's church and possibly others, as we have seen. In *Differences in Judgment* he
explained his reticence to meet, noting that *A Confession* was in print "before I
spake with any of you, or knew whether I might be accepted of you" (4:248). In
fact, he pleaded his own inadequacies as justification for his rejection of the invitation to confer:

> The reason why I came not amongst you, was partly because I consulted mine own
> weakness, and counted not my self, being a dull-headed man, able to engage so many
> of the chief of you, as I was then informed intended to meet me; I also feared, in per-
> sonal Disputes, heats and bitter contentions might arise, a thing my Spirit hath not

[113] *MW*, 4:xxxii; *CB*, 22–34; *The Mischief of Persecution Exemplified* (London, 1688), 8
(which indicates that Child was a Baptist for approximately twenty-six years).
[114] *CB*, 22.

pleasure in: I feared also, that both my self and words would be misrepresented; and that not without cause, for if they that Answer a Book will alter, and scrue Arguments out of their place, and make my Sentences stand in their own words, not mine, when (I say) my words are in a Book to be seen. What would you have done, had I in the least, either in matter or manner, though but seemingly miscarried among you? (4:248)

Bunyan personally knew some of the London Baptists, and presumably had a sense of what awaited him should he debate prominent Particular Baptists. Within the previous year, at a meeting in Lothbury, he had heard "Mr. D."—probably Daniel Dyke, Kiffin's co-minister—state the case for baptism as the initiating ordinance into the church (4:198).[115] The same argument was espoused by Bunyan's "much esteemed Friend Mr. D.A." in two conferences with him (4:198). This was very likely Henry Danvers, whose surname was sometimes spelled D'Anvers.[116]

For the most part, *Differences in Judgment* reasserts the position on baptism, church membership, and communion developed in Bunyan's *Confession*. Underwood fairly describes the book as rather plodding, and Bunyan's criticism of Paul's redundancy is equally true of his own book: "This is but round, round, the same thing, over and over" (4:xxxiii, 245). Only once did Bunyan give ground, if at all, asserting that even if all church members in Corinth, Galatia, Rome, and elsewhere had been baptized, it matters not, for nowhere in Scripture does it say that visible but unbaptized saints should be excluded from the church (4:243). In *Differences in Judgment* he clarified his stance on baptism by the Spirit, distinguishing between the Spirit's "coming from Heaven into us" and the Spirit's baptizing "*us into a Body, or Church*" (4:210). In contrast, he accords water-baptism minimal importance, insisting it is not part of the church's worship, having significance as a sign only for the person being baptized; it makes no one a saint, is not an initiatory ordinance into the church, and is not necessary for a church's well-being (4:200–202, 208, 214, 221). "He therefore that doth it according to his Light, doth well; and he that doth it not, for want of Light, doth not ill; for he approveth his heart to be sincere with God, even by that his forbearance" (4:220). Bunyan attached significantly more importance to the Lord's supper, which he reckoned part of church worship and a vehicle for the believer's union and communion with Christ (4:202, 223, 245). Presumably he continued the congregation's practice of observing this ordinance monthly or every third week.[117]

---

[115] Underwood posits two other possibilities, John Denne and Henry Danvers. *MW*, 4:400. For Dyke see *BDBR*, *s.v.*

[116] Underwood suggests Daniel Angier, at whose barn in Toft, Cambridgeshire, Bunyan had preached in 1659. *MW*, 4:400–401.

[117] *CB*, 35. The Stevington church observed the sacrament monthly. BLA, MS X239/1, fol. 26.

Because only visible saints are proper subjects of baptism, infants are not. "According to our Notion of [baptism], they only that have before received the Doctrine of the Gospel, and so shew it us by their Confession of Faith, they only ought to be baptized" (4:246). Plainly, infants cannot make such a confession and therefore are unqualified for baptism. Yet he was willing to permit those baptized as infants to join the church, refusing to let such an "infirmity" preclude them so long as they were visible saints. "We indulge them not; but being Commanded to bear with the Infirmities of each other, suffer it" (4:226). To enter the church without having been baptized as a believer is acceptable, though Bunyan hoped such people would eventually accept "our Notion" of believer's baptism (4:227). Indeed, he found a degree of unity with Paul in their shared conviction that only believing adults should be baptized.

Seeking support in this debate, Bunyan persuaded John Owen to write an epistle to *Differences in Judgment*. After several unidentified Baptists, probably including Kiffin, persuaded Owen to retract his promise, Bunyan, in London to deliver the manuscript to the printer John Wilkins, obtained a copy of Jessey's 5,000-word statement defending open-communion, open-membership principles (4:252, 272). Jessey had died in 1663, but Bunyan may have acquired his statement from their mutual friend, the bookseller Francis Smith.[118] Jessey had sent copies to some of the Baptists, though none had responded.

*Differences in Judgment* elicited replies from Paul and Danvers. Apparently no copy of Paul's work, not even the title, has survived, though its theses can be reconstructed from those points Bunyan refuted in *Peaceable Principles and True* (1674). Resorting to vituperative language, Paul called Bunyan a proud man and a liar as well as an "*ill Bird*" who betrayed his own nest, a reference to Bunyan's reputed disloyalty to the Baptists (*MW*, 4:270). The last point is worth noting, for it indicates that some people had regarded Bunyan as a Baptist before he wrote his *Confession*. According to Paul, Bunyan's assertion of open-membership, open-communion principles in print, a manifestation of his "*turbulent and mutineering Spirit*," stirred up considerable dissension in London among people of disparate persuasions who had hitherto enjoyed harmonious relations (4:270). Even some of the "sober Independents" had indicated their dislike of Bunyan's writings on this subject, though this is hardly surprising given his advocacy of believer's baptism. Paul portrayed himself as a champion of toleration who favored liberty for Presbyterians, Congregationalists, and "*mixt Communionists*" to worship according to their light (4:272), and he took pride in claiming he had no desire to impose his views on others, "*having not arrived unto such a peremptory way of Dictatorship, as what I render must be taken for Laws binding to others in Faith and*

---

[118]Greaves, *DUFE*, 211, 213. For Wilkins see Plomer, *DBP*, 315.

*Practice*" (4:282). With one exception, Paul reiterated his earlier views; his only change was his apparent willingness to accept baptism as the initiatory ordinance, ostensibly because of Danvers' influence and because his prior denial of this concept was inconsistent with his general argument. Interestingly, Danvers had told Bunyan he would speak to Paul on this point (4:210, 273).

Bunyan would have had this discussion with Danvers sometime between the publication of Paul's *Some Serious Reflections* in 1673 and his own *Peaceable Principles* the following year. The contact is noteworthy because Danvers was a known radical with a Fifth Monarchist background. His name was on a list of armed and "Dangerous persons" living in London during the fall of 1661; he was reportedly staying in Soper Lane, where the minister George Cokayne, also on the list, could be found. Responding to allegations, probably specious, that Danvers was implicated in the Tong conspiracy, the government issued a warrant for his arrest in February 1663, but he escaped. In the aftermath of the northern rebellion, another warrant was issued in December 1663, though he fled to Rotterdam.[119] Accused of treason for alleged involvement in the Rathbone plot to assassinate the king and restore the republic, he was apprehended in August 1665, but a crowd rescued him as he was being conveyed to the Tower. The following year the government received reports linking Danvers to Colonel Thomas Blood, another prominent conspirator, and further warrants for his arrest were forthcoming in March 1667 and May 1670. Not until January 1676 did the authorities finally seize and commit him to the Tower.[120] Thus Bunyan managed to see Danvers at a time when his movements must have been furtive; perhaps this meeting was possible because of contacts established in the 1650s when Bunyan was attracted to the Fifth Monarchists, whose members included Danvers and their mutual friend Cokayne.

In June 1673 Danvers published a substantive defense of believer's baptism in his *Treatise of Baptism*, which ignited a controversy with such paedobaptists as Obadiah Wills, Richard Baxter, and Richard Blinman.[121] To his *Treatise* Danvers appended a postscript refuting Bunyan's position and excoriating his "manifold *Absurdities*, Contradictions, unbrotherly Tauntings and Reflections, [and] Contemptuous traducing the wisdome of Christ."[122] Heaping on the invective, he accused Bunyan of violating the law of love, obscuring knowledge, and committing fundamental errors because of egregious ignorance. If pleading lack of light as

[119] PRO, SP 29/44/134; Greaves, *DUFE*, 116, 127–29, 203; Greaves, *EUHF*, 9.

[120] Greaves, *EUHF*, 32; Pepys, 6:184; Greaves, *SR*, 167–68; *HMC* 19, *Townshend*, 43; *HMC* 25, *Le Fleming*, 124. For Blood see *BDBR*, *s.v.*

[121] Baxter, *Calendar*, 2:166–67; Greaves, *SR*, 170–72. For Wills and Blinman see *Calamy Revised*, *s.vv.*

[122] H[enry] D[anvers], "A Postscript" to his *Treatise of Baptism* (London, 1673), 41 (emended to reflect the list of errata).

justification for not undergoing water-baptism were acceptable, he argued, the door was open to permit all sorts of corrupt doctrine and practice in the church.[123] Attributing considerably more importance to baptism than did Bunyan, Danvers reckoned it "the *Listing, Espousing, Covenanting, Ingrafting, Implanting* Ordinance," and thus the indispensable entryway to the church.[124] To reinforce his point he referred readers to Baxter's *Plain Scripture Proof of Infants Church-Membership and Baptism* (1651), notwithstanding their differences as to the proper subject and mode of baptism.[125] He also appealed to early works of the Baptists William Allen and Thomas Lamb, though he had to acknowledge that both men had subsequently repudiated their Baptist tenets.[126] In his postscript, Danvers' most creative point, which Paul also employed (*MW*, 4:284), was an analogy between baptism and marriage, the baptismal contract (or covenant) between Christ and the believer being no less essential for the latter to have church privileges than matrimony for a couple to enjoy conjugal rights.[127]

The tone of the Baptist attacks stunned Bunyan. Kiffin, Paul, Danvers, and Denne, he bitterly complained, "fell with might and main upon me; some comparing me to the Devil, others to a Bedlam, others to a sot and the like. . . . Nay, further, they began to cry out *MURDER*, as if I intended nothing less than to accuse them to the Magistrate, and to render them uncapable of a share in the Common-wealth" (*MW*, 4:286). Clearly, the ferocity of the assault had caught him off guard, inflicting personal pain. Yet Danvers had warned him about Paul's second book, which he thought would provoke Bunyan to an equally "beastly" counterattack. When some of Bunyan's friends saw Paul's second book, they urged Bunyan not to let the "bitter invectives" go unanswered, but he opted for a relatively restrained response in *Peaceable Principles*. "Railing for Railing, I will not render," probably because he was pleased that some traditional Baptists, whom he did not identify, had become more moderate during the course of the controversy (4:288). He knew but did not name some Baptists who were dismayed at Paul's books, and he must have been chary of alienating such people by a defamatory response (4:272). Moreover, some moderate Baptists, again unidentified, had made it known that Kiffin, Paul, and Danvers had not disproved Bunyan's key thesis that baptism by water must not be a door to or bar against communion with visible saints (4:287).

[123]Ibid., 42, 45, 48.
[124]Ibid., 44.
[125]Ibid., 45, 52.
[126] Ibid., 53–54. The works Danvers cited are William Allen, *Some Baptismal Abuses Briefly Discovered* (London, 1653), and Thomas Lamb, *Truth Prevailing Against the Fiercest Opposition* (London, 1655). For Allen and Lamb (d. 1686) see *BDBR, s.vv.*
[127]Danvers, "Postscript," 52–53.

Notwithstanding the title-page of *Peaceable Principles*, which portrays the book as a reply to both Paul and Danvers, the latter, with one exception, receives only token mention. Bunyan singled out Danvers' analogy between baptism and marriage for special attention, deeming it "very black" because it prohibits Christ and others from communing with visible but unbaptized saints. Such communion, according to the marital analogy, renders those who engage in it wicked. Repent, Bunyan counseled Danvers. "I wot that through ignorance, and a preposterous Zeal he said it: unsay it again with tears, and by a publick renunciation of so wicked and horrible words" (4:284–85). Apart from rejecting this analogy, Bunyan offered nothing new in *Peaceable Principles* to the substance of the debate. His emphasis was indisputably on the primacy of love over baptism, and the absence of any biblical precept that visible saints must be excluded from church membership and communion if they lack believer's (or any) baptism (4:280, 285–89).

At no point in the debate did Bunyan make a substantive effort to refute Denne's book, though he read it (4:279, 288). As justification he cited Denne's reputed immorality: "Considering him, and comparing his Notions with his Conversation [i.e., life-style], I count it will be better for him to be better in Morals, before he be worthy of an Answer" (4:285). Those who know Denne's life, surmised Bunyan, would "see little of Conscience in the whole of his Religion, and conclude him not worth the taking notice of" (4:288). Unfortunately, the church book of Denne's congregation at Caxton and Fenstanton for this period, which might have cast light on his reputed offenses, has not survived. Sometime before 1672 Denne moved to St. Ives, Huntingdonshire, where he was licensed to preach the same year. Margaret Spufford suggests that "some disaster" struck the Caxton part of the congregation in this period, for the church had no members there by 1676.[128] This crisis may have involved the immoral conduct of Denne to which Bunyan alludes.

*Peaceable Principles* offers additional insight about Bunyan. When Paul suggested he was disloyal to Baptists, Bunyan replied: "Since you would know by what Name I would be distinguished from others; I tell you, I would be, and hope I am, *a Christian*." In his judgment, denominational terms originated in hell and Babylon (4:270). On this, at least, he and Baxter, who described himself as "a MEER CHRISTIAN, . . . a CATHOLICK CHRISTIAN,"[129] agreed, though this is not to suggest either man influenced the other. Bunyan may have read something of Baxter's, for he referred in *Peaceable Principles* to Baxter's argument that baptism is the door of entry to the visible church. More likely, he learned about Baxter's

---

[128] Margaret Spufford, *Contrasting Communities: English Villagers in the Sixteenth and Seventeenth Centuries* (Cambridge: Cambridge University Press, 1974), 291–92.

[129] Richard Baxter, *Church-History of the Government of Bishops and Their Councils Abbreviated* (London, 1680), sig. b1r.

position in Danvers' *Treatise*.[130] Judging from his references to the concurrence between his views and Jessey's, Bunyan would like to have had more such support, and the failure to win "the sober" Dr. Owen's endorsement manifestly disappointed him. Yet he put a bold face on this, thinking that "*perhaps, 'twas more for the Glory of God, that Truth should go naked into the world, than as seconded by so mighty an Armour-bearer as he*" (4:272). Despite the personal nature of the attacks by Paul and Danvers, Bunyan retained his sense of humor. When Paul charged him with using the paedobaptists' arguments, Bunyan joked, "I know not what *Paedo* means; and how then should I know his Arguments" (4:282). Yet the pain was real enough. Had not Paul stigmatized him with scandal and reproach, Bunyan claimed, he would have ignored his critic (4:285). The poem, "Of the Love of Christ," appended to *Peaceable Principles* implicitly compares Bunyan with Jesus, who likewise suffered "abusive Carriages" from those who opposed his overtures of love (4:289–90). The suffering Christ is visibly and immediately juxtaposed to Bunyan the suffering servant, who signed his tract in these words: "*I am thine to serve thee, Christian, so long as I can look out at those Eyes, that have had so much dirt thrown at them by many*" (4:289).

*Peaceable Principles* elicited at least two responses. Apparently no copy of Denne's *Hypocrisie Detected, or Peaceable and True Principles* (1674) has survived. In *A Sober Discourse of Right to Church-Communion* (1681), Kiffin quoted and refuted Bunyan without mentioning his name. His epistle made it clear that he too hoped to heal the breach, stressing that love could unite those whose views on baptism differed. However, he was unwilling to compromise his view of the necessity of believer's baptism for church membership and communion, not least because baptism, more than any other ordinance, signifies new birth.[131] Thus Bunyan and Kiffin, though not relinquishing their tenets, ended the controversy on an irenic note. For his part, Danvers, finding himself embroiled in full-scale pamphlet warfare with paedobaptists, had no interest in a sustained debate with Bunyan.

### "Cumber-ground Professors"[132]: Prophetic Admonitions

Gathered congregations of visible saints had recurring problems with members whose lifestyle altered after they joined, often bringing disrepute on the church by critics anxious to discredit their rivals. Gathered churches conse-

---

[130] Danvers, *Treatise of Baptism*, 32, citing Baxter's *Plain Scripture Proof of Infants Church-Membership and Baptism*.

[131] William Kiffin, *A Sober Discourse of Right to Church-Communion* (London, 1681), 12, 38.

[132] *MW*, 5:9 (where the text uses the singular form).

quently found it essential to police themselves by counseling the wayward and, if necessary, excommunicating them. Bunyan's expanded sermon, *The Barren Fig-Tree*, entered in the Term Catalogues on 24 November 1673,[133] reflects the use of the pulpit as another way to deal with troublesome members, and is thus a logical extension of the views on the church enunciated in *A Confession*. His primary targets in *The Barren Fig-Tree* were the seemingly awakened but barren members of gathered congregations as well as hypocrites who feigned godliness in order to belong. The work also has a subtext, accessible only to his more discerning readers, relating to Parliament's opposition to the Declaration of Indulgence and its passage of the first Test Act in 1673.

Bunyan's text is the parable of the barren fig-tree in Luke 13:6–9, which he interprets to mean that God the father will examine his vineyard, the church, seeking fruit or good works. Having found none on a fig-tree—a professor of Christianity—for three years, he orders his vine-dresser, Christ, to cut it down, but the latter prevails with God to give him one more year to make the tree fruitful by loosening and fertilizing the soil, that is, by applying *"Gospel-helps"* (*MW*, 5:12–14). If after another year the tree is still barren, it will justly be removed, thereby suffering eternal damnation. In Bunyan's view, numerous barren professors belong to the church, and some will not respond to offers of gospel assistance, such as preaching and counseling, even when Christ endeavors to win them. The implication is that these professors willfully reject such help, bringing condemnation on themselves. Hints of election and reprobation appear in the text, as in Bunyan's contention that some professors are incurable and cannot repent or profit by the various means of divine grace. Indeed, once someone's day of grace has passed, God contrives his or her ruin and sends delusions (5:16, 26, 43, 60–61). The preacher's task is to alert barren professors to repent and become fruitful Christians while they still have time, though theologically only the elect can—and must—do so.

Drawing on his pastoral work, Bunyan made some interesting observations about gathered-church life. Momentarily switching metaphors, he cited Matthew 22:11–13, which relates the story of a king who found a man improperly attired at a wedding and had him bound and cast into darkness. Bunyan likened the offender to someone who had improperly become a church member, and to the thief in John 10:1 who had entered the sheepfold by some way other than the door. In such fashion did some people become members of gathered churches, as in the case of those who dissembled about their spiritual convictions or beguiled the church with false professions of humility and self-denial. Some were accepted into congregations because members were careless in examining their qualifica-

---

[133] Arber, *Term Catalogues*, 1:148.

tions, whereas others gained admission because of "falsness amongst *some* Pastors, either for the sake of carnal Relations, or the like." Understandably, he cited no contemporary examples, though he mentioned Tobiah the Ammonite, who had improperly obtained access to the temple from the priest Eliashib (Nehemiah 13:4–6) (5:16–17). Tobiah had previously mocked Nehemiah's exhortation that God's servants rebuild the wall around Jerusalem, claiming such an act amounted to rebellion against the king; to this, Nehemiah responded that God's people would arise and build (Nehemiah 2:17–20). Bunyan's point was that some ministers had accepted into church membership those who, blindly obeying the king and by implication Parliament, had ridiculed Christians determined to build the new Jerusalem, that is, most nonconformists.

In *The Barren Fig-Tree* Bunyan stressed that God has a right to require church members to produce good fruit, such as praying, fasting, and honest dealing (5:15–16). He lashed out against those who are devils and vipers at home but seemingly saints abroad, and those who, though ostensibly church members, are proud, ambitious, and gluttonous (5:25). Barren professors, he averred, can sometimes be identified by their inappropriate clothing, "the Lust-provoking Fashions of the times," as they parade "with stretched out Necks, naked Breasts, frizled Fore-tops, wanton Gestures, in gorgeous Apparel, mixt with Gold and Pearl, and costly array" (5:20). Hyperbolizing, he went so far as to warn that prosperity is a sign of impending divine wrath, not godliness (5:50). No less satisfactory than a barren fruit tree is one that bears bad fruit, and it too will be hewn down. Here again the picture he painted was drawn from his pastoral experience. By those who produced bad fruit he meant church members who begin to repent and reform but do not persevere; those who are suddenly "so awakened, so convinced, and so affected with their condition, that they shake the whole Family, the End-ship, the whole Town" before rapidly withering; those whose fruits are ill-tasting because their hearts are estranged from communion with the Holy Spirit; those whose actions are like wild fruit because their stock is not ingrafted in God's vineyard; and those whose fruit is ill-timed, appearing before the tree has sufficient roots, as are professors who fail to anticipate the hardships that confront the godly. A pattern of bad or no fruit, Bunyan warned, signifies a dreadful end (5:21–23).

Cutting down the barren tree—removing the fruitless professor from the church—can be undertaken, asserted Bunyan, by God or the congregation. Acting directly, God can oust the offender by delusions that beguile the soul with reprehensible doctrines. Bunyan has God say, "I will smite them with blindness, and hardness of heart, and failing of eyes, and will also suffer the Tempter to tempt and effect his hellish designs upon them." Presumably God does this because these souls are reprobate, yet Bunyan makes it clear that such action occurs only *after* wayward professors persist in their refusal to repent. According to Bunyan, God can also remove fruitless professors from the church by permitting them to embrace open profanity, beastly lusts, and ungodly company: "Thou art crouded into a Profession, art got among the Godly, and there art a scandal to the . . . Gospel, but withal so cunning, that . . . thou art too hard for the Church," prompting God to take direct action. Moreover, the congregation can deal with offenders, using the censures Christ provides as set forth in Matthew 18:17–18, 1 Corinthians 5:4–5, and 1 Timothy 1:20 (5:35–36). The Bedford church periodically exercised its right to excommunicate, as in the recent cases of Richard Deane and Robert Nelson (March 1671). Deane had "after a very ungodly manner separated himself from this congregation," engaged in fraudulent business practices, spoken contemptuously of the church, and used the names of Bunyan and Samuel Fenne without authorization to seek charity from the people of St. Neots, Huntingdonshire. For his part, Nelson had conformed to the Church of England, being "profanely bishopt, after the Antichristian order of that generation, to the great profanation of God's order." The church had been incredibly patient with Nelson, who had not attended its meetings for eight or nine years.[134]

For those cast out of the church, Bunyan warned, damnation would follow unless they repented. Their ability to do so depended on whether the day of grace had passed for them. This theme, which Bunyan mentions in many of his works, receives extended treatment in *The Barren Fig-Tree*. His major point is that the season of grace is limited, sometimes concluding well before a person dies. "Many there be that come not till the floud of Gods anger is raised, and too deep for them to wade through" (5:23, 36). He cites three scriptural cases: Cain, who killed Abel; Ishmael, who mocked the birth of Isaac; and Esau, whose day of grace terminated when he sold his birthright. Each man, though condemned by God, had more material possessions after the day of grace terminated than before (5:46–50). The idea that the day of grace can end during one's lifetime led to the inevitable question, how can one know if it has ceased? Bunyan suggested a series of signs by which one could answer this query. The first is an indication that God has lost patience with a barren professor, as reflected by a series of tragic events, such as the death of a spouse, children, or cattle. Another occurs when a fruitless believer acts without restraint, or when a professor's heart becomes too hard to repent. A fourth sign is when a professing believer turns from seemingly godly ways to pursue sinful actions, and the last is when a barren professor secretly determines to continue his or her evil ways and despises godly preachers (5:50–62). These are the points Bunyan would have made in counseling recalcitrant church members, some of whom apparently responded with scoffing and derision.

[134] *CB*, 63–64.

Once God has terminated the day of grace for the refractory, they are beyond all mercy, wandering like fugitives or vagabonds, bereft of hope. They may go where they will, traipsing from opinion to opinion, sect to sect, but they will never find grace and forgiveness. Their consciences seared, as if burned by a scalding iron, they are incapable of genuine remorse. God denies them the ability to repent, and their fate is like that of Spira, whose case had once haunted Bunyan himself (5:56–58, 64). In such cases, Bunyan explained, God has *"judicially hardened"* the hearts of the obstinately unrepentant (5:58). As Jude 13 suggests, they are like wandering stars, forever consigned to blackness, a punishment fit for those who have sinned "after some great Light received" (5:57, 59).

Taking advantage of the subject matter to drive home his message, Bunyan included two death tableaux. In the first, he personified death, symbolized by the axe in the parable from Luke 13. The passage's forcefulness and ebullience, which reflect the style already worked out in the as yet unpublished *Pilgrim's Progress*, are apparent from the outset, as this sampling manifests; the speaker is God:

> Death come, smite me *this* Fig-tree, and withal the Lord shakes this Sinner, and *whirls* him upon a Sick-bed, saying, *Take him Death*. . . . *Death, fetch away this Fig-tree to the fire,* fetch this barren Professor to Hell. At this, Death comes with *grim* looks into the Chamber, yea and Hell follows with him to the Bed-side, and both stare this Professor in the face, yea, begin to lay hands upon him; one smiting him with pains in his Body, with Head-ach, Heart-ach, Back-ach, Shortness of Breath, Fainting, Qualms, Trembling of Joints, Stopping at the Chest, and almost all the *Symptomes* of a man past all recovery. Now while *Death* is thus tormenting the Body, *Hell* is doing with the Mind and Conscience.

The vivid depiction of a personalized Death at the bed of a dying man is reminiscent of late medieval and early modern paintings of similar scenes. Perhaps Bunyan saw a wood-cut of such a tableau. In any event, on this occasion God, responding to the poor man's cries for mercy and vows to reform, stays Death's hand (5:51–52).

In the second deathbed tableau, the same personalized Death is accompanied by a huge cast of supporting characters, among them the dying man's "fruitless *Fruits*" and "*bands* and *legions* of his other wickedness" (5:63). Death's jaws gape, the doors of the Shadow of Death open, and the terrified man sees a narrow, dark entry through which he must pass into another world. As his conscience trembles, Want strikes him like a terrible army, crying in his ears that he lacks faith, love, repentance, and a new heart. Around him now stand Death's companions. God, Christ, and Pity have left him, and he must face Sin-against-Light virtually alone while Hope and Conscience lie dying beside him (5:63–64). "Death is at his work, *Cutting of him down*, hewing both bark and heart, both Body and Soul asunder; The man groans, but Death hears him not: He looks gastly, carefully, dejectedly; he sighs, he sweats, he trembles, but Death matters nothing." "An heart-string, an eye-string snaps asunder," and still Death relentlessly proceeds. The lungs no longer able to draw breath, the soul departs, to be seized immediately by the devils lurking in every hole of the death-chamber, ready to transport it to hell (5:64). These are powerful images, the force of which would have been striking when uttered from the pulpit by an eloquent preacher.

To be effective such imagery must be used selectively. Bunyan accomplished this by making as much as possible of the olive-tree metaphor, the development of which enabled him to use rustic language. The most striking illustration is the depiction of gospel-measures as fertilizing. In his preface to the reader he expressed hope that Christ, the vineyard's cultivator, will "*dig about thee, and dung thee, that thou maist bear* Fruit" (10). He repeated this metaphor several times, noting that Christ will apply "warm dung" to the professor's roots and enable him or her to "suck in the Gospel-dung" (5:42–43, 55). In a related metaphor, he described a woman tidying her garden in the spring, removing weeds and nettles, sweeping the walks, and pulling up the herbs and shoots that died during the winter (5:34–35). Like barren fig-trees or dead herbs and slips, fruitless, "Cumberground" professors will be cast on the rubbish heap (5:9, 37–39).

In *The Barren Fig-Tree* Bunyan also developed a second theme, this time in response to a major setback for Protestant nonconformists. Pressured by Parliament, Charles II rescinded the Declaration of Indulgence in 1673, and the same year Parliament passed the Test Act, requiring all clergy and holders of public office to subscribe to oaths of supremacy and allegiance.[135] The House of Commons in particular had opposed the king's reputed right to suspend penal laws in religion, but it also rejected a bill that would have provided toleration to Protestant dissenters. Henry Coventry, secretary of state for the north, couched Charles' retreat in terms that blamed the nonconformists: The declaration, he claimed, "had an Effect much different to what his Majesty intended it, and instead of composing the minds of the Dissenters . . . gave an occasion to some men to dispense such Jealousies in the Minds of very many of the Church, that it gave an Universall damp upon the Spirits of the Nation."[136] For years, local magistrates took differing positions on whether those licenses were still valid, and many opted not to

---

[135] Bodl., Tanner MSS 43, fol. 75r; 25 Car. II, c. 2; *Statutes of the Realm*, 5:782–85.

[136] Bodl., Carte MSS 79, fol. 72r-v; Bodl., Rawlinson Letters 51, fol. 39r; BL, Add. MSS 25,122, fol. 59r (quoted). In defensive tones, Charles explained to Parliament on 24 February 1673 that his intent in issuing the declaration was to secure the peace of the church and the realm. *CJ*, 9:256. One of his (anonymous) supporters defended the indulgence as legitimate because of the king's ecclesiastical authority as well as a means to honor his promise of liberty to tender consciences in the Declaration of Breda. Inner Temple Library, Petyt MSS 538, fols. 40v–41r.

prosecute nonconformists because of legal doubts about this issue. This was the case at such places as Bristol, Cambridge, Norwich, Great Yarmouth, Weymouth, and Melcombe Regis.[137] The task of suppressing dissent was now greater because of the numerical gains made by the nonconformists following the Declaration of Indulgence. In the diocese of Lincoln, which encompassed Bedford, Bishop William Fuller complained that licensed nonconformists had grown insolent and increased substantially. The Privy Council noted in June 1673 that the crown had received numerous reports "of disorders happening and animosityes increasing between [the king's] Subjects upon occasion of dissenting from the forme of Worship & discipline by Law Established."[138] Some magistrates lost no time in prosecuting nonconformists, as at Sherborne, Dorset, where "so many convictions will be made," reported the Congregationalist pastor Lewis Stucley, one of Wharton's correspondents, "as will bring in poverty upon many of the Lords people."[139] "There will be enmity between the seeds," he reflected, but there can be no thought of surrender: "Our cause is good, & the Lord will vindicate it in due time," asserted the Presbyterian minister Samuel Hieron, another member of Wharton's circle.[140] Bunyan was writing *The Barren Fig-Tree* about this time, and his subtext evinces the prevailing tension between dissenters and the state following the retraction of the Declaration of Indulgence.[141]

Having only recently been released from prison, Bunyan circumspectly responded to this renewed attack on nonconformists by including a subtext in *The Barren Fig-Tree* that probably would not have been obvious to casual readers. Using scriptural passages to make his points, he prophetically alerted England to the danger of continuing to be a nation of fruitless professors. He pointed to Luke 13:3–5, in which Jesus refers to the death of eighteen people on whom the tower of Siloam collapsed as a warning of the Hebrews' fate if they refuse to repent. The prophecy, Bunyan opined, was fulfilled in the reign of the Roman Emperor Titus when Jerusalem was overrun and many of its residents dispersed. "God gave them Sword, and Famine, Pestilence, and Blood, for their outrage against the Son of his Love" (5:11–12). Just as the Jews' claim to be the children of Abraham failed to save them from this calamity, so, by implication, England's

---

[137] PRO, SP 29/319/131; 29/335/13; 29/362/169; 29/363/25; Greaves, *EUHF*, 226.

[138] PRO, SP 29/312/195; 29/314/223; 29/319/65; 29/335/296.1 (quoted).

[139] Bodl., Rawlinson Letters 104, fol. 92r.

[140] Bodl., Rawlinson Letters 51, fols. 30r (quoted), 39r (quoted). For Stucley and Hieron see *Calamy Revised, s.vv.*

[141] Not all Anglicans welcomed a return to repressive ways. Isaac Archer, a vicar in Cambridgeshire, accepted the retraction of the Declaration of Indulgence as necessary to prevent the growth of Catholicism, but he preferred toleration for "sober & peaceable men." CUL, Add. MSS 8499, fol. 161.

avowal to be a Protestant nation would not prevent its overthrow. Bunyan likened the Jewish people to God's vineyard in the parable from Luke 13: Because fruit was not found among them, justice demanded that the people be cut down so another vineyard could be planted. His message to England was barely veiled: "This therefore must be your end, although you are planted in the Garden of God, for the barrenness and unfruitfulness of your Hearts and Lives, you must be cut off, yea rooted up, and cast out of the Vineyard" (5:12).

A nation that did no more than outwardly embrace Christian practices failed to meet the divine standard for being fruitful. Bunyan quoted Ezekiel 33:31 and Isaiah 58:2, which refer to the Jewish nation's pursuit of righteousness, desire to know God's ways, and interest in divine ordinances, but all this was external, for their hearts were corrupt and their motives impure (5:14). When the Jews brought the fruits of their obedience to God, they were too late, the day of grace having passed (5:23). For their fate—and by implication England's destiny—Bunyan quoted Jeremiah 15:1, in which God casts the Jewish people from his presence (5:33). He also cited Hebrews 3:10–11, where God expresses dissatisfaction with an entire generation that erred in their hearts, for which he excluded them from the promised land. For additional reinforcement, Bunyan also quoted Jude 5–6, with its affirmation that God, after bringing his people out of Egypt, destroyed those who refused to believe in him (5:45–46).

Bunyan's prophetic declamation belongs to a literary tradition that encompasses such disparate Protestant authors as John Knox, Stephen Marshall, and Edward Burrough.[142] In similar fashion, Bunyan sounded a prophetic warning that England, despite its external conformity to Protestant beliefs and practices, faced divine retribution as a nation unless it repented. As Jesus told the Jews in Matthew 21:43, the kingdom of God would be taken from them and given to another nation. "The *Jews* for their barrennes were *cut down*," Bunyan added, "and more fruitful people put in their room" (5:38). This, by implication, could be England's fate. In passing the Test Act Parliament stressed outward adherence to the king as head of the Church of England and to worship as stipulated in the Book of Common Prayer, but in Bunyan's judgment this was fundamentally wrong, for it ignored the only conformity that mattered—adherence to Christ's precepts. Although he was now more cautious, he remained resolute in his denunciation of the established church. Observance of the sacraments, performance

---

[142] For the earlier development of this genre among English Protestants see Mary Morrissey, "Elect Nations and Prophetic Preaching: *Types* and *Examples* in the Paul's Cross Jeremiad," in *The English Sermon Revised: Religion, Literature and History, 1600–1750*, ed. Lori Anne Ferrell and Peter McCullough (Manchester: Manchester University Press, 2000), 43–58.

of the liturgy, and obedience to the sovereign as head of the church were insufficient to avoid divine retribution since all this was mere formalism and akin to
hypocrisy. For England, as for the ancient Hebrew nation, the choice was "Fruit
or the Fire" (5:43).

## "Shie of Women"[143]: The Agnes Beaumont Episode

While Bunyan had his eyes on both the country's failure to meet God's standards and the barren members of gathered churches, some of his critics were
spreading scandalous tales about his alleged womanizing. He addressed these
rumors in the (lost) fourth or fifth edition of *Grace Abounding*, explicitly mentioning some of the sexual smears, namely, "that I had my *Misses*, my *Whores*, my
*Bastards*, yea, *two wives at once*, and the like" (*GA*, §309). Such allegations were
circulating, at least in the Bedford area, before an incident involving Agnes
Beaumont occurred. At age twenty-two she had joined the Bedford congregation
on 31 October 1672, the first member whose name Bunyan personally recorded.[144]
With her widowed father, the farmer John Beaumont the elder, she lived in the
village of Edworth, southeast of Biggleswade. Her brother John, who lived nearby,
attended at least some of the services with his sister, though he seems not to have
formally joined the Bedford church. He had been presented by the churchwardens at Edworth for recusancy in 1669.[145] Their father disapproved of Bunyan,
having heard scurrilous accounts of his conduct.[146] Agnes had attended services
for two years, though at times her father had prevented her from participating.

On a chilly winter Friday in February 1674, Agnes wanted to worship with the
congregation and observe the Lord's supper at Gamlingay, Cambridgeshire, some
seven miles away. In the past this sacrament "had been a sweet sealing ordinance
to [her] soul."[147] Having no spare horse for Agnes to use, her brother thought she
could ride with John Wilson, who in 1677 would become the pastor of a gathered
church at Hitchin. After Wilson failed to appear, a disconsolate Agnes found new
hope when Bunyan unexpectedly stopped at her brother's house. Too shy to ask
him for a ride, she prevailed on her brother to intercede. Knowing the elder

[143]*GA*, §315.

[144]*CB*, 75; *The Church Book of Bunyan Meeting 1650–1821: Being a Reproduction in Facsimile of the Original Folio*, intro. by G. B. Harrison (London: J. M. Dent and Sons, 1928),
fol. 53.

[145]Extracts from "The Narrative of the Persecution of Agnes Beaumont in 1674," in
*GA*, 179–80.

[146]Agnes Beaumont, *The Narratives of the Persecutions of Agnes Beaumont*, ed. Vera J.
Camden (East Lansing, MI: Colleagues Press, 1992), 44, 61.

[147]Ibid., 41.

Beaumont's hostility toward him, Bunyan initially refused, acquiescing only after repeated entreaties from Agnes and her brother.[148] Bunyan's reticence had deeper roots than mere concern for what the elder Beaumont thought, and rightly so, given the fact that a man and woman riding together on a horse sometimes fueled gossip in the seventeenth century. Although we can safely assume that the pious Agnes was hardly a threat to use Bunyan's genitalia as a pommel,[149] Bunyan by the early 1670s was keenly sensitive to physical contact with women because of the possibility of scandalous rumors that could undercut his message. He abhorred the commonplace kiss of greeting and even avoided touching a woman's hand. When others urged him to engage in "the holy kiss," he asked why they bestowed it only on the prettiest women (*GA*, §315). His unusual sensitivity toward *any* physical contact with women outside his family is not evidence of misogyny, but reflects an acute reaction against the slings and arrows that threatened his reputation.

At least on this occasion, Bunyan's concern was not misplaced. Had the elder Beaumont arrived at his son's farm in time, he undoubtedly would have pulled Agnes off the horse. As Bunyan and his passenger rode out of Edworth, the local Anglican minister, Anthony Lane, curate of Edworth and minister at Langford, Bedfordshire, looked at them "as if he would have stared his eyes out; and afterwards did scandalize us after a base manner, and did raise a very wicked report of us." Bunyan had given his foes a propaganda victory. Once at Gamlingay, he led the congregation in worship, Agnes' description of which provides a rare eyewitness account of the impact he could have:

> My soul was filled with consolation, and I sat under his shadow, with great delight, and his fruit was pleasant to my taste when I was at the Lord's table. I found such a return of prayer that I was scarce able to bear up under it. Oh, I had such a sight of Jesus Christ that brake my heart to pieces. Oh, how I longed that day to be with Jesus Christ; how fain would I have died in the place, that I might have gone the next way to him, my blessed Saviour. A sense of my sins, and of his dying love, made me love him, and long to be with him.[150]

If these feelings are representative of Bunyan's more intense followers, he was capable of inspiring a sense of spiritual ecstasy in them, and this must have been part of his appeal.

Following the service Agnes rode home with a maid, only to find herself

[148] Ibid., 42–44.

[149] Camden, in ibid., 17; G. R. Quaife, *Wanton Wenches and Wayward Wives: Peasants and Illicit Sex in Early Seventeenth Century England* (New Brunswick, NJ: Rutgers University Press, 1979), 48–49.

[150] Beaumont, *Narratives*, ed. Camden, 45.

locked out of the house by her father. After spending a frigid night in the barn, occupying herself in prayer, she failed to achieve a reconciliation with her father the following day. Her brother provided her with shelter on Saturday night, and the next afternoon she finally yielded to her father's demands, promising not to attend another of Bunyan's meetings while the father was alive unless he approved. Unexpectedly, the father died Tuesday night, apparently the victim of a heart attack. The yeoman Peter Feery, evidently angry because Agnes had rejected a proposed marriage to his son Thomas, accused her of poisoning her father at Bunyan's instigation. Although a coroner's inquest found her innocent of patricide, Agnes, and probably Bunyan too, continued to be the butt of ridicule.[151]

Continuing accusations of adultery and bigamy finally provoked Bunyan's angry retort in the fourth or fifth edition of *Grace Abounding*. "I know not whether there be such a thing as a woman breathing under the Copes of the whole Heaven but by their apparel, their Children, or by common Fame, except my Wife" (§315). His critics, he insisted, had missed their mark, for "if all the Fornicators and Adulterers in *England* were hang'd by the Neck till they be dead, *John Bunyan*, the object of their Envie, would be still alive and well" (§314). But his detractors *had* hit the mark, not because he was guilty of adultery or bigamy but because he felt compelled to defend himself in print against manifestly baseless allegations even while ignoring more implausible rumors that he was a witch, a Jesuit, or a highway robber (§307). One can imagine Bunyan, his face flushed, heatedly denying that he had mistresses and illegitimate children, to say nothing of relations with prostitutes (§309). The severity of his reaction was partly the consequence of the not unnatural attraction he felt toward women, undoubtedly those who, like Agnes Beaumont, were awed by his ministerial prowess. For Bunyan, as Neil Keeble has astutely observed, women were often seen as temptresses, especially to sexual indulgence.[152] When he initially refused to share his horse

---

[151] Ibid., 46, 48, 57–58, 65, 73–74, 80–83; Patricia L. Bell, "Agnes Beaumont of Edworth," *Baptist Quarterly* 35 (January 1993): 9, 11–12. The coroner's rolls are not extant. Beaumont's religious experience is discussed by Raymond Brown in "Bedfordshire Nonconformist Devotion: Another Look at the Agnes Beaumont Story," *Baptist Quarterly* 35 (July 1994): 310–23.

[152] N. H. Keeble, "'Here is her Glory, even to be under Him': The Feminine in the Thought and Work of John Bunyan," in *JBHE*, ed. Laurence, Owens, and Sim, 139. In a similar fashion, Tamsin Spargo has averred that Bunyan's response to the Beaumont episode was "to defend his pastoral, and patriarchal, authority by locating the threat of seduction within a dangerous female sexuality." *The Writing of John Bunyan* (Aldershot, Hants.: Ashgate, 1997), 40. To a point this is true, but Bunyan never denied the temptations that welled up within him. To assert, as does Margaret Thickstun, that he located "sexuality, and therefore evil" in the female body is misleading. He did situate lust in the

with Beaumont, he must have known what feelings, however unwanted, would well up within him as they rode for seven miles, her body rubbing against his, her hands clasped tightly around his waist. Whatever he felt from such close physical contact with this "attractive, dramatic, articulate" young woman, they "sometimes" conversed about religious matters as they rode to Gamlingay.[153] Although he knew he was innocent of improper conduct with Beaumont, the emotive force of his denials of sexual impropriety suggest discomfit stemming from his probable battle with carnal thoughts. This he virtually admitted: "Not that I have been thus kept [from sexual misbehavior], because of any goodness in me more than any other, but God has been merciful to me, and has kept me . . . from every evil way and work" (§316). However pious and gifted, Bunyan was also human.

---

female body, but this was but one aspect of sinfulness, the essence of which, for him, was rebellion against God. Eve's sin was disobedience, not lust. Margaret Olofson Thickstun, *Fictions of the Femine: Puritan Doctrine and the Representation of Women* (Ithaca, NY: Cornell University Press, 1988), 35 (quoted); *MW*, 4:306.

[153]Beaumont, *Narratives*, ed. Camden, 17, 44. The description of Beaumont is Camden's.

CHAPTER 8

# Evangelical Concerns

—◦•◦•◦—

Although Charles II had formally revoked the Declaration of Indulgence in 1673, disputes over the validity of the licenses compelled him to issue a proclamation on 3 February 1675 canceling them, an action the bishops in particular had been urging. This fresh signal of the king's support for the Church of England encouraged those determined to quash dissent. From Whitehall, however, Secretary of State Henry Coventry counseled moderation toward quiescent nonconformists, with severity reserved for the "Insolent and presumptuous."[1] The anticipation of renewed toleration gave some nonconformists reason for optimism and prompted complaints from ecclesiastical officials, but other dissenters were pessimistic. "Som expectations I had of what is now com upon us," Samuel Hieron reflected, "but did not think it would have com in such manner as to ruine us all, as they may now do."[2] In Bedford, the commissary of the archdeacon's court, William Foster, took this opportunity to obtain a warrant for Bunyan's arrest on 4 March 1675; signed by the justices of the peace, it charged him with having taught at a conventicle various times during the previous month. Under the terms of the Second Conventicle Act, if found guilty, Bunyan as a minister faced a fine of up to £20 for the first offense and double that for a second. Should he flee, his congregation would be liable for the fine, though no member could be compelled to remit more than £10. If the fine exceeded 10s., the accused had the right to a jury trial, which Bunyan presumably would have invoked had he been apprehended; the alternative was sentencing by a justice of the peace based on the accused's confession or the testimony of two sworn witnesses.[3]

[1] BL, Stowe MSS 207, fol. 114v; Bodl., Carte MSS 72, fols. 253r, 261v–262r; BL, Add. MSS 25,124, fol. 16r (quoted).
[2] Bodl., Tanner MSS 42, fols. 119r, 121r; Bodl., Rawlinson Letters 51, fol. 70r (quoted).
[3] 22 Car. II, c. 1; *Statutes of the Realm*, 5:648–51.

Rather than face a trial, Bunyan apparently went into hiding. A month later, on 10 April 1675, Foster and his deputy registrar, William Johnson, reported to the bishop of Lincoln that Bunyan "stands excommunicated, having been presented by the churchwardens for refusing to come to church and receive the sacrament."[4] An excommunicate was barred from pleading at law, recovering debts through litigation, or serving as an executor, and theoretically was ostracized from the community as well as excluded from the services and sacraments of the Church of England.[5] As a member of an alternative society that viewed the established church as Antichrist's, Bunyan must have preferred excommunication to a return appearance before magistrates. His epistle to *Instruction for the Ignorant*, published in 1675, explicitly states that he had been *"driven from you in presence, not affection,"* and he signed it, *"Yours, to serve you by my Ministry (when I can) to your Edification and Consolation"* (*MW*, 8:7). He was not in prison, for incarceration required the relatively unusual step of seeking a writ *de excommunicato capiendo* from the Chancery, a process that could not begin until forty days after excommunication.[6] Instead, he almost certainly fled from Bedfordshire to London, where he could work with his printers and find refuge in the nonconformist community.

Through informers the government attempted to monitor the dissenting congregations in the London area and elsewhere, but the task was daunting. At Taunton, Somerset, dissenters posted sentinels to warn them if magistrates were coming and barred the doors to prevent entry, and in a village near Wells nonconformists stationed nearly forty cudgel-bearing guards to protect their conventicle.[7] An incomplete report in 1676 listed 47 conventicles in London and Westminster, of which 17 can be identified as Presbyterian, 5 as Independent, 15 as Baptist, 6 as Quaker, and 2 as Fifth Monarchist; the remaining two cannot be firmly identified.[8] However, the Baptist historian W. T. Whitley noted the existence of approximately 34 Baptist churches in the greater London area, including several mixed-communion congregations, by this time.[9] The 1676 report also

[4] Quoted in Joyce Godber, "The Imprisonments of John Bunyan," *Transactions of the Congregational Historical Society* 16 (April 1949): 28.

[5] Spurr, *RCE*, 214–17; Bodl., Carte MSS 77, fol. 611r.

[6] Spurr, *RCE*, 217.

[7] Longleat, Coventry MSS 7, fols. 66r–v, 82v–83r.

[8] BL, Egerton MSS 3330, fols. 14r–v, 16r–17r. A printed version is available in *HMC* 22, *Eleventh Report*, appendix, pt. 7, 15–17. (Three conventicles are listed twice.) See also BL, Add. MSS 28,093, fols. 212r, 213v. Informers could be held accountable if errors were made in prosecuting nonconformists. Bodl., Tanner MSS 42, fol. 204r.

[9] W. T. Whitley, *The Baptists of London 1612–1928* (London: Kingsgate Press, 1928), 101–21.

omits such major churches as those of the Congregationalists Anthony Palmer, Thomas Brooks, John Owen, George Griffith, and George Cokayne.[10] Adequate surveillance of all these congregations and their members was manifestly more than the cash-strapped government could manage, making it feasible for Bunyan to stay in the London area for a time in 1675 and 1676. Judging from earlier contacts between the Bedford church and like-minded groups in London, he probably found hospitality among the Congregationalist ministers Cokayne, Griffith, Palmer, Owen, Ferguson, Meade, and Richard Lawrence (Meade's assistant at Stepney, Middlesex).[11] Henry Jessey's successor, James Fitten, was not among those with whom Bunyan presumably stayed, for in December 1676 the latter and others in the Bedford church wrote to Fitten's congregation, inquiring if it still held Jessey's principles on open membership and communion; it did not.[12] Had Bunyan contacted this church while he was probably taking refuge in London, his congregation would have known what principles Fitten's church espoused in 1676. In the aftermath of the baptismal controversy, Bunyan undoubtedly felt ill at ease with the Particular and General Baptist communities and thus would have sought out Congregationalists.

The Independent circles in which Bunyan likely moved in 1675–76 included prominent moderates and radicals. In 1669 Griffith and Owen had participated in a lectureship at Hackney with Brooks, Nye (d. 1672), Peter Sterry (d. 1672), and the Presbyterians William Bates and Thomas Watson. Griffith, Owen, Cokayne, Nye, Palmer, and John Loder were among a group of ministers who counseled Harvard College in February 1672, and the following month Griffith, Owen, and Palmer had an audience with the king to thank him for the Declaration of Indulgence. Yet only a year earlier, in June 1671, the government had issued a warrant to search the houses of Griffith, Palmer, and Cokayne for Richard Cromwell.[13] Griffith's patron, Lord Wharton, had fought against the royalists in the civil war, enjoyed good relations with Oliver Cromwell, and opposed the Clarendon Code and the Second Conventicle Act. In February 1677 Wharton would be sent to the Tower with the duke of Buckingham and the earls of Shaftesbury and Salisbury

---

[10]PRO, SP 29/387/132; 29/379/50. For Brooke see *BDBR, s.v.*

[11] For Lawrence see *Calamy Revised, s.v.* After being ejected as rector of Trunch with Swafield, Norfolk, he served for a time as pastor of a congregation in Amsterdam, and from him Bunyan could have learned more about Protestant activities on the continent.

[12]*CB*, 79–80; Tindall, 240. For Fitten see *BDBR, s.v.*

[13] C. E. Whiting, *Studies in English Puritanism from the Restoration to the Revolution, 1660–1688* (London: Society for Promoting Christian Knowledge, 1931), 75; *The Correspondence of John Owen (1616–1683): With an Account of His Life and Work*, ed. Peter Toon (Cambridge: James Clarke, 1970), 151–53; *CSPD, 1671–72*, 609; *CSPD, 1671*, 335. For Sterry and Loder see *BDBR, s.vv.*; for Watson see *Calamy Revised, s.v.*

for attempting to obtain the dissolution of the Cavalier Parliament on the grounds that it had been prorogued more than a year.[14] Moreover, he continued to be at the hub of a network of dissenting ministers, including Owen, Meade, Loder, Baxter, Thomas Yates, Samuel Clark, and Francis Wells.[15]

Palmer and Cokayne had Fifth Monarchist backgrounds. Although allegations linking Palmer and Danvers to the Tong plot are probably groundless, the two men were working together about late 1663 when Danvers was in hiding. The government issued a warrant for Palmer's arrest in early 1664, and in May 1670 it fined him £20 for preaching at a conventicle. In addition to his Fifth Monarchist activities in the early 1660s, Cokayne was exchanging prodigies, almost certainly critical of the government, with Jessey in 1661. The countesses of Anglesey and Peterborough and four or five knights attended an illegal service Cokayne held in London in August 1664. Earlier, in January of that year, he had been arrested for allegedly preaching at Cardington, Bedfordshire, that Charles I's beheading was justifiable.[16] Owen's congregation at Leadenhall Street was a magnet for such radicals as General Charles Fleetwood, Major-General John Desborough, Major-General James Berry, Lieutenant-Colonel Jeffrey Ellison, and Captain Griffith Lloyd, all of whom probably heard Bunyan preach. Fleetwood's son Smith and his son-in-law, Sir John Hartopp, whose aunt was married to Danvers, were also part of Owen's congregation. So too were Bridget Bendish, daughter of Henry Ireton and granddaughter of Oliver Cromwell, and William Steele, lord chancellor of Ireland in the late 1650s. In February 1676 an informer reported that Owen's congregation was very dangerous, "praying and preaching to the decrying of the present power and all authority to them contrary."[17] As Bunyan almost certainly associated with such churches during his visits to the London area, he would have been exposed to a ferment of views critical of the established church and its lay defenders.

[14] *BDBR, s.v.* Philip Wharton; Bodl., Carte MSS 79, fols. 27r–28v, 35r, 45r; Carte MSS 228, fol. 96r; Greaves, *EUHF*, 35, 151, 153, 233. Wharton was released in July 1677. Carte MSS 79, fol. 92r; 228, fol. 116r.

[15] Bodl., Rawlinson Letters 50, fol. 104r; Rawlinson Letters 51, fols. 9r, 19r–20v, 27r, 63r–64v, 105r, 160r. For Clark (of Bedfordshire) and Wells see *Calamy Revised, s.vv.* Wells was ejected and later conformed.

[16] Greaves, *DUFE*, 82, 97, 116, 203, 205, 213; Greaves, *EUHF*, 7, 128, 159; *BDBR, s.v.* George Cokayne; *CSPD, 1663–64*, 451.

[17] Greaves, *EUHF*, 128; *CSPD, 1675–76*, 571 (quoted). For Fleetwood, Desborough, Berry, Hartopp, and Steele see *BDBR, s.vv.*

*"Anathematised of God"*[18]: Enemies of the Faith

Against this background Bunyan wrote *Light for Them That Sit in Darkness: or, a Discourse of Jesus Christ*, which Roger L'Estrange licensed on 19 June 1675.[19] As a polemical work, it echoed Bunyan's previous attacks on Fowler and Penn, but the book's interest derives as well from its use of typology, which indirectly involved Bunyan in yet another controversy. In 1669 Samuel Parker, secretary to Gilbert Sheldon, archbishop of Canterbury, had denounced nonconformists for debasing religion "into unaccountable Fansies and Enthusiasms, drest it up with pompous and empty Schemes of Speech, and so embrace a few gawdy Metaphors and Allegories, instead of the substance of true and real Righteousness."[20] As used by nonconformists, he charged, metaphor and allegory were devices to undermine rationality and appeal to the multitude's savage, unreasonable instincts. Parker's primary thesis was a defense of royal authority in matters of church and state, the denial of which he deemed irrational. Toleration, therefore, was unacceptable, and dissenters must be silenced. Owen led the nonconformists' counterattack with *Truth and Innocence Vindicated* (1669), to which Parker replied in *A Defence and Continuation of the Ecclesiastical Politie* (1671). Owen's friend, Andrew Marvell, took up the case for toleration against Parker in the two parts of *The Rehearsal Transpros'd* (1672–73). Among the others who joined the fray was Owen's assistant, Robert Ferguson, initially with *A Sober Enquiry into the Nature, Measure, and Principle of Moral Virtue* (1673), and subsequently in *The Interest of Reason in Religion* (1675).[21] Licensed on 15 February 1675, the latter work antedated *Light for Them That Sit in Darkness* by four months.

In the meantime, William Sherlock, rector of St. George, Botolph Lane, London, whose views on justification were akin to Fowler's, accused Owen and Watson in 1674 of "jumbling metaphors, and Allegories, and Types, and Figures, altogether, and proving one thing from another in a most wonderful manner." Sherlock specifically accused Watson of using metaphors to assert the erroneous doctrine of justification by Christ's imputed righteousness. "All this," wrote Sherlock of the dissenters' employment of metaphorical language to make doctrinal points, "is the work of fancy and imagination, . . . nothing but phrase, and Religious tattle, the fruit of precarious *Hypotheses* . . . ; for at this Rate it were easie to make any thing of any thing, to find out some pretty words, and phrases,

[18] *MW*, 8:160.

[19] Arber, *Term Catalogues*, 1:209–10.

[20] Samuel Parker, *A Discourse of Ecclesiastical Politie* (London, 1670), 74.

[21] For an overview of the debate see Richard Ashcraft, *Revolutionary Politics and Locke's Two Treatises of Government* (Princeton, NJ: Princeton University Press, 1986), 41–74.

and allusions, types, or Metaphors, to countenance all the feats of Enthusiasm, and the more godly Romances of Popish Legends."[22] Thus the tangled skeins of the debate sparked by Parker included related attacks on justification by imputed righteousness and the use of types and allegories.

Bunyan probably arrived in London about the time Ferguson's *Interest of Reason in Religion* came from the press, and it is highly likely that he discussed at least some of the issues in the debate with his nonconformist friends, probably including Ferguson and Owen. By the time Bunyan completed the first part of *The Pilgrim's Progress*, the debate triggered by Parker was already under way, and some of the advice Bunyan received not to publish the allegory may have been occasioned by sensitivity to Parker's linkage of allegory with religious enthusiasm, irrationality, and the need for a policy of repression. Ferguson's *Interest of Reason in Religion* would have attracted Bunyan because the Scot devoted substantial attention to the appropriate use of metaphor and allegory. The Holy Spirit, Ferguson argued, utilizes metaphors and allegory in Scripture to help people grasp the gospel mysteries. Always, however, the Spirit somewhere reveals these teachings in plain words; hence metaphorical language and allegory are vehicles to illustrate faith's mysteries, not the primary means of their declaration. "Metaphors are not used to impregnate our Minds with gawdy Phantasms, but to adjust the Mysteries of Religion to the weakness of our Capacities." The interpretation of metaphorical and allegorical language must never be forced; indeed, Ferguson insisted that every biblical text has a literal meaning. He spent little time discussing types, though he clearly regarded them as part of the general subject of tropes. The Old Testament, he noted, employs types to prefigure Christ's priesthood and kingship, as in the depiction of Melchizedek as a type of the messiah. Beyond the interpretation of biblical tropes, Ferguson defended the preacher's right to use them in the pulpit as long as they were not abused. Metaphors can be employed when they aid memory, assist people to grasp scriptural principles, or compensate for a paucity of ordinary language to explain something. Metaphors and allegory, Ferguson asserted, cannot be used lightly, excessively, or in obscure and unintelligible ways, and the subject matter must not be sordid or otherwise inappropriate.[23] With his keen interest in allegory, Bunyan must have found Ferguson's views of interest, and he would also have discovered

[22] William Sherlock, *A Discourse Concerning the Knowledge of Jesus Christ* (London, 1674), 114 (quoted), 117 (quoted), 118–21. For Sherlock's attack on imputed righteousness and the necessity of repentance and reformation before justification, see 234, 266–68, 273, 312–13. For Sherlock see *DNB, s.v.*

[23] Robert Ferguson, *The Interest of Reason in Religion, with the Import & Use of Scripture-Metaphors* (London, 1675), 278, 280–83, 308–9, 312, 315, 343 (quoted), 353, 360–62, 367, 369–71, 393–94.

a kindred spirit in Ferguson, who took issue with Fowler's *The Principles and Practices, of Certain Moderate Divines of the Church of England* (1670).[24]

Bunyan's primary intent in *Light for Them That Sit in Darkness* was neither to refute Fowler and Penn nor to engage in the scholarly debate over metaphorical language, including typology and allegory. Instead, apparently expanding a sermon, he addressed church-goers whom he wanted to prevent from embracing the tenets of Latitudinarians, Quakers, or others who rejected salvation by Christ's imputed righteousness. The thesis explores the meaning of Christ's redemptive work, particularly as his death appeased God, and how his righteousness, imputed to the elect, facilitates their acceptance by God (*MW*, 8:83, 94, 108, 114, 128–29, 135, 149). Bunyan's doctrine of the atonement is Anselmic, resting on the premise that God, having threatened punishment for transgressing the divine will, cannot accept sinners, no matter how penitent, unless "Revenging Justice" has been satisfied (8:107–8).[25] But mere satisfaction, which Bunyan defined as "compleatly to answer a legal Demand for harms and injuries done," is insufficient to obtain God's love, for this only evens the ledger (8:108). Christ must go beyond his death, argued Bunyan, and "wash" the elect in his blood (8:109). "Now if we be redeemed, washed, purged, made nigh to God, have peace with God; if we stand just before God, are saved, reconciled, sanctified, admitted into the Holiest; if we have eternal Redemption by his Blood, and if his Blood will be the burden of our Song for ever: then hath Christ paid the full price for us by his Death; then hath he done more than made satisfaction for our Sins" (8:110). Any denigration of the sheer grandeur of Christ's salvific work by according a redemptive role to human righteousness as measured by repentance or other good works was unacceptable to Bunyan, and this more than anything else set him apart from Latitudinarians.

He was concerned that purveyors of feigned holiness such as Fowler, Penn, and perhaps Parker would attract the gullible, tempting them to commit the unpardonable sin. This he now defined as turning from knowledge of the gospel to "*Fables, Seducing-Spirits, and Doctrines of Devils through the Intoxications of Delusions, and the Witchcrafts of false Preachers*" (8:49). Regarding such a fall from the

---

[24]Ibid., 381 (mispr. 379). Ferguson explicitly referred to Fowler's derogatory comments about the Apostle Paul's style. Edward Fowler, *The Principles and Practices, of Certain Moderate Divines of the Church of England* (London, 1670), 261. The third part of Ferguson's *Interest of Reason in Religion* is an extensive defense, against Sherlock, of the idea that divine grace is infused into believers, uniting them with Christ and bringing regeneration. This theme is, of course, closely related to the doctrine of imputed righteousness.

[25]Bunyan may have learned the doctrine from Bayly's *The Practise of Pietie*, 692–93 (mispr. 668–69), 751. Penn had opposed the Anselmic doctrine in *The Sandy Foundation Shaken* (London, 1668), 16–21.

truth as *"the most dangerous and damning Miscarriage,"* he wrote this book to dissuade the endangered from succumbing to the allure of *"the crafty Children of darkness"* and thereby committing the fatal sin against the Holy Spirit (8:50). The significance of what he was saying should not be missed. The greatest of sins was now turning from the gospel of justification by faith and Christ's imputed righteousness to the pseudo-gospel of Latitudinarians and Quakers, with its call to sinners to begin reforming themselves, aided by grace, before they could be accepted by God. This pseudo-gospel, thundered Bunyan, despises the blood of the covenant and tramples Christ (8:50–51). Scathingly, he excoriated deluded preachers, "with their Tongues smoother than Oil," who rejected the core gospel principle that God made Christ to be sin for the elect by imputing their transgressions to him (8:92, 101). So important was this point that Bunyan refused to recognize those who rejected it as Christians (8:101), thereby relegating Quakers, Latitudinarians, and other Prayer-Book Protestants with similar views beyond the pale of Christianity. Once again, he sharply distinguished between visible saints and adherents of false doctrine in the Church of England.

The principal antagonists in the wide-ranging debate triggered by Parker had recourse to a galaxy of learned writers. Although Bunyan read more than he admitted, he was not equipped to engage in scholarly polemic of this nature, nor were writers such as Parker, Fowler, and Sherlock his intended audience. Instead he professed to emulate the Apostle Paul by delivering the gospel message in simple terms that enabled the people to remember it more readily. From experience he knew ministers had to cope with *"the Unaptness of the Minds even of the Saints themselves to retain [the gospel] without commixture."* Moreover, this was *"to say nothing of the Projects of Hell, and of the cunning craftiness of some that lie in wait to deceive, even the Godly themselves, as they are dull of hearing, so much more dull in receiving, and holding fast the simplicity of the Gospel"* (8:49). Simplicity, then, was Bunyan's goal in this book, enabling him to dismiss erudite citations to non-biblical authors as "Duncish Sophistry," an allusion to the specious reasoning popularly associated with the late medieval scholar Duns Scotus (8:91). The "high thoughts" and "Sophistical Reason" of Bunyan's learned opponents reputedly obscured the knowledge of God (8:49, 92). In this context he uttered one of his most explicit repudiations of reliance on the works of others, insisting that his doctrine came from the Bible, not libraries, and that he depended on the writings of no one apart from Scripture (8:51). He stopped short of claiming not to have read other works or counseling his audience not to read godly literature. However, without mentioning names he made it clear that writers such as Penn, Fowler, Parker, and Sherlock should be condemned because of "the revilings, despiteful sayings, and . . . Ungodly Speeches which these abominable Children of Hell, let fall in their Pamphlets, Doctrines, and Discourses" against Christ (8:144).

Although Bunyan likely discussed aspects of the Parker debate with Owen and Ferguson, he offered no theoretical justification for the use of allegory and typology. Nevertheless, *Light for Them That Sit in Darkness* displays more interest in typology than he had expressed in most of his earlier writings. *The Doctrine of the Law and Grace Unfolded* and *A Defence of the Doctrine of Justification* contain modest references to typology, but of Bunyan's earlier works only *The Holy City* had made substantial use of this mode of scriptural exegesis.[26] The renewal of his typological interests in early 1675 may have been spurred by discussions with Ferguson or reading his *Interest of Reason in Religion*. In any event, Bunyan's response to recent criticism of metaphor, allegory, and typology was a reassertion of typological exegesis. The defense of allegory and metaphorical language in general came some two years later, in his Apology for *The Pilgrim's Progress*:

> ... *must I needs want solidness, because*
> *By Metaphors I speak; was not Gods Laws,*
> *His Gospel-laws in older time held forth*
> *By Types, Shadows and Metaphors?*
>
> . . . .
>
> *Am I afraid to say that holy Writ,*
> *Which for its Stile, and Phrase, puts down all Wit,*
> *Is every where so full of all these things,*
> *(Dark Figures, Allegories,) yet there springs*
> *From that same Book that lustre, and those rayes*
> *Of light, that turns our darkest nights to days.* (PP, 4)

To the criticism of authors such as Sherlock and Parker, Bunyan retorted that the Bible provides ample precedent for tropes, allegories, and types. Indeed, sound scriptural exegesis requires the explication of such literary techniques, the use of which has been divinely sanctioned, as reflected by their presence in holy writ.

In *Light for Them That Sit in Darkness* Bunyan conventionally explained his understanding of typology, noting that the Old Testament is "filled with Promises of the Messias to come, Prophetical Promises, Typical Promises: For all the Types and shadows of the Saviour, are virtually so many Promises" (*MW*, 8:60). For Bunyan as for expositors of typology generally, Old Testament types fall into the categories of people, animals, and material objects, or what he called "Insensible Creatures." He cited eight men as types of Christ, including Adam, "the Head and Father of the first World," and Moses, a mediator and tabernacle-builder. Among the others, Aaron and Melchizedek are types as high priests, Samson as

[26]See, e.g., *MW*, 2:91, 93, 97, 104–6, 117, 160, 217, 219 (*The Doctrine of the Law and Grace Unfolded*); 3:78, 80, 83, 86, 116–17, 119, 121–22, 125–28, 132–33, 139, 172, 175, 188 (*The Holy City*); 4:33, 56, 70, 88, 108, 120 (*A Defence of the Doctrine of Justification*). For other examples see 1:34, 158; 3:216–17, 227, 240–41; 5:113; *GA*, §71.

Israel's deliverer through his death, Joshua as donor of the promised land to Israel, David as conqueror of Israel's enemies and its provider, and Solomon as
temple-builder and sovereign of a peaceful kingdom. For Bunyan, the typological
animals include the paschal lamb, the red cow in Numbers 19, and sacrificial
bulls, goats, and birds. Inanimate objects serving as biblical types encompass the
manna in the wilderness, the water-giving rock struck by Moses, and Mount Moriah (8:60–63, 112). Beyond these general categories he cited the passover as a type
of Christ and the holiest site in the temple as a type of heaven (8:106, 115). Essentially, the Old Testament is a vast storehouse of people, things, and events that
prefigure the great events in the New Testament which mark the drama of divine
redemption. Seen in this light, the Old Testament, though undeniably a historical
record for Bunyan, is a body of texts to be decoded as keys to understand God's
redemptive work. Bunyan's return to typological hermeneutics at a time when
such exegesis was under attack by Sherlock and others was his way of attesting to
the validity of such interpretation. In making his case, he trumped his erstwhile
opponents, their learned citations notwithstanding, by claiming God as the
source of his teaching: "*I have presented thee with that which I have received from
God, and the Holy Men of God, who spake as they were moved by the Holy Ghost do
bear me witness*" (8:51).

Although Bunyan's intended audience in this book comprised visible saints, he
also had an eye on his opponents. In part this is reflected in his assurance of ultimate triumph over them. The peace of God bestowed on saints gives them not only
inner calm, boldness, confidence, and a "Melodious" frame of mind, but the certainty of victory over their enemies (8:130). Bunyan depicts this spirit as "*the Triumph* that ariseth sometimes in the Hearts of the Believers; for they at times are able
to see Death, Sin, the Devil, and Hell, and all Adversity conquered by, and tied as
Captives at the Chariot-Wheels of Jesus Christ" (8:131). One of the more unrecog-
nized aspects of Bunyan's mature religious experience, this involved his triumph
over spiritual turmoil and melancholy, and subsequently his external enemies. He
still remembered his "afflicted Conscience" and the agonizing sense of being swallowed up by despair (8:156–57), but his preoccupation in early 1675 was with his external enemies. He reserved his closing words for them, noting "the Accursed Condition of those among the Religious in these Nations whose notions put them far off
from Jesus" (8:160). Although he refrained from naming his opponents in this
book, he must have been thinking of Fowler, Penn, Parker, and possibly Sherlock
when he wrote of "graceless men" whose knowledge of Christianity was merely notional, not experiential, and for whom religion was nothing more than a cloak for
wickedness (8:127–28). "These Men speak not by the Holy Ghost, for in the Sum,
they call *Jesus Accursed*; . . . many of them are *Anathematised of God, and shall stand
so*, till the Coming of the Lord Jesus" (8:160).

*"Wholsome Medicine"*[27]: Teaching the Basics

Shortly after completing *Light for Them That Sit in Darkness*, Bunyan prepared a catechism entitled *Instruction for the Ignorant*, also published in 1675 by Francis Smith. The sequence of the publications is evident from a list of Bunyan's books published by Smith and appended to *Light for Them That Sit in Darkness*. *Instruction for the Ignorant* is not among the ten works on the list, as it surely would have been had its publication preceded *Light*. This time the intended audience comprised the adults and children of the Bedford church. When he wrote, Bunyan was still away from Bedford, almost certainly in London, and to his friends at Bedford he remarked that he had been *"driven from [them] in presence, not affection"* (MW, 8:7). The catechism, he explained, was to remind them of *"first things,"* but he also hoped members of the Bedford church would give copies to their *"carnal"* relatives as a means of encouraging their conversion. Simultaneously he wrote the catechism—*"this wholsome Medicine"*—for all those who had heard him preach but remained unregenerate. Like so much of what he wrote, the catechism's *"awakening"* words were intended to convey the gospel message to those in the dark, and as such, *Instruction for the Ignorant* manifests the evangelical face of Bunyan's Calvinist theology.

The production of catechisms burgeoned in England between 1530 and 1740. For this period Ian Green has identified 1,043 catechisms, catechetical works, or new translations of such works, with the most productive decades being the 1640s (95 items) and the 1700s (79 items). Sixty works, including Bunyan's *Instruction for the Ignorant*, appeared in the 1670s, tying this decade for the eighth highest.[28] Green has identified three basic stages of development, the first of which extended from the 1530s to the 1560s. During this period catechetical authors relied extensively on the medieval heritage, generally failed to distinguish clearly between catechisms and dialogue, and were often influenced by continental models. Moreover, catechizing was relatively novel at this time. Extending from the 1570s to the mid-1640s, the second stage witnessed the triumph of the question-and-answer format over the declaratory, the clear distinction between dialogues and catechisms, and a growth in the number of dedications to bishops, aristocrats, and corporations. This stage saw an increase in the number of catechisms produced in England, a rise in new forms and often longer works, and evidence of improved catechetical techniques, such as simpler vocabulary and shorter sentences. In the final period, which began in the 1640s and continued into the

---

[27] MW, 8:7.

[28] Ian Green, *The Christian's ABC: Catechisms and Catechizing in England c.1530–1740* (Oxford: Clarendon Press, 1996), 51.

eighteenth century, polemical content became common, doctrinal variety increased owing to sectarian growth, overt political material appeared in some catechisms, and the employment of innovative techniques increased. These techniques included reliance on shorter questions and answers, briefer catechisms,
simpler language, snappy responses, the utilization of parallel full-scale and abbreviated catechisms, reduced amounts of material for daily memorization, the
use of verse, the employment of support devices such as broadsheets that could
be hung in homes, and a trend away from black letter to easier-to-read roman
type.[29]

English catechisms, according to Green, manifest substantial continuity in
content from the 1540s to the 1730s, with innovation restricted primarily to presentation techniques. Numerous similarities, he argues, marked conformist and
nonconformist catechisms in the mid-seventeenth century, even to the point that
conformists borrowed from dissenters, and the latter sometimes acknowledged
the worth of Anglican catechisms. Yet Green also notes that by the mid-1640s
some writers had begun incorporating polemical material into their catechisms.[30]
In February 1673, Archbishop Sheldon informed his suffragans that the king attributed the growth of sects and religious disorder to a neglect in educating
young people in Christian principles as interpreted by the Church of England,
and Sheldon directed the bishops to reinforce catechetical teaching. The same
month the House of Commons asked the attorney-general to draft a bill to require "all Persons that are in Ecclesiastical Preferment, under a Penalty, to cate-
chize and instruct the Youth . . . every *Sunday* in the Afternoon, in the Church
Catechism: And to explain the same; and expound thereupon to the Congregation."[31] Catechisms were clearly appreciated as valuable weapons in the struggle
for minds and souls, old as well as young. Sheldon deemed catechizing "the most
effectuall means to prevent the further increase of the growing Sects and disorders amongst us," and the rector of Winwick, Lancashire, Richard Sherlock, regarded a good catechism as a means of stemming the growth of sects, religious
divisions, and heterodox or heretical theological views. "We see by experience
that the most *fickle* and *giddy people* are commonly the most eager *hearers* of
many Sermons and several Preachers: and what's the reason, but that such Sermons as men ordinarily hear, being not first well *Catechized*, tender their mindes
like a *ship* without *ballast*, which cannot keep a steddy course."[32] Catechizing vac-

[29]Ibid., 59–86, 92, 246, 248–56.
[30]Ibid., 168–69, 299, 565.
[31]BL, Harleian MSS 7377, fol. 42v; *CJ*, 9:259 (quoted).
[32]BL, Harleian MSS 7377, fol. 55r (quoted); Richard Sherlock, *The Principles of the Holy
Christian Religion*, 6th ed. (London, 1663), sig. A3r–v (quoted). For Sherlock see *DNB, s.v.*

cinates against the virulent viruses of dissent, and those who saw catechisms in such light would not have been impressed by whatever degree of commonness existed between nonconformist and Anglican versions.

Until the 1580s most English catechisms were organized around four basic components: the Apostles' Creed, the Lord's prayer, the Ten Commandments, and the sacraments. In the late sixteenth century catechetical authors began to do more experimenting, focusing on one of these themes, dealing with three (typically excluding the Apostles' Creed), or adopting a wholly new structure while retaining much of the traditional material.[33] Bunyan's catechism is unusual in its six-part organization as well as the themes of those parts, namely, general doctrinal material, confession of sin, faith, prayer, self-denial, and conclusions similar to the "uses" with which he typically ended his sermons. Apart from the last section, he employed the commonplace question-and-answer format, though reversing the usual order by having the catechumens ask the questions rather than provide the answers, a methodology he may have borrowed from Henry Jessey's *Miscellanea Sacra: or, Diverse Necessary Truths* (1665). In size, *Instruction for the Ignorant* is moderate, running to approximately 13,000 words. Likewise moderate in comparison to other catechisms was Bunyan's decision to incorporate a modest number of scriptural citations in the text, though none in the margins. In technique his catechism evinces few of the more innovative pedagogical devices. Many of his answers are rather long, though most questions are relatively brief in keeping with his role reversal of catechumens and instructor. Language is generally simple, but answers are neither snappy nor susceptible to memorization. At times he forgot his medium and launched into a mini-sermon, as in the following answer (quoted only in part) to a question about why the ungodly could not be effectively punished in this world as an example to others:

> If the ungodly should with punishment have been rewarded in this World, it would in all probability have overthrown the whole order that God hath settled here among Men. For who could have endured here to have seen the flames of Fire, to have heard the groans, and to have seen the tears perhaps of damned relations, as Parents or Children. Therefore as Tophet of old was without the City, and as the Gallows and Gibbets are builded without the Towns; so Christ hath ordered that they who are to be punished with this kind of Torment, shall be taken away. . . . (8:14–15)

In style and content Bunyan returned here to *A Few Sighs from Hell. Instruction for the Ignorant* cannot have been intended for memorization, which is hardly surprising given his intense disapprobation of notional knowledge. In content, *Instruction for the Ignorant* is less a catechism than an instructional handbook or

---

[33] Green, *The Christian's ABC*, 283–89.

primer of the faith. Partly this may explain why it was not a commercial success, only one edition having been printed in his lifetime.[34]

Although not a polemical work, Bunyan's catechism contains assorted remarks implicitly critical of the Church of England. True worship, he argued, is diametrically opposed to that which is superstitious and profane, just as genuine prayer differs from that which is vain and repetitious (8:26, 36). As he asserted in *I Will Pray with the Spirit*, the Bible is the exclusive standard for worship (8:19). Such teachings implicitly condemn the Book of Common Prayer, with its reliance on tradition as well as Scripture, and its rote, repetitious prayers. To confess sins "through Custom, or Tradition" is meaningless, for genuine confession must be rooted in a conviction of guilt. Only the best preachers, he insisted, should be heeded, and he issued a stern admonition not to despise, reproach, or relate scandals about such men (8:25). In making the last point he must have had in mind the recent Agnes Beaumont affair as well as the more general criticism leveled by conformists against dissenting clergy. His warning also extended to those who persecuted godly clergy, an admonition directed against all those defenders of the Church of England who endorsed the government's repressive policy (8:16).

The doctrine of justification by Christ's imputed righteousness, for which Bunyan had contended against Fowler and Penn, is reiterated in the catechism, but without explicit identification of his antagonists. They were probably in his mind when he warned his catechumens against those who believe divine justice "is such as they can pacifie with their own good works," and those who aver that reformation should precede coming to Christ (8:20, 28). He also implicitly repudiated Fowler's attack on the doctrine of original sin:

> Q. *But do not some hold that we are sinners only by imitation?*
> A. Yes, being themselves deceived. But God's Word saith, we are Children of Wrath by Nature, that is, by Birth and Generation. (8:12)

For his part, Fowler leveled another criticism against Bunyan in a preface to John Worthington's catechism: "The *Christian Religion* is no *Speculative* but a purely *Practical* Science, and . . . *the* design and business thereof is (though those that would not have it so will not see it) to make men *inwardly* and *really* Righteous, to purify our souls . . . , and endue us with a God-like and divine nature."[35] As late as 1680 Fowler was still condemning reputed Antinomians on the grounds that they rejected the obligation of Christians to perform duties required by the

---

[34] Apparently only one copy of this edition is extant.

[35] Edward Fowler, epistle to John Worthington, *A Form of Sound of Words: or, a Scripture-Catechism* (London, 1673), sig. A7v.

moral law, thereby destroying gospel precepts.[36] However, Bunyan never used the doctrine of imputed righteousness to excuse licentious behavior, and his catechism makes it clear that the Christian life is characterized by godly living (8:34).

Bunyan's catechism is faithful to his Calvinist principles, but since it has an evangelical as well as a pedagogical purpose, he made no attempt to explicate the doctrine of predestination. Although he plead with his readers to come to Christ, he explained that those who will be regenerated must be "implanted into the Faith of Christ"; the initiative, in other words, is God's (8:28–29, 31). Reiterating a theme on which he had touched in *Light for Them That Sit in Darkness*, he maintained that God sometimes creates delusions in people's minds so "that they might believe lies, and be damned" (8:13, 147). These are the reprobate, though in the catechism he shied away from attributing their status to a pre-creation decision by God; instead the latter is depicted as giving "them up to their own hearts lusts, to blindness of mind also, and hardness of heart" (8:13).

The catalogue of the greatest sins, as Bunyan fashioned it, includes not only the obvious moral offenses, such as adultery, fornication, swearing, covetousness, and lying, but the crimes of murder and theft. Considering that children comprised a key portion of his intended audience, the inclusion of sedition, heresy, and witchcraft is surprising (8:15). Yet many of his works include passing references to witches and witchcraft, for which he could cite such scriptural passages as 1 Samuel 15:23, Galatians 5:19, and Revelation 21:8. How much instruction in such subjects he gave children is impossible to ascertain, but he indisputably attempted to terrify them with the penalties of sin and the possibility of an early death, "for there be little Graves in the Church-yard" (8:18). The picture of God he painted for children must have caused more than a little anxiety and perhaps some nightmares: "When the Flood came, he drowned all the little Children that were in the old World; he also burned up all the little Children which were in *Sodom*: and because upon a time the little Children at *Bethel* mocked the Prophet as he was a-going to worship God, God let loose two she-Bears upon them which tore forty and two of them to pieces" (8:17). Bunyan's ultimate goal, of course, was to entice or frighten his audience into embracing the gospel as he understood it, and he concluded his catechism with an unadulterated appeal to self-interest: "Consider how sweet the thought of Salvation will be to thee when thou seest thy self in Heaven, whilst others are roaring in Hell" (8:44). Still in forced absence from Bedford when he wrote these words, he must have envisioned Foster and his associates among those whose ultimate destination was such a fiery fate.

[36] Edward Fowler, *Libertas Evangelica: or, a Discourse of Christian Liberty* (London, 1680), 159–60.

"Holy-day Saints"[37]: Damned Professors

Bunyan was still away from Bedford, almost certainly in London, when in late 1675 he completed *The Strait Gate, or, Great Difficulty of Going to Heaven.* Licensed on 24 November 1675, it was published by Francis Smith in 1676.[38] Bunyan's new work, another expanded sermon, tendentiously contended that most professing Christians were destined for hell. In his epistle to the reader he remarked that as his text, Luke 13:24, "*calls for sharpness, so do the times, yea, the faithful discharge of my duty towards thee, hath put me upon it*" (*MW*, 5:69).

Bunyan's reference to the need for sharp measures because of "*the times*" pertained to increasing tension between conformists on the one hand and dissenters and their supporters on the other, particularly in Parliament and in London. During the spring of 1675 the earl of Danby and his allies had sought parliamentary approval of a bill to impose a Test on all members of Parliament and office-holders, requiring them to pledge not to seek any alteration in the government of church or state, and not to take up arms against the king or those he commissioned. The bill intended to restrict power to conformists. Despite opposition from the earl of Bedford, Lord Wharton, Lord Delamere, and others, the House of Lords approved the bill, but the Commons balked. On 9 June Charles prorogued Parliament until October. In this context, an anonymous author, either Shaftesbury or a close ally, composed *A Letter from a Person of Quality, to His Friend in the Country,* which appears to have been published in the first week of November 1675; it was publicly burned in London on 10 November. Arguing that the Test Bill would make the government arbitrary and absolute, the author warned that passage would render the established church's polity virtually unalterable.[39] Critics of the Court such as Shaftesbury and Buckingham also pushed unsuccessfully for the dissolution of the Cavalier Parliament and new elections. When Parliament reconvened in the fall, a motion in the Commons for the king to announce a dissolution date failed, as did a similar motion in the Lords, but in the latter only by two votes. On 16 November, about the time Bunyan probably finished *The Strait Gate*, Buckingham obtained the Lords' approval to introduce a bill to tolerate Protestant dissenters. Shaftesbury too favored such a bill on the grounds that people should not be deprived of their rights because of differences over "uncertain *Opinions* of *Religion*."[40]

[37] *MW*, 5:89 (where the text uses the singular form).

[38] Arber, *Term Catalogues*, 1:216.

[39] Lacey, 77–78; Ashcraft, *Revolutionary Politics*, 122–23; *A Letter from a Person of Quality, to His Friend in the Country* (n.p., 1675).

[40] Harris, *PULS*, 58–59; PRO SP 29/375/22; *Two Speeches. I. The Earl of Shaftsbury's Speech in the House of Lords the 20th. of October, 1675. II. The D. of Buckinghams Speech in the House of Lords the 16th. of November 1675* (Amsterdam, 1675), 14 (quoted).

In the meantime Bunyan probably observed political developments in London of major interest to nonconformists. Opponents of Danby were seeking support from Londoners at a time when the lord mayor, Sir Robert Viner, a staunch ally of the Court, was engaged in a struggle with the Common Council, which included fifty dissenters in 1675. At issue in the spring of that year was the mayor's claim to the right of appointment to the shrieval court; opposing him, the Common Council asserted a right to elect its members. Many of those battling Viner were nonconformists, among them Shaftesbury's friend Thomas Papillon, to whom Ferguson had dedicated *The Interest of Reason in Religion* earlier in the year. Owen, Ferguson's senior minister, was patronized at this time by Buckingham, Shaftesbury's ally, and he enjoyed close relations with the earl of Anglesey, who had ties to Buckingham and Shaftesbury. The latter was also associated with Kiffin.[41] Thus Bunyan, with known links to Owen and Kiffin, could have readily followed issues of interest to nonconformists in the City and Parliament through these contacts as well as more general sources of information.

Written against this background, *The Strait Gate* is both a sweeping condemnation of those pseudo-Christians Bunyan associated with the policy of repression and a wake-up call to embrace Christ and the visible saints. Near the end of his work, he asserted that his purpose was to awaken both churches and professing Christians, though most of the book is a sustained castigation of the latter, including many eminent persons (5:128). Such people "will in Gods day be counted fit for nothing but to be troden down as the mire in the streets" (5:111). Throughout the tract Bunyan emphasized that few would be saved (5:69, 103, 109, 119); "'tis the devil and sin that carry away the cart-loads, while Christ and his ministers come after a gleaning" (5:107). Even preachers will be among the damned, perishing, like other reprobates, in their own dung. Not surprisingly, Bunyan expected some readers to dislike this tract (5:69). In it he distinguished between two gates, the first of which is the door of grace opened by God to the gentiles, to wit, Jesus Christ, as indicated in Acts 14:27 and John 10:9 (5:74). In *The Strait Gate* Bunyan expounded on the second door, the entrance to heaven, the straightness of which he interpreted "mistically" rather than materially. "You are not to understand it, as if the entrance into heaven was some little pinching wicket," for the gate is wide enough to accommodate all who sincerely love Christ, but no

[41] Gary S. De Krey, "London Radicals and Revolutionary Politics, 1675–1683," in *The Politics of Religion in Restoration England*, ed. Tim Harris, Paul Seaward, and Mark Goldie (Oxford: Basil Blackwell, 1990), 134–37; De Krey, "The London Whigs and the Exclusion Crisis Reconsidered," in *The First Modern Society: Essays in English History in Honour of Lawrence Stone*, ed. A. L. Beier, David Cannadine, and James M. Rosenheim (Cambridge: Cambridge University Press, 1989), 464; Ashcraft, *Revolutionary Politics*, 112–14. For Papillon see *BDBR, s.v.*; for Viner see *DNB, s.v.*

one else (5:76). At the last judgment, when the gate's straightness will be manifest to everyone, the swarms of prayerless, slothful professors, saddled by their lusts, will find no entry into God's kingdom (5:82–84, 97, 111).

With a keen eye for recognizing fundamental but disparate characteristics, Bunyan divided barren professors into a dozen groups. One comprises the *talkers*, whose religion goes no deeper than their speech, and who differ from the rest of the world's "rabble" only because they can discuss religious matters. *Covetous professors* embrace religion for monetary purposes, finding that it has "a good trade at the end of it," whereas *wanton professors* twist Scripture so they can maintain their pride, idolatry, and lust. Among the wanton are those who eat gluttonously, pretending to strengthen their frail bodies or maintain their health while in reality satiating their lusts. *Opinionists* make incidentals—*adiaphora* in the language of contemporary academics—essential for true believers. Presumably Bunyan included the Particular and General Baptists in this group because of their insistence on believer's baptism, though it also incorporated Anglicans, for "with this sort this kingdom swarms at this day." Prayer-Book Protestants, in his estimation, would also have been among the *formalists*, who embrace only the shell of religion, having neither the power nor the spirit of godliness. Beside them are the *legalists*, whose religion comprises a series of duties, and the *libertines*, who oppose "forms, and duties, as things that gender to bondage, neglecting the order of God." As Bunyan defined them, libertines pretend to pray perpetually, but in fact never pray, and claim to keep the sabbath every day, a pretense they employ to reject all set times of worship (5:85, 124–25).

Among the other groups of fruitless professors are the *Latitudinarians*. With Fowler undoubtedly still in his mind, Bunyan described "the *temporizing Latitudinarian*" as a person who has "no God but his belly, nor any religion but that by which his belly is worshiped." His religion is like a weathercock, twisting and turning on the steeple, and his conscience has been seared to numbness; he is "next door to a down right atheist." Yet other professors are *willfully ignorant*, afraid that learning more will lead to suffering for the cross; such people, maintained Bunyan, pick and choose what they believe and do, unwilling to hazard everything for Christ. Another group, the *comparators*, measure their religion by comparing themselves with others rather than the Bible, whereas *pliable professors* alter their views as fast as their companions, able to speak for both God and Baal and to "be *any* thing, for *any* company." In his final category Bunyan lumped various Protestants with whose tenets he disagreed, namely, *Arminians* because they reputedly deny the Holy Spirit's role in conversion, *Socinians* because they repudiate the doctrine that Christ's atonement satisfied God for the sins of humanity, and *Quakers* because they reject the tenet of Christ's two natures. All of these people, Bunyan insisted, will find themselves excluded from heaven (5:125–27).

*The Strait Gate* is a good example of Bunyan's embrace of Calvinism's evangelical face, or what is virtually a *de facto* 'pastoral Arminianism'. Scattered references to the elect appear in the book, though never does he discuss election in depth; indeed, this would have been impossible without altering the tenor of the work, which emphasizes the necessity of striving. The elect have divinely bestowed faith, which is "the effect of electing love, and of a new birth." Saving faith without election is an impossibility in Bunyan's theology. The kingdom of God belongs to the elect, he averred, and was prepared for them before the beginning of creation (5:100–101). He also made clear references to the reprobate, or non-elect, who have no saving faith and thus no holiness or perseverance (5:102, 108), and who manifest "the tokens of their damnation in their foreheads" (5:89). In the words of Jeremiah 6:30, such people are *"reprobate silver"* because God has rejected them; they are "the generation of his wrath" (5:109–10). Although they can believe faith in God, such faith is not a divine gift and thus has no soteriological worth (5:117–18). This is standard Calvinist fare, but the logical force of such doctrine is substantially mitigated by Bunyan's repeated emphasis on the necessity to strive, the implication of which is that people have a choice in deciding whether to exert themselves in religious matters. "Bend your selves to the work with all your might," as did Samson when he destroyed the Philistines or David when he provided for the building and beautification of the temple. "Thus must thou do if ever thou entrest into heaven" (5:80). Simultaneously, however, Bunyan maintained that only those who have given their hearts, minds, and wills to God are capable of striving. These are converted people, for a key part of effectual conversion, he argued, is turning the mind and will to Christ and loving heavenly things. Conversion in turn begins with conviction—with awakening—but not all awakened people have been converted (5:80–81, 121).

The crucial issue, then, is whether spiritually awakened individuals have the freedom and ability to turn to God—to strive to enter the kingdom. Bunyan did not explore this matter, opting instead to discuss what striving entails, and how and why his readers should exert themselves. He assumed they could respond to his exhortations by striving—by turning their minds, hearts, and wills, by running the Christian race, by fighting the good fight, and by laboring for everlasting life. Failure to contend means Satan "will assuredly have thee," for believers who cease striving will become reprobates. "Strive to believe, strive *for* the faith of the Gospel, for the more we believe the Gospel, and the realitie of the things of the world to come, with the more stomack and courage shall we labour to possess the blessedness" (5:80–85). Bunyan's primary audience is the awakened, convicted body of professors in the church who have not yet converted;[42] the force of his message urges them onward, as if the decision were theirs to make, but his Calvinist theology predicated that without election no amount of striving could enable someone to enter the straight gate.

Because the targeted audience constituted professing Christians, most of whom presumably thought of themselves as sufficiently religious to avoid eternal damnation, Bunyan took pains to distinguish between genuine awakenings, repentance, and faith on the one hand and their counterfeits on the other. Whereas awakenings drive the elect to Christ, they propel the reprobate to the law and ultimately to desperation. Although the two types of repentance are similar, the believer with saving repentance loathes sin because of its reprehensible nature, whereas one who lacks such repentance detests sin merely because it offends. The two types of faith differ in their nature, but often not in their visible manifestations. Because only God can infallibly discern between saving and imitative awakenings, repentance, and faith, the churches "sometimes hit, and sometimes miss" in determining whom to admit as members (5:115–19). Thus, not all visible saints are necessarily people with saving faith and repentance. This posed a fundamental problem, for if neither the church nor its leading members can determine with certainty who has the requisite faith and repentance, how can an individual have peace of mind with respect to eternal destiny? By striving, was Bunyan's pragmatic answer. "Idleness is natural to professors, they think to get to heaven by lying as it were on their elbows" (5:80). Undoubtedly reflecting his own devotional practices, he advised his readers to test their "graces," such as faith and repentance, to ascertain their soundness by seeking divine assistance, confessing and combating their inner corruptions, and praying for more graces (5:86–87). He also admonished them to avoid unprofitable debates and "vain ranglings," which, he thought, preoccupied many professors, and he warned against being susceptible to "every winde of doctrine" (5:82, 89). In so doing, they can find reasonable assurance of their eternal destiny.

*The Strait Gate* is an excellent example of Bunyan's tendency to recapitulate themes from his previous works. He touches here on his early controversy with the Quakers, his depiction of the new Jerusalem in *The Holy City*, the race motif in *The Heavenly Foot-Man*, and the last judgment, which he analyzed in depth in *The Resurrection of the Dead*. He makes more extended references to the role of the law, a theme he developed in *The Doctrine of the Law and Grace Unfolded*, and to the imagery of a vineyard and an unproductive fig tree, which he treated exten-

---

[42] In his conclusion, however, he does advise readers to pray for an awakened heart. *MW*, 5:129.

sively in *The Barren Fig-Tree.* Indeed, *The Strait Gate,* with its focus on fruitless professors, is essentially the latter's sequel. Moreover, its discussion of the sin against the Holy Spirit—the unpardonable sin—is the most substantive since he recorded his own fears of having committed this offense in *Grace Abounding.*[43]

Thematically, then, *The Strait Gate* blends effectively with Bunyan's earlier writings. Stylistically, however, it falls short of *The Heavenly Foot-Man* and *The Barren Fig-Tree,* primarily because of his detailed exposition of individual words, including "in": "Behold therefore what a great thing the Lord Jesus hath included by this little word, *in,* in this word is wrapt up an whole heaven, and eternal life: even as there is also by other little words in the holy Scriptures" (5:73). At times, Bunyan explicates the obvious, as in explaining that gates open and shut, admitting and excluding (5:74). His fondness for word patterns sometimes leads him to repeat excessively: "A remnant, a small remnant, a very small remnant: O how doth the holy Ghost word it, and all to shew you, how few shall be saved: every one knows, what a remnant is, but this is a *small* remnant, a *very* small remnant" (5:108).[44] Such repetition, perhaps effective in the pulpit, is numbing in print. In what Graham Midgley imaginatively calls "constipated crumbling," Bunyan's syntax occasionally breaks down: "First, An Intimation of the kingdom of heaven, for when he saith, *strive to enter in*; and in such phrases there is supposed a place or state or both to be enjoyed; enter *in,* enter into what, or whether but into a state or place or both"; the sentence continues for another eight lines (5:xliii, 73). Unlike *The Heavenly Foot-Man* and *The Barren Fig-Tree, The Strait Gate* lacks narrative possibilities, and Bunyan eschewed the opportunity to personalize some of his concepts, as he did with death in *The Barren Fig-Tree.* The Mosaic law appears fleetingly as a roaring lion, and armed porters guard the entry to heaven, but nothing is made of either possibility to create dramatic interest (5:77–79). One notable exception is his depiction of the doomed professors as they reach heaven's gate at the last judgment:

> Lord, Lord, *open unto us.* The devils are coming; Lord, Lord, the pit opens her mouth upon us: Lord, Lord there is nothing but hell and damnation left us, if Lord, Lord thou hast not mercy upon *us.* (5:98)

Another are the doleful, haunting words Bunyan puts in the mouth of a professor who mistakenly thinks he is destined for heaven:

> *I was at the gates of heaven, I looked into heaven, I thought I should have entered into heaven! O how will these things sting!* (5:129)

[43] *MW,* 5:75, 90, 99, 120–21 (last judgment); 78 (new Jerusalem); 79, 125 (law); 94 (unpardonable sin); 106 (race motif); 110, 120 (vineyard and fig tree); 127 (Quakers).

[44] I am indebted to Graham Midgley for his incisive remarks on Bunyan's literary style.

Few such passages grace the pages of *The Strait Gate*, making it one of Bunyan's more pedestrian works.

Stylistically, Bunyan's writings in general and his sermons in particular do not manifest a steady pattern of continued improvement, though nearly all have at least some passages that evince his literary skill and imagination. It is worth remembering that numerous pastoral responsibilities and his own devotional life made claims on his time, energy, and emotions. Although *The Strait Gate* is far from his most appealing works, it unambiguously reveals his somber assessment of the state of English religious life in 1675.

### "Venture Heartily"[45]: Preaching Grace

The emergence of a clearly articulated Country platform in Parliament and a civic opposition in London by late 1675 sharpened the rhetoric of discontent and prompted countermeasures by the state.[46] On 7 January 1676 the government issued a proclamation intended to repress seditious and scandalous libels by offering a reward of £20 to anyone who reported where they had been transcribed or printed, and £50 for information about the authors and those who delivered libels to printers or transcribers. The following day another proclamation gave coffeehouse proprietors two days to report those selling, reading, or distributing libels against the government or the Church of England. Within days the magistrates were searching for alleged offenders in the London area, and in March they seized bundles of reputedly seditious literature imported from the Netherlands.[47] By 16 January officials had apprehended one of Bunyan's acquaintances, the elusive Henry Danvers, and confined him in the Tower for treasonable offenses. Because of his ill health, the government ordered his release on payment of £1,000 security, though he was confined to his house, where Bunyan perhaps visited him. In the meantime, Secretary of State Joseph Williamson was monitoring the activities of Shaftesbury and his friends in London, including Sir Robert Clayton and Sir Robert Peyton. L'Estrange received instructions in March to seize all copies of *A Letter from a Person of Quality*, Shaftesbury's anonymously published *Two Seasonable Discourses Concerning This Present Parliament* (1675), and *Two Speeches* by Buckingham and Shaftesbury. Once again, the archbishop of Canterbury instructed the bishops in his province to inquire how many Protestant nonconformists as well as Catholic recusants lived in each parish, and in May the

[45] *MW*, 8:223.

[46] Harris, *PULS*, 58–59; De Krey, "London Radicals and Revolutionary Politics," 134–35.

[47] PRO, SP 29/378/35.1, 76, 77, 79; London *Gazette* 1059 (10–13 January 1676); *CSPD, 1675–76*, 503, 511; BL, Stowe MSS 745, fol. 113r.

magistrates arrested various dissenting preachers in London and closed some of the City halls in which they had been meeting.[48]

During this period Bunyan's father, Thomas, still a brazier at Elstow, died on 7 February 1676. There was some warning, for he had made his will, signing with a mark on 22 January; presumably he had been unable to read any of his son's works. To each of his children—John, Thomas, Mary, and Elizabeth—he left a shilling, with the remainder of his possessions to his wife Anne. He died in poverty, as reflected also by the fact that he had been exempted from the hearth tax in 1673–74.[49] Of Bunyan's thoughts on his father's death we know nothing, but one passage in the book he was writing at the time, *Saved by Grace: or, a Discourse of the Grace of God*, may reflect how he saw his father's final days. Interpreting the ministering spirits in Hebrews 1:14 as angels, he described how they take charge of the soul of the dying saint and "conduct it safely into *Abraham's* bosom: 'tis not our meanness in the world, nor our weakness of Faith that shall hinder this; nor shall the loathsomness of our Diseases make these delicate Spirits shy of taking this charge upon them." Of what, we wonder, did his father die? He may have perished in some spiritual distress, for Bunyan wrote that "Sick Bed Temptations are oft-times the most violent, because then the Devil plays his last Game with us." Although the will contains no hint of spiritual struggle, such documents often tended to be almost formulaic, and in any event there was ample time for doubt in the sixteen days between making the will and death. In the end the angels reputedly spirit the soul away, enabling Bunyan to think, perhaps, that his father has been taken to heaven (*MW*, 8:178). Whether he wrote this passage with his father in mind we may never know.

The government's crackdown on dissent in early 1676 may explain why *Saved by Grace* was an innocuous exposition of the doctrine of salvation *sola gratia*. Printed for Francis Smith, it was licensed on 12 June 1676.[50] Another expanded sermon, it entailed an exposition of Ephesians 2:5, articulating the thesis that God has freely chosen the elect to manifest divine glory in their salvation. For the most part, Bunyan addressed his remarks to the unconverted, reflecting his evangelical Calvinism. Fundamentally, however, he framed his comments in the context of the Reformed doctrine of predestination, with an emphasis on the elect. They are saved, he avers, even before God calls them; God "appointed them their portion and measure of grace, and that before the World began" (8:173). No one

---

[48] PRO, SP 44/28, fols. 148r, 153r; SP 29/379/39, 43; Bodl., Carte MSS 228, fol. 101r–v; *CSPD 1676–77*, 51; Bodl., Carte MSS 79, fol. 22r; BL, Harleian MSS 7377, fol. 61r; BL, Stowe MSS 209, fol. 237v. For Clayton see *BDBR*, *s.v.*

[49] Brown, 292–93.

[50] Arber, *Term Catalogues*, 1:245.

has the ability to believe on her or his own, for faith and repentance are divine gifts (8:173–74, 200, 218). God makes the elect believe while refusing grace to others, even blinding sinners to assure their damnation (8:195, 226). Yet, as Bunyan had done so often before, he did not let his predestinarian convictions keep him from suggesting to his audience that they could and should respond to the gospel of grace (8:198). The implication is clearly that people have the ability to repent, though such an assumption flies in the face of the Reformed doctrine of predestination that informs this work. Once the elect believe and repent, God's sustaining grace enables them to persevere; he is "engaged, either by power to keep them from falling, or by grace, to pardon if they fall, and to lift them up again" (8:175–76). Echoes of earlier controversies still reverberate, as in his denunciation of the Latitudinarian position on justification, his insistence on an Anselmic view of the atonement, his condemnation of the Quaker doctrine of the divine light in every person, his reiteration of the contrast between gospel simplicity and worldly sophistry, and his denunciation of unnecessary religious ceremonies (8:174, 193, 210, 214, 219, 221). He aimed the last of these points not only at Prayer-Book Protestants but also at Particular and General Baptists, for he likened certain contemporaries to "the false Apostles [who] urged Circumcision of old, saying, unless you do these things, ye cannot be saved" (8:221). As we have seen, traditional Baptists compared baptism to circumcision, the "visible door of entrance into the Old testament-church," as Danvers had argued.[51]

Saved by Grace is essentially autobiographical in its rendition of God's dealings with the elect. Bunyan's account moves from the initial conviction of sin and the sinner's preference for sports and pleasures, to an increasing sense of sin, and to the quest for peace through good works and superficial religiosity (8:202–4). "But all this while he is as ignorant of Christ, as the stool he sits on, and no nearer Heaven then was the blind *Pharisee*, only he is got in a cleaner way to Hell, than the rest of his Neighbours are" (8:204). Gaining a fuller realization of his "nothingness," the sinner plunges into despair, "and now he falls"—the same sickening sense of falling Bunyan had once experienced. Like a man with millstones on his shoulders, the sinner sinks further, dragged down by doubts and fear of damnation. "He sinks in his heart, he dies in his thoughts, he doubts, he despairs, and concludes, he shall never be saved" (8:204–5). Although God provides temporary relief through a sense of forgiveness, doubt and despair return, tormenting the sinner's mind "with a thousand fears of perishing, for he hears not a word from Heaven, perhaps for several Weeks together" (8:205). When the Devil warns of the futility of the tormented soul's efforts to be religious, the sinner loses virtually all hope. At last, the Holy Spirit bestows grace and pardon on

[51] H[enry] D[anvers], *Treatise of Baptism* (London, 1673), 27–28.

the sinner, who has "such a sight of the grace of God in Christ, as kindly breaks his heart with joy and comfort" (8:206). Calm and sunshine flood the soul, and though temporary apostasy is still possible, God will enable the believer to return to him and persevere (8:206–7). This passage effectively captures the essence of Bunyan's religious experience as recounted in *Grace Abounding*, and in so doing it provides a valuable example of how he utilized that experience to give his sermons an air of authority no less convincing—and perhaps more so—than the pulpit offerings of the formally learned.

Bunyan's preaching could also be compelling because at times he displayed an extraordinary sense of cadence. One particularly fine example merits quoting *in extenso*:

> Thou Son of the Blessed, What Grace was manifest in thy Condescention? Grace brought thee down from Heaven, Grace stript thee of thy Glory, Grace made thee Poor and Despicable, Grace made thee bear such burdens of Sin, such burdens of Sorrow, such burdens of God's Curse as is unspeakable: O Son of God! Grace was in all thy Tears, Grace came bubling out of thy side with the Blood, Grace came forth with every word of thy sweet Mouth. . . . Grace came out where the Whip smote thee, where the Thorns prickt thee, where the Nails and Spear pierced thee: O Blessed Son of God! Here is Grace indeed! Unsearchable Riches of Grace! Unthought of Riches of Grace! Grace to make Angels wonder, Grace to make Sinners happy, Grace to astonish Devils. (8:191)

Delivered with conviction and feeling, these words must have evoked responsive chords in Bunyan's audience.

Many of the themes in *Saved by Grace*, which Charles Doe later praised as "the best Book that was ever writ or I read, except the *Bible*,"[52] echo but add nothing to Bunyan's development of them in earlier works. However, he broke new ground when he postulated that in heaven the memories of the elect will recall "with unspeakable aptness . . . all God's Providences, all Sathan's Malice, all our own Weaknesses, all the rage of Men," and how God made everything work for divine glory and the saints' good (8:180). His persecutors, he believed, would live eternally in his memory even as they suffered hell's unfathomable horrors.

After completing *Saved by Grace*, Bunyan probably spent most of the remainder of 1676 in the London area. The records of the Bedford congregation do not mention him between 29 August 1672, when his absence was noted, and 11 December 1676, when his name, with others, is affixed to a letter to Fitten's congregation in London.[53] Generally the entries in this period deal with disciplinary matters and the admission of new members; hence the absence of his name does

---

[52] Charles Doe, *A Collection of Experience of the Work of Grace* (London, [1700]), 57.
[53] *CB*, 74–80.

not necessarily mean he was away from Bedford. However, he is likely to have stayed away throughout most of 1676 owing to his excommunication and the threat of a writ *de excommunicato capiendo*.

Bunyan's probable absence from Bedford and seclusion in the London area during the latter half of 1676 would explain why he ignored the challenge to debate John Child, a former member of the Bedford congregation. In 1658 Child had left that group to join the Baptists, and in the ensuing decades he preached in Bedfordshire, Buckinghamshire, and Hertfordshire.[54] In 1676 Benjamin Harris published Child's *A Moderate Message to Quakers, Seekers, and Socinians, by a Friend and Well-Wisher to Them All,* in which he defended the practice of baptism by water as a required duty for all Christians. His rationale for having left the Bedford congregation was his belief that removing or altering a gospel ceremony, such as believer's baptism, was dangerous because such action facilitated the introduction of innovations in worship. Defensive about his lack of ordination, he averred that this was not essential for a minister, citing the examples of John the Baptist, the apostle Paul, and the saints who preached after Stephen's death. On this point Bunyan would have concurred. Like the latter, Child was sensitive too about his lack of a formal theological education, for he closed the body of his book with a plea and a pun: "If any shall contest with me about the premises, I beseech them to do it as with a child, even a babe in Religion." Throughout the pamphlet he made no references to Bunyan, but he appended a postscript offering to debate three questions with him before any audience *"in City or Countrey"*: whether Christ "Instituted a certain order to be oberserv'd by his followers in the administration of Gospel ordinances"; whether baptism by water must precede participation in the Lord's supper; and, if so, whether Bunyan or others could presume to reject this order? There is no evidence to suggest that Bunyan accepted Child's challenge to dispute these issues.[55]

In the London area and perhaps beyond, Bunyan would have preached in 1676 when he had the opportunity. One such sermon may have been the nucleus of the tract *Of Justification by an Imputed Righteousness,* which was never published in his lifetime. From the history of *The Heavenly Foot-Man* and the first part of *The Pilgrim's Progress* we know that sometimes he delayed publication, and such was presumably the case with *Of Justification by an Imputed Righteousness.* The theme had been at the heart of his debate with Fowler, and he noted the

[54] James Jones, *Modesty and Faithfulness in Opposition to Envy and Rashness* (London, 1683), 2.

[55] John Child, *A Moderate Message to Quakers, Seekers, and Socinians, by a Friend and Well-Wisher to Them All* ([London], 1676), 3, 28, 51–52, 74–75 (quoted). Child had sufficient education to use syllogisms in his writing.

doctrine in other works of the early 1670s, ranging from his *Confession of My Faith* to *Saved by Grace*. Moreover, in *Of Justification* he refers to "our Adversaries" in the imputation debate, specifically their contention that the Bible does not impute righteousness to people unless they are truly so (*MW*, 12:301). He was alluding to the doctrinal positions of Fowler and Penn[56]; hence, *Of Justification* was very likely written in the 1670s rather than the 1680s. Noting the more systematic, comprehensive treatment of the doctrine in *Of Justification*, W. R. Owens cogently concludes that it postdates Bunyan's *Defence of the Doctrine of Justification* (12:xxv). *Of Justification* may provisionally be dated between about July and November 1676, following the completion of *Saved by Grace*.

Apart from the direct reference to his adversaries in the controversy over imputed righteousness, various passages in *Of Justification* echo that debate, particularly Bunyan's insistence that good works cannot make one righteous in God's sight, for "by this *we* should make *our selves* the Saviours, and jostle *Christ* quite *out* of doors" (12:296, 300). In contrast to his opponents, he continued to insist that any repentance not bestowed by God was worthless and a cause for remorse (12:316). Likewise, he remained firm in rejecting Fowler's belief that Jesus should be an exemplar "in keeping the Law for Life" (12:318) since righteousness was wholly a matter of undeserved grace. In fact, Bunyan typically disparaged the law, pronouncing it void of grace and mercy, and warning of its capacity "to delude, by its real Holiness, the Understanding, Conscience, and Reason of a Man" (12:327). As he knew from experience, the law, with its unrelenting demands for obedience, could overwhelm a soul with guilt and horror for its transgressions, imposing a veil that obscures the gospel's promises. What he wrote of David is fundamentally autobiographical: "When *David's* Guilt, for Murther and Blood, did roar by the Law in his Conscience, notwithstanding he knew much of the Grace of the Gospel, he could hear nothing else but Terror, the sound of *Blood*" (12:325). Although Bunyan had not sent anyone to his death, as David had Uriah, the law was terrifying simply because *any* infraction resulted in the same punishment—ultimate damnation. The influence of Luther's commentary on Galatians was still as much a part of his outlook in the 1670s as it had been two decades earlier. To obey the moral law as a condition of justification renders one accursed in God's judgment; indeed, the law and good works actually hinder justification (12:286, 333). Even beyond the process of justification, he believed God's people had "too much to do with the Law," for it "is now in the Conscience, imposing Duty upon the Carnal part: This is the Reason of the Noise that you hear, and of the Sin that you see, and of the Honour that you feel in your own Souls

---

[56] Edward Fowler, *The Design of Christianity* (London, 1671), 5, 19–20; [Fowler or his surrogate], *Dirt Wip't Off* (London, 1672), 48–49; Penn, *Sandy Foundation*, 24, 30.

when tempted" (12:316). At this point, Bunyan, driven by his sense of the law's ability to strike terror in susceptible hearts, was very close to Antinomianism.

Even in this rather formal work, autobiographical insights abound. So traumatic was his protracted conversion crisis that it shaped his preaching and writing throughout his career. His near drowning provided an analogy for those who, devoid of saving faith, clung to the law, while his battles with depression seem to have intensified his rendition of the law as a blinding force that keeps people in the depths of darkness and despair (12:324–26). "So long as Guilt is on the Conscience, so long remains the Blindness: For Guilt standing before the Soul, the Grace of God is intercepted, even as the Sun is hid from the sight of mine Eyes, *by the Cloud that cometh between*" (12:326). From the profound struggle with despondency came the imagery to warn his audience of the law's awesome power to hold sinners in a bondage as black as the darkest night. But as he also knew from experience, the law could instruct by persuading transgressors to admit their offenses: "This is a hard pinch, (I know what I say,) for a Man to fall down under the sense of Sin, by acknowledging them to be, what the Lord saith they are" (12:337).

Bunyan lightened the somber theological arguments in *Of Justification* with interest-catching analogies. We have embarked in a ship with Christ, he told believers (12:342). As the refuge of afflicted, sick, and wounded people, the church is a hospital (12:336). Unbelief, the sin that most easily besets Christians, is a finely spun thread, unlike the "grosser" offenses, whereas believing, to alter the analogy, is the noblest of actions because it crowns the head of grace (12:301, 343). Just as sparks fly when steel strikes flint, so sins become manifest when the law assails a carnal heart (12:316). Christ's fulfillment of the law for the elect is likened by Bunyan to an attorney who acts on behalf of his client, and the last judgment is the Great Assize (12:288, 348). Those who face that assize without having trusted in Christ are like a madman laden with combustible matter who runs headlong into a fire "upon a bravado" (12:351). Such easily remembered analogies enabled Bunyan to drive home his theological points.

Although he faced possible arrest if he returned to Bedford and ecclesiastical officials obtained a writ *de excommunicato capiendo*, Bunyan continued to make caustic remarks about the Church of England. He accused formalists of seeking vain glory: "They love to have Honour one of another; they love to be commended for their own vain-glorious Righteousness; and the Fools think, that because they are commended of Men, they shall be commended of God also" (12:349).[57] He was probably thinking of Fowler and the Cambridge Platonists

---

[57] Cf. Thomas Watson's reproof of a formalist as one "who puts all his Religion in gestures, and vestures, emblems of devotion," which are mostly "in punctilioes, and niceties." *Heaven Taken by Storm* (London, 1669), 96–97.

when he condemned legalists and merit-mongers who thought their seemingly moral acts were essential prerequisites for justification (12: 313, 317, 346). The false apostles in Paul's day who fraudulently called themselves ministers and misappropriated gospel language to preach their evil message were akin to contemporary Anglican clergy; by urging obedience to the law rather than relying wholly on Christ's imputed righteousness, such ministers poisoned the people, dishonored Christ, and were false spirits (12:327, 341). Those who take refuge in formal religiosity will ultimately perish: "He is a religious Man, for he prays; he is a seeking Man, a desiring Man, for he prays; But he halts between two, he leaneth to his Righteousness, and *committeth iniquity*. . . . Let not that Man think of receiving any thing from the Lord." Although such formally religious people are not openly profane, Bunyan warned that God will deal with them in the same manner as idolaters, murderers, liars, and fornicators (12:347). However, his criticism of the established church was less pronounced in *Of Justification* than some of his earlier works because of this book's more formal organization as a sustained argument. Ever the pastor, he concluded the book with an evangelical appeal, urging sinners to awake, cry to God for light, and seriously meditate on eternal judgment, implying that the choice of fate is theirs (12:348–49).

## "What Chaines So Heavy?"[58]: Evangelical Outreach

If *Of Justification* was written in late 1676, Bunyan was apparently thinking of returning to Bedford despite the risk of incarceration, for in the book he insists that wearing a chain for Christ is not shameful (12:342). If he was still in London in the latter half of 1676, as seems probable, he would have observed the increasing tension between Court and Country, partly over religious concerns. On 24 June Francis Jenks, a Cornhill linendraper, made a speech in the Guildhall exhorting the lord mayor to convene the Common Council with the intent of petitioning the king for a new Parliament. The Catholics, Jenks feared, were plotting to place James on the throne, thereby imperiling Protestantism, property, liberty, and lives. Rushed into print, the speech received widespread attention.[59] Jenks had the support of Sir Robert Peyton, Sir Thomas Player, and probably Buckingham, to whom he had been introduced by the erstwhile Leveller John Wildman. Jenks' father-in-law, William Walwyn, was another former Leveller leader. For more than three months Jenks was imprisoned in the Gatehouse, and on 9 July Sir Joseph Williamson ordered L'Estrange to search for and confiscate copies of

---

[58] *MW*, 8:269.

[59] PRO, SP 29/382/142; *CSPD, 1676–77*, 193–94; *Account of the Proceedings at Guild-Hall, London, . . . Held 24th. of June 1676* [London, 1676], 9–13.

the speech.[60] Jenks belonged to the Green Ribbon Club, whose membership included various nonconformists, critics of the Court, and friends of Buckingham and Shaftesbury. Another club member, John Freke, a Shaftesbury ally, had been committed to the Tower on charges of high treason on 28 May for having published *The Chronicle*, which harshly criticized the king.[61]

As the government stepped up surveillance, it monitored conventicles and cracked down on unlicensed publishing. In August government agents raided the shops of bookbinders and booksellers to seize unlicensed material and arrest offenders. Nevertheless, printed matter critical of the established church as well as the government continued to circulate, prompting Williamson to renew efforts to suppress it in October. Tighter control over the press may explain why *Of Justification* was not published, especially since Bunyan's preferred printer at this time, Francis Smith, had a record of trouble with the authorities. Still, *Of Justification* should not have incurred opposition from a licenser.[62]

By December 1676 Bunyan had returned to Bedford. Having not appeared in the archdeacon's court within forty days of his excommunication in April 1675, he was subject to arrest on a writ *de excommunicato capiendo*, which the bishop of Lincoln procured from the Chancery. The sheriff of Bedfordshire thereupon arrested him and confined him in jail. If this second imprisonment lasted six months, as Doe indicates, it would have commenced in December, probably sometime after the 11th when he signed a letter to Fitten's church in London. However, his name is also affixed to letters dated 7 February 1677 to the church at Braintree, Essex, and 29 March 1677 to the congregation at Hitchin, Hertfordshire.[63] Either Bunyan's confinement was not close, enabling him to attend various meetings during this period, or someone brought the letters to him in prison for his approval.

The writ *de excommunicato capiendo* under which Bunyan was incarcerated did not provide for relief by *habeas corpus*, and the imprisonment was consequently of indeterminate length. Legally, release was possible if the prisoner provided "caution," which in the late seventeenth century could entail taking an oath or having sureties post a bond with the bishop, typically in the amount of £10 or £20. To initiate the process a prisoner obtained a writ *de cautione admittenda*, which required the payment of fees and sometimes the filing of motions, a source

[60]De Krey, "London Radicals and Revolutionary Politics," 138–40; *CSPD, 1676–77*, 215. See also *CSPD, 1676–77*, 251–52, 285. For Player, Wildman, and Walwyn see *BDBR, s.vv.*; for Wildman see also *New DNB, s.v.*

[61] De Krey, "London Radicals and Revolutionary Politics," 142; Greaves, *SOK*, 98; PRO, SP 44/28, fol. 157r; BL, Stowe MSS 209, fols. 261r, 309r.

[62]*CSPD, 1676–77*, 274, 362; Hill, *TPM*, 286–87; Greaves, *EUHF*, 182.

[63]*CB*, 79–80, 82–83; Charles Doe, "The Struggler," in *MW*, 12:454; Brown, 241.

of additional expense. Once obtained, the writ was tendered to the bishop, and if he were unresponsive, to the sheriff, and as a last resort to the coroner. Depending largely on the attitude of the bishop and possibly the sheriff, the process of obtaining a release could entail substantial expense and delay. The abuses prompted demands to remove what someone in Wharton's circle called "a nationall guilt of Oppression upon us." He summarized the case for reform thus: "Multitudes are deprived of theire Liberty, theire familyes and Estates by it [are] ruined at the commands of the Civill magistrate (who hath never had the least Cognizance of the Causes) and to Justifie the Church mans abominable Profanation of a most solemne ordinance of God[,] I meane Excommunication pronounced by a Civill Lawyer in causes not to be warranted by Gods word, or any right Reason."[64] Presumably Bunyan would have concurred, and in any event these were the legal circumstances in which he now found himself.

It was probably during this incarceration that Bunyan revised *Grace Abounding* for the fourth edition.[65] Although no copy apparently survived, it is more conceivable that he made the substantive changes for this edition rather than the fifth, which appeared in 1680, partly because confinement again provided time for spiritual introspection, and partly because the most important change—the addition of twelve new paragraphs refuting slanderous allegations—is more likely to have been made within three years of the Agnes Beaumont episode than six. Among the new material are paragraphs dealing with his neighbors' amazement at his apparent conversion (§32) and the errors of the Quakers (§§124–25), but he also added accounts of a two-year period in which he sensed damnation (§142), his weariness with life yet his fear of dying (§149), and his recognition that God sometimes allows the elect to experience grievous temptations, though he was concerned that he was not among their number (§157). He also recounted the profound despair he experienced by reading about Spira (§163), and he provided additional details about looking to see if God were following him with a pardon in his hand (§173), the mysterious experience of hearing a voice like a rushing wind (§174), his preoccupation with thoughts of having committed the unpardonable sin (§183), and his ultimate realization that he had not (§188). Not all reaction to *Grace Abounding* was favorable, for he reported that some people thought his religious doubts were ridiculous (§184). The most striking new paragraphs deal with various allegations that had been made against him, including

[64] Bodl., Carte MSS 77, fols. 611r, 617r (quoted), 629r.
[65] The fact that the third edition was reprinted in 1679 (Arber, *Term Catalogues*, 1:363–64) does not rule out publication of a fourth edition about 1677. A version of the fifth edition of *The Pilgrim's Progress* was published in 1682, following the sixth and seventh editions in 1681.

charges that he was a witch, a Jesuit, and a highway robber. But his attention, as
we have seen, was dominated by accusations of sexual improprieties and bigamy,
which he attributed to efforts to render his preaching ineffectual. Seeking to turn
these charges to his advantage, he wore them like a badge of honor: "I bind these
lies and slanders to me as an ornament, it belongs to my Christian Profession, to
be villified, slandered, reproached and reviled: . . . I rejoyce in reproaches for
Christs sake" But the allegations and rumors had their effect, for he found himself reluctant even to touch a woman's hand or treat a woman pleasantly (§§306–
17).

Information about Bunyan's release from prison is found in the memoir of
John Owen by John Asty, whose source was Sir John Hartopp, Owen's close
friend.[66] According to Asty (who misdated the event to 1678 and erroneously associated it with Bunyan's lengthy period of incarceration), one of Bunyan's
friends persuaded Owen to give Thomas Barlow, bishop of Lincoln and Owen's
former tutor at Queen's College, Oxford, a letter or bond from the friend on
Bunyan's behalf. When Owen did so, Barlow demurred, insisting that Owen obtain an order from the chancellor, Heneage Lord Finch, directing the bishop to
release Bunyan after receipt of a cautionary bond. Fearing a hostile reaction from
his enemies, Barlow was unwilling to act on his own. Although reluctant to pursue this course because of the expense to Bunyan, Owen finally did so, obtaining
Finch's order for Barlow to liberate Bunyan.[67] In considering the case, Barlow
seems to have acquired copies of several of Bunyan's books, including *Light for
Them That Sit in Darkness* and *Instruction for the Ignorant*, which he subsequently
donated to the Bodleian Library. Some confirmation of Barlow's role is provided
by the author of "A Continuation of Mr. Bunyan's Life," appended to the seventh
edition of *Grace Abounding* (1692), in which he reported that Bunyan's patience
persuaded the bishop and other churchmen to free him.[68]

[66] Toon, *God's Statesman*, 5.

[67] John Asty, "Memoirs of the Life of John Owen, D.D.," in John Owen, *A Complete
Collection of the Sermons of the Reverend and Learned John Owen, D.D.* (London, 1721),
xxx.

[68] Brown, 242; *GA*, v; "A Continuation of Mr. Bunyan's Life," in *GA*, 168. In February
1680 Barlow offered to loan any of his books to the archbishop of Canterbury. If this was
his general practice, it raises the possibility that other Anglicans could have borrowed
some of Bunyan's books from him. Bodl., Tanner MSS 38, fol. 131r. An avid collector of
books and manuscripts, Barlow acquired a number of nonconformist works, including
volumes by Danvers, Knollys, Ferguson, Thomas Grantham, Jeremiah Burroughs, William Greenhill, George Whitehead, and Bunyan's erstwhile associate Nehemiah Coxe.
Bodl., Wood MSS 8535.

The cautionary bond for Bunyan's release, dated 21 June 1677, includes the names of two sureties, Thomas Kelsey (or Kelsay), the former Cromwellian major-general for Kent and Surrey, and Robert Blaney, clerk to the Haberdashers' Company from 1654 to 1662, an attorney, and now or somewhat later a member of the Green Ribbon Club. In February 1664 a government informer reported that Blaney was living in London, where dissidents consulted him frequently. An MP for Sandwich in 1654 and Dover in 1656 and 1659, Kelsey fled to the Netherlands at the Restoration. After obtaining a pardon in February 1672, he settled in London as a brewer and by February 1676 was attending Owen's congregation in Leadenhall Street. Earlier in his career he had been a member of John Simpson's congregation, which, as we have seen, was a place recommended by the Bedford church for members moving to London.[69] In 1677 Kelsey and Blaney lived in the parish of St. Giles, Cripplegate, where Cokayne ministered to a congregation in Red Cross Street. Cokayne may have been the friend who persuaded Owen to intervene with Barlow on Bunyan's behalf.[70] Shortly after Kelsey and Blaney provided security, Bunyan was released, thanks in part to a former Cromwellian major-general and an associate whose radical associations in the City would lead to his involvement in the Rye House conspiracy in the early 1680s.

Following his release Bunyan had to behave circumspectly, for his bond empowered Bishop Barlow, the archdeacon of Bedford, or the latter's assistant to summon and compel him to conform to the Church of England. Moreover, his congregation was again experiencing persecution, for the constables presented various members at the sessions in August 1677 for recusancy. In the absence of the relevant borough records it is impossible to ascertain whether Bunyan and other members living in the town were similarly affected, but some of the dissenters with whom he had been imprisoned in the 1660s, such as John Wright and George Farr of Blunham, were among those presented by the constables.[71] In

[69] Godber, "The Imprisonments of John Bunyan," 29–30; PRO, SP 29/93/3; *BDBR, s.v.* Thomas Kelsey; *CB*, 30. Blaney's name is not on the list of members for the period 1678–81 in "The Journall of the Green Ribbon-Clubb at the King's Head Taverne over against the Temple in Fleet-Street," Pepys Library, Cambridge, Misc. MSS 7, but following his arrest in 1685, Nathaniel Wade provided the names of other members, including Blaney. BL, Harleian MSS 6845, fol. 282r. For Wade see *BDBR, s.v.*

[70] Godber, "The Imprisonments of John Bunyan," 30. No membership list for Cokayne's church in the late 1670s is extant, making it impossible to ascertain if Kelsey and Blaney belonged to his congregation.

[71] BLA, MSS HSA 1677 S/10, 18. The members of Bunyan's congregation who were presented include Henry Man, William Langley, Edward Stratton (or Straton), John Croker, Ruth Beech, and Robert Holstock.

the county as a whole, the constabulary accused 124 people of recusancy, some of whom were Catholics, a substantial increase from the summer of 1670 (87) and especially that of 1672 (17), following the Declaration of Indulgence.[72]

Conditions in Bedford itself were probably not very hostile to nonconformity at this point, for in September 1677 Bunyan's colleague John Fenne became a member of the Common Council and was admitted to the office of chamberlain in the corporation after taking the oaths of allegiance and supremacy and subscribing the declaration against the Solemn League and Covenant. In taking the oath of supremacy he acknowledged that the king was the lawful head of the Church of England, thus seemingly conceding the legitimacy of the established church. Unless he meant nothing more than recognizing the king's headship of an institution *claiming* to be a church, this would have put him at variance with Bunyan, who had repeatedly denounced the Church of England, not least for its persecutory policies and unscriptural worship. The Bedford church book does not indicate how this difference in judgment—if one existed—was resolved, or even if it triggered dissension within the congregation. The church certainly did not excommunicate or censor Fenne, who continued to hold office in the corporation until September 1683—as bailiff in 1678–79 and 1680–81, and as a common councilman in 1679–80 and 1681–83.[73] The congregation's willingness to accommodate such service, which required Fenne to take the requisite oaths, suggests Bunyan's tolerance on this issue, perhaps because he recognized the value of having a dissenter's voice in the corporation.

Although the Bedford church book does not mention Bunyan's name until 2 November 1680, when the congregation condemned John Wildman of Bedford for slandering him, he probably continued his preaching. The king ordered conventicles prosecuted in November 1677, but again the task was substantial. At Taunton the followers of the Presbyterian George Newton physically threatened magistrates in the street, and one of them grabbed an officer by the cravat and struck him in the face. The bishop of Bath and Wells complained to Secretary of State Coventry that dissenters were throwing libels into the houses of Anglican magistrates and ministers, and he protested that the number of conventicles was actually growing in his diocese.[74]

Probably about this time, Bunyan, having decided to publish *The Pilgrim's*

[72] BLA, MSS 1670 S/1, 4; 1672 S/9, 10, 12; 1677 S/10–13, 15, 17, 18. Most of the time the constables did not distinguish between Protestant and Catholic recusants.

[73] BLA, Bedford Corporation Minute Book, 1664–1688, fols. 148, 150, 159, 162, 176, 186, 189, 200, 214.

[74] Longleat, Coventry MSS 7, fols. 128v, 130r, 132r; 11, fol. 185r; see also 7, fol. 126v. For Newton see *Calamy Revised, s.v.*

*Progress*, took the manuscript to Nathaniel Ponder in London. The son of the founder of the Independent church at Rothwell, Northamptonshire, in 1656, Ponder had helped many dissenting clergy obtain licenses in 1672, including one for John Whitman to preach at Cokayne's house in Cotton End, Bedfordshire. For printing Marvell's *Mr. Smirke; or, the Divine in Mode* in 1676, Ponder was indicted on 10 May, though he was released on the 26th after providing a bond of £500 and two sureties. Owen, whose works he published, perhaps introduced him to Bunyan.[75] The friends who read *The Pilgrim's Progress* and advised Bunyan about publishing it probably included Owen, Cokayne, Ferguson (owing to his relationship with Owen and his interest in metaphorical language), Griffith, and Palmer. As we have seen, the allegory was entered in the Stationers' Register on 22 December. While in London Bunyan may have heard reports of the crackdown on conventicles in western England, an announcement about which was made to Griffith's congregation. In conversations with Owen, Bunyan would have learned that the latter anticipated a period of major persecution: "I am persuaded, Brethren, the day is coming, the day is nowe at hand, wherein you will stand in need of all the Experiences that ever you had of the Presence of God with you, and his Protection of you." Word spread too about new instructions to the lord mayor regarding the suppression of illegal religious gatherings in London.[76] Conditions were not propitious for Bunyan to remain in London very long, yet his own congregation continued to face persecution. Although there is no evidence that he was personally affected by the new crackdown, this may again be due to the loss of the borough's legal records. Certainly some members of his church who lived outside Bedford were presented for recusancy at the sessions in March 1678,[77] and in the county as a whole the number of presentments continued to rise, this time to 157 people.[78]

Following his second imprisonment, Bunyan prepared a greatly expanded

[75] Hill, *TPM*, 289–90; Beth Lynch, "*Mr. Smirke* and 'Mr. Filth': A Bibliographic Case Study in Nonconformist Printing," *The Library*, 7th ser., 1 (March 2000): 51–52; Longleat, Coventry MSS 11, fol. 128r.

[76] DWL, MSS L6/3, sermon of John Owen on Psalm 90:11 (18 October 1677) (quoted); PRO, SP 29/398/131. Information compiled for the bishop of London in October identified sixteen Fifth Monarchist congregations in London and Southwark, but some of these appear to have been traditional Baptist groups. BL, Add. MSS 28,093, fol. 212.

[77] BLA, MSS HSA 1678 W/7, 8, 12, 15; Godber, "The Imprisonments of John Bunyan," 30–31; *CB*, 85; BL, Add. MSS 25,124, fol. 130r. The members of Bunyan's congregation presented in March 1678 included John Wildman (for operating an unlicensed school), Ruth Beech, Edward Stratton, William Langley, Benjamin Goodman, and possibly Sister Cooper of Clapham.

[78] BLA, MSS HSA 1678 W/6–9, 11–16.

version of his sermon *Come, & Welcome, to Jesus Christ* for the press. The composition of this work can be provisionally dated between July or August 1677 and March 1678. Initially published by Benjamin Harris,[79] it proved to be very popular, reaching six editions in the author's lifetime. An exposition of John 6:37, *Come, & Welcome* is a good specimen of Bunyan's evangelical Calvinism. While remaining faithful to the Reformed doctrine of predestination, he found a way to appeal to his audience, not by offering them a legitimate choice in determining their destiny, but by assuring them that if they had or would come to Christ they were among the elect. "Coming to Christ, is by vertue of the gift, promise, and drawing of the Father; but thou art a coming, therefore God hath given thee, promised thee, and is drawing thee to Jesus Christ" (*MW*, 8:352). The work's substantial popularity is explained by the extraordinary simplicity of Bunyan's answer to the question, How do I know I am one of the elect? He preserved the Reformed emphasis on the primacy of divine sovereignty in the work of salvation by subordinating all conditional promises, such as Jeremiah 4:1, Matthew 19:21, Ezekiel 18:30–32, and Romans 4:7–8, to the absolute promises grounded in the covenant between God the father and God the son (8:245, 275–77, 326). Conditional promises call for faith, repentance, a new heart, and holy living, but the absolute promises provide these things to the elect. Substantively and sequentially, Bunyan accords primacy to the absolute promises, guaranteeing that the conditional will be fulfilled. For instance, "the Absolute promise says, that Gods elect shall hold out to the end; then the Conditional follows with his blessing, *He that shall endure to the end, the same shall be saved*"; the biblical references are to 1 Peter 1:4–6 and Matthew 24:13 (8:277). By interpreting his core text, John 6:37, as an absolute promise, Bunyan could offer an almost iron-clad guarantee of salvation to anyone coming to Christ (8:277).

This doctrine provided Bunyan with ready answers to some of the more pressing questions facing a seventeenth-century pastor. To those concerned, as he had once been, with whether the day of grace had passed, he could point to their coming as proof it had not (8:269–70). The same answer was pertinent to those who had fallen from grace, though he warned that some offenses—"falls against Light, from the Faith to the despising of, and trampling upon Jesus Christ, and his blessed undertakings"—are incapable of pardon (8:271–72).

Bunyan carefully delineated the spiritual act of coming to Christ, as he understood it, from a formal but carnal reliance on patterns of worship or sacraments (8:255, 309–10). Coming, as used in the unconditional promise in John 6:37, means "*a moving of the mind towards [Christ] from a Sound Sense of the absolute want that a man hath of him for his Justification and Salvation*" (8:255). Believing

[79] For Harris see *BDBR, s.v.*

and coming are one (8:260). The sinner can only come to Christ by grace, not any human capacity; neither the will nor worldly wisdom plays any role, a position that once again set Bunyan apart from the Latitudinarians (8:273–74, 327, 330). One cannot come to Christ without being drawn by God; the elect receive the faith and repentance that enable them to come, and this they cannot resist (8:282, 288, 368). The act of coming thus means one has been divinely called and enabled to go to Christ (8:391). This was the message of the "Thundring Preachers," among whom Bunyan included himself (8:337).

Using a literary technique akin to his allegorical treatment of vices and virtues in *The Pilgrim's Progress*, Bunyan creatively personified two words of his text, "shall-come," which he defined as God's absolute promise. Shall-come will lead the elect from their transgressions, enable them to hear God's voice, liberate them from Satan's bondage, and make them willing to go to Christ. "We may see, what *shall-come* can do, when it comes to be fulfilled upon the Soul of a rebellious sinner" (8:279–80). At the appointed time, Shall-come takes the sinner in hand, turning the most stubborn to God like a dove to its nest. Shall-come has the power to enable the spiritually blind to see and understand the gospel message (8:280–82). Bunyan enlisted Shall-come in his battle against the purveyors of dangerous, damnable opinions that seemingly threaten the elect like quicksand. "A company of *Shall-comes* in the Bible" preserves the elect from such perils, and, changing the analogy, "break[s] those Chains and Fetters, that those given to Christ are intangled in" (8:283). Shifting metaphors again, Bunyan proclaimed that the sheep—the elect—would not hear the false voices of thieves because the former are "under the power of *shall come*" (8:284). Shall-come also plays a critical role in Scripture, liberating the body and soul of Abraham's daughter, exorcizing the seven devils from Mary Magdalene and a legion from a possessed man, humbling King Manasseh of Judah, converting the thief on the cross, and taming the rebellious Saul (8:278, 280–81). Thus two simple words from a straightforward Johannine text acquire a lively presence as exorcist, redeemer, and pastor, all of them manifestations of divine sovereignty in the elect's redemption. With Shall-come, the creative forces that enabled Bunyan to compose *The Pilgrim's Progress* spill over in imaginative pulpit rhetoric that stands in sharp contrast to his often humdrum biblical exposition.

Armed with his concordance, Bunyan could be deadly dull as he tirelessly explained the varied uses of a term or phrase in his text. One example, his explication of the phrase, "*to cast out*," will suffice:

> First, *To cast out*, Is to Slight, and Despise, and Contemn; as it is said of *Saul's Shield*, *It was vilely cast away*; that is, Slighted and Contemned. Thus it is with the Sinners, that come not to Jesus Christ; He Slights, Despises, and Contemns them; that is, *Casts them away*. . . .

> *Secondly*, Things cast away, are reputed as Menstruous Cloaths, and as the Dirt of the Street. . . . And thus it shall be with the Men, that come not to Jesus Christ; they shall be counted as Menstruous, and as the Dirt in the Streets.
>
> *Thirdly*, To be cast out, or off; it is, To be abhorred, not to be pityed; but to be put to perpetual Shame.  (8:316)

Because of his belief in the harmony of Scripture, Bunyan treated the Bible as a single work in two parts, overlooking the diversity of styles and linguistic usage, and paying little heed to historical development and context.

Bunyan's pulpit forte was not his pedestrian expository skills but an ability to draw on his personal experience to enliven his message and his wide-ranging analogies. Inasmuch as *Grace Abounding* went through six editions in his lifetime, many of his auditors and readers must have noticed at least some of the numerous autobiographical references in his sermons. Like *Saved by Grace, Come, & Welcome* has a rich store of such allusions, none of them explicitly identified, but virtually all of them unmistakable. When Bunyan queried his audience about the means through which providence operated to bring them to Christ, he asked: "was it thy casting of thine Eye upon some good Book," much as he had read Bayly, Dent, and especially Luther; "thy hearing of thy Neighbours talk of Heavenly Things," as he had listened to women from Gifford's congregation; "the beholding of Gods Judgments, as executed upon others," which he had contemplated in Spira's story; "thine own Deliverance from them," as in his escape from drowning or death in the civil war; "or thy being strangly cast under the Ministry of some Godly Man," as had Bunyan when he went to Gifford's church (8:334)? More powerful are the allusions to his psychological state. From personal experience he knew that those coming to Christ could be deemed victims of melancholy, much as Graceless was regarded as mentally ill at the outset of *The Pilgrim's Progress* (8:336). "The poor World, they Mock us, because, we are a dejected people; I mean, because we are sometimes so: But they do not know the cause of our Dejections" (8:363). Bunyan's description of the man assaulted with blasphemous thoughts as he wandered in a field is autobiographical, and he knew whereof he wrote when he recalled how Christ revealed himself "*when Providences are black and terrible*" (8:239, 266). Capturing his feelings when he recovered from depression, he described the coming sinner's periodic relief from guilt and despair: "Hast thou not sometimes as it were the very warmth of [Christ's] wings over-shadowing the face of thy Soul, that gives thee as it were a gload [a warming sensation] upon thy Spirit, as the bright beams of the Sun do upon thy body, when it suddenly breaks out in the midst of a cloud, though presently all is gone again?" (8:392). This was the voice of experience, particularly that of a man who knew just how welcome those warm rays of sunshine felt after the horrific depths of seemingly interminable blackness.

Bunyan also helped sustain interest in his message with abundant analogies and metaphors, probably a reflection of the fact that he was at this point considering whether to publish *The Pilgrim's Progress* and was discussing metaphors and allegory with some of his colleagues. The coming sinner's discouraging thoughts, he explained, are like the cold weather that numbs the senses (8:267), and people who refuse to embrace Christ are garbed "in the Filthy Rags of their own stinking Polutions, and shall be wrapt up in them, as in a Winding-sheet" (8:318). He also likened them to fugitives and vagabonds, and their unbelief to the churning waves of the sea (8:317, 378). In contrast, those who embrace Christ experience "a sweet, and stiff gale of the Spirit of God filling [their] sails with the fresh gales of his good Spirit; and thou ridest at those times, as upon the wings of the wind, being carried out beyond thy self, beyond the most of thy prayers, and also above all thy fears and temptations" (8:392). The hesitancy of a sinner coming to Christ, he thought, might be a sign of strong desire for the Savior, much like a young man afraid his overture of marriage will be rejected (8:345–46). Temptations are to the coming sinner what a portrait painter or a mirror is to a conceited person with an "ill-favoured" face, but a sense of unworthiness drives the sinner toward the Savior like a man with a broken arm to a bone-setter (8:348, 359). Christ's offer of mercy to the coming sinner is likened by Bunyan to a prince or noble's proffer of marriage to "some poor, sorry, beggarly scrub":

> Every thought of her pedigree confounds her; also her sense of want of beauty, makes her ashamed: and if she doth but think of being imbraced, the unbelief that is mixed with that thought, whirls her into tremblings: And now she calls her self fool for believing the Messenger, and thinks not to go: If she thinks of being bold, she Blushes, and the least thought that she shall be rejected, when she comes at him, makes her look as if she would give up the Ghost. (8:349, 350)

The analogy became a vignette, compelling in its simplicity, irresistible with its Cinderella appeal, and easily remembered, unlike much of Bunyan's bromidic hermeneutics.

*Come, & Welcome's* appeal also derives from its plentiful use of metaphorical and analogous animals. Bunyan sprinkled animals, especially lions, throughout his works,[80] but *Come, & Welcome* has a well-stocked menagerie, replete with dogs, bears, leopards, wolves, bulls, sheep, horses, flies, bees, the nearly omnipresent lions, and mythical dragons. As Sir Keith Thomas has remarked, this was an age when controversialists dehumanized their opponents by speaking of them as animals, implying that they should be treated as such. Human ascendancy over animals and birds was a common assumption.[81] Bunyan used animals with consider-

---

[80] For further discussion of Bunyan's use of animals, see Chapter 13.

[81] Keith Thomas, *Man and the Natural World: Changing Attitudes in England 1500–1800* (Oxford: Oxford University Press, 1983), 46–49.

able literary dexterity. Although a roaring lion can represent the Devil, to the reprobate Christ appears as "a Lyon Rampant," ready to tear them to pieces (8:264, 310, 319, 351). Lions, bears, wolves, leopards, and dragons—the wild beasts in the wilderness—are like the temptations and fears that daunt the coming sinner (8:357). Similarly, temptations are like a badly trained shepherd's dog that runs down the stray sheep, "pulls it down, Worries it, Wounds it, and grievously bedabbleth it with dirt and wet in the lowest places of the Furrows of the field: And not leaving it, untill it is half dead" (8:358). Bunyan had obviously observed such dogs in action. Fearing God would reject him owing to his vileness, the sinner, says Bunyan, sees himself as a dead dog (8:347). He also reminded his readers that Jesus had called a Canaanite woman "Dog" (8:298). A stubborn horse, ignoring spurring and kicking, serves as an analogy for a coming sinner's balking flesh, while the bees and flies darting about in warm sunshine provide an analogy for Christ's enlivening promise to accept a sinner, dispelling the discouraging, numbing thoughts (8:267–68). Finally, the coming sinner, sensitive to fleshly infirmities and desperate thoughts, "Flings and Tumbles like a Wild Bull in a net" (8:359). For the most part, in Bunyan's mind animals were neither good nor evil, but examples from a partly real, partly imaginary world of nature that illustrated some of his points. Despite his fascination with lions, as reflected in part in *The Pilgrim's Progress*, his most telling use of animals is arguably his likening of the temptations and anxieties that beset the coming sinner to the wild beasts of the forest, seemingly lurking on all sides to pounce on their hapless victims. The imaginary was more influential than the natural world in his expository use of animals, though the latter would figure prominently in *A Book for Boys and Girls* (1686).

One of the most dramatic passages in *Come, & Welcome* encapsulates material from Foxe's *Acts and Monuments*, which Bunyan continued to read after his imprisonment years. Indeed, his return to jail about December 1676 may have prompted renewed interest in Foxe. Apart from the New Testament martyr Stephen (Acts 7), the other seven martyrs to whom Bunyan refers, carefully selecting both men and women, belonged to the early but post-biblical church. In all cases they reflect what John Knott has called Bunyan's "fascination with the drama of martyrdom" and his use of martyrs as exemplars.[82] Coming sinners are exhorted to find strength in Eulalia, who kept her eyes on Christ as her tormentors ripped her joints apart, or Agnes, who welcomed a sword through her breast to facilitate her escape from the world's darkness to join Christ, her spouse. Rather than obey an imperial command to worship pagan deities, Julitta bade farewell to life, welcoming death. Bunyan also cites the example of Marcus Arethusius, who was hung in a basket, his lacerated flesh coated with honey to attract flies and bees, because he

[82] Knott, *DM*, 179.

had refused to pay taxes to support the state religion; readers could easily have deduced that rendering tithes to the Church of England was likewise evil. Ignatius,
Romanus, and the Egyptian Menas, all of whom defied the state's authority in the
name of conscience, were martyrs with whom Bunyan could identify (8:383–84).
In the 1680s he would pay serious attention to the Marian martyrs, but not now, in
the latter half of 1677 and early 1678, when Catholicism seemed not to threaten
England. The only direct reference in *Come, & Welcome* to the Catholics is a sarcastic comment that if life in Christ were "in the *Popes* hand, we should pay
soundly for it" (8:374). Given the fact that this is the only reference to Catholicism,
he must have completed *Come, & Welcome* before the spectacular allegations in
late 1678 of a Popish plot to assassinate Charles and James.

   Bunyan's principal foes in the late 1670s were not the Catholics but those
Protestants in England who crafted "false Christs" and espoused "damnable errors," including a denial of imputed righteousness (8:261). These were often the
people who relied on human wisdom, which he ranked among God's greatest
enemies (8:328). He challenged "the best Master of Arts on Earth" to disprove his
contention that John 6:37 is an absolute promise, and referred approvingly to
those in Acts 19:19 who, having used "Curious Arts," burned their "Curious
Books" when they came to Jesus (8:275, 380–81). Yet learning was not in itself
evil, for he quoted Luther in this work ("*When Christ speaketh, he hath a mouth as
Wide as Heaven and Earth*") and counted Owen, the former Oxford vice-chancel-
lor, among his friends (8:296). For Bunyan the greatest foe, at least in this period,
was probably unbelief, "*the White Devil*; for it often-times in its Mischievous doings in the Soul, shews as if it was an Angel of Light" (8:375). Among other perils
were atheism, blasphemy, and materialism, all of which were challenges familiar
to dissenting ministers.[83] In *Come, & Welcome* Bunyan combated the growing
secularization of his age by contributing to the spiritualizing of faith[84]—an emphasis on the sinner's coming, not to the institutionalized church, with its liturgy
and sacramental theology, but to Christ through spiritual rebirth. Because of the
communal setting provided by dissenting congregations, this is less the privatiz-
ing of religion[85] than its reorientation toward a less institutionalized, more personal relationship with God. This was the crux of Bunyan's evangelical Calvinist
message on the eve of a profound political and religious crisis in England involving the perceived threat of Catholicism, a bitter dispute over succession to
the crown, and the rights of subjects.

   [83] *MW*, 8:240, 265–66, 357, 360, 368.
   [84] C. John Sommerville, *The Secularization of Early Modern England: From Religious
Culture to Religious Faith* (New York: Oxford University Press, 1992), 178–79, 186.
   [85] Ibid., 186.

After Bunyan completed *Come, & Welcome*, he expanded *The Pilgrim's Progress* in the summer of 1678, an indication of its early success. The new passages in the second edition, published before 25 March 1679, embody some of the best-known episodes in the allegory, including Christian's relations with his family before leaving home (*PP*, 8–9), his meeting with Worldly-wiseman (16–20), his fear that Mount Sinai would fall on his head (20), Evangelist's counsel (20–25), and a recounting of all this to Good Will (26–27). Bunyan has Christian provide a fuller account of his family to Charity (50–52), and he has Evangelist return to engage in a discussion with Christian and Faithful in which they are warned of the danger they will face in Vanity Fair, a discourse they recall after arriving there (85–88, 92). Probably reflecting the dismay felt by nonconformists after the king was pressured to withdraw the declaration of indulgence, Bunyan added a paragraph identifying some of the inhabitants of the town of Fair-speech, including Lords Turn-about, Time-server, and Fair-speech, Mr. Facing-bothways, Mr. Anything, Mr. Smooth-man, and Parson Two-tongues (99). A discussion of the fate of Lot's wife and Sodom constitutes a prophetic warning to England, particularly its quest to increase wealth (108–10). In keeping with some of the changes introduced to the fourth edition of *Grace Abounding* in 1677, Bunyan substantially expanded the episode of Giant Despair and the experiences in his dungeon (114–17), but he balanced this by describing how the king's trumpeters and the pealing of bells greeted Christian and Hopeful as they approached the heavenly gate (160–61). As in *Come, & Welcome*, the fundamental message of the allegory is an invitation to embrace the offer of grace and embark on the Christian pilgrimage, and the addition of the musical welcome accorded to Christian and Hopeful at the end of their pilgrimage encouraged such a commitment.

CHAPTER 9

# Popery's Long Shadows

By the late seventeenth century, anti-Catholicism had been firmly woven into the English national fabric.[1] For the most part, the focus of this hostility was not Catholics in England but the papacy and its perceived international champions, Spain in the late sixteenth and early seventeenth centuries and more recently Louis XIV's France. Each year the English celebrated two holidays that helped sustain anti-Catholic sentiment, 5 November, commemorating the failure of the Gunpowder plot, and 17 November, honoring Elizabeth I's accession. On both days London crowds had begun burning effigies of the pope. The first such incineration was apparently on 5 November 1673, when an effigy of the Whore of Babylon, decorated with a triple crown, papal crosses, beads, and the symbolic keys, was borne through the streets in a torchlight parade, strung up in the Poultrey, used as a target for pistol-bearing celebrants, and finally lowered into a bonfire. The observance, remarked the Anglican minister Isaac Archer, "was kept with unusuall zeale in the city." On 17 November 1677 the crowd burned effigies of two devils as well as the pope, the latter's belly full of cats yowling in pain as the flames claimed the effigies.[2] Anti-Catholicism was also spurred by sermons and assorted publications, among the more prominent of which was the series of twenty-five sermons against popery by Nathaniel Vincent and other dissenters at Southwark in 1675.[3] Arguably the most influential book attacking Catholicism in this period was Marvell's *An Account of the Growth of Popery, and Arbitrary Government in England* (1677), which outlined an alleged conspiracy to establish ty-

---

[1] See especially Jonathan Scott, *England's Troubles: Seventeenth-Century English Political Instability in European Context* (Cambridge: Cambridge University Press, 2000).

[2] David Cressy, *Bonfires and Bells: National Memory and the Protestant Calendar in Elizabethan and Stuart England* (Berkeley: University of California Press, 1989), 175, 177; CUL, Add. MSS 8499, fol. 165 (quoted).

[3] [Nathaniel Vincent, ed.], *The Morning-Exercise Against Popery* (London, 1675).

rannical government and overthrow Protestantism. Unnamed perpetrators, Marvell alleged, were committing high crimes by seeking "to introduce a *French Slavery*, and . . . *Roman Idolatry*" (8). This was a topic thoroughly explored by the Green Ribbon Club, whose members complained about the nation being sold to the French and Whitehall's commitment to "Popery & arbitrary Government."[4]

Although fears of Catholicism may have been exaggerated, they were not without some justification. Protestants in France, Piedmont, Ireland, and the German states had suffered at the hands of Catholics, and reports of such travails in the English press reminded Protestants of the need for vigilance. Charles II's alliance with France likewise caused concern, particularly because the Sun King governed without recourse to the Estates General and was no friend of his Huguenot subjects. In late 1678 the House of Commons would learn that the repeated prorogations of Parliament that had so concerned Shaftesbury, Buckingham, Jenks, and others were in return for Louis' secret subvention of Charles, amply justifying earlier fears that the French alliance threatened England's traditional government. Fanned in press and pulpit, such concerns helped intensify the growing polarization between Court and Country. Although the Court, particularly as envisioned by the earl of Danby, the king's principal minister, viewed Catholicism as a threat, its policy of repressing Protestant nonconformists prompted the latter to suspect the Court of Catholic leanings.[5] In fact, the government had informers monitoring the activities of dissenting ministers, including Bunyan's friends Owen and Cokayne, in mid-1678.[6]

### "This Day of *Jacobs* Trouble"[7]: The Popish Plot and the Godly

On the eve of the disclosure of an alleged new Popish plot, dissenting ministers were speaking out against Catholicism and arbitrary government. On 26 May 1678, the Congregationalist Stephen Ford or his fellow Independent Jeremiah Marsden, preaching in London, likened the current persecution of God's people to the Marian fires at Smithfield, urged the auditors "to press forward" in their cause, and referred to "a great Duke [Lauderdale] that was a persecutor of Gods

[4] PRO, SP 29/411/22.

[5] Jonathan Scott, "England's Troubles: Exhuming the Popish Plot," in *The Politics of Religion in Restoration England*, ed. Tim Harris, Paul Seaward, and Mark Goldie (Oxford: Basil Blackwell, 1990), 117–19; Harris, *PULS*, 54, 70–71.

[6] PRO, SP 29/404/90, 253. More than a year earlier, in February 1677, the government had ordered the suppression of a conventicle at Pinners' Hall, London. *CSPD, 1676–77*, 547.

[7] *MW*, 12:359.

people."[8] A week later, on 3 June, Vincent addressed the theme of persecution, warning of a dark cloud on the horizon, and Owen had made the same point in sermons on 1 Peter 4:12 and 17 in March and May. Scottish preachers in London provided an international flavor by recounting the Highland Host's suppression of Presbyterians earlier in the year. Preaching on God's frustration of Haman's plot to exterminate the Jews, as reported in the book of Esther, one of the Scots drew attention as well to the failure of Ahithophel's plan to slay David and rout his army (2 Samuel 17). Knowledgeable listeners would probably have likened Ahithophel to Lauderdale, and Haman to either the duke or Danby. Other preachers, including the London minister and schoolmaster Josiah Basset and the Presbyterian Andrew Parsons, aimed their pulpit salvos at the bishops in England and Scotland. According to an informer, the dissenting ministers "generally speak against the Church Government, and Complain of their brethren being persecuted in the Country with imprisonment." Reflecting the heightening tension, Cokayne's congregation, with which Bunyan was personally familiar, physically expelled the same informer.[9] Comparing their persecutors to those responsible for the Marian burnings or such biblical malefactors as Haman and Ahithophel contributed to growing concern about Catholicism as well as the further polarization of Court and Country.

Against this background Londoners reacted with alarm when the corpse of Sir Edmund Berry Godfrey was discovered in a ditch on Primrose Hill on 17 October 1678. The previous month he had taken depositions from Titus Oates about an alleged conspiracy, funded by French Jesuits, to assassinate Charles and various well-known Protestants. In the ensuing weeks Godfrey feared for his own life, and his murder now seemingly corroborated the plot's reality. Testifying to the Privy Council on 28 September, Oates related his tale concerning Catholic plans for insurrections in England, Scotland, and Ireland, but the king was skeptical. Nevertheless he authorized an investigation by Danby, who viewed the allegations as an opportunity to advance Court interests. By 17 January 1679 Secretary of State Henry Coventry noted that "the busyness of the Conspiracy imployeth all our time [at court], we have dayly Evidence of a Conspiracy and a great one, but yet the particulars and where to fasten the Crime asketh some time to adjust." Extraordinary political theater ensued, including show trials, some thirty-five executions, the prosecution of more than 1,200 Catholics in London during 1679

[8] PRO, SP 29/404/13. The informer referred to Marsden by his alias, Ralphson. See Greaves, *DUFE*, 198. For Ford and Marsden see *BDBR, s.vv.*

[9] PRO, SP 29/404/13, 88, 167, 217 (quoted); DWL, MSS L6/3, sermons of Owen on 1 Peter 4:17 (13 March 1678) and 1 Peter 4:12 (30 May 1678). For Basset and Parsons see *Calamy Revised, s.vv.*

alone, and the publication of hundreds of anti-Catholic tracts. The scale of the reaction to Oates' fabrications was due partly to concern about the impact of Charles' French alliance on England's self-anointed role as the defender of Protestantism, and partly to the success of prior sermons and publications, including Marvell's *An Account of the Growth of Popery*, in shaping public opinion to heed the perils of popery and arbitrary government.[10] Bunyan was well placed to follow the unfolding allegations of the conspiracy. After Oates was expelled from the Catholic college at St. Omers in France, he returned to England, where he associated with the General Baptists William Radden, an attorney, and Thomas Parsons. Radden and Parsons were closely linked to Bunyan's long-time printer, Francis Smith, and Radden also had ties to Henry Danvers. Moreover, while Oates continued to reveal more and more reputed plotting to the government, he drew close to Danvers, who also had links to Bunyan. One of Bunyan's sureties in 1677, Robert Blaney, had served in Shaftesbury's household and remained loyal to the earl, who tenaciously investigated the plot after he became lord president of the Privy Council on 21 April 1679. In this endeavor Shaftesbury worked closely with Lord Wharton, a friend of Owen's.[11] Owen, whom Bunyan visited on his trips to London, believed in the conspiracy's reality, and while the investigations were under way he published a broad attack on Catholicism entitled *The Church of Rome No Safe Guide* (1679). His assistant, Robert Ferguson, believed Catholics were conspiring against Protestantism, the king, and the English people. Although there is no direct evidence that Bunyan discussed the plot with any of these people, the probability of his having done so is very high; Owen thought half the world was talking about the conspiracy in 1680.[12]

The Popish plot and the Court-Country rivalry against which the investigation played out affected Bunyan's printers. In early 1678 magistrates were searching for seditious, scandalous, and unlicensed books and pamphlets, including *An Account of the Growth of Popery*, but following Oates' initial allegations the focus temporarily shifted to Catholic works. By year's end, magistrates were looking for all sorts of illegal material, and in January 1679 Coventry explicitly ordered a

[10]BL, Add. MSS 25,119, fol. 141r (quoted). For the alleged conspiracy see John Kenyon, *The Popish Plot* (Harmondsworth, Middlesex: Penguin Books, 1974); Scott, "England's Troubles," 107–31.

[11]PRO, SP 29/420/36; 29/421/7, 30; Greaves, *SOK*, 6–8, 32; K. H. D. Haley, *The First Earl of Shaftesbury* (Oxford: Clarendon Press, 1968), 440; G. F. Trevallyn Jones, *Saw-Pit Wharton: The Political Career from 1640 to 1691 of Philip, Fourth Lord Wharton* (Sydney: Sydney University Press, 1967), 238.

[12] Peter Toon, *God's Statesman: The Life and Work of John Owen, Pastor, Educator, Theologian* (Grand Rapids, MI: Zondervan, 1973), 142; [Robert Ferguson], *A Letter to a Person of Honour, Concerning the Black Box* [London, 1680], 4; Owen, *Works*, 9:505.

search for unlicensed publications critical of the government or the Church of England.[13] As this broad search continued throughout the year, it led to Smith's arrest in December for having published allegedly seditious material pertaining to the Association drafted when Catholic plotters threatened Elizabeth I's life. Although freed within days on a writ of *habeas corpus*, he was rearrested on 7 January 1680 for having published *A New-Years-Gift for the Lord Chief in Justice Sc[rog]gs*; a second writ procured his liberty the following day.[14] A month later, on 7 February, the government tried Smith for having published *Some Observations upon the Trial of Sir George Wakeman*, an alleged plotter who had been found innocent along with three Benedictine monks. After pleading guilty, Smith was fined. For publishing *An Act of Common-Council of the City of London* he was indicted at a London session of the peace in September 1680, but three times the jurors returned verdicts of *ignoramus*. He was again in trouble in January 1681 for having published the *Speech Lately Made by a Noble Peer*, attacking the king as untrustworthy; the speech was believed to have been Shaftesbury's, though the earl never delivered it. The House of Lords ordered the work burned, but the jury trying Smith returned a verdict of *ignoramus*.[15]

Another of Bunyan's publishers, Benjamin Harris, was an associate of Shaftesbury's banker, Peter Percival. Beginning in July 1679, Shaftesbury and Oates sponsored Harris' newssheet, the *Domestick Intelligence*, which carried reports about the conspiracy. Following his arrest in October, Harris was tried on 5 February 1680 on charges of publishing *An Appeal from the Country to the City, for the Preservation of His Majesties Person, Liberty, Property, and the Protestant Religion* (1679). The work, which appeared anonymously, was by the Whig Charles Blount, who blamed Catholics for the great fire of London and the 1679 Covenanter rebellion in Scotland, which, he claimed, had been fomented by priests and papal emissaries. Found guilty, Harris was pilloried, fined £500, and required to provide security for his good behavior, and his newspaper ceased publication between 16 April

[13] PRO, SP 29/401/237; 44/54, p. 12; 44/334, pp. 457, 554–55, 596; London *Gazette* 1368 (26–30 December 1678).

[14] Luttrell, 1:28; London *Gazette* 1432 (7–11 August 1679); 1457 (3–6 November 1679); 1469 (15–18 December 1679); *CSPD, 1679–80*, 269; *Domestick Intelligence* 48 (19 December 1679); 49 (23 December 1679); 54 (9 January 1680). In 1677 or 1678, a year or two after Smith published *A Strait Gate* and *Saved By Grace*, the chaplain of the Fleet prison informed officials that Smith had spoken seditiously about the king and government, and he described him as a notorious dealer in libels. PRO, SP 29/442/49.

[15] Kenyon, *Popish Plot*, 192–201; London *Gazette* 1484 (5–9 February 1680); *Protestant (Domestick) Intelligence* 63 (10 February 1680); *True Protestant Mercury* 8 (18–22 January 1681); Luttrell, 1:35, 64; Timothy Crist, "Government Control of the Press After the Expiration of the Printing Act in 1679," *Publishing History* 5 (1979): 57, 64–65.

and 28 December 1680. He was arrested once more in February 1681, and two months later his newspaper was again suppressed.[16]

Bunyan was thus effectively positioned to obtain substantive information about the Popish plot. Through Smith and Blaney he was one step removed from Shaftesbury, and Harris was in direct contact with Shaftesbury's banker. More-over, through Harris and Danvers, Bunyan was one step removed from Oates, whereas Smith was tied to Oates' associates, Radden and Parsons. Finally, through Owen and Griffith, Bunyan was a step away from Wharton, a key ally of Shaftesbury in the investigation. Other than the seventh edition of *Sighs from Hell* (by 1686) and a reprint of the third edition of *Grace Abounding* (1679), Smith's last known work for Bunyan was *Saved by Grace* (June 1676), perhaps, as J. Sears McGee suggests, because Bunyan resented Smith's publication of books by Gen-eral Baptists (*MW*, 3:4). Bunyan may also have shied away from Smith following his release from prison because of the security Blaney and Kelsey had posted for him. Harris published *Come, & Welcome* in 1678 (and four later editions between 1684 and 1686). But Bunyan may have relied on Ponder, Dorman Newman, and Benjamin Alsop during the period of the Popish plot investigation and the ensu-ing crisis over popery and arbitrary government because Smith and Harris were preoccupied with publishing tracts concerning the crisis and, in Harris' case, newspapers, or because they were in frequent trouble with the authorities.[17] What is clear is that Bunyan felt the need to switch publishers. This may help to explain why a work that very likely dates from the winter of 1678–79, *Paul's Departure and Crown*, was not published during his lifetime.

Bunyan's only explicit reference to the Popish plot appears in *Israel's Hope Encouraged*, probably written, as we shall see, in the autumn of 1680 and the winter of 1680–81. Noting that England had experienced substantial trouble since the conspiracy's disclosure, he succinctly but revealingly described the plot's psy-chological impact: "We began to fear cutting of Throats, of being burned in our beds, and of seeing our Children dashed in pieces before our Faces" (*MW*, 13:21). Others made similar observations. In a letter to Edward Clarke dated 22 January 1679, his cousin William Clarke reported that the discovery of the plot had made people "mightily afrayd of Popery, and ill Times," and Isaac Archer acknowl-

---

[16]Luttrell, 1:33–34, 36; London *Gazette* 1484 (5–9 February 1680); 1486 (12–16 February 1680); *Protestant (Domestick) Intelligence* 65 (17 February 1680); Bodl., Carte MSS 228, fol. 145r; *CSPD, 1679–80*, 392, 397; Longleat, Coventry MSS 11, fol. 436r; Crist, "Government Control," 56–57; *BDBR, s.v.* Harris tried to obtain his release in September 1681 by reveal-ing the names of authors of objectionable books and pamphlets, but Bunyan was not en-dangered since the only book of his that Harris had published was *Come, & Welcome*. Luttrell, 1:127.

[17]For Alsop see *BDBR, s.v.*; for Newman see Plomer, *DBP*, 217.

edged that "the feares of Popery, & massacre, with which the land was alarmed, made mee serious & my heart was enlarged to plead for the poore nation fervently." Rumors were rampant. Armed bands reportedly engaged in surreptitious movements in southern Wiltshire between midnight and 2:00 A.M., and similar accounts reached the government from other areas. From Whitby came allegations about plans to blow up Tynemouth Castle, and reports of bombs in churches, Catholics secretly acquiring weapons, and Spanish and French landings were rife. Londoners worried about another fire, especially since some people blamed Catholics for the conflagration in 1666. Trained bands guarded the City day and night, and chains blocked major streets to deter would-be rebels.[18] Tracts and newspapers pouring from the press fed the fears, intensifying concern that Protestant lives and properties were in peril. The fear described by Bunyan that throats might be cut, houses incinerated in the night, and children brutally slain echoed the stories that had spread following the reputed massacre of Protestants by the Irish in the fall of 1641.

*Paul's Departure and Crown* explicitly speaks to such fears, exhorting the godly—especially ministers—to stand firm in defense of the gospel. No work of Bunyan is more directed at fellow ministers than this one, though his audience also encompassed the rest of the visible saints. Particularly in the first part of the book, his primary concern was to ensure that the godly did not retreat from their profession of the gospel for fear of martyrdom. Common sense, he argued, indicates that the Catholics, if there were a plot, could not slaughter all Protestants. As he knew from his immersion in Foxe, the most likely targets of a bloody persecution included ministers. To encourage them to remain steadfast, Bunyan cited the example of Paul, who had refused to cower in the face of persecution, instead remaining faithful to the end, fighting the good fight, and dying with the assurance of receiving a crown of righteousness (2 Timothy 4:6–8). He interpreted Paul's indication that he was "ready to be offered" as evidence "that his death and martyrdom for the Gospel should be both sweet in the Nostrils of God, and of great profit to his Church in this World" (*MW*, 12:360–61). In Paul's example he found "encouragement to those that are yet in the storm" (12:360), and he clearly expected some of these people to die brutally, as had earlier martyrs at the hands of Catholics. Yet such suffering has a worthy purpose: "How hath the Headship and Lordship of Christ, with many other Doctrins of God, been taken away from the Pope by the sufferings of our Brethren before us?" (12:362). With

---

[18] Somerset Record Office, MSS DD/SF 3109 (quoted); CUL, Add. MSS 8499, fol. 185r (quoted); PRO, SP 29/408/4; 44/29, p. 303; *CSPD, 1678*, 542; Luttrell, 1:9, 12; Barry Coward, *The Stuart Age: England, 1603–1714*, 2nd ed. (London: Longman, 1994), 327; Greaves, *EUHF*, 46; Bodl., English Letters C328, fol. 509v.

the time of such persecution seemingly at hand, Bunyan exhorted the saints to face it with Pauline courage, undeterred by popish massacres. "The murders and out-rage that our Brethren suffer at the hands of wicked Men, should not discourage those that live, from a full and faithful performance of their duty to God and Man, whatever may be the consequence thereof" (12:358, 361).

The godly must not only be resolute in the face of persecution but embrace martyrdom. Anticipating the possibility of a Catholic seizure of power through a popish conspiracy, Bunyan articulated the standard for the godly's response: "When we see our Brethren before us fall to the Earth, by death, through the violence of the enemies of God for their Holy and Christian profession, we should covet to make good their ground against them, though our turn should be the next" (12:358–59). Freely using such terms as sacrifice and suffering in describing the obligations of visible saints, he expected such actions to have manifold benefits, including the recovery of divine truth "buried in Antichristian Rubbish," a reference to the pseudo-gospel propounded by the Church of England (12:362). Although such suffering is "hard labor," it wins converts and purifies the church and its teachings (12:364). "While [the martyrs'] flesh did fry in the flames, the Word of God was cleansed, and by such means purified in these their Earthen Furnaces, and so delivered to us" (12:362). Seen in this light, to suffer for righteousness is a sign of divine favor, and the godly should therefore emulate Paul by taking pleasure in persecution (12:363). Sometimes, Bunyan explained, God decides that "his best People" should be afflicted, and he chastens those he loves "for trial and for the exercise of grace received" (12:380, 394). Because this is God's decision, Catholics can operate only within divinely sanctioned parameters. "They with all their raging Waves, have Banks and Bounds set to them, by which they are limited with in their range" (12:365). For Bunyan the Popish plot could succeed only with God's permission, though he also noted that persecuting visible saints provokes God to wreak vengeance against the "Butchers" (12:363–64).

Previously I suggested that Bunyan did not publish *Paul's Departure and Crown* in part because of the legal difficulties in which Harris and Smith found themselves, but other factors also played a role. Although one passage seems to suggest Bunyan's respect for monarchy, in fact he alludes only to what most English subjects felt. Note his carefully selected words:

> Be it in acted by the Kings most Excellent Majesty, is in the head of every Law, because that Law should therefore be reverenced by, and be made glorious and beautiful to all. And we see upon this very account what Power and place the precepts of Kings do take in the hearts of their Subjects, every one loving and reverencing the Statute because there is the name of their King. Will you rebel against the King, is a word that shakes the world. (12:376)

But statute had legalized the burning of Protestants in Mary Tudor's reign, as Bunyan knew, and he therefore went on to make the point that God is wiser than any earthly monarch, and divine commands consequently take precedence over those of any worldly government. The Bible, not statute, is "the line and rule whereby we must order and govern all our actions" (12:376–77).

Sensitive to the possible return of Catholic rule, Bunyan repeatedly urged the godly to resist such a government. In a striking embellishment on 1 Thessalonians 3:3, he counseled his readers not to be moved by persecution but to endure by "resisting even unto blood" (12:359). Paul had described his ministry as "a good fight," and Bunyan reiterated the imagery, casting the struggle as a war against the Beast, Antichrist (12:360). But as expressed in this book, the battle—the resistance—stops short of taking up arms, for the blood shed in defiance is entirely that of Christians, whom he exhorted to suffer patiently.[19] Although he referred to such resistance in terms of sacrificing oneself, he also resorted to militant imagery, likening ministers to soldiers, the summons to embrace persecution to a trumpet call to war, and Christians who retreat in the face of affliction to cowards who take refuge in a garrison instead of engaging the enemy (12:366–67). "We should valiantly do in this matter as is the Custom of Soldiers in Wars; take great care that the ground be maintained, and the front kept full and compleat" (12:359). The godly are Christ's soldiers, their sacrifice that of troops dying in combat for a worthy cause. To his fellow dissenting pastors Bunyan issued a call to "stand up . . . like valiant Worthies as the Ministers of my God, and fly not every Man to his own, while the cause and ways and Brethren of our Lord are buffeted and condemned by the World" (12:359). Moreover, he likened Paul, the role model for nonconforming ministers, to "those mighty Men of *Solomon*, that were ready prepared for the War, and waited on the King, fit to be sent at any time upon the most sharp and pinching service" (12:366). In this context, the analogous king is not Charles II but Christ. Such militant imagery and calls for resistance may well have given a censor or a publisher pause, especially if Bunyan sought a printer before the expiration of the Licensing Act on 13 March 1679. Even in the absence of the Licensing Act, seditious literature was still illegal.

Although Bunyan's primary concern was the resolve of the godly, especially ministers, to resist a Catholic regime should another one be established in England, he did not cease to criticize the Church of England. He castigated its time-serving, self-saving clergy, particularly those whose itching ears attracted false professors filled with an ungodly spirit and enmity to sound doctrine. The reference to itching ears was borrowed from Deuteronomy 28:27, which describes

[19] *MW*, 12:363–64; see also 358–59, 361, 381–82, 388.

God's threat to inflict misery and illness, including incurable diseases, on those who refuse to obey the divine commandments (12:357–58). Any biblically knowledgeable reader would have understood Bunyan's warning that the Church of England's adherents could expect to suffer from the host of divine punishments vividly depicted in Deuteronomy 28:15–68, including their ultimate destruction and scattering among the nations. Viewed in this context, Catholic conspirators were agents to effect divine judgment. He also lashed out against the established church because of its idolatry; its members "go a whoring from under their God" (12:359).

Expecting visible saints to stand up and be counted, Bunyan issued a chilling admonition to those who, like Edward Fowler, had turned away from their seeming commitment to the gospel and made their peace with the Church of England: "Let this therefore smight with conviction those that in this day of *Jacobs* trouble, have been false with God, his cause and people; I say those first and especially as the chief ringleaders of this cowardliness, who have done it against light, profession and resolutions" (12:359). People who desert God "in a day when his truth is cast down to the ground" will pay dearly for affronting divine majesty. Pointedly, he recounted the story of the wayward prophet in 1 Kings 13, who denounced Jeroboam for his idolatrous practices, but then failed to heed a divine command not to eat or drink on his return journey. Because of the prophet's disobedience, a lion killed him, leaving the carcass as a gruesome warning to others. To avoid such a fate, Bunyan declaimed, ministers must fight the good fight (12:359–60). *Paul's Departure and Crown* is a ringing summons to spiritual combat against God's enemies, whoever they are.

To his fellow nonconformists Bunyan issued a call for total commitment. Religion, he declared, must be "the only business to take up thy thoughts and time," for it is no "by-business" or stalking horse for gain (12:377–78). "Indifferency in Religion" is intolerable (12:360, 378); this is the gospel of struggle, affliction, and rugged endurance. In this cosmic campaign, ministers must not look to the government to implement divine law, for "the Ministers of the Gospel have each of them all that authority that belongs to their calling and office, and need not to stay for power from Man to put the Laws of Christ in his Church into due and full Execution" (12:358). This was nothing less than a ringing summons to civil disobedience and a rejection of all forms of worship that contravene divine commands.

Although Bunyan remained faithful to his doctrine of justification by Christ's imputed righteousness (12:387, 390), in *Paul's Departure and Crown* he placed considerable emphasis on good works and the eternal rewards that will ensue (12:386, 389–97). Included among these works was relief for the poor. His exhortation to be generous provides a glimpse of what the indigent probably received when they knocked at his door: "Deal thy Bread to the hungry, bring the poor that are cast out, into thine House . . . ; say not to such messengers, go and come again to morrow, if thou hast it by thee, now the opportunity is put into thy hand, delay not to do it" (12:384). Perhaps not since he wrote *A Few Sighs from Hell* did Bunyan aver so explicitly that few of the wealthy, the nobility, and the powerful embrace the gospel (12:383).

Like many preachers, Bunyan employed deathbed scenes to drive home his message. One of the most unusual examples occurs in *Paul's Departure and Crown*, where he reiterated a story he heard about a dying saint whose passing was accompanied by ethereal music. While he lay dying, the mourners reportedly heard "such blessed and ravishing musick as they never heard before." As his soul departed, the music slowly faded, seemingly accompanying him to his heavenly reward. Never questioning the story, Bunyan used it here and in *The Life and Death of Mr. Badman* to illustrate how dying could be made an easy rite of passage by the presence of other saints (12:396; *BM*, 144). He probably found this story alluring because of his love of music, an enjoyment manifested throughout most of his writings. Elsewhere in *Paul's Departure and Crown* he likened gospel sermons in which only grace is preached to pleasant songs (12:379). In his fertile mind, heaven is a musical kingdom where saints sing the songs of Moses and the Lamb while playing "the Harps of God" (12:360). Such blissful melodies stand in sharp contrast to "the noyse that doth sound in sinners Souls . . . when they are departed hence" (12:397). To Bunyan, music is a foretaste of heavenly bliss, a welcome relief from the din of battle against God's enemies in this life. Like light and darkness, music and noise symbolize both the cosmic struggle and the believer's individual combat with the forces of evil.

After completing *Paul's Departure and Crown*, Bunyan revised *The Pilgrim's Progress* for the third edition, which Ponder published in 1679. He made only one substantive change, the addition of a lengthy discussion between By-ends and his companions, and their ensuing discourse with Christian and Hopeful. The thrust of the new material struck at the acquisitive spirit evinced by Hold-the-world, Mony-love, and Save-all, the gentry friends of By-ends, and their demeaning attitude toward the godly, whom they adjudge to be "*righteous over-much.*" The best sort of religion, as Hold-the-world describes it, supports the amassing of worldly goods, "the security of Gods good blessings." Bunyan also incorporated a jibe at Anglican clerics who altered their principles in order to attain more rewarding benefices. Denouncing all who held such materialistic views, he referred to them as heathens, hypocritical Pharisees, devils such as Judas, and witches (*PP*, 100–106). He was clearly in no mood to compromise with his Anglican opponents.

"Good Coin in the Best of Tryals"[20]: A Sense of Impending Danger

About the time Bunyan was probably completing *Paul's Departure and Crown* and revising *The Pilgrim's Progress*, the first so-called exclusion Parliament was meeting, having convened on 6 March 1679. The issue of the succession and assurances for Protestant ascendancy had not been resolved in the final months of the Cavalier Parliament owing at least partly to growing mistrust of Danby, suspicion of the Court's intentions, and disunity within the Court itself. Sir Robert Southwell effectively captured the prevailing mood of the political nation:

> No man is able to foretell where all this Wind, that is heard, rumbling in the bowells of the Mountain, will at last breake out and what it may beare away before it. Popery is thought so Universaly to have been the Infection upon all things that have been amiss, that less than persecution of it, and all its Members, can hardly cleer a man from being a partaker with them; and by how much the Court is of different Sentiment, by so much certaine opposition or distance may wee calculate the Court and Parliament to bee at.

Seeking reconciliation with his parliamentary critics, Charles removed Danby and some of his key allies in April, replacing them in the Privy Council with Shaftesbury, the earl of Essex, and others. Riven by faction, the remodeled Council was largely ineffective. On the contentious issue of the succession, various options were possible, including James' exclusion. Placing limitations on a Catholic king, giving James the title of king but not the power, urging Charles to provide a Protestant successor by annulling his marriage to Catherine and taking a Protestant wife, and legitimating Monmouth were other possibilities, and it was even rumored that James might convert to Protestantism. Because Charles would have agreed to limitations, that option was the most promising, but it foundered, partly because many MPs refused to trust the Court, and partly because Shaftesbury, jockeying for power, finally threw his support to the exclusionists.[21]

The succession was not the only contentious issue that involved religion in the spring of 1679. Concern was voiced as well about Lauderdale's repression of the Scottish Covenanters, the government's reluctance to execute Catholic priests and prosecute the Catholic peers held in the Tower of London, and the security of Protestants in the face of reputed Catholic plotting. Nevertheless, Charles' de-

---

[20] *MW*, 9:97.

[21] Bodl., Carte MSS 39, fol. 21r (quoted); BL, Add. MSS 70,013, fol. 10r; Mark Knights, *Politics and Opinion in Crisis, 1678–81* (Cambridge: Cambridge University Press, 1994), 32–36, 40–41, 45, 47–48, 50–52. Southwell's point is effectively illustrated by an Anglican cleric at Christ Church, Oxford, who complained that those who opposed "the violent encroachments of Fanaticisme, & Sedition" were accused of popery. BL, Sloane MSS 1008, fol. 289r.

cision to prorogue Parliament on 27 May was prompted by concern over an exclusion bill which had received a second reading in the House of Commons six days earlier, on which occasion the Court's supporters lost a division 207 to 128. The leading proponents of limitations, Essex, Halifax, and Sunderland, persuaded the king to prorogue Parliament, and its dissolution ensued in early July.[22] Yet the Court was unsure of its next move: "We are here so troubled with apprehensions of Tempests from Contrary Corners," admitted Coventry, "that we are not without Difficulties how to set our Rigging." As the threat of Catholicism seemed to loom larger and the succession became a matter of increasing concern, Shaftesbury was the focus of much nonconformist hope. The Congregationalist Christopher Ness, pastor of a church in Fleet Street, London, dedicated *A Distinct Discourse and Discovery of the Person and Period of Antichrist* to the earl in August, urging him "to pull down this cursed *Antichrist*," by which he meant Catholicism. Shaftesbury, he said, was "an Honourable Patriot, yea, and in this sad conjuncture of Affairs, you have shone forth (through the good hand of God upon you) as a Star of the first Magnitude in our *British* Horizon."[23]

Results of the elections for a new House of Commons, which occurred between 6 August and 14 October 1679, amounted to a significant setback for the Court, thanks in part to the fact that nonconformists more firmly supported Country candidates than they had in the first election of 1679. The election was fought largely over such issues as popery, arbitrary government, and the candidates' relationship to the Court; although the election did not center primarily around exclusion, broad concern about Catholicism was evident. The key issue was concern about popery and arbitrary government, including the treatment of Protestant nonconformists. In Shaftesbury's words, "Popery & Slavery Like two Sisters go hand in hand." In London and Southwark, where the election was held in early October, later than most polls, succession played a greater role, particularly since the king had become ill in late August, necessitating James' return from the Continent. The duke of York's successful attempt to have Monmouth exiled increased concern about the Court's apparent pro-Catholic leanings. Buckingham attempted to increase his support in London by accusing Lord Chief Justice Sir William Scroggs of possessing surreptitious instructions to favor Catholics, but when faced with prosecution the duke fled to the Continent. Sir Robert Clayton fared better, winning the lord mayorship with the support of dissenters and others, as did Sir Thomas Player, who won a seat in the House of

[22] BL, Add. MSS 70,013, fol. 13v; Knights, *Politics and Opinion*, 52–53, 56.
[23] BL, Add. MSS 25,119, fol. 145r (quoted); Christopher Ness, *A Distinct Discourse and Discovery of the Person and Period of Antichrist* (London, 1679), sigs. A2v (quoted), A3v (quoted). For Ness (or Nesse) see *BDBR*, *s.v.*

Commons in part by appealing to nonconformists. Belief in the Popish plot's reality remained strong among these people at a time when others had doubts.[24]

During the fall of 1679 the Court responded to the rising sentiment against it in various ways. Roger L'Estrange received instructions on 24 September to confiscate seditious books, and a series of arrests ensued in October, followed on the 31st by a royal proclamation to suppress all treasonable literature. Among the apprehended was Bunyan's former printer, Benjamin Harris, who, as we have seen, was arrested for publishing Blount's *An Appeal from the Country to the City*. Blount's identification of the enemy as "young beggarly Officers, Courtiers, overhot Church-men, and Papists" effectively encapsulated the Country's concerns.[25] Faced with such sentiment, Charles accepted James' recommendation to prorogue the new Parliament on 17 October. The duke of York also supported an illconceived attempt to frame Shaftesbury and his supporters. Elizabeth Cellier, a midwife with ties to James' wife, had her agent, Thomas Dangerfield (alias Willoughby), plant forged documents in the chamber of Colonel Roderick Mansell, Buckingham's steward, and then "discover" them. A suspicious Privy Council ordered a search of Cellier's house, which turned up incriminating documents in a meal tub, and her arrest and that of other Catholics ensued.[26] Fears of Catholic plotting once again soared, as reflected partly by the huge throngs that attended the pope-burnings on 5 and 17 November, the latter funded in part by the Green Ribbon Club. On those occasions the flames also claimed replicas of bishops adorned with surplices, copes, hoods, and rochets. In the eyes of the more dissident nonconformists, such imagery must have linked the Church of England to Catholicism.[27]

Given his friendship with Bunyan, Owen's outlook in this period is noteworthy. The views he expressed to his congregation underscore the extent to which he regarded the time as one of great trials and danger. In a sermon delivered on 8 January 1680, he announced that all of the ministers with whom he was conversing—Bunyan would have been among them—thought God was about to impose a period of darkness on England, and they disagreed only as to its length. Ensuing sermons reiterated this theme, pointing to the imminent "Night and Dawning of Judgment."

[24] Bodl., Carte MSS 72, fol. 470r (quoted); Knights, *Politics and Opinion*, 214–20, 222–23, 226.

[25] *A Proclamation for the Suppressing of Seditious and Treasonable Books and Pamphlets* (London, 1679); [Charles Blount], *An Appeal from the Country to the City, for the Preservation of His Majesties Person, Liberty, Property, and the Protestant Religion* (London, 1679), 5.

[26] Knights, *Politics and Opinion*, 224–25; Bodl., Carte MSS 228, fol. 157r; Greaves, *SOK*, 10; Haley, *Shaftesbury*, 554–55. For Cellier and Dangerfield see *DNB*, s.vv.

[27] Knights, *Politics and Opinion*, 225; Harris, *LC*, 123–24.

Now the Ax is layd at the Root of the Tree. You have had many Branches lopped off
. . . and many Captivityes, and many Desolations; . . . unless you do Repent, the whole
Tree will be cutt downe, the whole Judaicall Church shall be destroyed.

This message of impending judgment was directed to England in general as well
as to the godly.[28] In *The Church of Rome No Safe Guide* (1679) Owen lashed out
against the use of force to compel religious beliefs, warning that such methods
would characterize Catholic rule if papists gained ascendancy in England. Any
attempt to impose Catholicism on the country without the people's consent was
intolerable, for "the *Insupportable Yoke* this Guide puts *on Kings* and *Soveraign
Princes*, on pretence of its divine Right of an universal Guidance of them and all
their Subjects, deserves the Consideration of them that are concerned, before
they give themselves unto it."[29] Popery, arbitrary government, Protestantism's security, and the succession concerned Owen, and it is not surprising to see him
join Baxter, John Howe, Thomas Jacombe, John Griffith, and Daniel Bull in organizing petitions for a new Parliament in the late spring or early summer of
1679. Hoping to placate the nonconformists, on 15 July Charles invited these
clergy to confer with him. Owen enjoyed close contact with several members of
Parliament, including Wharton in the Lords and Sir John Hartopp, MP for
Leicestershire and a member of his congregation, in the Commons. Owen's assistant, Ferguson, was suspected of treasonable activities in the fall, prompting
the king on 1 December to order his arrest upon his return from the Netherlands.[30]

Against this background, including renewed concern about the Catholic
threat following the Meal Tub plot's disclosure in October, Bunyan composed *A
Treatise of the Fear of God*, which apparently was an expanded version of a sermon on Revelation 14:7, "Fear God, and give glory to him; for the hour of his
judgment is come. . . ."[31] The probable period of composition was between
August 1679 and January 1680. Like many good preachers, he took advantage of a
topic on people's minds—the fear stemming from further disclosure of alleged

[28] DWL, MSS L6/4, discourse of Owen at a church meeting (5 December 1679), and
sermon of Owen on Jeremiah 13:16 (8 January 1680); L6/3, sermon of Owen on Luke
19:41–44 (4 February 1680) (quoted).

[29] John Owen, *The Church of Rome No Safe Guide* (London, 1679), 42–43, 45–46. See
also [John Owen], *An Account of the Grounds and Reasons on Which Protestant Dissenters
Desire Their Liberty* [1680], 1–2.

[30] Lacey, 138; *BDBR, s.v.* Sir John Hartopp; PRO, SP 44/56, p. 22. For Jacombe and Bull
see *Calamy Revised, s.vv.*; for Griffith see *DNB, s.v.*

[31] E. Beatrice Batson has postulated that fear is the predominant tone in Bunyan's
sermons. "The Artistry of John Bunyan's Sermons," *American Baptist Quarterly* 7 (December 1988): 494–95.

Catholic conspiracy—as the setting for his sermon. He had relatively little to say about Catholicism itself, at least explicitly. Much of the book deals with the wrong kinds of fear, including that which stems from conscience, or what Bunyan calls the light of nature, and that which causes people to tremble before God and yet be devoid of repentance and faith (*MW*, 9:22–23). The latter fear, which he deemed ungodly, was at the root of Catholicism, though it extended far beyond Catholics. "*This ungodly fear of God*, is that which will put men upon adding to the revealed Will of God, their own inventions, and their own performances of them as a means to pacifie the anger of God" (9:29). As he had explained in *I Will Pray with the Spirit*, this would encompass Prayer-Book Protestants, who in general terms are among his targets in *A Treatise of the Fear of God*. He singled out the idolatrous Israelites in 2 Kings 17, the Pharisees, and the Catholics as examples of those who manifest ungodly fear. For centuries, he averred, the Catholics had been wracked and tortured by such fear, as evinced by their penance, self-flagellation, recitations of the rosary, pilgrimages, confession to priests, purchase of pardons, sackcloth, and "creeping to the Cross." "Could they be brought to believe this Doctrine, that Christ was delivered for our offences, and raised again for our justification, and to apply it by faith with Godly boldness to their own souls, this fear would vanish, and so consequently all those things with which they so needlessly and unprofitably afflicted themselves, offend God, and grieve his people" (9:29). Bunyan also accused Catholics of fostering the fear that holds transgressors in perpetual bondage (9:31–39). Such is the case, he averred, with those who adhere to "that profane and Popish doctrine, forgiven to day, unforgiven to morrow, a child of God to day, a child of Hell to morrow" (9:35).

Elsewhere in this book Bunyan attacked the Catholics implicitly, as in his insistence that the power of binding and releasing was divinely vested in Scripture, not in the papacy (9:19). Catholics were in his mind when, implicitly evoking his readings in Foxe, he praised the invincible spirit of those who had suffered for the gospel at the stake and in prison, by the sword and on the gallows. Addressing Catholics and persecuting Anglicans, he contrasted the martyrs with "your great, ranting, swaggering Roysters," ignorant of the saving fear of God (9:105–6). Catholics must have been in his thoughts when he excoriated hypocrites who make merchandise of souls and sell God's word, but he also directed this denunciation against a powerful English figure, pointedly asking, "Why should the saints look for any good from thee?" (9:132). The barbed comment was probably aimed at Buckingham, whose secret dealings with the French were becoming known by the fall of 1679.[32] If Bunyan heard such reports on one of his visits to

---

[32] *HMC* 36, *Ormonde*, 5:242; Richard Ashcraft, *Revolutionary Politics & Locke's Two Treatises of Government* (Princeton, NJ: Princeton University Press, 1986), 132–34.

London, he would have been enraged. In *The Greatness of the Soul* (1682) he would refer sympathetically to exiled Huguenots (*MW*, 9:235), and his affinities with the Country involved deep-seated antipathy to popery and arbitrary government such as that in France. Despite Buckingham's record of support for toleration, his fraternizing with Louis XIV's government would have been ample provocation for Bunyan to have denounced such hypocrisy.

A sense of impending danger was on Bunyan's mind in late 1679. In Lamentations he found a biblical model for the church under affliction, an archetype that resonated in his own day. The Jews, he noted, complained that a fiercely angry God had punished them for their transgressions, treading "under foot her mighty men" and summoning the heathen to oppress them. In the face of a reputed, internationally sanctioned conspiracy to tyrannize England, this passage must have struck a responsive chord among his readers. The suffering Jewish "Church," Bunyan added, believed that God "had covered her with a cloud in his anger, that he was an enemy, and that he had hung a chain upon her, . . . [and] shut out her prayer, broken her teeth with gravel stones, and covered her with ashes, and . . . utterly rejected her." Yet the Jews managed to cling to their faith, and this Bunyan exhorted his readers to do, no matter how severe the impending persecution (9:47). Should the Catholics seize power, he expected little sympathy for visible saints from most people. Like David, the Israelites, and Jesus, the godly would find those around them rejoicing at their misery (9:97–98). This was hardly surprising, given Bunyan's view of England as a land, like ancient Judah, wallowing in sin (9:95).

He urged the godly not to worry about temporal perils, for God will deliver them from their enemies if they rightly fear him (9:111, 124). Reports of armed Catholics riding through the night should cause the godly no terror, he counseled, for one angel can slay 185,000 men in a single night, a reference to Isaiah 37:36. God "hath given charge to the armies of Heaven to look after, take charge of, to camp about, and to deliver thee"; each person has an assigned angel (9:80–81, 118). "We little think of this, yet this is the priviledge of them that fear the Lord, yea if need be [the angels] shall all come down to help them, and to deliver them, rather then contrary to the mind of their God they should by any be abused" (9:81). Heaven's armies of angels are thus the greatest military force, capable of defending the godly's interests much as they did Elisha's with horses and chariots of fire (2 Kings 6:17) (9:80). In the face of anticipated Catholic repression, Bunyan assured the faithful that God would never abandon them to their foes' subtlety and power, though he also explained that God might subject them to fires, dungeons, and other frightful torments as chastisements (9:44–45, 77). In such circumstances, the persecutory forces act as divine agents, however unwittingly. "In the hottest of this battel," Christians can be certain only of ultimate victory, not freedom from pain and persecution (9:47, 83). God offers no guarantees against a return of the travail suffered by Protestants during Mary Tudor's reign.

In late 1679 Bunyan was not prepared to accept the possibility of a Catholic takeover without resistance. Pointedly, he recounted the story of the Hebrew midwives who disobeyed the pharaoh's command to slay newly born Hebrew males (Exodus 1:15–20). As long as they acted in the proper fear of God, Bunyan adjudged their resistance legitimate, and this, he contended, was the key to deliverance (9:110). Although implicit, the parallel with England in 1679 was obvious. He was also implicitly addressing the English scene when he commented on godly fear as a qualification for positions of trust, such as Joseph had exercised in Egypt or Daniel and Mordecai in Babylon. Special circumstances necessitated that power be vested in the hands of those who rightly fear God:

> True, when there is no special matter, or thing to be done by God in a Nation for his people, then who will, that is, whether they have grace or no, may have the dispose of those things: but if God has any thing in special to bestow upon his people of this worlds good, then he will intrust it in the hands of men fearing God. (9:107)

For Protestants the years of the Catholic threat and widespread concern over Protestantism's security and arbitrary government made this such a special time. Bunyan would hardly have seen the openly Catholic duke of York as a man filled with godly fear, but he may have been thinking of Monmouth as a possible successor. On 9 November 1678 Londoners had circulated a rumor that the king had informed the House of Commons he would name Monmouth, the "protestant duke," his successor. Crowds celebrated with bonfires and toasted the health of Charles, Monmouth, and Shaftesbury. Even after the duke had been temporarily exiled by the king, London crowds drank to his health in September 1679. When Monmouth returned to England in November, church bells rang, more cups were lifted in toasts, and fires of celebration were lit—more than sixty along the Strand alone.[33] Bunyan must have known of such activities, perhaps even observing or participating in them. Certainly any of Monmouth's supporters who read Bunyan's remarks on the need for rulers with godly fear would have had no trouble applying them to their Protestant duke.

Bunyan likened the present enemies of the godly to the Amalekites who ambushed the Israelites after they left Egypt, slaughtering the feeble and weary who lagged behind the main body (Deuteronomy 25:17–18). Late seventeenth-century Amalekites acted similarly against the saints, smiting them in all manner of ways, ranging from physical punishment, fines, and expropriations to slander and alle-

---

[33] Knights, *Politics and Opinion*, 36; Harris, *LC*, 159–60.

gations of scandal (9:94). He lashed out as well against such favorite targets as sorcerers, adulterers, oppressive employers, and false swearers, in whose company he presumably included the informers who continued to submit reports about nonconformist meetings to the government (9:97).

Theologically, *A Treatise of the Fear of God* rests on an understanding of the covenants delineated in *The Doctrine of the Law and Grace Unfolded*. Those who possess efficacious fear[34] have a divinely bestowed gift because of their inclusion in the covenant of grace originally formulated between God the father and God the son. Such people are no longer subject to the conditions of the covenant of the law but are now governed by the principles of the new covenant. Nevertheless, Bunyan was still chary of being identified as an Antinomian because of this concept; hence near the outset of the work he castigated those "light, frothy professors in the world, that carry it under that which they call the presence of God, more like to *Anticks*, than sober sensible Christians" (9:10). The life of grace is not one of wantonness, but neither is it a life free from the proper fear of God.[35]

From a doctrinal standpoint another significant passage in *A Treatise of the Fear of God* deals with the will, which Bunyan defines as "*That chief and great faculty of the soul.*" Whichever way it "goes, all goes," whether to heaven or hell (9:124). Yet he refused to attribute a full range of choices to the human will. Grace is limited, and those on whom it is bestowed have no power to resist it, nor can those without it believe, repent, and fear God efficaciously. Only when Christians have this grace can they freely fear God: "Fearing of God is a voluntary act of the *will*" (9:124). Yet the voluntarism is deceptive, for it is beyond the reprobate's ability to fear God in an acceptable manner. Bunyan's apparent voluntarism is real only in the sense that the elect are free *temporarily* to cease fearing God, for once the will has been infused with grace and efficacious fear, the believer is "kept from final, and damnable apostasy" (9:125).

Late in 1679 Bunyan was also pondering the theme he subsequently developed in his second allegory, *The Holy War*, namely, the heart as "the main *FORT* in the mystical world, *man*." Using the analogy of a king who takes precautions to secure a town by garrisoning its fort with well-armed troops, he depicted the heart as the principal fortress of what he would later call Mansoul. The most effective way for the godly to secure their hearts, their fortresses, is to fill them with godly fear, which keeps the soul perpetually on watch against enemy attack (9:124–26). When the Israelites arrived in Canaan, Bunyan reflected, they made a

[34]In a sermon on Psalm 90:11 preached on 18 October 1677, Owen too had stressed the importance of the proper fear of God. He and Bunyan may have discussed this theme before the latter wrote *A Treatise of the Fear of God*. DWL, MSS L6/3.

[35]This paragraph and that which follows are adapted from *MW*, 9:xxx–xxxi.

covenant with the native Gibeonites without seeking God's counsel. "But would they have done so, think you, if at the same time *the fear of God*, had had its full play in the soul, in the Army?" (9:126). Thus the kernel of *The Holy War* began to develop in the context of a country tense with concern about popery and arbitrary government, and far from united with respect to the nature of and potential solutions for these perceived threats.

### "O Debauchery, Debauchery"[36]: Restoration Society and the Reprobate

Ponder obtained licenses for *A Treatise of the Fear of God* and *The Life and Death of Mr. Badman* as well as the fourth edition of *The Pilgrim's Progress* in February 1680.[37] The only changes Bunyan made in the new edition of his allegory were the addition of some marginal notes and biblical references, and assorted minor alterations in wording. Unlike the other two books, *A Treatise* was dated 1679 on the title-page, indicating that it appeared prior to 25 March 1680. Bunyan apparently worked on *Mr. Badman* off and on between the spring of 1678 and its completion in January 1680. Intended as a foil to *The Pilgrim's Progress* (*BM*, 1), *Mr. Badman* reflected, in part, some of the disciplinary cases of the Bedford congregation, particularly between 1676 and 1679, though Bunyan also drew on people he had observed or met on his preaching forays and his time in London.

During these years the Bedford church handled eight disciplinary cases, beginning in May 1676 with those of Susanna Cooper, who was received back into full communion after repenting of unspecified offenses, and Sarah Caine, who was publicly admonished for inappropriate conduct with young men, neglecting her vocation, and slighting the church. The following January Oliver Thodye acknowledged various misdeeds, including sabbath-breaking and brawling with neighbors.[38] In late 1677 the congregation withdrew communion—the step preliminary to expulsion—from William Gardiner of Gamlingay for "wicked light speches and carages" toward a village woman, which had exposed the church to infamy and reproach.[39] Unacceptable behavior brought similar punishment for another Gamlingay man, Edward Dent, in early 1678 because he mismanaged his sister's employment, contracted excessive debt, defrauded people, and failed to pay his bills on time. A full confession prompted the church to welcome him back in March of the same year. That month Bunyan and his congregants withdrew communion from William Man at Cotton End, Bedfordshire, because of his improper behavior toward a woman, including kissing and attempted inter-

[36] *BM*, 7.
[37] Arber, *Term Catalogues*, 1:381–82.
[38] *CB*, 81.
[39] *CB*, 82.

course; by May he had confessed to fornication with several women, for which the congregation "cast him out of the Church, and deliver[ed] him up to Satan, for the destruction of the flesh, and that his sperit may be saved in the day of the Lord Jesus."[40] For spreading rumors of an untrue scandal reputedly involving another church member and for unspecified additional offenses, Mary Fosket was publicly admonished in July 1678, and the following year the church finally expelled John Stanton, who had repeatedly beaten his wife "for very light matters."[41]

The behavior of one other miscreant, John Wildman, may have begun before Bunyan completed *Mr. Badman*, though the church took up his case only on 2 November 1680 after he had filed a written complaint. Finding this grievance objectionable (the content is unspecified), the church deemed remarks Wildman had made to the minister John Gibbs about Bunyan and the congregation slanderous. According to the church book, Wildman "did desperately charge our brother and pastor, John Bunyan, with calling the sisters to know ther husband's estates, in order to put a levy open them, wher in he was proved before the whole congregation an abominable lyer and slanderer of our beloved brother Bunyan." Unanimously the congregation withdrew communion from Wildman, but his case dragged on past Bunyan's death.[42] In the meantime Wildman began worshiping with the neighboring congregation at Stevington, where he quickly became the focal point of a related controversy. When Oliver Scott, a member of Bunyan's church who had been preaching to the Stevington group, criticized one of Wildman's supporters in his dispute with Bedford, the Stevington congregation rebuked Scott. However, it refused to admit Wildman to membership and permit him to preach until he resolved his differences with Bunyan's church.[43] Most of the Wildman case occurred after Bunyan had finished *Mr. Badman*, but its early stages and the other disciplinary problems may have helped to persuade him of the need for a book describing the behavior and ultimate destiny of the ungodly.

In addition to drawing on misconduct in his own congregation, Bunyan found ample material for *Mr. Badman* in those he observed beyond the community of visible saints (probably including some of those with whom he had been imprisoned), in accounts from people he respected, and in printed material. Six of his stories are borrowed nearly verbatim from Samuel Clarke's *A Mirrour or Looking-Glass Both for Saints & Sinners, Held Forth in Some Thousands of Examples* (4th ed., 1671), and he may also have read Thomas Beard's *The Theatre of*

[40] *CB*, 83.
[41] *CB*, 84.
[42] *CB*, 85–86, 88–90.
[43] BLA, MS X239/1, fols. 21–25.

*Gods Judgements* (rev. ed., 1631) and John Reynolds' *The Triumphs of Gods Revenge Against the Crying and Execrable Sinne of (Wilful and Premeditated) Murther* (4th ed., 1663) (*BM*, xix, xxii, xxiv).[44] To the extent that *Mr. Badman* incorporates such subject-matter, it is another entry in the list of judgment-books, though such material has only secondary, illustrative purpose for Bunyan. In his epistle to the reader he went so far as to claim he had *"as little as may be, gone out of the road of mine own observation of things."* To the best of his memory he thought everything he discussed, *"as to matter of fact, [had] been acted upon the stage of this World, even many times before mine eyes"* (*BM*, 1). Presumably he was referring to the numerous types of inappropriate conduct discussed in the work—incidents similar to some of his borrowed accounts. His palpable intent in making this claim was to give his book a measure of authority through the evocation of personal observation as well as the standard reliance on scriptural material.

Bunyan did not write *Mr. Badman* primarily for entertainment, though he made no attempt to hide the fact that the reader's enjoyment was a consideration in his selection of a dialogue format. *"I have . . . put it into the form of a Dialogue, that I might with more ease to my self, and pleasure to the Reader, perform the work"* (1). Because writing an interesting book was a conscious decision, critics have legitimately assessed Bunyan's success—or more often the lack of it—in composing a fictive work. Yet his principal goals in *Mr. Badman* were evangelical, providing readers with a handbook by which to assess their conduct and ascertain *"whether thou thy self art treading in his path"* to hell (1); theological, using Badman's story to explicate the doctrine of providence and the practical outworking of the divine decree of predestination; and reformist, assessing Restoration society in terms of the New Testament's demanding standards of conduct.[45] He did not intend *Mr. Badman* to be a fictional work except in the limited sense in which he made Badman a composite of observable behavioral patterns, for he deemed Badman's life true to experience. In Bunyan's mind, the illustrative ma-

---

[44] For Clarke, Beard, and Reynolds (*ad cal.* John Reynolds, epigrammatist) see *DNB*, s.vv. The first of the eventual six books of Reynolds' work was published in 1621. I see no evidence that Bunyan borrowed any material from Reynolds, but the latter's book helped whet the public's appetite for such material. Anne Dunan suggests that Bunyan may have been influenced by books written for English youth, such as Thomas Vincent's *Words of Advice to Young Men* (London, 1668) and Thomas Gouge's *The Young Man's Guide* (London, 1670). "*The Life and Death of Mr. Badman* as a 'Compassionate Counsel to all Young Men': John Bunyan and Nonconformist Writings on Youth," *BS* 9 (1999–2000): 50–68.

[45] See J. G. Randall's discussion of *Mr. Badman* in the context of the conduct-book tradition. "Against the Backdrop of Eternity: Narrative and the Negative Casuistry of John Bunyan's *The Life and Death of Mr Badman*," *Baptist Quarterly* 35 (July 1994): 347–59.

terial drawn from Clarke and others validated the veracity of his composite of reprobate behavior. Thus *Mr. Badman* was never intended to be primarily a fictional work but an account "*of the Life and Death of the Ungodly*" designed to benefit the reader (1, 169). The evangelical purpose could not be more manifest: "*My endeavour is to stop an hellish Course of Life, and to save a soul from death*" (5).

As Bunyan tells it, the story of Badman's life is relatively straightforward, with his fate implied in the title and explicitly stated virtually at the outset: "He died that he might die, he went from Life to Death, and then from Death to Death, from Death Natural to death Eternal" (14). Given his reprobate status, his ultimate destiny could be no other, and in this there is no mystery. The book's compelling interest does not derive from suspense about a possible deathbed conversion but instead from curiosity, perhaps even fascination, about Badman's relentlessly immoral behavior. Aberrant conduct is more likely to claim the headlines than pious living. Badman's struggles are fundamentally different from Christian's in *The Pilgrim's Progress*, for his battles are waged from the perspective of the wicked combating the good, particularly in the form of his first wife and her fellow visible saints, but also his godly parents, his honest customers, and his one God-fearing child (of seven). Badman struggles too in finding the material resources to fund his dissolute life, with the diseases that finally wrack his body, and with a second wife whose proclivity to evil living fully equals his own. Where there is struggle, there is suspense.[46] Stricken in mid-life by a serious illness, Badman wrestles with the prospect of death and is seemingly on the verge of genuine conversion, but when his demise does come, there is no replay of this travail, for his commitment to depravity, ingrained in his nature from birth, is total (17). He belongs to Mephistopheles, a fate freely chosen yet eternally destined. Divine mercy has not intruded to save him from himself, nor would he have wanted God to do so. This is precisely the fascination of Badman, whose life represents the triumph of human nature's darker side, a relentless march to the abyss.

In Bunyan's depiction of the unbridgeable gulf between the reprobate and the elect, one crucial distinction is the former's inability to recognize the role of divine providence in ordering the world's affairs. "Instead of honouring of God, and of giving glory to him for any of his Mercies, or under any of his good Providences towards him (for God is good to all, and lets his Sun shine, and his Rain fall upon the unthankful and unholy,) [Badman] would ascribe the glory to other causes" (127). Badman's "Crosses," as he describes them, are not attributed to di-

---

[46] For a contrary view see Hill, *TPM*, 231; Mullett, *JBC*, 213. See also Sharrock, *JB*, 106–7.

vine oversight but to misfortune, bad luck, poor management, his neighbors' ill-will, or the time his first wife spent in religious pursuits, whereas he takes credit for the good things that happen in his life (127). In other words, in Bunyan's judgment he lacks the divine gift that enables the elect to discern the working of providence. Should a visible saint go bankrupt, Bunyan provided a series of questions to be asked and answered, all of them based on the assumption that the bankruptcy was ultimately attributable to providence (93–94). Likewise, when people are preserved from the potentially disastrous consequences of their actions, such as escaping serious accidents when riding a horse while inebriated, "protecting" providence is responsible (132). At root, *Mr. Badman* is a lesson in reading everything in life, ranging from health and weather to financial matters, through the lens of providence.[47]

Bunyan sought to teach his readers that no simple correlation exists between someone's actions and the apparent consequences. Although he filled his book with accounts of immediate divine punishment of people whose offenses are akin to Badman's, in many cases Badman seemingly escapes such retribution, even dying quietly in the company of like-minded friends. Bunyan's point is that providence's apparent vicissitudes are not an infallible guide to eternal destiny, though the elect, with the capability of reading providence, can grasp God's shaping of events and use their understanding to help their own pursuit of godliness. For Bunyan the consequence of this understanding of providence was a tendency to see life in supernatural terms rather than natural causes and effects.[48] At times, however, he gravitated toward a modern notion of causality, as when he attributed Badman's venereal disease to sexual promiscuity or recognized the physical damage caused by alcoholism. "*Many times these diseases come through mans inordinate use of things*"; in Badman's case, his death is the result of "his *Cups* and his *Queans*" (148).[49]

In addition to providing an account of the rake's progress, *Mr. Badman* is a sustained critique of the persecutory society Bunyan rendered in *The Pilgrim's*

[47] See U. Milo Kaufmann, "Spiritual Discerning: Bunyan and the Mysteries of the Divine Will," in *John Bunyan*, ed. Keeble, 181–87; and for general context, Alexandra Walsham, *Providence in Early Modern England* (Oxford: Oxford University Press, 1999), 8–15.

[48] Philip Henry's diaries provide useful examples of how such a view of providence shaped the interpretation of events. *Diaries and Letters of Philip Henry, M.A. of Broad Oak, Flintshire A.D. 1631–1696*, ed. Matthew Henry Lee (London: Kegan Paul, Trench and Co., 1882), e.g. 104–6, 144–45, 159.

[49] Bunyan's references to prostitutes evinced the growing interest of polite society in such women. In the eighteenth century such fascination was evident in Samuel Richardson's *Pamela* and *Clarissa*, Charlotte Lennox's *The Female Quixote*, Frances Burney's *Evelina*, Eliza Haywood's *Betsy Thoughtless*, and Daniel Defoe's *Roxana*.

*Progress* as Vanity Fair—"the Restoration *beau monde*" and its preoccupation "with forms of civility and etiquette, with status and hierarchy, with fashion, dress, and manners."[50] Hostile to godly values, generally inhospitable to visible saints, and profoundly at odds with New Testament principles, Restoration England was, in Bunyan's judgment, a nation desperately in need of heeding the prophetic message of repentance and reform. "England *shakes and totters already, by reason of the burden that Mr.* Badman *and his Friends have wickedly laid upon it*" (2). Like a flood, wickedness was about to drown England in a sea of iniquity, its turbulent, roiling waters engulfing young and old in debauchery. "*What hast thou done in* England! *Thou hast corrupted our Young men, and hast made our Old men beasts; thou hast deflowered our Virgins, and hast made Matrons Bawds.*" So heavy was the burden of transgression on England that the country was likely to sin and rise no more, an analogy Bunyan borrowed from Isaiah 24:20 (7). "*O! that I could mourn for* England, *and for the sins that are committed therein, even while I see that without repentance, the men of Gods wrath are about to deal with us, each having his slaughtering weapon in his hand*"; this time Bunyan found his inspiration in Ezekiel 9:1–2, but he was also referring to the perceived threat of a Catholic invasion. He likened his words to the coastal beacons that warned of sea-borne invaders. Body and soul, estate and country faced destruction from sin's malignity, a plague with the potency to overwhelm kingdoms (8). "*Bad men . . .* make *bad times*" (13). Badman's seamy portrait is framed in a jeremiad whose stark message of impending doom contrasts sharply with his carefree, irresponsible embrace of depravity. The jeremiad is a pointed reminder that providence governs nations no less than individuals, indeed, that England, like Badman, may perish.

As he surveyed a nation in peril, Bunyan continued to evince disenchantment with most of the powerful and wealthy. Badman, who for a time is very rich, is compared to Dives, evoking the theme of Bunyan's early work, *A Few Sighs from Hell* (139). To swear is described as "Gentleman-like" (27), and Bunyan noted the extortionate practices of office-holders through fees, rewards, and (implicitly) bribes, though he thought extortion was more commonly the practice of tradesmen (108). Among his examples of sexual offenders are various people of status, including a "great man" who, when warned that his womanizing threatened his vision, replied, "*Nay then,* said he, *farewell sweet Sight*" (50–51). In the 1650s another man had advised his mistress to tell the magistrate she had been impreg-

[50]N. H. Keeble, "'Till one greater man / Restore us . . .': Restoration Images in Bunyan and Milton," in *Awakening Words*, ed. Gay, Randall, and Zinck, 41. The phrase "rake's progress" was popularized by William Hogarth's series of engravings under that title in 1735, though Henry More had used the term "rake" in this sense in 1653 (*Oxford English Dictionary*).

nated by the Holy Spirit should she become pregnant. Bunyan thought about reporting this offender, but remained silent because "he was a great man, and I was
poor" (54–55).[51] From a fellow minister Bunyan learned how the former's mother, a midwife, had been taken to a stately home by "a brave young Gallant on
horseback" to help his gentry lover give birth. "Now there was made in a Room
hard by, a very great Fire: so the Gentleman took up the Babe, went and drew the
coals from the stock, cast the Child in, and covered it up, and there was an end of
that" (52–53). Earlier, Bunyan had made his point in a terse marginal comment
no reader could miss: "Sins of great men dangerous" (49). Subsequently expanding on this, he explained that providence protects the poor more than the
wealthy. "A poor condition has preventing mercy attending of it. The poor, because they are poor, are not capable of sinning against God as the rich man does"
(94).

Medical doctors also attracted Bunyan's criticism. When Badman becomes
seriously ill, fearing death, he expresses remorse and seeks the comfort of his first
wife's ministers, but as he recovers, his doctor attributes his religious *"fears and
Out-cries"* to distemper. Reckoning his physician a savior, Badman returns to his
former ways, making lust his deity. In the margin Bunyan caustically noted,
"ignorant physicians kill souls while they cure bodyes" (138). He also recounted a
report about a physician in the Colchester area who helped his mistress murder
their three or four illegitimate children (53).

Sexual offenses play a substantial role in *Mr. Badman*, partly, I suspect, because of the prurient interests they aroused, partly because of Bunyan's desire to
warn of the health risk in licentious behavior, and partly because he seems to
have felt the strong lure of sexual temptation in his own life. This is *not* to suggest
that he was unfaithful to his wife or in any way sexually aberrant, but merely to
recognize that he sensed "the enchanting and bewitching pleasures" of sex (53).
Proverbs 7 provided him with a cautionary tale against the allures of a temptress,
her tapestry and linen-covered bed perfumed with spices, and her offer to make
love until dawn seemingly irresistible. "The very hands, words and ways of such,
are all snares and bands to youthful, lustful fellows" (49–50). "A whore is commonly a deep ditch, few recover," as Philip Henry bluntly put it.[52] Bunyan's
ringing denunciation of fashionable low necklines and bare female shoulders that

[51] Similar stories had been attributed to mid-century radicals, notably the Ranter
Mary Adams and the millenarian John Robins. Anon., *The Ranters Monster: Being a True
Relation of One Mary Adams* (London, 1652); John Taylor, *Ranters of Both Sexes, Male and
Female* (London, 1651), title-page, 2.
[52] CUL, Add. MSS 7338, commenting on Genesis 38.

incite lust has the ring of experience, particularly when he lashes out against the "bewitching and tempting" garments worn by professing Christians (125). Once again, he located sexual lust in the female body. As he battled unwanted feelings of sexual arousal, he found inspiration in the biblical story of Joseph, who withstood the daily enticements of the beautiful wife of a captain of the guard and her invitations to make love. Bunyan read his own resolve to resist such temptations into Joseph's mind, averring that the young man would "not defile himself, sin against God, and hazard his own eternal salvation" (55). Although Bunyan assigned ample blame to women who lured men into sexual misdeeds, he apportioned some of the responsibility for England's plague of lust to men who made whores of honest women by enticing them into sexual intercourse with false promises of marriage (55–56). At a deeper level he attributed sexual misconduct to one's reprobate status, making the offenses a consequence of God's pretemporal decision to withhold grace and mercy from the perpetrator. "Men are given up to this sin, because they are abhorred of God, and because abhorred, therefore they shall fall into the commission of it" (54).

The horrific nature of venereal disease was at once repulsive and, in a morbid sense, fascinating to Bunyan. Although gonorrhea was more common than syphilis in England by the seventeenth century—James Boswell would contract gonorrhea at least seventeen times in the next century[53]—Bunyan's description of "*the Foul Disease*, now called by us the *Pox*," refers to syphilis, with its chancres (painless sores) and rash (51). Badman suffered from "a tang of the Pox in his bowels," which Bunyan rightly associated with syphilis, the second stage of which can include a rectal rash. He identified the disease with the "reproach [that] shall not be wiped away" in Proverbs 6:33 and the "strange punishment" in Job 31:3. Graphically, he depicted the illness as "a disease so nauseous and stinking, so infectious to the whole body (and so intailed to this sin,) that hardly are any common with unclean Women, but they have more or less a touch of it to their shame" (51). As he noted, the illness can lead to a diminution of strength, a multitude of illnesses, and even blindness. Although syphilis-induced blindness is rare, the disease can cause paralysis, numbness in the legs, impaired balance, and dementia. Bunyan had carefully observed the symptoms or paid close attention to descriptions of the afflicted, at least one of whom he personally knew; that man, he recalled, had "*rotted away with it*," whereas another "*had his Nose eaten off, and his Mouth almost quite sewed up thereby*" (51). Earlier in the century the poet Sir William Davenant had suffered a similar fate after contracting syphilis

[53] Lawrence Stone, *The Family, Sex and Marriage in England 1500–1800*, abridged ed. (New York: Harper and Row, 1979), 378–79.

(176). Bunyan probably learned much of what he knew about the disease during his visits to London.[54]

Swearing, to which Bunyan had been prone in his younger days, also receives prominent attention in *Mr. Badman*. He distinguished between cursing, whereby someone unjustly wishes evil on another person, and swearing, which is done in the name of someone, typically God, or something, such as idols, the Catholic mass, animals, or birds (29). Badman curses others, wishing them severe beatings, broken necks, syphilis, or the plague, but he also curses himself, ostensibly desiring to be hanged, burned, or snatched by Satan. Consequently Bunyan included him among "the *Damme* Blades" (30). Unlike the Friends and some Baptists,[55] Bunyan accepted swearing as legitimate to attest the truth in God's name, but not when such oaths were unnecessary, even if the matter was true. Badman is particularly obnoxious to Bunyan because he made cursing and swearing a badge of honor and a sign of masculinity. Consequently, Bunyan exhorted his readers not to engage in commerce with such people (27–29). Among the most vivid judgment accounts in *Mr. Badman* are two that deal with swearing, including the story of Dorothy Mately of Ashover, Derby. A notorious swearer, curser, and liar, Mately, while sifting tailings at a lead mine, stole two pence from a boy's pocket, "for he had laid his Breeches by, and was at work in his Drawers." When accused of the theft, she heatedly denied it, wishing the ground would swallow her if she were lying. According to the Ashover parish register, a cave-in claimed her life, and Bunyan averred that the missing money was found in her pocket (33).[56] Clearly, he attributed her mishap to providence rather than a mining accident. This was also the case with the mentally ill Ned, whose father encouraged the boy to curse and swear as entertainment for alehouse customers. As Bunyan tells the story, when Ned urged the Devil to take his father, Satan responded, possessing the father and moving at will through his tortured body. The Devil "*would lye like an hard bump in the soft place of his chest, (I mean, I saw it so,) and so would rent and tare him, and make him roar.*" A doctor failed to expurgate the

---

[54] The parish of St. Botolph without Aldgate had twelve recorded deaths from the so-called French pox between 1583 and 1599, nine of them in the years 1594–99. Thomas Rogers Forbes, *Chronicle from Aldgate: Life and Death in Shakespeare's London* (New Haven, CT: Yale University Press, 1971), 101, 105–6.

[55] Underwood, *PRLW*, 96–97.

[56] J. Charles Cox, *The Parish Registers of England* (London: Methuen, 1910), 133. Tindall (199) has traced the Mately story to *Mirabilis Annus* (1661), the author of which was probably Cokayne or Danvers. Bunyan could have heard the account, which he embellished, from either of them. Greaves, *DUFE*, 213. Philip Henry read the story and noted it in his diary. *Diaries*, 105. See also Maurice Hussey, "John Bunyan and the Books of God's Judgements: A Study of *The Life and Death of Mr. Badman*," *English* 7 (Spring 1949): 166.

Devil by nearly suffocating the victim with fumes from a pan of coals, and shortly thereafter the man died "according to the cursed Wishes of his Son" (35, 37). In Bunyan's world, divine and satanic agencies freely interacted to accomplish, through providence, God's decrees of election and reprobation. Natural causality was subordinate to and a vehicle of this providence.

Not only is Badman a prolific user of profanity, but he is also an alcoholic, a condition Bunyan called "Swinish" because of its beastly nature. As with syphilis, he recognized the physical damage caused by excessive drinking, including premature death. To such behavior he also attributed dissipated estates, the ruination of families, destroyed reputations, and the damnation of souls. Alcoholism "so stupifies and besotts the soul, that a man that is far gone in Drunkenness, is hardly ever recovered to God" (45–47). A habitue of taverns, Badman, in a drunken stupor, breaks his leg when his horse throws him, but Bunyan quickly added that he had heard of many whose necks had been snapped under similar circumstances. In passing, he noted that a man in the Bedford area had "died in his drink," apparently a victim of alcohol poisoning (131–32). From Clarke, Bunyan borrowed three more stories of drunken fatalities, including a Salisbury man who toasted the Devil and shortly thereafter disappeared from a tavern's upstairs room, leaving behind a shattered window, its iron bar bowed and bloody. Bunyan seems to have had no doubt that Satan claimed the man, who was never seen again. Once more, the supernatural's full array is accepted as wholly real, the story's verisimilitude enhanced by such details as "a hideous noise" and "a stinking savour," both of them, as we have previously seen, associated with evil in Bunyan's mind (134–35).

By making Badman a merchant, Bunyan set the stage for a critique of Restoration economic practices. Some of his most astute commentators have missed a fundamental point in assessing his economic views. Like R. H. Tawney, who associated Bunyan's economic ideas with those of medieval Christianity, W. Y. Tindall regarded the economic tenets of Bunyan, Baxter, and the Friends as "the last moral vestiges of the Middle Ages."[57] In turn, Michael Mullett saw Bunyan's business ethics as an expression of small-town artisans and traders, whereas Roger Sharrock argued that Bunyan had an aversion to a money economy.[58] Whatever the similarity of his views to those of medieval friars or contemporary small-town traders and artisans, Bunyan based his critique of England's economy primarily on New Testament principles. He had no interest in defending traditionalism for its own sake, opposing commercial development per se, or espous-

[57] R. H. Tawney, *Religion and the Rise of Capitalism: A Historical Study* (London: John Murray, 1926), 8, 269; Tindall, 111–12.

[58] Mullett, *JBC,* 222; Sharrock, *JB,* 112.

ing any particular form of economic organization, nor was he against all forms of a capitalist economy. Instead he constructed his code of economic behavior on a series of key biblical precepts: Jesus' exhortation to treat others as you would have them deal with you (Matthew 7:12); Paul's counsel to undertake everything with love, which never seeks its own advantage (1 Corinthians 13:5 and 16:14); his admonition to speak truthfully (Ephesians 4:25); and the Pauline expostulation to undertake everything with a conscience free from offense to God and humanity (Acts 24:16). To this corpus of core texts Bunyan added two from the Old Testament, namely, the command to buy and sell based on fair prices (Genesis 23:9), and the injunction not to oppress others (Leviticus 25:14). In terms of both medieval and seventeenth-century practices, these were radical principles, much like those of the Quakers,[59] for they focus on conscientious concern for the welfare of others, with all transactions undertaken in love and honesty, eschewing every opportunity to take advantage of another party. To prey on someone else's ignorance, need, or desire for one's goods is unconscionable, but this does *not* prohibit fair profits or a capitalist economy per se (111–14). "There may be and is sin in trading," he noted in the marginalia, but he was not arguing that *all* commerce is evil (113). Bunyan's standards preclude *excessive* profit rather than legitimate gain, with both parties benefitting through an honest arrangement: "If it be lawful for me alway to sell my commodity as dear, or for as much as I can, then 'tis lawful for me to lay aside in my dealing with others, good conscience, to them, and to God: but it is not lawful for me, in my dealing with others, to lay aside good conscience, *&c.*" (110). His prohibition excludes unbridled profit, not reasonable gain.

To be sure, some of Bunyan's economic principles echo those of earlier reformers and preachers. Usury is wrong, though he focused his discussion solely on the poor, who are victimized by its practitioners, including pawnbrokers, "*the pest and Vermin of the Common-wealth*" (109–10). He made no attempt to prohibit interest in other areas, such as commercial trade, though he was chary of indebtedness: "A Professor should not owe any man any thing, *but love*" (98). Yet this prohibition is not absolute, for he thought that some debt is legitimate; Christians must beware of going so far into debt that they cannot pay their obligations, "for the further in, the greater fall" (99). Moreover, he rejected the medieval notion of the just price, recognizing that in commerce the cost of everything ebbs and flows, like the tide (115).

Like so many reformers before him, Bunyan decried fraudulent weights and measures, extortion, double billing, hoarding, and falsely creating the impression

[59] Richard L. Greaves, *Dublin's Merchant-Quaker: Anthony Sharp and the Community of Friends, 1643–1707* (Stanford, CA: Stanford University Press, 1998), 196–97.

of scarcity (100, 107–9, 117). Among the offenders he cited were people of substance ("Masters or Dames") who charged excessive prices to the poor when the latter could not afford the loss of a day's wages to shop in a market town. "In this the Women are especially faulty, in the sale of their Butter and Cheese, &c." With his keen sensitivity to the indigent's suffering, Bunyan opposed any oppressive economic activity, for preying on their needs, in his judgment, was tantamount to buying and selling the poor themselves (109).

Badman epitomizes virtually everything Bunyan deemed unacceptable in economic dealings. An oppressor of the poor, Badman trades dishonestly, uses fraudulent weights and measures, keeps false accounts, double-bills his customers, sells inferior goods at exorbitant prices, exploits his customers' needs, and goes heavily into debt. Moreover, he employs "the new Engine of *Breaking*," by which Bunyan meant the fraudulent use of bankruptcy, a practice Samuel Pepys considered common in the late seventeenth century.[60] When Badman's debts exceed £4,000, he deceives his creditors, sustaining a high volume of sales by disposing of his goods below cost. Simultaneously he places his possessions beyond his creditors' reach before declaring bankruptcy. To avoid arrest, he uses an agent to negotiate with the creditors, offering to settle his debts for two and a half shillings in the pound (12.5 percent), and finally agreeing to twice this amount. By this process he nets several thousand pounds (88–89). In Bunyan's judgment, "*this way of breaking*, it is nothing else but a more neat way of Thieving," and no one who "has conscience to God or man, can ever be his Crafts Master in this Hellish art" (90). He recognized that Christians could fall into bankruptcy through mismanagement or divine judgment, as was apparently the case with several members of his congregation,[61] in which case he advised them to deal with their creditors by seeking forgiveness, offering all their possessions toward repayment, and expressing a willingness to go to prison or serve the creditors as long as necessary in return only for enough to sustain their families (90, 93–95).

In addition to his knavery as a businessman, Badman is exceptionally proud, and Bunyan was convinced that such people are persecutors. One of the obvious signs of such arrogance is an addiction to fashionable and opulent attire, jewelry, and coiffure. Pointing to gold and pearl jewelry, costly raiment, pleated hair, and "other fools baubles" as signs of spiritual defilement, he was especially troubled by the recourse of some believers to such practices, not least because this hardened the ungodly to the gospel message (118, 121–22). "I have seen many my self, and those Church-members too, so deckt and bedaubed with their Fangles and Toyes, and that when they have been at the solemn Appointments of God, in the

---

[60] Pepys, 8:450.
[61] *CB*, 76, 83.

way of his Worship, that I have wondred with what face such painted persons could sit in the place where they were without swounding" (122). This must have been particularly true when he visited London churches, especially Owen's congregation, which included such persons of prominence and wealth as Sir John and Lady Elizabeth Hartopp, Charles Fleetwood, Frances Lady Haversham, daughter of the earl of Anglesey, and Benjamin and Mary Shute, whose son became the first Viscount Barrington. Owen himself hoped "that the Woomen who profess Godliness in this day would seriously enquire whither their Appearances in Publick and in the Assemblye of Gods People, be Fitt to meet the Lord in the Way of his Judgmente."[62] Why, Bunyan wondered, should people take pride in the clothing intended to cover the shame of their nudity (124–25)? Had it been within his power, he would probably have implemented standards for attire nearly as severe as those espoused by Quakers.

> What can be the end of those that are proud, in the decking of themselves after their antick manner? why are they for going with their Bulls-foretops [hair piled high on the front of the head], with their naked shoulders, and Paps hanging out like a Cows bag? why are they for painting their faces, for stretching out their necks, and for putting of themselves into all the Formalities which proud Fancy leads them to? . . . It is . . . to please their lusts, to satisfie their wild and extravagant fancies.[63]

Likening the Restoration's fashionable raiment to a harlot's attire, Bunyan was pained that some godly ministers winked and connived at such clothing (123).

He also addressed visible saints when he used Badman's story to champion endogamous marriage, a practice valued by nonconformist ministers and probably many of their followers.[64] By feigning piety, expressing remorse for his transgressions, speaking highly of godly ministers, taking notes during sermons, and giving one or two religious books to the pious woman whose hand he sought, Badman persuades her to marry him, but shortly thereafter "he hangs his Religion upon the hedge" (66–69). Her parents are deceased, and she entered into matrimony without seeking the godly's counsel, relying only on "her own poor,

---

[62] Toon, *God's Statesman*, 153; DWL, MSS L6/3, sermon of Owen on 1 Peter 4:17 (13 March 1678) (quoted). Hanserd Knollys similarly complained about the attire of London dissenters. *The World That Now Is; and the World That Is to Come* (London, 1681), pt. 1, 87–88.

[63] *BM*, 125. For Quaker standards of dress see Richard L. Greaves, *God's Other Children: Protestant Nonconformists and the Emergence of Denominational Churches in Ireland, 1660–1700* (Stanford, CA: Stanford University Press, 1997), 318–20; Greaves, *Dublin's Merchant-Quaker*, 204–9. Bunyan may have been influenced on this subject by Arthur Dent, *The Plaine Mans Path-Way to Heaven* (London, 1601), 40, 45–60.

[64] See, e.g., Philip Henry, CUL, Add. MSS 7388, commenting on Genesis 24; John Howe, DWL, MS 24.18, fols. 44–45.

raw, womanish Judgment" (73). For this mistake she pays with a life of misery, unequally yoked to a thoroughly obnoxious husband. In Bunyan's opinion, young people are prone to think themselves wise enough to select their own spouses (67).[65] He was not defending arranged marriages, but arguing for the necessity of obtaining the counsel of mature Christians. Marriages between believers and unbelievers, he insisted, are not only unwise but contrary to biblical precepts. Such unions can even cause the seemingly godly partner to turn from true religion, though his predestinarian theology would dictate that such persons had never been among the elect. Still, his warning implies that mixed marriages can alter eternal destinies: "Many that have had very hopefull beginnings for heaven, have by vertue of the mischiefs that have attended these unlawfull marriages, miserably and fearfully miscarried" (74–75).[66]

As diametrically opposed as Badman and his first wife are, both die quietly, though in very different spiritual estates and with opposite eternal destinies (141–45, 148–57). As Michael Mullett has observed, Bunyan could not utilize the traditional elements of the medieval *hora mortis*, such as sacramental ritual and a belief in free choice, to depict a tense, dramatic battle for a soul (227–28). Predestination ruled out a cosmic struggle for the dying, yet he could interiorize that battle, depicting a contest between faith and despair of the sort experienced by Christian as he crossed the river. But neither Badman nor his first wife undergo such a struggle. Although Badman's death differs from the horrific demises common in judgment books, writers such as Richard Greenham, Robert Bolton, Arthur Dent, and Thomas Jackson had discussed the peaceful deaths of sinners, as had Bunyan himself in *A Few Sighs from Hell* and *The Pilgrim's Progress*, where Ignorance perishes without a struggle.[67] There is no deathbed conversion in *Mr.*

[65] From George Griffith Bunyan may have learned about the case of Lord Wharton's daughter, Anne, who married without her father's consent, an act that led to Griffith's efforts to heal the resulting rupture in family relations. Bodl., Rawlinson Letters 50, fol. 121r.

[66] The endogamous ideal was nicely expressed by Philip Henry's daughter, Ann Hulton, in February 1695: "How good has Almighty God bin to us in providing so comforitably for us, so that wee are not unequaly yoked." BL, Add. MSS 42,849, fol. 15r.

[67] Robert Bolton, *The Workes of the Reverend, Truly Pious, and Judiciously Learned Robert Bolton* (London, 1641), 244–45; Richard Greenham, *The Workes of the Reverend and Faithfull Servant of Jesus Christ M. Richard Greenham*, 2nd ed. (London, 1599), 144; *MW*, 1:269–72; Arthur Dent, *A Sermon of Repentaunce* (London, 1582), sigs. D7v-D8r; Thomas Jackson, *The Raging Tempest Stilled* (London, 1623), 194–96. In contrast, Thomas Jenner asserted that the wicked die "*either Suddenly, Sullenly or desperately.*" *Divine Mysteries That Cannot Be Seene, Made Plain by That Which May Be Seene* (London, 1651), poem 15. For Greenham and Bolton see *DNB, s.vv.*

*Badman* because Badman is one of the reprobate, but Bunyan in any event put little stock in sickbed and deathbed repentance, and he had no reason to encourage such practices in this book. Badman's seemingly near conversion occurs well before his death, in connection with a grave illness (135–40), and Bunyan eschewed the opportunity to tease his readers with a sense of drama by reiterating such feigned religiosity in the death chamber. In assigning Badman a quiescent demise, Bunyan's point was that "there is no Judgment to be made by a quiet death, of the Eternal state of him that so dieth" (157). He was *not* suggesting that all reprobate perish so calmly. Earlier in the book he had recounted the story of an adulteress who died in considerable emotional distress, damning herself as a whore, labeling her children bastards, and sensing the Devil at the foot of her bed, waiting to claim her soul (53). A similar end had befallen a man who lived about twelve miles from Bedford and wrote a manuscript attacking Christ and the Bible. As he lay dying "a sense of his evil in writing of it . . . tore his Conscience as a Lyon would tare a Kid." Overwhelmed by guilt, he sought to take his own life by jumping from a window, only to be restrained by friends (136). Bunyan incorporated other stories of the wicked dying in anguish, all of which serve as counterpoints to Badman's death (160). Still, a sinful life and a calm demise are "the common high-way to Hell" (164).

The most glaring exception to this generality are those who commit suicide, an act for which Bunyan had nothing but abhorrence. As we have seen, during his own intense battles with depression he entertained suicidal thoughts but took no action because of his intense fear of death and the judgment that would ensue. In *Mr. Badman* he made it clear that anyone who commits suicide is destined for hell, like those who live wickedly and perish in utter despair (158, 160). To illustrate his point he related the stories of three suicides, two of whom slit their throats. The third case, involving John Cox of Brafield on the Green, Northamptonshire, occurred about 1667. A poor man, Cox became depressed when relentless ill health threatened his ability to provide for himself and his wife. With a razor he slashed his side, reached in, and pulled out entrails, throwing them around his bedchamber. Still alive, he slit his throat with the razor, at which point his wife heard him gasping for breath, discovered what he had done, and called neighbors for help; one of them subsequently told Bunyan about the suicide. When the neighbors implored Cox to repent, he responded that it was too late. Urged to pray for forgiveness,

> he seemed much offended, and in angry manner said, *Pray!* and with that flung himself away to the wall, and so after a few gasps died desperately. When he had turned him of his back, to the wall, the blood ran out of his belly as out of a boul, and soaked quite through the bed to the boards, and through the chinks of the boards it ran pouring down to the ground. Some said, that when the neighbours came to see him,

he lay groaping with his hand in his bowels, reaching upward, as was thought, that he might have pulled or cut out his heart. 'Twas said also, that some of his Liver had been by him torn out and cast upon the boards, and that many of his guts hung out of the bed on the side thereof. (159)

The detail, carefully recorded to establish verisimilitude, paints a gory picture of an evil death that stands sharply juxtaposed to Badman's demise. Bunyan's gripping account provokes only revulsion, not sympathy for this victim of insidious depression. Despite his own turbulent experience, he could not or would not recognize that Cox was afflicted with the same sense of futility and blackness that had once virtually overwhelmed him, though ostensibly for different reasons. Instead, Cox's fate, like everyone else's, is the result of providence. Bunyan may have responded to suicide so harshly because intuitively he sensed that his own despair, had it not been for providence, might have driven him to an equally abhorrent end.

In the substantial critique of Restoration society that fills the pages of *Mr. Badman*, Bunyan made room for one particularly odious character—the informer. Many magistrates would not have shared Bunyan's view of what to him was a nefarious activity, but nonconformists must have responded favorably to his inclusion of informers with drunkards, adulteresses, prostitutes, dishonest merchants, swearers, pawnbrokers, and the haughty. However devoted to the Church of England they might be, informers were part of Bunyan's rogues' gallery, and his attack on them was another aspect of his assault on the ecclesiastical establishment. He shared this hostility toward informers with other dissenters, including his friend John Owen, who considered them people of obnoxious character. In late 1674 hundreds of Presbyterians at Norwich had beaten and chased an informer, crying "Fall on & Kill the Rogue," and at Great Yarmouth an informer died after nonconformists dragged him and a colleague through a hog sty and a pond.[68] In *Mr. Badman* Bunyan described the spying activities of one W. S.—William Swinton, sexton of St. Cuthbert's—who diligently searched for dissenting meetings day and night, in the woods and fields, even climbing trees to observe his quarry. In due course he evinced the symptoms of a stroke—faltering speech, drooling, and an inability to hold his head upright. Ultimately he lost the ability to speak and even fell from a church steeple. "But after that he also walked about, till God had made him a sufficient spectacle of his Judgment for his sin, and then on a sudden he was stricken and dyed miserably" (82). Bunyan also reported the fate of another informer, an employee of a gentleman who lived near St. Neots, Huntingdonshire. For his zealous pursuit of dissenters, providence claimed him through a dog bite that became gangrenous, slowly and painfully

[68] Greaves, *EUHF*, 155, 226 (quoted).

rotting his flesh until he died.[69] In Bunyan's estimation, similar stories about divine judgment against informers could be related from most English counties—"True stories, that are neither *Lye*, nor *Romance*" (82).

He could have made a similar observation about the accounts of other offenders with which he sprinkled *Mr. Badman*, underscoring the seriousness with which he regarded his critique of Restoration society and all those people whose lives embodied the traits and vices of Badman.[70] In delineating Badman's character and ways, Bunyan effectively divided England into two camps, the visible saints and their enemies, the elect and the reprobate (though the correlation was imperfect). For him there was no middle ground: "Only the Godly that are in the world have a Sanctuary to go to" (168).

After *Mr. Badman* was completed, Bunyan devoted time in early or mid-1680 to prepare the fifth editions of *Grace Abounding* and *The Pilgrim's Progress*. If most or all of the last substantive changes had been undertaken for the fourth edition of *Grace Abounding*, as I have suggested, little was done now. Likewise, he made only token changes in the fifth edition of *The Pilgrim's Progress*. Both books were now essentially as he wanted them, and he made no substantive alterations in future editions.

### "The *Drum* in the Day of Alarum"[71]: England in Crisis

While Bunyan was finishing *Mr. Badman* during the winter of 1679–80, England plunged deeper into a crisis involving fears of arbitrary government and popery in the present and, owing to James' likely succession, the future. The king had sent Monmouth, James' principal rival, to the Netherlands in September, and the duke of York himself to Scotland in November. Charles also dismissed Shaftesbury from the Privy Council, and his decision to prorogue Parliament led two of his key ministers, Essex and Halifax, to indicate their displeasure, Essex by resigning from the Treasury and Halifax by withdrawing from court. In the aftermath of the Meal Tub plot, which heightened concern about Catholics, Shaftesbury and others mounted a petitioning campaign aimed especially at persuading Charles to summon Parliament, but instead the king continued to prorogue it until October 1680. In London a "monster" petition with almost 16,000 signatures—nearly 18,000 if one calculates the likely number on the missing pages—

---

[69] Brown, 211. Badman refrained from becoming an informer because of potentially negative repercussions for his business, an indication that dissenters retaliated where possible (*BM*, 79).

[70] Cf. Stuart Sim, *Negotiations with Paradox: Narrative Practice and Narrative Form in Bunyan and Defoe* (New York: Harvester Wheatsheaf, 1990), 73, 87–88.

[71] *MW*, 13:8.

was presented to the king on 13 January by Sir Gilbert Gerard, Titus Oates, and others. It urged that Parliament sit in late January and called for the trials of Danby and the five Catholic peers in the Tower, but it said nothing about exclusion. Mark Knights has estimated that at least 700 of the signatories were nonconformists, and that the actual number may run into the thousands. At least thirty-five dissenting ministers are among the signers, and others almost certainly would have been among those who signed the missing sheets. Owen's name is not on the surviving portion of the petition, but those of his three assistants— Ferguson, Isaac Loeffs, and John Danson—are. Other signers were George Cokayne, another friend of Bunyan's, and the Congregationalist John Ryther, who was associated with Ferguson and thus may have known Bunyan. Among the other ministerial signatories were the Congregationalists Thankful Owen, Stephen Ford, and Stephen Lobb; the Presbyterians Vincent Alsop and Andrew Parsons; and the Baptists Nehemiah Coxe, Laurence Wise, and Daniel Dyke. Bunyan's printers were well represented on the petition, which includes the names of Francis Smith, Dorman Newman, George Larkin, Benjamin Harris, and Benjamin Alsop (who would soon join their ranks). Moreover, Thomas Kelsey and Robert Blaney, Bunyan's sureties in 1677, also signed.[72] Bunyan must have been familiar with the petition, and his name, like Owen's, may have been among the estimated 2,000 missing ones.

Petitions came as well from outside London, and although none appear to have survived, their themes were reported in newspapers, newsletters, pamphlets, and correspondence. At least one country petition averred that the hope of a Catholic succession had emboldened the Popish plotters, and another urged further investigation of the Popish plot and greater security against a French invasion. Rather than unifying the nation, the petitioning exacerbated division, partly because Charles not only refused to yield but in late January brought James back to England, and partly because many people feared the petitioners might incite another civil war. The bishop of Norwich told the archbishop of Canterbury on 6 February that no petitions had been submitted from Norfolk or Suffolk, where

---

[72] Luttrell, 1:30; Mark Knights, "London's 'Monster' Petition of 1680," *Historical Journal* 36 (1993): 40, 44, 48–51, 58–59, 67; Knights, *Politics and Opinion*, 227–40; Bodl., Carte MSS 228, fols. 140r, 146r, 164r; Haley, *Shaftesbury*, 563. Blaney signed immediately preceding R[ichard] Halford, who frequently visited Oates. Professor Knights kindly provided the information about Blaney in a personal communication. Philip Henry described the petition as being 300 feet long and containing 60,000 signatures, an example of how accounts of it were quickly exaggerated. Henry, *Diaries*, 283. For Loeffs and Vincent Alsop see *Calamy Revised, s.vv.*; for Gerard, Ryther, Thankful Owen, and Wise see *BDBR, s.vv.*; for Lobb see *DNB, s.v.*; for Coxe see *The Records of a Church of Christ in Bristol, 1640–1687*, ed. Roger Hayden, Bristol Record Society's Publications, vol. 27 (1974), 41, 70, 185, 191, 287.

the gentry fiercely opposed them and clergy were generally unsupportive.[73] Beginning in the spring of 1680, loyalists began submitting addresses abhorring the petitioners' endeavors, and for months they spread rumors that the "Presbyterians" were conspiring against the government. In an angry retort, the Presbyterian minister John Collings protested to Wharton that "a company of Pseudo-protestants" was using all possible means "to cast the plot upon persons of the same [Protestant] religion."[74] The growing ideological divide led conservatives to publish Sir Robert Filmer's *Patriarcha* (1680), written half a century earlier, which in turn prompted John Locke, whose patron was Shaftesbury, to begin writing his *Two Treatises of Government.*

In this explosive atmosphere, Shaftesbury and Essex presented evidence of a supposed Irish plot to the Privy Council in March. During the summer Shaftesbury, Essex, and Wharton worked closely with Titus Oates and Israel Tong to investigate the alleged conspiracy. Meanwhile, on 26 June Shaftesbury and a group of parliamentary supporters accused James of being a Catholic recusant before the Middlesex grand jury, and for good measure they also charged the king's mistress, the duchess of Portsmouth, with prostitution and serving as a French agent; although Charles ordered the jury's dismissal before it could act, the brazen attempt further inflamed the situation. So too did Monmouth's triumphal progress during the summer from Reading to Bristol and Exeter, followed by a tumultuous reception at Oxford in September.[75]

These years witnessed the emergence of political parties, the essence of which was a commitment to a core of common tenets, an endeavor to obtain and exercise political power, and a sense of shared identity recognizable to a party's adherents as well as outsiders. Parties evolved, and in this period lacked a formal leadership structure, formal membership, disciplinary procedures, and official propaganda. The roots of party are found in London and various towns, including Gloucester and Great Yarmouth. For the Whigs the key principles were relief for Protestant nonconformists, parliamentary sovereignty, and the accountability of rulers to the people, whereas Tories stressed the defense of the established church and penal laws, Parliament's subordination to the monarch, and the latter's responsibility to God. The Tories depicted themselves as defenders of the rule of law against the threat of Catholic, arbitrary government, but the Whigs painted them in different hues, accusing them of seeking "to alter the Constitution of the Government, and to give the Protestant Religion its fatal blow." However, the Tories insisted royal prerogatives were grounded in law, that a Catholic

[73] Bodl., Tanner MSS 38, fol. 121r.
[74] Bodl., Carte MSS 77, fol. 635r (quoted); 228, fol. 146r. For Collings see *BDBR, s.v.*
[75] Greaves, *SOK*, 13; Bodl., English Letters C328, fol. 519r–v.

succession was legal, and that Protestant rights under a Catholic monarch were guaranteed by law. In the Tories' view, nonconformists were republicans who, like Catholics, were attempting to destroy the established church and the crown. A degree of shared rhetoric existed, with both parties insisting they were defending the rule of law.[76]

In London these divisions were evident in the campaigns for the mayoralty and shrievalty. The lord mayor for 1679–80, Sir Robert Clayton, a Shaftesbury ally, refused Charles' request in January 1680 to postpone the Common Council's consideration of a petition for a new Parliament. In the 1680 elections the Whigs enjoyed substantial success, making Sir Patience Ward lord mayor and Slingsby Bethel and Henry Cornish sheriffs. Like Clayton, Ward supported exclusion, petitioning, and efforts to remove George Jeffreys as London's recorder because he opposed exclusion. A man of republican sympathies and a dissenter, Bethel had ties to Buckingham, and Cornish too was a nonconformist. As sheriffs they empaneled grand juries that typically refused to indict their supporters. The Whigs retained the shrievalty in the 1681 election, won by Samuel Shute, a friend of Ferguson's, and Sir Thomas Pilkington, who selected the jury that refused to indict Shaftesbury. However, the Tory Sir John Moore won the mayoral election, and the following year Tory candidates captured all three offices.[77] As we shall see, these elections have a direct bearing on the dating of one of Bunyan's posthumously published books, *Israel's Hope Encouraged*.

The king finally permitted Parliament to convene on 21 October 1680. This time the House of Commons passed an exclusion bill, but in the Lords, with the king present, Halifax helped to inspire a successful charge against it. When the Commons responded by offering Charles supply in the amount of £600,000 if he would accept exclusion, he refused to yield. Denied funds, the irate king dissolved Parliament on 18 January 1681, incidentally killing a bill to repeal the Elizabethan Conventicle Act (35 Eliz. I, c. 1), though he probably would not have signed it in any event owing to his anger toward nonconformists because of their support of James' exclusion. Two days later he summoned another Parliament to

[76] Tim Harris, "Party Turns? Or, Whigs and Tories Get Off Scott Free," *Albion* 25 (Winter 1993): 613–16; Richard L. Greaves, "Great Scott! The Restoration in Turmoil, or, Restoration Crises and the Emergence of Party," ibid., 611–18; Jonathan Scott, "Restoration Process. Or, If This Isn't a Party, We're Not Having a Good Time," ibid., 629; anon., *A Tory Plot* (London, 1682), sig. A2r (quoted).

[77] *BDBR, s.vv.* Sir Robert Clayton, Patience Ward, Slingsby Bethel, Henry Cornish, Sir Thomas Pilkington; Gary S. De Krey, "London Radicals and Revolutionary Politics, 1657–1683," in *The Politics of Religion,* ed. Harris, Seaward, and Goldie, 141–46; Bodl., Carte MSS 39, fol. 160r; Greaves, *SOK,* 27. For Moore see *DNB, s.v.*

convene in March at Oxford, where the university was a Tory bastion.[78] The case against James had been forcefully made to the House of Lords during the second exclusion Parliament by Shaftesbury, whose speech was subsequently published by Smith. In it the earl blamed James for the Popish plot, protested against Tory attempts to fabricate a Presbyterian conspiracy, and called on Charles to change his principles as well as his court.[79] "We are not far from breaking out into hostility," observed the bishop of Oxford; "I pray God restrain the minds of unquiet & tumultous men."[80]

While the second exclusion Parliament was in session, Owen preached a powerful sermon on Jeremiah 51:5 in which he likened England to Israel and Judah, and the Catholic church to Babylon. Preached on 22 December 1680, the sermon embodies some of the same themes that Bunyan was developing in *Israel's Hope Encouraged*, suggesting, perhaps, that they may have discussed England's situation in late 1679. Owen was convinced that the country had avoided a return to civil war only through divine intervention: "There hath beene such a dissolution of mutual Trust and all ordinary ligaments of the politick Union of a Nation, that if God had not powerfully grasped the whole in his hand, we had long since beene in Confusion, and every mans sword had been in the side of his Brother and his Neighbour." He hoped to refocus the nation's attention on what he deemed to be the fundamental problem—the desolation and destruction with which England was threatened by the Roman church, the perceived fount of idolatry and persecution. The discovery of the Popish plot was proof in his eyes that God had not forsaken England, but he warned that this would happen unless there were firm evidence of repentance and a sincere effort to reform. He also lashed out at those responsible for preventing godly ministers from functioning as well as Church of England clerics who attempted to monopolize the ministry but were either unable to perform their responsibilities or negligent in doing so. As in the case of *Israel's Hope Encouraged*, Owen's sermon was only published posthumously.[81]

Bunyan probably composed *Israel's Hope Encouraged* about the time the second exclusion Parliament met, completing it in the winter of 1680–81, following the Lords' rejection of the exclusion bill on 15 November. In the key passage for

[78] Luttrell, 1:63; Lacey, 144.

[79] [Anthony Ashley Cooper, earl of Shaftesbury], *Speech Lately Made by a Noble Peer* (n.p., [1681]).

[80] BL, Add. MSS 29,582, fol. 3r.

[81] DWL, MSS L6/3, sermon of Owen on Jeremiah 51:5 (22 December 1680). It was published in 1690 as *Seasonable Words for English Protestants*.

dating purposes, he complains that good people are prone to hope for things other than God, which he thought was "the case of *Israel* [England] now."

> We have seen a great deal of this in our days; our days indeed have been days of trouble, especially since the discovery of the Popish Plot, for then we began to fear cutting of Throats, of being burned in our beds, and of seeing our Children dashed in pieces before our Faces. But looking about us, we found we had a gracious King, brave Parliaments, a stout City, good Lord Maiors, honest Sherifs, substantial Laws against them [Catholics], and these we made the object of our Hope. (*MW*, 13:21)

With the rejection of the exclusion bill, that hope proved to have been misplaced. The brave Parliaments must have been those of 1679 and 1680–81 (at least through 14 November), not the abortive one at Oxford in March 1681, which was dismissed before it could pass legislation dealing with the succession. The good mayors would have been the Whigs Clayton and Ward, and the honest sheriffs, the Whigs Bethel and Cornish. An analogy depicting great traders, their chapmen, and the identifying marks placed on goods sold by the former to the chapmen suggests the work may have been written in London; at the least, the analogy reflected Bunyan's knowledge of commercial practices in the City (13:19).

Several passages in this work reflect the Whiggish views prevalent among Bunyan's principal friends in London. "The old Laws, which are the *magna charta*, the sole basis of the Government of a Kingdom, may not be cast away," he asserted, "for the pet that is taken by every little Gentleman against them" (13:53). Shaftesbury regarded Magna Carta as a source of English freedom, and Ferguson, with whom Bunyan may have discussed the subject, appealed to both the ancient constitution and natural law as the basis for such liberties.[82] Bunyan's view of Magna Carta differed sharply from that of the Leveller William Walwyn, who deemed it a "messe of pottage" because it was only part of the people's rights and liberties, having been "wrestled out of the pawes of those Kings, who by force had conquered the Nation, changed the lawes and by strong hand held them in bondage."[83] For Bunyan, Magna Carta's glory was its binding nature and exclusive place as *the* authoritative basis for English government. He likened Magna Carta to the "foundation of Salvation" in which "the Kingdom, Government and Glory of Christ is wrapped up." If we transpose the analogy back to the political realm, he was evincing his conviction that the kingdom, government, and glory of Eng-

[82] Ashcraft, *Revolutionary Politics*, 209–11.

[83] William Walwyn, *Englands Lamentable Slaverie*, in *Tracts on Liberty in the Puritan Revolution 1638–1647*, ed. William Haller, vol. 3 (New York: Columbia University Press, 1933), 313–14. The Tories countered by arguing that the Whigs were attempting to destroy the liberties guaranteed by Magna Carta. Harris, *LC*, 136.

land were enveloped in Magna Carta. He was undoubtedly familiar with the fact that nonconformists such as Nicholas Lockyer had argued that religious repression violated Magna Carta, and he may have known that some conservatives complained bitterly about the use of Magna Carta by dissidents to bolster their demands for reform.[84]

The radical overtones of another passage are more subtle and perhaps unintended. In explaining how God "breaketh his People" because of their transgressions, Bunyan paraphrased Hosea 2:15, asserting that *the valley of Achor must be given for a door of Hope.*" In Achor, he explained, Achan had been stoned because of his dishonesty, an act that rendered Israel impotent to resist its enemies (Joshua 7:11–26). Because the Israelites purged themselves of this covenant-breaker, God ceased to be angry with them, hence the notion of hope as a consequence of radical reformation. Like Israel, England was being divinely chastened, and hope was possible, in Bunyan's view, only if major reforms were enacted (13:34). In 1660 the former Leveller John Rhye had written *The Valley of Achor*, defending the regicide of 1649 and the legitimacy of deposing tyrannical rulers, and three years later the Congregationalist Edward Richardson used the same theme for the declaration of the northern rebels, *A Door of Hope Opened in the Valley of Achor for the Mourners in Sion out of the North.*[85] For some readers, Bunyan's use of the Achor theme may have suggested radical reformation.

The most intriguing radical passage, presented in the guise of a similitude, has significant implications in the context of the exclusion debate. Some Whigs championed Monmouth as Charles' successor, though their case was considerably weakened by the duke's illegitimacy. Rumors had circulated as early as 1662 that the king had secretly married Lucy Walters, Monmouth's mother, but little was made of this until 1680, when another rumor alleged that Dr. John Cosin, bishop of Durham, had given a black box containing the marriage contract to his son-in-law, Sir Gilbert Gerard. Ferguson, whom Bunyan surely knew, tried to give the rumor credence in *A Letter to a Person of Honour, Concerning the Black Box* (1680), as did an anonymous publication of the same year, *A Full Relation of the Contents of the Black Box*. Although government agents seized large quantities of Ferguson's *Letter* in May 1680, copies continued to circulate in London and elsewhere, thanks to the financial support of Monmouth and Shaftesbury. Smith also helped spread the story of the black box, and another Bunyan publisher, Benjamin Harris, printed an account of the duke's reputed cure of a young woman afflicted with the king's evil (scrofula), a clear allusion to his royal line-

[84] [Nicholas Lockyer], *Some Seasonable and Serious Queries upon the Late Act Against Conventicles* [London, 1670], 5; Inner Temple Library, Petyt MSS 538, fol. 42r.

[85] BL, Add. MSS 38,856, fols. 79r–80r; Greaves, *DUFE*, 178–79, 211.

age.[86] In the context of his Whiggish associations, Bunyan's similitude was pregnant with political meaning:

> There was a King that adopted such an one to be his Child, and Cloathed him with the Attire of the Children of the King, and promised him that if he would fight his Fathers Battels, and walk in his Fathers ways, he should at last share in his Fathers Kingdom. He has received the adoption, and the Kings Robe, but not yet his part in the Kingdom; but now Hope of a share in that, will make him fight the Kings Battels, and also tread the Kings Paths. Yea, and tho' he should meet with many things that have a Tendency to deter him from so doing, yet Thoughts of the Interest promised in the Kingdom, and hopes to enjoy it, will make him cut his Way through those difficulties, and so save him from the Ruins that those destructions would bring upon him, and will in conclusion, usher him into a Personal Possession and Enjoyment of that Inheritance. (13:8)

This passage can obviously be read in a spiritual context as a reference to the believer's adoption by Christ, but in late 1680 it *also* had unmistakable political meaning for anyone cognizant of the titanic struggle in which Monmouth and his supporters were engaged. At this point Bunyan's sympathies were manifestly with the duke, though he recognized that the Whigs could triumph only if, sustained by hope, they were prepared to "wade through a Sea of Blood," enduring everything because of "the Joy that is set" before them (13:8). The suggestion that England might have to undergo another round of bloody civil war—"a Sea of Blood"—may be the reason Bunyan's book was not published in 1681.[87]

Most of *Israel's Hope Encouraged* deals with the less contentious issues of reform as well as hope for individual believers and more generally the nation. Bunyan expounds on a verse from Psalm 130, the intensely personal cry of the psalmist beseeching God to hear his voice. In the seventh verse, which is Bunyan's text, the psalmist urges people to hope in the Lord, the fount of mercy and redemption. The final verse in the Authorized Version blends the personal and corporate in a reference to Israel's redemption from "his" iniquities. This interchangeability of the individual and the corporate under the appellation of Israel provided Bunyan with the opportunity to deal variously with England (the contemporary Israel) and the Christian, the contemporary Israel(ite). Readers acquainted with the full psalm were thus prepared to look for Bunyan's double meaning. For those less familiar with the Bible, Bunyan provided an explicit key, referring to England as "*Israel* now" (13:21).

The double reference is evident in one of the book's principal themes, the af-

[86] Greaves, *SOK*, 19–20; BL, Add. MSS 62,453, fol. 99.

[87] Following the Oxford Parliament the government regained control of the press. Apparently Bunyan was unable to get *Israel's Hope Encouraged* in print before control tightened. Crist, "Government Control," 67.

fliction of Israel and its people (13:34). The sole way to overcome these difficulties, Bunyan argued, was through the grace of hope (13:14). Despite his reference to a sea of blood, he restricted the believers' role in the impending trials to suffering adversity, sustained by hope and the solace of experiencing unity with prophets, apostles, martyrs, and, indeed, all saints (13:7, 9). Sensitive to the Tories' defense of the penal laws, he sought to steel the godly to withstand continuing persecution: "Men of a persecuting Spirit, because of their Greatness, and of their Teeth, the Laws, are said to be a Terror, and to carry amazement in their doings; and Gods People are apt to be afraid of them, . . . and to forget God their Maker; and this makes Hoping hard work." As he knew from personal experience, Satan could make a jail seem like hell, or banishment and execution intolerable, rendering hope extremely difficult (13:14). Because of hope, believers could face death on the scaffold, knowing they would die bravely, innocently, and boldly (13:16). This was a far cry from the fear of dying badly that had plagued Bunyan as a neophyte believer. His emphasis on suffering and endurance was partly a recognition that a Tory triumph would mean no end to state persecution, partly a manifestation of the fear caused by the prospect of even worse affliction with a Catholic on the throne. The church, he insisted, must be patient in tribulation, secure in the conviction that it could withstand anything (13:35, 54). Although "Enemies lie in wait for Poor *Israel* in every Hole," not even the specter of French domination daunted Bunyan. He even sneered that persecutors were no more than the Devil's scarecrows (13:57).

Sprinkled throughout *Israel's Hope Encouraged* are caustic comments about many of Bunyan's long-time enemies, who were not forgotten even amid the strife between Tories and Whigs. In fact, his broadsides against the "Carnal Gospelers" who populated the Church of England included the Tories as champions of that establishment. To Bunyan, they were Christians "only in their own Fancies and Conceits," and their profession was a lie (13:25). Because these people deluded themselves, they were the worst deceivers of all (13:26). Among Bunyan's other targets in this work are Socinians, Latitudinarians, atheists, Muslims, heathen philosophers, and William Penn (13:18, 75, 81, 85, 87). From Luther, whose commentary on Galatians he apparently re-read about 1679, he adopted the term "justiciary" to condemn "the Self-Justiciary" who thinks he or she can obtain justification by meritorious works (13:88).[88] Likewise, Bunyan continued to contrast those who relied on the gospel with those who depended on carnal reason and "the doltish wisdom of this World" (13:12, 71, 75, 92). Such references to all

[88] Luther, *Galatians*, 41. Bunyan quoted from Luther's commentary in *Mr. Badman* (105).

these "brain-sick-fellows" indicate that he kept his enemies in mind through the years, aware that none of them were vanquished (13:53).

The theme of hope prompted Bunyan to draw on his own intense psychological and religious experiences as a young man to illustrate hope's importance to those mired in despair. The darkness of the soul and a feeling of having been deserted by God are intolerable burdens, like a profound sense of sin's guilt (13:12–13). In Bunyan's judgment, eternal life without God is a terrifying prospect because it means an existence replete with desolation, impenetrable gloom, horror, and profound sorrow—despondency without relief, without end, something so terrifying that only the victim of depression can sense the indescribable blackness (13:23). Even life in this world, if devoid of hope and subjected to tribulation, is, for Bunyan, filled with despair, fear, and a tumultuous raging within the soul (13:35). As late as 1681, he may still have suffered from recurring, if less severe, melancholic moods, but if so, he now knew how to combat them by clinging fiercely to hope. Citing Paul's warning that believers should be cautious lest they fall (1 Corinthians 10:12) and the admonition in Hebrews 4:1 to beware of coming short of the promise to enter God's rest, Bunyan cautioned against "the evil of Despair, . . . [for] we at times are incident to it; our daily Weaknesses, our fresh Guilt, our often Decays, our aptness to forget the Goodness of God, are direct Tendencies unto this evil, of which we should beware" (13:32). This passage has the ring of autobiographical authenticity, surpassing the reflections of a pastor ruminating on his flock's experiences. From personal knowledge Bunyan knew that some people are far more troubled by the conviction of sin than others. Such individuals

> are driven by the *greatness* of Sin into despairing Thoughts, hotter than Fire: These have the greatness of their Sin betwixt God and them, like a great Mountain; yea, they are like a Cloud, that darkneth the Sun and Air. This Man stands under *Cain's* Gibbet, and has the Halter of *Judas*, to his own thinking, fastned about his Neck. (13:42–43)

Bunyan had wrestled with exactly such despair, the remedy for which was hope grounded in the divine promise of mercy, and the faith that bathes the soul in sunshine (13:38–39, 93).

Should the Tories and their persecutory policies triumph, or should English Protestants again be subjected to the persecution of a Catholic monarch, Bunyan exhorted the godly to ground themselves firmly in hope. "It is for want of Hope, that so many brisk Professors that have so boasted and made brags of their Faith, have not been able to endure the *Drum* in the day of Alarum and Affliction" (13:8). *Israel's Hope Encouraged* was intended to prepare the saints for a period of severe persecution at the hands of Tories or Catholics. Neither Bunyan nor his intended readers had the comfort of knowing that James II's reign would not revive the fires of Smithfield.

One passage in *Israel's Hope Encouraged* appears to relate to the death of Bunyan's stepmother, Ann, who was buried at Elstow on 25 September 1680,[89] about the time he began writing this book. In June 1644 she had married his father a mere two months after his mother's death, but whatever strain that caused had apparently dissipated, for he now looked forward to the time when "all our Relations, as Wife, Husband, Child, Father, Mother, Brother or Sister, that have died in the Faith" will meet in heaven. "How gloriously they will look when we shall see them, and how gloriously we shall love when we are with them, it is not for us in this World to know" (13:10). This too was cause for hope, the offspring of faith, "the Mother Grace" (13:7).

[89]Brown, 293.

# CHAPTER 10

# Holy Warfare

————◦✦◦————

Although Charles II waited only two days to summon a new Parliament following his dissolution of the second exclusion Parliament on 18 February 1681, Whig and nonconformist concerns intensified in the ensuing months. For one thing, the new Parliament would meet in Oxford, where loyalist sentiment was strong within the university community and nearly 700 government troops could more easily maintain order. Charles also signaled a tougher stance by dismissing Essex, the earl of Sunderland, and Sir William Temple from the Privy Council on 24 January because they had opposed the dissolution. The following day, Essex gave the king a petition signed by sixteen peers, including Monmouth, Shaftesbury, and the earls of Salisbury and Clare, asking that Parliament convene in London rather than Oxford, "where neither lords nor commons can be in safety, but will be daily exposed to the swords of the papists, and their adherents, of whom too many are crept into your majesty's guards."[1] For again challenging Charles, Essex was removed as lord-lieutenant of Hertfordshire on the 28th. Emotions ran high among some on both sides, as reflected in an exchange between the earl of Fever-sham, who expressed a willingness to march through London with 20,000 men in support of the king, and Sir Thomas Player, who replied that he would stop him in Cheapside with twenty good men.[2]

Frustrated by the inability to resolve their concerns through peaceful means, some of the Whigs began to consider violence. "To dye in Freedome," proclaimed one, "is preferable to Life in Chains." Shortly after the House of Lords rejected the exclusion bill in November 1680, Shaftesbury suggested using arms to compel Charles to bar his brother from the succession, but Monmouth, Lord

---

[1] *HMC 36, Ormonde*, n.s., 5:563; *A Collection of Scarce and Valuable Tracts . . . of the Late Lord Somers*, ed. Walter Scott, 13 vols. (London, 1809–15), 8:282–83 (quoted).

[2] *CSPD, 1680–81*, 149; PRO, SP 29/415/50. For Player see *BDBR*, s.v.

William Russell, Ford Lord Grey, and Sir Thomas Armstrong were unwilling to support such action at this point.[3] When Shaftesbury traveled to Oxford for the parliamentary session accompanied by approximately 200 well-armed men, he chose to enter the town on horseback, with pistols prominently displayed, rather than in the customary coach. Some of the other Whigs likewise came well armed, perhaps believing themselves in danger, perhaps only wanting to create such an impression for propaganda purposes. Many Whigs had ribbons on their hats emblazoned with the words, "No Popery, No Slavery," and the London joiner Stephen College distributed printed material satirizing Charles, James, and the Tories, associating all of them with popery.[4]

In his opening speech to the Oxford Parliament on 21 March, Charles proposed to resolve the succession dispute by guaranteeing that the administration of the government would remain in Protestant hands when James became king. While leaders in the Commons discussed whether to renew their demand for exclusion or pursue a compromise with the king, Shaftesbury advocated that Charles designate Monmouth as his successor. To this the king retorted that he would defend the royal prerogative, the law, and the established church, blaming the attempt to subvert the succession on Presbyterianism. Rejecting a compromise based on a regency during James' reign, the Commons opted to introduce an exclusion bill. This had only received a first reading when, on 28 March, Charles dismissed Parliament. With the possible exception of the king, no one knew at this time that no Parliament would meet again during Charles' reign, and this undoubtedly contributed to the relative calm that greeted news of the dissolution. "We have not been so much an University here of late," opined a Tory-Anglican at Oxford, "as a Stage; upon which very suddain . . . changes of State affairs have been acted; but what denomination the Drama must have, cannot appear till the event; for the Last Act is not yet come, & we must expect other revolutions."[5] Petitioning resumed with heightened intensity, though much of it was undertaken by Tories grateful for the king's pledge to preserve the government and church as established by law. "'Tis endeavoured to raise the people to discontent," noted one Tory, "but 'tis hoped they will be silent and quiet: all

[3] Letter of P. H., Bodl., Carte MSS 66, fol. 604r (quoted); Ford Lord Grey, *The Secret History of the Rye-House Plot: and of Monmouth's Rebellion* (London, 1754), 3; Greaves, *SOK*, 99–101. For Grey and Armstrong see *New DNB, s.vv.*

[4] K. H. D. Haley, *The First Earl of Shaftesbury* (Oxford: Clarendon Press, 1968), 631–32. For College see *BDBR, s.v.*

[5] Mark Knights, *Politics and Opinion in Crisis, 1678–81* (Cambridge: Cambridge University Press, 1994), 96–102; Haley, *Shaftesbury*, 632–34; BL, Egerton MSS 2985, fols. 280–81; BL, Sloane MSS 1008, fol. 305r (quoted).

good Protestants resolve to be so."[6] If not, suggested one of the archbishop of Dublin's correspondents, "the hot headed Zealots" in England should be transplanted to Ireland in exchange for that country's "bloody minded" youth.[7]

## "The Alarm of War"[8]: The Campaign to Repress Dissent

A more confident government began to strike selectively at its enemies. For allegedly having insisted that he would continue to publish the news until England was free, Bunyan's former printer, Francis Smith, was committed to Newgate on 15 April on charges of high treason. He would remain there until 1 June, when he was released on a writ of *habeas corpus*; he was finally discharged in July.[9] In June the state tried Edward Fitzharris, an Irish Catholic and government informer who had endeavored to plant treasonable documents on Whig leaders. Attempting to save himself, he expressed a willingness to testify that James, Catherine of Braganza, and Danby had been involved in Sir Edmund Godfrey's murder. Charged with having written *The True Englishman*, which castigated Charles for governing arbitrarily, Fitzharris was found guilty and executed on 1 July. Shortly after his arrest, his wife had accused Lord Howard of Escrick of having written *The True Englishman*, and on 11 June he was arrested, but the state soon dropped the charges for lack of evidence.[10] Moreover, during the evening of the day Fitzharris was executed, the king ordered Shaftesbury's arrest on charges of high treason, sparking rumors that the apprehension of Monmouth, Essex, Salisbury, and others might follow.[11] While Shaftesbury and Howard, who had been rearrested and charged with treasonable conduct during the third Dutch war, were confined in the Tower, on 8 July the government accused Stephen College of conspiring to seize the king; the grand jury, nominated by the Whig sheriffs Samuel Shute and Thomas Pilkington and assisted by the undersheriff Richard Goodenough, a prominent member of the Green Ribbon Club, issued a verdict of *ignoramus*.[12] Rather than release College, the government procured an indict-

---

[6] BL, Sloan MSS 1008, fols. 303r (quoted), 309r; BL, Egerton MSS 2985, fol. 235; Haley, *Shaftesbury*, 638–40; Harris, *LC*, 174.

[7] Bodl., Carte MSS 72, fol. 525r.

[8] *HW*, 60.

[9] Luttrell, 1:75, 92, 109; HMC 36, *Ormonde*, n.s., 6:35.

[10] Greaves, *SOK*, 22–26. For Howard see *New DNB, s.v.*; for Fitzharris see *DNB, s.v.*

[11] Haley, *Shaftesbury*, 654–55.

[12] Ibid., 657–58; HMC 36, *Ormonde*, n.s., 6:96; Gary S. De Krey, "London Radicals and Revolutionary Politics, 1675–1683," in *The Politics of Religion in Restoration England*, ed. Tim Harris, Paul Seaward, and Mark Goldie (Oxford: Basil Blackwell, 1990), 145. For Goodenough see *BDBR, s.v.*

ment against him at Oxford, where he was tried and convicted on 17 and 18 August, and executed on the 31st. Shaftesbury remained in the Tower while the government sought additional evidence against him, but these efforts were in vain, for on 24 November the jury issued a verdict of *ignoramus*; four days later he was released. During the ensuing celebration in London, Pilkington refused to obey orders from the lord chief justice to arrest the leaders of the demonstrations, and Shute encouraged the festivities.[13] Through his contacts in the City, Bunyan would have followed these developments, undoubtedly sharing concern about Shaftesbury's safety and the perceived threat of Catholicism to England.

Bunyan would likewise have been aware of the government's crackdown on conventicles in 1681. In some places efforts at suppression had begun earlier, as at Exeter and Bristol, in Herefordshire and Westmorland, and in the diocese of Norwich.[14] Indeed, various members of Bunyan's congregation had been presented for recusancy at the sessions in March and July 1680,[15] although the number in the county as a whole declined nearly 75 percent from the winter of 1678, dropping to 43 (of whom at least 15 were Catholics) in the summer of 1680.[16] In the autumn of 1680 the earl of Anglesey, chiding the mayor of Gloucester for not treating dissenters with leniency, referred to the "undisturbed libertie in the great city of the kingdome ministers & people of that persuasion under the very eye of king & counsell have of late yeares enjoyed, because upon good experience [they were] found to be otherwise peaceable people & loyall subjects."[17] Referring to this tolerance, Sir Leoline Jenkins bemoaned the fact that the opportunity to repress "Sectaries" had passed because of the danger posed by Catholics; dissenters,

[13] Haley, *Shaftesbury*, 663, 673–80, 682; De Krey, "London Radicals," 145; *CSPD, 1680–81*, 611. Bunyan's former publisher, Francis Smith, was responsible for issuing *A Ra-ree Show*, a ballad satirizing Charles which College wrote or at least distributed. Greaves, *SOK*, 28–29; Luttrell, 1:309, 311.

[14] Bodl., Tanner MSS 37, fols. 17r, 38r, 114r, 142r; Bodl., Carte MSS 77, fols. 604r, 606r, 615r; BL, Add. MSS 70,013, fol. 52r. Among those accused of recusancy was the minister Thomas Jollie (November 1678 and November 1679). DWL, MS 12.78, fol. 148. To some degree, enforcement throughout the period was a matter decided by local magistrates. In August 1679 the bishop of Chester was pleased to inform the archbishop of Canterbury about a neighboring magistrate who was suppressing conventicles. Tanner MSS 38, fol. 71r.

[15] BLA, MSS HSA 1680 W/13, 19; HSA 1680 S/19. The members presented in March included Ruth Beech, Henry Man, Edward Stratton, William Langley and his wife, John Barker, and Grace Cooper of Clapham. Beech and William Langley were also accused in July.

[16] BLA, MSS HSA 1680 W/13–15, 17, 19–21; 1680 S/13, 15–22. The number of presentments at the winter sessions was 86.

[17] PRO, SP 29/414/109.

he complained, had put conformists on the defensive.[18] Sensitive to Covenanter unrest in Scotland, the king ordered deputy lieutenants in Northumberland to suppress mixed conventicles of Scots and English dissenters in January 1681, and the following month magistrates in Wiltshire prosecuted nonconformists. Vigorous repression was under way in parts of Essex in March.[19] Rumors abounded in April that Charles would enforce the laws against nonconformists to obtain the revenue he needed, but others questioned whether the Elizabethan Conventicle Act (35 Eliz. I, c. 1) could still be enforced.[20] During the spring, security concerns continued to drive the suppression of conventicles in Northumberland, including some in the garrison town of Berwick. Yet as late as the summer of 1681, dissenters in London, emboldened by the London grand jury's verdict of *ignoramus* in College's first trial, were building several new meetinghouses, prompting one justice of the peace to propose arresting some of the followers of Bunyan's friend Matthew Meade in order to discourage the nonconformists.[21] Although justices of the peace and gentry at the quarter sessions at Exeter in April resolved to enforce the penal statutes against dissenters, the strength of the conventicles had not been diminished by July, prompting the bishop of Exeter to complain that the tolerance shown to London nonconformists was a bad example.[22] Again in July 1681 the constables filed charges against some members of Bunyan's church for not attending parish services,[23] though the number of presentments in the county remained relatively low.[24]

At Canterbury and Dover in August 1681, magistrates began to repress conventicles,[25] and similar efforts were soon under way in Norfolk, Leicestershire, Middlesex, and Shropshire, and at Bristol, Canterbury, and Rye.[26] Endeavors to quash conventicles intensified during November and December in such places as

[18] PRO, SP 44/62, p. 103.

[19] PRO, SP 44/62, p. 125; *Protestant (Domestick) Intelligence* 97 (15 February 1681); 107 (22 March 1681).

[20] Luttrell, 1:72, 76.

[21] PRO, SP 44/62, p. 145; SP 29/415/125; 29/416/49.

[22] Bodl., Tanner MSS 36, fols. 11r, 62r, 91r.

[23] BLA, MS HSA S/16. The members included William Langley, Ruth Beech, Edward Stratton, and Henry Man.

[24] The number of presentments in the winter of 1681 was 83, followed by 49 in the summer, figures that virtually replicated those of the preceding year. BLA, MSS 1681 W/7–16; 1681 S/11–19.

[25] PRO, SP 29/416/117, 126, 134, 173, 173.1, 174; 29/417/68; 44/62, p. 282; *CSPD, 1680–81*, 428.

[26] *True Protestant Mercury* 70 (3–7 September 1681); 76 (24–28 September 1681); *Impartial Protestant Mercury* 44 (20–23 September 1681); BL, Add. MSS 70,013, fol. 90v; Luttrell, 1:125, 140.

Marlborough, Plymouth, Reading, Salisbury, York, London, and Middlesex, and in Bristol magistrates confiscated a pulpit, pews, and galleries in a meetinghouse.[27] Elsewhere, as at Lyme Regis and Windsor and in Monmouthshire and Wiltshire, loyalists pleaded for the government to take action against illegal meetings.[28] The crackdown spread in January and February, targeting nonconformists in such locales as Cornwall, Dorset, Somerset, Gloucester, Cheshire, Hertfordshire, Surrey, Huntingdonshire, and the Isle of Ely, and it was reportedly very severe in Middlesex and Bristol. In Middlesex, justices of the peace threatened the indigent with loss of relief if they refused to attend the parish churches.[29] Feelings ran high; in the diocese of Chichester Bishop Guy Carleton complained that dissenters were insolent, speaking boldly as if they were about to draw their swords.[30] The crackdown was beginning to attain its objective in some areas, for the bishop of Gloucester reported that illegal meetings in his diocese were decreasing, and the bishop of Exeter observed that attendance was rising in parish churches, though he renewed his complaint about London's deleterious example.[31]

If Bunyan read some of the newspapers, he would have known about the intensifying campaign against dissenters, and his trips to London would have kept him apprized of events there and elsewhere. By mid-September 1681, Middlesex justices of the peace had suppressed activities at recently built meetinghouses and schoolhouses, and in October Sir George Jeffreys told the Middlesex quarter sessions that nonconformists and Catholics were equally troublesome to church and state. In directing the Middlesex grand jury to execute the laws against conventiclers and Catholic recusants in December, Sir William Smith admitted he had not prosecuted Protestants for recusancy, but their attendance at illegal meetings was a different matter because this weakened church and state, not least by making a "Prince and a Pope in every Congregation." Gentry at the quarter sessions

[27] PRO, SP 44/62, pp. 354–55, 358, 365–66, 370–71; 29/417/130; Bodl., Tanner MSS 36, fol. 196r; *Impartial Protestant Mercury* 67 (9–13 December 1681); *True Protestant Mercury* 101 (21–24 December 1681); *CSPD, 1680–81*, 636; Luttrell, 1:151–53. However, the *Impartial Protestant Mercury* 59 (11–15 November 1681) reported that constables at Stepney were afraid to execute warrants against nonconformists for fear of violating the law governing sabbath observance.

[28] PRO, SP 29/417/96, 171, 182, 274.

[29] PRO, SP 29/418/26, 26.1, 27.1, 43, 72, 83, 110; Bodl., Tanner MSS 36, fols. 212r–214r, 218r; *True Protestant Mercury* 110 (21–25 January 1682); 119 (22–25 February 1682); Chester City Record Office, MSS QSF/82, fol. 270r; *Impartial Protestant Mercury* 88 (21–24 February 1682); London *Gazette* 1686 (12–16 January 1682); PRO, SP 44/68, pp. 18–19; Luttrell, 1:156, 162, 165, 167.

[30] Bodl., Tanner MSS 36, fol. 222r.

[31] Bodl., Tanner MSS 36, fols. 235r, 251r.

in Norfolk pledged to enforce the laws against dissenters, but in Plymouth the constables refused to serve warrants against nonconformists. On 29 October magistrates throughout the country received orders to quash all conventicles. Two weeks earlier pub and alehouse keepers were threatened with the loss of their licenses if they attended illegal religious services, and the indigent were told to expect no further relief if they went to conventicles.[32] As late as 15 November the earl of Longford knew of no illegal meetings in the City that had been disturbed, but within two weeks, eleven dissenting ministers, including Bunyan's friends Owen and Meade, his almost certain acquaintance Robert Ferguson, and Thomas Watson and John Collings, were subpoened on charges of recusancy and violating the Five-Mile Act (by coming within five miles of where they had previously ministered or any incorporated town); they reportedly faced possible cumulative fines of £4,840. A subsequent list, prepared on or shortly before 12 December, named twenty-two ministers, including Owen, Meade, Ferguson, Danvers, and Nathaniel Vincent, with projected fines, if levied, of £9,680.[33] In an understatement, the diarist Narcissus Luttrell observed in September that "there is a great division and animosity between those that call themselves church of England men and those that are dissenters."[34] That description certainly was applicable to Bunyan.

Vincent appears to have given magistrates the most difficulty, for he refused to obey their orders to cease preaching in his Southwark meetinghouse, citing the King of Kings as his authority. On another occasion he eluded arrest, instructing his congregants to remain behind and sing psalms. The more the justices commanded his people to disperse, the louder they sang. Although Vincent prayed for Charles, he adamantly refused to cease preaching and was finally arrested, but the grand jury returned a verdict of *ignoramus*. When magistrates again sought to arrest him in early February, they found "almost every seat that adjoins to the Sides of the Conventicle has a door like the Sally Port of a Fire-ship to [enable worshipers to] make their escape by. And in each door, a smal Peep-hole like to Taverns & Alehouses door[s], to Ken the person before they let them in."[35]

Generally, attempts to quash dissent in 1681 and early 1682 were greater in the

---

[32] *HMC* 36, *Ormonde*, n.s., 6:155; Luttrell, 1:132, 134, 136, 140; *The Proceedings at the Sessions of the Peace Held at Hicks Hall for the County of Middlesex December 5. 1681* (London, 1682), 4 (quoted); *True Protestant Mercury* 86 (29 October–2 November 1681); London *Gazette* 1660 (13–17 October 1681).

[33] *HMC* 36, *Ormonde*, n.s., 6:229; PRO, SP 29/417/122, 144; Luttrell, 1:148.

[34] Luttrell, 1:124.

[35] *True Protestant Mercury* 100 (17–21 December 1681); *HMC* 36, *Ormonde*, n.s., 6:264, 271; PRO, SP 29/417/156, 158; 29/418/89 (quoted); *CSPD, 1680–81*, 640; *CSPD, 1682*, 78–79; *Impartial Protestant Mercury* 75 (6–10 January 1682).

areas around the City than within its precincts, thanks to the Whig sheriffs and allies such as Sir Robert Clayton, who were reluctant to prosecute and sometimes gave dissenters advance warning that magistrates intended to disrupt their gatherings. This occasioned some complaint. On 1 February the grand jury at Westminster even refused to receive presentments regarding conventiclers.[36] Wharton's papers contain documents explaining how justices of the peace could effectively ignore informers' reports regarding conventicles and avoid enforcing the Five-Mile Act, in both cases without subjecting themselves to legal penalties; presumably this information was provided to sympathetic magistrates.[37] Yet religious assemblies at a number of guild halls, including those of the pewterers, turners, cordwainers, and cutlers, were soon suppressed.[38] At Stepney, magistrates disrupted Meade's congregation on 12 January 1682, but an unidentified guest was preaching; given his growing reputation by this time, the minister was probably not Bunyan, but the officers were clearly tolerant, taking down the name of only one conventicler. Owen fared about as well when three people were dispatched by a justice of the peace to observe his conventicle on 19 February; they reported only that he preached on Song of Solomon 1:7–8, and that he failed to mention the king or the government in his pre-sermon prayer.[39] Bunyan himself was attacked in a pamphlet attributed to Cave Underhill, who asserted that the tinker of Bedford, the Presbyterians Thomas Doelittle and William Farrington, and unnamed others proclaimed that it was "their priviledge to bind Kings in Chains, and their Nobles in Links of Iron" as well as to eradicate any power or interest that "sets it self up against our *Zion*." With or without cause, they "cry out, *Popery, Popery*," and they claim to follow King David or "pragmatical young *Absalom*," an allusion to Monmouth. Underhill accused them as well of denouncing bishops and deans as servants of the whore of Babylon and decrying episcopacy as antichristian.[40] The idea of linking Bunyan to Doelittle and Farrington presumably was inspired by their preaching to sizable London congregations.[41]

---

[36] PRO, SP 29/418/30, 110, 114; *True Protestant Mercury* 102 (24–28 December 1681); 113 (1–4 February 1682). For the areas outside London see PRO, SP 29/417/25, 28, 73, 140; *CSPD, 1682*, 27.

[37] Bodl., Carte MSS 77, fols. 627r–v, 633r–634r.

[38] Bodl., Tanner MSS 36, fol. 257r.

[39] *True Protestant Mercury* 107 (11–14 January 1682); PRO, SP 29/418/106, 127.

[40] [Cave Underhill], *Vox Lachrymae: A Sermon Newly Held Forth at Weavers-Hall, upon the Funeral of the Famous T. O. Doctor of Salamancha* (Frankfurt, 1681; repr. London, 1682), 6–8. Oates did not die until July 1705. For Underhill see *DNB, s.v.*

[41] Farrington preached to nearly a thousand at the Old Theatre, Vere Street, and Doelittle addressed dissenters at a meetinghouse in Mugwell (now Monkwell) Street. *Calamy Revised, s.vv.*

Some sense of what Bunyan probably discussed when he visited London may be gleaned from Owen's *An Humble Testimony unto the Goodness and Severity of God in His Dealing with Sinful Churches and Nations*, issued by Ponder in 1681, and a revised edition of the Particular Baptist Benjamin Keach's *Sion in Distress*, published by George Larkin the same year. Bunyan, of course, knew Ponder and Larkin, if not necessarily Keach, but the latter's strident anti-Catholicism was characteristic of nonconformist feeling at this time. Why, Keach wondered, must the throats of those who hate the "*Rotten Whore*" of Rome be cut, or why

> Must flaming *Smithfield* belch out *Fire* and Smoke
> Of Martyr'd *Saints*?

His caustic reference to "*Monkish Torys*" who possess English land had a double meaning, referring not only to Irish Catholics but also to those English Tories who supported the persecution of dissenters.[42] Political meaning was evinced as well in Keach's condemnation of those aristocrats who failed to stand up against Catholicism:

> What pity is't that Dukes and Noble Peers,
> With other *Heroes*, should for many years
> Thus truckle to that Proud, Usurping *Whore*,
> And for her sake inslave themselves?[43]

Indeed, he accused such nobles of engaging in "*Hellish Plots*," an interesting charge in light of the fact that by year's end Essex, Howard of Escrick, Sir Patience Ward, Slingsby Bethel, Henry Cornish, and others were interviewing witnesses in an attempt to prove James, Catherine of Braganza, the earls of Clarendon, Feversham, Peterborough, and Halifax, the marquess of Worcester, and others had encouraged the allegations of a reputed "presbiterian" plot.[44] Keach posed the crucial question of what action should be taken to preserve Protestantism and the nation from popery's threat:

> Shall we (indanger'd by her Plots) arise
> To curb this Whore, that our great God defies?
> Why should her Treasons any more annoy
> Thy precious Saints and Nations thus destroy?[45]

---

[42] [Benjamin Keach], *Sion in Distress: or, the Groans of the Protestant Church*, 2nd ed. (London, 1681), 40.

[43] Ibid., 64.

[44] PRO, SP 29/417/145; *HMC 36, Ormonde*, n.s., 6:262–63. Cf. PRO, SP 29/417/155. For Ward see *BDBR, s.v.*

[45] [Keach], *Sion in Distress*, 68.

The answer was to take no action until the forces of the godly were mighty enough to prevail:

> At present you must keep your selves retir'd
> Make no attempts untill the Lord on high,
> Does give you strength this *Babel* to defie.[46]

The message was cautiously restrained, though with a clearly militant overtone.

Owen shared Keach's fear that "*England's* black *Catastrophe* is near,"[47] expressing concern in *An Humble Testimony* for the divisions he saw rending the country asunder as well as the "*Contrivances of our Adversaries*" which seemed to threaten ruin.[48] Not surprisingly, he noted, people were concerned with deliverance from the anticipated public calamities, but the means they proposed were contradictory, thereby exacerbating the danger and increasing the likelihood of ruin. Owen's solution was to exhort the nation to embrace "universal Reformation" as the only way to avoid disaster, for only if the country endorsed this course could it surmount the "present *mutual destructive Animosities.*"[49] He was not suggesting a *modus vivendi* with Catholicism, for as he made clear in 1682, "the Church of *Rome* is that *Idolatrous Antichristian State*" foretold in the Bible. Given the expectation of James' succession to the throne, he pointedly warned that by reconciling with Rome, princes would "bring a Bondage on themselves and their Subjects."[50] The unity he sought would unite English Protestants against any ruler who threatened their freedom by returning the nation to Catholicism. Owen went one step further than Keach, explicitly arguing for the right of Christians to take up arms in self-defense against a government that endeavored to destroy their rights and religion.[51] This work was published in the same year as Bunyan's *Holy War*, and by Benjamin Alsop, who, with Dorman Newman, issued the new allegory.[52] Alsop had been Ponder's apprentice and in 1685 would serve as a

---

[46] Ibid., 69.

[47] Ibid., 37.

[48] John Owen, *An Humble Testimony unto the Goodness and Severity of God in His Dealing with Sinful Churches and Nations* (London, 1681), 117.

[49] Ibid., sig. A3r–v. His sermons continued to deal with the theme of imminent judgment, but he offered hope that the church's prayers could mitigate the impact of "publick Calamityes." DWL, MSS L6/3, sermons of Owen on James 5:16 (25 March 1681) (quoted) and Amos 4:12 (8 April 1681).

[50] John Owen, *A Brief and Impartial Account of the Nature of the Protestant Religion* (London, 1682), 19 (quoted), 31 (quoted).

[51] Ibid., 12.

[52] Although Newman published radical works, he served as churchwarden in the parish of St. Mildred, Poultry, from 1680 to 1682. GL, MS 9060A, vol. 2, churchwardens' lists from June 1680 to May 1682.

captain in Monmouth's rebel army. Against this background, Bunyan wrote *The Holy War*, an allegory that spoke especially to nonconformists and Whigs enmeshed in a struggle against the perceived Catholic threat to their religion and liberties.

"New Modelling the Town"[53]: Efforts to Control the Boroughs

The inspiration for the setting of Bunyan's new allegory, composed between approximately March 1681 and January 1682,[54] was the government's renewed interest in enforcing the Corporation Act of 1661, which required all municipal officials to swear the oaths of allegiance, supremacy, and non-resistance; make a declaration against the Solemn League and Covenant; and take the sacrament of the Lord's supper in the Church of England. Control of the corporations was essential if the government was to restrict religious and political disaffection and enhance the likelihood of returning members to the House of Commons who would support its policies. Remodeling a town's charter—recalling the existing document and issuing a new one—was the most intrusive method of interference from Westminster because it enabled the king to nominate a new recorder, town clerk, and aldermen, and, particularly in the 1680s, exercise a veto over unacceptable nominees for subsequent recorders and clerks. In the early 1680s such control was especially important because the government wanted to secure juries that would convict nonconformists.[55]

As a young man Bunyan could have followed a series of changes that affected the exercise of power in Bedford. In January 1650, when Parliament approved annual elections and reduced the privileges of burgesses, eight members of the new council of eighteen were members or associates of the recently formed Bedford congregation. After the Bedford Council abolished the distinction between burgesses and freemen in April 1650, it sought to renew the town's charter, though nothing seems to have come of this. The council tried again in January 1653, seeking additional privileges, but without success. Attempting to strengthen the

---

[53] *HW*, 18.

[54] To have composed the 102,000-word allegory in ten months, Bunyan would have had to average approximately 475 words a day if he wrote five days a week. Neil Keeble believes that planning and writing such a complex epic would have taken two years. Bunyan probably thought about the fundamental themes before he began composing the epic, and we also have firm evidence that he could write very rapidly. For Keeble's position see "Christiana's Key: The Unity of *The Pilgrim's Progress*," in *Pilgrim's Progress*, ed. Newey, 7–8.

[55] G. C. F. Forster, "Government in Provincial England Under the Later Stuarts," *Transactions of the Royal Historical Society*, 5th ser., 33 (1983): 44; Harris, *PULS*, 122.

godly's position, Major-General William Boteler purged the Bedford Corporation in 1656, removing the mayor, a bailiff, and four councilors for misdemeanors
or "malignancy."[56] At the Restoration the council restored the distinction between
burgesses and freemen, and, in 1662, removed Bunyan's fellow church member,
John Eston, who had thrice been mayor, and another alderman from office. This
action accorded with the king's wishes as reflected in letters to a number of corporations urging the readmission of officials ousted during the revolution and the
expulsion of their replacements. Following the passage of the Corporation Act,
the government's efforts focused on purging the boroughs by enforcing the law's
provisions, and relatively little interest was shown in remodeling charters until
the powers of the commissioners implementing the statute expired in March 1663
and a bill to renew them died in committee. *Quo warranto* proceedings, the process of recalling a charter, had been implemented against Bristol in 1660 and Preston, Lancashire, and Taunton, Somerset, in 1661. In 1663–64 many towns petitioned for new charters, in some cases anticipating *quo warranto* proceedings and
in others because newly appointed officials sought to consolidate their positions.[57] Bedford, against which a *quo warranto* proceeding was instigated in 1663,
was an example of the former. Its new charter empowered the crown to approve
appointments to the offices of recorder and clerk. Although Bunyan was a prisoner during these developments, his association with Eston and his friends would
have kept him abreast of developments. He would have known, too, that four of
the justices of the peace who had sent him to prison—Sir John Kelynge, Sir
Henry Chester, Sir William Becher, and Sir George Blundell—were admitted to
the Bedford Corporation as burgesses in 1661.[58] As he sat in his prison cell, Bunyan had ample time to reflect on the importance of remodeling corporations.

Between 1664 and 1680 Charles was generally content to rely on the Corporation Act to keep dissident religious and political activities in the boroughs within
tolerable bounds,[59] though some towns received new charters. Among them were
Leicester in 1664–65 and Maidstone in 1666. Threatened with proceedings,
Gloucester succumbed in 1671, and the government moved against Poole in
1675.[60] Bedford was fortunate in escaping such action, for in 1678 its mayor, Wil-

---

[56] Hill, *TPM*, 255; *Minute Book*, ed. Parsloe, xxiii, 35–37, 71–72; *BDBR*, *s.v.* William
Boteler.

[57] *Minute Book*, ed. Parsloe, xxiii; John Miller, "The Crown and the Borough Charters
in the Reign of Charles II," *English Historical Review* 100 (January 1985): 56–57, 63–64, 66;
Jennifer Levin, *The Charter Controversy in the City of London, 1660–1688, and Its Consequences* (London: Athlone Press, 1969), 13.

[58] *Minute Book*, ed. Parsloe, xxiii, 147–48, 154, 176–77.

[59] See, e.g., Luttrell, 1:19, 66.

[60] Miller, "Crown and Borough Charters," 67; Levin, *Charter Controversy*, 14–16.

liam Fenne, the father of Bunyan's fellow church members John and Samuel
Fenne,[61] did not swear the required oaths, and Robert Audley, the new deputy recorder, was tolerant of nonconformists. In 1679 Lord William Russell, whose political views were those of the Country, was elected to the House of Commons for
Bedfordshire, replacing Lord Bruce, son of the first earl of Ailesbury. The earl
was no friend of nonconformists, and his chaplain, Thomas Pomfret, vicar of
Luton, would on 11 March 1682 preach a sermon at the assizes in Ampthill condemning "seditious Pamphlets" that proclaimed the right of dissenters to disobey
the government on conscientious grounds. Among the targets may have been
*The Holy War*, published the preceding month, for its message clearly fit the target of Pomfret's attack: "The whole Rout of Dissenters, all of them with one
mouth declare against our Laws, that they are not agreeable to the Word of
God."[62]

Commencing in 1679 the government began removing the more zealous
Country supporters from commissions of the peace, but still it clung to the hope
of controlling the boroughs by enforcing the Corporation Act. The Privy Council's letters in March 1680 ordering such enforcement were largely ignored,
prompting the court to threaten *quo warranto* proceedings. In fact, the government moved against Worcester the same year.[63] Bunyan probably heard reports
of the government's threats, and he must have known about the Council's inquiry in April 1681 as to whether municipal officials had complied with the Corporation Act. In Bedford the result was the ouster of two chamberlains who had
not taken the sacrament in the Church of England and had reportedly indulged
conventicles, undoubtedly including Bunyan's congregation.[64] By this point he
had almost certainly begun writing *The Holy War*, and he may have found additional inspiration from events in neighboring Northampton, the first town to receive a new charter in a fresh wave of remodeling that would result in fifty-one
new charters during the remainder of Charles' reign and another forty-seven in
the first three months of James'. Given his friendship with Ponder, who had close
ties with Northampton, Bunyan probably heard about the pomp surrounding the
delivery of its new charter by the earl of Peterborough, the county's lord lieutenant, and his party of nobles and gentry on 25 September. They were greeted by
the mayor, aldermen, bailiffs, and burgesses, and the mayor kneeled to receive

[61] BLA, MSS 1679 W/5, 62, 64.

[62] Michael Mullett, "'Deprived of Our Former Place': The Internal Politics of Bedford
1660 to 1688," *PBHRS* 59 (1980): 12–16; Thomas Pomfret, *Subjection for Conscience-Sake
Asserted in a Sermon Preached at the Assizes Held at Ant-hill in Bedfordshire* (London,
1682), 2 (quoted), 18 (quoted).

[63] Miller, "Crown and Borough Charters," 72; Levin, *Charter Controversy*, 16.

[64] Hill, *TPM*, 257; *HW*, xxii.

the new charter. In November the government began preparing for *quo warranto* proceedings against London, which received the writ on 21 December; the Common Council appointed a committee to defend the charter on 18 January 1682.[65] Also in December, while Bunyan was still working on *The Holy War*, Audley, Bedford's deputy recorder, was cited before the Privy Council on charges of being an enemy of the established church and the government as well as one who tolerated conventicles. When Ailesbury pressed for the removal of Audley and others because of their failure to comply with the Corporation Act, Audley appealed to the Council, citing his service as a royalist officer in the civil war and insisting he had never attended a conventicle, though he noted that he had heard reports of trenchant preaching at such meetings. The Privy Council did not remove Audley from office, but shortly thereafter he was deprived of a vote in the Bedford Common Council. *The Holy War* was published well before the remodeling of Bedford's charter in 1684, or even the addition of seventy-six new burgesses, including Sir Francis Wingate and William Foster, in October and November 1683.[66] The timing of *The Holy War* was thus propitious, but the allegory was not based on the remodeling of Bedford's charter. Although the Northampton experience in 1681 probably encouraged Bunyan's resolve as he worked on the allegory, his perspective was informed by events that stretched back to the 1660s and possibly the 1650s. Certainly, as he wrote, Tories throughout the country were rallying to the king's call to defend the Church of England.

### "*Blood, Blood, Nothing but Blood*"[67]: The Plot of *The Holy War*

*The Holy War* begins with the conspiracy of Diabolus, the "*Gyant* . . . King of the *Blacks* or *Negroes*" and his fallen angels to conquer Mansoul as revenge for their ouster from heaven.[68] After seducing the Mansoulians and slaying Captain

---

[65] Ronald Hutton, *Charles the Second, King of England, Scotland, and Ireland* (Oxford: Clarendon Press, 1989), 433; David Ogg, *England in the Reign of Charles II*, 2nd ed. (Oxford: Oxford University Press, 1956), 635–36; Levin, *Charter Controversy*, 23.

[66] Brown, 316–17; *HW*, xxiii–xxiv. The Bedford council voted to surrender the corporation's charter on 8 January 1684, and the surrender formally occurred the following month. BLA, Bedford Corporation Minute Book, 1664–1688, fols. 236–37; BL, Add. MSS 70,013, fol. 172r.

[67] *HW*, 34.

[68] Bunyan's apparent racial prejudice is also reflected in his depiction of the offspring of Affection and Carnal Lust as the black boys Impudent, Blackmouth, and Hate-reproof. Their sisters, Scorn-truth, Slight-God, and Revenge must also have been black. *HW*, 23. Hill argues that the racial theme in *The Holy War* "can be explained by the allegory," though I am less inclined to do so inasmuch as racial implications are evident in some of his other works. Hill, *TPM*, 370. In *A Book for Boys and Girls*, those who depend on obedi-

Resistance, the Diabolonians seize the town, their way made easier by the death of Lord Innocency. Accepting the crown of Mansoul, the tyrannical Diabolus appoints Lord Willbewill his second in command and replaces the mayor, Lord Understanding, with Lord Lustings, and the recorder, Mr. Conscience, with Forget-good. New burgesses, aldermen, and common councilors are selected, and the image of Shaddai, lord of the universe, is replaced with that of Diabolus, the debasing of the former undertaken by No-truth. Diabolus also "spoiled the old Law Books" (*HW*, 26), promoting lasciviousness and godliness in their place and encouraging the circulation of atheistic pamphlets and obscene ballads and romances. Informed of Mansoul's fall, Shaddai dispatches an army of more than 40,000 under the command of Captains Boanerges, Conviction, Judgment, and Execution, each with a banner and an escutcheon emblazoned with a telling symbol: thunderbolts, a flaming law-book, a fiery furnace, and a barren tree with an axe at its base respectively. After sustaining casualties, including the deaths of the aldermen Swearing, Whoring, Fury, Stand-to-lies, Drunkenness, and Cheating, Diabolus endeavors to negotiate a peace that will permit Shaddai to be nothing more than a titular prince while Mansoul retains the legal right to live in lewdness and vanity. Finding the terms unsatisfactory, the besiegers request reinforcements from Shaddai, who responds by sending another army under the command of his son, Emanuel, the warrior Christ, and his captains, Credence, Good-hope, Charity, Innocent, and Patience.

As his troops take up their positions outside Mansoul, Emanuel signals his intentions by successively flying the white flag of grace, the red flag of justice, and the black flag of defiance, but the Mansoulians refuse to surrender, citing their obligation to obey Diabolus' royal prerogative. Emanuel therefore attacks. When he pauses amid the fighting to offer grace to Mansoul, Diabolus proposes peace terms, pledging to "bend Mansoul *to thy bow*" (83), become Emanuel's deputy,

---

ence to the law for salvation are compared to Moses' wife, "a swarthy Ethiopian"; they will "be left a Black-a-more." In contrast, the King of Kings is "white, and ruddy." *MW*, 6:236, 258. Bunyan likens people without grace to black parents who are unable to give birth to a white child, which is analogous to good. *MW*, 13:114. In *The Pilgrim's Progress* Flatterer is a black man (133–34). All of these allusions can be explained away, but Bunyan's decision to employ them when alternatives were available is suggestive. Cf. Charles Doe's assertion that the Devil appeared to him "in the Shape of a black Man." *A Collection of Experience of the Work of Grace* (London, [1700]), 34. Bunyan would have seen blacks in London, and he probably accepted the popular belief that they were descendants of Ham (Genesis 10), who had been punished with dark skin because of their sexual profligacy. Ruth Cowhig, "Blacks in English Renaissance Drama and the Role of Shakespeare's Othello," *The Black Presence in English Literature*, ed. David Dabydeen (Manchester: Manchester University Press, 1985), 1, 5–7.

and establish an adequate ministry in the town if the prince withdraws. Renewing their assault, but concentrating on the Diabolonians rather than the Mansoulians, Emanuel's troops break into the town, capture Diabolus, tie him to Emanuel's chariot wheels for a triumphal ride through the streets, and finally exile him to "parched places in a salt land" (93). Mansoul is now remodeled, with a reformed Lord Willbewill placed in charge of the militia, Lord Understanding restored as mayor, and Mr. Knowledge appointed recorder. A policy of iconoclasm replaces the image of Diabolus with those of Shaddai and Emanuel, and the Diabolonians Atheism, Lustings, Forget-good, False-peace, No-truth, Pityless, and Haughty are tried, convicted, and crucified, a biblical punishment as well as another manifestation of Bunyan's use of violence to punish those people or temptations that have assaulted him, whether in body or in spirit.[69] Mansoul receives a new charter embodying forgiveness for all offenses, holy laws, free access for petitioners, and authority to destroy all Diabolonians in the town.

However, the Mansoulians fail to locate and eradicate the Diabolonians who lurk in the town, particularly Carnal Security, whose insidious lies beguile the citizens. At last a dismayed Emanuel withdraws, opening the way for the Diabolonians to plot their return to power with counsel from hell. Although the government spy, Mr. Prywell, discovers the conspiracy, the Mansoulians are no match for the army of more than 20,000 doubters Diabolus dispatches to retake the town. Overrunning all of Mansoul except for the castle, which Lord Willbewill and Godlyfear successfully defend, the invaders burn, rape, slaughter children, and slay the unborn in their mothers' wombs. Aided by Emanuel's Lord Chief Secretary, the besieged castilians petition the prince to return, and the secretary appoints Captain Credence lord lieutenant to command the forces in Mansoul that will fight on Emanuel's behalf. In a fierce battle on the plains outside the town, the armies of Emanuel and the Mansoulians trap the Diabolonian forces, killing all the doubters, though Diabolus and "the Lords of the Pit" escape (222). Unbowed, Diabolus assembles a new army composed of 10,000 men from the land of Doubting to the north, between the land of darkness and the valley of the shadow of death, and 15,000 bloodmen from the country of Loathgood, whose captains are Cain, Nimrod, Ishmael, Esau, Saul, Absalom, Judas, and Pope. Commanded by General Incredulity, these forces besiege Mansoul, but this time Emanuel's forces put most of the doubters to flight and capture the bloodmen.

[69] John R. Knott, "Bunyan and the Cry of Blood," in *Awakening Words*, ed. Gay, Randall, and Zinck, 65. In *The Holy War* Bunyan's trial scenes reflect contemporary judicial practice. See Clarence Eugene Dugdale, "Bunyan's Court Scenes," *University of Texas Studies in English* 21 (8 July 1941): 64–78; Diane Parkin-Speer, "John Bunyan's Legal Ideas and the Legal Trials in His Allegories," *Baptist Quarterly* 35 (July 1994): 327–30.

Another round of trials leads to the conviction and execution of Evil-questioning, Election-doubter, Vocation-doubter, and Grace-doubter, and a diligent search results in the apprehension of Fooling, Letgoodslip, Clip-promise, Carnal-sense, Wrong-thoughts-of-Christ, Self-love, Live-by-feeling, and Legal-life. However, Unbelief manages to elude arrest, as do "some few more of the subtilest of the *Diabolonian* tribe" (244). As Emanuel explains in his closing oration, he permits these Diabolonians to remain in the town to keep the Mansoulians alert: "*My design is that they should drive thee, not further off, but nearer to my Father, to learn thee war, to make Petitioning desirable to thee, and to make thee little in thine own eyes*" (249).

The visual setting for this epic could have been inspired by several places, including London, which was defended during the civil war by an eighteen-foot-high earthen wall, eleven miles in circumference, with a ditch in front.[70] In this case the Tower would have been the model for Mansoul's castle. Closer to home, Northampton, which received its new charter while Bunyan was writing his allegory, still had its castle and town walls during the civil war, though they were demolished after the Restoration. In Bedford itself a fort was erected on the old castle mound during the civil war, but fortifications here were hardly substantial enough to provide a model for Mansoul.[71] Nor were those in Newport Pagnell, with its earthworks and trenches during the civil war. Three years before completing *The Holy War*, Bunyan had depicted the heart as "the main *FORT* in the mystical world, *man*" (*MW*, 9:124), and the imagery of a walled town had been developed in *The Holy City* (*MW*, 3:98–101), but the attention to physical details in *The Holy War* suggests that he was also thinking of London or Northampton as he wrote.

Likewise, Bunyan's military experience informed his writing, though he freely intermixed elements he remembered from his pre-conversion reading and such scriptural images as the breastplate of righteousness, the shield of faith, and the sword of the Spirit. Diabolus arms the men of Mansoul with swords, shields, breastplates, and helmets as well as mauls, arrows, and firebrands, and his army of doubters goes into battle with the latter group of weapons. Emanuel's men wield swords, and at least some troops on both sides have arquebuses (the ancestor of the musket) and pikes. Expectations that both sides will "come to push a *Pike*" (*HW*, 40) reflect the tactic of sending massed bodies of pikemen, who wear helmets and breastplates, against enemy fortifica-

[70]Charles Carlton, *Going to the Wars: The Experience of the British Civil Wars, 1638–1651* (New York: Routledge, 1992), 159.

[71] Joyce Godber, *History of Bedfordshire 1066–1888* (Bedford: Bedfordshire County Council, 1969), 262.

tions.[72] Bunyan's account of "the *Forlorn hope*" (200) also evoked contemporary experience, for these were the men in the vanguard of an attack who typically sustained heavy casualties. The two great guns mounted on the tower over Eargate are cannons or culverins, not the smaller demiculverins used in the field (50, 65). The involvement of reformades—voluntary officers—is another contemporary reference (69), as is the post of scoutmaster-general held by Prywell (183–84). Bunyan's depiction of Emanuel's troops before Mansoul—"*they marched, they counter-marched*" (110)–may have been inspired by his drills in the parliamentary garrison at Newport Pagnell.

Parts of Bunyan's epistle to the reader capture some of the sights and sounds he would have experienced had he been at the siege of Oxford:

> *I saw the* Princes *armed men come down*
> *By troops, by thousands, to besiege the Town.*
> *I saw the* Captains, *heard the* Trumpets *sound,*
> *And how his forces cover'd all the ground.*
>
> . . .
>
> *I saw the* Colours *waving in the wind.*
>
> . . .
>
> *I heard the cries of those that wounded were,*
> *(While others fought like men bereft of fear)*
> *And while they cry, kill, kill, was in mine ears.*
>
> . . .
>
> *Indeed the* Captains *did not always fight,*
> *But then they would molest us day and night;*
> *Their cry,* up, fall on, *let us take the Town,*
> *Kept us from sleeping, or from lying down.* (2–3)

Yet the siege equipment and techniques in *The Holy War* are antiquated. Whereas contemporary besiegers used cannons and sappers, and tunneled under walls before attempting to bring them down with explosives,[73] Bunyan's warriors rely primarily on slings, stones, and battering rams, though he mentions trenches in passing (57). In contrast, the importance attached by Bunyan to standards emblazoned with symbols was characteristic of contemporary practice, for they served as rallying points and a means to distinguish friend from foe.[74] He varied slightly

---

[72] For the use of pikes and arquebuses see Geoffrey Parker, *The Military Revolution: Military Innovation and the Rise of the West, 1500–1800* (Cambridge: Cambridge University Press, 1988), 16–19; Brent Nosworthy, *The Anatomy of Victory: Battle Tactics, 1689–1763* (New York: Hippocrene Books, 1990), 10–11, 17–18, 21.

[73] Ibid., 13–14.

[74] Carlton, *Going to the Wars*, 83; C. H. Firth, *Cromwell's Army*, 4th ed. (London: Methuen and Co., 1962), 45–46; contrary to Mullett, *JBC*, 233.

from contemporary practice in not using the fife and drums to sustain soldiers' morale, preferring the employment of trumpets by Emanuel's forces and a hideous-sounding drum by Diabolus' troops. In contemporary warfare the cavalry utilized trumpets whereas the foot relied on the fife and drum.[75] Bunyan's account of military matters is thus highly eclectic.

### "*If Thou Wouldest Know My Riddle*"[76]: Interpreting the Allegory— Soteriology and Personal Experience

*The Holy War* is a technically sophisticated allegory that explores multiple levels of meaning, the most fundamental and consistent of which is soteriological, particularly with reference to Bunyan's own religious experience. But the allegory is not merely a different recounting of his experience, for soteriology makes it relevant to all Christians. He signals the allegory's transcendence of gender by referring to Mansoul as feminine in his epistle to the reader, but thereafter as a gender-neutral town with a male name (*HW*, 1–5).[77] In soteriological terms, the unfinished history of Mansoul is the story of Christ's redemption of the elect through unmerited grace and their subsequent sanctification, a lifelong process plagued by periodic backsliding but undergirded by grace sufficient to sustain them through recurring battles with Diabolonian temptations. Mansoul's fall from its original Edenic state of innocence made it a wholly corrupt place, the inheritance of original sin evident in the names of the town's streets: Blackmouth Lane, Blasphemers Row, Flesh Street, All-base Lane, Flesh Lane, Nauseous Street, Filth Lane, Folly Yard, and Bad Street. An omniscient Shaddai foresaw the fall and provided a remedy through a covenant with Emanuel (28–29, 32). Bunyan managed to convey his Calvinist tenets by damning Election-doubters—Diabolus' life-guard—as well as the Arminian Vocation-doubters and the mostly Catholic Grace-doubters who believe good works are requisite for salvation (220, 240–41).[78] Theological correctness was important for Bunyan, whose long-stand-

---

[75] *HW*, 188, 218–19; Carlton, *Going to the Wars*, 102.

[76] *HW*, 5. Bunyan used riddles as an interpretive strategy. Sharon Achinstein suggests that learning to interpret Samson's riddles (Judges 14:5–8) may have given Bunyan's audience "an experience of active resistance through reading, to signal their commitment" to the spiritual world. "Honey from the Lion's Carcass: Bunyan, Allegory, and the Samsonian Moment," in *Awakening Words*, ed. Gay, Randall, and Zinck, 78.

[77] According to Sim and Walker (211), Bunyan may have been indicating that Mansoul's lack of resolve to resist Diabolus was the result of female "'weakness'"; they note the town's subsequent dependence on Lord Willbewill to fight on its behalf, much as Greatheart defended Christiana and her party.

[78] I differ from Sharrock, who argued that the assorted doubters represent forms of

ing hostility toward unorthodox belief, as he defined it, is evident in *The Holy War* by his inclusion of Mr. Heresy among the Diabolonians (145). Any interpretation of the allegory that is discordant with his theology is therefore incorrect. Indeed, Emanuel cautions the recorder to "take heed that he receive not any Doctrine, or point of Doctrine, that are not communicated to him by his superiour teacher" (142). Bunyan's Calvinist principles exclude any possibility of reading the concept of double conversion into the allegory based on Emanuel's two occupations of Mansoul, an interpretation that ignores the fate of the Perseverance-doubters.[79] In fact, Bunyan carefully distinguished between Emanuel's first conquest, which included town and castle, and the second, when only the town had to be recaptured, the castle (heart) having remained in the possession of Emanuel's allies. Theologically, Mansoul's fate is never in doubt, but Bunyan infused tension into his epic by dramatizing the believer's struggles with Diabolonian temptations. His point is that sanctification is a process entailing the ebb and flow—but never the loss—of faith, not a simple progression of ever greater degrees of grace and certitude. Unbelief and some of his evil confederates lurk within Mansoul's dark corners, plotting to regain power when given the slightest opportunity. Emanuel's final exhortation to Christians is thus to "hold fast till I come" (250).

The soteriological theme of *The Holy War* is heavily influenced by Bunyan's personal experience. Indeed, the frontispiece of the first edition is a full portrait of Bunyan imposed on a rendition of Mansoul. Like *The Pilgrim's Progress*, *The Holy War* has a claim to be included among *Ego-Dokumente*, the first-person texts that encompass more than traditional autobiographies. Bunyan's allegories are personal documents that incorporate his experience as their very bedrock, a point he explicitly makes in his epistle to the reader:

---

despair regarding salvation rather than theological positions (*JB*, 124). Hill suggests that Bunyan is targeting proponents of free will, especially Ranters, Quakers, and Latitudinarians (*Tinker*, 247).

[79] Vincent Newey and Anne Hawkins interpret *The Holy War* as embodying double conversion. Newey, "'With the eyes of my understanding': Bunyan, Experience, and Acts of Interpretation," in *John Bunyan*, ed. Keeble, 214; Hawkins, "The Double Conversion in Bunyan's *Grace Abounding*," *Philological Quarterly* 61 (Summer 1982): 259–76. Beth Lynch plausibly contends that readers should "experience" the text of *The Holy War*, thereby avoiding the pitfall of treating the narrative and the doctrinal as dialectical rather than "mutually constitutive." However, Bunyan would have rejected any reading shaped by "experience" if it contradicted his fundamental theological tenets. "'Rather Dark to Readers in General': Some Critical Casualties of John Bunyan's *Holy War* (1682)," *BS* 9 (1999–2000): 45.

> For my part I (my self) was in the Town,
> Both when 'twas set up, and when pulling down,
> I saw Diabolus in his possession,
> And Mansoul also under his oppression.
> Yea, I was there when she own'd him for Lord,
> And to him did submit with one accord. (2)

Bunyan was there because this is *his* story, the account of the fearful combat waged within *his* soul and the ensuing battles with scheming, skulking Diabolonians. The claim to have seen and heard this epic struggle validates his account, imparting an air of authenticity reinforced by the biblical citations in the marginalia. Consequently the reader is led to accept the accuracy of the eyewitness account because it accords with Scripture.[80]

*The Holy War* does not objectify Bunyan's psychological and spiritual struggles as recorded in *Grace Abounding* any more than *The Pilgrim's Progress* does. As Leo Damrosch has argued, "the experience of *Grace Abounding* is continuous with that of the allegories, rather than being raw material from which nobler substances are refined."[81] This is not to suggest that the episodes in *The Holy War* closely parallel those in *Grace Abounding*, but that the allegory effectively captures the core themes of the spiritual autobiography, such as the soul's wrestling with anxiety, terror, despair, and false peace. Periodically, to be sure, unmistakable parallels between the two works are evident, as in the two-and-a-half-year reoccupation of the town of Mansoul (though not its castle), an episode inspired by that period in Bunyan's life when he "could not be delivered nor brought to peace again until well-nigh two years and an half were compleatly finished" (*GA*, §198). Shaddai's force of 40,000 recalls Bunyan's likening of the biblical sentences that bombarded him to an army of 40,000 men (§246). His dread of the law in his early religious experience (§130) is evinced in *The Holy War* when Mr. Conscience, the recorder, partially succumbs to Diabolus but yet is terrified when he reads Shaddai's laws (*HW*, 18–19), and again when he interprets Emanuel's response to Mansoul's petition as "*a messenger of death*," causing Mansoul to become "a terrour to it self" (97–98). Trepidation is again evident when Mansoulian

---

[80] Some interesting similarities (as well as differences) exist between Bunyan's spiritual autobiography and allegories on one hand and the artisan autobiographies analyzed by James S. Amelang on the other. The artisans also made eyewitness claims, tended to embrace radical religious views, and wrote out of a sense of duty. *The Flight of Icarus: Artisan Autobiography in Early Modern Europe* (Stanford, CA: Stanford University Press, 1998).

[81] Damrosch, *GP*, 141. Sharrock has a different interpretation (*JB*, 157), as does Crawford Gribben, who claims that "*Grace Abounding* became *The Holy War*." *The Puritan Millennium: Literature & Theology, 1550–1682* (Dublin: Four Courts Press, 2000), 197.

prisoners appear before Emanuel with ropes on their heads, shaking and trembling (104–5; cf. *GA*, §251).

The sense of dread inevitably causes anxiety like that manifest throughout much of *Grace Abounding*. After Diabolus' initial expulsion from Mansoul, Captains Boanerges and Conviction generated such dread "that they kept the Town under continued heart-aking, and caused (in their apprehension) the well-being of *Mansoul* for the future, to hang in doubt before them, so that (for some considerable time) they neither knew what rest or ease, or peace, or hope meant" (*HW*, 93–94). This is an effective synopsis of much of what Bunyan experienced in his period of psychological and religious turmoil. Anxiety is evinced as well when Desires-awake, returning to imprisoned Mansoulians to report on Emanuel's response to their petition for forgiveness, finds the recorder quaking and the frightened mayor "white as a clout" (96). When even a third petition failed to convince Emanuel to issue a pardon, their perturbation deepened and "death seem'd to sit upon some of their *Eyebrows*" (103). In general such anxieties no longer troubled Bunyan, as reflected in his confident rendition of Emanuel's rout of the army of doubters. Yet Bunyan was still wary, recognizing that seeds of Diabolonian disbelief lurked within, keeping him from total victory over disquietude even in what would be the last decade of his life. Attempting to displace this apprehension by identifying it as an intruding Diabolonian agent helped him to understand what he felt and to transfer the blame for his lingering disquietude to the cosmic warfare between God and the Devil.[82]

A crucial part of Bunyan's turbulent early religious experience—aptly described in *The Holy War* "as a ball tossed, and as a rolling thing before the whirlwind" (92)—was his struggle with melancholy. Not surprisingly, signs of that turmoil are found throughout *The Holy War*, though Bunyan, apparently untroubled by the illness in these years, dealt with it confidently. Early in the allegory, Diabolus tries to persuade the Mansoulians that Mr. Conscience is insane, depicting his language as raving, calling him a madman, and subjecting him to the sort of substantive mood swings Bunyan himself once experienced (19–20). Before long, the contemplation of Shaddai's holiness plunges Mansoul into despondency (64), but shortly thereafter, Emanuel tells Mansoul not to despair of life (76). Mansoul is unable to embrace this proclamation, and deep despondency periodically reasserts itself as the allegory unfolds. Bunyan was prepared to accept a degree of melancholy as spiritually healthy, and he condemned Pityless for having attempted to cheer up a miserable Mansoul after it had "apostatized from her rightful King" (130). Undoubtedly recalling how his neighbors had misjudged him when he was burdened with a profound sense of guilt, he casti-

[82] Cf. Damrosch, *GP*, 145–46, 149.

gated people who "call all those melancholy that have serious thoughts how that state [of damnation] should be shunned by them" (130). But he had difficulty distinguishing between the keen sense of remorse experienced by the elect, which some of his contemporaries diagnosed as melancholy, and the profound feeling of despair that constitutes depression. The draining physical weakness that often accompanies depression is recalled when Bunyan describes Mansoulians after they regressed as staggering and panting, their knees feeble, their hands weak, their faces pale; physically languishing, they nearly faint (158). The scheming Mr. Deceit, recognizing that the greatest threat to the Mansoulians is despair, proposes that if the Diabolonians "could drive them into desperation, that would knock the nail on the head" (167), thereby enabling the Diabolonians to regain the town. The clouds over Mansoul become increasingly blacker as its petitions to Shaddai go unanswered (171). When Prywell discovers the scheming Diabolonians within Mansoul, he tells his fellow citizens, "the sickness is now in the Town, and we have been made weak thereby" (182). One of the captains in the army of doubters descending on the town is Past-hope, whose "Ancient-bearer" is Mr. Despair and whose scutcheon is emblazoned with a hot iron and a hard heart. Among Past-hope's fellow captains are Torment, No-ease, and Brimstone (186–87), names that evoke Bunyan's earlier traumatic psychological struggles. The sense of oppressive weight experienced by the depressed is reflected in Bunyan's description of the Mansoulians after the Lord Secretary refused to join them in petitioning Shaddai for relief, for his decision fell "like a milstone upon them; yea, it crushed them so that they could not tell what to do" (191). Diabolus gloats as he observes the Mansoulians' *"hard, dark, troublesome and heart-afflicting hours,"* a phrase that blurs spiritual remorse and melancholy (193). Black clouds return when the Diabolonian forces storm the town, bringing a powerful sense of imminent ruin (204). Mansoul now seems to be "a place of total darkness," every one of its corners swarming with doubters (204–5). But Bunyan knew from his own experience that deliverance from the abyss of despair is possible, and this is the thrust of the lord mayor's message as Captain Credence returns (211).

The play of light and dark that characterized Bunyan's psychological struggles is incorporated in *The Holy War.* Identifying light with good and black with evil is obviously a biblical theme, but given his previous emotional state, the importance he attached to light and darkness was experiential as well as biblical in inspiration. When Diabolus initially captures Mansoul, he builds a tall fortified tower that blocks the sun's light from the lord mayor's palace, casting it into total blackness and rendering the mayor virtually blind as well as a prisoner (18). Blackness is thus coupled with constriction and made antithetic to freedom. This too is characteristic of a depressed mood. Similarly, the "Hold of *Defiance*" is built near Eyegate, and Midnight stronghold, whose governor is Love-no-light, is erected to plunge both of them into darkness (26). After Mansoul's fall to the Diabolonians, Lord Willbewill can no longer endure even a candle's light (23), and Diabolus, who speaks the language of the "black pit," now rules Mansoul (72). Once the town had been liberated and the Mansoulian prisoners pardoned, the latter received new attire that "lightened" the streets, and the citizens beseeched Emanuel to "*let light go before, and let love come after*" (109, 112). When the Mansoulians yielded to the Diabolonians, preserving only their castle for Emanuel's men, "now was it a day gloomy and dark, a day of clouds and of thick darkness" (157). The sense of pervasive gloom and "thick darkness" captures what the depressed undergo. Describing the two-and-a-half-year occupation by the Diabolonians, Bunyan, undoubtedly reminded of his own dark night, asked, "What Sun could shine upon it?" (206). When at last a radiant Emanuel returned to Mansoul, "the Sun shone comfortably upon them for a great while together" (225).

The light/dark motif is paralleled by another dealing with music and noise, much as in *The Pilgrim's Progress*.[83] Bunyan distinguished between the noise emitted by remorseful sinners and the cacophony of evil. When the Mansoulian prisoners appeared before Emanuel in mourning garb, "their Chains still mixing *their dolorous notes*, with the cries of the prisoners, made the noise more lamentable" (104). Far worse is the tolling of the "*Dead-mans-bell*" in hell, which rings on the occasion of Mansoul's backsliding. By making this tolling part of Mansoul's "horrible ceremony," Bunyan was parodying the mass, perhaps more specifically a requiem (164). For him noise was synonymous with evil. When Diabolus and his cohorts received word that his forces had retaken Mansoul, "*our yauning hollow bellied place, where we are, made so hideous and yelling a noise for joy, that the mountains that stand round about* Hellgate-hill, *had like to have been shaken to pieces at the sound thereof*" (176). Hell, then, is the place of ear-splitting din featuring the devilish "*Hell-drum*," hideous to hear and capable of frightening people as far as seven miles away (188, 200). At night, "no noise was ever heard upon earth more terrible, except the voice of *Shaddai* when he speaketh," an allusion to the divine voice of judgment (189). After the Diabolonians retake Mansoul, the town is filled with repellent noises and vain songs (205). Bunyan even suggests that the ungodly cannot appreciate true music, for alderman Hard-heart thinks wronging others is musical (125).

In contrast, genuine music is typically associated in *The Holy War* with spiritual and psychological well-being. The major exception occurs early in the epic,

[83] For the sounds of the period see Bruce R. Smith, *The Acoustic World of Early Modern England* (Chicago: University of Chicago Press, 1999).

when the Mansoulians decide to resist Shaddai's army, evincing their misplaced self-confidence by ringing bells, making merry, and dancing on the walls (49).[84] In virtually all other instances, bells, trumpets, pipes, tabors, and voices signal joy and spiritual triumph. When Emanuel binds Diabolus in chains, trumpets sound and soldiers sing (92–93), and when the prince pardons the Mansoulian prisoners, music rings out "in the upper region," followed by their appearance before their fellow townsfolk accompanied by the melodious sounds of a pipe and tabor (105–8). As news of their pardon spreads, every house in Mansoul is filled with joyous music, the bells peal, and in the camp of Emanuel's army the trumpets sound (109–10). Emanuel's entry into Mansoul is preceded by dancing elders and accompanied with the sound of trumpets (113). A heavenly choir entertains at the gala banquet hosted by Emanuel for Mansoul, after which the people sing about the prince in their homes, even as they sleep; for a time at least, nightmares are non-existent (115–16).[85] After Mansoul's new charter was read in the marketplace, bells ring, minstrels play, trumpets sound, and people dance (138). The prince himself is attended by "singing-men and singing-women," and while he rules Mansoul its women and children work and sing from morning to night (149–50). When the Diabolonians mount another attack on Mansoul, its people counter the terrible beating of the drum with "the melodious noise of their Trumpets," and they sing psalms while they execute some of the Diabolonians (198). News that Emanuel will come to Mansoul's rescue prompts Captain Credence to dispatch the royal trumpeters to the castle's battlements, where they make "the best musick that heart could invent" (218). Emanuel's second entry into Mansoul is accompanied with songs by the town's most skilled musicians, the trumpets so beloved by Bunyan, and women playing timbrels (223), and this processional is followed by more music, dancing, and peeling bells (225). Music, then, symbolizes spiritual and psychological well-being, a sense that one is at peace with one's self and God. The abundant music in *The Holy War* and Bunyan's confident handling of the episode of Mansoul's black despair suggest that he was now in robust health, psychologically as well as spiritually, though still wary of furtive Diabolonians within his mind and soul.

[84] For Bunyan dancing is neutral. Another instance of dancing in an evil context occurs when Mr. Profane carries a message to Diabolus in hell. The lords of the place arranged a dance for his entertainment, and when Mansoul turned from Shaddai its residents danced "after the Giants pipe" (*HW*, 20, 172).

[85] After the prisoners' pardon was proclaimed, no one slept that night for joy (*HW*, 108). This sleeplessness is in sharp contrast with that which afflicted Bunyan in his depressed state.

*"Things of Greatest Moment Be"*[86]: Millenarian and Historical Concerns

In addition to the soteriological interpretation of *The Holy War*, so firmly rooted in Bunyan's religious experience, the allegory invites other levels of explication. Interpreters have suggested readings focused on millenarianism, world history, the history of the Christian church, English history from the "tyranny" of Charles I to the projected overthrow of Charles II, and the history of the Bedford Corporation.[87] Apart from the soteriological, the other levels do not operate continuously, but this does not necessarily mean that Bunyan's execution was flawed. Multiple meanings enabled him to address disparate concerns ranging from a soul's spiritual needs to the problems of an endangered nonconformist community. When dealing with contemporary political circumstances in the charged atmosphere of 1679–82, prudence dictated relative obliquity, yet his critique of the Tory-Anglicans and Restoration society is both forceful and pervasive in this work. In the preface he made it clear that readers should consciously seek to interpret his "*riddle*," finding manifold "*inward Rarities*" among the work's "*mysteries.*" He left no doubt that in its deeper meanings *The Holy War* is a book for the initiated:

> . . . *if a Christian, thou wilt see*
> *Not small, but things of greatest moment be.* (5)

The closest biblical parallel is the book of Revelation, composed for the persecuted Christians of the late first century and pregnant with meaning no outsider could penetrate.[88] Insofar as possible *The Holy War* should be read and assessed from the standpoint of a late seventeenth-century nonconformist, who presumably would have had little difficulty decoding the millenarian and historical themes. This is not to suggest that other readers would have had difficulty understanding the epic as an allegory of the Christian life.

If *The Holy War* is interpreted in millenarian terms, *The Holy City* provides the necessary chronological framework: the fall and pre-Christian history; Christ and the apostolic church; the church's decline and captivity, followed by a period of altar-work (Wyclif, Hus, and the Protestant Reformation) and another of temple-work (the era of gathered churches); Antichrist's fall, the church's emergence from captivity, and the millennium; and finally Christ's return and the last judgment. Using Bunyan's schema as a guide, *The Holy War* incorporates the broad

---

[86] *HW*, 5.

[87] See, e.g., Tindall, chap. 7; Talon, 242–56; Sharrock, *JB*, 118–28; Sharrock and Forrest, in *HW*, xxv–xxxix; Hill, *TPM*, 240–50, 254–59; Gribben, *Puritan Millennium*, 177–93.

[88] Lord Understanding was to govern by daily consulting the book of Revelation, "the *Revelation* of Mysteries" (*HW*, 117–18).

swath of Christian history in a millenarian framework, commencing with humanity in its Edenic purity, Diabolus' plot to seize control of Mansoul, and the ensuing fall. Emanuel's initial conquest and the appointment of the Lord Chief Secretary (the Holy Spirit) as the principal teacher represent the apostolic church and pentecost, and Diabolus' reconquest of the town symbolizes the church's decline and captivity throughout the medieval era, the fourth monarchy of Daniel 7. The besieged castilians who petition Emanuel to return signal the period of altar-work, "a season of Grace" (211). This leads into the time of temple-work, when Captain Credence summons Mansoulians to the field against the Diabolonians (218). Just as Diabolus was initially defeated when Christ triumphed over death, so now Emanuel is again victorious as Diabolus' armies are vanquished. The millennium now commences, a time when Emanuel rules, but *not* in person, for his closing exhortation bids the redeemed Mansoulians to hold fast until he returns (250). The last judgment and Christ's final return remain in the future, as does the transfiguration of redeemed Mansoul, when Emanuel promises to dismantle and rebuild it in heaven (247).[89]

Bunyan provides various clues to indicate that he deems Emanuel's second conquest to be the commencement of the millennium, the chief of these being Emanuel's closing promise to have such communion with Mansoul in heaven "*as is not possible here to be enjoyed. Nor ever could be, shouldest thou live in* Universe *the space of a thousand years*" (247). Another millennial reference is Emanuel's bestowal of white garments on the Mansoulians (225), a reference to Revelation 7:14. The final battle with the bloodmen (228–33) is compatible with Revelation 17:14 and 19:19–21, and the transformed Mansoul reflects Revelation 21:2–3. Even the final words of the epic are an unattributed quotation of Revelation 2:24–25.

[89]This interpretation substantially agrees with that of Sharrock, *JB*, 126; Sharrock and Forrest, in *HW*, xxxiii; and the second of three proposed millenarian scenarios suggested by Tindall, 156. See also W. R. Owens, "John Bunyan and English Millenarianism," in *Awakening Words*, ed. Gay, Randall, and Zinck, 91–92. It differs from that which I proposed in *JBEN*, 147; cf. Tindall's first interpretation (156). To avoid some of the inconsistencies suggested by Tindall, Donald Mackenzie confines the "apocalyptic" to "specific moments." "Rhetoric *versus* Apocalypse: The Oratory of *The Holy War*," *BS* 2 (Spring 1990), 38. For another view see Aileen Macleod [Ross] Sinton, "Millenarianism in the Works of John Bunyan" (Ph.D. diss., University of Alberta, 1986), chap. 6; Aileen M. Ross, "Paradise Regained: The Development of John Bunyan's Millenarianism," in *Bunyan in England and Abroad*, ed. M. van Os and G. J. Schutte (Amsterdam: VU University Press, 1990), 73–89. Gribben contends that in *The Holy War* the millennium does not commence at the end, as I have argued, but is "the experience of the believer within time," and is thus similar to the "realized" eschatology of the Quakers. This interpretation is at odds with the framework laid out by Bunyan in *The Holy City*. *Puritan Millennium*, 184, 192.

Millennial references are, of course, scattered elsewhere in the allegory, as in the description of Mansoul's pardon as a parchment with seven seals (106; Rev. 5:1) and the engraving of Emanuel's name in Mansoul (118; Rev. 3:12).

Efforts to interpret *The Holy War* as an allegory of Stuart and republican rule beginning in 1625 are not persuasive. William York Tindall identified the first reign of Diabolus with Charles I's government, Emanuel's initial reign with the rule of the saints, Mansoul's decline with the Protectorate, Diabolus' return with the Restoration, and Emanuel's second coming with the inauguration of the fifth monarchy.[90] In contrast, Jack Lindsay likened the first Diabolonian attack to the civil war, the initial rule of Emanuel to the commonwealth, the second Diabolonian assault to a feudal reaction under Charles II, and Emanuel's ultimate victory to a prophecy of the 1688 revolution.[91] Such readings mistake Bunyan's plentiful sprinkling of historical references, both biblical and English, throughout his epic. Sensitive to such usage, a perceptive reader can approximate what a contemporary might have been reminded of as he or she read. The effect is to create a vivid sense of the battle to preserve England for Protestantism in the wider context of the cosmic warfare between the forces of Christ and those of Antichrist. Because those hostilities are ongoing, the epic cannot conclude with a sense of finality, other than Emanuel's promise that he will come again. Although Bunyan's theological convictions, including his millenarianism, provided the answers about the ultimate conclusion of the cosmic struggle, his concern with the English political and religious scene, which he could not accurately predict, necessitated leaving the work unfinished. Critics who fault Bunyan for this[92] miss the point of what he was endeavoring to do, something his nonconformist readers were unlikely to have done.

Although allusions to English history are not developed in any systematic or chronological manner, it would be erroneous to conclude that they are accidental or even non-existent. When the Diabolonian privy council contemplated blowing up Mansoul with "*the Gun-powder of pride*" (165), the contemporary reader must have been reminded of the infamous Gunpowder plot, and Emanuel's claim to have often delivered Mansoul "*from the designs, plots, attempts, and conspiracies of* Diabolus" (248–49) probably evoked memories of the recent alleged Popish and Meal Tub conspiracies as well as earlier ones including the army plots of 1641 and the Gunpowder plot. In heaven, Bunyan pointedly averred, there would be no more conspiracies (247). When Captain Boanerges and his men assault Eargate, the marginal note explains that he "plays the man" (81), an echo of

[90] Tindall, 156–57.

[91] Lindsay, 219.

[92] E.g. James Anthony Froude, *Bunyan* (New York: Harper and Brothers, 1880), 148.

Hugh Latimer's exhortation to Nicholas Ridley when the two men were about to be burned as martyrs in Mary I's reign. The day of fasting proclaimed by Conscience after Mansoul regressed and another one after Mr. Prywell discovered the Diabolonian conspiracy (158–59, 183) recall the fasts during the civil war. Diabolus warns Mansoul that Shaddai will destroy Mansoul "*root and branch*," borrowing a descriptor used tellingly in the campaign of the early 1640s to destroy episcopacy, but now placed in the mouth of the satanic prince (33). Diabolus set up his standard in the north, much as Charles I had done at Nottingham in August 1642 (189). Led by Boanerges, Shaddai's army "lived upon the Kings cost in all the way they went" (38), a probable jab at Charles I's quartering of troops in citizens' homes. Christopher Hill sees a parallel between the Diabolonian intruders and the Norman invaders, and thus reinforcement of the myth of the Norman yoke, and he also suggests a possible echo of the Declaration of Breda in the speeches of Diabolus and Ill-pause at Eargate (14–16).[93] Sensitive to the possibilities, a contemporary reader probably saw numerous allusions to historical events in England, ranging from the obvious, such as the plague, to the recondite.

Jack Lindsay has described *The Holy War* in broad strokes as a commentary on "absolutism against the liberties of the people."[94] Although such an interpretation cannot be sustained, Bunyan is unquestionably interested, as were his contemporaries, in the theme of freedom and slavery. In his epistle to the reader he announces that this is an allegory about how Mansoul "*was lost, took captive, [and] made a slave*" (1). Freedom, however, is a theme embraced by Diabolus as much as Emanuel. To live in fear of punishment for committing trivial offenses, Diabolus argues, is slavery. "*You are not a free people*," he tells the Mansoulians, but "*are kept both in bondage and slavery*," captives in "*a dark and stinking cave*" (15). From the beginning, Diabolus proclaims a message of freedom, admonishing the Mansoulians to beware of having their privileges taken away after he liberates them (17). Whereas Mansoulians in their Edenic state were "a pen'd up people," Diabolus promises to impose no laws on them (20–21). Once he acquires control of the town, he urges his subjects to resist Emanuel forcefully, for "*it is better to dye valiantly, than to live like pitiful Slaves*" (34). Shaddai's subjects are "so inslaved in all places" that "none in the *Universe* [are] so unhappy as they, none so trampled upon as they" (63). In putting such words in Diabolus' mouth, Bunyan was almost certainly criticizing his Tory-Anglican opponents, for their message entailed not only a defense of the established church but also a claim to support the rule of law against arbitrary government. No less than the Whigs,

---

[93] Hill, *TPM*, 241, 244.
[94] Lindsay, 216.

they sought to make the language of freedom their own.[95] But he made it clear that Diabolus' message was fraudulent, for the Mansoulians become slaves and vassals after Resistance and Innocency—a revealing combination—perish in the unsuccessful attempt to defend the town against the Diabolonians (17). As the epic unfolds, the call to liberty is proclaimed by the forces of Shaddai, who announce their mission as the end of Mansoul's enslavement to Diabolus' tyranny (42, 64). Bunyan recognizes that the Mansoulians are not seeking liberation, but are content "to abide in the Chains of the Tyrant *Diabolus*" (71). The task of Emanuel's forces is thus one of enlightenment as well as liberation.

In *The Holy War* the ongoing battle between opposing forces, each of which claims the banner of freedom, is related to Bunyan's fascination with plotting. In the charged atmosphere of the Popish plot and succession crisis this was not unusual. Charles' critics suspected his prorogation and dismissal of Parliaments were part of a conspiracy to prevent an investigation of the Popish plot,[96] and suspicion of ongoing Catholic scheming seems to have been widespread. In 1680 Ferguson warned of "the obnoxiousness of the Papists to the Law, for their many and continued Conspiracies against his Majesties Person, the Lives of the People, the Protestant Religion, and the Peace and Safety of the Government."[97] About the time Bunyan began writing *The Holy War*, the Irish Catholic Edward Fitzharris was arrested, as we have seen; the *True Protestant Mercury* reported that he had attempted to enlist confederates "to Exasperate Dissenters into some Disorders, perswade them to buy Arms, or proceed to any rash Actions that might Create Suspicions of them." Failing this, Fitzharris alleged, Catholics pretending to be Protestant nonconformists would feign a rising, setting the stage for a Catholic insurrection. As fanciful as this reputed scheme was, Whigs were prepared to believe that their enemies were determined to implicate them in a "Sham plot."[98] Likewise, Tories suspected Whigs of conspiring against the government and threatening the established church.[99]

This poisonous atmosphere of fear and suspicion is reflected in *The Holy War*. After Emanuel's initial conquest of the town, its residents evince concern that the Diabolonians lurking within are engaging in "designs, plots, or contrivances" (112), and Emanuel underscores the danger when he warns that the intent of such scheming is to reduce the Mansoulians to servitude more severe than that

[95] Harris, *PULS*, 98–101.
[96] PRO, SP 29/411/16.
[97] [Robert Ferguson], *A Letter to a Person of Honour, Concerning the Black Box* [London, 1680], 4.
[98] *True Protestant Mercury* 19 (26 February–2 March 1681); Greaves, *SOK*, 22–23.
[99] Morrice, 1:326.

experienced by the ancient Hebrews in Egypt (144). Indeed, after a disappointed Emanuel withdraws from the town, the Diabolonians meet at the home of Mr. Mischief to plot Mansoul's ruin with Diabolus' help (162–63, 166). In developing this theme Bunyan describes how the cabal had Lords Covetousness, Anger, and Lasciviousness disguise themselves as Mansoulians and foster feelings of despair among the residents (167–71). As the conspiracy develops, Diabolus resolves to send an army of doubters against Mansoul (175–76), but Mr. Prywell finally discovers the plot and reports it to the mayor, Lord Understanding, and the town preacher, Mr. Conscience. The lecture-bell is rung, the people are apprized of the conspiracy, petitions are sent to Shaddai seeking his assistance, and security measures are implemented, including a house-to-house search (181–83). Bunyan's allegory reflects the atmosphere of suspected conspiracies, particularly after allegations of the Popish plot. In depicting Mr. Prywell he may have been thinking of Sir Edmund Godfrey, the magistrate who first heard those allegations, or possibly the earl of Shaftesbury, arguably the most relentless investigator of the reputed conspiracy—"the great Giant that speaks to all," in Sir Robert Southwell's apt description.[100] Similarly, the lecture-bell may have been inspired by the series of twenty-five morning lectures against popery organized in Southwark by Vincent in 1675 and subsequently published.[101]

Another theme with a sense of historical immediacy in *The Holy War* is petitioning, which contemporary readers would have seen against the background of the Whig and Tory petitioning campaigns of 1680–81. When the allegory is interpreted in strictly religious terms, petitioning obviously refers to prayer, but when the epic is read in its historical context the allusions to the petitioning campaigns are apparent. The captains of Shaddai's army petition him to send troops to facilitate the conquest of Mansoul (65–66), and Lord Understanding and other residents subsequently petition Emanuel, confessing their offenses (90). After Emanuel reconquers the town and incarcerates Willbewill, Conscience, and Understanding, the people have to petition the prince three times, on the last occasion sending their plea with Desires-awake and Wet-eyes, the son of Repentance (94–100). After Mansoul regresses, the townsfolk heed Godly-fear's advice to petition repeatedly, but Emanuel does not respond until the Lord Secretary drafts a petition (159–61, 180, 191, 207–8). By this point Diabolus is determined to prohibit the petitioning, accusing the Mansoulians of treachery (209). At last, Emanuel replies positively to the petitioners (213) and takes possession of the town. When Diabolus sends his army of bloodmen and doubters to besiege Mansoul, the peo-

---

[100] Bodl., Carte MSS 38, fol. 678r. Reflections of Shaftesbury are manifest in Lord Willbewill, as shall be seen.

[101] [Nathaniel Vincent, ed.], *The Morning-Exercise Against Popery* (London, 1675).

ple again petition Emanuel, and once more he comes to their aid (231). Bunyan's message is that petitioning, although not always effective, can produce the desired results if people are persistent.

Several commentators have argued for the presence of yet another historical theme—hostility toward the landed aristocracy—in *The Holy War*.[102] In fact, the forces of righteousness in the allegory are monarchical and hierarchical (28, 30), yet the number of explicitly named evil lords is much larger than the few good ones with names. Prince Emanuel's allies include the Lord Chief Secretary, Lord Innocent, unnamed "high Lords" and noble princes at Shaddai's court (28, 30), and, after their redemption, Lords Willbewill and Understanding and the gentry of Mansoul (156, 224). Late in the allegory Self-denial is ennobled (244). The impression Bunyan creates by naming more than twenty of the peers who serve Diabolus is that most nobles, especially those in Charles II's reign, are opponents of the godly. Among them are Lords Belial, Deceit, Evil-eye, Blasphemy, Covetousness, Beelzebub, Apollyon, Brisk, Murmer, Pragmatick, Lustings, Fornication, Adultery, Murder, Anger, and Lasciviousness. As Bunyan undoubtedly knew, the Tories enjoyed a majority in the House of Lords, where they blocked efforts to exclude the duke of York from the succession. By creating the impression that so many nobles in the cosmic struggle are evil, he managed to convey his criticism of those who, in his view, endangered England and Protestantism, and yet signal that some peers, such as Shaftesbury, were supporters of the godly. In fact, Bunyan may have had Shaftesbury in mind when he drew the portrait of Lord Willbewill, who limped, as did the earl. (Willbewill's clerk, Mr. Mind, would then have been John Locke.) In his expectations of the nobility, Bunyan adhered to the concept of *noblesse oblige*, for the clerk at Lord Lustings' trial told him "*the higher the better you should have been*" (121).

Bunyan also avoided typing other social strata as godly or evil. The latter include Mansoul's vagabonds and some of the "meaner sort" (199, 202), but he also mentions the godly poor (148). Wealth *per se* is not bad if properly used. Bunyan proposes that the riches of Mr. Letgoodslip, a merchant or trader, be expropriated and given to Mr. Meditation, the husband of Mrs. Piety, "to improve for the common good" (243). When the Diabolonians conspire to seize Mansoul's castle, they intend to make the town so prosperous that its residents will use the castle as a warehouse instead of an anti-Diabolonian garrison (216–17). Evoking a theme from *The Life and Death of Mr. Badman* Bunyan castigated those dishonest merchants who were "playing the Bankrupt" (75), but he manifested no hostility toward honest commerce. At the end of the epic Mansoul "minded her trade that

---

[102] Lindsay, 219–20; Tindall, 117, 148; Hill, *TPM*, 250 (though he also notes the role of godly gentry, p. 246).

she had with the Country that was a far off, also she was busie in her *Manufac-ture*" (244). A godly society on earth was not one devoid of social stratification but one in which everyone kept "close to his own imployment" (149–50).

"Turn the World Upside Down"[103]: Challenging Unregenerate England

The radical nature of *The Holy War* is not the espousal of a revolutionary so-cial vision but its attack on Charles II and the Tory-Anglicans, an assault veiled to many readers (and some modern commentators[104]) but in all likelihood not to nonconformists. The recurring depiction of Diabolus as a tyrant could not have been missed by readers steeped in the rhetoric about an England endangered by arbitrary government and popery. "Our Lives and Estates are not [to be] sub-jected to the arbitrary and despotick Pleasure of a Sovereign, nor left to the Dis-cretion of Judges," Ferguson protested in 1682. In the same month *The Holy War* was published, an anonymous critic of the king boldly wrote: "We the People of England (finding our Parliaments dissolved) do, in the name of God, demand of Thee Charles Stewart, Quo Warranto art thou King of England?"[105] The separa-tion of the man from the office of kingship recalled the House of Commons' resolution of 7 January 1642 asserting that (the first) Charles Stuart's bringing of troops to arrest members of Parliament was an illegal act against king and Par-liament. As the anonymous pamphlet *Vox populi, vox Dei* (1681) made clear, much of the rhetoric was directed against the duke of York, whose succession was believed to be tantamount to the establishment of tyranny: "The people seem to cry out with one Voice, *No Popish Successor*, no *Idolater*, no Queen *Mary* in Breeches, no Tyrant over the Conscience."[106] Thus in the opinion of the Whigs, Charles, in his determination to have his brother succeed him, abetted the estab-lishment of tyranny, as did his infamous alliance with Louis XIV. As a threat to Mansoul's spiritual *bene esse*, Diabolus could be read as a stand-in for Charles, an interpretation reinforced by Bunyan's depiction of Diabolus making havoc of Shaddai's laws, spoiling the law books, and establishing "his own vain Edicts,

[103] *HW*, 40.

[104] E.g. Lynn Veach Sadler, who contends that "time and again Bunyan demonstrates that he is not politically controversial." *John Bunyan* (Boston: Twayne Publishers, 1979), 84. Cf. Newey, "'With the eyes of my understanding,'" 215. Mullett rightly asserts that *The Holy War* is "more than a coded attack on governmental policies of centralization and Tory control," but Bunyan's critique is not merely occasional, as Mullett avers. *JBC*, 232 (quoted), 235.

[105] [Robert Ferguson], *The Second Part of No Protestant Plot* (London, 1682), 19 (quoted); PRO SP 29/418/88 (quoted).

[106] Anon., *Vox populi, vox Dei* (n.p., 1681), 1.

Statutes and Commandments" (24). In the eyes of nonconformists, using the laws to persecute them and depriving them of perceived legal rights were cardinal offenses of Charles' regime during the succession crisis. As Ferguson declared in 1682, "whensoever Laws cease to be a security unto men, they will be sorely tempted to apprehend themselves cast into a state of War."[107]

The tyranny against which Bunyan warns in *The Holy War* is intimately linked to the perceived threat of Catholicism. His concern may have been heightened by the publication of *The Increase of Popery in England* by his late friend William Dell. L'Estrange had prevented its publication in 1667, but someone carefully preserved the manuscript and got Richard Janeway to publish it in 1681. In it Dell warned that Catholicism's dual aim was to destroy Protestantism in England and then eradicate all people of English blood, replacing them with French and other emigrants who would restore the country "to its former *Popish Splendor*." Ferguson made a similar point, contending that Catholics are "obliged by the Principles of their Religion, to extirpate all Christians, who have withdrawn from the Communion of their Church."[108] It is not surprising to find Bunyan expressing analogous views in *The Holy War*. Various reminders of Catholicism are in the allegory, most notably the role of Captain Pope as a commander in the Diabolonian army of persecuting bloodmen; his scutcheon bears the image of a godly man being burned at the stake (*HW*, 229), a grim reminder of what some Protestants feared should James become king. The maul wielded by Diabolus is another way of underscoring the threat of persecution (35). When Lord Understanding warns that Diabolus and Incredulity might set Mansoul afire as they leave the town (60), Bunyan's readers probably recalled the rumors that Catholics had been responsible for the great fire in London.[109] In addition, he satirized Catholics when he had Lord Cerberus welcome Mr. Profane to Hell-gate Hill with an oath: "By St. *Mary* I am glad to see thee" (171). Catholics and conformists alike were the butt of satire regarding their observation of Lent, for Bunyan had Lord Willbewill invite Lord Lasciviousness, disguised as the servant Harmless-mirth, into his household near the end of the Lenten season (168).

Bunyan leavened *The Holy War* with caustic allusions to the Restoration state and society, as in his introductory observation that

> . . . Mansoul *trampled upon things Divine,*
> *And wallowed in filth as doth a swine.* (2)

[107] [Ferguson], *Second Part*, 1–2.

[108] William Dell, *The Increase of Popery in England* (London, 1681), 3–4; [Robert Ferguson], *The Third Part of No Protestant Plot* (London, 1682), 1.

[109] Greaves, *EUHF*, 46.

When Mansoul is under Diabolus' sway, red-coated troops and black-coated clergy teem in its streets (205), poignant symbols of the state's power to persecute dissent. This was the government that sought to make traitors of nonconformists, accusing them of disturbing the people's tranquility. Denouncing Lord Under-standing for treason when he wants to accept the terms offered by Shaddai's army, Incredulity, echoing the Tory-Anglican line, calls for *"the quieting of the people, whom by your unlawfull actions, you have this day set to mutiny against us"* (59). Similarly, Shaddai's troops are described by Mansoul's debased inhabitants as "the men that turn the World upside down" (40). When Incredulity is finally apprehended and put on trial, he is unrepentant, faithful to his belief—so typical of the Tories—that his fundamental duty is to obey his sovereign: "I thought it my duty to be true to my trust, and to do what I could to possess the minds of the men of *Mansoul* to do their utmost to resist strangers and foreigners" (123).

For the most part, Bunyan depicts the Tory-Anglicans as a hodgepodge of turncoats, persecutors, conformists, and spies. Those who broke with the godly to conform at the Restoration are portrayed in *The Holy War* as Tradition, Hu-man-wisdom, and Man's Invention, all of whom served under Boanerges before their capture. After telling Diabolus "that they did not so much live by *Religion*, as by the fates of *Fortune*," they are assigned to the company of Captain Anything (52), a deliberate slap at their perceived lack of principles. The bloodmen, who come from the country of Loath-good, particularly the counties of Blindman-shire, Blindzealshire, and Malice, represent persecutors (227–28, 233). Their cap-tain is Nimrod, the biblical figure who sometimes serves as a type for tyrants (229). Like the residents of Vanity Fair in *The Pilgrim's Progress*, many of the Dia-bolonians—or Tory-Anglicans—appear to be "very rife and hot for Religion" (145–46). Appearing in the guise of an angel of light, Diabolus offers to establish ministers and lecturers, a none too subtle identification of the Restoration Church of England with the Diabolonians. Although they may be superficially religious, the Diabolonians and their unregenerate Mansoulian friends read "Odious Atheistical Pamphlets and filthy Ballads & Romances full of baldry" (31). The licenser of such material is Mr. Filth, an unmistakable allusion to Roger L'Estrange, the surveyor of the press who did his utmost to repress dissenting lit-erature.[110] L'Estrange worked in tandem with government informers, who appear in *The Holy War* as Diabolonian spies (5–9, 67). Bunyan even made use of the

[110] *HW*, 257; Keeble, *LCN*, 102–10; Beth Lynch, "*Mr. Smirke* and 'Mr. Filth': A Biblio-graphic Case Study in Nonconformist Printing," *The Library*, 7th ser., 1 (March 2000): 49–50; Greaves, *DUFE*, 216–25; Greaves, *EUHF*, 167ff, 176ff, 182f, 231f; Greaves, *SOK*, 42–48 *passim*.

emerging political parties to describe a Mansoul divided between those who supported Mr. Incredulity (the Tory-Anglicans) and the adherents of Lord Understanding (the Whigs and their nonconformist allies) (61).

Among the crowd of Tory-Anglicans who populate *The Holy War*, one of the most significant for Bunyan is Mr. False-peace, whom Diabolus appoints to the bench of aldermen after his initial conquest of Mansoul (25). At his trial following Emanuel's capture of the town, he insists his name is Mr. Peace, a man who loves to live quietly, serve as a peacemaker, and uphold virtue (126). In other words, he is like those ostensibly decent citizens of Vanity Fair. According to one witness, False-peace believes that "peace, though in a way of unrighteousness is better than trouble with truth" (128). In the words of the indictment, he kept rebellious Mansoul "*in a false, groundless and dangerous peace, and damnable security, to the dishonour of the King, the transgression of his Law, and the great damage of the Town of* Mansoul" (126).[111] To nonconformists Bunyan was making the point that peace at any price—peace grounded on lies—is not only deceitful but damning (128). Simultaneously he was lashing out against those who, like Mr. Incredulity, opposed Shaddai and his followers because they posed a threat to a tranquil society (49). In the jaundiced estimation of Incredulity, the army of dissenters is "some Vagabond Runagate Crew, that having shaken off all obedience to your King, have gotten together in tumultuous manner" (48). Lest any reader miss his point, Bunyan explicitly noted in the marginalia that Satan was urging the Mansoulians to defy the godly ministers marching against the town (39–40).

If peace at any price were intolerable, then Bunyan was prepared to expound a doctrine of resistance. That he should have done so is not surprising, given the fact that this was a subject discussed in the circles with which he was affiliated. When Ferguson asserted in 1682 that subjects deprived of the law's protection are "cast into a state of War," he concluded that they are "justified in having recourse to the best means they can for their shelter and defence."[112] As he went on to argue the following year, to resist a ruler who prohibits what God has enjoined or commands what God has banned is not to oppose legitimate authority but a usurper. "Nor is the dethroning those who have invaded the Right and Authority of their Maker, a deposing of Governours, but a delivering our selves from conspirators against their as wel as our King." When a prince fails to uphold his contract with his subjects, the latter are freed from their fealty to him, making resistance legitimate.[113] Owen, a

---

[111] For the literary background of vices disguised as virtues, see Roger Sharrock, "The Trial of Vices in Puritan Fiction," *Baptist Quarterly* 14 (January 1951): 3–12, 48.

[112] [Ferguson], *Second Part*, 1–2.

[113] [Robert Ferguson], *An Impartial Enquiry into the Administration of Affair's in England* (n.p., 1683), 3–4 (quoted), 28.

friend of both Ferguson and Bunyan, stopped short of this avowal of the people's right to resist, asserting instead Calvin's argument for the right of magistrates to take up arms against monarchs who betray the people's freedom.[114] In the same year Bunyan published *The Holy War*, Owen defended the right of potentates, princes, and magistrates to protect themselves and their subjects in the profession of Protestantism. Since the Reformation, he averred, "no instance can be given of any people defending themselves in the Profession of the Protestant Religion by Arms, but where together with their Religion their Enemies did design and endeavour to destroy those Rights, Liberties and Priviledges."[115] As long as resistance is led by magistrates in defense of Protestantism, Owen accepted its legitimacy. Thus, while Bunyan was composing his allegory, resistance was a subject of discussion in the London circles with which he was acquainted. That he talked about this subject during his visits to London is highly likely.

In *The Holy War* Bunyan espouses a doctrine of resistance compatible with Owen's. Early in the allegory Diabolus is more afraid of Captain Resistance, the only man of war in Mansoul, than the rest of the town combined. At Diabolus' behest, Tisiphane, one of the classical Furies, kills the captain, leaving Mansoul "naked of Courage" and devoid of the will to resist (13, 15–16). This sets the stage for Diabolus and Mansoul to rebel against Shaddai (27, 44), a clever attempt by Bunyan to turn objections to resistance against his enemies by making them mutineers. This was his response to those Tory-Anglicans who were doing their utmost to tar Whigs and dissenters with the brush of sedition. L'Estrange, for instance, would contend in 1683 that "this *Doctrine* of *Resistance* in case of *Religion*, is the *Source* of all our *Feares*, and *Jealousies, Seditions* and *Conspiracies*."[116] Bunyan countered proponents of such views by distinguishing between those who rebel against God and "*the Government of the Captains, and of* Shaddai *their King*" (58) on one hand and those who resist tyranny and the repression of godly worship on the other. Legitimate resistance entails a willingness to die if necessary (65). When Emanuel mounts his assault on Mansoul, Mr. Conscience regrets that in the past he transgressed by perverting instead of executing justice and by keeping silent when he should have condemned Diabolonian rule; such inactivity, Bunyan insists, constitutes true rebellion as well as treason (89). Diabolus, not the dissenter or Whig who resists, is the real rebel (101). For Bunyan, the correct position is enunciated by the mayor, Lord Understanding, when he an-

[114] John Calvin, *Institutes of the Christian Religion*, ed. John T. McNeill and trans. Ford Lewis Battles, 2 vols. (Philadelphia: Westminster Press, 1960), 2:1519.

[115] Owen, *Brief and Impartial Account*, 12.

[116] [Roger L'Estrange], *Considerations upon a Printed Sheet Entituled the Speech of the Late Lord Russel to the Sheriffs* (London, 1683), sig. A2v.

nounces to Diabolus that *"we are resolved to resist thee as long as a Captain, a man, a sling, and a stone to throw at thee, shall be found in the Town of Mansoul"* (210). In his closing oration, Emanuel asks the people of Mansoul to stand with him against the Diabolonians, having already made clear that in this warfare there is no room for compromise (78, 80, 250). The Mansoulians, he stresses, have been taught *"to watch, to fight, to pray, and to make war against [his] foes"* (250). Resistance is therefore not only permissible but mandated by Emanuel. The role of the captains in *The Holy War* suggests that Bunyan expected such resistance to be led by a coalition of magistrates and ministers, much as Owen and Calvin had advocated. He stopped short of calling on nonconformists to rebel, but if their leaders should mount an insurrection to defend Protestantism and oppose what they saw as tyranny, he clearly expected dissenters to support them. In 1681–82 Bunyan's usual militancy of the spirit was on the verge of embracing militancy of the sword.

# CHAPTER 11

# The Struggle with Evil

When Bunyan took the manuscript of *The Holy War* to Dorman Newman and Benjamin Alsop about January 1682, the campaign against nonconformists was intensifying in various parts of the country. The same month the Middlesex quarter sessions ordered the laws against conventicles enforced, and *The True Protestant Mercury* reported in March 1682 that several counties, among them Nottinghamshire, Cheshire, and Somerset, were following the lead of Middlesex in prosecuting dissenters. In ordering a comparable effort, the grand jury in Devon condemned nonconformist clergy on 25 April for attempting to "debauch" people with the doctrines responsible for civil war in the 1640s.[1] Action was undertaken against dissenters at Newcastle in May, but the mayor of Reading found their ministers too elusive, Canterbury's mayor refused to curtail illegal religious meetings, and some jurors were sympathetic to nonconformists.[2] Magistrates in London had trouble when their attempts to suppress conventicles sparked tumults and physical assaults on informers in June, though they had experienced some success the previous month in fining those who attended the services of Thomas Doelittle and William Jenkyn.[3] Although several London conventicles were suppressed in July, another informer was beaten and a group of conventi-

---

[1] LMA, MS MJ/SBB/394, fols. 45–46; *True Protestant Mercury* 124 (11–15 March 1682); 126 (18–22 March 1682); PRO, SP 29/418/97, 132, 181; *CSPD, 1682*, 145; Luttrell, 1:172.

[2] *True Protestant Mercury* 141 (10–13 May 1682); PRO, SP 29/419/19, 97, 98. The mayor of Deal also refused to suppress a conventicle in December 1682. PRO, SP 29/421/127.

[3] BL, Add. MSS 63,776, fol. 3v; *CSPD, 1682*, 255, 272; *True Protestant Mercury* 148 (3–7 June 1682). See also *Impartial Protestant Mercury* 115 (26–30 May 1682); Jeaffreson, 4:161; Luttrell, 1:190, 193, 196. For Jenkyn see *Calamy Revised, s.v.* The author of a newsletter dated 22 June 1682 clearly misread the situation in London when he expected few if any conventicles to meet in the future. BL, Add. MSS 63,776, fol. 6r.

440       THE STRUGGLE WITH EVIL

clers offered resistance. Two months later, worshipers in Exchange Alley were kicked and beaten.[4]

The authorities were now endeavoring to quash dissent by the imposition of heavy financial penalties. Among those fined at the Middlesex assizes for illegal preaching were the Congregationalists Stephen Lobb (£140 in August) and Matthew Meade (£180 in November) and the Presbyterians Benjamin Agas (Anglesey's former chaplain, who was fined £840 between August and November), Joseph Read (fined at least £460 in the same period), Andrew Parsons (£280 in the same period), John Quick (£140 in the same period), John Humfrey (£100 in August), and William Bates (£100 in November). In the autumn an informer claimed to have more than fifty men in his employ searching for conventicles in the London area, and to have obtained convictions in the preceding six months that resulted in fines in excess of £10,000 in the City and £7,000 in Westminster. Elsewhere, dissenters in Bristol, where more than 1,500 awaited prosecution in August, faced fines of £200, reportedly forcing more than 500 families to leave their homes. In Herefordshire magistrates were reportedly seizing two-thirds of the estates of some dissenters,[5] but in London many nonconformists fought back, coming to the archdeaconry court as many as 300 or 400 at a time. Numerous dissenters instituted legal action against their adversaries, including complaints to Chancery, hoping to strain the financial resources of the church and clog the legal system. They enjoyed a degree of success, for some of these cases were still pending in 1687.[6]

The outlook for nonconformists in London dimmed as a result of the Common Council elections in December 1681, when Tories won enough seats to leave the body evenly divided. As we have seen, magistrates had the meetings of two of Bunyan's friends, Meade and Owen, under observation on 12 January and 19 February respectively.[7] When Bunyan was in the City about this time he must have discussed the dissenters' plight with his ministerial colleagues. Among them may have been Ferguson, who was furious with the king's recent dissolution of parliaments and concerned about the duke of York's perceived temper and penchant for arbitrary power. He was worried too about the government's willingness to punish dissenters at home while turning a blind eye to the predicament of Prot-

[4] *True Protestant Mercury* 158 (8–12 July 1682); 162 (22–26 July 1682); 180 (23–27 September 1682); Luttrell, 1:202, 209, 213. At Chichester an informer was murdered in October 1682. Luttrell, 1:228.

[5] *True Protestant Mercury* 175 (6–9 September 1682); 187 (21 October 1682); Jeaffreson, 4:175–90; BL, Add. MSS 63,776, fol. 9r; Luttrell, 1:213, 216, 229; *Calamy Revised, s.vv.*; PRO, SP 29/421/52.

[6] Bodl., Tanner MSS 30, fol. 200r–v.

[7] *True Protestant Mercury* 107 (11–14 January 1682); PRO, SP 29/418/106, 127.

estants abroad.[8] Griffith's sympathies were with the Whigs, whose leaders, he said, comprised "that Intrest & Division of Nobles, & Gentry, that are True Lovers of the Protestant profession."[9] Owen, who apparently knew various Whigs were considering active resistance against the government, had called instead for national repentance and reformation: "Whereas they fix themselves on various and opposite *Ways* and *Means* . . . [to avoid '*publick Calamities*'], the Conflict of their *Counsels* and *Designs* encreaseth our Danger, and is like to prove our Ruine."[10] However, he was careful to refrain from naming those to whom he referred.

During the early months of 1682 Owen's sermons evinced his reaction to the growing persecution. The church's responsibility, he told his congregation in February, was to wait patiently and quietly as God imposed his judgment, and the following month he outlined the signs that heralded the public calamities which would befall "the whole State of the Jewish Church." Among them were the failure to expiate innocent blood, the violent persecution of the saints, and the dissolution of public tranquility because of "the restless, incurable Commotion of the Minds of men," a reference to the recent political turmoil. Incensed, like Bunyan, that at least some of the persecution was the work of those who professed to be Christians, he proclaimed that God's people would not be intimidated, even if their own blood were shed. Suffering, he explained to his congregation in May, should be regarded as commonplace, and they should concentrate on the spiritual blessings made possible by travail rather than worry about incarceration, financial ruin, or even death. Much of what he said was couched in the context of a possible revival of persecution by Catholics, but in June the implications for the Church of England were inescapable when he distinguished between "the prophane, hypocritical, persecuting Church, and . . . the Church of the Elect." God, he promised, would deliver the faithful, much as he did when the Hebrews were liberated from captivity by Cyrus and Babylon was ruined. Owen may well have been thinking of Monmouth as the latter-day Cyrus, for he pointedly remarked that the Hebrews' deliverance was "not unsuited to Our present Condition."[11]

[8] Robert Ferguson, *A Just and Modest Vindication of the Proceedings of the Two Last Parliaments* [London? 1681], 24–25, 30–31, 46–47.

[9] Bodl., Rawlinson Letters 104, fol. 37r.

[10] John Owen, *An Humble Testimony unto the Goodness and Severity of God in His Dealing with Sinful Churches and Nations* (London, 1681), sig. A3r–v. See also Owen's "The Chamber of Imagery in the Church of Rome Laid Open," in *Works*, 8:587: "It is our duty, on all occasions, to apply ourselves unto [Christ] by faith, for all supplies, reliefs, and deliverances."

[11] DWL, MSS L6/3, Owen's sermons on Isaiah 26:9 (10 February 1682); Luke 21:7 (10 March 1682) (quoted); Luke 21:7 (31 March 1682); 1 Peter 4:14 (5 May 1682); L6/1, Owen's

Owen probably knew no details, but from Ferguson or Shaftesbury he seems to have had an indication that the latter was considering the use of force to coerce Charles to exclude his brother from the line of succession. As we have seen, such an option was first pondered by Shaftesbury after the House of Lords rejected the exclusion bill in November 1680, but Monmouth, Lord William Russell, and others were not supportive at that time. Further consideration was given to the idea in mid-1681, but again it was shelved. Circumstances changed when the earl of Argyll fled in secrecy to London following his escape from Edinburgh Castle on 20 December 1681. When Charles became ill in May, Shaftesbury, Monmouth, Ford Lord Grey, and Sir Thomas Armstrong began considering a plan to compel Parliament to convene and resolve the succession crisis if the king died. The discussion halted when Charles recovered, but in the summer of 1682 Argyll met secretly with Shaftesbury and then with Monmouth in an attempt to obtain money for an insurrection in Scotland, but these initial endeavors were unsuccessful and Argyll went to the Netherlands later that year. His intelligence network included Bunyan's former printer, Francis Smith, who was then living in Rotterdam.[12]

About this time Bunyan was in the London area and preached at Newington Green, near Stoke Newington, north of the City. On this occasion his audience included students from the nonconformist academy of Charles Morton, who had recommended that his pupils hear Bunyan preach, and who apparently was present himself. At the academy his students read works by Owen, Baxter, Milton, William Ames, Stephen Charnock, and Samuel Rutherford, but there is no evidence that they studied anything of Bunyan's. Among the students who heard "Friend Bunnian" preach was Samuel Wesley, whose father, John, had been ejected as rector of Winterborne Whitchurch, Dorset, in 1662. The younger Wesley, who had studied with Owen before attending Morton's academy, was critical of Bunyan because he lacked formal ordination. Looking back on the academy in 1703, he described it in harsh terms as a place where Church of England clergy and episcopacy were denounced, "the King-killing Doctrines" defended, and the regicides generally remembered in positive terms. Wesley's recollection was challenged by Samuel Palmer, who claimed the dissenting academies had abhorred the execution of Charles I as the barbaric act of a standing army, though he acknowledged their opposition to the use of the dispensing power by mon-

---

sermon on Isaiah 45:11 (30 June 1682) (quoted). Letters to his church (composed while he was staying with Wharton) and Lady Hartopp also deal with the importance of withstanding persecution. DWL, MSS L6/1, letters 4 and 8. See also the sermon by John Colling asserting the significance of embracing affliction. DWL, MSS L4/2, sermon of 10 December 1682.

[12] Greaves, SOK, 99–105.

archs as akin to the practices of Louis XIV, Julius Caesar, and Cyrus. Given Owen's recommendation of Morton, the prevailing political views at the academy must have been Whig. Morton himself was repeatedly in legal trouble for his nonconformity in 1683. In Bunyan he recognized a minister whose pulpit oratory was of pedagogical value for his students.[13]

## "Tyranny of the Antichristian Generation"[14]: Antichrist and the Tory-Anglicans

Bunyan's reactions to the increasingly tense political conditions are reflected in *Of Antichrist, and His Ruine,* which was not published in his lifetime, though it was very likely composed between February 1682, after he completed *The Holy War,* and late spring of the same year, when he began writing *The Greatness of the Soul.*[15] Internal evidence, including Bunyan's assertion that churches and their members had been degenerating in their principles and practice for twenty years (1662, when the Great Ejection occurred, to 1682), points to this period (*MW,* 13:427). The treatise could not have been written before 1677 because Bunyan refers to the repeal of the writ *de haeretico comburendo* (29 Car. II, c. 9) in April of that year (13:440). More generally, he mentions the persecution of the Huguenots, which was under way in France, though Louis XIV would not repeal the Edict of Nantes until 1685 (13:426). Bunyan would make the same point in his next work, *The Greatness of the Soul* (*MW,* 9:235). Moreover, *Of Antichrist, and His Ruine* cannot have been composed after April 1687, when James II issued his first Declaration of Indulgence, for Bunyan appeals in his treatise for religious freedom of the kind King Artaxerxes granted to Ezra and his fellow Jews, "such liberty, to wit, that God's People should be directed in their Temple-Building, and Temple-Worship, as they find it in the Law of their God, without the additions of Man's Inventions." Bunyan explicitly states that this was the wish of the Protestant nonconformists: "We desire only that this Letter of the King [referring

[13] [Samuel Wesley], *A Letter from a Country Divine to His Friend in London* (London, 1703), 5–7, 13–15; [Samuel Palmer], *A Defence of the Dissenters Education in Their Private Academies* (London, 1703), 6, 10–12; Wesley, *A Defence of a Letter Concerning the Education of Dissenters in Their Private Academies* (London, 1704), 48; GL, MS 9060, fols. 9v, 18v, 28r, 33v, 57v, 66v. Edward Harley was interested in Morton's academy as a school for his son, Edward. BL, Add. MSS 70,013, fol. 81r. Daniel Defoe studied at Morton's academy from 1674 to 1679. For Morton and John Wesley (Westley) see *BDBR, s.vv.* Samuel Wesley's son, John, founded the Methodist movement.

[14] *MW,* 13:447.

[15] This alters the date I suggested in *MW,* 9:xxiii. See also W. R. Owens, "The Date of Bunyan's Treatise *Of Antichrist," Seventeenth Century* 1 (July 1986): 153–57.

to Artaxerxes' order] might be considered of, and we left to do as is there licens'd and directed" (*MW*, 13:425). In short, he was appealing for an indulgence, an act that would have been unnecessary after April 1687.

No less important internal evidence for dating the treatise is Bunyan's assertion in the epistle, "A Premonition to the Reader," that nonconformists must not take up arms on their own initiative: "It displeases [God] that any should seek, or go about to revenge their own Injuries, or to work their own Deliverances; for that is the work of God, and he will do it by the Kings" (13:426–27). Until this time the godly must exercise patience (13:426). This is the point Owen had made in 1681 in his preface to *An Humble Testimony* (quoted above), a work indicating his own interest in Antichrist's destruction,[16] and informal discussions about resistance would have occurred throughout mid and late 1681 and 1682. The issue would soon be very much to the fore during and after the gathering of dissenting ministers at Tunbridge Wells in July 1682. Whether Bunyan was among the many ministers in attendance is impossible to ascertain, though he certainly knew about the spas at Tunbridge, Bath, and Epsom; the Church Book has no entries for this month, and he may therefore have been absent from Bedford (*MW*, 7:217; 13:185). Work on *Of Antichrist* would have been completed prior to the Tunbridge Wells gathering, but the epistle manifests the concern Owen shared about militant endeavors against the government. Bunyan cautioned dissenters not to lay the blame for their predicament "in the badness of the Temper of Governours," especially the king, for monarchs "seldom trouble Churches of their own Inclinations." Yet he took cover in the traditional refuge of those attacking the crown by accusing the king's evil advisors rather than the monarch *per se*: Sovereigns "*see* with other Mens Eyes, *hear* with other Mens Ears, and *act* and *do* by the Judgments of others." The root of the nonconformists' suffering, he argued, was not in the king but in their own sins (13:428). He prudently closed his epistle with an affirmation of loyalty to the king (13:429), though too much must not be made of this inasmuch as many English rebels had made similar professions.

Perceptive readers would have noticed that Bunyan's view of the Stuarts was very critical—hardly what one modern commentator has described as conservative.[17] In reciting the accomplishments of England's ostensibly Protestant monarchs, he praised Henry VIII, Edward VI, and Elizabeth I, but conspicuously ig-

---

[16]Owen, *An Humble Testimony*, 53–54.

[17]Aileen M. Ross, "Paradise Regained: The Development of John Bunyan's Millenarianism," in *Bunyan in England and Abroad*, ed. M. van Os and G. J. Schutte (Amsterdam: VU University Press, 1990), 73. Sim and Walker (113–25) present a strong case for an opposing reading.

nored the Stuarts (13:441).[18] The opening lines of his epistle refer to Nebuchadnezzar and his sons as tyrannical enslavers; against the background of the charged rhetoric of the period 1679–82, readers, had the work been published, could easily have compared Nebuchadnezzar to Charles I, and to have hoped for an Artaxerxes (most likely Monmouth) to provide them with the liberty that would end "their long and tedious Captivity" (13:421). Bunyan's reference to the "wicked Antichristian Penal Laws" currently in force was a harsh indictment of the government (13:440), as was his comment about the "Tyranny of the Antichristian Generation," with its persecutory practices (13:447).

Yet he held out hope that Charles II, whose Declaration of Indulgence in 1672 had released him from a long imprisonment, might be another Artaxerxes. Pointedly, he reminded his readers that Charles was "a better Saviour of us than we may be aware of, and may have delivered us from more Deaths than we can tell how to think," clearly an allusion to the government's prosecution of the alleged Popish plotters (13:488). With this in mind, Bunyan exhorted his audience to pray that God would disclose all conspiracies against the king and his government (13:489), a recommendation he might have been less inclined to express following the disclosure of the Rye House plot and the Monmouth cabal in June 1683, and the government's interrogation of some of his friends. In 1682 he was proposing that people not rush to condemn Charles because of the succession crisis and the campaign against dissent, but to remember the king's defense of Protestantism against the alleged Popish plotters. "Be not angry with them [kings], . . . but consider, if they go not on in the Work of Reformation so fast as thou wouldest they should, the fault may be thine; know that thou also hast thy cold and chill frames of heart, and sittest still when thou shouldest be up and doing" (13:488). The hope that Charles might prove to be a modern Artaxerxes provides the context for Bunyan's description of himself as an old-fashioned Christian who fears God and honors the king. Some of his colleagues had misinterpreted his position, thinking he would support violent action against the government without qualification, but this he sought to correct in *Of Antichrist*: "I would shew my Brethren that I also am one of them; and to set them right that have wrong Thoughts of me as to so weighty Matters as these" (13:489). Solidarity with other dissenters did not require the unqualified endorsement of violence or preclude hope that the king might liberate nonconformists from their bondage. Neither, however, did it mean that he was unalterably opposed to resistance led by prominent nobles and magistrates to compel Charles to assure a Protestant

[18] He praised Henry VIII for having overthrown antichristian worship, but the liturgical reform embodied in the Book of Common Prayer first occurred during Edward's reign.

succession, as he had indicated in *The Holy War*. Like Calvin and Owen, he repudiated an insurrection of the people, but not resistance led by men of rank and authority, although it is also clear that he hoped for a peaceful resolution of the crisis.

No theme in *Of Antichrist* is more significant than the role of monarchs in the divine plan, a subject directly relevant to the debate over succession. In Bunyan's judgment monarchs had been, and some continued to be, instruments of Antichrist, yet he was unwilling to hold them fully accountable, for they had been bewitched by false promises, specious doctrines, and "causeless Curses" (13:433, 496). Indeed, they had been *forced* to act in such a capacity, and thus deserve pity rather than condemnation (13:496–97). Among those whom he considered as instruments of Antichrist was Charles II:

> *Antichrist* has, where she rules, put all out of order; and no wonder, for she has *bepuddled* the Word of God; no wonder, then, I say, if the Foundations of the World be out of course. 'Tis She that hath turned the Sword of the Magistrate against those that keep God's Law: 'Tis She that has made it the Ruine of the Good and Vertuous, and a Protection to the Vile and Base. (13:495–96)

Bunyan certainly believed that Charles' regime was employing the magistrate's sword against the godly, yet rather than call for the ouster of monarchs, he envisioned them as the divinely ordained agency for Antichrist's overthrow (13:427, 440, 461–63, 485–86, 496). "*Antichrist shall not down but by the Hand of Kings*" (13:462). This work, Bunyan insisted, will not be done without the church's cooperation, but its role is to slay Antichrist's soul through preaching, prayer, and holy living, whereas monarchs, utilizing the physical forces at their disposal, will destroy Antichrist's body (13:462, 485–86). He was careful to explain that not all sovereigns will help topple Antichrist, for some will remain bewitched to the end. Referring to the activities of Protestant rulers, he averred that the work of assaulting Antichrist had already commenced in England, Scotland, the Netherlands, Germany, France, Sweden, Denmark, and Hungary (13:435–36, 463, 488). Presumably he was thinking of Henry IV's reign in France, yet he believed that in time God would make Louis XIV hate Antichrist (13:426). In espousing his role of monarchs in the toppling of Antichrist, Bunyan was not breaking new ground, for similar views had been advocated by such Protestants as Martin Bucer, John Foxe, John Napier, Arthur Dent, Henry Barrow, Leonard Busher, and more recently Hanserd Knollys and Christopher Ness.[19] He claimed he had not read mil-

---

[19] Hanserd Knollys, *Mystical Babylon Unvailed* ([London], 1670), 30–31; *MW*, 13:xxxi–xxxiii. Cf. Knollys, *The World That Now Is; and the World That Is to Come* (London, 1681), pt. 2, 45–46. For Busher see *New DNB*, *s.v.*; for Barrow see *DNB*, *s.v.*

lenarian works by such authors (13:476), but these views would have been spread through sermons and informal discussions.

The latter-day Artaxerxes for whom Bunyan looked in England did not have to be one of the godly or even a Protestant. Monmouth would have fit the bill, but Charles II could serve as well if he provided dissenters with the requisite freedom and ordered his subordinates not to impede nonconformist worship. The crown's officers, Bunyan contended, must provide the godly with what they need to undertake their work and impose no tolls or tribute on ministers. Like Artaxerxes, the English monarch must leave dissenters free of any state-imposed doctrines, liturgy, priesthood, or tithes. However, whereas Artaxerxes subjected his officials to execution, incarceration, fines, or banishment if they hindered Ezra and his fellow Jews, Bunyan diplomatically insisted that nonconformists did not seek such remedies (13:424–26).

In *Of Antichrist* Bunyan made no attempt to provide a definitive statement about the possibility of James' succession. If God could ultimately make Louis XIV detest Antichrist, presumably James too could become an instrument for Antichrist's overthrow. Yet Bunyan, like most English Protestants, left no doubt that Catholicism was the religion of Antichrist, and in this context the possibility of James' succession can only have been foreboding. Bunyan recited a litany of the characteristics of antichristian religion, all of them unmistakable components of Catholicism in the minds of at least most English Protestants: sacrilegious rites and unscriptural worship, reliance on tradition (as well as the Bible) as authoritative, superstitious legends and fraudulent miracles, "Pretences to *Infallibility*," the "filthy Equivocations" of priests, friars, and Jesuits, unbiblical church polity and discipline, and the councils and convocations that blasphemously attributed their actions to the Holy Spirit (13:435, 437, 442, 493–94). He also denounced the Catholic church's sale of pardons, indulgences, and preferments (13:497–98). "Popish Edicts," he averred, "are the support of the Religion of *Antichrist* now" (13:440). In the minds of Protestants such edicts served as authority for the long, bloody record of persecution associated with Catholicism. Antichrist's church has "waded through a Sea of innocent Blood" to promote its blasphemous ceremonies, idolatry, and superstition (13:494). Bunyan directly addressed the Catholic fear that drove much of the opposition to James when he vividly recalled the Marian persecution, though not without finding in it an opportunity for the godly to embrace the ethic of suffering because of the positive effects it could produce: "In the *Maryan* days here at home, there was such sweet Songs sung in the Fire, such sweet Notes answering them from Prison, and such Providences, that Coals of burning Fire still dropped here and there upon the Heads of those that hated God; that it might, and doubtless did make those that did wisely consider of God's Doings, to think God was yet near, with, and for, a despised and afflicted People" (13:427). He also reminded his readers of the Spanish Inquisition, noting that similar persecution had recently occurred in France, Ireland, Piedmont, and elsewhere (13:439, 495). The blood of saints and martyrs had made the sovereigns who imbibed it inebriated (13:433). Should James become king, this, Bunyan was implying, could again be the lot of English Protestants.

Whereas Bunyan's attack on Catholicism is painted in bold, stark colors, his criticism of the Church of England is less pronounced in this treatise. Picking up on the elements common to Catholicism and the established church, he castigated all human additions to the simplicity of divinely prescribed worship (13:425). Antichrist's ordinances are depicted as fallen leaves, devoid of reason and nourishment; likened to stagnant pools fit only for hatching frogs; and castigated as vehicles to conjure devils. Most of Bunyan's examples are from Catholicism—masses, prayers for the dead, pilgrimages, monkish vows, and clerical celibacy—but several—images and "sinful" fasts—were also part of the Church of England (13:437–39). When he criticized the use of books (other than the Bible) as a means of worship, he implicitly included the Book of Common Prayer as well as mass books, and his castigation of convocations applied to the Church of England as well as the Catholic church (13:490, 493). He was also denouncing both traditions when he condemned their ecclesiastical titles, which he likened to idols, but he was cautious on this point, leaving his readers to ascertain which titles were obnoxious (13:441–42). The Church of England's willingness to persecute the godly likewise linked its adherents with Catholics as the bloody, superstitious, idolatrous people of Antichrist (13:445). Thus associated in infamy, these "Antichristian Churches [were] otherwise called the Daughters of the Mother of Harlots, and Abominations of the Earth" (13:451–52).

The other major theme in this treatise is Bunyan's explication of Antichrist's fall, a subject only briefly discussed in *The Holy City*. In the latter book he indicated that Antichrist would be overthrown at the conclusion of the period of temple-work, just before the millennium—the era of city-work—commenced. *Of Antichrist* is primarily about the latter stages of this time of temple-work (cf. 13:425, 501), which will culminate with Antichrist's destruction, the necessary precondition to the establishment of God's kingdom on earth (13:502). Like Owen and Danvers,[20] Bunyan refused to predict the date, insisting that the saints could

[20] Owen, *Works*, 9:510 (in a sermon preached on 7 May 1680); Henry Danvers, *Theopolis, or the City of God* (London, 1672), 46. Hanserd Knollys gave serious consideration to starting the 1,260 days (i.e., years) in 407, 409, 410, or by 428 in keeping with some of the prior scholarship on Revelation. *An Exposition of the Eleventh Chapter of the Revelation* ([London?], 1679), 13.

do no more than guess; such conjectures, in his judgment, were harmful because they encouraged the ungodly to reject the gospel message when the dates proved incorrect (13:456–57). He may have been thinking of John Harrison's prognosis of 1630 as the time, though Joseph Mede's projected date of 1736 was still in the future.[21] Although Bunyan refused to predict the date, he did maintain that Antichrist's demise would occur over a substantial period of time, gradually melting, he suggested, like grease: "For the Lord Jesus shall consume him, and cause him to melt away; not all at once, but *now* this part, and *then* that; now his *Soul*, and after that his *Body*, even until Soul and Body are both destroyed" (13:435; cf. 449). The work was already under way, asseverated Bunyan, who counseled his readers to compare Antichrist's condition 400 or 500 years ago with that of their own day, paying heed to the destruction of various diabolical rites, the recovery of gospel truths, and the recapture of England, Scotland, and other countries from Satanic sway (13:435–36).

Although Bunyan refused to project the date of Antichrist's final demise, he tentatively identified five signs that would indicate its approach. "Whether I shall hit right, as to these, that I must leave to Time to make manifest; and in the mean while to the *wise in heart* to judge" (13:456). The first sign is the expulsion of the godly from their havens, a time when no monarchs will provide refuge for the saints. Visible churches will be completely overcome, their members universally and simultaneously exposed to the enemies' rage. The period of the church's utter destruction will last three and a half days in apocalyptic time, after which the millennium will commence (13:458–61). The second sign will be the nations' newfound ability to see their baseness and abhor Antichrist as they awaken from the "deep sleep" into which he (or she, for Bunyan uses both pronouns) bewitched them. Now some monarchs will take up arms against Antichrist, much as Protestant sovereigns have already done (13:461–63). When the people of God totally forsake Antichrist, leaving her adherents isolated, "she will soon be hissed out of the World." This dramatic act of forsaking, which is the third sign, entails the unqualified repudiation of "the Church and Members of *Babylon*" by Christians everywhere (13:463–65).

The fourth and fifth signs pertain to the slaying of the two witnesses mentioned in Revelation 11. According to this passage they will prophesy 1,260 days, after which the beast from the bottomless pit will slay them, and three and a half days later they will be resurrected by the Holy Spirit. Like a number of other Protestant commentators, including John Bale, Dent, Mede, and Knollys, Bunyan believed the slaying of the two witnesses would occur over a long period of

---

[21] Katharine R. Firth, *The Apocalyptic Tradition in Reformation Britain 1530–1645* (Oxford: Oxford University Press, 1979), 216–17. For Mede (as Mead) see *DNB, s.v.*

time stretching into the future, when their resurrection would take place.[22] Rather than identify the two witnesses as specific individuals, as did Lodowick Muggleton and John Reeve (referring to themselves),[23] he thought they were "a Succession of good Men," "a successive Church, or the Congregation of God abiding for him against *Antichrist*" (13:471, 473). This view was similar to Dent's, who interpreted the witnesses to be all faithful preachers and professors—past, present, and future—opposed to the papacy and Catholicism, whereas Knollys limited the witnesses to Christ's ministers and prophets. Mede thought the two witnesses would be interpreters and defenders of divine truth in accord with the pattern established by Moses and Aaron, Elijah and Elisha, and Zerubbabel and Jeshua.[24] According to Bunyan, their death will not be corporeal but mystical, resulting in the destruction of the true visible church. The fourth sign, then, is the end of congregations of visible saints (13:468–73), and the final sign is the rejoicing of Antichrist and his disciples at this event (13:478–79). Their joy is premature because the resurrection and ultimate triumph of the witnesses—the visible saints—are assured (13:484).

In the dark days of 1682 Bunyan thus predicted intensified persecution as the end time for Antichrist nears (13:473). Although he hoped that Charles might be a latter-day Artaxerxes, should James inherit the throne and plunge the three kingdoms into persecution severe enough to eradicate Protestantism, this could be the slaying of the witnesses prophesied in Revelation 11, the essential prerequisite for the inauguration of the millennium. Bunyan did not spell this out, partly because he was unwilling to predict dates, partly because he held out hope of England finding an Artaxerxes, and probably because he realized that such an interpretation might be deemed treasonable. His message was already provocative because of his identification of Antichrist as an evil conglomerate comprising the

---

[22] John Bale, *The Image of Both Churches*, in *Select Works of John Bale, D.D.*, ed. Henry Christmas, Publications of the Parker Society, vol. 1 (Cambridge: Cambridge University Press, 1849), 387–98; Arthur Dent, *The Ruine of Rome* (London, 1644), 145–50; Joseph Mede, *The Key of the Revelation*, trans. Richard More, 2nd ed. (London, 1650), pt. 2, 13, 15; Knollys, *Exposition*, 18–23; W. Adams, DWL, MSS 12.78, fol. 198.

[23] Lodowick Muggleton, *The Acts of the Witnesses: The Autobiography of Lodowick Muggleton and Other Early Muggletonian Writings*, ed. T. L. Underwood (New York: Oxford University Press, 1999), 12–13.

[24] Dent, *Ruine*, 177–80, 183–84; Knollys, *Exposition*, 9–10; Mede, *Key*, 7. Unlike Bunyan, Dent provided concrete examples of such witnesses, including Wyclif, Huss, Savonarola, and Peter Waldo. William Aspinwall's interpretation was akin to Dent's, whereas Thomas Tillam diverged sharply by identifying the witnesses as the Old and New Testaments. Aspinwall, *An Explication and Application of the Seventh Chapter of Daniel* (London, 1654), 40–44; Tillam, *The Two Witnesses* (London, 1651), 23–24.

Devil as the head, "the Synagogue of Satan"—the reprobate—as the body, and the spirit of iniquity as the soul (13:432). Reflecting an interpretation going back to the early church,[25] Antichrist is thus the collective embodiment of evil wherever it is found, but Bunyan also posited the existence of many Antichrists. Implicitly their numbers included persecuting magistrates, Jesuits, priests, and the reprobate wherever they exist, even among one's neighbors. "The *many* maketh but *one* Great Antichrist, *one* Man of Sin, *one* Enemy, *one* great Whore, *one* Son of Perdition" (13:431). Ness made the same point, referring both to many Antichrists—all those opposed to Christ—and "one *grand-prince-Antichrist.*"[26] Given the fact that serious interest in Antichrist declined substantially after 1660, particularly outside nonconformist circles, Bunyan's *Of Antichrist* is a remarkable treatise.[27]

When Bunyan completed this work, probably in the late spring of 1682, either he opted not to publish it or his publisher at this time, Benjamin Alsop, declined to print it. The latter possibility seems less likely than the former, for Alsop, in the words of the bookseller John Dunton, was "a wild sort of a spark."[28] Bunyan may have withheld publication out of concern that his remarks might further divide nonconformists or prompt the government to curtail his preaching in light of his barely disguised criticism of the established church and his damning indictment of Catholicism at a time when the heir to the throne was an avowed Catholic. Certainly defenders of the established church bitterly resented assertions linking elements of their religion to Catholicism. In the words of William Lloyd, bishop of St. Asaph, "these [dissenters] by a fatal mistake, calling all Forms & Ceremonies Popery, and hunting about for a purer way of Worship, have run out into Schism, & some into damnable Heresies: & branding every thing that they do not Understand or dislike with the Name of Popery, they have not only divided and weakened our Church, but they have added wonderfully to the Strength & Credit of Popery." Such people, he added, foment rebellion.[29] In the face of such hostility, particularly the charge that attacks on Catholic elements in the Church of England promoted insurrection, Bunyan probably decided not to publish *Of Antichrist* at this time.

[25] Bernard McGinn, *Antichrist: Two Thousand Years of the Human Fascination with Evil* (New York: Harper San Francisco, 1994), 54–56.

[26] Christopher Ness, *A Distinct Discourse and Discovery of the Person and Period of Antichrist* (London, 1679), 7.

[27] Christopher Hill, *Antichrist in Seventeenth-Century England,* rev. ed. (London: Verso, 1990), 146–60; McGinn, *Antichrist,* 225–26.

[28] *BDBR, s.v.* Benjamin Alsop. For Dunton see *DNB, s.v.*

[29] Bodl., Tanner MSS 33, fol. 7r.

"Vipers Will Come"[30]: Maintaining Priorities amid Political Turmoil

In the spring of 1682 Bunyan traveled to London, where he preached at Pinners' Hall, one of a number of common halls of city companies in which nonconformist congregations were meeting. At Pinners' Hall the preachers included Owen and Daniel Bull. The latter had been assisting John Howe minister to a congregation at Haberdashers' Hall, and Howe was also preaching at Cordwainers' Hall in 1682. About the same time Bunyan's friend George Griffith was preaching at Plasterers' Hall. Other groups met in the common halls of the pewterers, bricklayers, embroiderers, and saddlers.[31] In London the magistrates were watching Pinners' Hall, where Richard Wavel ministered to a Congregational church, having succeeded Anthony Palmer, who died on 26 January 1679. Beginning in 1672 the Merchants' Lectures were also given in Pinners' Hall by Presbyterians and Congregationalists, including Owen, Howe, Baxter, Jenkyn, Bates, and John Collins.[32]

In his sermon at Pinners' Hall Bunyan primarily targeted the unconverted, attempting to persuade them that nothing was more valuable than their souls' welfare. References to ascertaining costs, profit and loss, the misguided belief that "mony answereth all things," the relationship of price to intrinsic worth, the treatment of customers, trade with the Indies, and the threat of North African pirates to commerce indicate his sensitivity to a City audience (*MW*, 9:138, 142–43, 162, 170, 201). So too does his reference to the arrival of a Moroccan delegation in December 1681, though his reaction was anything but open-minded, for he described its members as "men of strange faces, in strange habit, with strange gestures and behaviours, monsters to be behold" (9:235).[33] His intent, of course, was not the improvement of diplomatic relations but the conversion of souls, and his rationale for citing the Moroccan visit was to draw an analogy between the reaction to the delegates as foreign and the way secular-minded people viewed thoughts of salvation and eternal life. In a politically charged atmosphere he sought to focus his audience's attention on first principles. Implicitly this was a message as relevant to his fellow dissenters as it was to Londoners caught up in

---

[30] *MW*, 9:244.

[31] *Calamy Revised*, s.v. Daniel Bull; PRO, SP 29/421/176, 177.

[32] *Calamy Revised*, s.vv. Anthony Palmer and Richard Wavel; Roger Thomas, "Parties in Nonconformity," in *The English Presbyterians: From Elizabethan Puritanism to Modern Unitarianism* (London: George Allen and Unwin, 1968), 99; Walter Wilson, *The History and Antiquities of Dissenting Churches and Meeting Houses, in London, Westminster, and Southwark*, 4 vols. (London: For the Author, 1808–14), 2:252–53. Meade replaced Owen as a Merchants' lecturer following the latter's death in 1683.

[33] For the Moroccan visit see *CSPD, 1680–81*, 650, 694; *CSPD, 1682*, 28, 39, 61, 305–6.

the world of commerce, for in his judgment the salvation of souls takes precedence over all other issues, whether commercial or political. At root, *The Greatness of the Soul*, which he probably composed between June and October 1682, is
about prioritizing. Here again Bunyan espoused his evangelical Calvinist message,
with its hope of arousing sinners from their "Beds of ease, security and pleasure,
and fetch[ing them] down upon [their] knees before [God], to beg of him Grace
to be concerned about the Salvation of [their] Souls." But he was also doing this
to free himself of responsibility for their eternal destiny: "I have taken upon me
to do this, that I may deliver, if not you, yet my self; and that I may be clear of
your blood" (9:138). He felt a sense of urgency that probably was heightened by
concern that James' succession could bring repression severe enough to eradicate
Protestantism, as he had explained in his treatise on Antichrist.

In making his case that the soul's welfare is the greatest consideration, Bunyan drew on his own experience. Although he evinced no signs of recurring depression at this time, he remembered what it had felt like to be plunged into the
depths of despair. These memories became useful descriptors of what he believed
the damned undergo in hell: "Here all the powers, sences, and passions of the
Soul must be made self-burners, self-tormentors, self-executioners by the just
judgement of God; also all that the *will* shall do in this place, shall be but to wish
for ease, but the wish shall only be such, as shall only seem to lift up, for the Ca-
ble rope of despair shall with violence pull him down again" (9:173). As the
damned realize the reasons for their perdition, they will sink under their guilt
(9:185, 205). Again he recalled his sense of utter despondency to contrast the
darkness of hell, its raging fires notwithstanding, with the warming, welcoming
light of heaven. In hell the damned are "swallowed up in the thickest darkness,
and griped with the burning thoughts of the endlessness of that most unutterable
misery" (9:240). Even in this life the soul insensitive to the ways and commands
of God is described by Bunyan as "darkned . . . with such thick and stupefying
darkness" that it cannot perceive the things of greatest concern (9:164–65). The
desperation and blackness reminded him anew of Francesco Spira (9:167). For
Bunyan, these experiences were now in the past, but the insight he gained from
having undergone them gave his preaching and writing heightened poignancy.

As he had in *A Few Sighs from Hell*, Bunyan dwelled on hades, candidly acknowledging his recourse to terror in an attempt to frighten people into embracing the gospel message (9:238). His literary creativity is evident in the vivid
imagery he employed to make his points. The reprobate are tormented with an
infernal zoo whose denizens include biting cockatrices, gnawing vipers, soul-
sucking worms, vicious hornets, and lashing scorpions (9:173–74, 177, 182, 243–
45). In hell the groans of the damned peal like thunderclaps, and curses perpetually rain down as thick as hail and as heavy as millstones (9:174, 182, 239). For the

damned, memory is a red-hot iron, its pain akin to scalding lead poured down the throat; fearful thoughts are riveted in place, with no capacity to forget and nothing to serve as diversions from the searing, ceaseless pain (9:172, 174). Devoid of hope, the reprobate drink their own tears as coals hang from their burning lips (9:186, 210). Like houses ablaze, with flames spewing from doors, windows, and chimneys, the damned have fire raging in every orifice, but unlike a log that burns itself out, this conflagration blazes eternally (9:210, 223). "Down, down, down they go, and nothing but down, down still," deeper and deeper into "the yawning panch, and belly of Hell" (9:240). The worse the sinner, the further into the depths of hell, where the chambers of death await. Like Dante, Bunyan believed in differing degrees of eternal punishment. "Why should a poor silly, ignorant man tho' damned, be punished with the same degree of torment that he that has lived a thousand times worse shall be punished with?" (9:240–41).

Although the principal thrust of the sermon is Bunyan's attempt to terrorize sinners into seeking redemption, he did not overlook the opportunity to continue his attack on the established church. The reprobate, he argued, had made the fatal mistake of rejecting God's messengers, the dissenting ministers, and for this there will be divine retaliation, "scorn for scorn, repulse for repulse, contempt for contempt" (9:178–80). Just as people are scrupulous in selecting guardians for their children and executors for their wills, they should be judicious in determining what spiritual shepherds to follow. He warned against "Idol Shepherds," citing Zechariah 11:17, where the connotation is idle clergy, but the verse could also have been read in Bunyan's context as an attack on ministers who worship idols. Clearly he was distinguishing between Church of England clerics and dissenting ministers who nourished their flocks; to the latter "thou shouldest commit thy Soul for teaching and for guidance" (9:227–28). He would not have said this about clergy committed to the Book of Common Prayer, which he detested. His critical view of Anglican clergy was not without some foundation, for in May 1686 Thomas White, bishop of Peterborough, reported to the archbishop of Canterbury about Church of England clerics in Bedfordshire: "One part of the Clergy is very vicious in their manners, the other very unconformable in discharge of their offices."[34] Yet the clergy in the town of Bedford seem to have been an exception, for in September 1681 Robert Beaumont had informed the archbishop of Canterbury that its churches were supplied with very able and conscientious ministers.[35]

[34] Bodl., Tanner MSS 30, fol. 47r. Five years earlier William Lloyd, bishop of Peterborough, reported that much of his diocese was not in order, including some ministers who were very careless. Tanner MSS 36, fol. 185r.

[35] Bodl., Tanner MSS 36, fol. 111r. Beaumont also informed the archbishop about Sir George Carteret's legacy for the reading of divine service at Bedford each day.

To the godly, Bunyan remarked in *The Greatness of the Soul* on the importance of remaining firm in their commitment notwithstanding the expectation of persecution, mindful that "God counteth it a righteous thing to recompence tribulation to them that trouble you" (9:140–41). In this light, the sustained commentary on the horrors of eternal perdition has direct relevance to the Tory Reaction, for he made it clear that those who persecute dissenters would ultimately be subject to harsh but just divine retribution. This, then, was his message to those who ignored the call to repent and repressed the godly, and by delivering it he could "stand quit, as to you, before God, when you shall for neglect be damned" (9:138).

## "The Rage of the Enemy"[36]: Battling Persecution

The plight of Whigs and nonconformists in London worsened as a result of the shrieval election in July 1682. When the Whig candidates, John Dubois and Thomas Papillon, were elected, the Privy Council rejected the tallies. Using questionable procedures, the lord mayor recognized the election of the Tory candidates, Dudley North and Ralph Box. When the latter opted not to serve, another Tory, Peter Rich, replaced him in September. Jury selection in London was now in the hands of Tories, substantially increasing the likelihood of convicting Whig and nonconforming dissidents.[37] "Where is the man of Wisdome now to save the Citty?" Owen publicly wondered.[38] Concerned for their lives, Shaftesbury, Monmouth, Russell, and Armstrong resumed discussions, probably in July, about a general insurrection. On the 17th of that month Henry Hills, the king's printer, reported having seen Russell and many dissenting ministers, including Bunyan's friends Meade and Griffith, at Tunbridge Wells, Kent, discussing the twin perils of popery and arbitrary government and possessing printed material critical of the government. Whether Russell canvassed the ministers about their views on how to respond to the growing threat, particularly whether they would support a recourse to arms, is impossible to ascertain, but Monmouth would subsequently claim that Meade, Griffith, Owen, "& all the considerable Nonconformist Ministers knew of the Conspiracy."[39] As Bunyan's treatise *Of Antichrist, and His Ruine* suggests, he too seems to have known that militant means were being considered by some of the leading Whigs, though this is not to suggest that he necessarily approved of them.

Efforts to quash dissent continued throughout various parts of the country in

---

[36] *MW*, 12:236.
[37] Greaves, *SOK*, 96–97; Bodl., Carte MSS 39, fol. 602v.
[38] DWL, MSS L6/3, Owen's sermon on Malachi 3:7 (22 September 1682).
[39] Greaves, *SOK*, 106; PRO, SP 29/429/162; 29/434/98 (quoted).

the fall of 1682. On 3 October the Cheshire quarter sessions ordered churchwardens and constables to execute the penal laws to the fullest extent, similar action was undertaken at the sessions in Norfolk, and scattered prosecutions occurred in Surrey and Dorset the same month.[40] The pattern of enforcement varied; at Plymouth the constables refused to serve warrants against dissenters, but the bishop of St. Asaph boasted that every "separatist" in his diocese was being prosecuted or had been given additional time to conform.[41] From Canterbury the archbishop's chaplain reported regularly on efforts in the church courts to compel dissenters, particularly Baptists and Quakers, to conform, but both groups reacted contemptuously to excommunication, and he thought they would willingly pay the 12d. per Sunday recusancy fine and "be glad to purchase non conformity at soe cheap a rate."[42]

In the London area the prosecution of dissent was vigorous in the fall of 1682. By mid-September Vincent Alsop's Presbyterian congregation in Westminster, having "found it very hazardous to enjoy our liberty with security in the Lords Supper in our publick places," had begun meeting in smaller groups and in secret to avoid detection.[43] Griffith anticipated the increased persecution, telling Lady Wharton in September that he expected each Sunday to be his last in the pulpit, for "Bonds will attend mee, & others in the like Circumstances. . . . Things seeme to hasten towards the actuall bringing on of those sufferings on Christes behalf, that have long hoverd over our Heads."[44] Among those indicted for nonconformity in October and November were Bunyan's friends Owen, Griffith, Cokayne, and Meade as well as other ministers he almost certainly knew, such as Danvers, Ferguson, and Richard Lawrence. Baxter, Doelittle, Howe, and Jacombe were also among the indicted. Bunyan's former colleague at Bedford, Nehemiah Coxe, as well as Hanserd Knollys and Thomas Plant were also accused of preaching at conventicles in October.[45] On the 13th of that month, Sir John Shorter, a former sheriff, was presented at the Old Bailey for having attended a conventicle at Pinners' Hall, and upon conviction he was suspended from the Court of Aldermen

[40] Jeaffreson, 4:165–90; PRO, SP 29/420/150.1; Bodl., Tanner MSS 35, fols. 107r, 118r; CSPD, 1682, 461. Cf. PRO, SP 29/421/43; Bodl., Tanner MSS 35, fol. 115r. Reports of the persecution prompted concern as far away as New England. DWL, MSS 12.78, fol. 198.

[41] Bodl., Tanner MSS 35, fols. 118r, 151r, 162r.

[42] Bodl., Tanner MSS 33, fols. 213r, 216r, 217r, 220r, 221r, 222r (quoted).

[43] Bodl., Rawlinson Letters 52, fol. 294r (quoted); R. A. Beddard, "Vincent Alsop and the Emancipation of Restoration Dissent," Journal of Ecclesiastical History 24 (April 1973): 168, 182.

[44] Bodl., Rawlinson Letters 51, fol. 296r.

[45] LMA, MS MJ/SBB/400, fols. 60–61; CLRO, Conventicle Box 2, no. 6; Morrice, 1:343; PRO, SP 29/421/177; Luttrell, 1:230, 232, 237.

in December.[46] Shorter seems to have thought well of Bunyan's preaching, though an old tradition that Bunyan served as his chaplain is without foundation.[47] However, Shorter may have heard Bunyan preach his sermon on the greatness of the soul earlier in the year.[48]

Conditions for nonconformists in London worsened following vigorous demonstrations on Monmouth's behalf in conjunction with the annual celebration of deliverance from the Gunpowder Plot. The trained bands had to be called out to suppress unruly crowds shouting "noe Yorke[,] noe Yorke[,] a Monmouth[,] a Monmouth." In the aftermath, the Middlesex grand jury on 30 November called for the enforcement of laws against conventicles and other illegal forms of association on the grounds that "Fanaticism" was as much a threat to the kingdom as popery.[49] Pursuing this theme, the grand jury declared on 4 December that "Conventicles are destructive to the Interest of this Kingdome, They publish our divisions to Princes abroad and consequently the weaknesse of the Kingdome and will inevitably perpetuate the unhappy separation which is amongst us."[50] About this time William Kiffin faced a fine of £300 for having attended fifteen conventicles, but his attorney found errors made by the informers and got the case dismissed. As Bunyan would have learned, his friend Meade was not so fortunate; after he was fined £180 at the Middlesex assizes for preaching to five conventicles between 1 October and 5 November, a magistrate took "a strong guard" to Stepney in December, pulled down his pulpit, and smashed the benches on which worshipers sat. A Monmouth supporter, Meade was now a marked man; six justices descended on his conventicle in December to arrest him, but someone else was in the pulpit, and the magistrates left that person alone.[51] Physical damage also occurred when magistrates raided the meetinghouses of Stephen Lobb, another Monmouth supporter, and Samuel Annesley the same month. Such destruction may have been triggered at least in part by the reaction of Tory-Anglicans against the Monmouth demonstrations. The issuance of fifty warrants to distrain nonconformists' goods at Hackney and another for the arrest of the minister William Bates on 14 December as well as the excommunication of hundreds in

---

[46]*CSPD, 1682*, 471, 583; PRO, SP 44/66, p. 180; 29/421/177.

[47]Brown, 368, 380.

[48]The Church Book records a general meeting on 4 October, and then only "several Church meeting[s]" between that date and 20 April 1683. *CB*, 88.

[49]PRO, SP 29/421/67 (quoted); *CSPD, 1682*, 528, 556–57 (quoted).

[50]PRO, SP 29/421/109.

[51]Jeaffreson, 4:182; William Kiffin, *Remarkable Passages in the Life of William Kiffin*, ed. William Orme (London: Burton and Smith, 1823), 51; HMC 2, *Third Report*, 269 (quoted); Morrice, 1:349.

London were further manifestations of the fact that leading Tory-Anglicans in London and Middlesex had virtually declared war on dissent, something Bunyan could not have failed to notice.[52]

As the campaign continued, on 4 January 1683 the king ordered a halt to the use of the London companies' common halls for nonconformist meetings on the grounds that conventiclers pursued seditious, evil designs which threatened the security of Protestantism and the peace of the realm. The Council of Aldermen responded with a proclamation ordering the suppression of illegal meetings,[53] and the same month the earl of Clare was convicted of permitting sixteen conventicles to meet in the Old Playhouse.[54] On 21 January Lobb's congregation was again disrupted and two other ministers were arrested, but no meetings were disturbed a week later, suggesting that magistrates were selective in their targets or remiss in obeying. Consequently the Council of Aldermen directed officials to prohibit all nonconformist meetings on 11 February or arrest the violators.[55] This time its instructions were carried out, sometimes with the assistance of parties of armed men, although those who apprehended the Congregationalist minister John Faldo had to repulse a physical assault by more than 200 people. The preceding Tuesday the Merchants' Lecture at Pinners' Hall had been suppressed, and by month's end the General Baptist John Griffith had been arrested and sentenced to banishment as a three-time offender.[56] The same month the Seventh-Day Baptists Francis Bampfield, John Belcher, and Edward Stennett were presented for having participated in conventicles.[57] Narcissus Luttrell reported that some dissenters had decided to conform, but "multitudes" of others were being excommunicated and incarcerated.[58] Owen was among those who urged his followers not to yield on the grounds that taking communion in the Church of England would not only endorse the Book of Common Prayer but condemn the present generation of dissenters and all who had similarly suffered in the past. Like Bunyan, he re-

---

[52] Morrice, 1:348–49; Luttrell, 1:242. Luttrell reported that some dissenting artisans fled overseas to avoid persecution (1:245–46). For Annesley see *Calamy Revised, s.v.*

[53] PRO, SP 44/66, pp. 187–88; BL, Add. MSS 46,960A, fol. 22r; Luttrell, 1:246.

[54] LMA, MS MJ/SBB/408, fols. 63–64, 71.

[55] Morrice, 1:352, 354–55. The ministers arrested in Lobb's congregation were Marmaduke Roberts and William Pearse. For the latter see *Calamy Revised, s.v. A List of the Conventicles or Unlawful Meetings within the City of London and Bills of Mortality* (London, 1683) noted 40 conventicles in London, 23 in Westminster and the outlying areas in Middlesex, and 9 in Southwark.

[56] Morrice, 1:357, 360; PRO, SP 29/422/79; 29/423/115; *CSPD, 1683 (1)*, 50; CLRO, Conventicle Box 2, no. 6; Luttrell, 1:250.

[57] CLRO, Conventicle Box 2, no. 6.

[58] Luttrell, 1:250–51.

mained adamantly opposed to compromise with the established church,[59] a position that set them apart from moderate nonconformists such as Baxter and Henry, who attended some services in parish churches.[60] Despite the efforts of such moderates to bridge the gap between conformity and dissent, a sense of foreboding pervaded the nonconformist community: "There is a Judgment hangs Over us at this day, that is incomparably worse then All that hath befallen us. . . . The Clouds are gathering," warned David Clarkson, Owen's assistant and a minister whom Bunyan would have known, "and They look black and dismall upon us."[61]

The campaign against dissenters in the London area continued throughout the late winter and spring, though not with the intensity some Tory-Anglicans preferred. As long as conventicles—those "nurseries of Rebellion"—continued to meet, averred one of Secretary of State Leoline Jenkins' correspondents, conspiracies against the monarchy would continue.[62] South of the Thames a grand jury at the Surrey quarter sessions in January urged the justices to halt conventicles, and Vincent was convicted at the same sessions for having violated the 1593 act Bunyan had been accused of disobeying in 1660.[63] On 19 April the grand jury for London, complaining bitterly that seditious sectaries were spreading "the poysonous Principles of Schism and Rebellion," presented seventeen ministers, including Owen, Danvers, Cockayne, Plant, Jacomb, and Howe, for preaching to conventicles.[64] Outside the greater London area, attacks on nonconformists con-

[59]DWL, MSS L6/4, sermon of Owen on Ezra 9:13–14 (23 December 1682). See also MSS L6/4, Owen's sermon on Hebrews 12:15 (undated), fols. 31r–37v; L6/4, David Clarkson's sermon on Psalm 50:15 (22 September 1682); L6/4, Clarkson's sermon on 2 Chronicles 7:14 (2 June 1683); L6/4, Owen's "case of conscience," a sermon on this issue (30 April 1678). For Clarkson see BDBR, s.v.

[60]The Anglican response to moderate dissenters was varied. Francis Turner, bishop of Ely, denounced Baxter's participation in Anglican communion as spiritual fornication, whereas Isaac Archer, whose theological studies had included works by the puritans Richard Sibbes and William Perkins, made a point of hearing Baxter preach in London and was favorably impressed. Bodl., Rawlinson Letters 98, fol. 174v; CUL, Add. MSS 8499, fols. 183, 203, 207.

[61]DWL, MSS L6/4, sermon of Clarkson on Isaiah 1:25 (12 March 1683). In the same spirit Collins asked his congregation if they were willing to undertake their share of suffering and be companions with the other saints in tribulation. DWL, MSS L4/2, sermon of 24 December 1682.

[62]PRO, SP 29/422/142. Cf. SP 29/423/24, 115; 44/68, p. 237; BL, Add. MSS 46,960A, fol. 109v; HMC 63, Egmont, 2:131.

[63]PRO, SP 29/422/22; Morrice, 1:351; Luttrell, 1:246.

[64] The Presentment for the City of London at the Sessions of Peace and Gaol Delivery (London, 1683), 2–3; manuscript original, CLRO, MS SM 53. Among those accused in May

tinued to be sporadic, particularly because magistrates were reluctant to act, but also because William Sancroft, archbishop of Canterbury, was disinclined to "proceed to extremitys" according to his own chaplain.[65] The bishop of Bristol fumed when he learned that the chief constable in a Dorset hundred was himself a dissenting minister and had been treated leniently by a justice of the peace: "Such trashing of the Execution of the Laws will ruine us." The conventicle in question was soon suppressed, and the bishop resolved to quash those in Bristol itself, though this effort never succeeded. Elsewhere the bishop of Chichester was vigorously suppressing illegal religious meetings.[66] Unlike some of his colleagues, Bunyan was apparently left alone in Bedford, but his sense of responsibility for Protestantism in the country as a whole virtually assured that his pen would remain active in responding to the campaign against nonconformists. So too did the fact that constables continued to present some of his church members at the sessions for refusing to attend parish services as required by law.[67] He would have known as well that the number of people accused of recusancy in Bedfordshire had risen sharply in the summer of 1682.[68]

In the meantime, Monmouth and his associates continued to ponder a general uprising to force Charles to exclude his brother from the succession. Monmouth's tour through Staffordshire and Cheshire in September 1682 had drawn enthusiastic crowds, many of whom shouted "A Monmouth, a Monmouth," and "Let Munmouth reigne." Nonconformists played a major role in these demonstrations.[69] Alarmed by this show of popular support for the duke, Charles ordered his arrest on 20 September for allegedly having incited a riot at Chester. Although Monmouth and Shaftesbury were apparently willing to take up arms at this point, Russell was opposed because preparations were incomplete and a manifesto announcing their goals had not been prepared. Briefly incarcerated, Monmouth was released after filing a writ of *habeas corpus* and posting a bond. More cautious after this experience, he nevertheless met with Shaftesbury, Rus-

---

of participating in conventicles were Richard Rumbold and Charles Bateman, who were involved at that point in the Rye House plot. LG, MS 9060, fol. 5r; CLRO, Conventicle Box 2, no. 6.

[65] PRO, SP 29/421/127; 29/422/107; 29/424/16, 22, 23; 44/68, pp. 217–18, 259–61; Bodl., Tanner MSS 33, fol. 228r (quoted).

[66] Bodl., Tanner MSS 35, fols. 163r (quoted), 173r, 221r; Tanner MSS 34, fol. 302 (280)r.

[67] BLA, MSS HSA 1682 S/13, 14. The members presented included Oliver Scott and Widow Cooper of Clapham. The returns for the winter of 1682 are missing.

[68] BLA, MSS HSA 1682 S/8–16. The number of recusants presented at the sessions in the summer of 1682 was 132, of whom at least eight were Catholics.

[69] PRO, SP 29/420/60, 66 (quoted), 81 (quoted); John Rylands Library, Legh of Lyme MSS (deposition of Edward Sherman, 20 September 1682).

sell, and Grey in late September to reconsider an insurrection. At this time they decided to take no action, though discussions continued in October. Early that month Shaftesbury, now in hiding following the installation of Tory sheriffs in London on 28 September, stayed in Ferguson's house for a week before going to Wapping, where he expected substantial support. According to Ferguson, the earl, increasingly frustrated by the procrastination of Monmouth and his closest allies, pondered assassination as a means of attaining his aims, but nothing came of this.[70]

Monmouth and Shaftesbury finally agreed to mount a rebellion on 19 November 1682, at which time thousands of their supporters would supposedly rendezvous at various sites in London, including four or five nonconformist meetinghouses. Secretary Jenkins had received a report in October that two members of Meade's congregation, possibly recruits for the planned uprising, were boasting they would soon "pull downe Babylon and all the greate ones." However, about 15 or 16 November the plotters, having received no word that their supporters in the southwest were ready to rise, postponed the rebellion. Dismayed by this turn of events and worried about another attempt by the government to file charges against him, particularly with Tory sheriffs in London, Shaftesbury fled to the Netherlands with Ferguson.[71]

Following Shaftesbury's death on 21 December, Monmouth, Russell, and four colleagues—Essex, Algernon Sidney, John Hampden, and Lord Howard of Escrick—began exploring the possibility of an insurrection in conjunction with an uprising by Argyll's supporters in Scotland.[72] To that end a group of dissident Scots, including Sir John Cochrane of Ochiltree and Sir Hugh Campbell of Cessnock, traveled to London in April and May 1683. Monmouth and his collaborators allegedly decided to loan the Scots £10,000 to purchase arms and recruit men with a view to launching an uprising by the end of June. These plans never materialized, partly because magistrates, acting on a tip from an upholsterer, arrested Monmouth's ally, Lord Grey, on 11 May and seized between 80 and 90 firelock muskets and armor concealed in his London house. Released after he and two sureties provided recognizances totaling £20,000, he retired to his estate in Sussex.[73]

The government received another break when, on 11 June, Josiah Keeling, an excommunicated Baptist, disclosed the Rye House plot to assassinate Charles and James. Loosely linked to Monmouth's group, the Rye House conspirators in-

---

[70] Greaves, *SOK*, 110–12, 115–19.
[71] Ibid., 119–27; PRO, SP 29/421/30 (quoted).
[72] Greaves, *SOK*, 136–39. For Hampden and Essex see *New DNB, s.vv.*
[73] Greaves, *SOK*, 163–70. For Cochrane and Campbell see *New DNB, s.vv.*

cluded a number of attorneys, among them Robert West and Robert Blaney, who
had assisted Bunyan in obtaining release from prison in 1677. Ferguson, who had
returned to England in February, had acted as an intermediary between the cabals
of Monmouth and West. With his colleagues, West had planned to kill Charles
and James near the Rye House in Hertfordshire as they came back from the races
at Newmarket, but their plans were foiled when a fire caused the royal entourage
to return to Westminster earlier than anticipated. Undeterred, the group continued to discuss assassination schemes and an uprising in London, but nothing had
been finalized when Keeling, a minor co-conspirator, informed authorities. As
the ensuing investigation widened, the government, having also learned about the
Monmouth cabal, implemented security measures in all three kingdoms, and in
late June, Russell, Sidney, Grey, Campbell of Cessnock, and others were apprehended.[74]

Until the Rye House plot was publicized, Bunyan almost certainly knew
nothing about it, nor does anything in his teachings indicate he would have sanctioned assassination. On this point he was manifestly at odds with Blaney and
Ferguson. However, he may have had a general sense that Monmouth was considering some form of action to compel the king to exclude James from the succession. The duke undoubtedly hoped for substantial backing from nonconformists in London and elsewhere, and his subsequent confession that Owen,
Meade, Griffith, and other prominent dissenting ministers knew about the proposed insurrection probably referred only to general inquiries as to whether they
and other nonconformists would participate in an uprising intended to manifest
popular support for exclusion, not overthrow Charles.[75] Because of his ties to
Ferguson, the Rye House plotter Zachary Bourne, and John Nisbet, an agent of a
radical group of Scottish Covenanters known as the United Societies, Meade may
have known more about the proposed rebellion than Owen and Griffith. If Bunyan was cognizant of anything at all—and his writings suggest he was—he had
only a general idea that nonconformist support was sought on the duke's behalf,
possibly for armed intervention to force Charles to exclude his brother from the
succession. Under the right circumstances, the key being the status of the men
leading the rebellion and their aims, Bunyan would have endorsed such an endeavor, though his preference was unmistakably for a peaceful solution. His
carefully guarded statements about resistance in *Of Antichrist* and his exposition
of Genesis are difficult to explain if he was wholly unaware that nonconformist
backing had been sought for armed insurrection.

Against this background it is possible to date another of Bunyan's posthu-

---

[74]Greaves, *SOK*, 171–96. For Keeling see *DNB, s.v.*
[75]BL, Lansdowne MSS 937, fol. 68r.

mously published works, *An Exposition on the Ten First Chapters of Genesis, and Part of the Eleventh*. In this work he mounted a sustained attack on persecutors, a theme that would not have been at the forefront of his concerns after James II issued a Declaration of Indulgence in April 1687. Nor would it have been prudent for Bunyan to have criticized Catholics as harshly as he does in this work once James was on the throne. Bunyan, then, must have written his commentary before Charles' death in February 1685. More precise dating is possible because of Bunyan's expectation that God would stir up the high and mighty to deliver the church from persecution: "When the *Great Ones* of this World begin to discover themselves to the Church, by way of Encouragement, it is a Sign that the Waters [of persecution] are now decreasing" (*MW*, 12:227). After the exposure of the Rye House plot and the Monmouth cabal, persecution intensified and dissenters had no friends powerful enough to ameliorate their plight, at least in the short term. When Bunyan anticipated the possibility of improved circumstances for nonconformists, he was very likely thinking of Monmouth, whose popularity was evident during his tour of Staffordshire and Cheshire in September 1682, but whose influence was vastly diminished following the Rye House revelations. Thus Bunyan probably began his commentary in October or November, about the time he finished *The Greatness of the Soul*, and ceased working on it in June 1683, when the sensational revelations about the Rye House conspiracy and Monmouth's cabal created a climate in which it was perilous to publish his harsh criticisms of Catholicism and tyrannical government and unrealistic to express hope that powerful people would secure better conditions for nonconformists. For the rest of his life, circumstances were not conducive to finishing the commentary, which abruptly ceases with Genesis 11:6.

Whether Bunyan had recourse to other biblical commentaries as he composed this work cannot be known with certitude, though he probably did. He certainly made use of the Geneva Bible, with its marginal annotations, but he manifested little interest in the major debates in which commentators had long engaged, such as Eden's location, the identity of the four rivers, the serpent's ability to speak, the possibility of salvation for animals, and the language Adam and Eve spoke. When writing about the mark God gave to Cain, Bunyan averred that he did not know how others interpreted this (12:173), but he attacked those who argued that Adam was the first Jew, not the first man (12:152). This denunciation of the pre-Adamite position suggests he may have been looking at other commentaries.[76] So too does his statement about propounding his "private thoughts" when positing that Zacharias was a contemporary of Christ, not an

[76] Philip C. Almond, *Adam and Eve in Seventeenth-Century Thought* (Cambridge: Cambridge University Press, 1999), 49–60.

early Hebrew (12:167). Again, he may have been referring to published commentaries when he attacked those who contended that people were vegetarians prior to the great flood (12:249).[77]

With one notable exception Bunyan's hermeneutics are straightforward and uncritical, in keeping with his belief that Christians must interpret Scripture in a manner consistent with its simplicity, shunning "devilish and delusive Arguments." Confusion over the interpretation of texts is the Devil's doing. As Bunyan recalled from his protracted conversion experience, "Satan doth not first of all *deny*, but makes a *doubt* upon the word, whether it is to be taken in this or another sence; and so first corrupting the Mind with a doubt about the *simplicity* of the true sence, he after brings them [i.e., readers] to a denial thereof" (12:128). This methodology enabled Bunyan to accept his text without asking most of the questions that perturbed other commentators, such as the source of light prior to the sun's creation. For him it was sufficient to assert that light originated with God (12:113–14).

The exception to Bunyan's insistence on hermeneutic simplicity is his conviction that the Old Testament is a vast storehouse of types. His commentary on the early chapters of Genesis is a sustained exercise in typology. While he was clearly interested in the text's spiritual lessons, he was intrigued by the typological meanings he could tease out of the text. Adam, the tree of life, the ark, Noah, and his altar are types of Christ (12:116, 122, 201, 231, 241), whereas Eve is a type of the church, and the trees in Eden, of the saints (12:126, 137). One object can serve as multiple types, as in the case of the flood, which represents the church's enemies, water-baptism, and the end of the world (12:204, 218–19). Similarly, the ark is a type of the church and works of faith as well as Christ (12:201–2). In the firmament the sun is a type of Christ; the moon, a type of the church; and the stars represent the saints (12:113), whereas in the sea the "beasts" are a type of persecutors, and whales, a type of the devils (12:115). In short, Bunyan found types virtually everywhere, though occasionally he sensed he might be speculating, as in his interpretation of Genesis 1:2: "The *Deep* here, might be a Type of the Heart of Man before Conversion; and so *Solomon* seems to intimate" (12:108).

The account of the creation of light in Genesis 1 provided Bunyan with an opportunity to probe the conflict between light and darkness that had been such a prominent part of his experience, but other concerns were now paramount, and demonic darkness no longer threatened his well-being. Indeed, he moved rather quickly through his exposition of light and darkness, with much of the subject matter of *Grace Abounding* reduced to a single, matter-of-fact sentence: "So it is in the New Creation; before the light of the Glorious gospel of Christ appears,

[77] Ibid., 118–26.

there is Night, all Night in the Soul; but when that indeed doth shine in the Soul, then for Night there is Day in the Soul." Light and darkness duel near the dawn of creation in their own holy war, reminding Bunyan that before a Christian can oppose Antichrist, "he findeth a struggling in his own Soul between the light and the darkness that is there" (12:110). The godly are the children of light, the ungodly, of the night. The entire passage is handled with an assurance that indicates the traumatic struggles with melancholy were no threat at his time. Referring to the divine activity in dividing the waters from the land as well as light from darkness, he remarked, "dividing Work is difficult Work" (12:112). This he certainly knew from personal experience.

As he had in *Of Antichrist*, Bunyan boldly denounced Catholicism, perhaps even daringly given the fact that the heir to the throne was a Catholic. The pope, he averred, was a "cursed Monster" who had striven to become prince of the world. To find a type for him Bunyan had recourse to the king of Tyrus in Ezekiel 28:13–18, who had been cast from Eden by God for his offenses (12:123). Nimrod, an enforcer of idolatry and superstition, was no less useful as a biblical prototype of the popes, for Babel, Bunyan explained, was the first great seat of oppressors after the universal flood. Like the popes, Nimrod revolted against the gospel's simplicity (12:269). Just as he rebelliously and wickedly had Babel and other cities built for his glorification, so his imitators and successors, especially the popes, had strongholds—churches—erected to enhance their personal grandeur, and by such means "*Nimrod's* Invention could not be kept at Rome" (12:269–70). Obeying orders from "the *Apostolical Sea*" in "*Romish Babel*," these emulators espouse "pretended Religion." Lest there be any misunderstanding as to the object of Bunyan's attack, he referred explicitly to Augustine's mission on Rome's behalf to erect Nineveh in England, adding that he and others like him were "Brats of *Babel*" (12:270). Making no attempt at subtlety in his assault on Catholicism, Bunyan remarked as well on "the Degenerators course in the days of general Apostasy, from the true Apostolical Doctrine, to the Church of our *Romish Babel*" (12:277).[78]

The possessive pronoun in the last sentence is suggestive, ostensibly linking the contemporary Church of England to its Catholic roots. Earlier Bunyan had brazenly cited Revelation 16:19 as proof that *all* national churches would eventually fall, "and Great *Babylon*, their Inventer and Founder," would receive the cup of wrath from God (12:270–71). Almost imperceptibly, he segued from a frontal offensive against Catholicism to a less pronounced attack on the Church of England. He also slipped in a caustic depiction of Anglican clerics when he averred that the locusts of Egypt "were a Type of our *graceless Clergy*, that have covered

[78]Cf. Knollys' exposition of papal Rome as the mystical Babylon. *Mystical Babylon*, 1–4.

the ground of our Land" (12:223). The image of clerical locusts devouring every-thing in sight is both powerful and provocative. His remarks on mixed com-munion were likewise directed primarily against the Church of England. The depth of his opposition to this practice is manifest in his assertion that God's first major quarrel with the church involved its "holding unwarrantable Communion with others" (12:192; cf. 199), an offense that subsequently brought the apostolic church under divine punishment (12:276). He was also castigating the Church of England when he articulated the difference between the godly and their adver-saries in terms of worshiping according to faith as opposed to relying on human inventions (12:160). A substantial gulf thus existed between the established church and congregations of visible saints.

More generally, the Church of England, because of its close affinity with the persecutive Stuart regime, was subject to the sustained attack on persecutors that is the commentary's dominant theme. Woven throughout most of the work, Bun-yan's comments on persecution are less about the ethic of suffering (though this is not ignored) than a withering denunciation of oppressors. He traced the roots of persecution, along with war, tyranny, treachery, and rapine, to Eve's disobedience in Eden and Adam's willingness to eat the forbidden fruit (12:133). Subsequently, from Cain came a "Brood" of persecuting lords and rulers, whereas Abel's progeny are the persecuted (12:162). The chain of oppressors stretches through time, en-compassing the infamous Nimrod, against whose reputation for cruelty all later persecutors are compared, ultimately culminating in "the great *Persecutors* of the Church in the latter Days," Gomer, Magog, Meshech, and Tubal, the apocalyptic figures of Ezekiel 38:2, 6 and Revelation 20:8 (12:267, 269).

At root, Bunyan believed Satan was responsible for persecution. If his minis-ters, who bewitchingly preach righteousness and espouse "a divine and holy Wor-ship," fail to entice people to embrace his false religion, he incites "the hellish rage of Tyrants" to oppress the true church in the hope of frightening the godly to join his cause (12:144). Here again Bunyan reiterated the crucial point he had made in the Vanity Fair episode: Among the most insidious persecutors are those who profess to be Christians and lead superficially godly lives. They can materi-alize in the most unexpected places, which is one of the points of the Cain and Abel account: "Subtil Persecutors love not to bite, till they can make their Teeth to meet; for which they observe their time and place" (12:164). Ultimately their efforts will fail, no matter how extensive their repression in the interim, for "there is yet a *Seth*, another Seed behind, that God hath appointed to stand in the stead of his Brethren, by whom you will certainly be put to flight" (12:180).

Repeatedly Bunyan warned persecutors that they faced punishment for their invidious actions. Their lot is that of Cain and Corah, for God, heeding the cries of blood from their victims, will wreak vengeance (12:166, 175, 225). In a pointed comment about the campaign of repression in the early 1680s, Bunyan insisted that not even reasons of state justify persecution (12:251). Indeed, repressing the godly is a more heinous offense than running a sword through a royal portrait, an interesting point considering that West, Bourne, and their cohorts were at this very time discussing assassination (12:252). Bunyan undoubtedly knew nothing of their scheming, but he was alluding to an incident that had occurred in London in January when someone slashed the duke of York's portrait in the Guildhall.[79] No passage in this commentary is more arresting than Bunyan's questioning of whether gospel ministers can properly extend the promise of grace and forgiveness to persecutors, for their offense is the unpardonable sin (12:169), a quite different definition than the one with which he had wrestled in the 1650s. "They above all Men are prepared unto Wrath," that is, they are reprobate and must not be the objects of prayer (12:169, 172). Given the fact that numerous English magistrates were arresting nonconformists, prohibiting conventicles, and fining or imprisoning offenders, Bunyan's relegation of them to reprobate status is striking. Inasmuch as the king personally ordered or sanctioned some of these activities, the implications for him are obvious.

Bunyan also had harsh words for tyrannical rulers, and to some extent for monarchs in general. In explicating Genesis 2:10 he interpreted the four heads formed by the river flowing out of Eden as a type of "the four great Monarchs of the World." "While Men abide in the Church of God, there is not by them a seeking after the Monarchies of this World; but when they depart from thence, then they seek and strive to be Heads." After Cain murdered Abel, he sought to become a monarch, building a city to preserve his name and posterity and governing tyrannically (12:123, 162). Yet Bunyan never suggested that monarchies should be replaced with republics. He accepted monarchical government, convinced that God can moderate the dealings of princes toward the church (12:225), but he did not hide his hatred of absolute monarchy, the origin of which in the post-deluge era he traced to Nimrod, the cruelest "Monster" (12:267–68). Others, "big with desires of Ostentation," emulated "the Tyranny and Pollution of *Nimrod* and *Babel*" (12:269–70, 274).[80] Religion imposed by tyrants, no matter whether undertaken in God's name, is abominable because of its association with shedding the blood of innocent people (12:163–64).

---

[79] Luttrell, 1:160; CLRO, MS SF 298, entry for 6 May 1682.

[80] For Nimrod as a figure depicting a tyrant see John Tillinghast, *Mr. Tillinghasts Eight Last Sermons* (London, 1655), sigs. A2v-A3r; [Thomas Venner *et al.*], *A Door of Hope: or, a Call and Declaration for the Gathering Together of the First Ripe Fruits unto the Standard of Our Lord, King Jesus* [London, 1661], 1; Philip Henry, CUL, Add. MSS 7338, commenting on Genesis 10.

In the face of tyranny and persecution, the godly must stand their ground *and resist* (12:164):

> The way to weary out God's Enemies, it is to maintain, and make good the Front against them: *Resist the Devil, and he will flie* [James 4:7]. Now if the Captain, their King *Apollion* be made to yield, how can his Followers stand their ground? The *Dragon*, the Devil, Satan, he was *cast out into the earth*, and his Angels were cast out with him [Rev. 12:9]. But how? It was by fighting. (12:179)

Bunyan was not proposing that the godly take up arms against the repressive Stuart regime on their own, for their responsibility was to entreat God for vengeance against tyrants and persecutors (12:167). Suffering saints, as he had taught in his earlier works, must learn to undergo tribulation patiently, leaving revenge to God, for the quarrel is between him and persecutors (12:172, 225). Resistance means "hold[ing] up the Bucklers against the Kingdom of the Devil and Hell," particularly by preaching (12:183, 204). He pointed to Noah's ability to find peace of mind by declaring God's ultimate overthrow of the ungodly, and this, he insisted, did not render Noah guilty of treason or rebellion (12:201, 203). He also cited Daniel's refusal to obey a royal decree by continuing to pray, and Paul's denunciation of imperial Roman religion (12:203–4). Acceptable resistance means that laws against the church must not be obeyed, a principle pregnant with meaning for those tempted to comply with the penal laws against Protestant dissent (12:145).

Recourse to physical force by nonconformists acting alone is unacceptable, "for the Gospel knows no other Compulsion, but to force by Argumentation" (12:266). Those who take it upon themselves to exercise judgment on persecutors will themselves be punished sevenfold, for as Matthew 26:51–52 indicates, those who wield the sword will perish by it (12:173). Moreover, if the godly act precipitously, their affliction will increase. Nor must they undertake things alone, but opt instead for collective endeavor; Bunyan consequently issued an appeal for the "Church of God in *England*, which art now upon the waves of Affliction, and Temptation," to act in concert (12:239). Instead of doing something on their own, the saints must look to the high and mighty to deliver them from tyranny and persecution, much as Josias and Cyrus had done for the ancient Hebrews (12:227). Here again, Bunyan was probably thinking of Monmouth, although with circumspection. "Though it be too much below a Christian to place his Confidence in Men; yet when God shall raise up a *Josias*, or a *Cyrus*, we may take Encouragement at this Working of God." Still, he was cautious, for saints must "look not to them but when God discovers them," and this will happen only when the waters of persecution "begin to cease their raging" (12:227). Presumably he hoped that the duke would be the contemporary Josias, but only time would tell.

Until the appearance of such a deliverer, the godly must practice the ethic of suffering, knowing that the more spiritually productive the church, the greater the persecution. The divine purpose of such afflictions is not punishment for offenses but reminders of the necessity to pursue godly lives (12:147), a subject to which Bunyan would soon turn in his next work, *A Holy Life*. To witness to the truth is hazardous as long as Cain's offspring remain in the world, and not until the millennium, which will commence 6,000 years after the creation according to Bunyan's reckoning, will the church be free of persecution (12:119, 180, 183). In the meantime God will sustain the church as it is "tossed upon the Waves of the Rage and Fury of the World," like Noah's ark on the universal deluge, a type of the church's persecution (12:208, 218–20, 223). The more repression, the higher the ark is lifted toward heaven, a point also made by Philip Henry.[81] Bunyan was convinced that periods of peace and liberty are far more dangerous for Christians than are times of affliction, for the latter are more likely to make believers remember their spiritual obligations (12:261–62, 277).

Divine use of the cross for purgative and instructional purposes does not excuse the persecutors. Bunyan employed the typology of the raven that flew from Noah's ark to indicate their fate. The raven, he argued, represents those worldly professors in the church who will ultimately feast on the flesh of monarchs and mighty men. "They will *eat Flesh* and *Fat*, till they be *full*, and *drink the Blood*, till they be *drunk*." By this he meant that such professors will devour "the Carkasses, the Kingdoms and Estates of the Antichristian Party" (12:229–30). Although he numbered these professors among the visible saints, he averred that their goal was to attain worldly honor and material ease, at which time he expected them to leave the church (12:230–31). Uncertain of Monmouth and some of those around him, he was apparently suspicious enough of their motives to think their intentions were at root different from those of the godly. This would help explain his cautious reaction to the duke and his political allies.

One final theme in the commentary—Bunyan's assertion of female inferiority and subordination—merits attention as the prelude to a work he would write later in 1683, *A Case of Conscience Resolved*. According to Bunyan, women's inferiority is not a consequence of Eve's succumbing to temptation in Eden, as Luther argued,[82] for she was *created* in a subordinate position to Adam. Had she not

---

[81] CUL, Add. MSS 7338, commenting on Genesis 7.

[82] Martin Luther, *Luther's Works*, ed. Jaroslav Pelikan and Helmut T. Lehmann, 56 vols. (St. Louis: Concordia Publishing House; Philadelphia: Muhlenberg Press; Philadelphia: Fortress Press, 1958–74), 1:203. If Eve had not sinned, Luther contended, women would not have been subjected to their husbands' rule. Philip Henry's interpretation of Genesis 2 emphasizes Adam and Eve's mutual love; Eve was created from Adam's rib, "no higher, lest shee should despise him, no lower, lest hee should despise her, near his Heart,

sinned, she would still have had to obey him as a fundamental duty. Because women are weaker and more subject to the Devil's enticements, they are more prone than men to vanity "and all mis-orders in the matters of God" (12:147). Relying on the Bible for proof, Bunyan depicted women as "fantastical and unstable Spirits" who are less likely than men to be in the right (12:148–49). Eve was specifically faulted for having engaged the serpent when it was Adam's responsibility to have done so given his greater capability, and Adam in turn was admonished for having yielded his authority to Eve (12:128, 148). Bunyan's negative treatment of Eve thus stands in sharp contrast to Margaret Fell's earlier rehabilitation of her as part of the campaign to assert a leadership role for women in the Quaker movement.[83] The account of the events in Eden, as Bunyan interpreted it, was about power relationships as well as disobedience to God. Because of Eve's offense, God commanded women to be silent and learn from their husbands, as Paul directed in 1 Corinthians 14:34–35, "a Command that is necessary enough for that simple and weak Sex." Although Bunyan refrained from citing examples, he asserted that some of his female contemporaries meddled with "potent Enemies, about the great and weighty Matters that concern Eternity" (12:128). Had some of the dissenting women taken it upon themselves to engage the Quakers or adherents of the Church of England? In any event he was not without some sympathy for Eve (and implicitly her female successors, as he would make evident in the second part of The Pilgrim's Progress): "O poor Eve! Do we wonder at thy Folly! Doubtless we had done as bad with half the Argument of thy Temptation" (12:130).

### "A Place to Fight and Wrestle in"[84]: Repudiating Iniquity

When the government learned about the conspiracies of the Monmouth and West cabals in June, it implemented widespread security measures and ordered numerous arrests, including those of Bunyan's ministerial colleagues, Ferguson, Owen, and Meade, and the Whig attorney Robert Blaney. After being arrested Owen was examined at Whitehall on 27 June 1683, but he denied any knowledge of the plotting other than what had been announced in a royal proclamation. He

---

that they might bee taught to love and tender each other." CUL, Add. MSS 7338, commenting on Genesis 2 (the leaf is bound with the commentary on chapter 26).

[83] Margaret Fell, Womens Speaking Justified, Proved and Allowed of by the Scriptures (London, 1667); Marilyn Serraino Luecke, "'God hath made no difference such as men would': Margaret Fell and the Politics of Women's Speech," BS 7 (1997): 77–93.

[84] MW, 9:296.

was released, but less than two months later, on 24 August, "the Bell-weather of Independents," as Jenkins described him, was dead.[85] Two days before his demise he wrote, "I am leaving the Ship of the Church in a Storme. But whilst the great *Pilot* is in it, the loss of a poor Under-rower will be inconsiderable."[86] The government also arrested his brother, Colonel Henry Owen, who had frequently been with Ferguson in the spring of 1683, had unsuccessfully attempted to meet with Monmouth at the earl of Anglesey's house in late May or early June, and had allegedly told an ex-army officer in Dublin in June that between 80,000 and 100,000 "fighting" dissenters were in London. According to Colonel John Rumsey, who was part of the Monmouth cabal and associated with West's group as well, Colonel Owen had provided funds to send the Whig attorney Aaron Smith to Scotland with an invitation for leading dissidents to come to London and explore the possibility of coordinated uprisings in the two countries.[87]

On the day John Owen was examined, the government ordered Meade's arrest. Apprehended as he attempted to flee to the Netherlands with the Rye House conspirator Zachary Bourne and the dissenting minister Walter Cross, he was initially examined on 2 July. He admitted that John Nisbet had lived in his house eight or nine months, and he also confessed that he had been in contact with Ferguson. Although Meade claimed to know nothing of any conspiracy, he probably had at least a general idea that Monmouth was contemplating an uprising, possibly in connection with Scottish Covenanters. He remained in prison until 30 July, when he was freed after posting a bond of £2,000 and providing two sureties.[88] The Scottish minister William Carstares, an intermediary between Argyll and his supporters on one hand and the Monmouth group on the other, later admitted having told Meade, John Owen, and Griffith of the proposed insurrection, thus confirming Monmouth's allegation that the three ministers knew such plans were being considered. Moreover, Carstares asserted that Meade, Owen, and Griffith had approved of an uprising. He also claimed that Danvers, with whom Bunyan was acquainted, had known about efforts of Scottish dissidents to raise money in England for an uprising on Argyll's behalf, though he had this information second-hand. These accusations were subsequently reinforced by the Rye House

---

[85] PRO, SP 29/425/102; 63/341, p. 158 (quoted); *HMC 29, Portland*, 2:236; Morrice, 1:371. Noting Owen's death, Bishop Barlow called him a remarkable man. BL, Add. MSS 29,582, fol. 59v.

[86] DWL, MSS L6/1, no. 11.

[87] PRO, SP 29/425/83, 103, 156; 29/427/34; Greaves, *SOK*, 190–91. For Rumsey see *BDBR, s.v.*

[88] *CSPD, 1683 (1)*, 357; *CSPD, 1683 (2)*, 14–15, 54, 57, 214; PRO, SP 29/427/25, 98; BL, Add. MSS 4107, fol. 39r; Luttrell, 1:265.

plotter Richard Goodenough, who implicated Meade, Danvers, and Colonel Owen.[89] According to West, Ferguson told the Rye House cabal that some dissenting ministers approved of their scheme, whereas others suspected something illegal was being planned and urged him to desist lest all nonconformists suffer reproach.[90] If this secondhand report is accurate, it is tempting to think that Bunyan might have been in the latter group.

Blaney confessed to having attended a meeting in late December 1682 with a number of alleged Rye House conspirators—including West, Rumsey, Richard Goodenough, John Row, and Christopher Battiscombe—at which the assassination of Charles and James was discussed. West confirmed Blaney's presence at this meeting.[91] Bunyan's former surety was thus involved in the scheming.

Among those who escaped were the ministers Ferguson and Lobb, both of whom Bunyan almost certainly knew. Lobb, the pastor of a Congregationalist church in Fetter Lane, London, and a relative of Carstares' wife, was eventually apprehended in early August, but Ferguson, who had been extensively involved in the plotting, fled to the continent.[92] Information about Lobb was provided by Bourne, who confessed that Lobb had told him he intended to liberate two of his imprisoned followers because they would prove useful to Bourne. Moreover, West asserted that Bourne had told the other Rye House conspirators that Lobb and his congregation had approved a plan to recruit insurgents in London. Of questionable value is the testimony of a reputed conspirator named Norwich Salisbury, who alleged that John Owen and Meade had recommended Lobb. Also of indeterminate worth is the confession of Edmund Massey, a man with assorted radical connections who reinforced Salisbury's accusation that Lobb was involved. According to Massey, Lobb had encouraged various dissidents to remain firm and prayed that God would deliver the king into their hands that he might

---

[89] PRO, SP 29/430/40; *The Deposition of Mr. William Carstares* (Edinburgh and London, 1684), 1, 4; BL, Lansdowne MSS 1152, fol. 227v. Another conspirator, Norwich Salisbury, likewise testified that Owen, Meade, and Griffith knew an uprising was under consideration. PRO, SP 29/431/108. For Carstares see *DNB, s.v.*

[90] BL, Add. MSS 38,847, fol. 105r.

[91] PRO, SP 29/425/138, pp. 25–26; *Copies of the Informations and Original Papers Relating to the Proof of the Horrid Conspiracy Against the Late King, His Present Majesty, and the Government*, 3rd ed. (London, 1685), 32–33, 48. Cf. BL, Lansdowne MSS 1152, fol. 250v. For Row see *New DNB, s.v.*

[92] BL, Add. MSS 28,875, fols. 261r, 265r; NUL, MSS PwV95, fol. 300; Luttrell, 1:275. Ferguson was included in the proclamation of 28 June calling for the apprehension of Monmouth, Grey, and Sir Thomas Armstrong. BL, Add. MSS 62,453, fols. 102–3; London *Gazette* 1838 (28 June–2 July 1683).

no longer be an enemy of the saints.[93] Whether or not Lobb was involved in the plotting, he was certainly a suspect and, prior to his arrest, a fugitive.

Thus a number of men with whom Bunyan had demonstrable or probable links were suspected of treasonable activity in the summer of 1683: John Owen, Meade, Griffith, Blaney, Ferguson, Danvers, and Lobb. Moreover, the name of Dorman Newman, publisher of *The Holy War*, appeared on a list of dissidents to be disarmed in June, and all meetinghouses linked to suspected conspirators, in some of which Bunyan would have preached, were to be searched.[94] In addition to Danvers, William Kiffin, another minister with whom Bunyan had debated the subject of baptism, was under suspicion, for government agents searched his house and seized his weapons. Although the state could find no one to testify against Kiffin, his name was discovered in a code in the possession of Lieutenant-Colonel Abraham Holmes, a co-conspirator of Argyll's; the portion of the cipher containing Kiffin's name is in Carstares' handwriting.[95] In July the government ordered the arrest of two of Bunyan's publishers, Newman and Alsop, along with others for allegedly having issued treasonable and scandalous material, though all went into temporary hiding.[96] This is not to suggest that Bunyan was party to the plotting, but his ties to these men made it imprudent for him to go to London during the summer of 1683, let alone publish anything overtly critical of the regime or the established church.

The security measures may also have dissuaded Bunyan from spending time in London. On 20 June Secretary Jenkins instructed London's lord mayor to take appropriate measures for the City's security, and comparable orders were sent to the earl of Craven for Middlesex and Southwark as well as London. Three days later Jenkins directed all lords lieutenant to assure that militia officers were in a state of readiness and that people suspected of involvement in the conspiracies be disarmed. The mayor also received orders to dispatch representatives to meet with the king on the 28th and report what measures had been implemented.[97] The garrison in the Tower was reinforced, companies of royal and City guards were strategically positioned in the London area, the houses of Parliament and the adjacent buildings were carefully inspected, dissenters and dissidents were dis-

---

[93] PRO, SP 29/427/114; 29/430/157; 29/431/76, 108; *Copies*, 93; Greaves, *SOK*, 162–69, 189.

[94] PRO, SP 29/425/43.

[95] Kiffin, *Remarkable Passages*, 52; *State-Papers and Letters, Addressed to William Carstares*, ed. Joseph McCormick (Edinburgh, 1774), 108–9; [George Mackenzie], *A True and Plain Account of the Discoveries Made in Scotland, of the Late Conspiracies Against His Majesty and the Government* (Edinburgh, 1685), 19. For Holmes see *BDBR, s.v.*

[96] NUL, MSS PwV95, fols. 255–56.

[97] PRO, SP 44/68, pp. 293–94, 301; 44/69, p. 39.

armed, and suspicious places were searched.[98] Concerned that fugitives were being hidden by Anglesey, who had strong ties to Monmouth and Essex as well as
various nonconformists, including Owen, the government had his London house
searched; troops arrived at midnight, forced open most of his doors, and scattered his papers and books.[99] Magistrates seized numerous weapons from the
Buckinghamshire home of Wharton's son, Thomas.[100] Searches were undertaken
and weapons confiscated in Bedfordshire and other counties where Bunyan ministered, including Cambridgeshire, Northamptonshire, Leicestershire, Hertfordshire, Suffolk, and Middlesex.[101] In Bedfordshire special attention was focused on
Leighton Buzzard because one of West's fellow conspirators, Francis Goodenough or his brother Richard, had gone there.[102] This, then, was a climate in
which Bunyan was well advised to be cautious.

Circumspection with respect to what he wrote was further suggested in light
of the action taken by Oxford University on 21 July. Its convocation promulgated
a decree asserting the duty "to search into, and lay open those Impious Doctrines, which . . . gave rise and growth to these Nefarious Attempts" by the West
and Monmouth cabals. Among the twenty-seven propositions convocation denounced were those asserting that civil authority is derived from the people, that
there is a contract between a ruler and his subjects discharging the latter from
obedience if the ruler does not fulfill his responsibilities, that tyrants forfeit their
right to govern, and that subjects can enter into covenants to defend themselves
and their religion contrary to their rulers' commands. Books allegedly espousing
these tenets were publicly burned, among them works by Owen, Milton, Baxter,
John Knox, Christopher Goodman, Thomas Cartwright, Walter Travers, Fifth
Monarchists, and Quakers.[103]

Against this background, Bunyan wrote *A Holy Life*, probably between late
June and August 1683. It was entered in the Stationers' Register on 10 August

[98] PRO, SP 44/54, p. 182; 44/68, pp. 326–27; 44/335, pp. 7–9, 14, 20–21; NUL, MSS
PwV95, fols. 248, 257.

[99] BL, Add. MSS 18,730, fols. 20r, 36r, 63r, 67r, 73r, 81v, 88v–89v, 91v, 92v, 95r, 98r, 100r–
101r, 102r–103v, 103v, 105v; PRO SP 44/335, p. 8. Angelsey also had ties to Shaftesbury, Lord
Grey, Sir Thomas Armstrong, Lord Howard of Escrick, and John Hampden. BL, Add.
MSS 18,730, fols. 58v, 81v, 86r, 95r, 102r.

[100] Bodl., Carte MSS 81, fols. 727r, 730r.

[101] PRO, SP 29/425/149; 29/430/131, 146; 29/433/67; 44/56, p. 103; NUL, MSS PwV95, fol.
277.

[102] PRO, SP 44/68, p. 301; 44/335, p. 10.

[103] PRO, SP 29/429/107, 107.1; London *Gazette* 1845 (23–26 July 1683); *The Judgment and
Decree of the University of Oxford Past in Their Convocation July 21. 1683, Against Certain
Pernicious Books and Damnable Doctrines* (Oxford, 1683).

(perhaps an early draft Bunyan subsequently decided to expand) and 6 October and in the Term Catalogue in November. In his "Advertisement" for the book Alsop mentioned Bunyan's "inconvenient distance" from London.[104] Given Bunyan's association with some of those suspected of involvement in the plotting and the security measures that had been implemented, he probably decided it was unwise to travel to London and left the publication of A Holy Life solely in Alsop's care.

In part, Bunyan discreetly used A Holy Life to condemn the conspirators by expounding on Paul's exhortation to depart from iniquity (2 Timothy 2:19). Bunyan argued that most professors of the gospel in England were nothing more than superficial Christians wedded to evildoing. A reader who studied the text with care could have recognized the mostly subtle criticism of the plotters, a theme woven throughout the book, though not its principal focus. He clearly signaled his position when he used an analogy based on the government's search for the conspirators:

> Would the King count him a Loyal subject, who would hide in his house, nourish in his Bed, and feed at his Table, one that implacably hateth and seeketh to murder his Majesty? Why, sin is *such* an enemy to the Lord Jesus Christ: therefore as Kings command that Traitors be delivered up to Justice; so Christ commands, *that we depart from iniquity*. (*MW*, 9:311)

Bunyan's stance can be contrasted with that of the Presbyterian minister Henry Newcome, who helped Ferguson escape.[105]

Ferguson probably headed the list of those whose conspiratorial conduct Bunyan found reprehensible because it compromised the dissenters' position. He must have been chagrined to learn as well of the arrest of Owen, Meade, Lobb, and some of the other alleged conspirators, though never did he condemn any of them by name, at least in print. They were undoubtedly on his mind when he discussed the futility of attempting to pursue both "the designs of the Gospel, and their own worldly and fleshly designs." He expected believers to uphold the gospel's reputation in the world, an allusion to the fact that the plotters had brought dissenters into disrepute (9:300). "They that name the name of Christ should depart from iniquity . . . that his name may not be evil spoken of by men: for our holiness puts a lustre and a beauty upon the name of Christ, and our *not* departing from iniquity draws a cloud upon it" (9:299). His elucidation of why those who were once enlightened subsequently returned to worldly ways helped to explain the actions of plotters such as Ferguson, the Baptist Thomas Walcott, who had been closely allied to Shaftesbury, and some of West's co-conspirators, in-

---

[104] Arber, *Transcript*, 3:180, 199; Arber, *Catalogues*, 2:41; *MW*, 9:xviii.
[105] Hill, *TPM*, 313–14. For Newcome see *Calamy Revised*, *s.v.*

cluding the Congregationalist Nathaniel Wade and the Baptists Richard Rumbold, Josiah Keeling (though excommunicated), and Thomas Lee, who sometimes worshiped with the Congregationalists, as did William Hone.[106] Such dissenters "joyn[ed] in confederacy with the world again" because their hearts had never become receptive to the gospel or estranged from their lusts, and they lacked the grace of the fear of God. As soon as they began to return to their wicked ways, God "force[d] their hearts to comply with bad things" (290–91), yet he cannot be faulted for withdrawing grace from these people, partly because he is a free agent who can do as he likes: "Why may not God, since these Rebels had such working with them, as that their minds, by their understandings, their will and affections, by their judgment and consciences were somewhat taken and allured, cause a withdrawing of these for tryal, and to see if they would cry after him to return" (9:287–88). On the one hand Bunyan held out hope that such rebels would repent, but on the other he rigorously denounced those who deceived others, masking their erroneous principles with a moral life; these people—he probably included Ferguson among them—are "the more mischievous, dangerous, and damnable" (9:267). The depth of his abomination of "carnal Gospellers" is manifest in his closing observation that God raises some people to heaven before he casts them into hell "that their fall may be the greater, and their punishment the more intolerable" (9:351).

Although Bunyan provided ample scriptural citations in the margins, he made it clear that he was writing about men he had *personally* seen profess Christ devoutly, only to turn their backs on him and embrace iniquity (9:264). In his judgment these nefarious apostates, lacking "holy faith," used their profession of Christianity as a cloak for evil designs (9:280). Far from being exempt from such strictures, certain visible saints were his target: "How many are there in our day, since the Gospel is grown so common, that catch up a notion of good things, and from that notion make a profession of the name of Christ, get into Churches, and obtain the title of a Brother, a Saint, a member of a Gospel congregation, that have clean escaped *repentance?*" The churches, he maintained, swarm with such pseudo-professors (9:281). To his godly readers Bunyan offered candid advice: To avoid "evil matter[s]," stay away from those who defile (9:275).

The revelations of the conspiracies prompted him to embed a jeremiad in *A Holy Life.* God, he warned, is angry with England because of the sins of professing Christians who profane his name and use his word and ordinances for their own ends. Because they pollute his name with their idols—a clear allusion to the Church of England[107]—they profane God. Although the people sense imminent

---

[106] Greaves, *SOK*, 335. For Walcott see *New DNB, s.v.;* for Wade see *DNB, s.v.*

[107] He was also attacking the Church of England when he castigated ministers who

judgment, they lack the justifying faith capable of saving them:

> We are every one looking for something; even for something that carrieth terrour and dread in the sound of its Wings as it comes, though we know not the form nor visage thereof. One cries out, another has his Hands upon his Loyns, and a third is made mad with the sight of his Eyes, and with what his Ears do hear. . . . Yet where is the Church, the House, the Man that stands in the gap for the Land to turn away this Wrath by Repentance, and amendment of Life? (9:256)

Everything done by God to England has been insufficient to cause reformation and humility, and now, Bunyan surmised, it might be too late (9:257). He also had a special message for the godly, whom he urged to remain faithful to their covenant with God. If they failed to do so, they faced punishment at the hands of the wicked, who could justifiably defend their persecutive actions by claiming to be God's agents (9:260).

The involvement of dissenters in the scheming seems to have prompted Bunyan to address the broader problem of abundant "Wooden, and Earthy professors" in England (9:279). Among men only one in a thousand manifested genuine repentance, he thought, reflecting his gender bias, but the problem was substantially worse among women, only one in 10,000 of whom evinced this grace (9:282). The numbers were for rhetorical effect, but his concern was genuine: "It is marvelous to me to see sin so high amidst the swarms of Professors that are found in every corner of this Land" (9:256). He likened them to brambles, fit only for burning, despite their prayers, pious reading, attendance at sermons, participation in church fellowship, and observance of the sacraments, for in every other way they are "as black as others, even in their whole Life and Conversation" (9:251, 254). Because these professors refuse to depart from wickedness, they scandalize religion (9:306–7), much as the actions of the nonconformist conspirators had. In urging genuine believers to evade these carnal gospelers, Bunyan acknowledged that no saint is capable of perfection in this life, a point on which he differed from the Quakers.[108]

In addition to denouncing the multitudinous carnal gospelers and exhorting the faithful to wage ceaseless war against evil, he provided readers with precepts for holy living. Much of this was in keeping with standard Protestant fare, par-

---

preached with a view to preferment or praise, though the latter was applicable to dissenters as well (329). His condemnation of "half-priests" who could not teach people the entire gospel for fear of condemning themselves was aimed at clergy of the established church (284); Bunyan never used the term "priest" for a dissenting minister.

[108] For the Quaker position on perfection see Underwood, PRLW, 60–61; Richard L. Greaves, Dublin's Merchant-Quaker: Anthony Sharp and the Community of Friends, 1643–1707 (Stanford, CA: Stanford University Press, 1998), 232, 234, 240.

ticularly as expressed in the puritan and nonconformist traditions, and covered such topics as relations between spouses, parents and children, and masters and servants.[109] His sensitivity to the responsibility of adult children toward their elderly parents is noteworthy (9:319–24). Like many other Protestant ministers he recommended moderation in apparel and home decoration, avoidance of lascivious behavior, and greater charity for the indigent (9:282–83, 318). His admonition not to take pride in one's library is unusual. "'Tis better to have no books, and depart from iniquity, than to have a thousand, and not to be bettered in my soul thereby" (9:324). This is not to suggest that he owned no books, though his library may have been small; he was certainly an avid reader. He was still reading, or at least remembering, Foxe's *Acts and Monuments*, for he cited John Philpot's brazen remark to the ecclesiastical commissioners accusing them of dancing with bare buttocks in a net, unable to see the evil of their ways (9:309).[110] He was offended by professing Christians in London who spent more time in coffeehouses than closet devotions or who hurried off in the morning to pursue business without first spending time in prayer (9:325). The virtues he valued can be summarized as an embrace of the cross, self-denial, charity, and purity of life and conversation, all of which he thought were rare among professing Christians (9:346–47).

As nonconformists embraced the cross, the persecution they suffered moved Bunyan to urge greater unity among dissenting Protestants. He counseled them to beware of being so wedded to the distinctive tenets of Presbyterians, Congregationalists, or Baptists that they refused to commune with saints of other persuasions. To shun this wider communion, in his estimation, was to make too much of one's opinions: "The more a man stands upon his points to justifie himself, and to condemn his holy brethren: the more danger he is in of becoming overcome of divers evils" (9:327–28). Although Bunyan saw much to criticize in London, he also found concrete examples of ecumenical cooperation among some nonconformists, as in the Merchants' Lectures, and men of a similar outlook, among them Owen and Lobb. Given the persecution that characterized the Tory Reaction, closer relations among dissenters made sense.

[109] See, e.g., Richard L. Greaves, *Society and Religion in Elizabethan England* (Minneapolis: University of Minnesota Press, 1981), 251–67, 274–87, 314–25. Bunyan's articulation of the social responsibilities of the godly is similar to that espoused by Thomas Collier, *A Discourse of the True Gospel Blessedness in the New Covenant* (London, 1659), 126–28.

[110] For Bunyan's reading habits see the Epilogue.

# CHAPTER 12

# Nonconformity and the Tory Backlash

As newspapers, newsletters, and other forms of communication recounted allegations of the Rye House plotting and Monmouth's discussions about a general insurrection, and as the state tried the accused and executed some of them, moderate Whigs and nonconformists as well as Tory-Anglicans reacted with revulsion against the reputed conspirators. Declarations of loyalty and gratitude for the failure of the plots poured in, some from as far afield as Jamaica, Nevis, New Plymouth, Connecticut, and Virginia.[1] Tory-Anglicans seized the opportunity to tar nonconformists and Whigs with the brush of sedition. "The Herd of Dissenters," observed White Kennet, the future bishop of Peterborough, are "vigerously compared to Josephs Coat, A garment of divers colours dipd in bloud," an obvious allusion to the assassination schemes.[2] An address from Cambridge denounced the "Machinations of Republicans and Dissenters," and the Somerset grand jury not only condemned the conspirators' designs as devilish but also pledged to suppress all conventicles and riotous assemblies. The perceived connection between sedition and dissent was vividly rendered in an address from the people of Hereford: "From those Hives of Faction the Conventicles, did swarm these Hellish Monsters of Rebellion and Treason, and will still do so, since in them Divisions are made and Fomented, and a Disaffection to [the king's] Person and Government taught."[3] An address from Buckinghamshire blamed the

---

[1] London *Gazette* 1839 (2–5 July 1683); 1844 (19–23 July 1683); 1846 (26–30 July 1683); 1847 (30 July–2 August 1683); 1853 (20–23 August 1683); 1857 (3–6 September 1683); 1872 (25–29 October 1683); 1886 (13–17 December 1683); 1894 (10–14 January 1684); 1908 (28 February–3 March 1684); 1912 (13–17 March 1684); 1927 (5–8 May 1684); 1979 (3–6 November 1684); BL, Egerton MSS 2985, fols. 303r, 305r.

[2] BL, Lansdowne MSS 937, fol. 46v.

[3] London *Gazette* 1855 (27–30 August 1683) (quoted); 1856 (30 August–3 September 1683); PRO, SP 29/430/115. See also Bodl., English Letters C12, fol. 156r.

plotting on unreasonable men who had cast aside all sense of loyalty and religion while zealously professing both. Elsewhere, grand juries in Dorset and Wiltshire castigated dissenters and Catholics who bore arms as a threat to the government, though the spirit of the Catholics generally improved as criticism focused on Protestant nonconformists.[4] The Tory Reaction of which these declarations were a part constituted a wave of popular support for crown and church that left many Whigs demoralized and nonconformists feeling increasingly more embattled. In this context Bunyan found some diversion in writing the second part of *The Pilgrim's Progress*, addressing the role of women in the church, and responding to the challenge posed by seventh-day sabbatarians, but he also published an exposition of the ethic of suffering, very much a tract for the times.

## "To Set You Right"[5]: Defining Women's Place

About September 1683, after Bunyan had completed *A Holy Life*, he responded to an attack by someone he identified only as Mr. K. concerning his opposition to women's prayer meetings, an issue that went to the heart of his views on women. By 1681 the Bedford congregation had instituted such gatherings, but after reflecting on the relevant scriptural passages Bunyan concluded that such meetings had no biblical warrant. When he explained his reasoning to the church the women agreed to cease gathering separately for prayer, "so subject to the *Word* were our Women, and so willing to let go what by *that* could not be proved a duty for them" (*MW*, 4:297). Some two years later, in 1683, a group of women who had held such meetings for a substantial period of time, probably in London,[6] sent Mr. K.'s refutation to Bunyan in care of S.F. at Bedford. S.F. and S.B. forwarded the critique to Bunyan with a covering note explaining that Mr. K. expected a written response (4:297). Bunyan did not identify S.B. and S.F. other than to refer to them as Mr. K.'s women. Although he professed to know nothing about Mr. K.'s educational background, he assumed formal training, which he forthrightly contrasted with his own lack thereof: "I am not ashamed to Confess, that I neither know the *Mode* nor *Figure* of a Sylogism, nor scarce which is *Major* or *Minor*" (4:300). This may suggest that Mr. K. was Hanserd Knollys, a Particular Baptist minister in London who had studied at Catherine Hall, Cambridge, and published guides to the study of Greek, Hebrew, and Latin. Another possibility is William Kiffin, against whom Bunyan had defended the principles of

---

[4] London *Gazette* 1854 (23–27 August 1683); PRO, SP 29/416/62, 69; BL, Add. MSS 70,013, fol. 158v.

[5] *MW*, 4:329.

[6] At the end of the pamphlet Bunyan chided London Christians for ceasing their "Morning-Closet-Prayers." *MW*, 4:330.

open membership and communion in the early 1670s, and who attacked those who espoused such tenets in *A Sober Discourse of Right to Church-Communion* (1681).[7] A third possibility is Benjamin Keach, a Particular Baptist minister at Horsleydown, Southwark, whose preaching forays into such areas as Essex, Suffolk, and Hertfordshire may have won converts who included S.F. in Bedford. Moreover, in October 1691 a breakaway group from Keach's church would fault him for having permitted women "to speake and sing, to teach and admonish in the Worship and servis of God in his Church."[8]

The issue of women's participation in Independent and Baptist churches was not new. At a meeting of the Abingdon Association of Particular Baptists in April 1658, the delegates had agreed that women could not teach, hold a ruling office, pass judgment on doctrine or disciplinary cases, or "speake in prayer as the mouth of the church." Women could confess their faith, express their desire to be baptized and join the church, testify in a disciplinary hearing, publicly repent, and report anything that would render a candidate for membership unfit. The governing principle was that women "may not so speake as that their speaking shall shew a not acknowledging of the inferioritie of their sexe and so be an usurping authoritie over the man."[9] This language was largely borrowed from the records of the Midland Association of Particular Baptists in June 1656, which had also permitted a woman to speak in church if she had been sent as a messenger to another congregation.[10] As John Child expressed the Baptist position, "Women have Authority to Minister according to ability and occasion, (though not in the Church, or to Usurp)." Peter Chamberlen's Baptist congregation at Lothbury Square, London, explicitly recognized the right of a prophetess, though not other women, to speak, prophesy, and pray aloud in the church as long as she wore a veil.[11] In the 1650s John Rogers' open-membership, open-communion congrega-

---

[7] The Oxford editor of *A Case of Conscience Resolved*, T. L. Underwood, suggests Kiffin as the possible author, citing Bunyan's reference to him in *Peaceable Principles and True* as Mr. K. *MW*, 4:xliii. Bunyan's mention of Mr. K.'s prior assertion of "Rigid Principles" (316) may allude to his defense of closed-membership, closed-communion Baptist views. For Kiffin and Knollys see *BDBR, s.vv.*

[8] Quoted in Patricia Crawford, *Women and Religion in England 1500–1720* (London: Routledge, 1993), 198. For Keach see *BDBR, s.v.*

[9] *Association Records of the Particular Baptists of England, Wales and Ireland to 1660*, ed. B. R. White, 3 vols. (London: Baptist Historical Society, n.d.), 3:185.

[10] Ibid., 1:28.

[11] John Child, *A Moderate Message to Quakers, Seekers, and Socinians, by a Friend and Well-Wisher to Them All* ([London], 1676), 62 (quoted); Claire Cross, "The Church in England 1646–1660," in *The Interregnum: The Quest for Settlement 1640–1660*, ed. G. E. Aylmer (Hamden, CT: Archon Books, 1972), 116–17. For Chamberlen see *BDBR, s.v.*

tion in Dublin permitted women to speak and vote in the church in keeping with their Christian liberty and the dictates of their consciences. Questioning whether the admonition in 1 Timothy 2:12 that women should be silent in church was a standing precept or a temporary expedient, Rogers reluctantly accepted the ban on women preaching and their prophesying as ministers or officers, but he predicted that they would one day be able to prophesy in the church and enjoy greater freedom than they currently enjoyed. During the previous decade Thomas Edwards had received reports of women preaching in Lincolnshire, Ely, Hertfordshire, Kent, and London, and another that Independents in Somerset believed that women could speak in church if led by the Spirit.[12]

Proponents of severe restrictions on women's role in the church cited biblical passages as their rationale, but their stance was also culturally conditioned and a practical reflection of the fact that women outnumbered men in most dissenting congregations, comprising 62 percent of the Baptists and 61 percent of the Congregationalists in the late seventeenth century. The proportion was even higher in London, where 68 percent of the members of Baptist and Congregational churches were female.[13] The issue was thus one of control as well as biblical precedent and conformity with cultural mores. Bunyan made no attempt to hide the fact that his goal was to keep women in their place (4:329).

As summarized by Bunyan in *A Case of Conscience Resolved*, the thrust of Mr. K.'s argument was that scriptural rules governing prayer do not discriminate by gender. If women can praise God for his mercy, they can also pray together. Mr. K. contended that women in peril had prayed for and received forgiveness and deliverance. Moreover, because God bestowed his Spirit on women in gospel times, they have a duty to pray together, and if such gatherings were acceptable in the early church, they remain so. Women who pray together experience spiritual blessings, indicating divine approval. With all this in mind, Mr. K. counseled pious women that "*what God hath Born Witness to, and approved of, let no Man deter you from*" (4:299).

Bunyan was frankly irritated with Mr. K., whom he denounced as "a Man of Conceit," for having resurrected the issue in the Bedford congregation because it could have "*set us into a Flame*" (4:296, 327). By encouraging women to withdraw

---

[12] John Rogers, *Ohel or Beth-Shemesh: A Tabernacle for the Sun* (London, 1653), 463 (mspr. 563)–77; Thomas Edwards, *Gangraena*, 2nd ed. (London, 1646), 116–21, 217–18 (mspr. 117–18). See also Phyllis Mack, *Visionary Women: Ecstatic Prophecy in Seventeenth-Century England* (Berkeley: University of California Press, 1992), 87–124; Dorothy P. Ludlow, "Shaking Patriarchy's Foundations: Sectarian Women in England, 1641–1700," in *Triumph over Silence: Women in Protestant History*, ed. Richard L. Greaves (Westport, CT: Greenwood Press, 1985), 93–108.

[13] Crawford, *Women and Religion in England*, 189.

into their own prayer meetings Mr. K., Bunyan alleged, was setting the stage for schism and countenancing women to be unruly and headstrong (4:318–19). He even chided Mr. K. for being "*Nunnish*" and flattering women by "making of them the Judges in their own cause" (4:299, 307).

Bunyan's case against Mr. K. sought to prove that no biblical passage supports the right of women to worship or pray in meetings separate from men: "In all the Scripture, I find not that the Women of the Churches of Christ, did use to separate themselves from their Brethren, and as so separate, performe Worship together among themselves or in that *their* Congregation: or that they made, by allowance of the Word, appointment so to do" (4:301). In the absence of such evidence, he adjudged women's prayer meetings a human invention that the church had no authority to institute, however good its intentions. He likened such gatherings to monasticism, mendicant orders, and mandatory vows of celibacy, which had also been established with the best of intentions, yet without divine authority (4:322). Although admitting that biblical women such as Miriam, Deborah, Huldah, Anna, Priscilla, the daughters of the evangelist Philip, and the women who assisted Paul taught, prophesied, and had the authority to call believers together, he insisted they were special cases. Even so, these women, he argued, were inferior to male prophets, as Paul had underscored when he insisted they must cover their heads while praying or prophesying in the church (4:326, referring to 1 Corinthians 11:5). Rather condescendingly, Bunyan averred that "none of our Women will pretend" to be prophetesses, thus rendering, in his mind, the scriptural examples of extraordinary women irrelevant as precedents for his own time (4:310). In his judgment, the essential gifts were rarely found in women (4:328).

Unlike the Midland and Abingdon associations, Bunyan concentrated on proscribing those things women could not do, including separate prayer meetings. In mixed assemblies they were not to pray aloud but were limited to approaching God in their hearts with inner groans and tears (4:303, 324). In such services they must cover their faces, be silent, and recognize that they have no authority to teach or even ask questions because they lack the ability provided to men by the Holy Spirit (4:304, 306, 325, 328–29). If women want to learn, they must ask their husbands at home, as Paul stipulates in 1 Corinthians 14:35, not meet together to teach one another (4:309). Women who think their separate gatherings for prayer have resulted in positive responses from God are to be pitied (4:320), and even praying aloud in church is something women are prohibited from doing: "I do not believe they should Minister to God in Prayer before the whole Church, for then I should be a Ranter or a Quaker" (4:305). Nor can women exercise any role in church government, as they did in Rogers' congregation (4:323).

In Bunyan's judgment, godly women "should be content to wear this *Power*, or badge of your inferiority, since the cause thereof, arose at first from your selves" (4:325). Owing to Eve's transgression every woman "must wear tokens of her *Underlingship* in all Matters of Worship" just as she must undergo the pain of childbirth. A woman's spiritual empowerment is the acceptance of her shame and inferiority (4:325). As Bunyan had taught in his commentary on Genesis, even before the fall Eve was inferior to Adam, whose headship in worship had been divinely created. Recognizing Eve's weakness, the serpent tempted her, causing the corruption of all humanity through her disobedience. This, averred Bunyan, is why Paul told Timothy that women must not teach or usurp authority over men in the church (4:306–7). Men are "the more noble part in all the Churches of Christ," manifestly superior in authority and ability, though he acknowledged that many women had exceeded men in their piety (4:295, 317). To permit women to have a voice in the church is dangerous because they are more prone to doctrinal error than are men (4:324).

In making his case Bunyan anticipated a hostile reaction from the women who had sent him Mr. K.'s manuscript. They would, he surmised, make him run the gauntlet, undergo verbal scourging, and face condemnation as an opponent of prayer and prayer meetings, yet he insisted he was seeking only to edify, not cause contention (4:296, 330). He certainly struck no blows on behalf of women, though he was undoubtedly sincere in his conviction that women who held gender-segregated prayer meetings were engaging in "*Will-Worship*" which contravened divine law (4:327). Their assemblages, he contended, shamed the churches to which they belonged by manifesting the latter's inability to govern female members (4:328). Respectability was not an irrelevant consideration, for he completed his pamphlet and took it to Benjamin Alsop for publication—probably in late September[14]—as people continued to hear about the conspiracies in which various nonconformists had allegedly been engaged. This was not a propitious time for some dissenting women to be claiming an expanded voice in the church, thereby reinforcing the notion that nonconformists were a threat to social stability. As Tamsin Spargo has argued, *A Case of Conscience Resolved* embodies "an implied recognition of the threat to existing power relations posed by women in the church, both to local structures and to an entire metaphysical framework,"[15]

---

[14]The work is entered in the Stationers' Register under the date 2 October 1683. Arber, *Transcript*, 2:197.

[15]Tamsin Spargo, *The Writing of John Bunyan* (Aldershot, Hants.: Ashgate, 1997), 78. Spargo notes that Bunyan was responding to the threat posed by women such as Margaret Fell. It is an intriguing suggestion, though I have found no firm evidence to support it other than the rough parallel between the women's meetings of the Quakers and the women's gatherings for prayer that concerned Bunyan.

and it was also an endeavor to dampen concerns of conservatives that nonconformity endangered social and political stability. Bunyan's emphasis on keeping women in their place contributed to the efforts of most dissenters to project an image of social respectability,[16] a theme he had already touched on in *A Holy Life*. Although he had other things he wanted to say about women, he postponed them for another occasion (4:330). The result may have been the second part of *The Pilgrim's Progress*.

## "Kiss the Rod"[17]: Survival and the Ethic of Suffering

In the months following disclosure of the plotting, the nonconformists experienced the full force of the Tory Reaction. Tim Harris has determined that nearly 4,000 different nonconformists were bound over, indicted, or convicted for attending conventicles in the London area in the 1680s. Many of them suffered more than once; moreover, this figure does not include those accused of recusancy or refusal to take the oaths of allegiance.[18] So numerous had prosecutions become by this time that magistrates in the London area were printing substantial numbers of forms with blanks to insert the offenders' names, the dates, and the places where the conventicles had met. Using only the Great Book of Sufferings, Craig Horle has counted 401 Quakers against whom legal action was undertaken for meeting in conventicles in London and Middlesex during 1683, up from five in 1682; the number would increase to 440 in 1684 before declining to 209 in 1685. The Middlesex grand jury urged justices of the peace to repress conventicles and compel people to attend services in the parish churches, and the justices, frustrated by constables who refused to perform their duty, imposed fines on the recalcitrant.[19] Among the London-area ministers accused of nonconformity in 1683 were the Congregationalist Stephen Lobb, the Baptists Laurence Wise, Thomas Plant, and Bunyan's former protagonist John Denne, and

---

[16] For the tendency among nonconformists to curb some of the religious activities of women during the Restoration era, see Robert B. Shoemaker, "Separate Spheres? Ideology and Practice in London Gender Relations, 1660–1740," in *Protestant Identities: Religion, Society, and Self-Fashioning in Post-Reformation England*, ed. Muriel C. McClendon, Joseph P. Ward, and Michael MacDonald (Stanford, CA: Stanford University Press, 1999), 273–74.

[17] *MW*, 10:35.

[18] Harris, *LC*, 66.

[19] LMA, MSS MJ/SBB/406, fols. 75–76; MJ/SBB/408, fols. 65–66; MJ/SBB/410, fols. 29, 56; *The Proceedings of His Majesties Justices of Peace, at the Sessions of Oyer and Terminer . . . September the 6th, 1684* (London, 1684).

the Presbyterians Samuel Annesley, Thomas Doelittle, William Jenkyn, Vincent Alsop, and John Humfrey. Sir John Shorter was also among the accused.[20]

Bunyan undoubtedly learned that some of his ministerial friends were in trouble, among them George Griffith, who was incarcerated in the autumn of 1683 and fined for illegal preaching in 1684 and 1685.[21] At the Middlesex sessions in December 1683 Meade was charged with recusancy and attending conventicles, and in October and November Cockayne was presented for having preached illegally.[22] In June of that year, Bunyan's former printer Francis Smith was tried at the Guildhall for having published *A Ra-ree Show*, found guilty, fined £500, and sentenced to the pillory at Westminster, the Temple, and the Royal Exchange, and the radical printer Henry Care was charged with recusancy in May 1683 and again in May 1684.[23] To relieve some of the dissenting ministers, the earl of Bedford and others gave money to Baxter to distribute as he deemed appropriate, but Baxter himself was accused of participating in a conventicle in July 1684.[24] When the Baptist schoolmaster and printer Thomas Delaune complained that the nonconformists' lives, liberties, and estates were being unjustly destroyed, he was imprisoned in Newgate, where he, his wife, and children subsequently died.[25] Among the other Baptists in legal difficulties in 1684 and early 1685 were Plant, Knollys, John Griffith, and John Belcher.[26] Such repression created concern that "the Hazzard of Our Liberty or Estate," in the words of Clarkson, might become "more dreaded, then the Hazzard of the Light of the Gospel."[27]

Substantial persecution occurred beyond the London area. In Norfolk the number of convicted nonconformists rose from 213 in 1680 to 666 in 1684, but

[20] LMA, MSS MR/RC/3, fols. 230–32, 237–39; MR/RC/5, fol. 2; MR/RC/6, fols. 27, 34, 62; GL, MS 9060, fols. 26r, 50v, 74r; CLRO, Conventicle Box 2, no. 6.

[21] LMA, MS MJ/SBB/408, fol. 72; CLRO, Conventicle Box 1, no. 3; *New DNB, s.v.; Calamy Revised, s.v.*

[22] LMA, MSS MR/RC/3, fols. 191–95; MJ/SBB/409, fol. 46; Morrice, 1:407; *New DNB, s.v.* Matthew Meade; CLRO, Conventicle Box 1, no. 3.

[23] Bodl., Carte MSS 72, fol. 532r; GL, MS 9060, fols. 97r, 108v; Luttrell, 1:309, 311.

[24] Baxter, *Calendar*, 2:257–58; Bodl., Rawlinson Letters 109, fol. 8r; CLRO, Conventicle Box 2, no. 2.

[25] [Thomas Delaune], *A Plea for the Non-Conformists, Giving the True State of the Dissenters Case* (London, 1684), 11; Keeble, *LCN*, 101. In the same year Delaune published another provocative work, *The Image of the Beast* (1684), in which he compared the Catholic church to the "pagan" religion of the Roman Empire, and identified the dissenters as the true Christian church. The Church of England was not mentioned, leaving readers to associate it with Catholicism.

[26] CLRO, Conventicle Box 1, no. 3; Conventicle Box 2, no. 2.

[27] DWL, MSS L6/4, sermon of Clarkson on 2 Thessalonians 3:1 (21 October 1683).

the percentage of those who were Catholic dropped from 20 in 1680 to 6.5 in 1684, down from 61 percent in 1677.[28] Judging from incomplete records, Bunyan's congregation was apparently not hit hard at the summer sessions in 1683, although several of his former fellow prisoners, John Wright and George Farr of Blunham, were accused of recusancy at the Bedfordshire sessions.[29] In the county as a whole, however, the number of presentments for recusancy dramatically increased, exceeding 200 in the summer of 1683 and again in the winter of 1684, and remaining nearly as high in the summer of 1684 and the winter of 1685.[30] In 1684 the constables struck much harder at the Bedford church, citing, among others, Bunyan's brother Thomas in both the winter and summer sessions.[31] Among the victims of the repression was Francis Holcroft, a Congregationalist minister in Cambridge who had preached to the Bedford church in the early 1660s; arrested on 28 June 1683, he was fined £140 for recusancy and imprisoned in the Fleet.[32] "The Root of all our Grievances is conventicles," proclaimed the *Observator* in July, but in *The Nonconformist's Vindication: or, Mr. Furguson's Fault No General Crime* (1683), an anonymous author protested against the punishment of dissenting clergy who had nothing to do with the plotting. As arrests mounted and meetinghouses were closed, fear gripped many nonconformists.[33] Zealous royalists destroyed pulpits and seats in the meetinghouses at Lyme Regis and Bridport, Dorset, in July, and magistrates at Taunton, Somerset, wreaked substantial damage in two meetinghouses, burning the doors, seats, pulpits, and galleries in the town marketplace.[34] The bishop of Gloucester reported in early September that conventicles in his diocese had generally been suppressed, and by the following

---

[28] Craig W. Horle, *The Quakers and the English Legal System, 1660–1688* (Philadelphia: University of Pennsylvania Press, 1988), 284; John Miller, *Popery and Politics in England, 1660–1688* (Cambridge: Cambridge University Press, 1973), 191.

[29] BLA, MSS HSA 1683 S/8, 10. From Bunyan's congregation William Man was presented. Two others may have been members of his church, viz. Edward Sutton of Northill (if he is the Brother Sutton in the church book) and Thomas Langley of Wilshamstead, who was charged for permitting a conventicle to meet in his house. MS HSA 1683 S/12.

[30] BLA, MSS HSA 1683 S/9–17, 27–29; 1684 W/13–30; 1684 S/9–11, 13–18, 44, 58; 1685 W/20–23.

[31] BLA, MSS HSA 1684 W/28–30; HSA 1684 S/16–18, 58. In addition to Thomas Bunyan, the members who were presented included William Man, Oliver Scott, Widow Cooper, John Spenser, and (in winter only) Robert Disher. At the winter sessions Thomas Langley was again charged with holding a conventicle in his house at Wilshamstead. HSA 1684 W/27, 56.

[32] PRO, SP 29/436/83; *CB*, 38. For Holcroft see Greaves, *JBEN*, 90–96; *Calamy Revised, s.v.*

[33] *Observator* 377 (19 July 1683); PRO, SP 29/425/63; 29/429/30, 139.

[34] Bodl., Tanner MSS 34, fol. 81 (75)v; PRO, SP 29/427/117; 29/428/177; 29/430/96.

spring the Presbyterian Joseph Boyse had received word in Dublin that most nonconformist meetinghouses in England were no longer in use.[35]

In this atmosphere many Tory-Anglicans denounced the nonconformists. Narcissus Luttrell noted in his diary that on 9 September 1683, the official day of thanksgiving for Charles' deliverance from the plots, some preachers "were violent against the dissenters."[36] Although magistrates at Taunton could not prevent nonconformists from meeting in private homes, the mayor, Stephen Timewell, gloated that he had "fought with Thousands of the beasts of Ephesus & . . . overcome them."[37] The parson at Greystoke, Cumberland, was probably typical of most conformist ministers in condemning dissenters for putting "a public affront upon the Lawes" by their conventicles and implying that the liturgy was unfit by their recusancy.[38] Dissenters, averred the author of a newsletter in March 1684, are "ill weeds, and if any of them be left, will in their own time spring out and poison the land."[39] Kennet belittled them by making nonconformists the butt of sarcastic humor: "The reason why Conventicle[r]s sitt with their hats on one side of their head, because what comes at one ear should not goe out of t'other."[40] At the quarter sessions in Exeter on 2 October 1683 the justices of the peace not only ordered a more rigorous enforcement of the laws against nonconformists but also offered a reward of 40s. for every dissenting preacher who was arrested. These justices were typical of many in believing that "the Nonconformist Preachers are the Authors and Fomenters of this Pestilent Faction, and the implacable Enemies of the Established Government, and to whom the late Execrable Treasons . . . are principally to be imputed." In Bedfordshire the grand jury held a similar view, promising the king on 7 November 1683 that it would present all conventiclers as well as members of "Clubs and Cabals . . . whose Religion or Loyalty is much and justly to be doubted."[41] The bishop of Lincoln, Thomas Barlow, whose diocese included Bedfordshire, felt it necessary in May 1684 to defend himself against a charge of having accorded excessive favor to nonconformists. With some exaggeration, he informed Archbishop Sancroft that he had always encouraged his officials to execute the laws against dissenters, and he recounted how he had told nonconformists who complained to him of persecution that they were being

---

[35] Bodl., Tanner MSS 34, fol. 130 (125)r; *Letters of Eminent Men, Addressed to Ralph Thoresby, F.R.S.*, 2 vols. (London: Henry Colburn and Richard Bentley, 1832), 1:54.

[36] Luttrell, 1:279.

[37] PRO, SP 29/430/37; 29/431/81; 29/432/89 (quoted); 29/433/78.

[38] PRO, SP 29/432/76.

[39] *HMC 36, Ormonde*, n.s., 7:203.

[40] BL, Lansdowne MSS 937, fol. 46v.

[41] DWL, MS 31.J, entry 1691.2; *Ad General. Quarterial. Session. Pacis Dom. Regis tent. apud Castr. Exon.* (London, 1683) (quoted); London *Gazette* 1875 (5–8 November 1683).

justly punished for their seditious and rebellious behavior, including their sepa-ration from the Church of England.[42] Bunyan himself was now the target of mag-istrates who *"often searched and laid wait for him, and sometimes narrowly miss'd him,"* according to Charles Doe.[43]

Bunyan forcefully distanced himself from the plotting and more fully articu-lated his ethic of suffering in *Seasonable Counsel: or, Advice to Sufferers*, published by Alsop in 1684. He very likely wrote this book between October 1683 and Janu-ary 1684 following the completion of *A Case of Conscience Resolved*. *Seasonable Counsel* had a tripartite purpose: to assert his innocence of any complicity in trea-sonable activity, to urge nonconformists to eschew opposition to the govern-ment, even verbally, and to provide an ethic of suffering to sustain the godly no matter how fierce the persecution. He was sensitive to the fact that his manu-script might be read by government agents investigating the conspiracies: "Be-cause I appear thus in publick, and know not into whose hands these lines may come, therefore thus I write" (*MW*, 10:40). This was said with respect to his effu-sive professions of loyalty, an outpouring intended to distance him from the con-spirators and other harsh critics of the Stuarts. He was not alone in doing so. In *The Loyal Baptist: or an Apology for the Baptized Believers* (1684) the General Bap-tist Thomas Grantham noted that many had ruined themselves by seeking changes in secular government and stressed the duty of Christians to obey mag-istrates, "knowing how impossible it would be to propagate the Profession of Christianity, if Christians did not adorn their Profession with a meek and harm-less Conversation towards all Men, and especially by their Obedience to those in Authority." Armed resistance was out of the question, even if rulers violated the rights of their subjects or ordered things that contravened God's will.[44] In Taun-ton, which an under-sheriff deemed one of the most disloyal, factious towns in the kingdom, prominent Whigs publicly testified of their allegiance to the crown, and the townsfolk held festivities in September that featured toasts to Charles II and the royal family.[45]

Several of Bunyan's statements suggest caution in taking his strong profes-sions of support for the crown at face value. If interpreted literally, they almost

[42] Bodl., Tanner MSS 32, fol. 54r–v. To some extent Barlow was vulnerable to criticism because of his friendship with Essex and Anglesey in the years prior to the disclosure of the Monmouth conspiracy. Inner Temple Library, Petyt MSS 538, fols. 293r, 298r; BL, Add. MSS 18,730, fols. 28v, 34v, 80r, 101v. He also had ties to Wharton. Bodl., Rawlinson Letters 52, fol. 244r.

[43] *MW*, 12:454.

[44] Thomas Grantham, *The Loyal Baptist: or an Apology for the Baptized Believers* (London, 1684), sig. A3r (quoted), 35–36, 39.

[45] PRO, SP 29/432/54.

amount to a *volte-face* from the criticism of the regime in *The Holy War*, the treatise on Antichrist, and the commentary on Genesis. The quotation by him in the preceding paragraph reveals his need to explain why he was now so keenly supporting the government. The phrase "thus I write" suggests a deliberate fashioning of his language to avoid problems with the authorities during the far-flung investigation of the plotting. Moreover, he explicitly stated that he knew no one engaged in any conspiratorial activity, and his denial was immediately preceded by a statement that clearly referred to the Rye House and Monmouth cabals:

> The Devil . . . can send forth such Spirits into the World as shall not only disturb Men, but Nations, Kings, and Kingdoms, in raising divisions, distractions and rebellions. And can so manage matters, that the looser sort of Christians may also be dipt, and concerned therein.

He followed this statement with a reference to 2 Samuel 15:10–11, which explains how 200 men from Jerusalem followed Absalom *"in their simplicity, not knowing any thing,"* as he rebelled against his father (10:32). Monmouth, of course, was now widely seen as the modern-day Absalom. Bunyan's selection of this passage is notable because it virtually exonerated Absalom's (Monmouth's) supporters as simple-minded men unaware of what they were undertaking. Especially revealing is Bunyan's ensuing claim, "I know of no such men, nor thing" (10:32), an assertion he subsequently reiterated: "I speak not these things, as knowing any that are disaffected to the Government" (10:40). As we have seen, this was simply untrue, for he was acquainted with the Rye House plotter Robert Blaney and Matthew Meade, who very likely knew something about the planning of the Monmouth group, as well as John Owen and George Griffith, who were apparently aware, without necessarily approving, that Monmouth and his allies were considering armed intervention. He must have known the conspirator Robert Ferguson during the latter's service as Owen's assistant and possibly later, and he probably was acquainted with Stephen Lobb, who was linked to the plotting. Twice his former printer Francis Smith had been arrested for treason in 1681,[46] and the government ordered the apprehension of Newman and Alsop in July 1683 during the investigation of the two conspiracies.[47] He also knew Danvers, who had a long record of dissident activity.

---

[46] The first arrest occurred in April. *CSPD, 1680–81*, 137; Morrice, 1:295; London *Gazette* 1608 (14–18 April 1681). He was rearrested in November 1681 and found guilty of misdemeanor and libel for having once again printed the *Speech Lately Made by a Noble Peer*. PRO, SP 29/417/83; Morrice, 1:317; *CSPD, 1680–81*, 564; London *Gazette* 1668 (10–14 November 1681).

[47] Another former Bunyan printer, George Larkin, was a marked man for having printed an exclusionist newspaper for Richard Janeway, but by June 1683 he was cooperating with the government. PRO, SP 29/419/8; 29/424/151.

By his denials Bunyan may have meant only that he knew nothing of the alleged involvement of these men in conspiratorial activities, though his selection of words does not support such an interpretation. He may have made the statements to protect himself and assist the accused, hoping not to be interrogated about them, or he may have thought of these men as the counterpart to the 200 simple folk misled by Absalom. Had he admitted knowing that leading Whigs were pondering some form of armed endeavor, or even that some of his ministerial colleagues had known as much, he would have been subject to arrest and pressure to testify against his fellow pastors and Blaney. Bunyan was thus in the difficult position of having to choose between absolute honesty and possibly the lives of his dissenting friends.

His denunciation of the plotting was uncompromising, but a close reading indicates a measure of understanding for the alleged perpetrators. He likened the would-be assassins to David's companion Abishai, who would have killed Saul while he slept had David approved. In Bunyan's judgment Abishai was a good man who would have assassinated the king as a matter of conscience and out of love for David, but such an act could have resulted in "publick justice and shame." Had David reported the incident to Saul, Bunyan reflected, Abishai would likely have been executed as a traitor (10:32, referring to 1 Samuel 26:7–8). However, David did not divulge Abishai's willingness to commit the crime but retained him in his service, as biblically literate readers would have known. Bunyan also cited the example of Peter, who drew his sword to defend Jesus, but was instructed to sheath it instead (10:32, referring to Matthew 26:51–52). Both cases— and the contemporary ones—elicited a degree of understanding: "Oppression makes a wise man mad; and when a man is mad, what evils will he not do?" (10:32).[48] Nevertheless, the conspirators had brought reproach on Christ and the Christian faith, and for this Bunyan chastised them. In an apparent reference to the alleged suicide of Monmouth's ally, the earl of Essex, as he awaited trial, Bunyan averred that "the guilt and shame that evil actions will load the conscience with at such a time, can hardly be stood under" (10:33).[49] As the plotters faced their deaths on the scaffold, Bunyan surmised that the conscience of each man was plagued with guilt for what he had done. "His *cause* will not bear him out, his heart will be clogged with guilt, innocency and boldness will take wings and fly

[48] See the thoughtful analysis of Sharon Achinstein, "Honey from the Lion's Carcass: Bunyan, Allegory, and the Samsonian Moment," in *Awakening Words*, 74–75.

[49] Essex was probably murdered by Major Webster and John Holland at the behest of James, duke of York, and Robert Spencer, earl of Sunderland. However, the government pronounced his death a suicide, a verdict Bunyan apparently believed. Greaves, *SOK*, 219–29.

from him." The conspirators might talk about religion on the scaffold, but Bunyan, undoubtedly reflecting his own feelings, thought the godly would be embarrassed to hear evil-doers speak in such fashion (10:33, 104). He may have been thinking of Lord Russell's scaffold speech, in which he wished that all sincere Protestants would love one another, or that of the Baptist Thomas Walcott, Shaftesbury's ally, who professed he would "die religiously."[50] Although Bunyan thought such men could be pitied, he was more concerned that "a thing so much unbecoming Christianity, should be suffered to shew the least part of it self among any of those that profess the Gospel" (10:38). In contrast, Griffith offered solace to Lady Rachel Russell, assuring her that whatever her husband had done, "he did it faithfully as unto god, and upon that beleif [you] may safely ground a hope he was lifted from a prison to a throne."[51]

The counsel Bunyan provided his readers now focused on nearly total obedience to the state. Monarchs and magistrates, he explained, are divinely appointed ministers who are not only ordained but governed by God, and Christians must therefore render themselves subject to secular rulers (10:32, 34, 39). He exhorted the godly to pray for everyone in authority, mind their own business while leaving magistrates free to do their work, and refrain from criticizing their actions (10:5, 33, 35–36, 38). No disdainful language must be used about those in authority, nor must the saints make jokes about them. "Take heed of being offended with Magistrates, because by their State-Acts they may cross thy inclinations." Subjects who do not approve of what their rulers do must meekly and patiently suffer. "Discontent in the mind, sometimes puts discontent into the mouth; and discontent in the mouth, doth sometimes also put a halter about the neck" (10:39). To quarrel with superiors is the hallmark of a captive of one's passions and prejudice rather than their master (10:103). Because God as the supreme governor manages the world's affairs for the church's ultimate benefit, Christians must not interfere with the work of monarchs and magistrates: "If the work that these men do, is that which God will promote and set up for ever, then you cannot disannul it." Rulers will fall only at the time appointed by God, and it is not appropriate for Christians to wish for their destruction, even if monarchs and magistrates are persecutors. Subjects who profess to act against the government in the name of justice, the gospel, or the suppression of wickedness are motivated by "a preposterous zeal" or such factors as anger, a desire to preserve estates and finances, or impatience under the cross (10:99–100). The Christian, Bunyan averred, must practice self-denial, not "*self-revenge*" (10:103). In articulating this

[50] *Cobbett's Complete Collection of State Trials and Proceedings*, ed. W. Cobbett, T. B. Howell, *et al.*, 34 vols. (London: R. Bagshaw, 1809–28), 9:674 (quoted), 683.

[51] BL, Add. MSS 19,399, fol. 132r–v (Lady Russell quoting Griffith's letter to her).

position he placed himself at odds with those, such as Samuel Johnson, Lord Russell's chaplain, who argued that passive obedience was tantamount to "Popery established," for "as soon as ever a Popish Successor shall give the Word, Popery is as surely established by the Imperial Laws [i.e., the royal prerogative], as it can be by ten thousand Political Acts of Parliament. . . . We may be driven to *Smithfield* by Droves, and be piled up, and burnt, like Loads of Faggots."[52]

The submission Bunyan advocated was only possible if believers embraced an ethic of suffering. Nonconformists generally espoused such an ethic, though he was unusual in the fulness of his exposition. Dissenters typically agreed that the godly must suffer in return for spiritual benefits such as a greater infusion of grace, a manifestation of divine love and election, means to increase humility and holy living, and an enhanced sense of Christ's presence. Nonconformists believed suffering should be willingly undergone with patience, humility, and cheerfulness, for it is a badge of the saint and evidence of one's faithfulness, not an indication that God has abandoned the elect. To suffer is to follow in the steps of Jesus, accepting the necessity of tribulation as a precondition to reigning with Christ.[53]

In most respects, Bunyan's ethic of suffering harmonized with that of other nonconformists. The Christian does not suffer by chance or human will but divine appointment; God determines who will suffer, as well as when, where, at whose hands, and for how long (10:67–70).[54] "It is not what enemies will, nor what they are resolved upon, but what God will, and what God appoints, that shall be done" (10:66). The tribulations of the godly are recorded in "Gods Book," though in characters seemingly unreadable to them (10:68). For those called to undergo affliction, it is a duty (10:11–12). Although Bunyan believed it was "the will of God that they that go to heaven should go thither hardly or with difficulty," he exempted some Christians from the necessity of the most grievous suffering by making it a special badge of honor (10:73). Not all saints, he argued, are deemed worthy to suffer for Christ's cause (10:72), yet undergoing persecution is necessary both for the soul's health and to demonstrate faith and patience.

---

[52] [Samuel Johnson], *Julian the Apostate: Being a Short Account of His Life* (London, 1682), vi–vii.

[53] Greaves, *JBEN*, 177–79; Keeble, *LCN*, 190–91.

[54] Others made the same point. The Presbyterian John Angier, for example, asserted that "the evil of affliction cannot befall the Christian unless God be the principal agent." Oliver Heywood, *Life of John Angier of Denton: Together with Angier's Diary*, ed. Ernest Axon, Publications of the Chetham Society, n.s., vol. 97 (Manchester, 1937), 131. See also Thomas Watson, *A Divine Cordial* (London, 1663), 35, 39; sermons of Thomas Jollie, BL, Add. MSS 54,185, fol. 42v; and [Thomas Goodwin], *Patience and Its Perfect Work, Under Sudden & Sore Tryals* (London, 1666), 91.

Because affliction is preferable to sin, the suffering saint should thank the persecutor and "*pay the messenger*" (10:6–7).[55]

On the enigmatic question of whether to confront or flee from persecution,
Bunyan left the decision to each believer, who must act in accord with conscience
(10:73). "A man, though his *cause* be good, ought not by undue ways to run himself into suffering for it," a course contrary to nature and divine law (10:50). The
latter, Bunyan insisted, does not require the believer to put himself "into the
mouth of his enemy," for on occasion both Jesus and Paul escaped magistrates.
Acceptable suffering requires a divine call. To flee because of slavish fear, to escape physical punishment, to preserve material possessions, or to deny the gospel
is wrong, yet in appropriate circumstances flight is "an ordinance of God, opening a door for the escape of some" by providence. A minister can elude a magistrate to preach elsewhere, yet when suffering is divinely ordained, no Christian
can escape. Those who try to flee and are caught should laugh, realizing that "the
scales are still in Gods hand" (10:74). A more mellow Bunyan was less willing to
seek a confrontation than he had been when he courted arrest at Lower Samsell
in 1660. As he neared his fifty-sixth birthday, he was "*not for running my self into
sufferings*" (10:8). He would endure affliction rather than relinquish his right to
preach and worship as his conscience dictated, and he would do this as a duty,
but he refused to sanction reckless bravado. This explains why he now eluded arrest when magistrates were looking for him.[56]

Like other dissenters, Bunyan extolled the benefits of suffering, the "*bitter
pills*" of which purge the saints of impurities. "*I still have need of these Tryals*," he
remarked in a personal aside (10:6). Despite having spent more time in prison
than almost any other nonconformist, he could still attest that God can make a
jail more beautiful than a palace by the honeyed sweetness of his word and the
glory of his presence; yet he knew from experience that prison could appear "as
black as *Hell*" without divine assistance (10:17, 21, 23). Suffering is a manifestation
of God's love, not wrath, a point Luther had tellingly made in his commentary on
Galatians: "When the cross is abolished, and the rage of tyrants and heretics
ceaseth on the one side, and all things are in peace, the devil keeping the entry of
the house, this is a sure token that the pure doctrine of God's word is taken

---

[55] The Presbyterian George Swinnock also described affliction as a messenger. *The
Christian Man's Calling*, pt. 2 (London, 1663), 364. I have adapted this paragraph and the
four that follow from my *JBEN*, 180–82.

[56] *MW*, 12:454 (quoted above). For similar views on whether to flee persecution see
Vavasor Powell, *The Bird in the Cage, Chirping* (London, 1661), 38–39; R[ichard] A[lleine],
*Heaven Opened* (London, 1666), 52–53; Philip Henry, CUL, Add. MSS 7338, commenting
on Genesis 8.

away."[57] Through tribulation, Bunyan explained, spiritual graces are experienced in greater intensity; there is, for instance, "*a rejoycing in hope, when we are in tribulation, that is, over and above that which we have when we are at ease and quiet*" (10:6, 96–97). "Righteousness thriveth best in affliction, the more afflicted, the more holy man; the more persecuted, the more shining man" (10:61), a point also made by Philip Henry.[58] Bunyan intended to make suffering less forbidding in the hope of decreasing the likelihood that those who experienced it would react violently to their persecutors (10:96), and he especially wanted nonconformists to avoid the impression that they would persecute others if they attained power: "What will men say, if you *shrink* and *whinch*, and take your sufferings unquietly: but that if you your selves were uppermost, you would persecute also? . . . Be quiet then," and turn the other cheek (10:102).

Bunyan distinguished himself from most other nonconformists by the rigid conditions he imposed for efficacious suffering. It must not be undertaken to seek approval from others, for fear of reproach, or because of a dislike of the persecutors and a "scorn to submit" (10:57). The cause must be worthy or suffering is meaningless; by a good cause he meant morality (for which tribulation is rare) or evangelical righteousness and worship (10:43–44). Suffering must be "not only for *truth*, but of love to truth; not only *for* God's word, but *according* to it: to wit in that holy, humble, meek manner as the word of God requireth" (10:30). This ruled out any recognition of the executed Rye House plotters as martyrs; they may have acted in defense of God's word, but not, in Bunyan's judgment, in the manner it stipulated, and under these circumstances magistrates were justified in holding them accountable for their actions (10:31).

Enduring meekly, patiently, quietly, and in a biblical manner is only part of a Christian's duty, for the saint is also expected to suffer *willingly*. Bunyan distinguished between passive tribulation, as inflicted on the murdered children of Ireland, France, and Piedmont because of their parents' religion, and active suffering, which requires the victim's approval. Because active suffering necessitates the consent of the will, the believer must kiss the chastising rod and love it, knowing that tribulation is divinely imposed (10:35, 41–42). In effect, suffering is a fundamental aspect of worship, and as any reader of Foxe's *Acts and Monuments* knew, it is also a telling pedagogical act. With his flair for the dramatic, Bunyan expressed it thus: "A man when he suffereth for Christ, is set upon an *Hill*, upon a *Stage*, as in a *Theatre*, to play a part for God in the World" (10:62).

As he expounded on this ethic of suffering, Bunyan was again reading *Acts and Monuments*. In broad terms, the idea that the saints are a suffering people

[57] Luther, *Galatians*, 477.
[58] CUL, Add. MSS 7338, commenting on Genesis 41.

whose tribulations are divinely ordered to test and fortify them is a cardinal theme of Foxe. Bunyan recounted the deaths of Thomas Haukes, a gentleman burned at Coggeshall, Essex, on 10 June 1555, and James Bainham, a lawyer burned at Newgate in 1532, as proof that God can make the intense heat of the flames bearable (10:22), and the case of Dr. Rowland Taylor, minister of Hadleigh, Suffolk, as evidence that God can empower martyrs to dance in joy as they approach their deaths and anticipate entry into heaven (10:81). The martyr-dom of Richard Atkins of Hertfordshire, who traveled to Rome in 1581 to testify against the city's wickedness, was retold by Bunyan as an example of one who had received an extraordinary call from God to suffer for righteousness (10:55). Bunyan's deep aversion to apostates prompted him to warn believers that re-canting, even in the face of the severest persecution, betrays their souls, their profession of faith, and their cause, but he cited the cases of Peter, Origen, Jerome of Prague, Thomas Cranmer, James Bainham, and Cicely Ormis of East Dereham, Norfolk, as examples of Christians who briefly recanted before reaf-firming their faith and becoming martyrs (10:63–64). He referred his readers to the *Acts and Monuments* for examples of martyrs who died variously for "the Godhead," Christ's manhood, the ordinances (sacraments), and their fellow be-lievers (10:69). He also buttressed his discussion of affliction with historical refer-ences, twice referring to massacres in Ireland, Paris, and Piedmont (10:25, 41), and more generally to the lengthy history of persecution in France, Spain, Germany, and Italy (10:48). Two emperors are mentioned: "that Lyon *Nero*," who examined Paul, and Julian the Apostate (10:24, 102).[59]

In *Seasonable Counsel* Bunyan drew the line between suffering and obedience to the state at the point where the latter prescribed worship that was not wholly in accord with New Testament principles. In keeping with the stand he took in 1660–61, he would not compromise on this issue, which continued to leave him firmly opposed to the Church of England even as he now stressed obedience to the monarch and his magistrates. Bunyan thought most of the godly who suffered did so because they refused to act in such a fashion "that sin should cleave to the worship of God," and he urged them to persevere in divinely instituted worship whatever the cost (10:28, 56). His synopsis of the argument against conformity in *adiaphora* applied equally to Catholicism and the Church of England, once again damning the latter by associating it with the former:

> Carnal men . . . much delighted in the notion of things . . . will first, count [Christ's] Testament, though good, a thing *defective*, and not of fulness sufficient to give in all particular things, direction how they should to their own content, perform their glo-rious Doctrine. For *here*, and *there*, and in *another* place, cry they, there is something

---

[59] Both emperors are discussed by Foxe, *Acts and Monuments*, 1:91, 100–104, 176, 286–87.

> wanting. Here, say they, is nothing said of those *places, vestures, gestures,* shews, and outward greatness that we think seemly to be found in, and with those that worship Jesus. Here wants sumptuous ceremonies, glorious ornaments, new fashion'd carriages, all which are necessary to adorn worship withall. (10:47–48)

Such *adiaphora,* Bunyan insisted, derive from human institution, and their advocates have no legitimate authority to impose them on the godly (10:48).

The saints must resist any attempt to force them to embrace such forms of worship, Bunyan's exhortations to obey rulers notwithstanding. The kind of resistance he envisioned was exemplified by Daniel, Esther's cousin Mordecai, and the three men in the lion's den, Shadrach, Meshach, and Abednego, but he also cited David's willingness to confront Goliath (10:37, 51–52). Although David engaged in physical combat, Bunyan now argued against the use of any weapons other than Scripture, faith, and prayer—the Christian's artillery. Rather than employ physical weapons to resist persecution, the godly must seek the graces of the Spirit that will enable them to withstand the ordeal (10:96–97). In pressing them to resist "*unto blood,*" he meant the shedding of their own blood, not violence against their oppressors (10:56). Nor did resisting unto blood entail "striving to deliver our selves from the affliction," but instead a refusal to engage in unacceptable worship regardless of the penalties (10:34).

Although Bunyan was unalterably opposed to the worship of the Church of England and was prepared to die rather than accept it, he insisted, with an eye on the government, that the principles of Christianity are innocuous. "Christianity is so harmless a thing, that be it never so openly professed, it hurts no man," including rulers (10:51). For this to be so, Christians must embrace only non-maleficent principles and not meddle in the business of others (10:5). Although Christ has made each Christian a monarch according to Revelation 5:10, each person's dominion extends only over himself or herself, and the weapons at the believer's disposal are not carnal but spiritual. To those who might have been considering militant action against the Stuart regime, Bunyan offered forthright advice:

> Let him bring down, if he must be bringing down, his own high imaginations. . . . If he must be a Warrior, let him *levy* War against his own unruly passions. . . . If thou wilt needs be a Ruler, thou hast a tongue, rule that; Lusts, rule them; Affections, govern them. (10:34)

In a gesture of peace toward the regime, Bunyan indicated that he was amazed at Charles II's favor toward his subjects (10:35), a sentiment at odds with his mostly veiled but harsh criticism of the Stuart regime in *The Holy War,* the treatise on Antichrist, and the commentary on Genesis. Sensitive to critics who tarred nonconformists with the brush of treason in the aftermath of the plotting, Bunyan countered by observing that enemies of the gospel had perverted the words of Jesus and Luther, adjudging them seditious and against both God and Caesar (10:45). Like other innocent nonconformists he could say, "I am counted a *Rebel*, and yet am *Loyal*" (10:75). He was also considerably more restrained in his attitude toward the government than he had been before the conspiracies were revealed.

### "*To Friends, Not Foes*"[60]: A Return to *The Pilgrim's Progress*

In concluding *A Case of Conscience Resolved* Bunyan indicated he had more to say about women, and this may have been a motive for his decision to write a second part of *The Pilgrim's Progress*. Income too may have been a factor for him or Ponder, for the first part was a publishing success, having won acclaim, according to Bunyan, in France, Flanders, the Netherlands, and New England, and among Scottish Highlanders and "Wild-Irish" (*PP*, 169). In 1681 Thomas Sherman commented on its "Universal esteem and commendation."[61] The first Dutch edition was issued by Johannes Boekholt in 1682 and reached a fifth edition in 1687.[62] Pirated editions in English were a problem as early as 1680, causing Ponder to complain in the fourth edition (1680) about "*Land Pirates*," including the printer Thomas Braddyl. In the epistle to the second part Bunyan protested against the imitations that had begun to appear:

> 'Tis true, some have of late, to Counterfeit
> My *Pilgrim*, to their own, my Title set;
> Yea others, half my Name and Title too. (168)

Among such works was Sherman's *The Second Part of the Pilgrim's Progress, from This Present World of Wicke[d]ness and Misery, to an Eternity of Holiness and Fidelity* (1682), which professed to correct four major defects in Bunyan's allegory: an absence of commentary on the state of humanity before the fall; the lack of an appropriate discussion of humankind's misery in its lapsed state; insufficient attention to the methods of grace in convincing, converting, and reconciling sinners; and inadequate use of serious, spiritual language.[63] John Dunton, who is-

---

[60] *PP*, 171.

[61] T[homas] S[herman], *The Second Part of the Pilgrim's Progress, from This Present World of Wicke[d]ness and Misery, to an Eternity of Holiness and Fidelity* (London, 1682), sig. A7v.

[62] J. B. H. Alblas, *Johannes Boekholt (1656–1693): The First Dutch Publisher of John Bunyan and Other English Authors* (Nieuwkoop: De Graaf Publishers, 1987), 85–88.

[63] Sherman, *Second Part*, sigs. A7v-A8r. Published by Thomas Malthus, Sherman's work actually appeared in 1683; it is listed in the Stationers' Register with the date 12 May 1683, and

sued Sherman's work, also published Keach's *The Travels of True Godliness* in the spring of 1683 and *The Progress of Sin; or the Travels of Ungodliness,* which was roughly comparable to *The Life and Death of Mr. Badman,* Bunyan's intended sequel to his own allegory, a year later.[64] Dunton published his own imitative works, *The Pilgrim's Guide from the Cradle to His Death-Bed,* in the spring of 1684,[65] and *An Hue and Cry after Conscience: or the Pilgrim's Progress by Candle-Light* the following year. In 1684 Thomas Passinger issued an unauthorized twenty-two-page abridgement of the first part of Bunyan's *Pilgrim's Progress,* and numerous other derivative works followed.[66]

Bunyan likely wrote the second part between February and early October 1684. It is listed in the Stationers' Register for 22 November 1684, though the Term Catalogues advertised it in June of the same year.[67] In an apparent attempt to head off sales of imitations, Ponder must have advertised the sequel in June, perhaps expecting the manuscript well before Bunyan was ready to submit it. In any event, Ponder did not have copies to sell until January 1685, for the reverse of the title-page carries this statement: "I appoint Mr. *Nathaniel* Ponder, But no other to Print this Book. *John Bunyan.* January 1. 1684 [i.e., 1685]" (*PP,* xcix).[68]

For the second part Bunyan's intended audience comprised "*Friends, not foes*" (171), a point he made in the opening lines of the preface:

> *Go, now my little Book, to every place,*
> *Where my first* Pilgrim *has but shewn his Face.* (167)

He expected readers of the sequel to have read *The Pilgrim's Progress,* and with that in mind he regularly reminded them of Christian's adventures. Christiana

---

in the Term Catalogues in June 1683. A second edition is listed in the latter in November 1683 and May 1684. Arber, *Transcript,* 3:154; Arber, *Term Catalogues,* 2:26, 55–56, 78.

[64] *The Travels of True Godliness* appears in the Stationers' Register under the date 12 June 1683. Arber, *Transcript,* 3:162. A sixth edition was published in 1684. The epistle to *The Progress of Sin* was dated 28 April 1684.

[65] Dunton's allegory is listed in the Stationers' Register under 12 June 1684. Arber, *Transcript,* 3:242. It was dedicated in part to a Mrs. Mead of St. Mary's parish, Bedford (*op. cit.,* sig. A2r). Albert B. Cook, III, has argued that Bunyan's complaint was most likely directed at Dunton. "John Bunyan and John Dunton: A Case of Plagiarism," *Papers of the Bibliographical Society of America* 71 (1977): 11–28.

[66] See the Epilogue and the discussion by Susan Cook, "Pilgrims' Progresses: Derivative Texts and the Seventeenth-Century Reader," in *Awakening Words,* ed. Gay, Randall, and Zinck, 186–201. For Passinger see Plomer, *DBP,* 145.

[67] Arber, *Transcript,* 3:262; Arber, *Term Catalogues,* 2:90. The Term Catalogues published trade announcements and were an early form of advertising. Philip Gaskell, *A New Introduction to Bibliography* (Oxford: Clarendon Press, 1972), 182–83.

[68] Mullett, *JBC,* 111, erroneously dates the publication of the second part in 1683.

and her four sons are routinely identified in relationship to Christian, and her experiences at the major sites during the pilgrimage are compared to his. The second part is the only one of Bunyan's books that cannot stand on its own, and he never intended that it should do so. Convinced that more can be learned from the pilgrimage theme, he has Christiana and her fellow pilgrims visit most of the places her husband had been, but many of their experiences are substantially different for a variety of reasons: disparate personalities, divergences in age and gender, the presence of a powerful pastoral guide (Great-heart) in the second part, and a general shift in *emphasis* from the heroic individual to the communal. The dissimilarities notwithstanding, "the correspondence of details" between the first and second parts underscores "the universality of Christian's experience."[69] Bunyan used the second part to explore both the universal nature of the fundamental Christian experience, as he defined it, and the richness of individual responses to the challenges and opportunities presented to pilgrims.[70]

As the second part unfolds, Bunyan piques the reader's interest by revisiting nearly all the familiar places made memorable by Christian's pilgrimage, but varying the responses of Christiana and her companions. The dominant question in part two is not whether Christiana's party will reach the Celestial City but how they will react to the assorted challenges and opportunities, and the form those challenges and opportunities take. In part two the by-paths of formality and hypocrisy have been blocked with chains, posts, and a ditch, making it much more difficult for wayward pilgrims to mistake them for the correct route (215). Whereas Christian had a titanic battle with Apollyon in the Valley of Humiliation, Christiana's party finds it a fruitful ground abloom with lilies in the summer. In this place of serene beauty, where Jesus once had a country house, no foul fiends or evil spirits dwell, and the truly humble can meet angels or find pearls (236–39). In contrast, the Valley of the Shadow of Death is still a place of horror, "great stinks and loathsome smells," but Christiana and her fellow pilgrims have an easier passage because of Great-heart, who provides light and repulses the Devil (242–43).

The presence of Great-heart, an experienced guide, means Christiana and her fellow pilgrims have someone not only to vanquish or repel the enemies but also to warn of impending dangers as they approach, whereas Christian and his com-

---

[69] N. H. Keeble, "Christiana's Key: The Unity of *The Pilgrim's Progress*," in *Pilgrim's Progress*, ed. Newey, 14. The first part of the allegory also has communal elements, as in the episodes involving the House Beautiful and the shepherds in the Delectable Mountains. Robert Archer, "Like Flowers in the Garden: John Bunyan and His Concept of the Church," *Baptist Quarterly* 36 (April 1996): 287–89.

[70] See the perceptive essay by Keeble, "Christiana's Key," 1–18.

panions, who had longer advance notice, tended to forget (288). Because Great-heart is leading Christiana's party, the three robbers who victimized Little-faith avoid the pilgrims (258). Vanity Fair is a less hostile place, though Bunyan could not decide whether many or few good people now live there (274, 277). When the pilgrims reach the Delectable Mountains and Great-heart requests hospitality for them, the shepherds welcome the disparate group, assuring them that "we have for the *Feeble*, as for the *Strong*" (284). As Christiana's group nears the end of the pilgrimage, they learn that the River of Death rises and falls, enabling some to cross when it is nearly dry, whereas for others the river, surging over its banks, is a terrifying experience (304).

The perspective of the second part differs from its predecessor, partly because of the focus on the dissenting pastor, Great-heart, who provides leadership, protection, edification, and above all the voice of experience. He knows what to expect, offers counsel on how to deal with it, and functions as a heroic protector. In contrast, Evangelist, who made only scattered appearances in part one, played a less substantial role. Like Christian, the character of Great-heart is autobiographical, yet he is not Christian "at another stage of his growth, . . . the fully mature pilgrim."[71] Instead he is Bunyan the minister, and by extension every committed dissenting pastor. Great-heart is not a role model for believers, or even male ones, but for ministers of gathered churches, and his function in the allegory is to underscore the importance of looking to such men for spiritual leadership.

The perspective of the second part is also different because Bunyan has been free for some time of the anxiety and despair that once plagued him, a struggle that gave psychological intensity to the first part. Christiana remembers that her husband had been "over run with Melancholy Humours," and her own guilt "would have drawn [her] into the *Pond*," that is, driven her to suicide had she not experienced a dream in which her husband is well and his king invites her to join them (178, 205). In describing her condition or remembering his own, Bunyan conveys no sense of intense struggling but rather a mood of detachment. This is true as well of the episode at the Slough of Despond, which Christiana, her sons, and Mercy find in worse condition because so many people have dumped excrement and refuse into it. Although Mercy and the boys get "staggeringly over," Christiana nearly falls in several times, but the reader has little sense of the peril or psychological trauma that Christian experienced. Bunyan had not forgotten his own experience, which he utilized in drawing the character of Mr. Fearing:

[71] Henri A. Talon, "Space and the Hero in *The Pilgrim's Progress*: A Study of the Meaning of the Allegorical Universe (1961)," in Bunyan, *The Pilgrim's Progress: A Casebook*, ed. Roger Sharrock (London: Macmillan, 1976), 165.

> *Tell them also how Master* Fearing *went*
> *On Pilgrimage, and how the time he spent*
> *In Solitariness, with Fears and Cries,*
> *And how at last, he won the Joyful Prize.* (172)

This was the dark side of the younger Bunyan, a side that had still troubled him in the 1660s, and the Bunyan who, like Mr. Fearing, found the Slough of Despond so difficult. "He lay roaring at the *Slow of Dispond*" until "one sunshine Morning, I do not know how, he ventured, and so got over. . . . He had, I think, a *Slow of Dispond* in his Mind" (249). At this point Bunyan was describing himself as he had once been, though much of Mr. Fearing, including the ease with which he entered the Valley of Humiliation (252), is not autobiographical.

Bunyan knew he was now well, and he attested to that realization in the sequel. In one of the second part's most revealing episodes, Great-heart kills and beheads Giant Despair while Old Honest fells Diffidence, the giant's wife, with a single blow. With the aid of Old Honest and Christiana's sons, Great-heart demolishes Doubting Castle, liberating two prisoners, Despondencie and his daughter, Much-afraid, and finding numerous corpses and skeletal remains in the castle yard and dungeon. Giant Despair's head is erected on a pole by the road to warn other pilgrims not to enter the still perilous grounds, but depression itself has been slain (281–83). Bunyan was testifying here to his own victory over (or recovery from) bleak despondency, but he was also making the point that Great-heart the pastor is a spiritual physician capable of helping others overcome despair. The insomnia that plagued Bunyan during his illness is now transformed into the sleeplessness of joy such as Mercy experiences (207); so too do the pilgrims in the land of Beulah, where the ceaseless sound of trumpets and bells prevents sleep, though the wayfarers are as refreshed as if they had slept soundly (303). Bunyan recognized that some believers are prone to dejection, or, as Despondencie put it, to slavish fears akin to ghosts relentlessly seeking entertainment. Not until he reaches the River of Death is Despondencie able to put the black moods behind him, his final words being "*Farewel Night, welcome Day*" (308).

The keen sensitivity to light and darkness Bunyan gained from his psychological struggles is reflected in the second part, as in the first. Prudence explains to Christiana that the birds which cheerily sing when "the Sun shines warm . . . are very fine Company for us when we are *Melancholy*," and she teaches Christiana's son Matthew that sunlight is an analogue for Christ's bestowal of grace and love (231, 235). For Christiana's party most of the passage through the Valley of the Shadow of Death, "where the Light is Darkness," occurs in daylight, but darkness, which Great-heart likens to a descent into the ocean's depths, finally enshrouds them. Because Great-heart has been through the valley he knows deliverance is possible only by praying for light, which finally comes (242–43, 293). So great is Mr. Fearing's dejection that he lays outside the interpreter's house a long time despite the long, dark nights (250). When Gaius comes to the rescue of Mr. Feeble-mind, whose temperament is like that of Mr. Fearing, Bunyan likens the event to sunshine piercing a black cloud (269). For a time in the treacherous Enchanted Ground the pilgrims are enveloped in darkness, yet Great-heart's leadership enables them to make "a pretty good shift to wagg along," particularly after he lights a lantern at their request (296–99). Soon they are in the land of Beulah, where the sun shines night and day, an affirmation by Bunyan that believers can attain freedom from despair in this life (303).

In addition to exploring varieties of religious experience in the second part, Bunyan had more he wanted to say about women, although it would be a serious mistake to read the second part as if it were concerned exclusively or even primarily with this subject. In *A Case of Conscience Resolved* he explained why women should not hold separate meetings for worship or prayer, and he firmly asserted women's subordinate status, tracing it to the moment of their creation. In the second part of *The Pilgrim's Progress* he neither recanted nor modified this position. As the church is the bride of Christ and subordinate to him, so Christiana is subservient to Great-heart, whose pastoral voice is that of Christ as manifested through Scripture. Christiana does not become a pilgrim to assert her independence of male authority but because of guilt about how she responded to Christian's spiritual awakening and out of a desire to return to him and thus to his patriarchal dominion. Yet the very act of expressing ultimate loyalty to Christ created a situation in which some women had to defy the authority of ungodly spouses, and all nonconformist women had to disobey the authority of a state that insisted on conformity to the established church. As Stuart Sim and David Walker have observed, "almost unwittingly, it would seem, nonconformism provides the basis for at least a measure of female liberation."[72] The necessity to take sides in the religious disputes presumed a degree of liberty.

Christiana's subordination to Christian is social rather than spiritual, for Bunyan made no gender distinction when he attested to the primacy of the divine word for all Christians. The entourage Great-heart leads includes both men and women, young and old. Submissiveness to Great-heart is required of the male pilgrims as well as their female counterparts. Depictions of the pilgrim band as a collection of the weak and feeble are inaccurate, for Great-heart's retinue includes the young and courageous Mr. Valiant-for-Truth, Stand-fast, and Old Honest, who take up arms in the assault on Giant Despair and his wife, as well as Masters Fearing, Feeble-mind, Ready-to-Halt, and Despondencie. Nor are all of

[72] Sim and Walker, 159.

these characters as wholly opposite as their names suggest, for Mr. Fearing is cheered by the cross and sepulcher, undaunted by the lions and Hill Difficulty, and ready to fight the men of Vanity Fair whose "fooleries" he opposes (251–52). In contrast, Mr. Feeble-mind, a pilgrim *true of Heart, tho weak in grace,* has no strength of body or mind, must be carried up Hill Difficulty, and when caught by a giant mugger in Assault Lane refuses to fight, longing instead for a cordial (172, 267–68). Feeble-mind is a better example than Fearing of "the underside of heroic wayfaring."[73]

Christiana compares herself to Fearing (254), who is in some ways a person of valor as well as a paragon of humility. Neil Keeble has likened him to Christian, whom most commentators describe as heroic. The affinity Christiana sees between herself and Fearing, and the extent to which Fearing reflects Christian, should caution us against any simplistic contrasting of Christian's epic heroism and Christiana's supposed domesticity.[74] Christiana and Mercy manifest courage in their own right, not least by setting out on their pilgrimage accompanied only by four boys. When Mercy is not admitted through the princely gate with Christiana, she summons her courage and knocks boldly (189–91). Mrs. Timorous makes the case that going on a pilgrimage with all its dangers is unwomanly, insane, and a threat to one's children, but such reasoning deters neither Christiana nor Mercy (181–83). The disdain in which Bunyan held Mrs. Timorous' logic is reflected in the friends he gave her: Bats-eyes, Inconsiderate, Light-mind, and Know-nothing (184). Yet Mercy herself holds a view similar in some ways to that of Mrs. Timorous. When Mercy learns that Simple, Sloth, and Presumption have been hanged, she rejoices, for *"who knows else what they might a done to such poor Women as we are?"* (214). As Great-heart prepares to leave the pilgrims after escorting them to the porter's lodge, Christiana remonstrates with him, though saying nothing about her gender, but Mercy returns to her sense of female weakness: "How can such poor Women as we, hold out in a way so full of Troubles as this way is, without a Friend, and Defender?" (220). Bunyan's point is not that women lack the courage or the ability to be pilgrims, but that in their spiritual lives they must submit to pastoral authority. Because women were excluded from the pastorate, this necessitated submission to masculine control.

*A Case of Conscience Resolved* focused on what women could not do, whereas in the second part of *The Pilgrim's Progress* Bunyan concentrated on showing women what they *can* accomplish, especially if they take advantage of pastoral leadership. The key passage comes well into the story when Christiana's party arrives at the inn of Gaius, whose biblical namesake had been Paul's host at Corinth

---

[73] Swaim, *PP*, 158.
[74] Keeble, "Christiana's Key," 5, 17.

(Romans 16:23) and a man Paul baptized (1 Corinthians 1:14). Bunyan thus se-lected a character linguistically tied to a disciple of Paul, author of the well-known strictures on the place of women in the church, to articulate his own view of women. To a biblically literate audience he was associating his stance with Paul, implicitly evoking the apostle's blessing for a statement exhorting women to continue the exemplary work for the gospel undertaken by their scriptural predecessors. Gaius begins by declaring his intent to "speak on the behalf of Women, to take away their Reproach," a reference to Eve's yielding to the ser-pent's enticements in Eden. He moves quickly to explain that as Eve's action brought death and a curse on humankind, so Mary has given birth to the messiah who offers life and health. Women were the first to rejoice in the savior's arrival and the only ones who "ministered to him of their Substance," the men giving not a single groat.

> 'Twas a Woman that washed his Feet with Tears, and a Woman that anointed his Body to the Burial. They were Women that wept when he was going to the Cross; And Women that followed him from the Cross, and that sat by his Sepulcher when he was buried. They were Women that was first with him at his Resurrection *morn*, and Women that brought Tidings first to his Disciples that he was risen from the Dead. (261)

Without women the gospel story would have been radically different, for they went places and did things on behalf of Jesus while men—even the disciples—either manifested indifference or cowered in fear. In the events surrounding the passion and resurrection women monopolized bravery. To Bunyan these exam-ples meant that women are "highly favoured, and . . . sharers with us in the Grace of Life" (261).

Thus it is not the case that one must be male to be a pilgrim.[75] The thrust of Bunyan's message is that subordination does not mean exclusion, a point rein-forced by his insistence that the two essentials required of a pilgrim are courage and a holy life, neither of which is limited to men (276). He developed a deeper, more subtle perspective on gender by having Mercy embody what Kathleen Swaim has termed "a modified version of Christian's spiritual history." Mercy "echoes, subsumes, and elevates elements of Christian's heroism . . . on the way to becoming a full realization or embodiment of the practice and principle of

---

[75] As asserted by Keeble, "'Here is her Glory, even to be under Him': The Feminine in the Thought and Work of John Bunyan," in *JBHE*, ed. Laurence, Owens, and Sim, 143; and Luxon, 200–207. Such readings, in my judgment, overemphasize gender and accord insufficient weight to personality differences, disparate ages, the impact of a pastoral guide in the second part, and the change in emphasis from individual to communal. The second part is about much more than gender.

Christian Charity inscribed in her name."[76] This underscores both the fundamental core of Christian experience that is not gender specific and the fact that assorted elements of Christian experience can be shared by some male and female believers but not others; some traits cut across gender, as Bunyan's pilgrims effectively illustrate.

The gender-based differences Bunyan perceived must therefore have been secondary. Never did his female pilgrims take up arms, and never could he say of them what he did of Christian in his battle with Apollyon, namely, that he "did here play the Man," proving to be as stout as Hercules (240). Great-heart describes Christian and Faithful as "Lyon-like Men," and the pilgrims reflect on the latter's "manly Suffering" (272, 279). Female pilgrims do not wield weapons because they lack courage but because they are physically weaker than men. Nevertheless they face challenges requiring fortitude and stamina. After Christiana's party left Mnason's house the women and children, "being weakly, . . . were forced to go as they could bear," eliciting sympathy from Ready-to-halt and Feeble-mind (279). In lumping the women's physical limitations with the religious deficiencies of these two men Bunyan nearly undermined his basic argument about women's spiritual valor. Almost immediately, however, the pilgrims are reunited, and they remain so until they reach the entry to By-path Meadow, where Great-heart, Old Honest, and Christiana's sons break away to attack Giant Despair (281). This is warfaring, and that part of the pilgrimage, at least allegorically, is man's work.[77] While Great-heart's party makes its assault on Giant Despair, Feeble-mind and Ready-to-halt are left to guard the women, prompting Aileen Ross to observe that "the least male is to be preferred to the best female" by the misogynist Bunyan.[78] His point, however, is underscored by a quotation from Isaiah 11:6 coupled with his own contingent phrase: "They keeping in the Road, *A little Child might lead them*" (281). Isaiah 11 is not about gender or age but the promised salvation of the remnant of God's people, "the root of Jesse," the outcasts of Israel and the dispersed of Judah; as they travel on God's Highway, they are beyond danger because the wolf and the lamb, the leopard and the kid, and the calf and the lion live together in peace. No guard is necessary, which is

[76] Kathleen M. Swaim, "Mercy and the Feminine Heroic in the Second Part of *Pilgrim's Progress*," *Studies in English Literature* 30 (Summer 1990): 388, 397–98. Maureen Quilligan notes that Mercy "does not personify God's grace itself, but represents the lowly object of his grace." *The Language of Allegory: Defining the Genre* (Ithaca, NY: Cornell University Press, 1979), 129.

[77] For militant imagery in part two see *PP*, 208, 218–19, 244–45, 252, 278, 289–91, 296.

[78] Aileen Ross, "'Baffled, and Befooled': Misogyny in the Works of John Bunyan," in *Awakening Words*, ed. Gay, Randall, and Zinck, 167.

why the least qualified male pilgrims can serve in what is a merely symbolic role.[79] Moreover, as John Knott has observed, as the second part comes to a conclusion, Great-heart fades and Christiana becomes the dominant figure, though this is partly the result of Bunyan not wanting to imply that the role of the ministry will somehow perish.[80]

The second part of *The Pilgrim's Progress* is as much about the church and pastoral leadership as women. The remarkably varied company of pilgrims that gathers around Christiana as her travels progress is, in Bunyan's analogy, akin to a garden in which flowers differ in height, quality, color, and smell; they live in order and harmony, for "where the Gardiner has set them, there they stand, and quarrel not one with another" (202). In its communal orientation the allegory's second part reflects the pastoral experience Bunyan gained since his release from prison in 1672—a perspective he lacked when he wrote the first part.[81] Through participation in the pilgrim community the travelers find spiritual sustenance, as in the meals at the interpreter's house, the arbor on Hill Difficulty, the porter's lodge, Gaius' inn, and Mnason's house; doctrinal instruction from Great-heart (210–11); catechizing for the boys from Prudence, another indication of the important role of women (224–26); hermeneutic lessons in such subjects as Eve's apple and Jacob's ladder (233); and, perhaps above all, the fellowship that sustains them throughout the lengthy journey.

Sacraments—Bunyan preferred to call them ordinances—play at most a minimal role in the second part unless one interprets the many communal meals as celebrations of the Lord's supper. This seems implausible given their role in ministering spiritual sustenance and the varied menus, none of which comprises the bread and wine that would have signaled the communion service. Instead the pilgrims dine on honeycomb, pomegranates, lamb in a sauce, and bottles of spirit

[79] For Bunyan, no matter how talented, women cannot serve as officers in the church, and in this context Ross' point is valid.

[80] Knott, *DM*, 214. Margaret Olofson Thickstun offers a different reading, according to which Bunyan has Stand-fast, "the male perfection of the idea of the feminine," displace Christiana and all other women as the spouse of Christ. However, in the second part of the allegory the church, apart from its pastoral leadership, is not gendered, and there is no evidence to indicate that Bunyan intended Stand-fast to be a symbol of the church. Instead Stand-fast personifies Emanuel's advice to Mansoul at the conclusion of *The Holy War*: "Hold fast till I come" (*HW*, 250). In theological terms, Stand-fast represents perseverance. Thickstun, *Fictions of the Feminine: Puritan Doctrine and the Representation of Women* (Ithaca, NY: Cornell University Press, 1988), 103–4.

[81] The communal orientation is stressed by Melissa D. Aaron in "'Christiana and her train': Bunyan and the Alternative Society in the Second Part of *The Pilgrim's Progress*," in *Awakening Words*, ed. Gay, Randall, and Zinck, 169–85.

(216–17, 221). Wine, "red as Blood," is served at Gaius' inn, but instead of bread the rest of the menu consists of meat, milk, apples, nuts, and blended butter and honey (262–63). Moreover, the biblical verses cited in the marginalia, including those for the wine—Deuteronomy 32:14, Judges 9:13, and John 15:1—do not include the classic New Testament passage in 1 Corinthians 11 concerning the Lord's supper. Bunyan, it seems, took pains to indicate that communal meals were *not* allegorical representations of the Lord's supper.[82] Various critics have suggested that Matthew's pills are an analogy for the Lord's supper,[83] but this is dubious inasmuch as he alone takes them, three at a time and with salt; the Lord's supper in gathered churches is a communal experience, and the puritans had earlier criticized private communion. In connection with the pills Bunyan quotes the phrase *ex Carne & Sanguine Christi* (229), but this may refer to the infusion of divine grace, which is not restricted to sacramental observance in his thought. It is certainly a tongue-in-cheek allusion to the tradition of eucharistic medicinal imagery.[84] Bunyan's parenthetical sentence, "You know Physicians give strange Medicines to their Patients" (229), reinforces the notion of a spoof, and so too did the experiences of readers with purging pills. Taken in conjunction with "some Vomitts," for instance, they provided Edward Harley with limited relief from headaches, flatulence, impaired vision, ringing in the left ear, and vertigo, and Sir William Boothby reported that purging pills made him very sick "but yet worked well."[85] Some commentators have explained the bath taken by the pilgrims at the interpreter's house as an allegory of baptism,[86] but this too poses problems, for the damsel Innocent tells the travelers that "they must wash and be clean" (207). Elsewhere in his writings Bunyan argued at length that bap-

[82] For a contrary view see Swaim, *PP*, 208; Tindall, 64–65; John R. Knott, Jr., "Bunyan and the Holy Community," *Studies in Philology* 80 (Spring 1983): 219; Ken Simpson, "'For the Best Improvement of Time': *Pilgrim's Progress* and the Liturgies of Nonconformity," in *Awakening Words*, ed. Gay, Randall, and Zinck, 113–26; Margaret Spufford, "The Importance of Religion in the Sixteenth and Seventeenth Centuries," in *The World of Rural Dissenters, 1520–1725*, ed. Spufford (Cambridge: Cambridge University Press, 1995), 93–94. Spufford sees a sacramental analogy in the bottle of wine presented to Christiana by the lord of the Palace Beautiful (*PP*, 234), but the pilgrims also receive corn and pomegranates, and in addition the boys are given figs and raisins. All of this signifies spiritual sustenance, not communion. Spufford, "The Importance of Religion," 93–94.

[83] Frye, *GMS*, 155–56; Tindall, 65; Knott, "Bunyan and the Holy Community," 219; Gordon S. Wakefield, "'To be a Pilgrim': Bunyan and the Christian Life," in *John Bunyan*, ed. Keeble, 125.

[84] J. H. Alexander notes the latter context, but interprets it as a serious statement. "Christ in *The Pilgrim's Progress*," *BS* 1 (Spring 1989): 28.

[85] BL, Add. MSS 70,013, fol. 131r (quoted); Add. MSS 71,689, fol. 100r.

[86] Sharrock, in *PP*, 343–44; Swaim, *PP*, 208; Tindall, 65.

tism was *not* compulsory[87]; to make it so in *The Pilgrim's Progress* would go against the position he defended in the 1670s. Moreover, his own marginal notation explains that the bath mandated by Innocent is sanctification, a process essential to the Christian life, unlike baptism.[88] The second part of the allegory provides explicit examples of the holy kiss of charity, which Old Honest bestows on the other pilgrims as Paul commanded in Romans 16:16 (248), and the ritual of foot-washing, which the gatekeeper administers (193), but neither baptism nor the Lord's supper.

The best illustration of the gathered church in part two is Gaius' inn, where entry is restricted to pilgrims (believers). In this context Bunyan articulated his ideal of endogamous marriage, "the way to preserve . . . a posterity in the Earth" (261). So important is such marriage to the community's well-being that he provided four examples (269, 277), thereby giving it a greater role in the Christian community than the sacraments, at least as far as the allegory is concerned. For Bunyan, ritual is not at the heart of the communal experience, or even a necessary part of it. Instead the holy community is bound together by the shared experience of the pilgrimage, a deeply rooted determination to reach the Celestial City, and a sense of spiritual communion.

Although ritual has virtually no place in Bunyan's pilgrim community, music does. Music is pervasive in both parts, though more so in the second, with its generally brighter tone. Christian sang following his pleasant experiences in the House Beautiful, a restful meadow, and the Delectable Mountains, and upon his arrival in the Celestial City (53, 110–11, 123, 162), but more often after his escapes: from the Valley of the Shadow of Death, the villain Shame, Vanity Fair, Demas' enticements, Doubting Castle, and the Flatterer's net (66, 74, 97–98, 108, 118–19, 134). In keeping with the communal emphasis in the second part, Bunyan has the pilgrim party periodically function as a chorus, singing as they leave the interpreter's house (208–9), as they depart from the porter's lodge (235), after they bid farewell to the shepherds in the Valley of Humiliation (289), and in response to a recounting of Stand-fast's escapades (303). Like an oratorio composer, Bunyan assigned arias to a number of his characters, both major and minor: Early in the pilgrimage Christiana sings an ebullient song about setting out on her journey (193), a minstrel vocalizes about the Lord's support (204), Mercy gives musical

[87]Greaves, *JB*, 139–43.
[88]Ibid., 87–89. Thickstun's comparison between the bath of sanctification and mikvah, the Jewish rite of purification for women before marriage and after menstruation and childbirth, founders because the boys in Christiana's party were also bathed (*PP*, 207). Her attempt to explain the boys' participation in the bath in terms of original sin is foreign to Bunyan's doctrine of sanctification. *Fictions*, 98.

expression to her relief that Simple, Sloth, and Presumption have been hanged (214), Prudence, playing the virginals, sings about Eve's apple, Jacob's ladder, and a golden anchor (233–34), a shepherd boy exalts humbleness in the Valley of Humiliation (238), and in the allegory's best-known lines Valiant-for-Truth offers a paean to valor (295).[89] The songs of the second part evince Bunyan's dexterity in employing his verse in a way the first part did not.[90] Music provides a fitting way to contrast the youthful prowess of Valiant-for-Truth, who could sing about the pilgrim's *"avow'd* Intent" and fearlessness when confronted with giants and lions, and the doleful, monotonous notes of Mr. Fearing's sackbut (253, 295). In the controversy over hymn-singing that engaged Baptists, Bunyan, as we shall see, probably sided with Benjamin Keach judging from the prominence of music in the allegory.[91]

The mostly cheerful music of the second part contrasts sharply with the suffering nonconformists were undergoing during the Tory Reaction, and Bunyan may have included so much joyous music as a morale booster. Like its predecessor the second part is sensitive to the historical context in which it was composed. Bunyan's dismay over the extent to which Monmouth and his close allies had gone in considering a general insurrection is reflected in his comment that Madam Bubble pitted Absalom against his father David. John Dryden's poem *Absalom and Achitophel* (1681) had done much to popularize the identification of Absalom with Monmouth, and it was an easy step to interpret Madam Bubble's nefarious deed as having incited the duke against Charles II. "She makes Variance betwixt Rulers and Subjects, betwixt Parents and Children," Bunyan pointedly wrote (302).

As in part one, persecution remains a dominant theme, only this time the focus is on its impact on the godly community and the role of the dissenting clergy, represented by Great-heart, in helping the pilgrims withstand oppression. With his sword, helmet, and shield, Great-heart the pastor and conductor is a divine agent leading the resistance against the persecuting powers (208). Bunyan intriguingly juxtaposes numerous examples of resistance, mostly led by Great-

---

[89] Writing of Christian's songs, U. Milo Kaufmann observes that Bunyan wrote this verse with an eye to easy memorization. *The Pilgrim's Progress and Traditions in Puritan Meditation* (New Haven, CT: Yale University Press, 1966), 223. This would also be true of the songs in part two.

[90] Graham Midgley has observed that the poems in part two constituted "a breakthrough in Bunyan's poetical career," enabling him to surpass Thomas Sternhold, the well-known versifier of psalms. *MW*, 6:lvi–lvii.

[91] Hill, *TPM*, 260–66; Knott, Jr., "Bunyan and the Holy Community," 219. Bunyan's position on music in the church is discussed in Chapter 14.

heart, with the interpreter's analogy of sheep quietly and patiently waiting to be killed in a slaughter-shop:

> You must learn of this Sheep, to suffer: And to put up wrongs without murmurings and complaints. Behold how quietly she takes her Death, and without objecting she suffereth her Skin to be pulled over her Ears. Your King doth call you his Sheep. (202)

The image of saints awaiting slaughter like sheep is reinforced by Gaius' assertion that many of Christiana's progenitors were martyrs: the biblical leaders Stephen, James, Paul, and Peter, and their successors Ignatius of Antioch, who was thrown to the lions, Marcus of Arethusa, whose lacerated flesh was coated with honey and exposed to bees and flies, and Romanus and Polycarp of Smyrna, who were burned to death. Once more Bunyan drew on Foxe to buttress his scriptural evidence and exhort the faithful to undergo whatever persecution might await. The juxtaposition of resistance and suffering was not a manifestation of inconsistency, for evil in all its forms must be resisted, even if this means undergoing a martyr's death. Moreover, the Christian's response is situational, depending on the possibilities at hand. As Roland Frye has noted, Bunyan believed that "both passive suffering and overt assault upon evil, as circumstances may require, are appropriate for the Christian who makes his way through this world to the celestial city."[92]

The giants engaged in battle by Great-heart represent persecutors and are, as John Knott has suggested, an analogue of the army of bloodmen in *The Holy War*.[93] Backed by Giant Grim, the lions are a greater threat to pilgrims in the second part, and consequently the king's highway is largely overgrown with grass owing to minimal use. This is a commentary on the persecution of the early 1680s, a point Bunyan reinforced by giving Grim the alias Giant Bloody-man.[94] Defiantly claiming to be a mother in Israel, a reference to Deborah (Judges 5:6–7), Christiana, like Deborah, refuses to be forced into a detour by Grim. Bunyan's association of Christiana with Deborah is noteworthy, for Deborah was regarded as an exception to the exclusion of women from positions of authority,[95] and Bunyan had explicitly indicated in *A Case of Conscience Resolved* that he knew of no such women in the contemporary church. Before Christiana's defiant expression, Great-heart attempted to reason with Grim, but seemingly inspired by her

[92] Frye, *GMS*, 123–24.

[93] Knott, *DM*, 209.

[94] Hill's interpretation of Giant Grim as justices of the peace who defended enclosure (the grassy highway) is not persuasive. *TPM*, 217.

[95] See, e.g., John Knox, *On Rebellion*, ed. Roger A. Mason (Cambridge: Cambridge University Press, 1994), 32–38.

resolve he leads the armed resistance, ultimately killing Grim, though not the lions, who remain in chains (218–19, 276). When Great-heart prepares to resist another lion in the Valley of the Shadow of Death, it retreats (242).

Giant Maul, who lives in a cave as did Giant Pope, represents a different kind of threat, for whereas Pope killed pilgrims, Maul tricks young pilgrims with sophistry and chastises Great-heart for refusing to obey, a likely reference to the penal laws. The inspiration for Giant Maul may have come from Luther's commentary on Galatians, though Luther had God wield the maul against the unrepentant conscience and the presumption that good works and righteousness were not rooted in the fear of God.[96] The linkage between Giants Pope and Maul effectively associates the repressive policies of the Tory-Anglicans with Catholicism, and the comment about sophistry, which was popularly associated with the Jesuits, points to the threat posed by James' succession. In 1678 Titus Oates charged that the Jesuits had held a consult (a triennial business meeting) in London in April to discuss the king's assassination, and the government subsequently obtained evidence that the Jesuits had indeed met, though for other purposes, in the duke of York's apartments at Whitehall.[97] For the perceptive reader, Giant Maul thus represented both the Catholic threat personified in James and the penal laws against dissent that had an affinity with historic Catholic persecution. Once again, Great-heart rises to the occasion and in fierce combat ultimately beheads his adversary. Seemingly forgetting that the women and children displayed courage in undertaking this journey and that Christiana's defiance emboldened Great-heart to slay Giant Grim, Bunyan wrote derisively that they "did nothing but sigh and cry all the time that the Battle did last," that is, they prayed weakly to God (244–45).

When the pilgrims reach Gaius' inn, they learn about Giant Slaygood, a cave-dwelling cannibal who devours pilgrims. Although Great-heart takes others with him, the women and children remain at the inn. Sensitive to the persecution of nonconformists during the Tory Reaction as well as martyrs at the hands of Catholics, Bunyan pronounced vengeance on those responsible: "We are come," Great-heart informs Slaygood, "to revenge the Quarrel of the many that thou hast slain of the Pilgrims." In a manner familiar to those who had seen the severed heads of the plotters publicly displayed, Great-heart does likewise with Slaygood's head after killing him (266–67).

As Bunyan neared the end of the second part, the persecution of the Tory Reaction had begun to ebb, a development reflected in the visit of Christiana's party

[96] Luther, *Galatians*, 303, 324.

[97] John Kenyon, *The Popish Plot* (Harmondsworth, Middlesex: Penguin Books, 1974), 64–65, 144.

to Vanity Fair. They find the residents "far more moderate" than in Christian's time, when Faithful was burned. Some now regard religion as honorable, and the godly can again show themselves, presumably a reference to an easing of attempts to repress conventicles (275). Yet the threat of Catholicism remained, as Bunyan made clear in his depiction of the monster that menaces the town; borrowing the apocalyptic language of Revelation 17:3 he described the beast as having seven heads and ten horns. The woman who controls the beast, as biblically literate readers knew, is Babylon, the mother of harlots and abominations—the papacy. Intent on protecting the town, Great-heart enters into a covenant with the pilgrims to engage the monster. The beast's assaults are periodic, but each time the "valiant Worthies" repulse it, gradually leaving it lame from injuries. "It is verily believed by some, that the Beast will die of his Wounds." The valiant worthies to whom Bunyan referred were the dissenting ministers and their allies who remained loyal to their principles throughout the recurring persecution of the Restoration era.[98] Each time, Bunyan believed, they had repelled the threat (277–78). Inasmuch as he had already associated the penal laws with the Catholics' persecutive practices in the episode of Giant Maul and elsewhere, the threat posed by the beast to the faithful cannot be limited to Catholicism alone. Although the monster is beaten back, danger remains, prompting the male pilgrims to travel through the Enchanted Ground with their swords drawn, prepared to fight against evil (296).[99] Whereas the battles of the second part are less dramatic than those of the first, the persecution to which they refer is no less real, nor is the struggle against it any less central to the pilgrimage.

Despite the disclosures about Monmouth, Russell, and their confederates, Bunyan did not lose faith that some members of the aristocracy would continue to play a role in this struggle. Springs sometimes flow from the tops of high hills, Prudence explains, because the Spirit "shall spring up in *some* that are Great and Mighty, as well as in *many* that are Poor and low" (231). Sagacity, Old Honest, and Despondencie are gentlemen, though Madams Bubble and Wanton are gentlewomen (174–75, 185, 246, 283, 301). The God-fearing shepherd boy, Bunyan opined, has more "*Hearts-ease*" than those who dress in silk and velvet (238). In the second part his empathy is again palpably with the poor. Mercy is a maiden who sews clothing and hosiery for the indigent, and her sister, Bountiful, was

[98] Sharrock suggested that the valiant worthies were the preachers of the twenty-five sermons against popery by Nathaniel Vincent and other dissenters at Southwark in 1675, whereas Hill interprets the episode as an analogue of Protestant solidarity during the period of the Popish plot investigations. Sharrock, in *PP*, 350; Hill, *TPM*, 218. Both overlook the point that the monster's attacks are recurring.

[99] Valiant-for-Truth, who "*resisted unto Blood*," provides another example of militant resistance (*PP*, 289–91).

thrown out of her home by her husband for doing the same (227–28). Fond of lavish banquets, Madam Bubble scorns the poor while extolling the wealthy (302). "As poor as a *Howlet*," Stand-fast has no material bequest to leave at his death, nor do Ready-to-Halt (other than his crutches), Feeble-mind, Despondencie, Old Honest, and Valiant-for-Truth (apart from a sword). Other than giving a ring to Stand-fast, Christiana leaves what little she possesses to the poor (301, 305, 307–10). The pilgrim band is characterized by its general poverty rather than its supposed feebleness. Several times in the second part, Bunyan commented favorably on communal property, as at the outset of the pilgrimage when Christiana promises Mercy to hold "all things in common" between them (185). Laboring people can obtain good estates in the Valley of Humiliation, and the country of Beulah is "common for Pilgrims," who enjoy free access to its orchards and vineyards (237, 303). In times of persecution, when nonconformists faced the possibility of ruinous fines or the distraint of their property, the godly community, Bunyan seems to have been suggesting, should share its material goods with those in need.

As he composed the second part, he found such pleasure in poetry that he stopped long enough to write a short piece in verse, *A Caution to Stir up to Watch Against Sin*. Ponder published it as a broadside in or before April 1684, charging a penny for it. In the poem sin takes on life, much like many of the virtues and vices in the allegories, though sin is more remarkable because of its many guises: as beggar, briber, flatterer, lying witness, tyrant, deceiver, and assassin (an interesting rendition given the recent Rye House plot, with its focus on assassination). Second in power only to God, sin has the ability, Bunyan warned, to make vices of virtues, impose laws "where God has made Man free," and break laws that are binding (*MW*, 6:179). As in so much of Bunyan's work, here too there is an allusion to witchcraft in his portrayal of sin riding its victims "as the Devil rides his Hagg" (6:180). Some of the imagery of the second part of *The Pilgrim's Progress* found expression in *A Caution*, notably the representation of sin as both a lion and a giant (6:180–81). Readers who had been following accounts of the trials of the Rye House and Monmouth conspirators would have noticed echoes in the twelfth stanza:

> SIN will accuse, will stare thee in the face,
> Will for its Witnesses quote time and place
> Where thou committedst it; and so appeal
> To Conscience, who thy facts will not conceal;
> But on thee as a Judge such Sentence pass,
> As will to thy Sweet bits, prove bitter Sawce. (6:181)

The trials of the conspirators and the general opprobrium cast on nonconformists—those "Fantastical Fools," as Mrs. Inconsiderate called Christian and

Christiana—had an impact on Bunyan (*PP*, 184). In *A Holy Life*, the second part of *The Pilgrim's Progress*, and *A Caution* he pulled back from his attack on the tyranny of the Stuart regime, focusing instead on sin as the mighty tyrant (*MW*, 9:295; 6:179; *PP*, 225). In late 1683 and 1684 he remained staunchly opposed to persecution, but he prudently toned down his attack on those responsible for it. To his readers he offered hope that God would

> Keep thee from Enemies external,
> Help thee to fight with those internal. (*MW*, 6:182)

## "His Own Executioner"[100]: The Suicide of John Child

In 1684 Bunyan had an opportunity to draw on his earlier experience with depression to assist his former colleague, John Child, who was wrestling with suicidal tendencies and despair. He had known Child since the 1650s, when both belonged to the Bedford congregation and were active on its behalf, but Child, a man of "austere countenance and piercing eye," subsequently joined the Particular Baptists and preached in the region. According to James Jones, minister of a Particular Baptist church in Southwark, by 1683 Child had been a separatist for thirty years, though in the latter part of that period he increased his financial resources, "decayed in his Christianity," and altered some of his principles.[101] By his own account, composed in 1676, Child was a "Latitude man" who loved all "sincere Professors of Religion." At this point he began attempting to convert "some of the extravagant strains too apparently found in many well-meaning Dissenters," including their depiction of the Church of England as antichristian.[102] He was still a Baptist when he moved to London about 1669 at the invitation of Thomas Plant and joined the congregation of Edward Harrison in Petty France, but he was disappointed when that church did not select him as its minister following Harrison's retirement or death in 1674. About 1676 he became the pastor of a small congregation in Gracechurch Street, but it soon terminated his responsibilities. For a time he wandered, variously attending both conventicles and services in the established church.[103] A London constable mistakenly cited him for

---

[100] *MW*, 11:66.

[101] James Jones, *Modesty and Faithfulness in Opposition to Envy and Rashness* (London, 1683), 2 (quoted); anon., *A Warning from God to All Apostates* (London, 1684) (quoted).

[102] Child, *Moderate Message*, 2 (quoted); Child, *A Second Argument for a More Full and Firm Union Amongst All Good Protestants* (London, 1683), 1–2 (quoted). *A Second Argument* was licensed on 26 March 1683. Arber, *Transcript*, 3:139.

[103] W. T. Whitley, *The Baptists of London, 1612–1928* (London: Kingsgate Press, n.d.), 105, 117; Jones, *Modesty and Faithfulness*, 2. Child's name appears on jury lists in January and September 1682. CLRO, MSS SM 52; SM 53.

not having taken the Lord's supper in a parish church, but the charge was dismissed in June 1683.[104]

In that year Child made a public appeal to dissenters, urging them to take communion in the Church of England and hear its ministers preach. One of his fundamental points in *A Second Argument for a More Full and Firm Union Amongst All Good Protestants* (1683) was that the state church embodied the four essentials necessary for salvation: a good catechism, a well-composed form of prayer to guide worship, the preaching of learned, upright men, and moral precepts by which to regulate one's life. To take communion in this church was acceptable because such an act was neither prohibited by God nor harmful, but was instead spiritually good as well as in conformity with English law. In Child's judgment the Church of England must either be the synagogue of Satan, a position he deemed indefensible, or the church of God, in which case its celebration of the Lord's supper was legitimate. The clergy of the established church, he asserted, could not be surpassed anywhere in the world with respect to their profound learning, admirable sermons, holy living, and abundant charity, and it was therefore wrong to refuse to worship with them. Those who contended that communing with the Church of England was spiritually dangerous must deny its legitimacy or denounce it as antichristian, but the soundness of its theology rendered such a conclusion untenable.

According to Child, most sectaries (by whom he meant nonconformists) espoused principles that were heretical and "Abusive of the most Holy and Blessed God." He went on to assert that "Sectaries cannot be a Church in the best sense, because they are so giddy and foolish, as they want Wit and Policy for Church Government, and so penurious and covetous, that they will not allow what is requisite to the keeping up of a Church State." As proof he cited their opposition to episcopacy, Anglican clergy, mandatory tithes and poor rates, and the universities because of their supposed opposition to the Spirit's teaching. In place of the archbishoprics of Canterbury and York, they reputedly proposed to substitute "a *Tinker* and a *Taylor*, men of great confidence and long standing," a reference to Bunyan and Samuel How (who is named) respectively. A waterman, a shoemaker, a coffee-man, and a hat-dresser would replace the bishops of London, Winchester, Ely, and Durham, and men of inferior rank, education, and ability would oust the rest of the clergy. He went on to denounce the covetousness of the nonconformists, chiding them for having failed to establish free schools or banks, ignoring the needs of the poor, and leaving their ministers in penury. In Child's opinion the dissenters were not the true church, and if their repudiation

[104]GL, MS 9060, fol. 26r.

of the Church of England were accepted, the Catholics would be left to claim that status, which he found intolerable.[105]

Jones retorted in *Modesty and Faithfulness in Opposition to Envy and Rashness* (1683), castigating Child's *Second Argument* as "a Childish wandering Pamphlet full of Pernitious matter," and likening the author to the unclean spirit in Matthew 12:43–45 who perpetually roamed without finding rest. On the crucial issue of communion, Jones asserted that ordinances "must be performed by a people of good hearts, and good lives" in order to be accepted by God. Although he acknowledged that some Anglican clerics were holy, humble, and charitable, he contended that members of the true church must live godly lives in order to be fit for communion, and he insisted that its members congregated voluntarily rather than being compelled to do so by laws of the state. The Church of England, in Jones' judgment, was neither antichristian nor the true church, but something in between. Child's attack had clearly offended dissenters, and Jones responded in kind, denouncing him as a hypocrite, a false brother, a forger (because of his spurious charges), and a liar, and warning the Church of England to "beware of a False *CHILD*."[106]

Apparently stung deeply by the reaction of nonconformists, Child soon plunged into the bogs of despair, though his depressed moods extended "some years past" according to an anonymous account of his demise.[107] At his wife's urging, he began to consult in July 1684 with various dissenting ministers, some of whom came from "distant places." To them he recounted "the horrors of his mind," including his fear that he had committed the unpardonable sin against the Holy Spirit by writing *A Second Argument*, and his conviction that he had been motivated to leave the Baptists by pride, hypocrisy, covetousness, and a love of this world.[108] According to the account by Benjamin Dennis[109] and Thomas Plant, a Particular Baptist minister at the Barbican, London, he consulted first with a Mr. D., who may have been Dennis himself. He conferred next with his friend Benjamin Keach, who urged him to seek the assistance of ministers he had once esteemed, and then on several occasions with Hercules Collins, minister of a Particular Baptist church at Wapping. Child also exchanged letters with J. J., proba-

---

[105] Child, *A Second Argument*, 3–9, 11–16 (quoted at 9, 11, 13).

[106] Jones, *Modesty and Faithfulness*, 1, 3, 5–7, 12–14 (quoted at 1, 5, 14).

[107] Anon., *Sad and Lamentable News from Brick-Lane in the Hamlet of Spittle-Fields* (London, [1684]). This work ignores Child's apostasy, possibly to associate his death with nonconformity. *A Warning from God* compares Child's suicide to Spira's.

[108] *A Warning from God*; *Sad and Lamentable News* (quoted).

[109] In September 1693 Dennis obtained a certificate for a Congregationalist meeting at Sawbridgeworth, Hertfordshire. GL, MS 9579, vol. 1.

bly James Jones or Jonathan Jennings of the General Baptist church at White's Alley, London, and meetings transpired as well with E. P., who may have been Edward Price, Particular Baptist minister at Hereford. In a conference with Bunyan (J. B.[110]), Henry Danvers (H. D.), Edward Man (E. M.), the Particular Baptist minister at Houndsditch, London, and Mr. F. (probably Henry Forty, Jessey's successor), he replied in the negative when asked if he had acted in malice against the Trinity and the saints. In their judgment he had not committed the unforgivable sin, although they thought he had attempted "too much to advance Freewill, and the power of the Creature," for which God had permitted him to fall. However, Child insisted he was unable to repent. He also sought help from Thomas Wilcocks (T. W.), pastor of a Baptist church at Little Maze Pond, Southwark, A. B., and F. M., possibly Francis Mence, a Congregationalist pastor at Wapping. Still deeply enmeshed in despair, he turned to Plant, but again he found no relief.[111] Writing a retraction of what he had said in *A Second Argument* failed to dispel the depression, though the ministers, presumably including Bunyan, were optimistic about his recovery. His wife frustrated his first attempt to kill himself, but on 13 October, while she slept, he fashioned a noose from a leather strap and hanged himself.[112] Bunyan's reaction to the news is unrecorded, though he may have offered a prayer of thanks that his own psychological and spiritual travail in the 1650s had not resulted in a similar end.

[110] I base the identification of J. B. as Bunyan on the grounds of his prior relationship with Child, Keach's recommendation that Child seek the assistance of ministers he had once valued, the fact that some of the ministers came from areas outside London, and Child's acknowledgment that in the past he had "run down your opinions," referring to those of Mr. B., Mr. J., and Collins. In 1676, as we have seen, he had attacked Bunyan in print. *A Relation of the Fearful Estate of Francis Spira . . . To Which Is Added, Some Account of the Miserable Lives and Deaths of John Child & George Edwards*, ed. W. C. Brownlee (Philadelphia: Andrew Morgan and D. Hogan, 1814), 73, 77.

[111] Thomas Plant and Benjamin Dennis, *The Mischief of Persecution Exemplified* (London, 1688); Brownlee, ed., *A Relation*, 65–102. *The Mischief of Persecution Exemplified* was listed in the Term Catalogues in May 1688. Arber, *Term Catalogues*, 2:222. Keach, Price, Man, and Collins were signatories of the 1689 Particular Baptist confession. William L. Lumpkin, *Baptist Confessions of Faith* (Philadelphia: Judson Press, 1959), 239. For Jones, Jennings, Man, Forty, Wilcocks, Plant, and Collins see Whitley, *Baptists of London*, 102, 104–5, 108, 112, 113, 120; for Collins see also *DNB, s.v.*; for Mence see *Calamy Revised, s.v.* See also Michael MacDonald and Terence R. Murphy, *Sleepless Souls: Suicide in Early Modern England* (Oxford: Clarendon Press, 1990), 67–68.

[112] Plant and Dennis, *The Mischief of Persecution*; *A Warning from God*; *Sad and Lamentable News*.

"The Christians *Market-day*"[113]: Repulsing the Seventh-day Sabbatarians

In *Seasonable Counsel* Bunyan defended the Christian's right to worship in full accord with the dictates of the New Testament, an argument aimed principally at the Church of England, but "instituted Worship," as he called it (*MW*, 4:338), was threatened as well by sabbatarians who believed that Saturday rather than Sunday was the divinely prescribed day of worship. He had conversed with some of these seventh-day sabbatarians, though he never identified them or indicated where they resided (4:386). Historians have found no evidence of seventh-day sabbatarians in Bedfordshire, although some were in counties Bunyan visited, including Suffolk, Essex, and Berkshire.[114] More likely, he came into personal contact with sabbatarians in London, where three Seventh-day Baptist congregations were in existence by this time. The church at East Smithfield, which numbered approximately eighty members and was ministered to by Henry Soursby, had moved from Whitechapel in 1673 and traced its origins to at least 1661. Soursby's predecessor, William Saller, had composed *An Examination of a Late Book Published by Doctor Owen, Concerning a Sacred Day of Rest* (1671) in reply to Owen's *Exercitations Concerning the Name, Original, Nature, Use and Continuance of a Day of Sacred Rest* (1671). Although deeming Owen a man of piety and "*so Learned a Scribe*," Saller accused him of having dishonored Christianity in his book. Under the leadership of John Belcher, a second congregation had moved from Fenchurch Street to Wentford Street in 1683, and the last church, founded by Francis Bampfield, had relocated from Great Moorfields to Pinners' Hall in 1681.[115]

Because Bunyan preached at Pinners' Hall about June 1682, he probably met some of Bampfield's followers and possibly the erudite Bampfield himself. Like Bunyan, Bampfield had undergone a lengthy imprisonment, from July 1663 to May 1672, and while incarcerated at Dorchester he had embraced Baptist and seventh-day sabbatarian tenets. His views were attacked by Baxter in *The Divine Ap-*

---

[113] *MW*, 4:382.

[114] Bryan W. Ball, *The Seventh-Day Men: Sabbatarians and Sabbatarianism in England and Wales, 1600–1800* (Oxford: Clarendon Press, 1994), 5, 168–72, 266–67, 276–87, 351–52, 355; David S. Katz, *Sabbath and Sectarianism in Seventeenth-Century England* (Leiden: E. J. Brill, 1988), 108, 178. For Bunyan's activity in these counties see Greaves, *JBEN*, 95–99. Bunyan knew Henry Jessey, who had observed the Saturday sabbath, possibly in the late 1650s. Mark R. Bell, *Apocalypse How? Baptist Movements During the English Revolution* (Macon, GA: Mercer University Press, 2000), 65–66.

[115] Ball, *Seventh-Day Men*, 83–85, 105, 111, 113–15; William Saller, *An Examination of a Late Book Published by Doctor Owen, Concerning a Sacred Day of Rest* ([London], 1671), 1 (quoted). For Belcher see *BDBR, s.v.*

*pointment of the Lords Day Proved* (1671) and William Benn, a dissenting minister at Dorchester, in *The Judgment of Mr. Francis Bampfield* (1672). After moving to London in 1674, Bampfield began preaching in his house at Bethnal Green, and subsequently relocated his congregation to Great Moorfields and then Pinners' Hall. In 1681 he published both his autobiography, *A Name, an After-One*, and proposals for educational reform, *The House of Wisdom*. For illegally preaching he was arrested on 13 February 1683 and again a week later, tried at the Old Bailey on 17 March, and sentenced to incarceration for life or during the king's pleasure. Following Bampfield's death in Newgate prison on 16 February 1684, Edward Stennett became the pastor of his church on 25 October.[116] Bunyan may have seen Bampfield's death as an opportunity to make overtures to his congregation in a new book, *Questions about the Nature and Perpetuity of the Seventh-Day-Sabbath*, almost certainly written in October and November 1684. The Term Catalogues list it in November, but the published volume has the date 1685, suggesting that Ponder may not have had it in print until late March or April.[117] Bunyan may also have been motivated by the appearance of *A Discourse of the Sabbath* (1683) by Soursby and Mehetabel Smith, a member of his church.[118]

The seventh-day sabbatarians contended that the Saturday sabbath had been instituted before the fall of Adam and Eve (Genesis 2:2–3) and was part of natural and moral law. From the beginning, therefore, it was binding on both Jews and Gentiles. The Ten Commandments embody natural and moral law, and the fourth, governing the sabbath, remains perpetual and fully in force; it is not ceremonial. All of the Ten Commandments, Bampfield averred, remain a rule for Christians to obey: "The whole of the Christian Religion for Doctrines, Graces, Duties, Priviledges, and such like parts of that Religion, is one and the same under both the Old and New Testament." Seventh-day sabbatarians found no biblical command instructing believers to move the sabbath from the seventh day to the first, and they noted that Jesus, who adhered to the Saturday sabbath, had taught that every jot and tittle of the law will remain until heaven and earth have passed away (Matthew 5:18).[119]

---

[116] Greaves, *SR*, 187–207; *New DNB*, *s.v.*; Katz, *Sabbath and Sectarianism*, 90–124; Ball, *Seventh-Day Men*, 119. Numerous dissenters were present for Bampfield's funeral. *HMC* 36, *Ormonde*, n.s., 7:198. For Benn and Stennett see *BDBR*, *s.vv.*

[117] Arber, *Term Catalogues*, 2:95.

[118] Soursby and Smith's *A Discourse of the Sabbath* was repudiated by J. B. (an M.A., not Bunyan) in *The Morality of the Seventh-Day-Sabbath Disproved* (London, 1683).

[119] Henry Soursby and Mehetabel Smith, *A Discourse of the Sabbath* (London, 1683), 2–3, 5, 25–41, 59–65, 79–100; Francis Bampfield, *The Seventh-Day-Sabbath the Desirable-Day* ([London], 1677), 4, 19, 98–101 (quoted), 108, 112–13, 116–17, 123, 126–27; Bampfield, *The Judgment of Mr. Francis Bampfield*, ed. William Benn (London, 1672), 4r–7r; Edward

In entering the lists in favor of a Sunday sabbath Bunyan knew many works had been published on this theme (4:335). Owen may have told him about his book, and he may have seen some of the other contributions, including Thomas Grantham's *The Seventh-Day-Sabbath Ceased as Ceremonial* (1667), William Russell's *No Seventh-Day-Sabbath Commanded by Jesus Christ in the New-Testament* (1663), Thomas Collier's *The Seventh Day Sabbath Opened and Discovered* (1658), and Jeremiah Ives' *Saturday No Sabbath* (1659). Bunyan must have read other authors, for he remarked that "our Protestant Writers" had offered good reasons why the moral law includes a provision requiring time to worship God but not a specified day (4:353). His goal in writing *Questions about the Nature and Perpetuity of the Seventh-Day-Sabbath* was to provide a book small enough to meet the needs of those who "*have but* shallow *Purses*, short *Memories, and but* little *Time to spare, which usually is the lot of the mean and poorest sort of men.*" Given the fact that the work required 156 duodecimo pages, brevity was not attained, but the thematic layout of five questions and answers was straightforward. In addition to providing instruction for those who observe Sunday worship without fully understanding why, he hoped to persuade sabbatarians to embrace his arguments (4:335). The latter, he hoped, would not "take it ill" that he expressed himself so freely—an understatement given his attack on these "Jewish Gentiles": "Those Gentile-professors that adhere thereto, are Jewifi'd, Legaliz'd, and so far gone back from the authority of God" (4:388–89). Three times he followed references to their sabbatarian beliefs with the inflammatory phrase, "oh stupidity!" (4:381, 383–84). That he should then have asked seventh-day sabbatarians to consider his arguments "without prejudice to my person" was rather brazen, yet he seems to have been genuinely concerned that "Fictions and Fancies" had become the basis of factions that mitigated against love and unity (4:389).

Bunyan was troubled by nonconformists who advocated a return to various Jewish practices, including circumcision, polygamy, and sacrifices. He had personally engaged in discussions "with some pretending to Christianity, who have said, *and affirmed*, as well as they could, that the Jewish Sacrifices must be up again" (4:386).[120] Similar views had been asserted in the 1660s by Thomas Tillam,

---

Stennett, *The Seventh Day Is the Sabbath of the Lord* (n.p., 1664), 2, 27, 35–38, 45; William Saller, *Sundry Queries Formerly Tendred to the Ministers of London* [London? 1660]; Saller, *A Preservative Against Atheism and Error* (London, 1664), 14–15, 17–19; Saller, *An Examination*, 3, 13, 36–37, 48–49; Thomas Tillam, *The Seventh-Day Sabbath Sought out and Celebrated* (London, 1657), 1, 6, 10, 19, 113–14. See also *MW*, xlix–l.

[120] One such person may have been John Cowell, who reported the practices of Tillam and Pooley in the Palatinate (discussed below); later he may have known John Owen, whose *Exercitations Concerning the Name, Original, Nature, Use and Continuance of a Day of Sacred Rest* (London, 1671) he found of great value. Cowell, *The Snare Broken* (London, 1677), 53.

a Seventh-day Baptist who had been associated earlier in his career with Hanserd Knollys and John Simpson. With the assistance of Christopher Pooley, Tillam founded a millenarian community in the Palatinate that adopted Jewish rites, including circumcision, ceremonial laws, and sacrifices, and reputedly allowed polygamy and the communal ownership of property. After Tillam's death, reportedly in 1674, Pooley returned to England. In 1667, Belcher, Stennett, Arthur Squibb, and other Seventh-day Baptists had renounced Tillam's extremism in *A Faithful Testimony Against the Teachers of Circumcision and the Legal Ceremonies*,[121] but views akin to Tillam's were apparently still held in the early 1680s. In Bunyan's opinion such sectaries had succumbed to "Jewish Fables" (4:386). If these people "did either believe, or think of the incoherence that this [seventh] day with its Rites and Ceremonies has with the Ministration of the Spirit, our New-Testament Ministration, they would not so stand in their own light as they do" (4:388).

Like that of Ives, Baxter, and William Aspinwall,[122] Bunyan's strategy in repudiating the seventh-day sabbath was to associate it with the Mosaic ceremonial law, not the law of nature or Christ's precepts for worship. If the Saturday sabbath is not part of the natural law, he argued, it cannot be obligatory for all people, and the Gentiles never observed it. Moreover, natural law reveals nothing about "instituted Worship," which can be prescribed only through revelation. If natural law prescribes what God will eventually reveal, and if that law is present in every person, as the Quakers assert, there would have been no need for prophets, their writings, or revelation (4:338). The moral law, Bunyan argued, requires that time be set aside to worship God but provides no specifics as to when this should be (4:350). "The *Law* of Nature then calls for Time; but the *God* of Nature assigns it" (4:353).[123] Thus natural law does not impose a Saturday sabbath.

In his commentary on Genesis Bunyan had explained the seventh day, on which God rested after the creation (Genesis 2:2–3), both as a type of the repose the saints will enjoy following the end of the world and as a type of Christ, in whom the Gentiles will have rest. Using Hebrews 4:4–11 as the hermeneutic key to the meaning of the seventh day, he interpreted the sabbath as "the Seventh

---

[121] Cowell, *The Snare Broken*, 2, 5, 59, 82; Capp, *FMM*, 201–2, 266; Ball, *Seventh-Day Men*, 274, 345; PRO, SP 29/181/116, 116.1. For Tillam, Pooley, and Squibb see *BDBR*, s.vv.

[122] Jeremiah Ives, *Saturday No Sabbath* (London, 1659), 83, 85–86, 105; Richard Baxter, *The Divine Appointment of the Lords Day Proved* (London, 1671), 74–75; William Aspinwall, *The Abrogation of the Jewish Sabbath* (London, 1657), 10, 12–13.

[123] This was also the position of Thomas Grantham, *The Seventh-Day-Sabbath Ceased as Ceremonial* (London, 1667), 1–2; Ives, *Saturday No Sabbath*, 93, 215–16; Owen, *Exercitations*, 147–51; Baxter, *Divine Appointment*, 72, 203–13; and James Durham, *A Practical Exposition of the X . Commandements* (London, 1675), 188–95.

thousand of Years, which are to follow immediately after the World hath stood Six thousand first." The seventh year—or day, since a day is as a thousand years with God—will conclude with the last judgment and is thus the millennium (*MW*, 12:119). Grantham found no clear scriptural evidence for this view,[124] but Bunyan incorporated it in *Questions about the Nature and Perpetuity of the Seventh-Day-Sabbath*, using typology to drive his exposition. He interpreted the seventh day as a type of Christ the redeemer, and as with all types, once "the thing signified, or substance, is come, the signe or thing shadowing ceaseth" (*MW*, 4:348, 353–54). This logic effectively ruled out the Saturday sabbath, but in the commentary on Genesis he had also used the seventh-day rest as a type of the millennium, which still lay in the future. To solve this enigma in a way that would not preserve the Saturday sabbath, he made Christ's first coming the beginning of the rest that will culminate after the last judgment: This "Rest begins in Christ *now*, and shall be consummated *in glory*" (4:355).

Bunyan still had to explain why God had sanctified the seventh day (Genesis 2:3). Some defenders of the Sunday sabbath, such as Owen, Baxter, and Aspinwall, interpreted this as the origin of the sabbath,[125] but Bunyan argued that God sanctified the seventh day only for himself and did not impose it on humankind. "'Tis one thing for God to sanctifie this or that thing to an use, and another thing to command that that thing be forthwith in being to us" (4:340–41). Not until the time of Moses, he contended, did God require sabbath observance, and Moses received the command by revelation, not through tradition (4:342). In the 2,000 years between Adam and Moses, there was no "*stated* and *stinted* Worship" in the church, for that commenced only when the Hebrews were in the wilderness. Until that time, as Grantham also argued,[126] no sabbath existed (4:343).

When God instituted the seventh-day sabbath at Sinai, it was not part of the moral law, for the latter applied to all people, not the Jews alone (4:346–47). In Bunyan's judgment, God provided the seventh-day sabbath to the Jews as a sign that he had chosen them as a special people: "He had given to them (his own Rest) a Figure and Pledge of his sending his Son into the world to redeem them from the Bondage and Slavery of the Devil" (4:348).[127] Because the Gentiles were not part of this promise, the command to observe the sabbath did not apply to them, a point also made by Ives.[128] Had the precept been applicable to Gentiles,

---

[124] Grantham, *The Seventh-Day-Sabbath Ceased*, 11.

[125] Owen, *Exercitations*, 55–60; Baxter, *Divine Appointment*, 73; Aspinwall, *Abrogation*, 31.

[126] Grantham, *The Seventh-Day-Sabbath Ceased*, 13.

[127] Grantham regarded the seventh-day sabbath as a sign of sanctification to the Jews. Ibid., 10.

[128] Ives, *Saturday No Sabbath*, 15.

Bunyan contended, God would have imposed two forms of acceptable worship, both requiring sabbath observance, but with only the Jews being accountable for their distinctive rites, and this he deemed ridiculous (4:346–47). Nor was he willing to regard the command to observe a Saturday sabbath as part of the moral law, for it was not incorporated in the Sermon on the Mount (4:339, 343). Moreover, the moral law is eternal, whereas the precept establishing a seventh-day sabbath is finite (4:345, 349). Like Grantham,[129] Bunyan distinguished between the nature of the law, which is moral, and its ministration, which is "*shadowish* and *figurative*" and includes the command to keep the sabbath on the seventh day. Like the law of nature, the moral law requires only a day of rest, but does not stipulate which one (4:348, 350). When the ministration of the law prescribed to the Hebrews in the wilderness ended with the redeeming work of Christ, the seventh-day sabbath terminated, and rightly so in Bunyan's estimation, for it was associated with condemnation and death (4:350–52), a point driven home forcefully in Luther's commentary on Galatians.[130] Bunyan recognized that relinquishing the Saturday sabbath was difficult for those in whom "an old Religion" had obtained "*footing* and *rooting*," but he reminded his readers that Luther had striven mightily "to get his Conscience clear from all those *roots* and *strings* of inbred errour" (4:379–80).

For Bunyan Sunday is the divinely appointed day of worship because on that day the church at Jerusalem met, Pentecost occurred, and Gentile congregations gathered as Paul commanded (4:364–65, 368–70, 379). Sunday is the day of Christ's resurrection and his personal rest, the day on which he revealed himself to his disciples, and the day on which various sleeping saints awoke to commence their eternal sabbath (4:360, 364). Sunday is thus a special day, the only one that can properly be called the Lord's day (4:363). It is "the Christians *Market-day*, that which they so solemnly trade in for sole provision for all the week following." On this day, believers gather manna, the essential spiritual nourishment for Christian living (4:382, 385).

Bunyan's tract on the sabbath provided him with an opportunity to address concerns raised by earlier authors about proper behavior on that day,[131] but this he opted not to do other than to underscore the importance of providing for the poor (4:370–72). Sunday is a time for weighty spiritual matters and a respite from

[129] Grantham, *The Seventh-Day-Sabbath Ceased*, 1.

[130] See, e.g., Luther, *Galatians*, 143, 181–85, 426–27.

[131] Kenneth L. Parker, *The English Sabbath: A Study of Doctrine and Discipline from the Reformation to the Civil War* (Cambridge: Cambridge University Press, 1988), chaps. 2–7; Richard L. Greaves, *Society and Religion in Elizabethan England* (Minneapolis: University of Minnesota Press, 1981), 395–419; Winton U. Solberg, *Redeem the Time: The Puritan Sabbath in Early America* (Cambridge, MA: Harvard University Press, 1977), 27–80.

worldly affairs (4:336, 388), not petty regulations such as the Judaic prohibitions against kindling fires, preparing food, or leaving one's home on the sabbath (referring to Exodus 16:23, 29; 35:3). His primary concern in this tract was not conduct appropriate to the Lord's day but the distinction between the seventh-day sabbath, the observance of which requires adherence to the regulations in the Torah, and the Christian Sunday, when believers are required to worship in conformity with New Testament principles (4:387–88). Indeed, like Grantham[132] he contended that "a Seventh-day-Sabbath pursued according to its imposition by Law" would require stoning violators to death as God had commanded Moses (4:386–87, referring to Numbers 15:32–36). In their "preposterous zeal," proponents of a seventh-day sabbath misled others as well as themselves (4:388). Professing to have more to say on this subject, Bunyan teased his readers with the prospect of a second part to attack the "wild notions" of the seventh-day sabbatarians (4:386, 388–89), but in the meantime he hoped his book would tip the scales in favor of Sunday as the Lord's special day (4:335). Given the harsh language he used against his opponents and his reference to the Jews as "Christs deadliest Enemies" (4:388), perhaps it was best that he wrote no sequel.

[132] Grantham, *The Seventh-Day-Sabbath Ceased*, 15.

# CHAPTER 13

# Facing a Catholic Monarch

When James II succeeded his brother on 6 February 1685, he inherited a king-dom in which Whigs and dissenters were on the defensive and Tory-Anglicans exercised substantial influence. The campaign to purge the borough corpora-tions in the early 1680s had achieved considerable success, and the Whigs had only fifty-seven seats in the 525-member House of Commons that convened on 19 May. In Bedford, however, the Tory success was achieved, according to Nar-cissus Luttrell, by holding the election without general notice and at night.[1] Al-though the new king promised to preserve the established government in church and state, he signaled his preferred religious policy by ordering the release of Catholics incarcerated for recusancy or refusal to take the oaths and the return of their fines. According to William Lloyd, bishop of Peterborough, some non-conformists, believing "the Bishops domineering tyme is over," were hopeful the new Parliament would issue an indulgence, but most MPs were of a different mind. On 27 May a grand committee on religion in the Commons recom-mended that Parliament urge James to enforce the penal laws against both Catholics and Protestant nonconformists. When the king indicated his opposi-tion to such action, the Commons rejected the committee's recommendation. The depth of hostility toward nonconformists in some circles was manifest in Roger L'Estrange's vitriolic *Observator*, which accused them of having an "*In-curable Aversion* to a Monarchy" in church and state, described them as secret enemies of the kingdom who sucked the blood of royalists, and blamed them for the civil war and demise of Charles I. Seemingly few nonconformists or Catho-lics were intimidated, and Guy Carleton, bishop of Chichester, observed on 5 July that conventicles were meeting in most of the towns of his diocese and

[1]Luttrell, 1:341. Despite the remodeling, Bishop Compton of London worried about the possible choice of "factious and turbulent Spirits" as MPs. CUL, Add. MSS 5, fol. 185r.

Catholics were proselytizing.[2] "Our feares for religion were great," noted the Anglican minister Isaac Archer.[3]

"As if fire had been set to powder," news of Charles' death prompted a spate of activity among dissident exiles on the continent,[4] and in the spring they made preparations to invade Scotland and England. Argyll's force, pledging to establish a new government and suppress popery and prelacy in Scotland, sailed from Amsterdam on 2 May. An inept commander, Argyll, having failed to attract enough Scottish recruits and squandered valuable time, suffered defeat on 16 June. Captured two days later, he was tried and executed on the 26th. Plagued by delays, Monmouth's small force did not disembark near Lyme Regis until 11 June. The duke's key allies in London, John Wildman, Henry Danvers, and Matthew Meade, failed to mount an uprising after James committed troops to the southwest, nor did Monmouth's fellow peers in Cheshire, the earl of Macclesfield and Lords Brandon and Delamere.[5] Following his defeat at Sedgemoor, Monmouth was executed on 15 July. The state tried nearly 1,300 of his supporters, of whom approximately 250 were executed and 850 transported to the West Indies. Lord Chief Justice George Jeffreys and four colleagues presided over the trials, handling 385 of the accused at Taunton in one day, and 541 at Wells on another. "We are sending presents to all the Whiggish Townes of rogues to be hanged there," exulted a royalist at Wells.[6]

A small number of nonconformist ministers or their immediate relatives, some of whom Bunyan knew, were associated in varying degrees with Monmouth's insurrection. Ferguson, who had sailed with the exiles and drafted the duke's manifesto, escaped to the Netherlands, as did Danvers and Meade.[7] Two other ministers, the Particular Baptist Sampson Larke and the Presbyterian John Hickes, were caught and executed, as were Benjamin and William Hewling, the two deeply religious grandsons of William Kiffin.[8] For preaching a thanksgiving

[2] Bodl., Tanner MSS 31, fols. 19r (quoted), 128r; *Observator*, vol. 3, no. 8 (25 February 1685), and no. 9 (26 February 1685).

[3] CUL, Add. MSS 8499, fol. 206.

[4] John Erskine, *Journal of the Hon. John Erskine of Carnock. 1683–1687*, ed. Walter Macleod, Publications of the Scottish Historical Society, 14 (Edinburgh: T. and A. Constable, 1893), 180.

[5] For Delamere, Brandon, and Macclesfield see *BDBR, s.vv.*

[6] Bodl., Carte MSS 40, fol. 420v.

[7] Robin Clifton, *The Last Popular Rebellion: The Western Rising of 1685* (London: Maurice Temple Smith; New York: St. Martin's, 1984), chaps. 5–8; Greaves, *SOK*, 278–93; BL, Add. MSS 41,820, fol. 87r; 41,823, fol. 33r; *A Further Account of the Proceedings Against the Rebels in the West of England* (London, 1685).

[8] BL, Lansdowne MSS 1152, fol. 238v (Larke's examination); Michael R. Watts, *The*

sermon extolling Monmouth's supposed victory, the Presbyterian minister Joseph Bennet was charged with high treason but escaped with his life. Stephen Towgood, the Congregationalist minister at Axminster who had led a group of his members to Monmouth, retreated after he saw the bloodshed but continued to hold field conventicles. Andrew Gifford, pastor of a Particular Baptist church in Bristol who had collected money and ammunition for Monmouth, avoided detection. Gifford had links to the Bedford church, for he had been ordained in August 1677 by the Particular Baptist Daniel Dyke, who was Kiffin's co-pastor, and Nehemiah Coxe, Bunyan's former associate at Bedford, who had become a co-pastor with the Congregationalist John Collins in London. After Bunyan's death, his widow gave a silver tankard to Gifford, clearly an indication of some prior relationship, probably between him and her husband.[9]

Although nonconformists probably did not comprise a majority of the Monmouth rebels, the duke's manifesto called attention to them by demanding the repeal of penal laws against Protestant dissenters. Not surprisingly, nonconformists were among the hundreds of suspected dissidents arrested during and after the rebellions.[10] In the *Observator* L'Estrange accused "the *Whole Body*" of them of having supported Monmouth and reiterated the charges that Owen, Meade, Griffith, Ferguson, Lobb, and others had been party to the duke's plotting in 1683. "It will tend very much to the preserving our future peace," insisted the bishop of Oxford, "if the little remaining incendiaries be glean'd up, especially the Scotch firebrand Ferguson, who can not live out of a conspiracy." The king's instructions to his lords lieutenant concerning the apprehension of disaffected and suspicious people called for special attention to dissenting ministers and those who

---

*Dissenters: From the Reformation to the French Revolution* (Oxford: Clarendon Press, 1978), 257; William Kiffin, *Remarkable Passages in the Life of William Kiffin*, ed. William Orme (London: Burton and Smith, 1823), 53–54, 60, 62, 80. Judge Jeffreys rejected Kiffin's offer to pay £3,000 for his grandsons' release. For Hickes see *BDBR, s.v.*

⁹ *Calamy Revised, s.v.* Joseph Bennett; B. R. White, *The English Baptists of the Seventeenth Century* (London: Baptist Historical Society, 1983), 133; Clifton, *Last Popular Rebellion*, 191, 272; Peter Earle, *Monmouth's Rebels: The Road to Sedgemoor 1685* (New York: St. Martin's Press, 1977), 65, 143; Frank Mott Harrison, "John Bunyan and Andrew Gifford," *Baptist Quarterly* 10 (1940–41): 139–45 . For Collins see Alexander Gordon, ed., *Freedom After Ejection: A Review (1690–1692) of Presbyterian and Congregational Nonconformity in England and Wales* (Manchester: Manchester University Press; London: Longmans, Green and Co., 1917), 240–41. For Gifford see *BDBR, s.v.*; for Towgood (or Toogood) see *Calamy Revised, s.v.* The Bristol Baptist church subscribed to the 1692 folio edition of some of Bunyan's works.

¹⁰ Clifton, *Last Popular Rebellion*, 272–74; BL, Add. MSS 42,849, fol. 2r; Greaves, *SOK*, 417.

had been in arms against his father and brother.[11] Among the imprisoned ministers were the Presbyterians Francis Tallents and Philip Henry, who were confined in Chester Castle with clergy from Lancashire; Henry had opposed Monmouth's rebellion, convinced that God would not work through the duke. Baxter was also under house arrest, having been confined in January or February 1685 for refusing to take the oath of allegiance, and his sentence was not remitted until November 1686.[12] Lingering support for Monmouth may have existed in or near Bunyan's congregation, for at the Bedfordshire sessions in the summer of 1685 the Bedford tailor John Gale, possibly the husband or brother of Elizabeth Gale, a church member, was accused of having spoken favorably of the duke.[13] In February 1686 the government seized three meetinghouses in London, converting two of them into barracks for soldiers from the Tower of London and the other for a hospital. The Congregationalist minister Thomas Jollie, who had to appear before an assize in the late summer of 1685 and was temporarily forced from his home, aptly described the period following the Monmouth rebellion as a time of darkness and "grievous sufferings" for nonconformists.[14] Looking back on 1685–86, Henry remembered that "the coming in of Popery upon us . . . [had been] like a flood, a correction, a threatening, a scourge."[15] Meade's retrospect was similar: "How desperate was our Case, not only with respect to Rights and Properties, but with respect to Religion and the Worship of God; all things being fitted to let in Popery upon us like a Flood."[16]

[11] *Observator*, vol. 3, no. 57 (11 July 1685), and no. 62 (22 July 1685); BL, Add. MSS 29,582, fol. 274r (quoted); PRO, SP 31/2, pp. 18, 36, 38, 41; BL, Add. MSS 71,691, fol. 89r.

[12] BL, Add. MSS 42,849, fol. 1r; Philip Henry, *Diaries and Letters of Philip Henry, M.A. of Broad Oak, Flintshire A.D. 1631–1696*, ed. Matthew Henry Lee (London: Kegan Paul, Trench and Co., 1882), 325; *CSPD, 1684–85*, 293; Geoffrey F. Nuttall, *Richard Baxter* (London: Thomas Nelson and Sons, 1965), 109–11; Baxter, *Calendar*, 2:272, 281–82; Luttrell, 1:345, 350; Morrice, 1:472. Baxter's colleague, William Jenkyn, died in Newgate in January 1685. Luttrell, 1:316, 325. For Tallents see *Calamy Revised, s.v.* Among others charged with participating in London conventicles in early 1685 were Kiffin and the Presbyterians Thomas Watson, Matthew Sylvester, and Thomas Doelittle. CLRO, Conventicle Box 1, no. 4; Conventicle Box 2, no. 1.

[13] BLA, MS HSA 1685 S/38. Matthew Hobbs was also accused of having spoken dangerous words, probably in support of Monmouth, but I have found nothing to link him to the Bedford congregation. MS HSA 1685 S/54. Once the duke launched his rebellion, it was treasonable to assert his legitimacy. BL, Add. MSS 70,070, unbound newsletter of 16 June 1685.

[14] PRO, SP 44/164, p. 297; Thomas Jollie, *The Note Book of the Rev. Thomas Jolly A.D. 1671–1693*, Chetham Society Publications, new ser., 33 (Manchester, 1894), 71–72.

[15] Henry, *Diaries*, 254 (from a fast day sermon preached on 9 August 1693).

[16] Matthew Meade, *The Vision of the Wheels Seen by the Prophet Ezekiel* (London, 1689),

"These Pretended Righteous Men"[17]: Denouncing
Hypocritical, Persecuting Conformists

Charles II was in the final months of his reign when Bunyan began writing
*A Discourse upon the Pharisee and the Publicane* about December 1684. After
referring in *Seasonable Counsel* to the parable of the widow and the unjust judge
who agreed to avenge her against an adversary (*MW*, 10:88; Luke 18:1–8), he
returned to this story in his new book before launching into a substantive exposition of the accompanying parable concerning a Pharisee and a publican
(Luke 18:9–14). By this time the sustained persecution of the Tory Reaction was
clearly troubling Bunyan, who cited the parable of the widow to comfort saints
"under hard usages, by reason of evil Men, their *Might*, and *Tyranny*." The unjust judge was transformed into "an *unmerciful and hard-hearted Tyrant*" on
whom God would ultimately wreak vengeance, and Bunyan held out hope to
the afflicted that God would eventually provide relief from "cruel Tyrants" (10:
113–14). In his powerful opening paragraphs, which contain three references to
tyrants and tyranny, he palpably had the Stuarts in mind. The ire toward the
court manifest in *The Holy War*, the treatise on Antichrist, and the commentary
on Genesis again surfaced, but given the political climate during the winter of
1684–85 he was undoubtedly prudent to shift his attention to the second parable
in Luke 18.

In Bunyan's judgment, Jesus intended the story of the Pharisee and the publican as a means of relieving those burdened by a guilty conscience, though his
own focus in explicating the parable was largely elsewhere (10:114). Concentrating
primarily on the Pharisee, he implored his audience to "*read thy self*" in the book
and reserve judgment about the author until they had finished it (10:111). With
good reason he expected to anger some readers, for the Pharisee was a symbol of
those who prided themselves on superficial, ineffectual religiosity. These were the
residents Christian and Faithful had met in Vanity Fair—the outwardly religious,
inwardly corrupt people who, in Bunyan's view, were loyal to the rituals of the
established church and the regime that enforced its supremacy. Although he
never ruled out the possibility that dissenting congregations had Pharisees in
their midst, his primary target was the Church of England. His hostility was very
likely heightened by the publication of a broadside from the general sessions of
Bedford magistrates, dated 14 January 1685, ordering the penal laws against nonconformists enforced, and an accompanying statement from Bishop Barlow en-

---

97. Clarkson espoused a similar perspective, referring to the return of "the House of
Bondage." DWL, MSS L6/4, sermon on Amos 5:15 (1 March 1686), fol. 114r.
    [17] *MW*, 10:143.

dorsing the use of force to compel uniformity and accusing dissenters of schism.[18]

That the established church was the primary object of Bunyan's withering critique of the Pharisee is evident in several respects, particularly his condemnation of its ritual. "Great is the formality of Religion this day, and little the power thereof." Nothing is more conducive to hypocrisy, he insisted, than an emphasis on formality at the expense of substance (10:129). The pharisaical mistakenly elevate ceremony over faith, love, and hope, confusing true righteousness with "a few lean and *lowsie* Formalities" (10:143, 146). As in *I Will Pray with the Spirit*, he praised extempore prayer, though noting that even these prayers were meaningless if not moved by the Holy Spirit, a slap at some nonconformists (10:128–29). Those who impose regulations for posture during prayer, including kneeling and standing, are innovators, and such rules foster hypocrisy rather than sincere prayer (10:221–22). Prayers devoid of a keen sense of sin and a desire for divine mercy are "the floatings of Pharisaical fancies" (10:235). He warned that "Hypocrisie and a spirit of Errour will so *besmut* Gods Ordinances," including prayer and the sacraments, that he will "take no pleasure in them" (10:224).

Bunyan had the Church of England in mind when he denounced the "hotheaded zeal" of those who add human laws and traditions to what God has appointed for worship, implying by their action that the divinely ordained is imperfect. This, Bunyan thundered, is arrogance and blasphemy, the indefensible attitude of the Tory-Anglicans who punish dissenters for refusing to conform to human traditions. "Why do'st thou Rage, and Rail, and Cry out when men keep not thy Law, or the rule of thine Order, and Tradition of thine Elders? and yet shut thine eyes, or wink with them, when thou thy self shalt live in the breach of the Law of God?" (10:142–43). In his judgment the preposterous zeal of the persecutors was rooted in their misguided sense of righteousness: "What else means thy madness, and the rage thereof, against men as good as thy self?" He had harsh words for lawyers who prosecuted the godly, and for those who allied with attorneys in this endeavor, all of them acting on the basis of a simulated, deficient righteousness tinged with madness (10:142).

The references to treason, trials, and pardons in *A Discourse* suggest that Bunyan was following newspaper reports of the government's prosecution of the conspirators. He likened the soul's sudden apprehension of its loss to the startled sensation caused by the arrival of the king's sergeant-at-arms or a bailiff to make an arrest (10:232), and several times he used the analogy of the king pardoning a traitor (10:184, 210–11), as Charles had done for Monmouth and Lord Howard of Escrick in 1683. Another illustration almost certainly adapted from the newspapers refers to a man indicted for treason who received a royal pardon despite insisting that his

[18]Brown, 323–24.

crimes had been petty in nature (10:209); Bunyan was probably thinking of Monmouth's treatment in 1683. He also noted the diverse behavior of defendants, indicating that one acknowledged guilt in a capital case in the hope of avoiding the death sentence, whereas another, likewise admitting culpability, refused to plead for mercy but cited privilege or promised to lead a good life (10:213, 215). In drawing legal analogies from the contemporary scene, Bunyan also likened the disrepute in which publicans (tax collectors for the Romans) were held by biblical Jews to the vile reputation of informers and bailiffs in his own day (10:118).[19]

Bunyan juxtaposed his condemnation of the Pharisee's superficial righteousness with another exposition of justification by Christ's imputed righteousness. This time, however, he changed his mind with respect to the relation of faith to justification. Hitherto, he had argued that faith is the instrumental cause of justification, making the latter temporally subsequent to faith: In *A Defence of the Doctrine of Justification, by Faith,* he had told Fowler that believers are justified by faith in Christ's blood, and that faith must "go first to the Blood of Christ for Justification, and must bring this home to the Defiled Conscience, before it be delivered from those dead Works that are in it" (*MW*, 4:90). Again, in *Of Justification by an Imputed Righteousness* he averred that the effects of the imputation of Christ's righteousness are found in the godly through the electing love of God and the believer's faith; in Pauline terms, the elect are justified by faith (*MW*, 12:331, 334; Galatians 2:16). Seeking to put as much distance as possible between the works-based pseudo-righteousness of the Pharisees—implicitly, the persecuting Tory-Anglicans—and Christ's imputed righteousness bestowed on the elect, Bunyan reversed his earlier position on the order of salvation by proclaiming in *A Discourse* that justification precedes faith. This means that the elect can be justified without realizing it and in the absence of faith (*MW*, 10:194). Whether knowingly or not, he allied himself with the Antinomians on this point[20] against the position of Calvinist ministers such as Owen, Baxter, Collier,

---

[19] He also compared the publican to a Dutch citizen who had collected taxes for the French occupiers (119), a reference to the war of 1672–78; apart from Maastricht, the Dutch drove most of the French from their country by 1674.

[20] Tobias Crisp, *Christ Alone Exalted* (London, 1690), 85–96. Crisp died in 1643. Three of Bunyan's friends, Cokayne, Griffith, and John Gammon, were among the twelve authors of a preface to this work attesting Crisp's authorship. An epistle, dated 13 April 1646 and written by Cokayne alone, praised Crisp's sermons as "*a full vindication of the truth of Christ*" and "*the sole exaltation of the Lord Jesus in Saints and Duties, and the debasing and trampling upon all flesh that shall aspire to the seat of Christ.*" If these sermons represented Antinomianism, Cokayne asserted, all preaching should be Antinomian (sig. Aaaa3r–v). To the extent that Bunyan displayed some affinity with the Antinomians, he may have been influenced by Cokayne as well as Luther. Cf. Greaves, *JB*, 116–17. He may

Thomas Goodwin, and Stephen Geree.[21] According to Bunyan, "he then that is justified by Gods Imputation, shall believe by the power of the Holy Ghost; for that *MUST* come, and work Faith, and strengthen the Soul to act it, because imputed righteousness has gone before" (10:196). Faith is now the sign of justification but no longer an instrument in God's hands to convey it. The effect was to place as much distance as possible between pharisaical human efforts intended to manifest faith and earn justification on the one hand and the divinely infused righteousness of Christ given solely to the elect on the other. Bunyan found that conveying this message to proponents of the former, "our glorious Justiciaries," provoked an explosive reaction, for those who heard their virtue condemned as worthless felt like "kill[ing] the man that so slighteth and disdaineth his goodly righteousness" (10:161, 166). Thus a direct link existed between the persecution suffered by the godly and their repudiation of the pretended rectitude of latter-day Pharisees.

Bunyan probably finished *A Discourse* in April or early May 1685; it appears in the Term Catalogues under the date 21 May.[22] This time the publisher was John Harris, possibly a relative of Benjamin Harris, for he issued the third through the tenth editions of *Come, & Welcome*, first published by the latter (*MW*, 8:232–37). John Harris wrote a poem about the late Lord Russell and was a partner of Thomas Malthus, who became part of the exile community in the Netherlands in November 1685.[23] John Harris himself would go there in the spring of 1686, joining his brother Samuel, who was well-connected to other dissidents, including Sir John Thompson, Anglesey's son-in-law; Thompson's wife had been a member of Owen's congregation.[24] In the Netherlands John Harris also associated with Wildman, who had links to Meade before Monmouth's ill-fated invasion. Bunyan and John Harris were friends of George Larkin.[25]

---

have been rereading Luther's commentary about this time for he quoted it in this book (10:135; Luther, *Galatians*, 64). Pieter De Vries denies that Bunyan reversed the order of faith and justification in *A Discourse* but offers no evidence. *John Bunyan on the Order of Salvation*, trans. C. van Haaften (New York: Peter Lang, 1994), 151.

[21] Owen, *Works*, 10:276–77; Richard Baxter, *Plain Scripture Proof of Infants Church-Membership and Baptism* (London, 1651), 100, 224; Thomas Collier, *The Body of Divinity* (London, 1674), 19, 187–88; Thomas Goodwin, *The Works of Thomas Goodwin, D.D.*, 4 vols. (London, 1681–97), 4, pt. 1, 104–7; 1, pt. 2, 210–11; Stephen Geree, *The Doctrine of the Antinomians by Evidence of Gods Truth Plainely Confuted* (London, 1644), 99–100; Jeremiah Marsden and John Puckering, DWL, MSS 12.78, fols. 174–75; John Howe, sermon on James 2:23 (17 September 1693), DWL, MS 24.20, fols. 10–11.

[22] Arber, *Term Catalogues*, 3:284.

[23] *MW*, 10:107; Plomer, *DBP*, 146–47; Hill, *TPM*, 289; Greaves, *SOK*, 302, 420. For Harris and Malthus see Plomer, *DBP*, 146–47, 196.

[24] Greaves, *SOK*, 296, 298, 301; Lacey, 448. For Thompson see *DNB*, s.v.

[25] BL, Add. MSS 41,819, fol. 60r–v; *MW*, 10:107.

About the time Bunyan took the manuscript of *A Discourse* to John Harris, he preached a sermon on Proverbs 11:23 in the open-communion church of Stephen More in Southwark. A cloth merchant, More had succeeded Samuel How as pastor of the church in 1640, and seven years later he was commissioned chaplain to Colonel John Barkstead's regiment of foot, which at that time was stationed in London; however, there is no evidence that he served. He died in prison in 1685.[26] Hearing that Bunyan was going to preach to More's congregation, the comb-maker Charles Doe, who had read some of Bunyan's books, made it a point to attend. At first he was put off by the text, having "newly come into *New Testament* Light, in the Love of God, and the Promises, [and] having had enough for the present of the Historical," but Bunyan preached "so *New-Testament*-like, that he made [Doe] admire and weep for Joy, and give him [his] Affections." Doe would subsequently hear other sermons of Bunyan's, finding them relevant to his spiritual state, peppered with apt similitudes, and capable of moving him to tears of delight. "By a Letter I introduced my self into his Acquaintance; and indeed I have not since met with a Man I have lik'd so well."[27]

The first sermon Doe heard Bunyan preach was the nucleus of *The Desire of the Righteous Granted*, which he probably wrote between about June and August 1685. In it he defined the righteous as those who have been made so by the imputation of Christ's righteousness and possess a principle of rectitude that enables them to live virtuously (*MW*, 13:115). Linkage to *A Discourse* is provided by a reminder of the parable of the Pharisee and the publican and a reassertion of his recently developed view that justification precedes faith: "To say, That an unjustified Man, has Faith . . . is to overthrow the Gospel. For what need of Christ's Righteousness, if a Man may have Faith and the Spirit of Christ without it?" (13:107, 111). Walking in Christ—acting virtuously—is no more possible without Christ's imputed righteousness than for black parents to beget white children (13:111–12, 114). It is no less true, argued Bunyan, that without evidence of sanctification one cannot have been justified (13:115). To be acceptable to God, the desires of the righteous must be essential to the soul's well-being or intrinsically good, such as wanting an increase in grace (13:153–54). He cautioned, however, that "the more Grace, . . . the greater Trials." With a newly enthroned Catholic king, he thought it worthwhile to emphasize that "new Work, new Tryals, new

---

[26] Murray Tolmie, *The Triumph of the Saints: The Separate Churches of London, 1616–1649* (Cambridge: Cambridge University Press, 1977), 36, 40, 66; Anne Laurence, *Parliamentary Army Chaplains, 1642–1651* (Woodbridge, Suffolk: Boydell Press, for the Royal Historical Society, 1990), 155; W. T. Whitley, *The Baptists of London, 1612–1928* (London: Kingsgate Press, [1928]), 105.

[27] Charles Doe, *A Collection of Experience of the Work of Grace* (London, [1700]), 52.

Sufferings" would bring substantial infusions of grace to assist the godly (13:157–58). Simultaneously he insisted that it was unlawful for the faithful to desire the lives of their enemies (13:153), a principle that implicitly repudiated the Argyll and Monmouth rebels.

Believers can legitimately seek liberty to enjoy divine ordinances, which Bunyan described as God's love-letters and love-tokens (13:124–25, 130). In this context he used the term "ordinance" broadly to encompass not only the sacraments but also the broader communion of saints in church-fellowship, and he noted how God's people had historically ventured everything, including their lives, for these ordinances "in their purity" (13:131). Implicitly this was yet another indictment of the established church, which lacked purity of worship and was unable to engage in such fellowship because it made no attempt to restrict membership to visible saints. This church and its defenders, he said, were now kicking the saints around like footballs (13:134). Likening formalists to sluggards whose piety "lies in a few of the *shells* of Religion," he warned that hypocrites would perish in their own excrement (13:102, 144–45). Not surprisingly, Bunyan or one of his publishers presumably decided that it would be imprudent to print this book in late 1685 or 1686, and once James had issued a declaration of indulgence in April 1687, such criticism would have been impolitic. Moreover, at that point there was no longer a need to seek liberty to enjoy God's ordinances. For whatever reason, Bunyan set aside the manuscript, which remained unpublished in his lifetime.

## "God's Iron Whip"[28]: Seeking Hope Amid Persecution

The assizes to try the Monmouth rebels commenced on 26 August, about the time Bunyan finished *The Desire of the Righteous Granted*, and concluded on 23 September, though executions continued into November.[29] In the meantime magistrates cracked down on nonconformists, creating considerable apprehension and fear. Cokayne and Plant were among those accused of participating in conventicles. "The Persecution grew very hot, that great Meetings were all scattered and divided in private," observed Charles Doe, who owed £280 in recusancy fines by the time the king issued a declaration of indulgence in April 1687.[30] Bunyan's old nemesis, Edward Fowler, now rector of St. Giles, Cripplegate, London, proudly informed the archbishop of Canterbury that he had been successful in "bringing over abundance of people from the Separation" to the Church of England.[31] In this context Bunyan turned from his attack on pharisaical conformists

---

[28] *MW*, 13:387.
[29] Clifton, *Last Popular Rebellion*, 233–39.
[30] CLRO, Conventicle Box 2, nos. 1 and 6; Doe, *A Collection*, 51 (quoted).
[31] Bodl., Tanner MSS 31, fol. 225r.

to a work offering comfort and hope to the dissenting community. He probably started his new book, posthumously published as *The Saints Knowledge of Christs Love*, in September 1685 against the backdrop of Jeffreys' assizes and completed it by year's end. Because the work was written during a period of substantial persecution, it cannot have been composed after the promulgation of a declaration of indulgence in April 1687.

At the outset Bunyan set the tone by interpreting his text, Ephesians 3:18–19, as Paul's prayer that the saints could see how they "are secured from the evil of the worst that might come upon them" (*MW*, 13:339). Apart from the closing paragraph, which addresses non-believers, this work was composed to assist the godly at a time when it might have seemed that "the whole face of Heaven" was hidden; in his estimation, they had two options: despair and die, or apprehend the astounding scope of divine love and mercy. The breadth of God's love, he stressed, "overmatcheth that spreading and *over spreading* Rage of Men" that seemingly threatens to engulf the entire church. Whatever the trials confronting the saints, Bunyan was convinced that divine grace is more than sufficient to sustain and relieve the persecuted (13:343).

In developing this theme Bunyan addressed the role of monarchs and magistrates, including judges, a timely touch given the assizes over which Jeffreys and his colleagues were presiding. The fundamental principle was straightforward: "Who ever is set up on earth, they are set up by our Lord," and once established, they govern within divinely established parameters, lacking the freedom to pursue their own will without restraint. Holding the bridle in his hands, Christ "giveth reins, or check, even as it pleaseth him" (13:378). Monarchs and magistrates persecute the saints only if God permits, but in doing so they place themselves squarely in the path of divine vengeance. Bunyan referred his readers to Isaiah 8:8–10, in which the prophet foretold the Assyrian conquest of Judah, an example of the rage of rulers against the godly (13:343). Biblically literate readers would have known that two chapters later (10:26–27) Isaiah prophesied the overthrow of Assyrian domination, comparing it to the punishment inflicted on the Egyptians when Moses lifted his rod and the waters engulfed the pharaoh and his army. Bunyan used this account (Exodus 14) in a passage charged with political overtones:

> The *Greatness* of God, . . . if rightly considered, . . . will support the spirits of those of his people that are frighted with the greatness of their Adversaries. For here is a greatness against a greatness. *Pharaoh* was great, but God more great. (13:341)

God "collered with him, overcame him, and cast him down" (13:412), and he could do the same with James.

In this work Bunyan's primary concern was providing comfort and guidance to the godly during this period of persecution, not denouncing James' regime. Referring to the solace provided by God during his own tribulations, he assured his coreligionists that divine assistance would "always come in for your help against them that contend with you" (13:341). The key to understanding tribulation, he explained, is providence, for it uses the cross to purge fleshly desires inimical to godliness; trials are thus a divine blessing and a gift that brings believers closer to the throne of grace. The persecuted are "the best sort of Christians," not least because "the afterwards of affliction doth yield the peaceable fruits of righteousness to them that are exercised thereby" (13:357–58). He hoped visible saints could find solace in recognizing that Christ had "so disabled our Foes, that they cannot now accomplish their designed enmity upon us," and he urged them to focus on the last judgment when they will join Christ in sentencing the wicked to everlasting perdition (13:394–95).

To fear oppressors, he declaimed, is to forget God, but to be remiss in observing divine ordinances is to be careless in a time of peril (13:361). The problem, of course, was that repressive magistrates were endeavoring to bar access to nonconformist preaching, administration of the sacraments, and church fellowship. As Bunyan presumably knew from his pastoral experience, consciences deprived of spiritual nourishment could become tormented with temptation and guilt (13:345–46). What he witnessed in late 1685 reminded him of his spiritual turmoil in the 1650s, though the circumstances were quite different. Christians, he observed, "have sometimes their sinking Fits, and are as if they were alwaies descending" (13:347), not least because of their sensitivity to recurring temptations and the virtual impossibility of upholding the highest Christian moral standards without lapses. Guilt can toss a soul like a ship in a tempest, but so can the experience of persecution, even to the point of utter despair (13:345, 413). One of the more intriguing aspects of *The Saints Knowledge of Christ's Love* is Bunyan's juxtaposition of the despair caused by persecution with that triggered by a profound sense of spiritual guilt. The latter, he recognized, can drive a person to contemplate suicide (13:409). For both kinds of despair the cure is identical: grasping the fact that Christ's love is infinite and incomprehensible (13:384, 388). "The help for a stay from utter despair is at hand," namely, "the love of Christ which passeth knowledge," in the words of Bunyan's text (13:402).

He included some subtle comments pertaining to political developments in the mid-1680s. Tory-Anglican efforts to associate nonconformists with the recent conspiracies and invasions were countered with the assertion that Jesus himself had been accused of being a rebel against the state, and Bunyan's reference to the Devil's "Plottings, Contrivings and designs and attempts" made Satan the arch conspirator (13:373, 388). In addition to implicitly associating James with a pharaoh and Assyrian monarchs, Bunyan made a powerful political comment near the end of the book. Referring to the governing powers, he wrote: "If the shields of the earth be the Lords, then he can wield them for the safeguard of his Body the Church; or if they are become uncapable of being made use of any longer in that way, and for such a thing, can he not lay them aside, and make himself new ones? Men can do after this manner, much more God" (13:412–13). Monmouth and Argyll had not been the "new ones," but Bunyan did not relinquish his belief that God could supplant any regime once it had "become uncapable of being made use of any longer." James II could be replaced.[32] These were daring words in the fall of 1685, and that fact may explain why Bunyan or his publisher decided not to print the work.

About the time Bunyan completed *The Saints Knowledge of Christ's Love* he drafted a deed of gift dated 23 December 1685, sealed with a two-pence piece, and witnessed by four members of his church, including John Gifford's son-in-law, William Hawkes. Describing himself as a brazier living in St. Cuthbert's parish, Bunyan, in consideration of "the natural affection and love which I have and bear into my well-beloved wife," gave Elizabeth ownership of all his money, rings, apparel, household goods, and other possessions as well as responsibility for his debts. He hid the document in their house, and Elizabeth apparently forgot about it or did not know where it was hidden, for after his death the archdeacon's court treated him as having died intestate. The document was not found until the nineteenth century.[33] The decision to transfer ownership of all possessions to his wife as opposed to bequeathing them to her at his death suggests a concern that he might be rearrested and have his property confiscated, and this would help to explain his wariness about publishing manuscripts critical of the government or the established church in the 1680s.

### "*Catching Girls and Boys*"[34]: Homely Rhymes and Poetic Diversions

Bunyan found diversion from his ministerial challenges and the plight of nonconformity in music and poetry, which appear to have been his principal pastimes. Among his ministerial colleagues, Henry Jessey, Benjamin Keach, and Hanserd Knollys shared his love of verse.[35] Bunyan gave voice to poetry and mu-

---

[32] Mullett's assessment of this book is sharply divergent. In his view, "there is an almost complete absence of political commentary and what there is is innocuous enough." Mullett, *JBC*, 281.

[33] The document is reproduced in Brown, 338–39.

[34] *MW*, 6:191.

[35] Examples of Keach's poetry are quoted in Chapter 10. Knollys copied poems, including a dialogue between body and soul, in a commonplace book. BL, Add. MSS 29,921,

sic in both parts of *The Pilgrim's Progress* and again in *A Book for Boys and Girls: or, Country Rhimes for Children*. Published by Ponder, the latter was in print by 12 May 1686, when a purchaser recorded the date on the title-page of the copy now in the British Library.[36] Since the poems have no logical progression, they were probably composed over a substantial period of time and then finalized for the printer in the early months of 1686.[37] Bunyan intended the volume to serve in part as a handbook for parents who were teaching their children to read, for it begins with black letter, roman, and italic alphabets, a guide to vowels and consonants, brief comments on spelling and syllables, a list of people's first names as a spelling guide, and lists of arabic and roman numerals (*MW*, 6:194–96). The remainder of the book comprises seventy-four poems of varying quality, ranging in length from four lines to more than two hundred. Rosemary Freeman's harsh verdict—the verse is "amateurish rather than positively bad, bearing some of the marks of genius working in a wrong medium"—is excessive, particularly in light of the wit displayed in the emblem of the spider and the emotional force in the emblem of a disobedient child. Bunyan has fared better with more recent critics: Kathleen Swaim found the poems "lively, direct, effective, and multileveled," and Graham Midgely opined that this verse "shows Bunyan at his best and most adventurous as a poet, and expresses more completely the many sides of his personality," including his love of children, his gentleness, his country pursuits, and his keen observation of nature.[38] However, the substantial variations in quality make any generalization problematic.

Most of the poems are emblems, a tradition developed by Catholic and Protestant writers primarily for meditation and moral edification in ways that delighted readers. Emblems imaginatively link two disparate ideas; "an *Embleme* is but a silent Parable," explained Francis Quarles.[39] The emblem was particularly useful for Protestants engaged in the practice of occasional meditation; Bunyan used them to encourage this practice, which his fellow dissenter, William Bates,

---

fols. 4r–36r. For Jessey's poetry see *Miscellanea Sacra: or, Diverse Necessary Truths* (London, 1665).

[36] According to the title-page the work was licensed, though it does not appear in the Stationers' Register.

[37] Roger Sharrock thought Bunyan was probably collecting animal parables in the 1680s, particularly after including the emblems of the spider and the robin with a spider in its mouth in the second part of *The Pilgrim's Progress*. "Bunyan and the English Emblem Writers," *Review of English Studies* 21 (April 1945): 116.

[38] Rosemary Freeman, *English Emblem Books* (London: Chatto and Windus, 1948), 215; Swaim, *PP*, 243; *MW*, 6:lvii.

[39] Francis Quarles, *Emblemes*, 4th ("2nd") ed. (Cambridge, 1643), sig. A3r.

thought was rare among Christians.[40] Seventeenth-century Protestant authors found the subject matter for emblems in Scripture, nature, personifications, abstract symbols, and fables. Religious writers also developed emblems that focused on the heart and its regeneration; in the hands of Protestants this meant God's working on the heart through grace.[41] Bunyan may have read the works of the last major practitioners of this literary form in England, George Wither's *A Collection of Emblemes, Ancient and Moderne* (1635) and Quarles' *Emblemes* (1635) and *Hieroglyphikes of the Life of Man* (1638). If so, the influence was probably not great, at least in the case of Quarles, for Bunyan's emblems manifest a rustic simplicity that contrasts with Quarles' complexity, ingenuity, and visual riddles. Nor did Bunyan emulate Quarles' practice of beginning an emblem with a biblical verse. Presumably he would have found Wither, with his simpler style and emphasis on ethical virtues, more to his liking.[42] There is no firm evidence that Bunyan borrowed from Thomas Jenner's *The Soules Solace, or Thirtie and One Spirituall Emblems* (1626), which drew its inspiration from sermons, incorporated homely examples, and addressed readers in a colloquial style.[43] With a focus on creatures and simple dialogue, a popular, colloquial version of Aesop's fables, such as *The Fables of Aesop* (1634), John Ogilby's *The Fables of Aesop Paraphras'd in Verse* (1665), or *Aesop Improved or, Above Three Hundred and Fifty Fables* (1673), probably had an impact on Bunyan. *The Fables of Aesop* blend the fable and the emblem, and all three adaptations employ a simple, colloquial style much like that found in *A Book for Boys and Girls*.[44] If anything, Bunyan's verse was even simpler and his themes were equally elementary.

He wrote for children of all ages, including, as he put it, boys with beards and girls as large as elderly women (*MW*, 6:190). Conscious of his evangelical responsibilities, he was more concerned that his message strike home than with impressing readers by a polished style:

[40] William Bates, *A Discourse of Divine Meditation*, in *The Spirituality of the Later English Puritans: An Anthology*, ed. Dewey D. Wallace, Jr. (Macon, GA: Mercer University Press, 1987), 100.

[41] Barbara Kiefer Lewalski, *Protestant Poetics and the Seventeenth-Century Religious Lyric* (Princeton, NJ: Princeton University Press, 1979), 184–96; Freeman, *English Emblem Books*, 3; Swaim, *PP*, 243. For the problem of defining 'emblem' see Peter M. Daly, *Literature in the Light of the Emblem: Structural Parallels Between the Emblem and Literature in the Sixteenth and Seventeenth Centuries*, 2nd ed. (Toronto: University of Toronto Press, 1998), 3–9.

[42] *MW*, 6:xxxvii; Freeman, *English Emblem Books*, 114–32, 140–47. For Wither see *DNB*, s.v.

[43] *MW*, 6:xxxix–xl; Freeman, *English Emblem Books*, 87.

[44] *MW*, 6:xl–xliii.

> *I could, were I so pleas'd, use higher Strains,*
> *And for Applause, on Tenters stretch my Brains,*
> *But what needs that? The Arrow out of Sight,*
> *Does not the Sleeper, nor the Watchman fright.* (6:192)

The "*Foolish,*" he thought, would prefer his homely rhymes, and these are the people God has chosen, an allusion to Luke 10:21. In this case "*Foolish Things*" are the simple devices God and his messengers employ to convey gospel teachings, much as Jesus used "familiar Speech." Emphasizing that his content was weighty notwithstanding the simplicity of his means (6:191–92, 235), Bunyan envisioned his audience as all those who are childlike—the minimally educated and culturally unsophisticated. With such people in mind, he crafted emblems that began as word-pictures (unlike most emblem books, which included engravings or wood-cuts), following these with easily understood moral lessons. Whereas the emblems of writers such as Quarles are "intricately contrived problem-picture[s]" that require skillful interpretation, Bunyan's were taken from daily life and embodied meanings readily accessible to his intended audience (6:xxxviii).

Composing the poems in *A Book for Boys and Girls* provided an opportunity for Bunyan to meditate on nature, music, and the light-and-darkness motif he found so intriguing. As we saw in Chapter Eight, animals, birds, and other creatures populate nearly all of his writings, reflecting both their biblical importance and his interest in the natural realm. Sir Keith Thomas has noted that animals, including cows and pigs as well as the obvious dogs and horses, were ubiquitous in towns, and in London poulterers kept thousands of live fowl in their attics and cellars.[45] All of these creatures appear in Bunyan's works, as do those popularly envisioned as the monarchs of their respective realms—the lion, the eagle, and the whale.[46] Most of the creatures identified by Thomas as the privileged species of the age are found in Bunyan's writings: horses, hawks, dogs, cats, monkeys, lambs, nightingales and larks (valued as cage-birds), and robins, a sort of honorary pet.[47] He also included such domesticated animals as hogs, sheep, oxen, asses, and goats as well as such objects of the hunt as the fox and the hart. He referred to rats, mice, and moles; to wolves, boars, and otters; to bears and bulls, often the objects of baiting in early modern England; and to exotic animals, including camels, leopards, tigers, and apes.[48] The reptiles in his works include tortoises and

---

[45]Keith Thomas, *Man and the Natural World: Changing Attitudes in England, 1500–1800* (Oxford: Oxford University Press, 1983), 95.

[46]Ibid., 60.

[47]Ibid., 100–120.

[48] Unlike Bunyan, Philip Henry distinguished between birds and animals which are "profitable" to humanity, including sheep, oxen, and pigs, and those which are "hurtfull," including tigers, bears, and wolves. CUL, Add. MSS 7338, commenting on Genesis 7.

serpents, with specific mention of asps and adders, and amphibians are represented by frogs and toads. Like serpents and amphibians, insects were widely disliked in early modern England;[49] Bunyan found places for grasshoppers and locusts, bees and hornets, butterflies and moths, flies and fleas, and ants. From the
realm of arachnids came spiders and scorpions, and he also found meaning in
worms, maggots, and snails. In addition to eagles, hawks, robins, nightingales,
jackdaws, and larks, his writings include references to sparrows, doves, ravens,
crows, owls, swallows, cuckoos, wrens, and vultures as well as partridges (including pheasants), pelicans, storks, ostriches, and peacocks. He apparently had little
knowledge of or interest in fish, other than to mention them in general terms,
though he knew the seas contained "small and great Beasts," including fish of
prey (*MW*, 12:115). Finally, his "Book of Creatures" (*MW*, 13:360) included mythical dragons and cockatrices.

Quarles asked, "What are the Heavens, the Earth, nay every Creature, but
*Hieroglyphicks* and *Emblems* of [God's] Glory?"[50] Bunyan concurred, and *A Book
for Boys and Girls* evinces his belief that God is revealed in the Book of Creatures,
the Book of Nature, and the Book of Providences as well as the Bible (13:360). All
the creatures mentioned in his works have something to teach humankind about
God, and the emblems Bunyan wrote were intended to instruct his audience how
to "read" the natural world. He provided them with a methodology for learning
from the Books of Creatures and Nature as well as the specific lessons embodied
in the emblems.

> *Wise* Solomon *did Fools to Piss-ants send,*
> *To learn true Wisdom, and their Lives to mend.*
> *Yea, God by Swallows, Cuckows, and the Ass,*
> *Shews they are Fools who let that season pass,*
> *Which he put in their hand. . . .* (*MW*, 6:192)

This is, then, a book of instruction and meditation, a guide to "reading" nature as
well as the ABCs. Given the fact that it includes poetic versions of the Ten Commandments, the Lord's prayer, and the creed as well as poems on the sacraments,
Christ's love, the spouse of Christ, and human nature, *A Book for Boys and Girls*
served almost as a catechism in verse.

The longest poem in the book comprises a dialogue between a spider and a
scoffing sinner in which the former functions rather like Interpreter in the first
part of *The Pilgrim's Progress*, teaching the sinner about the different paths to hell
(the varied places the spider spins its web), the snares laid by the Devil (the spider's trapping of flies), and the importance of boldly seeking entrance to Christ's

---

[49]Thomas, *Man and the Natural World*, 57.
[50]Quarles, *Emblemes*, sig. A3r.

kingdom, much as the spider has found its way into a royal palace. "*They learn may, that to Spiders go to School.*" Although allusions to the contemporary political scene are rare in this book, Bunyan did incorporate one in the sinner's response to the spider's depiction of him as filthy:

> *God has possessed me with humane Reason,*
> *Speak not against me, lest thou speakest Treason.*

Bunyan's point was that the spider had been accurate in its characterization of the sinner, a fact the latter could not cloak by wrapping himself in treason statutes. In fact, the spider retorted by calling the sinner a traitor to God (6:214–21). There was a political point here for those who cared to ponder it: The real traitors are not those who denounce the mighty as sinners but those who cover their evil by accusing their critics of sedition. Another political allusion is found in the emblem of the rose bush, which uses its thorns to spill the blood of those lured too close by its flowers: "This looks like a Treppan, or a Decoy," alluding to government spies who encouraged plotters for the purpose of entrapping them (6:238). A third allusion is found in the emblem of the horse and drum; whereas some horses are so skittish that the sound of a drum scares them away, others hold their ground, as do Christians who stand firm in the face of persecution (6:252–53).

Bunyan took advantage of popular perceptions of creatures to make some of his points. The frog was widely seen as ugly and filthy,[51] a point he reinforced by describing it as damp and cold, with an oversized mouth and belly and a penchant to sit in gardens croaking unpleasantly. To Bunyan the frog was like a big-mouthed, cold-natured hypocrite:

> And though he seeks in Churches for to croak,
> He neither loveth Jesus, nor his Yoak.  (6:240)

Bunyan derided cuckoos, whose spit some people thought was poisonous,[52] because they could not sing like robins and wrens or herald the spring, but only suck eggs and make unwelcome noise:

> The Formalist we may compare her to,
> For he doth suck our Eggs and sing Cuckow.  (6:222–23)

The allusions to the frog and the cuckoo were directed primarily toward adherents of the Church of England. He was partial toward the lark, for the fowler who attempted to trap it was an emblem of the Devil, "his Nets and Whistle, Figures of all evil" (6:225–26). In popular lore swallows nesting under eaves brought

---

[51] Thomas, *Man and the Natural World*, 57.
[52] Ibid., 74.

luck,[53] and Bunyan, who admired their singing and graceful flight, likened their wings to faith and their chirping notes to songs of peace (6:207). He could also counter popular views, as in his treatment of the snail, which many associated with putrefied matter.[54] In the snail's resolve to reach its objective, he saw an emblem of a sinner intent on finding and feeding on Christ (6:256–57). Like so many of his countrymen, he deemed ants and bees instructive, the former because of their diligent work in storing food for the coming winter, but whereas contemporaries observed similar qualities in bees,[55] he viewed them as an emblem of sin because of their capacity to sting and kill (6:207–8). He passed up an opportunity to portray moles as emblematic of blind Catholics,[56] using them instead to portray unregenerate people too in love with the world to see heaven's glory (6:221–22). As he observed folks with phobias about frogs, dogs, cats, rats, mice, worms, lice, or flies, he noted the irony, for "Man by Creation was made Lord of all,/But now he is become an Underling" (6:263). From the tone of this poem one suspects that he did not share these fears but instead found such creatures intriguing because of the lessons they could teach about things divine.

In this collection Bunyan's love of music finds expression in verse about bell-ringing and musical instruments in skilled and unskilled hands. Two other poems—on a child and a bird, and on a rose bush—have accompanying tunes he either composed or borrowed. The range of both is high, perhaps suggesting he was a tenor, though he may have been composing with the flute or violin in mind. Like Owen, he was a flautist, reportedly carving a flute from a chair leg while in prison, and he may also have made the metal violin on which is inscribed "John Bunyan, Helstowe."[57] He probably knew something about the virginal as well, for a fellow church member, William Whitbread, owned one.[58] Although the first tune is nondescript, the second, as Midgley indicates, has a religious modal character (6:338). Of the three emblems dealing with musical themes, one depicts an unskilled musician playing out of tune or clumsily breaking a string on his instrument, the emblem of a novice in religious matters who abuses the Bible and fails to make truth shine (6:242–43). In contrast, the talented player is an emblem of a gospel minister who "rightly preacheth (and doth Godly pray)" (6:259–60).

[53] Ibid., 76.
[54] Ibid., 55.
[55] Ibid., 63–64.
[56] Ibid., 64.
[57] Percy A. Scholes, *The Puritans and Music in England and New England: A Contribution to the Cultural History of Two Nations* (London: Oxford University Press, 1934), 384–86 (which includes illustrations of the flute and violin).
[58] Joyce Godber, *History of Bedfordshire, 1066–1888* (Bedford: Bedfordshire County Council, 1969), 291.

The best of the musical emblems draws on Bunyan's enjoyment of bell-ringing:

> When Ringers handle them with Art and Skill,
> They then the ears of their Observers fill,
> With such brave Notes, they ting and tang so well
> As to out strip all with their ding, dong, Bell.

Likening the bells to the powers of his soul, he envisioned the clappers as the passions of his mind, the bell-ropes as promises, and his body as the steeple.

> My Graces they which do ring ev'ry Bell:
> Nor is there any thing gives such a tang,
> When by these Ropes these Ringers ring them well.

As they peal, the bells' glorious sound drowns "the tempting tinckling Voice of Vice," but when mischievous boys (his lusts) sneak into the belfry and pull the ropes, the cacophony shakes the very belfry; "from such Ringers of Musick there's no hopes." Bunyan briefly recalled his psychological trauma and the absence of musical enjoyment that characterizes the silent depths into which the depressed plunge:

> Lord! when my Bells have gone, my Soul has bin
> As 'twere a tumbling in the Paradice!

In religious terms the perceived deprivation of graces (divine promises) pitches the soul into seemingly hopeless disequilibrium, a state devoid of the musical harmony characteristic of skillfully played bells (6:231–32).

Ten of the poems deal with the motif of light and darkness, a theme of particular interest to Bunyan since his bouts with despondency. His treatment of the motif in this work lacks the intensity of some of his earlier writing, partly because of his distance from the melancholic episodes, and partly owing to the childlike audience he was addressing. A meditation before sunrise looks emblematically for Christ, "whose goodly face doth warm and heal,/And shew us what the darksome nights conceal" (6:221). The first hint of light at daybreak is symbolic of those unsure whether they are divinely blessed (light) or cursed (darkness), but once the sun has risen, "the night is gone, the shadow's fled away," and believers, bathed in light, have no more reason to doubt divine grace and love (6:205, 228). Light is associated with assurance, life, and hope, whereas the gloom of night is indicative of doubt, despair, and death, not rest.[59] Instead of the sunset being a

---

[59] Quarles too had mostly negative connotations for night and darkness, though he also associated the onset of darkness with rest: "And the descending damp doth now prepare /T' uncurl bright *Titans* hair;/Whose western wardrobe now begins t' unfold/Her purples,

thing of beauty, one of nature's crowning glories, to Bunyan it had bad connotations, which in religious terms he likened to God's withdrawal of grace. "Let not the voice of night-Birds us afflict" (6:239). A cloudy day, however, might bring hope if the black clouds are rimmed with the sun's silvery, shimmering light.

> Unto the Saints sweet incense or their Prayer,
> These Smoaky curdled Clouds I do compare.
> For as these Clouds seem edg'd or lac'd with Gold,
> Their Prayers return with Blessings manifold.  (6:213)

The rays of sunlight piercing the heavy overcast on a rainy morn are emblems of gospel light, tinging the clouds like the blood of Christ, the rain symbolizing the tears of penitent sinners (6:209).

The light of candles and lanterns offered Bunyan additional opportunities to explore this motif. In an emblem about candles that had fallen on the floor in the darkness, the one still in its place was lit (Christ) in order to find the others (the elect "in their lapst State") (6:245). Working with the same theme in another emblem, he made the point that candles cannot light themselves anymore than souls can infuse themselves with grace. The larger the candle, the greater the light, "as Grace on biggest Sinners shines most bright." Christians are like candles in the night, their light showing "others how their course to steer." In a storm—in tribulation—a candle will burn unsteadily, flickering as if to be extinguished, much as Christians "in a Tempest [are apt] to despair" (6:210–12). This linkage between the threat of darkness and the onset of despair may have been evoked by memories of his earlier psychological and spiritual turmoil. In another emblem he used the familiar image of the moth attacking and finally being destroyed by the candle flame to symbolize the ultimate failure of persecutors to extinguish the light of the gospel (6:224–25). Bunyan's embrace of light as a symbol of life, warmth, and comfort—a theme that is experientially as well as biblically based—is patent in these emblems.

Experience of a different sort is reflected in his emblem about a disobedient child, a subject uncomfortably close to Bunyan during the winter of 1679–80. Two counterfeiters, pretending to be button-makers, set up shop in Bedford and began passing bad coins with the assistance of William Robinson, a stonemason's son. They were arrested and incarcerated in the county jail, where they met Edward Cooke, a thief. To facilitate the release of Cooke and Robinson, presumably local men, Thomas Bunyan, the minister's younger son by his first marriage,[60]

---

fring'd with gold, / To cloath his evening glory, when th' alarms / Of rest shall call to rest...."
*Hieroglyphikes of the Life of Man, ad cal. Emblemes* (London, 1660), 375. For examples of Quarles' negative connotations of night see *Emblemes*, 57–58, 65, 129–30, 225–26.

[60] This Thomas Bunyan is not to be confused with his uncle of the same name. The

Thomas Hunilove, whose father (of the same name) belonged to Bunyan's congregation, and Thomas Brancklin, an apprentice to Robinson's father, allegedly schemed to obtain money to pay the jailer's fees by robbing travelers at night. After learning of the plan, magistrates made young Bunyan find two sureties, one of whom was his brother John, the pastor's eldest son and a metal-worker. Thomas was to have been indicted at the next assizes on charges of soliciting Brancklin to steal horses for use in committing the highway robberies, but the records do not indicate the case's disposition. Perhaps the elder Bunyan employed an attorney to assist his son. The fact that sons of two leading members of the church had reputedly become embroiled in such conduct and associated with men of disrepute must have caused a scandal and embarrassed their fathers.[61] Bunyan would undoubtedly have agreed with Philip Henry that "the Miscarriages of children doe oftentimes reflect reproch upon their Innocent parents."[62]

The emblem of a disobedient son was almost certainly inspired by Thomas and evinces his father's deep pain and bitterness.

> Children become, while little, our delights,
> When they grow bigger, they begin to fright's.

Rejecting a father's grave instructions, children take the counsel of libertines, engage in pursuits harmful to their souls, and reckon themselves masters over their parents.

> How many Children, by becoming Head,
> Have brought their Parents to a peice of Bread.
> Thus they who at the first were Parents Joy,
> Turn that to Bitterness, themselves destroy.

Having begun this poem with a reference to children's sinful nature, Bunyan offered no moral, opting instead to let his pain drive the verse to its disconsolate conclusion:

> For their Indulgent Love, and tender Care,
> All is forgot, this Love he doth despise,
> They brought this Bird up to pick out their Eyes. (6:264–65)

---

latter joined his brother's church in July 1673, lived at Northill, and became a preacher. *CB*, 75, 96.

[61] BLA, MSS HSA 1680 W/8, 57, 77–78; Patricia Bell, "Thomas Bunyan and Mr Badman," *BS* 2 (Spring 1990): 47–50. Thomas Bunyan had to post a recognizance of £20, and his brother John and the tailor William Linford each posted £10 on his behalf. The latter may have been related to Mary Linford, a member of Bunyan's congregation. *CB*, 22, 214.

[62] CUL, Add. MSS 7338, commenting on Genesis 34. Henry thought excessive affection on the parents' part "causes too much Affliction." Ibid., commenting on Genesis 37.

Thomas apparently never became a member of his father's congregation, turning instead to the Church of England, where his son Steven would be baptized at St. Cuthbert's, Bedford, on 14 November 1687, his daughter Elizabeth (by a second wife) on 29 January 1693, and another son, Stephen (the first having died), on 25 December 1696. John Bunyan's youngest child, Joseph, would pursue a similar religious path, marrying at St. Paul's, Bedford, in December 1694, and having his children, Chernock and Ann, baptized there in October 1695 and October 1696 respectively.[63] Bunyan had died well before these landmarks in Joseph's life, but he had probably seen enough of Thomas' proclivities to conclude, in dismay, that he delighted "in Paths that lead to Hell" (6:264). Bunyan's oldest son, who shared his father's name and trade, joined the Bedford church, but not until 27 June 1693.[64]

### "Take Shelter"[65]: Christ as Refuge

When Bunyan took the manuscript of *A Book for Boys and Girls* to London about March 1686, Parliament was no longer in session, for James had prorogued it on 20 November. In a session of less than two weeks it had attacked the standing army raised by the king during the summer, preferring that he restore the militia instead. Controversy also erupted over James' dispensing of the Test for nearly ninety Catholics whom he commissioned as officers in the army. The king was in the House of Lords on the 19th when it debated the question of Catholic officers, and the harsh criticism was undoubtedly a factor in his decision to prorogue Parliament.[66] Protestant concern heightened as news of Louis XIV's revocation of the Edict of Nantes spread and as people learned about the bishop of Valence's speech exhorting Louis and James to cooperate in eradicating heresy in their realms. Alarmed Anglican leaders, including Henry Compton, bishop of London, engaged in an anti-Catholic campaign in the press and pulpit as well as through catechizing, prompting the king to issue directions in March 1686 ordering the clergy to avoid controversial subjects, not meddle in matters of state, and focus on practical divinity.[67] About the same time, the king, thanks largely to the endeavors of William Penn, issued a general pardon for religious offenses to those for whom judgment was pending, and he ordered the release of approxi-

---

[63] Brown, 391–92.

[64] *CB*, 98; Brown, 388–89.

[65] *MW*, 13:170.

[66] John Miller, *James II: A Study in Kingship* (Hove, East Sussex: Wayland Publishers, 1977), 146–47; Lois G. Schwoerer, *"No Standing Armies!": The Antiarmy Ideology in Seventeenth-Century England* (Baltimore: Johns Hopkins University Press, 1974), 140–45.

[67] Miller, *James II*, 154; Harris, *PULS*, 125; *CSPD*, *1686–87*, 56–58.

mately 1,600 Quakers from prison, though Friends continued to suffer well after this.[68]

Generally, the scale of persecution began declining in 1686. In London and Middlesex the number of Quakers prosecuted for attending conventicles dropped from 209 in 1685 to 83 in 1686, down from 401 and 440 in 1683 and 1684 respectively.[69] For many other nonconformists, however, persecution continued. Edward Ange, the royal agent responsible for collecting recusancy fines, received orders in December 1685 to prosecute conventiclers and excommunicates unless they possessed loyalty certificates. In January the Congregationalist Thomas Jollie was fearful about his impending appearance at an assize, having heard reports that the judges intended to deal severely with dissenters; the people of God, he noted, were suffering. For attending conventicles in Middlesex, several thousand people were arrested between February and June 1686 alone, among them the Presbyterian Samuel Annesley, the Baptist Laurence Wise, and the Fifth Monarchist Walter Thimbleton. In May, soldiers in London disrupted a Presbyterian service but left Quakers alone and protected a Catholic chapel in Lime Street.[70] Magistrates struck repeatedly at the conventicle in Stoke Newington whose members included Sir John Hartopp, Charles Fleetwood, his son Smith Fleetwood, and Samuel Danvers; this group, with which Owen had been associated, fought back in the courts, achieving some success.[71] The number of dissenting ministers charged with illegal preaching would have been greater had informants not professed ignorance as to the identity of the preachers on so many occasions, perhaps deliberately if their real targets were neighbors they disliked.[72] In light of his contacts in Leicester, Bunyan may have heard that soldiers raped Quaker women at sword-point in that town in October 1686 when the latter refused to

[68] H. Larry Ingle, *First Among Friends: George Fox and the Creation of Quakerism* (New York: Oxford University Press, 1994), 280; John Miller, *Popery and Politics in England, 1660–1688* (Cambridge: Cambridge University Press, 1973), 210. In some cases, such as that of Friends in Southwark, release took months. As late as November 1686 the earl of Sunderland had to order Lord Morley not to prosecute Quakers. PRO, SP 44/56, p. 353; SP 44/337, pp. 32–33.

[69] Craig W. Horle, *The Quakers and the English Legal System, 1660–1688* (Philadelphia: University of Pennsylvania Press, 1988), 284.

[70] LMA, MS MJ/SBB/437, fols. 40, 43; Jeaffreson, 4:301–9; Miller, *Popery and Politics*, 205; Lacey, 176. Thimbleton was also charged with preaching to a conventicle in London in May 1686, and Plant was cited for the same offense in May and June. CLRO, Conventicle Box 2, nos. 2 and 6.

[71] LMA, MSS MR/RC/9, fols. 10–57, 73–78, 110–28; MJ/SBB/437, fol. 46; MJ/SBB/439, fols. 50, 55; MJ/SBB/441, fols. 27–28; MS/SBB/443, fol. 28; BL, Add. MSS 38,856, fol. 98r.

[72] See, e.g., CLRO, Conventicle Box 2, no. 2; LMA, MSS MR/RC/10, fols. 5–37 *passim*; MJ/SBB/404, fols. 45–49; MJ/SBB/439, fol. 59; BL, Add. MSS 38,856, fol. 97.

drink a toast to the king's health.[73] Generally, however, by late 1686 nonconformists could hold meetings if they applied for licenses, following the lead of Baptists at Abingdon (July) and Tewkesbury (August). Congregationalists and Presbyterians generally refused to petition, opposing the king's intent to tolerate Catholics. Despite James' move toward tolerating nonconformists, some Anglicans continued to view them harshly. Dissenters who blamed their repressive treatment on the government were ridiculed in L'Estrange's *Observator*: "There's not a *Verse* in the whole *Bible*, against *Persecution*, but makes them Shake their Heads at the *Government*."[74]

Bunyan wrote two works, both posthumously published, that very likely date from this period, *Christ a Compleat Saviour* and *The Saints Privilege and Profit*, based on texts from Hebrews—7:25 and 4:16 respectively. Both books are almost certainly expanded sermons and deal in part with persecution, a topic still relevant in 1686. *Christ a Compleat Saviour* includes an analogy to the Monmouth rebellion, "a desperate venture" that led to the erection of gallows, the binding over of prisoners in chains until their judgment day, and the appointment of a special judge (*MW*, 13:315). In the same work Bunyan used an analogy of James' councils to depict the last judgment, which "will be the Day of breaking up of *Closet*-Councils, *Cabinet*-Councils, *Secret* purposes, [and] *hidden* Thoughts" (13:298). By 1685 the Privy Council's functions had become primarily formal, and the principal advisory functions were handled by the smaller cabinet council, all members of which were Protestant at James' accession. However, he soon relied on an unofficial council—Bunyan's "*Closet*-Council"—comprised of Catholics to discuss religious matters, and this soon became the most important advisory body.[75] In Charles II's reign cabinet-councils had acquired a reputation for secrecy, which Bunyan reflects in linking them with hidden thoughts and serpentine purposes. Thus *Christ a Compleat Saviour* can be assigned provisionally to the period from about April to July 1686, and its companion work, *The Saints Privilege and Profit*, to approximately the four ensuing months.

Composed in a period of persecution, *Christ a Compleat Saviour* discusses Christ's work as an intercessor with God on behalf of those who seek his assistance. As in the epistle to the Hebrews, Christ is depicted as a priest in perpetuity. In keeping with his Calvinist theology, Bunyan restricted Christ's priestly benefits to the elect, who alone share the promise of ultimate glory and receive the graces of faith, hope, love, humility, godly zeal, reverence, and simplicity (13:257–60,

[73] Morrice, 1:643.
[74] Jolly, *Note Book*, 75; Miller, *Popery and Politics*, 210–12; *Observator*, vol. 3, no. 202 (21 August 1686).
[75] Miller, *James II*, 149.

277–79). As in various earlier works, Bunyan reiterated his belief in justification by Christ's imputed righteousness, explicitly rejecting justification by obedience to precepts and laws (in conjunction with faith), which the Catholics taught; by adherence to the pattern of holiness provided by Jesus, as Fowler and others espoused; or by conformity to the light within, as the Quakers believed (13:287, 295, 318). With the righteousness imputed by God come the graces of the Spirit, the greatest of which is faith, "the *Mother* Grace, the *root* Grace, the grace that hath *all others* in the *Bowels* of it, and *that*, from the which all others *flow*" (13:259, 277). He was thus reasserting his conviction, expressed in *A Discourse upon the Pharisee and the Publicane*, that justification precedes faith.

As Bunyan had observed, particularly in the 1680s, the godly manifested an inclination "to faint under the Cross," falling back on their own resources rather than the intercessory work of Christ and the spiritual graces it makes available (13:277). He reminded the saints that Jesus had been assailed by the Devil and that he too had been accused of attempting to overthrow the government (13:261, 313, 327). Both the Jews who had opposed Jesus and Paul (Saul) in his pre-conversion days were filled with madness (Luke 6:11), prompting Bunyan to ask, "how many, at this day, must be counted exceeding *mad*, who yet count themselves the *only* sober Men?" (13:314). This question directly targeted the Tory-Anglicans who continued to favor the persecution of dissenters. The passage is critical to a correct understanding of his recommendation that the godly pray "for Magistrates, and that God would make speed to set them all to that work that is so desireable to his Church, that is, to hate the Whore, to eat her Flesh, to make her desolate, and burn her with Fire" (13:306). He was looking expectantly to that time *in the future* when, he believed, God would use magistrates to overthrow Antichrist, but at the time he wrote, this was not the case, for magistrates had been enforcing the penal laws against the saints. His other key point is that Christ did not die to prevent his followers from being persecuted in this life. On the contrary, "God has reserved a power to punish with temporal punishments the best and dearest of his people, if need be" (13:270). Christ's intercessory work does not protect the godly from repression but provides the means—the spiritual graces—to enable them to withstand it. An understanding of Christ as intercessor is thus a crucial source of strength for persecuted believers, who must realize that they have "Salvation from those ruins that all the Enemies of our Souls *would* yet bring us unto, but cannot: for the Intercession of Christ preventeth" (13:267). Like *Seasonable Counsel*, *Christ a Compleat Saviour* is a book for the persecuted.

Bunyan made some interesting observations about contemporary religious life in this book. His keen sense of obligation for the poor was offended by wealthy saints whose slighting of the indigent betrayed their professions of piety. Although they spent money for toys and "Fool's Baubles" for their children, they had little or nothing for the poor, and instead of donating excess food to the needy, they let it rot so completely that not even their dogs and cats would consume it. "Ah! love is cold in these frozen days." He complained as well about professing Christians who were very attentive to customers in their shops but slept or let their minds wander during sermons. "The heads also, and hearts of most hearers *are* to the *Word*, as the *Sieve* is to *Water*, they can hold no Sermons, remember no Texts, bring home no proofs; produce none of the Sermon to the edification and profit of others" (13:278–80). As a pastor Bunyan was palpably experiencing some frustration.

He was struggling as well in his spiritual life, though only because of the high standards he set for himself. In a revealing aside he wished that Christians who were not living in the fear of God and repudiating iniquity might "feel for three or four months something of what I have felt for several years together for base sinful thoughts" (13:282). The temptations that had been troubling him for several years were probably among the five types of "personal, sinful imperfections" he discusses in this book. The first of these ranged widely, encompassing "unbelief, fear, mistrust, doubting, despondings, murmurings, blasphemies, pride, lightness, foolishness, avarice, fleshly lusts, heartlesness to good, wicked desires, low thoughts of Christ, too good thoughts of sin, and, at times, too great an itching after the worst of immoralities." An inclination to accept doctrinal errors, which comprised the second category, was unlikely to have tempted him, nor was a tendency to dissemble and say improper things to avoid persecution. The final categories—weariness in performing religious duties and improperly using lawful things such as food, sleep, clothing, and personal relationships—may have enticed him, but his renewed battle with "base sinful thoughts" probably involved such things as doubting, despondency, pride, and a perceived lack of gravity. Unlike the Quakers, he did not believe perfection could be attained in this life, but he was deeply sensitive of his spiritual shortcomings (13:276–77).

In the companion volume, *The Saints Privilege and Profit*, Bunyan again focused on Christ's priestly work, developing the idea of the throne of grace as a place where saints can take refuge from the fury of the wicked (*MW*, 13:170). From this throne come streams of grace—the water of life, a theme on which he would expound a year later in a book of that name (13:173, 183–86, 206). His intent was to encourage the godly, especially embattled saints, to approach this throne boldly, like princes, though he cautioned them that God might enshroud it to test their sincerity and resolve. "Faith if it be strong, will play the Man in the dark, will like a metled Horse flounce in bad way, will not be discouraged at Tryals, at many or strong Tryals" (13:203). For Bunyan the Christian life is always a struggle to some degree, for "in the general, all the days of our Pilgrimage here, *are evil*, yea, *every day* has a sufficiency of evil in it to destroy the best Saint that breatheth, were it not for the Grace of God" (13:235). Yet he never encouraged a religiosity focused on a recurring cycle of guilt and pardon; such Christians, he thought, "have their Heads so often in a Bag," failing to seek the divine assistance that can bring them spiritual peace and better lives (13:246). How far he attained this goal in his own life is impossible to know, though his struggling with "base sinful thoughts" in the mid-1680s suggests that complete inner peace eluded him.

In *The Saints Privilege and Profit* Bunyan included a revealing autobiographical passage explaining how he enjoyed playing with children, virtually acting as a child himself. On one occasion he met a child with a finger so sore that the entire hand was incapacitated. When the child came to him for comfort, he responded teasingly by asking if he should amputate the finger and replace it with a golden one, whereupon the child "no more cared to be intimate" with him. As he reflected on the incident, he made it a virtual emblem, with the child's "tenderness to the most Infirm" part of his body an analogy of Christ's concern for the "afflicted Members" of his church:

> Ah! who would not make many Supplications, Prayers and Intercessions for a Leg, for an Eye, for a Foot, for a Hand, for a Finger, rather than they will lose it? And can it be imagined that Christ alone should be like the foolish *Ostrich*, hardned against his young, yea, against his Members! it cannot be.

Bunyan could find something emblematic even as he played with a child, extracting, as he phrased it, honey from a sore finger (13:230). He discovered an emblem of a different sort in the sons of gentry dressed "in their *lowzy* hue" rather than finery appropriate to their social rank; instead of seeking the help of their fathers, they wore threadbare jackets as well as hose and shoes with the heels worn away, emblematic of Christians reluctant to approach the throne of grace with their spiritual needs (13:244–45).

Bunyan mounted a substantive attack on Catholicism in *The Saints Privilege and Profit*. The criticism was in keeping with the campaign led by Bishop Compton, though obviously not part of it. Christ's role as high priest provided Bunyan with an opportunity to discuss the altar on which he offered his sacrifice. To some commentators the altar was the cross,[76] but Bunyan rejected this interpretation on

[76] Bunyan may have encountered the alternate interpretation in sermons, private discussions, or his reading. For the altar as a type of the cross see Edward Dering, *M. Derings Workes* (London, 1597), sig. X2r. For the altar as a type of Christ see William Gouge, *Commentary on Hebrews* (Grand Rapids, MI: Kregel Publications, 1980), 1085 (specifically Christ's divine nature); John Owen, *An Exposition of the Two First Chapters of the Epistle of Paul the Apostle unto the Hebrews* (London, 1668), 65; Owen, *A Continuation of the Exposition of the Epistle of Paul the Apostle to the Hebrews* (London, 1680), 191; and, implicitly, George Lawson, *An Exposition of the Epistle to the Hebrewes* (London, 1661), 347.

the grounds that the altar must be greater than the offering. "Since the Gift was the Body and Soul of Christ, for so saith the Text, *He gave himself for our Sins* [Galatians 1:4]: The Altar must be something else than a sorry bit of Wood, or than a cursed Tree." The altar is not the cross but Christ's divine nature, which sanctifies his offering of himself. Consequently those who worship the cross, an allusion to reverence of the crucifix, are guilty of idolatry and blasphemy, and so too are those who venerate physical altars, as do the Catholics. "Let Men have a care how in their Worship, they make Altars, upon which, as they pretend they offer the Body of Christ; and let them leave off foolishly to dote upon the Wood, and the works of their Hands" (13:218–20). Bunyan's criticism extended to the Church of England, whose communicants kneeled at railed altars hung with tapestries and colored cloth, atop which were the communion plate, a Bible, and sometimes a pair of candlesticks.[77] In his mind such veneration was tantamount to adoration of the altar itself. Certainly his attack on the physical altar and the cross can be read as such, probably making publication of the book more of a risk than he was prepared to take in late 1686, particularly since he equated reverence for the physical altar and the cross with blasphemy and idolatry.

## "Sack-cloth, Tears and Affliction"[78]: The Church in the Wilderness

During the latter part of 1686 nonconformists were increasingly divided in response to the court's evolving religious policy. In August the king dispatched Sir John Baber to gauge the Presbyterians' likely response to a grant of religious liberty by statute, and the same month he used his prerogative authority to halt legal proceedings against Baptists who had violated the penal laws. Various nonconformists, especially Quakers and some Baptists, supported James' use of his prerogative to dispense with the penal laws and his plans for a statute to terminate them, but other Baptists as well as Congregationalists and Presbyterians were chary of any policy that included toleration for Catholics. Alarmed Anglicans vigorously suppressed nonconformists, but the king countered in November by permitting dissenters to purchase licenses exempting them from legal prosecution for their religious beliefs. On a trip to Chester, other places in Cheshire, and Liverpool in the fall, Thomas Jollie found that some groups were meeting openly while others gathered secretly because of the presence of soldiers and government persecution; not until after the declaration of indulgence was issued in April 1687 could he preach in Chester. Presbyterians and Congregationalists generally opted not to acquire licenses but met illegally, whereas Baptists tended to obtain dis-

[77] Spurr, *RCE*, 350.
[78] *MW*, 7:130.

pensations. By the end of 1686 most Anglicans were pitted against the court and many dissenters, while the latter were split among themselves over the question of whether toleration of Catholics was too high a price for religious liberty.[79] All of this took place as Huguenot suffering increased in France following revocation of the Edict of Nantes and some sought refuge in England.

In this context Bunyan wrote one of his most powerful works, *A Discourse of the House of the Forest of Lebanon*, during the winter of 1686–87. His interest in typology, which had been evident since his earliest writings, peaked in the 1680s with his commentary on Genesis, his book on the house of the forest of Lebanon, and its successor, *Solomon's Temple Spiritualiz'd*. Typology is also prominent in *The Saints Privilege and Profit*: Melchizedek and the high priest as types of Christ, priestly robes and the rainbow as types of Christ's righteousness, the priesthood and its laws as types of the eternal covenant, and the mercy-seat as a type of the throne of grace. Among others identified by Bunyan were the covenant of mercy with Noah as a type of the covenant of grace, Solomon's ivory throne as a type of the deity's, and the burnt offering and the sin-offering as types of Christ's sacrifice. He also interpreted the molten sea as a type of the remission of sins by Christ's blood, the altar of incense as Christ's intercessory prayers, the tabernacle as a type of the church, and so forth.[80] These antitypes relate primarily to Christ's redemptive work, but in *A Discourse of the House of the Forest of Lebanon* Bunyan developed a typology that refers to the church's struggles, particularly in what he believed were the late stages of history. In this respect *The House of the Forest of Lebanon* is similar to *The Holy City* and *Of Antichrist, and His Ruine* rather than *The Saints Privilege and Profit* and *Solomon's Temple Spiritualiz'd*.

*The House of the Forest of Lebanon* was not published until 1692, when Doe included it in his partial edition of Bunyan's works. Midgley has plausibly suggested that this work and *Solomon's Temple Spiritualiz'd*, which was published in 1688, were composed in close proximity because both books take their texts from 1 Kings, use a similar hermeneutic method, and deal with closely related subjects. Because *The House of the Forest of Lebanon* includes numerous detailed references to Solomon's temple, he surmises that Bunyan may have composed it after *Solomon's Temple Spiritualiz'd* (*MW*, 7:xv). His argument for sequential composition is sound, but the content of the two works in relation to the historical context indicates that *The House of the Forest of Lebanon* was composed during the winter of 1686–87, probably about December to February, when persecution of dissenters was recent and still a threat, whereas *Solomon's Temple Spiritualiz'd*, with a

[79]Lacey, 177–79; Jolly, *Note Book*, 79, 82. The Tories were likewise divided over the toleration issue. Bodl., English Letters C12, fol. 158v.

[80]*MW*, 13:168, 173–74, 177–81, 196, 198, 208–9, 216.

positive view of kings consistent with James' issuance of a declaration of indulgence in April 1687, was likely written from about March to June of that year. The theme of an embattled church which dominates *The House of the Forest of Lebanon* would not have been directly relevant to the last seventeen months of Bunyan's life.

From an expository standpoint the work is flawed by Bunyan's misreading of his primary text, 1 Kings 7:2–6, which describes the house of the forest of Lebanon constructed by Solomon. Some interpreters, Bunyan remarked, had erroneously identified the building with the temple in Jerusalem, a mistake disproved by comparing the disparate measurements of the two structures (7:121).[81] On this point his reasoning was solid, but the building was part of the palace complex in Jerusalem and was so named because of its forest-like cedar pillars supporting the roof; it was not a building in a forest or in Lebanon.[82] He was probably influenced by the Geneva Bible, in which the marginal note to 1 Kings 7:2 describes the building as Solomon's summer house and compares it to Mount Lebanon in Syria because of "the beautie of the place and great abundance of cedre trees that went to the buylding thereof." Although Bunyan might have seen one of the editions of this Bible,[83] including those of 1560, 1579, and 1599, that includes cuts of a Renaissance-style aristocratic house amid trees, some editions lacked them; one of the illustrations situates the structure "in the wood of Lebanon."[84] By accepting Lebanon as the location of the palatial house, Bunyan, employing his usual hermeneutic principles, combed the pages of Scripture for references to Lebanon regardless of whether the passages mention the house in question: "Nor need we stumble, because this word *House* is not subjoyned in every particular place, where this sorrow, or joy of *Lebanon* is made mention of; for it is an usual thing

[81] The major commentaries by John Diodati, John Downame, and John Trapp correctly identified the house as part of the palace complex. Diodati, *Pious and Learned Annotations upon the Holy Bible,* 3rd ed. (London, 1651), sig. Gg1r–v; [Downame], *Annotations upon All the Books of the Old and New Testament* [2nd ed.], vol. 1 (London, 1651), sig. Cccc 3r–v; Trapp, *Annotations upon the Old and New Testament, in Five Distinct Volumes,* vol. 1 (London, 1662), 332–33.

[82] *MW,* 7:xxxviii–xxxix; Charles Gore, Henry Leighton Goudge, and Alfred Guillaume, eds., *A New Commentary on Holy Scripture Including the Apocrypha,* 2 vols. (London: Society for Promoting Christian Knowledge, 1943), 1:255; Gwilym H. Jones, *1 and 2 Kings,* vol. 1 (Grand Rapids, MI: William B. Eerdmans Publishing Co., 1984), 173–76; Burke O. Long, *1 Kings with an Introduction to Historical Literature* (Grand Rapids, MI: William B. Eerdmans Publishing Co., 1984), 88–90; Richard D. Nelson, *First and Second Kings* (Louisville: John Knox Press, 1987), 44–45.

[83] As Midgley suggests; *MW,* 7:xxxix.

[84] Among the editions without the illustrations were those of 1581, 1598, 1608, and 1614.

with the Holy Ghost, when he directs his speech to a Man, to speak as if he spake to a Tree; and when he directs his voice to a King, to speak as if he intended the Kingdom; so when he speaks of the House, to speak as to the Forest of *Lebanon*" (7:126–27). Employing the same methodology, he cited Isaiah 10:34, 33:9, and 37:34, Zechariah 11:1–2, and Habakkuk 2:17, which depict violence against Lebanon, as attacks on the house of the forest of Lebanon (7:123–25, 129). Similarly, he envisioned the house in a Lebanon forest as a defensive outpost designed to protect Jerusalem from Assyrian invasion, and the king of Assyria as a type of the beast in the book of Revelation (7:123).

Bunyan interpreted the house of the forest of Lebanon as a type of the church in the wilderness, contrasting it with the temple as a type of the church under the gospel. The book reveals his state of mind during the winter of 1686–87 by portraying a church "assaulted for her worship, as she is persecuted for the same." Like the woman in labor in Revelation 12:1–6, the church has fled into the wilderness, "a desolate, a tempted, an afflicted, a persecuted state," in the hope of escaping the seven-headed red dragon waiting to devour her child as soon as it is born (7:122–24). He drew on dynamic, violent imagery to describe a church—his church—as the target of aggression, its members being cut down and burned like Lebanon's mighty cedars, its people "in a state of Sack-cloth, Tears and Affliction" while the "*Dads* of Antichristianism" inflict maximum damage (7:124, 130, 146). The church in the wilderness—"*so* persecuted, *so* distressed, *so* oppressed, and made the Seat of *so* much War, *so* much Blood, of *so* many Murders of her Children"—drinks the bitter cup of affliction (7:156). He also likened the church in its wilderness state to a beautiful, delicate woman whom men of raging passion are intent on raping; thwarted by her armed guards, their "fleshly love" is transformed into cruel rage, and "because she complies not with their desires, they prepare War against her" (7:142–43). These images of a church under siege are a telling indicator of his outlook in the winter of 1686–87.

Although feeling besieged, he was not prepared to yield, finding inspiration in his belief that the house of the forest of Lebanon had been willing to defend Jerusalem against the Assyrian invaders at all costs. The only refuge for the elect in this world, the house—the church—is a heavily fortified, well-armed tower capable of causing attackers to cringe in terror, yet "it is the *Terror*, or Majesty and Fortitude, which God has put upon the Church in the Wilderness, that makes the Gentiles so bestir them to have her under foot" (7:129, 149). Although Bunyan thought the church had been constructed to withstand assault and launch attacks of its own, he stressed its defensive posture, insisting it would use its weapons only if assailed (7:124, 128, 134, 152). The Assyrians might set the pillars afire, but the building would not be consumed because its defenders, themselves mighty pillars, are giants of grace with leonine faces. "*No* Prince, *no* King, *no* Threat, *no*

Terror, *no* Torment, could make them yield," and they laugh in their enemies' faces as they triumph amid the flames (7:130, 135). The blaze may scorch and kill some of the towering pillars, but they remain in place, structurally solid, even as new pillars join them, providing continual support to the church (7:134–35). The burned pillars are the church's martyrs, making the Assyrian besiegers in this context the Catholics. With a Catholic on the throne and reports circulating about the plight of Huguenots in France, Bunyan's thoughts were on martyrdom (7:131, 169). Once again he turned to Foxe's *Acts and Monuments*, particularly to a letter of the Italian martyr Pomponius Algerius, who had been burned at the stake in Rome in 1555. Bunyan quoted at length from the letter, in which Pomponius wrote movingly of the martyrs who had been crucified, stoned, quartered, thrown to ferocious animals, roasted on grates, skinned alive, or broiled in cauldrons, or had their eyes bored, their tongues cut out, and their hands and feet amputated. The heroic resolve with which Pomponius, a pillar in the house of the forest of Lebanon, engaged in combat with the forces of darkness was a source of both solace and inspiration for Bunyan (7:159–64). In one telling quotation he indicted the Church of Rome, one of whose adherents sat on the English throne, of heinous offenses against Christianity. Seemingly undaunted by the threat the Roman behemoth posed to visible saints, he was prepared to fight in their defense, convinced that "the Church is God's Tower, or Battery, by which he beateth down Antichrist" (7:167).

The fighting Bunyan advocated in this book was strictly spiritual in nature,[85] though he described the church as a place for "war-like-men" prepared to endure adversity, not people who insist on sleeping in beds of down (7:133). This is the gospel of militancy, fit for a church that is "the Seat of Spiritual War" (7:138). Instead of carnal weapons the church, explained Bunyan, relies on divine armor— the sword of God's word and the shield of faith (7:129, 150–52, 155). The Fifth Monarchist views that had interested him as a young man he now categorically repudiated:

> There are *extravagant* opinions in the World, about the Kingdom of Christ, as if it consisted in temporal glory, in part, and as if he would take it to him by carnal weapons, and so maintain it in its greatness and grandeur; but I confess my self an alien to these notions, and believe and profess the quite contrary, and look for the coming of Christ to Judgment personally, and 'twixt this and that, for his coming in Spirit, and in the power of his Word to destroy Antichrist, to inform Kings, and so to give quietness to his Church on Earth. (7:172)

He was probably thinking especially of Danvers, who had been allied with Monmouth in 1685, though he and Meade had failed to launch an uprising in London

[85] For a different interpretation see Hill, *TPM*, 330.

on the duke's behalf. Although the Fifth Monarchist movement was nearly a spent force by the 1680s, some adherents remained active, including Robert Perrott, who was executed for fighting in the battle of Sedgemoor; Thomas Venner the younger, who fought with Monmouth but escaped and joined a small band of Fifth Monarchist exiles in the Netherlands; John Patshall, who was allegedly involved in the Rye House plot but eluded arrest; Walter Thimbleton, who associated with Danvers and may have been involved with him in discussing a London insurrection; and William Medley, who welcomed Shaftesbury to Amsterdam.[86] Bunyan prudently took care to distance himself from such men, assuring monarchs and potentates that they had nothing to fear from visible saints, for they knew their places and were peaceful as long as they could profess their faith and worship God according to scriptural dictates (7:151, 172).

In Bunyan's judgment governments persecuted the church because they erroneously assumed it was "for destroying Kings, for subverting Kingdoms, and for bringing all to desolation," yet neither Christ nor his church "is for doing them any Hurt" (7:128). Because Christ's kingdom is not of this world, he and his followers covet no temporal power, and the church's privileges, concerned exclusively with the soul, infringe on no one's liberties. Although Christians are physically maltreated, they endanger no one, leaving God to avenge the wrongs done to the elect (7:124–26, 129, 153). The Assyrians, Bunyan surmised, deemed the house of the forest of Lebanon a threat, much as the church's size and prowess, "by reason of her inherent fortitude, and the valorous acts that she hath done, by Suffering, by Prayer, by Faith, and a constant induring of hardship for the Truth, doth force into the World a Belief, thorow their own guilt and clamours of Conscience against them for their Debaucheries, that this House of the Forest of *Lebanon* will destroy them all, when she shall be delivered from her servitude" (7:129).

Bunyan's disavowal of physical weapons and seditious undertakings was unconditional, but he made no pretense of eschewing militancy: The church in the wilderness is like "an Army terrible with Banners," fighting to defend its worship (7:155). Borrowing the potent imagery of Revelation 11:5, he warned that if the church were attacked, it would spew fire from its mouth, devouring its adversaries; those who hurt the church will be slain by the sword of the Spirit (7:129). Despite his insistence that the church responds only when assailed, he was sympathetic to those who go on the offensive: "Suppose they were the truly godly that made the first assault, can they be blamed?" The boar must be expelled from the vineyard, a sinful man from a holy temple, and a dragon (Antichrist) from

[86] Greaves, *SOK*, 183, 276, 288–89, 313, 407; Capp, *FMM*, 220–21. For Perrott, Patshall, Thimbleton, and Medley see *BDBR, s.vv.*

heaven. By choice, Bunyan's weapons were words; his battles, disputations (7:139). "Let us practise then our Religion in peace . . . and vindicate it *by way of Contention*" with monarchs, magistrates, and judges (7:154–55).

The war of words in which Bunyan engaged in *The House of the Forest of Lebanon* was fought on two fronts—against Catholics, as reflected especially in the references to Pomponius Algerius and other martyrs, and against the repressive practices of the Church of England and its allies. As Midgley has observed, the context determines which agent of persecution Bunyan is attacking (7:xxxix). His sustained development of the theme of an embattled church relates to oppression by Catholics, particularly in places such as France and Piedmont, and Anglicans. However, James' accession complicated the situation in England, where some Anglicans were taking a prominent part in the campaign against Catholics. At various times in the reign of Charles II, especially during the debate over liberty of conscience and the investigation of the alleged Popish plot, some dissenters, including Owen and Baxter,[87] had sought varying degrees of common ground with the Church of England, and more recently others, such as the Presbyterian John Corbet, the Particular Baptist Benjamin Keach, and the General Baptist Thomas Grantham, had addressed Protestant unity, as had Bunyan himself in his *Confession* of 1672. Arguing that Protestant divisiveness benefits only the Catholics, Keach called for cooperation among those who agree on theological fundamentals, and Grantham favored fellowship among Protestants while restricting full communion to those sharing unity in doctrine and practice in all essential matters.[88] In 1685 Stephen Lobb went further, calling for unity based on a national church and recognizing that the government has a legitimate interest in religion because of the negative impact of religious disorder on the state. Lobb wanted all Protestants to take the oaths of supremacy and allegiance and subscribe to the Thirty-nine Articles, with the exception of those dealing with polity and ceremonies. According to his plan each dissenting congregation would be permitted to administer the sacraments and impose discipline as it deemed appropriate, and to use or reject the liturgy as it saw fit.[89] Interested only in unity

[87] John Owen, *A Peace-Offering in an Apology and Humble Plea for Indulgence and Libertie of Conscience* (London, 1667), 12–13; Owen, *The Church of Rome No Safe Guide* (London, 1679), 2–3; Richard Baxter, *The Cure of Church-Divisions* (London, 1670), sigs. A2r–v, A4v, B3r–v, B4v, C2r, and 45–47, 50–51, 67–68, 75, 252, 296.

[88] John Corbet, *An Account Given of the Principles & Practises of Several Nonconformists* (London, 1682 [published posthumously]), 7, 23, 29; [Benjamin Keach], *Sion in Distress: or, the Groans of the Protestant Church*, 2nd ed. (London, 1681), 30–31; Thomas Grantham, *The Loyal Baptist: or an Apology for the Baptized Believers* (London, 1684), 15, 39. For Corbet see *Calamy Revised, s.v.*

[89] [Stephen Lobb], *A True Dissenter* (n.p., 1685), 134–41.

among visible saints, Bunyan never espoused such a scheme. However, despite the drumbeat of criticism against the Church of England in many of his works, not least because of its persecuting ways, he held out the possibility that its membership might include some who are genuine believers.

In *The House of the Forest of Lebanon* Bunyan explained how some of the elect had become members of the established church. God, he argued, permits the forces of Antichrist to proclaim their darkness as the true light and simultaneously denigrate the genuine light, though eventually they will fail because "*black sets off white, and darkness light, so error sets off truth.*" Both sides, he averred, claim to be the true church but differ in their doctrines, ordinances, and polity, and each accuses the other of destroying religion (7:140–41).

> Because the chast Matron, the Spouse of Christ, would not allow this *Slut* to run away with this name [of church], therefore [the whore] gets upon the back of her Beast, and by him pushes this woman [the church] into the dirt; but because her faith and love to her Husband remains, she turns again, and pleads by her titles, her features, and ornaments, that she, and she only, is she whose square [i.e., perfection] answereth to the square of her figure, and to the Characters which her Lord hath given of his own; and so the game began. (7:144)

In the contest between competing churches, Antichrist, responding to the beauty of the true church, made herself attractive with purple and scarlet finery as well as precious stones, a reference to Revelation 17:3–4. As she attracted supporters, she employed them in an attempt to turn everything in the church topsy-turvy. "Thus has the beauty of God's Church betrayed her into the hands of her lovers, who loved her for themselves, for the Devil, and for the making of her a Seat, a Throne for the Man of Sin" (7:144).

Following Antichrist's introduction of her "figments" into Christ's church, some of the godly, finding them alluring, were "much damnified" thereby, that is, they were seriously corrupted. As the smell of smoke lingers in a house charred by fire, many Christians, in Bunyan's opinion, have been born and raised in a church filled with the smoke of antichristian darkness. Although this darkness is proclaimed as the true light, it dims the vision of believers. "The Doctrines, Traditions, and Rudiments of the World, took more hold there, and spread themselves more formidably over the face of that whole Church." Acknowledging that he knew people whose religion was nurtured in these "smokey-holes," he explained that they have been misled because of their impaired sight, the cause of differences among Christians (7:145–46). In the early church antichristian darkness opposed Christian light, but now the murk has "got into the Christians," pitting them against each other. "Witness the *jarrs*, the *oppositions*, the *contentions, emulations, strifes, debates, whisperings, tumults* and *condemnations* that like *Cannon-shot* have so frequently on all sides been let fly against one another."

Most of these divisions, he thought, involve matters of lesser import, such as disputes over the extent of the atonement, whether Christ's power extends into the secular sphere, and whether the Bible alone is a sufficient guide in religious matters (7:147). In the wilderness, the church possesses adequate light to ascertain "the substantials" notwithstanding disagreement over incidental matters (7:137). Bunyan did not explicitly acknowledge the presence of "true worshippers" in the Church of England (7:146), but his belief that such people could be found in smokey holes opened the door to this possibility, though apparently stopping short of the search for common ground among Protestants for the purpose of Christian fellowship.

For Bunyan the one fundamental belief that cannot be sacrificed is the doctrine of the Trinity: "That's the substance, that's the ground and fundamental of all." Rather than expressing this doctrine in formal theological terms, he explained it as the love of the father in giving his son, the love of the son in giving himself, and the love of the Spirit in regenerating believers. "By this Doctrine, and by this *only*, the man is made a Christian: and he that has not this Doctrine, his Profession's not worth a button" (7:137). Bunyan briefly addressed this doctrine in another posthumous work, *Of the Trinity and a Christian*, which cannot be dated, though he may have composed it about the same time as *The House of the Forest of Lebanon*. A very short work, possibly intended for publication as a broadside, it was written to assist neophyte believers struggling to understand the Trinity. Rather than marshal theological arguments, he counseled young converts to accept the absolute authority of every word in the Bible regardless of how obscure or contradictory it might seem. To expect to understand everything in Scripture is arrogant, he insisted, for a Christian is a believer, not a doubter, a reasoner, or a perverse disputer. The Bible speaks of father, son, and Spirit, but Deuteronomy 6:4 and Mark 12:29 also make it clear that God is one. For Bunyan this was sufficient proof to believe in "one God consisting of three Persons" (*MW*, 12:403–5). In his reluctance to embrace credal formulas he was close to the position advocated by the Anglican Richard Salter, who deemed it preferable to leave "the confessed mysteryes of religion" as they are revealed in Scripture rather than require adherence to theological doctrines framed by fallible people.[90]

For Bunyan, if there is to be fellowship among Protestants, it must be grounded on this doctrine, particularly as it relates to the threefold manifestation of redeeming love. Now aged fifty-eight, he clung to this conviction, resolved to undergo martyrdom if necessary rather than surrender his beliefs. In Pomponius Algerius he had found his own man for all seasons, a model for the behavior he

[90] CUL, Add. MSS 1, no. 21. Unlike Bunyan, Salter pursued the logic of his position by querying the usefulness of the concept of heresy.

thought might be necessary because England was once again ruled by a Catholic monarch. But by the time he finished *The House of the Forest of Lebanon*, probably about February 1687, he may have begun to see the glimmering of the light he so dearly loved—"liberty growing upon us," as Thomas Jollie had expressed it in January.[91] With tension easing, Bunyan set aside his finished manuscript on the house of the forest of Lebanon, possibly because he could find no one to publish it. The difficulty should not be underestimated, for even the bishop of Lincoln could not obtain a printer for his manuscript attacking the idolatry of the Catholic church.[92] For his part, Bunyan now gave free rein to his fascination with typology by exploring the ways in which Solomon's temple is a type of important things to come.

[91] Jollie, *Note Book*, 81.
[92] BL, Add. MSS 29,584, fol. 66r.

# CHAPTER 14

# Toleration Renewed:
# Bunyan's Final Months

The policy of courting nonconformists inaugurated by James in 1686 led on 4 April 1687 to a Declaration of Indulgence suspending the Test and Corporation Acts and the penal laws against Protestant nonconformists and Catholics. Candidly acknowledging that he wished all inhabitants of his realms were members of the Catholic church, the king nevertheless professed to believe that consciences should not be constrained, for the use of force in religion, he argued, is inimical to trade, depopulates countries, discourages immigration, and has never attained its objectives. Desirous of easing Anglican concerns, he pledged to protect the Church of England and its possessions. In granting his subjects the right to meet freely for worship, he asked that gatherings be peaceful and public, that justices of the peace be informed where services would be held, and that nothing be preached or taught that would alienate the people's affections from him and his government. Finally, he incorporated a pardon for all subjects accused of having violated the penal laws governing religion.[1]

Most prelates, including William Sancroft, archbishop of Canterbury, reacted negatively and discouraged their clergy from submitting statements of appreciation and support to the king. Others, including Samuel Parker, bishop of Oxford, and Nathaniel Crew, bishop of Durham, were somewhat more accommodating; Crew and the dean and chapter of Durham, for instance, pointedly thanked James for promising to preserve the established church. Addresses of thanks came as well from Thomas Barlow, bishop of Lincoln, Thomas Wood, bishop of Coventry and Lichfield, Thomas Cartwright, bishop of Chester, and the dean and chapter of Ripon, yet Wood made his opposition to toleration clear when he boasted in August 1687 that he had kept Lichfield free of conventicles. Sir John Reresby, a staunch Anglican, rightly observed that many defenders of the Church

---

[1] J. P. Kenyon, ed., *The Stuart Constitution, 1603–1688: Documents and Commentary* (Cambridge: Cambridge University Press, 1969), 410–12.

of England regarded the declaration as a threat to the security of their institution.[2] Fearing the king's policy would overthrow the Anglican church, an anonymous critic regarded the bestowal of toleration on nonconformists as a feint to disguise James' underlying goal of imposing persecutory Catholicism on his realms: "All the celebrated kindness to the Fanaticks is only to use them as the cats paw for pulling the chestnutt out of the fire."[3] The declaration was part of James' policy of forging a new alliance with Catholics and dissenters at the expense of the Tory-Anglicans, a policy that contributed heavily to another revolution in the autumn of 1688. By that point Bunyan had died, but the final seventeen months of his life were played out in the context of James' endeavors to make his policy work. Like all nonconformists, Bunyan had to decide whether toleration was worth the price of cooperating with a Catholic sovereign.

## "Liberty . . . to Eat Freely"[4]: Dissent and the Lure of Toleration

The response of nonconformists to James' Declaration of Indulgence was mixed. From the diocese of Norwich Sancroft received a report that dissenters had "gredily swallowed the bayt & every where expressed thier Joy with bells & bonefiers," but from Chichester came word that nonconformists were divided in their reaction. Because Baxter favored the comprehension of moderate dissenters in the Church of England rather than toleration, he opposed the indulgence: "I have these 35 yeares made Love, Concord & Peace the maine study of my life: And I dare not now violate it causelessly with the body of the Conforming Clergie."[5] The Presbyterian George Trosse availed himself of the freedom to preach but would have suffered rather "than have pleaded the *King's Licence*, which I thought contrary to the *Subjects* Liberty establish'd by Law, and as having a direct Tendency to overthrow *our Religion*." The Presbyterians John Howe and William Bates were likewise critical, as was Daniel Williams, who persuaded a group of dissenting ministers in London not to submit an address of thanksgiving on the grounds that suffering was preferable to destroying England's liberties.[6] Other

---

[2] London *Gazette* 2243 (16–19 May 1687); 2256 (30 June–4 July 1687); 2257 (4–7 July 1687); 2258 (7–11 July 1687); BL, Add. MSS 34,487, fol. 5r; 45,974, fol. 23v; Bodl., Tanner MSS 29, fol. 59r; Sir John Reresby, *Memoirs of Sir John Reresby*, ed. Andrew Browning (Glasgow: Jackson, Son and Co., 1936), 462.

[3] BL, Add. MSS 45,974, fol. 27v.

[4] *MW*, 7:81.

[5] Bodl., Tanner MSS 29, fols. 9r, 10r (quoted); Baxter, *Calendar*, 2:286.

[6] George Trosse, *The Life of the Reverend Mr. George Trosse: Written by Himself, and Published Posthumously According to His Order in 1714*, ed. A. W. Brink (Montreal: McGill-Queen's University Press, 1974), 125; Michael R. Watts, *The Dissenters: From the Reforma-*

Presbyterians, including some in Westminster, Bristol, Norwich, Dublin, Colchester, Macclesfield, Hull, King's Lynn, Maidstone, Derbyshire, Nottinghamshire, and Wales, submitted statements thanking James.[7] Although the king received approximately eighty such addresses from nonconformists, none of which explicitly endorsed the use of the prerogative to suspend laws, many expressed hope that Parliament would confirm toleration by statute. The declaration itself had encouraged the expectation that Parliament would concur in the king's actions when it next met. James had the London *Gazette* publish the addresses, and when they did not arrive unsolicited in sufficient numbers, he had agents prompt reluctant parties, reportedly even quartering dragoons in Carlisle to exert pressure.[8]

As Reresby noted, "the design was well understood, viz., to devide the Protestant churches, that the popish might find less opposition." With the exception of the Quakers, every religious group was split. Among the Baptists the opponents included William Kiffin and Joseph Stennett, but some Baptists in the London area pledged "to give that proof of our Duty and Fidelity to Your Majesty, that You may never have occasion to repent of Your Princely Favour towards us."[9] Baptists throughout much of the country submitted addresses, sometimes, as in Bristol and Gloucester, in conjunction with Congregationalists.[10] Richard Stretton, a Congregationalist, opposed the indulgence, whereas Stephen Lobb approved it.[11] So too did Henry Nye, son of Philip Nye, who published his father's manuscript, written in conjunction with the 1672 Declaration of Indulgence, *The King's Authority in Dispensing with Ecclesiastical Laws, Asserted and Vindicated* (1687); in an epistle to this work the younger Nye thanked James for

---

tion to the French Revolution (Oxford: Clarendon Press, 1978), 258. For Trosse and Williams see *DNB, s.vv.*

[7] London *Gazette* 2238 (28 April–2 May 1687); 2246 (26–30 May 1687); 2248 (2–6 June 1687); 2253 (20–23 June 1687); 2265 (1–4 August 1687); 2274 (1–5 September 1687); 2278 (15–19 September 1687); 2287 (17–20 October 1687); 2289 (24–27 October 1687); 2295 (14–17 November 1687). Vincent Alsop played a leading role in the Westminster address. R. A. Beddard, "Vincent Alsop and the Emancipation of Restoration Dissent," *Journal of Ecclesiastical History* 24 (April 1973): 176.

[8] Lacey, 181; Kenyon, ed., *Stuart Constitution*, 411; John Miller, *James II: A Study in Kingship* (Hove, East Sussex: Wayland Publishers, 1977), 172.

[9] Reresby, *Memoirs*, 452 (quoted); Lacey, 180; London *Gazette* 2234 (14–18 April 1687) (quoted). For Stennett see *BDBR, s.v.*

[10] London *Gazette* 2241 (9–12 May 1687); 2243 (16–19 May 1687); 2244 (19–23 May 1687); 2246 (26–30 May 1687); 2252 (16–20 June 1687); 2255 (27–30 June 1687).

[11] Lobb was not a Quaker as Mark Goldie asserts. "The Roots of True Whiggism 1688–94," *History of Political Thought* 1 (Summer 1980): 207. For Stretton see *Calamy Revised, s.v.*

issuing "so compassionate an Indulgence." The Congregationalist Thomas Jollie, while appreciative of the declaration, had reservations, partly because Catholics were involved in its implementation. Congregationalists in London, Norwich, Great Yarmouth, Hitchin and Hertford, Macclesfield (in conjunction with the Presbyterians), and the counties of Suffolk, Norfolk, and Monmouthshire sent statements of support,[12] and many came from groups of dissenters identified only by locale. Nonconformists in Essex, including Braintree, where Bunyan had contacts, lavishly praised James for saving his subjects "from the jaws of Ruine" and confirming their religious and civil rights.[13] Dissenters in London, some of whom Bunyan undoubtedly knew, likened James to Moses because he had delivered the people "from the Yoak and Bondage of *Penal Laws*, a Slavery and Darkness worse than that which punished *Egypt*."[14] In Bedfordshire, with the exception of the Baptists, who participated in a sixteen-county address thanking James for toleration and expressing hope that Parliament would enact appropriate legislation,[15] and the Quakers, who were included in a statement from the Yearly meeting, nonconformists refrained from submitting a declaration to the king.

Following the leadership of William Penn, the Friends enthusiastically endorsed the indulgence, as reflected in their address of 25 May. Quakers in Scotland, Ireland, New England, and Wales also sent addresses.[16] Penn, who led the Quaker delegation that presented a statement from the Yearly Meeting to the king, wrote pamphlets defending toleration and the use of the royal prerogative to grant it; they included *A Perswasive to Moderation to Church Dissenters* (1686), in which he urged the king and Privy Council to "Try a True Liberty" (A3r); *Good Advice to the Church of England, Roman Catholick, and Protestant Dissenter* (1687), which condemned the penal laws and tests as "*the greatest Yoke a Nation can well Suffer under*" (A2r); and *Som Free Reflections upon Occasion of the Public Discourse about Liberty of Conscience* (1687). In *A Third Letter from a Gentleman in the Country, to His Friends in London, upon the Subject of Penal Laws and Tests* (1687), he argued that an indulgence in 1685 would have prevented the Monmouth re-

[12] DWL, MSS 12.78, fol. 199; Lacey, 180; London *Gazette* 2238 (28 April–2 May 1687); 2242 (12–16 May 1687); 2250 (9–13 June 1687); 2265 (1–4 August 1687); 2272 (25–29 August 1687); 2274 (1–5 September 1687); 2295 (14–17 November 1687).

[13] London *Gazette* 2258 (7–11 July 1687).

[14] London *Gazette* 2270 (18–22 August 1687).

[15] London *Gazette* 2255 (27–30 June 1687).

[16] BL, Add. MSS 70,014, fol. 38r; London *Gazette* 2245 (23–26 May 1687); 2252 (16–20 June 1687); 2270 (18–22 August 1687); 2273 (29 August–1 September 1687); 2282 (29 September–3 October 1687); HMC 75, *Downshire*, 1:237; H. Larry Ingle, *First Among Friends: George Fox and the Creation of Quakerism* (New York: Oxford University Press, 1994), 280–81.

bellion and that attending a conventicle or believing in transubstantiation did not mean a man lacked the qualifications to serve as a magistrate. Ridiculing the fears of massacres and persecution that preceded James' accession, he claimed that the Church of England was more secure in 1687 "than any other worldly support she can flatter her self with." Dismissing the constitutional objections to the indulgence, he averred that the declaration was "no more than a *Royal Bill without Doors*" that prepared Parliament to discuss the issue in its next meeting. In dispensing with the penal statutes governing nonconformity, the king had not suspended "a fundamental Law."[17] These arguments did not play well among many common people, as Penn discovered when he attempted to expound his views at Shrewsbury and was shouted down by a crowd.[18] "Father Penn and Father Peters" (a reference to Father Edward Petre, a Jesuit and member of the Privy Council) became a handy target for those who feared or resented the indulgence's impact on the Church of England.[19]

Prior to May 1688 the absence of an address that included Bunyan and his congregation is noteworthy. He had to have been aware of the propaganda campaign and very likely knew some of those who submitted addresses, particularly those from dissenters in London, Northampton, Cambridge, Hitchin, Reading, Leicestershire, and Essex; from Congregationalists in London and Suffolk; and from Baptists in Bedfordshire and Middlesex. If his congregation discussed whether to thank James, it left no record, though the church book has only ten entries between 21 November 1683 and 4 September 1688.[20]

Encouraged by the addresses and his tour of the west midlands, James, having formally dissolved Parliament on 2 July, began preparing for a new one. He instructed his lords lieutenant to pose three questions to their deputies and justices of the peace: if elected, would they vote to repeal the tests and the penal statutes; would they support the election of candidates who would do so; and would they live peacefully with those of a different faith? The questions were also tendered to former MPs, office-holders in corporations, numerous minor officials, and members of the London livery companies. For refusing to pose the queries, approximately half the lords lieutenant were dismissed. John Miller has calculated that of 1,311 JPs in thirty-two English counties, 375 responded negatively, 132 wanted to hear the issues debated in Parliament before deciding, 100 had doubts or were

---

[17] William Penn, *A Third Letter from a Gentleman in the Country, to His Friends in London, upon the Subject of Penal Laws and Tests* (London, 1687), 5–6 (quoted), 8 (quoted), 9–10, 14.

[18] *HMC* 13, *Tenth Report*, Appendix 4, 376.

[19] BL, Add. MSS 34,487, fol. 15v.

[20] *CB*, 88–89.

evasive, 180 answered affirmatively, and 104 registered qualified approval; of the remainder, 203 were recently appointed Catholics and 217 were absent or did not reply. Those whose answers were unsatisfactory were replaced with dissenters or Catholics. Comparable efforts were made in the boroughs, and in London approximately 3,500 men were ousted between September 1687 and February 1688.[21]

In Bedfordshire, where Thomas Bruce, earl of Ailesbury, tendered the questions, the responses were not encouraging from the crown's standpoint. William Foster, who had examined Bunyan following his arrest in 1660, was an exception, promising to submit everything to the king's pleasure. Sir John Cotton indicated he would go to the Commons prepared to be convinced by the best arguments, which he hoped would favor repeal of the penal laws, whereas Sir George Blundell refused to commit himself until he had heard the parliamentary debate.[22] When Ailesbury presented the replies to the earl of Sunderland, the latter was furious, and subsequently the court looked increasingly for help with Bedfordshire to Henry Mordaunt, earl of Peterborough, who had converted to Catholicism in March. Peterborough's agent in Bedford was John Eston, whose father (of the same name) had been a founding member of the church Bunyan subsequently joined. Although the younger Eston is not listed as a church member, the records are incomplete, for neither of Bunyan's wives appears in the church book. Eston, who died in 1697, was probably the father of the John Eston received into fellowship in January 1700.[23]

At Peterborough's suggestion, Eston conferred with leading dissenters in Bedford, particularly Bunyan and Thomas Margetts, MP for Bedford in 1656 and judge advocate under General George Monck. He found "them all to be unanimous for Electing only such members of Parliament as will certainly vote for repealing all the Tests and penal-Laws touching Religion; and they hope to steere all their friends and followers accordingly." When Eston proposed the names of two possible parliamentary candidates to Bunyan and Margetts, they expressed a preference for Eston and Robert Audley, who had previously served as deputy recorder and been "very indulgent to all Dissenters." Because Audley had gone to Lincolnshire, they recommended Sir Edmund Gardiner, believing he would support repeal. In this they were mistaken, for Gardiner's response to the three questions indicated he would decide according to his conscience only after hear-

[21] Miller, *James II*, 178–79.

[22] Bodl., Rawlinson MSS 139A, fols. 134r–135v. The responses are printed in Sir George Duckett, *Penal Laws and Test Act: Questions Touching Their Repeal Propounded in 1687–8 by James II* (London: n.p., 1883), 47–55.

[23] Luttrell, 1:398; *CB*, 15, 121.

ing the parliamentary debate. Optimistic that the election of suitable MPs could be carried if Peterborough used his influence with "the Church-party," Eston concluded his letter of 22 November to the earl with an enthusiastic profession of loyalty to the king's policy: "My zeal against the Tests and penal Laws is so fervent, that I cannot but strenuously endeavour, in my sphere, to promote the electing such members of parliament as will certainly damn them."[24]

Knowing Gardiner's position was noncommittal, Peterborough was presumably responsible for suggesting that Foster stand with Eston. The latter soon discovered that the Anglican clerics and several corporation officers opposed the election of the two men, though "the Dissenters are firm for us." Eston placed much of the blame for the opposition he and Foster confronted on "the common people": "So much Democracie is mixed in the Government, that therby the Exercise of the Soveraign power" is restricted. Without Peterborough's assistance, he pleaded, he and Foster would be defeated.[25] After Eston sent this letter to the earl on 6 December, the latter informed the king that Eston and Foster were fit to serve. As recorder of Bedford, Ailesbury relayed Peterborough's judgment to the corporation, but on the 19th the corporation replied that the town's popular franchise meant the corporation did not control elections; members promised only to support candidates of "undoubted loyalty" who would be "serviceable to the King and Kingdome."[26]

Responding to the recalcitrance, the king and the Privy Council ordered a partial purge of the corporation in March 1688, ousting Thomas Underwood, mayor and alderman, and six others, including John Fenne, Bunyan's co-pastor since 1672, and alderman William Faldo the elder, possibly related to the Sister Faldo who had joined Bunyan's congregation in February 1675. Fenne, as we have seen, had served as an officer of the corporation from September 1677 to September 1683, and he was again named bailiff in September 1686, at which time he took the oaths of supremacy and allegiance and subscribed to the declaration against the Solemn League and Covenant. He was among those selected for the Common Council in September 1687, the position from which he was removed in March 1688.[27] Of the newly appointed members, two—John Spenser, an alderman, and John Rush, a prisoner with Bunyan in 1665 and now a common councilman, belonged to Bunyan's church; moreover, Eston may have, and

---

[24] Bodl., Rawlinson MSS 139A, fol. 20r. The evidence does not support Mark Goldie's contention that Gardiner was an ally of Bunyan. "James II and the Dissenters' Revenge: The Commission of Enquiry of 1688," *Historical Research* 66 (February 1993): 63.

[25] Ibid., fol. 21r.

[26] Brown, 351.

[27] BLA, Bedford Corporation Minute Book, 1664–1688, fols. 274–75, 281, 283–84, 289; *CB*, 78.

James Veale had provided security for Samuel Fenne in 1669. Anglicans still controlled the corporation at this point, but a further purge ensued in mid-April. Five more members of Bunyan's congregation were added to the corporation, William Nicholls and Thomas Woodward as aldermen, and John Bardolph, Henry Clarke, and William Hawkes as common councilmen. At this point, three of the seven aldermen and four of the nine common councilmen belonged to Bunyan's flock.[28] This time the government apparently attained its objectives, for in May the corporation sent James an address thanking him for promising to secure the Church of England, protect dissenters' civil rights and the free exercise of their religion by law, and work for the election of two men who would support the indulgence policy in the next Parliament. The declaration came early in a second wave of addresses that began in the *Gazette*'s issue for 30 April–3 May 1688 and continued into the autumn.[29] The change in attitude may have been affected in part by James' re-issuance of the Declaration of Indulgence on 27 April with a pledge to summon Parliament in November to enact it as a statute.

Writing in the aftermath of the revolution of 1688–89, the author of the continuation of Bunyan's life appended to *Grace Abounding* attempted to distance him from the failed policy of indulgence and cooperation with James. According to this writer Bunyan possessed a "piercing wit [that] penetrated the Veil, and found it was not for the Dissenters sake they were so suddenly freed from the Prosecutions that had long lain heavy upon them." Yet he availed himself of the freedom to continue preaching, believing God is "the only Lord of Conscience." This author alleged that Bunyan entertained doubts about the crown's remodeling of the Bedford Corporation, expressed "his Zeal with some weariness [i.e., wariness], as foreseeing the bad consequence that would attend it," and counseled his congregation "to prevent their being imposed on in this kind."[30] But this interpretation fails to account for the fact that Spenser, Rush, Bardolph, Clarke,

---

[28] BLA, Bedford Corporation Minute Book, 1664–1688, fols. 289–94; Michael Mullett, "'Deprived of Our Former Place': The Internal Politics of Bedford 1660 to 1688," *PBHRS* 59 (1980): 25–32. Norwich faced a more difficult decision when the government ordered the admission of several Quakers to the corporation; the mayor and aldermen refused to comply. BL, Add. MSS 34,487, fol. 19v.

[29] BLA, Bedford Corporation Minute Book, 1664–1688, fols. 295–96; London *Gazette* 2343 (30 April–3 May 1688) *et seq.*; Luttrell, 1:440. Bedford's address appeared in the *Gazette* 2351 (28–31 May 1688). After the birth of the prince in June, some of the statements referred to that event.

[30] "A Continuation of Mr. Bunyan's Life," *ad cal. GA*, 169–70. Sharrock notes that the "Continuation" has been attributed to Bunyan's ministerial colleague and friend George Cokayne, a fellow Bedfordshire man (*GA*, xlii), but the ascription is unlikely inasmuch as the anonymous author considerably misdates Bunyan's death.

Nicholls, Hawkes, and Woodward, each of them a member of Bunyan's church, were appointed to the corporation, or that Eston, who had family ties to the congregation and may have been a member or regular attender, was heavily involved in the political maneuvering. The name of another member, William Whitbread, is on a list of men to be considered for appointment as justices of the peace in 1687.[31] Fenne's dismissal might suggest that Bunyan was reticent to embrace the indulgence, but his ouster probably resulted from outspoken criticism of Catholics rather than opposition to an indulgence for Protestant dissenters.

The anonymous author also claims that "a great man" came to Bedford to offer Bunyan "a place of publick Trust," though the latter refused to meet with him. John Brown has suggested that this agent may have been Ailesbury, but this is improbable given his dislike of the purging.[32] If the report is credible, the "great man" was probably Peterborough or one of his agents, and the place of trust may have been membership in the corporation. The evidence does not support the claim that Bunyan was "most unwilling to have anything to do with the king's plans,"[33] for the involvement of his church members in the remodeled corporation indicates he pursued a policy of cautious cooperation. Eston undoubtedly exaggerated Bunyan's support for the indulgence in his letters to Peterborough, but Bunyan must have expressed at least qualified approval for the grant of toleration to Protestant dissenters and the election of MPs who would support the repeal of the penal laws governing religion and the tests. Had Eston fabricated the report of Bunyan's endorsement, Ailesbury or one of his allies would presumably have elicited his denial, but that never happened. Moreover, had Bunyan opposed the indulgence and remodeling, one could expect some indication of dissension within the Bedford congregation, especially since seven of its members were appointed to the corporation and Whitbread was being considered for the commission of the peace, but the church book is silent. The evidence, then, indicates that Bunyan's lengthy campaign against persecution inclined him to reply warily but positively when Eston sounded him out concerning the indulgence and plans to elect two MPs who would support the king's policy. Such a response was compatible with his belief that God would use monarchs to accomplish his goals.[34]

---

[31] Bodl., Rawlinson MSS 139A, fol. 132r–v. As we have seen, Whitbread belonged to the gentry; an ancestor of the same name was described as a gentleman in 1615. BLA, MS HSA 1671 W/17; Joyce Godber, *History of Bedfordshire, 1066–1888* ([Bedford]: Bedfordshire County Council, 1969), 304.

[32] "A Continuation of Mr. Bunyan's Life," *ad cal. GA*, 170; Brown, 353; Mullett, *JBC*, 27.

[33] Mullett, *JBC*, 28.

[34] Two of Bunyan's close colleagues, Cokayne and Griffith, would be among a small group of ministers summoned by James in October (by which point Bunyan was dead) to inform them of William's expected invasion and to assert that the infant James was in fact

"Watchman, Watchman, Watch"[35]: Reinforcing the Faithful

By the time James issued his first Declaration of Indulgence, Bunyan had probably begun work on the last volume of his trilogy on typology, *Solomon's Temple Spiritualiz'd or Gospel-Light Fetcht out of the Temple at Jerusalem, to Let Us More Easily into the Glory of New-Testament-Truths.* Published by George Larkin on 21 May 1688,[36] this work was also the first of a pair dealing with the church, a relevant topic at a time when all groups in the Christian tradition could compete openly in Britain. Bunyan likely wrote *Solomon's Temple Spiritualiz'd* from about March through June 1687, following this with *A Discourse of the Building, Nature, Excellency, and Government of the House of God*, probably composed in July and August 1687 and published by Larkin in 1688.[37] In addition to developing the theme of the church addressed in *Solomon's Temple Spiritualiz'd*, *A Discourse* returns to some of the objects prominently discussed in its predecessor, such as the altar, laver, holy temple, chains, carved work, sapphire-decorated foundation, censers, pomegranates, and holy water.

*Solomon's Temple Spiritualiz'd* contains two political allusions that help to date its composition. The first is an assertion that monarchs and "the *mighty* of the earth" will be attracted by the church's glory and bring it presents, though Gentile kings are not permitted entry. The church's visible goodness "allureth others to fall in love with their own Salvation, and makes them fall in with Christ against the Devil, and his Kingdom" (*MW*, 7:33–34). The key to this passage is Bunyan's reference to Psalm 68:29 and 31, which indicate that princes from Egypt and Ethiopia will bring gifts to God because of the temple at Jerusalem, though as uncircumcised people they will be unable to enter the temple. Bunyan was reaffirming his belief that near the end times God will utilize monarchs to defeat Antichrist. In 1687 the gift from James II must be the Declaration of Indulgence, an example, in Bunyan's eyes, of how God can use a non-Christian king in the spiritual warfare against Antichrist. In the second passage Bunyan refers to the account of the ark's relocation in 1 Chronicles 13:9–10: "When *Uzza* put forth his hand to *stay the Ark*, when *the Oxen shook it*, as despairing of GOD's protecting of it, without a humane help, *he died before the Lord*: even so will all those do (without repentance) who use unlawful means to promote Christ's Religion, and to support it in the World" (7:97). References to Matthew 26:52 and Revelation

---

his legitimate son. Virtually to the end the king hoped for support from dissenting clergy. Morrice, 2:309; Lacey, 219–20.

[35] *MW*, 7:42.

[36] *Publick Occurrences Truly Stated* 14 (22 May 1688).

[37] Larkin also published the sixth edition of *Grace Abounding* in 1688.

13:10, which admonish believers not to wield the sword in religious matters, underscore Bunyan's point. This passage was both a reminder of the fate of Monmouth, who died like Uzza for employing unlawful means in a well-intentioned effort to help the church, and a warning not to use such methods in the future.[38]

Unlike *The House of the Forest of Lebanon*, *Solomon's Temple Spiritualiz'd* contains only a few passing references to persecution, as one would expect for a work composed during a period of toleration. Whereas the saints in heaven enjoy the calm and security of being moored in a harbor, Bunyan noted, those still in this life are in a storm; from another perspective the former are at rest while the latter are in a wilderness (7:86). The chambers for hiding and security in Solomon's temple are types of the safety believers have in Christ from the world's rage, and the temple's chains are a type of the godly's obligation to suffer in God's cause (7:49, 52). Whatever hesitation Bunyan felt about embracing James' policy of indulgence reflected his wariness of "the mischievous Designs of the Enemies of God's church" (7:114).

In analyzing Solomon's temple Bunyan was dealing with a much discussed subject. Among earlier works were Thomas Fuller's *A Pisgah-Sight of Palestine and the Confines Thereof, with the History of the Old and New Testament Acted Thereon* (1650), a folio volume replete with maps and illustrations (see 355–404); John Lightfoot's *The Temple: Especially as It Stood in the Dayes of Our Saviour* (1650), which uses Hebrew liberally as well as some Greek and which surveys the temple's history after Solomon; and Samuel Lee's *Orbis miraculum, or the Temple of Solomon, Pourtrayed by Scripture-Light* (1659), a folio volume of 371 pages, with illustrations and citations in Hebrew and Greek. Unlike Bunyan's book, these volumes include references to learned authors.[39] The temple seems to have been a popular subject in some circles judging from the success of an exhibition in London in February 1675 featuring models of Solomon's temple and Moses' tabernacle constructed by a Jewish rabbi.[40]

Intending his work for godly readers, Bunyan strove for simplicity of exposition as opposed to the "*lofty, airy Notions*" he so despised, alluding to the ponderous scholastic thinking that in his estimation encouraged vain speculation (7:39–40). He took pride in asserting that he had not "fished in other mens *Wa-*

---

[38] Essentially the same point is made in a book Bunyan may have read, Thomas Grantham's *St. Paul's Catechism* (London, 1687), 61. See Richard L. Greaves, "A John Bunyan Signature," *Baptist Quarterly* 25 (October 1974): 379.

[39] A much shorter work was Jacob Jehudah Leon's *A Relation of the Most Memorable Thinges in the Tabernacle of Moses, and the Temple of Salomon, According to Text of Scripture* (Amsterdam, 1675); Solomon's temple is discussed on pp. 13–27. For Lee see *BDBR*, s.v.; for Fuller and Lightfoot see *DNB*, s.vv.

[40] *MW*, 7:xxx.

*ters*, my Bible and Concordance are my only Library in my writings" (7:9).[41] This, of course, was not true, as the lengthy quotation from Foxe in *The House of the Forest of Lebanon*, to cite an obvious example, proves. He may have written *Solomon's Temple Spiritualiz'd* without recourse to expository material, but a comment about the temple's pinnacles suggests he had seen other commentaries: "What men say of their number and length, I wave, and come directly to their signification" (7:39). Admitting he may have made some errors in his interpretation, he asked his readers "lovingly" to set such material aside and concentrate on passages that would benefit them (7:9). Sensitive that he might have been speculating when he interpreted the temple's chargers (large plates) as a type of the Bible in which meat (gospel doctrine) and sauce (repentance and prayer) are served, he offered this challenge:

> He that will scoff at this, let him scoff. The *Chargers* were a type of some thing, and he that can shew a fitter Antitype then is here proposed to consideration, let him do it, and I'l be thankful to him. (7:81)

Ferreting out the mysteries of typology was an hermeneutic exercise that clearly fascinated Bunyan, even if he was uncertain about some of his findings. In a sense this was sacred sport, his concordance serving as a storehouse of clues to decipher divine mysteries. Much of the enjoyment was in the hunt.

As a sustained exercise in typology, *Solomon's Temple Spiritualiz'd* demonstrates diligence and a degree of creativity, though it lacks inspiration. Its seventy sections are formulaic, each commencing with an explication of the nature, appearance, and use of part of the temple or one of its objects, with scriptural documentation, followed by a discussion of the antitype and sometimes spiritual counsel. Bunyan's purpose is straightforward: "Now because . . . there lies, as wrapt up in a Mantle, much of the Glory of our Gospel-matters in this Temple which *Solomon* builded; therefore, I have made, as well as I could, by comparing Spiritual Things with Spiritual, this Book upon this Subject" (7:8). He proceeded on the conviction that everything in the temple, including the decorations, doors, staircases, and building materials as well as the spoons, censers, bowls, cups, snuff-dishes, and snuffers has a spiritual signification for Christians because each detail has been divinely inspired (7:6–8). Many aspects of the temple, such as its location on Mount Moriah, its builder, the brazen altar, the doors, the veil, the ark of the covenant, and the mercy-seat, are types of Christ (7:13–14, 22–23, 42, 89, 95, 104). The Christological focus is dominant, as in this example:

[41] For a time Bunyan probably used the concordance prepared by Vavasor Powell and recommended by John Owen. A copy at Bristol Baptist College includes Bunyan's signature, but Joyce Godber attributes it to his son of the same name. "John Bunyan's Signature," *Bedfordshire Magazine* 6 (Autumn 1957): 47–49.

> For *Aaron* was a type of *Christ*; his *Offering*, a type of Christ's Offering his *Body*; the *Blood* of the Sacrifice, a type of the *Blood* of Christ; his *Garments*, a type of Christ's *Righteousness*; the *Mercy-seat*, a type of the *Throne* of *Grace*; the Incense, a type of Christ's *Praise*; and the *sprinkling* of the Blood upon the *Mercy-seat*, a type of Christ's *pleading* the vertue of his Sufferings for us in the presence of God in Heaven. (7:106)

Bunyan did not restrict each type to a single antitype, but employed an elastic methodology that enabled him to range freely and creatively, meditating on virtually every aspect of the temple to ascertain its spiritual significance. The golden nails, for example, are a type of Christ's everlasting priesthood and the words of God that abide eternally, whereas the palm trees carved on the temple doors are a type of Christ's assurance of the saints' ultimate triumph (7:90–93).

*Solomon's Temple Spiritualiz'd* was intended to reinforce the faithful as the church moved into an era of toleration. Bunyan reminded believers that the only acceptable church is a congregation of visible saints, entry into which is "according to a *prescript Rule*" (7:43, 83). Its worship must be based on apostolic doctrine as expressed in Scripture, not on human inventions (7:6, 8, 55). Reasserting his conviction that the church must provide ample latitude for all who agree on the fundamentals, he used the temple's spacious porch to underscore the importance of maintaining "a wide bosom for reception of all that come thither to worship" (7:35). Although he shared a belief in gathered churches with Congregationalists and Baptists of all types, he remained convinced that baptism must not be a bar to church membership or communion. No less significant was his commitment to church discipline, especially when toleration increased the likelihood that church members could become lax. With the lapse in persecution the threat was now as much internal as external, and the example of the lukewarm church at Laodicea (Revelation 3:14–19) was in his mind. God, he warned, could be driven from a church, leaving it with bare walls and lifeless traditions, a likely thrust at the Church of England (7:13). Discipline therefore had to be maintained in the church through the minister's admonitions and rebukes and the congregation's censures, the antitype of the temple's snuff-dishes (7:66–68). The ultimate penalty inflicted by a congregation, Bunyan explained, is withdrawal of communion, "the *holy compulsion* of the Church" (7:82). This penalty had recently been imposed by his congregation on Henry Man after he failed to show remorse for frequent lying and dishonest dealings in his occupation, but the sanction could be lifted after due penitence, as had recently happened in the case of Mary Fosket, who repented of the "horrid scandall" she had spread about another church member.[42]

The singers associated with Solomon's temple provided Bunyan with an op-

[42]*CB*, 89.

portunity to address the role of music in worship. He interpreted the songs used in the temple as a type of those sung in the church, by which he meant songs of redemption, offered by the redeemed in spiritual joy as a manifestation of the grace in their hearts. The church is "to sing *now, new* Songs, with *new* hearts, for *new* mercies," lifting up their voices in response to deliverance from hardships and iniquity, revelations of God to the soul, and "*new* frames of heart." Like prayer, singing must be done in the Spirit and with understanding. "To sing to God, is the highest Worship we are capable to perform in Heaven; and 'tis much if sinners on Earth, without grace, should be capable of performing it, according to his Institution, acceptably" (7:83–85). On the crucial question of whether hymns as well as psalms could be sung, Bunyan's endorsement of new songs aligned him with Benjamin Keach, Hanserd Knollys, and others who accepted hymn-singing, unlike the Quakers, who approved only spontaneous singing in the Spirit, and some members of Keach's congregation. Like Knollys, Bunyan accepted new words and tunes as long as worshipers sang with the Spirit and understanding, and for edification.[43]

A final theme of note in *Solomon's Temple Spiritualiz'd* is Bunyan's reiteration of the importance of charity, a cardinal concern throughout his career and a reflection of his deep-rooted sympathy for the poor. The temple's capacious porch is a type of "the Churches *bosom for Charity*," and its gates are rarely closed, suggesting that the church's compassion should always be extended to those in need. Charity beautifies the church. He reckoned that the porch was four times taller than the rest of the temple, teaching Christians that charity, "if it be rich, runs up from the Church like a *Steeple*, and will be seen afar off," visible from church to church and a cause of their acclamation (7:35–36). The orphans and the indigent presumably found relief at Bunyan's door, but unfortunately the Bedford church book, unlike that of the General Baptist church at White's Alley, London, for instance, does not record donations to the poor, making it impossible to ascertain whether Bunyan's congregation acquired the reputation for charity he considered so important. Nor is it possible to determine whether Bunyan's congregation provided relief to prisoners, as did the White's Alley church.[44] Bunyan's friend, Matthew Meade, earned a reputation as an effective money-raiser for "Christs

---

[43] Hanserd Knollys, *The World That Now Is; and the World That Is to Come* (London, 1681), pt. 1, 76, 78–80; Rosemary Moore, *The Light in Their Consciences: Early Quakers in Britain, 1646–1666* (University Park: Pennsylvania State University Press, 2000), 152–53. David W. Music has identified five places in Bunyan's works where he used Sternhold and Hopkins' psalter, but no specific references to hymns. However, Bunyan's interest in new songs would not have referred to psalms unless he meant new psalm tunes. "John Bunyan and Baptist Hymnody," *Baptist History and Heritage* 27 (April 1992): 7–8.

[44] GL, MS 592/1.

poor," on one occasion obtaining £300 for impoverished ministers at a Pinners' Hall lecture.[45]

For the most part, *A Discourse of the House of God* is a commentary in verse on most of the key subjects discussed in *Solomon's Temple Spiritualiz'd*. Bunyan's last poem, it is technically his best, though the content breaks no new ground and tends to be shallow. Graham Midgley plausibly suggests that this work took shape while Bunyan wrote *Solomon's Temple Spiritualiz'd* (*MW*, 6:lix), and he probably withheld both from publication while he polished the poetry and pondered some of the antitypes about which he was uncertain in his explication of Solomon's temple. Like *Solomon's Temple Spiritualiz'd*, *A Discourse* was directed primarily to visible saints, with the exception of a substantive appeal to prodigals at the end (6:314–17). This entreaty was probably intended especially for those who had left the gathered churches during the persecution of the early and mid-1680s. In some places the indulgence led to a sharp increase in the number of people attending nonconformist services, and these returnees would have been a likely target for Bunyan. In April 1687 John Evelyn observed "a wonderfull concourse at the Dissenters meeting house" at Upper Deptford, Kent, "and the Parish-Church left exceeding thinn." The meetinghouse to which he referred was that of the Congregationalist Henry Godman, whose congregation would number 500 in 1690.[46] Elsewhere, a Northamptonshire minister, plaintively recounting how some of his parishioners had taken advantage of the indulgence to become dissenters, described how they walked through the churchyard while he was preaching or paused to catch a few words of his sermon before hurrying away.[47] Bunyan may also have hoped to reach those who did not return to dissenting churches despite the indulgence. In Yorkshire, for example, several observers remarked that most people continued to attend the established church following the declaration.[48]

In *A Discourse* Bunyan amplified his discussion of the gathered church by surveying its officers, beginning with a portrayal of ministers as watchmen and shimmering stars. Recognizing Christ and the Holy Spirit as the church's principal governors, he depicted ministers as subordinate officers who are "not only here to *Rule*, but wait at *Table*." Returning to militant imagery to portray the

---

[45] DWL, MS 38.18, fol. 15.

[46] John Evelyn, *The Diary of John Evelyn*, ed. E. S. de Beer, 6 vols. (Oxford: Clarendon Press, 1955), 4:546; *Calamy Revised, s.v.* Deptford may have had a General Baptist church as well. W. T. Whitley, *The Baptists of London, 1612–1928* (London: Kingsgate Press, [1928]), 119. See also BL, Add. MSS 70,014, fol. 62r–v, noting the growth of Daniel Burgess' Presbyterian congregation, especially among "the common people."

[47] BL, Egerton MSS 2570, fol. 129r–v.

[48] Reresby, *Memoirs*, 582; HMC 29, *Portland*, 3:403–4 (a letter of Robert Harley's).

church, he poetically described the pastors' supervisory oversight:

> . . . they have power
> To mount on high and to ascend the *Tower*
> Of this brave Fabrick, and from thence to see
> Who keeps their ground, and who the straglers be.  (6:282–85)

He also characterized pastors as stewards responsible for distributing the word of grace as well as the church's funds, overseers of the congregation's well-being and security against intruders and false doctrines, and chefs who prepare milk for babes and meat for mature believers. He likened them as well to assistant physicians who diagnose the spiritual state of their patients and help cure the ill, prophets capable of telling people whether they are heading for heaven or hell, and guides to show saints the proper path (6:285–89). Essentially, he was writing his own job description.

Bunyan also addressed deacons and widows in this tract. The deacons' principal responsibility was distributing funds to the deserving poor, and they were also in charge of preparations for the Lord's supper. A deacon's marital situation was an important consideration in assessing his fitness to serve:

> The *Wife* must answer here as Face doth Face,
> The Husbands fitness to his work and place,
> That ground of *Scandal* or of *Jealousie*
> Obstructs not proof that he most zealously
> Performs his Office well. . . .  (6:290)

Bunyan regarded the widows' role as a service but not a church office. To be appointed, women had to be elderly, trustworthy, meek, and "*Pitiful.*" Their duties included teaching younger women what is "proper to their Sex and State, [and] what not," and caring for the ill. In return for their service they received food and clothing from the deacons (6:291–92). *A Discourse* thus incorporated a brief handbook in church management.

Bunyan expanded his commentary on charity, primarily by emphasizing that relief must be channeled to the sick, the elderly, the maimed, and the blind, but not the idle (6:290). Those who refuse to work must not eat, for idleness

> . . . gives great occasions
> To th' *Flesh*, to make its *rude* and *bold* invasions
> Upon good *Orders*. . . .

Including the idle rich in his target, he expected those who had no need to toil for their own food and attire to work for the destitute. To reinforce his point he had recourse to a familiar emblem:

> No *Drone* must hide himself under those Eaves;
> Who *sows* not, will in Harvest Reap *no* Sheaves:
> The *sloathful* man himself, may plainly see,
> The *Honey*'s gotten by the *working Bee*. (6:305)

Convinced that sloth and sin are handmaidens, he displayed no patience with those who live pampered lives, lolling on beds of ease and imbibing things that enflame their lusts (6:306). The social outrage that had burned fiercely in *A Few Sighs from Hell* still flared three decades later.

Again expanding on a theme articulated in *Solomon's Temple Spiritualiz'd*, Bunyan urged toleration with respect to minor matters and issues unessential to the faith.

> For those that have *private* opinions too
> We must *make* room, or shall the Church undo;
> Provided they be *such* as don't impair
> Faith, Holiness, nor with good Conscience jarr;
> Provided also *those that hold them shall*
> Such Faith hold to themselves, and not let fall
> Their fruitless Notions in their Brothers way. (6:310–11)

In these words Midgley has seen evidence of a gentler, more tolerant Bunyan, particularly as contrasted with his attacks on the Quakers in the late 1650s (6:lxii), but this passage is fully compatible with his position in his controversy with other Baptists in the 1670s. Since the Quakers did not keep their views to themselves, they were not among those to whom Bunyan offered an olive branch. In the communion he envisioned, his embrace extended to everyone who shared his faith, lived as a visible saint, and accepted all like-minded people in the bonds of Christian fellowship. Aside from the Friends, this presumably covered much of the spectrum of mainline Protestant nonconformity.

## "A *Voice from the Throne*"[49]: Grace as a River, Christ as an Advocate

Following completion of his trilogy on typology, Bunyan turned to an extended development of water as an emblem of divine grace. A favorite theme, this motif had been previously used in such works as *The Holy City, The Pilgrim's Progress, The Saints Privilege and Profit,* and *Solomon's Temple Spiritualiz'd.*[50] In *A Discourse of the House of God* he touched briefly on

> . . . those *goodly springs* of lasting grace,
> Whose *Christal Streams* minister Life to those
> That here of Love to her, make their repose. (*MW*, 6:278)

---

[49] *MW*, 7:195.
[50] *MW*, 3:178–84; 7:102–3; 8:255–56; 13:173, 183–87; *PP*, 110–11.

His new work, *The Water of Life: or, a Discourse Shewing the Richness and Glory of the Grace and Spirit of the Gospel*, was the logical culmination of his interest in this theme. Midgley has cogently argued that the similarity of detail in *The Saints Privilege and Profit* and *The Water of Life* suggests they were written in reasonably close proximity (*MW*, 7:xlv). I have proposed August to November 1686 as the period of composition for the former work, and Bunyan probably wrote the latter about September and early October 1687, after he had finished *A Discourse of the House of God*. Published by Ponder, *The Water of Life* was entered in the Stationers' Register on 9 January 1688.[51]

Allusions to contemporary events in *The Water of Life* are few. As befitting a time of general toleration, persecution is mentioned only in passing. Everything that happens to Christians, Bunyan asserts, is "turned into Grace" for Christ's sake (7:201). Implicitly he articulated the basis for his cautious acceptance of James' policy of indulgence by asserting that it was dangerous to reject, oppose, or despise those in authority. Convinced that it was preferable to speak against twenty subjects rather than one person exercising dominion, he reminded his readers of the aphorism in Proverbs 16:14 that a king's wrath is like a messenger of death. Referring to a royal pardon for treason to make his point, he noted that refusal to accept such an offer was an inflammatory act: "To dispise Grace, to refuse Pardon, to be unwilling to be saved from the Guilt and Punishment due to Treasons the *King's* way, since that also is the *best* way, how will that provoke?" (7:194–95). This argument may reflect Bunyan's concern that rejecting James' indulgence might induce the king to react harshly toward dissenters. Similarly, Bunyan's belief that the king's way is best may have been a factor in his decision to cooperate circumspectly with the government. This is not to suggest that his *principal* concern in making these arguments was anything other than an attempt to warn readers not to provoke divine wrath by repudiating the tender of grace and pardon, yet he deliberately employed an analogy with contemporary political overtones.

Taking Revelation 22:1 as his text, he developed the image of the water of life as a pure, crystal-clear river of enormous proportions flowing from the throne of God and the lamb: "Its nature is excellent, its quantity abundant, its head-spring glorious, and its quality singularly good" (7:215).[52] The water is dispensed by

---

[51] Arber, *Transcript*, 3:328.

[52] Midgley argues that Bunyan was probably influenced in his exposition of this text by Benjamin Keach's *A Key to Open Scripture Metaphors* (London, 1682). *MW*, 7:xliv–xlv. The inspiration may have come from Keach, but the latter's treatment is somewhat different. He compares the Holy Spirit to water, which is "free and cheap," accessible to all, and essential for life; water cools, cleanses, quenches thirst, and makes the earth fruitful. Keach, *Tropologia; A Key to Open Scripture Metaphors, in Four Books* (London: City Press, 1855), 516–18.

Christ the physician without charge to the poor and needy, not to the rich who haughtily drink wine from bowls. Bunyan's sympathy for the poor is again at the fore (7:179, 185, 190). Like a mighty river that carries away filth, grace is an ever flowing source of utmost purity, unlike the water that accumulates in ponds, pools, and cisterns. Without the continual infusion of fresh grace, believers would become malodorous and putrid (7:187–88). Although grace is akin to a mighty river, it purges gently, and its pristine waters provide a mirror in which people can see reflections of God's son as well as divine glory and the habitation prepared by God for his people (7:211, 216). This river of grace is all sufficient:

> Grace can justifie freely, *when* it will, *who* it will, from *what* it will. Grace can continue to pardon, favour and save *from* falls, *in* falls, *out* of falls. Grace can comfort, relieve and help those that have hurt themselves. And Grace can bring the Unworthy to Glory. (7:198)

In short, grace is the keystone of Bunyan's theology.[53]

With a deft touch of humor Bunyan parodied the sales pitches of those who purveyed miraculous cures of the sort advertised in handbills and the *City Mercury*. One such trumpeted "*the true Elixir Proprietatis*, And the perfect use thereof in all or most diseases, with printed directions how to take it, which is an effectual Medicine against the Griping of the Guts, Small Pox, and Measles, an incomparable Medicine against Wind and Vapours, and a general Cordial in most diseases, especially for Women in Childbirth."[54] In the opening line of his epistle to the reader he playfully suggested that people could call his book "*Bunyan's* Bill of his Masters Water of Life," and he promised to tell them who had been cured by the water of life, what their diseases had been, and what "*Liquors and Preparations*" had been concocted for that purpose (7:179). Playfulness is evident too in his reference to this water of life as *aqua vitae*, a term commonly used for alcoholic spirits or a remedy for those about to faint. "*Aqua vitae* . . . hath a quality inherent in it, but keep it stopt up in a Bottle & then who will may faint notwithstanding; but apply it, apply it fitly, and to such as have need thereof, and then you may see its quality by the Operation" (7:184, 203). Many, he noted, had invented medicinal waters for the body's health or to heal its ills, hawking their products as cure-alls with extravagant claims. Reciting a litany of such assertions, he applied them to the water of life as if he were drafting the text for his own handbill:

[53] This thesis is developed in Greaves, *JB*.

[54] *City Mercury* 14 (3–10 February 1676). For two more examples see *MW*, 7:233. For an analysis of magical healing see Keith Thomas, *Religion and the Decline of Magic* (New York: Charles Scribner's Sons, 1971), chap. 7.

This Water is *Probatum est*. It has been proved times without number: it never fails, but where 'tis not taken. No Disease comes amiss to it, it cures blindness, deadness, deafness, dumbness. *It makes the lips of them that are asleep to speak*. This is the *RIGHT* Holy Water (all other is counterfeit) it will drive away *Devils* and *Spirits*, 'twill cure *Inchantments*, and *Witchcrafts*, it will heal the *Mad* and *Lunatick*: it will cure the most desperate *Melancholy*, it will *dissolve* doubts, and *mistrusts* . . . : It will make you *speak* well, it will make you have a *white* Soul. . . . It will make you *tast* well, it will make you *disrelish* all hurtful Meats; it will beget in you a *good* appetite to that which is *good*; 'twill remove Obstructions in the *Stomach* and *Liver*. (7:215)

Contemporary readers would have recognized this as partly a parody of the elixirs hawked to cure physical and psychological ills, though Bunyan stressed that his remedy is free. Moreover, unlike the stylish spas at Tunbridge, Bath, and Epsom, the water of life is available everywhere (7:187, 217). The employment of such clear parody reflects the continuing development of Bunyan as an author, particularly his interest in experimenting with literary genres.

In contrast to his preceding two books, *The Water of Life* is addressed to the unregenerate as well as believers, with the emphasis on the former. Whereas *Solomon's Temple Spiritualiz'd* contains frequent references to the elect (7:48, 52, 63, 84, 100, 110, 112–13) and *A Discourse of the House of God* is directed to visible saints, *The Water of Life* manifests Bunyan's evangelical Calvinism, or what I have described as his "pastoral Arminianism." The unmistakable thrust of his message is that the water of life is freely available to all who ask: "Sinner, Sick-sinner, what sayest thou to this? wouldest thou *wade*, wouldst thou *swim*? here thou mayest *wade*, here thou mayest *swim*, 'tis *deep*, yet fordable at first entrance" (7:185). Citing the open-ended invitation in Revelation 22:17, Bunyan explained that anyone can drink freely of the water of life (7:186). The responsibility to accept this grace and be saved or reject it and be damned is wholly the individual's (7:194–95, 199). "If ye will enquire, enquire, return, come" (7:216). To those who despair of being the beneficiaries of grace, he held out assurance, promising a sufficiency of grace for all who seek it. "Thou therefore hast nothing to do, I mean as to the curing of thy Soul of its doubts and fears, and dispairing thoughts, but to drink and live for ever" (7:219). Whatever the religious problems with which he had wrestled in recent years, he was once again brimful of assurance.

The water motif offered Bunyan an opportunity to underscore the significance of doctrinal purity. In the second part of *The Pilgrim's Progress* Christiana and her party reach the spring at the base of Hill Difficulty and find that it has been muddied by the feet of those intent on keeping pilgrims from quenching their thirst (7:214–15). Bunyan provided commentary in *The Water of Life*, likening dirty water to doctrines fouled by "the false *glosses* and *sluttish* opinions of erroneous Judgments." He had in mind reliance on tradition and superstition, a critique that targeted both Catholics and Anglicans. Just as the appearance of fish is affected by the quality and impurities of the water in which they swim, so professing Christians are colored by the doctrines, traditions, and superstitions to which they are exposed. "If their Doctrines are clear, so are their Notions, for their Doctrine has given them a *clear* understanding of things" (211). Because the water of life is like crystal, one can judge doctrines by their clarity, rejecting those that have been fouled by the corruption of human traditions. The secret to finding pure water is to obtain it at its source, for the nearer the spring, the cleaner the water. With more ministers able to preach freely because of the indulgence, Bunyan felt obliged to advise his readers to "take heed how you hear what you hear, for . . . by your colour 'twill be seen what Waters you swim in" (7:218).

After finishing *The Water of Life* Bunyan wrote a companion volume to the still unpublished *Saints Privilege and Profit*. Whereas the latter is devoted to Christ's priestly office, *The Advocateship of Jesus Christ, Clearly Explained, and Largely Improved, for the Benefit of All Believers* deals with the relatively ignored topic of his role as an attorney. Dorman Newman, publisher of *The Holy War*, brought out *The Advocateship* and a second issue, entitled *The Work of Jesus Christ, as an Advocate, Clearly Explained . . .*; the second issue is listed in the Term Catalogues for May 1688 and May 1689.[55] The change of title was apparently an attempt to increase sales by simplifying the language. Other than a revised table of contents, the book's substance was not altered. Bunyan probably wrote it between late October 1687 and the end of February 1688, and the first issue must have appeared shortly thereafter.

Although the title-page indicates that Bunyan is addressing all believers, his primary focus is on recent converts and those with doubts about their spiritual destiny. Given his traumatic experiences as a young man, he sympathized with "the sinking Christian" and endeavored in this work to prevent the spiritual despondency triggered by undue preoccupation with one's depravity (*MW*, 11:99–100, 110, 115). To counter such feelings he counseled his readers to ponder Christ's role as a barrister who skillfully pleads the saints' cause before the supreme judge in the celestial court, an analogy based on 1 John 2:1: "And if any man sin, we have an advocate with the Father, Jesus Christ the righteous." Because the godly have no status to defend themselves against Satan's charges, Christ, working alone, pleads their case, though not by disputing the charges. Using the new law of the covenant of grace, he transfers his own righteousness to the accused, paying their debt and winning their acquittal. Christ is an attorney only for the children of God, whom he serves without charge, and Satan's accusations are upheld against all others, resulting in guilty verdicts and eternal damnation.[56]

[55] Arber, *Term Catalogues*, 2:222–23, 247.
[56] In discussing *The Advocateship* I have drawn in part on my introduction to this work

In developing this similitude Bunyan displayed a level of legal knowledge equaled nowhere else in his works. In *The Doctrine of the Law and Grace Unfolded* he referred to praemunire, replevy, and indenting, and in *A Relation of the Imprisonment* he adverted to sureties, bonds, a mittimus, a bill of indictment, and a writ of error.[57] His time in prison had increased the legal knowledge he acquired in the late 1650s, and thereafter he continued to expand his understanding of the law, perhaps in part through his acquaintance with the attorney Robert Blaney, one of the two men who posted bond for him in June 1677, and other London contacts. In *The Advocateship* he used a variety of legal concepts to make his points, including the impounding of stray or trespassing cattle and the owner's recourse to an action of replevin to reclaim them. If Christ's sheep are "pounded by the Law, he delivereth them by Ransom; if pounded by the Devil, he will replevy them, stand a Tryal at Law for them, and will be against their Accuser, their *Advocate* himself" (11:132–33). Bunyan also referred to the devices employed by barristers to delay legal proceedings, such as motions and writs of supersedeas (11:154). He mentions as well the demurrer, which terminates legal action on the grounds that the plaintiff is not entitled to relief. After Christ has successfully pleaded the new law on a client's behalf, the Devil as prosecuting attorney cannot "find any Ground for a *Demurr* to be put in against [his or her] present Discharge in open Court" (11:164). Unlike attorneys who are unprepared and let their poorer clients be "nonsuited," the ever vigilant Christ pleads cases in a timely manner and prevents his clients from having uncontested judgments rendered against them (11:169). Bunyan portrayed Christ as a feofee in trust—a trustee for property, in this case the saints' inheritance (11:184). With respect to property Bunyan cited estate deeds, leases, mortgages, and bonds (11:152, 185–86), and he understood that a husband had the right of disposition over his wife's real property (11:163). Moreover, he seems to have been familiar with the concept of equity in English law (11:135), and he certainly knew about the process by which the poor could appeal to the government *in forma pauperis*, obtaining writs and legal counsel without charge (11:190–91, 205).

---

in *MW*, 11:xxxii–xliii. As in the case of the water of life, the idea of Christ as an advocate was developed in Keach's *Tropologia*, which may have inspired Bunyan to expound the theme. In Keach's simpler exposition the advocate is learned and entrusted with weighty causes, which he undertakes on his client's behalf. He is faithful to his client, observant of the court's procedures, freely accessible, and respected by the judge. Moreover, he diligently pleads the cause of the poor and will not accept cases for which no remedy exists. *Tropologia*, 408–13. Like the water of life, the basic concept of an advocate is biblical, and Bunyan did not need Keach as an intermediary. Cf., e.g., Philip Henry: "If the same that is to bee our Judge, bee our Advocate, there's no Danger, all shal bee wel." BL, Add. MSS 42,849, fol. 6r.

[57] *MW*, 2:139, 143; "Relation," 107–8, 112–13, 128.

The level of legal knowledge and the technical vocabulary in this book indicate that in social terms the intended audience comprised nonconformists of substance. They must have had some familiarity with the legal process, although it required little imagination to think of oneself "at God's Bar" in need of a very good defense attorney (11:118). Despite the legal theme, he made no attempt to propose legal reforms, including some that might have assisted the indigent, nor is there any substantive notice of his audience's social obligations for the poor. Christ pleads for the indigent and needy, but the context is spiritual and the alms are heavenly (11:191, 203). The sharp social criticism characteristic of some of his other works is likewise absent, and his analogy between the titles accorded to Christ on one hand and those at the upper echelons of the social hierarchy and the government on the other is conservative in its implications: "'Tis common also to call Men in great Places by their Titles rather than by their Names, yea it also pleases such great ones well" (11:194). All of this underscores the atypicality of *The Advocateship*, a work Bunyan intended for people of means and a modest acquaintance with the legal process. Perhaps ironically, the book proved to be quite popular, with at least ten editions in the eighteenth century (11:98).

One of the more intriguing features of *The Advocateship* appears in the table of contents in the first issue, which refers to a passage in the body of the text in which Bunyan recounts a religious story from a source he could not recall. As he remembered the account in the text, a corpse being carried on a bier to the grave cried out, "*I am accused before the just Judgment of God*," and shortly thereafter, "*I am condemned before the just Judgment of God*." Bunyan recollected that this man had been a strict observer of "the Religion that was then on Foot in the World," a subtle jab at Catholicism (11:214). The table of contents in the first issue provides a fuller account of the story, including a third exclamation on the third day. This is followed by the sentence, *Vide vitam Brunonis* (11:108), an apparent citation of Giacomo Desiderio's *Vita di S. Bruno* (1657), a biography of Bruno of Cologne (d. 1101), founder of the Carthusian order. According to the traditional account, Bruno was converted when Raymond Diocrès, a canon at the Cathedral of Notre Dame in Paris, uttered the sentences on his bier. The story was included in the Roman Breviary until Pope Urban VIII ordered its deletion in the early seventeenth century.[58] Although Bunyan used a handful of Latin phrases in his writings, he could not read the language and must have seen the story in a secondary source or heard an oral account. Since he claimed he could not remember his source, the fuller account in the table of contents, with the instruction to see the *Vita Brunonis*, was probably added by Newman without Bunyan's knowledge.

---

[58] *MW*, 11:xxxvi; Sabine Baring-Gould, *The Lives of the Saints*, rev. ed., 16 vols. (Edinburgh: John Grant, 1914), 11:141–51.

When the latter saw it in print, he presumably ordered it struck, which would explain the altered table of contents in the second issue. One or more readers of the first issue may have objected to the reference to a Catholic saint, or Bunyan may have been embarrassed to learn that the story had been associated with a prominent Catholic.

*The Advocateship* contains several significant autobiographical passages, the most important of which is Bunyan's observation that he was once "much taken" with a sect that typically referred to Jesus as "*the blessed King of Glory*" (11:194), a reference to the Fifth Monarchists.[59] In the winter of 1687–88 he recalled his earlier attraction to this group to make the point that the godly should revive the practice of regularly referring to Jesus as the blessed king of glory, thus recognizing kingship as one of his principal offices. "The very calling of him by this or that Title, or Name belonging to this or that Office of his, giveth us Occasion, not only to think of him as exercising that Office, but to enquire by the Word, by Meditation, and one of another, *what there is in that Office*, and what by his exercising of that, the Lord Jesus profiteth his Church" (11:194). This was the rationale for Bunyan's extended discussions of Christ's priesthood in *The Saints Privilege and Profit* and his advocateship in this work.[60] Another important autobiographical insight is Bunyan's confession that he, like most believers, looked "over the Scriptures too slightly, and [took] too little Notice" of the timeliness of biblical expressions, "the *Season of administring* of Ordinances," and the numerous honors bestowed by God on Christ (11:195). As familiar with the Bible as he was, his feeling of guilt about not having devoted more consideration to these scriptural themes is a revealing insight into the spiritual standards he set for himself and his periodic concern about falling short. His sense of inadequacy and failing to attain his standards reflects Matthew Meade's belief that "the highest communion that grace is capeable of[,] it will not satisfye for it is but weake, & imperfect, & arbitrary, & . . . liable to the uncomfortable interoptions of sin." If Meade was right, the greater Bunyan's sense of fellowship with the divine, the more he longed for a fuller experience of it.[61]

Bunyan may have written *Of the Law and a Christian*, which was published posthumously, about this time. Like *Of the Trinity and a Christian*, it cannot be dated, but it too is a very brief work, possibly intended for publication as a

[59] See Chapter 2.

[60] Bunyan underscores the linkage of the two themes by his frequent references to Christ's priesthood in *The Advocateship* (99, 116–17, 119, 124–25, 135, 137, 141–45, 159–60, 163, 166, 169, 173, 186–87, 189, 194–95, 212, 214–16).

[61] Bodl., Rawlinson MSS E120, fols. 12v–13r. In the same sermon Meade asserted that "grace is a pleasant path to walk in, but an ill bed to rest in" (fols. 15v–16r). Since the two men were friends, they may have discussed Bunyan's concern about falling short.

broadside. In *The Advocateship of Jesus Christ* he had described how Christ employed the new law of the covenant of grace to transfer his righteousness to the accused, remitting their debt and procuring their acquittal. This may have prompted the need for a broadside that outlined the use of the law in the Christian life. In the covenant of works, he explained, the law sentences unbelievers to damnation, but in the covenant of grace it serves as a rule or guide for those who have been justified by Christ. The believer can therefore say, "I may not, will not, cannot, dare not make it my Saviour and Judg, nor suffer it to set up its government in my conscience; for by so doing I fall from Grace, and Christ Jesus doth profit me nothing" (*MW*, 12:412). As in *The Advocateship of Jesus Christ*, Bunyan employed the analogy of a wife's legal status, explaining that when a woman in debt marries, her husband assumes her financial obligations, enabling her to be released from debtors' prison. Similarly, the Christian is liberated from the law "as it thundreth and burneth on *Sinai*, or as it bindeth the conscience to wrath and the displeasure of God for Sin" (12:413). Thereby freed, the believer can appreciate the law as a guide that is holy, just, and good. In contrast to his treatment of this theme in *The Doctrine of the Law and Grace Unfolded* some three decades earlier, he now emphasized the law's usefulness in Christian living, thereby moving away from the inclinations toward Antinomianism that had been present in his religious thought.

## "Where Promises *Swarm*"[62]: The Quest for Jerusalem Sinners

While Bunyan continued to write and preach in what would be the final year of his life, James pressed forward with his policy of indulgence. Addresses of thanksgiving still appeared in the London *Gazette*, although Jonathan Trelawney, bishop of Bristol, reported that in his diocese they had "faln like water upon oyl cloath, . . . goeing off without making any impression." Some of the Presbyterian laity, he noted, were angry because their names had been affixed to an address without their knowledge or permission.[63] In December 1687 the king ordered a review of deputy lieutenants and justices of the peace with a view to removing those opposed to repeal of the penal laws and tests, and by the following spring fourteen of twenty-four lords lieutenant and three-quarters of all JPs had been dismissed.[64] Using commissions and writs of *quo warranto* the government purged the town corporations of approximately 1,200 members. Narcissus Luttrell observed of the purge in November 1687 that "generally it falls heavy on the

---

[62] *MW*, 11:65.
[63] Bodl., Tanner MSS 29, fols. 42r, 147r (quoted).
[64] Luttrell, 1:423, 426, 429, 431, 439; David L. Smith, *A History of the Modern British Isles, 1603–1707: The Double Crown* (Oxford: Blackwell Publishers, 1998), 279–80.

church of England men; and the dissenters now are only favour'd and caress'd" in order to secure the indulgence.[65] Implementing the policy was not easy, for some dissenters refused to serve, and in London insufficient numbers of nonconformists were willing to administer the companies.[66]

In April 1687 the king had indicated he wanted restitution made to nonconformists for their suffering. On 5 December a warrant was issued to establish commissions to ascertain what fines had been levied or property confiscated from nonconformists and recusants since September 1677 for which an accounting had not been made to Westminster. Bedfordshire was included in a commission that was also responsible for Buckinghamshire, Berkshire, and Oxfordshire. Appointed in December, March, and July, commissioners altogether numbered more than 300, most of whom were gentry, lawyers, and other leaders among the urban elite. Of those appointed from Bedfordshire, the only one known to have had a relationship with Bunyan was John Eston, though the former may also have been acquainted with Sir Edmund Gardiner, who was appointed to the commission for Huntingdonshire. Records survive only for the commission in Devon, but commissioners were evidently active in London, Essex, Cambridgeshire, Nottinghamshire, and elsewhere.[67] Church officials in London vehemently protested, citing the fact that some of the proceeds had been used to build St. Paul's, for charitable and pious purposes, and to help cover the cost of prosecuting nonconformists beginning in 1682; moreover, the authorities had returned the bonds to some dissenters after they promised to conform.[68] Whether commissioners were active in Bedfordshire is not known, but if they were, Eston would surely have wanted to interview Bunyan.

During his visits to London Bunyan would have followed events with considerable interest. Among the newly appointed aldermen was the Baptist William Kiffin, and Sir John Shorter, who was elected mayor in 1687, was a prominent nonconformist and a member of Richard Wavel's congregation. In early November Shorter heard Matthew Meade preach to a conventicle in Grocers' Hall, and later the same day he listened to a sermon by John Howe. The following month he was among the congregation in Grocers' Hall that heard the dissenter Samuel

[65]Luttrell, 1:421 (quoted), 426–27, 429, 431, 438; Smith, *History*, 279–80.

[66]Mark Knights, "A City Revolution: The Remodelling of the London Livery Companies in the 1680s," *English Historical Review* 112 (November 1997): 1166–67.

[67]Luttrell, 1:398, 429; *Calendar of Treasury Books, 1685–1689*, vol. 8, 4 parts (London: His Majesty's Stationery Office, 1923), pt. 3, 1695–97, 1803–6; pt. 4, 1981–83, 2028, 2034–35; Mark Goldie, "James II and the Dissenters' Revenge," 55, 59, 61–62, 66, 80–88; John Miller, *Popery and Politics in England, 1660–1688* (Cambridge: Cambridge University Press, 1973), 216.

[68]Bodl., Tanner MSS 30, fol. 200r–v.

Slater preach. Although the Ecclesiastical Commission had no objection to Shorter having nonconformist services in the Guildhall chapel, the court of aldermen successfully blocked him. Dissenters were permitted to meet in Skinners' Hall, which the king had leased. Stephen Lobb was dubbed "the Jacobite Independent" because he enjoyed frequent access to James, and in February 1688 the king remitted a fine imposed on Bunyan's former printer, Francis Smith, for illegal publishing.[69] For his part, Bunyan continued his circumspect approval of the indulgence, much as Thomas Jollie and some of his fellow Congregationalists did: "Wee shall be cautious," they explained, "lest wee give offence to any, or any way expose the liberty which wee doe enjoy allready."[70] In *The Advocateship* Bunyan incorporated yet another passage with political overtones, cautioning readers that a person who "troubled his Neighbour and . . . , in the Face of the Country, cast Contempt upon the highest act of Mercy, Justice, and Righteousness" would be subject to "sound and severe snibs, from the Judge" (11:128–29). He may have been thinking in part of those who opposed the king's offer of toleration. Among them was George Griffith, who, with Howe and Bates, supported Church of England clerics when they refused to read the second Declaration of Indulgence in their pulpits. When the prelates who led the opposition were acquitted of seditious libel, Bedford celebrated, though Bunyan and his congregation may have been of a different mind.[71]

In keeping with his conviction that God would use monarchs in the battle against Antichrist during the end times, Bunyan seems to have held out hope that James might be converted. This is the import of his discussion of Manasseh, son of Hezekiah and king of Judah, who seduced his people to commit evil, erected altars, and shed innocent blood (2 Kings 20:21–21:18; 2 Chronicles 32:33–33:20). "So long as he was a ringleading Sinner, the great Idolater, and chief for Devilism, the whole Land flowed with wickedness," but after he was converted, the idols and the altars of Baal were replaced with "true Religion in much of the Power and Purity of it." Most, possibly all Protestants would have associated idolatry and altars with Catholicism and thus recognized Bunyan's suggestion that God might convert James. After all, Bunyan's major theme in *Good News for the Vilest of Men, or, a Help for Despairing Souls* was that Jesus offered mercy to the biggest sinners first (*MW*, 11:36).

As the king continued his quest to forge a pro-government alliance of non-

---

[69] Luttrell, 1:411, 414, 419, 424–25, 427–28, 432; *HMC 75, Downshire*, 1:276, 279; Morrice, 2:227; DWL, MS 38.18, fol. 38 (quoted); Knights, "A City Revolution," 1165. For Slater see *BDBR, s.v.*

[70] DWL, MSS 12.78, fol. 209.

[71] Greaves, *SR*, 94; Luttrell, 1:449.

conformists and Catholics, Bunyan pressed ahead with his writing, turning now to an exposition of Luke 24:47, in which Christ commands his disciples to preach repentance and forgiveness of sins to all nations beginning in Jerusalem. *Good News*, which Bunyan wrote between about March and mid-May 1688, was published by Larkin the same year.[72] An evangelical work in the tradition of *Come, & Welcome* and *The Water of Life*, *Good News* explores God's offer of grace and mercy to the greatest offenders—the Jerusalem sinners—first. Those at Jerusalem were responsible for crucifying Jesus and thus, Bunyan argued, unequaled in their wickedness. Jerusalem was "the very Slaughter-shop for Saints," the place where the prophets, Christ, and his people were persecuted and murdered. Those who were not killed were driven "into the utmost Corners" (11:14–15). The apostle Paul, the self-described chief of sinners, had also been a persecutor as well as a blasphemer and *"an injurious Person"* (11:32). Bunyan's depiction of the worst sinners as persecutors made a polemical point, and his renewed concern with this subject reflected the fact that cases of persecution were again being reported, the royal policy of toleration notwithstanding. He could have read about them in the weekly newspaper *Publick Occurrences Truly Stated*, published by Larkin and Henry Care, and he could also have discussed such cases with Larkin when he visited London. *Publick Occurrences* reported that in February 1688 magistrates in Southwark distrained the goods of nonconformists, and in early March the "Rabble" disrupted two meetings of dissenters in York. Early the same year an Anglican cleric at Chelmsford, Essex, preached six sermons justifying the lawfulness of prosecuting nonconformists, and at Mildenhall, Suffolk, another Church of England minister harassed dissenters, dispersing one meeting with the aid of a constable and his assistants. On another occasion, while a nonconformist minister was preaching at Mildenhall, windows in the meetinghouse were broken. Similarly, at Sandwich, Kent, a nonconformist meetinghouse was damaged on 29 March and again on 2 April, and the pulpit, seats, and cloth on the communion table were destroyed at a dissenting church in Ryegate, Surrey, in April.[73] Such incidents fell well short of the more severe persecution experienced in the early 1680s, but they evinced the hostility that continued to seethe in some circles despite the policy of toleration. In February 1689 Meade looked back on the 1680s as a time of "incessant vexations, by *Suits*, by *Fines*, by *illegal House-breakings*, by

[72] The second edition was published by Larkin under the title *The Jerusalem Sinner Saved*. The title-page has the date 1689, but Larkin advertised it in *Publick Occurrences Truly Stated* 30 (11 September 1688).

[73] *Publick Occurrences Truly Stated* 3 (6 March 1688); 4 (13 March 1688); 6 (27 March 1688); 7 (3 April 1688); 9 (17 April 1688); 11 (1 May 1688). See also 23 (24 July 1688). For Care see *DNB*, s.v.

*Plundering and Spoil*, by *Imprisonments*, by *Prosecution for Life*, by *Wandering in a strange Land*."[74]

In addition to renewing his attack on persecutors, Bunyan criticized Catholics and conformists alike for espousing worship that contravened scriptural precepts. Scathingly, he denounced their forebears, the religious leaders at Jerusalem and their followers, for their decay, degeneration, and apostasy. Rejecting the rules of worship and the "weighty Ordinances" in the Bible, they established their own religious traditions, defacing truth and embracing hypocrisy (11:14). The greatest of Jerusalem sinners, he insisted, were priests, "the Inventors and Ringleaders" in the rejection and crucifixion of Jesus (11:22). He went on to accuse Satan of disguising his clergy as ministers of righteousness and having them "set up fond Names and Images" in Christ's place, an obvious attack on the liturgy and iconography of the churches of England and Rome (11:74). More subtly, he hinted at the difference between the contemporary Catholic church and its first-century predecessor. Referring to the dramatic conversion of Jerusalem sinners in Acts 4:32–35, he suggested that God "took them up betwixt the Earth and the Heavens," where they conversed about "the Church of *Rome*, and set her in her Primitive state, as a Patern, and Mother of Churches" (11:45). Such criticism of the Catholics was Bunyan's way of maintaining his distance from them even as he approved the king's policy of toleration.

Christ wants to save the greatest sinners first, Bunyan contended, because they are the colonels and captives in Satan's army as well as ringleaders in vice (11:35, 48). "Sin swarms and lieth by Legions, and whole Armies, in the Souls of the biggest Sinners, as in Garrisons" (11:35). Once converted, they become monuments and mirrors of mercy, the beneficiaries of the greatest love and forgiveness (11:37, 40). To Christ such converts are booty (11:7). Just as dry wood burns the brightest, so grace shines most brilliantly in the greatest sinners once they have been redeemed (11:45). Having recently discussed Christ as priest and advocate, Bunyan now depicted him as a physician intent on curing the worst sinners in order to spread his fame and encourage others to seek his treatment.

> Physicians get neither Name nor Fame by pricking of *Wheals* [pimples] or picking out *Thistles*, or by laying of Plaisters to the scratch of a *Pin*. Every old Woman can do this. But if they will have a Name and a Fame, if they will have it quickly, they must, as I said, do some great and desperate Cures. Let them fetch one to Life that was Dead; let them recover one to his Wits, that was Mad; let them make one that was born Blind, to See; or let them give ripe Wits to a Fool; these are notable Cures; and he that can do thus, and if he doth thus first, he shall have the *Name* and *Fame* he desires; he may lye a Bed till Noon. (11:27)

[74]Matthew Meade, *The Vision of the Wheels Seen by the Prophet Ezekiel* (London, 1689), sigs. A3v-A4r.

Just as physicians advertise dramatic cures in handbills, so Christ publishes his successes, such as David, Solomon, Peter, and Mary Magdalen, in the Bible (11:28).

Extending the offer of mercy to the greatest sinners first, which Bunyan counseled ministers to do (11:36), raised two substantive enigmas: Did this not discourage those who were not among the most depraved, and did this not countenance licentiousness? He dealt with the first issue by averring that someone can be a comparatively modest sinner and yet be "sensibly a great one." As in his own religious experience, thoroughness of conviction is more significant than the extent of one's sinful behavior. The key is "the *grievousness* of the [sinner's] Cry" (11:71–72). He thought "one of the comliest Sights in the world, [is] to see a little Sinner commenting upon the greatness of his sins; multiplying, and multiplying them to himself; till he makes them in his own eyes *bigger* and *higher* than he seeth any other mans sins to be in the World," much as he had done during his own turbulent conversion experience (11:73). In response to the second question Bunyan insisted that without repentance there can be no remission of guilt, for sinning that grace might abound is not an option (11:68–69). Although he acknowledged that some people might regard his doctrine as Antinomian, he firmly rejected any notion that extending the offer of grace to the greatest sinners first is conducive to loose living (11:40, 82).

As in *Grace Abounding* Bunyan used himself as a case study in the salvation of Jerusalem sinners. "I have been Vile *myself*," he explained, "but have obtained Mercy" (11:7). He likened himself to a breeder of lice who had infected all the youth of Elstow—at least his neighbors thought so—yet after he converted, nearly everyone in the village, he claimed, "went out to hear at the place where I found good" (11:35–36). Still vividly remembering his own spiritual and psychological turmoil, he recounted his eventual triumph over despair:

> I would say to my Soul; O my Soul! *this* is not the place of Despair, *this* is not the *time* to despair in: As long as mine eyes can find a Promise in the Bible; as long as there is the least mention of Grace, as long as there is a moment left me of breath or life in this World; so long will I wait and look for Mercy; so long will I fight against Unbelief and Despair. (11:66)

To preach so powerfully in autobiographical tones must have enabled Bunyan to hold congregations nearly spellbound. Indeed, he acknowledged he had enjoyed considerable success preaching on the subject of mercy for the chief of sinners, undoubtedly because he incorporated his own experience (11:7).

With its ring of autobiographical authenticity, evangelical fervor, optimistic spirit, and effective use of anecdotes and homely similitudes, *Good News* was one of Bunyan's more successful works. As one of his last acts he prepared a second

edition, published posthumously in 1689 by Larkin, with a new title, *The Jerusa-
lem-Sinner Saved: or, Good News for the Vilest of Men.* By 1728 it had reached the
tenth edition, and editions were published in Wales (1721), Boston, Massachusetts
(1733), Scotland (1765), and Amherst, New Hampshire (1798). In the second edition Bunyan added a section amplifying his comments on the unpardonable sin
and offering spiritual counsel to those afraid they had committed it.

In the first edition he had mentioned the unpardonable sin in passing, though
it was clearly implicit in his assertion that forlornness "drives a man to the study
of his own ruine, and brings him at last to be his own Executioner" (11:54, 66). As
a young man Bunyan had been troubled by the despair and suicide of Francesco
Spira (*GA*, §163), but now he must have been pondering anew the recent case of
John Child. When Thomas Plant and Benjamin Dennis published their account
of Child, *The Mischief of Persecution Exemplified* (1688), possibly after interviewing Bunyan, they must have stirred interest in the unpardonable sin. Probably
because Bunyan had been one of those who unsuccessfully ministered to Child, a
much fuller version of whose story was now in print, he decided to expand his
comments on the unpardonable sin in the second edition of *Good News.* In
dealing with people concerned that they might have committed this sin, he explained that those who seek salvation cannot be guilty of the offense because this
would negate the biblical promise that no one who comes to Christ will be
turned away. Those guilty of the unforgivable sin cannot go to him because they
deem him a magician or a witch whose powers derive from the Devil. Moreover,
no one can commit this heinous offense without first having been spiritually enlightened, and the repudiation of that light must be done publicly (*MW*, 11:89–
91). "Words, and Wars, and Blasphemies against this Son of Man are pardonable;
but then they must be done ignorantly and in unbelief" (11:92). However, Bunyan did warn his readers that the offer of free grace is temporally limited, a point
he illustrated with the analogy of a royal pardon that has an expiration date. Yet
even here he softened the message by averring that those for whom the day of
grace is past are usually beyond the point of experiencing guilt. Merely to ask if it
is too late to repent is evidence that the offer of grace remains open (11:83, 85).
The entirety of this discussion was conducted in the spirit of evangelical Calvinism that was one of Bunyan's trademarks.

## "Ah! Pride, Pride!"[75]: A Transcript of the Heart

The king's policy of indulgence made it possible for Bunyan to preach to
large crowds in London, and even Archbishop Sancroft was instructing his clergy

[75] *MW*, 12:47.

in July 1688 to have "a very tender Regard" toward nonconformists.[76] According to Charles Doe some 3,000 people came to hear Bunyan preach on Sunday at "*a Townsend Meeting-house, so that half were fain to go back again for want of room, and then himself was fain at a back-door to be pull'd almost over people to get up stairs to his Pulpit.*" Doe only knew Bunyan approximately two years, so this occasion must have occurred after James' first Declaration of Indulgence was issued. The capacious meetinghouse was that of Matthew Meade in Stepney, reportedly the largest church in the London area. Doe attested that Bunyan could pack London meetinghouses to overflowing on a day's notice, and he also reported an assemblage of some 1,200 people for a lecture in London on a weekday during the winter.[77] *The Pilgrim's Progress*, the tenth and eleventh editions of which appeared in 1685 and 1688 respectively, had made Bunyan a celebrity, and his printed sermons suggest he was at times a powerful orator. He belonged to that tradition of preaching to which Peter Mews, bishop of Bath and Wells, referred in 1673 when he indicated that some Presbyterians could be "out preached . . . by Bottle makers and Tanners."[78] Bunyan's simple themes, homely anecdotes, colloquial language, and abundant repetition contributed to his pulpit success, though his published sermons vary in quality, and the redundancy that facilitated ease of comprehension in an oral format can become tedious in print.

This was the case with his last significant work, an expanded sermon on Psalm 51:17: "The sacrifices of God are a broken spirit: a broken and a contrite heart, O God, thou wilt not despise." Written from about mid-May to July 1688, the manuscript was delivered by Bunyan to Larkin shortly before the former's death (*MW*, 12:11), and it was published the following year under the title, *The Acceptable Sacrifice: or the Excellency of a Broken Heart*. In the book's preface, dated 21 September 1688, Cokayne succinctly captured its spirit, remarking that the work had been "Transcribed out of the Author's heart" (12:11). Cokayne, who knew Bunyan well, thought pride was the temptation that most discomfited him, adding that he periodically needed a thorn in the flesh to keep him humble. God, surmised Cokayne, "was still Hewing and Hammering [Bunyan] by his Word,

[76] *The Articles Recommended by the Arch-Bishop of Canterbury* (London, 1688); a copy is bound in Bodl., Tanner MSS 28, fols. 131r–132v. Several prominent Anglicans conferred with dissenters in July about ways to improve their relations. The former were willing to recognize that the state has no right to persecute people for matters of conscience regarding faith and worship, though they insisted that the government can legitimately regulate times and places of meetings and the number of people allowed to assemble (as the Conventicle Acts did). BL, Add. MSS 71,692, fol. 13v; 45,974, fol. 37r.

[77] Doe, "The Struggler," in *MW*, 12:456, 460; DWL, MS 38.18, fol. 15.

[78] Longleat, Coventry MSS 7, fol. 18v. He continued: "The Players and Rope Dancers will have more company than their Lecturers."

and sometimes also by more than ordinary Temptations and Desertions" (12:7). Interpreting Bunyan's spiritual trials as God's way of keeping his spirit contrite, Cokayne confirmed what Bunyan had noted about recurring temptations in *Christ a Compleat Saviour*. As a transcript of his religious experience, *An Acceptable Sacrifice* is at root autobiographical, and it reflects nothing of the historical drama being played out in England and the Netherlands that would culminate in the revolution of 1688–89.

In *The Acceptable Sacrifice* Bunyan argued that no sinner could be saved nor an apostate returned to grace without a broken spirit and a contrite heart. To an extent his own experience became the pattern for all, though he acknowledged that people undergo differing degrees of spiritual perturbation in both intensity and longevity (12:79). Still, every person who "truly comes to *God*" must have a broken, penitent heart and experience qualms and "*sinking fits*"; such a person "oftimes *dies away* with pain and fear," pining in her or his iniquity (12:18, 70). Bunyan described this "sinking of the whole Man" in medical terms, returning to the theme of God or Christ as the physician who heals the spiritually sick and despondent (12:18, 29, 61–62, 79). God must first make patients aware they suffer from a deadly ailment. Like the mentally ill in Stuart England, "they must be taken, they must be separated from men; they must be laid in Chains, in Darkness, Afflictions and Irons: They must be blooded, half starved, whipped, purged, and be dealt with, as mad People are dealt with," and this must continue until their cries for relief result in deliverance from darkness and the shadow of death (12:55). In the twilight of his life, the memories of what he had undergone in the 1650s remained vivid, for he still knew what it meant to feel the "*lashes of Conscience*" as they burned like a whip on lacerated flesh (12:49). Piling images one upon another, he described how "the Arrows of the Almighty" pierce the soul, the relentless blows of God's hammer strike the heart until it is broken, the pestle of the law grinds the sinner in God's mortar, and the burden of guilt weighs intolerably on the spirit (12:29, 45). If neither the rod nor reasoning breaks the sinner's spirit, God administers a posset of offenses so foul-tasting, bitter to the soul, and loathsome to the mind that the sinner will repent or be left with "*Tobacco-Pipe-Heads*," an allusion to the story of a Bedford girl prone to eat pipe bowls until a doctor broke her of the habit by having her father boil pipe bowls in milk and make her drink the foul brew (12:52). For some of the elect, Bunyan reflected, the way to heaven is dreadful, made so by the visible manifestation of divine wrath, "a Home-charge from Heaven of the guilt of Sin to the Conscience" (12:21, 35). As he well knew, the soul's anguish is excruciatingly painful, eliciting cries of agony from the afflicted (12:37, 39). In the end, the broken, contrite heart is no more likely to take pleasure in sin than a man with broken bones is to play in a football match (12:28).

Wrestling with pride in his own spiritual life, Bunyan warned that it pumped sinners full of self-conceit, causing them to reckon themselves a thousand times better than they are. Because of pride they spurn warnings and admonitions, mistaking their false sense of righteousness for grace. Pride "lies most hid, most deep in *Man* as to his Soul Concerns," preventing him from recognizing the futility of reliance on natural goodness, human wisdom, and honesty. "If a man be proud of his Goodness, a broken Heart will maul him." So powerful a force was pride in Bunyan's experience that he likened it—using the imagery of Leviticus 26:19 and Psalm 73:6—to an iron sinew or chain, deliverance from which can only come after God has broken one's spirit (12:46–48).

For Bunyan, pride is intimately related to self-righteousness, as great an iniquity as any immoral act. For a self-righteous person to be saved, he asserted, is virtually impossible, for such a person is "but a *painted Satan*, or *a Devil in fine Cloathes*," someone with a holier-than-thou attitude (12:80). In a final broadside at the Church of England he denounced its "*pretended divine Services*" as stumbling blocks, the ineffectual product of vain minds. All merely external worship is unavailing because it is performed by people devoid of contrite spirits (12:78, 82). Christopher Hill has aptly observed that Bunyan was nearly obsessed with the corruption of those who formally profess Christianity but in their self-righteousness lack genuine redemption.[79] Throughout history, Bunyan opined, "great flocks of such Professors" have always existed, but they reek of gangrene and rotting flesh; like crows devouring carrion, they remain oblivious to the nauseous odors of the evil they devour (12:30, 78). His preoccupation with purveyors of pseudo-righteousness reflects his life-long battle against the Church of England, but it may also evince a struggle within himself against self-righteousness. "A mans goodness," he wrote, perhaps revealingly, "is that which blinds him most, is dearest to him, and hardly parted with; and therefore when such an one is converted . . . there is required a great deal of breaking work upon his heart" (12:80). Arguably more so than in any other published sermon, in *An Acceptable Sacrifice* he was addressing his own needs as well as those of his audience.

Shortly after completing this book, Bunyan was approached in mid-August by a neighbor who had quarreled with his father and was in danger of being disinherited. Asked to intercede, Bunyan rode to Reading and effected a reconciliation. While traveling on to London he was drenched in a storm and soon "fell sick of a violent Feavor." On the 19th, possibly before he became ill, he preached to the open membership congregation of John Gammon in Boar's Head Yard, off Petticoat Lane, on John 1:13: "which were born, not of blood, nor of the will of

---

[79] Christopher Hill, "Bunyan, Professors and Sinners," *BS* 2 (Spring 1990): 7–25, especially 7, 20.

the flesh, nor of the will of man, but of God."[80] W. R. Owens has suggested that his notes may have been the basis for the printed version, *Mr. John Bunyan's Last Sermon*, published by Larkin in 1689 (*MW*, 12:85). However, this seems implausible since the sermon contrasts rather strikingly with earlier ones in the evangelical Calvinist tradition, such as *Good News, The Water of Life*, and *Come, & Welcome*. In the sermon to Gammon's congregation the Calvinist doctrine of predestination is presented starkly, without Bunyan's typical softening of the edges with at least the illusion of an offer of grace to all comers. Instead, in this sermon he—or the note-taker—asserted that although even the most wicked people at some point desire salvation, God withholds grace from certain of them despite their yearning for redemption. For them the water of grace is not freely available. "I am not a Free-willer, I do abhor it," he reportedly said, referring to the Arminian doctrine of individual choice (12:88). Such a statement was consistent with his Calvinist tenets, but the tone of the predestinarian comments is jarring when juxtaposed with some of his earlier pulpit oratory.

Much of the sermon is taken up with a similitude between the spiritual new birth on the one hand and childbirth and infant care on the other. In developing the analogy, as in *The Acceptable Sacrifice*, he was insensitive to women. In the latter work he asked, "Would one in his *Wits*, think to make himself fine or acceptable to men, by arraying himself in *Menstruous Clothes*, or by painting his Face with *Dross* and *Dung*?" (12:54). Similarly, in his last sermon he compared "the dark Dungeon of Sin" to "the dark dungeon of [a] Mothers Womb" (12:89). Although sometimes strained, the rest of the analogy is more palatable. He suggested similarities between childbirth and Christ's resurrection from the grave, the cries of an infant and those born of God, an infant's craving for a mother's breast and the newly converted Christian's hunger for the milk of God's word, and fine swaddling clothes and the righteousness that envelops the Christian (12:89–93). Judging from the printed text, the sermon was not distinguished by its creativity or captivating anecdotes, but the published version may have been a pale reflection of what Bunyan actually said or of what the text might have looked like had he revised and expanded it. It would be unwise to accord much weight to it.

After the service Bunyan returned to the home of the grocer John Strudwick in Holborn, where his physical condition deteriorated. He died on Saturday, 31 August, of what Doe called "*a sweating Distemper*."[81] According to a newsletter

---

[80] Anon., "A Continuation of Mr. Bunyan's Life," *ad cal. GA*, 173; Whitley, *Baptists of London*, 120–21; GL, MSS 9579, vol. 1, entry for 21 July 1693.

[81] Doe, "The Struggler," in *MW*, 12:454. The principal accounts of Bunyan's death are problematic. The author of "A Continuation of Mr. Bunyan's Life" asserts that he was sick for ten days prior to his death, which he erroneously gives as 12 August (174). Doe

dated 9 June 1688, distemper had reached epidemic proportions, though few perished. Robert Harley blamed it on north winds, adding that it had struck France as well. According to one observer, writing on 14 June, "it seises like a giddiness in the head and . . . ague throwout the whole body. They say three parts of the City have had it."[82] The illness that claimed Bunyan was probably influenza, though pneumonia is also a possibility. Of his funeral service we know virtually nothing, although Cokayne, Strudwick's pastor, probably officiated; he must have been thinking in part of this service when, on 21 September, he referred to the "unexpressible Grief of many precious Souls" as they mourned Bunyan (*MW*, 12:11). On 2 September he was buried in Strudwick's vault in Bunhill Fields, Finsbury, a burial ground where Thomas Goodwin and John Owen as well as other dissenters were interred, but so too were conformists and Catholics. His wife Elizabeth, who would die in 1691, survived him, as did his sons John, Thomas, and Joseph, and his daughters Elizabeth and Sarah. His blind daughter Mary had predeceased him. Unlike Owen, who reportedly left an estate worth £2,000, Bunyan died in very modest circumstances, leaving goods valued at £42 19s.[83] The Bedford church book records the stunned reaction of his congregation: "Wedensday the 4th of September was kept in prayre and huemilyation for this heavy stroak upon us, the death of dare brother Bunyan. Apoynted allso that Wednsday next be kept in praire and humilitaion on the same account."[84]

---

provides the correct date, but states that Bunyan had been ill for "*some weeks*" (*MW*, 12:454). Contrary to Brown (374), 31 August was a Saturday.

[82] *HMC* 29, *Portland*, 3:409–11; *HMC* 35, *Fourteenth Report*, Appendix 4, 192 (quoted). William Lloyd, bishop of Norwich, was among the infected, though he recovered. Bodl., Tanner MSS 28, fol. 48r.

[83] Doe, "The Struggler," in *MW*, 12:454; Brown, 376; NUL, MSS PwV95, p. 328; Hill, *TPM*, 367. Bunyan's funeral was apparently modest in contrast with that of Owen, whose hearse had been accompanied by "a very great number of Noblemen's and Gentlemen's coaches with six horses each, and many Gentlemen on horseback." John Asty, "Memoirs of the Life of John Owen, D.D.," in *A Complete Collection of the Sermons of the Reverend and Learned John Owen, D.D.* (London, 1721), xxxiii.

[84] *CB*, 89

# Epilogue

---

"*Ah Goodman* Bunyan!"[1]: A Retrospect

As described by a contemporary, Bunyan was a tall, stout, strong-boned man with reddish hair, sparkling eyes, and a ruddy complexion. Robert White's portrait, sketched in pencil when Bunyan was fifty, shows him with shoulder-length, wavy hair, thick eyebrows, a mustache, and plain attire, and Thomas Sadler's portrait in oil, painted in 1685, is very similar. Two of Bunyan's colleagues in the ministry, John Wilson and Ebenezer Chandler, referred to him as "*Christ's Soldier*" and observed that "*his Countenance was grave and sedate*," his wit sharp and quick, and his memory tenacious. He was, they averred, "*a Son of Thunder*" when preaching to "*secure and dead Sinners*," but when administering the Lord's supper he wept. They also recognized his facility with language, remarking on his "*peculiar Phrase*" and noting that "*his Fancy and Invention were very pregnant, and fertile.*"[2] A powerful orator, he used homely metaphors and colloquial language with telling effect,[3] though his most important asset was a talent for utilizing his own religious and psychological experiences to give his message the ring of conviction and a compelling sense of authority. The intense inner turmoil of the 1650s contributed immeasurably to his success in the pulpit and with the pen, and without

---

[1] *MW*, 12:40.

[2] Samuel Wilson and Ebenezer Chandler, epistle to Bunyan, *Works* (1692), sigs. A1r-A2r. Of Bunyan's surviving sermons (all in printed form), none were devoted to the Lord's supper, although he may have preached on this topic. John Collins preached a series of nineteen sermons on the sacrament. DWL, MSS L4/2.

[3] Roger Pooley rightly asserts that Bunyan's use of colloquial English is discerning. "It is not that he is an unconscious artist, whose rude untutored English issued in a masterpiece because of some inherent vitality in colloquial language." "Plain and Simple: Bunyan and Style," in *John Bunyan*, ed. Keeble, 107.

those experiences *Grace Abounding* and *The Pilgrim's Progress* are virtually unimaginable.

Bunyan's spiritual and psychological experiences in the 1650s are the key to his career as a minister and author. Accurately analyzing the emotional state and behavior of the dead is challenging under the best of circumstances, and in Bunyan's case the difficulty is compounded by the fact that the core evidence is in the form of a spiritual autobiography. That parallels, especially in structure, exist between *Grace Abounding* and contemporaneous works in the same genre has been firmly established, yet this does not mean that he necessarily wrote for effect or in a fictive manner, using the spiritual autobiographies of others to determine the content of his own. On the contrary, the substantial extent to which echoes of the experiences recorded in *Grace Abounding* are found in many of his other works underscores their reality. This is unlikely to have been the case if his spiritual autobiography were merely imitative and his experiences molded if not created by a perceived need to conform to a literary genre. Moreover, Bunyan's account evinces so many symptoms of depression that it is improbable that he contrived them. The evidence suggests that he suffered from mood disorders in the 1650s and that the melancholy recurred, especially in late 1663 and 1664. *Grace Abounding* also manifests unmistakable signs of Bunyan's anxiety, which first appeared in the pre-adolescent nightmares of exclusion and punishment he still remembered a quarter of a century later.

*Grace Abounding* is a powerful literary work precisely because it captures Bunyan's profound struggle with depression as well as his turbulent quest for acceptance by God. The force of his prose is rooted in life-altering experiences that plunged him into a black abyss whose depths only the victims of depression truly plumb. He was not donning the mask of fashionable melancholy or engaging in an imitative exercise to demonstrate his spiritual credentials, though *Grace Abounding* served the latter function long after the experiences it records. What he underwent was chillingly real, and it shaped how he understood life as well as religion. His works evince a keen, perceptive sensitivity to the psychological importance of light and darkness that is traceable to his melancholic moods.

*The Pilgrim's Progress* acquires a new dimension when read as the work of an author who battled these mood disorders. The Slough of Despond, the caged man in Interpreter's house, the confrontation with Apollyon, the frightful passage through the Valley of the Shadow of Death, the sensation of nearly drowning in the inky blackness of By-path-meadow, the episode involving Giant Despair and Doubting Castle, and Christian's terrifying experience crossing the River of Death reflect Bunyan's psychological struggles. The fact that so much of the allegory deals with doubt, despair, and pervasive feelings of sadness is not accidental, for it is heavily indebted to *Grace Abounding*. Recognizing that many pilgrims make their journeys without being plummeted into the black depths of utter despair, he composed the second part. In his own life he eventually experienced relief, gaining deeper appreciation of the importance of light, warmth, and acceptance—and of music, for the world of the depressed is often eerily silent. Light, warmth, music, and a sense of finally being accepted by God were crucial elements in Bunyan's recovery. So too was his ability to relate his experiences from the pulpit and in his books, and in this way he brought his creative talents to bear in regaining his health. Perhaps the almost unbroken regimen of composition that commenced in 1665 resulted in part from an intuitive recognition that writing helped stave off debilitating melancholy.

Bunyan's arduous work ethic and the significance he attributed to writing as a fundamental part of his ministry meant that his pen was in regular use. As the history of *A Defence of the Doctrine of Justification, by Faith in Jesus Christ* demonstrates, he could write quickly. After obtaining a copy of Fowler's *The Design of Christianity* on 13 January 1672, he read it and wrote a refutation of approximately 46,500 words, completing it on 27 February. Thus he could write more than a thousand words a day. I have suggested that he averaged approximately 425 words a day, writing five days a week for ten months, in composing *The Holy War*. If my provisional dating of Bunyan's works is reasonably accurate, there were at most seven periods of five months or more when he was not writing: January to December 1657, May 1659 to December 1660, September 1661 to early 1662 (other than letters), late June 1663 to late 1664 (other than *A Mapp*), October 1669 to April 1670, possibly April to September 1671, and the winter of 1673–74. The longest gaps occurred early in his career, when he lacked confidence in his writing ability (*MW*, 2:16; *GA*, §§282–83), and between late June 1663 and late 1664, when he almost certainly suffered from a recurrence of despondency. He was indisputably a disciplined author, with a preference for preaching and writing rather than counseling, exercising church discipline, and conducting the congregation's administrative affairs. The scattered entries in the church book and the absence of records for collections, disbursements, and poor relief underscore his lack of interest in administrative details. His world revolved around the pulpit and the study.

One of the most enduring myths about Bunyan is something he perpetuated when he asserted that the Bible and a concordance were the only library he used in his writing (*MW*, 7:9). In 1723 Thomas Hearne reinforced this myth when he recounted how a friend had visited Bunyan's study, which "consisted only of a Bible and a parcell of Books (the Pilgrim's Progress chiefly) written by himself."[4]

---

[4]Thomas Hearne, *The Remains of Thomas Hearne: Reliquiae Hernianae*, ed. John Bliss and rev. by John Buchanan-Brown (Carbondale: Southern Illinois University Press, 1966), 251.

In fact, Bunyan was an avid reader well before his conversion, evincing an early preference for ballads, newspapers, and medieval romances, including *Bevis of Southampton* and the tale of St. George, which he probably read in Richard Johnson's *The Most Famous History of the Seven Champions of Christendome* (1597). The early interest in newspapers indicates an appetite for current events that continued throughout his life, although he never again acknowledged reading such material. His early penchant to read about "curious arts" was likely a reference to manuals on alchemy and witchcraft, and his belief in the latter was life-long (1:333). Fables were also among his youthful preferences, and these he must have enjoyed in a version of Aesop, such as *The Fables of Aesop* (1634).

Among his earliest religious reading were the two books that comprised his first wife's dowry, Arthur Dent's *The Plaine Mans Path-Way to Heaven* and Lewis Bayly's *The Practise of Pietie*. Luther's commentary on Galatians had a profound impact on shaping his early spiritual experience, and he also sampled Ranter works, probably Jacob Bauthumley's *The Light and Dark Sides of God* (1650) and Lawrence Clarkson's *A Single Eye All Light, No Darkness* (1650). Amid his spiritual and psychological trials he also read *A Relation of the Fearful Estate of Francis Spira, in the Year 1548* (1649), a work that struck daggers into his soul and still impressed him late in life (*GA*, §163; *MW*, 9:167).

By the late 1650s Bunyan was reading Foxe's *Acts and Monuments*, a copy of which he later had with him in prison, and a work to which he referred on numerous occasions. Its influence, as John Knott has observed, was "more pervasive than specific references reveal and can be found throughout his career."[5] By the late 1650s Bunyan was also studying John Dod and Robert Cleaver's *A Plaine and Familiar Exposition of the Ten Commaundements* and unidentified biblical commentaries (*MW*, 2:35; 1:39–40). His interest in commentaries is evident elsewhere, particularly in his exposition of Genesis but probably also in his discussions of Revelation, Hebrews 4:16, 1 Kings 7:2–6, and Solomon's temple. We can reasonably assume that he read other commentaries as well. He certainly made regular use of the Authorized and Geneva Bibles, and the extensive marginalia in the latter provided a running commentary in its own right. In *The Acceptable Sacrifice* he also referred to a translation of Psalm 51:17 by William Tyndale, by which he may have meant the so-called Matthew Bible, which was the work of John Rogers (12:27, 426). Given the pronounced interest in typology displayed throughout his career, he probably read one or more of the three major studies of the subject available in the late 1650s: William Guild's *Moses Unveiled* (1620), Thomas Taylor's *Christ Revealed* (1635; published as *Moses and Aaron* in 1653), and John Ever-

---

[5]Knott, *DM*, 179.

ard's *The Gospel-Treasury Opened* (1657). In learning to preach he may have had recourse to a manual such as William Perkins' *The Arte of Prophecying* (1592), the most popular guide among those who became nonconformists.

A visitor to Bunyan during his imprisonment reported that his library consisted solely of his Bible and Foxe's *Acts and Monuments*, but this assertion, which was recorded by an anonymous author after Bunyan's death, was another version of the myth.[6] He probably shared books with the ministers incarcerated with him, and his wife or friends may well have borrowed books for him to read. He definitely consulted Perkins' *A Golden Chaine, or, the Description of Theologie* (1612) and probably religious ballads (which influenced his prison poetry) and Vavasor Powell's *Common-Prayer-Book No Divine Service* (1660, 1661). While in prison he learned to write verse using iambic pentameter couplets, perhaps by reading Thomas Jenner's *The Soules Solace, or Thirtie and One Spirituall Emblems* (1626; published as *Divine Mysteries That Cannot Be Seene* in 1651). Among the sources that may have influenced *The Pilgrim's Progress* are Quarles' *Emblemes*, Richard Bernard's *The Isle of Man* (1627), and Geoffrey Whitney's *A Choice of Emblemes* (1586), all of which would have helped to pass the dreary days in the Bedford county jail.

Bunyan certainly read a variety of controversial works, the first of which was Edward Burrough's *The True Faith of the Gospel of Peace Contended for, in the Spirit of Meekness* (1656). He presumably read Burrough's response to his *Vindication*, entitled *Truth (the Strongest of All) Witnessed Forth in the Spirit of Truth, Against All Deceit* (1657), though he declined to reply. He read and refuted Fowler's *The Design of Christianity* (1671) and William Penn's *The Sandy Foundation Shaken* (1668), and the most likely source for his references to Edmund Campion was Alexander Nowell and William Day's *A True Report of the Disputation . . . with Ed. Campion Jesuite* (1583). In the course of the baptismal debate he read Thomas Paul's *Some Serious Reflections* (1673), a second work by the same author that is not extant, Henry Danvers' *Treatise of Baptism* (1673), and John Denne's *Truth Outweighing Error* (1673). His decision to enter the lists against the seventh-day sabbath may have been prompted in part by Henry Soursby and Mehetabel Smith's *A Discourse of the Sabbath* (1683), and his own views on this subject were shaped by "our Protestant writers" (4:353). Although he did not identify which of their books he read, the likeliest possibilities are John Owen's *Exercitations Concerning the Name, Original, Nature, Use and Continuance of a Day of Sacred Rest* (1671), Thomas Grantham's *The Seventh-Day-Sabbath Ceased as Ceremonial* (1667), William Russell's *No Seventh-Day-Sabbath Commanded by*

---

[6]Brown, 154.

*Jesus Christ* (1663), Thomas Collier's *The Seventh Day Sabbath Opened and Discovered* (1658), and Jeremiah Ives' *Saturday No Sabbath* (1659). The important point is that Bunyan acknowledged having read Protestant works on this topic.

We know too that he read and borrowed from Samuel Clarke's *A Mirrour or Looking-Glass Both for Saints & Sinners* (4th ed., 1671), and as background for *Mr. Badman* he may also have consulted Thomas Beard's *The Theatre of Gods Judgements* (rev. ed., 1631) and John Reynolds' *The Triumphs of Gods Revenge Against the Crying and Execrable Sinne of (Wilful and Premeditated) Murther* (4th ed., 1663). He definitely read an unidentified volume discussing Martha and Mary and a book that referred to the conversion of Bruno of Cologne (11:42–44, 108), and he perhaps owned and read a copy of Grantham's *St. Paul's Catechism* (1687). Benjamin Keach's *A Key to Open Scripture Metaphors* (1682) is also a volume Bunyan apparently perused. Roland Frye has suggested that he may have seen a print of a copy or an imitation of Dürer's 1498 painting of the apocalypse, part of which shows an angel, with heaven in the background, sending the Devil into a hole leading to hell. The scene is somewhat similar to the fate of Ignorance at the conclusion of *The Pilgrim's Progress*.[7] Although much of what Bunyan read cannot be identified with certainty, he was clearly an ardent reader as well as a prolific author, and it is probably an exaggeration to claim that there is "no intellectual—and certainly no literary—intermediary between Bunyan and the Bible, or Satan, or Christ."[8]

Bunyan's pattern of reading and writing necessitates a re-evaluation of assertions that he was unlearned.[9] Early in his career John Gifford and John Burton thought it necessary to comment on his minimal formal education, though both insisted that he had been instructed by the Holy Spirit, which they thought far more important (1:11–12, 243–44). After his death his ministerial colleagues Wilson and Chandler claimed that "*like the Spider, all came from his own Bowels.*"[10] Bunyan himself fostered the myth that he was uneducated, as in his claim to have forgotten "that little I learned" about reading and writing "long before the Lord did work his gracious work of conversion upon my Soul" (*GA*, §53). He made the

[7] Roland Mushat Frye, "Bunyan, Dürer, and the Byway to Hell," *English Literary Renaissance* 1 (Autumn 1971): between 288 and 289.

[8] Keeble, *LCN*, 160. Keeble's ensuing sentence—"all act with an immediacy whose forcefulness only images of physical irresistibility can convey"—effectively describes nearly all of the experiences recorded in *Grace Abounding*, though even during this period Bunyan was reading Dent, Bayly, and Luther.

[9] David Seed makes the point that Bunyan's skillful use of dialogue also demonstrates that he was not "a semi-literate 'mechanick'." "Dialogue and Debate in *The Pilgrim's Progress*," in *Pilgrim's Progress*, ed. Newey, 69–90.

[10] Wilson and Chandler, epistle to Bunyan, *Works* (1692), sig. A1r.

same complaint about boys who attended grammar school and then promptly forgot what they had learned (*MW*, 13:91), perhaps suggesting he had briefly gone to such a school. In any event he knew no Latin and was clearly self-educated beyond the basics of reading and writing. This was a process that had begun well before his conversion experience, for in the midst of these trials he was able to read and understand Luther's commentary on Galatians, a book many modern university students would find challenging. By the time he came across Luther's volume he had read Dent and Bayly with his wife. Although he was already enjoying newspapers, romances, and ballads, his first serious introduction to religious literature must have come under his wife's tutelage. She seems to have been biblically literate, for in the throes of his spiritual and psychological struggles he turned to her for help with a message he thought might be from Scripture (*GA*, §263). She deserves more credit than she customarily receives for helping him understand fundamental religious concepts, particularly through their shared reading of Dent and Bayly.

Bunyan's success as a preacher and author rendered him particularly susceptible to pride. Cokayne remarked on this in his epistle to *The Acceptable Sacrifice*, noting that Bunyan was cognizant of this weakness (*MW*, 12:7). Periodically he struggled in his spiritual life, partly because of the high standards he set for himself, and partly because he could never permanently free himself of despondency and self-doubt. In the early 1660s, and perhaps longer, he still found it difficult to pray. During his later years he experienced more periods of spiritual tranquility, but permanent inner peace eluded him. Sensing that he fell short in the nearly constant battle against temptations, he attributed this weakness to an insufficiently rigorous spiritual regimen and a lack of gravamen. Time was something he hated to waste, a precious commodity to be devoted to the pursuit of God's work. He found relaxation in music and poetry, but even here he framed his pastimes in religious terms, seeking to use these diversions to advance the gospel and enrich his devotional life. Bell-ringing as a source of pleasure for its own sake triggered guilt, but the bells could peal if they welcomed pilgrims and the trumpets could sound if they called Christians to battle in the war against evil.

Bunyan's values were fundamentally other-centered. The work ethic he embraced was not intended to acquire wealth or further commerce, and he never seems to have envisioned his writing as a source of income. The very modest estate he left indicates either a comparably modest income or the generous distribution of whatever wealth he acquired to the indigent. The poor had a special place in his heart, and he never lost his sense of outrage at the way the rich treated them or the irresponsible wastefulness of the wealthy. He was no social leveler, he articulated no program of radical economic reform, and he never exhorted the indigent to demonstrate or act illegally no matter how desperate their plight. The most effective way to redress their needs, in his judgment, was to persuade people of substance to fulfill their gospel responsibilities. Part of the appeal of *The Pilgrim's Progress* to the masses was Bunyan's sensitivity to the poor, the supreme exemplar of which is Graceless, who left the City of Destruction in rags but finished his journey with a princely welcome to a realm of plenty. Bunyan's vision was not the embodiment of medieval ideals, though he echoed the social protests of medieval reformers, nor was it an endorsement of capitalism and its acquisitive spirit, but an alternative culture rooted in spiritual values and characterized by other-centeredness. Hold-the-world, Mony-love, Save-all, and By-ends represent the antithesis of the values he cherished, and the hypocrisy that characterized their lives was anathema to him. Opposed to absolute monarchy, he spoke in defense of Magna Carta, but he displayed no interest in the sort of political platform the Levellers had once championed. The world was a vast stage on which the forces of evil contended with the godly for ultimate supremacy, their values and their allegiances starkly opposed despite the subterfuge of piety in which Antichrist's minions cloaked themselves.

For Bunyan religion entails conflict as well as devotion and service. As circumstances changed he altered his position on the nature of resistance, but the core principle remained the same: The Christian has an obligation to resist evil regardless of the consequences. What altered was the *form* resistance could take. When he went to prison in 1660, it was not as a passive resister, for he had deliberately violated the Elizabethan statute against conventicles and eschewed opportunities to evade a confrontation by preaching at another time or place. Although he courted this confrontation, during the Tory Reaction he took steps to elude would-be captors. *The Pilgrim's Progress* is about warfaring as well as wayfaring, and its message includes the importance of standing up to a repressive state, defying its oppressive laws, and accepting the fact that spiritual acts have secular connotations because of the state's claims to spiritual authority. Until the early 1680s Bunyan espoused a message of active resistance short of violence. When Charles and Parliament failed to agree on excluding James from the line of succession or severely restricting his authority if he became king, Bunyan cautiously endorsed the use of arms to prevent England from a possible return to Catholic persecution, but only if opposition were led by nobles or magistrates, as Calvin had argued. Nonconformists could not take up arms on their own. When the Rye House conspiracy and Monmouth's scheming were disclosed, he reverted to his earlier position, rejecting violent means but retaining his gospel of spiritual militancy. Yet as late as the winter of 1686–87, with James on the throne, he displayed sympathy, but not support, for those who go on the offensive against a persecutory regime (*MW*, 7:139).

Unlike his position on resistance, Bunyan's hostile view of the Church of England remained unchanged from 1660 until his death. In late 1656 he had lashed out against professional clergy (1:127–28, 205, 216–17), implicitly contrasting them with godly ministers such as Gifford, but at the Restoration he shifted his target to the established church, henceforth including it among the false churches of the world. He was willing to acknowledge that some members of the Church of England were godly, but the number was small—less than 2.5 percent, he thought, in 1662 (2:240; 7:144–46). Unlike Philip Henry and Richard Baxter, who favored comprehension within the established church, Bunyan thoroughly opposed even the possibility of communion between congregations of visible saints and Anglican churches. Because it supported a policy of persecution he likened the Church of England to the Catholics, and he denounced its "rabling counterfeit Clergy," who were "profanely bishopt," and pronounced it contaminated with "Antichristian Rubbish" and the smoke of antichristian darkness (4:100; 7:145–46; 12:362; CB, 64). In his judgment the Church of England was awash in "Carnal Gospelers" and its liturgy was a stumbling block created by vain minds (13:25; 12:78). In short, it was a barren fig tree, rife with formalism and hypocrisy. In The Pilgrim's Progress he subjected the established church and its adherents to withering criticism, most poignantly in the Vanity Fair episode, where Faithful and Christian are persecuted by religious, law-abiding people, but also in such figures as the church-goer Worldly Wiseman, Formalist, Hypocrisie, the parson Two-tongues and his nephew By-ends, Facing-bothways, and Mony-love, who defended ministers in search of more lucrative benefices. Ironically, many of those Bunyan attacked missed his criticism when they read the allegory, failing to see themselves as he intended and identifying instead with the godly pilgrims. In this respect The Pilgrim's Progress was arguably a failure.

Nearly twelve years in prison did not persuade Bunyan to soften his hostility to the Church of England, but he learned how to express it more subtly. Interwoven throughout most of his works is the message that persecution, formalism, and mandatory forms of worship not expressly sanctioned in Scripture are wrong. The state imprisoned him to halt the spread of his views, but instead confinement provided him with an opportunity to develop his tenets through reading, writing, and discourse with some of his fellow prisoners. In the Bedford jail he initiated a writing regimen and learned how to use a concordance as a tool to mine the Bible, treating it as a storehouse of divine truths while generally ignoring critical issues of historical context and authorship. His best works, the first part of The Pilgrim's Progress and Grace Abounding, were composed in prison, and there too he developed his millenarian ideas, formulated his confession of faith, and learned how to express his religious message in verse. The cold chains of bondage pro-

vided both the opportunity and the motivation to write extensively and sometimes powerfully, and as a result, the message a repressive government sought to
stifle eventually spread throughout the world, carried by the tale of a pilgrim who
would not be denied.

*"To Every Place"*[11]: Bunyan and His Pilgrims Through the Ages

Although Bunyan spent much of his career attacking the Church of England,
memorial windows commemorate him in Westminster Abbey and Southwark
Cathedral, and these monuments are not the only examples of Anglican embrace.
In 1847, for instance, the evangelical Anglican minister Charles Overton published
thirty lectures on the first part of *The Pilgrim's Progress*, followed three years later
with twenty-three more on the second part.[12] From the opposite wing of the
Church of England J. M. Neale prepared an edition of Bunyan's classic for children, making alterations to enhance the role of the sacraments and good works,
transform Giant Pope into Giant Mahometan, and eliminate Legality and Worldly
Wiseman because of the aspersions they cast on traditional morality.[13] The dean of
Westminster, A. P. Stanley, delivered an address at the unveiling of Bunyan's
statue at Bedford in 1874, and the archbishop of Dublin called for a celebration at
London's Mansion House in 1928 to commemorate the tercentenary of Bunyan's
birth.[14] In another ceremony on that occasion, the archbishop-designate of Canterbury lauded Bunyan, not least for his belief that life's basic lesson is each soul's
solitary pilgrimage to God.[15] The same year the bishop of Durham not only praised
Bunyan for being free of sectarian bias but also urged Anglicans to study him because of his emphasis on the Bible's power to educate and motivate, his stress on
the importance of religion, and his downplaying of polity.[16] A popular commen-

[11] *PP*, 167.

[12] Charles Overton, *Cottage Lectures: or, the Pilgrim's Progress Practically Explained*
(London and Hull: Seeleys, 1847); *Christiana and Her Children: or, the Second Part of Cottage Lectures on Pilgrim's Progress* (Philadelphia: American Sunday-School Union, 1850).

[13] *The Pilgrim's Progress of John Bunyan*, ed. J. M. Neale (Oxford: John Henry Parker,
1853). Neale's edition was attacked in the anonymous *The Pilgrim: or, John Bunyan's Apparition, in the Bed-Room of the Rev. J. M. Neale* (London: J. Nisbet and Co., 1854).

[14] A. P. Stanley, "The Character of John Bunyan: Local, Ecclesiastical, Universal," in
*The Book of the Bunyan Festival*, ed. W. H. Wylie (London: James Clarke and Co.; Bedford: Rowland Hill and Sons, 1874); anon., "The Bunyan Tercentenary," *British Weekly*
(29 November 1928): 195.

[15] Anon., "Bunyan Tercentenary," *Baptist Times* (29 November 1928): 868.

[16] H. Hensley Henson, "An Anglican's Reflections on Bunyan's Career," *Review of the
Churches* 5 (July 1928): 313–18; Henson, "John Bunyan," *Christian World Pulpit* 114 (6 December 1928): 270–72.

tary on *The Pilgrim's Progress* by an Anglican appeared in 1931, and Robert Runcie, archbishop of Canterbury, preached at Bunyan Meeting, Bedford, for the tercentenary commemorations of the publication of *The Pilgrim's Progress* and Bunyan's death.[17]

Other religious groups, including some that Bunyan had attacked, have found meaning in his work. As early as 1691 the Quaker Stephen Crisp adapted *The Pilgrim's Progress* for Friends, calling it *A Short History of a Long Travel, from Babylon, to Bethel*. Catholic editions of *The Pilgrim's Progress* were published in France in 1772 and 1847, although in 1909 a Catholic critic faulted Bunyan for having rejected medieval theology and only tardily recognizing the spiritual life of women.[18] The prominent Bunyan scholar of the twentieth century, Roger Sharrock, was a Catholic. From a very different religious perspective, the Universalist D. J. Mendle adapted *The Pilgrim's Progress*, publishing it in 1838 as *The Adventures of Search for Life: A Bunyanic Narrative, as Detailed by Himself*. Although closer to Bunyan in spirit and doctrine than Anglicans, Catholics, and Universalists, John Wesley altered Bunyan's theology when he abridged the first part of *The Pilgrim's Progress* (1743), revising Faithful's explanation of the work of grace in the soul, stressing joy in Hopeful's description of his conversion, and modifying the dialogue between Christian and Ignorance. His edition of *The Holy War* (1750) deleted the trial of the Doubters because of its predestinarian doctrine.[19] Despite such revisions, these adherents of other religious traditions responded positively to Bunyan's fundamental motif of spiritual struggle and the hope of ultimate victory in the pilgrimage of faith.

The extent of Bunyan's appeal beyond the dissenting tradition is attested both by the sales of his twelve best-selling works and by the extraordinary popularity of *The Pilgrim's Progress*. By 1740, approximately 155 editions of his dozen best sellers had been issued, accounting for perhaps 200,000 copies and indicating an audience that extended well beyond dissenters.[20] Twenty-two editions of *The Pil-*

---

[17] Claude Dunbar Paterson, *Are You a Pilgrim? An Introduction to the Study of John Bunyan's "Pilgrim's Progress"* (London: A. R. Mowbray and Co., 1931); W. R. Owens and Stuart Sim, "Some Tercentenary Publications from Bedfordshire," *BS* 1, no. 2 (Spring 1989): 68

[18] Katherine Brégy, "The Pilgrim's Progress and Some Pre-Reformation Allegories," *Catholic World* 89 (April 1909): 96–102; 89 (May 1909): 166–76.

[19] See the discussion in Isabel Rivers, *Reason, Grace, and Sentiment: A Study of the Language of Religion and Ethics in England, 1660–1780* (Cambridge: Cambridge University Press, 1991), 218–19.

[20] I. M. Green, "Bunyan in Context: The Changing Face of Protestantism in Seventeenth-Century England," in *Bunyan in England and Abroad*, ed. M. van Os and G. J. Schutte (Amsterdam: VU University Press, 1990), 19–20, 27. By 1700 Doe had sold ap-

*grim's Progress* had been published by 1700, seventy by 1800, and more than 1,300 by 1938. Neil Keeble has estimated that in the seventeenth century approximately 30,000 copies were printed, and Joyce Godber noted that the allegory has been translated into more than 200 languages. Between 1682 and 1996 the Dutch alone published some 125 editions.[21] The imperial powers' insatiable appetite for territory and the westward expansion of the United States prompted numerous editions for the African peoples and the native Americans. David Livingstone's call for a world crusade based on commerce, Christianity, and civilization to open the whole of Africa[22] led to new editions of *The Pilgrim's Progress* in languages and dialects such as Fanti, Yoruba, Douala, Xosa, Efik, Congo, Basa, Chuana, and Kafin, and native American editions were published for the Dakota, Cree, and Cheyenne. An 1853 Chinese edition of the allegory was imported into Japan in the same decade, and the first Japanese edition appeared in 1876.[23] *The Pilgrim's Progress* was the first English literary work translated into Polish; undertaken in 1728, it was published at Königsberg in 1764. A ployglot edition, with texts in English, Welsh, and French, was printed in 1876, in part because William Gladstone, whose papers include brief notes on the allegory, wanted the people of Wales to learn English.[24] A phonetic edition, *Pilgrimz Progres*, appeared in 1849, and the allegory has been issued in braille.

Adaptations of *The Pilgrim's Progress* have been prepared to increase its accessibility to children.[25] An early eighteenth-century Dutch broadside reduced the story to sixteen small woodcuts featuring such landmarks as dykes and dams, and

proximately 3,000 copies of Bunyan's books, but he could not market *The Pilgrim's Progress*. Doe, *A Collection of Experience of the Work of Grace* (London, [1700]), 57.

[21] Keeble, *LCN*, 128, 134; Jacques B. H. Alblas, "The Bunyan Collection of the Vrije Universiteit, Amsterdam," *BS* 6 (1995–96): 78, 82; Frank Mott Harrison, Introduction, *The Pilgrim's Progress* (Bedford: Sidney Press, 1939), iii–iv; Joyce Godber, *John Bunyan of Bedfordshire* (Bedford: Bedfordshire County Council, 1972), 9.

[22] Thomas Pakenham, *The Scramble for Africa, 1876–1912* (New York: Random House, 1991), xxii.

[23] Kazuko Nishimura, "John Bunyan's Reception in Japan," *BS* 1, no. 2 (Spring 1989): 49–50.

[24] Wiktor Weintraub, "Bunyan in Poland," *Canadian Slavonic Papers* 4 (1959): 35–41; Renée J. Fulton, "The Polyglot Edition of *Pilgrim's Progress*: A Historical Note on Modern Language Methodology," *Modern Language Journal* 34 (May 1950): 381–83; BL, Add. MSS 44,792, fol. 97. Gladstone's notes mention the Valley of Humiliation, Mr. Fearing, Ready-to-Halt's dance on learning of Giant Despair's death, Stand-fast, and "Mutual Recognition hereafter."

[25] E.g., Katharine K. C. Walker, *The Pilgrim's Progress for the Little Ones* (New York: J. J. Little and Co., 1869). A similar adaptation of Bunyan's other allegory is *The History of the Holy War* (London, 1817) by an anonymous editor.

accompanying verse explains how Christians can overcome these barriers.[26] In contrast, Isaac Taylor's adaptation of the allegory, *Bunyan Explained to a Child* (1824–25), required two volumes, whereas an 1858 edition by Joseph Curdall, *The Story of the Pilgrim's Progress Told for Young People*, pared the theological content and eliminated the perceived redundancy. A decade earlier George Sargent had written a biography of Bunyan for children,[27] and Charlotte Tucker's *On the Way: Places Passed by Pilgrims* (1868) was a work of fiction for young people. Neale's High Church edition of the allegory was, of course, intended for children. Recent adaptations by Rhoda Coulridge and Jean Gray indicate a continuing interest in making the allegory accessible to young people.[28]

The *Pilgrim's Progress* has been recast in verse,[29] adapted for the stage, set to music, and performed on television. The pseudonymous versifier of *The Pilgrim's Passage in Poesie* (1697–98) admitted that the original appeared "far better in his plain Cloaths, than by all the Lacing, Pricking, and Pinning, that I could afford him."[30] Taking a different approach, an early nineteenth-century author penned 104 poems to explain the allegory.[31] By 1941 more than 150 poetic or dramatic versions of *The Pilgrim's Progress* had been published.[32] Most of the dramatic renditions were intended for the theater,[33] but a 1934 adaptation of part two was de-

---

[26] Alblas, "The Bunyan Collection," 82–83.

[27] George E. Sargent, *The Bedfordshire Tinker: or the History of John Bunyan* (Philadelphia: Presbyterian Board of Publication, 1848).

[28] Rhoda Couldridge, *Christian's Journey, John Bunyan's "Pilgrim's Progress" Retold* (Nashville, TN: Abingdon Press, 1979); Jean Gray, *A Children's Pilgrim's Progress* (Leominster, Herefordshire: Gracewing, 1990).

[29] E.g., Francis Hoffman, *The Pilgrim's Progress* (London, 1706); J. S. Dodd, *The Pilgrim's Progress* (Dublin, 1794); George Burder, *Bunyan's Pilgrim's Progress Versified* (London: T. Williams, and Button and Son, 1804); Isaac James, *The Pilgrim's Progress* (Bristol: Mary Brian, 1815); T. Dibdin, *Bunyan's Pilgrim's Progress, Metrically Condensed* (London: Harding and King, 1834). E. J. rendered *The Holy War* in verse (London: Robert Hardwicke, 1859).

[30] "Ager Scholae," *The Pilgrim's Progress in Poesie*, 2 vols. (London, 1697–98), 1: sig. A2r.

[31] Victory Purdy, *Poetical Miscellanies* (Bristol: John Wansbrough, 1825), 159–252.

[32] Frank Mott Harrison, "Editions of *The Pilgrim's Progress*," *Library*, 4th ser., 22 (June 1941): 73–81.

[33] E.g., Mrs. Duncan Pearce, *Christiana & Her Children: A Mystery Play* (London: Longmans, Green and Co., 1914); Walter Stephens, *The Pilgrim's Progress: A Sacred Drama in Four Acts* (London: Francis Griffiths, 1914); E. U. Ouless, *Scenes Dramatized from Bunyan's Pilgrim's Progress* (Kelly, Lifton, Devon: Village Drama Society, 1923); Bernard C. Clausen and Florence L. Purington, *Pilgrim's Progress in Pageant* (New York: American Tract Society, 1928), for use in churches; John Dalley, *John Bunyan's Pilgrim's Progress* (London: Independent Press, 1928). See also R. I., "Bunyan Dramatized," *Notes and Que-*

signed specifically for churches, and there is even an edition for presentation as a
dramatic sermon.[34] G. G. Collingham's play, performed at London's Olympic
Theatre in December 1896, merited a review by George Bernard Shaw, and Hugh
Ross Williamson's adaptation was staged at the prestigious Royal Opera House,
Covent Garden.[35] One of the more bizarre renditions was a 1928 play featuring a
dialogue between Cinderella and Bunyan, with most of the latter's lines taken
from his works.[36] Against the background of the Napoleonic Wars, *The Siege of
Mansoul*, a play in five acts by an anonymous female writer, was published in
1801. Adapted for television, *The Pilgrim's Progress* was fittingly broadcast as
"Dangerous Journey."[37]

Musical settings of *The Pilgrim's Progress* date at least to 1870, when a Welsh
harpist prepared a rendition of the first part.[38] A setting of both parts by Mrs.
George MacDonald, a minister's wife, was undertaken in 1877, though not published until 1925.[39] Following the armistice ending the fighting in World War I,
the B.B.C. broadcast a musical setting of the first part of the allegory, but Sir Edward Elgar never used a libretto for a symphonic drama prepared for him the
same year.[40] In 1923 John Foulds incorporated some of Bunyan's work in "A
World Requiem," which also included material from the requiem mass, the Bible, and the Muslim poet Kabir, a combination Bunyan would presumably have
found offensive. For the 1928 tercentenary, the B.B.C. broadcast Bowker An-
drews' adaptation of the text of the first part, set to music by Sir Granville Ban-

*ries*, 3rd ser., 7 (10 June 1855): 458; P. N. Furbank, "Pilgrim's Progress on the Stage," *BS* 4
(Spring 1991): 92–95.

[34] Hugh Parry, *Christiana: A Morality* (London: Richard James, 1934); Robert C. Hal-
lock, *The Great Drama of Pilgrim's Progress* (New York: American Tract Society, 1928).

[35] George B. Shaw, "Better Than Shakespeare," *Saturday Review of Politics, Literature,
Science and Art* 83 (2 January 1897): 11–12; D. Woodruff, "The Literary Pedigree of John
Bunyan," *Tablet* 192 (31 July 1948): 75.

[36] Alicia Amy Leith, "Bunyan's Cinderella: A Mystery Play," *Quest* 20 (October 1928):
57–70.

[37] *Dangerous Journey* (London: Marshall, Morgan and Scott; Grand Rapids, MI: Eerdmans, 1985) was published to accompany the televised version.

[38] Thomas Aptommas, *The Pilgrim's Progress: Music Written to Bunyan's Allegory of the
Life of a Christian* (London: The Composer, *c.* 1870).

[39] Mrs. George MacDonald, *Dramatic Illustrations of Passages from the Second Part of
the Pilgrim's Progress* (London: Oxford University Press, Humphrey Milford, 1925); Ar-
leane Ralph, "'They do such Musick make': *The Pilgrim's Progress* and Textually Inspired
Music," *BS* 5 (Autumn 1994): 65–66.

[40] Granville Bantock, *The Pilgrim's Progress . . . Set to Music* (London: Swan and Co.,
1918); R. A. Streatfeild, "*The Pilgrim's Progress*: A Mystery," (1918), typescript in the British
Library.

tock.[41] Ralph Vaughan Williams' stage version of *The Pilgrim's Progress* was performed at the Royal Opera House, Covent Garden, as part of the Festival of Britain in 1951 and at Cambridge University in 1954; the B.B.C. broadcast the work in 1970, and it was recorded in 1972 and 1992, on the latter occasion at performances by the Royal Northern College of Music.[42] Texts by Bunyan, William Blake, Christina Rossetti, Thomas Hardy, and others were employed in a song-cycle featuring children's voices by a late twentieth-century composer.[43]

*The Pilgrim's Progress* has attracted writers determined to improve it, add a third part, or imitate it. Attempting to make the allegory acceptable to the culturally sophisticated, an early nineteenth-century editor elucidated supposed obscurities, deleted redundancies, and revised the phraseology, whereas an edition published in 1884 amputated eighty percent of the work on the grounds that it was repetitious and verbose.[44] The first attempt to continue the allegory appears to have been Thomas Sherman's second part, published under his initials in 1682 and reprinted the following year. The historian Joseph Ivimey, for many years minister of a Particular Baptist church in London, wrote *Pilgrims of the Nineteenth Century: A Continuation of the Pilgrim's Progress* (1827), in which he extended the allegory to the City of Toleration, and James Edward Walker entitled his continuation *The Story of Matthew and Mary, Being a Third Part to Bunyan's Pilgrim's Progress* (1911).

Of the many imitations, one of the earliest was a work in verse, *The Heavenly Passenger, or, the Pilgrim's Progress* (1687), by one M. S.,[45] and another was Francis Bugg's account of his conversion from the Society of Friends to the Church of England, *The Pilgrim's Progress, from Quakerism, to Christianity* (1698). Among the numerous imitations that followed were *A New Pilgrim's Progress* (1760), John Mitchell's *The Female Pilgrim* (1762), Mary Anne Burges' *The Progress of the Pilgrim Good-Intent, in Jacobinical Times* (1800), *The Pilgrimage of Theophilus to the City of God* (1812) by John Marten Butt or Joseph Gilpin, and Mark Twain's *The New Pilgrim's Progress; A Book of Travel in Pursuit of Pleasure* (1870). While she was in the East Indies Mary Martha Sherwood composed *The Infants Progress*

---

[41] Ralph, "'They do such Musick make,'" 65.

[42] Ibid.; Robert Manning, "*The Pilgrim's Progress*: A Vindication and Celebration of Vaughan Williams's Neglected Masterpiece," *BS* 6 (1995–96): 70–77.

[43] Howard Blake, *All God's Creatures: A Song-Cycle for Children's Voices and Orchestra (or Piano)* (London: Highbridge Music, 1997). See also David Diamond, *Shepherd Boy Sings in the Valley of Humiliation* (New York: Southern, *c.* 1949), for voice and piano.

[44] *The Pilgrim's Progress*, ed. Joshua Gilpin (Wellington: F. Houlston and Son, 1811); *Pilgrim's Progress*, ed. Mary Godolphin; foreword by Robert Lawson (Philadelphia and New York: J. B. Lippincott, 1939).

[45] Entered in the Stationers' Register on 9 March 1687. Arber, *Transcript*, 3:317.

*from the Valley of Destruction to Everlasting Glory* (1821). Hoping to elevate the morality of the lower classes in the Netherlands, the teacher Johannes Samuel Swaan wrote *Levensgeschiedenis van eenen Christen, of Eens Christens Reize naar de Eeuwigheid* (The History of a Christian, or a Christian's Journey to Eternity, 1807), the hero of which is a tailor.[46] North America provided the setting for various imitations, the first of which was Joseph Morgan's *The History of the Kingdom of Basaruah* (1715), in which the pilgrims travel through the wilderness to the Celestial City. A Congregationalist minister, Morgan drew on *The Holy War* as well as *The Pilgrim's Progress*, and made the millennium, which he called *Ta Chilia Ete* (the thousand years), a key doctrine. Another American millennial work, *Pilgrim's Progress in the Last Days* (1843), attacks a host of perceived evils, including slavery, transcendentalism, classical humanism, progress, rationalism, and revivalism. In *The California Pilgrim* (1853), set in the context of the gold rush, Joseph Benton sent his hero trekking from the east coast to California, where the journey's final leg was on a coastal steamer. California would become the New Jerusalem, but only after being cleansed by an apocalyptic fire, and cities such as San Fastopolis (San Francisco) and Slough-Port (Sacramento) are portrayed as dens of iniquity.[47] Among the more inelegant imitations are Frank Thompson's *Bob's Hike to the Holy City: The Adventures of a Boy Scout and His Sister on the Hill Trail* (1927) and Joseph and Elizabeth Robins Pennell's *Two Pilgrims' Progress; from Fair Florence to the Eternal City of Rome* (1899) on a bicycle.

Many of these imitations are novels, such as George Cheever's *The Hill Difficulty, and Some Experiences of Life in the Plains of Ease* (1849). In the same author's *A Reel in a Bottle, for Jack in the Doldrums* (1852) the pilgrims sail to the heavenly country. Cheever's millenarian narrative attacks businessmen, scientists (especially geologists), railroads, insurance companies, deists, transcendentalists, Unitarians, and slavery.[48] In George Wood's *Modern Pilgrims* (1855), two couples leave New York, the City of Destruction, to pursue their journey on a train; among his targets are the Catholic Church, liberal theology, Unitarianism, and the women's rights movement. Sallie Rochester Ford wrote an imaginative novel, *Mary Bunyan, the Dreamer's Blind Daughter* (1860), and Bunyan inspired Charlotte Tucker's novels, *The Young Pilgrim* (1857) and *The City of Nocross and Its Famous Physician* (1873).

[46] Jacques B. H. Alblas, "The Reception of *The Pilgrim's Progress* in Holland During the Eighteenth and Nineteenth Centuries," in *Bunyan in England and Abroad*, ed. van Os and Schutte, 127–29.

[47] David E. Smith, *John Bunyan in America* (Bloomington: Indiana University Press, 1966), 6–10, 25–37.

[48] Ibid., 37–41.

If imitations and adaptations are testimonies to the popularity of Bunyan's allegory and its hold over plebian imagination, so too are the spurious works that unscrupulous publishers marketed as the product of Bunyan's prolific pen. Of these the only one whose authorship can be seriously contested is *Reprobation Asserted: or the Doctrine of Eternal Election & Reprobation*, published by G. L. Although Charles Doe surmised that the undated volume appeared in 1674, his dating is sometimes inaccurate.[49] The initials suggest George Larkin, but he published nothing of Bunyan's between the first or (lost) second edition of *Grace Abounding* (c. 1667–68) and three of his works in 1688. Although there is no record that Larkin did business at Turn-Stile-Alley, Holborn, where *Reprobation Asserted* was sold, the second edition (1696) was printed by George Larkin the younger, suggesting that his father was the publisher of the first. Theologically, the author of *Reprobation Asserted* subscribed to a doctrine of general atonement, which Bunyan rejected, and the book's style is unlike his. The author's language is sometimes philosophical and generally lacking in popular phraseology and colorful metaphors. Thus *Reprobation Asserted* is probably a spurious work.[50] About the suppositious authorship of *Exhortation to Peace and Unity Among All That Fear God* (1688) there can be no doubt, though one of Bunyan's publishers, Jonathan Robinson, who issued the first and second editions of *The Barren Fig-Tree*, included the *Exhortation* with the latter. The internal evidence against Bunyan's authorship is unimpeachable: the assertion that baptism is essential to church communion, a view Bunyan repudiated (9–11); references to Machiavelli (28), Agesilaus and Lacedaemon (29, 41), Plutarch (30), Camden's *Britannia* and Augustine of Canterbury (32), "the Learned [Edward] *Stillingfleet*" (36–37), and Gnostics (48–49); a description of the Bible as *terra incognita* (54); and the Latin closing, *Vale* (64).

Bunyan's name was attached to a number of other spurious works, one of the earliest of which was *Mr. John Bunyan's Dying Sayings* (1688), the provenance of which is unknown, though it cannot reliably be traced to him.[51] The same year the publisher Joseph Blare issued *The Saints' Triumph* by J. B., with a portrait of Bunyan to suggest the author's identity. Blare would subsequently publish *Scriptural Poems* (1700) in Bunyan's name; in this work the author claimed to have attended a grammar school, something Bunyan never asserted. In 1701 Blare issued *Meditations on the Several Ages of Man's Life*, again ascribing it to Bunyan,

---

[49] In Bunyan, *Works* (1692), [871].

[50] Richard L. Greaves, "John Bunyan and the Authorship of 'Reprobation Asserted,'" *Baptist Quarterly* 21 (July 1965): 125–31. For a well-argued opposing view see Paul Helm, "John Bunyan and *Reprobation Asserted*," *Baptist Quarterly* 28 (April 1979): 87–93.

[51] Brown, 432–33.

and four years later he published a version of Bunyan's allegory under the title, *The Progress of the Christian Pilgrim*. In 1725 his successor, Edward Midwinter, published *The Visions of John Bunyan, Being His Last Remains*, a work by Larkin first issued in 1699 and reprinted in 1711 as *The World to Come*. Another unprincipled publisher issued *Heart's Ease in Heart's Trouble* under Bunyan's name in 1762, failing to note that the epistle, taken *verbatim* from the original 1690 edition, was dated March 1690, a year and a half after Bunyan's death; in fact, the author was James Birdwood, a dissenting minister in Devon.[52] Another version of Bunyan's reputed deathbed sayings appeared in 1725, this time under the title *Rest for a Weary Soul: or, the Pilgrim at His Journey's End*, probably by James Handley, author of the prefatory epistle. Other supposititious books followed, among them an undated work in verse entitled *Death and the Lady: A Solemn Dialogue*, the crudely named *The Shove to a Heavy A—d Christian* (*c.* 1760), and *The Advantages and Disadvantages of the Marital State as Enter'd into with Religious or Irreligious Persons* (1775), delivered in the similitude of a dream and complete with a portrait of Bunyan.[53] Collectively these attempts to profit by the misappropriation of Bunyan's name underscore the recognition he enjoyed, primarily as the author of *The Pilgrim's Progress*. To capitalize on his fame, ballads by J. B. with 'Pilgrim' in their titles were hawked in the mid-1680s.[54] Moreover, the spurious third part of the allegory, first published in 1693, reached a twenty-third edition in 1778. In modern terms, Bunyan's name had acquired the status of a well-known brand, the use of which enticed people to purchase products associated with his name.

The ability of *The Pilgrim's Progress* to capture imaginations extended beyond the world of books, plays, and musical performances. With a children's audience in mind, in 1790 publishers in London and Leeds began selling an engraved jig-saw puzzle depicting Christian's pilgrimage. Mount Sinai, a large wood, dark mountains, the Valley of the Shadow of Death, Vanity Fair, the Country of Conceit, hell, and Beulah are prominently depicted, as is Christian's combat in the Valley of Humiliation.[55] A set of picture cards to aid in learning the story appeared in 1858, and a coloring book dealing with *The Pilgrim's Progress* in 1996.[56] A panorama of

[52] *Calamy Revised, s.v.*

[53] Frank Mott Harrison, *A Bibliography of the Works of John Bunyan* (Oxford: Oxford University Press for the Bibliographical Society, 1932), 76–77.

[54] Keeble, *LCN*, 245.

[55] A photograph of the puzzle, which is in the British Library, was printed in the London *Times* (3 March 2000).

[56] R. D. Ringo, *The Pilgrim's Progress Coloring Book* (Dobbins, CA: Orion's Gate, 1996).

the allegory was exhibited in American cities in the 1850s, and again in 1999–2000 at Montclair, New Jersey; Wichita, Kansas; and Portland, Maine.[57] In 1887 Mark Twain (Samuel Clemens) thought substantial money could be made by costuming actors to represent such allegorical figures as Great-Heart and Apollyon, and photographing them in such places as Paris (Vanity Fair), a wild gorge (the Valley of the Shadow of Death), and Zululand. He suggested that twenty interesting cities, including Constantinople, Cairo, and Venice, would make interesting backgrounds for pilgrims wearing distinctive garb, and the project, he mused, would take three years and cost $10,000.[58] Had photographers and actors undertaken this enterprise, they would have found that copies of *The Pilgrim's Progress* in French (1685), Italian (1853), Arabic (1834), Greco-Turkish (1879), Armeno-Turkish (1881), and assorted African languages and dialects had preceded them.[59] In the nineteenth century the tinker of Bedford became John Bunyan of the world.

## "*As Fancy Leads the Writers*"[60]: Bunyan's Literary Reputation

The astounding success of *The Pilgrim's Progress* did not automatically translate into literary prestige for Bunyan. Even in the last decade of his life, when the allegory was in print, reaction to him varied. His admirers numbered ministers such as Owen, Cokayne, and Chandler, and laity such as Agnes Beaumont, Charles Doe, and Sir John Shorter.[61] Even Charles II reportedly inquired of Owen about him. In Richard Baxter's judgment, however, Bunyan's doctrine of law and grace subverted the gospel, and Fowler was not among those who thought well of him. Little firm evidence suggests that leading ministers read his works—even *The Pilgrim's Progress*. Of the 400 subscribers to Doe's 1692 edition comprising a dozen of his unpublished works, approximately thirty were ministers (*MW*, 12:458). The large library of Samuel Lee, a Presbyterian who served as co-pastor of a congregation in Holborn, London, before moving to New England in 1686, included works by Owen, Meade, Joseph Caryl, Thomas Manton, Jeremiah Bur-

---

[57] *The Grand Moving Panorama of Pilgrim's Progress* (Montclair, NJ: Montclair Art Museum, n.d.).

[58] Samuel Langhorne Clemens, *Mark Twain's Notebook*, ed. Albert Bigelow Paine (New York: Harper and Bros., 1935), 192.

[59] The earliest Turkish edition appears to have been the one published in 1905.

[60] *HW*, 1.

[61] In recounting his early religious experience, Doe provided one of the earliest surviving reactions to *The Pilgrim's Progress*: "By my thus going to work for Life; I was not less a Christian than him that Mr. *John Bunyan*, in his *Progress*, calls Christian, that went to *Mount Sinai* to be helpt off with his heavy Burthen." *A Collection*, 39.

roughs, John Preston, Samuel Rutherford, Richard Sibbes, and others, but nothing by Bunyan.[62] Yet the historian and antiquarian Anthony Wood thought some of his books, including *The Pilgrim's Progress*, were useful, and John Dunton averred that Bunyan was "as well known for an Author thro'out England, as any I have mention'd, by the many Books he has Publish'd, of which the Pilgrim's Progress bears away the Bell."[63] The avid book-collector Sir William Boothby, a justice of the peace since 1660 and a devout Anglican who had the Book of Common Prayer read twice daily in his chapel, acquired a copy of Bunyan's *A Holy Life* and Thomas Sherman's spurious second part of *The Pilgrim's Progress*, and he undoubtedly owned other works by Bunyan since he instructed his agent in 1684 to send him copies of all printed pamphlets, sermons, and discourses.[64] The first biography of Bunyan, an anonymous work entitled *An Account of the Life and Actions of Mr. John Bunyan*, was issued in 1692, the same year the publisher Stephen Marshall began selling large portraits of Bunyan for 6d.; he had become a celebrity.[65] Across the English Channel the anonymous author of the epistle to *Voyage d'un Chrestien vers l'Eternité* (1685) introduced Bunyan to French readers as a saintly man whose religious knowledge was experientially based.

In sharp contrast, during the early eighteenth century Bunyan was harshly criticized by the Anglican cleric John Lewis, minister at Margate, Kent, who set about to revise the second edition of *A Brief History of the Rise and Progress of Anabaptism in England* (1738). He faulted Bunyan for not seeking the counsel of his parish minister during his spiritual turmoil, for succumbing instead to the influence of three or four Antinomian women, and for never reflecting on his "ignorance and want of learning." Lewis erred on several points, including his assertion that Bunyan regarded the laying on of hands after baptism as a duty, but he was close to the mark in averring that Bunyan was "very strongly prejudiced against the Religion of the Church of England, [and] That he called their houses of prayer &c. High-places as if he thought the Worship performed in them was

[62] *The Library of the Late Reverend and Learned Mr. Samuel Lee* (Boston, 1693). In the early 1680s the library of John Percivale, which included works by Anglicans such as Jeremy Taylor, Edward Stillingfleet, and Lancelot Andrewes, and Baxter's *Saints Everlasting Rest*, had nothing of Bunyan's. BL, Add. MSS 47,024, fols. 81v–83v.

[63] Anthony Wood, *Athenae Oxonienses*, ed. Philip Bliss, 4 vols. (London: Lackington, Hughes *et al.*, 1813–20), 4:613; John Dunton, *Letters Written from New England A.D. 1686*, ed. W. H. Whitmore (Boston: Prince Society, 1867), 159 (quoted).

[64] BL, Add. MSS 71,690, fols. 34r, 81v, 92v–93r, 108r; 71,691, fols. 56v, 66v. His extensive library also included works by Milton, Baxter, Thomas Goodwin, Ferguson, Owen, Penn, and Nathaniel Vincent. Add. MSS 71,690; 71,691; and 71,692 *passim*.

[65] Bunyan, *Works* (1692), 868.

Idolatrous."[66] It would be interesting to know whether similar views were shared by other parish clergy in the eighteenth century, and, if so, to what extent.

From Cokayne, Beaumont, and Doe to the present, Bunyan has had admirers because of the religious views he espoused. In the eighteenth century such writers included the mystic Pierre Poiret, who found a spiritual affinity with Bunyan, the religious enthusiast Howel Harris, who read Bunyan frequently, and the Methodist leaders John Wesley, who edited and adapted several of Bunyan's works, and George Whitefield, who praised his catholic spirit, admired his defense of Christian liberty, and thought he exemplified the biblical teaching that the foolish confound the wise.[67] Nineteenth-century evangelicals, such as William Raymond Weeks, Daniel Warr, George Cheever, the Bunyan editor George Offor, and the Baptist preacher Charles Haddon Spurgeon, found in Bunyan a kindred spirit, using him both to propagate their own tenets and to denounce the views of liberals and others with whom they disagreed.[68] This tradition was continued in the twentieth century by such authors as Alexander Whyte, whose four volumes exploring Bunyan's characters were published between 1893 and 1908, the biographer William Nelson, and the evangelical literary scholar Beatrice Batson.[69] By the

---

[66] Bodl., Rawlinson MSS C409, fols. 26r, 34r–35v (quoted).

[67] Pierre Poiret, *Bibliotheca Mysticorum Selecta, Tribus Constans Partibus* (Amsterdam, 1708), 328; Geoffrey F. Nuttall, *Howel Harris, 1714–1773: The Last Enthusiast* (Cardiff: University of Wales Press, 1965), 26, 63; George Whitefield, *George Whitefield's Journals* (London: Banner of Truth Trust, 1960), 583; Whitefield, "Recommendatory Preface," in *The Works of That Eminent Servant of Christ, Mr. John Bunyan*, 2 vols. (London, 1767), 1:iii–iv.

[68] [William Raymond Weeks], *The Pilgrim's Progress in the Nineteenth Century*, 2 vols. (New York: Cornelius Davis, 1826); Daniel Warr, *A Course of Lectures Illustrative of the Pilgrim's Progress* (London: Richard Baynes, 1825); George Barrell Cheever, *Lectures on the Pilgrim's Progress, and on the Life and Times of John Bunyan* (New York: Wiley and Putnam, 1844); *The Works of John Bunyan*, ed. George Offor, 3 vols. (Glasgow: Blackie and Son); Charles H. Spurgeon, *Pictures from Pilgrim's Progress . . . : A Commentary on Portions of John Bunyan's Immortal Allegory* (London: Passmore and Alabaster, 1903).

[69] Alexander Whyte, *Bunyan Characters in the Pilgrim's Progress*, 2 vols. (Edinburgh and London: Oliphants, 1893, 1897); Whyte, *Bunyan Characters: The Holy War* (Edinburgh and London: Oliphant, Anderson and Ferrier, 1902); Whyte, *Bunyan Characters: Bunyan Himself as Seen in His 'Grace Abounding'* (Edinburgh and London: Oliphant, Anderson and Ferrier, 1908); William Hamilton Nelson, *Tinker and Thinker: John Bunyan, 1628–1688* (Chicago and New York: Willett, Clark and Colby, 1928); E. Beatrice Batson, "Old Games, New Players," *Presbyterian Journal* (7 May 1969): 9; Batson, "John Bunyan and the Contemporary Student," *Christianity Today* 14 (11 September 1970): 1067–69; Galen Johnson, "'Be not extream': The Limits of Theory in Reading John Bunyan," *Christianity and Literature* 49 (Summer 2000): 447–64. For Batson's work as a literary scholar, see *John Bunyan: Allegory and Imagination* (London: Croom Helm; Totowa, NJ: Barnes and Noble, 1984).

latter half of the twentieth century, scholarly studies of Bunyan had become as prevalent as works intended to perpetuate evangelical religious views.

The decline in published evangelical sermons and commentary generally paralleled and was probably triggered by a decrease in the number of readers exposed to Bunyan's work. In the early eighteenth century accessibility was encouraged by the distribution of free copies of his sermons, and cheap editions of his popular works were available well into the nineteenth century for 1s. or less. During that period teachers used *The Pilgrim's Progress* to provide instruction in reading and vocabulary.[70] Bunyan, Thomas Paine, William Cobbett, and Robert Owen "contributed most to the stock of ideas and attitudes which make up the raw material of the [English working-class] movement from 1790–1850," according to E. P. Thompson, who described *The Pilgrim's Progress* and the *Rights of Man* as the "foundation texts" of the movement. In the eyes of the Chartist Thomas Cooper, Bunyan's classic was the "book of books."[71] Yet in 1886 a survey of what the working class read reported a sharp decline in the allegory's audience primarily because of the popularity of Sunday newspapers:

> Years ago, had one walked into almost any poor but respectable man's room in the kingdom, one would probably have found two books at least—the Bible and the *Pilgrim's Progress*. Both were held in extreme veneration. Now it is to be feared that very few working men and women read the *Pilgrim's Progress*.[72]

The decline had commenced, although this assessment perhaps erred on the gloomy side.

Early twentieth-century reports were likewise pessimistic. A writer in the *Catholic World* asserted in the spring of 1909 that *The Pilgrim's Progress* had lost its influence and become a literary curiosity, and in November London's *Daily Graphic* reported that few now read the allegory.[73] The English Association included *The Holy War* but not *The Pilgrim's Progress* on its list of recommended reading for secondary schools.[74] Yet the allegory's impact was still manifest in the letters and diaries of British troops in World War I, who found meaning in the

[70] Alexander Pope, "Letter to Henry Cromwell," in *English Letters and Letter-Writers of the Eighteenth Century*, ed. Howard Williams (London: G. Bell and Sons, 1886), 357; David Vincent, *Literary and Popular Culture: England, 1750–1914* (Cambridge: Cambridge University Press, 1989), 69, 89, 209.

[71] E. P. Thompson, *The Making of the English Working Class*, rev. ed. (Harmondsworth, Middlesex: Penguin, 1980), 34.

[72] Quoted in Vincent, *Literary and Popular Culture*, 179.

[73] Brégy, "The Pilgrim's Progress," 96; C. T. B., "Is Bunyan Read To-day?" London *Daily Graphic* (6 November 1909).

[74] E. Sharwood Smith, "English Literature in Schools," *Journal of English Studies* 1 (September 1912): 118.

Slough of Despond and the Valley of the Shadow of Death. They recognized an affinity between the burden on Christian's back and the knapsacks on their own, and in the righteousness of Christian's cause they saw their own mirrored.[75] To these men Bunyan was neither unknown nor irrelevant. The Church Army, an organization of lay evangelists in the Church of England, did its part to keep this imagery alive, producing a lantern lecture in 1917 that depicted Bunyan as a world hero.[76] In the same year Edith Charter's *Some Daily Thoughts on the Pilgrim's Progress* provided day-by-day readings from the first part of the allegory accompanied by meditations and poetry. After the war a handbook for English teachers in American intermediate and high schools made the case for teaching *The Pilgrim's Progress* and explaining it with passages from *Grace Abounding*.[77] The tercentenary breathed new life into Bunyan, in part by the publication of at least twenty biographies in 1927–28, among them a revised version of John Brown's classic, edited by Frank Mott Harrison. But the infusion of new energy was short-lived. Whereas allusions to *The Pilgrim's Progress* were common among both the well-educated and those of more modest training during World War I, in World War II the allegory was almost never invoked or read. An exception occurred in June 1944, when the epilogue from part one was read at a memorial service in Italy for the 11th Battalion of the King's Royal Rifles.[78] By the late 1980s fewer than one in seven American seventeen-year-olds could answer a multiple-choice question about *The Pilgrim's Progress* correctly,[79] yet the continued publication of select Bunyan works by mostly Christian presses in America and Britain as well as the availability of his writings on the internet indicate the presence of a limited reading public beyond academia.[80]

Among literary critics and academics Bunyan's reputation followed a differ-

[75] Paul Fussell, *The Great War and Modern Memory* (New York: Oxford University Press, 1975), 137–44.

[76] Anon., *John Bunyan, the Bedfordshire Tinker, His Life and Times* (Oxford: Church Army Press, 1917).

[77] Sterling Andrus Leonard, *Essential Principles of Teaching Reading and Literature in the Intermediate Grades and the High School* (Philadelphia, Chicago, London: J. A. Lippincott, 1922), 52, 253.

[78] Paul Fussell, *Wartime: Understanding and Behavior in the Second World War* (New York: Oxford University Press, 1989), 232.

[79] Diane Ravitch and Chester E. Finn, Jr., *What Do Our 17-Year-Olds Know? A Report on the First National Assessment of History and Literature* (New York: Harper and Row, 1987), 96, 103. The number who correctly answered the multiple-choice question on *The Pilgrim's Progress* was 13.4 percent, well within the scope of random guessing.

[80] Cheryl V. Ford's *The Pilgrim's Progress Devotional: A Daily Journey Through the Christian Life* (Oxford: Bible Reading Fellowship, 1999) is an example of the continuing pious interest in the allegory.

ent trajectory. The response to his work in the early eighteenth century was mixed. Gottfried Arnold, a German historian of mysticism, referred to Bunyan in his work, and Jonathan Swift remarked that he had been more informed and better entertained by a few pages of *The Pilgrim's Progress* than by lengthy discourses on the will and intellect.[81] Joseph Addison offered a preview of the often harsh reaction to Bunyan in literary circles during the mid-eighteenth century when he caustically observed that the reception accorded the works of Bunyan and Quarles meant that any author could become as popular as John Dryden and John Tillotson.[82] As the upper classes looked disdainfully on popular culture, Bunyan's reputation in learned circles declined. Samuel Richardson adjudged him more suited for the multitude than were culturally polished authors, a view shared by the critic John Dennis.[83] In 1757 Edmund Burke unfavorably compared Bunyan's style to Virgil's *Aeneid*, though admitting it was energetic, and the same year David Hume proclaimed that there was no more equality of genius and elegance between Addison and Bunyan than between Teneriffe and a molehill, or the ocean and a pond. Those who liked Bunyan, he sniffed, were guilty of bad taste.[84] To Alexander Pope, Bunyan's style was tedious, and Elizabeth Montagu referred to *The Pilgrim's Progress* and Quarles' *Emblemes* as "classics of the artificers in leather."[85]

As the eighteenth century wore on, Bunyan's reputation began to rise in some literary circles. Laurence Sterne hoped *The Life and Opinions of Tristram Shandy, Gentleman* (1759) would be as widely read as *The Pilgrim's Progress*, an anonymous article in *Gentleman's Magazine* lauded the allegory as a work of genius, and Augustus Toplady favorably compared the allegory, with its "rich fund of

[81] Gottfried Arnold, *Gottfrid Arnolds Historie und Beschreibung der mystichen Theologie oder geheimen Gottes Gelehrtheit* (Frankfurt, 1703); Jonathan Swift, *The Works of the Rev. Jonathan Swift, D.D.*, new ed., 24 vols., ed. Thomas Sheridan and John Nichols (New York: William Durell and Co., 1812–13), 8:20.

[82] Joseph Addison, *The Works of the Right Honourable Joseph Addison*, ed. Richard Hurd, 6 vols. (London: Henry G. Bohn, 1854–56), 4:375.

[83] Samuel Richardson, *Selected Letters*, ed. John Carroll (Oxford: Clarendon Press, 1964), 57; John Dennis, *The Critical Works of John Dennis*, ed. Edward Niles Hooker, 2 vols. (Baltimore: Johns Hopkins University Press, 1939, 1943), 2:29–30.

[84] Edmund Burke, *A Philosophical Inquiry into the Origin of Our Ideas of the Sublime and Beautiful; with an Introductory Discourse Concerning Taste*, ed. Abraham Mills (New York: Harper and Bros., 1846), 31; David Hume, *Of the Standard of Taste and Other Essays*, ed. John W. Lenz (Indianapolis and New York: Bobbs-Merrill, 1965), 7.

[85] Alexander Pope, *The Correspondence of Alexander Pope*, ed. George Sherburn, 5 vols. (Oxford: Clarendon Press, 1956), 1:426–27; Elizabeth Montagu, *The Letters of Mrs. Elizabeth Montagu, with Some of the Letters of Her Correspondents*, vol. 4, ed. Matthew Montagu (London: T. Cadell and W. Davies, 1813), 77–78.

heavenly experience, life, and sweetness" to the lifeless, ponderous imitation of Simon Patrick.[86] Samuel Johnson praised Bunyan's allegory for its imagination and inventiveness, Horace Walpole likened Edmund Spenser's work to a rhymed version of Bunyan's, and Benjamin Franklin collected Bunyan's works.[87] Several critics offered a balanced assessment. *The Pilgrim's Progress* and *Robinson Crusoe* were very popular with "the vulgar," noted Henry Home, Lord Kames, who deemed the blend of drama and narrative in these works as effective as Homer's. Although Bunyan's language was coarse and vulgar, he did not deserve ridicule, asserted James Granger.[88] The derision was real enough, for William Cowper, who admired Bunyan's ability to combine fiction and truth and his simple style, humor, and wit, avoided mentioning his name lest it "move a sneer at thy deserved fame." Perhaps the unkindest cut was John Arbuthnot's characterization of Bunyan's work as that of a Grub Street hack.[89]

The generally polarized strands of eighteenth-century literary opinion carried into the early decades of the nineteenth century. Whereas John Dunlop decried Bunyan's coarse taste, illiberal theology, and execrable poetry, a pseudonymous author, reflecting the positive reception accorded Bunyan in the Evangelical Revival, extolled him as the Shakespeare of theology.[90] The latter point of view was

[86] Laurence Sterne, *The Life and Opinions of Tristram Shandy, Gentleman: The Text*, 3 vols., ed. Melvyn New and Joan New (Gainesville: University Presses of Florida, 1978–84), 1:5 ; anon., "Some Account of the Imprisonment of John Bunyan, Minister of the Gospel at Bedford, in November 1660," *Gentleman's Magazine* 35 (April 1765): 168–71; Augustus M. Toplady, *The Works of Augustus M. Toplady*, new ed., 6 vols. (London: William Baynes and Son; Edinburgh: H. S. Baynes, 1825), 1:40 (quoted).

[87] James Boswell, *The Life of Samuel Johnson, LL.D.*, ed. Edward Malone, 2 vols. (London: Oxford University Press, Humphrey Milford, 1927), 1:501; Horace Walpole, *Horace Walpole's Correspondence with William Mason*, 2 vols., ed. W. S. Lewis, Grover Cronin, Jr., and Charles H. Bennett (New Haven, CT: Yale University Press, 1955), 2:256; Benjamin Franklin, *The Writings of Benjamin Franklin*, 10 vols., ed. Albert Henry Smyth (New York: Macmillan, 1907), 1:238, 251.

[88] Henry Homes, Lord Kames, *Sketches of the History of Man*, 2 vols. (Edinburgh, 1774), 1:134; James Granger, *A Biographical History of England, from Egbert the Great to the Revolution*, 5th ed., 6 vols. (London: William Baynes and Son, 1824), 3:347–48.

[89] William Cowper, *Poems by William Cowper, Esq., Together with His Posthumous Poetry*, 3 vols. in 1, ed. John Johnson (Boston: Phillips, Sampson, and Co., 1849), 2:158–59. For the views of Arbuthnot, Thomas Brown, William Congreve, John Gay, and others see N. H. Keeble, "'Of him thousands daily Sing and talk': Bunyan and His Reputation," in *John Bunyan*, ed. Keeble, 246–47.

[90] John Colin Dunlop, *The History of Fiction: Being a Critical Account of the Most Celebrated Prose Works of Fiction*, 2nd ed., 3 vols. (Edinburgh: J. Ballantyne and Co.; London: Longman, Hurst, Rees, Orme, and Brown, 1816), 2:293; Mitis, "Critical Essays on the

closer to the Romantic assessment of Bunyan, with its appreciation of originality, unfettered genius, meditation, and matters of the heart. Leading the way were Sir Walter Scott, whose works include numerous allusions to Bunyan, and Samuel Taylor Coleridge, who in 1818 argued that Bunyan's dominant literary characteristic is originality.[91] Twelve years later Coleridge articulated an interpretive motif that guided much subsequent Bunyan scholarship—the triumph of his genius over his piety, of the Bunyan of Parnassus over the Bunyan of the conventicle.[92]

A landmark in Bunyan scholarship and his literary reputation—Robert Southey's biography—was published the same year, 1830. In a balanced assessment, the poet-laureate awarded Bunyan high marks for his homespun style and intelligible vocabulary while noting that he made no demands on the mind or imagination. Bunyan, he thought, was "the Prince of all allegorists in prose," though he concluded that the second part was not the equal of the first. Dismayed by what he deemed the hypocrisy and fanaticism of the seventeenth century, he denounced Bunyan's view of the Book of Common Prayer as intolerant and irrational, yet he praised Bunyan's catholicity of spirit, contrasting it with the sectarian preoccupations of other dissenters.[93] Among the reviewers of Southey's biography were Scott, who compared Bunyan favorably to Spenser, and the prominent Whig historian Thomas Babington Macaulay, who observed that mentioning Bunyan's name no longer produced sneers. Together Southey, Scott, and Macaulay elevated *The Pilgrim's Progress* to the status of an English classic. In the seventeenth century, according to Macaulay, "there were only two minds which possessed the imaginative faculty in a very eminent degree"—Milton's and Bunyan's.[94] Convinced that Southey had not gone far enough in praising Bunyan, Coleridge objected to his critical remarks about Bunyan's style and diction. *The*

---

Genius and Writings of Bunyan," *London Christian Instructor, or Congregational Magazine* 1 (December 1818): 632–35.

[91] Keeble, "'Of him thousands daily Sing and talk'," 253–55.

[92] *Coleridge on the Seventeenth Century*, ed. Roberta Florence Brinkley (Durham, NC: Duke University Press, 1955), 475–76.

[93] Robert Southey, "The Life of John Bunyan," in *The Pilgrim's Progress* (London: John Murray and John Major, 1830), v–c.

[94] [Sir Walter Scott], review of *The Pilgrim's Progress, with a Life of John Bunyan*, by Robert Southey, *Quarterly Review* (October 1830): 469–94; Thomas Babington Macaulay, review of *The Pilgrim's Progress, with a Life of John Bunyan*, by Robert Southey, *Edinburgh Review* 108 (December 1831): 450–61. Scott's suggestion that Bunyan was a gypsy sparked an interminable debate. See the entries noted in the index (423–24) in James F. Forrest and Richard Lee Greaves, *John Bunyan: A Reference Guide* (Boston: G. K. Hall and Co., 1982).

*Pilgrim's Progress*, he averred, is "the best *Summa Theologiae Evangelicae* ever produced by a writer not miraculously inspired."[95]

The Victorian Age was not of one mind regarding Bunyan's literary reputation, a more critical tone having been established virtually at the outset by John Ruskin. In 1845 he pronounced many of Bunyan's feelings insane and labeled *Grace Abounding* dangerous because it creates a misleading impression of God's dealings with people, foments heresy and schism, and causes insanity. Unlike George Herbert, who understood God intellectually, Bunyan, opined Ruskin, approached the deity through his liver. Having mellowed by the 1880s, Ruskin expressed appreciation for Bunyan's imaginative teaching, resolute faith, and deep insight into the nature of sin, concluding that in these respects he could be compared with Dante.[96] The philosopher Josiah Royce also saw Bunyan's religious experiences in the 1650s as the manifestation of a troubled psychological state. In his opinion, Bunyan suffered from morbidly insistent impulses and depression triggered by preoccupation with the unpardonable sin, yet by imposing a regimen on himself he staved off insistent temptations and deep depression.[97] Other scholars have explored Bunyan's psychological state, most notably William James, whose assessment has been discussed in Chapter Two, and Esther Harding, whose *Journey into Self* (1956) applies the psychoanalytical insights of Carl Gustav Jung to Bunyan.

As the Victorian Age waned, the evangelical tradition remained enthusiastic in its embrace of Bunyan, but beyond these circles reaction to his work remained divided. The literary scholar Richard Garnett offered a balanced appraisal, extolling *The Pilgrim's Progress* as a major work of English realism though prosaic when compared with Dante's *Comedy*. In Garnett's estimation *Grace Abounding* is similar to a host of other spiritual autobiographies with the exception of its vigorous prose, *Mr. Badman* lacks imagination, and *The Holy War* is dependent on *Paradise Lost*.[98] The satirist and novelist Samuel Butler offered a harsher judgment, denouncing *The Pilgrim's Progress* as "a series of infamous libels upon life and things" as well as "a blasphemy" against the traditional morality validated by conscience. In a similar vein Robert Bridges, after informally surveying the re-

---

[95] Samuel Taylor Coleridge, *The Literary Remains of Samuel Taylor Coleridge*, ed. Henry Nelson Coleridge, 4 vols. (London: William Pickering, 1836–39), 3:392.

[96] John Ruskin, *The Works of John Ruskin*, ed. E. T. Cook and Alexander Wedderburn, 39 vols. (London: George Allen; New York: Longmans, Green and Co., 1903–12), 4:348–49; 35:13; Ruskin, *The Stones of Venice*, vol. 2 (Orpington, Kent: George Allen, 1881), 189, 198.

[97] Josiah Royce, *Studies of Good and Evil: A Series of Essays upon Problems of Philosophy and of Life* (New York: D. Appleton and Co., 1898), 29–75.

[98] Richard Garnett, *The Age of Dryden* (London: George Bell and Sons, 1895), 233–44.

action of children to the allegory, concluded that it lacks educational value because it neglects practical morality.[99] Bunyan fared better at the hands of George
Bernard Shaw, who found that he, unlike Shakespeare, understood virtue and
courage; Shaw regarded Bunyan as the "greatest English dramatizer of life."[100]

The twentieth century was less concerned with assessing Bunyan's reputation
than examining his historical context, literary techniques, theology, perception of
women, and interpretive strategies. Simultaneously the body of popular literature
devoted to him increased substantially in the century's early decades, particularly
in connection with the tercentenary of his birth. As in the nineteenth century,
when he was a source of inspiration for abolitionists, some writers continued to
look to him for imagery and inspiration in espousing their causes. In 1917
Rudyard Kipling's poem "The Holy War" drew on Bunyan's allegory of the same
name to inspire British pilgrims battling the German Diabolus.[101] As the world
faced the totalitarian threat in the late 1930s, several authors appealed to Bunyan's
example in support of their appeals not to take up arms but instead to endure
suffering. Yet in 1940 a Catholic writer who envisioned World War II as a holy
war found him relevant.[102]

In the century that followed Coleridge's pronouncement that the Bunyan of
Parnassus had triumphed over the Bunyan of the conventicle, the latter continued to receive scant attention apart from the mostly unhistorical and uncritical
use of his writings by evangelicals. James Anthony Froude anointed him "the
Poet-apostle of the English middle classes, imperfectly educated like himself,"
and the prominent Whig historian George Macaulay Trevelyan described Bunyan
in 1928 as an unconscious artist, "the representative Puritan," and a perfect representative of evangelical religion.[103] Macaulay's was the last great articulation of the

[99] Samuel Butler, *The Note-Books of Samuel Butler, Author of "Erewhon,"* ed. Henry
Festing Jones (London: A. C. Fifield, 1912), 188–93, 326–27; Robert Bridges, *Collected Essays, Papers &c. of Robert Bridges* (Oxford: Oxford University Press, Humphrey Milford,
1934), 115–29.

[100] Shaw, "Better Than Shakespeare," 11–12; Shaw, *Three Plays for Puritans: The Devil's
Disciple, Caesar and Cleopatra, and Captain Brassbound's Conversion* (London: Constable
and Co., 1901), xxiv–xxv; Shaw, *Man and Superman* (London: Brentano's, 1920), xxxi–
xxxvi. However, Shaw thought *The Holy War* was absurd and barely readable. *Androcles
and the Lion Overruled Pygmalion* (New York: Brentano's, 1916), xxxvi, xcviii–xcix.

[101] Rudyard Kipling, "The Holy War," *Public Opinion* (14 December 1917): 428–29.

[102] Harold Butcher, "John Bunyan for Today," *Christian Century* 55 (31 August 1938):
1036–38; William Ralph Inge, *A Pacifist in Trouble* (London: Putnam, 1939), 280–84;
Christopher Hollis, "The City of Mansoul," *Tablet* 175 (29 June 1940): 638.

[103] James Anthony Froude, *Bunyan* (New York: Harper and Brothers, 1880), 173;
George Macaulay Trevelyan, "Bunyan's England," *Review of the Churches* 5 (July 1928):
319–25.

Romantic view of Bunyan, although vestiges of that tradition will probably linger in perpetuity. Coleridge's dictum was first substantively challenged by William York Tindall, whose *John Bunyan: Mechanick Preacher* (1934) forcefully restored Bunyan to his historical context—a world of religious enthusiasts, uneducated preachers, and sectaries. In dramatic contrast to the Romantic tradition, with its concentration on his solitary genius, Tindall stressed his resemblance to other lay preachers, especially those of the Baptists. By immersing himself in the pamphlet literature of the period, Tindall made a powerful case for the necessity of contextualizing Bunyan.

Scholars influenced by the Marxist tradition have likewise found the Romantic view inadequate. In *John Bunyan: Maker of Myths* (1937) Jack Lindsay interpreted Bunyan in the context of contemporary social forces, particularly the conflict between the Levellers' espousal of birthrights and capitalism. Bunyan went to prison, Lindsay argued, as part of the bourgeoisie's attempt to quash democratic ideals. Lindsay explained Bunyan's allegories in terms of myth and literature, with the celestial city representing the dream that all England, or even the world, will be united in harmony. To Lindsay, *The Holy War* depicts the strife between an absolutist monarch and the people in quest of their liberties. Writing in the same tradition, Alick West in the 1950s contended that Bunyan reveals the creative energy of revolution, and he interpreted the allegories as manifestations of the conflict between rich and poor (*The Pilgrim's Progress*) and monarchy and people (*The Holy War*). In the Vanity Fair episode, according to West, the pilgrims resolutely oppose the unjust, inhumane capitalist market, valuing instead the human soul.[104] From his Marxist roots Christopher Hill gained a keen appreciation of the revolutionary forces that shaped Bunyan's youth. With a deep grounding in contemporary literature that surpassed Tindall's, he brought his formidable historical skills to bear in situating Bunyan in a context fully informed by contemporary literature as well as political and social history. Instead of Coleridge's unsatisfactory dichotomy, Hill portrayed Bunyan as "a representative Puritan artisan who was also a writer of genius," and *The Pilgrim's Progress* as "the epic of the dissent which grew out of and discarded the revolutionary radicalism of the 1640s and 1650s but retained much of its popular ideology."[105]

Charting editions of *The Pilgrim's Progress*, assessing Bunyan's popular im-

---

[104]Alick West, "*The Holy War* and *The Pilgrim's Progress*," *Modern Quarterly* 8 (Summer 1953): 169–82; West, *Mountain in the Sunlight: Studies in Conflict and Unity* (London: Lawrence and Wishart, 1958), 11–57. For a fuller survey see David Herreshoff, "Marxist Perspectives on Bunyan," in *Bunyan in Our Time*, ed. Robert G. Collmer (Kent, OH: Kent State University Press, 1989), 161–85.

[105] Hill, *TPM*, 368, 378. Coleridge's dichotomy is defended by Ian Fletcher, "Mimic Heavens: Milton's Century," *Encounter* 55 (July 1980): 69–79.

pact, and tracking his literary reputation among critics and academics are not the only ways to measure Bunyan's influence. Another is to determine his impact on major authors and artists.[106] The earliest such writer may have been Daniel Defoe, in whose Roxana some have seen a female Mr. Badman, and another was Benjamin Franklin, whose autobiography acknowledges Bunyan's engaging blend of narrative and dialogue.[107] Among the early voices in what became a great chorus of literary appreciation in the nineteenth century were those of the poet John Keats and the essayist Charles Lamb.[108] Nathaniel Hawthorne adapted *The Pilgrim's Progress* to satirize liberalism in *The Celestial Rail-Road*, *The Scarlet Letter* reflects the allegory's influence, and the second part may have helped to inspire *The Blithedale Romance*. Charles Dickens' *Oliver Twist* and *The Old Curiosity Shop* owe something to Bunyan, as do Herman Melville's *Moby Dick*, William Makepeace Thackeray's *Vanity Fair*, Charlotte Bronte's *Jane Eyre*, and Louise May Alcott's *Little Women*. In *Silas Marner* and *Middlemarch* George Eliot (Mary Anne Evans) drew on Bunyan, whose style she admired as simple, rhythmic, and rigorous.[109] Dorothy Wordsworth, Christina Rossetti, and Henry David Thoreau referred or alluded to Bunyan.[110] In Robert Louis Stevenson's judgment *The Pilgrim's Progress* is full of beauty and profitable emotion, George Bernard Shaw acknowledged Bunyan's influence on his style, and Mark Twain and Virginia Woolf read Bunyan. The twentieth-century Italian author Beppe Fenoglio, who detested the Fascists and participated in the Italian resistance, found inspiration in seven-

---

[106] Bunyan's impact on those without literary or artistic reputations is reflected in diaries and autobiographies such as those of Hannah Heaton, an eighteenth-century Connecticut farm-wife, and Samuel Lane, an eighteenth-century New Hampshire tanner, shoemaker, and surveyor. James S. Amelang, *The Flight of Icarus: Artisan Autobiography in Early Modern Europe* (Stanford, CA: Stanford University Press, 1998), 131, 298, 308.

[107] James Sutherland, *Daniel Defoe: A Critical Study* (Cambridge, MA: Harvard University Press, 1971), 133, 211–13; Franklin, *Writings*, 1:251.

[108] John Keats, *The Letters of John Keats*, ed. Maurice Buxton Forman, 4th ed. (New York: Oxford University Press, 1952), 37, 420; Charles Lamb, *The Letters of Charles Lamb, to Which Are Added Those of His Sister Mary Lamb*, 3 vols., ed. E. V. Lucas (New Haven, CT: Yale University Press, 1935), 3:178–80, 269.

[109] George Eliot, *George Eliot's Life as Related in Her Letters and Journals*, vol. 2, ed. J. W. Cross (Boston: Dana Estes and Co., 1884), 161; Robert P. Lewis, "The Pilgrim Maggie: Natural Glory and Natural History in *The Mill on the Floss*," *Literature & Theology* 12 (June 1998): 121–34.

[110] Dorothy Wordsworth, *Journals of Dorothy Wordsworth*, ed. E. de Selincourt, 2 vols. (New York: Macmillan, 1941), 1:105, 208; Marjory Amelia Bald, *Women-Writers of the Nineteenth Century* (Cambridge: Cambridge University Press, 1923), 30, 244; Kenneth Walter Cameron, *Companion to Thoreau's Correspondence* (Hartford, CT: Transcendental Books, 1964), 57, 59–60, 66, 70.

teenth-century England, including the New Model Army and *The Pilgrim's Progress*, and the twentieth-century novelists John Buchan and Margaret Drabble reflect the influence of *The Pilgrim's Progress* in their work.[111]

The galaxy of those who found reason to appreciate Bunyan is expansive. Among the major poets John Greenleaf Whittier praised his literary accomplishments, devotion to liberty, and imagination, and Robert Browning's "Ned Bratts, a Poem on Bunyan" explores his incarceration. Ralph Waldo Emerson took time to annotate a copy of *Grace Abounding*, Walt Whitman was influenced by Bunyan, and Matthew Arnold was inspired by *The Pilgrim's Progress* in writing his poem "Rugby Chapel."[112] The Irish novelist James Joyce parodied Bunyan's style in the "Oxen of the Sun" episode in *Ulysses*, and E. E. Cummings' *The Enormous Room* has been described as "an intentional *Pilgrim's Progress*."[113] The Russian poet Alexander Pushkin's "The Wanderer" reflects the opening scene of *The Pilgrim's Progress*, and the allegory may have been one of the models for Vladimir Nabokov's novel *Transparent Things*.[114] So profound was the impact of *The Pilgrim's Progress* on the nineteenth-century Indian poet Krishna Pillai that he converted to Christianity,[115] which probably would have pleased Bunyan more than

---

[111] Robert Louis Stevenson, "Books Which Have Influenced Me," *British Weekly* (13 May 1887): 18; George Bernard Shaw, *Shaw: An Autobiography, 1856–1898*, ed. Stanley Weintraub (New York: Weybright and Talley, 1969), 59–60; Mark Twain (Samuel L. Clemens), *Adventures of Huckleberry Finn* (New York: Charles L. Webster and Co., 1884), 137; Juliet Dusinberre, "Bunyan and Virginia Woolf: A History and a Language of Their Own," *BS* 5 (Autumn 1994): 15–46; Mark Pietralunga, *Beppe Fenoglio and English Literature: A Study of the Writer as Translator* (Berkeley: University of California Press, 1987), 3, 30–32, 127–40; Kathleen M. Swaim, "Mercy and the Feminine Heroic in the Second Part of *Pilgrim's Progress*," *Studies in English Literature* 30 (Summer 1990): 388; Jeremy Idle, "The Pilgrim's Plane-Crash: Buchan, Bunyan and Canonicity," *Literature & Theology* 13 (September 1999): 249–58.

[112] John Greenleaf Whittier, *Old Portraits and Modern Sketches* (Boston: Ticknor, Reed and Fields, 1850), 1–32; Walter Harding, *Emerson's Library* (Charlottesville: University Press of Virginia, 1967), 44; Kenneth W. Cameron, "Bunyan and the Writers of the American Renaissance," *American Transcendental Quarterly* 13 (Supplement, Part One, Winter 1972): 1; Michael V. DiMassa, "'On to the City of God': The Influence of *The Pilgrim's Progress* on 'Rugby Chapel'," *English Language Notes* 35 (December 1997): 44–61.

[113] James Joyce, *Ulysses* (New York: Random House, 1918), 388–89; Smith, *John Bunyan in America*, 105 (quoted). See also W. Todd Martin, "*The Enormous Room*: E. E. Cummings' Modern Rendering of John Bunyan's *The Pilgrim's Progress*" (Ph.D. diss., Baylor University, 1998); Martin, "Cummings's *The enormous room*," *Explicator* 58 (Fall 1999): 33–36.

[114] Robert Alter, "Mirrors for Immortality," *Saturday Review* 55 (December 1972): 72–74, 76.

[115] D. Yesudhas, "*The Pilgrim's Progress* and *iratcaniya yaattirikam*," *Proceedings of the*

all the literary accolades. Among the sources for the first black South African novel in English, Sol T. Plaatje's *Mhudi*, were Bunyan and Shakespeare.[116]

In the world of art William Blake's twenty-nine watercolors illustrating *The Pilgrim's Progress* take pride of place among numerous depictions of the allegory. Bunyan's impact on Vincent Van Gogh is less obvious, though in 1875 he repudiated secular literature, proclaiming instead that he wanted only three books, *The Pilgrim's Progress*, the Bible, and Thomas à Kempis' *Imitation of Christ*. Bunyan seems to have influenced his understanding of life as trial and ordeal, the escape from which is provided by death. Kathleen Powers Erickson has seen Bunyan's impact in the importance Van Gogh attached to journeying, as in "The Artist on the Road to Tarascon," "Road with Cypress and Star," and "The Bridge at Trinquetaille."[117] The British artist Barry Burman, best known for his paintings of psychotics and their victims, rendered perhaps the most unusual series inspired by *The Pilgrim's Progress*.[118]

Influence of a different sort is evident in the many ways proponents of political agendas or other causes have appropriated Bunyan's work. These applications are comments on his reputation, for there is little point in citing obscure literature to win adherents to a cause or reinforce the faithful. In 1741 an anonymous author parodied *The Pilgrim's Progress* in *The Statesman's Progress: or, a Pilgrimage to Greatness* to satirize Sir Robert Walpole. Slave-owners and their agents employed *The Pilgrim's Progress* to acculturate their slaves, only to see them embrace Bunyan's imagery to express their flight from servitude; the South became the City of Destruction, and England the Great City.[119] The abolitionists too found relevance in Bunyan; *Pilgrim's Progress in the Last Days* depicted a holy war between Christian Abolition and Giant Slavery.[120] In the 1850s and early 1860s freedom of a different sort was the goal of the Taiping rebels, whose leader, Hong Xiuquan, regarded the Bible and *The Pilgrim's Progress* as his two favorite books. Tolstoy thought the Dukhobors, a peasant religious sect that rejected the authority of the Russian state and the established church, were attracted to *The Pilgrim's*

---

*First International Conference Seminar of Tamil Studies*, vol. 2, ed. Xavier S. Thani Nayagam *et al.* (1966), 232–36.

[116] Stephen Gray, "Two Sources of Plaatje's *Mhudi*," *Munger Africana Library Notes* 37 (1975): 6–28.

[117] Kathleen Powers Erickson, "Pilgrims and Strangers: The Role of *The Pilgrim's Progress* and *The Imitation of Christ* in Shaping the Piety of Vincent van Gogh," *BS* 4 (Spring 1991): 7–36.

[118] Glyn Hughes, "Barry Burman's *Pilgrim's Progress*," *BS* 9 (1999–2000): 69–76.

[119] Stephen Butterfield, *Black Autobiography in America* (Amherst: University of Massachusetts Press, 1974), 47, 53, 115.

[120] Smith, *John Bunyan in America*, 15.

*Progress.*[121] But Bunyan also had admirers with very different political outlooks, such as Theodore Roosevelt, whose heroes included Cromwell, Bunyan, and Milton,[122] and the British imperialists who packed the allegory in their trunks and transported it throughout much of the world. Bunyan, boasted Augustine Birrell in the *Empire Review*, was "as good an Imperialist as it is possible for any Christian man to be."[123] The empire fell, but Bunyan's books live on, their coverage far exceeding the furthest reaches of British dominion at its peak.

By any standard *The Pilgrim's Progress* has had a remarkable history. It served slave-owners and imperialists as a tool to teach their subjects to accept servitude, but it also inspired abolitionists and slaves in their struggle against bondage. In its pages British pacifists, Chinese rebels, Russian sectaries, and German mystics have found meaning, and its symbols have been embraced or adapted by temperance campaigners,[124] British troops, political pundits, and evangelical preachers. Novelists and poets in Britain, Ireland, the United States, Russia, India, and South Africa have felt its influence. Bunyan has been employed in the disparate causes of proletarian unity, imperialism, anti-Catholicism, and opposition to insurance companies, railroads, modern science, big business, women's rights, and liberal theology. Although he spent much of his career attacking the Church of England, the Catholic Church, and the Quakers, he has been toasted as an apostle of Christian unity.[125] Comparisons have been drawn between Bunyan and a host of diverse figures, among them Ignatius Loyola,[126] St. John of the Cross,[127] Augustine,[128] George Fox,[129] Friedrich Nietzsche, Henrik Ibsen, Richard Wagner,[130]

[121] Hill, *TPM*, 375–76.

[122] Theodore Roosevelt, *Oliver Cromwell* (New York: C. Scribner's Sons, 1900), 232.

[123] Augustine Birrell, "Links of Empire—Books (IX): 'The Pilgrim's Progress'," *Empire Review* 47 (February 1928): 87.

[124] James Miller, *Communion Wine and Intemperance: Bunyan's Pilgrim's Progress and Intoxicating Liquors* (Boston: Lee and Shepard, 1877).

[125] Charles Bernard Cockett, *Broken Things (A Plea for Unity)* (London: Arthur H. Stockwell, 1932), 24. Cf. Elmo Howell, "Bunyan's Two Valleys: A Note on the Ecumenic Element in *Pilgrim's Progress*," *Tennessee Studies in Literature* 19 (1974): 1–7.

[126] Joseph Rickaby, "St. Ignatius and John Bunyan," *American Catholic Quarterly Review* 27 (April 1902): 294–313.

[127] Howell, "Bunyan's Two Valleys," 1–7.

[128] E. Glenn Hinson, "Midwives and Mothers of Grace," *Theological Education: A Journal of Theology and Ministry* 43 (Spring 1991): 65–79; Philip H. Pfatteicher, "Plashing Pears in Augustine and Bunyan," *Literature & Theology* 9 (March 1995): 24–29.

[129] Hugh Barbour, "The 'Openings' of Fox and Bunyan," in *New Light on George Fox, 1624–1691*, ed. Michael Mullett (York: William Sessions, Ebor Press, [1993]), 129–43.

[130] Shaw, *Man and Superman*, xxxii–xxxiii.

Aesop,[131] the Muslim mystic Al-Ghazzali, the early monk Macarius of Egypt,[132] Teresa of Avila,[133] Samuel Beckett,[134] and James Bond's Agent 007.[135] A resemblance has even been seen between Bunyan's work and *Star Wars.*[136]

Bunyan's literary success ultimately rests on his extraordinary ability to rouse the imaginations of his readers—an ability rooted in his intense spirituality and powerful creativity, and given emotive force by his deep sympathy for the poor and oppressed and his fierce commitment to the principle that truth must be free.[137] Two periods in prison, one lasting more than eleven years (with a brief respite in 1666), failed to crush his spirit or his will to resist a government resolved to impose its religious system on its subjects. Unbroken and undeterred, he emerged from confinement to continue his preaching and writing, having honed a regimen of composition in prison that continued to serve him well as a free man. No less significant was his triumph over the debilitating, harrowing depressive moods that plunged him into the depths of black despair in the 1650s and early 1660s, leaving him with a keen sensitivity to the importance of light, warmth, and love, all of which ultimately helped him to hold back the dark. In the end his potent creativity enabled him to turn his experiences into a gripping spiritual autobiography and two major allegories that attest to his triumph over crippling despair and a repressive government.

[131] Alexander Smith, preface to John Bunyan, *Divine Emblems* (London: Bickers and Son, 1864).

[132] John T. McNeill, *A History of the Cure of Souls* (New York: Harper and Brothers, 1951), 64, 105–6.

[133] José María Ruiz Ruiz, "El lenguaje figurativo en la obra literaria de Teresa de Ávila y John Bunyan" (Ph.D. dissertation, University of Valladolid, 1974).

[134] Ronald R. Thomas, "The Novel and the Afterlife: The End of the Line in Bunyan and Beckett," *Modern Philology* 86 (May 1989): 385–97.

[135] Ann S. Boyd, "James Bond: Modern-Day Dragonslayer," *Christian Century* 82 (May 1965): 644–47.

[136] Alison White, "Children and Their Books," *Canadian Home Economics Journal* 28 (October 1978): 254–57.

[137] Unlike Penn, Bunyan never asserted that the liberty he sought extended to Catholics, let alone adherents of other religions. His unqualified condemnation of Catholicism did nothing to dampen the heritage of anti-Catholicism subsequently manifest in the Gordon riots in 1780. He had sympathy for the Huguenots but not the "Wild-Irish" (*PP*, 169)

# Reference Matter

# Appendix

————◆————

*Provisional Dating of Bunyan's Publications*

| Title | Ed. | Pub. date | Publisher | Stationers' register[1] | Term catalogues[2] | Provisional date of composition |
|---|---|---|---|---|---|---|
| Some Gospel Truths | 1 | 1656 | John Wright, Jr.; J. W. & M. Cowley | | | late summer 1656 |
| Vindication of Gospel Tr. | 1 | 1657 | Matthias Cowley | | | Oct. to Dec. 1656 |
| A Few Sighs from Hell | 1 | 1658 | M. Wright | | | Jan. to July 1658[3] |
| Law and Grace Unfolded | 1 | 1659 | M. Wright & M. Cowley | | | Aug. 1658 to Mar./Apr. 1659[4] |
| Profitable Meditations | 1 | [1661] | Francis Smith | | | Jan. to Aug. 1661 |
| Relation of My Imprisonment | 1 | 1765 | James Buckland | | | five letters, Nov. 1660 to Mar. 1662[5] |
| I Will Pray | 1 | [1662?] | [The Author?] (no copy) | | | mid-1662 |
| Prison Meditations | 1 | [1663] | Francis Smith | | | winter 1662–63 |
| Christian Behaviour | 1 | 1663 | Francis Smith | | | early 1663[6] |
| I Will Pray | 2 | 1663 | The Author | | | — |
| Sighs from Hell | 2 | [early 1660s?] | Francis Smith | | | [some revision] |
| A Mapp | 1 | [1663–64] | no copy | | | between late June 1663 & late 1664 |
| The Holy City | 1 | 1665 | J. Dover; F. Smith; n.p. | 6/28/69 (1:12) | | Dec. 1664 to May 1665 |
| One Thing Is Needful | 1 | [1665?] | (no copy) | | | May/June 1665 |
| Resurrection of the Dead | 1 | [1665?] | Francis Smith | | | July to Oct 1665 |
| Ebal and Gerizzim | 1 | [1665?] | (no copy) | | | Oct./Nov. 1665 |
| Prison Meditations | 2 | 1665 | n.p. | | | [prob. some revisions] |
| Grace Abounding | 1 | 1666 | George Larkin | | | Dec. 1665 to Feb. 1666[7] |
| A Pocket Concordance | 1 | ? | (may not have been published) | | | May 1666 to Aug. 1667, & possibly Apr. to Sept. 1671 |
| Grace Abounding | 2 | between 1667 & 1671 | (no copy) | | | ? Sept. to Nov. 1667 |

| Title | Ed. | Pub. date | Publisher | Stationers' register[1] | Term catalogues[2] | Provisional date of composition |
|---|---|---|---|---|---|---|
| Sighs from Hell | 3 | late 1660s? | Francis Smith | | | — |
| One Thing Is Needful; Ebal and Gerizzim | 2 | before 1672 | Francis Smith | | | [modest revision] |
| Christian Behaviour | 2 | between 1664 & 1671 | Francis Smith | | | [minor revision] |
| Heavenly Foot-man | 1 | 1698 | Charles Doe | | | Dec. 1667 to Feb. 1668 |
| Pilgrim's Progress | 1 | 1678 | N. Ponder | 12/22/77 (3:49) | 2/18/78 (1:299) | Mar. 1668 to Sept. 1669; May 1670 to Mar. 1671 |
| The Holy City | 1* | 1669 | Francis Smith | | 6/28/69 (1:12) | *new issue |
| Confession of My Faith | 1 | 1672 | Francis Smith | | | Oct. to Dec. 1671 |
| Defence of Justification | 1 | 1672 | Francis Smith | | 11/21/72 (1:116) | 13 Jan. to 27 Feb. 1672 |
| One Thing Is Needful; Ebal and Gerizzim | "3" [2a] | 1672 | Francis Smith | | | — |
| Grace Abounding | 3 | [1672?] | Francis Smith | | | late 1672 or winter 1672–73 |
| Christian Behaviour | 3 | [by 1672] | Francis Smith | | | — |
| Differences in Judgment | 1 | 1673 | John Wilkins | | | Mar. to July 1673 |
| Barren Fig-Tree | 1 | 1673 | Jonathan Robinson | | 11/24/73 (1:148) | Aug. to Oct. 1673 |
| Peaceable Principles | 1 | 1674 | (no title-page) | | | sometime in 1674 |
| Sighs from Hell | 4 | 1674 | Francis Smith | 5/18/74 (2:481) | 7/6/74 (1:182) | — |
| Light in Darkness | 1 | 1675 | Francis Smith | | 6/19/75 (1: 209–10) | early 1675 |
| Instruction for Ignorant | 1 | 1675 | Francis Smith | | | June/July 1675 |
| Sighs from Hell | 5 | 1675 | Francis Smith | | | — |
| Strait Gate | 1 | 1676 | Francis Smith | | 11/24/75 (1:216) | Aug. to Nov. 1675 |
| Saved by Grace | 1 | [1676] | Francis Smith | | 6/12/76 (1:245) | early 1676 |
| Of Justification by Imputed Righteousness | 1 | 1692 | Charles Doe | 8/3/92 (3:406) | June 1694 (2:506) | July to Nov. 1676 |
| Grace Abounding | 4 | [1677?] | (no copy) | | | during 2nd imprisonment, Dec. 1676 to June 1677 |
| Come, & Welcome | 1 | 1678 | Benjamin Harris | | | July/Aug. 1677 to Mar. 1678 |
| Pilgrim's Progress | 2 | 1678 | N. Ponder | | | summer 1678 |
| Grace Abounding | 3 | 1679 | Francis Smith | | June 1679 (1:363–64) | reprint |
| Paul's Departure | 1 | 1692 | Charles Doe | 8/3/92 (3:406) | June 1694 (2:506) | winter 1678–79 |
| Pilgrim's Progress | 3 | 1679 | N. Ponder | | | mid-1679 |
| Sighs from Hell | 6 | between 1676 & 1685 | Francis Smith | | | — |

| Title | Ed. | Pub. date | Publisher | Stationers' register[1] | Term catalogues[2] | Provisional date of composition |
|---|---|---|---|---|---|---|
| Treatise of the Fear of God | 1 | 1679 | N. Ponder | | Feb. 1680 (1:381–82) | Aug. 1679 to Jan. 1680 |
| Mr. Badman | 1 | 1680 | N. Ponder | | Feb. 1680 (1:382) | off and on from spring 1678 to Jan. 1680 |
| Pilgrim's Progress | 4 | 1680 | N. Ponder | | Feb. 1680 (1:382) | — |
| Grace Abounding | 5 | 1680 | N. Ponder | | | early to mid-1680 |
| Pilgrim's Progress | 5 | 1680 | N. Ponder | | | early to mid-1680 |
| Israel's Hope Encouraged | 1 | 1692 | Charles Doe | 8/3/92 (3:406) | June 1694 (2:506) | fall 1680 & winter 1680–81 |
| Pilgrim's Progress | 6 | 1681 | N. Ponder | | | — |
| Pilgrim's Progress | 7 | 1681 | N. Ponder | | | — |
| Pilgrim's Progress | 5a | 1682 | N. Ponder | | | — |
| Holy War | 1 | 1682 | Dorman Newman & Ben. Alsop | | Feb. 1682 (1:469) | Mar. 1681 to Jan. 1682 |
| Pilgrim's Progress | 8 | 1682 | N. Ponder | | Feb. 1682 (1:478) | — |
| Of Antichrist | 1 | 1692 | Charles Doe | 8/3/92 (3:406) | June 1694 (2:506) | Feb. to May 1682 |
| Greatness of the Soul | 1 | 1682, 1683 | Benjamin Alsop | | Nov. 1682 (1:504) | June to Oct. 1682 |
| Exposition of Genesis | 1 | 1692 | Charles Doe | 8/3/92 (3:406) | June 1694 (2:506) | Oct./Nov. 1682 to June 1683 |
| A Holy Life | 1 | 1684 | Benjamin Alsop | 8/10/83; 10/6/83 (3:180, 199) | Nov. 1683 (2:41) | late June to Aug. 1683 |
| Case of Conscience | 1 | 1683 | Benjamin Alsop | 10/2/83 (3:197) | | Sept. 1683 |
| Pilgrim's Progress | 9 | 1683 | N. Ponder | | | — |
| Prison Meditations | 3 | 1683 | n.p. | | | Substantial changes, though probably made in the 2nd ed. |
| One Thing Is Needful | 3 | 1683 | N. Ponder | | | — |
| Seasonable Counsel | 1 | 1684 | Benjamin Alsop | | | Oct. 1683 to Jan. 1684 |
| Come, & Welcome | 2 | 1684 | Ben. Harris | 3/11/84 (3:228) (?) | | Minor changes |
| Holy War | "2" | 1684 | Dorman Newman | | May 1684 (2:78–79) | Spurious (Sharrock and Forrest) |
| Pilgrim's Progress, Part II | 1 | 1684 | N. Ponder | 11/22/84 (3:262) | 6/84 (2:90) | Feb. to Oct. 1684 |
| Caution to Stir Up | 1 | 1684 | N. Ponder | | | by Apr. 1684 |
| Pilgrim's Progress | 9a | 1684 | N. Ponder | | | — |
| Questions about Sabbath | 1 | 1685 | N. Ponder | | Nov. 1684 (2:95) | Oct./Nov. 1684 |

| Title | Ed. | Pub. date | Publisher | Stationers' register[1] | Term catalogues[2] | Provisional date of composition |
|---|---|---|---|---|---|---|
| Pharisee and Publican | 1 | 1685 | John Harris | 5/21/85 (3:284) | | Dec. 1684 to early May 1685 |
| Pilgrim's Progress | 10 | 1685 | N. Ponder | | May 1685 (2:132) | — |
| Mr. Badman | 2 | 1685 | N. Ponder | | | no copy |
| Law and Grace Unfolded | 2 | 1685 | N. Ponder | | | token changes |
| I Will Pray | 3 | [1685] | The Author | | | — |
| Desire of the Righteous | 1 | 1692 | Charles Doe | 8/3/92 (3:406) | June 1694 (2:506) | June to Aug. 1685 |
| Come, & Welcome | 3 | 1685 | B. Harris for J. Harris | | | token changes |
| Saints Knowledge of Christ's Love | 1 | 1692 | Charles Doe | 8/3/92 (3:406) | June 1694 (2:506) | Sept. to Dec. 1685 |
| Sighs from Hell | 7 | [by 1686] | Francis Smith | | | — |
| Book for Boys and Girls | 1 | 1686 | N. Ponder | | | Jan. to Mar. 1686; pub. by 12 May |
| Come, & Welcome | 4 | 1686 | B. Harris for J. Harris | | | — |
| Christ a Compleat Saviour | 1 | 1692 | Charles Doe | 8/3/92 (3:406) | June 1694 (2:506) | Apr. to July 1686 |
| Saints Privilege and Profit | 1 | 1692 | Charles Doe | 8/3/92 (3:406) | June 1694 (2:506) | Aug. to Nov. 1686 |
| Come, & Welcome | 5 | 1686 | B. Harris for J. Harris | | | — |
| Pilgrim's Progress, Part II | 2 | 1686, 1687 | N. Ponder | | 12/13/86 (2:184) | fall 1686; minor additions |
| Discourse of the House of the Forest of Lebanon | 1 | 1692 | Charles Doe | 8/3/92 (3:406) | June 1694 (2:506) | Dec. 1686 to Feb. 1687 |
| Of the Trinity | 1 | 1692 | Charles Doe | 8/3/92 (3:406) | June 1694 (2:506) | ? winter of 1686–87 |
| Solomon's Temple | 1 | 1688 | George Larkin | | | Mar. to June 1687 |
| Discourse of House of God | 1 | 1688 | George Larkin | | | July/Aug. 1687 |
| Water of Life | 1 | 1688 | N. Ponder | 1/9/88 (3:328) | | Sept./Oct. 1687 |
| Advocateship of Jesus Christ | 1 | 1688 | Dorman Newman | | | late Oct. 1687 to Feb. 1688 |
| Come, & Welcome | 6 | 1688 | John Harris | 2/17/88 (3:329) | | — |
| Of the Law and a Christian | 1 | 1692 | Charles Doe | 8/3/92 (3:406) | June 1694 (2:506) | ? Feb./Mar. 1688 |
| Good News | 1 | 1688 | George Larkin | | | Mar. to mid-May 1688 |
| Work of Christ as an Advocate | 2 | 1688 | Dorman Newman | | May 1688 (2:222–3) | — |
| Grace Abounding | 6 | 1688 | N. Ponder | | | — |
| Pilgrim's Progress | 11 | 1688 | N. Ponder | | | — |
| Mr. Badman | "2" | 1688 | N. Ponder | | | reprint |

| Title | Ed. | Pub. date | Publisher | Stationers' register[1] | Term catalogues[2] | Provisional date of composition |
|---|---|---|---|---|---|---|
| Barren Fig-Tree | 2 | 1688 | J. Robinson | | Dec. 1688 (2:238) | — |
| Acceptable Sacrifice | 1 | 1689 | George Larkin | | | mid-May to July 1688 |
| Jerusalem Sinner Saved | 2 | 1689 | George Larkin | | | early Aug. 1688 |
| Last Sermon | 1 | 1689 | George Larkin | | | notes prepared before 19 Aug. 1688 |

[1]Publishers had their books entered in the Stationers' Register to secure their rights. In most cases the manuscripts were entered prior to publication, and the date refers to the license rather than the date of publication. Ronald B. McKerrow, *An Introduction to Bibliography for Literary Students* (Oxford: Clarendon Press, 1927), 136–37; Philip Gaskell, *A New Introduction to Bibliography* (Oxford: Clarendon Press, 1972), 183–84.

[2]Entries in the the Term Catalogues, which were trade announcements, normally appeared about the time of publication or a short time before. McKerrow, *Introduction*, 138–39; Gaskell, *New Introduction*, 182–83.

[3]The British Library copy has September written on the title-page. Advertised in *Commonwealth Mercury* (2–9 Sept. 1658).

[4]The British Library copy has May written on the title-page.

[5]The last event described in a "Relation" occurred on 19 Mar. 1662.

[6]The epistle is dated 17 June 1663.

[7]*GA*, §319, states that Bunyan wrote this about five and a quarter years after his imprisonment (12 Nov. 1660), i.e. about Feb. 1666.

# Bibliography of Primary Sources

Manuscripts

BEDFORDSHIRE AND LUTON ARCHIVES
Bedfordshire Corporation Minute Book, 1664–1688
MSS HSA S[ummer] 1661 through S[ummer] 1685 (jail calendars, presentments, recognizances, and depositions for Bedfordshire)
MS X239/1 (Stevington church book)

BODLEIAN LIBRARY
Add. MSS C307 (papers of Gilbert Sheldon)
Carte MSS 38–40 (Ormond papers, 1673–89)
Carte MSS 66, 79, 81 (Wharton papers)
Carte MSS 72 (newsletters and parliamentary proceedings)
Carte MSS 77; 228 (Huntingdon and Wharton papers)
English Letters C12
English Letters C328
Rawlinson Letters 49–53, 104 (Wharton correspondence)
Rawlinson Letters 98 (correspondence and papers of Francis Turner, bishop of Ely)
Rawlinson Letters 109 (letters to John Thornton)
Rawlinson MSS 139A (documents regarding James II's 'three questions', 1687–88)
Rawlinson MSS C409 (papers of John Lewis)
Rawlinson MSS C719 (miscellaneous legal records)
Rawlinson MSS D1352 (unpublished nonconformist tracts)
Rawlinson MSS E120 (sermon notes of Matthew Meade)
Rawlinson Poetry 58 (poems copied by Stephen Thompson, including Bunyan's *Prison Meditations* and *One Thing Is Needful*)
Tanner MSS 28–38, 42–43 (primarily correspondence of William Sancroft)
Wood MSS 8535 (Anthony Wood's catalogue of printed material in Thomas Barlow's library)

BRITISH LIBRARY
Add. MSS 4107 (Weymouth's diary)
Add. MSS 18,730 (earl of Anglesey's diary, 1667–75)

Add. MSS 19,399 (letters of monarchs and nobles)

Add. MSS 22,576 (correspondence of John Palmer, archdeacon of Northampton, and Joseph Henshaw, bishop of Peterborough)

Add. MSS 25,119 (correspondence of Sir Leoline Jenkins)

Add. MSS 25,122; 25,124 (Coventry papers)

Add. MSS 28,093 (miscellaneous papers)

Add. MSS 28,875 (Ellis papers, 1672–86)

Add. MSS 29,571; 29,572; 29,582; 29,583 (Hatton-Finch papers)

Add. MSS 29,584 (correspondence of English bishops; Hatton-Finch papers)

Add. MSS 29,921 (commonplace book of Hanserd Knollys)

Add. MSS 33,498 (miscellaneous papers)

Add. MSS 34,487 (Macintosh collection)

Add. MSS 34,769 (Moseley and Rolleston correspondence)

Add. MSS 37,719 (commonplace book of Sir John Gibson, 1655–60)

Add. MSS 38,847 (Robert West's confession)

Add. MSS 38,856 (Hodgkin papers)

Add. MSS 39,865 (Richard Farnworth, "Truth Cleared from Scandalls," 1653)

Add. MSS 41,819; 41,820; 41,823 (Middleton papers)

Add. MSS 42,849 (papers of Philip Henry)

Add. MSS 44,792 (Gladstone papers)

Add. MSS 45,974 (papers of Oliver Heywood)

Add. MSS 46,960A (Egmont papers)

Add. MSS 47,024 (letter-book of John Percivale)

Add. MSS 54,185 (sermons of Thomas Jollie)

Add. MSS 61,681; 61,682 (Boteler papers; Blenheim manuscripts)

Add. MSS 62,453 (documents relating to Monmouth's rebellion)

Add. MSS 63,776 (Preston papers)

Add. MSS 70,013; 70,014; 70,070 (Portland manuscripts)

Add. MSS 71,689 (diary of Sir William Boothby)

Add. MSS 71,690; 71,691; 71,692 (letter-books of Sir William Boothby)

Egerton MSS 786 (letter-book of Sir Samuel Luke)

Egerton MSS 2539; 2543 (Nicholas papers)

Egerton MSS 2570 (Baxter manuscripts)

Egerton MSS 2985 (Heath and Verney papers)

Egerton MSS 3330 (Leeds manuscripts)

Harleian MSS 3784 (correspondence of Gilbert Sheldon)

Harleian MSS 6845 (documents relating to Monmouth's rebellion)

Harleian MSS 7377 (letter-book of Gilbert Sheldon)

Lansdowne MSS 937 (correspondence of White Kennett)

Lansdowne MSS 1152 (examinations of Monmouth rebels)

Sloane MSS 1008 (correspondence of Edmund Borlase)

Stowe MSS 185 (state papers)

Stowe MSS 186 (transcripts of state papers)

Stowe MSS 190 (letter-book of Sir Samuel Luke)

Stowe MSS 207; 209 (Essex papers)

Stowe MSS 745 (correspondence of Sir Edward Dering)

CAMBRIDGE UNIVERSITY LIBRARY

Add. MSS 1; 5 (Strype correspondence; Baumgartner papers)

Add. MSS 40 (John Gibson's revelation, etc.)

Add. MSS 90 (record of nonconformist licenses, 1672)

Add. MSS 6375 (letters of Thomas Mariott)

Add. MSS 7338 (Philip Henry's sermon notes on Genesis)

Add. MSS 8499 (diary of Isaac Archer)

CHESTER CITY RECORD OFFICE

MSS QSF/82 (quarter sessions' files).

CORPORATION OF LONDON RECORD OFFICE

MSS SM 52; SM 53 (London sessions minute books, 1681–85)

MSS SF 297; SF 298; SF 299 (London sessions files, 1682–84)

DR. WILLIAMS'S LIBRARY, LONDON

MSS 12.78 (correspondence and papers of Thomas Jollie)

MSS 24.7

MSS 24.18–20 (sermons and papers of John Howe)

MSS 31.J (Morrice manuscripts)

MS 38.18 (A. B., "A View of the Dissenting Intrest in London of the Presbyterian & Independent Denominations from the Year 1695 to the 25 of December 1731 with a Pos[t]-script of the Present State of the Baptists")

MSS 89.32 (Turner manuscripts)

MSS L4/2 (sermons and notes of John Collins)

MSS L6/1 (letters and a sermon of John Owen transcribed by Sir John Hartopp)

MSS L6/3 (sermons of John Owen transcribed by Sir John Hartopp)

MSS L6/4 (sermons of John Owen, David Clarkson, et al. Transcribed by Sir John Hartopp)

Roger Morrice, "Entr'ing Book, Being an Historical Register of Occurrences from April, Anno 1677 to April 1691"

FRIENDS' LIBRARY, LONDON

Swarthmore MSS, vol. 3 (Quaker letters)

GUILDHALL LIBRARY, LONDON

MS 592/1 (church book of General Baptist church, White's Alley, London)

MS 9060 (assignation book for proceedings against dissenters, archdeaconry of London, 4 May 1683–17 December 1684)

MS 9060A, vol. 2 (visitation book, archdeaconry of London, 1678–83)

MSS 9579, vol. 1 (certificates of dissenters)

HENRY E. HUNTINGTON LIBRARY
MS STT 524 (Stowe manuscripts)

INNER TEMPLE LIBRARY, LONDON
Petyt MSS 538 (vol. 17)

JOHN RYLANDS LIBRARY
Legh of Lyme MSS (deposition of Edward Sherman, 20 September 1682)

LONDON METROPOLITAN ARCHIVES
MSS MJ/SBB/394–443 (sessions of the peace, oyer and terminer books, Middlesex, 1681–87)
MSS MR/RC/3–10 (certificates of convictions for participation in conventicles, 1682–87)

LONGLEAT
Coventry MSS 7, 11

NOTTINGHAM UNIVERSITY LIBRARY
MSS PwV95 (Portland manuscripts)

PEPYS LIBRARY, CAMBRIDGE
Misc. MSS 7 (records of Green Ribbon Club)

PUBLIC RECORD OFFICE, LONDON
SP 29 (state papers, Charles II)
SP 31 (state papers, James II)
SP 44 (entry books)
SP 63 (state papers, Ireland)


Printed Primary Sources

Account of the Life and Actions of Mr. John Bunyan (London, 1692), ad cal. The Pilgrim's Progress, 3rd part. London, 1693.
Account of the Proceedings at Guild-Hall, London, . . . Held 24th. of June 1676. [London, 1676].
Acts and Ordinances of the Interregnum, 1642–1660, ed. C. H. Firth and R. S. Rait, 3 vols. London: His Majesty's Stationery Office, 1911.
Ad General. Quarterial. Session. Pacis Dom. Regis tent. apud Castr. Exon. London, 1683.
Aesop. Aesop Improved or, Above Three Hundred and Fifty Fables. London, 1673.
———. The Fables of Aesop. London, 1634.
"Ager Scholae." The Pilgrim's Progress in Poesie, 2 vols. London, 1697–98.
A[lleine], R[ichard]. Heaven Opened. London, 1666.
Allen, William. Some Baptismal Abuses Briefly Discovered. London, 1653.
The Arraignment and Tryall with a Declaration of the Ranters. [London], 1650.
The Articles Recommended by the Arch-Bishop of Canterbury. London, 1688.
Aspinwall, William. The Abrogation of the Jewish Sabbath. London, 1657.

———. *A Brief Description of the Fifth Monarchy*. London, 1653.

———. *An Explication and Application of the Seventh Chapter of Daniel*. London, 1654.

———. *Thunder from Heaven Against the Back-Sliders and Apostates of the Times*. London, 1655.

———. *The Work of the Age*. London, 1655.

*Association Records of the Particular Baptists of England, Wales and Ireland to 1660*, ed. B. R. White, 3 vols. London: Baptist Historical Society, n.d.

Asty, John. "Memoirs of the Life of John Owen, D.D." In John Owen, *A Complete Collection of the Sermons of the Reverend and Learned John Owen, D.D.* London, 1721.

B., J. *The Morality of the Seventh-Day-Sabbath Disproved*. London, 1683. [not by John Bunyan]

Bale, John. *The Image of Both Churches*, in *Select Works of John Bale, D.D.*, ed. Henry Christmas, Publications of the Parker Society, vol. 1. Cambridge: Cambridge University Press, 1849.

Ball, John. *A Treatise of the Covenant of Grace*. London, 1645.

Bampfield, Francis. *The House of Wisdom*. London, 1681.

———. *The Judgment of Mr. Francis Bampfield*, ed. William Benn. London, 1672.

———. *A Name, an After-one*. London, 1681.

———. *The Seventh-Day-Sabbath the Desirable-Day*. [London], 1677.

*Baptist Confessions of Faith*, ed. William L. Lumpkin. Philadelphia: Judson Press, 1959.

Bates, William. *A Discourse of Divine Meditation*, in *The Spirituality of the Later English Puritans: An Anthology*, ed. Dewey D. Wallace, Jr. Macon, GA: Mercer University Press, 1987.

Bauthumley, Jacob. *The Light and Dark Sides of God*. London, 1650.

Baxter, Richard. *Calendar of the Correspondence of Richard Baxter*, ed. N. H. Keeble and Geoffrey F. Nuttall, 2 vols. Oxford: Clarendon Press, 1991.

———. *Catholick Theologie*. London, 1675.

———. *A Christian Directory*. London, 1673.

———. *Church-History of the Government of Bishops and Their Councils Abbreviated*. London, 1680.

———. *The Cure of Church-Divisions*. London, 1670.

———. *A Defence of Christ, and Free Grace*. Part 2 of *The Scripture Gospel Defended, and Christ, Grace and Free Justification Vindicated Against the Libertines*. London, 1690.

———. *The Divine Appointment of the Lords Day Proved*. London, 1671.

———. *An End of Doctrinal Controversies*. London, 1691.

———. *How Far Holinesse Is the Design of Christianity*. London, 1671.

———. *Plain Scripture Proof of Infants Church-Membership and Baptism*. London, 1651.

———. *The Scripture Gospel Defended, and Christ, Grace and Free Justification Vindicated Against the Libertines*. Part 1: *A Breviate of the Doctrine of Justification*. London, 1690.

———. *Short Instructions for the Sick*. London, 1665.

Bayly, Lewis. *The Practise of Pietie*, 3rd ed. London, 1613.

Beard, Thomas. *The Theatre of Gods Judgements*, rev. ed. London, 1631.

Beaumont, Agnes. *The Narratives of the Persecutions of Agnes Beaumont*, ed. Vera J. Camden. East Lansing, MI: Colleagues Press, 1992.

*Bedfordshire County Records: Notes and Extracts from the County Records Being a Calendar of Volume I. of the Sessions Minute Books 1651 to 1660*, ed. Hardy and Page, vol. 2. Bedford: C. F. Timaeus, n.d.

[Belcher, John, *et al.*]. *A Faithful Testimony Against the Teachers of Circumcision and the Legal Ceremonies.* [London? 1667].

Bernard, Richard. *The Isle of Man.* London, 1627.

[Bethel, Slingsby]. *The Present Interest of England Stated.* London, 1671.

Beza, Theodore. *Theodori Bezae Vezelii, Volumen . . . Tractationum Theologicarum*, 3 vols. Geneva, 1570–82.

Blackley, James. *Strange & Terrible Newes from Cambridge, Being a True Relation of the Quakers Bewitching of Mary Philips.* London, 1659.

Blake, Thomas. *Vindiciae Foederis.* London, 1653.

[Blount, Charles]. *An Appeal from the Country to the City, for the Preservation of His Majesties Person, Liberty, Property, and the Protestant Religion.* London, 1679.

*A Blow at the Root.* London, 1650.

Bolton, Robert. *The Workes of the Reverend, Truly Pious, and Judiciously Learned Robert Bolton.* London, 1641.

Boteler, Sir William. "The Papers of Sir Will. Boteler, 1642–1655," ed. Herbert Fowler, *PBHRS* 18 (1936).

Bugg, Francis. *The Pilgrim's Progress, from Quakerism, to Christianity.* London, 1698.

Bunyan, John. *Grace Abounding to the Chief of Sinners*, ed. Roger Sharrock. Oxford: Clarendon Press, 1962.

———. *The Heavenly Foot-Man: or, a Description of the Man That Gets to Heaven.* London, 1698.

———. *The Holy War*, ed. Roger Sharrock and James F. Forrest. Oxford: Clarendon Press, 1980.

———. *The Life and Death of Mr. Badman*, ed. James F. Forrest and Roger Sharrock. Oxford: Clarendon Press, 1988.

———. *The Miscellaneous Works of John Bunyan*, general editor, Roger Sharrock, 13 vols. Oxford: Clarendon Press, 1976–94.

  Vol. 1, ed. T. L. Underwood and Roger Sharrock. 1980.

  Vol. 2, ed. Richard L. Greaves. 1976.

  Vol. 3, ed. J. Sears McGee. 1987.

  Vol. 4, ed. T. L. Underwood. 1989.

  Vol. 5, ed. Graham Midgley. 1986.

  Vol. 6, ed. Graham Midgley. 1980.

  Vol. 7, ed. Graham Midgley. 1989.

  Vol. 8, ed. Richard L. Greaves. 1979.

  Vol. 9, ed. Richard L. Greaves. 1981.

  Vol. 10, ed. Owen C. Watkins. 1988.

  Vol. 11, ed. Richard L. Greaves. 1985.

  Vol. 12, ed. W. R. Owens. 1994.

  Vol. 13, ed. W. R. Owens. 1994.

———. *The Pilgrim's Progress from This World to That Which Is to Come*, ed. James Blanton Wharey and Roger Sharrock. Oxford: Clarendon Press, 1960; reprinted with corrections, 1967.

———. "A Relation of the Imprisonment of Mr. John Bunyan," *ad cal. Grace Abounding to the Chief of Sinners*, ed. Roger Sharrock. Oxford: Clarendon Press, 1962.

———. *The Works of That Eminent Servant of Christ, Mr. John Bunyan*, ed. Charles Doe. London, 1692.

Burrough, Edward. *The Memorable Works of a Son of Thunder and Consolation*. N.p., 1672.

Burton, Robert. *The Anatomy of Melancholy*, ed. Thomas C. Faulkner, Nicolas K. Kiessling, and Rhonda L. Blair, 3 vols. Oxford: Clarendon Press, 1989–94.

*Calendar of State Papers, Domestic Series*.

*Calendar of State Papers, Ireland, 1647–60*.

*Calendar of State Papers, Venetian, 1659–61*.

*Calendar of the Clarendon State Papers Preserved in the Bodleian Library*, vol. 5: 1660–1726, ed. F. J. Routledge. Oxford: Clarendon Press, 1970.

*Calendar of Treasury Books, 1685–1689*, vol. 8, 4 parts. London: His Majesty's Stationery Office, 1923.

Calvin, John. *Institutes of the Christian Religion*, ed. John T. McNeill and trans. Ford Lewis Battles, 2 vols. Philadelphia: Westminster Press, 1960.

Canne, John. *A Seasonable Word to the Parliament-Men*. London, 1659.

———. *The Time of the End*. London, 1657.

Carpenter, Richard. *The Anabaptist Washt and Washt, and Shrunk in the Washing*. London, 1653.

———. *The Downfal of Anti-Christ*. London, 1644.

Carstares, William. *The Deposition of Mr. William Carstares*. Edinburgh and London, 1684.

Cary, Mary. *The Little Horns Doom & Downfall*. London, 1651.

———. *A New and More Exact Mappe or, Description of New Jerusalems Glory*, *ad cal. The Little Horns Doom & Downfall*.

Caryl, Joseph, Philip Nye, *et al.*, *A Renuntiation and Declaration of the Ministers of Congregational Churches and Publick Preachers*. London, 1661.

*Certain Quaeres Humbly Presented in Way of Petition*. London, 1648 [February 1649].

Cheare, Abraham. *Words in Season*. London, 1668.

Child, John. *A Moderate Message to Quakers, Seekers, and Socinians, by a Friend and Well-Wisher to Them All*. [London], 1676.

———. *A Second Argument for a More Full and Firm Union Amongst All Good Protestants*. London, 1683.

*The Church Book of Bunyan Meeting 1650–1821: Being a Reproduction in Facsimile of the Original Folio*, intro. by G. B. Harrison. London: J. M. Dent and Sons, 1928.

*City Mercury* (1676).

Clarke (or Clark), Samuel. *A Mirrour or Looking-Glass Both for Saints & Sinners, Held Forth in Some Thousands of Examples*, 4th ed., 2 vols. London, 1671.

Clarkson, Lawrence. *The Lost Sheep Found*. London, 1660.

———. *A Single Eye All Light, No Darkness; or Light and Darkness One*. London, [1650].

*Cobbett's Complete Collection of State Trials and Proceedings*, ed. W. Cobbett, T. B. Howell, *et al.*, 34 vols. London: R. Bagshaw, 1809–28.

*A Collection of Scarce and Valuable Tracts . . . of the Late Lord Somers*, ed. Walter Scott, 13 vols. London, 1809–15.

*A Collection of the State Papers of John Thurloe*, ed. Thomas Birch, 7 vols. London, 1742.

Collier, Thomas. *The Body of Divinity.* London, 1674.

———. *A Discourse of the True Gospel Blessedness in the New Covenant.* London, 1659.

———. *A Looking-Glasse for the Quakers, Wherein They May Behold Themselves.* London, 1657.

"A Continuation of Mr. Bunyan's Life," *ad cal. Grace Abounding,* ed. Roger Sharrock.

[Cooper, Anthony Ashley, earl of Shaftesbury]. *Speech Lately Made by a Noble Peer.* [N.p., 1681].

[———]. *Two Seasonable Discourses Concerning This Present Parliament.* Oxford [Amsterdam?], 1675.

Cooper, Anthony Ashley, earl of Shaftesbury, and George Villiers, duke of Buckingham. *Two Speeches. I. The Earl of Shaftsbury's Speech in the House of Lords the 20th. of October, 1675. II. The D. of Buckinghams Speech in the House of Lords the 16th. of November 1675.* Amsterdam, 1675.

*Copies of the Informations and Original Papers Relating to the Proof of the Horrid Conspiracy Against the Late King, His Present Majesty, and the Government.* 3rd ed. London, 1685.

Corbet, John. *An Account Given of the Principles & Practises of Several Nonconformists.* London, 1682.

Cowell, John. *The Snare Broken.* London, 1677.

Cradock, Walter. *Gospel-Libertie, in the Extensions [and] Limitations of It.* London, 1648.

———. *Mount Sion* (London, 1649), *ad cal. Gospel-Holinesse.* London, 1651.

Crisp, Tobias. *Christ Alone Exalted.* London, 1690.

Danvers, Henry. *Theopolis, or the City of God.* London, 1672.

[———]. *Treatise of Baptism.* London, 1673.

*Debates of the House of Commons from the Year 1667 to the Year 1694,* ed. Anchitel Grey, 10 vols. London, 1763.

*A Declaration of Several of the Churches of Christ, and Godly People in and about the Citie of London.* London, 1654.

*The Declaration of the Gentlemen, Free-Holders and Inhabitants of the County of Bedford.* London, 1659 [1660].

[Delaune, Thomas]. *The Image of the Beast.* N.p., 1684.

[———]. *A Plea for the Non-Conformists, Giving the True State of the Dissenters Case.* London, 1684.

Dell, William. *Christ's Spirit, a Christians Strength.* London, 1651.

———. *The Doctrine of Baptismes, Reduced from Its Ancient and Moderne Corruptions.* London, 1648.

———. *The Increase of Popery in England.* London, 1681.

———. *A Plain and Necessary Confutation of Divers Gross and Antichristian Errors.* London, 1654.

———. *Power from on High.* London, 1645.

———. *Right Reformation.* London, 1646.

———. *A Testimony from the Word Against Divinity-Degrees in the University, ad cal. A Plain and Necessary Confutation.*

———. *The Tryall of Spirits Both in Teachers & Hearers.* London, 1660.

———. *Uniformity Examined.* London, 1646.

———. *The Way of True Peace and Unity in the True Church of Christ.* London, 1651.

Denne, Henry. *The Doctrine and Conversation of John Baptist.* London, 1642.

———. *The Quaker No Papist, in Answer to the Quaker Disarm'd.* London, 1659.

Denne, John. *Truth Outweighing Error.* London, 1673.

Dent, Arthur. *The Plaine Mans Path-Way to Heaven.* London, 1601.

———. *The Ruine of Rome.* London, 1644.

———. *A Sermon of Repentaunce.* London, 1582.

*Depositions from the Castle of York, Relating to Offences Committed in the Northern Counties in the Seventeenth Century,* ed. J. Raine, Surtees Society, vol. 40 (1861).

Dering, Edward. *M. Derings Workes.* London, 1597.

Dering, Sir Edward. *The Parliamentary Diary of Sir Edward Dering 1670–1673,* ed. Basil Duke Henning. New Haven, CT: Yale University Press, 1940.

Diodati, John. *Pious and Learned Annotations upon the Holy Bible,* 3rd ed. London, 1651.

*Dirt Wip't Off: or a Manifest Discovery of the Gross Ignorance, Erroneousness and Most Unchristian and Wicked Spirit of One John Bunyan, Lay-Preacher in Bedford.* London, 1672.

Dod, John. *Old Mr. Dod's Sayings.* London, 1671.

Dod, John, and Robert Cleaver. *A Plaine and Familiar Exposition of the Ten Commaundements.* London, 1605.

Doe, Charles. *A Collection of Experience of the Work of Grace.* London, [1700].

———. "The Struggler," in *MW,* 12:453–60.

*Domestick Intelligence* (1679–80).

[Downame, John]. *Annotations upon All the Books of the Old and New Testament,* 2nd ed., vol. 1. London, 1651.

Dunton, John. *An Hue and Cry after Conscience: or the Pilgrim's Progress by Candle-Light.* London, 1685.

———. *Letters Written from New England A.D. 1686,* ed. W. H. Whitmore. Boston: Prince Society, 1867.

———. *The Pilgrim's Guide from the Cradle to His Death-Bed.* London, 1684.

Durham, James. *A Practical Exposition of the X . Commandements.* London, 1675.

Dyve, Sir Lewis. "The Tower of London Letter-Book of Sir Lewis Dyve, 1646–47," *PBHRS* 38 (1958).

Edwards, Thomas. *Gangraena,* 2nd ed. London, 1646.

———. *Gangraena,* part 3. London, 1646.

Erbery, William. *The Testimony of William Erbery, Left upon Record from the Saints of Succeeding Ages.* London, 1658.

Erskine, John. *Journal of the Hon. John Erskine of Carnock. 1683–1687,* ed. Walter Macleod, Publications of the Scottish Historical Society, 14 (Edinburgh: T. and A. Constable, 1893).

Evelyn, John. *The Diary of John Evelyn,* ed. E. S. de Beer, 6 vols. Oxford: Clarendon Press, 1955.

Everard, John. *The Gospel-Treasury Opened.* London, 1657.

*The Faithfull Narrative of the Late Testimony and Demand Made to Oliver Cromwell . . . in the Name of the Lord Jehovah (Jesus Christ,) King of Saints and Nations.* N.p., 1654.

Farnworth, Richard. *Witchcraft Cast out from the Religious Seed and Israel of God.* London, 1655.

Ferguson, Robert. *The Impact and Use of Scripture-Metaphors.* 1675.

[————]. *An Impartial Enquiry into the Administration of Affair's in England.* N.p., 1683.

————. *The Interest of Reason in Religion, with the Import & Use of Scripture-Metaphors.* London, 1675.

————. *A Just and Modest Vindication of the Proceedings of the Two Last Parliaments.* [London? 1681].

[————]. *A Letter to a Person of Honour, Concerning the Black Box.* [London, 1680].

[————]. *The Second Part of No Protestant Plot.* London, 1682.

————. *A Sober Enquiry into the Nature, Measure, and Principle of Moral Virtue.* London, 1673.

[————]. *The Third Part of No Protestant Plot.* London, 1682.

*The Fifth Monarchy, or Kingdom of Christ, in Opposition to the Beasts.* London, 1659.

Firmin, Giles. *The Liturgical Considerator Considered,* 2nd ed. London, 1661.

Fowler, Edward. *The Design of Christianity.* London, 1671.

————. *Libertas Evangelica: or, a Discourse of Christian Liberty.* London, 1680.

————. *The Principles and Practices, of Certain Moderate Divines of the Church of England.* London, 1670.

Fox, George. *A Declaration of the Ground of Error.* London, 1657.

————. *The Great Mistery of the Great Whore Unfolded: and Antichrists Kingdom Revealed unto Destruction.* London, 1659.

————. *The Journal of George Fox,* ed. Norman Penney, 2 vols. Cambridge: Cambridge University Press, 1911.

————. *Something in Answer to the Old Common-Prayer-Book.* London, 1660.

Fox, George, and John Burnyeat. *A New-England-Fire-Brand Quenched. The Second Part.* [London], 1679.

[Fox, George, *et al.*]. *A Declaration from the Harmles & Innocent People of God Called Quakers, Against All Plotters and Fighters in the World.* London, 1660 [1661].

Foxe, John. *The Acts and Monuments of John Foxe,* ed. George Townsend, 8 vols. New York: AMS Press, 1965.

Fuller, Thomas. *A Pisgah-Sight of Palestine and the Confines Thereof, with the History of the Old and New Testament Acted Thereon.* London, 1650.

*A Full Relation of the Contents of the Black Box.* [London?], 1680.

*A Further Account of the Proceedings Against the Rebels in the West of England.* London, 1685.

Gauden, John. *Considerations Touching the Liturgy of the Church of England.* London, 1661.

Geree, Stephen. *The Doctrine of the Antinomians by Evidence of Gods Truth Plainely Confuted.* London, 1644.

Gilpin, John. *The Quakers Shaken: or, a Fire-Brand Snatch'd out of the Fire.* Gateside, 1653.

Goodwin, John. *The Agreement & Distance of Brethren.* London, 1652.

————. *Redemption Redeemed.* London, 1651.

Goodwin, Thomas. *Most Holy and Profitable Sayings of That Reverend Divine, Doctor Tho. Goodwin.* [London, 1680].

[————]. *Patience and Its Perfect Work, Under Sudden & Sore Tryals.* London, 1666.

————. *A Sermon of the Fifth Monarchy.* London, 1654.

————. *The Works of Thomas Goodwin, D.D.,* 4 vols. London, 1681–97.

Gouge, William. *Commentary on Hebrews.* Grand Rapids, MI: Kregel Publications, 1980.

————. *Of Domesticall Duties,* 2nd ed. London, 1626.

Grantham, Thomas. *The Loyal Baptist: or an Apology for the Baptized Believers.* London, 1684.

————. *The Seventh-Day-Sabbath Ceased as Ceremonial.* London, 1667.

————. *St. Paul's Catechism.* London, 1687.

Greenham, Richard. *The Workes of the Reverend and Faithfull Servant of Jesus Christ M. Richard Greenham,* 2nd ed. London, 1599.

Grey, Ford Lord. *The Secret History of the Rye-House Plot: and of Monmouth's Rebellion.* London, 1754.

Guild, William. *Moses Unveiled.* London, 1620.

*The Happy Successe of the Parliaments Armie at Newport and Some Other Places.* London, 1643.

Harvey, Christopher. *The Synagogue, or, the Shadow of the Temple.* London, 1640.

Hearne, Thomas. *The Remains of Thomas Hearne: Reliquiae Hernianae,* ed. John Bliss and rev. by John Buchanan-Brown. Carbondale: Southern Illinois University Press, 1966.

Henry, Philip. *Diaries and Letters of Philip Henry, M.A. of Broad Oak, Flintshire A.D. 1631–1696,* ed. Matthew Henry Lee. London: Kegan Paul, Trench and Co., 1882.

Heywood, Oliver. *Life of John Angier of Denton: Together with Angier's Diary,* ed. Ernest Axon, Publications of the Chetham Society, n.s., vol. 97 (Manchester, 1937).

*Historical Collections of Private Passages of State,* ed. John Rushworth, 6 vols. London, 1680–1701.

*Historical Manuscripts Commission, Reports*: 2, *Third Report*; 6, *Seventh Report*; 7, *Eighth Report*; 13, *Tenth Report*; 19, *Townshend*; 22, *Eleventh Report*; 25, *Le Fleming*; 29, *Portland*; 35, *Fourteenth Report*; 36, *Ormonde*; 63, *Egmont*; 75, *Downshire.*

H[obson], P[aul]. *A Discoverie of Truth: Presented to the Sons of Truth.* N.p., 1645.

————. *The Fallacy of Infants Baptisme Discovered.* London, 1645.

————. *A Garden Inclosed, and Wisdom Justified Only of Her Children.* London, 1647.

*The Humble and Serious Testimony of Many Hundreds, of Godly and Well Affected People in the County of Bedford, and Parts Adjacent, Constant Adherers to the Cause of God and the Nation.* N.p., 1657.

[Humfrey, John]. *A Case of Conscience.* London, 1669.

[————]. *Two Points of Great Moment, the Obligation of Humane Laws, and the Authority of the Magistrate, About Religion, Discussed.* [London], 1672.

*Impartial Protestant Mercury* (1681–82).

Ives, Jeremiah. *Saturday No Sabbath.* London, 1659.

Jackson, Thomas. *The Raging Tempest Stilled.* London, 1623.

Jelinger, Christopher. *The Resolution-Table.* London, 1676.

Jenner, Thomas. *Divine Mysteries That Cannot Be Seene, Made Plain by That Which May Be Seene.* London, 1651. (Originally published as *The Soules Solace.*)

————. *The Soules Solace, or Thirtie and One Spirituall Emblems.* London, 1626.

Jessey, Henry. *A Looking-Glass for Children.* London, 1672.

[————]. *The Lords Loud Call to England.* London, 1660.

————. *Miscellanea Sacra: or, Diverse Necessary Truths.* London, 1665.

————. *A Storehouse of Provision, to Further Resolution in Severall Cases of Conscience.* London, 1650.

Johnson, Richard. *The Most Famous History of the Seven Champions of Christendome*. London, 1596.

[Johnson, Samuel]. *Julian the Apostate: Being a Short Account of His Life*. London, 1682.

Jollie, Thomas. *The Note Book of the Rev. Thomas Jolly A.D. 1671–1693*, ed. Henry Fishwick, Chetham Society, new ser., vol. 33 (1894).

Jones, James. *Modesty and Faithfulness in Opposition to Envy and Rashness*. London, 1683.

*Journals of the House of Commons*. 1742ff.

*Journals of the House of Lords*. 1767ff.

*The Judgment and Decree of the University of Oxford Past in Their Convocation July 21. 1683, Against Certain Pernicious Books and Damnable Doctrines*. Oxford, 1683.

Keach, Benjamin. *A Golden Mine Opened*. London, 1694.

———. *The Progress of Sin; or the Travels of Ungodliness*. London, 1684.

[———]. *Sion in Distress: or, the Groans of the Protestant Church*, 2nd ed. London, 1681.

———. *The Travels of True Godliness*, 3rd ed. London, 1684.

———. *Tropologia; A Key to Open Scripture Metaphors, in Four Books*. London: City Press, 1855.

Kenyon, J. P., ed., *The Stuart Constitution, 1603–1688: Documents and Commentary*. Cambridge: Cambridge University Press, 1969.

Kiffin, William. *Remarkable Passages in the Life of William Kiffin*, ed. William Orme. London: Burton and Smith, 1823.

———. *A Sober Discourse of Right to Church-Communion*. London, 1681.

*Kingdomes Intelligencer* (1661).

Knollys, Hanserd. *An Exposition of the Eleventh Chapter of the Revelation*. [London?], 1679.

———. *Mystical Babylon Unvailed*. [London], 1670.

———. *The World That Now Is; and the World That Is to Come*. London, 1681.

Knox, John. *On Rebellion*, ed. Roger A. Mason. Cambridge: Cambridge University Press, 1994.

Lamb, Thomas. *Truth Prevailing Against the Fiercest Opposition*. London, 1655.

Lawson, George. *An Exposition of the Epistle to the Hebrewes*. London, 1661.

Lee, Samuel. *Orbis miraculum, or the Temple of Solomon, Pourtrayed by Scripture-Light*. London, 1659.

Leon, Jacob Jehudah. *A Relation of the Most Memorable Thinges in the Tabernacle of Moses, and the Temple of Salomon, According to Text of Scripture*. Amsterdam, 1675.

[L'Estrange, Roger]. *Considerations upon a Printed Sheet Entituled the Speech of the Late Lord Russel to the Sheriffs*. London, 1683.

*A Letter from a Person of Quality, to His Friend in the Country*. N.p., 1675.

*A Letter from Colonell Harvie, to His Excellency Robert Earle of Essex*. London, 1643.

*Letters of Eminent Men, Addressed to Ralph Thoresby, F.R.S.*, 2 vols. London: Henry Colburn and Richard Bentley, 1832.

*The Library of the Late Reverend and Learned Mr. Samuel Lee*. Boston, 1693.

*The Life and Death of Mr. Vavasor Powell*. London, 1671.

Lightfoot, John. *The Temple: Especially as It Stood in the Dayes of Our Saviour*. London, 1650.

*A List of the Conventicles or Unlawful Meetings within the City of London and Bills of Mortality*. London, 1683.

Llanvaedonon, William. *A Brief Exposition upon the Second Psalme.* London, 1655.

[Lobb, Stephen]. *A True Dissenter.* N.p., 1685.

[Lockyer, Nicholas]. *Some Seasonable and Serious Queries upon the Late Act Against Conventicles.* [London, 1670].

London *Gazette* (1668–88).

Luke, Sir Samuel. *The Letter Books 1644–45 of Sir Samuel Luke: Parliamentary Governor of Newport Pagnell,* ed. H. G. Tibbutt. London: Her Majesty's Stationery Office, 1963.

Lumpkin, William L. *Baptist Confessions of Faith.* Philadelphia: Judson Press, 1959.

Luther, Martin. *A Commentary on St. Paul's Epistle to the Galatians,* ed. Philip S. Watson. Cambridge: James Clarke and Co., 1953.

———. *Luther's Works,* ed. Jaroslav Pelikan and Helmut T. Lehmann, 56 vols. St. Louis: Concordia Publishing House; Philadelphia: Muhlenberg Press; Philadelphia: Fortress Press, 1958–74.

Luttrell, Narcissus. *A Brief Historical Relation of State Affairs from September 1678 to April 1714,* 6 vols. Oxford: Oxford University Press, 1857.

[Mackenzie, George]. *A True and Plain Account of the Discoveries Made in Scotland, of the Late Conspiracies Against His Majesty and the Government.* Edinburgh, 1685.

Marvell, Andrew. *An Account of the Growth of Popery, and Arbitrary Government in England.* Amsterdam, [1677].

———. *The Rehearsal Transpros'd.* London, 1672–73.

Meade, Matthew. *The Vision of the Wheels Seen by the Prophet Ezekiel.* London, 1689.

Mede, Joseph. *The Key of the Revelation,* trans. Richard More, 2nd ed. London, 1650.

*Mercurius Civicus* (1645).

*Mercurius Publicus* (1660–61).

*Middlesex County Records,* ed. John Cordy Jeaffreson, 4 vols. London: Middlesex County Records Society, 1886–92.

M[ilton], J[ohn]. *Of True Religion, Haeresie, Schism, Toleration, and What Best Means May Be Us'd Against the Growth of Popery.* London, 1673.

———. *Paradise Regain'd: . . . to Which Is Added Samson Agonistes.* London, 1671.

*The Minute Book of Bedford Corporation, 1647–1664,* ed. Guy Parsloe, *PBHRS,* 26 (1949).

*The Minutes of the First Independent Church (now Bunyan Meeting) at Bedford 1656–1766,* ed. H. G. Tibbutt, *PBHRS,* 55 (1976).

*Mirabilis Annus, or the Year of Prodigies and Wonders.* [London], 1661.

*The Mischief of Persecution Exemplified.* London, 1688.

More, John. *A Trumpet Sounded.* N.p., 1654.

Ness, Christopher. *A Distinct Discourse and Discovery of the Person and Period of Antichrist.* London, 1679.

*A New-Years-Gift for the Lord Chief in Justice Sc[rog]gs.* [London, 1679].

Nowell, Alexander, and William Day. *A True Report of the Disputation . . . with Ed. Campion Jesuite.* London, 1583.

Nye, Philip. *The King's Authority in Dispensing with Ecclesiastical Laws, Asserted and Vindicated.* London, 1687.

———. *The Lawfulnes of the Oath of Supremacy, and Power of the King in Ecclesiastical Affairs.* London, 1683.

*Observator* (1683–86).

*The Observator Observ'd* (1681).

Ogilby, John. *The Fables of Aesop Paraphras'd in Verse.* London, 1665.

*An Ordinance of the Lords and Commons Assembled in Parliament: For the Erecting and Maintaining of a Garrison at Newport-Pagnell.* London, 1643.

*An Ordinance of the Lords and Commons Assembled in Parliament, for the Maintenance and Pay of the Garrisons of Newport Pagnel, Bedford, Lyn Regis.* London, 1645.

*An Ordinance of the Lords and Commons Assembled in Parliament: For the Sleighting and Demolishing of Severall Garrisons Under the Power of the Parliament.* London, 1646.

*Original Letters and Papers of State Addressed to Oliver Cromwell,* ed. John Nickolls. London, 1743.

*Original Records of Early Nonconformity Under Persecution and Indulgence,* ed. G. L. Turner, 2 vols. London: T. Fisher Unwin, 1911.

[Owen, John]. *An Account of the Grounds and Reasons on Which Protestant Dissenters Desire Their Liberty* [N.p., 1680].

———. *The Branch of the Lord, the Beauty of Sion.* London, 1650.

———. *A Brief and Impartial Account of the Nature of the Protestant Religion.* London, 1682.

———. *The Church of Rome No Safe Guide.* London, 1679.

———. *A Continuation of the Exposition of the Epistle of Paul the Apostle to the Hebrews.* London, 1680.

———. *The Correspondence of John Owen (1616–1683): With an Account of His Life and Work,* ed. Peter Toon. Cambridge: James Clarke, 1970.

———. *A Declaration of the Glorious Mystery of the Person of Christ, God and Man.* London, 1679.

[———]. *A Discourse Concerning Liturgies, and Their Imposition.* [London], 1662.

———. *The Doctrine of Justification by Faith Through the Imputation of the Righteousness of Christ.* London, 1677.

———. *Exercitations Concerning the Name, Original, Nature, Use and Continuance of a Day of Sacred Rest.* London, 1671.

———. *An Exposition of the Two First Chapters of the Epistle of Paul the Apostle unto the Hebrews.* London, 1668.

———. *An Humble Testimony unto the Goodness and Severity of God in His Dealing with Sinful Churches and Nations.* London, 1681.

[———]. *Indulgence and Toleration Considered in a Letter unto a Person of Honour.* London, 1667.

[———]. *A Peace-Offering in an Apology and Humble Plea for Indulgence and Libertie of Conscience.* London, 1667.

———. *Salus Electorum, Sanguis Jesu.* London, 1648.

———. *A Treatise of the Dominion of Sin and Grace.* London, 1688.

[———]. *Truth and Innocence Vindicated.* London, 1669.

———. *The Works of John Owen, D.D.,* ed. William H. Gould, 16 vols. London: Johnstone and Hunter, 1850–53.

[Palmer, Samuel]. *A Defence of the Dissenters Education in Their Private Academies.* London, 1703.

[Parker, Samuel]. *A Defence and Continuation of the Ecclesiastical Politie.* London, 1671.

———. *A Discourse of Ecclesiastical Politie.* London, 1670.

P[aul], T[homas]. *Some Serious Reflections on That Part of Mr. Bunion's Confession of Faith: Touching Church Communion with Unbaptized Persons.* London, 1673.

P[enn], W[illiam]. *Good Advice to the Church of England, Roman Catholick, and Protestant Dissenter.* [London], 1687.

———. *The Great Case of Liberty of Conscience.* [London], 1670.

———. *A Perswasive to Moderation to Church Dissenters.* [London, 1686].

———. *The Sandy Foundation Shaken.* London, 1668.

———. *Som Free Reflections upon Occasion of the Public Discourse about Liberty of Conscience.* London, 1687.

———. *A Third Letter from a Gentleman in the Country, to His Friends in London, upon the Subject of Penal Laws and Tests.* London, 1687.

Pepys, Samuel. *The Diary of Samuel Pepys,* ed. Robert Latham and William Matthews, 11 vols. Berkeley: University of California Press, 1970–83.

Perkins, William. *The Arte of Prophecying,* trans. Thomas Tuke. London, 1607.

———. *Christian Oeconomie: or, a Short Survey of the Right Manner of Erecting and Ordering a Familie, According to the Scriptures.* London, 1609.

———. *A Golden Chaine, or, the Description of Theologie,* trans. Robert Hill. London, 1612.

[Perrinchief, Richard]. *A Discourse of Toleration.* London, 1668.

Petto, Samuel. *The Difference Between the Old and New Covenant Stated and Explained.* London, 1674.

Plant, Thomas, and Benjamin Dennis. *The Mischief of Persecution Exemplified.* London, 1688.

Pomfret, Thomas. *Subjection for Conscience-Sake Asserted in a Sermon Preached at the Assizes Held at Ant-hill in Bedfordshire.* London, 1682.

Powell, Vavasor. *The Bird in the Cage, Chirping.* London, 1661.

———. *Christ and Moses Excellency.* London, 1650.

———. *Common-Prayer-Book No Divine Service.* London, 1660. 2nd ed. London, 1661.

———. *The Golden Sayings, Sentences and Experiences of Mr. Vavasor Powell.* [London, 1675?].

———. *A New and Useful Concordance to the Holy Bible.* London, 1671. 2nd ed. London, 1673.

*The Presentment for the City of London at the Sessions of Peace and Gaol Delivery.* London, 1683.

*The Proceedings at the Sessions of the Peace Held at Hicks Hall for the County of Middlesex December 5. 1681.* London, 1682.

*The Proceedings of His Majesties Justices of Peace, at the Sessions of Oyer and Terminer . . . September the 6th, 1684.* London, 1684.

*A Proclamation for the Suppressing of Seditious and Treasonable Books and Pamphlets.* London, 1679.

*Protestant (Domestick) Intelligence* (1680–81).

*Publick Occurrences Truly Stated* (1688).

*Quakers Are Inchanters and Dangerous Seducers.* London, 1655.

Quarles, Francis. *Emblemes,* 4th ("2nd") ed. Cambridge, 1643.

———. *Hieroglyphikes of the Life of Man, ad cal. Emblemes.* London, 1660.

*The Ranters Monster: Being a True Relation of One Mary Adams.* London, 1652.

*The Ranters Religion.* London, 1650.

[Reading, John]. *The Ranters Ranting.* London, 1650.

*The Records of a Church of Christ in Bristol, 1640–1687,* ed. Roger Hayden, Bristol Record Society's Publications, vol. 27 (1974).

*Records of the Churches of Christ, Gathered at Fenstanton, Warboys, and Hexham, 1644–1720,* ed. Edward Bean Underhill. London: Hanserd Knollys Society, 1854.

*A Relation of the Fearful Estate of Francis Spira . . . To Which Is Added, Some Account of the Miserable Lives and Deaths of John Child & George Edwards,* ed. W. C. Brownlee. Philadelphia: Andrew Morgan and D. Hogan, 1814.

Reresby, Sir John. *Memoirs of Sir John Reresby,* ed. Andrew Browning. Glasgow: Jackson, Son and Co., 1936.

Reynolds, John. *The Triumphs of Gods Revenge Against the Crying and Execrable Sinne of (Wilful and Premeditated) Murther.* 4th ed. London, 1663.

Rogers, John. *Jegar-Sahadutha: An Oyled Pillar.* N.p., [1657].

———. *Ohel or Beth-Shemesh: A Tabernacle for the Sun.* London, 1653.

*The Routing of th[e] Ranters.* [London, 1650].

Rutherford, Samuel. *A Survey of the Spirituall Antichrist.* London, 1648.

S., M. *The Heavenly Passenger, or, the Pilgrim's Progress.* London, 1687.

*Sad and Lamentable News from Brick-Lane in the Hamlet of Spittle-Fields.* London, [1684].

*The Saints Freedom from Tyranny Vindicated.* London, 1667.

Saller (Sellers), William. *An Examination of a Late Book Published by Doctor Owen, Concerning a Sacred Day of Rest.* [London], 1671.

———. *A Preservative Against Atheism and Error.* London, 1664.

———. *Sundry Queries Formerly Tendred to the Ministers of London.* [London? 1660].

Saltmarsh, John. *Free-Grace,* 2nd ed. London, 1646.

Sherlock, Richard. *The Principles of the Holy Christian Religion,* 6th ed. London, 1663.

Sherlock, William. *A Discourse Concerning the Knowledge of Jesus Christ.* London, 1674.

S[herman], T[homas]. *The Second Part of the Pilgrim's Progress, from This Present World of Wicke[d]ness and Misery, to an Eternity of Holiness and Fidelity.* London, 1682.

Sibbes, Richard. *Divine Meditations and Holy Contemplations.* Wilmington, DE, 1797.

[Smith, Francis, *et al.*]. *Sions Groans for Her Distres'd.* [London], 1661.

Smith, Thomas. *A Gagg for the Quakers, with an Answer to Mr. Denn's Quaker No Papist.* London, 1659.

[———]. "A Letter Sent to Mr. E. of Taft," *ad cal. The Quaker Disarm'd.* London, 1659.

Soursby, Henry, and Mehetabel Smith. *A Discourse of the Sabbath.* London, 1683.

Spittlehouse, John. *An Answer to One Part of the Lord Protector's Speech.* London, 1654.

———. *Certaine Queries Propounded to the Most Serious Consideration of Those Persons Now in Power.* London, 1654.

*State-Papers and Letters, Addressed to William Carstares,* ed. Joseph McCormick. Edinburgh, 1774.

*Statutes of the Realm.* 11 vols. London, 1820–28.

Stennett, Edward. *The Seventh Day Is the Sabbath of the Lord.* N.p., 1664.

*Strange & Terrible Newes from Cambridge, Being a True Relation of the Quakers Bewitching of Mary Philips.* London, 1659.

*Strange Newes from Newgate and the Old-Baily.* London, 1651.

Swinnock, George. *The Christian Man's Calling*, pt. 2. London, 1663.

Taylor, Jeremy. *The Rule and Exercises of Holy Living.* London, 1650.

Taylor, John. *Ranters of Both Sexes, Male and Female.* London, 1651.

Taylor, Thomas. *Christ Revealed: or the Old Testament Explained.* London, 1635. Republished as *Moses and Aaron, or the Types and Shadows of Our Saviour in the Old Testament.* London, 1653.

*A Testimony from the People of God, Called Quakers, Against Many Lying and Slanderous Books.* London, 1670.

Tillam, Thomas. *The Seventh-Day Sabbath Sought out and Celebrated.* London, 1657.

———. *The Two Witnesses.* London, 1651.

Tillinghast, John. *Mr. Tillinghasts Eight Last Sermons.* London, 1655.

Tomkins, Thomas. *The Inconveniences of Toleration.* London, 1667.

*To the Parliament of the Commonwealth of England: The Humble Representation and Desires of Divers Freeholders and Others Well Affected to the Commonwealth of England, Inhabiting Within the County of Bedford.* London, 1659.

Trapnel, Anna. *A Legacy for the Saints.* London, 1654.

Trapp, John. *Annotations upon the Old and New Testament, in Five Distinct Volumes*, vol. 1. London, 1662.

Trosse, George. *The Life of the Reverend Mr. George Trosse: Written by Himself, and Published Posthumously According to His Order in 1714*, ed. A. W. Brink. Montreal: McGill-Queen's University Press, 1974.

*A True and Impartial Narrative of Some Illegal and Arbitrary Proceedings.* N.p., 1670.

*True Protestant Mercury* (1681–82).

[Underhill, Cave]. *Vox Lachrymae: A Sermon Newly Held Forth at Weavers-Hall, upon the Funeral of the Famous T. O. Doctor of Salamancha.* Frankfurt, 1681; reprinted, London, 1682.

Underhill, Thomas. *Hell Broke Loose: or an History of the Quakers Both Old and New*, 2nd ed. London, 1660.

Vane, Sir Henry. *A Healing Question Propounded and Resolved.* London, 1656.

[Venner, Thomas, et al.]. *A Door of Hope: or, a Call and Declaration for the Gathering Together of the First Ripe Fruits unto the Standard of Our Lord, King Jesus.* [London, 1661].

[Vincent, Nathaniel, ed.]. *The Morning-Exercise Against Popery.* London, 1675.

*Vox populi, vox Dei.* N.p., 1681.

Walwyn, William. *Englands Lamentable Slaverie*, in *Tracts on Liberty in the Puritan Revolution 1638–1647*, ed. William Haller, vol. 3. New York: Columbia University Press, 1933.

*A Warning from God to All Apostates.* London, 1684.

Watson, Thomas. *A Divine Cordial.* London, 1663.

———. *Heaven Taken by Storm.* London, 1669.

*Weekly Account* (1645).

Weemes, John. *The Christian Synagogue.* London, 1623.

Wesley, Samuel. *A Defence of a Letter Concerning the Education of Dissenters in Their Private Academies.* London, 1704.

[———]. *A Letter from a Country Divine to His Friend in London.* London, 1703.

Whitehead, George. *The Christian Progress of That Ancient Servant and Minister of Jesus Christ, George Whitehead.* London, 1725.

Whitney, Geoffrey. *A Choice of Emblemes and Other Devises.* Leyden, 1586.

*The Whole Duty of Man Laid Down in a Plain Way for the Use of the Meanest Reader.* London, 1659.

Wilkins, John. *Of the Principles and Duties of Natural Religion.* London, 1675.

Williams, Roger. *George Fox Digg'd out of His Burrowes, or an Offer of Disputation.* Boston, 1676.

[Wilson, John]. *Nehushtan: or, a Sober and Peaceable Discourse.* London, 1668.

Wither, George. *A Collection of Emblemes, Ancient and Moderne.* London, 1635.

Wollebius, John [Johannes Wolleb]. *The Abridgment of Christian Divinitie,* 3rd ed. London, 1660.

[Wolseley, Sir Charles]. *Liberty of Conscience, the Magistrates Interest.* London, 1668.

[————]. *Liberty of Conscience upon Its True Proper Grounds Asserted & Vindicated.* London, 1668.

Wood, Anthony. *Athenae Oxonienses,* ed. Philip Bliss, 4 vols. London: Lackington, Hughes et al., 1813–20.

Worthington, John. *A Form of Sound of Words: or, a Scripture-Catechism.* London, 1673.

# Index of Biblical References

————◆————

# General Index

The religious affiliation of subjects is indicated by the following abbreviations: Cf = Conformist (Anglican); P = Presbyterian; C = Congregationalist (Independent); GB = General Baptist; PB = Particular Baptist; OCB = Open Communion, Open Membership Baptist; Q = Quaker (Friend); FM = Fifth Monarchist; RR = reputed Ranter; SDB = Seventh-Day Baptist. The designation for a printer or bookseller is PBS. An asterisk indicates a member of the Bedford church. In this index an "f" after a number indicates a separate reference on the next page, and an "ff" indicates separate references on the next two pages. *Passim* is used for a cluster of references in close but not consecutive sequence.

Xiuquan, Hong, 632

Yates, Thomas (C), 316
Yeamans, Sir Robert, Bristol councilor,
269
Yorkshire: general, 277, 578; Darfield, 129;

Draw-well, 115; Hull, 269, 566; Welburn,
67; York, 406, 591
Young, Thomas, puritan, 156

Zacharias, father of John the Baptist, 463–64
Zerubbabel, governor of Judah, 450